THE ANNALS OF AMERICA

THE ANNALS OF AMERICA

Volume 4

1797 - 1820

Domestic Expansion and Foreign Entanglements

William Benton, *Publisher*

ENCYCLOPÆDIA BRITANNICA, INC.

Chicago London Toronto Geneva Sydney Tokyo Manila

Printed in the U.S.A.
Library of Congress Catalog Card Number: 68-20888

The editors wish to express their gratitude for permission to reprint material from the following sources:

The Arthur H. Clark Company for Selection 53, from *A Documentary History of American Industrial Society,* ed. by John R. Commons *et al.*

Columbia University Press for Selection 148, from *Robert Mills, Architect of the Washington Monument, 1781-1855,* H. M. Pierce Gallagher, ed.

Helen Hartness Flanders for Selection 78, from *Ballads Migrant in New England,* New York: Farrar, Straus & Young, 1953.

Harvard University Press for Selections 119 and 133, from *This Was America,* Oscar Handlin, ed., Copyright 1949 by the President and Fellows of Harvard College.

The Manning Association for Selection 18, from *The Key of Libberty: Shewing the Causes Why a Free Government Has Always Failed, and a Remidy Against It.*

Maryland Historical Society for Selection 51, from MS in its possession.

Princeton University Press and The American Philosophical Society for Selection 49, from *Letters of Benjamin Rush,* ed. by L. H. Butterfield, Vol. II, Copyright 1951 by the American Philosophical Society.

CODED SOURCES IN THIS VOLUME

Butterfield	*Letters of Benjamin Rush.* Edited by L. H. Butterfield. In 2 vols. covering the years 1761-1813. Princeton, 1951.
C. F. Adams	*The Works of John Adams, Second President of the United States, with a Life of the Author.* Edited by Charles Francis Adams. In 10 vols. Boston, 1850-1856
Commons	*A Documentary History of American Industrial Society.* Edited by John R. Commons *et al.* In 10 vols. Cleveland, 1910-1911.
1 Cranch 137	*Reports of Cases Argued and Adjudged in the Supreme Court of the United States.* Edited by William Cranch. Vol. 1, Washington, 1804, pp. 137ff.
Debates	[Annals of Congress] *The Debates and Proceedings in the Congress of the United States with an Appendix Containing Important State Papers and Public Documents and All the Laws of a Public Nature; with a Copious Index.* In 42 vols. Washington, 1834-1856.
Elliot	*The Debates In the Several State Conventions on the Adoption of the Federal Constitution, etc., etc.* Edited by Jonathon Elliot. 2nd edition in 5 vols. Philadelphia, 1861. Vol. 4 reprinted 1876.
Ford	*The Writings of Thomas Jefferson.* Edited by Paul L. Ford. In 10 vols. New York and London, 1892-1899.
H. A. Washington	*The Writings of Thomas Jefferson: Being his Autobiography, Correspondence, Reports, Messages, Addresses and Other Writings, Official and Private.* Edited by H. A. Washington. In 9 vols. Washington, 1853-1854. Vol. 6, New York, 1884. Vol. 8, Philadelphia, 1871.
J. C. Hamilton	*The Works of Alexander Hamilton, etc., etc.* Edited by John C. Hamilton. In 7 vols. New York, 1850-1851.
Randolph	*Memoirs, Correspondence, and Private Papers of Thomas Jefferson.* Edited by Thomas Jefferson Randolph. In 4 vols. London (and Charlottesville, Va.), 1829.

Richardson	*A Compilation of the Messages and Papers of the Presidents 1789-1897.* Edited by James D. Richardson. In 10 vols. Washington, 1896-1899. New edition extended to 1908. Washington, 1909.
Statutes	*The Public Statutes at Large of the United States of America from the Organization of the Government in 1789, etc., etc.* In 79 vols. as of August 1966. 1845 *et seq.* Vol. 1-3 edited by Richard Peters. Boston, 1853, 1856.
TWA	*This Was America.* Edited by Oscar Handlin. Cambridge, 1949.
WGW	*The Writings of George Washington.* Edited by Worthington C. Ford. In 14 vols. New York, 1889-1893.
4 Wheaton 400 4 Wheaton 551 4 Wheaton 624	*Reports of Cases Argued and Adjudged in the Supreme Court of the United States.* Edited by Henry Wheaton. Vol. 4, New York, 1819, pp. 400ff.; 551ff.; 624ff.

Contents

Introduction, xviii
Chronology, 1797-1820, xxiii
Maps, xl

SELECTIONS

1797

1. Moses Austin: *Exploring the Ohio Valley,* 1
2. James Smith: *The Rich Land of the Frontier,* 10
3. *An Act to Prevent the Spreading of Contagious Sickness,* 13
4. Albert Gallatin: *A Profit Sharing Agreement,* 19

1798

5. Tadeusz Kosciuszko: *American Will and Testament,* 21
6. Benjamin H. Latrobe: *Thoughts on Education,* 22
7. Benjamin Rush: *Independence and Education,* 28
8. Timothy Dwight: *On the Duty of Americans at the Present Crisis,* 33
9. Charles Brockden Brown: *On the Essential Equality of the Sexes,* 40
10. Edward Livingston: *Against the Alien Act,* 49
11. *Debate on the Sedition Act,* 53
    "Long John" Allen: For the Sedition Act
    Albert Gallatin: Against the Sedition Act

12. *The Suppression of "Foreign" Opinion,* 59
The Alien Act
The Sedition Act

13. *The Kentucky and Virginia Resolutions of 1798,* 62
The Kentucky Resolutions
The Virginia Resolutions

14. FISHER AMES: *Undeclared War and Self-Defense,* 68

15. GEORGE WASHINGTON: *On the Disloyalty of Army Officers,* 71

16. *Opposition to a Standing Army,* 72

17. *Songs of Patriotism,* 73
JAMES HEWITT: "New Yankee Doodle"
ROBERT TREAT PAINE: "Adams and Liberty"
JOSEPH HOPKINSON: "Hail, Columbia!"

18. WILLIAM MANNING: *How the Few and Many Differ in Their Interests,* 76

1799

19. ALEXANDER HAMILTON: *The Beginnings of Expansion,* 101

20. *Massachusetts' Reply to the Kentucky and Virginia Resolutions of 1798,* 102

21. *The Kentucky Resolutions of 1799,* 106

22. JOHN WARD FENNO: *Our Economic Interests in the Caribbean,* 107

23. WILLIAM DUANE: *The Army and a Free Press,* 112

24. THOMAS JEFFERSON: *On Science and the Perfectibility of Man,* 113

25. GEORGE WASHINGTON: *Last Will and Testament,* 115

26. GOUVERNEUR MORRIS: *Appeal to Washington to Return to Public Life,* 119

1800

27. "Down in the Valley," 121

28. James Madison: *The Freedom of the Press,* 122

29. *Land Act of 1800,* 129

30. Tunis Wortman: *Despotism and the Freedom of Political Discussion,* 131

31. Benjamin Nones: *The Right To Be Poor and Radical,* 138

32. Thomas Jefferson: *A Simple and Inexpensive Government,* 140

1801

33. "Jefferson and Liberty," 142

34. Thomas Jefferson: *First Inaugural Address,* 143

35. *A Plan of Union for Protestant Churches,* 146

36. Thomas Jefferson: *On Accommodating the Negroes,* 147

1802

37. Thomas Jefferson: *The Threat of the French in Louisiana,* 150

38. Gouverneur Morris: *On the Union of Talents and Property,* 153

39. François André Michaux: *Frontier Kentucky,* 154

1803

40. Thomas Jefferson: *The Lewis and Clark Expedition,* 158
    Confidential Message to Congress
    Instructions to Meriwether Lewis

41. John Marshall: *Marbury* v. *Madison,* 165

42. Thomas Jefferson: *The Politics of the Louisiana Purchase,* 171
    Letter to John Breckinridge, August 12
    Letter to Breckinridge, August 18
    Proposed Constitutional Amendment

43. Thomas Jefferson: *On the Admission of New States,* 173

44. Samuel White: *Opposition to the Louisiana Purchase,* 175

1804

45. Timothy Pickering: *On Northern Secession,* 189

46. Abigail Adams: *On Presidential Appointments,* 191

1805

47. Red Jacket: *Against White Missions Among the Indians,* 194

48. John Adams: *On a Natural History of the Country,* 196

49. Benjamin Rush: *On Political Parties and the Romance of History,* 199

50. Fisher Ames: *The Passions and Tyranny of the Many,* 201

1806

51. Benjamin H. Latrobe: *Gentlemen-Architects and Building-Mechanics,* 204

52. Lorenzo Dow: *The Jerks,* 208

53. *The Trial of the Journeymen Boot- and Shoe-Makers,* 210

1807

54. *Act to Prohibit the Importation of Slaves,* 216

55. Thomas Jefferson: *On Misreporting by the Press,* 219

56. Fortescue Cuming: *A Tour to the Western Country,* 221

57. Joel Barlow: *Preface and Postscript to* The Columbiad, 227

58. *The Embargo Act,* 233

1808

59. Thomas Jefferson: *On the Civil and Religious Powers of Government,* 234

60. George Hay: *Aaron Burr's Conspiracy,* 235

1809

61. JACOB HENRY: *Private Belief and Public Office,* 239

62. THOMAS CAMPBELL: *Christian Union,* 242

1810

63. JOHN RANDOLPH: *Against Trade Restrictions,* 248

64. ALBERT GALLATIN: *The State of Manufacturing,* 259

65. THOMAS JEFFERSON: *On Authorities Beyond the Law,* 268

66. CHARLES J. INGERSOLL: *The National Character of Americans,* 270

67. TIMOTHY DWIGHT: *The Restless Frontiersman,* 278

1811

68. *State Aid for Jewish Schools,* 282

69. JOSIAH QUINCY: *Against the Admission of New States,* 283

70. JAMES MADISON: *The Civil and Religious Functions of Government,* 287

71. *On a Northern Confederation,* 288
    Benjamin Waterhouse to John Adams
    Adams to Waterhouse

72. *Debate Over War with England,* 291
    FELIX GRUNDY: War as a Means of Continental Expansion
    RICHARD M. JOHNSON: For War with England
    JOHN RANDOLPH: Against War with England

1812

73. DAVID HOSACK: *On the Progress of Medical Education,* 307

74. JOHN ADAMS: *Thoughts on Current Politics,* 311

75. JAMES MADISON: *War Message,* 314

76. OBADIAH GERMAN: *Unprepared for War with England,* 319

77. John Adams: *Party Divisions in America*, 324

78. "Ye Parliament of England," 325

1813

79. Henry Clay: *For a Vigorous Prosecution of the War*, 327

80. *Opposed Views on Aristocracy*, 331
    John Adams to Thomas Jefferson, July 9
    Adams to Jefferson, August
    Adams to Jefferson, September 2
    Jefferson to Adams, October 28
    Adams to Jefferson, November 15

81. Thomas Jefferson: *Isolation and Independence*, 340

1814

82. John Taylor: *True and False Aristocracies*, 342

83. Thomas Jefferson: *On the Censorship of Religious Books*, 348

84. Thomas Jefferson: *Elementary, General, and Professional Schools*, 350

85. Francis Scott Key: "The Star-Spangled Banner," 353

86. Daniel Webster: *Against Conscription*, 355

1815

87. *New England and the Union*, 371

88. Noah Worcester: *War and Popular Delusion*, 375

89. Thomas Jefferson: *The Sphere of Religion*, 383

90. Richard Rush: *Jurisprudence and the Common Law*, 385

91. Thomas Jefferson: *On the Constitutional Powers of the Branches of Government*, 390

92. Thomas Jefferson: *On the Balance of Power in Europe*, 391

93. Robert Finley: *National Uniformity in Textbooks and Curricula*, 393

94. Hezekiah Niles: *National Unity and Prosperity,* 397

95. Hugh H. Brackenridge: *Should Beasts Vote?,* 400

96. "Hunters of Kentucky," 405

97. Alexander J. Dallas: *Proposal for a National Bank,* 406

1816

98. Thomas Jefferson: *On the Present Need to Promote Manufacturing,* 412

99. Thomas Jefferson: *The Rulers and the Ruled,* 414

100. Thomas Jefferson: *On Republican Government,* 416

101. Thomas Jefferson: *On Civil and Natural Rights,* 419

102. William Plumer: *State Control of Dartmouth College,* 420

103. Thomas Jefferson: *The Roots of Democracy,* 422

104. John Randolph: *Against a Protective Tariff,* 427

105. *Hints to Emigrants from Europe,* 429

106. Jacob Bigelow: *The Future of the Arts and Sciences,* 449

107. *Displacement of Free Negroes,* 451

1817

108. John C. Calhoun: *Roadways and Waterways,* 457

109. James Madison: *On the Commerce Clause,* 462

110. John Quincy Adams: *On the Revolutions in Latin America,* 464

1818

111. John Adams: *The Meaning of the American Revolution,* 465

112. Elias Pym Fordham: *Opportunities in the West,* 470

113. *Land Sale Advertisement,* 473

114. *An Irish Colony in Illinois,* 476

115. DANIEL WEBSTER: *Contracts and Corporate Charters,* 477

116. HENRY CLAY: *Internal Improvements and the Powers of Congress,* 482

117. HENRY CLAY: *Recognition for Latin American Governments,* 488

118. THOMAS JEFFERSON: *The Education of Women,* 490

119. BARON DE MONTLEZUN: *American Women and American Character,* 492

120. *French Emigrants to America,* 495

121. ROBERT LEE: *A Society for a National Literature,* 497

122. ANONYMOUS: *Opposition to Paper Money,* 500

123. JAMES MADISON: *Agriculture and Conservation,* 503

124. *A Christian Indictment of Slavery,* 507

125. *Report on the Proposed University of Virginia,* 510

126. *Public Works in the State of Virginia,* 515

1819

127. JOHN MARSHALL: *Dartmouth College* v. *Woodward,* 522

128. *Apprentice Labor Act,* 528

129. JOHN MARSHALL: *M'Culloch* v. *Maryland,* 530

130. SPENCER ROANE: *Defense of the Power of State Courts,* 539

131. WILLIAM ELLERY CHANNING: *An Attack on Orthodox Calvinism,* 544

132. HENRY M. BRACKENRIDGE: *A Vindication of Civil Rights for Jews,* 552

133. GIOVANNI ANTONIO GRASSI: *Observations on the United States,* 560

134. WILLIAM COBBETT: *A Year in the United States,* 567

135. EMMA HART WILLARD: *Education and the Weaker Sex,* 574

136. RUFUS KING: *Against the Extension of Slavery to the New States,* 579

137. ANONYMOUS: *Against Restriction of Slavery to the Southern States*, 587

1820

138. JOHN QUINCY ADAMS: *Slavery and the Constitution*, 589

139. *Missouri Enabling Act*, 591

140. THOMAS JEFFERSON: *A Firebell in the Night*, 603

141. *Against a Protective Tariff*, 604
Fredericksburg Remonstrance
Salem Memorial

142. HENRY CLAY: *Manufacturing and a Protective Tariff*, 612

143. DANIEL RAYMOND: *The Role of Labor in the National Wealth*, 623

144. JAMES FLINT: *The Panic in Indiana*, 632

145. DANIEL WEBSTER: *Property and Political Power*, 634

146. *For Wider Suffrage*, 640

147. JOHN QUINCY ADAMS: *On America and European Alliances*, 642

148. ROBERT MILLS: *The Beginnings of American Architecture*, 645

149. JAMES KIRKE PAULDING: *On the Scarcity of Romantic Fiction in America*, 648

150. JOSEPH RODMAN DRAKE: "The American Flag," 650

Index of Authors, 652

CONSOLIDATION OF THE REPUBLIC
In Pictures

Images of American Life 87-100

The government was moved to the new capital at Washington, D.C., but Philadelphia remained the country's cultural center. In the South a new demand for cotton fortified the slave-labor system and aroused interest in Indian land in Alabama and Mississippi.

Exploring the West 177-188

Acquisition of the Louisiana Territory more than doubled the size of the United States. Fur traders and official government explorers were the first to chart these regions, which served as an outlet for Indians driven west by the migration of Americans into Ohio and the Northwest Territory.

Politics 251-258

Before the War of 1812 political argument centered on relations with England and France and the economic problems of an insecure international position. Diverse sectional interests compounded these issues and increasingly dominated domestic policy after the war.

War of 1812 299-306

Even though the war was militarily inconclusive, peace brought an end to harrassment of American shipping and to British-supported Indian resistance in Ohio.

City and Farm 359-370

Commercial prosperity in the major port cities freed some for theater-going and leisure activities, but life in the towns and villages remained largely unchanged.

Commerce and Enterprise 439-448

While sea trade and whaling brought wealth to Northern ports, technological innovation created the foundations for industry and revolutionized the agricultural economy.

Transition in the Arts 593-602

With few domestic traditions to draw on, ambitious American artists sought inspiration on the Continent. The first distinct school of American architecture was inspired almost entirely by classical models.

Introduction

These were the years of the nation's adolescence, when it tried out its inventions of constitutional government and federalism on the stage not only of the continent but of the world. It was an era of trials, from most of which the country emerged strengthened rather than weakened, as its enemies (and some of its friends) expected; it was an era of achievement, too, during which the younger generation of Revolutionary leaders inherited the mantle of rule, and, sobered by office, converted youthful zeal into mature policy. But all was not sobriety and wisdom in these eventful years. Indeed, a note of experimentation, not to say recklessness and bravado, pervades the epoch and helps to give it its characteristic youthfulness. Americans acted then as if insoluble problems did not face the country — and thereby, perhaps, made the problems soluble.

One of the problems was the vast area of land beyond the Alleghenies, into which a few hardy souls had been venturing for a generation, but into which the many now began to pour. Volume 4 opens with two selections that are typical of the time. Moses Austin's report of a journey in the Ohio Valley in 1797 (Selection 1) is somewhat less than enthusiastic; this was frontier country then, and the natural obstacles to travel encountered in a wilderness were magnified by the ever-present danger of lurking Indians — or "aborigines," as Austin called them. But the obstacles and dangers were more than balanced, in the view of men like James Smith (see Selection 2), by the almost incredible riches to be found along those pure streams, on those empty plains and hillsides, and under that quiet sky. In the end, as we now know, the Smiths outnumbered the Austins, for by 1820 — the terminal date of this volume — most of the Ohio Valley, and much of the land beyond it to the west, had been flowed over by the wave of settlement, and Americans were beginning to look even farther west.

Thomas Jefferson was one of the most enthusiastic of all. President from 1801-1809, he is the author of no less than twenty-six selections in the volume, and the subject of many more. The letters, official documents, and other writings of Jefferson reprinted here reveal the extraordinary range and power of his mind — he had an opinion on everything, and almost always an interesting one — but there was nothing, perhaps, that interested *him* more than the great vacuum on the western side of the mountains, on the eastern slopes of which stood his lovely home, Monticello. His was a grand vision, and partly as a result of that, and partly as a result of Napoleon's troubles with the British Navy, Jefferson gained for the nation its largest single territorial acquisition up to that time, and possibly the most valuable single acquisition ever gained by any country in the history of the world: the so-called Louisiana Territory. Jefferson, indeed, was so anxious to purchase Louisiana that he was not above practising what he suspected were some unconstitutional shenanigans in order to do it. (The nation has found it easy to forgive him.) In addition, he asked one of his friends, Meriwether Lewis, who in turn asked *his* friend, William Clark, to go out and take a look at what he had bought. They reported back, in effect, that the pig that had been purchased in the poke was a paradise. (For discussion of the Louisiana Purchase and the Lewis and Clark Expedition, see, among others, Selections 40, 42, 43, and 44.)

There were other problems that could not be solved so easily, in this period that saw the establishment of the party system in American politics. The differences between Hamilton's Federalist Party and Jefferson's Democratic-Republican had already attained serious proportions during Washington's second term (from 1793 to 1797), and they increased markedly during the administration of our second President, the Federalist John Adams (1797-1801). Much of the strife was caused by domestic difficulties, but it was exacerbated by the war raging in Europe, for the Federalists tended on the whole to support England, and the Republicans to support France (partly out of gratitude for French assistance in the Revolution). The European belligerents could not, or at least did not, consider American views to be very important, and both, but especially the French, treated our vessels cavalierly on the high seas. The Federalist-dominated Congress, in response to some particularly high-handed actions on the part of the French, passed the notorious Alien and Sedition Acts of 1798 (Selection 12). Jefferson, moved to some extent by partisan feeling but mainly by his deep and abiding faith in liberty, drafted the Kentucky Resolutions of 1798, and got his protégé James Madison to draft the Virginia Resolutions of the same year (Selection 13). Both resolutions expressed strong opposition to the Alien and Sedition Acts, which had been used by the Federalists to silence some Republican newspaper editors, and even went so far as to hint at, if not explicitly to state, the doctrine of "nullification" that rose again to torment the Union in the era before the Civil War. The doctrine, summarized, was that any state that disapproved of a federal law or policy could declare it null and void, at least within the state's territorial bounds. It was fraught with obvious dangers that Jefferson himself recognized. (For the controversy about the Alien and Sedition Acts, and about the question of a standing army for protection against an expected French and/or British attack, see also Selections 8, 10, 16, 20, 21, and 26.)

Diplomatic difficulties with both England and France troubled Jefferson's two terms. By 1812, with Jefferson retired and his successor Madison in the White House, the villain had clearly become Britain and not France, and the question arose once more of war. War had been avoided in 1798-1799, but this time it could not be, or at least was not, owing in part to Madison's courage (some called it criminal recklessness). He knew the country to be unprepared, and yet he plunged it into war — as other Presidents have been accused of doing, in other times. Madison threw forward the flag of the country, as he later put it, sure that the people would follow. Perhaps, however, it was not such a gamble after all. Anyone who read the newspapers could not fail to know that Britain had her hands full with Napoleon.

The conflict, not unlike several others in which we have been involved, was one in which we lost most of the battles (Washington was sacked, the Capitol burned, in 1814) but ended up winning the war. It was hardly a notable victory, but it gave notice to Europe that the young nation was not to be trifled with and helped establish the succeeding period as the Era of Good Feelings — so called because of the general optimism that prevailed during President Monroe's first term (1817-1821). The war also had two other memorable results. The young lawyer Francis Scott Key stayed up all night on September 13-14, 1814, to watch the British bombardment of Fort McHenry, in Baltimore, and improved the long hours by composing the verses that became our national anthem. And on January 8, 1815, General Andrew Jackson won the Battle of New Orleans and established himself as the most compelling national hero since Washington. (For differing views of the events leading up to the War of 1812, reports of some notable occurrences of the conflict, and a few of its results, see Selections 72, 74-79, 81, 85, 86, 88, and 92.)

The greatest problem of all was not caused by foreign difficulties but rather by the very nature of the country's situation and its prospects. The Constitution had been adopted in 1791 by the thirteen original states, strung up and down the Atlantic coast, and all of them east of the mountains. As the settlers filled the empty lands west of the mountains, the pressure on the government to create new states and to absorb them into the federal organization grew intense. In 1811-1812 New England began to be disturbed. The importance of the transmontane region was not yet great, but what would happen to the delicate federal balance when the new states in the South and West grew populous, and were furthermore filled with people who had very different interests from those in the states along the Atlantic seaboard? One possibility — it was a threat that was only partly veiled — was secession, and the formation of a New England Confederation (see Selections 69, 71, and 87).

The crisis did not come to a head at the time, mainly because of the war, but the problem arose again with the application for statehood by the Missouri Territory. This administrative change might have proceeded smoothly were it not for the action of James Tallmadge, a congressman from New York, who on February 13, 1819, moved to prohibit the further introduction of slaves into the Louisiana Purchase. The motion, supported by many Northern senators and representatives, threatened to upset the even balance of slave and free states admitted alternately, by tacit agreement, since 1802, and the ensuing controversy was only resolved by the Missouri Compromise (March 3, 1820), according to which the admission of Missouri as a slave state was balanced by the admission of free Maine. But the Compromise went further, and included in its terms a provision that slavery should henceforth be excluded north of latitude 36°30′, the *southern* boundary of Missouri and roughly the *northern* boundary of North Carolina, Tennessee, and Arkansas.

The separation of New England from the rest of the country had been primarily geographical. This new line of division was not geographical but ideological. All of the great distinguishing features of North American geology run north and south, but this line ran east and west, and divided the country on the basis not of physical differences between regions but of a principle. As such, it alarmed Jefferson, as he put it, "like a firebell in the night." He went on to predict the most dire consequences of the decision. "I considered it at once," he wrote, "as the knell of the Union. . . . A geographical line, coinciding with a marked principle, once conceived and held up to the angry passions of men, will never be obliterated; and every new irritation will make it deeper and deeper" (Selection 140. For other views of the Missouri Compromise, see Selections 136, 137, 138, and 139.)

All was not problems — it never is. This volume of *Annals* contains many comments on matters of less immediate import than foreign war and civil strife. Education, for example — see Selections 6, 7, 24, 73, 84, 93, 102, and 127. Women: see Selections 9, 118, 119, and 135. Religion: see Selections 35, 47, 52, 59, 61, 83, and 89. Civil rights: see especially Selections 28, 30, and 101. And both natives and visitors, then as now, were considering the question of whether there is any such thing, after all, as an *American* character. Charles J. Ingersoll's thoughts on the subject in 1810 (Selection 66) are of particular interest, for he had much to say that anticipated the conclusions of the great Frenchman, Alexis de Tocqueville, who would arrive on the scene twenty years later.

Several other subjects are notable among the many that are discussed by the authors represented in the volume. Some Americans believed that the United States could survive without a formally recognized aristocracy — either of birth or of talents. A number of writers discoursed on the question, among them William Manning, in 1798 (Selection 18), who was a spokesman for the many, Fisher Ames, in 1805 (Selection 50), a spokesman for the few, and John Taylor, in 1814 (Selection 82), who drew some needed distinctions. But it was John Adams and Thomas Jefferson who had the most memorable things to say. One-time political opponents, these two men, once leaders and later the "grand old men" of their respective sections of the country, found each other again in a long and wonderful correspondence after years of angry silence. They wrote to each other about anything and everything; in the summer and fall of 1813 they exchanged a series of letters (Selection 80) on aristocracy that will repay anyone the time spent in reading them.

One other incidental note, but a prophetic one. Jacob Bigelow was installed in the Rumford chair of application of science to the useful arts at Harvard in 1816, and gave an inaugural lecture (see Selection 106) in which he reviewed past American attainments in the arts and science, and predicted future ones; he also urged that practicality rather than elegance be adopted as the criterion of achievement in such endeavors. Thus far, many in the era agreed with him. But Bigelow went further, and in the course of his teaching of mechanics, for which he is said to have had a passion, invented the word "technology."

The particular political troubles of the period covered by this volume of *Annals* may have long been forgotten. But the principles that underlie them remain as relevant as ever, and their viability has been tested, perhaps above all, by the phenomenon for which Bigelow found a name.

Chronology: 1797 - 1820

1797

May 31. XYZ Affair. President John Adams appoints three-man commission consisting of Charles Cotesworth Pinckney, American Minister to Britain, John Marshall and Elbridge Gerry to seek treaty of commerce and amity with France. The French Directory, convinced that Jay's Treaty shows U.S. partiality toward Britain, has refused to receive Pinckney in December 1796 and has regularly interfered with American shipping (over 300 vessels have been lost in one year). **Oct. 4.** Commissioners arrive in Paris and are visited on October 18 by three agents of French Foreign Minister Talleyrand (identified in commission reports as X, Y, and Z). Agents suggest a U.S. loan to France and a $240,000 bribe for Talleyrand himself; they also threaten war between France and U.S. Commission refuses emphatically.

Preaching of James McGready, leader of camp meeting movement, is beginning of great religious revival on Western frontier.

1798

March 19. President Adams reports to Congress only that French mission has failed and says that America must prepare for war. **April 3.** Strong pro-French and anti-British protest forces Adams to submit XYZ correspondence to Congress, swinging public opinion against France. **March-July** In preparation for war, Congress passes 20 measures to strengthen national defense. **July 2.** George Washington is called from retirement to serve as commander in chief with Alexander Hamilton as second in command. **May 3.** Navy Department is established. **July 7.** Existing treaties with France are repealed. **Nov. 20.** Two years of undeclared war begin; isolated engagements include capture of French *L'Insurgente* by U.S. frigate *Constellation* on February 9, 1799.

Fear of war with France results in suspicion of aliens in U.S. **June-July.** Naturalization Act of June 18, Alien Act of June 25, Alien Enemies Act of July 6, and Sedition Act of July 14 passed by Federalist majority in Congress restrict activities (including freedom of speech) of citizens and European refugees, among whom are prominent supporters of Jefferson's party. Ten Republican newspaper editors are convicted, fined, and jailed for sedition.

November-December. Virginia and Kentucky Resolutions, framed by James Madison and Thomas Jefferson passed by Virginia and Kentucky legislatures; Resolutions declare that Alien and Sedition Acts are unconstitutional and that in such a case, states are "duty bound to interpose."

Calder v. *Bull* declares that prohibition against *ex post facto* laws (laws passed after a crime is committed) in Article I, Section 10 of Constitution applies only to criminal, not civil, laws.

Organization of Mississippi Territory, region between Georgia's western border and Mississippi River, opens this area to settlement, but most colonization is delayed by hostility of Indians and by Spanish control of West Florida ports.

Benjamin Thompson, Count Rumford, Loyalist exile, reports on his experiments in England involving heat as a form of motion.

Words of "Hail Columbia" by Joseph Hopkinson set to music of "The President's March" (*c.* 1793) thought to be work of Philip Roth or Philip Phile. Robert Treat Paine writes words of song "Adams and Liberty."

1798 - 1800

1798. Eli Whitney begins manufacture of 10,000 muskets for U.S. **1800.** Whitney devises system of interchangeable gun parts which, with additional machinery, makes it possible to use comparatively inexperienced workmen in his factory.

1799

Feb. 18. President Adams averts war with France by nominating William Vans Murray new minister to France on Talleyrand's assurance of respectful reception; thwarts prowar faction among Federalists by appointing new members to former Commission, two of whom are Federalists.

February. John Fries and several hundred Pennsylvania men rebel against payment of property tax established in 1798 in anticipation of French War. Fries resists U.S. marshal, is convicted of treason, but is pardoned by President Adams.

Dec. 14. George Washington dies at Mount Vernon, after catching a cold that develops into a severe sore throat. He is buried at Mount Vernon.

Publication of *The Practical Navigator,* which remains a classic work of reference for seamen, by Nathaniel Bowditch; also *Arthur Mervyn,* a fictionalized but accurate account of Philadelphia's yellow fever epidemic, by Charles Brockden Brown.

First Negro minstrel act is shown in the play *Oroonoko,* produced in Boston, when an actor made up in black-face sings "The Gay Negro Boy," accompanying himself on banjo.

1800

April 4. First federal bankruptcy law, applying only to merchants and traders, allows release from prison of Robert Morris, Revolutionary superintendent of finances who personally arranged for payment of the armed forces. Financially ruined in various land speculations, he had been confined to debtor's prison since 1798.

May 10. Land Act of 1800, also known as Harrison Land Act, reduces minimum purchase of public lands from 640 to 320 acres (half sections), establishes liberal credit terms. Resulting sales in first 18 months of enactment are 400,000 acres, as compared with less than 50,000 sold under Act of 1796, but much of the purchasing is by speculators rather than settlers.

Sept. 30. Convention of 1800 (Treaty of Morfontaine) is signed by France and the

U.S.; it abrogates U.S.-French Revolutionary alliance, brings French crisis of 1797-1800 to an end. Split in Federalist Party occurs over Adams' handling of French situation.

Oct. 1. Napoleon Bonaparte forces Spain to cede Louisiana to France by secret Treaty of San Ildefonso as move to revive French colonial empire in North America; France does not take possession.

Nov. 17. Congress convenes for first time in Washington, D.C.

Second U.S. census shows population of 5,308,000, an increase of 35 percent since 1790; figure includes 43,000 immigrants.

United Brethren in Christ founded by Martin Boehm and Philip E. Otterbein, who are first bishops.

Thomas Jefferson donates his private library to the federal government as initial collection in establishing Library of Congress.

Clergyman-bookseller Mason Locke ("Parson") Weems writes his widely popular but historically inaccurate *The Life and Memorable Actions of George Washington.*

1800 - 1802

1800. Cowpox vaccination to prevent smallpox introduced by Dr. Benjamin Waterhouse in Philadelphia. **Oct.-Nov. 1802.** Boston Board of Health experiments prove safety and effectiveness of vaccine.

1801

Jan. 20. John Marshall appointed Chief Justice of the Supreme Court in one of President Adams' last official acts.

Feb. 11. Count of ballots of presidential electors (cast December 3, 1800) shows a tie between Democratic-Republicans Jefferson and Aaron Burr each with 73 votes. Federalists John Adams, Charles Cotesworth Pinckney, and John Jay receive 65, 64, and 1 vote respectively. **Feb. 17.** House of Representatives, with one vote per state, elects Jefferson third President of the U.S. on thirty-sixth ballot by vote of 10 to 6 when Hamilton uses his influence against Burr, whom he considers the greater evil. Burr is elected Vice-President.

Feb. 27. Judiciary Act reduces number of Supreme Court justices to five, creates sixteen new circuit judgeships as well as positions for attorneys, marshals, and clerks. President Adams places Federalists in these positions in "midnight" appointments lasting until 9 P.M. on March 3, his last day in office, in effort to maintain Federalist power after losing presidency.

March 4. Jefferson inaugurated; first President to take office in District of Columbia. Inaugural address sets forth Democratic-Republican program, stressing economy and need for limits to power of central government.

May 14. Naval conflict with Tripoli begins when Tripolitan Pasha, demanding increase in tribute customarily paid to pirates of the Barbary States by foreign ships, declares war on U.S. President Jefferson dispatches naval vessels to Mediterranean, where blockade eventually brings war to an end. Peace treaty is signed by U.S. and Tripoli, but tribute payments to other Barbary States (Algiers, Tunis, and Morocco) are made until 1816.

New York Evening Post, Federalist newspaper, founded by Alexander Hamilton and others.

1801 - 1802

U.S. economic prosperity of 1789-1800, due largely to European wartime demand for U.S. products, is halted briefly by Peace of Amiens, temporary lull in European war.

1802

March 8. Judiciary Act of 1801 repealed in spite of opposition of Vice-President Burr. **April 29.** Act is replaced by measure that reduces number of circuit judges to six from sixteen and restores to six the number of Supreme Court judges previously reduced to five.

March 16. U.S. Military Academy established by Act of Congress; training school formally opens at West Point on July 4.

Benjamin Silliman, appointed Yale's first professor of chemistry and natural history, begins long career as influential teacher and popularizer of science.

1802 - 1809

Jefferson administration's retrenchment policy, planned and carried out by Secretary of the Treasury Albert Gallatin, increases customs duties, makes it possible to repeal excise taxes in 1802, and still reduces national debt from $83 million to $57 million by 1809.

1803

Feb. 24. Supreme Court voids an act of Congress for the first time in *Marbury* v. *Madison,* thus establishing its right to rule on the constitutionality of U.S. laws. No other congressional act is declared unconstitutional until 1857.

March 1. Ohio admitted to the Union as seventeenth state. Formerly eastern part of Northwest Territory, and still called Northwest Territory after western region became Indiana Territory in 1800, population has grown to 70,000 since peace with Indians in 1794. Slavery is prohibited.

April 30. France cedes Louisiana (the western half of the Mississippi Valley) to U.S. for $11,250,000 plus $3,750,000 debt to U.S. citizens owed by France and assumed by U.S. Purchase of 828,000 square miles, or more than 500 million acres, doubles area of U.S. Purchase of foreign territory is resisted by Federalists as not provided for in the Constitution but is approved by Senate on October 20, eventually upheld by Supreme Court in 1828. **Dec. 20.** U.S. takes formal possession of area.

1803 - 1806

Aug. 31, 1803. Captain Meriwether Lewis, President Jefferson's secretary, and William Clark begin exploration of lands west of the Mississippi River, authorized by Congress at President Jefferson's request. Expedition follows Ohio, Missouri, and Columbia rivers to Pacific Ocean, and returns by similar route, a total of 8,000 miles. **Sept. 23, 1806.** Expedition ends on return to St. Louis, having demonstrated that an overland route to the Far West is practicable.

1804

March 12. U.S. Senate removes Judge John Pickering from his post as federal district judge in New Hampshire as unfit to serve. Justice Samuel Chase, associate justice of the Supreme Court, is impeached on charge of bias, but acquitted in trial in Senate next year. Latter case finally frustrates Jefferson's efforts to assert authority over Federalist judiciary.

March 26. Land Act of 1804 reduces minimum cash payment for Western lands from $2 an acre to $1.64, permits minimum purchase of a quarter section (160 acres).

Group of extremist New England Federalists, the Essex Junto, plan to organize a separate New England Confederacy (including New York and New Jersey) in alliance with Aaron Burr. **April 25.** Plan is frustrated when Burr is defeated in attempt to become governor of New York through efforts of Alexander Hamilton. **July 11.** Burr's demand for explanation of slur on his character leads to Hamilton-Burr duel in which Hamilton is mortally wounded, dying on the following day.

Sept. 25. Twelfth Amendment to Constitution, proposed by Congress in 1803, is declared ratified, providing separate voting for President and Vice-President.

Dec. 5. In first election with separate presidential and vice-presidential balloting, Jefferson is overwhelmingly reelected, with George Clinton of New York as Vice-President, both by vote of 162 to 14. Federalist opponents are Charles Cotesworth Pinckney and Rufus King.

Louisiana Purchase land is divided; area of present-day Louisiana is organized as Territory of Orleans; remainder becomes District of Louisiana.

1805

Northern section of Indiana Territory organized as Michigan Territory. District of Louisiana becomes Louisiana Territory.

Free School Society (later Public School Society) is founded in New York as a private philanthropic body concerned with establishing an alternative to the pauper school system. De Witt Clinton, mayor of New York City, is first president of board of trustees.

Lorenzo da Ponte arrives in U.S.; Italian poet, librettist of Mozart's *Don Giovanni,* he becomes professor of Italian literature at Columbia College, and actively promotes Italian opera in U.S.

Boston Athenaeum is built to house George Washington's library, bought by a group of Boston citizens.

1805 - 1806

Aug. 9, 1805-April 30, 1806. Lieutenant Zebulon Montgomery Pike explores the upper Mississippi River on orders of General James Wilkinson, commander of U.S. forces in the Mississippi Valley, but fails to find the true source of the river. He sights Pikes Peak, Colorado, in second expedition of 1806-1807, but does not climb it.

1806

Jan. 25. Secretary of State James Madison reports to Congress on results of resumption of Napoleonic wars (1803); British have renewed efforts to close French ports to neutral shipping, which results in interference (restrictions, seizures, impressment of American seamen into British service) with American vessels. **Feb. 12.** Senate passes resolution attacking "unprovoked aggression," which Britain ignores. **April 18.** Congress passes Non-Importation Act prohibiting purchase of British goods, but this is suspended after a month at President Jefferson's request. **May 16.** British declare a general blockade of European Continent. **Nov. 21.** Napoleon responds with Berlin Decree blockading British Isles and authorizing seizure of blockade-running vessels.

Dec. 31. Monroe-Pinkney Treaty is negotiated in London by Minister to Britain James Monroe and special envoy William Pinkney, who threaten to enforce Non-Importation Act; treaty achieves no significant British concession, is never submitted to the Senate by President Jefferson, who continues to seek a more favorable agreement.

Trial of striking Philadelphia Cordwainers is first prosecution of trade union as common-law conspiracy; union is disbanded.

1807

June 22. U.S. frigate *Chesapeake* is attacked by British frigate *Leopard* off Norfolk, Virginia, after British commander demands surrender of four seamen alleged to be British subjects, and American commodore refuses to allow search. **July 2.** President Jefferson orders British warships from U.S. territorial waters. **Oct. 17.** British respond with announcement of intention to pursue impressment of British seamen from neutral ships even more rigorously.

Aug. 3-Sept. 1. Aaron Burr tried for treason after he is arrested while on mysterious western expedition thought to have as its aim either the formation of a Western empire through seizure of Spanish possessions in Mexico and the Southwest (a misdemeanor) or separating the Western states from the U.S. (treason). Tried for treason before Chief Justice Marshall, sitting in Circuit Court at Richmond, Virginia, Burr is acquitted on Marshall's narrow construction, afterward a settled principle, of U.S. law of treason. After trial, Burr goes to Europe to avoid prosecution for murder of Hamilton in New York and New Jersey and treason in Ohio, Louisiana, Mississippi, and Kentucky.

Aug. 17. First successful steamboat, the *Clermont,* built by Robert Fulton with two side paddlewheels and a Watt steam engine, sails from New York; it reaches Albany in 32 hours; return trip is made in 30 hours.

Nov. 11. British retaliate against Napoleon's Berlin Decree of 1806 by Orders in Council prohibiting all trade with ports closed to British ships and requiring duty paid at British ports from vessels bound to European ports still open. **Dec. 17.** Napoleon, in turn, issues Milan Decree declaring forfeit any shipping that obeys the Orders in Council.

Dec. 18. In response to British and French trade restrictions, President Jefferson recommends an embargo to Congress prohibiting further commerce with any foreign nation. **Dec. 22.** Act is passed by Southern and Western votes over objection of commercial states.

Eli Terry and Seth Thomas of Connecticut begin manufacture in quantity of clocks with interchangeable parts.

Agricultural fair movement, important for spread of scientific farming, begins under sponsorship of Elkanah Watson with exhibit of Merino sheep in Pittsfield, Massachusetts.

1808

Jan. 1. African slave trade prohibited by act of Congress, but illicit trade persists (estimated import of slaves from 1808 to 1860 is 250,000). By date of act, sale of unneeded slaves within U.S. from agriculturally exhausted areas to fertile ones has become more profitable than soil cultivation.

Jan. 9 and March 12. Additional embargo acts, strengthening Act of 1807, are ineffectual as domestic opposition leads to smuggling and other illegal trade. **April 17.** Napoleon, on pretext that embargo is effective, issues Bayonne Decree authorizing seizure of U.S. shipping in continental ports as presumptively British vessels with false papers; $10 million in U.S. goods and vessels is confiscated by French in 1808 and 1809. British economy is largely unaffected by embargo, since South America is alternative source of supply and British commerce thrives without American competition.

Dec. 7. President Jefferson, having declined to run for a third term, supports James Madison, who is elected to the presidency with 122 electoral votes over Federalist Charles Cotesworth Pinckney (47 votes) and over Vice-President George Clinton (6 votes), nominated by anti-embargo Eastern Republicans. Clinton, who also runs for the vice-presidency, is reelected.

John Jacob Astor incorporates American Fur Company, the first of several companies founded by him in the West that make him the dominant figure in the industry and, at his death, the richest man in the U.S.

1809

Stimulus to New England manufactures from embargo is outweighed by heavy shipping losses. **Jan.-Feb.** Economic distress inspires protests by town meetings and state legislatures, especially those of Massachusetts and Connecticut. State governors refuse cooperation for enforcement.

March. 1. Illinois Territory formed; region was originally part of "Territory Northwest of the River Ohio," and subsequently part of Indiana Territory.

March 1. President Jefferson, beset by criticism from both Federalists and dissidents in his own party, signs Non-Intercourse Act, repealing embargo and reopening trade with all nations except France and England as one of his last official acts before leaving office. **April 19.** On assurances by British Minister David M. Erskine that Orders in Council will be repealed, President Madison proclaims resumption of trade with Britain. **Aug. 9.** Non-Intercourse Act is revived when British government repudiates Erskine.

Publication of popular satire, *A History of New York . . . by Diedrich Knickerbocker,* the work of Washington Irving.

1810

May 1. Over solid Federalist opposition, Congress passes Macon's Bill Number 2, authorizing President Madison to reopen trade with France and England and stipulating that if either country removes its commercial restrictions before March 3, 1811, Non-Intercourse Act may be revived against the other. Napoleon, acting through French Foreign Minister the Duc de Cadore, then deceives Madison into believing that Berlin and Milan decrees are canceled, though in fact they are implemented by a fresh decree signed August 5 ordering seizure of U.S. vessels that have called at French ports before passage of Macon's Bill. **Nov. 2.** President Madison reopens trade with France and revives Non-Intercourse Act against Britain, voted by Congress March 2, 1811.

Sept. 26. Uprising of Southern expansionists against Spanish rule results in capture of fort at Baton Rouge in West Florida and proclamation of area's independence as the Republic of West Florida. **Oct. 27.** President Madison annexes West Florida (present-day southern parts of Mississippi, Alabama, and Louisiana) and announces military occupation and absorption into Orleans Territory on ground of consent by local authority.

Third U.S. census shows population of 7,239,000 — a gain of 36.4 percent since

1800; figure includes 60,000 immigrants arrived since 1800 and about 1,200,000 slaves, almost entirely in the South.

Boston Philharmonic Society, first regularly performing symphony orchestra in United States, founded by Gottlieb Graupner; it is discontinued in 1824.

1811

Jan. 24-Feb. 20. Administration attempts to renew charter of Alexander Hamilton's Bank of the United States (chartered in 1791 for 20 years), but fails when combination of Old Republicans (strict Jeffersonians), Anglophobes, who resent largely British ownership of bank stock, and state banking interests anxious to remove federal competition allows recharter bill to die in House and defeats it in Senate. Lack of a federal bank leaves U.S. in financial straits during War of 1812.

May 1. British frigate *Guerrière* forcibly removes and impresses an American sailor from American vessel off Sandy Hook. **May 16.** U.S. frigate *President,* in search of *Guerrière,* mistakenly engages and disables British corvette *Little Belt,* causing 32 British casualties, upon her refusal to identify herself. **Nov. 1.** U.S. offers to compensate, but makes condition that British revoke Orders in Council.

Nov. 4. Congressional elections bring Western "War Hawks" to Congress; among them are Henry Clay and Richard M. Johnson of Kentucky, John C. Calhoun, Langdon Cheves, and William Lowndes from South Carolina, Felix Grundy from Tennessee, and Peter B. Porter from western New York. Strongly nationalist in temper, they advocate U.S. expansion, including conquest of Canada, and take the lead in protesting outrages to U.S. shipping, though the South and West are not especially affected by them. **Nov. 5.** President Madison's message to Congress encourages drive toward war with England when he requests preparations for national defense.

Tecumseh, chief of the Shawnees, actively supported by Canadian governor and furtraders, attempts to organize a defensive confederacy of Indian tribes on Northwestern frontier to resist white settlement. **Nov. 8.** General William Henry Harrison, governor of Indiana Territory, takes advantage of Tecumseh's temporary absence to destroy, with heavy losses, the Indian capital village at Tippecanoe Creek after having been attacked by Indians the previous day. Conflict inflames Western feeling against British, who are believed to supply Indians with arms from Canada.

Beginning of Cumberland Road (the National Road) at Cumberland, Maryland. By 1840, road has reached Vandalia, Illinois, and cost $7 million. An important western route during era of westward expansion, it is present-day Highway 40.

Sidewheeler *New Orleans* is built in Pittsburgh, first steamboat built west of the Alleghenies; it makes voyage from Louisville to New Orleans, beginning Western steamboat navigation.

New York law is first to substitute general incorporation provisions for special charters from state legislatures; this leads to similar laws in other states that encourage growth in business corporations, especially those involved in transportation.

Niles Weekly Register (Whig), founded at Baltimore by Hezekiah Niles, is noted until its discontinuation in 1849 for factual reporting and the national influence of Niles' editorials.

1812

April. President Madison, in diplomatic exchange with England, insists wrongly that French commercial restrictions have been removed; Britain correctly denies that Napoleon has revoked them. **May 11.** Britain's stand on refusing to annul Orders in Council is weakening because of severe economic hardships when Prime Minister Spencer Perceval is assassinated, causing delay in considering question. **June 16.** Britain reluctantly and too late revokes Orders in Council (effective June 23). **June 18.** U S. Congress, ignorant of the revocation, declares war against England over Federalist and other opposition; Southern and Western "War Hawks" assure passage by vote of 79 to 49 in House and 19 to 13 in Senate.

April 30. Louisiana (Territory of Orleans) is admitted to the Union as the eighteenth state; state constitution allows slavery.

June 4. Name of Louisiana Territory changed to Missouri Territory.

July 2 and Aug. 5. Governors of Connecticut and Massachusetts refuse to supply militia to the federal government. **Aug. 5.** In New Hampshire, Daniel Webster prepares Rockingham memorial, which calls government measures "hasty, rash, and ruinous" and hints at disunion. **Aug. 25.** Massachusetts House of Representatives terms war against the public interest and discourages volunteers except for defensive purposes.

President Madison's War Message says nothing about Canada, listing only maritime grievances, but first U.S. effort is Canadian invasion as part of attempt to drive British from North America. **Aug. 16.** Poorly trained and badly equipped militia under General William Hull are surrendered to Canadian force under General Isaac Brock at Detroit after a disastrous campaign that persuades Northwest Indians under Tecumseh to join the British and loses U.S. control of Lake Erie and the Michigan country. **Oct. 13.** Despite death of General Brock, their ablest leader, Canadians also defeat U.S. forces at Fort George on Niagara River, when New York militia refuse to leave New York State and cross into Canada. **Nov. 19.** U.S. effort collapses when militia under General Henry Dearborn likewise refuse to cross the frontier near Plattsburgh.

U.S. military failures are partially compensated by naval victories. **Aug. 19.** U.S. frigate *Constitution* destroys British frigate *Guerrière*. **Oct. 17.** U.S. sloop-of-war *Wasp* defeats British brig *Frolic* off Virginia. **Oct. 25.** U.S. frigate *United States* commanded by Captain Stephen Decatur captures British frigate *Macedonian*. **Dec. 29.** The *Constitution* also destroys British frigate *Java* off Brazil, earning herself the nickname "Old Ironsides" by her performance.

Aug. 24. U.S. attempts peace feeler that requires suspension of impressment and "paper" blockades and asks compensation for losses to U.S. shipping. **Aug. 29.** British Foreign Secretary Castlereagh rejects proposal. **Sept. 30.** British offer of armistice is unimplemented when Secretary of State James Monroe demands end of impressment as a condition of agreement.

Dec. 2. President Madison, Southern Republican candidate, reelected over De Witt Clinton of New York, candidate of antiwar Republicans and Federalists, by vote of 128 to 89. Elbridge Gerry of Massachusetts is elected Vice-President, succeeding George Clinton who had died in office on April 20. Vote is Gerry, 131, Charles Jared Ingersoll, Federalist, 86. Antiwar coalition wins in all

New England and Middle States except Vermont and Pennsylvania; Federalists double their strength in Congress.

Diseases of the Mind by Benjamin Rush is published, a pioneer work that contains the seeds of modern psychoanalysis.

First life insurance company in U.S., incorporated in Philadelphia, is called Pennsylvania Company for Insurance on Lives and Granting Annuities.

1813

February-August. U.S. attempt to retake Detroit and Fort Dearborn (present-day Chicago) in expedition led by General William Henry Harrison results in stand-off for lack of control of Lake Erie.

April 15. U.S. occupies West Florida, western half of which had been annexed in 1810, by taking Spanish fort at Mobile.

April 27. U.S. effort to gain control of Lake Ontario by taking York (present-day Toronto) results in destruction of the town by fire, giving British their excuse for burning Washington, D.C., in 1814. **April-November.** Campaign to conquer upper Canada, especially Montreal, fails of its object after several battles, when U.S. forces fall back on Plattsburgh, New York, for winter quarters. **Dec. 18.** British take Fort Niagara and encourage Indians to plunder Lewiston and surrounding settlements. **Dec. 30-Jan. 1, 1814.** Buffalo is burned by British along with other towns along frontier.

British blockade Chesapeake and Delaware bays, cutting off commerce, and carry out raids along coasts of Chesapeake Bay. **May 26.** Blockade is extended to ports of New York, South Carolina, Georgia, and Louisiana. **Nov. 19.** British blockade Long Island Sound, leaving only New England ports open, in effort to encourage New England protest against war. When New England fails to break away from Union, blockade is extended to New England ports in following year.

May 8. President Madison sends peace commissioners Albert Gallatin and James A. Bayard to St. Petersburg, Russia, upon hearing of Czar Alexander's offer of September 1812 to mediate war. **July 5.** British Foreign Secretary Lord Castlereagh refuses Russian offer. **Nov. 4.** Castlereagh, concerned about British defeats in Lake Erie region, sends James Monroe, secretary of state, offer of direct negotiations. President Madison accepts immediately.

June 1. U.S. frigate *Chesapeake,* with raw crew, is disabled and captured by British frigate *Shannon* off Boston. Last words of dying U.S. Captain James Lawrence, "Don't give up the ship!" are later inscribed on battle flag of flagship *Lawrence* commanded by Captain Oliver Hazard Perry, who defeats British in Battle of Lake Erie on September 10, and sends message, "We have met the enemy and they are ours." Engagement regains control of the lake and reopens prospects for conquest of Canada.

Sept. 18. Because of Perry's victory, British are forced to evacuate Detroit. **Oct. 5.** U.S. triumphs at Battle of the Thames River, north of Lake Erie. Death of Tecumseh in this battle results in collapse of Indian confederacy in Northwest, depriving British of Indian allies. U.S. regains territory lost in 1812.

Dec. 9. President Madison requests new embargo in effort to prevent sale of supplies to British forces in Canada and in New England ports by New York and New England merchants. **Dec. 17.** Congress passes measure over strong opposition, and coastal trade is stopped, but frontier trade with the enemy persists.

Boston Manufacturing Company opens first textile factory to perform all cloth-making operations by power in Waltham, Massachusetts. Financed with large capital, company recruits New England farm girls as operatives, boards them in dormitories, and produces a standard coarse cotton cloth requiring minimum labor skill.

1814

Jan. 18. Senate confirms President Madison's nomination of James A. Bayard, John Quincy Adams, Henry Clay, and Jonathan Russell as U.S. peace commissioners. **Feb. 8.** Albert Gallatin is added to the commission. Ghent, in Flanders, is chosen for meeting of Americans and British.

March 27. Andrew Jackson, major general of Tennessee militia, with 2,000 volunteers, wins final victory at Horseshoe Bend of the Tallapoosa River in bloody Creek War fought in present-day Alabama since July 1813. **Aug. 9.** Creeks cede most of their lands to U.S. under Treaty of Fort Jackson. This ends Indian resistance in southern and western Alabama. **May 22.** Jackson is appointed major general in regular army.

March 31. President Madison, accepting failure of nearly 10 years of commercial restrictions, recommends repeal of Embargo and Non-Importation acts. **April 14.** Bill, passed by large majorities in Congress, is signed, and restrictions formally cease. U.S. trade with enemy continues, merchants paying duty to British at captured port of Castine, Maine.

Final defeat of Napoleon in April allows British to take offensive in U.S. war; 14,000 men of Duke of Wellington's veteran forces arrive during summer. Campaign of concerted attack on Lake Champlain, Chesapeake Bay, and New Orleans is planned. **July 5 and 25.** Thrust from Canada is prevented by U.S. offensive that leads to battles of Chippewa and Lundy's Lane. **Sept. 11.** Decisive victory on Lake Champlain is won by fleet of Commodore Thomas Macdonough near Plattsburgh, giving U.S. control of Great Lakes and convincing Wellington that war cannot be won.

Aug. 8. Peace negotiations begin at Ghent between U.S. and British envoys. U.S. demand for settlement on basis of prewar boundaries is met by British insistence on retaining territory acquired. **Nov. 26.** U.S. terms involving prewar boundaries are met when British hear of Macdonough's victory, and because of heavy British debt incurred in defeating Napoleon.

Aug. 19. British expeditionary force of 4,000 men lands at Chesapeake Bay, proceeds up the Patuxent River to Bladensburg and then to Washington, D.C. **Aug. 24-25.** Washington, undefended since U.S. Army has fled, is partially burned. **Sept. 12-14.** British meet greater resistance at Baltimore and are forced to withdraw; bombardment of Fort McHenry on night of September 13-14 inspires composition of "The Star Spangled Banner" by Francis Scott Key, an eyewitness.

Dec. 15. Unaware of progress of peace negotiations, Federalist representatives of Connecticut, Rhode Island, Massachusetts, New Hampshire, and Vermont meet at Hartford, Connecticut, for secret convention called on October 17 by Massachusetts legislature. Convention considers, with threat of possible disunion, revision of the Constitution that will prevent further national dominance of the sort that has led to and sustained the unpopular war. Convention is dominated from the outset by moderates whose influence brings about resolutions and recommendations that are not extreme, but news of Treaty of Ghent and of Battle of New Orleans two weeks after the signing causes even the moderates to be ridiculed throughout the country and constitutes fatal blow to Federalist Party.

Dec. 24. Treaty of Ghent signed; treaty is actually silent on the specific issues that have led to war, but British do not claim various rights in North America contested since 1783. This constitutes U.S. victory, since it amounts to abandonment of last serious European challenge to future American development.

Henry M. Shreve navigates steamboat *Enterprise* from Pittsburgh down the Ohio and Mississippi rivers to New Orleans, carrying supplies to General Andrew Jackson; *Enterprise* is first steamboat to travel on upper waters of Ohio-Mississippi river system. On return trip in following year, Shreve is first to ascend Mississippi and Ohio rivers to Louisville successfully.

War overturns federal economies of 1800 to 1811; national debt rises from $83 million 1811 level to $127 million in 1814. In effort to meet expenses, Congress adds to list of internally taxed items, increases tariff, doubles taxes on land, dwellings, and slaves.

1815

Jan. 1. Sir Edward Pakenham with 7,500 British veterans, having landed at mouth of the Mississippi River on December 13, 1814, attacks General Andrew Jackson with 5,000 well-fortified and experienced troops defending New Orleans; British retire after severe artillery pounding. **Jan. 8.** After waiting for reinforcements, Pakenham attacks again and is thrown back with crushing British losses — more than 2,000 casualties as opposed to 21 Americans killed or wounded. Neither British nor Americans know that war is over and treaty terms have been agreed on two weeks earlier; victory is strategically meaningless, but for America psychologically important; it wipes out at one blow the war's failures and humiliations and makes Jackson the first popular American hero.

March 3. Congress authorizes hostilities against Dey of Algiers, who has declared war on U.S. during War of 1812, saying tribute payments from U.S. ships are not great enough. **June 19.** Flotilla under command of Captain Stephen Decatur, dispatched May 10 from New York, enters Algiers harbor with two captured Algerine warships. **June 30.** Decatur exacts treaty from Dey that ends piracy and wins similar treaties from Tunis on July 26 and Tripoli on August 6, ending hostilities.

July 3. Commercial convention with Great Britain wins trade concessions for U.S., eliminates discriminatory duties and allows U.S. trade with East Indies.

Beginning of peace brings renewed western expansion into eastern half of Mississippi Valley, from the Great Lakes to the Gulf of Mexico. Population west of the Appalachian Mountains increases from 1,080,000 in 1810 to 2,236,000 in 1820.

Imports, held down by War of 1812, rise from $13 million in 1814 to $100 million average in 1815 to 1820 period. Exports, similarly affected, rise from $7 million in 1814 to $70 million average in 1815 to 1820 period. Chief imports are woolen and cotton items, sugar, and coffee; principal export is cotton.

North American Review, distinguished intellectual periodical, founded in Boston by William Tudor; discontinued 1940.

1816

March 14. Financial plight of country, and financial needs, lead to passage of bill chartering Second Bank of the United States, which had been recommended by President Madison in message of December 5, 1815. Votes in House (80 to 71) and Senate (22 to 12) reflect opposition of both strict Jeffersonians and Federalists who represent recently developed private banking interests. Debate is first one led by Henry Clay, John C. Calhoun (both taking a nationalist, pro-bank position), and Daniel Webster, a young congressman from New Hampshire, who opposes the measure.

April 27. Tariff of 1816 is first one enacted to protect home industry (developed during embargo and war years) rather than to raise revenue. New manufacturing interests oppose commercial and agricultural sectors in debate, which keeps duties moderate. Tariff is ineffective, since lenient British credit more than compensates for higher cost of imported goods.

Dec. 4. Madison succeeded by James Monroe as fifth President of the U.S. after struggle for nomination with younger element supporting William H. Crawford, who is defeated in Republican caucus by 65 to 54. Vote in electoral college demonstrates feeling against Federalists: 183 to 34 for Monroe over Federalist Rufus King of New York. Republican Daniel D. Tompkins of New York is elected Vice-President.

Dec. 11. Indiana admitted to the Union as the nineteenth state; originally part of Northwest Territory, it had been Indiana Territory with approximately the same boundaries as the state since 1809. Population is 75,000; slavery is prohibited.

Supreme Court decision in *Martin* v. *Hunter's Lessee* affirms right of federal courts to review decisions of state courts, leads to controversy between Supreme Court and Virginia court led by Virginia Judge Spencer Roane.

First incorporated savings bank is chartered in Boston.

African Methodist Episcopal Church founded at Philadelphia, one of a number of churches founded by independent groups of Negroes in this period.

School for children as young as four years is established in Boston; it is included in the public school system in 1818.

1817

March 3. On his last day in office, President Madison vetoes Bonus Bill, sponsored by John C. Calhoun and passed on February 8 by the House by 86 to 84 and Senate by 20 to 15. Bill provides for federal financing of "internal improvements," chiefly roads and canals to connect the West with the Eastern Seaboard. Veto is on grounds that measure requires constitutional amendment.

March 4. President Monroe's inaugural address indicates that Jeffersonian party has adopted most of the old Hamiltonian-Federalist program involving a strong central government. **May-Sept.** President Monroe tours the Northeast and as far west as Detroit; he is enthusiastically received, which leads to characterization on July 12 of the period by a Boston newspaper as an "era of good feelings," in which political party controversies have given way to national unity.

April 28-29. Rush-Bagot Agreement, signed by Acting Secretary of State Richard Rush and Charles Bagot, British Minister to the U.S., brings to a halt naval armaments on the Great Lakes by limiting Britain and U.S. to eight lake ships each. Agreement implies gradual demilitarization of the Canadian frontier, but actually full disarmament of land fortifications does not take place until 1871.

Dec. 10. Mississippi Territory is divided; western part becomes Mississippi, admitted to the Union as the twentieth state, and eastern part becomes Territory of Alabama.

New York legislature authorizes construction of Erie Canal from Albany on the Hudson River to Buffalo on Lake Erie, a distance of about 360 miles. Canal, when completed in 1825, makes possible direct shipment of produce from Atlantic Ocean to Great Lakes region.

Beginning of iron production by process of puddling (to make impure pig iron more malleable) and rolling at Plumstock, Pennsylvania; method is adopted soon afterward by the industry at Pittsburgh.

First machine-made paper manufactured in U.S. is made by Thomas Gilpin near Wilmington, Delaware.

Asylum for the insane is opened in Frankford, Pennsylvania; others are opened in Boston (McLean Hospital) and New York (Bloomingdale) in 1818.

American Colonization Society for return of Negroes to Africa founded in Richmond, Virginia. Headed by a succession of distinguished Virginians, Society initially sends Negroes to Sierra Leone, then in 1822 purchases and establishes neighboring area named Liberia by Robert Goodloe Harper. Twelve thousand Negroes have been transported by 1860. Colonization movement, the early form of emancipation attempt, is widely pushed in the South until 1831, after which it sharply declines.

"Thanatopsis," poem composed by William Cullen Bryant in 1811, makes first appearance in *North American Review.*

1818

April 17-Nov. 28. After two years of intermittent conflict between Seminole Indians and U.S. forces along Georgia-Alabama border, General Andrew Jackson is dispatched to clear border area and eastern Florida of hostile Indians. He offers to take all of Spanish East Florida, but receives no reply from President Monroe. Without explicit orders, he marches into East Florida, occupies St. Marks and Pensacola and executes two British subjects, Alexander Arbuthnot and Robert Ambrister, whom he accuses of aiding the enemy. Action is condemned by the Cabinet (except for Secretary of State John Quincy Adams), the Senate, and the House, but popular approval persuades President Monroe not to punish Jackson. Adams, stating that campaign was for self-defense, sends ultimatum to Spanish government on November 28 insisting that it either control the Indians or cede the region to the U.S.

Dec. 3. Illinois becomes twenty-first state of the Union. Formerly part of Illinois Territory (present-day Illinois and Wisconsin), only southern part of state is settled, with 40,000 population, at time of admission. Slavery is prohibited.

U.S.-Canadian border is fixed at 49th parallel between Lake of the Woods and crest of the Rocky Mountains in convention between Britain and U.S.; convention leaves Oregon boundary question open to later settlement.

Transatlantic packet lines (under sail) begin operations between New York and Liverpool, England; average time in 1818 to 1822 period is 39 days.

1819

Feb. 2. *Trustees of Dartmouth College* v. *Woodward* establishes that private corporate charters are contracts within the meaning of the Constitution, and therefore may not be revised or controlled by state legislatures that have granted them.

Feb. 22. Spanish government cedes East Florida to the U.S. in Adams-Onís Treaty. Border of Louisiana Purchase is agreed to as running irregularly northwest from Sabine River on Gulf of Mexico to 42nd parallel and thence due west to the Pacific Ocean. Line excludes Texas, to which U.S. relinquishes claims, and eliminates Spanish claims to Oregon country, north of treaty line. U.S. assumes $5 million claims of its citizens against Spain.

March 6. Supreme Court in *M'Culloch* v. *Maryland* unanimously disallows attempt by states to tax Bank of the United States, ("the power to tax involves the power to destroy"). Opinion of Chief Justice Marshall upholds constitutionality of the Bank and expresses nationalist doctrine on the Constitution as a document of implied powers which are to be loosely constructed: If the end is legitimate and the means are not prohibited and are consistent with the letter and spirit of the Constitution, the means are constitutional.

May 24. The *Savannah,* first steamship to cross the Atlantic Ocean, leaves from Savannah, Georgia, arriving in Liverpool, England, on June 20.

Dec. 14. Alabama admitted to the Union as twenty-second state; region had been organized as Alabama Territory in 1817; at time of admission population is 128,000. State constitution allows slavery.

Financial panic, especially in Southern and Western states, occurs with collapse of credit on purchases, largely speculative, of Western lands. Crash is long-term result of liberal credit provisions of Land Act of 1800, but immediate cause is retraction of credit by Second Bank of the United States, which has been recklessly managed. Resulting pressure on state banks results in many failures and causes vast areas of Western land to become property of the Bank of the United States, which is henceforth characterized by Westerners as "The Monster." End of postwar European demand for U.S. food staples, sharply reducing land values, is contributing factor to what becomes general business depression lasting until 1822.

Arkansas Territory organized; area is southern part of Missouri Territory — present-day Oklahoma and Arkansas.

Because of high death rate among immigrants subjected to inhuman conditions during Atlantic crossings, federal law is passed to protect passengers; this and later acts of following thirty-five years are ineffective.

Cast-iron three-piece plow with interchangeable parts developed by Jethrow Wood of New York. Breechloading flintlock rifle invented by John Hall.

Sermon by William Ellery Channing of Boston delivered at Baltimore formulates liberal and humane Unitarian creed as opposed to orthodox Calvinist beliefs and leads to formation of Unitarian Church in Boston in 1820.

Washington Irving, during stay in England, writes *The Sketch Book of Geoffrey Crayon, Gent.*, containing, among other pieces, "Rip Van Winkle" and "The Legend of Sleepy Hollow."

American Farmer, first farm journal (discontinued 1897), founded by John P. Skinner at Baltimore. The *Texas Republican* published in Nacogdoches is first English-language Texan newspaper.

1819 - 1820

Feb. 13, 1819. Application of Missouri for statehood occasions move by Representative James Tallmadge of New York to prohibit further introduction of slaves (permitted by France and Spain before Louisiana Purchase) into Missouri as condition of admission. Motion threatens to upset even balance of slave and free states that has been maintained by tacit agreement since 1802 to admit free and slave states alternately. **March 3, 1820.** Extended debate and complex parliamentary maneuverings lead eventually to Missouri Compromise, in which admission of Missouri as a slave state is balanced by admission of free Maine, and which provides that slavery be henceforth prohibited in the Purchase north of latitude 36°30.' Controversy does not reflect abolitionist sentiment so much as sectional antagonism over the fact that slave states, though steadily falling behind in population and thus in House representation, maintain national power by equal representation in the Senate. With Maine (admitted on March 15, 1820) and Missouri (admitted on August 10, 1821, after extended debate about its constitution) the U.S. has 12 free and 12 slave states.

1820

April 24. Land Act of 1820 abolishes credit provisions of earlier act but reduces minimum purchase to 80 acres (⅛ section) and minimum price per acre to $1.25. General indebtedness in depression period makes act of benefit only to speculators, since settlers cannot usually pay full amount in cash.

Dec. 6. President Monroe, unopposed by any formal candidate for reelection as President, gains 231 out of 232 electoral votes cast; three electors abstain from voting and one vote is cast for John Quincy Adams (thought by some to retain for George Washington the honor of the only unanimous election). Daniel Tompkins is reelected Vice-President, with 218 votes.

Fourth National Census shows that population is 9,638,000, a gain of more than 33 percent since 1810; figure includes 98,000 immigrants arrived since 1810. New York is largest city, with population of approximately 124,000, followed by Philadelphia (113,000), Baltimore (63,000), Boston (43,000), and New Orleans (27,000). Urban population (in places of more than 2,500) is 7.2 percent.

Responding to various American boasts of the new country's cultural importance, Sydney Smith asks in *Edinburgh Review*, "Who reads an American book?" Result is Anglo-American "Pamphlet War" on respective manners, morals, and intellect.

Edmund Kean, English tragic actor, makes American debut in New York as *Richard III*. Edwin Forrest, first native-born actor to achieve distinction, appears in tragedy *Douglas* in Philadelphia.

A PORTFOLIO OF MAPS

Charting the West

Apart from the patchwork of Indian land cessions in the late 18th and early 19th centuries, territorial additions to the United States were normally very large: the Louisiana Purchase, the Mexican cessions, and the Oregon Territory. In all cases this was far more land than could be readily settled or even adequately explored. The territories were added because it seemed increasingly inevitable during the 19th century that the United States was destined to extend from the Atlantic to the Pacific. Eventually, with large population increases and a generous immigration policy, it was felt the whole continent would be settled.

The addition of the Louisiana Territory by purchase from France in 1803 nearly doubled the size of the United States. To learn something of this vast new acquisition, President Jefferson sent exploring parties west (Map 1). Most famous was the Lewis and Clark Expedition into the northern part of the Territory. Zebulon Pike and his party, in addition to following the Mississippi River northward, explored the central and southern regions, venturing into the Mexican territory claimed by the United States but not gained until the 1840s. Other explorations by smaller parties investigated the southern part of Louisiana.

The vast, unsettled, unorganized territory of the Northwest invited a free-for-all competition for the lucrative fur trade. Trading posts and forts were located throughout the region, and options were taken on territory by several nations, England, Spain, and the United States being the chief contenders (Map 2).

Beyond Louisiana, on the other side of the Rockies, most of the territory was of disputed ownership, and it was not until the 1840s, during President Polk's administration, that boundaries were agreed to in Oregon and the greater part of Mexico's territory was added to the United States by conquest. But disputed ownership never prevented the fur trappers from exploring and charting the West, opening up trade routes, and building trading posts. Other explorers followed the fur trappers: John C. Frémont, Joseph R. Walker, and Charles Wilkes are among the best known (Maps 3 and 4).

Maps prepared by Uni-Map Inc., Palatine, Ill.
for Encyclopaedia Britannica, Inc.

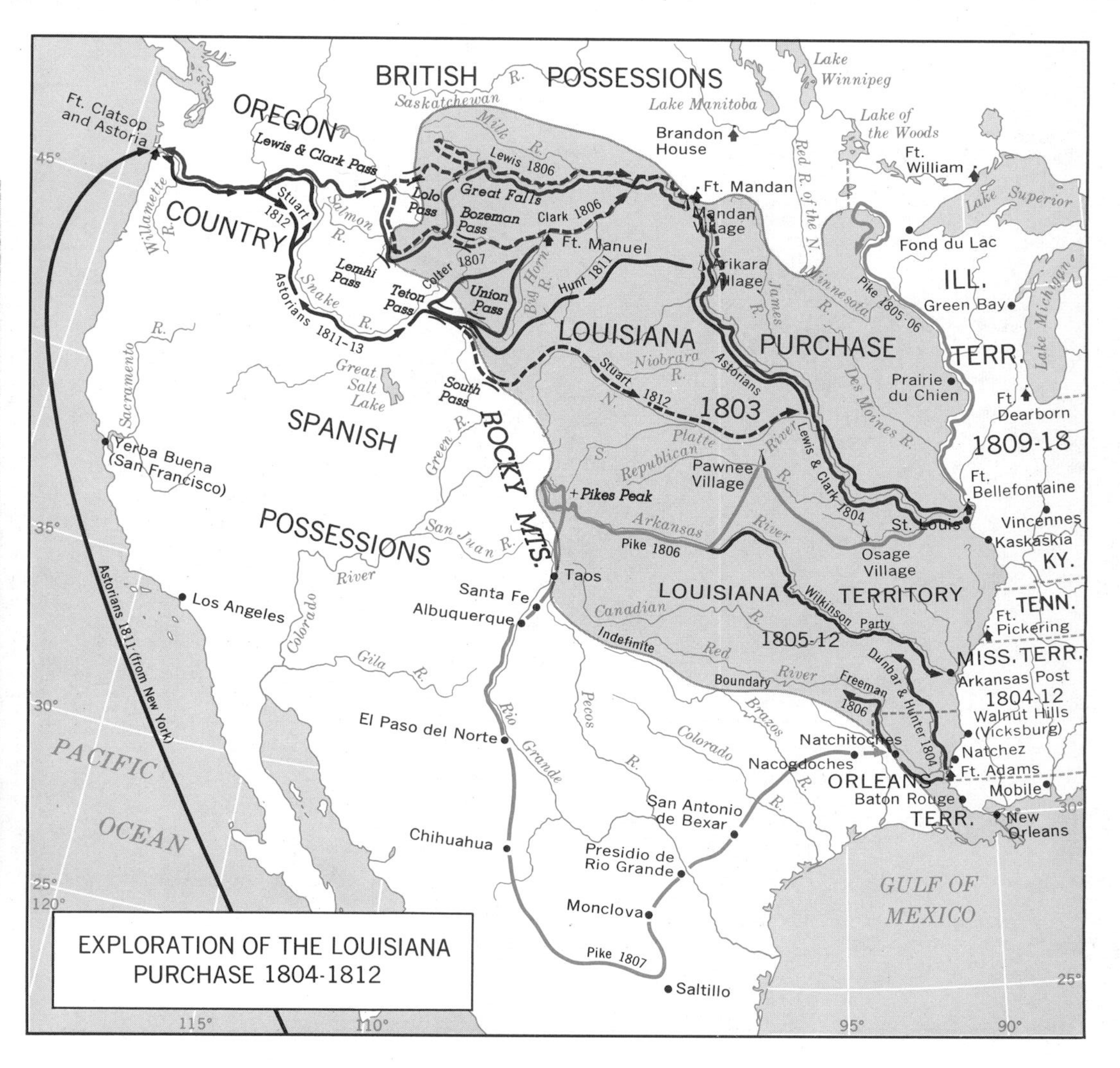

EXPLORATION OF THE LOUISIANA PURCHASE 1804-1812

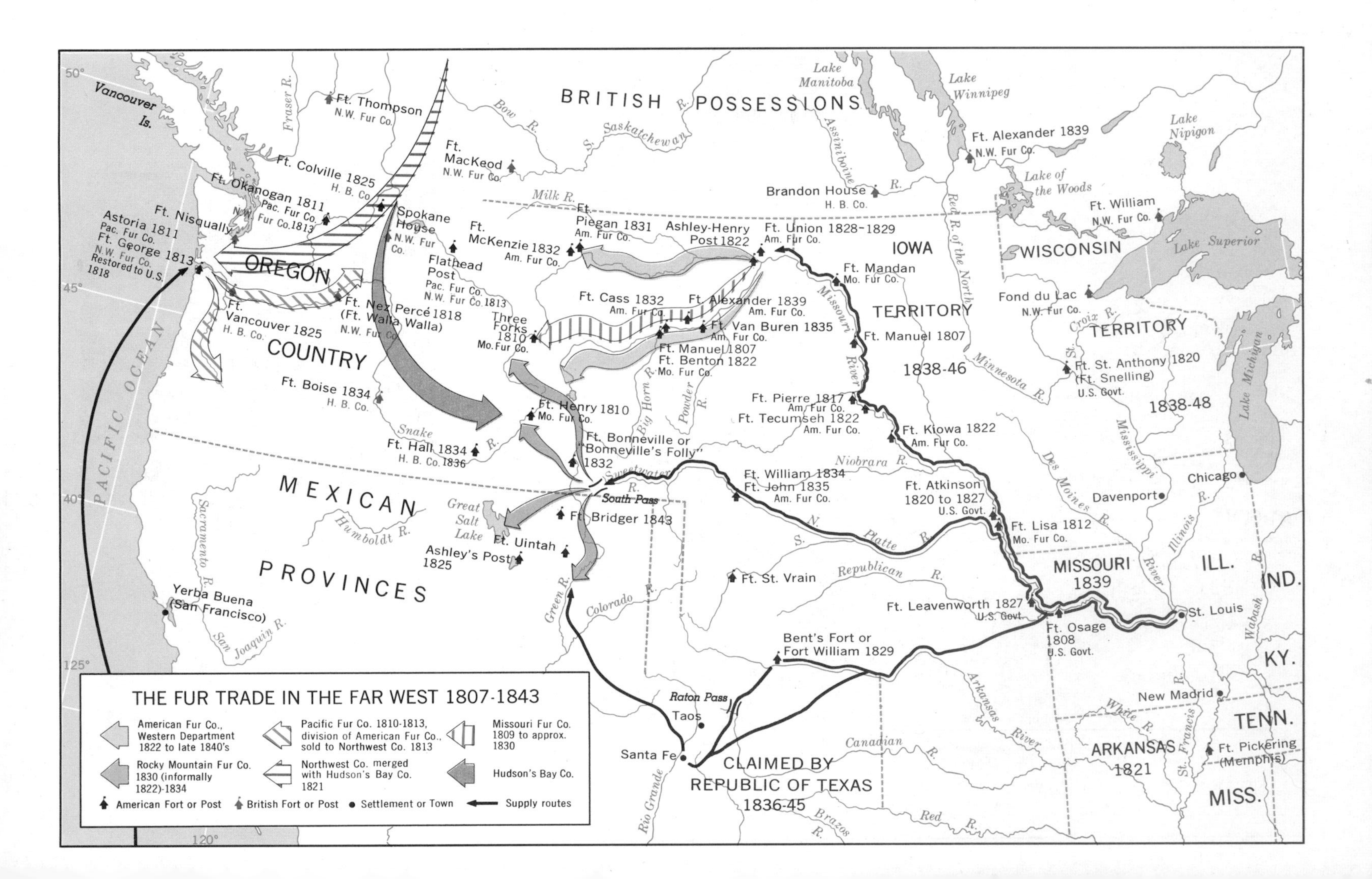

THE FUR TRADE IN THE FAR WEST 1807-1843
American Fur Co., Western Department 1822 to late 1840's
Rocky Mountain Fur Co. 1830 (informally 1822)-1834
Pacific Fur Co. 1810-1813, division of American Fur Co., sold to Northwest Co. 1813
Northwest Co. merged with Hudson's Bay Co. 1821
Missouri Fur Co. 1809 to approx. 1830
Hudson's Bay Co.
American Fort or Post
British Fort or Post
Settlement or Town
Supply routes
BRITISH POSSESSIONS
OREGON COUNTRY
MEXICAN PROVINCES
IOWA TERRITORY 1838-46
WISCONSIN TERRITORY 1838-48
MISSOURI 1839
ARKANSAS 1821
CLAIMED BY REPUBLIC OF TEXAS 1836-45
ILL.
IND.
KY.
TENN.
MISS.
Vancouver Is.
PACIFIC OCEAN
Astoria 1811 Pac. Fur Co. Ft. George 1813 N.W. Fur Co. Restored to U.S. 1818
Ft. Nisqually
Ft. Okanogan 1811 Pac. Fur Co. N.W. Fur Co. 1813
Ft. Colville 1825 H. B. Co.
Ft. Thompson N.W. Fur Co.
Ft. Vancouver 1825 H. B. Co.
Spokane House N.W. Fur Co.
Ft. Nez Percé 1818 (Ft. Walla Walla) N.W. Fur Co.
Ft. MacKeod N.W. Fur Co.
Ft. McKenzie 1832 Am. Fur Co.
Flathead Post Pac. Fur Co. N.W. Fur Co. 1813
Ft. Boise 1834 H. B. Co.
Ft. Hall 1834 H. B. Co. 1836
Three Forks 1810 Mo. Fur Co.
Ft. Henry 1810 Mo. Fur Co.
Ft. Piegan 1831 Am. Fur Co.
Ft. Cass 1832 Am. Fur Co.
Ashley-Henry Post 1822
Ft. Alexander 1839 Am. Fur Co.
Ft. Van Buren 1835 Am. Fur Co.
Ft. Manuel 1807
Ft. Benton 1822 Mo. Fur Co.
Ft. Bonneville or "Bonneville's Folly" 1832
South Pass
Ft. Bridger 1843
Ft. Uintah
Ashley's Post 1825
Great Salt Lake
Yerba Buena (San Francisco)
Ft. Union 1828-1829 Am. Fur Co.
Ft. Mandan Mo. Fur Co.
Ft. Manuel 1807
Ft. Pierre 1817 Am. Fur Co.
Ft. Tecumseh 1822 Am. Fur Co.
Ft. Kiowa 1822 Am. Fur Co.
Ft. William 1834
Ft. John 1835 Am. Fur Co.
Ft. Atkinson 1820 to 1827 U.S. Govt.
Ft. Lisa 1812 Mo. Fur Co.
Ft. St. Vrain
Ft. Leavenworth 1827 U.S. Govt.
Ft. Osage 1808 U.S. Govt.
Bent's Fort or Fort William 1829
Raton Pass
Taos
Santa Fe
Brandon House H. B. Co.
Ft. Alexander 1839 N.W. Fur Co.
Ft. William N.W. Fur Co.
Fond du Lac N.W. Fur Co.
Ft. St. Anthony 1820 (Ft. Snelling) U.S. Govt.
Chicago
Davenport
St. Louis
New Madrid
Ft. Pickering (Memphis)
Lake Manitoba
Lake Winnipeg
Lake Nipigon
Lake of the Woods
Lake Superior
Lake Michigan
Fraser R.
Bow R.
S. Saskatchewan R.
Assiniboine R.
Milk R.
Red R. of the North
Missouri River
Minnesota R.
St. Croix R.
Mississippi
Des Moines R.
Illinois River
Wabash R.
White R.
St. Francis
Arkansas River
Canadian R.
Red R.
Brazos R.
Rio Grande
Colorado R.
Green R.
Sweetwater R.
N. Platte R.
S. Platte R.
Republican R.
Niobrara R.
Big Horn R.
Powder R.
Snake R.
Humboldt R.
Sacramento R.
San Joaquin R.
50°
45°
40°
125°
120°

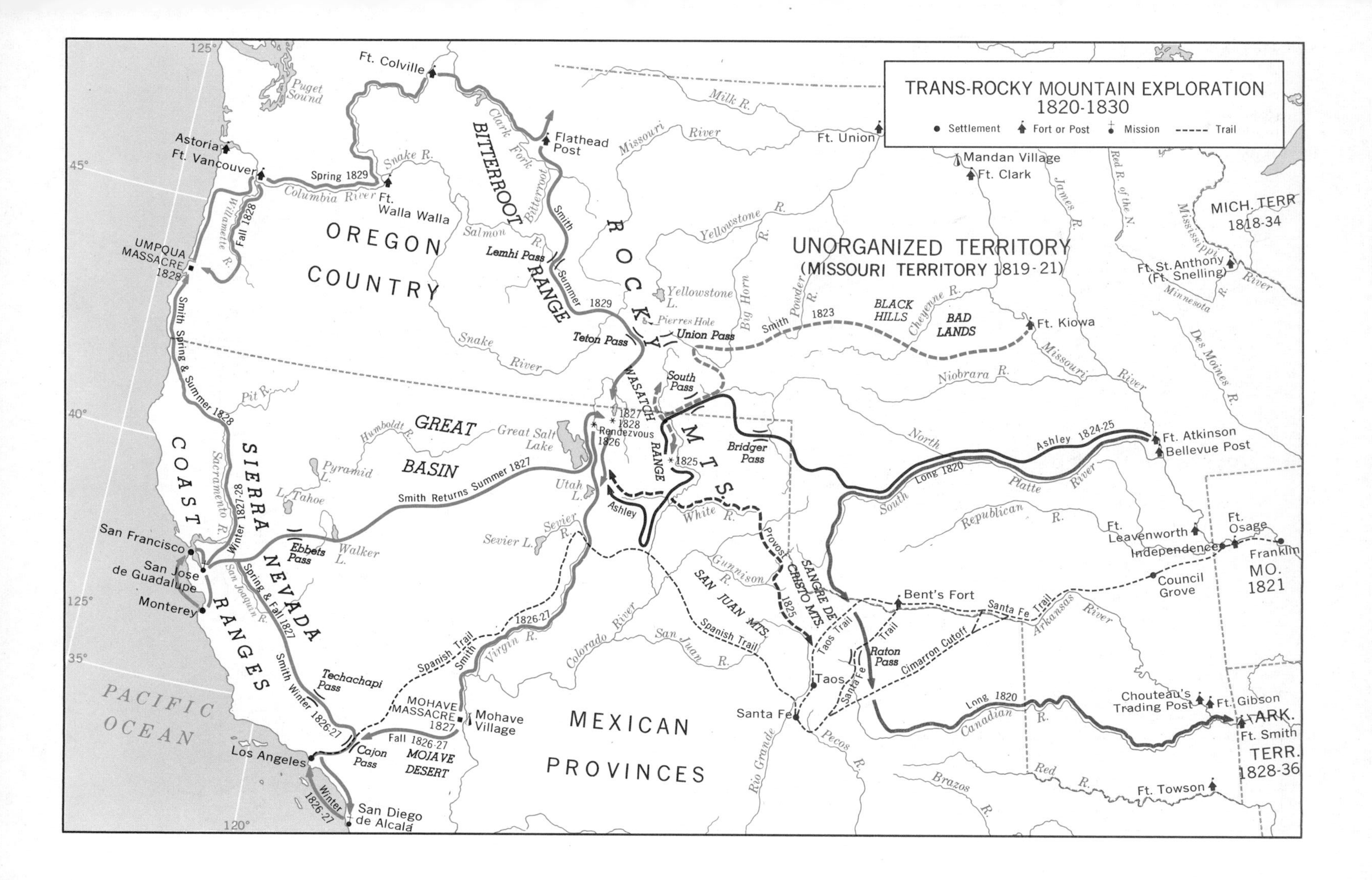

TRANS-ROCKY MOUNTAIN EXPLORATION
1820-1830
Settlement
Fort or Post
Mission
Trail
UNORGANIZED TERRITORY
(MISSOURI TERRITORY 1819-21)
OREGON COUNTRY
MEXICAN PROVINCES
MICH. TERR 1818-34
MO. 1821
ARK. TERR. 1828-36
GREAT BASIN
ROCKY MTS.
BITTERROOT RANGE
WASATCH RANGE
SIERRA NEVADA
COAST RANGES
SANGRE DE CRISTO MTS.
SAN JUAN MTS.
BLACK HILLS
BAD LANDS
MOJAVE DESERT
PACIFIC OCEAN
Ft. Colville
Astoria
Ft. Vancouver
Ft. Walla Walla
Flathead Post
UMPQUA MASSACRE 1828
Ft. Union
Mandan Village
Ft. Clark
Ft. St. Anthony (Ft. Snelling)
Ft. Kiowa
Ft. Atkinson
Bellevue Post
Ft. Leavenworth
Ft. Osage
Independence
Franklin
Council Grove
Bent's Fort
Taos
Santa Fe
Chouteau's Trading Post
Ft. Gibson
Ft. Smith
Ft. Towson
San Francisco
San Jose de Guadalupe
Monterey
Los Angeles
San Diego de Alcala
MOHAVE MASSACRE 1827
Mohave Village
Rendezvous 1826
1827
1828
1825
Lemhi Pass
Teton Pass
Union Pass
South Pass
Bridger Pass
Ebbets Pass
Techachapi Pass
Cajon Pass
Raton Pass
Pierres Hole
Spring 1829
Fall 1828
Smith
Summer 1829
Smith 1823
Ashley 1824-25
Long 1820
Ashley
Provost 1825
Smith Returns Summer 1827
Winter 1827-28
Spring & Fall 1827
Smith Winter 1826-27
Smith Spring & Summer 1828
1826-27
Fall 1826-27
Winter 1826-27
Santa Fe Trail
Cimarron Cutoff
Taos Trail
Spanish Trail
Puget Sound
Columbia River
Snake R.
Willamette R.
Clark Fork
Bitterroot
Salmon R.
Snake River
Missouri River
Milk R.
Yellowstone R.
Yellowstone L.
Big Horn R.
Powder R.
Cheyenne R.
Niobrara R.
James R.
Red R. of the N.
Mississippi River
Minnesota R.
Des Moines R.
North Platte River
South
Republican R.
Arkansas River
Canadian R.
Red R.
Brazos R.
Pecos R.
Rio Grande
San Juan R.
Colorado River
Gunnison R.
White R.
Virgin R.
Sevier R.
Sevier L.
Utah L.
Great Salt Lake
Humboldt R.
Pyramid L.
L. Tahoe
Walker L.
Pit R.
Sacramento R.
San Joaquin R.
125°
45°
40°
35°
120°

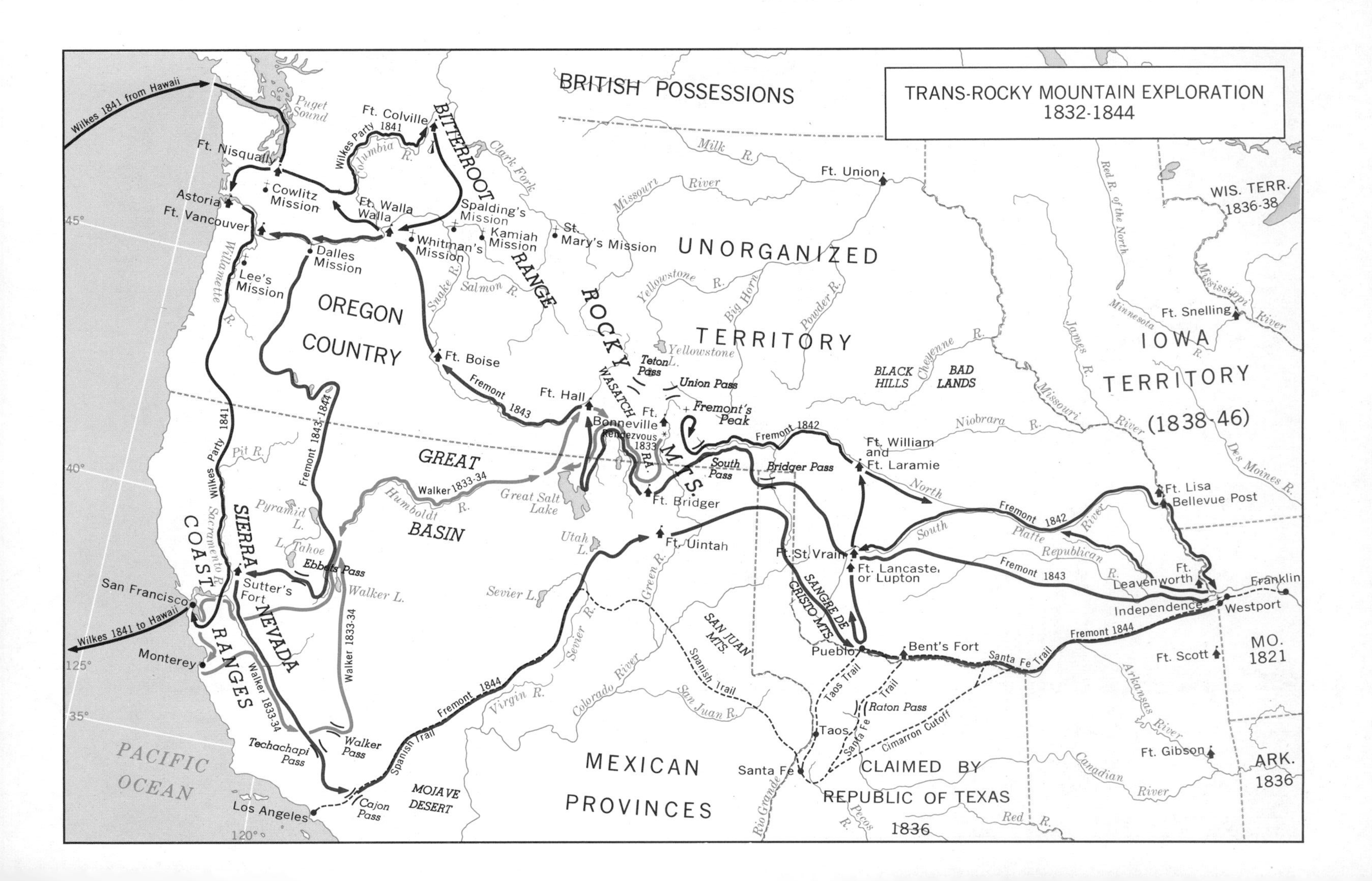
TRANS-ROCKY MOUNTAIN EXPLORATION
1832-1844
BRITISH POSSESSIONS
UNORGANIZED
TERRITORY
IOWA
TERRITORY
(1838-46)
WIS. TERR.
1836-38
OREGON
COUNTRY
GREAT
BASIN
MEXICAN
PROVINCES
CLAIMED BY
REPUBLIC OF TEXAS
1836
MO.
1821
ARK.
1836
PACIFIC
OCEAN
ROCKY
MTS.
WASATCH
RA.
BITTERROOT
RANGE
SIERRA
NEVADA
COAST
RANGES
SANGRE DE
CRISTO MTS.
SAN JUAN
MTS.
BLACK
HILLS
BAD
LANDS
MOJAVE
DESERT
Wilkes 1841 from Hawaii
Wilkes 1841 to Hawaii
Wilkes Party 1841
Fremont 1842
Fremont 1843
Fremont 1843-1844
Fremont 1844
Walker 1833-34
Santa Fe Trail
Spanish Trail
Taos Trail
Cimarron Cutoff
Ft. Nisqually
Astoria
Ft. Vancouver
Cowlitz
Mission
Ft. Colville
Ft. Walla
Walla
Spalding's
Mission
Kamiah
Mission
Whitman's
Mission
St.
Mary's Mission
Dalles
Mission
Lee's
Mission
Ft. Boise
Ft. Hall
Ft.
Bonneville
Rendezvous
1833
Ft. Bridger
Ft. Uintah
Ft. Union
Ft. Snelling
Ft. William
and
Ft. Laramie
Ft. St. Vrain
Ft. Lancaste,
or Lupton
Pueblo
Bent's Fort
Taos
Santa Fe
Ft. Lisa
Bellevue Post
Ft.
Leavenworth
Independence
Westport
Franklin
Ft. Scott
Ft. Gibson
Sutter's
Fort
San Francisco
Monterey
Los Angeles
Teton
Pass
Union Pass
Fremont's
Peak
South
Pass
Bridger Pass
Ebbets Pass
Walker
Pass
Techachapi
Pass
Cajon
Pass
Raton Pass
Puget
Sound
Milk R.
Missouri River
Clark Fork
Columbia R.
Snake R.
Salmon R.
Willamette R.
Yellowstone R.
Yellowstone L.
Big Horn
Powder R.
Cheyenne R.
Red R. of the North
Minnesota R.
Mississippi River
James R.
Missouri River
Niobrara R.
Des Moines R.
North
South
Platte River
Republican R.
Arkansas River
Canadian River
Red R.
Pecos R.
Rio Grande
San Juan R.
Colorado River
Green R.
Sevier R.
Sevier L.
Virgin R.
Utah L.
Great Salt
Lake
Humboldt R.
Pyramid L.
L. Tahoe
Walker L.
Pit R.
Sacramento R.
45°
40°
35°
125°
120°

1797

1.

Moses Austin: Exploring the Ohio Valley

The diaries, journals, and letters of pioneers and explorers are among the best, and often the only, accounts that we have of life on the frontier. One such explorer and reporter was the energetic and enterprising miner, Moses Austin. While traveling across the Ohio Valley to the Mississippi River in the 1790s, he encountered many men and women who had made their homes in the wilderness. The trials of the frontiersmen are reflected in Austin's account of his journey. The selection reprinted below was signed by Austin on March 25, 1797, after he had returned to Virginia, although it was probably written earlier.

Source: *American Historical Review,* Vol. V, pp. 523-542.

On December 8, 1796, in the evening, I left Austinville on horseback, taking Joseph Bell as an assistant, and a mule to pack my baggage; and that night went to Mr. James Campbell's, who, on the morning of the 9th, started with me for Kentucky. Nothing of note took place from Mr. Campbell's to Captain Cragg's, where we arrived on the 11th at evening, furnishing ourselves with blankets, etc., at Abington as we passed.

The morning of the 12th I left Captain Cragg, in company with a Mr. Wills from Richmond, bound to Nashville in the state of Tennessee. That night I arrived at the Block House, so called from being some years past used as such but at this time in the hands of Colonel Anderson, at whose house it was expected good accommodations could be had; more so in consequence of his being a friend of Mr. Campbell's. However, it was with great trouble that he admitted us under his roof or would allow us anything for our horses and mules. Colonel Anderson's is thirty-six miles from Captain Cragg's, which I left by daylight, taking the road through Powell's Valley.

At this place I parted with Mr. Wills, who took the road for Cumberland, which forked at this place. The road being bad and the weather uncommonly cold, I found it was with hard traveling that we reached the foot of Wallon's Ridge that night. From

Anderson's to Benedict Yancy's is thirty-four miles and an uncommon mountainous road. Fifteen miles from the Block House is Clinch Mountain and the river of the same name. I, the same day, passed a number of mountains and ridges, the most considerable of which are Copper Creek, Powell's, and Wallon's, as also several large creeks and Powell's River.

Mr. Yancy's is the entrance into Powell's Valley. A wagon road has lately been opened into and down the valley, and notwithstanding great pains and expense, the passage is so bad that at many of the mountains the wagoners are obliged to lock all the wheels and make fast a trunk of tree forty feet long to the back of the wagon to prevent it from pressing on the horses. In this manner many wagons have passed on to Kentucky.

It was late in the evening of the 13th that I arrived at the house of this Mr. Yancy, and the badness of the weather had made me determine not to go any farther, being then 8 o'clock and snowing fast. However, I found it was not so easy a matter to bring the old man and woman to think as I did; for when I demanded, or rather requested, leave to stay, they absolutely refused me, saying that we could go to a house six miles down the valley. Finding moderate words would not answer, I plainly told Mr. Yancy that I should not go any farther and that stay I would. Old Mrs. Yancy had much to say about the liberties some men take, and I replied by observing the humanity of others; and so ended our dispute. Our horse was stripped and some corn and fodder obtained. We soon found ways and means to make the rough ways smooth, and, taking out our provision bag, made a good supper; after which, placing our blankets on the floor with our feet to the fire, I slept well.

The 14th we started from Mr. Yancy's, and, the day being bad with snow and rain, we stopped at Mr. Ewing's, five miles below Lee's Court House and ten from Mr. Yancy's. At Mr. Ewing's we received the welcome of Mr. and Mrs. Ewing, at whose house we stayed until the morning of the 15th, when, after being furnished with everything we wanted and a good piece of beef to take with us, we took leave of Mr. and Mrs. Ewing and family and that night about sundown arrived at Cumberland Mountain. About half a mile before you pass this mountain you come into the road from Hawkins' Court House and Knoxville, which is said to be the best road.

After passing the mountain, which we did this night, we stopped at Mrs. Davis', who keeps a tavern down the mountain, and met with very good accommodations. Powell's Valley has lately been made a county by the name of Lee, taking all the country from Washington County to the Kentucky line. The Court House is about thirty miles up the valley from the pass of Cumberland Mountain, at which place is a small town of six or ten houses and two stores. Powell's Valley is, I am informed, about six miles broad and sixty in length. It is good land but so enclosed with mountains that it will be always difficult to enter with wagons. When the valley becomes well improved, it will be an agreeable place, but at this time it is thinly settled and [has] small farms.

On the 16th, by daylight, our horses being ready, we took our leave of Mrs. Davis, who I must take the liberty to say may be justly called Captain Molly of Cumberland Mountain, for she fully commands this passage to the New World. She soon took the freedom to tell me she was a come-by-chance — her mother she knew little of and her father, less. As to herself, she said pleasure was the only thing she had in view and that she had her ideas of life and its enjoyments, etc.

A Mr. Hay from Knoxville joined us this day. The weather still continued cold and the road which had been much broken up was now hard frozen. However, we arrived by dark at Ballinger's Tavern, thirty-seven miles from Cumberland Mountain. At this place I met with a number of gentlemen from Kentucky and a Doctor Rosse from the Illinois, with whom I had much conversation respecting that country. Our horses suffered this night, being obliged to make them fast to a tree and feed them on cane; but the accommodations for ourselves were good, considering the newness of the place.

The 17th, leaving Ballinger's, we traveled that day over an unpleasant road, passing several large waters and Cumberland River. We came at night to a small hut on Little Rock Castle, thirty miles from Richland or Ballinger's. At this place our accommodations were abominably bad. The house was about twelve feet square, and the night, which was distressingly cold, obliged all that were stopped at the place to take shelter in the hut — in all, women and children included, seventeen in number — nor can a more filthy place be imagined.

This night our horses suffered much. A few oats was all that the place afforded. After taking a supper from our provision bag, we took some rest on our blankets; and at daylight started on our journey, and in the evening arrived at the Crab Orchard, and took up our quarters at a Mr. Davis', twenty-three miles from Rock Castle, making in all ninety miles from Cumberland Mountain to the Crab Orchard. . . .

I cannot omit noticing the many distressed families I passed . . . traveling a wilderness through ice and snow; passing large rivers and creeks without shoe or stocking and barely as many rags as covers their nakedness; without money or provisions, except what the wilderness affords — the situation of such can better be imagined than described. To say they are poor is but faintly expressing their situation — Life, what is it, or what can it give, to make compensation for such accumulated misery? Ask these pilgrims what they expect when they get to Kentucky. The answer is land. "Have you any?" "No, but I expect I can git it." "Have you anything to pay for land?" "No." "Did you ever see the country?" "No, but everybody says it's good land."

Can anything be more absurd than the conduct of man? Here are hundreds, traveling hundreds of miles — they know not for what nor whither, except it's to Kentucky — passing land almost as good and easy obtained, the proprietors of which would gladly give on any terms. But it will not do. It's not Kentucky. It's not the Promised Land. It's not the goodly inheritance, the Land of Milk and Honey. And when arrived at this Heaven in Idea, what do they find? A goodly land, I will allow, but to them forbidden land. Exhausted and worn down with distress and disappointment, they are at last obliged to become hewers of wood and drawers of water. . . .

January 1, 1797, on Monday, I arrived at the town of St. Vincennes, which I found to be much larger than I had an idea of. The situation is quite charming, nor can fancy paint a more desirable spot.

From Harvies to Vincennes — five miles — is an open champaign country and extremely fertile, interspersed with islands of trees and plains or prairies quite to the banks of the Wabash. Two miles from the town are two mounds which overlook the country for some miles, as also the town and river. These mounds arise in the middle of a large plain and are said to be Indian burial grounds. However, I cannot suppose this to be true unless the world has been in being much longer than some pretend to say, and the destruction of the human family greater than we have any account of in this part of the world. However, I was told by a gentleman in Vincennes that he had taken human bones from out of the mounds and that he discovered many more in the ground. I suppose each of the mounds to be at least half a mile in circumference and from the common level of the plain to the summit, sixty feet. They are now well set with grass and have every appearance of the works of nature and not of art.

Vincennes may contain 200 houses in all, but they are small and generally one story and badly finished. The streets are narrow and very irregular. At this time not more than three-fourths of the houses are inhabited. The inhabitants, since the treaty made by General Wayne, are gone onto their farms. This place is said to have been settled in or about the year 1726 and has undergone many changes since that time, but was always a place of considerable trade and wealth until General Clark took possession of it in the year 1778 for the United States; from which time until within the last eighteen months it has been on the decline.

Vincennes is settled with French from the towns on the Mississippi and Canada. And after the town came into the hands of the United States, many of the most respectable and wealthy families left the place and either went to Detroit or the Spanish side of the Mississippi; but the natural advantage of the place and the beauty of the country will, if the Indians are peaceable, soon make Vincennes a place of consequence. The garrison at this place is commanded by Captain Parsters. It consists of fifty men. The fort or citadel commands the town and Wabash River, in which are four six-pounders.

The Wabash may be numbered among the beauties of nature. It is about 350 yards wide at the town. The banks are not high and the prairies on each side extend as far as the eye can command, forming a landscape, when viewed from the mounds back of the town, equal to anything of the kind I have ever seen. The God of this comely land has been lavish in finishing His work, for notwithstanding that the sovereign hand of winter had extended its terrific influence over all the face of creation, yet inexpressible charms could be discovered which the severity of winter could not change.

The navigation from the Ohio to Vincennes is said to be 130 miles safe and easy, upward from Vincennes, 150 miles for canoes; and the waters of the river in the spring may be navigated within a few miles of the Miami. The lands on this river are said to be equal to any in the world, forming large and extensive plains and groves of timber, and must at some time not long distant form a settlement equal to any in the United States. The west bank of the Wabash is said to overflow every spring, but the east bank, on which the town stands, is something higher and is not subject to overflow.

The aborigines which are settled on the Wabash, near Vincennes, are much reduced and some nations entirely extinct. The Piankishas [Piankashaws] had a town within one mile of St. Vincennes, but it is now destroyed and their number reduced to about 120 men. They have not any town or fixed place of residence but wander about from place to place, always calling Vincennes their home. The Wyatonas [Weas] are said to be 150 men and are settled up the Wabash, 200 miles from Vincennes. The Shakis [Sacs] I could get no information about, nor is there such a nation now known. If any of them are in being, they are united with some other nation.

I was directed to go to Colonel Small's for quarters, to which place I went and found good accommodations. The colonel and his lady were from home on a party of pleasure. And being informed of a Mr. Henry who was in town on his way to Illinois, I got a gentleman to direct me where he could be found; and calling at the house of Monsieur Dubois, I found Mr. Henry at table with a number of French gentlemen. I was unfortunate in not having letters to any gentlemen in Vincennes; however, the embarrassment I felt on this account was soon removed by the politeness of Monsieur Dubois, who, without ceremony, took me to the table and placed me beside the Roman priest. At Monsieur Dubois', I met with a number of Americans, and, notwithstanding I was a stranger to all, yet I found myself very agreeably situated.

After spending an agreeable afternoon, I returned to Colonel Small's and that evening went to a ball, where I was introduced to several gentlemen. Major Vanderburg, a man of some note, requested Mr. Henry and myself to take breakfast with him, which we did the next morning. I received much politeness from Colonel Small, Doctor Tisdale, and Monsieur Dubois, to all of whom I am much indebted, as well as Major Vanderburg. Colonel Small keeps the only tavern in Vincennes at which good accommodations can be had. There is a Catholic church at Vincennes, but the building is not of sufficient note to be known by strangers unless informed, but to whom this church is dedicated I did not learn. . . .

The morning of the 15th, Mr. Henry and myself crossed the Mississippi on the ice to St. Louis, and being told there was not any tavern in the town, I left Joseph Bell and the mule at Kahokia; nor was it without great trouble that I procured quarters for myself. And I believe I should have been obliged to have returned to Kahokia the same day had I not met with a man by the name of Drake, who spoke English and went with me to a Monsieur le Compt, who politely took Mr. Henry and myself into [his] house. After changing our dress, we immediately paid our respects to the commandant, Monsieur Zeno Trudeau, to whom we had letters. The commandant received us with much politeness and promised us all the assistance the nature of our business demanded. I had letters to a merchant, Monsieur Charles Gratiot, from whom I received much attention. Monsieur Gratiot spoke English well and was of great advantage to me as I could not speak French.

St. Louis is prettily situated on a rising spot of ground, and has a commanding prospect of the Mississippi for some distance up and down the river, and also the American side. The town of St. Louis is better built than any town on the Mississippi, and has a number of wealthy merchants and an extensive trade, from the Missouri, Illinois, and upper parts of the Mississippi. It is fast improving and will soon be a large place; the town at this time contains about 200 houses, most of which are of stone, and some of them large but not elegant. The exports of St. Louis are supposed to amount to £20,000 per annum. The trade of this place must increase, being within fifteen miles of the Missouri and thirty of the Illinois rivers.

The large settlements making on the Missouri by the Americans will be of great advantage to St. Louis, the wealth of which is so much greater than any other town on the Mississippi that it will take a long time to change the trade even from the American side to any other place. And the great advantages held out by the government of Spain will soon make the settlements on the Missouri formidable. Land has already been granted to 1,000 families, near 400 of which have arrived from different parts of the United States. Back of St. Louis is a small fort mounting four four-pounders. It is not of much strength, has a guard of twenty men only. The church is a frame building and makes but an indifferent appearance, has neither steeple nor bell.

The aborigines which trade to St. Louis are the Kakapoos [Kickapoos], Piankishas, Piorias [Peorias], Sioux, Shawanees [Shawnees] (west of the Mississippi), and Osages on the Missouri. There is none of the above Indians that confine their trade to St. Louis except the Osages. But St. Louis gets the best part of all as well as many other nations, both on the Mississippi and Missouri, which seldom or ever visit the town of St. Louis but have goods taken to them by traders employed by the merchants of St. Louis, who make their returns in the months of April and May.

The lands on the west side of the Mississippi are not equal to those on the American side, except on the Missouri River, which enters the Mississippi fifteen miles above St. Louis, and the Maramag [Meramec], ten miles below, and the Saline, six miles below St. Genevieve and sixty below St. Louis.

The River Maramag is navigable for batteaux thirty miles at all times in the year and in the spring much higher; it is about 100 yards wide at its mouth and keeps nearly its width until its forks, after which it loses its name and makes what is called the Grand River and the Mine Fork. Between the Mine Fork and Grand River are the lead mines known by the name of the Mines of Briton, which without doubt are richer than any in the known world. These mines are about forty miles from St. Louis, and thirty from St. Genevieve, and fifteen from the navigation of the Maramag. On the Maramag are several salt springs from which some salt is made, but the Saline will, it's most likely, furnish this country with salt, there being a great number of salt springs on its banks from which much salt is now made. And when the works are extended, it may furnish all the upper settlements on the Mississippi.

[On the] 16th I waited on the commandant and received letters from him to the commandant of St. Genevieve. Leaving St. Louis, I recrossed the Mississippi to Kahokia, and on the 18th arrived at the town of Kaskaskia. From Kahokia to Kaskaskia is about fifty miles and the best body of land in the world. The bottom, which extends from Kahokia to the mouth of the Kaskaskia, is in common five miles in width and, except immediately on the bank of the river and one-fourth of a mile out, is in order for any kind of farming use, being a natural meadow the whole way. Between the town of Kahokia and Kaskaskia you pass the village of Prairie Du Rocher, which has about sixty houses, as also the Little Village, which, I am told, when under the English, had fifty families and a good church, but at this time there are but three families in the town and the church is destroyed. The church at Prairie Du Rocher is a frame house and not large. It is much out of repair, has a small bell, [and] is dedicated to St. Joseph.

About thirty miles from Kahokia stands Fort Charter [Chartres]. It is a notable work, and the manner in which it is neglected proves how much this country has been and still is neglected by government. Fort Charter, when built, I am told, was a mile from the Mississippi, but the river has so changed its channel that it has demolished the west side of the fort entirely and it has fallen into the river. Each angle of the fort is 140 paces, or steps. It is built of stone taken from the Mississippi cliff; and where the walls are unhurt, they are about twenty feet high. But the south walls are much injured; the east and north are more perfect; the ditch which surrounds the fort is almost filled up. The gate was finished with hewn stone, but it is much defaced.

Within the walls of the fort is a range of stone barracks, within which is the parade. At the southeast corner of the fort stands the magazine, which is also of stone and not in the least injured. The arch appears to be as good as when finished. At the southwest corner stands the guardhouse, a part of which has fallen with the west wall into the Mississippi; between the guardhouse and the west range of barracks is a deep well walled up with hewn stone and is as good as when made. The woodwork of the barracks was destroyed, I am told, by fire. The last English garrison had orders to demolish the fort and turned their cannon against the walls for some days; however, the pieces were not sufficiently large to effect the destruction, but the walls are much injured.

The French from the Spanish side of the Mississippi have pillaged the windows and doors of the barracks of many of the best hewn stones and taken them up to St. Louis for private use. Fort Charter is said to be the best work of the kind in America.

It is not easy to account why this country has been neglected by the government of the United States; and when it is considered that it is not only a frontier as to the Indians but also as to Spain, who are taking every step to make their country formidable in case of an attack, it is not unreasonable to suppose that the executive of the United States have not a just idea of the importance of the Mississippi country or the trade they are daily losing, and which will soon be so fixed on the Spanish shore as to be hard to withdraw. Some of the standing laws of Congress as they respect the Illinois country are distressing and unjust in their operation. The law, which makes the property of all the people forfeited to the United States who have left the government of said States and do not return within five years, is cruel and severely unjust.

It ought to be remembered that in 1778 General Clark took the Illinois and left a small garrison at Kaskaskia only, who, instead of protecting the people, pillaged them at will; and when that garrison was withdrawn, which I believe was in the year '82, the whole settlement was unprotected. And notwithstanding, garrisons have been established from Georgia north for the protection of much smaller settlements, yet the Illinois have not received the least assistance from government from the time of Clark until the present moment; which obliged many families to take shelter under the Spanish government. And because they did not return and stand the scalping knife, they are to lose their property; for it is to be known that all the towns on the Mississippi have been at the mercy of the Indians until the treaty made by General Wayne. That government should take away the property of a people they could not or would not protect is something new, more especially a government like ours.

Kaskaskia, which is a place of the most consequence of any on the American side of the Mississippi and the county town of Randolph, is situated in about 38°48′ N and longitude 16° W from Philadelphia, on the banks of the River Kaskaskia, two miles from the Mississippi and five from the mouth of the Kaskaskia, in a level champaign country; and is overlooked by a hill on the opposite side of the Kaskaskia River, which commands an extensive prospect, as well of the country below as of the Mississippi and the Spanish villages of St. Genevieve and New Bourbon, forming all together a landscape beautiful and pleasing.

It is supposed to have been settled much about the same time as Philadelphia, or at least about a century ago; the oldest records in the office, which are dated in the year 1722, being marked with the number 1015, show that it was settled at an earlier period. It was formerly populous and in a flourishing condition. At present no more than from 500 to 600 souls are in the town, and it is much diminished in wealth as well as population. The many changes that have taken place in the government of this country have greatly contributed to this decay, and more especially the last when taken possession of by the Americans in the year 1778; from which time to the year 1790 it was in a manner left without any civil authority, which induced numbers of the most wealthy of the inhabitants to remove to the Spanish dominions. It is now the capital of the county of Randolph, having in the year 1795 been detached from the county of St. Clair. . . .

The Illinois country is perhaps one of the most beautiful and fertile in America and has the peculiar advantage of being interspersed with large plains or prairies and woodlands, where a crop can be made the first year without the trouble and expense of felling the timber, which in every other part of America exhausts the strength and purse of a new settler. The Mississippi affords an easy and certain conveyance for his produce, at all seasons of the year, to New Orleans, which place or some other on the lower parts of the river bids fair to be one of the greatest marts in the world. Nature has undoubtedly intended this country to be not only the most agreeable and pleasing in the world but the richest also. Not that I suppose there are many, if any, silver mines or gold dust. Nor do I consider either of them sufficient to make a country rich.

But the Mississippi has what is better — she has a rich landed country. She has the richest lead mines in the world, not only on the Maramag and its waters but also on the banks of the Mississippi, about 700 miles up from St. Louis at a place called Prairie du Chien, or Dog Prairie, at which place, or near it, is also a copper mine of malleable copper, the veins of which are more extensive than any of the kind heretofore found. She has salt springs on each side of the river and also iron ore in great quantities. These minerals are more useful in a country than gold or silver. A country thus rich by nature cannot be otherwise than wealthy with a moderate share of industry. It is also to be remembered that all the wealth of this extensive world may be warfted [shipped] to a market, at any time of the year, down the Mississippi, at an easy expense.

The 19th I passed the Mississippi on ice to St. Genevieve, which is about two miles from the bank of the river, which at this place is about a mile over. I presented my letters from the commandant of St. Louis to Monsieur Valle, the commandant of St. Genevieve, who received me with much politeness and promised me all the assistance in his power. And on the 21st, being furnished with a carryall and two horses, I left St. Genevieve in company with a Mr. Jones of Kaskaskia for the Mines of Briton; and on the 23rd, arrived at the place. I found the mines equal to my expectation in every respect. The weather turning warm, we were obliged to make a quicker return than I wished. However, I satisfied myself as to the object I had in view and returned to St. Genevieve on the 26th.

The Mines of Briton, so called in consequence of their being found by a man of that name, are about thirty miles from the town of St. Genevieve. There is a good wagon road to the place, and all the lead that has been made at them is by making a fire over the ore with large logs, which melts some of the ore, by which means about two-thirds of the lead is lost. Notwithstanding the imperfect manner in which they melt the ore, yet at the Mines of Briton last summer was made 400,000 pounds of lead; and from an experiment I made, the same quantity of ore that was made use of to make the 400,000 pounds would have made 1,200,000 pounds of lead, if I was rightly informed as to the quantity of ore they took to make 1,000 pounds of lead in the log fires. The ore at the Mines of Briton covers about forty acres of ground and is found within three feet of the surface of the earth in great plenty and better quality than any I have ever seen, either from the mines in England or America.

The town of St. Genevieve is about two miles from the Mississippi on the high land from which you have a commanding view of the country and river. The old town stood immediately on the bank of the river in an extensive plain. But it being sometimes overflowed by the Mississippi and many of the houses washed into the river by the falling of the bank, it was thought advisable to remove the town to the heights. The place is small, not over 100 houses, but has more inhabitants than Kaskaskia and the houses are in better repair and the citizens are more wealthy. It has some Indian trade; but what has made the town of St. Genevieve are the lead and salt that are made near the place, the whole of which is brought to town for sale, and from thence shipped up and down the Mississippi River, as well as up the Ohio to Cumberland and Kentucky. And when the lead mines are properly worked and the salt springs advantageously managed, St. Genevieve will be a place of as much wealth as any on the Mississippi.

One mile from St. Genevieve, down the river, is a small village called New Bourbon, of about twenty houses. At this place I was introduced to the Chevalier Pierre Charles de Hault de Lassus, a French nobleman, formerly of the Council of the late king of France. Chevalier de Lassus told me he had an estate in France of 30,000 crowns, but was obliged to make his escape to America and leave all, which has since been taken by the present government. Madame de Lassus had an estate of half that sum per annum, so that the yearly income of the family, besides the sums allowed him by the king, amounted to 45,000 crowns per annum. Madame de Lassus did not appear to support the change of situation so well as the chevalier. I was examining a large piece of painting, which was in Madame de Lassus' bedchamber, representing a grand festival given by the citizens of Paris to the queen on the birth of the dauphin and a parade of all the nobles on the same occasion. She came to me and putting her finger on the picture pointing out a couch: "There," said she, "was I on that happy day. My situation is now strangely changed."

After taking leave of Chevalier de Lassus, I recrossed the river to Kaskaskia; and on the 8th of February took my leave of the good people of Kaskaskia, taking a Frenchman by the name of Degar as a guide to Fort Massac, setting my face homeward. After rafting and swimming several rivers, I arrived at the Ohio about eighteen miles above Fort Massac, where a number of Frenchmen were camped for hunting. With much trouble and danger I swam my horses over the Ohio, getting another Frenchman as a guide.

I, on the 17th day of February, arrived at the town of Nashville, on [the] Cumberland River in the state of Tennessee. At this place I rested myself and horses six days. And then, in company with fourteen others, some women and some men, took the wilderness for Knoxville; and without meeting anything uncommon, arrived at Knoxville on the 4th day of March, where I stayed but a night; and on the 9th day of the month arrived at the village of Austinville after an absence of three months and nine days, making a journey of upward of 2,000 miles, 960 of which was a wilderness, and the snow most of the way two feet deep. Five days of the time I was without provisions.

I have made these few observations of my journey to the Mississippi for the use of my son, should he live to my age, not doubting but by that time the country I have passed in a state of nature will be overspread with towns and villages; for it is not possible a country which has within itself everything to make its settlers rich and happy can remain unnoticed by the American people.

The dark and bloody ground.

Anon.; the words are the translation of the Indian name, Kentucky

2.

James Smith: The Rich Land of the Frontier

James Smith, a member of a family of wealthy Virginia planters, explored parts of Pennsylvania and the present Kentucky and Ohio during the years from 1783 to 1797. A Methodist minister, Smith devoted himself to the task of bringing the word of Christ to the settlers in these wilderness regions. Only a few years before his death, he began to explore the land northwest of the Ohio River. The excerpts, reprinted here from his journals of 1795 and 1797, exhibit his enthusiasm for this country from which slavery was excluded by the Northwest Ordinance of 1787. Although Smith employed slaves on his plantation, his was one of the strongest antislavery voices prior to the Abolitionist movement of the 1840s.

Source: *Ohio Archaeological and Historical Publications,* Vol. XVI: "Tours into Kentucky and the Northwest Territory."

Having now finished my tour through the territory northwest of the Ohio, it may not be amiss to speak in general terms of the country through which I have passed. From Cincinnati we found the lands near the river broken, not very rich, a little sand and some small pebble stones. Five or six miles from the river the lands were level, clear of stone, soil rich, water good, and clear and serene air. As we advanced farther the lands continued level, but were not as well watered as they were a little back. Within about nine or ten miles of Hamilton the lands, I think, are the richest I ever saw. The growth is mostly walnut, sugar tree [sugar maple], etc., tied together by clusters of grapevines, which in this country grow amazingly large. From this to Hamilton is the most beautiful level that ever my eyes beheld; the soil is rich, free from swampy or marshy ground, and the growth mostly hickory.

Near Hamilton we saw several *pararas* [prairies], as they are called. They are large tracts of fine, rich land, without trees and producing as fine grass as the best meadows. From Hamilton down the Miami River to the Ohio, the lands exceed description. Indeed, this country of all others that I ever saw seems best calculated for earthly happiness. If you have a desire to raise great quantities of corn, wheat, or other grain, here is perhaps the best soil in the world, inviting your industry. If you prefer the raising of cattle or feeding large flocks of sheep, here the beautiful and green *parara* excites your wonder and claims your attention. If, wearied with toil, you seek the bank of the river as a place to rest; here the fishes sporting in the limpid stream invite you to cast in your hook and draw forth nourishment for yourself and your family. The most excellent fowl perch in the trees and flutter in the waters, while these immense woods produce innumerable quantities of the most excellent venison. Amidst this rich, this pleasing variety, he must be undeserving the name of man who will want the common comforts of life. Glad should I have been to have had a little more time to have pleased my eyes with a view of this delightful country. But circumstances call me hence. I must now take off mine eyes and turn them another way and for the present bid adieu to this delightful land.

LIBERTY AND SLAVERY

I CANNOT, HOWEVER, on this occasion conceal the warm emotions of my heart. Long have I wished to see a land, sacred to liberty, nor stained with the crimson dye of blood. A land where slavery, the present disgrace and the future scourge of America, should not be permitted to come. This ardent wish I at length see accomplished and in this infant country behold the features of true felicity and greatness. Here I see genuine liberty and national happiness growing up together, on the firm foundation and under the guardian protection of constitutional authority.

Yes, I anticipate, O land, the rising glory of thy unequaled fame. Thy forests, now wild and uncultivated, soon shall the hand of industry sow with golden grain. Thy unequaled soil, cultivated by the fostering hands of freemen, shall e'er long display its beauties and yield an increase worthy a land of liberty. Thy stately trees, habituated for ages to lie and rot, shall e'er long raise the lofty dome and be fashioned into curious workmanship by the hand of the ingenious artist. Thy large and noble rivers, which silently flow in gentle currents, shall e'er long waft thy rich products to distant markets in foreign climes; and thou, beautiful Ohio, shalt stand an impenetrable barrier to guard this sacred land. And though the tears of the oppressed on thy southeastern border may help increase thy crystal tide, yet the galling yoke, should it attempt to cross thy current, shall sink beneath thy wave and be buried in thy bosom. The voice of the oppressor may spread terror and dismay throughout the eastern and southern states, but farther than thy delightful banks it cannot, it dare not, it shall not be heard. Yes, in thee, O thrice happy land, shall be fulfilled an ancient prophecy.

> The wilderness and the solitary place shall be glad and the desert shall rejoice, and blossom as the rose . . . the glory of Lebanon shall be given unto it, the excellency of Carmel and Sharon . . . for in the wilderness shall waters break out, and streams in the desert. . . . There the weary prisoners shall rest together and hear not the voice of the oppressor *(Isaiah 35. Job 3.)*.

I must now leave this fair land of happiness with offering to Heaven this humble request: May the foot of pride never come against thee, nor human blood stain thy lovely plains. May the scourge of war never desolate thee, nor cruel tyrants raise their banners here. May thy aged never feel the loss of liberty, nor the yoke of slavery rest on the necks of thy children. May thy gates remain open to the oppressed of all nations and may those that flock thither be the excellent ones of the earth; and if the still continued oppressions of enlightened Virginia should at length bring down the just judgments of an incensed Deity, may it be when I or those that pertain unto me have found an asylum in thy peaceful borders. . . .

DESCRIPTION OF THE COUNTRY NORTHWEST OF THE OHIO

HAVING NOW TRAVELED between 300 and 400 miles through this country, I think I can form a tolerable judgment of the same and will as concisely as possible give a general description of the same before I leave it. The land naturally claims the first place. Bordering on the rivers, the land exceeds description. Suffice it to say that the soil is amazingly rich, not subject to overflow, unbroken with gulches and gutters, as level as a bowling plain, and vastly extensive. Leaving the rivers, a high hill skirts the low ground. Here the land is still amazingly fertile, covered with a heavy growth of timber, such as white and red oak, hickory, ash, beech, sugar tree, walnut, buckeye, etc. Here a number of small streams take their rise, then gently creep along through the winding valleys; and in their course these winding streams form a great quantity of excellent meadowland. These streams uniting increase their consequence; the meadows enlarge and extend themselves, till they discharge their crystal streams into the rivers.

As to mountains, there are properly speaking none; there are, however, high hills from which a beautiful view of the adjoining country presents itself. There is generally but little stone. Quarries of freestone are plenty on the Scioto and limestone in many places. The land is generally very light, soft and easy to cultivate. Indian corn grows to great perfection; wheat, oats, rye, etc., thrive amazingly well. All kinds of roots, such as potatoes, turnips, and the like, grow extremely well. Cotton also grows very well, and hemp and flax come to great perfection.

Grass of the meadow kind grows all over this country and white clover and bluegrass grow spontaneously wherever the land is cleared. A country so famous for grass must of course be excellent for all kinds of stock. Here I saw the finest beef and mutton that I ever saw, fed on grass. Hogs also increase and fatten in the woods in a most surprising manner. Exclusive of tame cattle, great numbers of wild beasts, as bears, buffalo, deer, elk, etc., shelter in these immense woods. The rivers produce an infinite number of fish; besides geese, ducks and the like, turkeys, pheasants, partridges, etc., are produced in great plenty and get exceedingly fat on the produce of the forest. Honey itself is not wanting to make up the rich variety. Incredible numbers of bees have found their way to this delightful region and in vast quantities deposit their honey in the trees of the woods, so that it is not an uncommon thing for the people to take their wagon and team and return loaded with honey.

The water of this country is generally very good. The rivers are clear as crystal and the springs are bold, good, and in considerable plenty.

The air appears clear and serene, not subject to dampness and vapors which render a country unwholesome. Neither does it appear subject to those sudden changes and alterations which are so pernicious to health and prejudicial to fruits and vegetables. When these things are duly considered, the country which possesses these natural advantages surely merits notice. But when we recollect this country is the asylum of liberty; that cruelty has not stained the country with blood; that freedom and equality are the precious boon of its inhabitants; and that this is to be the case in the future, surely this of all countries is most worthy of our attention and esteem.

3.

An Act to Prevent the Spreading of Contagious Sickness

Smallpox epidemics reached serious proportions in America in the eighteenth century. Public health organizations were virtually nonexistent, but some local communities took ad hoc *measures to combat epidemics. These included the quarantine of individuals and even whole villages that were suspected of harboring the disease and occasional stringent restrictions on commerce and travel. Massachusetts pioneered, toward the end of the century, in state-wide health programs, and on June 22, 1797, the state legislature passed the following public health law.*

Source: *Report of a General Plan for the Promotion of Public and Personal Health,* Boston, 1850, pp. 326-332.

Section 1. *Be it enacted by the Senate and House of Representatives, in General Court assembled, and by the authority of the same,* that for the better preventing the spreading of infection, when it shall happen that any person or persons coming from abroad, or belonging to any town or place within this state, shall be visited, or shall lately before have been visited with the plague, smallpox, pestilential or malignant fever, or other contagious sickness, the infection whereof may probably be communicated to others; the selectmen of the town where such person or persons may arrive or be are hereby empowered to take care and make effectual provision in the best way they can for the preservation of the inhabitants, by removing such sick or infected person or persons and placing him or them in a separate house or houses, and by providing nurses, attendance, and other assistance and necessaries for them; which nurses, attendance, and other assistance and necessaries shall be at the charge of the parties themselves, their parents or masters (if able), or otherwise at the charge of the town or place whereto they belong; and in case such person or persons are not inhabitants of any town or place within this state, then at the charge of the commonwealth.

Section 2. *And be it further enacted,* that any person or persons coming from any place out of this state, where the smallpox or other malignant distemper is prevailing, into any town within this state, shall, when thereto required by the selectmen of such town, within the space of two hours from the time they shall be first informed of their duty by law in this particular, give notice to one or more of the selectmen, or the clerk of such town, of their coming there, and of the place from whence they came, upon pain of forfeiting, in case of neglect, the sum of $100.

And such person or persons, if not disabled by sickness, shall, within the space of two hours after warning given to him or them by the selectmen of such town for that purpose, depart from this state in such manner, and by such road, as the said selectmen shall direct; and in case of refusal, it shall be lawful for any justice of the peace in the county where such town may lie, by warrant directed to a constable or other proper officer, or other person whom the justice shall judge proper, to cause such person or persons to be removed into the state from whence he or they may have come.

And any person removed by warrant as aforesaid, who, during the prevalence of such distemper, shall presume to return into any town of this state without liberty first obtained from such justice, shall forfeit and pay the sum of $400; and any inhabitant of this state who shall entertain in his house any person warned to depart as aforesaid, for the space of two hours after notice given him of such warning by one or more of the selectmen aforesaid, shall forfeit and pay the sum of $200.

Section 3. *And be it further enacted,* that it shall and may be lawful for the selectmen of any town near to, or bordering upon either of the neighboring states, to appoint, by writing, under their hands, some meet [suitable] person or persons to attend at ferries or other places by or over which passengers may pass from such infected places; which person or persons so appointed, shall have power to examine such passengers, as they may suspect to bring infection with them, and, if need be, to hinder and restrain them from traveling, until licensed thereto by a justice of the peace within such county, or by the selectmen of the town in which such person or persons may come.

And any passenger who, coming from such infected place, shall (without license as aforesaid) presume to travel within this state, unless it be to return by the most direct way to the state from whence he came, after he shall be cautioned to depart by the person or persons appointed as aforesaid, shall forfeit and pay the sum of $100; the several forfeitures aforesaid to be recovered by action of debt in any court of record proper to try the same, one moiety [a half] to and for the use of the town where the offense shall be committed and the other moiety to the use of the person who may sue for the same.

Section 4. *And be it further enacted,* that if need be, any two justices of the peace may make out a warrant directed to the sheriff of the county or his deputy, or constables of the town or place where any such sick person or persons may be, requiring them or any of them, in the name of the Commonwealth, with the advice and direction of the selectmen of the same, to remove such infected person or persons, or to impress and take up convenient houses, lodging, nurses, attendance, and other necessaries, for the accommodation, safety, and relief of the sick. And such sheriff, his deputy, and constable are hereby authorized and required to execute such warrant accordingly.

Section 5. *And be it further enacted,* that whenever there shall be brought into any town within this state, either from any other town therein or from parts without the state, any baggage, clothing, or goods of any kind whatsoever, and it shall be made to appear to the selectmen of the town to which such baggage, clothing, or other goods shall be brought, or by the major part of such selectmen, to the satisfaction of any justice of the peace, that there is just cause to suspect baggage, clothing, or other goods to be infected with the plague, smallpox, pestilential fever, or other malignant contagious distemper; it shall be lawful for such justice of the peace, and he is hereby required, in such case, by warrant under his hand and seal, directed to the sheriff or his deputy, or any constable of the town in which such baggage, clothing, or other goods shall be, requiring him to impress so many men as said justice shall judge necessary to secure such baggage, clothing, or other goods, and said men to post as a guard and watch over the house or other place or places where such baggage, clothing, or other goods shall be lodged. Which guard and watch are hereby required to take effectual care to prevent such baggage, clothing, or other goods being removed or intermeddled with by any persons whatsoever until due inquiry be made into the circumstances thereof, requiring likewise the said sheriff, his deputy, or the constable aforesaid, if it shall appear necessary, with the advice and direction of said selectmen, to impress and take up convenient houses or stores, for the receiving, lodging, and safekeeping of such baggage, clothing, or other goods, until the same shall be sufficiently cleansed from infection.

And in case it shall appear highly probable to the said justice that such baggage, clothing, or other goods are infected as aforesaid, he is hereby empowered and directed to issue his warrant in manner as aforesaid, requiring said sheriff, his deputy, or any constable, or other person therein specially named, to remove said baggage, clothing, or other goods to some convenient place where there shall be the least danger of the infection spreading; there to remain until the same shall be sufficiently aired and freed from infection, in the opinion of said selectmen.

And the said sheriff, deputy sheriff, or constable, in the execution of said warrants, are empowered and directed, if need be, to break up any house, warehouse, shop, or other place particularly mentioned in said warrant where such baggage, clothing, or other goods shall be; and in case of opposition, to require such aid as shall be necessary to effect the execution of said warrants and repel such opposition; and all persons are hereby required, at the commandment of either of the said officers, having either of the warrants aforesaid, under penalty of $10, to be recovered before any justice of the peace in the county where such opposition may happen, to assist such officer in the execution of the same warrant against any opposition as aforesaid; and the charges of securing such baggage, clothing, or other goods, and of airing and transporting the same, shall be borne and paid by the owners thereof at such rates and prices as shall be set and appointed by the selectmen of the town where such baggage, clothing, or other goods shall be, to be recovered by action of debt, by any person or persons who may have been employed in the business aforesaid, in any court of record proper to try the same.

Section 6. *And be it further enacted,* that inquiry shall be made by the officer or other person on duty at the Castle in the harbor of Boston of every vessel coming from sea and passing by the said Castle, whether any infectious sickness be on board, or has been on board since such vessel left the port from whence she last came; and if any such vessel has any sickness on board, or has had any on board since her leaving such port. In such case, orders shall be given by said officer or other person on duty to the master or commander of such vessel immediately to anchor and to remain at anchor until a certificate shall be obtained from the major part of the selectmen of the town of Boston that they are of opinion that such vessel may come up to the town without danger to the inhabitants, or until the said master or commander shall receive orders from the said selectmen to anchor his vessel near the hospital on Rainsford's Island, in the harbor of Boston.

And in case any master or commander of a vessel shall, by himself, or the people on board, make false answer when inquired of as aforesaid by the officer or other person on duty as aforesaid, or, after orders are given as aforesaid, shall neglect or refuse to anchor near the Castle as aforesaid, or come on shore, or suffer any passenger or other person belonging to the vessel to come on shore, or any goods to be taken out before the vessel shall have anchored, or without liberty from the selectmen as aforesaid; or in case any master or commander of a vessel ordered to anchor near the hospital aforesaid shall neglect or refuse so to do; in every such case, every master or commander so offending shall forfeit and pay for each offense the sum of $400, or suffer six months' imprisonment.

Section 7. *And be it further enacted,* that upon application made to the selectmen of the town of Boston by any master or commander of any vessel at anchor near the hospital as aforesaid, the said selectmen are hereby empowered to permit such passengers, goods, or lading, as they shall judge free from infection, to come on shore, or to be taken out and disposed of as the owners shall see fit; and such passengers and goods as shall not be permitted as aforesaid, shall remain on board, or be landed on said island.

And if any master or commander of any such vessel, for the time being, shall come on shore, or suffer any of his people or passengers to come on shore, or any boat to come on board, or suffer any goods to be taken out of his vessel, unless permitted as aforesaid, or shall come up to said town with his vessel until by a certificate under the hands of said selectmen, or the major part of them, it shall appear, that said vessel, company, and goods are clear of infection, and the orders for stopping the same be removed or taken off, he shall, for every such offense, forfeit the sum of $200; and in case he be not able to pay that sum, he shall suffer three months' imprisonment.

And if any sailors or passengers coming in said vessel shall, without the knowledge or consent of the master or commander, presume to come on shore, or up above the Castle aforesaid; or if any person shall knowingly presume to go on board from shore, or to go to the aforesaid house or island in time of infection there, without leave as aforesaid; or if any person put sick into the said house, or sent there on suspicion of being infected, shall presume to go off the said island without leave as aforesaid; any person offending in any of the particulars above mentioned shall forfeit the sum of $200; and in case such person be not able to pay said forfeiture, he shall suffer two months' imprisonment.

All prosecutions for offenses contrary to this and the preceding section shall be by indictment or information in the Supreme Judicial Court or Court of General Sessions of the Peace; and one moiety of all fines mentioned in said sections shall be to the use of the town of Boston, and the other moiety to the use of the selectmen of said town for the time being, whose particular duty it is hereby made to prosecute therefore.

Section 8. *And be it further enacted,* that whenever any ship or vessel wherein any infection or infectious sickness has lately been shall come to any harbor within this state, or whenever any person or persons belonging to, or that may either by sea or land come into, any town or place near the public hospital aforesaid, shall be visited, or shall lately before have been visited with any infectious sickness, two of the justices of the peace, or selectmen of such place, be and hereby are empowered immediately to order the said vessel and sick persons to the said hospital, there to be taken care of according to the directions of this act.

And where any such ship, vessel, or persons cannot, without great inconvenience and damage, be ordered to the aforesaid hospital; in any such case, the rules and directions are to be observed which are provided in the first enacting clause of this act.

And in case the master or mariners of any vessel ordered to the hospital as aforesaid shall refuse or delay for the space of six hours after such order being given to said master, or either of the owners of said vessel, or of the factors, or either of said owners of the goods, to come to sail, if wind and weather permit, in order to proceed to said hospital; such master so refusing shall forfeit and pay the sum of $400; and each mariner so refusing, the sum of $100; and in case they be not able to pay said sums, they shall suffer six months' imprisonment, one-half of said fine to be to the informer, and the other half to the poor of the town or district to which such port or harbor belongs; and to be recovered in any court of record proper to try the same, by indictment or information.

Section 9. *And be it further enacted,* that if any master, seaman, or passenger belonging to any vessel on board which any infection is or may have lately been, or suspected to have been, or which may have come from any port where any infectious, mortal distemper prevails, shall refuse to make answer on oath to such questions as may be asked him or them relating to such infection by the selectmen of the town to which such vessel may come (which oath the said selectmen are hereby empowered to administer) such master, seaman, or passenger so refusing shall forfeit the sum of $200; and in case he be not able to pay said sum, he shall suffer six months' imprisonment; said penalty to be adjudged on prosecution by indictment on information in any court proper to try the same, one moiety of said fine to the use of the town where the offense may be committed, and the other moiety to the use of the selectmen thereof, whose particular duty it is hereby made to prosecute therefor.

And the selectmen of Boston are hereby authorized and directed to provide nurses, assistance, and other necessaries for the comfort and relief of such sick persons as may be sent to said hospital as aforesaid, the charge thereof to be borne by the said persons themselves, if able; or if poor and unable, by the towns to which they respectively belong; or if not inhabitants of any particular town or other place within this state, then by the Commonwealth.

Section 10. *And be it further enacted,* that whenever the smallpox or other mortally infectious distemper shall prevail in any of the towns wherein the Supreme Judicial Court of this Commonwealth, the courts of Common Pleas or General Sessions of the Peace are to be held, at the times prescribed by law, or by their own adjournment, for their sitting in such town; the justices of the said courts, respectively, are hereby empowered to adjourn and hold said courts in any town within the same county, by proclamation to be made in the shire, town, or as near the same as safety will, in their opinion, permit.

Section 11. *Be it further enacted,* that each town or district in this Commonwealth may, at their meeting held in March or April annually, or at any other meeting legally warned for the purpose, when they shall judge it to be necessary, choose and appoint a health committee, to consist of not less than five nor more than nine suitable persons, or one person to be a health officer, whose duty it shall be to remove all filth of any kind whatever which shall be found in any of the streets, lanes, wharves, docks, or in any other place whatever within the limits of the town to which such committee or health officer belongs, whenever such filth shall, in their judgment, endanger the lives or the health of the inhabitants thereof; all the expenses whereof to be paid by the person or persons who placed it there, if known; or if not, by the town by which said committee or health officer was appointed.

And whenever any filth as aforesaid shall be found on private property, said committee or health officer shall notify and order the owner or occupier thereof, after twenty-four hours' notice, to remove the same, at their own expense; and in case said owner or occupier shall neglect to remove such filth from his or her property after the expiration of the time aforesaid, he or they so offending shall forfeit and pay a fine of $100, to be sued for and recovered, with costs of suit, by said committee or health officer, before any court proper to try the same, for the use of the poor of the town in which such offense is committed.

And said owner or occupier as aforesaid shall be liable and obliged to repay to said town all cost and charges which the said committee or health officer may have incurred in removing the filth from his or her property; and in case of refusal to pay the same, he or they may be sued in the same way as is provided in this act for the recovery of fines as aforesaid.

Section 12. *And be it further enacted,* that whenever any vessel shall arrive at any port other than Boston within this Commonwealth, having on board any person visited with the plague, smallpox, malignant fever, or any other pestilential disease, the master, commander, or pilot thereof shall not bring such vessel up near the town of the port where she first arrives until liberty be first granted, in writing, by the selectmen thereof; but they may bring such vessel to an anchor in such place below the town as will be most for the safety of the inhabitants thereof, and the preservation of the vessel and the people on board, there to wait for orders from the selectmen of such town, before any passenger or person belonging to, or anything on board the same, be brought on shore.

And any master or commander of such vessel who shall be found guilty of a breach of the law contained in this section shall forfeit and pay a fine of $200 for every such offense, upon conviction thereof before any court proper to try the same. And any pilot who may go on board any such vessel and pilot the same up to the town, without liberty first had and obtained from the selectmen thereof as aforesaid, shall, upon conviction in manner as aforesaid, forfeit and pay a fine of $50 for every such offense.

All which fines contained in this section may be sued for and recovered, with costs of suit, in manner as aforesaid, by the selectmen of the town where the offense is committed, to and for the use of the same town.

Section 13. *And be it further enacted,* that a law of this Commonwealth, made in the year 1701, providing in case of sickness; one other law made in addition thereto in the year 1751; one other law made in the year 1730, empowering courts to adjourn and remove from the towns appointed by law for holding courts, to other towns, in case of sickness by the smallpox; one other law made in the year of our Lord 1757, for regulating the hospital on Rainsford's Island, and further providing in case of sickness; one law passed the next year, in addition thereto; one other law made in the year 1742, to prevent the spreading of the smallpox and other infectious sickness, and to prevent the concealing the same, be and they are hereby repealed, except that the same shall remain in force for the purpose of recovering all fines incurred by force thereof.

I am an aristocrat. I love justice and hate equality.

John Randolph of Roanoke

4.

ALBERT GALLATIN: A Profit Sharing Agreement

The origins of profit sharing in American business have long been uncertainly traced to Albert Gallatin, the secretary of the treasury under Jefferson and Madison. "The democratic principle on which this nation was founded," Gallatin once wrote, "should not be restricted to the political processes but should be applied to the industrial operations as well." Though this statement is in keeping with Gallatin's known policies and actions, no proof that he actually practised profit sharing in his own business was available until recent scholarship uncovered the agreement reprinted here. It was signed in 1797 by Gallatin and his partners, who operated a glass factory, and a glass blower named George Kramer and his fellow workers. The contract also provided for a stock purchase plan, whereby the employees were able to buy into the business.

Source: Manuscript in the possession of the Council of Profit Sharing Industries, Chicago, Illinois.

THESE ARTICLES OF AGREEMENT entered into this 20th day of September, 1797, between the copartnership of Albert Gallatin, Louis Bourdillon, John Badollet, James W. Nicholson, and Charles A. Cazenove, trading under the firm of Albert Gallatin & Company of New Geneva in Fayette County, State of Pennsylvania, of the one part, and George Kramer, Adolphus Eberhart, Ludowitz Reitz, Christian Kramer, and George Repert, glassmakers, and now of Fayette County aforesaid, of the other part, do witness that the above-mentioned parties have entered into an association of copartnership for the purpose of erecting glassworks and establishing a manufacture of glass on the following conditions, that is to say:

First. The above-mentioned copartnership shall continue for the term of six years from the date of these presents.

Second. Albert Gallatin & Company shall advance the whole of the monies necessary to erect the buildings belonging to the said manufacture and for establishing and carrying on the said glassworks on the seat they have appropriated for that purpose of their land near New Geneva.

Third. The above-mentioned parties of the second part shall attend to and work at the said manufacture for the term of six years, for which work they shall be paid and allowed the usual rate and pay of such labor and work.

Fourth. The neat profits of the said works, after deducting all expenses (including in said expenses the pay of the above-mentioned parties of the second part as workmen according to the next preceding article), both as to erecting and carrying on the works, shall belong to and be equally divided between the parties of the first part and the parties of the second part, that is to say Albert Gallatin & Company shall be entitled to one half of the said profits and George Kramer and the other workmen his associates of the second part, for and in consideration of their attending and working at the said manufacture, and of refunding one half of the advances made by the said Albert Gallatin & Company in the manner hereafter mentioned, shall be entitled to the other half of the said neat profits.

Fifth. George Kramer and his associates, the parties of the second part, shall repay to Albert Gallatin & Company one half of all the advances made by said Albert Gallatin & Company, by virtue of the second article of these presents, for erecting and carrying on the said glassworks, out of the half of the neat profits allowed to them by the preceding articles, so that they shall not be entitled to receive any part of their said half until one half of all the advances thus made by Albert Gallatin & Company shall have been fully repaid and refunded to them out of the said half of neat profits thus allowed to the said George Kramer and his associates, the parties of the second part, but no interest shall be charged by said Albert Gallatin & Company on the advances thus made by them.

Sixth. In addition to the above, Albert Gallatin & Company also for and in consideration of the conditions entered into by the parties of the second part in these presents, will convey them in fee simple the five town lots in New Geneva this day agreed upon between the parties to this agreement, and also that spot of ground adjoining the glassworks which has been marked out and designated between the parties above-mentioned for that purpose, to the said George Kramer and his associates, the parties of the second part.

In witness whereof the above-mentioned parties have set their hands and affixed their seals to this and another instrument of writing of the same tenor and date, the day and year first above mentioned.

1798

5.

TADEUSZ KOSCIUSZKO: American Will and Testament

Though the French were among the most active supporters of the American Revolution, representatives of many other nationalities came to participate in the war. Tadeusz (Thaddeus) Kosciuszko was a Polish patriot who, following a tragic love affair, immigrated to America and became a colonel of engineers in the Revolutionary forces. His friend, Thomas Jefferson, once wrote that Kosciuszko was "the purest son of liberty . . . that I have ever known, the kind of liberty which extends to all, not only to the rich." Kosciuszko's hope for the liberty of all peoples is reflected in his will, which he wrote shortly before returning to Europe in 1798. The condition of Negro slaves prompted him to bequeath his lands in Ohio for the purpose of bettering their lot. The execution of this will was entrusted to Jefferson who, on May 5, 1798, incorporated Kosciuszko's wishes into legal language. The original words of the will, reprinted here, were written around April 20. Although the exact terms of Kosciuszko's bequest were never fulfilled, his estate was used in 1826 to found an American school for Negroes, the Colored School, at Newark, New Jersey.

Source: Massachusetts Historical Society, Jefferson Collection, [Miecislaus Haiman, *Kosciuszko: Leader and Exile*, New York, 1946, p. 76].

I BEG MR. JEFFERSON that in case I should die without will or testament he should buy out of my money so many Negroes and free them, that the restant [remaining] sum should be sufficient to give them education and provide for their maintenance. That is to say, each should know before the duty of a citizen in the free government; that he must defend his country against foreign as well as internal enemies who would wish to change the Constitution for the worse to enslave them by degree afterward; to have good and human heart sensible for the sufferings of others; each must be married and have 100 acres of land, with instruments, cattle for tillage, and know how to manage and govern it as well; to know how to behave to neighbors, always with kindness and ready to help them; to themselves [they must be] frugal; to their children give good education (I mean as to the heart and the duty to their country); [and] in gratitude to me, to make themselves happy as possible.

6.

Benjamin H. Latrobe: Thoughts on Education

Following the Revolution, there was a revival of interest in schooling. In newspaper articles and pamphlets, journalists and educators argued about what kind of education was most suitable for Americans. Many believed that the curriculum should be practical and should stress subjects such as arithmetic and grammar, rather than the traditional classics. Benjamin Latrobe, the architect and engineer, who had been educated in Latin and Greek literature, concurred in these more modern views. Writing from Richmond, Virginia, on May 28, 1798, he expressed his ideas about education to Ferdinand Fairfax, of Shannon Hall, Shenandoah.

Source: *The Journal of Latrobe,* New York, 1905: "Thoughts on National System of Education."

Education has been the subject of innumerable treatises. They have all, even those which are founded in the boldest and most original trains of thinking, received part of their character from the habits acquired by their authors from the mode which was fashionable in their own education. There is a fashion even of sentiment, and wherever there is fashion there is bigotry. I wish we could get rid of fashions in thinking. I think this age less addicted to them than the preceding have been. At all events, more fashions are suffered to live together as contemporaries than formerly, and we have a greater choice of them. They therefore improve by emulation. The old ones, which were seldom changed, and the absurdity of which was not so easily discovered for want of contrast, seldom ceased to be worn until they would no longer hang together.

While religion and law were the only paths of learning which led to riches and honor, and while priests occupied both professions, it was (exclusively of other circumstances which made the rest of barbarous Europe dependent upon the remnant of Roman civilization in Italy) good policy in the priests to entrench themselves in the Latin and Greek languages. How effectually the Latin religion and the Latin law of the centuries between the sixth and the fifteenth held Europe in the most abject subjection to ecclesiastical and political tyrants everybody knows. A mathematician was then a heretic, and a natural philosopher a wizard.

After the reformers had driven the priests from many of their strongholds, and Lord Bacon had pointed out by the way of experiment the true road to science or, which is synonymous, to truth, the habits of mankind, though their knowledge was increased, still continued to subsist. Accustomed to see pretended knowledge only in Greek and Latin dress, they could not bear to behold truth in the plain garb of a vernacular idiom, but tricked out the simple, chaste maiden in the foppery of the harlot.

Learning, in fact, within the remembrance of everyone who is above thirty, was another word for Greek and Latin. Oxford, and even Cambridge, are yet immense hospitals in which lingers, decrepit and mortally wounded, what remains of Greek and Latin ignorance in England; and within these forty years in Germany, to write upon any literary subject in German was to proclaim the ignorance of the author. Out of the pale, however, of the old seminaries whose crazy and diseased constitutions can never be repaired, and which may now be safely suffered to die a natural death, the men of letters, both in Europe and America, have shaken off the shackles of the dead languages, and quitting their study with the slavery of the schools, more useful knowledge employs their attention and their time. Now no man of genius or clear understanding devotes himself to the settling of doubtful readings in useless works or to the acquisition of the command of a language which he will never be required to speak or to write.

In the establishment of a new seminary in a country, the social and political duties of which are settled, it were much to be wished that every part of instruction should tend to render the citizen useful and the man happy. A republic would be ill served if its schools were only contrived to create a privileged class of men furnished with languages, to the acquirement of which in perfection a gregarious education of long continuance is absolutely necessary, which cannot be applied to the common transactions of life, and which, therefore, as we see of other things that are useless and rare, command reverence from those who want and feel pride in those who profess them.

As America took the lead in the practice of improved political theory in the organization of a community, I sincerely wish that she may set the example of a rational education of her citizens.

American citizens may be divided into only three classes — cultivators of the soil, artisans, and merchants. Of the practical sciences, the first have most occasion for a knowledge of chemistry, natural history, and national philosophy; the second, of those branches of mathematics called usually mechanics; and the third, of numeral mathematics. To each a general range of science is highly useful, but these ought, in my opinion, to be the leading objects of education in an American seminary. They may be acquired without the knowledge of Latin or Greek, although an acquaintance with these beautiful languages will greatly ease the memory in retaining the technical vocabulary and assist in comprehending the precise meaning of terms, most of which are taken from them. Young men, and of these there will always be a great number in a country circumstanced as ours is — young men who will have sufficient property to purchase philosophic leisure, whose business it is "to do little, but to observe everything," will, in such a course of study, be rendered capable of employing and amusing themselves usefully throughout their lives, while little can be expected from a mere knowledge of Greek and Latin toward the improvement of the enjoyments of American society.

I cannot, therefore, help regretting that your seminary has so far followed the beaten track of the old schools as to place knowledge of Greek and Latin at the head of your studies. I am by no means ignorant of all the advantages attending a critical knowledge of the ancient languages. They are included in the following heads:

1. In learning a dead language, or even a living one, which must be acquired not in loose conversation but in reading and analyzing authors who are perfectly correct in their diction and in composing by dint of inflexible rules, a general knowledge of language and of grammar becomes so imprinted upon the mind, at an age when permanent impressions are easily received, that it may never be effaced. This general knowledge comes into use whenever a living language is to be learned or the native language studied.

2. The dry, laborious study of words, uninteresting in themselves, inures the mind to labor and to the habits of attention.

3. So many useful and elegant works are written in these languages that it is worthwhile to expend much time in obtaining the key that unlocks these treasures.

4. A knowledge of Latin, and especially of Greek, renders it easy to understand the technical language of every science.

5. There is a time when it is difficult to employ boys in anything else, and when it is very indifferent what they are employed in, provided they be kept out of mischief. They may, therefore, as well be learning languages, which may perhaps become useful and never can be a burden.

The first argument, the importance of acquiring a perfect knowledge of grammar, has perhaps the most weight, and is the principal reason why, after all the useful sciences, I would recommend the study of Greek and Latin.

Second, if the minds of children generally were less capable of understanding mathematical truths or of retaining facts in natural history or philosophy than of remembering grammatical rules, for which no reasons can be assigned, and which do not interest the mind in any degree, I would agree that Greek and Latin should be forced into their memories at all hazards. But I believe the contrary to be the case generally. I know it from my own experience, and besides the presumption is highly reasonable. I think of a boy ten or twelve years old I could much sooner make a perfect botanist than a good Greek scholar; and I am sure the botanist would be happier, healthier, and less agitated by false notions of glory and honor than the expositor of Homer; nor do I believe his mind would have acquired less activity and vigor.

Third, if there be little weight in the other points, then this argument can have none, for all the good works of the ancients may be read in excellent translations.

Fourth, to comprehend and remember easily the technical terms of science, it is very true that a knowledge of the learned languages is highly useful, but a much slighter acquaintance with Greek and Latin is necessary than that proposed by the usual modes of education, and which is attainable in a much shorter space of time. Indeed, the knowledge of a science will lead to, and render pleasant, the study of its language, the latter being subordinate to the former.

Fifth, I am so ashamed of the fifth reason that were it not very commonly urged I should not have quoted it. It is answered under the second head.

My objection, therefore, goes not to teaching Greek and Latin but to the preference given to the Greek and Latin instruction. I should object even to its being upon a level with moral philosophy, mathematics, physics, or modern languages. . . .

I observe that with the instruction in Greek and Latin the elements of history, rhetoric, and poetry are to be connected. This is some atonement for the attention forced into the channel of the languages; and if the authors read in the Greek and Latin schools be more judiciously chosen than has been usual in the old schools, it is impossible not to combine the acquisition of the language with that of the useful knowledge conveyed in it. But then Terence, Phaedrus, Ovid, and other poets, from whom no one ever learned a single useful fact, should be rejected, and in their room it would be well to substitute Justin's epitome of the history of Trogus Pompeius, as being an easy and entertaining writer, and containing a tolerably good sketch of general history; Cornelius Nepos, Caesar's *Commentaries,* and for the more advanced scholars, Livy, and, above all, Tacitus, the most elegant and virtuous of historians. I would confine the study of poetry to Virgil and select pieces to Horace. In eloquence, Cicero's book *De oratore* stands for all that ever has been or will be written, and ought to be well digested by those who propose to plead at the bar or to serve their country or their party in the Senate. I believe the first Latin book which is studied appears to the student to be written in the easiest style; at least I have always thought Livy and Cicero to be the easiest of all Latin authors, because I first learned the language by reading their works. Many of my friends, however, think them more difficult than others whom I cannot read with equal ease. Should the observation be true, and it is reasonable, the book *De oratore* might be put into the hands of very young students as well as any other, and might upon the whole be the most useful to those who propose to read only a few ancient writers and to devote most of their attention to science.

In Greek the works of Xenophon are among the richest treasures of the language. I wonder his *Anabasis* is so little read in schools. It is highly entertaining and instructive, and as a composition nothing can be more elegant. The *Cyropaedia* is not less elegant and instructive, but boys will think much of it very dull. Plutarch has both the advantages of fixing the attention to his story and teaching the purest Greek by his style. Herodotus, with both those excellences — and without both no ancient author ought to be put into the hands of a scholar — has another of considerable importance. The subject of his work — the institutions of Egypt, which he has often been charged with disguising in fables — is daily more and more found to be faithfully copied from actually existing facts; and he conveys much important knowledge concerning the cradle of all the past and present religious systems which have been called Christianity. He is well translated by Beloe. Homer's *Iliad,* which no one can more admire as an effort of genius than myself, is, I think, the most improper book for a school. It poisons the minds of young men, fills them with a rage for military murder and glory, and conveys no information which can ever be practically useful. Sooner than suffer my pupil to learn to read without horror many beautiful passages he should read nothing but Theocritus and Anacreon. It is better to soften the mind of a boy of fifteen by a picture of a tender shepherdess hanging upon the neck of her lover than to set it on fire by a description of brains dashed out, bellies ripped open, blood streaming around, and convulsed heroes gnawing the earth in agony. But neither is necessary.

To the mathematical school there can be no objection, provided the trustees watch over it and prevent it becoming a mere ciphering school. Half the rules of the common books of arithmetic are useless to one who understands the principles of algebra. Arithmetic is generally a heavy study to boys, because it is rendered entirely a business of memory, no reasons being assigned for the rules. A schoolbook of arithmetic accompanied with demonstrations is much wanted. We do boys from seven to fifteen years old great injustice in supposing they cannot reason.

Natural philosophy and history ought to have a fair proportion of time. Moral science and political economy ought to have a separate school. Adam Smith's book, *The Wealth of Nations,* ought to be the groundwork of a very principal instruction. We much want a schoolbook upon this subject. It is a subject the most necessary for an American citizen.

Two more schools are allotted to languages, that is, to words. The time, class, or school allotted to English might include the French language, but under separate teachers.

I highly approve the degree, neither more nor less, of attention paid to writing. . . .

As an American republican I may ask what right has any human being to prescribe laws to the actions of any other unless they be injurious to him? What right has any American citizen to say to any other, "You shall get *quis, quae, quid* by heart by a certain time or you shall be punished?" What injury does the punisher receive from the neglect? Can he even plead the savage law of retaliation? But suppose the fault to be punished to be of the active kind. Suppose tricks be played, and squibs and crackers thrown in the school. Then punishment can only be just, as it is retaliation, as it is revenge. Punishment upon this principle — and my reasoning applies to all legislative punishment — is, in fact, a repetition of the offense, and most frequently it is a repetition with aggravation. If the punishment be, as we falsely say, *just,* or exactly adequate to the crime, that is if the pain, or evil, or inconvenience inflicted upon the criminal be equal to that occasioned by him, the moral nature of the act of punishment would stand in the place and be as *bad* as that of the crime if the crime had not preceded it. And will anyone say that moral actions are good or bad according to their succession in the order of time?

This reasoning appears to me to be mathematical, and by no means puts an end to social order and discipline. We have mistaken the moral rights of communities because we have mistaken the moral rights of man. We have taken it for granted that retaliation is a law of nature because it is the propensity of educated man. But can that be a law of nature that in its mildest form *doubles* the injury committed? Nor is it certain that the propensity is natural, because the desire of revenge may, by education, be rendered as perpetually absent from the mind of the dervish and the true Christian as it is perpetually present to that of the Cherokee and the Arab. We Christians who cherish laws of honor are in the situation of the Cherokee.

The original rights of man are bounded by his individual existence and his individual interests. They are self-preservation and self-defense. I cannot conceive a principle upon which they can be further extended. A society is an interchange and a union of these individual rights. Every individual has a right to enter into compact by mutual consent for mutual preservation and defense, and under this compact to observe certain laws. But what right have I to force any man or boy into my society and to make him observe its laws? If an individual of my society refuse to conform to its rules, let him be removed. If, after agreeing to abide by them, he is guilty of their violation, that act cancels his title to protection, and he ceases to be a member of it. The preservation and defense of the society require his removal, and the society has a right to remove him. A school is such a society, as far as the rights of one individual over the other extend. It is an institution for the good of its members, and my argument might be strengthened by considering the matter in another point of view, and deciding upon the morality of what is called punishment by its utility.

As far as punishment is the effect upon the punished and not the act of the punisher, so far is exclusion from the society the severest that can be suffered. It involves the society in no immoral act, and it makes unhappiness what it is in nature, in spite of human ingenuity to invert her order, synonymous with misconduct. This fact applies particularly to a school. Does a boy fear the ferule half as much as a temporary separation from his schoolmates? We all know the contrary.

If this be mere theory, look at experience. Crimes, she teaches us, abound in every state, in proportion to the multitude and severity of penal laws. This proves that if they be immoral, they are at the same time ineffectual. On the other hand, examine that great and first experiment in the moral science of mind — the penitentiary house at Philadelphia. I may be told that it is an insult to an academy to compare it to a prison. Is it not a greater to make it a place of execution, and to erect in it a whipping post? So much for the punishment. But as to the exception, it is worse than the rule. No boy of sixteen and upward is to receive corporeal punishment. Those under that age — the more innocent, the more incapable of resistance, those who being more ignorant are less guilty — they are to be punished!

The lenity of public and private admonition is very laudable. But I do not like the title of the *Book of Disgrace.* It will tend only to fix a stigma upon a boy, which he may not practically wipe off again by ever so good behavior. It betrays anger against those recorded in it and excites it in them. If such a book must be kept, why not call it what it is, the *Record of Misconduct.*

It occurs to me that in this country, however, such a record were improper, unless every boy on leaving the school could be satisfied that the record of his misconduct were destroyed. How most injuriously might not the youthful follies of a meritorious citizen be brought forward against him from such a record — from political or any other hostile motives! The intention of the book is obvious and good; but it appears to me to be very open to abuse in its application.

No master ought to be permitted to punish at his discretion, under the idea of punishment evidently established by these rules. He will punish promptly if he has the power. If punishment be admitted, it should be delayed and considered. The very act of punishment, though begun in the most philosophic temper and coldest blood, excites anger by the habitual association of angry feelings with inflicted blows, and the last strokes are always the severest. If begun while the irritation of the offense is fresh, the floggings will be, what, to the disgrace of humanity and of reason, it is in all the schools which I have ever known, the most flagitious act committed within their walls. I cannot bear the idea, besides, of tormenting the poor little boys and letting the strong fellows escape. The personal feeling of the master, operating by rules of capricious dislike or favoritism, will dictate the infliction and the measure of the punishment.

As I have already given you my sentiments so freely upon the bylaws as they are before me, I will add a few words more:

Nothing can be of greater importance than to render the study of language and science amusing to the scholars. The former is always disagreeable to the boys, especially at first. On this account the most entertaining authors ought to be put into their hands. I have, therefore, recommended such as I thought agreeable when I was very young. Much will, however, also depend upon the method of the master.

For the preservation of the morals of the boys, they should be under constant inspection. But this inspection should not be constant government. Therefore, the hours unoccupied by school ought to be devoted to established games of ingenuity and activity under the eye of the master or usher, whose sole interference should be to prevent dispute and decide doubtful cases of skill, unless he chose to play with them, which could not, I think, degrade the greatest philosopher under heaven. The rewards should be impressive trifles. Cricket, running, swinging, seesaw, and tops may be thus made moral amusements. If the boys be moderately fatigued by exercise in the day, they will be glad to go to bed and rest at night, when otherwise they would be planning adventures of fifty sorts. I know by my own experience much of the ingenuity of boys to contrive nocturnal rambles and meetings, and I believe they are everywhere alike and differ only according to their management.

But the most amusing and useful recreations to boys, and indeed a most important one to the community, would be their being trained to arms and military evolutions. While arms wound, and men, believing their separate interests to be different from those of the human race, have recourse to arms to decide their quarrels, every citizen ought to learn how to defend himself against, and repel, a hired soldier. If this be learned by the boy, it will never be forgotten by the man. Let their officers be chosen by themselves for a limited term so as to give each the chance of a turn. Let the principal, or the trustees, commission them. Their mothers will find them uniforms. If in every neighborhood throughout the state the boys from seven to fifteen were regimented, and called out to parade frequently, no useful labor would be lost, no public expense incurred, a well-trained and disciplined militia would be formed, always ready to act though unexercised for many years. Habits acquired at so early a period of life are never lost, as no one forgets how to dance, to swim, to ride, or to skate. This is enough for a hint.

7.

Benjamin Rush: Independence and Education

The new American republicanism was essentially an experiment in free, popular government, the success of which, as many post-Revolutionary writers pointed out, depended on the development of an effective educational system. At the same time, Americans were attempting to understand all of the implications of the constitutional separation of church and state, and the question of the place of religious education in the schools naturally came to the fore. Benjamin Rush, a staunch supporter of plans to use public funds to establish a national school system, wrote the following essay in 1798 on the proper relation, as he conceived it, of religion and education in a republic.

Source: *Essays, Literary, Moral and Philosophical,* Philadelphia, 1798: "Of the Mode of Education Proper in a Republic."

The business of education has acquired a new complexion by the independence of our country. The form of government we have assumed has created a new class of duties to every American. It becomes us, therefore, to examine our former habits upon this subject, and, in laying the foundations for nurseries of wise and good men, to adapt our modes of teaching to the peculiar form of our government.

The first remark that I shall make upon this subject is that an education in our own is to be preferred to an education in a foreign country. The principle of patriotism stands in need of the reinforcement of prejudice, and it is well known that our strongest prejudices in favor of our country are formed in the first one-and-twenty years of our lives. . . . Passing by, in this place, the advantages to the community from the early attachment of youth to the laws and constitution of their country, I shall only remark that young men who have trodden the paths of science together, or have joined in the same sports, whether of swimming, feating, fishing, or hunting, generally feel, through life, such ties to each other as add greatly to the obligations of mutual benevolence.

I conceive the education of our youth in this country to be peculiarly necessary in Pennsylvania, while our citizens are composed of the natives of so many different kingdoms in Europe. Our schools of learning, by producing one general and uniform system of education, will render the mass of the people more homogeneous, and thereby fit them more easily for uniform and peaceable government.

I proceed, in the next place, to inquire what mode of education we shall adopt so as to secure to the state all of the advantages that are to be derived from the proper instruction of youth; and here I beg leave to remark that the only foundation for a useful education in a republic is to be laid in religion. Without this there can be no virtue, and without virtue there can be no liberty, and liberty is the object and life of all republican governments.

Such is my veneration for every religion that reveals the attributes of the Deity, or a future state of rewards and punishments, that I had rather see the opinions of Confucius or Mohammed inculcated upon our youth than see them grow up wholly devoid of a system of religious principles. But the religion I mean to recommend in this place is that of the New Testament.

It is foreign to my purpose to hint at the arguments which establish the truth of the Christian revelation. My only business is to declare that all its doctrines and precepts are calculated to promote the happiness of society and the safety and well-being of civil government. A Christian cannot fail of being a republican. The history of the creation of man and of the relation of our species to each other by birth, which is recorded in the Old Testament, is the best refutation that can be given to the divine right of kings, and the strongest argument that can be used in favor of the original and natural equality of all mankind.

A Christian, I say again, cannot fail of being a republican, for every precept of the Gospel inculcates those degrees of humility, self-denial, and brotherly kindness which are directly opposed to the pride of monarchy and the pageantry of a court. A Christian cannot fail of being useful to the republic, for his religion teaches him that no man "liveth to himself." And lastly, a Christian cannot fail of being wholly inoffensive, for his religion teaches him in all things to do to others what he would wish, in like circumstances, they should do to him.

I am aware that I dissent from one of those paradoxical opinions with which modern times abound; and that it is improper to fill the minds of youth with religious prejudices of any kind, and that they should be left to choose their own principles after they have arrived at an age in which they are capable of judging for themselves. Could we preserve the mind in childhood and youth a perfect blank, this plan of education would have more to recommend it; but this we know to be impossible. The human mind runs as naturally into principles as it does after facts. It submits with difficulty to those restraints or partial discoveries which are imposed upon it in the infancy of reason. Hence the impatience of children to be informed upon all subjects that relate to the invisible world.

But I beg leave to ask, why should we pursue a different plan of education with respect to religion from that which we pursue in teaching the arts and sciences? Do we leave our youth to acquire systems of geography, philosophy, or politics till they have arrived at an age in which they are capable of judging for themselves? We do not. I claim no more then for religion than for the other sciences; and I add further that if our youth are disposed after they are of age to think for themselves, a knowledge of one system will be the best means of conducting them in a free inquiry into other systems of religion, just as an acquaintance with one system of philosophy is the best introduction to the study of all the other systems in the world.

Next to the duty which young men owe to their Creator, I wish to see a regard to their country inculcated upon them. . . . Our country includes family, friends, and property, and should be preferred to them all. Let our pupil be taught that he does not belong to himself, but that he is public property. Let him be taught to love his family, but let him be taught, at the same time, that he must forsake, and even forget, them when the welfare of his country requires it. He must watch for the state as if its liberties depended upon his vigilance alone, but he must do this in such a manner as not to defraud his creditors or neglect his family. He must love private life, but he must decline no station, however public or responsible it may be, when called to it by

Courtesy, Winterthur Museum; gift of Mrs. T. Charlton Henry

Portrait of Benjamin Rush by C. W. Peale, 1783

the suffrages of his fellow citizens. He must love popularity, but he must despise it when set in competition with the dictates of his judgment or the real interest of his country.

He must love character and have a due sense of injuries, but he must be taught to appeal only to the laws of the state, to defend the one and punish the other. He must love family honor, but he must be taught that neither the rank nor antiquity of his ancestors can command respect without personal merit. He must avoid neutrality in all questions that divide the state, but he must shun the rage and acrimony of party spirit. He must be taught to love his fellow creatures in every part of the world, but he must cherish with a more intense and peculiar affection the citizens of Pennsylvania and of the United States. I do not wish to see our youth educated with a single prejudice against any nation or country; but we impose a task upon human nature, repugnant alike to reason, revelation, and the ordinary dimensions of the human heart, when we require him to embrace, with equal affection, the whole family of mankind.

He must be taught to amass wealth, but it must be only to increase his power of contributing to the wants and demands of the state. He must be indulged occasionally in amusements, but he must be taught that study and business should be his principal pursuits in life. Above all he must love life and endeavor to acquire as many of its conveniences as possible by industry and economy, but he must be taught that this life "is not his own," when the safety of his country requires it. . . .

While we inculcate these republican duties upon our pupil, we must not neglect, at the same time, to inspire him with republican principles. He must be taught that there can be no durable liberty but in a republic; and that government, like all other sciences, is of a progressive nature. The chains which have bound this science in Europe are happily unloosed in America. Here it is open to investigation and improvement. While philosophy has protected us by its discoveries from a thousand natural evils, government has unhappily followed with an unequal pace. It would be to dishonor human genius only to name the many defects which still exist in the best systems of legislation. We daily see matter of a perishable nature rendered durable by certain chemical operations. In like manner, I conceive that it is possible to combine power in such a way as not only to increase the happiness but to promote the duration of republican forms of government far beyond the terms limited for them by history or the common opinions of mankind. . . .

From the observations that have been made, it is plain that I consider it is possible to convert men into republican machines. This must be done if we expect them to perform their parts properly in the great machine of the government of the state. That republic is sophisticated with monarchy or aristocracy that does not revolve upon the wills of the people, and these must be fitted to each other by means of education before they can be made to produce regularity and unison in government.

Having pointed out those general principles, which should be inculcated alike in all the schools of the state, I proceed now to make a few remarks upon the method of conducting what is commonly called a liberal or learned education in a republic.

I shall begin this part of my subject by bearing a testimony against the common practice of attempting to teach boys the learned languages and the arts and sciences too early in life. The first twelve years of life are barely sufficient to instruct a boy in reading, writing, and arithmetic. With these, he may be taught those modern languages which are necessary for him to speak. The state of the memory in early life is favorable to the acquisition of languages, especially when they are conveyed to the mind through the ear. It is, moreover, in early life only that the organs of speech yield in such a manner as to favor the just pronunciation of foreign languages.

Too much pains cannot be taken to teach our youth to read and write our American language with propriety and elegance. The study of the Greek language constituted a material part of the literature of the Athenians, hence the sublimity, purity, and immortality of so many of their writings. The advantages of a perfect knowledge of our language to young men intended for the professions of law, physic, or divinity are too obvious to be mentioned; but in a state which boasts of the first commercial city in America, I wish to see it cultivated by young men who are intended for the counting house, for many such, I hope, will be educated in our colleges. The time is past when an academical education was thought to be unnecessary to qualify a young man for merchandise. I conceive no profession is capable of receiving more embellishments from it.

The French and German languages should likewise be carefully taught in all our colleges. They abound with useful books upon all subjects. So important and necessary are those languages that a degree should never be conferred upon a young man who cannot speak or translate them.

Connected with the study of languages is the study of eloquence. It is well known how great a part it constituted of the Roman education. It is the first accomplishment in a republic, and often sets the whole machine of government in motion. Let our youth, therefore, be instructed in this art. We do not extol it too highly when we attribute as much to the power of eloquence as to the sword in bringing about the American Revolution.

With the usual arts and sciences that are taught in our American colleges, I wish to see a regular course of lectures given upon history and chronology. The science of government, whether it relates to constitutions or laws, can only be advanced by a careful selection of facts, and these are to be found chiefly in history. Above all, let our youth be instructed in the history of the ancient republics and the progress of liberty and tyranny in the different states of Europe.

I wish, likewise, to see the numerous facts that relate to the origin and present state of commerce, together with the nature and principles of money, reduced to such a system as to be intelligible and agreeable to a young man. If we consider the commerce of our metropolis only as the avenue of the wealth of the state, the study of it merits a place in a young man's education; but I consider commerce in a much higher light when I recommend the study of it in republican seminaries. I view it as the best security against the influence of hereditary monopolies of land, and, therefore, the surest protection against aristocracy. I consider its effects as next to those of religion in humanizing mankind. And lastly, I view it as the means of uniting the different nations of the world together by the ties of mutual wants and obligations.

Chemistry, by unfolding to us the effects of heat and mixture, enlarges our acquaintance with the wonders of nature and the mysteries of art; hence it has become, in most of the universities of Europe, a necessary branch of a gentleman's education. In a young country, where improvements in agriculture and manufactures are so much to be desired, the cultivation of this science which explains the principles of both of them should be considered as an object of the utmost importance.

Again, let your youth be instructed in all the means of promoting national prosperity and independence, whether they relate to improvements in agriculture, manufactures, or inland navigation. Let him be instructed further in the general principles of legislation, whether they relate to revenue or to the preservation of life, liberty, or property. Let him be directed frequently to attend the courts of justice, where he will have the best opportunities of acquiring habits of comparing and arranging his ideas by observing the discovery of truth in the examination of witnesses, and where he will hear the laws of the state explained, with all the advantages of that species of eloquence which belongs to the bar. Of so much importance do I conceive it to be to a young man to attend occasionally to the decisions of our courts of law that I wish to see our colleges established only in county towns.

But, further, considering the nature of our connection with the United States, it will be necessary to make our pupil acquainted with all the prerogatives of the national government. He must be instructed in the nature and variety of treaties. He must know the difference in the powers and duties of the several species of ambassadors. He must be taught wherein the obligations of individuals and of states are the same, and wherein they differ. In short, he must acquire a general knowledge of all those laws and forms which unite the sovereigns of the earth or separate them from each other.

I beg pardon for having delayed so long to say anything of the separate and peculiar mode of education proper for women in a republic. I am sensible that they must concur in all our plans of education for young men, or no laws will ever render them effectual. To qualify our women for this purpose, they should not only be instructed in the usual branches of female education but they should be taught the principles of liberty and government; and the obligations of patriotism should be inculcated upon them. The opinions and conduct of men are often regulated by the women in the most arduous enterprises of life; and their approbation is frequently the principal reward of the hero's dangers and the patriot's toils. Besides, the first impressions upon the minds of children are generally derived from the women. Of how much consequence, therefore, is it in a republic that they should think justly upon the great subjects of liberty and government!

The complaints that have been made against religion, liberty, and learning have been against each of them in a separate state. Perhaps, like certain liquors, they should only be used in a state of mixture. They mutually assist in correcting the abuses and in improving the good effects of each other. From the combined and reciprocal influence of religion, liberty, and learning upon the morals, manners, and knowledge of individuals, of these upon government, and of government upon individuals, it is impossible to measure the degrees of happiness and perfection to which mankind may be raised. For my part, I can form no ideas of the Golden Age, so much celebrated by the poets, more delightful than the contemplation of that happiness which it is now in the power of the legislature of Pennsylvania to confer upon her citizens by establishing proper modes and places of education in every part of the state.

8.

Timothy Dwight: On the Duty of Americans at the Present Crisis

The sweeping changes in the political, social, and religious ideas of the nation after the Revolution were scarcely perceptible in Massachusetts and Connecticut, which remained strongholds of conservatism. Men like Timothy Dwight, Congregational minister and president of Yale College, believed that Jeffersonian Republicanism was destroying the morals, the faith, and the order of New England society. Dwight was a prolific writer whose sermons and addresses attacking the "degeneration" of the times revealed views not dissimilar to those of his grandfather, Jonathan Edwards. The following excerpt from Dwight's sermon of July 4, 1798, titled The Duty of Americans, at the Present Crisis, *is a noteworthy example of the school of thought that refused to relinquish the rigid principles of Calvinism.*

Source: *The Duty of Americans, at the Present Crisis, Illustrated in a Discourse, Preached on the Fourth of July, 1798,* New Haven, 1798.

About the year 1728, Voltaire, so celebrated for his wit and brilliancy and not less distinguished for his hatred of Christianity and his abandonment of principle, formed a systematical design to destroy Christianity and to introduce in its stead a general diffusion of irreligion and atheism. For this purpose he associated with himself Frederick the II, king of Prussia, and Mess. D'Alembert and Diderot, the principal compilers of the *Encyclopédie,* all men of talents, atheists, and in the like manner abandoned. The principal parts of this system were:

1. The compilation of the *Encyclopédie*: in which with great art and insidiousness the doctrines of natural as well as Christian theology were rendered absurd and ridiculous; and the mind of the reader was insensibly steeled against conviction and duty.

2. The overthrow of the religious orders in Catholic countries, a step essentially necessary to the destruction of the religion professed in those countries.

3. The establishment of a sect of philosophists to serve, it is presumed as a conclave, a rallying point, for all their followers.

4. The appropriation to themselves, and their disciples, of the places and honors of members of the French Academy, the most respectable literary society in France, and always considered as containing none but men of prime learning and talents. In this way they designed to hold out themselves and their friends as the only persons of great literary and intellectual distinction in that country, and to dictate all literary opinions to the nation.

5. The fabrication of books of all kinds against Christianity, especially such as excite doubt and generate contempt and derision. Of these they issued by themselves and their friends who early became numerous,

an immense number; so printed as to be purchased for little or nothing, and so written as to catch the feelings, and steal upon the approbation, of every class of men.

6. The formation of a secret Academy, of which Voltaire was the standing president, and in which books were formed, altered, forged, imputed as posthumous to deceased writers of reputation, and sent abroad with the weight of their names. These were printed and circulated at the lowest price through all classes of men in an uninterrupted succession, and through every part of the kingdom.

Nor were the labors of this Academy confined to religion. They attacked also morality and government, unhinged gradually the minds of men, and destroyed their reverence for everything heretofore esteemed sacred.

In the meantime, the Masonic societies, which had been originally instituted for convivial and friendly purposes only, were, especially in France and Germany, made the professed scenes of debate concerning religion, morality, and government, by these philosophists who had in great numbers become Masons. For such debate, the legalized existence of Masonry, its profound secrecy, its solemn and mystic rites and symbols, its mutual correspondence, and its extension through most civilized countries furnished the greatest advantages.

All here was free, safe, and calculated to encourage the boldest excursions of restless opinion and impatient ardor and to make and fix the deepest impressions. Here, and in no other place, under such arbitrary governments, could every innovator in these important subjects utter every sentiment, however daring, and attack every doctrine and institution, however guarded by law or sanctity. In the secure and unrestrained debates of the lodge, every novel, licentious, and alarming opinion was resolutely advanced. Minds, already tinged with philosophism, were here speedily blackened with a deep and deadly dye; and those which came fresh and innocent to the scene of contamination became early and irremediably corrupted. A stubborn incapacity of conviction and flinty insensibility to every moral and natural tie grew of course out of this combination of causes; and men were surely prepared, before themselves were aware, for every plot and perpetration. In these hotbeds were sown the seeds of that astonishing revolution, and all its dreadful appendages which now spreads dismay and horror throughout half the globe.

While these measures were advancing the great design with a regular and rapid progress, Doctor Adam Weishaupt, professor of the canon law in the University of Ingolstadt, a city of Bavaria (in Germany), formed, about the year 1777, the order of Illuminati. This order is professedly a higher order of Masons, originated by himself, and grafted on ancient Masonic institutions. The secrecy, solemnity, mysticism, and correspondence of Masonry were in this new order preserved and enhanced; while the ardor of innovation, the impatience of civil and moral restraints, and the aims against government, morals, and religion were elevated, expanded, and rendered more systematical, malignant, and daring.

In the societies of Illuminati, doctrines were taught which strike at the root of all human happiness and virtue; and every such doctrine was either expressly or implicitly involved in their system.

The being of God was denied and ridiculed.

Government was asserted to be a curse, and authority a mere usurpation.

Civil society was declared to be the only apostasy of man.

The possession of property was pronounced to be robbery.

Chastity and natural affection were declared to be nothing more than groundless prejudices.

Adultery, assassination, poisoning, and

other crimes of the like infernal nature, were taught as lawful and even as virtuous actions.

To crown such a system of falsehood and horror, all means were declared to be lawful, provided the end was good.

In this last doctrine, men are not only loosed from every bond and from every duty but from every inducement to perform anything which is good and abstain from anything which is evil; and are set upon each other like a company of hellhounds to worry, rend, and destroy. Of the goodness of the end every man is to judge for himself; and most men, and all men who resemble the Illuminati, will pronounce every end to be good which will gratify their inclinations.

The great and good ends proposed by the Illuminati as the ultimate objects of their union are the overthrow of religion, government, and human society, civil and domestic. These they pronounce to be so good that murder, butchery, and war, however extended and dreadful, are declared by them to be completely justifiable if necessary for these great purposes. With such an example in view, it will be in vain to hunt for ends, which can be evil.

Correspondent with this summary was the whole system. No villainy, no impiety, no cruelty can be named which was not vindicated; and no virtue which was not covered with contempt.

The means by which this society was enlarged and its doctrines spread were of every promising kind. With unremitted ardor and diligence the members insinuated themselves into every place of power and trust, and into every literary, political, and friendly society; engrossed as much as possible the education of youth, especially of distinction; became licensers of the press and directors of every literary journal; waylaid every foolish prince, every unprincipled civil officer, and every abandoned clergyman; entered boldly into the desk, and with unhallowed hands and satanic lips polluted the pages of God; enlisted in their service almost all the booksellers and of course the printers of Germany; inundated the country with books replete with infidelity, irreligion, immorality, and obscenity; prohibited the printing and prevented the sale of books of the contrary character; decried and ridiculed them when published in spite of their efforts; panegyrized and trumpeted those of themselves and their coadjutors; and in a word made more numerous, more diversified, and more strenuous exertions than an active imagination would have preconceived. . . .

Among the particular duties required by this precept, and at the present time, none holds a higher place than the observation of the Sabbath. The Sabbath and its ordinances have ever been the great means of all moral good to mankind. The faithful observation of the Sabbath is, therefore, one of the chief duties and interests of men; but the present time furnishes reasons, peculiar, at least in degree, for exemplary regard to this divine institution. The enemies of God have by private argument, ridicule, and influence, and by public decrees, pointed their especial malignity against the Sabbath; and have expected, and not without reason, that, if they could annihilate it, they should overthrow Christianity. From them we cannot but learn its importance. Enemies usually discern, with more sagacity, the most promising point of attack than those who are to be attacked. In this point are they to be peculiarly opposed. Here, peculiarly, are their designs to be baffled. If they fail here, they will finally fail. Christianity cannot fall but by the neglect of the Sabbath.

I have been credibly informed that some years before the Revolution an eminent philosopher of this country, now deceased, declared to David Hume that Christianity would be exterminated from the American colonies within a century from that time. The opinion has doubtless been often de-

Yale University Art Gallery
Portrait of Timothy Dwight by J. Trumbull

clared and extensively imbibed, and has probably furnished our enemies their chief hopes of success. Where religion prevails, their system cannot succeed. Where religion prevails, Illuminatism cannot make disciples, a French directory cannot govern, a nation cannot be made slaves, nor villains, nor atheists, nor beasts. To destroy us therefore, in this dreadful sense, our enemies must first destroy our Sabbath and seduce us from the house of God.

Religion and liberty are the two great objects of defensive war. Conjoined, they unite all the feelings and call forth all the energies of man. . . . Religion and liberty are the meat and the drink of the body politic. Withdraw one of them and it languishes, consumes, and dies. If indifference to either, at any time, becomes the prevailing character of a people, one half of their motives to vigorous defense is lost, and the hopes of their enemies are proportionally increased. Here, eminently, they are inseparable.

Without religion we may possibly retain the freedom of savages, bears, and wolves, but not the freedom of New England. If our religion were gone, our state of society would perish with it and nothing would be left which would be worth defending. Our children, of course, if not ourselves, would be prepared, as the ox for the slaughter, to become the victims of conquest, tyranny, and atheism. . . .

Another duty to which we are also eminently called is an entire separation from our enemies. Among the moral duties of man none hold a higher rank than political ones, and among our own political duties none is more plain, or more absolute, than that which I have now mentioned. . . .

The two great reasons for the command are subjoined to it by the Savior — "that ye be not partakers of her sins; and that ye receive not of her plagues"; and each is a reason of incomprehensible magnitude.

The sins of these enemies of Christ and Christians are of numbers and degrees, which mock account and descriptions. All that the malice and atheism of the dragon, the cruelty and rapacity of the beast, and the fraud and deceit of the false prophet can generate, or accomplish, swell the list. No personal or national interest of man has been uninvaded; no impious sentiment or action against God has been spared; no malignant hostility against Christ and his religion has been unattempted. Justice, truth, kindness, piety, and moral obligation universally have been not merely trodden under foot — this might have resulted from vehemence and passion — but ridiculed, spurned, and insulted as the childish bugbears of driveling idiocy. Chastity and decency have been alike turned out-of-doors, and shame and pollution called out of their dens to the hall of distinction and the chair of state. Nor has any art, violence, or means been unemployed to accomplish these evils.

For what end shall we be connected with men of whom this is the character and conduct? Is it that we may assume the same character and pursue the same conduct? Is it that our churches may become temples of reason, our Sabbath a decade, and our psalms of praise Marseillaise hymns? Is it that we may change our holy worship into a dance of Jacobin frenzy, and that we may behold a strumpet personating a goddess on the altars of Jehovah? Is it that we may see the Bible cast into a bonfire, the vessels of the sacramental supper borne by an ass in public procession, and our children, either wheedled or terrified, uniting in the mob, chanting mockeries against God, and hailing in the sounds of "*Ca ira*" [song of the French Revolution, lit. "it will go on"] the ruin of their religion and the loss of their souls? Is it that we may see our wives and daughters the victims of legal prostitution; soberly dishonored; speciously polluted; the outcasts of delicacy and virtue and the loathing of God and man? Is it that we may see in our public papers a solemn comparison drawn by an American mother club between the Lord Jesus Christ and a new Marat; and the fiend of malice and fraud exalted above the glorious Redeemer?

Shall we, my brethren, become partakers of these sins? Shall we introduce them into our government, our schools, our families? Shall our sons become the disciples of Voltaire and the dragoons of Marat; or our daughters the concubines of the Illuminati? . . .

Should we, however, in a forbidden connection with these enemies of God, escape, against all hope, from moral ruin, we shall still receive our share of their plagues. This is the certain dictate of the prophetical injunction; and our own experience, and that of nations more intimately connected with them, has already proved its truth. . . .

France itself has been the chief seat of the evils wrought by these men. The unhappy and ever to be pitied inhabitants of that country, a great part of whom are doubtless of a character similar to that of the peaceable citizens of other countries and have probably no voluntary concern in accomplishing these evils, have themselves suffered far more from the hands of philosophists and their followers than the inhabitants of any other country.

General Danican, a French officer, asserts in his memoirs, lately published, that 3 million Frenchmen have perished in the Revolution. Of this amazing destruction, the causes by which it was produced, the principles on which it was founded, and the modes in which it was conducted are an aggravation that admits no bound. The butchery of the stall and the slaughter of the stye are scenes of deeper remorse and softened with more sensibility. The siege of Lyons, and the judicial massacres at Nantes stand, since the crucifixion, alone in the volume of human crimes. The misery of man never before reached the extreme of agony, nor the infamy of man its consummation. Collot d'Herbois and his satellites, Carrier and his associates, would claim eminence in a world of fiends, and will be marked with distinction in the future hissings of the universe. No guilt so deeply dyed in blood since the frenzied malice of Calvary will probably so amaze the assembly of the final day; and Nantes and Lyons may, without a hyperbole, obtain a literal immortality in a remembrance revived beyond the grave.

In which of these plagues, my brethren, are you willing to share? Which of them will you transmit as a legacy to your children?

Would you escape, you must separate yourselves. Would you wholly escape, you must be wholly separated. I do not intend that you must not buy and sell or exhibit the common offices of justice and goodwill; but you are bound by the voice of reason, of duty, of safety, and of God to shun all such connection with them as will interweave your sentiments or your friendship, your religion, or your policy with theirs. You cannot otherwise fail of partaking in their guilt and receiving of their plagues.

Another duty to which we are no less forcibly called is union among ourselves.

The same divine Person, who spoke in the Text, hath also said, "A house, a kingdom, divided against itself cannot stand." A divided family will destroy itself. A divided nation will anticipate ruin prepared by its enemies. . . .

The great bond of union to every people is its government. This destroyed or distrusted, there is no center left of intelligence, counsel, or action; no system of purposes or measures; no point of rallying or confidence. When a nation is ready to say, "What part have we in David, or what inheritance in the son of Jesse?" it will naturally subjoin, "Every man to his tent, O Israel!"

The candor and uprightness with which our own government has acted in the progress of the present controversy have forced encomiums even from its most bitter opposers, and excited the warmest approbation and applause of all its friends. Few objects could be more important, auspicious, or gratifying to Christians than to see the conduct of their rulers, such as they can, with boldness of access, bring before their God and fearlessly commend to his favor and protection.

In men possessed of similar candor, adherence to our government in the present crisis may be regarded as a thing of course. They need not be informed that the existing rulers must be the directors of our public affairs and the only directors; that their views and measures will not and cannot always accord with the judgment of individuals, as the opinions of individuals accord no better with each other; that the officers of government are possessed of better information than private persons can be; that if *they* had the same information, they would probably coincide with the opinions of their rulers; that confidence must be placed in men, imperfect as they are, in all human affairs or no important business can be done; and that men of known and tried probity are fully deserving of that confidence.

At the present time this adherence ought to be unequivocally manifested. In a land of universal suffrage where every individual is possessed of much personal consequence as in ours, the government ought, especially in great measures, to be as secure as may be of the harmonious and cheerful cooperation of the citizens. All success here depends on the hearty concurrence of the community; and no occasion ever called for it more.

But there are even in this state persons who are opposed to the government. To them I observe:

That the government of France has destroyed the independence of every nation which has confided in it;

That every such nation has been ruined by its internal divisions, especially by the separation of the people from their government;

That they have attempted to accomplish our ruin by the same means, and will certainly accomplish it if they can;

That the miseries suffered by the subjugated nations have been numberless and extreme, involving the loss of national honor, the immense plunder of public and private property, the conflagration of churches and dwellings, the total ruin of families, the butchery of great multitudes of fathers and sons, and the most deplorable dishonor of wives and daughters;

That the same miseries will be repeated here if in their power;

That there is under God no mean of escaping this ruin but union among ourselves and unshaken adherence to the existing government;

That themselves have an infinitely higher interest in preserving the independence of their country than in anything which *can* exist, should it be conquered;

That they must stand or fall with their country; since the French, like all other conquerors, though they may for a little time regard them as aids and friends with a seeming partiality, will soon lose that partiality in a general contempt and hatred for them as Americans. That should they, contrary to all experience, escape these evils, their children will suffer them as extensively as those of their neighbors; and

That to oppose or neglect the defense of their country is to stab the breast from which they have drawn their life.

I know not that even these considerations will prevail. If they do not, nothing can be suggested by me which will have efficacy. I must leave them, therefore, to their consciences and their God. . . .

We contend for all that is, or ought to be, dear to man. Our cause is eminently that in which "he who seeketh to save his life shall lose it, and he who loseth it," in obedience to the command of his Master, "shall find it" beyond the grave. To our enemies we have done no wrong. Unspotted justice looks down on all our public measures with a smile. We fight for that for which we can pray. We fight for the lives, the honor, the safety of our wives and children, for the religion of our fathers, and for the liberty "with which Christ hath made us free." "We jeopard our lives" that our children may inherit these glorious blessings, be rescued from the grinding insolence of foreign despotism, and saved from the corruption and perdition of foreign atheism.

I am a father. I feel the usual parental tenderness for my children. I have long soothed the approach of declining years with the fond hope of seeing my sons serving God and their generation around me. But from cool conviction I declare in this solemn place I would far rather follow them one by one to an untimely grave than to behold them, however prosperous, the victims of philosophism. What could I then believe but that they were "nigh unto cursing, and that their end was to be burned." . . .

Will you rely on men whose *principles justify falsehood, injustice, and cruelty?* Will you trust philosophists — men who set truth at nought, who make justice a butt of mockery, who deny the being and providence of God and laugh at the interests and sufferings of men? Think not that such men can change. They can scarcely be worse. There is not a hope that they will become better.

But perhaps you may be alarmed by the power and the successes of your enemies. I am warranted to declare that the ablest judge of this subject in America has said that if we are united, firm, and faithful to ourselves, neither France nor all Europe can subdue these states. Against other nations they contended with great and decisive advantages. Those nations were near to them, were divided, feeble, corrupted, seduced by philosophists, slaves of despotism, and separated from their government. None of these characters can be applied to us unless we voluntarily retain those which depend on ourselves.

Three thousand miles of ocean spread between us and our enemies to enfeeble and disappoint their efforts. They will not here contend with silken Italians, with divided Swiss, nor with self-surrendered Belgians and Batavians. They will find a hardy race of freemen, uncorrupted by luxury, unbroken by despotism, enlightened to understand their privileges, glowing with independence and determined to be free or to die; men who love and who will defend their families, their country, and their religion; men fresh from triumph and strong in a recent and victorious revolution. Doubled, since that revolution began, in their numbers and quadrupled in their resources and advantages at home, in a country formed to disappoint invasion and to prosper defense, under leaders skilled in all the arts and duties of war and trained in the path of success, they have, if united, firm, and faithful, everything to hope and, besides the common evils of war, nothing to fear.

9.

Charles Brockden Brown: On the Essential Equality of the Sexes

Charles Brockden Brown was the first novelist and journalist in America to devote his life solely to writing. He was highly influenced by European liberal thought and has been called a "left-wing Jeffersonian." His first work, Alcuin, *was a treatise on the rights of women, written as a dialogue between an unknown woman and himself. For all of its enlightened views about women at this early date, the work had no appreciable influence. A portion of the dialogue is reprinted here.*

Source: *Alcuin, A Dialogue,* 1798 [New Haven, 1935, pp. 21-59].

If I understand you rightly (said the lady), you are of opinion that the sexes are essentially equal.

It appears to me (answered I) that human beings are molded by the circumstances in which they are placed. In this they are all alike. The differences that flow from the sexual distinction are as nothing in the balance.

And yet women are often reminded that none of their sex are to be found among the formers of states, and the instructors of mankind — that Pythagoras, Lycurgus, and Socrates, Newton, and Locke were not women.

True; nor were they mountain savages, nor helots, nor shoemakers. You might as well expect a Laplander to write Greek spontaneously, and without instruction, as that anyone should be wise or skillful without suitable opportunities. I humbly presume one has a better chance of becoming an astronomer by gazing at the stars through a telescope than in eternally plying the needle, or snapping the scissors. To settle a bill of fare, to lard a pig, to compose a pudding, to carve a goose are tasks that do not, in any remarkable degree, tend to instill the love, or facilitate the acquisition of literature and science. Nay, I do not form prodigious expectations even of one who reads a novel or comedy once a month, or chants once a day to her harpsichord the hunter's foolish invocation to Phoebus or Cynthia.

Women are generally superficial and ignorant, because they are generally cooks and seamstresses. Men are the slaves of habit. It is doubtful whether the career of the species will ever terminate in knowledge. Certain it is, they began in ignorance. Habit has given permanence to errors, which ignorance had previously rendered universal. They are prompt to confound things, which are really distinct; and to persevere in a path to which they have been accustomed. Hence it is that certain employments have been exclusively assigned to women, and that their sex is supposed to disqualify them for any other. Women are defective. They are seldom or never metaphysicians, chemists, or lawgivers. Why? Because they are seamstresses and cooks. This is unavoidable. Such is the unalterable constitution of human nature. They cannot read who never saw an alphabet. They who know no tool but the needle cannot be skillful at the pen.

Yes (said the lady); of all forms of injustice that is the most egregious which makes the circumstance of sex a reason for excluding one-half of mankind from all those paths which lead to usefulness and honor.

Without doubt (returned I) there is abundance of injustice in the sentence; yet it is possible to misapprehend, and to overrate the injury that flows from the established order of things. If a certain part of every community must be condemned to servile and mechanical professions, it matters not of what sex they may be. If the benefits of leisure and science be, of necessity, the portion of a few, why should we be anxious to which sex the preference is given? The evil lies in so much of human capacity being thus fettered and perverted. This allotment is sad. Perhaps it is unnecessary. Perhaps that precept of justice is practicable which requires that each man should take his share of the labor, and enjoy his portion of the rest; that the tasks now assigned to a few, might be divided among the whole; and what now degenerates into ceaseless and brutalizing toil, might, by an equitable distribution, be changed into agreeable and useful exercise. Perhaps this inequality is incurable. In either case it is to be lamented, and, as far as possible, mitigated.

Now, the question of what sex either of those classes may be composed is of no importance. Though we must admit the claims of the female sex to an equality with the other, we cannot allow them to be superior. The state of the ignorant, servile, and laborious is entitled to compassion and relief, not because they are women, nor because they are men, but simply because they are rational. Among savage nations the women are slaves. They till the ground and cook the victuals. Such is the condition of half of the community — deplorable, without doubt; but it would be neither more nor less so, if the sexes were equally distributed through each class.

But, the burden is unequal (said Mrs. Carter) since the strength of the females is less.

What matters it (returned I) whether my strength be much or little, if I am tasked to the amount of it, and no more; and no task can go beyond.

But nature (said the lady) has subjected us to peculiar infirmities and hardships. In consideration of what we suffer as mothers and nurses, I think we ought to be exempted from the same proportion of labor.

It is hard (said I) to determine what is the amount of your pains as mothers and nurses. Have not ease and luxury a tendency to increase that amount? Is not the sustenance of infant offspring in every view a privilege? Of all changes in their condition, that which should transfer to men the task of nurturing the innocence and helplessness of infancy would, I should imagine, be to mothers the least acceptable.

I do not complain of this province. It is not, however, exempt from danger and trouble. It makes a large demand upon our time and attention. Ought not this to be considered in the distribution of tasks and duties?

Certainly. I was afraid you would imagine that too much regard had been paid to it; that the circle of female pursuits had been too much contracted on this account.

I, indeed (rejoined the lady), think it by far too much contracted. But I cannot give the authors of our institutions credit for any such motives. On the contrary, I think we have the highest reason to complain of our exclusion from many professions which might afford us, in common with men, the means of subsistence and independence.

How far, dear madam, is your complaint well grounded? What is it excludes you from the various occupations in use among us? Cannot a female be a trader? I know no law or custom that forbids it. You may, at any time, draw a subsistence from wages, if your station in life or your education has rendered you sufficiently robust. No one will deride you, or punish you for attempting to hew wood or bring water. If we rarely see you driving a team, or beating the anvil, is it not a favorable circumstance? In every family there are various duties. Certainly the most toilsome and rugged do not fall to the lot of women. If your employment be for the most part sedentary and recluse, to be exempted from an intemperate exertion of the muscles, or to be estranged from scenes of vulgar concourse might be deemed a privilege. The last of these advantages, however, is not yours; for do we not buy most of our meat, herbs, and fruit of women?

In the distribution of employments, the chief or only difference, perhaps, is that those which require most strength, or more unremitted exertion of it, belong to the males; and, yet, there is nothing obligatory or inviolable in this arrangement. In the country, the maid that milks and the man that plows, if discontented with their present office, may make an exchange, without breach of law or offense to decorum. If you possess stock by which to purchase the labor of others — and stock may accumulate in your hands as well as in ours — there is no species of manufacture in which you are forbidden to employ it.

But are we not (cried the lady) excluded from the liberal professions?

Why, that may admit of question. You have free access, for example, to the accounting house. It would be somewhat ludicrous, I own, to see you at the Exchange, or superintending the delivery of a cargo. Yet, this would attract our notice merely because it is singular, not because it is disgraceful or criminal; but if the singularity be a sufficient objection, we know that these offices are not necessary. The profession of a merchant may be pursued with success and dignity without being a constant visitor of the quay or the coffee house. In the trading cities of Europe, there are bankers and merchants of your sex to whom that consideration is attached, to which they are entitled by their skill, their integrity, or their opulence.

But what apology can you make for our exclusion from the class of physicians?

To a certain extent, the exclusion is imaginary. My grandmother was a tolerable physician. She had much personal experience; and her skill was, I assure you, in much request among her neighbors. It is true, she wisely forbore to tamper with diseases of an uncommon or complicated nature. Her experience was wholly personal. But that was accidental. She might have added, if she had chosen, the experience of others to her own.

But the law ——

True, we are not accustomed to see female pleaders at the bar. I never wish to see them there. But the law, as a science, is open to their curiosity, or their benevolence. It may be even practised as a source of gain, without obliging us to frequent and public exhibitions.

Well (said the lady), let us dismiss the lawyer and the physician and turn our eye to the pulpit. That, at least, is a sanctuary which women must not profane.

It is only (replied I) in some sects that divinity, the business of explaining to men their religious duty, is a trade. In such, custom or law, or the canons of their faith have confined the pulpit to men. Perhaps the distinction, wherever it is found, is an article of their religious creed, and, consequently, is no topic of complaint, since the propriety of this exclusion must be admitted by every member of the sect, whether male or female. But there are other sects which admit females into the class of preachers. With them, indeed, this distinction, if lucrative at all, is only indirectly so; and its profits are not greater to one sex than to the other. But there is no religious society in which women are debarred from the privileges of superior sanctity. The Christian religion has done much to level the distinctions of property, and rank, and sex. Perhaps, in reviewing the history of mankind, we shall find the authority derived from a real, or pretended, intercourse with Heaven pretty generally divided between them.

And, after all, what do these restrictions amount to? If some pursuits are monopolized by men, others are appropriated to you. If it appear that your occupations have least of toil, are most friendly to purity of manners, to delicacy of sensation, to intellectual improvement, and activity, or to public usefulness; if it should appear that your skill is always in such demand as to afford you employment when you stand in need of it; if, though few in number, they may be so generally and constantly useful as always to furnish you subsistence; or, at least, to expose you, by their vicissitudes, to the pressure of want as rarely as it is incident to men; you cannot reasonably complain, but, in my opinion, all this is true.

Perhaps not (replied the lady); yet I must own your statement is plausible. I shall not take much pains to confute it. It is evident that, for some reason or other, the liberal professions, those which require most vigor of mind, greatest extent of knowledge, and most commerce with books and with enlightened society are occupied only by men. If contrary instances occur, they are rare and must be considered as exceptions.

Admitting these facts (said I), I do not see reason for drawing mortifying inferences from them. For my part, I entertain but little respect for what are called the liberal professions, and, indeed, but little for any profession whatever. If their motive be gain, and that it is which constitutes them a profession, they seem to be, all of them, nearly on a level in point of dignity. The consideration of usefulness is of more value. He that roots out a national vice, or checks the ravages of a pestilence, is, no doubt, a respectable personage; but it is no man's trade to perform these services. How does a mercenary divine, or lawyer, or physician differ from a dishonest chimney sweep? The most that can be dreaded from a chimney sweep is the spoiling of our dinner, or a little temporary alarm; but what injuries may we not dread from the abuses of law, medicine, or divinity!

Honesty, you will say, is the best policy. Whatever it be, it is not the road to wealth. To the purposes of a profession, as such, it is not subservient. Degrees and examinations and licenses may qualify us for the trade; but benevolence needs not their aid to refine its skill, or augment its activity. Some portion of their time and their efforts must be employed by those who need, in obtaining the means of subsistence. The less tiresome, boisterous, and servile that task is which necessity enjoins, the less tendency it has to harden our hearts, to benumb our intellects, to undermine our health. The more leisure it affords us to gratify our curiosity and cultivate our moral discernment, the better. Here is a criterion for the choice of a profession, and which obliges us to consider the condition of women as preferable.

I cannot perceive it. But it matters nothing what field may be open, if our education does not qualify us to range over it. What think you of female education? Mine has been frivolous. I can make a pie, and cut out a gown. For this only I am indebted to my teachers. If I have added anything to these valuable attainments, it is through my own efforts and not by the assistance or encouragement of others.

And ought it not to be so? What can render men wise but their own efforts? Does curiosity derive no encouragement from the possession of the power and materials? You are taught to read and to write — quills, paper, and books are at hand. In-

Independence National Historical Park

Portrait of Charles Brockden Brown (1771-1810) by unknown artist

struments and machines are forthcoming to those who can purchase them. If you be insensible to the pleasures and benefits of knowledge, and are therefore ignorant and trifling, it is not for want of assistance and encouragement.

I shall find no difficulty (said the lady) to admit that the system is not such as to condemn all women, without exception, to stupidity. As it is, we have only to lament that a sentence so unjust is executed on, by far, the greater number. But you forget how seldom those who are most fortunately situated are permitted to cater for themselves. Their conduct, in this case, as in all others, is subject to the control of others who are guided by established prejudices, and are careful to remember that we are women. They think a being of this sex is to be instructed in a manner different from those of another. Schools and colleges and public instructors are provided in all the abstruse sciences and learned languages; but whatever may be their advantages, are not women totally excluded from them?

It would be prudent (said I), in the first place, to ascertain the amount of those advantages before we indulge ourselves in lamenting the loss of them. Let us consider whether a public education be not unfavorable to moral and intellectual improvement; or, at least, whether it be preferable to the domestic method; whether most knowledge be obtained by listening to hired professors, or by reading books; whether the abstruse sciences be best studied in a closet, or a college; whether the ancient tongues be worth learning; whether. since languages are of no use but as avenues to knowledge, our native tongue, especially in its present state of refinement, be not the best. Before we lament the exclusion of women from colleges, all these points must be settled; unless they shall be precluded by reflecting that places of public education, which are colleges in all respects but the name, are, perhaps, as numerous for females as for males.

They differ (said the lady) from colleges in this, that a very different plan of instruction is followed. I know of no female school where Latin is taught, or geometry, or chemistry.

Yet, madam, there are female geometricians, and chemists, and scholars, not a few. Were I desirous that my son or daughter should become either of these, I should not deem the assistance of a college indispensable. Suppose an anatomist should open a school to pupils of both sexes and solicit equally their attendance; would you comply with the invitation?

No; because that pursuit has no attractions for me. But if I had a friend whose curiosity was directed to it, why should I dissuade her from it?

Perhaps (said I) you are but little acquainted with the real circumstances of such a scene. If your disdain of prejudices should prompt you to adventure one visit, I question whether you would find an inclination to repeat it.

Perhaps not (said she); but that mode of

instruction in all the experimental sciences is not, perhaps, the best. A numerous company can derive little benefit from a dissection in their presence. A closer and more deliberate inspection than the circumstances of a large company will allow seems requisite. But the assembly need not be a mixed one. Objections on the score of delicacy, though they are more specious than sound and owe their force more to our weakness than our wisdom, would be removed by making the whole company, professor and pupils, female. But this would be obviating an imaginary evil at the price of a real benefit.

Nothing has been more injurious than the separation of the sexes. They associate in childhood without restraint; but the period quickly arrives when they are obliged to take different paths. Ideas, maxims, and pursuits, wholly opposite, engross their attention. Different systems of morality, different languages, or, at least, the same words with a different set of meanings are adopted. All intercourse between them is fettered and embarrassed. On one side, all is reserve and artifice; on the other, adulation and affected humility. The same end must be compassed by opposite means. The man must affect a disproportionable ardor; while the woman must counterfeit indifference and aversion. Her tongue has no office, but to belie the sentiments of her heart and the dictates of her understanding.

By marriage she loses all right to separate property. The will of her husband is the criterion of all her duties. All merit is comprised in unlimited obedience. She must not expostulate or rebel. In all contests with him, she must hope to prevail by blandishments and tears, not by appeals to justice and addresses to reason. She will be most applauded when she smiles with most perseverance on her oppressor, and when, with the undistinguishing attachment of a dog, no caprice or cruelty shall be able to estrange her affection.

Surely, madam, this picture is exaggerated. You derive it from some other source than your own experience, or even your own observation.

No; I believe the picture to be generally exact. No doubt there are exceptions. I believe myself to be one. I think myself exempt from the grosser defects of women, but by no means free from the influence of a mistaken education. But why should you think the picture exaggerated? Man is the strongest. This is the reason why, in the earliest stage of society, the females are slaves. The tendency of rational improvement is to equalize conditions; to abolish all distinctions but those that are founded in truth and reason; to limit the reign of brute force and uncontrollable accidents. Women have unquestionably benefited by the progress that has hitherto taken place. If I look abroad, I may see reason to congratulate myself on being born in this age and country. Women that are nowhere totally exempt from servitude, nowhere admitted to their true rank in society, may yet be subject to different degrees or kinds of servitude. Perhaps there is no country in the world where the yoke is lighter than here. But this persuasion, though in one view it may afford us consolation, ought not to blind us to our true condition, or weaken our efforts to remove the evils that still oppress us. It is manifest that we are hardly and unjustly treated. The natives of the most distant regions do not less resemble each other than the male and female of the same tribe, in consequence of the different discipline to which they are subject. Now, this is palpably absurd. Men and women are partakers of the same nature. They are rational beings; and, as such, the same principles of truth and equity must be applicable to both.

To this I replied, Certainly, madam, but it is obvious to inquire to which of the sexes the distinction is most favorable. In some respects, different paths are allotted to them, but I am apt to suspect that of the woman to be strewn with fewest thorns; to be beset with fewest asperities; and to lead, if not absolutely in conformity to truth and equity yet with fewest deviations from it. There are evils incident to your condition as women. As human beings, we all lie under considerable disadvantages; but it is of an unequal lot that you complain. The institutions of society have injuriously and capriciously distinguished you. True it is, laws, which have commonly been male births, have treated you unjustly; but it has been with that species of injustice that has given birth to nobles and kings. They have distinguished you by irrational and undeserved indulgences. They have exempted you from a thousand toils and cares. Their tenderness has secluded you from tumult and noise: your persons are sacred from profane violences; your eyes from ghastly spectacles; your ears from a thousand discords by which ours are incessantly invaded. Yours are the peacefulest recesses of the mansion; your hours glide along in sportive chat, in harmless recreation, or voluptuous indolence; or in labor so light as scarcely to be termed encroachments on the reign of contemplation. Your industry delights in the graceful and minute; it enlarges the empire of the senses, and improves the flexibility of the fibers. The art of the needle, by the luster of its hues and the delicacy of its touches, is able to mimic all the forms of nature, and portray all the images of fancy; and the needle but prepares the hand for doing wonders on the harp, for conjuring up the "piano" to melt, and the "forte" to astound, us.

This (cried the lady) is a very partial description. It can apply only to the opulent, and but to few of them. Meanwhile, how shall we estimate the hardships of the lower class? You have only pronounced a panegyric on indolence and luxury. Eminent virtue and true happiness are not to be found in this element.

True (returned I). I have only attempted to justify the male sex from the charge of cruelty. Ease and luxury are pernicious. Kings and nobles, the rich and the idle enjoy no genuine content. Their lot is hard enough; but still it is better than brutal ignorance and unintermitted toil; than nakedness and hunger. There must be one condition of society that approaches nearer than any other to the standard of rectitude and happiness. For this it is our duty to search; and, having found it, endeavor to reduce every other condition to this desirable mean. It is useful, meanwhile, to ascertain the relative importance of different conditions; and since deplorable evils are annexed to every state, to discover in what respects, and in what degree, one is more or less eligible than another. Half of the community are females. Let the whole community be divided into classes; and let us inquire whether the wives and daughters and single women of each class be not placed in a more favorable situation than the husbands, sons, and single men of the same class. Our answer will surely be in the affirmative.

There is (said the lady) but one important question relative to this subject. Are women as high in the scale of social felicity and usefulness as they may and ought to be?

To this (said I) there can be but one answer: No. At present they are only higher on that scale than the men. You will observe, madam, I speak only of that state of society which we enjoy. If you had excluded sex from the question, I must have made the same answer. Human beings, it is to be hoped, are destined to a better condition on this stage, or some other, than is now allotted them.

This remark was succeeded by a pause on both sides. The lady seemed more inclined to listen than talk. At length I ventured to resume the conversation.

Pray, madam, permit me to return from this impertinent digression and repeat my question — Are you a Federalist?

And let me (replied she) repeat my answer — What have I, as a woman, to do with politics? Even the government of our country, which is said to be the freest in the world, passes over women as if they were not. We are excluded from all political rights without the least ceremony. Lawmakers thought as little of comprehending us in their code of liberty as if we were pigs or sheep. That females are exceptions to their general maxims perhaps never occurred to them. If it did, the idea was quietly discarded, without leaving behind the slightest consciousness of inconsistency or injustice. If to uphold and defend, as far as woman's little power extends, the Constitution against violence; if to prefer a scheme of union and confederacy to war and dissention entitle me to that name, I may justly be styled a Federalist. But if that title be incompatible with a belief that, in many particulars, this Constitution is unjust and absurd, I certainly cannot pretend to it. But how should it be otherwise? While I am conscious of being an intelligent and moral being; while I see myself denied, in so many cases, the exercise of my own discretion; incapable of separate property; subject, in all periods of my life, to the will of another on whose bounty I am made to depend for food, raiment, and shelter; when I see myself, in my relation to society, regarded merely as a beast, or an insect; passed over, in the distribution of public duties, as absolutely nothing by those who disdain to assign the least apology for their injustice — what though politicians say I am nothing, it is impossible I should assent to their opinion, as long as I am conscious of willing and moving. If they generously admit me into the class of existence, but affirm that I exist for no purpose but the convenience of the more dignified sex; that I am not to be entrusted with the government of myself; that to foresee, to deliberate and decide, belongs to others, while all my duties resolve themselves into this precept, "listen and obey"; it is not for me to smile at their tyranny, or receive, as my gospel, a code built upon such atrocious maxims. No, I am no Federalist.

You are, at least (said I), a severe and uncommon censor. You assign most extraordinary reasons for your political heresy. You have many companions in your aversion to the government, but, I suspect, are wholly singular in your motives. There are few, even among your own sex, who reason in this manner.

Very probably; thoughtless and servile creatures! but that is not wonderful. All despotism subsists by virtue of the errors and supineness of its slaves. If their discernment was clear, their persons would be free. Brute strength has no part in the government of multitudes; they are bound in the fetters of opinion.

The maxims of constitution makers sound well. All power is derived from the people. Liberty is everyone's birthright. Since all cannot govern or deliberate individually, it is just that they should elect their representatives. That every one should possess indirectly, and through the medium of his representatives, a voice in the public councils, and should yield to no will but that of an actual or virtual majority. Plausible and specious maxims! but fallacious. What avails it to be told by anyone that he is an advocate for liberty? We must first know what he means by the word. We shall generally find that he intends only freedom to himself and subjection to all others. Suppose I place myself where I can conveniently mark the proceedings at a general election: "All," says the code, "are free. Liberty is the immediate gift of the Creator to all mankind and is unalienable. Those that are subject to the laws should possess a share in their enaction. This privilege can be exercised, consistently with the maintenance of social order, in a large society only in the choice of deputies." A person advances with his ticket. "Pray," says the officer, "are you twenty-one years of age?" — "No." — "Then I cannot receive your vote; you are no citizen." Disconcerted and abashed, he retires. A second assumes his place. "How long," says the officer, "have you been an inhabitant of this State?" — "Nineteen months and a few days." — "None has a right to vote who has not completed two years' residence." A third approaches, who is rejected because his name is not found in the catalogue of taxables. At length, room is made for a fourth person. "Man," cries the magistrate, "is your skin black or white?" — "Black." — "What, a sooty slave dare to usurp the rights of freemen?" The way being now clear, I venture to approach. "I am not a minor," say I to myself. "I was born in the state, and cannot, therefore, be stigmatized as a foreigner. I pay taxes, for I have no father or husband to pay them for me. Luckily, my complexion is white. Surely my vote will be received. But, no, I am a woman. Neither short residence, nor poverty, nor age, nor color, nor sex exempt from the jurisdiction of the laws." "True," says the magistrate, "but they deprive you from bearing any part in their formation." "So I perceive, but I cannot perceive the justice of your pretentions to equality and liberty, when those principles are thus openly and grossly violated."

If a stranger question me concerning the nature of our government, I answer that in this happy climate all men are free; the people are the source of all authority; from them it flows, and to them, in due season, it returns. But in what (says my friend) does this unrivaled and precious freedom consist? Not (say I) in every man's governing himself, literally and individually; that is impossible. Not in the control of an actual majority; they are by much too numerous to deliberate commodiously, or decide expeditiously. No, our liberty consists in the choice of our governors.

All, as reason requires, have a part in this choice, yet not without a few exceptions; for, in the first place, all females are excepted. They, indeed, compose one half of the community; but, no matter, women cannot possibly have any rights. Second, those whom the feudal law calls minors, because they could not lift a shield or manage a pike, are excepted. They comprehend one half of the remainder. Third, the poor. These vary in number, but are sure to increase with the increase of luxury and opulence, and to promote these is well known to be the aim of all wise governors. Fourth, those who have not been two years in the land; and, last, slaves.

It has been sagely decreed that none but freemen shall enjoy this privilege, and that all men are free but those that are slaves. When all these are sifted out, a majority of the remainder are entitled to elect our governor; provided, however, the candidate possess certain qualifications, which you will excuse me from enumerating. I am tired of explaining this charming system of equality and independence. Let the black, the young, the poor, and the stranger support their own claims. I am a woman. As such, I cannot celebrate the equity of that scheme of government which classes me with dogs and swine.

Asking one of the states to surrender a part of her sovereignty is like asking a lady to surrender a part of her chastity.

John Randolph of Roanoke

10.

EDWARD LIVINGSTON: Against the Alien Act

The American political climate of the later 1790s was in large measure determined by the French Revolution. Generally sympathetic to the goals of the Revolution, if not to the practices of the revolutionaries, and thus pro-French, were the liberal Jeffersonian Republicans; antagonistic to the Revolution and thus pro-British were the conservative Hamiltonian Federalists. A balance of forces was achieved early in the administration of President John Adams that prevailed even after France and Britain went to war and began to interfere with American shipping. But in 1798 the French foreign minister Talleyrand indirectly attempted to collect a bribe from an American mission sent to France to try to negotiate protection for American trade. This maneuver, all of the details of which are probably still not known, became immediately famous as the XYZ Affair, so-called because Talleyrand was supposed to have been represented in the bribe demand by three anonymous subordinates. Whatever the truth of the matter, the Federalist majority in Congress was so enraged that in quick succession it passed four laws, the Alien and Sedition Acts, that were designed to safeguard the country against foreign — that is, French — influence. Prior to passage of the Alien Act, Edward Livingston of New York rose before Congress on June 21, 1798, to give this powerful speech.

Source: *Debates,* 5 Cong., pp. 2006-2015.

THE STATE OF THINGS, if we are to judge from the complexion of the bill, must be that a number of aliens enjoying the protection of our government, were plotting its destruction; that they are engaged in treasonable machinations against a people who have given them an asylum and support; and that there is no provision to provide for their expulsion and punishment. If these things are so and no remedy exists for the evil, one ought speedily to be provided, but even then it must be a remedy that is consistent with the Constitution under which we act; for, as by that instrument all powers not expressly given by it to the Union are reserved to the states, it follows that unless an express authority can be found, vesting us with the power, be the evil ever so great, it can only be remedied by the several states who have never delegated the authority to Congress. But this point will be presently examined, and it will not be a difficult task to show that the provisions of this bill are not only unauthorized by the Constitution but are in direct violation of its fundamental principles, and contradictory to some of its most express prohibitions. At present, it is only necessary to ask whether the state of things contemplated by the bill have any existence.

We must legislate upon facts, not on surmises; we must have evidence, not vague suspicions, if we meant to legislate with prudence. What facts have been produced? What evidence had been submitted to the House? I have heard, sir, of none; but if evidence of facts could not be procured, at least it might have been expected that reasonable cause of suspicion should be shown. Here again, gentlemen were at fault; they could not show even a suspicion why aliens ought to be suspected. We have, indeed, been told that the fate of Venice, Switzerland, and Batavia was produced by the interference of foreigners. But the instances were unfortunate, because all those powers have been overcome by foreign force, or divided by domestic faction, not by aliens who resided among them; and if any instruction was to be gained from those republics, it would be that we ought to banish not aliens but all those who did not approve of the executive acts. This, he believed, gentlemen were not ready to avow; but if this measure prevailed, he should not think the other remote; but if it had been proved that these governments were destroyed by the conspiracies of aliens, it yet remains to show that we are in the same situation, or that any such plots have been detected, or are even reasonably suspected here.

Nothing of this kind has been yet done. A modern Theseus, indeed, has told us he has procured a clue that will enable him to penetrate the labyrinth and destroy this monster of sedition. Who the fair Ariadne is who so kindly gave him the ball he has not revealed; nor, though several days have elapsed since he undertook the adventure, has he yet told us where the monster lurks. No evidence then being produced, we have a right to say that none exists, and yet we are about to sanction a most important act; and on what ground — our individual suspicions, our private fears, our overheated imaginations. Seeing nothing to excite those suspicions, and not feeling those fears, I could not give my assent to the bill, even if I did not feel a superior obligation to reject it on other grounds.

As far as my own observation goes, I have seen nothing like the state of things contemplated by the bill. Most of the aliens I have seen were either triumphant Englishmen or Frenchmen, with dejection in their countenances and grief at their hearts, preparing to quit the country and seek another asylum. But if these plots exist, if this treason is apparent, if there are aliens guilty of the crimes ascribed to them, an effectual remedy presents itself for the evil. We have already wise laws, we have upright judges and vigilant magistrates, and there is no necessity of arming the executive with the destructive power proposed by the bill now on your table. The laws now in force are competent to punish every treasonable or seditious attempt.

But grant, sir — what, however, has not been supported by fact — grant that these fears are not visionary, that the dangers are imminent, and that no existing law is sufficient to avert them, let us examine whether the provisions of the bill are conformable to the principles of the Constitution. If it should be found to contravene them, I trust it will lose many of its present supporters; but if not only contrary to the general spirit and the principles of the Constitution, it should also be found diametrically opposite to the most express prohibitions, I cannot doubt that it would be rejected with that indignant decision which our duty to our country and our sacred oath demands.

The 1st Section provides, that it shall be lawful for the president "to order all such aliens as he shall judge dangerous to the peace and safety of the United States, or shall have reasonable grounds to suspect are concerned in any treasonable or secret machinations against the government thereof, to depart out of the United States, in such time as shall be expressed in such order."

Our government, sir, is founded on the establishment of those principles which constitute the difference between a free Constitution and a despotic power; a distribution of the legislative, executive, and judiciary powers into several hands; a distribution strongly marked in the three first and great divisions of the Constitution — by the first, all legislative power is given to Congress; the second vests all legislative functions in the president; and the third declares that the judiciary powers shall be exercised by the Supreme and inferior courts. Here then is a division of the governmental powers strongly marked, decisively pronounced, and every act of one or all of the branches that tends to confound these powers, or alter this arrangement, must be destructive of the Constitution. Examine then, sir, the bill on your table and declare whether the few lines I have repeated from the 1st Section do not confound these fundamental powers of government, vest them all in the more unqualified terms in one hand, and thus subvert the basis on which our liberties rest.

Art Commission of the City of New York
Portrait of Edward Livingston by John Trumbull

Legislative power prescribes the rule of action; the judiciary applies that general rule to particular cases; and it is the province of the executive to see that the laws are carried into full effect. In all free governments these powers are exercised by different men and their union, in the same hand, is the peculiar characteristic of despotism. If the same power that makes the law can construct it to suit his interest, and apply it to gratify his vengeance; if he can go further and execute, according to his own passions, the judgment which he himself has pronounced, upon his own construction of laws which he alone has made, what other features are wanted to complete the picture of tyranny? Yet all this and more is proposed to be done by this act; by it the president alone is empowered to make the law, to fix in his mind what acts, what words, what thoughts or looks, shall constitute the crime contemplated by the bill, that is the crime of being "suspected to be dangerous to the peace and safety of the United States." He is not only authorized to make this law for his own conduct but to vary it at pleasure, as every gust of passion, every cloud of suspicion, shall agitate or darken his mind. The same power that formed the law, then, applies it to the guilty or innocent victim, whom his own suspicions, or the secret whisper of a spy, have designated as its object. The president, then, having made the law, the president having construed and applied it, the same president is by the bill authorized to execute his sentence, in case of disobedience, by imprisonment during his pleasure. This, then, comes completely within the definition of despotism — a union of legislative, executive, and judicial powers.

But this bill, sir, does not stop here; its provisions are a refinement upon despotism, and present an image of the most fearful tyranny. Even in despotisms, though the monarch legislates, judges, and executes, yet he legislates openly; his laws, though oppressive, are known; they precede the offense, and every man who chooses may avoid the penalties of disobedience. Yet he judges and executes by proxy, and his private interests or passions do not inflame the mind of his deputy.

But here the law is so closely concealed in the same mind that gave it birth — the crime is "exciting the suspicions of the president," but no man can tell what conduct will avoid that suspicion — a careless word, perhaps misrepresented, or never spoken, may be sufficient evidence; a look may destroy, an idle gesture may insure punishment; no innocence can protect, no circumspection can avoid the jealousy of suspicion; surrounded by spies, informers, and all that infamous herd which fatten under laws like this, the unfortunate stranger will never know either of the law, of the accusation, or of the judgment until the moment it is put in execution. He will detest your tyranny and fly from a land of desolators, inquisitions, and spies. . . .

Judiciary power is taken from courts and given to the executive; the previous safeguard of a presentment by a grand inquest is removed; the trial by jury is abolished; the "public trial" required by the Constitution is changed into a secret and worse than inquisitorial tribunal. Instead of giving "information on the nature and cause of the accusation," the criminal, ignorant of his offense and the danger to which he is exposed, never hears of either until the judgment is passed and the sentence is executed; instead of being "confronted with his accusers," he is kept alike ignorant of their names and their existence; and even the forms of a trial being dispensed with, it would be a mockery to talk of "proofs for witnesses," or the "assistance of counsel for defense" — thus are all the barriers which the wisdom and humanity of our country had placed between accused innocence and oppressed power at once forced and broken down. Not a vestige even of their form remains. No indictment; no jury; no trial; no public procedure; no statement of the accusation; no examination of the witnesses in its support; no counsel for defense; all is darkness, silence, mystery, and suspicion.

But, as if this were not enough, the unfortunate victims of this law are told in the next section that if they can convince the president that his suspicions are unfounded, he may, if he pleases, give them a license to stay. But, how remove his suspicions when they know not on what act they were founded? Miserable mockery of justice! appoint an arbitrary judge armed with legislative and executive powers added to his own! let him condemn the unheard, the unaccused object of his suspicion; and then to cover the injustice of the scene, gravely tell him, you ought not to complain — you need only disprove facts that you have never heard — remove suspicions that have never been communicated to you; it will be easy to convince your judge, whom you shall not approach, that he is tyrannical and unjust; and, having done this, we give him the power he had before, to pardon you if he pleases. . . .

Eternal Vigilance Is the Price of Liberty.

THOMAS JEFFERSON, inscription on National Archives Building, Washington

11.

Debate on the Sedition Act

The Sedition Act, termed by James Madison "a monster that must forever disgrace its parents," provoked heated debate in Congress before it was finally passed. "Long John" Allen, a Connecticut congressman and long-time proponent of suppressive legislation, spoke so persuasively to his colleagues that he is given at least partial credit for the bill's passage. Albert Gallatin, a naturalized citizen and one of the leading Republican congressmen, argued eloquently against its acceptance. What he considered the real purpose of the Sedition Act was revealed by Gallatin in two speeches, parts of which are reprinted here. Though the speeches failed to prevent passage, they ably stated the Jeffersonian position. Allen addressed the Congress on July 5, 1798, and Gallatin on July 5 and 10.

Source: *Debates,* 5 Cong., pp. 2093-2100, 2107-2109, 2161-2162.

I.

"Long John" Allen: For the Sedition Act

Mr. Allen: I hope this bill will not be rejected. If ever there was a nation which required a law of this kind, it is this. Let gentlemen look at certain papers printed in this city and elsewhere, and ask themselves whether an unwarrantable and dangerous combination does not exist to overturn and ruin the government by publishing the most shameless falsehoods against the representatives of the people of all denominations, that they are hostile to free governments and genuine liberty, and of course to the welfare of this country; that they ought, therefore, to be displaced, and that the people ought to raise an *insurrection* against the government.

In the *Aurora,* of the 28th of June last, we see this paragraph: "It is a curious fact, America is making war with France for *not* treating, at the very moment the minister for foreign affairs fixes upon the very day for opening a negotiation with Mr. Gerry. What think you of this, Americans!"

Such paragraphs need but little comment. The public agents are charged with crimes for which, if true, they ought to be hung. The intention here is to persuade the people that peace with France is in our power; nay, that she is sincerely desirous of it, on proper terms, but that we reject her offers and proceed to plunge our country into a destructive war.

This combination against our peace is extensive; it embraces characters whose stations demand a different course. Is this House free from it? Recollect what a few days ago fell from the very gentleman (Mr. Livingston), who now so boldly and violently calls on us to reject this bill at the instant of its coming before us, without suffering it to be read a second time. The gentleman proposed a resolution requesting the President to instruct Mr. Gerry to conclude a treaty with the French government; and declared that he believed a negotiation might be opened, and that it was probable a treaty might be concluded which it would

Library of Congress

Engraving of Matthew Lyon fighting Roger Griswold on floor of Congress, 1798; Lyon was later prosecuted under the Sedition Act

be honorable to the United States to accept. He did not wish to frustrate so happy an event by any punctilio, because they had refused to treat with three envoys, but were willing to treat with one.

This is in the very spirit of the malicious paragraph I just now read. It is pursuing the same systematic course of operations. The gentleman also said (what has not been published, however) that "the commission of the envoys being joint and several, Mr. Gerry had unquestionably ample powers to treat alone." Here are circumstances of what I call *a combination against the government,* in attempts to persuade the people of certain facts, which a majority of this House, at least, and of the people at large, I believe, know to be unfounded.

Who can say that Mr. Gerry has power to treat alone, or that the French government is willing to treat with him on fair and honorable terms? Gentlemen do not believe either, let them say what they will. Does such a commission empower one to exercise the functions of the whole in opposition to the opinions of his colleagues? It would produce the most inextricable confusion. The severalty of the powers is well known always to be a provision against such accidents as may prevent or disable a part of the commissioners from acting. I mention these things to show what false ideas gentlemen endeavor to impress the public mind with on this subject. . . .

In the *Aurora,* of last Friday, we read the following:

> The period is now at hand when it will be a question difficult to determine, whether there is more safety and liberty to be enjoyed at Constantinople or Philadelphia?

This, sir, is faithfully pursuing the system of the gentleman in announcing to the poor deluded readers of the factious prints the rapid approach of Turkish slavery in this country. Who can doubt the existence of a combination against the real liberty, the real safety of the United States?

I say, sir, a combination, a conspiracy against the Constitution, the government, the peace and safety of this country, is formed, and is in full operation. It embraces members of all classes; the representative of the people on this floor, the wild and visionary theorist in the bloody philosophy of the day, the learned and ignorant. And the paper from which I have so often read, with three or four others, furnishes demonstrations without number of the truth of the accusation. Each acts its part; but all are in perfect unison. Permit me to read a paragraph from the *Timepiece,* a paper printed in New York:

> When such a character attempts by antiquated and exploded sophistry, by Jesuitical arguments, to extinguish the sentiment of liberty, 'tis fit the mask should be torn off from this meaner species of aristocracy than history has condescended to record; where a person without patriotism, without philosophy, without a taste for the fine arts, building his pretensions on a gross and indigested compilation of statutes and precedents, is jostled into the chief magistracy by the ominous combination of old Tories with old opinions, and old Whigs with new, 'tis fit this mock monarch, with his court, composed of Tories and speculators, should pass in review before the good sense of the world. Monarchies are seen only with indignation and concern; at sight of these terrible establishments, fears accompany the execrations of mankind; but when the champion of the well-born, with his serene court, is seen soliciting and answering addresses, and pronouncing anathemas against France, it shall be my fault if other emotions be not excited; if to tears and execrations be not added derision and contempt.

Gentlemen contend for the liberty of opinions and of the press. Let me ask them whether they seriously think the liberty of the press authorizes such publications? The president of the United States is here called "a person without patriotism, without philosophy, and a mock monarch," and the free election of the people is pronounced "a jostling him into the chief magistracy by the ominous combination of old Tories with old opinions, and old Whigs with new."

If this be not a conspiracy against government and people, I know not what to understand from the "threat of tears, execrations, derision, and contempt." Because the Constitution guarantees the right of expressing our opinions and the freedom of the press, am I at liberty to falsely call you a thief, a murderer, an atheist? Because I have the liberty of locomotion, of going where I please, have I a right to ride over the footman in the path? The freedom of the press and opinions was never understood to give the right of publishing falsehoods and slanders, nor of exciting sedition, insurrection, and slaughter, with impunity. A man was always answerable for the malicious publication of falsehood; and what more does this bill require?

In the *Aurora,* of last Tuesday, is this paragraph:

> Where a law shall have been passed in violation of the Constitution, making it criminal to expose the crimes, the official vices or abuses, or the attempts of men in power to usurp a despotic authority, is there any alternative between an abandonment of the Constitution and resistance?

The gentleman (Mr. Livingston) makes his proclamation of war on the government in the House, on Monday, and this infamous printer (Bache) follows it up with the tocsin of insurrection, on Tuesday. While this bill was under consideration in the Senate, an attempt is made to render it odious among the people. "Is there any alternative," says this printer, "between an abandonment of the Constitution and resistance?" He declares what is unconstitutional, and then invites the people to "resistance." This is an awful, horrible example of "the liberty of opinion and freedom of the press." Can gentlemen hear these things and lie quietly on their pillows? Are we to see all these acts practised against the repose of our country and remain passive? Are we bound hand and foot that we must be witnesses of these deadly thrusts at our liberty? Are we to be the unresisting spectators of these exertions to destroy all that we hold dear? Are these approaches to revolution and Jacobinic domination to be observed with the eye of meek submission? No, sir, they are indeed terrible; they are calculated to freeze the very blood in our veins. Such liberty of the press and of opinion is calculated to destroy all confidence between man and man; it leads to a dissolution of every bond of union; it cuts asunder every ligament that unites man to his family, man to his neighbor, man to society and to government. God deliver us from such liberty, the liberty of vomiting on the public floods of falsehood and hatred to everything sacred, human and divine!

II.

Albert Gallatin: Against the Sedition Act

Mr. Gallatin wished that the bill had been committed before any debate had taken place, as, in its present stage, any observations on details susceptible of amendment would be out of order; and he must now confine himself to the general question: Does the situation of the country, at this time, require that any law of this kind should pass? Do there exist such new and alarming symptoms of sedition as render it necessary to adopt, in addition to the existing laws, any extraordinary measure for the purpose of suppressing unlawful combinations, and of restricting the freedom of speech and of the press? For such were the objects of the bill, whatever modifications it might hereafter receive.

The manner in which the principle of the bill had been supported was perhaps more extraordinary still than the bill itself. The gentleman from Connecticut (Mr. Allen), in order to prove the existence of a combination against the Constitution and government, had communicated to the House — what? a number of newspaper paragraphs; and even most of those were such as would not be punishable by the bill as it now stands.

The object of that gentleman in wishing a bill of this nature to pass extended far beyond the intention of the Senate, who had sent down this bill; far beyond, he would venture to say, the idea of any other member upon this floor, besides himself. His idea was to punish men for stating facts which he happened to disbelieve, or for enacting and avowing opinions, not criminal but perhaps erroneous. Thus, one of the paragraphs most obnoxious to the gentleman from Connecticut was that in which the writer expresses his belief that Mr. Gerry may yet make a treaty with the French government, his powers being sufficient for that purpose. . . .

Was there anything criminal in that paragraph? It asserted that Mr. Gerry had powers sufficient to treat. The gentleman from Connecticut denies this to be true. Mr. Gerry would aver that it was an undeniable fact, as appears evidently from the documents now on the table. They showed that the powers given to the envoys were joint and several. And, if Mr. Gerry had powers to treat, how could it be criminal to say that he might treat? Or supposing the writer of the paragraph to have said that he believed Mr. Gerry would treat, could the opinion be charged with anything but being erroneous? When a paragraph of this nature was held out as criminal, what writings, what opinions could escape the severity of the intended law, which did not coincide with the opinions and which might counteract the secret views of a prevailing party?

The gentleman from Connecticut had also quoted an extract of a letter said to be written by a member of Congress from Virginia, and published in last Saturday's *Aurora.* The style and composition of that letter did the highest honor to its writer. It contained more information and more sense, and gave more proofs of a sound understanding and strong mind, than ever the gentleman from Connecticut had displayed, or could display, on this floor. So far he would venture to say, although he had given but a cursory reading to the letter, and he was altogether at a loss to know what was criminal in it, though he might easily see why it was obnoxious.

Was it erroneous or criminal to say that debts and taxes were the ruinous consequences of war? Or that some members in both houses of Congress uniformly voted in favor of an extension of the powers of the executive, and of every proposed expenditure of money? Was it not true? Gentlemen of that description avow that, in their opinion, the executive is the weakest branch of government; and they act upon the ostensible principle that, on that account, its influence and powers must be increased. Look at the laws passed during this session. Look at the alien bill, at the provisional army bill; look at the prodigious influence acquired by so many new offices, and then deny that the powers of the executive have not been greatly increased. As to the increased rate of expenditure, and the propensity of these gentlemen to vote money, they would not themselves deny it. Was it criminal to say that the executive is supported by a party, when gentlemen declared that it must be supported by a party; when the doctrine had been avowed on this floor that men of a certain political opinion, alone, ought to be appointed to offices; and when the executive had now adopted and carried into practice that doctrine in its fullest extent?

Mr. Gerry acknowledged that some of the newspaper paragraphs quoted by Mr. Allen were of a very different nature from that letter. One of them, taken from the *Timepiece,* was extremely exceptionable; most of them contained sentiments different from his own, and expressed in a style he never would adopt. Yet in almost every one of them there was a mixture of truth and error; and what was the remedy proposed by the gentleman from Connecticut in order to rectify and correct error? Coercion: a law inflicting fine and imprisonment for the publication of erroneous opinions.

New York Historical Society
Portrait of Matthew Lyon by unknown artist

Was the gentleman afraid, or rather was administration afraid, that in this instance error could not be successfully opposed by truth? The American government had heretofore subsisted, it had acquired strength, it had grown on the affection of the people, it had been fully supported without the assistance of laws similar to the bill now on the table. It had been able to repel opposition by the single weapon of argument. And, at present, when out of ten presses in the country nine were employed on the side of administration, such is their want of confidence in the purity of their own views and motives that they even fear the unequal contest, and require the help of force in order to suppress the limited circulation of the opinions of those who did not approve all their measures.

One of the paragraphs says that it will soon become a question whether there will be more liberty at Philadelphia or Constantinople. The gentleman from Connecticut bitterly complains of this as insinuating that some persons in government intend to establish a despotic power; and in order to convince the writer of his error, that gentleman not only supports the bill but avows principles perfectly calculated to justify the assertions contained in the paragraph. . . .

The only evidences brought by the supporters of this bill consist of writings expressing an opinion that certain measures of government have been dictated by an unwise policy, or by improper motives, and that some of them were unconstitutional. This bill and its supporters suppose, in fact, that whoever dislikes the measures of administration and of a temporary majority in Congress, and shall, either by speaking or writing, express his disapprobation and his want of confidence in the men now in power, is seditious, is an enemy, not of administration but of the Constitution, and is liable to punishment. That principle, Mr. Gerry said, was subversive of the principles of the Constitution itself. If you put the press under any restraint in respect to the measures of members of government; if you thus deprive the people of the means of obtaining information of their conduct, you in fact render their right of electing nugatory; and this bill must be considered only as a weapon used by a party now in power in order to perpetuate their authority and preserve their present places. . . .

The advocates of this measure must show to us its necessity for carrying into operation the powers vested in the president, or in either branch of the legislature — who are its objects. They must prove that the president dare not, cannot, will not execute the laws, unless the abuse poured upon him from certain presses is suppressed. If there be a majority of this House in favor of this law, are that majority ready to declare that that law is *necessary* in order to enable them to execute the powers vested in them by the Constitution? Are they ready to say that they are prevented from voting according to the dictates of their conscience, for voting is the only power belonging to them, by newspaper paragraphs? Are they ready to say that unless libels against them shall be punished; that unless they may obtain revenge from the insolence of the printers, they will not or dare not vote as they would otherwise do? But if they are ready to make those declarations; if they do believe this bill *necessary* in order to enable this House to do their duty, they must recollect that this House is composed of individuals, and that, according to their own doctrine, in order to insure a conscientious vote in the whole House, every individual, and not a majority of the House, ought to be equally sheltered by this law from the abuse of printers.

While, therefore, they support the bill in its present shape, do they not avow that the true object of the law is to enable one party to oppress the other; that they mean to have the power to punish printers who may publish against them, while their opponents will remain alone, and without redress, exposed to the abuse of ministerial prints? Is it not their object to frighten and suppress all presses which they consider as contrary to their views; to prevent a free circulation of opinion; to suffer the people at large to hear only partial accounts, and but one side of the question; to delude and deceive them by partial information, and, through those means, to perpetuate themselves in power?

12.

The Suppression of "Foreign" Opinion

Of the four laws (known collectively as the Alien and Sedition Acts) passed by Congress in 1798 under the threat of war with France, the first was a Naturalization Act that raised the residence requirement for naturalization from five to fourteen years; the next two gave the President summary authority over resident aliens; and the last, called the Sedition Act, gave the government wide powers to put down treasonable activities. In effect, the Alien Act of June 25 merely frightened hundreds of foreigners out of the country and was never enforced; but under the Sedition Act of July 14, twenty-five men, most of them editors of Republican newspapers, were arrested, while their newspapers were forced to close down. Of these twenty-five, ten were convicted. All four laws were controversial, and many questioned their constitutionality. So great was the public opposition to them, indeed, that they led indirectly to the election of the Republican Thomas Jefferson to the presidency in 1800. A portion of the texts of the Alien and Sedition Acts is reprinted here.

Source: *Statutes,* I, pp. 570-572, 596-597.

I.

The Alien Act

Section 1. *Be it enacted by the Senate and House of Representatives of the United States of America, in Congress assembled,* that it shall be lawful for the President of the United States at any time during the continuance of this act to order all such aliens as he shall judge dangerous to the peace and safety of the United States, or shall have reasonable grounds to suspect are concerned in any treasonable or secret machinations against the government thereof, to depart out of the territory of the United States within such time as shall be expressed in such order, which order shall be served on such alien by delivering him a copy thereof or leaving the same at his usual abode, and returned to the office of the secretary of state by the marshal or other person to whom the same shall be directed. And in case any alien so ordered to depart shall be found at large within the United States after the time limited in such order for his departure, and not having obtained a license from the President to reside therein, or having obtained such license shall not have conformed thereto, every such alien shall, on conviction thereof, be imprisoned for a term not exceeding three years, and shall never after be admitted to become a citizen of the United States.

Provided always, and be it further enacted, that if any alien so ordered to depart shall prove to the satisfaction of the President, by evidence to be taken before such person or persons as the President shall direct, who are for that purpose hereby authorized to administer oaths, that no injury or danger to the United States will arise from suffering such alien to reside therein, the President may grant a license to such alien to remain within the United States for such time as he shall judge proper, and at such place as he may designate. And the President may also require of such alien to enter into a bond to the United States, in such penal sum as he may direct, with one or more sufficient sureties to the satisfaction of the person authorized by the President to take the same, conditioned for the good behavior of such alien during his residence in the United States, and not violating his license, which license the President may revoke whenever he shall think proper.

Section 2. *And be it further enacted,* that it shall be lawful for the President of the United States, whenever he may deem it necessary for the public safety, to order to be removed out of the territory thereof any alien who may or shall be in prison in pursuance of this act; and to cause to be arrested and sent out of the United States such of those aliens as shall have been ordered to depart therefrom and shall not have obtained a license as aforesaid, in all cases where, in the opinion of the President, the public safety requires a speedy removal. And if any alien so removed or sent out of the United States by the President shall voluntarily return thereto, unless by permission of the President of the United States, such alien on conviction thereof shall be imprisoned so long as, in the opinion of the President, the public safety may require.

Section 3. *And be it further enacted,* that every master or commander of any ship or vessel which shall come into any port of the United States after the first day of July next shall immediately, on his arrival, make report in writing to the collector or other chief officer of the customs of such port of all aliens, if any, on board his vessel, specifying their names, age, the place of nativity; the country from which they shall have come, the nation to which they belong and owe allegiance, their occupation, and a description of their persons, as far as he shall be informed thereof; and, on failure, every such master and commander shall forfeit and pay $300, for the payment whereof on default of such master or commander such vessel shall also be held and may, by such collector or other officer of the customs, be detained. And it shall be the duty of such collector or other officer of the customs forthwith to transmit to the office of the Department of State true copies of all such returns.

Section 4. *And be it further enacted,* that the Circuit and District courts of the United States shall respectively have cognizance of all crimes and offenses against this act. And all marshals and other officers of the United States are required to execute all precepts and orders of the President of the United States issued in pursuance or by virtue of this act.

Section 5. *And be it further enacted,* that it shall be lawful for any alien who may be ordered to be removed from the United States, by virtue of this act, to take with him such part of his goods, chattels, or other property as he may find convenient; and all property left in the United States by any alien who may be removed, as aforesaid, shall be and remain subject to his order and disposal, in the same manner as if this act had not been passed.

Section 6. *And be it further enacted,* that this act shall continue and be in force for and during the term of two years from the passing thereof.

II.

The Sedition Act

Section 1. *Be it enacted by the Senate and House of Representatives of the United States of America, in Congress assembled,* that if any persons shall unlawfully combine or conspire together with intent to oppose any measure or measures of the government of the United States which are or shall be directed by proper authority, or to impede the operation of any law of the United States, or to intimidate or prevent any person holding a place or office in or under the government of the United States from undertaking, performing, or executing his trust or duty; and if any person or persons, with intent as aforesaid, shall counsel, advise, or attempt to procure any insurrection, riot, unlawful assembly, or combination, whether such conspiracy, threatening, counsel, advice, or attempt shall have the proposed effect or not, he or they shall be deemed guilty of a high misdemeanor, and on conviction before any court of the United States having jurisdiction thereof shall be punished by a fine not exceeding $5,000 and by imprisonment during a term not less than six months nor exceeding five years; and further, at the discretion of the court, may be held to find sureties for his good behavior in such sum and for such time as the said court may direct.

Section 2. *And be it further enacted,* that if any person shall write, print, utter, or publish, or shall cause or procure to be written, printed, uttered, or published, or shall knowingly and willingly assist or aid in writing, printing, uttering, or publishing any false, scandalous, and malicious writing or writings against the government of the United States, or either house of the Congress of the United States, or the President of the United States with intent to defame the said government, or either house of the said Congress, or the said President, or to bring them, or either of them, into contempt or disrepute; or to excite against them, or either or any of them, the hatred of the good people of the United States, or to stir up sedition within the United States, or to excite any unlawful combinations therein, for opposing or resisting any law of the United States, or any act of the President of the United States, done in pursuance of any such law, or of the powers in him vested by the Constitution of the United States, or to resist, oppose, or defeat any such law or act, or to aid, encourage or abet any hostile designs of any foreign nation against the United States, their people, or government, then such person being thereof convicted before any court of the United States having jurisdiction thereof shall be punished by a fine not exceeding $2,000 and by imprisonment not exceeding two years.

Section 3. *And be it further enacted and declared,* that if any person shall be prosecuted under this act, for the writing or publishing any libel aforesaid, it shall be lawful for the defendant, upon the trial of the cause, to give evidence in his defense, the truth of the matter contained in the publication charged as a libel. And the jury who shall try the cause shall have a right to determine the law and the fact, under the direction of the court, as in other cases.

Section 4. *And be it further enacted,* that this act shall continue and be in force until the third day of March, 1801, and no longer: *provided,* that the expiration of the act shall not prevent or defeat a prosecution and punishment of any offense against the law during the time it shall be in force.

Millions for defense but not a cent for tribute.

Robert Goodloe Harper, toast, June 18, 1798

13.

The Kentucky and Virginia Resolutions of 1798

Jefferson and Madison responded to the Alien and Sedition Acts by drafting resolutions of protest for consideration by the Virginia and Kentucky state legislatures. Those drawn up by Madison, while the same in substance as Jefferson's, came six weeks later and were characteristically the more restrained of the two. Passed by the Virginia legislature on December 24, 1798, they affirmed state authority to determine the validity of federal legislation and declared the Acts unconstitutional. The Kentucky resolutions, passed by that state's legislature on November 16, 1798, were written anonymously by Jefferson and sponsored by his friend, John Breckinridge. Jefferson's principal arguments were that the national government was a compact between the states, that any exercise of undelegated authority on its part was invalid, and that the states had the right to decide when their powers had been infringed, and to determine the mode of redress. The Kentucky resolutions thus declared the Alien and Sedition Acts to be "void and of no force." These ideas have often been invoked under the name of "states' rights." In fact, however, Jefferson, like Madison, sought not to frustrate government but instead to reform it; his interest was in the future of freedom rather than in the preservation of the status quo.

Source: Elliot, IV, pp. 540-544, 528-529.

I.

The Kentucky Resolutions

1. *Resolved,* that the several states composing the United States of America are not united on the principle of unlimited submission to their general government; but that, by compact, under the style and title of a Constitution for the United States, and of amendments thereto, they constituted a general government for special purposes, delegated to that government certain definite powers, reserving, each state to itself, the residuary mass of right to their own self-government. And that whensoever the general government assumes undelegated powers, its acts are unauthoritative, void, and of no force; that to this compact each state acceded as a state and is an integral party; that this government, created by this compact, was not made the exclusive or final judge of the extent of the powers delegated to itself, since that would have made its discretion, and not the Constitution, the measure of its powers; but that, as in all other cases of compact among parties having no common judge, each party has an equal right to judge for itself, as well of infractions as of the mode and measure of redress.

2. *Resolved,* that the Constitution of the United States having delegated to Congress a power to punish treason, counterfeiting

the securities and current coin of the United States, piracies and felonies committed on the high seas, and offenses against the laws of nations, and no other crimes whatever; and it being true, as a general principle, and one of the amendments to the Constitution having also declared "that the powers not delegated to the United States by the Constitution, nor prohibited by it to the states, are reserved to the states respectively, or to the people"; therefore, also, the same act of Congress, passed on the 14th day of July, 1798, and entitled "An Act in Addition to the Act Entitled 'An Act for the Punishment of Certain Crimes Against the United States,' " as also the act passed by them on the 27th day of June, 1798, entitled "An Act to Punish Frauds Committed on the Bank of the United States" (and all other their acts which assume to create, define, or punish crimes other than those enumerated in the Constitution), are altogether void and of no force; and that the power to create, define, and punish, such other crimes is reserved, and of right appertains, solely and exclusively, to the respective states, each within its own territory.

3. *Resolved,* that it is true, as a general principle, and is also expressly declared by one of the amendments to the Constitution, that "the powers not delegated to the United States by the Constitution, nor prohibited by it to the states, are reserved to the states respectively, or to the people;" and that no power over the freedom of religion, freedom of speech, or freedom of the press, being delegated to the United States by the Constitution, nor prohibited by it to the states, all lawful powers respecting the same did of right remain, and were reserved to the states, or to the people; that thus was manifested their determination to retain to themselves the right of judging how far the licentiousness of speech, and of the press, may be abridged without lessening their useful freedom, and how far those abuses, which cannot be separated from their use, should be tolerated rather than the use be destroyed. And thus also they guarded against all abridgment, by the United States, of the freedom of religious principles and exercises, and retained to themselves the right of protecting the same, as this, stated by a law passed on the general demand of its citizens, had already protected them from all human restraint or interference; and that, in addition to this general principle and express declaration, another and more special provision has been made by one of the amendments to the Constitution, which expressly declares that "Congress shall make no laws respecting an establishment of religion, or prohibiting the free exercise thereof, or abridging the freedom of speech, or of the press," thereby guarding, in the same sentence, and under the same words, the freedom of religion, of speech, and of the press, insomuch that whatever violates either throws down the sanctuary which covers the others; and that libels, falsehood, and defamation, equally with heresy and false religion, are withheld from the cognizance of federal tribunals. That, therefore, the act of the Congress of the United States, passed on the 14th of July, 1798, entitled "An Act in Addition to the Act Entitled 'An Act for the Punishment of Certain Crimes Against the United States,' " which does abridge the freedom of the press, is not law, but is altogether void and of no force.

4. *Resolved,* that alien friends are under the jurisdiction and protection of the laws of the state wherein they are; that no power over them has been delegated to the United States, nor prohibited to the individual states, distinct from their power over citizens; and it being true, as a general principle, and one of the amendments to the Constitution having also declared, that "the powers not delegated to the United States by the Constitution, nor prohibited to the states, are reserved to the states, respectively, or to the people," the act of the Con-

gress of the United States, passed the 22nd day of June, 1798, entitled "An Act Concerning Aliens," which assumes power over alien friends not delegated by the Constitution, is not law, but is altogether void and of no force.

5. *Resolved,* that, in addition to the general principle, as well as the express declaration, that powers not delegated are reserved, another and more special provision inserted in the Constitution from abundant caution has declared, "that the migration or importation of such persons as any of the states now existing shall think proper to admit shall not be prohibited by the Congress prior to the year 1808." That this commonwealth does admit the migration of alien friends described as the subject of the said act concerning aliens; that a provision against prohibiting their migration is a provision against all acts equivalent thereto, or it would be nugatory; that to remove them, when migrated, is equivalent to a prohibition of their migration, and is, therefore, contrary to the said provision of the Constitution, and void.

6. *Resolved,* that the imprisonment of a person under the protection of the laws of this commonwealth, on his failure to obey the simple order of the president to depart out of the United States, as is undertaken by the said act, entitled, "An Act Concerning Aliens," is contrary to the Constitution, one amendment in which has provided, that "no person shall be deprived of liberty without due process of law;" and that another having provided, "that, in all criminal prosecutions, the accused shall enjoy the right of a public trial by an impartial jury, to be informed as to the nature and cause of the accusation, to be confronted with the witnesses against him, to have compulsory process for obtaining witnesses in his favor, and to have assistance of counsel for his defense," the same act undertaking to authorize the president to remove a person out of the United States who is under the protection of the law, on his own suspicion, without jury, without public trial, without confrontation of the witnesses against him, without having witnesses in his favor, without defense, without counsel, contrary to these provisions also of the Constitution, is therefore not law, but utterly void and of no force.

That transferring the power of judging any person who is under the protection of the laws from the courts to the President of the United States, as is undertaken by the same act concerning aliens, is against the article of the Constitution which provides, that "the judicial power of the United States shall be vested in the courts, the judges of which shall hold their office during good behavior," and that the said act is void for that reason also. And it is further to be noted that this transfer of judiciary power is to that magistrate of the general government who already possesses all the executive, and a qualified negative in all the legislative powers.

7. *Resolved,* that the construction applied by the general government (as is evident by sundry of their proceedings) to those parts of the Constitution of the United States which delegate to Congress power to lay and collect taxes, duties, imposts, excises; to pay the debts, and provide for the common defense and general welfare of the United States, and to make all laws which shall be necessary and proper for carrying into execution the powers vested by the Constitution in the government of the United States, or any department thereof, goes to the destruction of all the limits prescribed to their power by the Constitution; that words meant by that instrument to be subsidiary only to the execution of the limited powers, ought not to be so construed as themselves to give unlimited powers, nor a part so to be taken as to destroy the whole residue of the instrument; that the proceedings of the general government, under color of those articles, will be a fit and necessary

subject for revisal and correction at a time of greater tranquility, while those specified in the preceding resolutions call for immediate redress.

8. *Resolved,* that the preceding resolutions be transmitted to the senators and representatives in Congress from this commonwealth, who are enjoined to present the same to their respective houses and to use their best endeavors to procure, at the next session of Congress, a repeal of the aforesaid unconstitutional and obnoxious acts.

9. *Resolved,* lastly, that the governor of this commonwealth be, and is, authorized and requested to communicate the preceding resolutions to the legislatures of the several states, to assure them that this commonwealth considers union for special national purposes, and particularly for those specified in their late federal compact, to be friendly to the peace, happiness, and prosperity, of all the states: that, faithful to that compact, according to the plain intent and meaning in which it was understood and acceded to by the several parties, it is sincerely anxious for its preservation.

That it does also believe, that, to take from the states all the powers of self-government and transfer them to a general and consolidated government, without regard to the special government, and reservations solemnly agreed to in that compact, is not for the peace, happiness, or prosperity of these states; and that, therefore, this commonwealth is determined, as it doubts not its co-states are, to submit to undelegated and consequently unlimited powers in no man, or body of men, on earth; that, if the acts before specified should stand, these conclusions would flow from them.

That the general government may place any act they think proper on the list of crimes, and punish it themselves, whether enumerated or not enumerated by the Constitution as cognizable by them; that they may transfer its cognizance to the President, or any other person, who may himself be the accuser, counsel, judge, and jury, whose suspicions may be the evidence, his order the sentence, his officer the executioner, and his breast the sole record of the transaction; that a very numerous and valuable description of the inhabitants of these states, being, by this precedent, reduced, as outlaws, to absolute dominion of one man, and the barriers of the Constitution thus swept from us all, no rampart now remains against the passions and the power of a majority of Congress, to protect from a like exportation, or other grievous punishment, the minority of the same body, the legislatures, judges, governors, and counselors of the states, nor their other peaceable inhabitants, who may venture to reclaim the constitutional rights and liberties of the states and people, or who, for other causes, good or bad, may be obnoxious to the view, or marked by the suspicions, of the President, or be thought dangerous to his or their elections, or other interests, public or personal.

That the friendless alien has been selected as the safest subject of a first experiment; but the citizen will soon follow, or rather has already followed; for already has a Sedition Act marked him as a prey. That these and successive acts of the same character, unless arrested on the threshold, may tend to drive these states into revolution and blood, and will furnish new calumnies against republican governments, and new pretexts for those who wish it to be believed that man cannot be governed but by a rod of iron; that it would be a dangerous delusion were a confidence in the men of our choice to silence our fears for the safety of our rights; that confidence is everywhere the parent of despotism; free government is founded in jealousy, and not in confidence; it is jealousy, and not confidence, which prescribes limited constitutions to bind down those whom we are obliged to trust with power; that our Constitution has accordingly fixed the limits to which, and no farther, our confidence may go; and let the honest advocate of confidence read the Alien and Sedition Acts, and say if the Constitution has not been wise in fixing limits to the government it created, and whether we should be wise in destroying those limits. Let him say what the government is, if it be not a tyranny, which the men of our choice have conferred on the President, and the President of our choice has assented to and accepted, over the friendly strangers to whom the mild spirit of our country and its laws had pledged hospitality and protection; that the men of our choice have more respected the bare suspicions of the President than the solid rights of innocence, the claims of justification, the sacred force of truth, and the forms and substance of law and justice.

In questions of power, then, let no more be said of confidence in man, but bind him down from mischief by the chains of the Constitution. That this commonwealth does therefore call on its co-states for an expression of their sentiments on the acts concerning aliens, and for the punishment of certain crimes herein before specified, plainly declaring whether these acts are or are not authorized by the federal compact. And it doubts not that their sense will be so announced as to prove their attachment to limited government, whether general or particular, and that the rights and liberties of their co-states will be exposed to no dangers by remaining embarked on a common bottom with their own; but they will concur with this commonwealth in considering the said acts as so palpably against the Constitution as to amount to an undisguised declaration, that the compact is not meant to be the measure of the powers of the general government, but that it will proceed in the exercise over these states of all powers whatsoever. That they will view this as seizing the rights of the states, and consolidating them in the hands of the general government with a power assumed to bind the states, not merely in cases made federal but in all cases whatsoever, by laws made, not with their consent but by others against their consent. That this would be to surrender the form of government we have chosen, and live under one deriving its powers from its own will, and not from our authority; and that the co-states, recurring to their natural rights not made federal, will concur in declaring these void and of no force, and will each unite with this commonwealth in requesting their repeal at the next session of Congress.

II.

The Virginia Resolutions

Resolved, that the General Assembly of Virginia does unequivocally express a firm resolution to maintain and defend the Constitution of the United States, and the constitution of this state against every aggression, either foreign or domestic; and that they will support the government of the United States in all measures warranted by the former.

That this Assembly most solemnly declares a warm attachment to the union of the states, to maintain which it pledges its powers; and that, for this end, it is their duty to watch over and oppose every infraction of those principles which constitute the only basis of that union, because a faithful observance of them can alone secure its existence and the public happiness.

That this Assembly does explicitly and peremptorily declare that it views the powers of the federal government as resulting from the compact to which the states are parties, as limited by the plain sense and intention of the instrument constituting that compact, as no further valid than they are authorized by the grants enumerated in that compact; and that, in case of a deliberate, palpable, and dangerous exercise of other powers, not granted by the said compact, the states who are parties thereto, have the right, and are in duty bound to interpose for arresting the progress of the evil, and for maintaining, within their respective limits, the authorities, rights, and liberties, appertaining to them.

That the General Assembly does also express its deep regret that a spirit has, in sundry instances, been manifested by the federal government to enlarge its powers by forced constructions of the constitutional charter which defines them; and that indications have appeared of a design to expound certain general phrases (which, having been copied from the very limited grant of powers in the former Articles of Confederation, were the less liable to be misconstrued) so as to destroy the meaning and effect of the particular enumeration which necessarily explains and limits the general phrases, and so as to consolidate the states, by degrees, into one sovereignty, the obvious tendency and inevitable result of which would be to transform the present republican system of the United States into an absolute or, at best, a mixed monarchy.

That the General Assembly does particularly protest against the palpable and alarming infractions of the Constitution in the two late cases of the Alien and Sedition Acts, passed at the last session of Congress; the first of which exercises a power nowhere delegated to the federal government, and which, by uniting legislative and judicial powers to those of executive, subverts the general principles of free government, as well as the particular organization and positive provisions of the federal Constitution; and the other of which acts exercises, in like manner, a power not delegated by the Constitution, but, on the contrary, expressly and positively forbidden by one of the amendments thereto, a power which, more than any other, ought to produce universal alarm, because it is leveled against the right of freely examining public characters and measures, and of free communication among the people thereon, which has ever been justly deemed the only effectual guardian of every other right.

That this state having, by its Convention, which ratified the federal Constitution, expressly declared that, among other essential rights, "the liberty of conscience and the press cannot be canceled, abridged, restrained, or modified, by any authority of the United States," and from its extreme anxiety to guard these rights from every possible attack of sophistry and ambition, having, with other states, recommended an amendment for that purpose, which amendment was, in due time, annexed to the Constitution, it would mark a reproachful inconsistency and criminal degeneracy if an indifference were now shown to the most palpable violation of one of the rights thus declared and secured, and to the establishment of a precedent which may be fatal to the other.

That the good people of this commonwealth, having ever felt, and continuing to feel, the most sincere affection for their brethren of the other states; the truest anxiety for establishing and perpetuating the union of all; and the most scrupulous fidelity to that Constitution, which is the pledge of mutual friendship and the instrument of mutual happiness; the General Assembly does solemnly appeal to the like dispositions in the other states, in confidence that they will concur with this commonwealth in declaring, as it does hereby declare, that the acts aforesaid are unconstitutional; and that the necessary and proper measures will be taken *by each* for cooperating with this state, in maintaining unimpaired the authorities, rights, and liberties, reserved to the states respectively, or to the people.

That the governor be desired to transmit a copy of the foregoing resolutions to the executive authority of each of the other states, with a request that the same may be communicated to the legislature thereof and that a copy be furnished to each of the senators and representatives representing this state in the Congress of the United States.

14.

Fisher Ames: Undeclared War and Self-Defense

Probably the most vexing problem that faced President John Adams was the undeclared naval war with France. Caught in the middle, he felt himself called upon to fend off the bellicose demands of his own party, the Federalists, on the one hand, and to resist the pro-French policies of Jefferson's Republicans, on the other hand. During Adams' term of office the army and navy were expanded and all treaties with France were repealed, but the President appointed George Washington commander of the army, hoping that the venerated general and ex-President would be able to stand up to those who did not want to wait for France to make the first move but instead wished to attack her immediately. One such advocate of war was Fisher Ames, the so-called Sage of Dedham (Massachusetts), who feared that Jeffersonian Republicanism would bring upon the country the "open hell" that he saw in France, torn by revolution and civil strife. Ames, no longer a congressman but a close friend and supporter of the Essex Junto, a group of influential Federalists, vociferously promoted a plan to strengthen the national government and to aid Great Britain to her struggle with the French. In a letter dated July 10, 1798, Ames urged Secretary of State Timothy Pickering to move for an immediate declaration of war.

Source: *Works of Fisher Ames,* Seth Ames, ed., Boston, 1854, Vol. I, pp. 232-235.

Half measures are seldom generally intelligible, and almost never safe, in the crisis of great affairs. The answers of the President have elevated the spirit and cleared the filmy eyes of the many. The people have risen *gradatim;* every answer was a step upstairs. But Congress follows too slowly, and unless they make haste to overtake the people, the latter, I fear, will begin to descend. I should be absolutely certain of this collapsing and sinking of the public if I did not depend on the friendly profligacy of the French. They will kick us into courage. Their plan allows us no retreat. The southern congressmen will be obliged, at last, to feel French blows, with some pain, through their thick skins, although hitherto what has wounded others only tickles them. To us, the wrongs of France are whips of scorpions; to them, the strokes of a feather.

As France aims at empire, and will exact compliances unexpected even by Democrats; as she wants cash, and will insist on more than they will freely give — I calculate on her doing for us, at last, that which Congress seems resolved shall not be attributable to the energy and wisdom of our counsels. If, in the interim of our infatuated torpor and indecision, she should condescend to resort to fraud and flattery, we should even yet be lost. But as her violence and arrogance happily lessen our fears on that head, I calculate on the eventual resort of Congress to measures of force. Internal foes can do us twice as much harm as they could in an open war. The hope of peace is yet strong enough to furnish the means of popular influence and delusion; at any rate, it chills the spirit of the citizens, and distracts them in the exercise of duty.

I wish, therefore, impatiently, to see Congress urged to proceed to steps which will have no such ambiguity in them. A declaration of war would be such a step. But it is the very one that their imbecility would reluct at; it is the very one that demands something like unanimity. I think this very reluctance might be used to advantage. Instead of *declaring* war in form, could they not be persuaded, even some of the Demos, to *enact* penal laws, *as if* it was war? To do something short of duty, something tamer than energy, suits the foible of the weak, temporizing, trimming members.

I should imagine a number who would flinch from a *declaration of war* would urge the enacting, one by one, the effects of a state of war. Not being on the spot, I can judge only from my knowledge of some characters, and the color of their conduct and speeches; with such materials I may be deceived in my conclusion. I think it probable, however, that several votes could be gained for strong measures from the dread of being urged to adopt still stronger. Energy is a word of comparison, and to vote *as if* we were in war, might seem a halfway business, compared with *a declaration* of war.

In this way they may authorize the burning, sinking, and destroying French ships and property *gradatim,* till no case is left which is to shelter them from hostility. As every armed French vessel takes our vessels, every armed French vessel should be prize, everyone on board a prisoner; correspondence with the French, adhering to our enemies, etc. I need not detail the consequences of this idea, as they will occur to you, nor discriminate the odds between a formal declaration of war, which would instantly draw after it all the consequences of a state of war, and a series of acts of Congress, which would annex to our state of peace all those consequences, one by one.

Harvard University, gift to Harvard College by I. P. Davis

Portrait of Fisher Ames by Gilbert Stuart

The difference of effect on the public mind is also worth computation and deliberation.

To declare is to choose war; it is voluntarily changing our condition, which, however urgent the reasons and motives of the change may be, leaves a door open for blame on the government; it is, no doubt, a change at all times involving a high responsibility. Disasters in the conduct of a war would aggravate first ill impressions, and give a malcontent party a specific text of sedition. Ripe as the citizens are for self-defense, they reluct at offense; they would yield much, far too much, for peace; and this hope would delude them, if proud France would condescend to hold it out.

Now why should not we play off against our foe a part of their own policy? Wage war, and call it self-defense; forbear to call it war; on the contrary, let it be said that we deprecate war, and will desist from arms, as soon as her acts shall be repealed, etc., grounding all we do on the necessity of self-preservation, etc. We should need no negotiation to restore peace; at least we should act, as the *salus Reipublicae* [well-being of the Republic] demands we should, instantly, and there would be little balancing among the citizens, and the spirit would grow warmer in its progress. But a formal declaration would perhaps engender discords; all the thinking would come first, the action after. I would reverse this order. Not that I would conceal from the country its duties or its dangers. No, they should be fully stated and enforced. I would, however, oppose art to art, and employ, in self-defense against French intrigue, some of those means of influence which we may lawfully use, and which her party will so much abuse if we do not first possess them.

My long letter amounts to this: we must make haste to *wage war*, or we shall be lost. But in doing it, and, I might premise, to induce Congress to do it, and that without its ordinary slowness, we had better begin at the tail of the business and go on enacting the consequences of war, instead of declaring it at once. The latter might be the bolder measure; its adaptedness to the temper of Congress, and even of the country, is not equally clear. Something energetic and decisive must be done soon. Congress fiddles while our Rome is burning. America, if just to her own character, and not too frugal of her means, can interdict France the ocean. Great Britain will keep her close in her European ports. We can clear our coasts, and, before long, the West Indian seas.

My faith is that we are born to high destinies. The length of this letter, and the fear of being too officious, restrains me from descanting on our prospects, as to our government, and as to any alliance with England. As to the former idea, governments are generally lost from bashfulness. Great occasions like the present either overturn or establish them.

"George," said his father, "do you know who killed that beautiful little cherry tree yonder in the garden?" This was a tough question; and George staggered under it for a moment; but quickly recovered himself: and looking at his father with the inexpressible charm of all-conquering truth, he bravely cried out, "I can't tell a lie, Pa; you know I can't tell a lie. I did cut it with my hatchet." — "Run to my arms, you dearest boy," cried his father in transports, "run to my arms; glad am I, George, that you killed my tree; for you have payed me for it a thousand fold. Such an act of heroism in my son is more worth than a thousand trees, though blossomed with silver, and their fruits of purest gold."

MASON LOCKE WEEMS, *The Life of George Washington.* The story appeared for the first time in the fifth edition of the work.

15.

George Washington: On the Disloyalty of Army Officers

After his appointment by President Adams as commander of the army in 1798, George Washington insisted upon selecting his own subordinates, foremost among whom was Alexander Hamilton. Hamilton, who had continuously influenced Washington when he was President, now convinced him that the Jeffersonian Republicans were subverting the principles of the Constitution and would even take measures "to make this country a province of France." It is no wonder that Washington, whose advisors were anti-Jefferson Federalists, feared disloyalty among his troops. In the following letter, dated September 30, 1798, to Secretary of War James McHenry, Washington suggested that men of Republican sentiments be deprived of their commissions. This plan was put into effect when, on November 10, Washington, Hamilton, and Charles Pinckney met to organize the army. One of those who did not receive a commission on political grounds was the famed foe of Hamilton, Aaron Burr. This deprivation is said to be one of the reasons why Burr challenged Hamilton to the duel in 1804 that resulted in the latter's death.

Source: WGW, XIV, pp. 104-105.

I have lately received information, which, in my opinion, merits attention. It is that the brawlers against governmental measures in some of the most discontented parts of this state have all of a sudden become silent; and, it is added, are very desirous of obtaining commissions in the army about to be raised.

This information did not fail to leave an impression upon my mind at the time I received it; but it has acquired strength from a publication I have lately seen in one of the Maryland gazettes (between the author of which and my informant there could have been no interchange of sentiments to the same effect). The motives ascribed to them are that, in such a situation, they would endeavor to divide and contaminate the army by artful and seditious discourses, and, perhaps, at a critical moment, bring on confusion. What weight to give to these conjectures you can judge as well as I. But, as there will be characters enough of an opposite description who are ready to receive appointments, circumspection is necessary. For my opinion is of the first that you could as soon scrub the blackamoor white as to change the principle of a professed Democrat, and that he will leave nothing unattempted to overturn the government of this country.

Finding the resentment of the people at the conduct of France too strong to be resisted, they have in appearance adopted their sentiments, and pretend that, notwithstanding the misconduct of government have brought it upon us, yet, if an invasion should take place, it will be found that *they* will be among the first to defend it. This is their story at all elections and election meetings, and told in many instances with effect.

Whether there be little, much, or nothing in the information, I shall not take upon me to decide; but it appeared to me to be of sufficient moment to apprise you thereof.

16.

Opposition to a Standing Army

In 1798 the army was increased from 3,500 to 12,000 men, with an additional reserve of 20,000 men that the President was empowered to call up should an emergency arise. Many Jeffersonians feared that a standing army would be used by the Federalists to enforce the hated Sedition Act and to suppress domestic unrest. President Adams, though himself a Federalist, opposed the army when Hamilton, one of the chief advocates of war with France, was appointed second in command by Washington, whom the President had earlier made commander in chief. Adams feared that a standing army would "make the government more unpopular than all [its] other acts." His fears were justified when resolutions were drafted in numerous local meetings denouncing the existence of a standing army. The following resolutions of Dinwiddie County, Virginia, appeared in the Philadelphia Aurora *at the end of the year.*

Source: *Philadelphia Aurora,* December 6, 1798.

Resolved, as the opinion of this meeting, that a militia, composed of the body of the people, is the proper, natural, and safe defense of a free state, and that regular armies, except in case of an invasion, or the certain prospect of an invasion, are not only highly detrimental to the public welfare but dangerous to liberty.

Detrimental to the public welfare; because industrious men are heavily taxed to support those who do nothing; because indolence among the poor is publicly encouraged; the army being an asylum for all who do not choose to labor; because the young men who form the mass of an army, instead of being a drawback on the productive labor of the community might be more beneficially employed in supporting, by their industry, themselves and their families and paying their proportions of the public debt; because the same object, immediate defense against a sudden invasion, might be attained infinitely cheaper by putting arms into the hands of every man capable of bearing them; and because the spirit which leads to war, the cause and the disgrace of humanity, is greatly augmented by standing armies, to whose leaders it opens a prospect of greater wealth and higher military honors; and,

Dangerous to liberty; because, when numerous, they have tyrannized, as the experience of all ages has proved, both over the people and the government; and when limited, have always been subservient to the views of the Executive Department, from which they derive their honors and emoluments; because these honors and emoluments furnish an ample fund, by means of which the executive is enabled to reward its partisans and increase the number of its adherents; because a people, accustomed to look for protection from external violence to a standing army, become abject, debased, and gradually enslaved; but knowing themselves to be the only defenders of their country, soon acquire that discipline and courage which insure safety, not only from foreign enemies but domestic tyrants; and because military establishments are in their nature progressive, the vast expense attending them, producing discontent and disturbances, and these furnishing a pretext for providing a force still more formidable; thus finally occasioning the oppression, the ruin, the *slavery* of the people.

17.

Songs of Patriotism

Political divisions in the Union brought about by wars in Europe and by the Alien and Sedition Acts and other governmental policies gave rise to a number of patriotic songs that sought to revive the spirit of unity of 1776. One was "New Yankee Doodle," by James Hewitt, an English-born composer, who wrote new words, appropriate for the times, to the famous old tune of "Yankee Doodle." Another was "Adams and Liberty," by a Bostonian poet and son of a signer of the Declaration of Independence of the same name, Robert Treat Paine. "Adams and Liberty" became immediately popular and is said to have swept the country. A third was "Hail, Columbia!" by Joseph Hopkinson. Gilbert Fox, a popular singer and friend of Hopkinson, was in need of new material to sing at a benefit performance for which ticket sales were lagging. He asked his friend, a lawyer, to write words for Philip Philes' "The President's March," which had been played at George Washington's first inauguration in 1789. "Hail, Columbia!" was well publicized, and a full house received it with great enthusiasm, calling for numerous encores. The song became an American favorite in the nineteenth century.

Source: "New Yankee Doodle," New York, [1801?].
The American Musical Miscellany: A Collection of the Newest and Most Approved Songs Set to Music, Northampton, Mass., 1798, pp. 211-218.
Famous Songs and Those Who Made Them, New York, 1895, pp. 252-253.

NEW YANKEE DOODLE

Columbians all the present hour
As brothers should unite us,
Union at home's the only way
To make each nation right us;
Yankee Doodle, guard your coast,
Yankee Doodle Dandy,
Fear not then, nor threat, nor boast,
Yankee Doodle Dandy.

The only way to keep off war,
And guard 'gainst persecution,
Is always to be well prepared,
With hearts of resolution.
Yankee Doodle, let's unite,
Yankee Doodle Dandy,
As patriots, still maintain our right,
Yankee Doodle Dandy.

Great Washington, who led us on,
And liberty effected,
Shall see we'll die or else be free —
We shall not be subjected.
Yankee Doodle, guard your coast,
Yankee Doodle Dandy,
Fear not then or threat or boast,
Yankee Doodle Dandy.

A band of brothers, let us be,
While Adams guides the nation;
And still our dear-bought freedom guard,
In ev'ry situation.
Yankee Doodle, guard your coast,
Yankee Doodle Dandy,
Fear not then or threat or boast,
Yankee Doodle Dandy.

May soon the wish'd for hour arrive,
When peace shall rule the nations,
And commerce, free from fetters prove
Mankind are all relations.
Then Yankee Doodle, be divine,
Yankee Doodle Dandy,
Beneath the fig tree and the vine,
Sing Yankee Doodle Dandy.

James Hewitt

ADAMS AND LIBERTY

Ye sons of Columbia, who bravely have fought,
For those rights, which unstained from your sires had descended,
May you long taste the blessings your valor has bought,
And your sons reap the soil which your fathers defended.
Mid the reign of mild peace,
May your nation increase,
With the glory of Rome, and the wisdom of Greece;
And ne'er may the sons of Columbia be slaves,
While the earth bears a plant, or the sea rolls its waves.

In a clime, whose rich vales feed the marts of the world,
Whose shores are unshaken by Europe's commotion,
The trident of commerce should never be hurled,
To incense the legitimate powers of the ocean.
But should pirates invade,
Though in thunder arrayed,
Let your cannon declare the free charter of trade,
For ne'er shall the sons of Columbia be slaves,
While the earth bears a plant, or the sea rolls its waves.

Let fame to the world sound America's voice;
No intrigue can her sons from their government sever;
Her pride is her Adams — his laws are her choice,
And shall flourish, till liberty slumber forever!
Then unite, heart and hand,
Like Leonidas' band,
And swear to the God of the ocean and land,
That ne'er shall the sons of Columbia be slaves,
While the earth bears a plant, or the sea rolls it waves.

ROBERT TREAT PAINE

HAIL, COLUMBIA!

Hail Columbia, happy land!
Hail ye heroes, heav'n-born band
Who fought and bled in freedom's cause,
Who fought and bled in freedom's cause;
And when the storm of war was gone,
Enjoyed the peace your valor won.
Let independence be your boast,
Ever mindful what it cost,
Ever grateful for the prize,
Let its altar reach the skies.

Chorus:

Firm, united let us stand,
Rallying round our liberty;
As a band of brothers joined,
Peace and safety we shall find.

Immortal patriots, rise once more!
Defend your rights, defend your shore!
Let no rude foe with impious hand,
Let no rude foe with impious hand
Invade the shrine where sacred lies,
Of toil and blood, the well-earned prize.
While off'ring peace, sincere and just,
In heav'n we place a manly trust
That truth and justice may prevail,
And ev'ry scheme of bondage fail.

Sound, sound the trump of fame!
Let Washington's great name
Ring through the world with loud applause,
Ring through the world with loud applause;
Let ev'ry chime to freedom dear
Listen with a joyful ear.
With equal skill, with steady pow'r,
He governs in the fearful hour
Of horrid war, or guides with ease
The happier time of honest peace.

Behold the chief who now commands!
Once more to serve his country stands
The rock on which the storm will beat,
The rock on which the storm will beat;
But armed in virtue, firm and true,
His hopes are fixed on heav'n and you.
When hope was sinking in dismay,
When gloom obscured Columbia's day,
His steady mind, from changes free,
Resolved on death or liberty.

JOSEPH HOPKINSON

18.

William Manning: How the Few and Many Differ in Their Interests

Underlying many of the political disputes between the Republicans and the Federalists was the issue of aristocracy versus democracy. Jefferson and his fellow Republican leaders, though democratic in principle and more representative of the farmers and workers than the Federalists, nevertheless belonged to the wealthier and better educated class in society. Relatively few Americans believed in a hereditary aristocracy such as Britain's, but many, including Jefferson, held to the view that there was a natural aristocracy of men of talent, who were obligated, and should be asked, to rule the rest. William Manning, a yeoman farmer of Billerica, Massachusetts, was a follower of Jefferson but, like many other farmers, he distrusted professional men and, indeed, government in general. Though not well educated, Manning wrote a number of essays for the Republican Boston Independent Chronicle. *The paper's editor rejected the articles mainly because Manning called for a nation-wide union of farmers and urged that this union should publish its own journal. The excerpt from Manning's* Key of Libberty *reprinted here exemplifies the conception of democracy held by many farmers of the time.*

Source: *The Key of Libberty,* Billerica, Mass., 1922, pp. 14-54.

I HAVE OFTEN THOUGHT it was impossible ever to support a free government, but, firmly believing it to be the best sort and the only one approved of by Heaven, it was my unwearied study and prayers to the Almighty for many years to find out the real cause and a remedy; and I have for many years been satisfied in my own mind what the causes are and what would in a great measure prove a remedy, provided it was carried into effect.

But I had no thoughts of publishing my sentiments on it until the adoption of the British treaty [of 1794] in the manner it has been done. But seeing the unwearied pains and the unjustifiable measures taken by large numbers of all orders of men who get a living without labor in elections and many other things to injure the interests of the laborer and deprive us of the privileges of a free government, I came to a resolution (although I have neither learning nor leisure for the purpose) to improve on my constitutional right and give you my sentiments on what the causes are and a remedy.

In doing which I must study brevity throughout the whole and but just touch on many things on which volumes might be written, but hope I shall do it so as to be understood. And as I have no room for compliments and shall often make observations on sundry orders of men and their conduct, I beg leave once for all to observe that I am far from thinking any orders of men who live without labor are entirely needless or that they are all chargeable with blame. But, on the contrary, I firmly believe that there is a large number in all orders who are true friends to liberty and that it is from them that liberty always has and always will receive its principal support.

But I also believe that a large majority of them are actuated by very different principles. Also, as I am not furnished with documents and other information that would be useful, I may represent some things different from what they really are and so desire that they may be taken only as my opinion and believed no further than they appear evident. . . .

SHOWS HOW THE FEW AND MANY DIFFER IN THEIR INTERESTS IN ITS OPERATION

In the sweat of thy face shalt thou get thy bread, until thou return to the ground, is the irreversible sentence of Heaven on man for his rebellion. To be sentenced to hard labor during life is very unpleasant to human nature. There is a great aversion to it perceivable in all men; yet it is absolutely necessary that a large majority of the world should labor, or we could not subsist. For labor is the sole parent of all property; the land yields nothing without it, and there is no food, clothing, shelter, vessel, or any necessary of life but what costs labor and is generally esteemed valuable according to the labor it costs. Therefore, no person can possess property without laboring unless he gets it by force or craft, fraud or fortune, out of the earnings of others.

But from the great variety of capacities, strength, and abilities of men, there always was and always will be a very unequal distribution of property in the world. Many are so rich that they can live without labor — also the merchant, physician, lawyer, and divine, the philosopher and schoolmaster, the judicial and executive officers, and many others who could honestly get a living without bodily labors. As all these professions require a considerable expense of time and property to qualify themselves therefor, and as no person after this qualifying himself and making a pick on a profession by which he means to live can desire to have it dishonorable or unproductive, so all these professions naturally unite in their schemes to make their callings as honorable and lucrative as possible.

Also, as ease and rest from labor are reasoned among the greatest pleasures of life, pursued by all with the greatest avidity, and when attained at once create a sense of superiority; and as pride and ostentation are natural to the human heart, these orders of men generally associate together and look down with too much contempt on those that labor.

On the other hand, the laborer, being conscious that it is labor that supports the whole, and that the more there are that live without labor, and the higher they live or the greater their salaries and fees are, so much the harder he must work or the shorter he must live — this makes the laborer watch the other with a jealous eye and often has reason to complain of real impositions.

But before I proceed to show how the few and the many differ in money matters, I will give a short description of what money is. Money is not property of itself but only the representative of property. Silver and gold are not so valuable as iron and steel for real use, but receive all their value from the use that is made of them as a medium of trade. Money is simply this: a thing of lighter carriage than property that has an established value set upon it either by law or general consent. For instance, if a dollar, or a piece of paper, or a chip would pass throughout a nation or the world for a bushel of corn or any other property to the value of said corn, then it would be the representative of so much property.

Also, money is a thing that will go where it will fetch the most as naturally as water runs downhill; for the possessor will give it where it will fetch the most; also when there is an addition to the quantity or an extraordinary use of barter and credit in commerce, the prices of property will rise. On the other hand, if credit is ruined and the medium is made scarcer, the price of all kinds of property will fall in proportion. Here lies the great shuffle between the few and the many.

As the interests and incomes of the few lie chiefly in money at interest, rents, salaries, and fees that are fixed on the nominal value of money, they are interested in having money scarce and the price of labor and produce as low as possible. For instance, if the prices of labor and produce should fall one-half, it would be just the same to the few as if their rents, fees, and salaries were doubled, all of which they would get out of the many. Besides, the fall of labor and produce and scarcity of money always bring the many into distress and compel them into a state of dependence on the few for favors and assistance in a thousand ways.

On the other hand, if the many could raise the price of labor, etc., one-half and have money circulate freely, they could pay their debts, eat and drink, and enjoy the good of their labor without being dependent on the few for assistance. Also, high prices operate as a bounty on industry and economy; an industrious and prudent man may presently lay up something against time of need, when prices are high. But if a person leaves off work and lives high when prices are up, his money or property will last him but a little while.

But the greatest danger the many are under in these money matters is from the judicial and executive officers, especially so as their incomes for a living are almost wholly gotten from the follies and distress of the many — they being governed by the same selfish principles as other men are. They are the most interested in the distresses of the many of any in the nation; the scarcer money is and the greater the distresses of the many are, the better for them. It not only doubles the nominal sum of their pay but it doubles and triples their business, and the many are obliged to come to them, cap in hand, and beg mercy, patience, and forbearance.

This gratifies both their pride and covetousness, when, on the other hand, money is plenty and prices high, they have little or nothing to do. This is the reason why they ought to be kept entirely from the legislative body; and unless there can be wisdom enough in the people to keep the three departments of government entirely separate, a free government cannot be supported. For in all these conceived differences of interests, it is the business and duty of the legislative body to determine what is justice, or what is right and wrong; and it is the duty of every individual in the nation to regulate his conduct according to their decisions. And if the many were always fully and fairly represented in the legislative body, they never would be oppressed or find fault so as to trouble the government, but would always be zealous to support it.

The reason why a free government has always failed is from the unreasonable demands and desires of the few. They cannot bear to be on a level with their fellow creatures, or submit to the determinations of a legislature where (as they call it) the swinish multitude is fairly represented, but sicken at the idea, and are ever hankering and striving after monarchy or aristocracy, where the people have nothing to do in matters of government but to support the few in luxury and idleness.

For these and many other reasons, a large majority of those that live without labor are ever opposed to the principles and operation of a free government; and though the whole of them do not amount to one-eighth part of the people, yet, by their combinations, arts, and schemes, have always made out to destroy it sooner or later — which I shall endeavor to prove by considering:

THE MEANS BY WHICH THE FEW DESTROY IT

THIS I WILL ENDEAVOR TO DO by making a few remarks on the doings of the few on the eight following things, viz.: on the ignorance of the many; on the combinations of the few; on learning; on knowledge; on constitutions; on money or the medium; on elections; on wars.

On the Ignorance of the Many

Solomon said: Train up a child in the way he should go; and when he is old, he will not depart from it. And it is as true that if a child is trained up in the way he should not go, when he is old, he will keep to it. It is the universal custom and practice of monarchical and despotic governments to train up their subjects as much in ignorance as they can in matters of government; and to teach them to reverence and worship great men in office; and to take for truth whatever they say without examining for themselves.

Consequently, whenever revolutions are brought about and free governments established, it is by the influence of a few leading men, who, after they have obtained their object (like other men), can never receive compensation and honors enough from the people for their services. And the people, being brought up from their youth to reverence and respect such men, go on old ways and neglect to search and see for themselves and take care of their own interests. Also, being naturally very fond of being flattered, they readily hear to measures proposed by great men who, they are convinced, have done them good services. This is the principal ground on which the few work to destroy a free government.

On the Combinations of the Few

In a free government, the few, finding their schemes and views of interest borne down by the many, to gain the power they cannot constitutionally obtain, always endeavor to get it by cunning and corruption, conscious at the same time that usurpation, when once begun, the safety of the usurper consists only in grasping the whole. To effect this, neither cost nor pain is spared, but they first unite their plans and schemes by associations, conventions, and correspondences with each other. The merchants associate by themselves; the physicians by themselves; the ministers by themselves; the judicial and executive officers are by their professions often called together and know each other's minds; and all literary men and the overgrown rich, that can live without laboring, can spare time for consultation. All being bound together by common interest — which is the strongest bond of union — join in their secret correspondence to counteract the interests of the many and pick their pockets, which is effected only for want of the means of knowledge among them.

On Learning

Learning is of the greatest importance to the support of a free government; and to prevent this the few are always crying up the advantages of costly colleges, national academies, and grammar schools in order to make places for men to live without work, and so strengthen their party; but are always opposed to cheap schools and women's schools, the only or principal means by which learning is spread among the many.

On Knowledge

The greatest and best means of obtaining the knowledge necessary for a free man to have is by the liberty of the press or public newspapers. To counteract and destroy this privilege, the few spare no pains to make them as costly as possible and to contradict everything in them that favors the interests of the many, putting darkness for light and light for darkness, falsehood for truth and truth for falsehood, etc.

On Constitutions and Laws

The few have a great advantage over the many in forming and constructing constitutions and laws, and are highly interested in having them numerous, intricate, and as inexplicit as possible. By this, they take to themselves the right of giving them such explanations as suits their interests, and make places for numerous lawyers and judicial and executive officers, which adds greatly to their strength by numbers.

On the Medium of Trade

Money or a medium of trade is of such a nature that there are innumerable ways by which the few can manage it to the injury of the many, such as erecting banks and using partiality in remittances, ruining public and private credit, and stopping the circulation of money, etc.; by which they can bring the many into distress and set them to quarreling and suing one another, and so make a plenty of business for their party.

On Elections

This is a great object with the few to carry their points in elections, this being the only means by which the many can support their rights. Consequently, the few all unite in extolling the goodness and abilities of their candidates, and of running down and blackguarding the candidates on the other side. Also, they will appeal to the electors in a variety of ways. Some they will flatter by promises of favors, such as being customers to them or helping them out of debt or other difficulties, or help them to a good bargain, or treat them, or trust them, or lend them money, or even give them a little money if they will vote for such and such a man. Others they will threaten: "If you don't vote for such and such a man," or "If you do, you shall pay me what you owe me," or "I will sue you," or "I will turn you out of my house" or "off of my farm"; "I won't be your customer any longer"; "I will wager a guinea that you dare not vote for such a man; if you do you shall have a bloody nose for it." Or they will hire somebody to communicate these things to the electors. Also, they will hinder votes from being counted or returned right, and often will themselves (or hire others to) put in two or three votes apiece. All these things have been practised and may be again.

On Wars

So apt are mankind to be wrought up into a passion by false reports and slight offenses that it is an easy matter for cunning men to set peaceable families and friends at variance where there is no ground for it on either side. In the same manner, towns, states, and nations may be set at war against each other; and I have no doubt but that it has been the case many a time that thousands and millions have been slain on both sides, equally thinking that they have been fighting in a good cause, when the whole matter in dispute would have made little or no dispute between honest neighbors. Nor do I dispute but that it has been agreed upon by rulers of nations to make war on each other only that they might have a pretense to raise and keep up standing armies to deprive their own subjects of their rights and liberties. This is a great object with the few, and when they attain it, it adds so much to their number, strength, and importance that they have but little to fear; and the many have but little reason to expect that they can maintain their liberties long.

In the foregoing remarks I have but just touched on the principal means by which the few destroy free governments. I shall now proceed:

TO ILLUSTRATE THEM BY SUNDRY REMARKS ON THE OPERATION OF THESE CAUSES IN OUR OWN GOVERNMENTS

I SHALL NOT HERE ATTEMPT TO SAY ANYTHING on the want of knowledge among the people, supposing that it will fully appear by the remarks I shall make on the combinations and doings of the few.

Remarks on the Society of Cincinnati

Toward the close of the late war, the officers of the Continental Army were considerably borne upon by not being paid according to contract, and many of them thought they were not notified enough in the framing of the state constitutions. At the close of the war, they formed themselves into a society by the name of Cincinnati. This institution caused great alarm, and many pointed publications in newspapers considered it as a dangerous body.

This uneasiness caused them, at their first general meeting, to make very essential alterations in their constitution, which they published together with a very plausible circular letter, endeavoring in it to make the world believe that they never would nor could prove any harm. But, from that time, there was a continual noise and writing, from one end of the continent to the other, against the badness of public credit and the weakness and insufficiency of the federal government. When the Shays affair happened in Massachusetts, it was headed by one of this order, and many of the rest of them put under pay to suppress it.

Immediately after, a convention was called to amend the federal government, when a hard tussle was made, chiefly by this order, to establish a monarchical government in order to have their president made king. But though they failed in that, yet, by some means or other, they have wriggled themselves into almost all the posts of profit and honor in the federal government. And from this order also originated the funding system, by which those that labor for a living will have millions and millions of dollars to pay, for which the public never received, nor the possessor never gave, one single farthing.

Also from this order originated the Indian war, which has cost us thousands of lives and $6 million, without the least advantage to us. From this order also originated the breach of the federal Constitution and a breach of the French alliance, by making the British treaty, which has brought us almost to the brink of ruin.

When I charge these things to Cincinnati, I do not mean that they did them alone but as planners and leaders in them; for to them also may be charged the organization of almost all the orders of the few who follow after and support them in their diabolical measures — which I will remark upon separately, as follows:

On Speculators, Stock and Landjobbers

These orders of men are made up principally of Cincinnati, and, by the funding system, have risen like a black cloud over the continent and have gained wealth like the nabobs of the East. They have got the principal command of our funds, and not only swindle honest individuals out of their property but, by their bribery and corruption, have great influence in our elections and agitate our public councils. By their land speculations and bribery, they shook the government of Georgia almost to its foundation, and agitated the federal government so that one of the senators challenged one of the representatives to a duel, right in the midst of one of the most important debates they ever were or ever will be engaged in.

On Doctors

The doctors have established their medical societies and have both their state and county meetings, by which they have so nearly annihilated quackery of all kinds that a poor man cannot get such great cures from them now for a guinea as he could fifty years ago from an old squaw for half a pint of rum. The business of a midwife could be performed fifty years ago for half a dollar, and now it costs a poor man five whole ones.

On Merchants

The merchants have organized themselves and have their chambers of commerce and correspondence from one end of the continent to the other. Although they are in many respects a great advantage to the many, by making vent for our produce and furnishing us with necessaries and conveniences from other countries, yet, if we should be drawn into a war by their adventures, we should pay very dear for all the advantages we receive from them. Besides, foreign trade not well regulated is the most dangerous to the interest of the many of anything we have to fear. Our money may be all carried off from among us for that which will do us no good.

Foreign manufactures may be cheapest at first cost, but not in the long run. Merchants may grow rich on the ruins of our mechanics and manufactures, and bring us into as bad a condition as we were in 1786, for they look only to their own interests. It is evident that a large part of the merchants were in favor of the British treaty and fond of carrying on a trade with that sinking nation, which trade leaves a balance against America of more than $4 million annually, which will ruin us in a few years unless it is stopped.

On Literary Men and Colleges

The true principles of republicanism and a free government may be taught to the youth in some of our colleges and academies for aught I know; but it is evident that other political principles are admitted in many of them, or we should not be stunned with exhibitions in favor of monarchies and running down republican principles as we often be. One thing is pretty certain: that the scholars are taught to keep up the dignity of their professions; for if we apply for a preacher or a schoolmaster, we are told the price is so much, and they cannot go under, for it is agreed upon and they shall be disgraced if they take less, let their abilities for the service be what they will.

On Ministers of the Gospel

The ministers of the Congregational order, and others for aught I know, have formed themselves into societies, and many of them are incorporated and have their state and county meetings which may be of great service or absolutely necessary in their sacred functions. But it is no breach of charity to suppose that they have some political purposes in them, nor do I deny their right to meddle in politics. But as they receive their support for teaching piety, religion, morality, and things relative to another world, and their hearers being not all of them capable of discerning between divinity and politics, they ought, whenever they teach obedience to the civil laws or reprove for disobedience, etc., to teach and explain to them the true principles of our free government as established in our constitutions.

Instead of preaching about and praying for officers of government as infallible beings, or so perfect that we ought to submit to and praise them for all they do (when in fact they are all our servants and at all times accountable to the people), they ought to teach their hearers to be watchful of men in power, and to guard their own rights and privileges with a jealous eye, and teach them how to do it in a constitutional way.

If their principles forbid this, they had better let politics entirely alone, for if they use their great influence to mislead and prejudice their hearers against the true principles of a free government (as many of them have done of late) by praising our executive for making the British treaty, and, in short, by praising monarchical and despotic government and running down and blackguarding republican principles and the French nation, they are in fact acting a treasonable and rebellious part and doing all in their power to destroy the government, and their hearers ought not to attend on such teachings. It is this conduct in ministers that is the principal reason for the neglect of public worship and religious institutions that is so much complained of by the ministers now.

Ministers have it more in their power to turn the minds of their hearers to right or wrong than any other order of men; and it has been the general practice of all arbitrary governments to prostitute religion to political purposes and make a handle of this order of men to mislead, flatter, and drive the people, by the terrors of the other world, into submission to their political schemes and interests. Consequently, they ought to be watched and guarded above all other orders, especially when they preach politics. . . .

On Lawyers

The lawyers have established their bar meetings and become the most formidable and influential order of any in the government; and though they are neither judicial nor executive officers but a kind of mule order, engendered by and many times overawing both. This order of men get their living entirely from the quarrels, follies, disputes, and distresses of the many and the intricacy of our laws; and it is from the arts and doings of these men that the judicial and executive officers are furnished with the chief of their business and employ. Consequently, they are bound together by the strongest bonds of union.

Many have been the complaints against the lawyers in years back and of the intricacy of our laws, and much time spent and pains taken by the legislature to remedy the evil. But all to little or no purpose, and the sole reason is because we send these fee officers as representatives to make our laws. Unless the people can be brought to calculate more upon the operation of these little selfish principles on mankind and purge the legislatures from fee officers, they cannot be governed by laws very long.

Thus we see all the orders of the few completely organized, and they have of late got so monstrously crowded with numbers that it is impossible for them all to get a living by their professions; and being in want of employ, they are aiding in all the plans and schemes of Cincinnati to influence the many.

I would not be understood to be against the associations of any orders of men, for to hinder it would hinder their improvements in their professions and hinder them from being serviceable to the many. They need only one society more being established, or proper means of information among the many, to hinder their being dangerous in politics. In order to promote those means of information among the people, there have been many societies established, by constitutional, democratic, and other names, made up of men of republican principles and great abilities, who did all in their power to enlighten the people into their true interests.

But for want of the society I have mentioned, or a proper channel of conveying their sentiments to the people, and by the joint exertions of a majority of the other orders I have mentioned to hinder their usefulness and prejudice the minds of the people against them, have brought them almost into disuse. But I have no doubt but that they will revive again when they think they can do any good.

But before I proceed to describe the society or means of knowledge I have mentioned, I must make sundry remarks on what has been, and probably may be done by the joint exertion of the few to enslave the many unless they meet with a check.

On Learning

No person who is a friend to liberty will be against a large expense in learning; but it ought to be promoted in the cheapest and best manner possible, which, in my opinion, would be: for every state to maintain as many colleges in convenient parts thereof as would be attended upon to give the highest degrees of learning; and for every county to keep as many grammar schools or academies in convenient parts thereof as would be attended to by both sexes, summer and winter; and no student or scholar to pay anything for tuition; and for the county schools to pay a particular attention to teaching the English language and qualifying its scholars to teach and govern common schools for little children; and for every town to be obliged to keep as much as six weeks of writing school in the winter and twelve weeks of a women's school in the summer in every part of the town, so that none should be thronged with too many scholars, nor none have too far to travel; and every person be obliged to send his children to school, for the public is as much interested in the learning of one child as another.

If this method of learning was established, we should soon have plenty of schoolmasters and mistresses as cheaply as we could hire other labor; and labor and learning would be connected together and lessen the number of those that live without work. Also, we should have plenty of men to fill the highest offices of state for less than half we now give. But instead of this mode of learning, the few are always striving to oblige us to maintain great men with great salaries, and to maintain grammar schools in every town to teach our children the ABC's, all of which is only to give employment to gentlemen's sons and make places for men to live without work. For there is no more need of a man's having knowledge of all the languages to teach a child to read, write, and cipher than there is for a farmer to know the mariner's art to hold a plow.

On Knowledge

The principal knowledge necessary for a free man to have is obtained by the liberty of the press or public newspapers. But this kind of knowledge is almost ruined of late by the doings of the few. But a few years ago we could have the whole news from one paper in a week, and could put some dependence on what was printed. But the few, being closely combined and determined to destroy our government, find it necessary to destroy the liberty of the press first. To effect this, they employ no printers but those that will adhere strictly to their views and interests, and use all the arts and rhetoric hell can invent to blackguard the republican printers and all they print; and strive to make the people believe falsehood for truths and truths for falsehood; and, as they have money and leisure, they have their papers every day in the week. Consequently, the republican printers double their papers so that a laboring man must now be at the expense of $3 or $4 annually and read and study half of his time, and then be at a loss to know what is true and what not. Thus the few have almost ruined the liberty of the press.

On Elections

The whole interest of the many lies in getting and keeping full and fair representation in the several branches of government; and this depends entirely on the electors having a knowledge of the character, abilities, and political sentiments of those they vote for; and it is impossible for all to have a personal knowledge of them. In large towns there are some instances where the electors do not all know those for whom they vote. The state senators are more unknown, the governor and federal representatives are further off still, and the electors of President, being chosen only for a single act and not accountable for his conduct in that all-important act. I have often wondered that, under the present means of knowledge and in opposition to the numerous arts of flattery, deception, threatenings, and falsehoods practised by the few in elections, the many get so fully represented as they do; and that there are so many representatives that expose themselves to the abuse of the few by supporting our cause when we support them so poorly; and all the hopes I have of supporting our liberties are by a reformation or improvement in this thing.

In our state elections for federal representatives and electors, although there were the greatest pains taken on both sides to collect all the votes they could, yet there were not half the people brought to act on either side, and I will appeal to the returns for evidence. For, according to the best calculations I can make, there are not short of 6,000 voters in every district for a federal representative, and in many of them they were chosen with less than 500 votes, and those collected chiefly by the influence of the few and their dependents, and from inconsiderate young men. The men of consideration, being at a loss who to vote for, chose not to act rather than be mortified afterward by finding that they had voted for those who did more hurt than good. . . .

On the Adoption of the British Treaty

A short revue of the combined doings of the few at the adoption of the British treaty will show the importance of which they viewed it to their interests.

When the monster came first into view, it was reprobated from one end of the continent to the other. Scarcely one dare say a single word in favor of it. But as it was an instrument that but few of the common people could comprehend, the petitions against it were chiefly from the seaport towns; and although they were almost unanimous and couched in humble terms, yet the President signed it and proclaimed it the supreme law of the land. Hence arose a great question, whether it was binding or not, and how we could get rid of it.

Great dependence was put on the state legislatures for a remedy, but as it had been very prosperous times for the many for some years, and the few had been borne upon by the high prices of labor and produce, and as prosperity is a time of inattention, and necessity the mother of invention, so the few, by close attention in elections, had got a large majority of the state legislatures, made up of lawyers and other fee officers, favorable to their interests. So that at their first meetings after the treaty was published, to our great surprise, the question of undiminished confidence in the President was put and carried in almost all the states.

Then all our hopes lay in the federal House of Representatives. When they met, the same question was put but met with a check; and when the question of the treaty came forward, there was a large number of the most powerful representatives advocated it, thundering out treason and rebellion against all those that dare say anything against it, declaring that it was constitutionally made. But to the immortal honor of the other side, after near twenty days of warm debate, they declared to the contrary by nearly two to one.

And here the monster must have died for want of supplies [appropriation of funds] had it not been for the most treasonable arts and doings of the few. But finding their characters, if not their lives, in danger, they racked their inventions to compel the house to grant supplies for said treaty. To effect this, circular letters were sent from the center, to every part of the continent, with a printed petition and memorial ready for signing, attended with a collection of the most horrid and frightful falsehoods that ever were invented by the devil. In order to fright the people to petition the House to grant said supplies, representing that the House were unconstitutionally withholding the supplies and trying to usurp all the powers of government to themselves, and that unless the treaty took place Britain would certainly make war with us, and that their power over us and vengeance upon us would be such that they would rouse off a great gun 3,000 miles distance and blow all our brains out if we stepped out to piss.

They also represented the certainty of a civil war in such a manner that we could almost hear the small arms crackle; and that the House of Representatives were led entirely by one [Albert] Gallatin, who was a vagrant foreigner and had no interest in this country, and was trying to overset the government, and had been the sole cause of the Pittsburgh insurrection, which had cost the government more than $1,200,000, and that the only choice we had was to follow this odious Gallatin, or the virtuous, wise, and glorious Washington, who had led us by the hand for twenty years, and had been the cause of all the blessings and prosperity we had received for eight years back; and that now was the only time to choose which of these characters we would follow; and if any person attempted to contradict them in these cursed lies, their eyes would sparkle, their chins quiver, and they would call them Jacobines, Shaysites, disorganizers, and enemies to all government.

I do not pretend to say that such representations were everywhere so, but they appeared so to me where I was; and I thought that if the swinish multitude had behaved so they would soon have had the adulterous Hamilton after them with 15,000 men; and though he could find nobody but men peaceably following their honest callings, yet he would have boasted of the expense of $1,200,000 and laid all the blame to Gabriel or some person as innocent, as he did the Pittsburgh insurrection to Mr. Gallatin.

But sad to relate, for want of the means of knowledge among the people, they were so frighted with these lies that they hastened to see which could get his name to the memorial first. And I asked many afterward what they signed for, and some would say they signed for the treaty; some for the good of the country; some to keep from war; some for Washington; and some to stand by the Constitution. And when I told them the true circumstances of the affair, they would, like lambs that are dumb after they are sheared, turn away and wish to hear no more about it.

But to return, these petitions, thronging in upon the House from all quarters, gave great courage to the minority and equally depressed the majority, so that, after a long resistance, a bare majority was gained and the supplies granted for the treaty. Thus, by the combinations of the few, with the order of Cincinnati at their head, a seal is put upon the breach of our Constitution.

Library of Congress

IMAGES OF AMERICAN LIFE

In 1786 the British rejected an American bid for a trade treaty with the comment that 13 separate treaties would more accurately mirror the reality of the American situation. The diversity and virtually incompatible sectional differences that the British comment reflected were the central problem facing the federal government and a primary reason for its establishment. Even locating the national capital presented problems. During the period of Congressional government, sessions of Congress had met at various times in Philadelphia, Princeton, N.J., Trenton, N.J., and New York City. During Washington's presidency the government sat first in New York and then in Philadelphia. Meanwhile, horse trading for a permanent site was going on between Southern and Northern representatives. Finally Hamilton's need for Jefferson's support on financial measures led to a "deal" that broke the deadlock in Congress and established the District of Columbia on lands turned over by Maryland and Virginia. The government moved to Washington in 1800.

Southern life, with its base in slave-labor and plantation agriculture, contrasted sharply with that of the North. Even within the South, there was conflict between the tidewater planters and the backwoods subsistence farmers. Charleston was the only major port city in the South until the spread of the plantation system into Alabama and Mississippi brought New Orleans into prominence. Cultural activity was largely confined to the individual plantations, and the wealthy continued to be educated at home or in private schools.

Philadelphia, by contrast, was one of several Northern cities thriving on commerce and trade. The city's population tripled between 1790 and 1820 to 112,000. This new population included a majority of working men: stevedores, laborers, construction and factory workers, and also a substantial number of free Negroes.

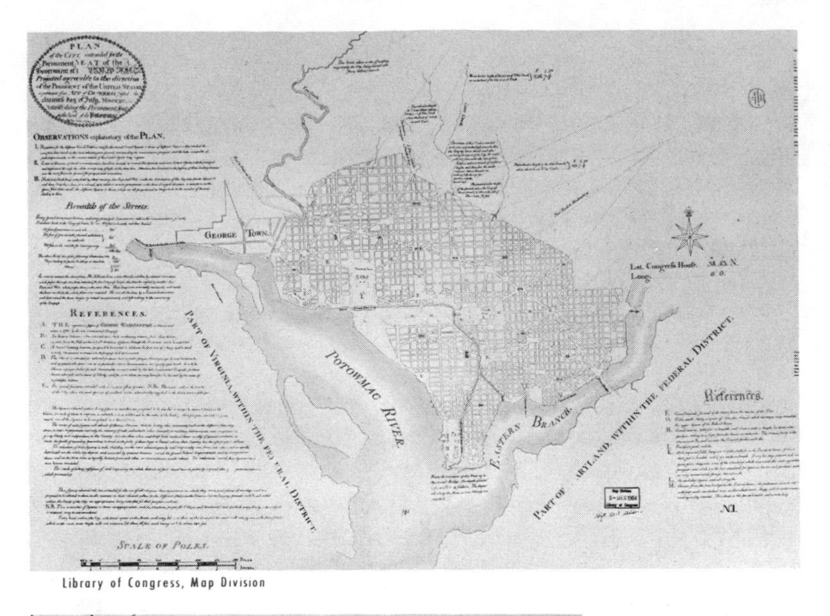

(Left) Redraft of L'Enfant's plan for the city of Washington showing location for the president's house, mall, and the Capitol, original drawn in 1791; (below left) Jefferson's sketch for development of land around the Capitol building, 1791

Library of Congress, Map Division

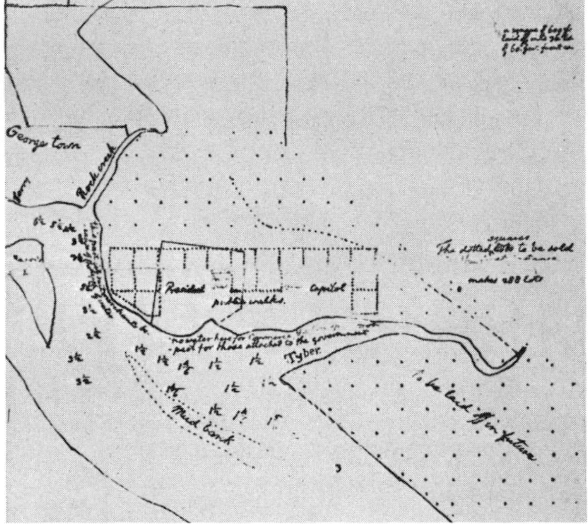

Library of Congress, Map Division

A Federal City

The original plan for Washington was drawn up by Pierre L'Enfant, a French-born officer in the American Revolutionary Army. His conception called for broad avenues and "magnificent vistas." Although L'Enfant was replaced after a year, much of his plan was eventually carried out. It was a long time, though, before Washington was much more than a country town with a few imposing buildings scattered through it. When the government moved to the new capital in 1800, construction was going on, and Mrs. Adams found the general atmosphere loathsome.

The White House in 1799, prior to occupancy by John and Abigail Adams
Library of Congress

Library of Congress

(Top) Senate wing of the Capitol, 1800; (right) view of the front of the President's house after the addition of the north and south porticos; watercolor by Latrobe, 1807; (bottom) the Capitol seen from Pennsylvania Ave. before it was burned by the British in 1814; watercolor by Latrobe

Library of Congress

Library of Congress

Stokes Collection, New York Public Library

(Above) Etching of Richmond, Va., by St. Memin, 1804; (below) the harbor at Norfolk, Va.; aquatint by J. Hill in "Picturesque Views of American Scenery" by Joshua Shaw, 1820

Library of Congress

The South

Cotton could claim to be king in the South only after Whitney's cotton gin made processing the harvest economical. Lack of large cities and an isolated plantation economy made the South develop in its own way. Elegant home life was stressed, and was feasible so long as Negro slaves were the foundation on which the stately mansions raised their pillars. Changes were slow in coming.

Baltimore in 1802, painting by Guy

The Brooklyn Museum

Library of Congress

Library of Congress

(Above) Montibello estate in Maryland; (right) interior of William Pennach's home, Norfolk, Va.

Courtesy, Edgar W. Garbisch

(Above) "Ceremonial at a Young Ladies Seminary," painting by an unknown artist, Virginia; (left) state house in Columbia, South Carolina, 1802; (below) rice plantation on the Cooper River, 1803

Ayer Collection, Newberry Library

Carolina Art Association

Maryland Historical Society

(Above) "Overseer Doing His Duty," watercolor by Latrobe; (right) Negro laborers in Philadelphia

Metropolitan Museum, Rogers Fund

The Black Man's America

Addison Gallery

A slave was three-fifths of a person for purposes of congressional apportionment. In most other legal dealings he was not a person at all, but property. House slaves, cooks, butlers, nurses, and chambermaids were privileged and often lived in a close, if involuntary, relationship with their owners from birth. Field hands, by far the majority, usually faced little but a short life of hard work. As cotton began to dominate the Southern economy, large work crews were required and conditions for field slaves worsened markedly. Free Negroes were discriminated against in both the North and South, often losing the few rights they had earlier enjoyed.

(Above) Portrait of a free Negro; "The Old Plantation" (1800) idealizes slave life

Rockefeller Coll., Colonial Williamsburg

New York Public Library

Valentine Museum

(Left) Negro laborer in New York; (above) Simeon Gilliat, a slave in Virginia, was well enough known as an entertainer for his name to be remembered today. He died in 1820

Library of Congress

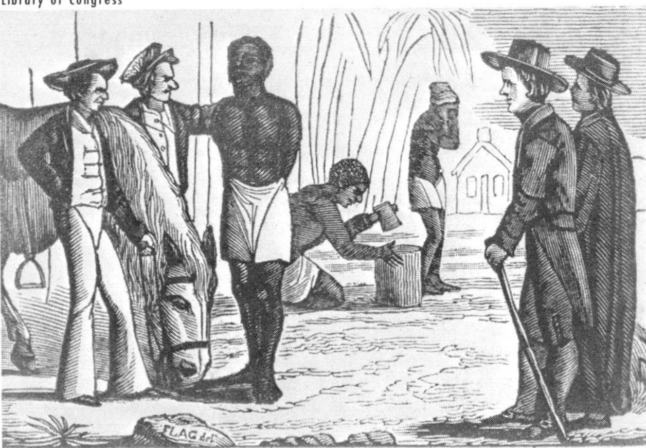

Bowdoin College Museum

(Above) A young Negro preacher; (above right) "Exchanging a Citizen for a Horse" is more representative of slavery than banjo playing; (right) a Negro, perhaps free, plays at an inn in the North about 1816

Metropolitan Museum, Rogers Fund

Library of Congress

Pennsylvania Academy of Fine Arts

(Above) Quakers going to meeting; (above right) William White, Episcopal bishop of Pennsylvania

Freedom to Worship

Virginia Historical Society

The prohibition of an established church and guarantees of the free exercise of religion resulted in a wide diversity of religious expression in the United States. Denominations and sects from all of Europe found homes in the new land, and individuals founded their own faiths as well. In addition to Protestant groups, Catholics and Jews also flourished.

Carolina Art Association

American Antiquarian Society

(Above left) James Madison, bishop of the Episcopal Church in Virginia and president of the College of William and Mary; (above) St. Andrew's Church, near Charleston, S.C.; (left) church at New Bedford, Mass., cut in half as result of quarrel among the congregation, 1816

Metropolitan Museum of Art, Rogers Fund

Library of Congress

(Top) Anabaptist immersion in Philadelphia, watercolor by Svinin; (above) Methodist camp meeting

Metropolitan Museum of Art, Rogers Fund

Library of Congress

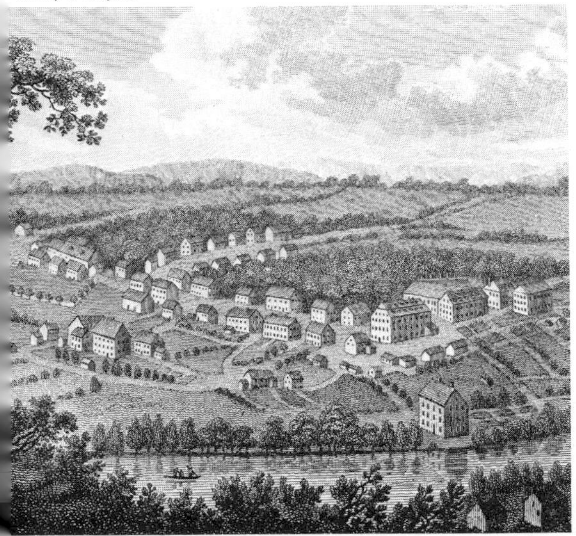

(Above) Negro Methodists holding a meeting in Philadelphia, watercolor by Svinin; (left) view of the Moravian settlement at Bethlehem, Pa., 1800; (below) Moravian sisters, watercolor by Svinin

Metropolitan Museum of Art, Rogers Fund

New York Public Library

Library of Congress

Philadelphia

By the time of the Revolution the Quaker City of Brotherly Love had become the largest city in the country. It kept that rank well into the nineteenth century. Philadelphia was the nation's chief cultural center, with Benjamin Franklin (died 1790) only the foremost in a long list of eminent scientists and writers.

Unlike Boston and New York, Philadelphia was nearly a hundred miles up river from the coast, and the Delaware was a treacherous river. But the astute city fathers saw its commercial possibilities and encouraged others to share the town's growing importance. Philadelphia was the nation's capital from 1790 to 1800, and became a banking center as well as the art and commercial center. But its leading role faded in the early part of the nineteenth century.

Stokes Collection, New York Public Library

Kean Archives

(All except center) Engravings by William Birch, 1800, showing various parts of Philadelphia; (left) High Street, with the First Presbyterian Church in the foregound; (center) Philadelphia, from the ferry at Camden, N.J.; by J. L. Bonquet de Woiseri, 1810

Library of Congress

Library of Congress

Library of Congress

Library of Congress

Library of Congress

Library of Congress

(Left) China Retreat, Pennsylvania; (right) Bush Hill, outside Philadelphia

Library of Congress

Covered bridge over the Schuylkill River, outside Philadelphia

(Left) Falls of the Schuylkill River; (right) the Penn estate Solitude

Library of Congress

Library of Congress

Maryland Historical Society

Road near Patterson, N. J., around 1800; watercolor by B. H. Latrobe

Travel

In 1796 a trip by coach between New York and Boston involved four days of jostling and discomfort. Even along the main post roads there were many fords and long stretches that were virtually impassable in bad weather. Road conditions forced most freight to be carried on the waterways and brought early pressure for canals and for federal highway programs.

Metropolitan Museum of Art, Rogers Fund

(Above) Stagecoach travel; (right) ferry on the Susquehanna, watercolors by Svinin

Metropolitan Museum of Art, Rogers Fund

"Mishap at the Ford," painting by Alvin Fisher, 1818

The Corcoran Gallery of Art

CITY-TAVERN.

THE SUBSCRIBER,

Respectfully informs his Friends and the Public in general, that he still occupies the noted stand, in Trenton, New-Jersey, *called the*

CITY TAVERN,

WHERE every attention, in the line of his business, will be paid to those who may please to favor him with their custom. His house is large and commodious, and being determined that every requisite necessary for the entertainment and accommodation of Travelers, shall be provided, he flatters himself he will be enabled to give general satisfaction to those of this, as well as every other description of customers.—He will be particularly enabled to accommodate travelers with lodging, as no stages put up at his house at night.

ALSO,

The best accommodations for Horses and Carriages. His stabling is large and in good repair, and every kind of the first quality provender is provided for horses, which will be under the care of the best Hostler, without exception, in the state of New-Jersey.

He likewise keeps

A Livery Stable,

Where Horses are taken in, and the strictest attention paid to their keeping.

Horses, Chairs, and a Coachee, to let, on the shortest notice, and most reasonable terms.

John Voorhees.

Trenton, August 8, 1801.

Warshaw Collection

Library of Congress

Waterloo Inn, along the route of the first stage between Baltimore and Washington

Litchfield Historical Society

(Above) Ad for City Tavern, Trenton, N.J.; (right) roadside inn in New England; (below) interior of an American inn in the early 19th century by John Lewis Krimmel

Toledo Museum of Art

1799

19.

Alexander Hamilton: The Beginnings of Expansion

By 1799, the threat of war with France had ended, owing to diplomatic concessions by both sides, and the domestic uprisings predicted by many Federalists had either not occurred or were inconsequential. Alexander Hamilton was thus left with a large standing army under his command but with no war to fight, and an army, furthermore, that was growing restless, and that President Adams feared would soon resort to "pillage and plunder" and to "debauching wives and seducing daughters." Hamilton, still seeking military glory, proposed to use the army to conquer lands in the West that were then occupied by the French and Spanish. In a letter dated January 26, 1799, to Harrison Gray Otis, a Federalist and Massachusetts congressman, Hamilton defended the maintenance of a large army, which, he argued, was necessary in order to support a policy of aggressive expansionism for the United States.

Source: J. C. Hamilton, VI, pp. 390-392.

You will recollect that I reserved for a future answer part of a letter which I had the pleasure of receiving from you some time since. These are my ideas on that subject.

I should be glad to see, before the close of the session, a law empowering the President, at his discretion, in case a negotiation between the United States and France should not be on foot by the 1st of August next, or being on foot should terminate without an adjustment of differences, to declare that a state of war exists between the two countries; and thereupon to employ the land and naval forces of the United States in such manner as shall appear to him most effectual for annoying the enemy, and for preventing and frustrating hostile designs of France, either directly or *indirectly through any of her allies.*

This course of proceeding, by postponing the event and giving time for the intervention of negotiation, would be a further proof of moderation in the government, and would tend to reconcile our citizens to the last extremity, if it shall ensue, gradually accustoming their minds to look forward to it.

If France be really desirous of accommodation, this plan will accelerate her measures to bring it about. If she have not that desire, it is best to anticipate her final vengeance, and to throw whatever weight we have into the scale opposed to her. This conduct may contribute to disable her to do the mischief which she may meditate.

As it is every moment possible that the project of taking possession of the Floridas and Louisiana, long since attributed to France, may be attempted to be put in execution, it is very important that the executive should be clothed with power to meet and defeat so dangerous an enterprise. Indeed, if it is the policy of France to leave us in a state of semihostility, it is preferable to terminate it, and, by taking possession of those countries for ourselves, to obviate the mischief of their falling into the hands of an active foreign power, and at the same time to secure to the United States the advantage of keeping the key of the western country. I have been long in the habit of considering the acquisition of those countries as essential to the permanency of the Union, which I consider as very important to the welfare of the whole.

If universal empire is still to be the pursuit of France, what can tend to defeat the purpose better than to detach South America from Spain, which is only the channel through which the riches of Mexico and Peru are conveyed to France? The executive ought to be put in a situation to embrace favorable conjunctures for effecting that separation. It is to be regretted that the preparation of an adequate military force does not advance more rapidly. There is some sad nonsense on this subject in some good heads. The reveries of some of the friends of the government are more injurious to it than the attacks of its declared enemies.

When will men learn to profit by experience?

20.

Massachusetts' Reply to the Kentucky and Virginia Resolutions of 1798

The states of the northeast, where the Federalist Party was dominant, did not support the Kentucky and Virginia Resolutions of 1798; and several, including Massachusetts, made their disapproval vocal. In the longest and most critical of the replies, Massachusetts asserted that the courts alone, and not the states, could decide questions involving the constitutionality of federal laws. The Reply of the Massachusetts Senate of February 9, 1799, appears below.

Source: Elliot, IV, pp. 533-537.

The legislature of Massachusetts, having taken into serious consideration the resolutions of the state of Virginia, passed the 21st day of December last, and communicated by his excellency the governor, relative to certain supposed infractions of the Constitution of the United States by the government thereof; and being convinced that the federal Constitution is calculated to promote the happiness, prosperity, and safety of the people of these United States, and to maintain that union of the several states so essential to the welfare of the whole; and being bound by solemn oath to support and defend that Constitution, feel it unnecessary to make any professions of their attachment to it or of their firm determination to support it against every aggression, foreign or domestic.

But they deem it their duty solemnly to declare that, while they hold sacred the principle that consent of the people is the only pure source of just and legitimate power, they cannot admit the right of the state legislatures to denounce the administration of that government to which the people themselves, by a solemn compact, have exclusively committed their national concerns.

That, although a liberal and enlightened vigilance among the people is always to be cherished, yet an unreasonable jealousy of the men of their choice and a recurrence to measures of extremity upon groundless or trivial pretexts have a strong tendency to destroy all rational liberty at home and to deprive the United States of the most essential advantages in relations abroad.

That this legislature are persuaded that the decision of all cases in law and equity arising under the Constitution of the United States, and the construction of all laws made in pursuance thereof, are exclusively vested by the people in the judicial courts of the United States.

That the people, in that solemn compact which is declared to be the supreme law of the land, have not constituted the state legislatures the judges of the acts or measures of the federal government but have confided to them the power of proposing such amendments of the Constitution as shall appear to them necessary to the interests, or conformable to the wishes, of the people whom they represent.

That, by this construction of the Constitution, an amicable and dispassionate remedy is pointed out for any evil which experience may prove to exist, and the peace and prosperity of the United States may be preserved without interruption.

But, should the respectable state of Virginia persist in the assumption of the right to declare the acts of the national government unconstitutional, and should she oppose successfully her force and will to those of the nation, the Constitution would be reduced to a mere cipher, to the form and pageantry of authority without the energy of power. Every act of the federal government which thwarted the views or checked the ambitious projects of a particular state, or of its leading and influential members, would be the object of opposition and of remonstrance, while the people, convulsed and confused by the conflict between two hostile jurisdictions, enjoying the protection of neither, would be wearied into a submission to some bold leader who would establish himself on the ruins of both.

The legislature of Massachusetts, although they do not themselves claim the right nor admit the authority of any of the state governments to decide upon the constitutionality of the acts of the federal government, still — lest their silence should be construed into disapprobation or at best into a doubt as to the constitutionality of the acts referred to by the state of Virginia, and as the General Assembly of Virginia has called for an expression of their sentiments — do explicitly declare that they consider the acts of Congress, commonly called the Alien and Sedition Acts, not only constitutional but expedient and necessary.

That the former act respects a description of persons whose rights were not particularly contemplated in the Constitution of the United States, who are entitled only to a temporary protection while they yield a temporary allegiance, a protection which ought to be withdrawn whenever they become "dangerous to the public safety" or are found guilty of "treasonable machination" against the government.

That Congress, having been especially entrusted by the people with the general defense of the nation, had not only the right but were bound to protect it against internal as well as external foes.

That the United States, at the time of passing the Act Concerning Aliens, were threatened with actual invasion; had been driven by the unjust and ambitious conduct of the French government into warlike preparations, expensive and burdensome; and had then, within the bosom of the country, thousands of aliens, who, we doubt not, were ready to cooperate in any external attack.

It cannot be seriously believed that the United States should have waited till the poniard had in fact been plunged. The removal of aliens is the usual preliminary of hostility and is justified by the invariable usages of nations. Actual hostility had unhappily long been experienced, and a formal declaration of it the government had reason daily to expect. The law, therefore, was just and salutary; and no officer could with so much propriety be entrusted with the execution of it as the one in whom the Constitution has reposed the executive power of the United States.

The Sedition Act, so-called, is, in the opinion of this legislature, equally defensible. The General Assembly of Virginia, in their resolve under consideration, observe that when that state by its convention ratified the federal Constitution, it expressly declared, "that, among other essential rights, the liberty of conscience and of the press cannot be canceled, abridged, restrained, or modified by any authority of the United States," and, from its extreme anxiety to guard these rights from every possible attack of sophistry or ambition, with other states, recommended an amendment for that purpose, which amendment was, in due time, annexed to the Constitution; but they did not surely expect that the proceedings of their state convention were to explain the amendment adopted by the Union. The words of that amendment on this subject are, "Congress shall make no law abridging the freedom of speech or of the press."

The act complained of is no abridgment of the freedom of either. The genuine liberty of speech and the press is the liberty to utter and publish the truth; but the constitutional right of the citizen to utter and publish the truth is not to be confounded with the licentiousness, in speaking and writing, that is only employed in propagating falsehood and slander. This freedom of the press has been explicitly secured by most if not all the state constitutions; and of this provision there has been generally but one construction among enlightened men — that it is a security for the rational use and not the abuse of the press — of which the courts of law, the juries, and people will judge; this right is not infringed but confirmed and established by the late act of Congress.

By the Constitution, the legislative, executive, and judicial departments of government are ordained and established, and general enumerated powers vested in them respectively, including those which are prohibited to the several states. Certain powers are granted in general terms, by the people, to their general government for the purposes of their safety and protection. The government is not only empowered but it is made their duty to repel invasions and suppress insurrections; to guarantee to the several states a republican form of government; to protect each state against invasion and, when applied to, against domestic violence; to hear and decide all cases in law and equity arising under the Constitution and under any treaty or law made in pursuance thereof, and all cases of admiralty and maritime jurisdiction, and relating to the law of nations. Whenever, therefore, it becomes necessary to effect any of the objects designated, it is perfectly consonant to all just rules of construction to infer that the usual means and powers necessary to the attainment of that object are also granted. But the Constitution has left no occasion to resort to implication for these powers; it has made an express grant of them, in Section 8 of Article I, which ordains,

> that Congress shall have power to make all laws which shall be necessary and proper for carrying into execution the foregoing powers, and all other powers vested by this Constitution in the government of the United States, or in any department or officer thereof.

This Constitution has established a Supreme Court of the United States, but has made no provision for its protection, even against such improper conduct in its presence as might disturb its proceedings, unless expressed in the section before recited. But as no statute has been passed on this subject, this protection is, and has been for nine years past, uniformly found in the application of the principles and usages of the common law. The same protection may unquestionably be afforded by a statute passed in virtue of the before-mentioned section, as necessary and proper for carrying into execution the powers vested in that department. A construction of the different parts of the Constitution, perfectly just and fair, will, on analogous principles, extend protection and security against the offenses in question to the other departments of government in discharge of their respective trusts.

The President of the United States is bound by his oath "to preserve, protect, and defend the Constitution"; and it is expressly made his duty "to take care that the laws be faithfully executed." But this would be impracticable by any created being if there could be no legal restraint of those scandalous misrepresentations of his measures and motives which directly tend to rob him of the public confidence; and equally impotent would be every other public officer, if thus left to the mercy of the seditious.

It is held to be a truth most clear that the important trusts before enumerated cannot be discharged by the government to which they are committed without the power to restrain seditious practices and unlawful combinations against itself, and to protect the officers thereof from abusive misrepresentations. Had the Constitution withheld this power, it would have made the government responsible for the effects, without any control over the causes which naturally produce them, and would have essentially failed of answering the great ends for which the people of the United States declare, in the first clause of that instrument, that they establish the same; viz.,

> to form a more perfect union, establish justice, insure domestic tranquillity, provide for the common defense, promote the general welfare, and secure the blessings of liberty to ourselves and our posterity.

Seditious practices and unlawful combinations against the federal government or any officer thereof in the performance of his duty, as well as licentiousness of speech and of the press, were punishable on the principles of common law in the courts of the United States before the act in question was passed. This act, then, is an amelioration of that law in favor of the party accused, as it mitigates the punishment which that authorizes and admits of any investigation of public men and measures which is regulated by truth. It is not intended to protect men in office, only as they are agents of the people. Its object is to afford legal security to public offices and trusts created for the safety and happiness of the people, and therefore the security derived from it is for the benefit of the people and is their right.

This construction of the Constitution, and of the existing law of the land, as well as the act complained of, the legislature of Massachusetts most deliberately and firmly believe results from a just and full view of the several parts of the Constitution; and they consider that act to be wise and necessary as an audacious and unprincipled spirit of falsehood and abuse had been too long unremittingly exerted for the purpose of perverting public opinion, and threatened to undermine and destroy the whole fabric of government.

The legislature further declare that in the foregoing sentiments they have expressed the general opinion of their constituents, who have not acquiesced without complaint in those particular measures of the federal government but have given their explicit approbation by reelecting those men who voted for the adoption of them. Nor is it apprehended that the citizens of this state will be accused of supineness or of an indifference to their constitutional rights; for while, on the one hand, they regard with due vigilance the conduct of the government; on the other, their freedom, safety, and happiness require that they should defend that government and its constitutional measures against the open or insidious attacks of any foe, whether foreign or domestic.

And, lastly, that the legislature of Massachusetts feel a strong conviction that the several United States are connected by a common interest, which ought to render their union indissoluble; and that this state will always cooperate with its confederate states in rendering that union productive of mutual security, freedom, and happiness.

21.

The Kentucky Resolutions of 1799

Jefferson was disheartened by the hostile replies from other states to the Kentucky and Virginia Resolutions of 1798. He thought that the Republican states, most of which lay below the Potomac, should "sever" themselves from the Union rather than give up their liberty. Accordingly, the further resolutions he prepared for Kentucky in 1799 not only restated his original position on constitutional matters but added an assertion of the right to "nullification" in "the several states." Under Madison's restraining influence, however, he made the language of these revised resolutions more temperate, and while he affirmed the right to nullify he pointedly refrained from urging that it be exercised. The revised resolutions, introduced by Jefferson's friend John Breckinridge, were adopted unanimously by the Kentucky legislature on November 22, 1799.

Source: Elliot, IV, pp. 544-545.

Resolved, that this commonwealth considers the federal Union, upon the terms and for the purposes specified in the late compact, conducive to the liberty and happiness of the several states. That it does now unequivocally declare its attachment to the Union and to that compact, agreeably to its obvious and real intention, and will be among the last to seek its dissolution. That if those who administer the general government be permitted to transgress the limits fixed by that compact, by a total disregard to the special delegations of power therein contained, an annihilation of the state governments and the creation, upon their ruins, of a general consolidated government will be the inevitable consequence.

That the principle and construction contended for by sundry of the state legislatures that the general government is the exclusive judge of the extent of the powers delegated to it, stop not short of despotism, since the discretion of those who administer the government and not the Constitution would be the measure of their powers. That the several states who formed that instrument, being sovereign and independent, have the unquestionable right to judge of the infraction; and, that a nullification by those sovereignties, of all unauthorized acts done under color of that instrument, is the rightful remedy.

That this commonwealth does, under the most deliberate reconsideration, declare that the said Alien and Sedition laws are, in their opinion, palpable violations of the said Constitution; and however cheerfully it may be disposed to surrender its opinion to a majority of its sister states in matters of ordinary or doubtful policy, yet, in momentous regulations like the present, which so vitally wound the best rights of the citizen, it would consider a silent acquiescence as highly criminal.

That although this commonwealth, as a party to the federal compact, will bow to the laws of the Union, yet it does, at the same time, declare that it will not now or ever hereafter cease to oppose, in a constitutional manner, every attempt, at what quarter soever offered, to violate that compact.

And finally, in order that no pretext or arguments may be drawn from a supposed acquiescence on the part of this commonwealth in the constitutionality of those laws, and be thereby used as precedents for similar future violations of the federal compact, this commonwealth does now enter against them its solemn protest.

22.

John Ward Fenno: Our Economic Interests in the Caribbean

The following selection appeared originally and at greater length in the form of an editorial in the Gazette of the United States, *a Federalist organ, on March 4, 1799. The ideas expressed in the editorial, though it was signed by the editor, John Ward Fenno, bear a striking resemblance to those contained in letters written several months later to various friends by Alexander Hamilton, on the same subject of a possible war with France. But the influence was almost certainly from Hamilton to Fenno and not the other way around. Fenno also argued for government reforms that included the abolition of the states as political entities. This was a notion that Hamilton had advanced as far back as the Federal Convention of 1787.*

Source: *Desultory Reflections on the New Political Aspects of Public Affairs in the United States of America, Since the Commencement of the Year 1799,* New York, 1800, pp. 18-24.

That the wavering and wanton conduct of this government must excite a very high degree of contempt in the British government and nation, every well-informed man will easily believe. That they will hold us very cheap, that they will regard our interests with an eye of perfect indifference, is equally probable. But that a state of war must inevitably arise out of these circumstances, I believe is credible only from the manifestations of our own government.

More than nine-tenths of the people of

America believe that Great Britain cannot or dare not go to war with them. What, say they, will become of her West-India islands, and other colonies, which depend on us for their bread, beef, and fish? What will become of her manufacturers and artisans? Strong in this confidence, they imagine that she will bear, with American tameness, every aggression that can be made upon her by this country, and, accordingly, outrage her, as a young scoundrel spendthrift and rake does the guardian of his estate.

But we shall find, to our cost, if this conduct be persisted in, that all such ideas are completely fallacious. The ties which ought to bind this country to Great Britain are very forcible ones; for we are dependent on her for various necessaries of life, while she is in every such respect essentially independent. Canada, and her other possessions in North America, are fully adequate to the supply, not only of her West-India possessions but of all her dominions, with every species of provisions. I have known seventeen ships, averaging 300 tons each, lying at Quebec at one time, laden with wheat, the produce of Canada, and of a quality equal to any that the earth can produce.

That this country presents a very extensive mart for the commodities of Great Britain is a very obvious fact. Equally obvious is it that those commodities are to us not only indispensable but derivable from no other source. Whence, but from the dominions of Great Britain, can America be supplied with cloths, linens, muslins, silks, hosiery, and woolens of all kinds; with hardware, metals of every species, and a variety even of raw materials? The *lien* therefore, the security for good behavior, is in her hands, and the calculations in this score, which have been so very current, are not only disgraceful but unfounded.

It is with this nation, so competent to every purpose of annoyance and distress to us, that so many of the people of this country, and so efficient a portion of its government, if a judgment may be formed from the stultiloquence in which they indulge, are willing to break off the ties of amity, and to rely on a broken reed in the power of her covenanted foe.

I shall not suppose the force of this infatuation to be such as to lead to actual or declared war. But I do sincerely believe that the train of measures which have been taken and which are still pursuing, will produce a chilling coldness towards America, in the British government and nation; among the consequences of which will be the excision of a trade to her Atlantic possessions, which employs annually more than 15,000 tons of American shipping; a suspension of the credits given by her merchants, and all the extensive consequences which must arise from the influence of her ill will in the Italian ports, in Portugal, Russia, Hamburg, and, in short, wherever her influence extends.

In such an extremity, what friendly power will there be left us to rely on? France! She needs our assistance but can afford us none; nay, among the least improbable of events is the sudden restoration of the king; and the least improbable consequence of that event, the ill will of the French court, who will most assuredly demand the repayment of the money which it loaned us.

These things, it will be said, are but contingencies; and different men, according to their different habits of thinking, will deem them more or less remote. But even allowing them to be contingencies, what evils avoided or what good in prospect have we to set off against them, to authorize us in encountering the hazard of these contingencies? It appears to me that the fatuity which is driving us into these straits will not leave us a title to so honorable an epitaph even as the foolish Spaniard, who, taking, while in sound health, medicine which destroyed him, had inscribed on his tomb, "I was well — would be better — now here I lie."

These sad scenes, these dire aspects, soon ceasing to be seen, in speculation only, will soon be present to our eyes in more ghastly deformity than is easy to conceive. The people, however, begin to feel these evils, and the beginning of fear is the beginning of wisdom. But our retrogression from the path of honor and safety toward this hideous precipice of danger, has been so rapid and so far elongated, that we are now almost at the extreme verge; and I tremble to think how much energy is requisite, and how little may be found, to retrieve our erratic steps.

The time is arrived when we must repudiate the author of our evils from any share in our confidence, and adopt all proper and honorable measures to thwart those future measures by which he may attempt to sacrifice the honor and safety of the country.

Under the auspices of a wise and prudent ruler, we may then proceed, by judicious provisions, to ward off in future similar disasters to those which have so nearly destroyed us. The arbitrary power now deposited in the hands of one man must be checked and regulated, somewhat after the manner of the British constitution, or by any better, if better can be devised by American ingenuity. Experience has shown us how entirely we have entrusted "our lives and sureties all" into the power of a single man; and if we have common wisdom, we shall profit by that experience to bar up in future every avenue to so dangerous and, in our case, so ruinous an exercise of an authority so inconsistent with the spirit of freedom or the nature of man, as that by which we have suffered.

Under the auspices of a wise and prudent ruler, we might proceed to other reformations absolutely essential to the continuance of our existence as a truly great, free, and independent nation. Those egregious baubles of sovereignty, those pestiferous incitements to demagogy — the state governments — might be abolished and their officers rendered dependent, as they ought to be, on the government of the United States, instead of having it in their power, as at present, to organize revolts against that government.

This would be a very admirable act for a new administration to commence its career with, the unfortunate people being in as distressful a situation amidst the jars and clashings of the multiplicity of jurisdictions as they would be placed between two globes, revolving in contact; so that a more popular or a more judicious step could not be adopted.

The present topographical location of the states would, in order the more effectually to abolish the memory of federalism, be totally changed, and the continent divided into ten, fifteen, or twenty counties, to be governed by a lieutenant, or prefect, appointed by the executive; certain subaltern appointments should be in his gift. These prefects would constitute as proper an Upper House for one branch of the legislature as could be well devised. I venture to confirm that it would be found a more proper and independent branch than that for which it would be substituted.

Under the auspices of a wise and prudent ruler, the elective franchise might be forever cut off from all paupers, vagabonds, and outlaws, and the legislation of the country placed in those hands to which it belongs — the proprietors of the country. At present we are the vassals of foreign outlaws. The frequency of elections, those elections being now entrusted to men of sense, men of principle, and men having interest connected with the interests of the country, declines of course, as the folly and danger of annual elections can now be securely remedied.

Thus will the public burdens be alleviated; thus will public dilapidations cease; thus will undue influences — corruption of the lowest and basest sort — be eradicated; while the people grow quieter, happier, and are better served, without a ruinous and useless expense.

The principle of federalism must be abolished or it will very soon destroy the principle of union. It is *influence* that sways the scepters of irregular or popular governments; and I will leave any man to decide what comparison the influence of the government of the United States will bear with the sixteen governments of the states: it is as sixteen to one.

But there should be gradual and secondary reformations; they are now only touched on, and that merely for the sake of committing to the public judgment opinions on which their welfare may very essentially depend, and which I have the pleasure to know, prevail in no inconsiderable extent.

The measure which most pressingly demands adoption is an immediate declaration of war against France and her dependencies, Spain and Holland. It is time, after having so long and so pusillanimously beheld England fighting our battles, while we have rather comforted and abetted the common enemy, than even wished well to the opposition to him. It is time, after having fattened so long upon the spoils of war, to bring our mite of contribution into the general chest, and to relieve, as we may effectually do, the generous asserters of the Christian cause.

The conquest of the remaining possessions of France, Spain, and Holland in the West Indies might be effected by this country, with very little expense or inconvenience. The naval force already extant is fully adequate, and the regular troops lately embodied through its intervention would have achieved the conquest without difficulty. This country possesses such advantages for carrying on expeditions against the West-India islands, as must render her cooperation in the cause very acceptable. In short, the contingent we could bring into the coalition would be such as to entitle us to assume the rank of a first-rate power, and to make stipulations, the fulfillment of which could not fail to fix us in a state of prosperity and to extend our empire and renown.

To instance, for our quota of 25,000 troops (which should act separately and independently) and a stipulated quantum of military stores, etc., Great Britain should guarantee to us the island of Cuba, or, which would be more convenient to our commerce, that of Puerto Rico. Either of these possessions would amply remunerate us for the most expensive exertions that the conquest of them could require. In the East, we might establish ourselves in the possession of Batavia or the Mauritius, and thus secure a footing in the Indian Ocean, highly essential to us, but now depending on the most precarious tenure.

It is in vain to attempt to disguise the truth, that America is essentially and naturally a commercial nation; and that from her location on the map of the world she must ever remain so. It ought, therefore, to be the undeviating care of the government, whether it be federal or Jacobinical, or true Columbian, to secure, on the most advantageous footing possible, our commercial intercourse with foreign nations. To procure admission to our flag in ports whence it is now excluded; to obtain it by right where it now rests on the ground of sufferance; and to establish it on a regular and permanent footing, in those cases where it is at present precarious and temporary, is not merely the province of the government but a duty, an obligation which its subjects have a right to hold it to.

We have a right to expect, and the government ought to exact from Spain, the opening of those of her ports in South America the most convenient for refitting our whalers on that coast. For the want of this privilege, our people are subjected to needless privations and hardships during voyages of two years' duration.

From Portugal, through the intervention of Great Britain, it could not be difficult to exact, for some adequate compensation which we could offer, the same privileges in Brazil, a station the most convenient to the whaling ground.

Pepper, spices, cottons of various kinds, and, above all, sugar and coffee are, whatever Negro-philanthropists may assert, undoubtedly necessaries of life. Whence are we to derive these, should our present precarious resources be cut off to us? Already, from the disadvantages to which we are subjected, do we pay three prices for them, and a state of things seems likely to arise in which they will be placed utterly without the reach of the middling and lower orders. Such a contingency, when we have it so fairly in our power, it would be the height of folly not to foreclose. Besides, while we deduce these commodities from the possessions of foreign powers, we can never be said to be truly independent. While we have to ask Great Britain, or France, or Denmark for supplies which we cannot dispense with, those nations have a *lien* upon us, a security for our good behavior, which is derogatory to our dignity and inconsistent with our self-will.

The attainment of these ends is believed with confidence to be neither impracticable nor difficult; for although our repulsive and jealous disposition toward Great Britain may cause her now to view us as aspiring to become a rival with her in certain branches of her commerce, yet, once entered on a footing of good intelligence and honorable confidence, the ground would be wholly changed, and by judicious playing into each other's hands, the two nations might and would concenter on their own ports the commerce of the whole world.

Under the auspices of such a system of action, what terrestrial power could interfere with us, what violence could jostle us, what unrevenged insult, degrade or annoy?

A national character is thus at once founded, and the American name, ceasing to be an opprobrium, shall pass abroad over the earth as the denomination of a race of men illustrious for their courage and the wisdom of their policy.

On this theme, I could dwell forever. It will be the salvation of the country. Nay, the country is otherwise doomed to irretrievable perdition. It is a long and a dark night that succeeds the going down of our sun, now just lingering above the horizon. There was a time, and opportunity too, which seized, had placed us far beyond the reach of those dire calamities which have assailed us, and those worse which threaten. But we were cast upon Time for deliverance, and Time has betrayed us; for the period of war is about to expire, and the circumstances and the relations of things by which we were to have profited expire along with it.

It is worthwhile to reflect on the condition in which a peace will probably place us.

We shall have upon our hands a controversy with Great Britain; which, being for no less an object than $21,000,000, can be regarded in no very trifling nor insignificant light. With regard to France, what better aspect would our circumstances wear? His Majesty, restored to the throne of his ancestors, can feel little disposition to amity with those who have uniformly aided and abetted the murderers of his princely brother. Nay, what is more likely than that he would demand the reimbursement of the money loaned us by the Crown?

It must be confessed that should we be swallowed up by this coalition of power, we shall have been accessory to our own destruction; for we have given to each and either mortal offenses enough to justify a war of extermination against us.

But the present deplorable aspects may brighten; there is yet an interval open for our rescue: and the people are and have long been ready and willing to embrace it. May there speedily arise those who are able and willing to lead them out of this dark valley of the shadow of death into the path of political salvation.

23.

William Duane: The Army and a Free Press

William Duane, editor of the Philadelphia Aurora, *was one of the more outstanding spokesmen for the Republicans. As a result of provocative articles in the* Aurora, *describing in sensational terms the army's suppression of Fries's Rebellion and other tumultuous incidents in the Pennsylvania countryside, a few soldiers took it upon themselves to avenge the army. In an article that appeared in the* Aurora *on May 16, 1799, Duane condemned the soldiers' actions.*

Source: *Philadelphia Aurora,* May 16, 1799.

After the conduct of the Lancaster Troop toward Mr. Schneider, printer, of Reading; after the vindication of that conduct by General Macpherson's aides-de-camp, it was hardly to be expected that any republican printer or editor should be exempt from similar violence.

The *Aurora* has been long an object of dread and abhorrence to the detestable faction that has labored with so much violence and dishonor to subject these free states to principles and institutions subversive of the republican form of government.

The late editor of the *Aurora* was publicly, unprovokedly assaulted, and the violator of public law was as publicly honored by an appointment on a public mission.

The present editor, without the advantage of being a descendant of the memorable founder of the American republic, could not hope to escape the hatred which must have arisen with increased force in proportion to the success with which the principles of republicanism and the spirit of resistance to oppression were sustained by him and with the same unabated zeal as by his predecessor.

This temper toward the present editor has been, on several occasions and in several modes, manifested to him. But the cowardice of those who hated would not suffer them to attack him individually — it would not suffer them to accept his repeated offers of satisfaction in the ordinary form which men of honor adjust differences which the laws do not embrace.

Yesterday, a band of those friends of good order and regular government, to the amount of near thirty, entered the office of the *Aurora,* and, while the editor was pursuing his business, assaulted him; while some of the band acted as sentinels on the compositors and pressmen, and others, with presented pistols, kept some persons who chanced to be in the office at bay, Peter Merkin, who was the principal of those dastards, with several others, seized the editor by violence [and] struck him several times on the head, while others held his hands. By force they dragged him downstairs into Franklin Court and there repeated their violence by reiterated blows from above ten different persons.

It was in vain that the editor offered personal satisfaction to any or to all of them successively, equally disregardful of the principles of honor as of the established laws; they had neither the courage to attack him singly nor to accept the resort of men of honor.

After having satiated their malice by blows which the editor was no longer able and could not from their number either effectually retaliate or repel, they sought to add what they conceived to be dishonor on the editor by several blows with a whip. Upon whom the dishonor rests, the public will determine; the editor neither feels it nor fears them, either collectively or individually.

If any circumstance could more deeply impress on his mind than the conviction of a mature and experienced judgment, the obligations which he is under to the public in his profession as editor, and in his principles as a citizen, and to himself as a man — the obligations which he is under to expose villainy to public censure, to expose despotic and wicked men to public execration, to guard with the vigilance of republican jealousy against the artifices, the intrigues, and the injustice of arbitrary men — this conduct would only more and more attach him to his principles. But he has never slackened since he has had the honor to hold his present situation; and while he holds it, his hand must perish or his vital principle must be suspended by the hand of some of those assassins before he will shrink from exposing villains and crimes to public obloquy.

24.

Thomas Jefferson: On Science and the Perfectibility of Man

Science and mathematics were high on the long list of subjects that interested Jefferson, and he thus took special care in replying to a letter from William Green Mumford, who had sought Jefferson's opinion of their importance. In the portion of his letter to Mumford of June 18, 1799, that is reprinted here, Jefferson related the study of science to the freedom and perfectibility of the human mind.

Source: "A Tribute to Philip May Hamer on the Completion of Ten Years as Executive Director, the National Historical Publications Commission," New York, December 29, 1960.

I have to acknowledge the receipt of your favor of May 14, in which you mention that you have finished the first six books of Euclid, plane trigonometry, surveying, and algebra, and ask whether I think a further pursuit of that branch of science would be useful to you. There are some propositions in the latter books of Euclid, and some of Archimedes, which are useful, and I have no doubt you have been made acquainted with them. Trigonometry, so far as this, is most valuable to every man; there is scarcely a day in which he will not resort to it for some of the purposes of common life.

The science of calculation also is indispensable as far as the extraction of the square and cube roots; algebra as far as the quadratic equation and the use of logarithms is often of value in ordinary cases. But all beyond these is but a luxury; a delicious luxury, indeed, but not to be indulged in by one who is to have a profession to follow for his subsistence. In this light I view the conic sections, curves of the higher orders, perhaps even spherical trigonometry, algebraical operations beyond the second dimension and fluxions.

There are other branches of science, however, worth the attention of every man: astronomy, botany, chemistry, natural philosophy, natural history, anatomy. Not indeed to be a proficient in them but to possess their general principles and outlines, so as that we may be able to amuse and inform ourselves further in any of them as we proceed through life and have occasion for them. Some knowledge of them is necessary for our character as well as comfort. The general elements of astronomy and of natural philosophy are best acquired at an academy where we can have the benefit of the instruments and apparatus usually provided there. But the others may well be acquired from books alone as far as our purposes require. I have indulged myself in these observations to you because the evidence cannot be unuseful to you of a person who has often had occasion to consider which of his acquisitions in science have been really useful to him in life, and which of them have been merely a matter of luxury.

I am among those who think well of the human character generally. I consider man as formed for society and endowed by nature with those dispositions which fit him for society. I believe also, with Condorcet, as mentioned in your letter, that his mind is perfectible to a degree of which we cannot as yet form any conception. It is impossible for a man who takes a survey of what is already known not to see what an immensity in every branch of science yet remains to be discovered, and that too of articles to which our faculties seem adequate.

In geometry and calculation we know a great deal. Yet there are some desiderata. In anatomy great progress has been made, but much is still to be acquired. In natural history we possess knowledge, but we want a great deal. In chemistry we are not yet sure of the first elements. Our natural philosophy is in a very infantine state; perhaps for great advances in it, a further progress in chemistry is necessary. Surgery is well advanced, but prodigiously short of what may be. The state of medicine is worse than that of total ignorance. Could we divest ourselves of everything we suppose we know in it, we should start from a higher ground and with fairer prospects.

From Hippocrates to Brown we have had nothing but a succession of hypothetical systems, each having its day of vogue, like the fashions and fancies of caps and gowns, and yielding in turn to the next caprice. Yet the human frame, which is to be the subject of suffering and torture under these learned modes, does not change. We have a few medicines, as the bark, opium, mercury, which in a few well-defined diseases are of unquestionable virtue; but the residuary list of the materia medica, long as it is, contains but the charlataneries of the art; and of the diseases of doubtful form, physicians have ever had a false knowledge, worse than ignorance. Yet surely the list of unequivocal diseases and remedies is capable of enlargement; and it is still more certain that in the other branches of science, great fields are yet to be explored to which our faculties are equal, and that to an extent of which we cannot fix the limits.

I join you, therefore, in branding as cowardly the idea that the human mind is incapable of further advances. This is precisely the doctrine which the present despots of the earth are inculcating and their friends here reechoing; and applying especially to religion and politics, "that it is not probable that anything better will be discovered than what was known to our fathers." We are to look backward, then, and not forward for the improvement of science, and to find it amidst feudal barbarians and the fires of Spitalfields. But thank heaven the American mind is already too much opened to listen to these impostures; and while the art of printing is left to us, science can never be retrograde; what is once acquired of real knowledge can never be lost.

To preserve the freedom of the human mind, then, and freedom of the press, every spirit should be ready to devote itself to martyrdom; for as long as we may think as we will and speak as we think, the condition of man will proceed in improvement.

The generation which is going off the stage has deserved well of mankind for the struggles it has made, and for having arrested that course of despotism which had overwhelmed the world for thousands and thousands of years. If there seems to be danger that the ground they have gained will be lost again, that danger comes from the generation your contemporary.

But that the enthusiasm which characterizes youth should lift its parricide hands against freedom and science would be such a monstrous phenomenon as I cannot place among possible things in this age and this country. Your college at least has shown itself incapable of it; and if the youth of any other place have seemed to rally under other banners, it has been from delusions which they will soon dissipate.

I shall be happy to hear from you from time to time, and of your progress in study, and to be useful to you in whatever is in my power.

25.

George Washington: Last Will and Testament

George Washington signed his last will and testament on July 9, 1799, five months before his sudden death. Among other provisions, the will directed that his slaves be freed (not, however, until the death of his wife) and that certain funds be used to establish a national university. The latter stipulation was never fulfilled.

Source: WGW, XIV, pp. 271-298.

I, George Washington of Mount Vernon, a citizen of the United States and lately President of the same, do make, ordain, and declare this instrument, which is written with my own hand and every page thereof subscribed with my name, to be my last will and testament, revoking all others.

Imprimus — All my debts, of which there are but few, and none of magnitude, are to be punctually and speedily paid, and the legacies hereinafter bequeathed are to be discharged as soon as circumstances will permit and in the manner directed.

Item — To my dearly beloved wife, Martha Washington, I give and bequeath the use, profit, and benefit of my whole estate, real and personal, for the term of her natural life, except such parts thereof as are specially disposed of hereafter. My improved lot in the town of Alexandria, situated on Pitt and Cameron streets, I give to her and her heirs forever, as I also do my household and kitchen furniture of every sort and kind, with the liquors and groceries which may be on hand at the time of my decease, to be used and disposed of as she may think proper.

Item — Upon the decease of [my] wife it is my will and desire that all the slaves which I hold in my own right shall receive their freedom. To emancipate them during her life would, though earnestly wished by me, be attended with such insuperable difficulties, on account of their intermixture by marriages with the dower Negroes, as to excite the most painful sensations, if not disagreeable consequences from the latter, while both descriptions are in the occupancy of the same proprietor; it not being in my power under the tenure by which the dower Negroes are held to manumit them. And whereas among those who will receive freedom according to this device, there may be some who from old age or bodily infirmities, and others on account of their infancy, that will be unable to support themselves, it is my will and desire that all who come under the first and second description shall be comfortably clothed and fed by my heirs while they live and that such of the latter description as have no parents living, or if living are unable or unwilling to provide for them, shall be bound by the court until they shall arrive at the age of twenty-five years; and in cases where no record can be produced whereby their ages can be ascertained, the judgment of the court upon its own view of the subject shall be adequate and final. The Negroes thus bound are (by their masters and mistresses) to be taught to read and write and to be brought up to some useful occupation, agreeably to the laws of the Commonwealth of Virginia, providing for the support of orphans and other poor children. I do hereby expressly forbid the sale or transportation out of the said commonwealth of any slave I may die possessed of, under any pretense whatsoever. And I do moreover most positively and most solemnly enjoin it upon my executors hereafter named, or the survivors of them, to see that this clause respecting slaves and every part thereof be religiously fulfilled at the epoch at which it is directed to take place without evasion, neglect, or delay after the crops which may then be on the ground are harvested, particularly as it respects the aged and infirm, seeing that a regular and permanent fund be established for their support so long as there are subjects requiring it, not trusting to the uncertain provisions to be made by individuals.

And to my mulatto man, William (calling himself William Lee), I give immediate freedom or, if he should prefer it (on account of the accidents which have befallen him and which have rendered him incapable of walking or of any active employment), to remain in the situation he now is, it shall be optional in him to do so. In either case, however, I allow him an annuity of $30 during his natural life, which shall be independent of the victuals and clothes he has been accustomed to receive, if he chooses the last alternative; but in full with his freedom, if he prefers the first; and this I give him as a testimony of my sense of his attachment to me and for his faithful services during the Revolutionary War.

Item — To the trustees (governors or by whatsoever other name they may be designated) of the academy in the town of Alexandria, I give and bequeath, in trust, $4,000, or, in other words, twenty of the shares which I hold in the Bank of Alexandria towards the support of a free school, established at and annexed to the said academy, for the purpose of educating such orphan children, or the children of such other poor and indigent persons as are unable to accomplish it with their own means, and who in the judgment of the trustees of the said seminary are best entitled to the benefits of this donation. The aforesaid twenty shares I give and bequeath in perpetuity, the dividends only of which are to be drawn for and applied by the said trustees for the time being, for the uses above mentioned, the stock to remain entire and untouched unless indications of a failure of the said bank should be so apparent or discontinuance thereof should render a removal of this fund necessary. In either of these cases the amount of the stock here devised is to be vested in some other bank or public institution whereby the interest may with regularity and certainty be drawn and applied as above. And to prevent misconception, my meaning is . . . that these twenty shares are in lieu of and not in addition to the £1,000 given by a missive letter some years ago in consequence whereof an annuity of £50 has since been paid toward the support of this institution.

Item — Whereas by a law of the Commonwealth of Virginia, enacted in the year 1785, the legislature thereof was pleased (as an evidence of its approbation of the services I had rendered the public during the Revolution — and partly, I believe, in consideration of my having suggested the vast advantages which the community would derive from the extension of its inland navigation, under legislative patronage) to present me with 100 shares of $100 each in the incorporated company established for the purpose of extending the navigation of James River from tidewater to the mountains, and also with 50 shares of £100 sterling each in the corporation of another company likewise established for the similar purpose of opening the navigation of the Potomac River from tidewater to Fort Cumberland — the acceptance of which, although the offer was highly honorable and grateful to my feelings, was refused as inconsistent with a principle which I had adopted and had never departed from, namely, not to receive pecuniary compensation for any services I could render my country in its arduous struggle with Great Britain for its rights — and because I had evaded similar propositions from other states in the Union, adding to this refusal, however, an intimation that if it should be the pleasure of the legislature to permit me to appropriate the said shares to public uses, I would receive them on those terms with due sensibility. And this it having consented to in flattering terms, as will appear by a subsequent law and sundry resolutions, in the most ample and honorable manner, I proceed after this recital for the more correct understanding of the case to declare:

That as it has always been a source of serious regret with me to see the youth of these United States sent to foreign countries for the purpose of education, often before their minds were formed or they had imbibed any adequate ideas of the happiness of their own, contracting too frequently not only habits of dissipation and extravagance but principles unfriendly to republican government and to the true and genuine liberties of mankind, which thereafter are rarely overcome. For these reasons it has been my ardent wish to see a plan devised on a liberal scale which would have a tendency to spread systematic ideas through all parts of this rising empire, thereby to do away local attachments and state prejudices as far as the nature of things would, or, indeed, ought to admit from our national councils. Looking anxiously forward to the accomplishment of so desirable an object as this is (in my estimation), my mind has not been able to contemplate any plan more likely to effect the measure than the establishment of a university in a central part of the United States to which the youth of fortune and talents from all parts thereof might be sent for the completion of their education in all the branches of polite literature in arts and sciences, in acquiring knowledge in the principles of politics and good government, and (as a matter of infinite importance in my judgment) by associating with each other and forming friendships in juvenile years, be enabled to free themselves in a proper degree from those local prejudices and habitual jealousies which have just been mentioned and which when carried to excess are never failing sources of disquietude to the public mind and pregnant of mischievous consequences to this country under these impressions so fully dilated.

Item — I give and bequeath in perpetuity the fifty shares which I hold in the Potomac Company (under the aforesaid acts of the legislature of Virginia) towards the endowment of a university to be established within the limits of the District of Columbia, under the auspices of the general government, if that government should incline to extend a fostering hand towards it; and until such seminary is established, and the funds arising on these shares shall be required for its support, my further will and desire is that the profit accruing therefrom shall, whenever the dividends are made, be laid out in purchasing stock in the Bank of Columbia or some other bank at the discretion of my executors, or by the treasurer of the United States for the time being under the direction of Congress, provided that honorable body should patronize the measure. And the dividends proceeding from the purchase of such stock is to be vested in more stock and so on until a sum adequate to the accomplishment of the object is obtained, of which I have not the smallest doubt before many years pass away, even if no aid or encouragement is given by legislative authority or from any other source.

Item — The 100 shares which I held in the James River Company I have given and now confirm in perpetuity to and for the use and benefit of Liberty Hall Academy in the county of Rockbridge, in the Commonwealth of Virginia. . . .

Item — To my nephew, Bushrod Washington, I give and bequeath all the papers in my possession which relate to my civil and military administration of the affairs of this country. I leave to him also such of my private papers as are worth preserving. At the decease of my wife, and before, if she is not inclined to retain them, I give and bequeath my library of books and pamphlets of every kind. . . .

To each of my nephews: William Augustine Washington, George Lewis, George Steptoe Washington, Bushrod Washington, and Samuel Washington, I give one of the swords or *cutteaux* of which I may die possessed, and they are to choose in the order they are named. These swords are accompanied with an injunction not to unsheath them for the purpose of shedding blood except it be for self-defense, or in defense of their country and its rights, and in the latter case to keep them unsheathed and prefer falling with them in their hands to the relinquishment thereof. . . .

And by way of advice, I recommended it to my executors not to be precipitate in disposing of the landed property (herein directed to be sold) if from temporary causes the sale thereof should be dull; experience having fully evinced that the price of land (especially above the falls of the rivers and on the western waters) have been progressively rising and cannot be long checked in its increasing value. I particularly recommend it to such of the legatees (under this clause of my will) as can make it convenient to take each a share of my stock in the Potomac Company in preference to the amount of what it might sell for, being thoroughly convinced myself that no uses to which the money can be applied will be so productive as the tolls arising from this navigation when in full operation (and this from the nature of things it must be before long) and more especially if that of the Shenandoah is added thereto.

The family vault at Mount Vernon requiring repairs, and being improperly situated besides, I desire that a new one of brick, and upon a larger scale, may be built at the foot of what is commonly called the Vineyard Enclosure, on the ground which is marked out, in which my remains, with those of my deceased relatives (now in the old vault) and such others of my family as may choose to be entombed there, may be deposited. And it is my express desire that my corpse may be interred in a private manner, without parade or funeral oration.

Lastly — I constitute and appoint my dearly beloved wife, Martha Washington; my nephews William Augustine Washington, Bushrod Washington, George Steptoe Washington, Samuel Washington, and Lawrence Lewis; and my ward, George Washington Parke Custis (when he shall have arrived at the age of twenty years), executrix and executors of this will and testament — in the construction of which it will readily be perceived that no professional character has been consulted or has had any agency in the draft — and that, although it has occupied many of my leisure hours to digest and to put it into its present form, it may notwithstanding appear crude and incorrect. But having endeavored to be plain and explicit in all the devises, even at the expense of prolixity, perhaps of tautology, I hope and trust that no disputes will arise concerning them; but if contrary to expectation the case should be otherwise from the want of legal expression or the usual technical terms, or because too much or too little has been said on any of the devises to be consonant with law, my will and direction expressly is that all disputes (if unhappily any should arise) shall be decided by three impartial and intelligent men, known for their probity and good understanding — two to be chosen by the disputants, each having the choice of one, and the third by those two — which three men thus chosen shall unfettered by law or legal constructions declare their sense of the testator's intention. And such decision is, to all intents and purposes, to be as binding on the parties as if it had been given in the Supreme Court of the United States.

In witness of all and of each of the things herein contained I have set my hand and seal this 9th day of July, in the year 1799, and of the independence of the United States, the twenty-fourth.

26.

Gouverneur Morris: Appeal to Washington to Return to Public Life

When George Washington retired at the end of his second term in the presidency, many were unhappy at the loss of this popular figure who alone was capable, they believed, of keeping within bounds the party strife that had already manifested itself in the politics of the day. Political differences became even more acute under John Adams, and the leaders of his Federalist Party began to realize that he was unlikely to be reelected in 1800. To men like Gouverneur Morris, the political views of the Republican opposition's leading candidate, Thomas Jefferson, were anathema. Morris, having served under Washington as minister to France, and believing the ex-President to be the only person who could unify the country, urged him, in a letter written on December 9, 1799, to return to public life. It is unlikely that Washington, who died on December 14, ever saw the letter.

Source: *The Life of Gouverneur Morris, etc., etc.,* Jared Sparks, ed., Boston, 1832, Vol. III, pp. 123-125.

During a late visit to New York, I learned that the leading characters, even in Massachusetts, consider Mr. Adams as unfit for the office he now holds. Without pretending to decide on the merits of that opinion, which will operate alike whether well or ill-founded, it appeared necessary to name some other person. You will easily conceive that his predecessor was wished for and regretted, nor will you be surprised that the doubt whether he would again accept should have excited much concern; for you are so perfectly acquainted with the different characters in America, and with the opinions which prevail respecting them, that you must be convinced, however painful the conviction, that should you decline, no man will be chosen whom you would wish to see in that high office.

Believing then that the dearest interests of our country are at stake, I beg leave to speak to you freely on this subject.

No reasonable man can doubt that after a life of glorious labor you must wish for repose, and it would not be surprising that a wish so natural should, by frequent disappointment, have acquired the force of passion. But is retirement in the strict sense of the word a possible thing? And is the half retirement, which you may attain to, more peaceful than public life? Nay, has it not the disadvantage of leaving you involved in measures which you can neither direct nor control? Another question suggests itself from another view of the subject. Will you not, when the seat of government is in your neighborhood, enjoy more retirement as President of the United States than as general of the army? And in the same view again, another question arises. May not your acceptance be the needful means of fixing the government in that seat?

There is a more important consideration. Shall the vast treasure of your fame be committed to the uncertainty of events, be exposed to the attempts of envy, and subject to the spoliation of slander? From envy and slander no retreat is safe but the grave, and you must not yet hide yourself behind that bulwark. As to the influence of events, if there be a human being who may look them fairly in the face, you are the man. Recollect, sir, that each occasion which has brought you back on the public stage has been to you the means of new and greater glory. If General Washington had not become a member of the Convention, he would have been considered only as the defender and not as the legislator of his country. And if the president of the Convention had not become President of the United States, he would not have added the character of a statesman to those of a patriot and a hero. Your modesty may repel these titles, but Europe has conferred them, and the world will set its seal of approbation when, in these tempestuous times, your country shall have again confided the helm of her affairs to your steady hand.

But you may perhaps say that you stand indirectly pledged to private life. Surely, sir, you neither gave nor meant to give such a pledge, to the extent of possible contingencies. The acceptance of your present office proves that you did not. Nay, you stand pledged by all your former conduct that when circumstances arise which shall require it, you will act again. These circumstances seem to be now imminent, and it is meet that you consider them on the broad ground of your extensive information.

Ponder them I pray you, and whatever may be the decision, pardon my freedom and believe me truly yours.

To the memory of the man, first in war, first in peace, and first in the hearts of his countrymen.

HENRY ("LIGHT-HORSE HARRY") LEE, eulogy on George Washington adopted by the Congress Dec. 26, 1799

The prevailin' weakness of most public men is to slop over. G. Washington never slopt over.

CHARLES FARRAR BROWNE ("ARTEMUS WARD"), *Fourth of July Oration*

1800

27.

"Down in the Valley"

The origins of "Down in the Valley" are uncertain. It is thought that the tune, at least, has been known in England for hundreds of years, and some of the song's verbal conceits go back more than two centuries. The familiar words reprinted below, or variants of them, were probably first sung in the hills of Kentucky, in areas settled mainly by English, Scotch, and Irish, around 1800. Verses have been added to the song at various times; the one in our version that refers to the Birmingham Jail could not have been sung before 1871, when Birmingham, Alabama, was founded. In fact, the song has usually contained such a verse making reference to a jail in the vicinity of the singer. Thus versions of the song exist in which the singer makes mention of "Powder Mill Jail," "Barbourville Jail," and so forth. The name hardly matters, for the point remains the same. In recent times, the song was a favorite of Carl Sandburg, who did much to bring about its modern revival.

DOWN IN THE VALLEY

Down in the valley, the valley so low,
Hang your head over, hear the wind blow.
Hear the wind blow, dear, hear the wind blow,
Hang your head over, hear the wind blow.

If you don't love me, love whom you please;
Throw your arms round me, give my heart ease.
Give my heart ease, dear, give my heart ease, etc.

Write me a letter, send it by mail;
Send it in care of the Birmingham Jail.
Birmingham Jail, dear, Birmingham Jail, etc.

Writing this letter, containing three lines,
Answer my question: "Will you be mine?"
"Will you be mine, dear, will you be mine?" etc.

Build me a castle, forty feet high,
So I can see her as she rides by.
As she rides by, dear, as she rides by, etc.

Roses love sunshine, violets love dew;
Angels in heaven know I love you.
Know I love you, dear, know I love you, etc.

28.

JAMES MADISON: The Freedom of the Press

Having been elected to the Virginia House of Delegates in 1799, Madison at once undertook to prepare a report defending his Virginia Resolutions of 1798 against the hostile replies of Federalist majorities in the northeastern states. His task was made easier in that, unlike Jefferson, whose Kentucky resolutions had asserted that any state legislature might "interpose" against the exercise of unauthorized powers by the national government, Madison had claimed such a right only for all the states together. A generation later, in 1832, when his and Jefferson's words were cited by the South Carolina nullifiers in support of their doctrine, Madison, then eighty-two, denied that there had been any intent actually to nullify either on his part or on that of his old friend. Could this "abuse" of the resolutions have been foreseen, Madison declared, their language "would doubtless have been varied." The portion of Madison's report reprinted here deals with the freedom of the press, particularly as it related to the suppressive Sedition Act. Madison wrote the report in December 1799, and the Virginia legislature approved it in January 1800.

Source: Elliot, IV, pp. 546-580.

THE NEXT POINT which the resolution requires to be proved is that the power over the press exercised by the Sedition Act is positively forbidden by one of the amendments to the Constitution.

The amendment stands in these words: "Congress shall make no law respecting an establishment of religion, or prohibiting the free exercise thereof; or abridging the freedom of speech or of the press; or the right of the people peaceably to assemble, and to petition the government for a redress of grievances."

In the attempts to vindicate the Sedition Act, it has been contended: (1) that the "freedom of the press" is to be determined by the meaning of these terms in the common law; (2) that the article supposes the power over the press to be in Congress, and prohibits them only from abridging the freedom allowed to it by the common law. . . .

The essential difference between the British government and the American constitutions will place this subject in the clearest light.

In the British government, the danger of encroachments on the rights of the people is understood to be confined to the executive magistrate. The representatives of the people in the legislature are not only exempt themselves from distrust but are considered as sufficient guardians of the rights of their constituents against the danger from the executive. Hence it is a principle that the Parliament is unlimited in its power; or, in their own language, is omnipotent. Hence, too, all the ramparts for protecting the rights of the people, such as their Magna Charta, their Bill of Rights, etc., are not reared against the Parliament but against the royal prerogative. They are merely legislative precautions against executive usurpations. Under such a government as this, an exemption of the press from previous restraint by licensers appointed by the king is all the freedom that can be secured to it.

In the United States the case is altogether different. The people, not the government, possess the absolute sovereignty. The legislature, no less than the executive, is under limitations of power. Encroachments are regarded as possible from the one as well as from the other. Hence, in the United States, the great and essential rights of the people are secured against legislative as well as against executive ambition. They are secured not by laws paramount to prerogative but by constitutions paramount to laws. This security of the freedom of the press requires that it should be exempt not only from previous restraint by the executive, as in Great Britain, but from legislative restraint also; and this exemption, to be effectual, must be an exemption not only from the previous inspection of licensers but from the subsequent penalty of laws.

The state of the press, therefore, under the common law, cannot, in this point of view, be the standard of its freedom in the United States. . . .

The nature of governments elective, limited, and responsible, in all their branches, may well be supposed to require a greater freedom of animadversion that might be tolerated by the genius of such a government as that of Great Britain. In the latter, it is a maxim that the king, a hereditary, not a responsible, magistrate, can do no wrong; and that the legislature, which in two-thirds of its composition is also hereditary, not responsible, can do what it pleases. In the United States, the executive magistrates are not held to be infallible nor the legislatures to be omnipotent; and both being elective are both responsible. Is it not natural and necessary, under such different circumstances, that a different degree of freedom in the use of the press should be contemplated?

Is not such an inference favored by what is observable in Great Britain itself? Notwithstanding the general doctrine of the common law on the subject of the press, and the occasional punishment of those who use it with a freedom offensive to the government; it is well known that with respect to the responsible measures of the government, where the reasons operating here become applicable there, the freedom exercised by the press and protected by the public opinion far exceeds the limits prescribed by the ordinary rules of law. The ministry, who are responsible to impeachment, are at all times animadverted on by the press with peculiar freedom; and during the elections for the House of Commons, the other responsible part of the government, the press is employed with as little reserve towards the candidates.

The practice in America must be entitled to much more respect. In every state, probably, in the Union, the press has exerted a freedom in canvassing the merits and measures of public men of every description which has not been confined to the strict limits of the common law. On this footing, the freedom of the press has stood; on this footing it yet stands. And it will not be a breach, either of truth or of candor, to say that no persons or presses are in the habit of more unrestrained animadversions on the proceedings and functionaries of the state governments than the persons and presses most zealous in vindicating the act of Congress for punishing similar animadversions on the government of the United States.

The last remark will not be understood as claiming for the state governments an immunity greater than they have heretofore enjoyed. Some degree of abuse is inseparable from the proper use of everything; and in no instances is this more true than in that of the press. It has accordingly been decided by the practice of the states that it is better to leave a few of its noxious branches to their luxuriant growth than, by pruning them away, to injure the vigor of those yielding the proper fruits. And can the wisdom of this policy be doubted by anyone who reflects that to the press alone, checkered as it is with abuses, the world is indebted for all the triumphs which have been gained by reason and humanity over error and oppression; who reflect that to the same beneficent source the United States owe much of the lights which conducted them to the rank of a free and independent nation, and which have improved their political system into a shape so auspicious to their happiness? Had sedition acts, forbidding every publication that might bring the constituted agents into contempt or disrepute, or that might excite the hatred of the people against the authors of unjust or pernicious measures, been uniformly enforced against the press, might not the United States have been languishing at this day under the infirmities of a sickly confederation? Might they not possibly be miserable colonies, groaning under a foreign yoke?

To these observations one fact will be added, which demonstrates that the common law cannot be admitted as the universal expositor of American terms, which may be the same with those contained in that law. The freedom of conscience and of religion are found in the same instrument which asserts the freedom of the press. It will never be admitted that the meaning of the former, in the common law of England, is to limit their meaning in the United States.

Whatever weight may be allowed to these considerations, the committee do not, however, by any means, intend to rest the question on them. They contend that the article of amendment, instead of supposing in Congress a power that might be exercised over the press, provided its freedom was not abridged, was meant as a positive denial to Congress of any power whatever on the subject.

To demonstrate that this was the true object of the article, it will be sufficient to recall the circumstances which led to it, and to refer to the explanation accompanying the article.

When the Constitution was under the discussions which preceded its ratification, it is well known that great apprehensions were expressed by many, lest the omission of some positive exception from the powers delegated, of certain rights, and of the freedom of the press particularly, might expose them to the danger of being drawn by construction within some of the powers vested in Congress, more especially of the power to make all laws necessary and proper for carrying their other powers into execution. In reply to this objection, it was invariably urged to be a fundamental and characteristic principle of the Constitution that all powers not given by it were reserved; that no powers were given beyond those enumerated in the Constitution and such as were fairly incident to them; that the power over the rights in question, and particularly over the press, was neither among the enumerated powers nor incident to any of them; and consequently that an exercise of any such power would be a manifest usurpation. It is painful to remark how much the arguments now employed in behalf of the Sedition Act are at variance with the reasoning which then justified the Constitution and invited its ratification.

From this posture of the subject resulted the interesting question in so many of the conventions, whether the doubts and dangers ascribed to the Constitution should be removed by any amendments previous to the ratification, or be postponed, in confidence that as far as they might be proper, they would be introduced in the form provided by the Constitution. The latter course was adopted; and in most of the states, the ratifications were followed by propositions and instructions for rendering the Constitution more explicit and more safe to the rights not meant to be delegated by it. Among those rights, the freedom of the press, in most instances, is particularly and emphatically mentioned. The firm and very pointed manner in which it is asserted in the proceedings of the convention of this state will be hereafter seen.

In pursuance of the wishes thus expressed, the first Congress that assembled under the Constitution proposed certain amendments, which have since, by the necessary ratifications, been made a part of it; among which amendments is the article containing, among other prohibitions on the Congress, an express declaration that they should make no law abridging the freedom of the press.

Without tracing farther the evidence on this subject, it will seem scarcely possible to doubt that no power whatever over the press was supposed to be delegated by the Constitution, as it originally stood; and that the amendment was intended as a positive and absolute reservation of it.

But the evidence is still stronger. The proposition of amendments made by Congress is introduced in the following terms:

> The conventions of a number of the states having at the time of their adopting the Constitution expressed a desire, in order to prevent misconstructions or abuse of its powers, that further declaratory and restrictive clauses should be added; and as extending the ground of public confidence in the government, will best ensure the beneficent ends of its institutions.

Here is the most satisfactory and authentic proof that the several amendments proposed were to be considered as either declaratory or restrictive, and whether the one or the other, as corresponding with the desire expressed by a number of the states and as extending the ground of public confidence in the government.

Under any other construction of the amendment relating to the press than that it declared the press to be wholly exempt from the power of Congress, the amendment could neither be said to correspond with the desire expressed by a number of the states nor be calculated to extend the ground of public confidence in the government.

Nay more; the construction employed to justify the Sedition Act would exhibit a phenomenon without a parallel in the political world. It would exhibit a number of respectable states as denying first that any power over the press was delegated by the Constitution; as proposing next that an amendment to it should explicitly declare that no such power was delegated; and finally, as concurring in an amendment actually recognizing or delegating such a power.

Is then the federal government, it will be asked, destitute of every authority for restraining the licentiousness of the press, and for shielding itself against the libelous attacks which may be made on those who administer it?

The Constitution alone can answer this question. If no such power be expressly delegated and it be not both necessary and proper to carry into execution an express power, above all, if it be expressly forbidden by a declaratory amendment to the Constitution, the answer must be that the federal government is destitute of all such authority.

And might it not be asked in turn whether it is not more probable, under all the circumstances which have been reviewed, that the authority should be withheld by the Constitution than that it should be left to a vague and violent construction; whilst so much pains were bestowed in enumerating other powers, and so many less important powers are included in the enumeration?

Might it not be likewise asked whether the anxious circumspection which dictated so many peculiar limitations on the general authority would be unlikely to exempt the press altogether from that authority? The peculiar magnitude of some of the powers necessarily committed to the federal government; the peculiar duration required for the functions of some of its departments; the peculiar distance of the seat of its proceedings from the great body of its constituents; and the peculiar difficulty of circulating an adequate knowledge of them through any other channel — will not these considerations, some or other of which produced other exceptions from the powers of ordinary governments, all together account for the policy of binding the hand of the federal government from touching the channel which alone can give efficacy to its responsibility to its constituents; and of leaving those who administer it, to a remedy for their injured reputations, under the same laws and in the same tribunals which protect their lives, their liberties, and their properties?

But the question does not turn either on the wisdom of the Constitution or on the policy which gave rise to its particular organization. It turns on the actual meaning of the instrument by which it has appeared that a power over the press is clearly excluded from the number of powers delegated to the federal government.

And in the opinion of the committee, well may it be said, as the resolution concludes with saying, that the unconstitutional power exercised over the press by the Sedition Act ought "more than any other, to produce universal alarm; because it is leveled against that right of freely examining public characters and measures, and of free communication among the people thereon, which has ever been justly deemed the only effectual guardian of every other right."

Without scrutinizing minutely into all the provisions of the Sedition Act, it will be sufficient to cite so much of section 2 as follows:

> And be it further enacted that if any shall write, print, utter, or publish, or shall cause or procure to be written, printed, uttered, or published, or shall knowingly and willingly assist or aid in writing, printing, uttering, or publishing any false, scandalous, and malicious writing or writings against the government of the United States, or either house of the Congress of the United States, or the President of the United States, with an intent to defame the said government, or either house of the said Congress, or the President, or to bring them, or either of them, into contempt or disrepute; or to excite against them, or either, or any of them, the hatred of the good people of the United States, etc. Then such person being thereof convicted before any court of the United States, having jurisdiction thereof, shall be punished by a fine not exceeding $2,000 and by imprisonment not exceeding two years.

On this part of the act, the following observations present themselves:

1. The Constitution supposes that the President, the Congress, and each of its houses may not discharge their trusts, either from defect of judgment or other causes. Hence, they are all made responsible to their constituents at the returning periods of elections; and the President, who is singly

entrusted with very great powers, is, as a further guard, subjected to an intermediate impeachment.

2. Should it happen, as the Constitution supposes it may happen, that either of these branches of the government may not have duly discharged its trust, it is natural and proper that, according to the cause and degree of their faults, they should be brought into contempt or disrepute and incur the hatred of the people.

3. Whether it has in any case happened that the proceedings of either or all of those branches evince such a violation of duty as to justify a contempt, a disrepute, or hatred among the people, can only be determined by a free examination thereof, and a free communication among the people thereon.

4. Whenever it may have actually happened that proceedings of this sort are chargeable on all or either of the branches of the government, it is the duty as well as right of intelligent and faithful citizens to discuss and promulgate them freely, as well to control them by the censorship of the public opinion as to promote a remedy according to the rules of the Constitution. And it cannot be avoided that those who are to apply the remedy must feel, in some degree, a contempt or hatred against the transgressing party.

5. As the act was passed on July 14, 1798, and is to be in force until March 3, 1801, it was of course, that during its continuance two elections of the entire House of Representatives, an election of a part of the Senate, and an election of a President were to take place.

6. That consequently, during all these elections, intended by the Constitution to preserve the purity or to purge the faults of the administration, the great remedial rights of the people were to be exercised and the responsibility of their public agents to be screened under the penalties of this act.

May it not be asked of every intelligent friend to the liberties of his country whether the power exercised in such an act as this ought not to produce great and universal alarm? Whether a rigid execution of such an act, in time past, would not have repressed that information and communication among the people, which is indispensable to the just exercise of their electoral rights? And whether such an act, if made perpetual and enforced with rigor, would not, in time to come, either destroy our free system of government or prepare a convulsion that might prove equally fatal to it?

In answer to such questions, it has been pleaded that the writings and publications forbidden by the act are those only which are false and malicious and intended to defame; and merit is claimed for the privilege allowed to authors to justify, by proving the truth of their publications, and for the limitations to which the sentence of fine and imprisonment is subjected.

To those who concurred in the act, under the extraordinary belief that the option lay between the passing of such an act and leaving in force the common law of libels, which punishes truth equally with falsehood and submits the fine and imprisonment to the indefinite discretion of the court, the merit of good intentions ought surely not to be refused. A like merit may perhaps be due for the discontinuance of the corporal punishment, which the common law also leaves to the discretion of the court. This merit of intention, however, would have been greater if the several mitigations had not been limited to so short a period; and the apparent inconsistency would have been avoided, between justifying the act at one time, by contrasting it with the rigors of the common law, otherwise in force, and at another time by appealing to the nature of the crisis, as requiring the temporary rigor exerted by the act.

But, whatever may have been the meritorious intentions of all or any who contributed to the Sedition Act, a very few reflections will prove that its baleful tendency is little diminished by the privilege of giving in evidence the truth of the matter contained in political writings.

In the first place, where simple and naked facts alone are in question, there is sufficient difficulty in some cases, and sufficient trouble and vexation in all, in meeting a prosecution from the government with the full and formal proof necessary in a court of law.

But in the next place, it must be obvious to the plainest minds that opinions, and inferences, and conjectural observations, are not only in many cases inseparable from the facts but may often be more the objects of the prosecution than the facts themselves, or may even be altogether abstracted from particular facts; and that opinions and inferences and conjectural observations cannot be subjects of that kind of proof which appertains to facts before a court of law.

Again — it is no less obvious that the *intent* to defame or bring into contempt, or disrepute, or hatred, which is made a condition of the offense created by the act, cannot prevent its pernicious influence on the freedom of the press. For, omitting the inquiry, how far the malice of the intent is an inference of the law from the mere publication, it is manifestly impossible to punish the intent to bring those who administer the government into disrepute or contempt without striking at the right of freely discussing public characters and measures; because those who engage in such discussions must expect and intend to excite these unfavorable sentiments so far as they may be thought to be deserved.

To prohibit, therefore, the intent to excite those unfavorable sentiments against those who administer the government is equivalent to a prohibition of the actual excitement of them; and to prohibit the actual excitement of them is equivalent to a prohibition of discussions having that tendency and effect; which, again, is equivalent to a protection of those who administer the government, if they should at any time deserve the contempt or hatred of the people, against being exposed to it by free animadversions on their characters and conduct. Nor can there be a doubt, if those in public trust be shielded by penal laws from such strictures of the press as may expose them to contempt, or disrepute, or hatred where they may deserve it, in exact proportion as they may deserve to be exposed, will be the certainty and criminality of the intent to expose them and the vigilance of prosecuting and punishing it; nor a doubt that a government thus entrenched in penal statutes against the just and natural effects of a culpable administration will easily evade the responsibility which is essential to a faithful discharge of its duty. . . .

The General Assembly were governed by the clearest reason, then, in considering the Sedition Act, which legislates on the freedom of the press, as establishing a precedent that may be fatal to the liberty of conscience; and it will be the duty of all, in proportion as they value the security of the latter, to take the alarm at every encroachment on the former.

Advertisements contain the only truth to be relied on in a newspaper.

Thomas Jefferson

29.

Land Act of 1800

The new government was faced in the early 1790s with a large national debt and with the problem of settling vast lands in the western public domain. Alexander Hamilton and many congressmen envisioned solving both problems at the same time by selling the land and absorbing the profits into the national treasury. To this end the Land Act of 1796 was passed, which provided for the sale of land at a minimum of $2 an acre. However, the expected onslaught of buyers did not materialize, and many of those who did purchase land were speculators, not settlers. By the end of 1799, it was clear that the 1796 law needed reevaluation. William Henry Harrison, a recently elected congressman from Indiana, was named chairman of a special committee to deal with the question. On March 31, 1800, the committee reported a bill that soon became law. The Land Act of 1800, reprinted here in part, extended credit to purchasers and established land offices to handle transactions, and otherwise gave needed assistance to buyers of small plots, to pioneers, and to farmers.

Source: *Statutes,* II, pp. 73-78.

Section 1. *Be it enacted, by the Senate and House of Representatives of the United States of America in Congress assembled,* that for the disposal of the lands of the United States directed to be sold by the act entitled "An act providing for the sale of the lands of the United States, in the territory northwest of the Ohio and above the mouth of Kentucky River," there shall be four land offices established in the said territory: one at Cincinnati, for lands below the Little Miami which have not heretofore been granted; one at Chillicothe, for lands east of the Scioto, south of the lands appropriated for satisfying military bounties to the late Army of the United States, and west of the fifteenth range of townships; one at Marietta, for the lands east of the sixteenth range of townships, south of the before-mentioned military lands, and south of a line drawn due west from the northwest corner of the first township of the second range, to the said military lands; and one at Steubenville, for the lands north of the last-mentioned line, and east or north of the said military lands.

Each of the said offices shall be under the direction of an officer to be called "The Register of the Land Office," who shall be appointed by the President of the United States, by and with the advice and consent of the Senate, and shall give bond to the United States, with approved security, in the sum of $10,000, for the faithful discharge of the duties of his office; and shall reside at the place where the land office is directed to be kept.

Section 2. *And be it further enacted,* that it shall be the duty of the surveyor general, and he is hereby expressly enjoined, to prepare and transmit to the registers of the several land offices, before the days herein appointed for commencing sales, general plats of the lands hereby directed to be sold at the said offices respectively, and also to forward copies of each of the said plats to the secretary of the treasury.

Section 3. *And be it further enacted,* that the surveyor general shall cause the townships west of the Muskingum, which by the above-mentioned act are directed to be sold in quarter townships, to be subdivided into half sections of 320 acres each, as nearly as may be, by running parallel lines through the same from east to west, and from south to north, at the distance of one mile from each other, and marking corners, at the distance of each half mile on the lines running from east to west, and at the distance of each mile on those running from south to north, and making the marks, notes and descriptions, prescribed to surveyors by the above-mentioned act. . . .

Section 4. *And be it further enacted,* that the lands thus subdivided (excluding the sections reserved by the above-mentioned act) shall be offered for sale in sections and half sections. . . . The sales shall remain open at each place for three weeks, and no longer. The superintendents shall observe the rules and regulations of the above-mentioned act, in classing and selling fractional with entire sections, and in keeping and transmitting accounts of the sales. All lands remaining unsold at the closing of either of the public sales may be disposed of at private sale by the registers of these respective land offices. . . .

Section 5. *And be it further enacted,* that no lands shall be sold by virtue of this act, at either public or private sale, for less than $2 per acre, and payment may be made for the same by all purchasers, either in specie or in evidences of the public debt of the United States, at the rates prescribed by the act entitled "An act to authorize the receipt of evidences of the public debt in payment for the lands of the United States"; and shall be made in the following manner, and under the following conditions, to wit:

1. At the time of purchase, every purchaser shall, exclusively of the fees hereafter mentioned, pay $6 for every section and $3 for every half section he may have purchased for surveying expenses, and deposit one-twentieth part of the amount of purchase money, to be forfeited if within forty days one-fourth part of the purchase money, including the said twentieth part, is not paid.

2. One-fourth part of the purchase money shall be paid within forty days after the day of sale as aforesaid; another fourth part shall be paid within two years; another fourth part within three years; and another fourth part within four years after the day of sale.

3. Interest, at the rate of 6 percent a year from the day of sale shall be charged upon each of the three last payments, payable as they respectively become due.

4. A discount at the rate of 8 percent a year shall be allowed on any of the three last payments, which shall be paid before the same shall become due, reckoning this discount always upon the sum which would have been demandable by the United States, on the day appointed for such payment.

5. If the first payment of one-fourth part of the purchase money shall not be made within forty days after the sale, the deposit, payment, and fees paid and made by the purchaser shall be forfeited, and the lands shall and may, from and after the day when the payment of one-fourth part of the purchase money should have been made, be disposed of at private sale, on the same terms and conditions and in the same manner as the other lands directed by this act to be disposed of at private sale: *Provided,* that the lands which shall have been sold at public sale and which shall, on account of such failure of payment, revert to the Unit-

ed States shall not be sold at private sale for a price less than the price that shall have been offered for the same at public sale. . . .

Section 15. *And be it further enacted,* that the lands of the United States reserved for future disposition may be let upon leases by the surveyor general, in sections or half sections, for terms not exceeding seven years, on condition of making such improvements as he shall deem reasonable.

Section 16. *And be it further enacted,* that each person who, before the passing of this act, shall have erected, or begun to erect, a gristmill or sawmill upon any of the lands herein directed to be sold, shall be entitled to the preemption of the section, including such mill, at the rate of $2 per acre: *Provided,* the person or his heirs, claiming such right of preemption, shall produce to the register of the land office satisfactory evidence that he or they are entitled thereto and shall be subject to and comply with the regulations and provisions by this act prescribed for other purchasers.

30.

Tunis Wortman: Despotism and the Freedom of Political Discussion

Alarmed at the growing popular support for the Jeffersonian Republicans, the Federalists enacted the Alien and Sedition Laws in 1798 partly with a view to secure the election of 1800. Widespread political persecution resulted from the legislation. Men were arrested and convicted for expressing anti-Federalist opinions in political discussions and writings. Republican leaders, some of whom were not citizens, were threatened with deportation. Republican editorial criticism of President Adams was suppressed. However, Federalist attempts to silence political discussion earned the Republicans much sympathy and raised questions about the legitimate role of public opinion in a democratic society. In the following chapters of his Treatise *(1800), Tunis Wortman, a lawyer, challenged the assumptions behind the Alien and Sedition Laws, arguing that the free exercise of public opinion is a safeguard of liberty.*

Source: *A Treatise, Concerning Political Enquiry, and the Liberty of the Press,* New York, 1800, pp. 149-205.

It is an important object of our inquiry to discover whether the interests of society require that any restraints should be imposed upon the freedom of political discussion; and to ascertain whether any judicious method can be adopted to guard against the evils of licentiousness on the one hand and those of despotism on the other.

In the first place, it is to be observed that the communication of truth, so far from being criminal, should ever be viewed as eminently meritorious. He who combats a pernicious error or destroys a dangerous falsehood may challenge a seat among the principal benefactors of mankind. The law which coerces the circulation of truth cannot be vindicated upon any principle of justice or reconciled to any rational theory of government.

Falsehood is constantly pernicious; willful defamation is invariably criminal. No man can have a right to utter an untruth concerning another; he is as little entitled to misrepresent the public measures of a government.

In the present state of society it would be fruitless to expect perfection. We are often reduced to the necessity of choosing between opposite evils. Whatever determination is most nearly allied to the general good should constantly be preferred. It cannot be denied that licentiousness is injurious; but it is extremely to be questioned whether the severity of criminal coercion is the most salutary and judicious corrective.

The reasoning of the present work will be exclusively confined to a consideration of the effects of misrepresentation in public or political transactions. The defamation of private character stands upon a separate and distinct foundation. Personal transactions are not the subject of general concern or notoriety; the individual whose reputation is aspersed sustains a personal injury. Attacks upon private character in general proceed from malignant or vindictive motives; they are calculated to affect our private avocations and property. The prosecution which is commenced to redress the injury entirely assumes a civil complexion; the object it embraces is reparation rather than punishment.

What are the evils to be apprehended from the aspersion of public characters, and from the misrepresentation of political transactions? It is usually observed with considerable vehemence "that the person of the civil magistrate should be regarded with reverence, and his reputation approached with deferential awe. How is it possible to separate the person of the public officer from that respect which is ever due to government? The consequence of attacking his reputation will be to render him odious and suspect. Remove that esteem which is challenged by his personal virtues and that confidence which should constantly reward his integrity and you will infallibly lessen or destroy his means of usefulness; his authority, instead of meeting with obedience, will become openly controverted and contemned, or perhaps expose him to insult and derision. The true foundation of the power of civil government is the respect and reverence with which it is generally contemplated; to strike at that foundation is to aim at the dissolution of order and peace in society."

Such is an epitome of the arguments generally advanced in support of the interposition of restriction, and such the alarming picture which they usually represent. Whatever speciousness may be attached to this reasoning, it exhibits a perpetual libel against the character and discernment of society. It argues a want of confidence in the energies of truth, and supposes that its evidences are less powerful and captivating than the dominion of prejudice and error. He who contends that misrepresentation will not invariably yield to the artless, simple, and unvarnished tale of truth is egregiously ignorant of the nature of understanding and the genuine principles of the human heart.

The government which is actuated by corrupt and ambitious views, it will be readily admitted, has everything to apprehend from the progress of investigation. The authority of such government is entirely founded in imposture and supported by public ignorance and credulity. It is, therefore, the interest of tyranny, as it values its existence, to deceive and hoodwink the multitude. The empire of despotism is founded upon delusion and is wholly irreconcilable with the liberty of political discussion. Corruption considers truth as her inveterate enemy; talents and virtues are regarded as her most formidable antagonists.

But shall it be contended that the perpetuation of imposture is to become the object of our anxious solicitude? Or that the interests of society will suffer by our ceasing to respect those fatal institutions to which probity and integrity are the devoted victims — those pernicious systems upon whose altars the liberties and happiness of the people are incessantly sacrificed?

Public good must constitute the exclusive object to the attainment of which our inquiries should ultimately be directed. To reverence oppression and imposture is wholly incompatible with considerations of general prosperity. The interests of society require that the dominion of despotism and error should become subverted. To sympathize with tyranny is a refinement in cruelty; it is to abandon every exalted feeling of our nature and every noble attribute of humanity. If it is the province of investigation to enlighten the public mind and destroy the abuses of political institution, it should be assiduously cherished and esteemed as the most powerful benefactor of mankind.

In examining the true merits of this subject, we should therefore confine our attention to a government which is uniformly actuated by the love of justice and impressed with a constant solicitude to promote the general happiness. Wherever such a government exists, it is plain that every proceeding which can embarrass its operations and diminish the respect to which it is justly entitled will lessen its authority and usefulness and materially injure the interests of society. It remains to be inquired whether a government of that description can entertain any serious apprehensions of the effects of misrepresentation; and whether a more judicious remedy than the coercion of a criminal code cannot with confidence become applied?

It is an incontrovertible position that a government which is steadily actuated by an earnest and sincere desire of promoting the public good must infallibly possess the confidence of the people. It has been already maintained to be impossible that society should ever become its own enemy. The will of a community must always be directed to the general benefit. If truth is sufficiently powerful to combat falsehood and error, it should become a principal task of the honest and enlightened statesman to present its evidences to public view.

Is it to be imagined that where an administration is possessed of the qualifications which must necessarily secure its popularity, any misrepresentation of its measures should obtain an extensive reception or become attended with mischievous consequences? Such supposition would inevitably imply either a want of integrity or remissness in duty. The idea of a government uniformly actuated by laudable and patriotic sentiments is diametrically opposed to mystery and concealment. Publicity is one of the principal characteristics of its proceedings; truth, sincerity, and justice are the pillars upon which it is supported. A stranger to artifice and dissimulation, it feels no apprehension from popular emotions; it shrinks not from the eye of general observation; it acknowledges responsibility to be an active, efficient, and substantial principle, and continually presents to public view a perspicuous and circumstantial history of its conduct. Fortified and emboldened by the consciousness of upright intention, it considers itself invulnerable and secure. Confidence is mutually reciprocated between the government and the people.

In proportion as the public mind becomes habituated to discussion, it is rendered more enlightened and informed. In proportion as political measures are accompanied with the evidences of rectitude and enforced by the energy of reasoning, the general mind becomes invigorated and corrected; and misrepresentation has little prospect of obtaining an extensive circulation or reception. There can be no room for jealousy and suspicion where nothing is mysterious and concealed. Faction is confounded and appalled by the powerful luster which surrounds a system of virtue. In vain shall malevolence direct its shafts at the venerable guardians of liberty and justice; those shafts will become enfeebled and shivered by the contact, or recoil with a redoubled momentum upon the hand by which they were propelled. Wherever sincerity is an acknowledged attribute of the government and the civil magistrate becomes accustomed to exhibit an undisguised and faithful account of his measures; wherever a community is accustomed to the uncontrolled exercise of political discussion, its confidence in the wisdom and integrity of its public officers will become strengthened and increased; and it will be impossible to stimulate the people to intemperate opposition, or to render them the dupes and the victims of designing conspirators.

It is true that every individual possesses an appropriate sphere of influence and activity, and that his sentiments, and even his errors, will possess a certain quantity of weight upon those with whom he is ordinarily conversant. But will it be maintained that the prejudices of a few individuals are sufficiently powerful to infect the general mass of opinion? Shall it be admitted that the erroneous sentiments of a limited circle can ever be dangerous to a government erected upon the solid adamant of political truth? Whatever might be the malevolent views of a few ambitious and interested conspirators, it is impossible that any respectable proportion of the community should become corrupted with hostile and treasonable designs. Nations can never become benefited by deception. It is their eternal interest to pursue the direction of truth and virtue; their errors, therefore, must continually appertain to the understanding and not belong to the heart.

What, then, are the most judicious means of preserving the government from the wanton attacks of licentiousness, and what the best security of public liberty against the hostile encroachments of ambition? It will be found, upon an accurate examination, that the same remedy is equally adapted to the removal of each of those evils.

Such remedy is to be found in the extensive dissemination of truth. But what is the most efficacious method of obtaining the universal reception of truth? It has hitherto been the practice of shortsighted policy to combat falsehood with force. Coercion may, indeed, be adequate to the purpose of punishment, but it never can be rendered the instructor of mankind. If you entertain the beneficent intention of removing my errors and correcting my mistakes; if you wish to banish my vices and purify my heart, assume the salutary office of the preceptor; speak to me with kindness and clemency; tell me in what I am wrong, and point to the path of rectitude. Under such circumstances, can it be possible that I should refuse to listen with complacency?

If you are sufficiently impressed with the importance of your subject, the generous glow of enthusiasm will animate your mind; and you will infallibly become imbued with captivating eloquence. There is a chord in every breast attuned to rectitude. Reason and argument, whenever they are properly applied, possess the power of penetrating into every understanding, but nothing can be more injudicious or more at war with its own purposes than the application of force. Instead of attracting, it perpetually repels; it engenders animosity and opposition and naturally inspires distrust. The penalties of positive law may awe me into silence; they may perpetually bear down the energies of mind; but they are better adapted to become an engine of oppression than a happy instrument for the promotion of political virtue.

Considered as the means of counteracting these injurious effects of falsehood, the interposition of a penal code is altogether unnecessary. On the other hand, it is invariably attended with the most pernicious and dangerous consequences to society; for most assuredly it is of equal importance that we should guard against the encroachments and abuses of government as that we should endeavor to prevent the evils of licentious misrepresentation. Criminal law is invariably liable to be exerted as an engine of power; it may be used as the instrument of an administration for the purpose of crushing those individuals whose sentiments are viewed as obnoxious.

Can we always be secure in the independence and impartiality of the tribunal by whom it is administered? Will judges never lean in favor of those constituted authorities which are the fountains of patronage and preferment? Will they never be inclined to sacrifice a victim upon the altars of power? Will they carefully abstain from vindictive incentives and from the infliction of aggravated and exorbitant penalties? In fine, are not more complicated and tremendous calamities to be apprehended from the introduction of coercive restriction than from the most unbounded licentiousness?

How, then, shall erroneous opinions or willful misrepresentations be combated by the wise and provident legislator? The proper answer to this inquiry is that government should by no means interfere, unless by affording such information to the public as may enable them to form a correct estimate of things. Let us suppose an idea is circulated that a certain measure of administration is likely to produce calamitous effects, or that it has originated from flagitious and dishonorable designs. It will be contended that such an idea will be injurious in proportion to the extent of its circulation. Admitted. But how shall such opinion be destroyed or its farther propagation prevented? By fair and argumentative refutation, or by the terrible dissuasive of a statute of sedition? By the convincing and circumstantial narrative of truth, or by the terrors of imprisonment and the singular logic of the pillory?

It is the constant tendency of licentiousness to defeat its own purposes. In a state of society which admits of continual and unrestrained discussion, the triumph of falsehood can never be of permanent duration. There is no character which excites general obloquy and detestation more readily than that of the malignant slanderer. In proportion as the public mind becomes inured to the exercise of investigation, its discriminating powers will be rendered discerning and correct; it will become enabled instantly to distinguish between truth and error; every man will be taught to reverence and fear the enlightened judgment of the community; detection will closely pursue the footsteps of misrepresentation; and none will dare to fabricate or utter the tale of falsehood with impunity.

The nature as well as the policy of civil government requires that confidence should be reposed in the wisdom and virtues of the people. Prudence as well as magnanimity will dictate that it should uniformly rely upon the established sanctity of its character. An extreme pertinacity in analyzing syllables and a jealous sensibility at the approach of censure naturally creates the suspicion that there is something vulnerable in its constitution, "something rotten in the state of Denmark." If it is in reality traduced, it will invariably possess the means of vindicating its honor without resorting to the ambiguous infliction of punishment. Any erroneous sentiment that may prevail with regard to its administration can readily be removed by the salutary application of argument. Error in the public sentiment respecting the affairs of government arises in every instance from the want of information in the community. It is, therefore, in a great measure, attributable to the mistaken polity of administration itself in concealing the necessary means of knowledge. Let a government accustom itself to the publication of a succinct and accurate detail of its measures, with their operation and inducements; no room will then remain for misrepresentation. Demagogues, who calumniate from criminal incentives, will become instantly silenced and confounded, and the honest but misguided victims of their artifice will relinquish their prejudices upon the first approach of the superior evidence of truth.

Besides, as far as we suppose that men are actuated by views of personal interest, government will never want its champions and vindicators. A crowd of panegyrists, like the Army of Pompey, will be readily collected by a stamp of the foot; for "wheresoever the carcass is, there will the eagles be gathered together." Patronage and office, that "hope of reward" which "sweetens labor," will always multiply the advocates of authority. Government will ever possess an imperious advantage in the argument without resorting to the auxiliary power of criminal jurisprudence. There are more that will always be ready to vindicate than to censure its measures from selfish or sinister considerations.

The restrictions which are enforced by the authority of a penal code will always possess an ambiguous character. In their nature they are liable to perpetual abuse; they can only be necessary to support a government whose measures cannot survive the contact of investigation. It is sufficiently apparent that the government whose established reputation of virtue has secured the veneration of the people is invulnerable to the shafts of calumny; it cannot, consequently, be driven to the expedient of obtaining security through the severity of its criminal system. Restrictions upon the freedom of investigation must, therefore, be repugnant to every rational theory of political institution, and pregnant with the most unsalutary consequences. . . .

Public opinion is the only check which can be judiciously opposed to the encroachments of prerogative. All other resistance would not only be ineffectual and perilous but subversive of every valuable principle of the social state. Disorder and violence should be severely discountenanced by every enlightened advocate of freedom. Let us fondly anticipate the gradual improvement of civil institution from the unrestricted progress of reason, for we have everything to dread from the licentious and unbridled intemperance of passion.

Public opinion should not only remain unconnected with civil authority but be rendered superior to its control. As the guardian of public liberty it will lose its powers and its usefulness the moment it is rendered dependent upon the government. The stream must flow in the direction to which it naturally inclines and not be diverted by subtlety or force. No superintendence should be introduced except what is exercised by the percipient faculties of society. Coercion will stamp an awe upon the mind which will infallibly destroy the freedom of public opinion. However innocent or correct may be our sentiments, we shall always remain uncertain with respect to the verdict to be pronounced upon them; we shall perpetually distrust the impartiality or discernment of the tribunal before which we are liable to be summoned. The consequences of mistake will be so fatal and destructive that we shall be driven to the pernicious alternative of silence and inexertion. The history of prosecutions for libel will constantly furnish us with the lesson that governments are impatient of contradiction; that they are not so zealous to punish falsehood from an enlightened and disinterested attachment to justice as they are ready to smother opinions that are unfavorable to their designs. The infliction of penalty, instead of being a wholesome corrective of falsehood, will be perpetually abused to answer the purposes of animosity, oppression, and ambition. It will infallibly destroy that censorial jurisdiction of society which is the only salutary preservative of public liberty and justice. . . .

It is a prejudice not unfrequently entertained that the advocates of public liberty are restless, turbulent, and seditious, perpetually addicted to the pursuit of novelty, and ever watchful for the opportunity of revolution. To remove a prejudice at once so fatal and delusive is a duty equally owing to the safety of the government and the permanent welfare of the people. Such an opinion may excite the apprehensions of administration and lead them to the adoption of measures creative of discontent and liable to terminate in the very evils they are studious to avoid; it may influence the weak, the timid, and the affluent, and induce them to oppose the benevolent efforts of melioration directed to the general benefit. Philosophical reformation is not a crude and visionary projector; rashness is not her attribute, nor physical force her weapon. Her province is to enlighten society by candid and argumentative addresses to the understanding. She is the benefactor of the human race, imbued with wisdom, moderation, and clemency, and not "the destroying angel," who would sacrifice one generation from uncertain prospects of benefit to the next. Her genuine task is to preserve the lives of millions, to respect the private possessions of the people, and forbid the sanguinary streams to flow. Her constant solicitude is not to invite mankind to assemble amid the ferocious din of arms but in the peaceful temple of reason and reflection.

We have already seen that the security of government and the conservation of public liberty rest upon the same common basis, public opinion. Those very sentiments of political rectitude which render a community solicitous for the preservation of every essential right will infallibly deter them from resorting to revolutionary measures for the redress of public grievances. It is, therefore, more dangerous for government to risk the destruction of that general mass of information which sustains the morals of society than to permit the most industrious activity and unbounded latitude of investigation.

If any case can possibly occur which can render the violence of revolution expedient, it must be when all hope of redress from any other remedy has completely vanished; it must be when the authority of government debars that mutual intercourse and communication of opinion which is essential to general knowledge and improvement. Of every possible mode of despotism there is none so pernicious, none from which the mind of man shrinks back with greater horror, than that which brutalizes his moral and percipient faculties and deprives him of the inestimable property of an intelligent being — freedom of speech and opinion. The habitude of reasoning and the liberty of communicating our sentiments are friendly alike to the rights of society and to the wholesome authority of government. Licentiousness is an evil infinitely less formidable than restriction.

31.

Benjamin Nones: The Right To Be Poor and Radical

An anonymous letter condemning democratic ideals, the poor, and certain minorities, in particular Jews and Negroes, appeared in the Federalist newspaper, the Gazette of the United States, *on August 5, 1800. Specific reference was made to Benjamin Nones, a recent immigrant, mocking him for not contributing to the cost of renting a meeting room for the Democratic Society of Philadelphia. Nones sent an eloquent defense of himself, of his people, and of democracy to the printer of the* Gazette, *Caleb F. Wayne. Wayne refused to print it. Nones then sent the letter to William Duane, editor of the Republican* Aurora, *stating that Wayne's "business appears to be to asperse and shut the door against justification." Duane published the letter in his paper on August 11, 1800.*

Source: *Publications of the American Jewish Historical Society,* No. 1, 2nd edition, 1905.

I hope, if you take the liberty of inserting calumnies against individuals for the amusement of your readers, you will at least have so much regard to justice as to permit the injured through the same channel that conveyed the slander to appeal to the public in self-defense. I expect of you therefore, to insert this reply to your ironical reporter of the proceedings at the meeting of the Republican citizens of Philadelphia, contained in your gazette of the 5th instant, so far as I am concerned in that statement.

I am no enemy, Mr. Wayne, to wit; nor do I think the political parties have much right to complain if they enable the public to laugh at each other's expense, provided it be managed with the same degree of ingenuity and some attention to truth and candor. But your reporter of the proceedings at that meeting is as destitute of truth and candor as he is of ingenuity, and I think I can show that the want of prudence of this Mr. Marplot in his slander upon me is equally glaring with his want of wit, his want of veracity, his want of decency, and his want of humanity.

I am accused of being a *Jew;* of being a *Republican;* and of being *poor.*

I *am* a *Jew.* I glory in belonging to that persuasion, which even its opponents, whether Christian or Mohammedan, allow to be of divine origin; of that persuasion on which Christianity itself was originally founded and must ultimately rest; which has preserved its faith secure and undefiled for near 3,000 years; whose votaries have never murdered each other in religious wars or cherished the theological hatred so general, so unextinguishable among those who revile them. A persuasion whose patient followers have endured for ages the pious cruelties of pagans and of Christians, and persevered in the unoffending practice of their rites and ceremonies, amidst poverties and privations, amidst pains, penalties, confiscations, banishments, tortures, and deaths, beyond the example of any other sect which the page of history has hitherto recorded.

To be of such a persuasion is to me no disgrace; though I well understand the inhuman language of bigoted contempt in which your reporter, by attempting to make me ridiculous as a Jew, has made himself detestable, whatever religious persuasion may be dishonored by his adherence.

But I am a Jew. I am so, and so were

Abraham and Isaac and Moses and the prophets, and so too were Christ and his apostles. I feel no disgrace in ranking with such society, however it may be subject to the illiberal buffoonery of such men as your correspondents.

I *am* a *Republican!* Thank God, I have not been so heedless and so ignorant of what has passed and is now passing in the political world. I have not been so proud or so prejudiced as to renounce the cause for which I have fought as an American throughout the whole of the Revolutionary War, in the militia of Charleston, and in Polafkey's Legion. I fought in almost every action which took place in Carolina, and in the disastrous affair of Savannah, shared the hardships of that sanguinary day, and for three-and-twenty years I felt no disposition to change my political, any more than my religious principles; and which in spite of the witling scribblers of aristocracy, I shall hold sacred until death as not to feel the ardor of republicanism.

Your correspondent, Mr. Wayne, cannot have known what it is to serve his country from principle in time of danger and difficulties, at the expense of his health and his peace, of his pocket and his person, as I have done; or he would not be as he is, a pert reviler of those who have so done. As I do not suspect you, Mr. Wayne, of being the author of the attack on me, I shall not inquire what share you or your relations had in establishing the liberties of your country. On religious grounds I am a Republican. Kingly government was first conceded to the foolish complaints of the Jewish people as a punishment and a curse; and so it was to them until their dispersion, and so it has been to every nation who have been as foolishly tempted to submit to it. Great Britain has a king, and her enemies need not wish her the sword, the pestilence, and the famine.

In the history of the Jews are contained the earliest warnings against kingly government, as anyone may know who has read the fable of Abimelich, or the exhortations of Samuel. But I do not recommend them to your reporter, Mr. Wayne. To him the language of truth and soberness would be unintelligible.

I am a Jew, and if for no other reason, for that reason am I a Republican. Among the pious priesthood of church establishments, we are compassionately ranked with Turks, infidels, and heretics. In the monarchies of Europe, we are hunted from society, stigmatized as unworthy of common civility, thrust out as it were from the converse of men; objects of mockery and insult to froward children, the butts of vulgar wit and low buffoonery, such as your correspondent, Mr. Wayne, is not ashamed to set us an example of. Among the nations of Europe we are inhabitants everywhere — but citizens nowhere unless in republics. Here, in France, and in the Batavian Republic alone, we are treated as men and as brethren. In republics we have *rights,* in monarchies we live but to experience *wrongs.* And why? Because we and our forefathers have *not* sacrificed our principles to our interest, or earned an exemption from pain and poverty, by the dereliction of our religious duties. . . .

How then can a Jew but be a Republican? in America particularly? Unfeeling and ungrateful would he be if he were callous to the glorious and benevolent cause of the difference between his situation in this land of freedom and among the proud and privileged lawgivers of Europe.

But I *am poor;* I am so, my family also is large but soberly and decently brought up. They have not been taught to revile a Christian because his religion is not so old as theirs. They have not been taught to mock even at the errors of good intention and conscientious belief. I trust they will always leave this to men as unlike themselves as I hope I am to your scurrilous correspondent.

I know that to purse-proud aristocracy poverty is a crime, but it may sometimes be accompanied with honesty even in a Jew. I was bankrupt some years ago. I obtained my certificate and I was discharged from my debts. Having been more successful afterwards, I called my creditors together, and eight years afterwards, unsolicited, I discharged all my old debts. I offered interest which was refused by my creditors, and they gave me under their hands, without any solicitations of mine, as a testimonial of the fact (to use their own language) "as a tribute due to my honor and honesty." This testimonial was signed by Messrs. J. Ball, W. Wister, George Meade, J. Philips, C. G. Paleske, J. Bispham, J.. Cohen, Robert Smith, J. H. Leuffer, A. Kuhn, John Stille, S. Pleasants, M. Woodhouse, Thomas Harrison, M. Boraef, E. Laskey, and Thomas Allibone, etc.

I was discharged by the insolvent act, true, because having the amount of my debts owing to me from the French Republic, the differences between France and America have prevented the recovery of what was due to me in time to discharge what was due to my creditors. Hitherto it has been the fault of the political situation of the two countries that my creditors are not paid; when peace shall enable me to receive what I am entitled to, it will be my fault if they are not fully paid.

This is a long defense, Mr. Wayne, but you have called it forth, and, therefore, I hope you at least will not object to it. The public will now judge who is the proper object of ridicule and contempt, your facetious reporter, or your humble servant.

32.

Thomas Jefferson: A Simple and Inexpensive Government

During the summer of 1800, the Republicans gathered their forces in an attempt to obtain the presidency for Thomas Jefferson. Though Jefferson did not campaign in the modern sense of the term, he did write many letters to friends and to newspaper editors, defending himself against the attacks of the Federalists. When Gideon Granger of Connecticut wrote to him that there would be some support for the Republican cause in that Federalist stronghold, Jefferson's reply of August 13, 1800, restated the main points of his political creed. In the portion of the letter reprinted here, he stressed his belief in strong state governments and in a weak federal government. In his understanding of the Constitution, "a few plain duties to be performed by a few servants" summed up the only way to avoid the distortion the document had undergone at the hands of Washington and Adams.

Source: Randolph, III, pp. 444-446.

I received with great pleasure your favor of June 4, and am much comforted by the appearance of a change of opinion in your state; for though we may obtain, and I believe shall obtain, a majority in the legislature of the United States, attached to the preservation of the federal Constitution, according to its obvious principles and those on which it was known to be received; attached equally to the preservation to the states of those rights unquestionably remaining with them; friends to the freedom of religion, freedom of the press, trial by jury, and to economical government; opposed to standing armies, paper systems, war, and all connection, other than commerce, with any foreign nation; in short, a majority firm in all those principles which we have espoused, and the Federalists have opposed uniformly, still, should the whole body of New England continue in opposition to these principles of government, either knowingly or through delusion, our government will be a very uneasy one. It can never be harmonious and solid while so respectable a portion of its citizens support principles which go directly to a change of the federal Constitution, to sink the state governments, consolidate them into one, and to monarchise that.

Our country is too large to have all its affairs directed by a single government. Public servants, at such a distance, and from under the eye of their constituents, must, from the circumstance of distance, be unable to administer and overlook all the details necessary for the good government of the citizens; and the same circumstance, by rendering detection impossible to their constituents, will invite the public agents to corruption, plunder, and waste. And I do verily believe that if the principle were to prevail, of a common law being in force in the United States (which principle possesses the general government at once of all the powers of the state governments, and reduces us to a single consolidated government), it would become the most corrupt government on the earth. You have seen the practices by which the public servants have been able to cover their conduct, or, where that could not be done, delusions by which they have varnished it for the eye of their constituents. What an augmentation of the field for jobbing, speculating, plundering, office building, and office hunting would be produced by an assumption of all the state powers into the hands of the general government!

The true theory of our Constitution is surely the wisest and best, that the states are independent as to everything within themselves, and united as to everything respecting foreign nations. Let the general government be reduced to foreign concerns only, and let our affairs be disentangled from those of all other nations, except as to commerce, which the merchants will manage the better the more they are left free to manage for themselves, and our general government may be reduced to a very simple organization, and a very unexpensive one — a few plain duties to be performed by a few servants. But, I repeat that this simple and economical mode of government can never be secured if the New England States continue to support the contrary system. I rejoice, therefore, in every appearance of their returning to those principles which I had always imagined to be almost innate in them.

In this state, a few persons were deluded by the X. Y. Z. duperies. You saw the effect of it in our last congressional representatives, chosen under their influence. This experiment on their credulity is now seen into, and our next representation will be as republican as it has heretofore been. On the whole, we hope that, by a part of the Union having held on to the principles of the Constitution, time has been given to the states to recover from the temporary frenzy into which they had been decoyed, to rally round the Constitution, and to rescue it from the destruction with which it had been threatened even at their own hands.

We must marry ourselves to the British fleet and nation.

Thomas Jefferson, 1802

1801

33.

"Jefferson and Liberty"

Emotions ran high during the months prior to the election of 1800. Many who felt that laws passed during President Adams' administration, particularly the Alien and Sedition Acts, had infringed on their constitutional rights now looked to Jefferson as a symbol of freedom from oppressive government. Jefferson was elected in what has been called the "Revolution of 1800." The feeling of many people for the President-elect is reflected in the following verses, which were sung to a traditional Irish tune.

Source: *Songs, Odes, and Other Poems on National Subjects,* compiled by Wm. McCarty, Philadelphia, 1842, pp. 172-175.

JEFFERSON AND LIBERTY

The gloomy night before us flies,
The reign of terror now is o'er;
Its gags, inquisitors, and spies,
Its herds of harpies are no more!
Chorus:
Rejoice! Columbia's sons, rejoice!
To tyrants never bend the knee;
But join with heart and soul and voice,
For Jefferson and Liberty.

His country's glory, hope, and stay,
In virtue and in talents tried,
Now rises to assume the sway,
O'er freedom's temple to preside.

No lordling here, with gorging jaws,
Shall wring from industry the food;
Nor fiery bigot's holy laws
Lay waste our fields and streets in blood

Here strangers, from a thousand shores,
Compelled by tyranny to roam,
Shall find, amidst abundant stores,
A nobler and a happier home.

Here art shall lift her laureled head,
Wealth, industry, and peace divine;
And where dark, pathless forests spread,
Rich fields and lofty cities shine.

From Europe's wants and woes remote,
A friendly waste of waves between,
Here plenty cheers the humblest cot,
And smiles on every village green.

Let foes to freedom dread the name;
But should they touch the sacred tree,
Twice fifty thousand swords would flame
For Jefferson and Liberty.

34.

Thomas Jefferson: First Inaugural Address

Thomas Jefferson, the third President of the United States, was the first one to be installed at Washington, a city that for all but the most elementary purposes had yet to be built. The Inaugural Address reprinted below was delivered March 4, 1801, in the Senate chamber, the only portion of the Capitol then completed. In addition to the Senate, there were present a number of federal judges and as many members of the House of Representatives as the crowded chamber could accommodate. On one side of the President as he rose to speak sat Vice-President Aaron Burr, a dubious supporter who had received the second largest number of votes for the presidency in the recent election; on the other side sat Chief Justice Marshall, an avowed enemy, who had been appointed to office by Jefferson's predecessor, John Adams, only six weeks before. Adams himself, bitter over the party struggles that had demolished his administration and caused him to retire, was absent. For eight years Jefferson had worked more or less deliberately to assemble an opposition to the Federalists, and now stood victorious at the head of a new Republican administration. He spoke as one seeking not to divide or oppose, but with the hope of uniting the Federalist and Republican faction.

Source: H. A. Washington, VIII, pp. 1-6.

Called upon to undertake the duties of the first executive office of our country, I avail myself of the presence of that portion of my fellow citizens which is here assembled to express my grateful thanks for the favor with which they have been pleased to look toward me, to declare a sincere consciousness that the task is above my talents, and that I approach it with those anxious and awful presentiments which the greatness of the charge and the weakness of my powers so justly inspire. A rising nation, spread over a wide and fruitful land, traversing all the seas with the rich productions of their industry, engaged in commerce with nations who feel power and forget right, advancing rapidly to destinies beyond the reach of mortal eye — when I contemplate these transcendent objects and see the honor, the happiness, and the hopes of this beloved country committed to the issue and the auspices of this day, I shrink from the contemplation and humble myself before the magnitude of the undertaking.

Utterly, indeed, should I despair did not the presence of many whom I here see remind me that in the other high authorities provided by our Constitution I shall find resources of wisdom, of virtue, and of zeal on which to rely under all difficulties. To you, then, gentlemen, who are charged with the sovereign functions of legislation, and to those associated with you, I look with encouragement for that guidance and support which may enable us to steer with safety the vessel in which we are all embarked amidst the conflicting elements of a troubled world.

During the contest of opinion through which we have passed, the animation of discussions and of exertions has sometimes worn an aspect which might impose on strangers unused to think freely and to speak and to write what they think; but this being now decided by the voice of the nation, announced according to the rules of the Constitution, all will, of course, arrange themselves under the will of the law, and unite in common efforts for the common good. All, too, will bear in mind this sacred principle, that though the will of the majority is in all cases to prevail, that will to be rightful must be reasonable; that the minority possess their equal rights, which equal law must protect, and to violate would be oppression.

Let us, then, fellow citizens, unite with one heart and one mind. Let us restore to social intercourse that harmony and affection without which liberty and even life itself are but dreary things. And let us reflect that, having banished from our land that religious intolerance under which mankind so long bled and suffered, we have yet gained little if we countenance a political intolerance as despotic, as wicked, and capable of as bitter and bloody persecutions. During the throes and convulsions of the ancient world, during the agonizing spasms of infuriated man, seeking through blood and slaughter his long-lost liberty, it was not wonderful that the agitation of the billows should reach even this distant and peaceful shore; that this should be more felt and feared by some and less by others and should divide opinions as to measures of safety. But every difference of opinion is not a difference of principle.

We have called by different names brethren of the same principle. We are all Republicans, we are all Federalists. If there be any among us who would wish to dissolve this Union or to change its republican form, let them stand undisturbed as monuments of the safety with which error of opinion may be tolerated where reason is left free to combat it. I know, indeed, that some honest men fear that a republican government cannot be strong, that this government is not strong enough; but would the honest patriot, in the full tide of successful experiment, abandon a government which has so far kept us free and firm on the theoretic and visionary fear that this government, the world's best hope, may by possibility want energy to preserve itself? I trust not. I believe this, on the contrary, the strongest government on earth. I believe it the only one where every man, at the call of the law, would fly to the standard of the law and would meet invasions of the public order as his own personal concern. Sometimes it is said that man cannot be trusted with the government of himself. Can he, then, be trusted with the government of others? Or have we found angels in the forms of kings to govern him? Let history answer this question.

Let us, then, with courage and confidence pursue our own Federal and Republican principles, our attachment to union and representative government. Kindly separated by nature and a wide ocean from the exterminating havoc of one-quarter of the globe; too high-minded to endure the degradations of the others; possessing a chosen country, with room enough for our descendants to the hundredth and thousandth generation; entertaining a due sense of our equal right to the use of our own faculties, to the acquisitions of our own industry, to honor and confidence from our fellow citizens, resulting not from birth but from our actions and their sense of them; enlightened by a benign religion, professed, indeed, and practised in various forms, yet all of them inculcating honesty, truth, temperance, gratitude, and the love of man; acknowledging and adoring an overruling Providence which by all its dispensations proves that it delights in the happiness of man here and his greater happiness hereafter; with all these blessings, what more is necessary to make us a happy and prosperous people?

Still one thing more, fellow citizens: a wise and frugal government, which shall restrain men from injuring one another, which shall leave them otherwise free to regulate their own pursuits of industry and improvement, and shall not take from the mouth of labor the bread it has earned. This is the sum of good government, and this is necessary to close the circle of our felicities.

About to enter, fellow citizens, on the exercise of duties which comprehend everything dear and valuable to you, it is proper you should understand what I deem the essential principles of our government and, consequently, those which ought to shape its administration. I will compress them within the narrowest compass they will bear, stating the general principle, but not all its limitations.

Equal and exact justice to all men, of whatever state or persuasion, religious or political; peace, commerce, and honest friendship with all nations, entangling alliances with none; the support of the state governments in all their rights, as the most competent administrations for our domestic concerns and the surest bulwarks against antirepublican tendencies; the preservation of the general government in its whole constitutional vigor, as the sheet anchor of our peace at home and safety abroad; a jealous care of the right of election by the people — a mild and safe corrective of abuses which are lopped by the sword of revolution where peaceable remedies are unprovided; absolute acquiescence in the decisions of the majority, the vital principle of republics, from which is no appeal but to force, the vital principle and immediate parent of despotism; a well-disciplined militia, our best reliance in peace and for the first moments of war till regulars may relieve them; the supremacy of the civil over the military authority; economy in the public expense that labor may be lightly burdened; the honest payment of our debts and sacred preservation of the public faith; encouragement of agriculture and of commerce as its handmaid; the diffusion of information and arraignment of all abuses at the bar of the public reason; freedom of religion, freedom of the press, and freedom of person under the protection of the habeas corpus, and trial by juries impartially selected.

These principles form the bright constellation which has gone before us and guided our steps through an age of revolution and reformation. The wisdom of our sages and blood of our heroes have been devoted to their attainment. They should be the creed of our political faith, the text of civil instruction, the touchstone by which to try the services of those we trust; and should we wander from them in moments of error or alarm, let us hasten to retrace our steps and to regain the road which alone leads to peace, liberty, and safety.

I repair, then, fellow citizens, to the post you have assigned me. With experience enough in subordinate offices to have seen the difficulties of this, the greatest of all, I have learned to expect that it will rarely fall to the lots of imperfect man to retire from this station with the reputation and the favor which bring him into it. Without pretensions to that high confidence you reposed in our first and greatest revolutionary character, whose preeminent services had entitled him to the first place in his country's love and destined for him the fairest page in the volume of faithful history, I ask so much confidence only as may give firmness and effect to the legal administration of your affairs. I shall often go wrong through defect of judgment. When right, I shall often be thought wrong by those whose positions will not command a view of the whole ground.

I ask your indulgence for my own errors, which will never be intentional, and your support against the errors of others, who may condemn what they would not if seen in all its parts. The approbation implied by your suffrage is a great consolation to me for the past, and my future solicitude will be to retain the good opinion of those who have bestowed it in advance, to conciliate that of others by doing them all the good in my power, and to be instrumental to the happiness and freedom of all.

Relying, then, on the patronage of your goodwill, I advance with obedience to the work, ready to retire from it whenever you become sensible how much better choice it is in your power to make. And may that Infinite Power which rules the destinies of the universe lead our councils to what is best and give them a favorable issue for your peace and prosperity.

35.

A Plan of Union for Protestant Churches

Though the era of the Great Awakening was marked by a revived interest in religious questions, it also gave rise to varying interpretations of the Bible and thus to a proliferation of small sects throughout the country. But the resulting diffusion of popular support made it almost inevitable that some efforts should be made to combine resources and endeavors. In 1801, the Congregational Association of Connecticut and the General Assembly of the Presbyterian Church joined forces for the stated purpose of multiplying churches and winning the unconverted throughout the northern states and territories. The so-called Plan of Union provided that Congregational ministers could serve in Presbyterian congregations and vice versa. Cooperation between these two churches was possible in part because of their common Calvinistic heritage. The Plan, which is reprinted below, was relatively short-lived, but it was a significant step toward understanding among the Protestant denominations.

Source: *A Collection of the Acts, Deliverances, and Testimonies of the Supreme Judicatory of the Presbyterian Church*, Samuel J. Baird, ed., Philadelphia, 1855, pp. 570-571.

Regulations adopted by the General Assembly of the Presbyterian Church in America, and by the General Association of the State of Connecticut (provided said Association agree to them) with a view to prevent alienation and promote union and harmony in those new settlements which are composed of inhabitants from these bodies.

1. It is strictly enjoined on all their missionaries to the new settlements to endeavor by all proper means to promote mutual forbearance and a spirit of accommodation between those inhabitants of the new settlements who hold the Presbyterian and those who hold the Congregational form of church government.

2. If, in the new settlements, any church of the Congregational order shall settle a minister of the Presbyterian order, that church may, if they choose, still conduct their discipline according to Congregational principles, settling their difficulties among themselves or by a council mutually agreed upon for that purpose. But if any difficulty shall exist between the minister and the church or any member of it, it shall be referred to the presbytery to which the minister shall belong, provided both parties agree to it; if not, to a council consisting of an equal number of Presbyterians and Congregationalists, agreed upon by both parties.

3. If a Presbyterian church shall settle a minister of Congregational principles, that

church may still conduct their discipline according to Presbyterian principles, excepting that if a difficulty arise between him and his church, or any member of it, the cause shall be tried by the association to which the said minister shall belong, provided both parties agree to it, otherwise by a council, one-half Congregationalists and the other half Presbyterians, mutually agreed upon by the parties.

4. If any congregation consist partly of those who hold the Congregational form of discipline and partly of those who hold the Presbyterian form, we recommend to both parties that this be no obstruction to their uniting in one church and settling a minister; and that in this case the church choose a standing committee from the communicants of said church whose business it shall be to call to account every member of the church who shall conduct himself inconsistently with the laws of Christianity, and to give judgment on such conduct. That if the person condemned by their judgment be a Presbyterian, he shall have liberty to appeal to the presbytery; if a Congregationalist, he shall have liberty to appeal to the body of the male communicants of the church. In the former case the determination of the presbytery shall be final, unless the church shall consent to a further appeal to the synod or to the General Assembly; and in the latter case, if the party condemned shall wish for a trial by a mutual council, the cause shall be referred to such a council. And provided the said standing committee of any church shall depute one of themselves to attend the presbytery, he may have the same right to sit and act in the presbytery as a ruling elder of the Presbyterian Church.

36.

Thomas Jefferson: On Accommodating the Negroes

The slave revolt on the island of Hispaniola that was led with remarkable brilliance by Toussaint L'Ouverture from 1791 until his betrayal into French hands in 1802 was an inspiration to Negro slaves in other colonies. Word of Toussaint's conquest of Santo Domingo in 1801 came to the vicinity of Richmond, Virginia, in the same year, and encouraged a slave named Gabriel and his nearly 1,000 followers to attempt a similar revolt. The uprising, however, was put down, and some twenty-five Negroes were executed. James Monroe, then governor of Virginia, expressed his concern in a letter to President Jefferson, and sought his advice on provisions for the remaining rebels. Jefferson replied on November 24, urging some form of colonization for the renegades.

Source: Ford, VIII, pp. 103-106.

I had not been unmindful of your letter of June 15, covering a resolution of the House of Representatives of Virginia, and referred to in yours of the 17th inst. The importance of the subject, and the belief that it gave us time for consideration till the next meeting of the legislature, have induced me to defer the answer to this date. You will perceive that some circumstances connected with the subject, and necessarily presenting themselves to view, would be improper but for yours and the legislative ear. Their pub-

White House Historical Association

Portrait of Thomas Jefferson by Rembrandt Peale, 1800

lication might have an ill effect in more than one quarter. In confidence of attention to this, I shall indulge greater freedom in writing.

Common malefactors, I presume, make no part of the object of that resolution. Neither their numbers nor the nature of their offenses seem to require any provisions beyond those practised heretofore and found adequate to the repression of ordinary crimes. Conspiracy, insurgency, treason, rebellion, among that description of persons who brought on us the alarm, and on themselves the tragedy of 1800 were doubtless within the view of everyone; but many perhaps contemplated, and one expression of the resolution might comprehend, a much larger scope. Respect to both opinions makes it my duty to understand the resolution in all the extent of which it is susceptible.

The idea seems to be to provide for these people by a purchase of lands; and it is asked whether such a purchase can be made of the U.S. in their western territory? A very great extent of country, north of the Ohio, has been laid off into townships, and is now at market, according to the provisions of the acts of Congress, with which you are acquainted. There is nothing which would restrain the state of Virginia, either in the purchase or the application of these lands; but a purchase, by the acre, might perhaps be a more expensive provision than the House of Representatives contemplated. Questions would also arise whether the establishment of such a colony within our limits, and to become a part of our Union, would be desirable to the state of Virginia itself, or to the other states — especially those who would be in its vicinity?

Could we procure lands beyond the limits of the U.S. to form a receptacle for these people? On our northern boundary, the country not occupied by British subjects is the property of Indian nations, whose title would be to be extinguished, with the consent of Great Britain; and the new settlers would be British subjects. It is hardly to be believed that either Great Britain or the Indian proprietors have so disinterested a regard for us as to be willing to relieve us by receiving such a colony themselves; and as much to be doubted whether that race of men could long exist in so rigorous a climate. On our western and southern frontiers, Spain holds an immense country, the occupancy of which, however, is in the Indian natives, except a few isolated spots possessed by Spanish subjects. It is very questionable, indeed, whether the Indians would sell, whether Spain would be willing to receive these people, and nearly certain that she would not alienate the sovereignty.

The same question to ourselves would recur here also, as did in the first case: should we be willing to have such a colony in contact with us? However our present interests may restrain us within our own limits, it is impossible not to look forward to distant times, when our rapid multiplication will expand itself beyond those limits and cover the whole northern, if not the southern, continent, with a people speaking the same language, governed in similar forms and by similar laws; nor can we contemplate with satisfaction either blot or mixture on that surface. Spain, France, and Portugal hold possessions on the southern continent, as to which I am not well enough informed to say how far they might meet our views. But either there or in the northern continent, should the constituted authorities of Virginia fix their attention, of preference, I will have the dispositions of those powers sounded in the first instance.

The West Indies offer a more probable and practicable retreat for them. Inhabited already by a people of their own race and color, climates congenial with their natural constitution, insulated from the other descriptions of men; nature seems to have formed these islands to become the receptacle of the blacks transplanted into this hemisphere. Whether we could obtain from the European sovereigns of those islands leave to send thither the persons under consideration, I cannot say; but I think it more probable than the former propositions, because of their being already inhabited more or less by the same race. The most promising portion of them is the island of Santo Domingo, where the black are established into a sovereignty *de facto* and have organized themselves under regular laws and government. I should conjecture that their present ruler might be willing, on many considerations, to receive even that description which would be exiled for acts deemed criminal by us, but meritorious, perhaps, by him.

The possibility that these exiles might stimulate and conduct vindicative or predatory descents on our coasts, and facilitate concert with their brethren remaining here, looks to a state of things between that island and us not probable on a contemplation of our relative strength, and of the disproportion daily growing; and it is overweighed by the humanity of the measures proposed and the advantages of disembarrassing ourselves of such dangerous characters. Africa would offer a last and undoubted resort, if all others more desirable should fail us.

Whenever the legislature of Virginia shall have brought its mind to a point so that I may know exactly what to propose to foreign authorities, I will execute their wishes with fidelity and zeal. I hope, however, they will pardon me for suggesting a single question for their own consideration. When we contemplate the variety of countries and of sovereigns toward which we may direct our views; the vast revolutions and changes of circumstances which are now in a course of progression; the possibilities that arrangements now to be made, with a view to any particular plan, may, at no great distance of time, be totally deranged by a change of sovereignty, of government, or of other circumstances, it will be for the legislature to consider whether, after they shall have made all those general provisions which may be fixed by legislative authority, it would be reposing too much confidence in their executive to leave the place of relegation to be decided on by *them*. They could accommodate their arrangements to the actual state of things in which countries or powers may be found to exist at the day; and may prevent the effect of the law from being defeated by intervening changes. This, however, is for them to decide. Our duty will be to respect their decision.

1802

37.

Thomas Jefferson: The Threat of the French in Louisiana

The province of Louisiana comprised the region between the Mississippi River and the Rocky Mountains, and between the Canadian border and approximately the northern boundary of what is now Texas. This vast territory had been claimed by France, but after her defeat by Great Britain in the French and Indian War, France was forced to cede it to Spain. When Napoleon came into power in 1799, he negotiated with Spain the secret treaty of San Ildefonso (1800), which gave France renewed dominion over the province. Napoleon's plan was to reoccupy New Orleans as a base from which to extend French political and commercial power on the American continent. When Jefferson heard of the secret agreement, he became deeply concerned about French control of the Mississippi trade routes, as well as the danger of a foreign empire adjacent to the United States. He enlisted the aid of James Monroe and Robert Livingston in negotiations to purchase the important strategic areas around the mouth of the Mississippi. The reasoning that inspired Jefferson to take a step that he feared was of doubtful constitutionality is revealed in the following letter of April 18, 1802, to Livingston, who had been appointed minister to France.

Source: Randolph, III, pp. 499-502.

The cession of Louisiana and the Floridas by Spain to France works most sorely on the United States. On this subject the secretary of state has written to you fully, yet I cannot forbear recurring to it personally, so deep is the impression it makes on my mind. It completely reverses all the political relations of the United States and will form a new epoch in our political course. Of all nations of any consideration, France is the one which, hitherto, has offered the fewest points on which we could have any conflict of right and the most points of a communion of interests. From these causes, we have ever looked to her as our natural friend, as one with which we never could have an occasion of difference. Her growth, therefore, we viewed as our own, her misfortunes ours.

There is on the globe one single spot, the

possessor of which is our natural and habitual enemy. It is New Orleans, through which the produce of three-eighths of our territory must pass to market, and from its fertility it will ere long yield more than half of our whole produce and contain more than half of our inhabitants. France, placing herself in that door, assumes to us the attitude of defiance. Spain might have retained it quietly for years. Her pacific dispositions, her feeble state, would induce her to increase our facilities there, so that her possession of the place would be hardly felt by us, and it would not, perhaps, be very long before some circumstance might arise which might make the cession of it to us the price of something of more worth to her. Not so can it ever be in the hands of France; the impetuosity of her temper, the energy and restlessness of her character, placed in a point of eternal friction with us, and our character, which, though quiet and loving peace and the pursuit of wealth, is high-minded, despising wealth in competition with insult or injury, enterprising and energetic as any nation on earth — these circumstances render it impossible that France and the United States can continue long friends when they meet in so irritable a position.

They, as well as we, must be blind if they do not see this; and we must be very improvident if we do not begin to make arrangements on that hypothesis. The day that France takes possession of New Orleans fixes the sentence which is to restrain her forever within her low-water mark. It seals the union of two nations, who, in conjunction, can maintain exclusive possession of the ocean. From that moment, we must marry ourselves to the British fleet and nation. We must turn all our attention to a maritime force for which our resources place us on very high ground; and, having formed and connected together a power which may render reinforcement of her settlements here impossible to France, make the first cannon which shall be fired in Europe the signal for tearing up any settlement she may have made, and for holding the two continents of America in sequestration for the common purposes of the united British and American nations.

This is not a state of things we seek or desire. It is one which this measure, if adopted by France, forces on us as necessarily as any other cause by the laws of nature brings on its necessary effect. It is not from a fear of France that we deprecate this measure proposed by her. For however greater her force is than ours, compared in the abstract, it is nothing in comparison of ours when to be exerted on our soil. But it is from a sincere love of peace and a firm persuasion that, bound to France by the interests and the strong sympathies still existing in the minds of our citizens, and holding relative positions which insure their continuance, we are secure of a long course of peace.

Whereas the change of friends, which will be rendered necessary if France changes that position, embarks us necessarily as a belligerent power in the first war of Europe. In that case, France will have held possession of New Orleans during the interval of a peace, long or short, at the end of which it will be wrested from her. Will this short-lived possession have been an equivalent to her for the transfer of such a weight into the scale of her enemy? Will not the amalgamation of a young, thriving nation continue to that enemy the health and force which are at present so evidently on the decline? And will a few years' possession of New Orleans add equally to the strength of France? She may say she needs Louisiana for the supply of her West Indies. She does not need it in time of peace, and in war she could not depend on them because they would be so easily intercepted. I should suppose that all these considerations might, in some proper form, be brought into view of the government of France. Though stated by us, it ought not to give offense, because we do not bring them forward as a menace but as consequences not controllable by us but inevitable from the course of things. We mention them not as things which we desire by any means but as things we deprecate; and we beseech a friend to look forward and to prevent them for our common interests.

If France considers Louisiana, however, as indispensable for her views, she might perhaps be willing to look about for arrangements which might reconcile it to our interests. If anything could do this, it would be the ceding to us the island of New Orleans and the Floridas. This would certainly, in a great degree, remove the causes of jarring and irritation between us and perhaps for such a length of time as might produce other means of making the measure permanently conciliatory to our interests and friendships. It would, at any rate, relieve us from the necessity of taking immediate measures for countervailing such an operation by arrangements in another quarter. But still we should consider New Orleans and the Floridas as no equivalent for the risk of a quarrel with France, produced by her vicinage.

I have no doubt you have urged these considerations on every proper occasion with the government where you are. They are such as must have effect if you can find means of producing thorough reflection on them by that government. The idea here is that the troops sent to Santo Domingo were to proceed to Louisiana after finishing their work in that island. If this were the arrangement, it will give you time to return again and again to the charge. For the conquest of Santo Domingo will not be a short work. It will take considerable time and wear down a great number of soldiers.

Every eye in the United States is now fixed on this affair of Louisiana. Perhaps nothing since the Revolutionary War has produced more uneasy sensations through the body of the nation. Notwithstanding temporary bickerings which have taken place with France, she has still a strong hold on the affection of our citizens generally. I have thought it not amiss, by way of supplement to the letters of the secretary of state, to write you this private one to impress you with the importance we affix to this transaction.

38.

Gouverneur Morris: On the Union of Talents and Property

By nature a man of aristocratic temperament, Gouverneur Morris corresponded frequently with such kindred spirits as George Washington, Alexander Hamilton, and Robert Livingston. Morris wrote the following letter to Livingston on October 10, 1802, when the latter, as minister to France, was handling the negotiations that culminated in the purchase of Louisiana. The letter reflects Morris' haughty distrust of democracy and popular government.

Source: *The Life of Gouverneur Morris, etc., etc.*, Jared Sparks, ed., Boston, 1832, Vol. III, pp. 171-173.

It is unnecessary to say, because you well know, that I accord with you in your ideas of men and things on your side of the water. I wish you at the same time to remember that those who dwell on this side of the water are men also.

The French government cannot, I think, respect either the government or people of the United States. What is it that renders a nation respectable? Power, courage, wisdom. Put out of view, for a moment, both France and America, and suppose yourself in the administration of Austria. What would be your estimation of the Turks? Of the Russians? Of Prussia? You would not, I think, inquire whether in those countries they have a habeas corpus act, a trial by jury, or a house of representatives, etc. You would seek information as to their fleets, their armies, and above all, the talents of those who are at the head of affairs. Now suppose, for a moment, that a European statesman (Monsieur Leuchesini, for instance) should make inquiries of you respecting such things in this country. Would your answers impress his mind with anything like respect?

I hope, as you do, that we may long continue free; but this hope involves the double idea of continuance and freedom. The duration of a government is perhaps the first consideration; for be it ever so good in other respects, if its texture be too frail to endure, it can be of but little value. Now it appears to me that the duration of our government must, humanly speaking, depend on the influence which property shall acquire; for it is not to be expected that men who have nothing to lose will feel so well disposed to support existing establishments as those who have a great interest at stake. The strongest aristocratic feature in our political organization is that which democrats are most attached to, the right of universal suffrage. This takes from men of moderate fortune their proper weight and will, in process of time, give undue influence to those of great wealth.

I know that this effect has not yet been produced, and I know the reasons why; but a different state of things seems to be approaching, and slight circumstances will perhaps decide whether we are to pass through a course of revolutions to military despotism, or whether our government is to be wound up, by constitutional means, to a tone sufficiently vigorous for the conduct of national concerns. Much will depend on the union of talents and property. There is a considerable mass of genius and courage, with much industrious cunning, now at work to overturn our Constitution. If these be not met by a phalanx of property under the guidance of our ablest men, I think there will be a scuffle, and that, in the course of it, many large estates will be put into the melting pot.

The engine by which a giddy populace can be most easily wrought on to do mischief is their hatred of the rich. If any one of these supposes he can climb into power by civil commotions, he will find himself mistaken. It seems, however, probable that the property in this country will continue to be divided on political questions, and if so, we may expect mischief. If you read our gazettes, they will show you the condition of parties in this state. The Clintonian faction will, I believe, preponderate, and their powerful adherents will be flattered, if not respected, until the Burrites shall be disposed of. When you return, you will be able to give many of your friends good advice; but whether you can give them so much of your experience as may induce them to follow that advice is not so certain. You will all, I believe, discover some time or other that in leaving the mother church of Federalism, you have brought yourselves into reprobation. I hope you will not have occasion to say with the poet, *facilis est descensus* [easy is the descent], etc.

This letter will be delivered to you by a very worthy priest who is returning to the care of souls of his parish, blessing God that he has redeemed his chosen seed by the hands of his servant Napoleon. M. Joulin will tell you all he knows about us. Pray remember me to those about you.

39.

François André Michaux: Frontier Kentucky

Many settlers moved to Kentucky after Daniel Boone's exploration of the area in 1769, and by 1775 a number of permanent communities had been established, and in 1792 the territory became a state. François Michaux, a French botanist, spent the summer of 1802 traveling in the region, and he described its lands, peoples, and customs in a book published in Paris in 1804. The selection reprinted here is taken from the English translation of the work, Travels to the West of the Alleghanies, *and gives a picture of Kentucky only ten years after it became a state.*

Source: *Early Western Travels 1748-1846*, Reuben Gold Thwaites, ed., Cleveland, 1904, Vol. III, pp. 243-250.

For some time past the inhabitants of Kentucky have taken to the rearing and training horses; and by this lucrative branch of trade they derive considerable profit, on account of the superfluous quantity of Indian corn, oats, and other forage of which they are deficient at New Orleans.

Of all the states belonging to the Union, Virginia is said to have the finest coach and saddle horses, and those they have in this country proceed originally from them, the greatest part of which was brought by the emigrants who came from Virginia to settle in this state. The number of horses, now very considerable, increases daily. Almost all the inhabitants employ themselves in training and meliorating the breed of these animals; and so great a degree of importance is attached to the melioration that the owners of fine stallions charge from $15 to $20 for the covering of a mare. These stallions come from Virginia, and, as I have been told, some were at different times imported from England. The horses that proceed from them have slim legs, a well-proportioned head, and are elegantly formed.

With draft horses it is quite different. The inhabitants pay no attention with respect to improving this breed, in consequence of which they are small, wretched in appearance, and similar to those made use of by the peasantry in France. They appeared to me still worse in Georgia and Upper Carolina. In short, I must say that throughout the United States there is not a single draft horse that can be in anywise compared with the poorest race of horses that I have seen in England. This is an assertion which many Americans may probably not believe, but still it is correct.

Many individuals profess to treat sick horses, but none of them have any regular notions of the veterinary art; an art which would be so necessary in a breeding country, and which has, within these few years, acquired so high a degree of perfection in England and France.

In Kentucky, as well as in the Southern states, the horses are generally fed with Indian corn. Its nutritive quality is esteemed double to that of oats; notwithstanding sometimes they are mixed together. In this state, horses are not limited as to food. In most of the plantations the manger is filled with corn, they eat of it when they please, leave the stable to go to grass, and return at pleasure to feed on the Indian wheat. The stables are nothing but log houses, where the light penetrates on all sides, the interval that separates the trunks of the trees with which they are constructed not being filled up with clay.

The Southern states, and in particular South Carolina, are the principal places destined for the sale of Kentucky horses. They are taken there in droves of fifteen, twenty, and thirty at a time, in the early part of winter, an epoch when the most business is transacted at Carolina, and when the drivers are in no fear of the yellow fever, of which the inhabitants of the interior have the greatest apprehension. They usually take eighteen or twenty days to go from Lexington to Charleston. This distance, which is about 700 miles, makes a difference of 25 or 30 percent in the price of horses. A fine saddle horse in Kentucky costs about $130 to $140.

During my sojourn in this state I had an opportunity of seeing those wild horses that are caught in the plains of New Mexico, and which descend from those that the Spaniards introduced there formerly. To catch them they make use of tame horses that run much swifter, and with which they approach them near enough to halter them. They take them to New Orleans and Natchez, where they fetch about $50. The crews belonging to the boats that return by land to Kentucky frequently purchase some of them. The two that I saw and made a trial of were roan-colored, of a middling size, the head large and not proportionate with the neck, the limbs thick, and the mane rather full and handsome. These horses have a very unpleasant gait, are capricious, difficult to govern, and even frequently throw the rider and take flight.

The number of horned cattle is very considerable in Kentucky; those who deal in them purchase them lean, and drive them in droves of from 200 to 300 to Virginia, along the River Potomac, where they sell them to graziers, who fatten them in order to supply the markets of Baltimore and Philadelphia. The price of a good milch cow is, at Kentucky, from $10 to $12. The milk in a great measure comprises the chief sustenance of the inhabitants. The butter that is not consumed in the country is put into barrels, and exported by the river to the Carribbees [Caribbean].

They bring up very few sheep in these parts; for, although I went upward of 200 miles in this state, I saw them only in four plantations. Their flesh is not much esteemed, and their wool is of the same quality as that of the sheep in the Eastern states. The most that I ever observed was in Rhode Island.

Of all domestic animals, hogs are the most numerous; they are kept by all the inhabitants; several of them feed 150 to 200. These animals never leave the woods, where they always find a sufficiency of food, especially in autumn and winter. They grow extremely wild, and generally go in herds. Whenever they are surprised, or attacked by a dog or any other animal, they either make their escape or flock together in the form of a circle to defend themselves. They are of a bulky shape, middling size, and straight-eared. Every inhabitant recognizes those that belong to him by the particular manner in which their ears are cut. They stray sometimes in the forests, and do not make their appearance again for several months. They accustom them, notwithstanding, to return every now and then to the plantation by throwing them Indian corn once or twice a week. It is surprising that in so vast a country, covered with forests, so thinly populated, comparatively to its immense extent, and where there are so few destructive animals, pigs have not increased so far as to grow completely wild.

In all the Western states, and even to the east of the Alleghenies, 200 miles of the seacoast, they are obliged to give salt to the cattle. Were it not for that, the food they give them would never make them look well; in fact, they are so fond of it that they go of their own accord to implore it at the doors of the houses every week or ten days, and spend hours together in licking the trough into which they have scattered a small quantity for them. This want manifests itself most among the horses; but it may be on account of their having it given them more frequently.

Salt provisions form another important article of the Kentucky trade. The quantity exported in the first six months of the year 1802 was 72,000 barrels of dried pork, and 2,485 of salt.

Notwithstanding the superfluity of corn that grows in this part of the country, there is scarcely any of the inhabitants that keep poultry. This branch of domestic economy would not increase their expense but add a pleasing variety in their food. Two reasons may be assigned for this neglect; the first is that the use of salt provisions (a use to which the prevalence of the scurvy among them may be attributed) renders these delicacies too insipid; the second, that the fields of Indian corn contiguous to the plantations would be exposed to considerable damage, the fences with which they are enclosed being only sufficient to prevent the cattle and pigs from trespassing.

The inhabitants of Kentucky, as we have before stated, are nearly all natives of Virginia, and particularly the remotest parts of that state; and exclusive of the gentlemen of the law, physicians, and a small number of citizens who have received an education suitable to their professions in the Atlantic states, they have preserved the manners of the Virginians. With them the passion for gaming and spirituous liquors is carried to excess, which frequently terminates in quarrels degrading to human nature. The public houses are always crowded, more especially during the sittings of the courts of justice. Horses and lawsuits comprise the usual topic of their conversation.

If a traveler happens to pass by, his horse is appreciated; if he stops, he is presented with a glass of whiskey, and then asked a thousand questions, such as: Where do you come from? Where are you going? What is your name? Where do you live? What profession? Were there any fevers in the different parts of the country you came through? These questions, which are frequently repeated in the course of a journey, become tedious, but it is easy to give a check to their inquiries by a little address, their only object being the gratification of that curiosity so natural to people who live isolated in the woods and seldom see a stranger. They are never dictated by mistrust; for from whatever part of the globe a person comes, he may visit all the ports and principal towns of the United States, stay there as long as he pleases, and travel in any part of the country without ever being interrogated by a public officer.

The inhabitants of Kentucky eagerly recommend to strangers the country they inhabit as the best part of the United States, as that where the soil is most fertile, the climate most salubrious, and where all the inhabitants were brought through the love of liberty and independence! In the interior of their houses they are generally very neat; which induced me, whenever an opportunity offered, to prefer lodging in a private family rather than at a public house, where the accommodation is inferior, although the charges are considerably higher.

The women seldom assist in the labors of the field; they are very attentive to their domestic concerns and the spinning of hemp or cotton, which they convert into linen for the use of their family. This employment alone is truly laborious, as there are few houses which contain less than four or five children.

Among the various sects that exist in Kentucky, those of the Methodists and Anabaptists are the most numerous. The spirit of religion has acquired a fresh degree of strength within these seven or eight years among the country inhabitants, since, independent of Sundays, which are scrupulously observed, they assemble, during the summer, in the course of the week, to hear sermons. These meetings, which frequently consist of 2,000 or 3,000 persons who come from all parts of the country within fifteen or twenty miles, take place in the woods and continue for several days. Each brings his provisions and spends the night round a fire. The clergymen are very vehement in their discourses. Often, in the midst of the sermons, the heads are lifted up, the imaginations exalted, and the inspired fall backwards, exclaiming, "Glory! glory!" This species of infatuation happens chiefly among the women, who are carried out of the crowd and put under a tree, where they lie a long time extended, heaving the most lamentable sighs.

There have been instances of 200 or 300 of the congregation being thus affected during the performance of divine service; so that one-third of the hearers were engaged in recovering the rest. While I was at Lexington I was present at one of these meetings. The better informed people do not share the opinion of the multitude with regard to this state of ecstacy, and on this account they are branded with the appellation of "bad folks."

Except during the continuance of this preaching, religion is very seldom the topic of conversation. Although divided into several sects, they live in the greatest harmony. And whenever there is an alliance between the families, the difference of religion is never considered as an obstacle; the husband and wife pursue whatever kind of worship they like best, and their children, when they grow up, do just the same, without the interference of their parents.

Throughout the Western country the children are kept punctually at school, where they learn reading, writing, and the elements of arithmetic. These schools are supported at the expense of the inhabitants, who send for masters as soon as the population and their circumstances permit; in consequence of which it is very rare to find an American who does not know how to read and write. Upon the Ohio, and in the Barrens, where the settlements are farther apart, the inhabitants have not yet been able to procure this advantage, which is the object of solicitude in every family.

1803

40.

THOMAS JEFFERSON: The Lewis and Clark Expedition

By 1800 nearly one million people had settled in the region between the Appalachians and the Mississippi. However, few Americans had ventured into the lands further west, and the Louisiana Purchase was negotiated with relatively little knowledge of what the area was like. Prior to the purchase, Jefferson had already made plans for its exploration. His interest was not only political; he was also moved by scientific curiosity, and he looked forward to fruitful commercial exploitation. "It is impossible," he had written in 1801, "not to look forward to distant times, when our rapid multiplication will . . . cover the whole northern, if not the southern continent." On January 18, 1803, the President secretly requested Congress to appropriate funds for an expedition to be led by Meriwether Lewis and William Clark. The money was forthcoming, and on June 20, 1803, Jefferson sent a letter to Lewis instructing him on his venture. The Lewis and Clark party left St. Louis later in the year. The text of Jefferson's message to Congress and instructions to Lewis are reprinted here.

Source: Ford, VIII, pp. 198-203.

I.

Confidential Message to Congress

Gentlemen of the Senate, and of the House of Representatives:

As the continuance of the act for establishing trading houses with the Indian tribes will be under the consideration of the legislature at its present session, I think it my duty to communicate the views which have guided me in the execution of that act, in order that you may decide on the policy of continuing it, in the present or any other form, or discontinue it altogether, if that shall, on the whole, seem most for the public good.

The Indian tribes residing within the limits of the United States have, for a considerable time, been growing more and more uneasy at the constant diminution of the territory they occupy, although effected by their own voluntary sales. And the policy has long been gaining strength with them of refusing absolutely all further sale, on any conditions; insomuch that, at this time, it hazards their friendship, and excites dangerous jealousies and perturbations in their minds to make any overture for the purchase of the smallest portions of their land.

A very few tribes only are not yet obstinately in these dispositions. In order, peaceably, to counteract this policy of theirs, and to provide an extension of territory which the rapid increase of our numbers will call for, two measures are deemed expedient. First, to encourage them to abandon hunting, to apply to the raising stock, to agriculture, and domestic manufacture, and thereby prove to themselves that less land and labor will maintain them in this better than in their former mode of living. The extensive forests necessary in the hunting life, will then become useless, and they will see advantage in exchanging them for the means of improving their farms, and of increasing their domestic comforts. Second, to multiply trading houses among them, and place within their reach those things which will contribute more to their domestic comfort than the possession of extensive, but uncultivated wilds. Experience and reflection will develop to them the wisdom of exchanging what they can spare and we want, for what we can spare and they want. In leading them to agriculture, to manufactures, and civilization; in bringing together their and our settlements, and in preparing them ultimately to participate in the benefits of our governments, I trust and believe we are acting for their greatest good.

At these trading houses we have pursued the principles of the act of Congress which directs that the commerce shall be carried on liberally, and requires only that the capital stock shall not be diminished. We, consequently, undersell private traders, foreign and domestic, drive them from the competition; and, thus, with the goodwill of the Indians, rid ourselves of a description of men who are constantly endeavoring to excite in the Indian mind suspicions, fears, and irritations toward us. A letter now enclosed shows the effect of our competition on the operations of the traders, while the Indians, perceiving the advantage of purchasing from us, are soliciting, generally, our establishment of trading houses among them. In one quarter this is particularly interesting.

The legislature, reflecting on the late occurrences on the Mississippi, must be sensible how desirable it is to possess a respectable breadth of country on that river, from our southern limit to the Illinois, at least, so that we may present as firm a front on that as on our eastern border. We possess what is below the Yazoo, and can probably acquire a certain breadth from the Illinois and Wabash to the Ohio; but, between the Ohio and Yazoo, the country all belongs to the Chickasaws, the most friendly tribe within our limits, but the most decided against the alienation of lands. The portion of their country most important for us is exactly that which they do not inhabit. Their settlements are not on the Mississippi but in the interior country. They have lately shown a desire to become agricultural; and this leads to the desire of buying implements and comforts. In the strengthening and gratifying of these wants, I see the only prospect of planting on the Mississippi itself the means of its own safety.

Duty has required me to submit these views to the judgment of the legislature; but as their disclosure might embarrass and defeat their effect, they are committed to the special confidence of the two houses.

While the extension of the public commerce among the Indian tribes may deprive of that source of profit such of our citizens as are engaged in it, it might be worthy the attention of Congress, in their care of individual as well as of the general interest, to point in another direction the enterprise of these citizens, as profitably for themselves and more usefully for the public.

The River Missouri, and the Indians inhabiting it, are not as well known as is rendered desirable by their connection with the Mississippi, and consequently with us. It is, however, understood that the country on that river is inhabited by numerous tribes, who furnish great supplies of furs and peltry to the trade of another nation, carried on in a high latitude, through an infinite number of portages and lakes shut up by ice through a long season. The commerce on that line could bear no competition with that of the Missouri, traversing a moderate climate, offering, according to the best accounts, a continued navigation from its source, and possibly with a single portage, from the western ocean, and finding to the Atlantic a choice of channels through the Illinois or Wabash, the lakes and Hudson, through the Ohio and Susquehanna, or Potomac or James rivers, and through the Tennessee and Savannah rivers.

An intelligent officer, with ten or twelve chosen men, fit for the enterprise and willing to undertake it, taken from our posts, where they may be spared without inconvenience, might explore the whole line, even to the western ocean; have conferences with the natives on the subject of commercial intercourse; get admission among them for our traders; as others are admitted, agree on convenient deposits for an interchange of articles; and return with the information acquired, in the course of two summers. Their arms and accoutrements, some instruments of observation, and light and cheap presents for the Indians would be all the apparatus they could carry, and, with an expectation of a soldier's portion of land on their return, would constitute the whole expense. Their pay would be going on, whether here or there. While other civilized nations have encountered great expense to enlarge the boundaries of knowledge by undertaking voyages of discovery and for other literary purposes, in various parts and directions, our nation seems to owe to the same object, as well as to its own interests, to explore this, the only line of easy communication across the continent, and so directly traversing our own part of it.

The interests of commerce place the principal object within the constitutional powers and care of Congress, and that it should incidentally advance the geographical knowledge of our own continent cannot be but an additional gratification. The nation claiming the territory, regarding this as a literary pursuit, which is in the habit of permitting within its dominions, would not be disposed to view it with jealousy, even if the expiring state of its interests there did not render it a matter of indifference. The appropriation of $2,500, "for the purpose of extending the external commerce of the United States," while understood and considered by the executive as giving the legislative sanction, would cover the undertaking from notice, and prevent the obstructions which interested individuals might otherwise previously prepare in its way.

II.

Instructions to Meriwether Lewis

Your situation as secretary of the president of the United States has made you acquainted with the objects of my confidential message of Jan. 18, 1803, to the legislature. You have seen the act they passed, which, though expressed in general terms, was meant to sanction those objects, and you are appointed to carry them into execution.

Instruments for ascertaining by celestial observations the geography of the country through which you will pass, have been already provided. Light articles for barter, and presents among the Indians, arms for your attendants, say for from ten to twelve men, boats, tents, and other traveling apparatus, with ammunition, medicine, surgical instruments, and provision you will have prepared with such aids as the secretary of war can yield in his department. And from him also you will receive authority to engage among our troops, by voluntary agreement, the number of attendants above mentioned, over whom you, as their commanding officer, are invested with all the powers the laws give in such a case.

As your movements while within the limits of the U.S. will be better directed by occasional communications, adapted to circumstances as they arise, they will not be noticed here. What follows will respect your proceedings after your departure from the U.S.

Your mission has been communicated to the ministers here from France, Spain, and Great Britain, and through them to their governments; and such assurances given them as to its objects as we trust will satisfy them. The country of Louisiana having been ceded by Spain to France, the passport you have from the minister of France, the representative of the present sovereign of the country, will be a protection with all its subjects. And that from the minister of England will entitle you to the friendly aid of any traders of that allegiance with whom you may happen to meet.

The object of your mission is to explore the Missouri River, and such principal stream of it, as, by its course and communication with the water of the Pacific Ocean may offer the most direct and practicable water communication across this continent, for the purposes of commerce.

Beginning at the mouth of the Missouri, you will take observations of latitude and longitude at all remarkable points on the river, and especially at the mouths of rivers, at rapids, at islands, and other places and objects distinguished by such natural marks and characters of a durable kind, as that they may with certainty be recognized hereafter. The courses of the river between these points of observation may be supplied by the compass, the logline, and by time, corrected by the observations themselves. The variations of the compass, too, in different places should be noticed.

The interesting points of the portage between the heads of the Missouri and the water offering the best communication with the Pacific Ocean should be fixed by observation and the course of that water to the ocean, in the same manner as that of the Missouri.

Your observations are to be taken with great pains and accuracy, to be entered distinctly and intelligibly for others as well as yourself to comprehend all the elements necessary, with the aid of the usual tables to fix the latitude and longitude of the places at which they were taken, and are to be rendered to the War Office for the purpose of having the calculations made concurrently by proper persons within the U.S. Several copies of these, as well as of your other notes, should be made at leisure times and put into the care of the most trustworthy of your attendants, to guard by multiplying them against the accidental losses to which they will be exposed. A further guard would be that one of these copies be written on the paper of the birch, as less liable to injury from damp than common paper.

The commerce which may be carried on with the people inhabiting the line you will pursue renders a knowledge of these people important. You will therefore endeavor to make yourself acquainted, as far as a diligent pursuit of your journey shall admit, with the names of the nations and their numbers; the extent and limits of their possessions; their relations with other tribes or nations; their language, traditions, monuments; their ordinary occupations in agriculture, fishing, hunting, war, arts, and the implements for these; their food, clothing, and domestic accommodations; the diseases prevalent among them, and the remedies they use; moral and physical circumstance which distinguish them from the tribes they know; peculiarities in their laws, customs and dispositions; and articles of commerce they may need or furnish and to what extent.

And considering the interest which every nation has in extending and strengthening the authority of reason and justice among the people around them, it will be useful to acquire what knowledge you can of the state of morality, religion, and information among them, as it may better enable those who endeavor to civilize and instruct them to adapt their measures to the existing notions and practices of those on whom they are to operate.

Other objects worthy of notice will be: the soil and face of the country, its growth and vegetable productions, especially those not of the U.S.; the animals of the country generally, and especially those not known in the U.S.; the remains and accounts of any which may be deemed rare or extinct; the mineral productions of every kind; but more particularly metals, limestone, pit coal, and saltpeter; salines and mineral waters, noting the temperature of the last and such circumstances as may indicate their character; volcanic appearances; climate as characterized by the thermometer, by the proportion of rainy, cloudy, and clear days, by lightning, hail, snow, ice, by the access and recess of frost, by the winds, prevailing at different seasons, the dates at which particular plants put forth or lose their flowers, or leaf, times of appearance of particular birds, reptiles, or insects.

Although your route will be along the channel of the Missouri, yet you will endeavor to inform yourself, by inquiry, of the character and extent of the country watered by its branches, and especially on its southern side. The North River, or Rio Bravo, which runs into the Gulf of Mexico, and the North River, or Rio Colorado, which runs into the Gulf of California, are understood to be the principal streams heading opposite to the waters of the Missouri, and running southwardly. Whether the dividing grounds between the Missouri and them are mountains or flatlands, what are their distance from the Missouri, the character of the intermediate country, and the people inhabiting it are worthy of particular inquiry.

The northern waters of the Missouri are less to be inquired after, because they have been ascertained to a considerable degree, and are still in a course of ascertainment by English traders and travelers. But if you can learn anything certain of the most northern source of the Mississippi, and of its position relative to the Lake of the Woods, it will be interesting to us. Some account, too, of the path of the Canadian traders from the Mississippi, at the mouth of the Ouisconsin [Wisconsin] River, to where it strikes the Missouri and of the soil and rivers in its course, is desirable.

In all your intercourse with the natives, treat them in the most friendly and conciliatory manner which their own conduct will admit; allay all jealousies as to the object of your journey, satisfy them of its innocence; make them acquainted with the position, extent, character, peaceable and commercial dispositions of the U.S., of our wish to be neighborly, friendly, and useful to them, and of our dispositions to a commercial intercourse with them; confer with them on the points most convenient, as mutual emporiums and the articles of most desirable interchange for them and us. If a few of their influential chiefs, within practicable distance, wish to visit us, arrange such a visit with them, and furnish them with authority to call on our officers, on their entering the U.S., to have them conveyed to this place at the public expense. If any of them should wish to have some of their young people brought up with us and taught such arts as may be useful to them, we will receive, instruct, and take care of them. Such a mission, whether of influential chiefs or of young people, would give some security to your own party.

Carry with you some matter of the kinepox [cowpox], inform those of them with whom you may be of its efficacy as a preservative from the smallpox; and instruct and encourage them in the use of it. This may be especially done wherever you may winter.

As it is impossible for us to foresee in what manner you will be received by those people, whether with hospitality or hostility, so is it impossible to prescribe the exact degree of perseverance with which you are to pursue your journey. We value too much the lives of citizens to offer them to probable destruction. Your numbers will be sufficient to secure you against the unauthorized opposition of individuals, or of small parties; but if a superior force, authorized or not authorized, by a nation should be arrayed against your further passage, and inflexibly determined to arrest it, you must decline its further pursuit, and return. In the loss of yourselves, we should lose also the information you will have acquired. By returning safely with that, you may enable us to renew the essay with better calculated means. To your own discretion, therefore, must be left the degree of danger you may risk, and the point at which you should decline, only saying we wish you to err on the side of your safety, and to bring back your party safe, even if it be with less information.

As far up the Missouri as the white settlements extend, an intercourse will probably be found to exist, between them and the Spanish posts at St. Louis, opposite Cahokia, or St. Genevieve opposite Kaskaskia. From still further up the river, the traders may furnish a conveyance for letters. Beyond that you may perhaps be able to engage Indians to bring letters for the government to Cahokia or Kaskaskia on promising that they shall there receive such special compensation as you shall have stipulated with them. Avail yourself of these means to communicate to us at seasonable intervals a copy of your journal, notes, and observations of every kind, putting into cipher whatever might do injury if betrayed.

Should you reach the Pacific Ocean, inform yourself of the circumstances which may decide whether the furs of those parts may not be collected as advantageously at the head of the Missouri (convenient as is supposed to the waters of the Colorado and Oregon or Columbia) as at Nootka Sound or any other point of that coast; and that trade be consequently conducted through the Missouri and U.S. more beneficially than by the circumnavigation now practised.

On your arrival on that coast, endeavor to learn if there be any port within your reach frequented by the sea vessels of any nation, and to send two of your trusted people back by sea, in such way as shall appear practicable, with a copy of your notes. And should you be of opinion that the return of your party by the way they went will be eminently dangerous, then ship the whole, and return by sea by way of Cape Horn or the Cape of Good Hope, as you shall be able.

As you will be without money, clothes, or provisions, you must endeavor to use the credit of the U.S. to obtain them; for which purpose open letters of credit shall be furnished you authorizing you to draw on the executive of the U.S. or any of its officers in any part of the world, in which drafts can be disposed of, and to apply with our recommendations to the consuls, agents, merchants, or citizens of any nation with which we have intercourse, assuring them in our name that any aids they may furnish you shall be honorably repaid and on demand. Our consuls, Thomas Howes at Batavia in Java, William Buchanan of the Isles of France and Bourbon, and John Elmslie at the Cape of Good Hope will be able to supply your necessities by drafts on us.

Should you find it safe to return by the way you go, after sending two of your party round by sea, or with your whole party if no conveyance by sea can be found, do so; making such observations on your return as may serve to supply, correct, or confirm those made on your outward journey.

In reentering the U.S. and reaching a place of safety, discharge any of your attendants who may desire and deserve it, procuring for them immediate payment of all arrears of pay and clothing which may have incurred since their departure; and assure them that they shall be recommended to the liberality of the legislature for the grant of a soldier's portion of land each, as proposed in my message to Congress; and repair yourself with your papers to the seat of government.

To provide, on the accident of your death, against anarchy, dispersion, and the consequent danger to your party, and total failure of the enterprise, you are hereby authorized, by any instrument signed and written in your own hand, to name the person among them who shall succeed to the command on your decease; and, by like instruments, to change the nomination from time to time, as further experience of the characters accompanying you shall point out superior fitness. And all the powers and authorities given to yourself are, in the event of your death, transferred to and vested in the successor so named, with further power to him, and his successors, in like manner, to name each his successor, who, on the death of his predecessor shall be invested with all the powers and authorities given to yourself.

41.

John Marshall: *Marbury* v. *Madison*

In 1801, shortly before he was to retire from office, President John Adams used an opportunity given him by the Congress to fill a number of newly created federal judgeships with Federalists. The incoming Republican President, Thomas Jefferson, thus found himself confronted with judges unfriendly to both his party and his program, especially in the Supreme Court itself, to which Adams had appointed as Chief Justice his former secretary of state, John Marshall. Marshall like Jefferson was a Virginian, and even a distant relative of the President, but the two men were bitter political antagonists. Adams had also appointed to a district judgeship a certain William Marbury, whose only claim to fame was that he figured prominently in one of Marshall's earliest decisions. For Marshall himself, in the confusion of the change of administration, had neglected to deliver Marbury's commission to him, and Marshall's successor as secretary of state, James Madison, was instructed by Jefferson to withhold it. Marbury therefore began proceedings in the Supreme Court to secure an order of mandamus *requiring the commission to be handed over. In his decision, handed down in February 1803, Marshall declared that the President had no* moral *right to keep back the commission. But Marshall also asserted that the section of the Judiciary Act of 1789 under which Marbury had brought suit was unconstitutional, and that the Court was therefore powerless to help him. By thus apparently limiting his own authority, Marshall actually extended it, since no Act of Congress had ever been declared unconstitutional before. He thereby delivered both a rebuke and a stern warning to the Jeffersonians, whose entire program was put on notice as being subject to judicial review — and by none other, in the last resort, than its most powerful enemy. Portions of Marshall's decision are reprinted here.*

Source: 1 Cranch 137.

It is . . . decidedly the opinion of the Court that when a commission has been signed by the President, the appointment is made; and that the commission is complete when the seal of the United States has been affixed to it by the secretary of state.

Where an officer is removable at the will of the executive, the circumstance which completes his appointment is of no concern, because the act is at any time revocable; and the commission may be arrested if still in the office. But when the officer is not removable at the will of the executive, the appointment is not revocable and cannot be annulled. It has conferred legal rights which cannot be resumed.

The discretion of the executive is to be exercised until the appointment has been made. But having once made the appointment, his power over the office is terminated in all cases where, by law, the officer is not removable by him. The right to the office is *then* in the person appointed, and he has the absolute, unconditional power of accepting or rejecting it.

Mr. Marbury, then, since his commission was signed by the President and sealed by the secretary of state, was appointed; and as the law creating the office gave the officer a right to hold for five years, independent of the executive, the appointment was not revocable, but vested in the officer legal rights, which are protected by the laws of his country.

To withhold his commission, therefore, is an act deemed by the Court not warranted by law but violative of a vested legal right. . . .

The power of nominating to the Senate and the power of appointing the person nominated are political powers to be exercised by the President according to his own discretion. When he has made an appointment, he has exercised his whole power, and his discretion has been completely applied to the case. If, by law, the officer be removable at the will of the President, then a new appointment may be immediately made, and the rights of the officer are terminated. But as a fact which has existed cannot be made never to have existed, the appointment cannot be annihilated; and, consequently, if the officer is by law not removable at the will of the President, the rights he has acquired are protected by the law and are not resumable by the President. They cannot be extinguished by executive authority, and he has the privilege of asserting them in like manner as if they had been derived from any other source. . . .

It is, then, the opinion of the Court:

First, that by signing the commission of Mr. Marbury, the President of the United States appointed him a justice of peace for the County of Washington, in the District of Columbia, and that the seal of the United States, affixed thereto by the secretary of state, is conclusive testimony of the verity of the signature, and of the completion of the appointment; and that the appointment conferred on him a legal right to the office for the space of five years.

Second, that, having this legal title to the office, he has a consequent right to the commission; a refusal to deliver which is a plain violation of that right for which the laws of his country afford him a remedy. . . .

This, then, is a plain case for a mandamus, either to deliver the commission or a copy of it from the record; and it only remains to be inquired whether it can issue from this Court.

The act to establish the judicial courts of the United States authorizes the Supreme Court "to issue writs of mandamus, in cases warranted by the principles and usages of law, to any courts appointed, or persons holding office, under the authority of the United States."

The secretary of state, being a person holding an office under the authority of the United States, is precisely within the letter of the description; and if this Court is not authorized to issue a writ of mandamus to such an officer, it must be because the law is unconstitutional and therefore absolutely incapable of conferring the authority and assigning the duties which its words purport to confer and assign.

The Constitution vests the whole judicial power of the United States in one Supreme Court and such inferior courts as Congress shall, from time to time, ordain and establish. This power is expressly extended to all cases arising under the laws of the United States and, consequently, in some form, may be exercised over the present case because the right claimed is given by a law of the United States.

In the distribution of this power it is declared that "the Supreme Court shall have original jurisdiction in all cases affecting ambassadors, other public ministers, and consuls, and those in which a state shall be a party. In all other cases, the Supreme Court shall have appellate jurisdiction."

It has been insisted, at the bar, that as the original grant of jurisdiction to the Supreme and inferior courts is general, and the clause assigning original jurisdiction to the Supreme Court contains no negative or restrictive words, the power remains to the legislature to assign original jurisdiction to that Court, in other cases than those specified in the article which has been recited, provided those cases belong to the judicial power of the United States.

If it had been intended to leave it in the discretion of the legislature to apportion the judicial power between the Supreme and inferior courts according to the will of that body, it would certainly have been useless to have proceeded further than to have defined the judicial power and the tribunals in which it should be vested. The subsequent part of the section is mere surplusage — is entirely without meaning — if such is to be the construction. If Congress remains at liberty to give this Court appellate jurisdiction, where the Constitution has declared their jurisdiction shall be original, and original jurisdiction where the Constitution has declared it shall be appellate, the distribution of jurisdiction made in the Constitution is form without substance.

Affirmative words are often, in their operation, negative of other objects than those affirmed; and in this case, a negative or exclusive sense must be given to them, or they have no operation at all.

It cannot be presumed that any clause in the Constitution is intended to be without effect; and, therefore, such a construction is inadmissable, unless the words require it.

If the solicitude of the convention, respecting our peace with foreign powers, induced a provision that the Supreme Court should take original jurisdiction in cases which might be supposed to affect them, yet the cause would have proceeded no further than to provide for such cases, if no further restriction on the powers of Congress had been intended. That they should have appellate jurisdiction in all other cases, with such exceptions as Congress might make, is no restriction, unless the words be deemed exclusive of original jurisdiction.

When an instrument organizing, fundamentally, a judicial system divides it into one Supreme and so many inferior courts as the legislature may ordain and establish, then enumerates its powers, and proceeds so far to distribute them as to define the jurisdiction of the Supreme Court by declaring the cases in which it shall take original jurisdiction and that in others it shall take appellate jurisdiction, the plain import of the words seems to be that in one class of cases its jurisdiction is original and not appellate; in the other, it is appellate and not original. If any other construction would render the clause inoperative, that is an additional reason for rejecting such other construction and for adhering to their obvious meaning.

To enable this Court, then, to issue a mandamus, it must be shown to be an exercise of appellate jurisdiction or to be necessary to enable them to exercise appellate jurisdiction.

It has been stated at the bar that the appellate jurisdiction may be exercised in a variety of forms, and that, if it be the will of the legislature that a mandamus should be used for that purpose, that will must be obeyed. This is true, yet the jurisdiction must be appellate, not original. It is the essential criterion of appellate jurisdiction that it revises and corrects the proceedings in a cause already instituted and does not create that cause. Although, therefore, a mandamus may be directed to courts, yet to issue such a writ to an officer for the delivery of a paper is, in effect, the same as to sustain an original action for that paper and, therefore, seems not to belong to appellate but

White House Historical Association

Portrait of John Marshall by John Wesley Jarvis, 1825

to original jurisdiction. Neither is it necessary in such a case as this to enable the court to exercise its appellate jurisdiction.

The authority, therefore, given to the Supreme Court by the act establishing the judicial courts of the United States to issue writs of mandamus to public officers appears not to be warranted by the Constitution; and it becomes necessary to inquire whether a jurisdiction so conferred can be exercised.

The question whether an act repugnant to the Constitution can become the law of the land is a question deeply interesting to the United States but, happily, not of an intricacy proportioned to its interest. It seems only necessary to recognize certain principles, supposed to have been long and well established, to decide it.

That the people have an original right to establish, for their future government, such principles as, in their opinion, shall most conduce to their own happiness is the basis on which the whole American fabric has been erected. The exercise of this original right is a very great exertion; nor can it, nor ought it, to be frequently repeated. The principles, therefore, so established are deemed fundamental. And as the authority from which they proceed is supreme and can seldom act, they are designed to be permanent.

This original and supreme will organizes the government and assigns to different departments their respective powers. It may either stop here or establish certain limits not to be transcended by those departments.

The government of the United States is of the latter description. The powers of the legislature are defined and limited; and that those limits may not be mistaken or forgotten, the Constitution is written. To what purpose are powers limited, and to what purpose is that limitation committed to writing, if these limits may, at any time, be passed by those intended to be restrained? The distinction between a government with limited and unlimited powers is abolished if those limits do not confine the persons on whom they are imposed, and if acts prohibited and acts allowed are of equal obligation. It is a proposition too plain to be contested that the Constitution controls any legislative act repugnant to it or that the legislature may alter the Constitution by an ordinary act.

Between these alternatives there is no middle ground. The Constitution is either a superior, paramount law, unchangeable by ordinary means, or it is on a level with ordinary legislative acts and, like other acts, is alterable when the legislature shall please to alter it.

If the former part of the alternative be true, then a legislative act contrary to the Constitution is not law; if the latter part be true, then written constitutions are absurd attempts, on the part of the people, to limit a power in its own nature illimitable.

Certainly, all those who have framed written constitutions contemplate them as forming the fundamental and paramount law of the nation, and, consequently, the theory of every such government must be that an act of the legislature repugnant to the Constitution is void.

This theory is essentially attached to a written constitution and is, consequently, to be considered by this Court as one of the fundamental principles of our society. It is not, therefore, to be lost sight of in the further consideration of this subject.

If an act of the legislature repugnant to the Constitution is void, does it, notwithstanding its invalidity, bind the courts and oblige them to give it effect? Or, in other words, though it be not law, does it constitute a rule as operative as if it was a law? This would be to overthrow in fact what was established in theory and would seem, at first view, an absurdity too gross to be insisted on. It shall, however, receive a more attentive consideration.

It is, emphatically, the province and duty of the Judicial Department to say what the law is. Those who apply the rule to particular cases must of necessity expound and interpret that rule. If two laws conflict with each other, the courts must decide on the operation of each. So if a law be in opposition to the Constitution, if both the law and the Constitution apply to a particular case, so that the court must either decide that case conformably to the law, disregarding the Constitution, or conformably to the Constitution, disregarding the law, the court must determine which of these conflicting rules governs the case. This is of the very essence of judicial duty. If, then, the courts are to regard the Constitution, and the Constitution is superior to any ordinary act of the legislature, the Constitution, and not such ordinary act, must govern the case to which they both apply.

Those, then, who controvert the principle that the Constitution is to be considered in court as a paramount law are reduced to the necessity of maintaining that courts must close their eyes on the Constitution and see only the law.

This doctrine would subvert the very foundation of all written constitutions. It would declare that an act which, according to the principles and theory of our government, is entirely void, is yet, in practice, completely obligatory. It would declare that if the legislature shall do what is expressly forbidden, such act, notwithstanding the express prohibition, is in reality effectual. It would be giving to the legislature a practical and real omnipotence, with the same breath which professes to restrict their powers within narrow limits. It is prescribing limits and declaring that those limits may be passed at pleasure.

That it thus reduces to nothing what we have deemed the greatest improvement on political institutions, a written constitution, would of itself be sufficient in America, where written constitutions have been viewed with so much reverence, for rejecting the construction. But the peculiar expressions of the Constitution of the United States furnish additional arguments in favor of its rejection.

The judicial power of the United States is extended to all cases arising under the Constitution. Could it be the intention of those who gave this power to say that, in using it, the Constitution should not be looked into? That a case arising under the Constitution should be decided without examining the instrument under which it arises?

This is too extravagant to be maintained. In some cases, then, the Constitution must be looked into by the judges. And if they can open it at all, what part of it are they forbidden to read or to obey?

There are many other parts of the Constitution which serve to illustrate this subject. It is declared that "no tax or duty shall be laid on articles exported from any state." Suppose a duty on the export of cotton, of tobacco, or of flour; and a suit instituted to recover it. Ought judgment to be rendered in such a case? Ought the judges to close their eyes on the Constitution and only see the law?

The Constitution declares that "no bill of attainder or ex post facto law shall be passed." If, however, such a bill should be passed and a person should be prosecuted under it, must the court condemn to death those victims whom the Constitution endeavors to preserve?

"No person," says the Constitution, "shall be convicted of treason, unless on the testimony of two witnesses to the same overt act, or on confession in open court." Here the language of the Constitution is addressed especially to the courts. It prescribes, directly for them, a rule of evidence not to be departed from. If the legislature should change that rule and declare one witness or a confession out of court sufficient for conviction, must the constitutional principle yield to the legislative act?

From these and many other selections which might be made, it is apparent that the framers of the Constitution contemplated that instrument as a rule for the government of *courts* as well as of the legislature.

Why, otherwise, does it direct the judges to take an oath to support it? This oath certainly applies, in an especial manner, to their conduct in their official character. How immoral to impose it on them if they were to be used as the instruments, and the knowing instruments, for violating what they swear to support!

The oath of office, too, imposed by the legislature is completely demonstrative of the legislative opinion on this subject. It is in these words:

> I do solemnly swear that I will administer justice without respect to persons, and do equal right to the poor and to the rich; and that I will faithfully and impartially discharge all the duties incumbent on me as ———, according to the best of my abilities and understanding, agreeably to the Constitution and laws of the United States.

Why does a judge swear to discharge his duties agreeably to the Constitution of the United States if that Constitution forms no rule for his government? If it is closed upon him and cannot be inspected by him? If such be the real state of things, this is worse than solemn mockery. To prescribe, or to take this oath, becomes equally a crime.

It is also not entirely unworthy of observation that in declaring what shall be the supreme law of the land, the Constitution itself is first mentioned, and not the laws of the United States generally, but those only which shall be made in pursuance of the Constitution have that rank.

Thus, the particular phraseology of the Constitution of the United States confirms and strengthens the principle, supposed to be essential to all written constitutions, that a law repugnant to the Constitution is void and that courts, as well as other departments, are bound by that instrument.

The rule must be discharged.

That most delicious of all privileges . . . spending other people's money.

John Randolph, of Roanoke, of the pleasures of governing

42.

Thomas Jefferson: The Politics of the Louisiana Purchase

When Napoleon was induced to sell the Louisiana Territory to the United States on April 30, 1803, many questions were raised by the purchase. The Constitution made no provision for a transaction of this nature, and many wondered whether the federal government had the right to increase the national domain through a negotiated sale with a foreign nation. If such power existed, did the government have the further right to promise statehood to persons living outside the original states? In a letter of August 12, 1803, Jefferson discussed these matters with John Breckinridge, his friend and political lieutenant, who had introduced his Kentucky Resolutions into the Kentucky legislature in 1798. Realizing that protests, especially from the Federalist camp, could block the congressional acceptance of the treaty, Jefferson beseeched Breckinridge, in a letter of August 18, not to divulge their correspondence. As a final preventive measure, in case the purchase was blocked on constitutional grounds, an amendment was prepared to incorporate the territory directly into the Union. The two Jefferson letters and the amendment are reprinted here.

Source: Randolph, III, pp. 519-521. *Magazine of American History,* August 1885, p. 199.

I.

Letter to John Breckinridge

The enclosed letter . . . gives me occasion to write a word to you on the subject of Louisiana, which, being a new one, an interchange of sentiments may produce correct ideas before we are to act on them.

Our information as to the country is very incomplete. We have taken measures to obtain it in full as to the settled part, which I hope to receive in time for Congress. The boundaries, which I deem not admitting question, are the highlands on the western side of the Mississippi enclosing all its waters, the Missouri, of course, and terminating in the line drawn from the northwestern point of the Lake of the Woods to the nearest source of the Mississippi, as lately settled between Great Britain and the United States. We have some claims to extend on the seacoast westwardly to the Rio Norte or Bravo [Rio Grande], and, better, to go eastwardly to the Rio Perdido, between Mobile and Pensacola, the ancient boundary of Louisiana. These claims will be a subject of negotiation with Spain and if, as soon as she is at war, we push them strongly with one hand, holding out a price in the other, we shall certainly obtain the Floridas, and all in good time.

In the meanwhile, without waiting for permission, we shall enter into the exercise of the natural right we have always insisted on with Spain, to wit, that of a nation holding the upper part of streams having a right of innocent passage through them to the ocean. We shall prepare her to see us practise on this, and she will not oppose it by force.

Objections are raising to the eastward against the vast extent of our boundaries, and propositions are made to exchange

Louisiana, or a part of it, for the Floridas. But, as I have said, we shall get the Floridas without, and I would not give one inch of the waters of the Mississippi to any nation because I see, in a light very important to our peace, the exclusive right to its navigation, and the admission of no nation into it, but as into the Potomac or Delaware, with our consent and under our police.

These Federalists see in this acquisition the formation of a new confederacy, embracing all the waters of the Mississippi on both sides of it, and a separation of its eastern waters from us. These combinations depend on so many circumstances which we cannot foresee that I place little reliance on them. We have seldom seen neighborhood produce affection among nations. The reverse is almost the universal truth. Besides, if it should become the great interest of those nations to separate from this, if their happiness should depend on it so strongly as to induce them to go through that convulsion, why should the Atlantic states dread it? But, especially, why should we, their present inhabitants, take side in such a question?

When I view the Atlantic states, procuring for those on the eastern waters of the Mississippi friendly instead of hostile neighbors on its western waters, I do not view it as an Englishman would the procuring future blessings for the French nation, with whom he has no relations of blood or affection. The future inhabitants of the Atlantic and Mississippi states will be our sons. We leave them in distinct but bordering establishments. We think we see their happiness in their union, and we wish it. Events may prove it otherwise; and if they see their interest in separation, why should we take side with our Atlantic rather than our Mississippi descendants? It is the elder and the younger son differing. God bless them both and keep them in union if it be for their good, but separate them if it be better.

The inhabited part of Louisiana, from Point Coupée to the sea, will of course be immediately a territorial government and soon a state. But, above that, the best use we can make of the country for some time will be to give establishments in it to the Indians on the east side of the Mississippi in exchange for their present country, and open land offices in the last, and thus make this acquisition the means of filling up the eastern side instead of drawing off its population. When we shall be full on this side, we may lay off a range of states on the western bank from the head to the mouth, and so, range after range, advancing compactly as we multiply.

This treaty must, of course, be laid before both houses, because both have important functions to exercise respecting it. They, I presume, will see their duty to their country in ratifying and paying for it so as to secure a good which would otherwise probably be never again in their power. But I suppose they must then appeal to the nation for an additional article to the Constitution, approving and confirming an act which the nation had not previously authorized. The Constitution has made no provision for our holding foreign territory, still less for incorporating foreign nations into our Union. The executive, in seizing the fugitive occurrence which so much advances the good of their country, have done an act beyond the Constitution. The legislature in casting behind them metaphysical subtleties, and risking themselves like faithful servants, must ratify and pay for it and throw themselves on their country for doing for them unauthorized what we know they would have done for themselves had they been in a situation to do it.

It is the case of a guardian investing the money of his ward in purchasing an important adjacent territory, and saying to him when of age, I did this for your good; I pretend to no right to bind you; you may disavow me, and I must get out of the scrape as I can; I thought it my duty to risk myself for you. But we shall not be disavowed by the nation, and their act of indemnity will confirm and not weaken the Constitution by more strongly marking out its lines.

II.

Letter to Breckinridge

I WROTE TO YOU on the 12th inst. on the subject of Louisiana and the constitutional provision that might be necessary for it. A letter received yesterday shows that nothing must be said on that subject which may give a pretext for retracting; but that we should do, *sub silentio*, what shall be found necessary. Be so good, therefore, as to consider that part of my letter as confidential; it strengthens the reasons for desiring the presence of every friend to the treaty on the first day of the session. Perhaps you can impress this necessity on the senators of the Western states by private letter.

Accept my friendly salutations and assurances of great respect and esteem.

III.

Proposed Constitutional Amendment

Resolved, by the Senate and House of Representatives of the United States, two-thirds of both houses concurring, that the following amendment to the Constitution of the United States be proposed to the legislatures of the several states, which, when ratified by three-fourths of the said legislatures, shall be valid to all intents and purposes as a part of the said Constitution:

Louisiana, as ceded by France to the United States, is made a part of the United States.

43.

THOMAS JEFFERSON: On the Admission of New States

Jefferson feared that the treaty with Napoleon that made the Louisiana Purchase legal might at any time be revised or even revoked. His attitude was summed up in 1808, when he declared that "to lose our country by a scrupulous adherence to written law, would be to lose the law itself." He expressed similar views in the following letter of September 7, 1803, to his friend Senator Wilson C. Nicholas of Virginia. In it, Jefferson outlined his understanding of the power the government had to admit new states — and thereby stretched his otherwise strict interpretation of the Constitution to the limit.

Source: Randolph, IV, pp. 2-4.

YOUR FAVOR OF THE 3rd was delivered me at court; but we were much disappointed at not seeing you here, Mr. Madison and the governor being here at the time. I enclose you a letter from Monroe on the subject of the late treaty. You will observe a hint in it to do without delay what we are bound to do. There is reason, in the opinion of our ministers, to believe that if the thing were to do over again, it could not be obtained, and that if we give the least opening, they will declare the treaty void. A warning amounting to that has been given to them, and an unusual kind of letter written by their minister to our secretary of state, direct. Whatever Congress shall think it necessary to do should be done with as little debate as possible, and particularly so far as respects the constitutional difficulty.

I am aware of the force of the observations you make on the power given by the Constitution to Congress, to admit new states into the Union, without restraining the subject to the territory then constituting the United States. But when I consider that the limits of the United States are precisely fixed by the Treaty of 1783, that the Constitution expressly declares itself to be made for the United States, I cannot help believing the intention was not to permit Congress to admit into the Union new states, which should be formed out of the territory for which, and under whose authority alone, they were then acting. I do not believe it was meant that they might receive England, Ireland, Holland, etc., into it, which would be the case on your construction. When an instrument admits two constructions — the one safe, the other dangerous; the one precise, the other indefinite — I prefer that which is safe and precise. I had rather ask an enlargement of power from the nation, where it is found necessary, than to assume it by a construction which would make our powers boundless. Our peculiar security is in the possession of a written constitution. Let us not make it a blank paper by construction.

I say the same as to the opinion of those who consider the grant of the treaty-making power as boundless. If it is, then we have no constitution. If it has bounds, they can be no others than the definitions of the powers which that instrument gives. It specifies and delineates the operations permitted to the federal government, and gives all the powers necessary to carry these into execution. Whatever of these enumerated objects is proper for a law, Congress may make the law; whatever is proper to be executed by way of a treaty, the president and Senate may enter into the treaty; whatever is to be done by a judicial sentence, the judges may pass the sentence. Nothing is more likely than that their enumeration of powers is defective. This is the ordinary case of all human works. Let us go on, then, perfecting it by adding, by way of amendment to the Constitution, those powers which time and trial show are still wanting. But it has been taken too much for granted that by this rigorous construction the treaty power would be reduced to nothing. I had occasion once to examine its effect on the French treaty, made by the old Congress, and found that out of thirty-odd articles which that contained, there were one, two, or three only which could not now be stipulated under our present constitution.

I confess, then, I think it important, in the present case, to set an example against broad construction by appealing for new power to the people. If, however, our friends shall think differently, certainly I shall acquiesce with satisfaction; confiding that the good sense of our country will correct the evil of construction when it shall produce ill effects.

44.

Samuel White: Opposition to the Louisiana Purchase

In purchasing the Louisiana Territory from France, Jefferson had doubled the size of the country with a stroke of his pen; but he had also performed an act wholly at variance with his own principles and those of his party, which advocated a strict construction of the Constitution. He thus alienated some of his supporters, but he could take comfort in the fact that the purchase was otherwise a diplomatic and political triumph. It ended the threat of war with France and opened up a vast new region to settlement. The latter, however, was the reason why Jefferson was not the only one to act out of character. The Federalists, who had traditionally favored a measured expansionism, now opposed the acquisition of Louisiana partly because it was a Jefferson coup, but mainly because they feared that the westward movement of settlers would eventually shift the balance of power away from the East, where they were strong. They also disliked the idea of negotiating a treaty with their bête noire, *Napoleon. Some of their arguments against the treaty, and therefore against the acquisition of Louisiana, were ably stated by Senator Samuel White of Delaware, who addressed the Senate on November 2, 1803.*

Source: *Debates,* 8 Cong., pp. 31-35.

Mr. [Samuel] White [Delaware] rose and made the following remarks:

Admitting then, Mr. President, that His Catholic Majesty [the King of Spain] is hostile to the cession of this territory to the United States, and no honorable gentleman will deny it, what reasons have we to suppose that the French prefect, provided the Spaniards should interfere, can give to us peaceable possession of the country? He is acknowledged there in no public character, is clothed with no authority, nor has he a single soldier to enforce his orders. I speak now, sir, from mere probabilities. I wish not to be understood as predicting that the French will not cede to us the actual and quiet possession of the territory. I hope to God they may, for possession of it we must have; I mean of New Orleans, and of such other positions on the Mississippi as may be necessary to secure to us forever the complete and uninterrupted navigation of that river.

This I have ever been in favor of; I think it essential to the peace of the United States and to the prosperity of our western country. But as to Louisiana, this new, immense, unbounded world, if it should ever be incorporated into this Union, which I have no idea can be done but by altering the Constitution, I believe it will be the greatest curse that could at present befall us; it may be productive of innumerable evils, and especially of one that I fear even to look upon. Gentlemen on all sides, with very few exceptions, agree that the settlement of this country will be highly injurious and dangerous to the United States; but as to what has been suggested of removing the Creeks and other nations of Indians from the eastern to the western banks of the Mississippi, and of making the fertile regions of Louisiana a howling wilderness, never to be trodden by the foot of civilized man, it is impracticable.

The gentleman from Tennessee [Mr. Cocke] has shown his usual candor on this subject, and I believe with him (to use his strong language) that you had as well pretend to inhibit the fish from swimming in the sea as to prevent the population of that country after its sovereignty shall become ours. To every man acquainted with the adventurous, roving, and enterprising temper of our people, and with the manner in which our western country has been settled, such an idea must be chimerical. The inducements will be so strong that it will be impossible to restrain our citizens from crossing the river. Louisiana must and will become settled if we hold it, and with the very population that would otherwise occupy part of our present territory. Thus our citizens will be removed to the immense distance of 2,000 or 3,000 miles from the capital of the Union, where they will scarcely ever feel the rays of the general government; their affections will become alienated; they will gradually begin to view us as strangers; they will form other commercial connections, and our interests will become distinct.

These, with other causes that human wisdom may not now foresee, will in time effect a separation, and I fear our bounds will be fixed nearer to our houses than the waters of the Mississippi. We have already territory enough, and when I contemplate the evils that may arise to these states from this intended incorporation of Louisiana into the Union, I would rather see it given to France, to Spain, or to any other nation of the earth upon the mere condition that no citizen of the United States should ever settle within its limits, than to see the territory sold for $100 million and we retain the sovereignty.

But however dangerous the possession of Louisiana might prove to us, I do not presume to say that the retention of it would not have been very convenient to France. And we know that at the time of the mission of Mr. Monroe, our administration had never thought of the purchase of Louisiana, and that nothing short of the fullest conviction on the part of the first consul that he was on the very eve of a war with England, that this being the most defenseless point of his possessions, if such they could be called, was the one at which the British would first strike, and that it must inevitably fall into their hands, could ever have induced his pride and ambition to make the sale. He judged wisely that he had better sell it for as much as he could get than lose it entirely. And I do say that under existing circumstances, even supposing that this extent of territory was a desirable acquisition, $15 million was a most enormous sum to give.

Our commissioners were negotiating in Paris; they must have known the relative situation of France and England; they must have known at the moment that a war was unavoidable between the two countries; and they knew the pecuniary necessities of France and the naval power of Great Britain. These imperious circumstances should have been turned to our advantage, and if we were to purchase, should have lessened the consideration.

Viewing, Mr. President, this subject in any point of light, either as it regards the territory purchased, the high consideration to be given, the contract itself, or any of the circumstances attending it I see no necessity for precipitating the passage of this bill. And if this motion for postponement should fail, and the question on the final passage of the bill be taken now, I shall certainly vote against it.

Library of Congress

EXPLORING THE WEST

Jeffersonian democracy was founded on the doctrine of agrarian supremacy. Mercantile and manufacturing interests were subordinated to the needs of the farmer. Only in the West was there unlimited land for planting and its allied economy, stock raising. Hence, Jefferson encouraged every move toward Westward expansion. He maneuvered the Louisiana Purchase, the largest single land acquisition in American history; and he organized expeditions to inventory the vast resources acquired. As early as 1792 he had urged the American Philosophical Society to sponsor a Western expedition. As President, he sent the Lewis and Clark expedition, and later Zebulon Pike, to chart the vast and unknown Western territories. For decades to come, this land would be chiefly the resort of buffalo hunters, trappers, traders, and those who disliked settled living. But to Jefferson this land was the key to the future of the infant United States. It would receive the migrants from the overpopulated seaboard states; it was also the key to the success of the Republican Party he had founded.

Mariners Museum

(Left) New Orleans 1803; (center) facade of the Public Bathe of New Orleans; (bottom left) first page of the Louisiana Purchase treaty, French copy; (bottom right) map of Mississippi River delta

Louisiana

By the purchase of the Louisiana Territory in 1803, the United States doubled in size. Jefferson authorized an expedition to explore the land between the Mississippi and the Pacific. Meriwether Lewis and William Clark led the party of about forty men, which headed up the Missouri in May 1804 and reached the mouth of the Columbia River in November 1805. In the wake of this expedition, trappers and traders began moving into the Rocky Mountains.

Louisiana State Museum

Bonaparte, Premier Consul,
au Nom du Peuple Français. Les Consuls de la République ayant vu et examiné le Traité conclu, arrêté et signé à Paris, le dix Floréal an onze (trente Avril Mil huit cent trois) par le Citoyen François Barbé Marbois, Ministre du Trésor Public, en vertu des pleins pouvoirs qui lui avaient été conférés à cet effet, avec les Sieurs Robert R. Livingston, Ministre Plénipotentiaire des Etats-unis d'Amérique et James Monroe, Ministre Plénipotentiaire et Envoyé extraordinaire des dits Etats, également munis de pleins pouvoirs, duquel Traité la teneur suit :

Traité
entre la République Française et les Etats-unis d'Amérique.

Le Premier Consul de la République Française, au nom du Peuple français, et le Président des Etats-unis d'Amérique, désirant prévenir tout sujet de mésintelligence relativement aux objets de discussion mentionnés dans les Articles 2 et 5 de la Convention du 8 Vendémiaire an 9 (30 Septembre 1800) et relativement aux droits reclamés pour les Etats-unis, en vertu du Traité conclu à Madrid le 27 Octobre 1795, entre Sa Majesté Catholique et les dits Etats-unis, et voulant fortifier de plus en plus les rapports d'union et d'amitié qui, à l'époque de la dite Convention, ont été heureusement rétablis entre les deux Etats, ont respectivement nommé pour Plénipotentiaires, savoir : Le Premier Consul, au nom du Peuple français, le Citoyen François Barbé Marbois,

Library of Congress

National Archives

Library of Congress

Independence National Historical Park

Library of Congress

Independence National Historical Park

(Top and center left) Two engravings from the third edition of "A Journal of the Voyage . . . of Capt. Lewis and Capt. Clarke . . ." by Patrick Gass, a member of the expedition

(Top right) Meriwether Lewis; (center right) William Clark, both portraits by C. W. Peale; (bottom) printed map copied from one drawn by Clark showing the area explored

Independence National Historical Park

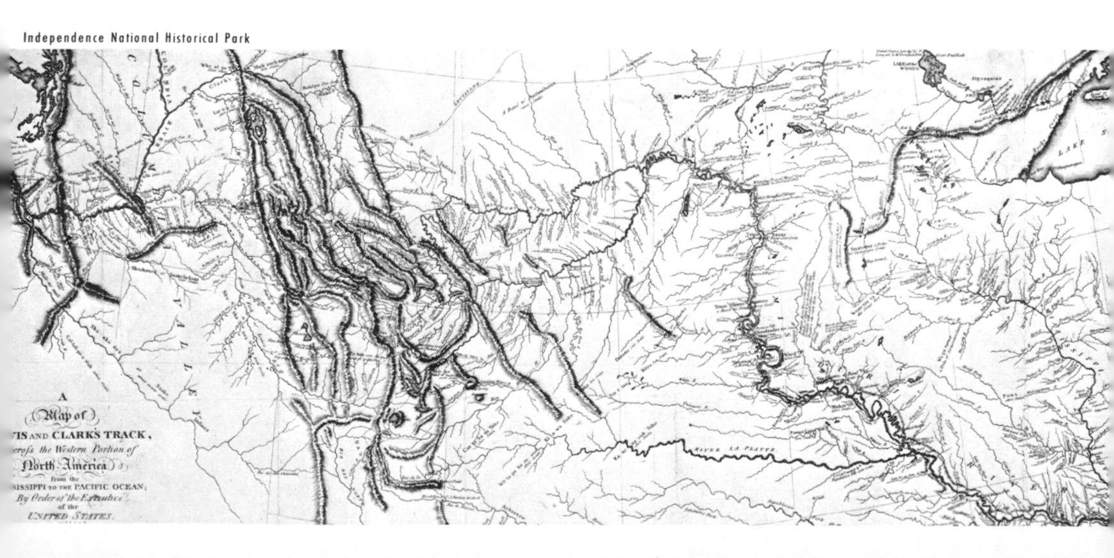

Virginia State Library

Shelburne Museum

Chicago Museum of Science and Industry

(Top) Lithograph of the Wilderness Road which went from Virginia to Kentucky and Tennessee through the Cumberland Gap; (left) "Conestoga Wagon on the Road" by Thomas Birch, 1814; (above and below) scenes on the road west in the early 19th century by Joshua Shaw

New States

In the short period between 1792 and 1803 the regions immediately west of the Appalachians were admitted to statehood, greatly increasing the area available for farming. Farmers who had toiled on depleted soil in the seaboard states could get a new start in fertile lands, especially along the rich Ohio River bottoms. Fresh land and the low taxes of the new states were a strong incentive, and thousands moved on, reaching Ohio and Kentucky by following the Ohio River downstream. Settlers came to eastern Tennessee chiefly by overland trails; some came down the Mississippi from the Ohio and settled around Memphis.

Chicago Museum of Science and Industry

American Antiquarian Society

Tennessee Historical Society

New York Public Library

Tennessee State Library

Library of Congress

(Top) John Sevier, first governor of Tennessee; (center left) Tennessee mountain valley with log house, sketch by Lesueur; (center right) Isaac Shelby, Kentucky's first governor; (bottom left) State House, Frankfort; (bottom right) splitting logs

Stokes Collection, New York Public Library

American Antiquarian Society

Chicago Museum of Science and Industry

Library of Congress

Library of Congress

(Top) Pittsburgh in 1796; engraving of a wash drawing by Joseph Warin; the Ohio River rises here from the Allegheny and Monongahela rivers; (center left) keelboat on the Ohio; (center right) pioneer axmen sketched by Joshua Shaw; (bottom left) Chillicothe courthouse in 1801; (bottom right) first courthouse in Greene County

(Top) Cleveland in 1800; located on the Cuyahoga River, Cleveland was founded in 1796 by Moses Cleaveland. It was the first settlement in northeastern Ohio but remained undeveloped until after the War of 1812. (Bottom left) Militia camp in Ohio during the war; (bottom right) Ohio, 1804; map by Rufus Putnam showing the major settlements and the remaining Indian lands in the northwestern region of the state

Western Reserve Historical Society

Library of Congress

Library of Congress

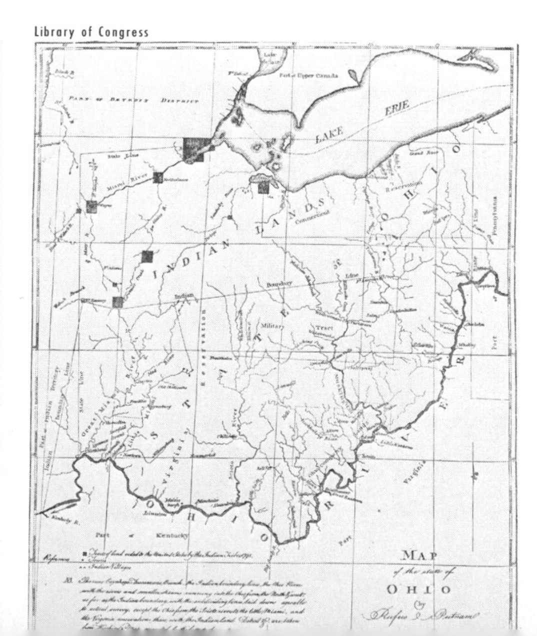

West Becomes Midwest

Independence National Historical Park

(Above) Arthur St. Clair, first governor of the Northwest Territory; (below) map of the Great Lakes region in 1816 by John Eddy

Before settlers could freely migrate west of the mountains, the Indians, reluctant to abandon ancestral lands, had to be crushed. Led by Tecumseh's brother, "The Prophet," the Shawnee engaged William Henry Harrison at the Tippecanoe River, near Lafayette, Ind. Harrison's victory opened Indiana and Illinois for settlement. At the close of the War of 1812, veterans and others settled the rich farmlands. Michigan and Wisconsin, less appealing to farmers, were largely reserved for hunting and trapping.

Indiana Historical Society

Library of Congress, Map Division

(Above) Prairie scene in Indiana, early 19th century; engraving from a painting by George Winter; (center left) the American Fur Company at Fond du Lac, Wisconsin territory; (center right) Detroit and the straits, 1804; (bottom left) Chicago in 1820; (bottom right) Fort Harrison, Indiana, in 1812

Library of Congress

Clements Library, University of Michigan

Chicago Historical Society

Library of Congress

Missouri Historical Society

Missouri Historical Society

(Above) St. Louis in 1817; (right) Manuel Lisa based his fur company in St. Louis with outposts all along the Missouri River

Explorer and Trader

The town of St. Louis, founded by the French near the confluence of the Missouri and the Mississippi, was a natural center for trade, especially in furs and hides. Manuel Lisa had fur-trading posts all along the Missouri as far northwest as Montana. One of his bitterest competitors, John Jacob Astor, chief trader in the territories of Michigan and Wisconsin, pushed west to the Pacific and established his Pacific Fur Company at Fort Astoria (at the mouth of the Columbia River). Competition was not limited to Americans: Hudson's Bay Company had its interests in the Northwest too. Meanwhile Zebulon Pike made two expeditions: in 1806 to the headwaters of the Mississippi, and in 1807 to the west, exploring what would later become Colorado and New Mexico. He discovered, but did not succeed in climbing, Pike's Peak.

The Granger Collection

(Below) Astoria as it was in 1813 before British troops from Canada forced the Americans to surrender the fort; (above right) John Jacob Astor, founder of the American Fur Company

Library of Congress

National Gallery of Canada

Yale University Library

(Above left) Alexander Mackenzie, leader of the 1793 expedition that crossed the continent through Canada; (above right) red sandstone cliffs near the Rocky Mountains, sketch by Seymour

Library of Congress

(Above) View of the insulated table lands at the foot of the Rocky Mountains; (below left) Zebulon Montgomery Pike, portrait by C. W. Peale

Independence National Historical Park

The Rocky Mountains as seen from the Platte River, 1823

Library of Congress

Yale University Library

American Philosophical Society

(Left) Kiowa encampment in the high plains; (right) "Western Engineer," Long's steamboat which carried his group to the expedition's winter camp at Council Bluffs

Independence National Historical Park

Yale University Library

(Above left) Stephen Long, portrait by C. W. Peale; (above right) Pawnee Council, sketched by Samuel Seymour; (below) American antelope, sketched by Titian Peale; Peale and Seymour were members of Long's survey group

Long Expedition

American Philosophical Society

In 1819 Stephen Long led an expedition to the source of the Mississippi and in 1820 he took a surveying party into the Colorado Rockies. Three men from Long's party were the first to climb Pike's Peak, but Long was unimpressed by the splendor of the Rockies and in his report called the area unfit for settlers. The government agreed, and viewed it as a good spot for relocating Indians displaced from their homes in the East. Long's expedition, like that of Lewis and Clark, was meant to blaze a trail for national expansion.

1804

45.

Timothy Pickering: On Northern Secession

Jefferson responded to Marbury *v.* Madison *by inciting his supporters in the House to attack the judiciary. The attack failed, but it convinced the extreme New England Federalists, such as Timothy Pickering of Massachusetts, the writer of the following letter, that Jefferson had no principles. Since these Federalists felt themselves already doomed to minority status by the Louisiana Purchase, which threatened them with an insuperable coalition of the South and West, they now became desperate. As Pickering's letter to Rufus King, dated March 4, 1804, indicates, they seriously considered bringing about the secession of at least New England and perhaps New York, as well. Pickering had been appointed secretary of state in 1795 and had continued in that position under John Adams until 1800. He was dismissed in the latter year for the persistent intrigues by which he had sought to bring on war with France. By 1804, when he wrote this letter, he had returned to Washington as Senator from Massachusetts.*

Source: *Documents Relating to New England Federalism, 1800-1815,* Henry Adams, ed., Boston, 1905, pp. 351-353.

I am disgusted with the men who now rule and with their measures. At some manifestations of their malignancy I am shocked. The cowardly wretch at their head, while, like a Parisian revolutionary monster, prating about humanity, would feel an infernal pleasure in the utter destruction of his opponents. We have too long witnessed his general turpitude, his cruel removals of faithful officers, and the substitution of corruption and looseness for integrity and worth.

We have now before the Senate a nomination of Merriweather Jones, of Richmond, editor of the *Examiner,* a paper devoted to Jefferson and Jacobinism; and he is now to be rewarded. Mr. Hopkins, commissioner of loans, a man of property and integrity, is to give room for this Jones. The commissioner may have at once $30,000 in his hands to pay the public creditors in Virginia. He is required by law to give bonds only in a sum from $5,000 to $10,000; and Jones's character is so notoriously bad that we have satisfactory evidence he could not now get credit at any store in Richmond for a suit of clothes! Yet I am far from thinking, if this evidence should be laid before the Senate, that his nomination will be negatived!

I am therefore ready to say, "Come out from among them, and be ye separate." Corruption is the object and instrument of the chief, and the tendency of his administration, for the purpose of maintaining himself in power and the accomplishment of his infidel and visionary schemes. The corrupt portion of the people are the agents of his misrule. Corruption is the recommendation to office; and many, of some pretensions to character but too feeble to resist temptation, become apostates. Virtue and worth are his enemies, and therefore he would overwhelm them. The collision of Democrats in your state promises some amendment; the administration of your government cannot well be worse.

The Federalists here, in general, anxiously desire the election of Mr. Burr to the chair of New York; for they despair of a present ascendancy of the Federal Party. Mr. Burr alone, we think, can break your Democratic phalanx; and we anticipate much good from his success. Were New York detached (as under his administration it would be) from the Virginian influence, the whole Union would be benefited. Jefferson would then be forced to observe some caution and forbearance in his measures. And, if a separation should be deemed proper, the five New England states, New York, and New Jersey would naturally be united. Among those seven states, there is a sufficient congeniality of character to authorize the expectation of practicable harmony and a permanent union, [with] New York the center.

Without a separation, can those states ever rid themselves of Negro presidents and Negro congresses, and regain their just weight in the political balance? At this moment, the slaves of the Middle and Southern states have fifteen representatives in Congress, and they will appoint that number of electors of the next president and vice-president; and the number of slaves is continually increasing. You notice this evil. But will the slave states ever renounce the advantage? As population is in fact no rule of taxation, the Negro representation ought to be given up. If refused, it would be a strong ground for separation, though perhaps an earlier occasion may present to declare it.

Courtesy, Museum of Fine Arts, Boston; Frederick Brown Fund
Pastel portrait of Timothy Pickering by St. Memmin

How many Indian wars, excited by the avidity of the Western and Southern states for Indian lands, shall we have to encounter, and who will pay the millions to support them? The Atlantic states. Yet the first moment we ourselves need assistance, and call on the Western states for taxes, they will declare off, or at any rate refuse to obey the call. Kentucky effectually resisted the collection of the excise; and of the $37,000 direct tax assessed upon her so many years ago, she has paid only $4,000, and probably will never pay the residue. In the meantime, we are maintaining their representatives in Congress for governing us, who surely can much better govern ourselves.

Whenever the Western states detach themselves, they will take Louisiana with them. In thirty years, the white population on the Western waters will equal that of the thirteen states when they declared themselves independent of Great Britain. On the census of 1790, Kentucky was entitled to two representatives; under that of 1800, she sends *six!*

P. S. I do not know *one reflecting* Nov-Anglian who is not anxious for the *great event* at which I have glanced. They fear, they *dread,* the effects of the corruption so rapidly extending; and that, if a decisive step be long delayed, it will be in vain to attempt it. If there be no improper delay, we have not any doubt but that the *great measure* may be taken, without the smallest hazard to private property or the public funds, the revenues of the Northern states being equal to their portion of the public debt, leaving that for Louisiana on those who incurred it.

46.

Abigail Adams: On Presidential Appointments

Following his defeat in 1800, John Adams and his wife Abigail retired to "Quincy," their Massachusetts farm. Like her husband, Mrs. Adams was a thoroughgoing Federalist, and she continued to be disturbed by the attacks on his administration, many of which she considered unfounded. In 1804, she wrote to Jefferson on the death of his daughter, of whom she had been fond in former days; but her letter, while full of what the President called "the tenderest expressions of concern at the event," carefully avoided any overtures of friendship toward himself. In reply, Jefferson expressed his appreciation for her concern, and went on to mention the strained relations between himself and her husband. In a further letter of July 1, 1804, which is reprinted here, Mrs. Adams took the opportunity to defend ex-President Adams' last-minute or "midnight" appointments, which had come under fire by the Republicans. Jefferson and Adams did not become epistolary friends again for another nine years.

Source: *Letters of Mrs. Adams,* Charles Francis Adams, ed., 4th edition, Boston, 1848, pp. 390-394.

Your letter of June 13 came duly to hand. If it had contained no other sentiments and opinions than those which my letter of condolence could have excited, and which are expressed in the first page of your reply, our correspondence would have terminated here. But you have been pleased to enter upon some subjects which call for a reply; and as you observe that you have wished for an opportunity to express your sentiments, I have given them every weight they claim.

"One act of Mr. Adams' life, and *one* only (you repeat) ever gave me a moment's personal displeasure. I did consider his last appointments to office as personally unkind;

they were from my most ardent political enemies."

As this act, I am certain, was not intended to give any personal pain or offense, I think it a duty to explain it, so far as I then knew his views and designs. The Constitution empowers the President to fill up offices as they become vacant. It was in the exercise of this power that appointments were made, and characters selected whom Mr. Adams considered as men faithful to the Constitution, and, where he personally knew them, such as were capable of fulfilling their duty to their country. This was done equally by General Washington in the last days of his administration, so that not an office remained vacant for his successor to fill upon his coming into office. No offense was given by it and no personal unkindness thought of.

But the different political opinions which have so unhappily divided our country must have given rise to the idea that personal unkindness was intended. You will please to recollect, sir, that at the time these appointments were made, there was not any certainty that the presidency would devolve upon you, which is another circumstance to prove that no personal unkindness was intended. No person, I am sure, was ever selected from such a motive, and so far was Mr. Adams from harboring such a sentiment that he had not any idea of the intolerance of a party spirit at that time. I know it was his opinion that if the presidency devolved upon you, except in the appointment of secretaries, no material change would be made.

I perfectly agree with you in opinion that those should be men in whom the President can repose confidence, possessing opinions and sentiments corresponding with his own; or if differing with him, that they ought rather to resign their offices than to cabal against measures which he may consider essential to the honor, safety, and peace of the country. Neither ought they to unite with any bold and daringly ambitious character to overrule the cabinet or to betray the secrets of it to friends or enemies. The two gentlemen who held the offices of secretaries, when you became President, were not of this character. They were persons appointed by your predecessor nearly two years previous to his retirement. They had cordially cooperated with him, and were gentlemen who enjoyed the public confidence. Possessing, however, different political sentiments from those which you were known to have embraced, it was expected that they would, as they did, resign.

I have never felt any enmity toward you, sir, for being elected President of the United States. But the instruments made use of and the means which were practised to effect a change have my utter abhorrence and detestation, for they were the blackest calumny and the foulest falsehoods. I had witnessed enough of the anxiety and solicitude, the envy, jealousy, and reproach attendant upon the office, as well as the high responsibility of the station, to be perfectly willing to see a transfer of it; and I can truly say that at the time of election, I considered your pretensions much superior to his who shared an equal vote with you. Your experience, I dare venture to affirm, has convinced you that it is not a station to be envied. If you feel yourself a freeman, and can conduct, in all cases, according to your own sentiments, opinions, and judgment, you can do more than either of your predecessors could, and are awfully responsible to God and your country for the measures of your administration.

I must rely upon the friendship you still profess to entertain for me (and I am conscious I have done nothing to forfeit it) to excuse the freedom of this discussion, to which you have led with an unreserve, which has taken off the shackles I should, otherwise, have found myself embarrassed with. And, now, sir, I will freely disclose to you what has severed the bonds of former friendship, and placed you in a light very different from what some viewed you in.

One of the first acts of your administration was to liberate a wretch who was suffering the just punishment of his crimes for publishing the basest libel, the lowest and vilest slander which malice could invent or calumny exhibit, against the character and reputation of your predecessor; of him for whom you professed a friendship and esteem, and whom you certainly knew incapable of such complicated baseness. The remission of Callender's fine was a public approbation of his conduct. If abandoned characters do not excite abhorrence, is not the last restraint of vice, a sense of shame, rendered abortive? If the chief magistrate of a nation, whose elevated station places him in a conspicuous light and renders his every action a concern of general importance, permits his public conduct to be influenced by private resentment, and so far forgets what is due to his character as to give countenance to a base calumniator, is he not answerable for the influence which his example has upon the manners and morals of the community?

Until I read Callender's seventh letter containing your compliment to him as a writer and your reward of $50, I could not be made to believe that such measures could have been resorted to, to stab the fair fame and upright intentions of one who, to use your own language, "was acting from an honest conviction in his own mind that he was right." This, sir, I considered as a personal injury; this was the sword that cut asunder the Gordian knot, which could not be untied by all the efforts of party spirit, by rivalry, by jealousy, or any other malignant fiend.

The serpent you cherished and warmed bit the hand that nourished him, and gave you sufficient specimens of his talents, his gratitude, his justice, and his truth. When such vipers are let loose upon society, all distinction between virtue and vice is leveled; all respect for character is lost in the deluge of calumny; that respect which is a necessary bond in the social union, which gives efficacy to laws, and teaches the subject to obey the magistrate, and the child to submit to the parent. . . .

This letter is written in confidence. Faithful are the wounds of a friend. Often have I wished to have seen a different course pursued by you. I bear no malice. I cherish no enmity. I would not retaliate if it was in my power; nay, more, in the true spirit of Christian charity, I would forgive as I hope to be forgiven.

Oh Burr, oh Burr, what has thou done,
Thou hast shooted dead great Hamilton!
You hid behind a bunch of thistle,
And shooted him dead with a great hoss pistol!

Poem dropped on Aaron Burr's doorstep and widely circulated. Burr killed Hamilton on the morning of July 11, 1804.

1805

47.

RED JACKET: Against White Missions Among the Indians

The missionary impulse to Christianize the Indians that marked the early Puritan settlers in America was also a major characteristic of the eighteenth-century religious revival known as the Great Awakening. Missionary societies, which continued to function into the nineteenth century, worked at the conversion of the red man with a single-minded zeal that could only be produced by the certainty of the eternal damnation that would otherwise be his lot. In the summer of 1805, a number of the principal chiefs and warriors of the Six Nations, principally Senecas, assembled at Buffalo Creek in the state of New York at the request of a certain Reverend Cram from the Boston Missionary Society. The following eloquent speech of the Seneca Chief, Red Jacket, was prompted by the somewhat tactless remarks and questions put to the Indians by Cram. Red Jacket, whose Indian name was Sagoyewatha, had little sympathy with the way in which the white man's customs were being foisted on his people.

Source: *A Library of American Literature*, Edmund C. Stedman and Ellen M. Hutchinson, eds., Vol. IV, New York, 1889, pp. 36-38.

FRIEND AND BROTHER, it was the will of the Great Spirit that we should meet together this day. He orders all things and has given us a fine day for our council. He has taken His garment from before the sun and caused it to shine with brightness upon us. Our eyes are opened, that we see clearly; our ears are unstopped, that we have been able to hear distinctly the words you have spoken. For all these favors we thank the Great Spirit, and Him only.

Brother, this council fire was kindled by you. It was at your request that we came together at this time. We have listened with attention to what you have said. You requested us to speak our minds freely. This gives us great joy, for we now consider that we stand upright before you and can speak what we think. All have heard your voice, and all speak to you now as one man. Our minds are agreed.

Brother, you say you want an answer to your talk before you leave this place. It is right you should have one as you are a great distance from home and we do not wish to detain you. But we will first look back a little and tell you what our fathers have told us and what we have heard from the white people.

Brother, listen to what we say.

There was a time when our forefathers owned this great island. Their seats extended from the rising to the setting sun. The Great Spirit had made it for the use of Indians. He had created the buffalo, the deer, and other animals for food. He had made the bear and the beaver. Their skins served us for clothing. He had scattered them over the country and taught us how to take them. He had caused the earth to produce corn for bread. All this He had done for his red children because He loved them. If we had some disputes about our hunting ground, they were generally settled without the shedding of much blood.

But an evil day came upon us. Your forefathers crossed the great water and landed on this island. Their numbers were small. They found friends and not enemies. They told us they had fled from their own country for fear of wicked men and had come here to enjoy their religion. They asked for a small seat. We took pity on them, granted their request; and they sat down amongst us. We gave them corn and meat; they gave us poison in return.

The white people, brother, had now found our country. Tidings were carried back and more came amongst us. Yet we did not fear them. We took them to be friends. They called us brothers. We believed them and gave them a larger seat. At length their numbers had greatly increased. They wanted more land; they wanted our country. Our eyes were opened and our minds became uneasy. Wars took place. Indians were hired to fight against Indians, and many of our people were destroyed. They also brought strong liquor amongst us. It was strong and powerful and has slain thousands.

Brother, our seats were once large and yours were small. You have now become a great people, and we have scarcely a place left to spread our blankets. You have got our country but are not satisfied; you want to force your religion upon us.

Brother, continue to listen.

New York Historical Society

Portrait of Red Jacket by Robert W. Weir, 1828

You say that you are sent to instruct us how to worship the Great Spirit agreeably to His mind, and, if we do not take hold of the religion which you white people teach, we shall be unhappy hereafter. You say that you are right and we are lost. How do we know this to be true? We understand that your religion is written in a book. If it was intended for us as well as you, why has not the Great Spirit given to us, and not only to us, but why did He not give to our forefathers the knowledge of that book, with the means of understanding it rightly? We only know what you tell us about it. How shall we know when to believe, being so often deceived by the white people?

Brother, you say there is but one way to worship and serve the Great Spirit. If there is but one religion, why do you white people differ so much about it? Why not all agreed, as you can all read the book?

Brother, we do not understand these things. We are told that your religion was given to your forefathers and has been handed down from father to son. We also have a religion which was given to our forefathers and has been handed down to us, their children. We worship in that way. It teaches us to be thankful for all the favors we receive, to love each other, and to be united. We never quarrel about religion.

Brother, the Great Spirit has made us all, but He has made a great difference between His white and red children. He has given us different complexions and different customs. To you He has given the arts. To these He has not opened our eyes. We know these things to be true. Since He has made so great a difference between us in other things, why may we not conclude that He has given us a different religion according to our understanding? The Great Spirit does right. He knows what is best for His children; we are satisfied.

Brother, we do not wish to destroy your religion or take it from you. We only want to enjoy our own.

Brother, you say you have not come to get our land or our money but to enlighten our minds. I will now tell you that I have been at your meetings and saw you collect money from the meeting. I cannot tell what this money was intended for, but suppose that it was for your minister, and if we should conform to your way of thinking, perhaps you may want some from us.

Brother, we are told that you have been preaching to the white people in this place. These people are our neighbors. We are acquainted with them. We will wait a little while and see what effect your preaching has upon them. If we find it does them good, makes them honest and less disposed to cheat Indians, we will then consider again of what you have said.

Brother, you have now heard our answer to your talk, and this is all we have to say at present. As we are going to part, we will come and take you by the hand and hope the Great Spirit will protect you on your journey and return you safe to your friends.

48.

John Adams: On a Natural History of the Country

The first settlers in America had been amazed at the richness and variety of the country's flora and fauna. But after nearly two centuries of habitation, during which many species must have perished and others departed from the Eastern Seaboard, none but sporadic attempts had been made to catalog, collate, and compare the abundant natural life. John Adams lamented these facts in the following letter, dated August 7, 1805, to his friend Benjamin Waterhouse. Waterhouse, who shared Adams' concern, lectured extensively on natural history for many years. However, the first systematic treatment of New England flora was Jacob Bigelow's Florula Bostoniensis, *which appeared in 1814.*

Source: *Statesman and Friend, Correspondence of John Adams with Benjamin Waterhouse 1784-1822,* Worthington C. Ford, ed., Boston, 1927, pp. 22-29.

From early youth I have heard it lamented among men of letters that we had neither a natural history of this country nor any person possessed of a taste for such inquiries. The science in general was not so much desired as a particular examination of the beasts, birds, fishes, trees, plants, flowers, fossils, etc., peculiar to North America. Mr. Hutchinson, at the close of the first volume of his *History of Massachusetts Bay,* page

486, says: "A natural history of the country will afford a volume of itself, and it is a work much wanted, and would entertain the curious. The botanical part would be very useful. I have not leisure and if I had, I have not a genius for such an undertaking. I wish some person who has both the one and the other would undertake it." This work was published in 1764 and I was very much pleased to see such an observation in it.

In 1774 on my journey to Congress, I was invited at Norwalk in Connecticut to see a collection made by a Mr. Arnold, an Englishman, of birds and insects, especially butterflies, made wholly in that neighborhood, and beautifully preserved. There was a great variety, and among many others which were very curious were twelve different species of owls. This cabinet was afterward sold to Governor Tryon of New York and by him sent to England and sold to Sir Ashton Lever, in whose possession I saw it again, ten or a dozen years afterward in London.

In 1778 I went to France, where I saw many cabinets, and some of more curiosity and magnificence than use. But they all served to impress upon my mind the utility of some establishment in America for collecting specimens of the works of nature peculiar to us. In 1779, in composing the frame of government for the state of Massachusetts, I thought it the best opportunity which might ever occur to promote a design of this kind and impress upon the minds of the people a sense of the importance of it. With this view, I inserted the second section of the fifth chapter in these words:

> Wisdom and knowledge, as well as virtue, diffused generally among the body of the people, being necessary for the preservation of their rights and liberties, and as these depend on spreading the opportunities and advantages of education in the various parts of the country, and among the different orders of the people, it shall be the duty of the legislatures and magistrates, in all future periods of this commonwealth, to cherish the interests of literature and the sciences, and all seminaries of them; especially the university at Cambridge, public schools, and grammar schools in the towns; to encourage private societies and public institutions, by rewards and immunities, for the promotion of agriculture, arts, sciences, commerce, trades, manufactures, and a natural history of the country; to countenance and inculcate the principles of humanity and general benevolence, public and private charity, industry and frugality, honesty and punctuality in their dealings, sincerity, good humor, and all social affections and generous sentiments among the people.

As the words flowed from my pen, from the heart in reality rather than the head, in composing this paragraph, I could not help laughing to myself, alone in my closet, at the oddity of it. I expected it would be attacked in the convention from all quarters, on the score of affectation, pedantry, hypocrisy, and above all economy. Many ideas in it implied expense, and I knew then as well as I have known since that too large a portion of the people and their representatives had rather starve their souls than draw upon their purses to pay for nourishment of them. And therefore no mercy was to be expected for a paragraph that I would not now exchange for a scepter, and wish may be engraved on my tombstone.

But to my great surprise, instead of objections, it was received with applause and adopted, I believe, with unanimity and without any amendment. Even the natural history of the country received no opposition.

I have a little more of anecdote to give you before I make the application. After my return from France in 1779, I was invited by the corporation to a dinner made at college in honor of the Chevalier de la Luzerne, the minister plenipotentiary from the king of France, and his suite, Mr. Marbois,

Mr. Otto, Mr. La Forest, the Captain De La Chaudière and his officers of the frigate *Le Sensible,* in which we all came over together. Happening to sit at table next to Dr. Cooper, I engaged him in conversation for the whole time on the subject of a natural history of the country and the means of promoting it. I suggested to him the plan of an American Academy of Arts and Sciences, to be established by the legislature as a corporation with capacity to receive donations in land and money. I told him that I had heard in France much conversation concerning the Philosophical Society in Philadelphia and their volume of transactions, which was considered as a laudable institution and an honor to our country. Massachusetts possessed many men of science and letters who would be capable of promoting knowledge and benefiting mankind as much as any others. The doctor was afraid it would injure the college; I thought it would serve it, for no doubt the principal officers of it would be members, and the meetings of the academy might, some of them at least, be at Cambridge. I earnestly importuned the doctor to think of it, converse with the governors of the college and members of the legislature on the subject, and promote the project if he found it practicable. This the doctor did to such effect that after my arrival in France the second time, in the next winter, the General Court established the American Academy of Arts and Sciences, out of which have grown the Society for the Promotion of Agriculture, the Historical Society, and, of late, the professorship of natural history.

I never was consulted directly nor indirectly about the establishment of this professorship until it was completed and the professor chosen. Two or three years ago, I mentioned to Dr. Willard that I had heard confused rumors of a design to purchase a botanical garden, and that I was pleased with the idea and should be willing to contribute my mite toward the subscription for it. The president gave me no answer and I heard no more of it till I was notified that Mr. Peck was appointed and that I was a visitor. Since that they have chosen me president of the visitors and president of the Agricultural Society. Who has been at the bottom of all this and what their motives or designs I know not. Although I never saw Mr. Peck till he was appointed a professor, I have a very good opinion of his talents, manners, and character. It is not impossible, however, that the whole might have been concealed from me till the professor was elected, from a jealousy that I should prefer Dr. Waterhouse, whom I knew, to Mr. Peck, whom I did not know.

The persons whom you designate the Essex Junto — and such a set exists in every state in the Union — have too much of an exclusive and monopolizing spirit, as I, as well as you, have experienced. But they are possessed of so much wealth and so great a portion of the talents of the country, and at the same time so many virtues and good principles, and are so nearly right, though not entirely so in system, that I am convinced, without them the people of America cannot preserve themselves from anarchy. Therefore, I am disposed to as little severity against them as possible, though, of all men in the world, I have the least obligation to them. To them I owe my motto, *sic vos non vobis mellificatis apes* [so you bees do not make honey for yourselves]. Even Mr. Pearson, who was very full of Mr. Lowell, and I knew not whom, but totally forgot; perhaps he was ignorant of the real author of it all.

I am glad to see you on the wings of mighty winds flying all abroad. But clouds and medusas must be the subject of another letter.

49.

Benjamin Rush: On Political Parties and the Romance of History

Benjamin Rush, who had been an active participant in the great years of 1774 to 1780, had become by 1805 a disillusioned critic of the factions and the party strife that troubled the country after the administration of Washington. In part, this may have been because Rush was not involved, as were some of his friends, in politics. His only public post in later life was that of treasurer of the U.S. Mint, to which he had been appointed by President Adams in 1797. In any event, writing to Adams on August 14, 1805, Rush severely questioned the accuracy of the histories of the Revolution that were already beginning to come out — but declared that he had abandoned any intention of publishing his own view of events. Later — in 1808 — Rush confessed, again to Adams, that he often wished that he had never signed the Declaration of Independence.

Source: Butterfield, II, pp. 900-903.

My dear old Friend,

Your letters are full of aphorisms. Every paragraph in them suggests new ideas or revives old ones. You have given a true picture of parties in our country. We have indeed no national character, and however much we boast of it there are very few true Americans in the United States.

We have four distinct parties in Pennsylvania: (1) old Tories; (2) honest Federalists; (3) violent Democrats; (4) moderate Republicans. The first united with the second in the struggle for the establishment of the general government. They were patronized by General Washington and Colonel Hamilton, probably from pure motives, and soon acquired a complete ascendancy over the party that had taken them by the hand. They discovered this in all their nominations for public appointments. It was their preference for one of themselves that threw Swanwick into Congress. Their English anti-Gallican prejudices against the peace you made with France first led the Federalists to see they were not a homogeneous party, for they were pleased with it. Ever since that time the Federalists ascribe their downfall to their union with the Tories. I predicted it when I saw those people flattering and almost worshiping Cobbett as the apostle of their restoration to Great Britain or to a kingly government in America. I now and then mention that prediction to persons who unjustly accused me at that time of a partiality for the detestable principles and conduct of France. The third and fourth parties united in the choice of Mr. McKean and Mr. Jefferson, but the late attack upon the constitution of our state has divided them. The moderate Republicans are few in number compared with the violent Democrats, and unless most of the honest Federalists join them at the next election, Mr. Snyder will be our governor, and Dr. Franklin's constitution will again be the constitution of Pennsylvania.

Ever since the Revolution, our state has been like a large inn. It has accommodated strangers at the expense of the landlord and his children, who have been driven by them from the bar and their bedrooms, and compelled at times to seek a retreat in their garret and cellar. In consequence of this state of things, everything not connected with individual exertions languishes in our state, particularly our commerce, which is tending fast to annihilation from the operation of a most absurd quarantine law, the result of Boeotian ignorance and disbelief. I am kept from feeling the anger and contempt which such conduct is calculated to create by considering our citizens as deranged upon the subject of their political and physical happiness.

I well remember your early cautions to your country upon the subject of treaties. In Baltimore you advised Congress to be careful how they threw themselves into the arms and power of France when they applied to her for aid, for "the time might come," you said, "when we should be obliged to call upon Britain to defend us against France." In being deprived of the credit of that just opinion as well as the honor of your accumulated services to your country, you share the fate of most of the patriots and benefactors to mankind that ever lived. I have lately seen a copy of an original letter from Columbus to the King of Spain written from Jamaica on his fourth and last voyage to the countries he had discovered. After describing his numerous sufferings of body and mind, he adds, "So that he who gave Spain another world has neither in *that* nor in the *old* world a cottage for himself or his wretched family." The French and American revolutions differed from each other in many things, but they were alike in one particular — the former gave all its *power* to a single man, the latter all its *fame*. The only credit which the other servants of the public in the successful contest for American independence possess with the world and will possess with posterity is and will be wholly derived from their imitating the example and carrying into effect the counsels of General Washington in the cabinet and the field. In reviewing the numerous instances of ingratitude of governments and nations to their benefactors, I am often struck with the perfection of that divine government in which "a cup of cold water" (the cheapest thing in the world), given under the influence of proper principles, "shall not lose its reward."

I once intended to have published a work to be entitled *Memoirs of the American Revolution*, and for that purpose collected many documents and pamphlets. But perceiving how widely I should differ from the historians of that event, and how much I should offend by telling the truth, I threw my documents into the fire and gave my pamphlets to my son Richard. Of the former I have preserved only a short account of the members of Congress who subscribed the Declaration of Independence, part of which I once read to you while you were President of the United States. From the immense difference between what I saw and heard of men and things during our Revolution and the histories that have been given of them, I am disposed to believe with Sir R. Walpole that all history (that which is contained in the Bible excepted) is a romance, and romance the only true history.

You remark in your last letter that the Tories have hunted down all the revolutionary characters of our country. To this, General Washington and Colonel Hamilton are exceptions. They are both idolized by them, and to their influence is owing the almost exclusive honor those gentlemen possess of having begun, carried on, and completed the American Revolution. Colonel Hamilton is indebted for much of his fame to his funding system, the emoluments of which centered chiefly in the hands of the Tories. They may say of him what Leo X impiously said of the Christian religion, *mutatis mutandis: "Quantas divitias peperit nobis hoc nomen Hamiltoni."* [How rich the name of Hamilton has made us!]

None of your letters are read out of my family. They deeply interest my son Richard. I have not seen T. Paine since his return to America. I do not know even the person of Wm. Duane, nor have I had the least intercourse with T. Coxe since the year 1800. He is at present out of the eye of the public and alike neglected and avoided by all the parties of the state.

Mr. Madison and his lady are now in our city. It gave me great pleasure to hear him mention your name in the most respectful terms a few days ago. He dwelt largely upon your "genius and integrity," and acquitted you of ever having had the least unfriendly designs in your administration upon the present forms of our American governments. He gave you credit likewise for your correct opinion of banks and standing armies in our country. Colonel Burr also in his visit to my family last spring spoke of your character to me with respect and affection. Your integrity was mentioned by him in the highest terms of commendation. For what virtue above all others would a good man wish to be generally known by the world and by posterity? I should suppose integrity.

This long letter has been written at three different sittings. I mention this fact as an excuse for its length and its want of correctness and method.

Adieu! my venerable and dear friend. My dear Mrs. Rush and son join me in affectionate remembrance of your excellent Mrs. Adams and all . . . your family.

50.

Fisher Ames: The Passions and Tyranny of the Many

The election of a Republican, and especially Thomas Jefferson, was a bitter pill for Fisher Ames, past Massachusetts representative, and his friends and former colleagues of the Essex Junto. Ultra-Federalists all, they felt that the belief in popular sovereignty, in the rule of "the many" rather than of "the few" who were educated, rich, and, in their view, best fitted for governing, was the way to anarchy. "It is the almost universal mistake of our countrymen," wrote Ames, "that democracy would be mild and safe in America." Nothing could be farther from the truth, he declared, and he predicted that the election of Jefferson was the beginning of a revolution that would proceed in much the same fashion as it had in France. The following selection is taken from Ames's "The Dangers of American Liberty," written in 1805, and published by his friends after his death. In it Ames argued, in a way reminiscent of Plato, for a view of democracy that was already becoming rare in his time, and that in the ensuing century and a half has become nearly extinct among Americans.

Source: *Works of Fisher Ames,* Seth Ames, ed., Boston, 1854, Vol. II, pp. 344-399.

Are not our people wholly engrossed by the pursuit of wealth and pleasure? Though grouped together into a society, the propensities of the individual still prevail; and if the nation discovers the rudiments of any character, they are yet to be developed. In forming it, have we not ground to fear that the sour, dissocial, malignant spirit of our politics will continue to find more to dread and hate in party than to love and reverence in our country? What foundation can there be for that political virtue to rest upon, while the virtue of the society is proscribed, and its vice lays an exclusive claim to emolument and honor? And as long as faction governs, it must look to all that is vice in the state for its force, and to all that is virtue for its plunder. It is not merely the choice of faction, though, no doubt, base agents are to be preferred for base purposes, but it is its necessity also to keep men of true worth depressed by keeping the turbulent and worthless contented.

How then can love of country take root and grow in a soil from which every valuable plant has thus been plucked up and thrown away as a weed? How can we forbear to identify the government with the country? And how is it possible that we should, at the same time, lavish all the ardor of our affection and yet withhold every emotion either of confidence or esteem? It is said that, in republics, majorities invariably oppress minorities. Can there be any real patriotism in a state which is thus filled with those who exercise and those who suffer tyranny? But how much less reason has any man to love that country in which the voice of the majority is counterfeited, or the vicious, ignorant, and needy are the instruments, and the wise and worthy are the victims of oppression? . . .

The party now in power . . . acted on the knowledge of what men actually are, not what they ought to be. Instead of enlightening the popular understanding, their business was to bewilder it. They knew that the vicious, on whom society makes war, would join them in their attack upon government. They inflamed the ignorant; they flattered the vain; they offered novelty to the restless; and promised plunder to the base. The envious were assured that the great should fall; and the ambitious that *they* should become great. The federal power, propped by nothing but opinion, fell, not because it deserved its fall but because its principles of action were more exalted and pure than the people could support. . . .

There is no society without Jacobins; no free society without a formidable host of them; and no democracy whose powers they will not usurp, nor whose liberties, if it be not absurd to suppose a democracy can have any, they will not destroy. A nation must be exceedingly well educated in which the ignorant and the credulous are few. . . .

A democracy cannot last. Its nature ordains that its next change shall be into a military despotism, of all known governments, perhaps, the most prone to shift its head and the slowest to mend its vices. The reason is that the tyranny of what is called the people and that by the sword both operate alike to debase and corrupt, till there are neither men left with the spirit to desire liberty, nor morals with the power to sustain justice. Like the burning pestilence that destroys the human body, nothing can subsist by its dissolution but vermin.

A military government may make a nation great, but it cannot make them free. There will be frequent and bloody struggles to decide who shall hold the sword; but the conqueror will destroy his competitors and prevent any permanent division of the empire. Experience proves that in all such governments there is a continual tendency to unity. . . .

The Federalists cannot command the consent of a majority, and they have no consular or imperial army to extort it. Everything of that sort is on the side of their foes, and of course an unsurmountable obstacle to their pretended enterprise. It will weigh nothing in the argument with some persons, but with men of sense it will be conclusive, that the mass of the Federalists are the owners of the commercial and moneyed wealth of the nation. Is it conceivable that such men will plot a revolution in favor of monarchy, a revolution that would make them beggars as well as traitors if it should miscarry; and if it should succeed ever so well, would require a century to take root and acquire stability enough to ensure justice and protect property?

In these convulsions of the state, property is shaken and, in almost every radical change of government, actually shifts hands. Such a project would seem audacious to the conception of needy adventurers who risk nothing but their lives; but to reproach the Federalists of New England, the most independent farmers, opulent merchants, and thriving mechanics, as well as pious clergy, with such a conspiracy requires a degree of impudence that nothing can transcend. As well might they suspect the merchants of a plot to choke up the entrance of our harbors by sinking hulks, or that the directors of the several banks had confederated to blow up the money vaults with gunpowder. The Catos and the Ciceros are accused of conspiring to subvert the commonwealth — and who are the accusers? The Clodii, the Antonies, and the Catilines. . . .

They are certainly blind who do not see that we are descending from a supposed orderly and stable republican government into a licentious democracy, with a progress that baffles all means to resist, and scarcely leaves leisure to deplore its celerity. The institutions and the hopes that Washington raised are nearly prostrate; and his name and memory would perish if the rage of his enemies had any power over history. But they have not — history will give scope to her vengeance and posterity will not be defrauded. But if our experience had not clearly given warning of our approaching catastrophe, the very nature of democracy would inevitably produce it.

A government by the passions of the multitude or, no less correctly, according to the vices and ambition of their leaders, is a democracy. We have heard so long of the indefeasible sovereignty of the people and have admitted so many specious theories of the rights of man, which are contradicted by his nature and experience, that few will dread at all, and fewer still will dread as they ought, the evils of an American democracy. They will not believe them near, or they will think them tolerable or temporary. Fatal delusion!

When it is said there may be a tyranny of the *many* as well as of the *few*, every democrat will yield at least a cold and speculative assent; but he will at all times act as if it were a thing incomprehensible, that there should be any evil to be apprehended in the uncontrolled power of the people. . . .

The people, as a body, cannot deliberate. Nevertheless, they will feel an irresistible impulse to act, and their resolutions will be dictated to them by their demagogues. The consciousness, or the opinion, that they possess the supreme power will inspire inordinate passions; and the violent men, who are the most forward to gratify those passions, will be their favorites. What is called the government of the people is in fact too often the arbitrary power of such men.

Here, then, we have the faithful portrait of democracy. What avails the boasted power of individual citizens? Or of what value is the will of the majority, if that will is dictated by a committee of demagogues, and law and right are in fact at the mercy of a victorious faction? To make a nation free, the crafty must be kept in awe and the violent in restraint. The weak and the simple find their liberty arise, not from their own individual sovereignty but from the power of law and justice over all. It is only by the due restraint of others that I am free.

1806

51.

BENJAMIN H. LATROBE: Gentlemen-Architects and Building-Mechanics

The functionalism of American colonial and frontier architecture was to a large extent transformed by the work as well as the theories of the British architect and engineer, Benjamin Latrobe, and his pupils. Latrobe eloquently decried the dilettante efforts of "gentlemen-architects," as he called them, and the restrictive influence of "building-mechanics" who, he felt, were tied to an outmoded tradition. Instead, he called for professionalism in architecture, and introduced into America the Graeco-Roman style that is apparent in the courthouses of many cities and towns throughout the United States. The following letter of advice to Latrobe's disciple, Robert Mills, was dated July 12, 1806.

Source: Manuscript in Maryland Historical Society.

THE PROFESSION OF ARCHITECTURE has been hitherto in the hands of two sorts of men. The first, of those who from traveling or from books have acquired some knowledge of the theory of the art but know nothing of its practice; the second, of those who know nothing but the practice and, whose early life being spent in labor and in the habits of a laborious life, have had no opportunity of acquiring the theory. The complaisance of these two sets of men to each other renders it difficult for the architect to get in between them, for the building mechanic finds his account in the ignorance of the gentleman-architect, as the latter does in the submissive deportment which interest dictates to the former.

It is therefore with sincere regret that I have observed your talents and information thrown into a sort of scramble between the two parties, in the designs of the churches you have given to the congregations at Charleston. You remember the faults I pointed out to you at an early period of your studies in my office, especially in the round church. You corrected them. Your design had, besides, very great and intrinsic merits of its own. What has been the event? Of all those who have contributed their ideas to that church you have been considered as the most ignorant. You have not even been permitted to correct your own errors, and in other points you have been overruled so far as to have been obliged to admit into your plan absolute absurdities, such as, for instance, the gallery within the cupola, which may probably be the cause why, within an interior circle of a certain diameter in the center of the church, the preacher's voice is said to be not perfectly heard.

Such a situation is degrading and would not be submitted to by any other member of a liberal profession, and scarcely by a mechanic whose necessities were not greater than his pride. In our country, indeed, the profession of an architect is in a great measure new. The building artisans, especially the carpenters, have been sufficiently informed to get through the business and supply the orders of a young country. Out of this state of infancy we are now emerging; and it is necessary that those who have devoted their best years and a very considerable expenditure to the attainment of that variety of knowledge which an architect ought to possess should take their legitimate rank themselves or not venture into that ocean of contact with all above and all below them into which a mistaken complaisance will throw them, but adopt some other profession sanctioned by the habits and opinions of the country.

It will be answered, "If you are paid for your designs and directions, he that expends his money on the building has an undoubted right to build what he pleases." If you are paid! I ask in the first place, are you paid? *No!* The custom of all Europe has decided that 5 percent on the cost of a building, with all personal expenses incurred, shall be the pay of the architect. This is just as much as is charged by a merchant for the transaction of business, expedited often in a few minutes by the labor of a clerk; while the architect must watch the daily progress of the work perhaps for years, pay all his clerk hire, and repay to himself the expense of an education greatly more costly than that of a merchant. But it was not my intention to enter at present into the question of compensation, for in your case, I believe that you have neither asked nor received anything but have given your advice *pour l'amour de dieu.* The question is in how far you ought to permit yourself to be overruled in your opinion by your employers, and in order to answer it, I have neither leisure nor inclination to go into a methodical disquisition but shall in a desultory manner proceed to the end of my letter which, as it is dictated only by friendship, will not be received by you as a regular treatise of the ethics of our profession but as proof of my goodwill.

If the most distinguished lawyer of our city, Mr. Rawle, for instance, or Mr. William L. Smith of South Carolina, were consulted as to the division, settlement, or alienation of a large estate, he would be informed by the parties concerned what it was that they actually wanted; the titles would be put into his hands; the shares, as to their amount and locality, perhaps, exactly defined; and the drafting of the instrument then would be committed to him.

As soon as the draft of the instrument were prepared, the parties would be called together; its nature, obligations, covenants, and general tendencies would be fully explained. In examining this draft, it would very probably occur that some intelligent person would discover that the intention of the parties had been mistaken, that the operation of the arrangement would be different perhaps than was expected, or that improvements in the settlements might be made. The lawyer consulted would not hesitate to redraw, to change his disposition until all parties were satisfied. But if, on hearing the deed read, any one of the party were to attempt to correct the technical phraseology, the terms of the conveyance, or to produce the opinions of the physician next door, or of the planter five miles off, or of some wonderfully ingenious young lady, or some person of surprising natural legal talents from the backwoods, as to the form of the deed, its construction, or its alteration, you would certainly hear no more from Mr. Rawle or Mr. Smith, excepting as to the amount of his charge for trouble already incurred.

In exactly this situation is an architect who is consulted on a public work. He should be first informed what it is that is wanted; what expense might be contemplated by his design; what are the particular views of the persons who have the management of the money devoted to the work.

There will be on the part of a sensible and good-tempered man no objection to any reasonable extent of revision or rerevision of a first design. Enlargement, contraction, alteration of arrangement, of construction and of decoration may be made by a man of talents in almost infinite variety, and suggestions from unprofessional men politely and kindly made are always acceptable. But no honest man will for a moment listen to the proposal that he shall lend his name to the contrivances of whim or of ignorance, or under the pretense of a cheap, give to the public a bad work. There is, as in most proverbs, a vast deal of good sense in the old Latin proverb . . . *in sua arte credendum* [he should believe in his own work]. We allow full faith to our plainest mechanics in their particular callings. No man thinks himself capable of instructing his shoemaker or his tailor. Indeed, we swallow what the physician orders with our eyes shut, and sign the deed the lawyer lays before us with very little inquiry. But every gentleman can build a house, a prison, or a city. This appears extraordinary, for when a gentleman sets about the work, he has the interests of all those he employs in array against his fortune, without any protection in his own knowledge. The mechanical arts employed in the erection of a capital building are more than twenty. Of these every architect has a competent knowledge, so as to judge of the quality as well as of the value and the amount of the work, but it is at least twenty to one against the gentleman who trusts only himself that he will lose 5 percent, at least.

Then as to the arrangement. Every architect who has been regularly educated knows what has been done before in the same line. This knowledge he necessarily acquires in the office in which he studies, not only from the books and designs which he finds there but in the instructions and actual practice of his principal, provided he be a man of intelligence, candor, and of business.

You are, on the subject of the difference between the professional and regular mode of conducting your works, as well as small buildings, and the desultory guessing manner in which they are otherwise managed, too well informed by experience to render it necessary for me to proceed further on this head. I will now give you with my accustomed frankness my opinion of the conduct you should pursue in respect to the proposed penitentiary house.

1. In the first place, do nothing gratuitously. The state of Carolina is infinitely better able to pay you well than you are to subscribe your time and your talents, which is your subsistence toward the annual revenue of the state — for this is the actual effect of gratuitous professional services. As far as you have hitherto promoted the very laudable design of the government by exhibiting the practicability of such a building as will be necessary, if the penitentiary law be enacted you have done well. For many people despair of the end unless they see the means. But further you ought not to go without a very clear understanding as to what is to be the reward of your labor. You know too well the course of my professional transactions to suppose that this advice is

the result of a mercenary disposition. The gratuitous services on a very great scale which I have given to unendowed public institutions for the promotion of religious or literary objects are well known to you, for you have had your share of the labors. But when a rich state is about to execute a project from which great public benefit is expected to result, compensation to those who assist in effecting that object is a thing so much of course that all I have said would appear superfluous, if the example of the donation of time and talent and expense had not in many instances been set by yourself. . . .

You must take it for granted that no liberality, that is, voluntary reward, is ever to be expected from a public body. Individuals, responsible only to themselves in the expenditure of their money, are often generous and reward handsomely, independently of stipulation; but a number of the same individuals, meeting as guardians of the public money, feel in the first place the necessity of pleasing their constituents, and in the second that of involving themselves in no unnecessary responsibility. And if at a public board, one or more individuals are willing at all hazards to act as they would in their own case, it is ten to one but they are a minority.

To balance this want of liberality in public boards, they have this advantage to offer over individual employment — that when a bargain is made for a salary or a commission, it is always rigidly adhered to, provided it be in writing and clearly expressed, for every ambiguity will always be interpreted for the public and against the individual.

In settling what shall be your compensation, on the presumption of your being employed, I would by all means advise you to prefer a salary to a commission. It will be both more certain to you and more satisfactory to your employers.

2. Take care that before the work begin, the plan is perfectly understood, and stipulate that no alteration but by mutual discussion and agreement shall be made.

3. Stipulate for the following points, all of which are most essential: no workman shall be employed to whom you object; no workman shall be allowed to apply to the board or individual to whom the state may delegate the management of the erection of the work but through you; no account shall be paid, unsanctioned by your signature.

With these powers you will have the mastery of all the operation, and you may do then justice to yourself and to the public, and as no money will pass through your hands, you will not labor under the temptation, the power, nor the suspicion of violating any point of pecuniary morality, that virtue which, like chastity in women, is in the general opinion supposed to be superior to all others and almost to render them unnecessary.

4. I fear you have already committed one blunder — that of leaving your drawings in the hands of the public. Of the honor and the gentlemanly feeling of the governor, far be it from me to suggest the slightest suspicion. But his very admiration of your design will produce its exhibition, and as the principles of the plan are the great merit of it, and these strike at one view, you have armed all those who see it or who hear it described with the weapons of competition against you. But this is not now to be remedied.

My time will not permit me to say more to you at present. In the conduct of the work should my experience be of any service to you, you will know how freely you may use it.

52.

Lorenzo Dow: The Jerks

At the beginning of the new century the religious life of many communities on the western frontier centered around an institution known as "camp meetings." Families would often travel twenty or thirty miles to spend a number of days camped together listening to traveling preachers and other messengers (sometimes self-appointed) of the word of God. It was not unusual, during these early revivals, for enthusiasts to succumb to erratic physical displays of "possession" — falling, jerking, rolling, barking, and laughing. Lorenzo Dow, an itinerant preacher and evangelist, who kept a journal describing his travels and conversions, has left us an account of his journey to Knoxville, Tennessee. It was here he first encountered the phenomenon known as the "jerks," an involuntary muscle reflex apparently caused by religious frenzy. Dow gives the following skeptical description in his journal entries for late February 1804. Dow's Travels *were first published in 1806.*

Source: *The Life, Travels, Labors, and Writings of Lorenzo Dow, etc., etc.*, Philadelphia, n.d., pp. 132-135.

I HAD HEARD about a singularity called the "jerks" or "jerking exercise," which appeared first near Knoxville in August last, to the great alarm of the people, which reports at first I considered as vague and false. But, at length, like the Queen of Sheba, I set out to go and see for myself, and sent over these appointments into this country accordingly.

When I arrived in sight of this town, I saw hundreds of people collected in little bodies, and, observing no place appointed for meeting, before I spoke to any, I got on a log and gave out a hymn; which caused them to assemble around in solemn attentive silence. I observed several involuntary motions in the course of the meeting, which I considered as a specimen of the jerks. I rode seven miles behind a man across streams of water and held meeting in the evening, being ten miles on my way.

In the night I grew uneasy, being twenty-five miles from my appointment for next morning at 11 o'clock. I prevailed on a young man to attempt carrying me with horses until day, which he thought was impracticable, considering the darkness of the night and the thickness of the trees. Solitary shrieks were heard in these woods, which he told me were said to be the cries of murdered persons. At day we parted, being still seventeen miles from the spot, and the ground covered with a white frost.

I had not proceeded far before I came to a stream of water, from the springs of the mountain, which made it dreadful cold. In my heated state I had to wade this stream five times in the course of an hour, which I perceived so affected my body that my strength began to fail. Fears began to arise that I must disappoint the people, till I observed some fresh tracks of horses, which caused me to exert every nerve to overtake them in hopes of aid or assistance on my journey; and soon I saw them on an eminence. I shouted for them to stop till I came up. They inquired what I wanted. I replied, I had heard there was a meeting at

Seversville by a stranger and was going to it. They replied that they had heard that a crazy man was to hold forth there and were going also; and perceiving that I was weary, they invited me to ride. And soon our company was increased to forty or fifty, who fell in with us on the road from different plantations.

At length I was interrogated whether I knew anything about the preacher. I replied, "I have heard a good deal about him and have heard him preach, but I have no great opinion of him." And thus the conversation continued for some miles before they found me out, which caused some color and smiles in the company.

Thus, I got on to meeting; and, after taking a cup of tea gratis, I began to speak to a vast audience, and I observed about thirty to have the jerks. Though they strove to keep still as they could, these emotions were involuntary and irresistible, as any unprejudiced eye might discern. Lawyer Porter, who had come a considerable distance, got his heart touched under the word, and, being informed how I came to meeting, voluntarily lent me a horse to ride near 100 miles and gave me a dollar, though he had never seen me before.

Hence to Marysville, where I spoke to about 1,500; and many appeared to feel the word, but about 50 felt the jerks. At night I lodged with one of the Nicholites, a kind of Quakers who do not feel free to wear colored clothes. I spoke to a number of people at his house that night. While at tea, I observed his daughter (who sat opposite to me at table) to have the jerks, and dropped the teacup from her hand in the violent agitation. I said to her, "Young woman, what is the matter?" She replied, "I have got the jerks." I asked her how long she had it. She observed, "A few days"; and that it had been the means of the awakening and conversion of her soul by stirring her up to serious consideration about her careless state, and so forth.

Sunday, February 19, I spoke in Knoxville to hundreds more than could get into the courthouse, the governor being present. About 150 appeared to have the jerking exercise, among whom was a circuit preacher (Johnson) who had opposed them a little before, but he now had them powerfully; and I believe he would have fallen over three times had not the auditory been so crowded that he could not unless he fell perpendicularly.

After meeting, I rode eighteen miles to hold a meeting at night. The people of this settlement were mostly Quakers, and they had said (as I was informed): "The Methodists and Presbyterians have the jerks because they *sing* and *pray* so much; but we are a still, peaceable people, wherefore we do not have them." However, about twenty of them came to the meeting to hear one, as they said, somewhat in a Quaker line. But their usual stillness and silence was interrupted, for about a dozen of them had the jerks as keen and as powerful as any I had seen, so as to have occasioned a kind of grunt or groan when they would jerk.

It appears that many have undervalued the great revival and attempted to account for it altogether on natural principles; therefore, it seems to me (from the best judgment I can form) that God has seen proper to take this method to convince people that He will work in a way to show His power and sent the jerks as a sign of the times, partly in judgment for the people's unbelief and yet as a mercy to convict people of divine realities.

I have seen Presbyterians, Methodists, Quakers, Baptists, Episcopalians, and Independents exercised with the jerks — gentleman and lady, black and white, the aged and the youth, rich and poor, without exception; from which I infer, as it cannot be accounted for on natural principles, and carries such marks of involuntary motion, that it is no trifling matter. I believe that those who are most pious and given up to God are rarely touched with it, and also those naturalists who wish and try to get it to philosophize upon it are excepted. But the lukewarm, lazy, halfhearted, indolent professor is subject to it; and many of them I have seen who, when it came upon them, would be alarmed and stirred up to redouble their diligence with God; and after they would get happy, were thankful it ever came upon them.

Again, the wicked are frequently more afraid of it than the smallpox or yellow fever; these are subject to it. But the persecutors are more subject to it than any; and they sometimes have cursed and swore and damned it while jerking. There is no pain attending the jerks, except they resist it; which if they do, it will weary them more in an hour than a day's labor, which shows that it requires the *consent* of the *will* to avoid suffering.

53.

The Trial of the Journeymen Boot- and Shoe-Makers

Shortly after 1800, craftsmen in various trades began to organize unions in order to improve their working conditions. The principal tactic used by craftsmen was refusing to work and attempting to block the work of others until their demands were met. According to the prevailing legal doctrine, which was drawn from English common law, such social and economic coercion was a criminal offense. The trial of journeymen boot- and shoe-makers of Philadelphia held between January and May of 1806, in which the craftsmen were found guilty of criminal conspiracy, set a legal precedent in the courts' handling of labor union cases that was upheld until 1842, when the Massachusetts Supreme Court overturned the doctrine of criminal conspiracy.

Source: *The Trial of the Boot and Shoemakers of Philadelphia*, Philadelphia, 1806, [Commons, III, pp. 61-71, 224-236].

For the Attorney General, Joseph Reed:

Witnesses annexed to the bill of indictment: Lewis Ryan, sworn; John Bedford, sworn; Job Harrison, sworn; James Comyns, sworn; Anthony Bennet, sworn; Andrew Dunlap, sworn; George Kemble, affirmed.

This prosecution has been commenced not from any private pique or personal resentment but solely with a view to promote the common good of the community, and to prevent in future the pernicious combinations of misguided men to effect purposes not only injurious to themselves but mischievous to society. Yet infinite pains have been taken to represent this prosecution as founded in very improper motives. Not only in private conversation and in public taverns but even the press has been employed in the work of misrepresentations.

The newspaper called the *Aurora* has teemed with false representations and statements of this transaction, and the most insolent abuse of the parties who have brought it before this tribunal, with a view (if not with the declared intention) to poison the public mind and obstruct the pure streams of justice flowing from the established courts of law. Yet we trust we shall be enabled to counteract the nefarious effects the publications alluded to were calculated to produce by a fair and candid exposure of all the circumstances. When the true nature of the case shall be explained, and the plain narrative of the facts shall be laid before you gentlemen of the jury, we feel confident that you will not be biased by newspaper attempts to delude and mislead you. It has been a common observation that newspaper accounts of the proceedings in our courts of law are filled with mistakes and misrepresentations. The publications alluded to are in conformity to this general character, which marks the ignorance or wickedness which gave them birth.

Let it be well understood that the present action is not intended to introduce the doctrine that a man is not at liberty to fix any price whatsoever upon his own labor; we disclaim the idea in the most unqualified terms: we declare that every man has a right to fix any price upon his commodities or his labor which he deems proper. We have no design to prevent him. We disclaim any such design. If any one of the defendants had thought proper to charge $100 for making a pair of boots, nobody would interfere if he could get his employer to give it, or could compel the payment. He would have a legal right to do so. Our complaint is not of that kind.

Our position is that no man is at liberty to combine, conspire, confederate, and unlawfully agree to regulate the whole body of workmen in the city. The defendants are not indicted for regulating their own individual wages, but for undertaking by a combination to regulate the price of the labor of others as well as their own.

It must be known to you that every society of people are affected by such private confederacies; that they are injurious to the public good and against the public interest. The law therefore forbids conspiracies of every kind which put in jeopardy the interest and well-being of the community. What may be lawful in an individual may be criminal in a number of individuals combined with a view to carry it into effect. The law does not permit any body of men to conspire or to undertake to do any act injurious to the general welfare. An act of conspiracy is an offense against the laws of this country, and that is the charge brought against these defendants, in the first count of the indictment. . . .

It is here stated that this confederacy was not only injurious to the community generally but also to other artificers and journeymen cordwainers; it is not alleged to be against the masters, for they are in no wise concerned; it is against such part of the fellow craft as do not wish to submit to the tyranny of the few. . . .

You will also please to observe that this body of journeymen are not an incorporated society, whatever may have been represented out-of-doors on that head; neither are they a society instituted for benevolent purposes. They are merely a society for compelling by the most arbitrary and malignant means the whole body of the journeymen to submit to their rules and regulations; it is not confined even to the members of the society, it reaches every individual of the trade, whether journeymen or master. It will appear from the evidence to be adduced before you to spread to an extent of which you cannot as yet form any idea. You will find that they not only determine the price of labor for themselves but compel everyone to demand that price and receive no other; they [also] refuse to hold communion with any person who shall disobey their mandates. . . .

There may be a number of young single men who may stand out for the wages required, but there are others with families who cannot subsist without work; these men are compelled to abstain from their employments and are reduced to the extreme of misery by the tyranny of the others. We shall show you that some journeymen with families have been forbidden to work at prices with which they were perfectly satisfied, and thereby been brought into deep distress.

We shall show you the nature of the

pains and penalties they affix to disobedience; we shall also show the mode by which they compel men to join their society, and the fetters with which they afterward bind them. A journeyman arriving from Europe, or any part of the United States, an apprentice who has served . . . his time must join the association or be shut out from every shop in the city if he presumes to work at his own price. Nay, every master shoemaker must decline to employ such journeyman or his shop will be abandoned by all the other workmen. A master who employs fifteen or twenty hands is called upon to discharge the journeyman who is not a member of the body; if he refuses they all leave him, whatever may be the situation of his business. This compulsion from its nature seldom fails. If the master discharges the nonconformist and he gets employed at another shop, the body pursue him and order the new master to drive him away, and threaten in case of refusal that they will draw off all the members of the society, and so on, until the persecuted man either joins their body or is driven from the city. The injury to the community is a very serious evil and demands at your hands to be redressed.

This is the chief charge in the indictment; and you now see that the action is instituted to maintain the cause of liberty and repress that of licentiousness. It is to secure the rights of each individual to obtain and enjoy the price he fixes upon his own labor.

In the progress of this case the evidence, the principles on which the prosecution is conducted, and the law arising thereon will respectively be laid before you, and you will ultimately decide for the prosecution of the defendants as shall in your judgment comport with the justice of the case. I have thought it necessary to say thus much that you might not suppose we are attempting to deprive any man of his constitutional rights and privileges as has been represented. I shall now proceed to call witnesses to establish the facts I have stated. . . .

The Recorder, Mr. Levy:

This laborious cause is now drawing to a close after a discussion of three days, during which we have had every information upon the facts and the law connected with them that a careful investigation and industrious research have been able to produce. We are informed of the circumstance and ground of the complaints, and of the law applicable to them. It remains with the court and jury to decide what the rule of law is and whether the defendants have or have not violated it. In forming this decision we cannot, we must not, forget that the law of the land is the supreme and only rule. We live in a country where the will of no individual ought to be, or is admitted to be, the rule of action: where the will of an individual or of any number of individuals, however distinguished by wealth, talents, or popular fame, ought not to affect or control, in the least degree, the administration of justice. There is but one place in which to determine whether violation and abuses of the law have been committed . . . it is in our courts of justice: and there only after proof to the fact and consideration of the principles of law connected with it.

The moment courts of justice lose their respectability — from that moment the security of persons and of property is gone. The moment courts of justice have their characters contaminated by a well-founded suspicion that they are governed by caprice, fear, or favor — from that moment they will cease to be able to administer justice with effect, and redress wrongs of either a public or a private nature. Every consideration, therefore, calls upon us to maintain the character of courts and juries, and that can only be maintained by undeviating integrity, by an adhesion to the rules of law, and by deciding impartially in conformity to them. . . .

This jury will act without fear or favor, without partiality or hatred; regardless whether they make friends or enemies by their verdict, they will do their duty; they will, after the rule of law has been investigated and laid down by the court, find a verdict in conformity to the justice of the case.

If this, gentlemen, is your disposition, there are only two objects for your consideration: first, what the rule of law is on this subject; second, whether the defendants acted in such a manner as to bring them within that rule. . . .

What are the offenses alleged against them? They are contained in the charges of the indictment. . . .

These are the questions for our consideration, and it lies with you to determine how far the evidence supports the charges, and how the principles of the law bear upon them.

It is proper to consider: Is such a combination consistent with the principles of our law, and injurious to the public welfare? The usual means by which the prices of work are regulated are the demand for the article and the excellence of its fabric. Where the work is well done, and the demand is considerable, the prices will necessarily be high. Where the work is ill done, and the demand is inconsiderable, they will unquestionably be low. If there are many to consume and few to work, the price of the article will be high; but if there are few to consume and many to work, the article must be low. Much will depend too, upon these circumstances: whether the materials are plenty or scarce; the price of the commodity will in consequence be higher or lower. These are the means by which prices are regulated in the natural course of things.

To make an artificial regulation is not to regard the excellence of the work or quality of the material, but to fix a positive and arbitrary price, governed by no standard, controlled by no impartial person, but dependent on the will of the few who are interested; this is the unnatural way of raising the price of goods or work. This is independent of the number of customers, or of the quality of the material, or of the number who are to do the work. It is an unnatural, artificial means of raising the price of work beyond its standard, and taking an undue advantage of the public. Is the rule of law bottomed upon such principles as to permit or protect such conduct? Consider it on the footing of the general commerce of the city. Is there any man who can calculate (if this is tolerated) at what price he may safely contract to deliver articles for which he may receive orders, if he is to be regulated by the journeymen in an arbitrary jump from one price to another? It renders it impossible for a man making a contract for a large quantity of such goods to know whether he shall lose or gain by it. If he makes a large contract for goods today, for delivery at three, six, or nine months hence, can he calculate what the prices will be then, if the journeymen in the intermediate time are permitted to meet and raise their prices, according to their caprice or pleasure? Can he fix the price of his commodity for a future day? It is impossible that any man can carry on commerce in this way. There cannot be a large contract entered into, but what the contractor will make at his peril. He may be ruined by the difference of prices made by the journeymen in the intermediate time.

What, then, is the operation of this kind of conduct upon the commerce of the city? It exposes it to inconveniences, if not to ruin; therefore, it is against the public welfare. How does it operate upon the defendants? We see that those who are in indigent circumstances and who have families to maintain and who get their bread by their daily labor have declared here upon oath that it was impossible for them to hold out; the masters might do it, but they could not. And it has been admitted by the witnesses for the defendants, that such persons, however sharp and pressing their necessities, were obliged to stand to the turnout, or never afterward to be employed. They were interdicted from all business in future, if they did not continue to persevere in the measures taken by the journeymen shoemakers.

Can such a regulation be just and proper? Does it not tend to involve necessitous men in the commission of crimes? If they are prevented from working for six weeks, it might induce those who are thus idle and have not the means of maintenance to take other courses for the support of their wives and children. It might lead them to procure it by crimes — by burglary, larceny, or highway robbery! A father cannot stand by and see, without agony, his children suffer; if he does, he is an inhuman monster; he will be driven to seek bread for them, either by crime, by beggary, or a removal from the city.

Consider these circumstances as they affect trade generally. Does this measure tend to make good workmen? No: it puts the botch incapable of doing justice to his work on a level with the best tradesman. The master must give the same wages to each. Such a practice would take away all the excitement to excel in workmanship or industry. Consider the effect it would have upon the whole community. If the masters say they will not sell under certain prices, as the journeymen declare they will not work at certain wages, they, if persisted in, would put the whole body of the people into their power. Shoes and boots are articles of the first necessity. If they could stand out three or four weeks in winter, they might raise the price of boots to $30, $40, or $50 a pair, at least for some time, and until a competent supply could be got from other places. In every point of view, this measure is pregnant with public mischief and private injury . . . tends to demoralize the workmen . . . and destroy the trade of the city, and leaves the pockets of the whole community to the discretion of the concerned. If these evils were unprovided for by the law now existing, it would be necessary that laws should be made to restrain them.

What has been the conduct of the defendants in this instance? They belong to an association, the object of which is that every person who follows the trade of a journeyman shoemaker must be a member of their body. The apprentice immediately upon becoming free, and the journeyman who comes here from distant places, are all considered members of this institution. If they do not join the body, a term of reproach is fixed upon them. The members of the body will not work with them, and they refuse to board or lodge with them. The consequence is that everyone is compelled to join the society. It is in evidence that the defendants in this action all took a part in the last attempt to raise their wages. . . . Keimer was their secretary, and the others were employed in giving notice, and were of the tramping committee. If the purpose of the association is well understood, it will be found they leave no individual at liberty to join the society or reject it. They compel him to become a member. Is there any reason to suppose that the laws are not competent to redress an evil of this magnitude? The laws of this society are grievous to those not inclined to become members . . . they are injurious to the community, but they are not the laws of Pennsylvania. We live in a community where the people in their collective capacity give the first momentum, and their representatives pass laws on circumstances and occasions which require their interference, as they arise.

But the acts of the legislature form but a small part of that code from which the citizen is to learn his duties, or the magistrate his power and rule of action. These temporary emanations of a body, the component members of which are subject to perpetual change, apply principally to the political exigencies of the day.

It is in the volumes of the common law we are to seek for information in the far greater number, as well as the most important causes that come before our tribunals. That invaluable code has ascertained and defined with a critical precision, and with a consistency that no fluctuating political body could or can attain, not only the civil rights of property but the nature of all crimes from treason to trespass; has pointed out the rules of evidence and the mode of proof; and has introduced and perpetuated, for their investigation, that admirable institution, the freeman's boast: the trial by jury. Its profound provisions grow up, not from the pressure of the only true foundations of all knowledge, long experience and practical observation at the moment, but from the common law matured into an elaborate connected system.

Law *is* by the length of time it has been in use and the able men who have administered it. Much abuse has of late teemed upon its valuable institutions. Its enemies do not attack it as a system but they single out some detached branch of it, declare it absurd or intelligible without understanding it. To treat it justly they should be able to comprehend the whole. Those who understand it best entertain the highest opinion of its excellence. . . . No other persons are competent judges of it. As well might a circle of a thousand miles diameter be described by the man whose eye could only see a single inch, as the common law be characterized by those who have not devoted years to its study. Those who know it know that it regulates with a sound discretion most of our concerns in civil and social life. Its rules are the result of the wisdom of ages. It says there may be cases in which what one man may do without offense, many combined may not do with impunity. It distinguishes between the object so aimed at in different transactions. If the purpose to be obtained be an object of individual interest, it may be fairly attempted by an individual. . . . Many are prohibited from combining for the attainment of it.

What is the case now before us. . . . A combination of workmen to raise their wages may be considered in a two-fold point of view: one is to benefit themselves . . . the other is to injure those who do not join their society. The rule of law condemns both. If the rule be clear, we are bound to conform to it even though we do not comprehend the principle upon which it is founded. We are not to reject it because we do not see the reason of it. It is enough that it is the will of the majority. It is law because it is their will — if it is law, there may be good reasons for it though we cannot find them out. But the rule in this case is pregnant with sound sense and all the authorities are clear upon the subject. . . .

It is now, therefore, left to you upon the law, and the evidence, to find the verdict. If you can reconcile it to your consciences to find the defendants not guilty, you will do so; if not, the alternative that remains is a verdict of guilty.

The jury retired about 9 o'clock and were directed by the court to seal up their verdict. . . . Next morning the following circumstances took place.

Mr. Franklin requested the jury to be polled.

It was granted by the court.

On calling over the jury list, Mr. Wm. Henderson, the fifth on the roster, said, "The clerk will find a paper enclosed in the bill of indictment containing the verdict of the jury, subscribed with their names." The clerk then read the paper referred to.

The reporter took it down in these words: "We find the defendants guilty of a combination to raise their wages," subscribed by the twelve jurors. (Note by the reporter.)

Calling at the clerk's office, this 21st May, 1806, he learned the paper above mentioned was destroyed or missing, and to convince him such paper was of no importance, Mr. Serjeant tore up two verdicts of a similar nature, in the presence of him and another person, saying the court takes no cognizance of these sealed verdicts. But after all, the verdict was entered on the back of the bill of indictment — guilty.

And the court fined the defendants $8 each, with costs of suit, and to stand committed till paid.

1807

54.

Act to Prohibit the Importation of Slaves

In his initial draft of the Declaration of Independence, Jefferson had condemned the slave trade, but the clause was struck from the final version. The matter was raised again in the Federal Convention of 1787, when several delegates urged constitutional abolition of the importation of slaves, but Southern slave owners, who were joined by Northern slave traders, won a stay of twenty years. As the end of this period approached, Jefferson, now President, urged Congress to act. "I congratulate you, fellow citizens," he declared in his sixth annual message (1806), "on the approach of the period at which you may interpose your authority constitutionally to withdraw the citizens of the United States from all further participation in these violations of human rights, which have been so long continued on the inoffending inhabitants of Africa." Several bills were accordingly introduced in the House, and the following one was passed on March 2, 1807. The new law, though it made the slave trade illegal, did not end it; the smuggling of slaves, who grew more and more valuable as the supply dwindled, continued sporadically until 1860.

Source: *Statutes,* II, pp. 426-430.

Be it enacted, by the Senate and House of Representatives of the United States of America in Congress assembled, that from and after the 1st day of January, 1808, it shall not be lawful to import or bring into the United States or the territories thereof, from any foreign kingdom, place, or country, any Negro, mulatto, or person of color with intent to hold, sell, or dispose of such Negro, mulatto, or person of color as a slave, or to be held to service or labor.

Section 2. *And be it further enacted,* that no citizen or citizens of the United States, or any other person, shall, from and after the 1st day of January, in the year of Our Lord 1808, for himself, or themselves, or any other person whatsoever, either as master, factor, or owner, build, fit, equip, load, or otherwise prepare any ship or vessel, in any port or place within the jurisdiction of the United States, nor shall cause any ship or vessel to sail from any port or place within the same, for the purpose of procuring any Negro, mulatto, or person of color from any foreign kingdom, place, or country, to be transported to any port or place whatsoever within the jurisdiction of the United States, to be held, sold, or disposed of as slaves, or to be held to service or labor. And if any ship or vessel shall be so fitted out for the purpose aforesaid, or shall be caused to sail so as aforesaid, every such ship or vessel, her tackle, apparel, and furniture shall be forfeited to the United States and shall be liable to be seized, prosecuted, and condemned in any of the circuit courts or district courts for the district where the said ship or vessel may be found or seized. . . .

Section 4. *And be it further enacted,* if any citizen or citizens of the United States, or any person resident within the jurisdiction of the same, shall, from and after the 1st day of January, 1808, take on board, receive, or transport from any of the coasts or kingdoms of Africa, or from any other foreign kingdom, place, or country, any Negro, mulatto, or person of color, in any ship or vessel, for the purpose of selling them in any port or place within the jurisdiction of the United States as slaves, or to be held to service or labor, or shall be in any ways aiding or abetting therein, such citizen or citizens, or person, shall severally forfeit and pay $5,000, one moiety thereof to the use of any person or persons who shall sue for and prosecute the same to effect. And every such ship or vessel in which such Negro, mulatto, or person of color shall have been taken on board, received, or transported as aforesaid, her tackle, apparel, and furniture, and the goods and effects which shall be found on board the same shall be forfeited to the United States and shall be liable to be seized, prosecuted, and condemned in any of the circuit courts or district courts in the district where the said ship or vessel may be found or seized.

And neither the importer, nor any person or persons claiming from or under him, shall hold any right or title whatsoever to any Negro, mulatto, or person of color, nor to the service or labor thereof, who may be imported or brought within the United States, or territories thereof, in violation of this law, but the same shall remain subject to any regulations not contravening the provisions of this act, which the legislatures of the several states or territories at anytime hereafter may make for disposing of any such Negro, mulatto, or person of color.

Section 5. *And be it further enacted,* that if any citizen or citizens of the United States, or any other person resident within the jurisdiction of the same, shall, from and after the 1st day of January, 1808, contrary to the true intent and meaning of this act, take on board any ship or vessel from any of the coasts or kingdoms of Africa, or from any other foreign kingdom, place, or country, any Negro, mulatto, or person of color with intent to sell him, her, or them for a slave, or slaves, or to be held to service or labor, and shall transport the same to any port or place within the jurisdiction of the United States and there sell such Negro, mulatto, or person of color so transported as aforesaid for a slave, or to be held to service or labor, every such offender shall be deemed guilty of a high misdemeanor and, being thereof convicted before any court having competent jurisdiction, shall suffer imprisonment for not more than ten years nor less than five years, and be fined not exceeding $10,000, nor less than $1,000.

Section 6. *And be it further enacted,* that if any person or persons whatsoever shall, from and after the 1st day of January, 1808, purchase or sell any Negro, mulatto, or person of color for a slave, or to be held to service or labor, who shall have been imported or brought from any foreign kingdom, place, or country, or from the dominions of any foreign state immediately adjoining to the United States into any port or place within the jurisdiction of the United States, after the last day of December, 1807, knowing at the time of such purchase or sale such Negro, mulatto, or person of color was so brought within the jurisdiction of the United States, as aforesaid, such purchaser and seller shall severally forfeit and pay for every Negro, mulatto, or person of color so purchased or sold as aforesaid $800, one moiety thereof to the United States and the other moiety to the use of any person or persons who shall sue for and prosecute the same to effect: *Provided,* that the aforesaid forfeiture shall not extend to the seller or purchaser of any Negro, mulatto, or person of color who may be sold or disposed of in virtue of any regulation which may hereafter be made by any of the legislatures of the several states in that respect, in pursuance of this act, and the Constitution of the United States.

Section 7. *And be it further enacted,* that if any ship or vessel shall be found, from and after the 1st day of January, 1808, in any river, port, bay, or harbor, or on the high seas, within the jurisdictional limits of the United States, or hovering on the coast thereof, having on board any Negro, mulatto, or person of color for the purpose of selling them as slaves, or with intent to land the same in any port or place within the jurisdiction of the United States, contrary to the prohibition of this act, every such ship or vessel, together with her tackle, apparel, and furniture, and the goods or effects which shall be found on board the same, shall be forfeited to the use of the United States and may be seized, prosecuted, and condemned in any court of the United States having jurisdiction thereof.

And it shall be lawful for the President of the United States, and he is hereby authorized, should he deem it expedient, to cause any of the armed vessels of the United States to be manned and employed to cruise on any part of the coast of the United States, or territories thereof, where he may judge attempts will be made to violate the provisions of this act, and to instruct and direct the commanders of armed vessels of the United States to seize, take, and bring into any port of the United States all such ships or vessels, and moreover to seize, take, and bring into any port of the United States all ships or vessels of the United States, wheresoever found on the high seas, contravening the provisions of this act, to be proceeded against according to law. And the captain, master, or commander of every such ship or vessel so found and seized as aforesaid shall be deemed guilty of a high misdemeanor, and shall be liable to be prosecuted before any court of the United States having jurisdiction thereof; and being thereof convicted, shall be fined not exceeding $10,000, and be imprisoned not less than two years and not exceeding four years.

She'll never run! She'll never run!

Kibitzers' cry as Robert Fulton attempted to start the engines of the *Clermont,* Sept. 4, 1807. As soon as the steamboat started to move upriver, the crowd on the bank began to shout, "She'll never stop! She'll never stop!" To his uneasy passengers, Fulton announced: "Gentlemen, you need not be uneasy; you shall be in Albany before twelve o'clock tomorrow." They were.

55.

Thomas Jefferson: On Misreporting by the Press

Thomas Jefferson, whose election to the presidency had been hailed as the "revolution of 1800," was constantly denounced during his two administrations (1801-1809) by the Federalist press. He was accused of everything from atheism to a desire to make America a French satellite. His consequent dim view of the press, which he retained to the end of his life, is expressed in this letter to John Norvell, dated June 14, 1807.

Source: *The Writings of Thomas Jefferson,* A. A. Lipscomb and E. A. Bergh, eds., Washington, 1905, pp. 415-419.

Your letter of May 9 has been duly received. The subject it proposes would require time and space for even moderate development. My occupations limit me to a very short notice of them. I think there does not exist a good elementary work on the organization of society into civil government. I mean a work which presents in one full and comprehensive view the system of principles on which such an organization should be founded, according to the rights of nature. For want of a single work of that character, I should recommend Locke on *Government,* Sidney, Priestley's *Essay on the First Principles of Government,* Chipman's *Principles of Government, The Federalist.* Adding, perhaps, Beccaria on crimes and punishments because of the demonstrative manner in which he has treated that branch of the subject. If your views of political inquiry go further, to the subjects of money and commerce, Smith's *Wealth of Nations* is the best book to be read, unless Say's *Political Economy* can be had, which treats the same subject on the same principles, but in a shorter compass and more lucid manner. But I believe this work has not been translated into our language.

History, in general, only informs us what bad government is. But as we have employed some of the best materials of the British constitution in the construction of our own government, a knowledge of British history becomes useful to the American politician. There is, however, no general history of that country which can be recommended. The elegant one of Hume seems intended to disguise and discredit the good principles of the government and is so plausible and pleasing in its style and manner as to instill its errors and heresies insensibly into the minds of unwary readers. Baxter has performed a good operation on it. He has taken the text of Hume as his groundwork, abridging it by the omission of some details of little interest, and wherever he has found him endeavoring to mislead, by either the suppression of a truth or by giving it a false coloring, he has changed the text to what it should be, so that we may properly call it Hume's history republicanized. He has, moreover, continued the history (but indifferently) from where Hume left it, to the year 1800. The work is not popular in England because it is republican; and but a few copies have ever reached America. It is a single quarto volume. Adding to this Ludlow's *Memoirs,* Mrs. Macauley's and

Belknap's histories, a sufficient view will be presented of the free principles of the English constitution.

To your request of my opinion of the manner in which a newspaper should be conducted so as to be most useful, I should answer, "by restraining it to true facts and sound principles only." Yet I fear such a paper would find few subscribers. It is a melancholy truth that a suppression of the press could not more completely deprive the nation of its benefits than is done by its abandoned prostitution to falsehood. Nothing can now be believed which is seen in a newspaper. Truth itself becomes suspicious by being put into that polluted vehicle. The real extent of this state of misinformation is known only to those who are in situations to confront facts within their knowledge with the lies of the day. I really look with commiseration over the great body of my fellow citizens who, reading newspapers, live and die in the belief that they have known something of what has been passing in the world in their time; whereas the accounts they have read in newspapers are just as true a history of any other period of the world as of the present, except that the real names of the day are affixed to their fables. General facts may indeed be collected from them, such as that Europe is now at war, that Bonaparte has been a successful warrior, that he has subjected a great portion of Europe to his will, etc., but no details can be relied on. I will add that the man who never looks into a newspaper is better informed than he who reads them, inasmuch as he who knows nothing is nearer to truth than he whose mind is filled with falsehoods and errors. He who reads nothing will still learn the great facts, and the details are all false.

Perhaps an editor might begin a reformation in some such way as this. Divide his paper into four chapters, heading the first, Truths; the second, Probabilities; the third, Possibilities; the fourth, Lies. The first chapter would be very short, as it would contain little more than authentic papers and information from such sources as the editor would be willing to risk his own reputation for their truth. The second would contain what, from a mature consideration of all circumstances, his judgment should conclude to be probably true. This, however, should rather contain too little than too much. The third and fourth should be professedly for those readers who would rather have lies for their money than the blank paper they would occupy.

Such an editor, too, would have to set his face against the demoralizing practice of feeding the public mind habitually on slander and the depravity of taste which this nauseous aliment induces. Defamation is becoming a necessary of life, insomuch that a dish of tea in the morning or evening cannot be digested without this stimulant. Even those who do not believe these abominations still read them with complaisance to their auditors, and instead of the abhorrence and indignation which should fill a virtuous mind, betray a secret pleasure in the possibility that some may believe them, though they do not themselves. It seems to escape them that it is not he who prints but he who pays for printing a slander who is its real author.

These thoughts on the subjects of your letter are hazarded at your request. Repeated instances of the publication of what has not been intended for the public eye, and the malignity with which political enemies torture every sentence from me into meanings imagined by their own wickedness only, justify my expressing a solicitude that this hasty communication may in nowise be permitted to find its way into the public papers. Not fearing these political bulldogs, I yet avoid putting myself in the way of being baited by them, and do not wish to volunteer away that portion of tranquillity which a firm execution of my duties will permit me to enjoy.

56.

FORTESCUE CUMING: A Tour to the Western Country

Irish-born Fortescue Cuming was educated in Europe before coming to New York in the 1780s. In 1806 he purchased acreage in Ohio and the following year set out on a two-year journey that took him throughout much of the backwoods country east of the Mississippi. He wrote a detailed account of his travels entitled Sketches of a Tour to the Western Country *that was published in 1810 at Pittsburgh. The work gives excellent, and for the most part, accurate descriptions of the political and social conditions of the frontier. The portion reprinted here tells of his arrival in Pittsburgh.*

Source: *Early Western Travels 1748-1846,* Reuben Gold Thwaites, ed., Cleveland, 1904, Vol. IV, pp. 70-87.

THE 1st OF FEBRUARY, AT 4 A.M., I left Somerset in a sleigh, a good deal of snow having fallen the day before. One of the gentlemen and the little girl having quitted the stage, my companions now were only a Mr. McKinley, of West Liberty near Wheeling in Virginia, one of the representatives in the state assembly, returning home from Richmond; and a Mr. Archer of Centreville in Ohio, returning home, also, from a circuitous voyage and journey to New Orleans and Baltimore, during which he had visited the Havana, and New Providence in the Bahamas. As we all possessed some information different from each other, we beguiled our journey by conversation pleasantly enough, except when politics were introduced, on which, my fellow travelers being of opposite sentiments, I was sometimes under the necessity of starting some new subject to prevent their being wrought up to an irritation of temper, which not only prevented cool argument but sometimes, in spite of my endeavors to the contrary, arose to such a height as to nearly approach to personalities.

Politics, throughout the whole of this country, seems to be the most irritable subject which can be discussed. There are two ruling or prevailing parties; one, which styles itself *Federal,* founded originally on the federal league or constitution which binds the states to each other, in contradistinction to a party which attempted to prevent the concurrence of the states to the present Constitution, and after it was agreed to, made some fruitless attempts to disorganize it, and was called *Antifederal.* The opposite party is one which has since sprung up and styles itself the *Democratic Republican.* Since the federal Constitution has been established, the first party exists no longer except *in name. That* which assumes it stickles for the offices of government being executed with a high hand, and is, therefore, accused of aristocratic and even of monarchic sentiments by its opponents, who in their turn are termed factious, and disorganizers, by the Federalists.

They nickname each other *Aristocrats* and *Democrats,* and it is astonishing to what a height their mutual animosity is carried. They are not content with declaiming against each other in Congress, or in the state legislatures, but they introduce the subject even at the bars of the judicial courts, and in the pulpits of the places of religious worship. In some places, the males, who might otherwise be on terms of friendship with each other, are, merely on account of their diversity of sentiment on politics, avowed and illiberal enemies; and the females carry the spirit of party into their coteries, so far as to exclude every female whose husband is of a different political opinion, however amiable and ornamental to society she may be. The most illiberal opinions are adopted by each party, and it is sufficient with a Federalist that another man is a Republican to pronounce him capable of every crime; while the Republican takes care not to allow the Federalist the smallest of the attributes of virtue. Their *general* difference of opinion, at last becomes *particular,* and a mistaken point of honor frequently hurries the one or the other maniac into a premature grave.

The political wheel is kept in constant motion by those two parties, who monopolize it to themselves to the exclusion of the moderate, well-disposed, and best informed part of the community, who quietly pursue their several avocations, lamenting at, yet amused by, the bickerings, disputes, and quarrels of the turbulent and ambitious leaders of the parties, and their ignorant, prejudiced and obstinate tools — satisfied with the unexampled prosperity they enjoy as a people and a nation — and equally watchful perhaps to guard against tyranny or licentiousness, with the violent and avowed opponents of both.

After traveling seven miles through the glades, a rather barren and thinly settled plain, we crossed a bridge over Laurel Hill Creek, a mile beyond which we began to ascend Laurel Hill, which we continued to do two miles farther to Evart's tavern, where we breakfasted. Six miles more brought us to the beginning of the descent westerly, there being several settlements on each side the road between the ridges of the mountain in that distance. From this point we had an extensive view as far west as the eye could reach, over and beyond Chesnut Hills. After descending two miles, we crossed Indian Creek at the foot of the mountain. I now remarked that the woods were much thicker, and the trees larger and taller than the same species to the eastward. A mile from Indian Creek, Mr. McKinley pointed out one of the finest farms between Philadelphia and Pittsburgh, owned by one McMullen, an Irishman.

At 10 A.M. we changed horses and our sleigh for a stagewagon, two miles from McMullen's, at McGinnis', perhaps the dirtiest tavern on the whole road. We then continued ten miles over a very broken hilly country, with rich valleys, crossing a high ridge called Chesnut Hills, from whence the Western country is spread out under the view like an immense forest, appearing flat from the height we were at, though it is in fact, as we found it, very hilly. We crossed the River Sewickly, a fine millstream, by a bridge, ten miles from McGinnis'; and eight miles farther we arrived at Greensburgh, the capital of Westmoreland County, which we had entered at the eastern foot of Laurel Hill.

Greensburgh is a compact, well-built, snug little town, of about a hundred houses, with a handsome courthouse, a Presbyterian meetinghouse, and a market house.

On entering Habach's tavern, I was no little surprised to see a fine coal fire, and I was informed that coal is the principal fuel of the country fifty or sixty miles round Pittsburgh. It is laid down at the doors here for six cents a bushel.

After supper we were joined by a Mr. Holly, a doctor, and another gentleman, residents of the town, according to the custom of the country where the inhabitants are in habits of collecting what information they can from travelers. We had a long political discussion, originating on the subject of Colonel Burr's projects; and among the six present, there were no two who agreed in sentiment. Indeed, in this country, every man thinks for himself, or at least he imagines he does, and would suppose himself insulted was another to attempt *openly* to bias his opinion; but notwithstanding this supposed liberty of sentiment, superior talents, when united to ambition, seldom fail of drawing the mass after them. The conversation of this evening was both amusing and instructive; some of the party, particularly Mr. Holly, a New England man, being possessed of very good information, and the arguments were conducted with cool, dispassionate reasoning.

About 8 o'clock, the landlord, who was a German, came into the room and offered to light us to bed. My fellow travelers complied, but I told him I should sit up two hours longer. The old man repeated my words, "two hours," shrugged up his shoulders, and went off, while I literally kept my word, amused by a series of three or four of the last *Baltimore Federal Gazettes*. On going to bed, and finding the bedclothes very light, I added the covering of another bed in the room to mine, which I left so in the morning as a hint to the house.

At five o'clock next morning, we resumed our journey and found very little snow on the road, though there was so much on the mountains behind us.

The aspect of the country is similar to what it is between the Laurel Hills and Greensburgh. Hills running in ridges from north to south, heavily wooded with white oak, walnut, sugar tree, and other timber natural to the climate; and the valleys narrow, but rich and all settled.

At eight miles from Greensburgh, we passed on our right an excellent house and fine farm of a Colonel Irwin, one of the assistant judges; and three miles farther, we stopped to change horses and breakfast at Stewart's, where we were charged only a quarter of a dollar each.

We soon after entered Allegheny County. The weather was cold and clear, and very pleasant for the season, but the country afforded no variety, being still, hill, dale, woods, and scattering farms. At nine miles from Stewart's, we descended a very long and steep hill, by a shocking road, crossed Turtle Creek at the bottom, which runs to the southward to join the River Monongahela, twelve miles above its confluence with the Allegheny. We then ascended another hill by an equally bad and dangerous road. It is astonishing that in so fine and so improving a country more attention is not paid to the roads. A turnpike is projected from Pittsburgh to Harrisburgh, which I am clearly of opinion might be kept in repair by a reasonable toll; and then wagons with goods may travel between the two places in a third less time than they do now, and without the present great risks of breaking down; and the mails may be delivered at the post offices one-half sooner.

When about seven miles from Pittsburgh, we had a picturesque view of the Monongahela on the left, which was soon hid again by the intervening hills; and when within three miles of that town, the view was beautiful over the fine, low, cultivated level, or bottom, as it is called, which skirts the River Allegheny from thence to Pittsburgh, which is seen at the confluence of that river with the Monongahela; beyond which, the high and steep coal hill crowned by a farmhouse most romantically situated seems to impend directly over the glass manufactory, on the bank of the river opposite the town.

The last two miles was along the fine level above mentioned, passing on the right, between the road and the Allegheny, the handsome seat of Mr. John Woods, a respectable lawyer; and immediately after, we passed Fort Fayette, a stockaded post on the right, entered Pittsburgh, and put up at Wm. McCullough's excellent inn.

The appearance of Pittsburgh in the winter is by no means pleasing, notwithstanding its fine situation, as none of the streets being paved except Market Street, they are so extremely miry that it is impossible to walk them without wading over the ankle, except during frosty weather, which rarely continues many days successively from its lying so low and being so well sheltered by the surrounding hills. This, though unpleasant now, is in reality in favor of the place, as when the streets are all paved that inconvenience will be obviated, and the advantage of shelter from the bleak wintry winds will still remain, without its being followed by an exclusion of fresh air during the summer, as the rivers at that season act as ventilators, a refreshing breeze always drawing up or down one of them, increasing with the elevation of the sun until noon and then gradually subsiding into a calm toward sunset; while at a little distance from those air conductors (the rivers), even in high situations, an oppressive heat not rarified by the most gentle zephyr prevails during the same time.

Another cause of the unprepossessing appearance of Pittsburgh proceeds from the effect of one of the most useful conveniences and necessaries of life, which it enjoys in a preeminent degree; namely, fuel, consisting of as fine coal as any in the world; in such plenty, so easily wrought, and so near the town that it is delivered in wagons, drawn by four horses, at the doors of the inhabitants at the rate of five cents per bushel.

A load of forty bushels, which costs only $2, will keep two fires in a house a month; and, in consequence, there are few houses, even among the poorest of the inhabitants, where at least two fires are not used — one for cooking and another for the family to sit at. This great consumption of a coal abounding in sulfur, and its smoke condensing into a vast quantity of lampblack, gives the outside of the houses a dirty and disagreeable appearance, even more so than in the most populous towns of Great Britain, where a proportionably great quantity of coal is used; which must be caused by a difference of quality, which appears in the grate to be in favor of the coal of this country.

The winter being too far advanced for boats to descend the Ohio, I preferred remaining in Pittsburgh, until I should have an opportunity of continuing my journey to the westward by water, to going on immediately by land, as I wished to see the banks of that celebrated river, as far as it lay in my route. . . .

Several musical amateurs are associated here under the title of the Apollonian Society. I visited it by invitation at the house of Mr. F. Amelung, the acting president; and was most agreeably surprised to hear a concert of instrumental music performed by about a dozen gentlemen of the town, with a degree of taste and execution which I could not have expected in so remote a place.

I was particularly astonished at the performance on the violin of Mr. Gabler, a German, employed at General O'Hara's glasshouse, and who is one of the society. His natural talents for music were so great that he could not bear the trammels of a scientific acquisition of it, and, therefore, never learned a note, yet he joins a correct extempore harmony to the compositions of Haydn, Pleyel, Bach, Mozart, and the other celebrated composers, particularly in their lively movements. He is not quite so happy in his accompaniments of Handel, or of grand or solemn music generally. His execution of waltzes is in a sweet and tasty style, and he has composed by ear and committed to memory several pieces, which impress the hearer with regret that they must die with their author. Indeed, he now (when too late) regrets himself that he had not in his youth, and when he had great opportunities, added science to natural taste.

The Apollonian Society is principally indebted for its formation to the labors of Mr. S. H. Dearborn, a New England man, who came here about a year ago to exercise the profession of a portrait painter; and being a very versatile genius, and having some knowledge of and taste for music, he soon discovered all the respectable people who were harmoniously inclined, and succeeded in associating them into a regular society, which meets one evening every week, and consists not only of those who can take parts but also of many of the most respectable inhabitants of the town who do not play but who become members for the sake of admission for themselves and families to the periodical concerts.

There are also two dramatic societies in Pittsburgh, one composed of the students of law, and the other of respectable mechanics. They occasionally unite with each other in order to cast the pieces to be performed with more effect. The theater is in the great room of the upper story of the courthouse, which, from its size, and having several other contiguous apartments which serve for green room, dressing rooms, etc., is very well adapted to that purpose. It is neatly fitted up under the direction of Mr. Dearborn, whose mechanical genius has rendered him a useful associate of the disciples of Thespis; whether as machinist, dresser, scene painter and shifter, or actor; particularly in the part of the garrulous Mrs. Bulgruddery in "John Bull," which he performs with much respectability.

Mr. W. Wilkins excels in genteel comedy; Mr. Johnston does justice to the part of an Irishman; Mr. Haslet, to that of a Yorkshire farmer or country squire; Mr. Linton in low comedy is the Edwin of Pittsburgh; and Mr. Van Baun would be an ornament to any established theater, either in the sock or the buskin, he being equally excellent in Octavian as in Fribble. The female characters, being sustained by young men, are deficient of that grace and modest vivacity which are natural to the fair sex, and which their grosser lords and masters vainly attempt to copy.

On the whole, however, the dramatic societies exhibit, in a very respectable manner, a rational entertainment to the inhabitants of Pittsburgh about once monthly through the winter. They have, hitherto, confined themselves to the comic walk, but I have no doubt that if they appear in the buskin, they will do equal credit to tragedy.

Some of the gentlemen of the bar resident here are very respectable in the profession of the law. Mr. Ross, formerly a senator, and set up in unsuccessful opposition to Mr. McKean for governor of the state, is an orator of the first abilities — his oratory being clear, intelligible, and impressive. Mr. Mountain, to deep learning adds careful investigation of the cause of his client, and is apt and happy in his quotations. Mr. W. Wilkins is by nature an orator. His person, action, and gesture are favorable to him; his words flow at will in a style of manly and bold oratory which commands attention. He has no occasion to study his periods; they form themselves. He enters in earnest into the cause of his client, and rarely fails to give it its full weight; but perhaps he sometimes works himself up into too great warmth of language, which may be occasioned by the glowing impulse of youth operating on a fertile fancy — he apparently not exceeding twenty-five years of age. Mr. Addison, Mr. Semple, Mr. Woods, Mr. Baldwin, and Mr. Collins are spoken of as very able practitioners, but as I had not the pleasure of witnessing their exertions at the bar, I cannot take it upon me to describe their talents, even was I adequate to it.

There are five societies of Christians, which have each an established minister — Mr. Steele, the pastor of one of the Presbyterian societies, possesses all that liberality of sentiment and Christian charity inculcated by the divine founder of his religion, and dignifies the pulpit by his clear and pleasing exposition of the Scriptures. Mr. Taylor, the Episcopal minister, is an able mathematician, a liberal philosopher, and a man of unaffected simplicity of manners. His discourses from the pulpit are good moral lectures, well adapted to the understanding of his hearers. He is an assistant teacher in the academy. Of Mr. Boggs, the minister of the other Presbyterian society, or of Mr. Black, the minister of a large society of a sect of Presbyterians called Covenanters, I am not adequate to speak, not having yet heard either officiate. Mr. Sheva, pastor of a congregation of German Lutherans, is a man of liberal morality and a lively social companion.

There are here several Roman Catholics, Methodists, and Anabaptists, who have as yet no established place of worship, but who occasionally meet to profit by the exhortations of some of their spiritual directors who travel this way. On the whole, the religious sects appear to be more free here, than in most places I have visited, from those illiberal and antichristian prejudices which render Christianity the scoff of even the ignorant Indians, whom we term savages.

But though difference of religious opinions does not cause any animosity here, politics have reduced society to a most deplorable state. There are two parties, which style themselves Federal Republicans, and Democratic Republicans, but who, speaking of each other, leave out the word "Republican," and call each other Federalists and Democrats. I have already described their opinions, which are argued with more warmth and are productive of more rancor and violence in Pittsburgh than perhaps in any other part of America. There are very few neutrals, as it requires a bold independence of sentiment to prevent a person from attaching himself to one or other party; and besides, to a man who has not resources for the employment of time within himself, the alternative of not being of one or other party is insupportable, as he is shunned equally by both, and, in this populous town lives, with respect to society, as though he were in a desert.

This may be one cause that Pittsburgh is not celebrated for its hospitality; another (which is equally applicable to most new settled towns) is that it is inhabited by people who have fixed here for the express purpose of making money. This employs the whole of their time and attention, when they are not occupied by politics, and leaves them no leisure to devote to the duties of hospitality. Another cause, which one would scarcely suspect, is pride. Those, who from the adventitious circumstance of having settled here at an early period and purchased, or became possessed of, landed property when, from its very low value, it was obtained in the most easy manner for a mere trifle, now find themselves rich suddenly from its rapid increase in value. Those who came after them had not the same opportunities, and, of course, were not so fortunate. Wealth, acquired suddenly, generally operates on the ignorant to make them wish to seem as if they had always been in the same situation; and, in affecting the manners and appearance of the great, they always overact their part and assume airs of superiority even over the really well-born and well-bred part of the community, who have been reduced from a more affluent situation, by misfortune, or who have not been so fortunate as themselves in acquiring what stands the possessor in lieu of descent, and all the virtues and accomplishments.

This accounts for the pride which generally pervades the fortunate first settlers, but it is carried to such extravagant excess, that I have been credibly informed that some of the females of this class have styled themselves and their families the "well-born," to distinguish them from those not quite so wealthy, forgetting that some among them could not tell who had been their ancestors in the second generation. This is all matter of ridicule and amusement to a person possessed of the least philosophy.

There is also a very numerous class which assumes a certain air of superiority throughout this whole country — I mean the lawyers. They (even their students and pupils) arrogate to themselves the title or epithet of esquire, which the uninformed mass of the people allow them; and as, by intrigue, they generally fill all the respectable offices in the government as well as the legislature, they assume to themselves a consequence to which they are in no other way entitled.

The profession of physic is also on a very respectable footing in this town, there being four established physicians — Doctors Bedford, Richardson, Stevenson, and Mowry — all of considerable practice, experience, and reputation.

I shall defer an account of the situation, history, and present state of Pittsburgh until I have finished my tour to the westward, when I shall have obtained more information on so important a subject.

57.

Joel Barlow: Preface and Postscript to *The Columbiad*

The desire to write "the great American epic" had seduced many ambitious writers. At an early age, Joel Barlow envisioned a great philosophic poem that would exalt the magnanimity, the vastness, and the dignity of the America he so dearly cherished. In 1779, he began The Vision of Columbus *and for the next eight years devoted his leisure time to this project. In 1787, the nine-volume work appeared and was well received by many who were delighted with this huge epic depicting in couplets the discovery and grand future of America. In 1804, Barlow began revising and rewriting the work, determined to produce a final version equal in scope to the whole of America. The ten volumes and 3,675 couplets of* The Columbiad *were published in 1807. The following selection comprises the Preface and Postscript of Barlow's work.*

Source: *The Columbiad*, Philadelphia, 1807.

PREFACE

In preparing this work for publication it seems proper to offer some observations explanatory of its design. The classical reader will perceive the obstacles which necessarily presented themselves in reconciling the nature of the subject with such a manner of treating it as should appear the most poetical, and at the same time the most likely to arrive at that degree of dignity and usefulness to which it ought to aspire.

The Columbiad is a patriotic poem; the subject is national and historical. Thus far it must be interesting to my countrymen. But most of the events were so recent, so important, and so well known as to render them inflexible to the hand of fiction. The poem therefore could not with propriety be modeled after that regular epic form which the more splendid works of this kind have taken and on which their success is supposed in a great measure to depend. The attempt would have been highly injudicious; it must have diminished and debased a series of actions which were really great in themselves and could not be disfigured without losing their interest.

I shall enter into no discussion on the nature of the epopee, nor attempt to prove by any latitude of reasoning that I have written an epic poem. The subject indeed is vast; far superior to any one of those on which the celebrated poems of this description have been constructed; and I have no doubt but the form I have given to the work is the best that the subject would admit. It may be added that in no poem are the unities of time, place and action more rigidly observed; the action, in the technical sense of the word, consisting only of what takes place between Columbus and Hesper, which must be supposed to occupy but few hours, and is confined to the prison and the mount of vision.

But these circumstances of classical regularity are of little consideration in estimating the real merit of any work of this nature. Its merit must depend on the importance of the action, the disposition of the parts, the invention and application of incidents, the propriety of the illustrations, the liveliness and chastity of the images, the suitable intervention of machinery, the moral tendency of the manners, the strength and sublimity of the sentiments; the whole being clothed in language whose energy, harmony, and elegance shall constitute a style everywhere suited to the matter they have to treat.

It is impossible for me to determine how far I may have succeeded in any of these particulars. This must be decided by others, the result of whose decision I shall never know. But there is one point of view in which I wish the reader to place the character of my work before he pronounces on its merit: I mean its political tendency. There are two distinct objects to be kept in view in the conduct of a narrative poem: the *poetical* object and the *moral* object. The poetical is the fictitious design of the action; the moral is the real design of the poem. . . .

In the poem here presented to the public, the objects, as in other works of the kind, are two: the fictitious object of the action and the real object of the poem. The first of these is to soothe and satisfy the desponding mind of Columbus; to show him that his labors, tho ill-rewarded by his contemporaries, had not been performed in vain; that he had opened the way to the most extensive career of civilization and public happiness; and that he would one day be recognized as the author of the greatest benefits to the human race. This object is steadily kept in view; and the actions, images and sentiments are so disposed as probably to attain the end. But the real object of the poem embraces a larger scope; it is to inculcate the love of rational liberty, and to discountenance the deleterious passion for violence and war; to show that on the basis of the republican principle all good morals, as well as good government and hopes of permanent peace, must be founded; and to convince the student in political science that the theoretical question of the future advancement of human society, till states as well as individuals arrive at universal civilization, is held in dispute and still unsettled only because we have had too little experience of organized liberty in the government of nations to have well considered its effects.

I cannot expect that every reader, nor even every republican reader, will join me in opinion with respect to the future progress of society and the civilization of states; but there are two sentiments in which I think all men will agree: that the event is desirable, and that to believe it practicable is one step toward rendering it so. This being the case they ought to pardon a writer, if not applaud him, for endeavoring to inculcate this belief.

I have taken the liberty, notwithstanding the recency of the events, to make some changes in the order of several of the principal battles described in this poem. I have associated the actions of Starke, Herkimer, Brown and Francis in the Battle of Saratoga, tho they happened at some distance from that battle, both as to time and place. A like circumstance will be noticed with respect to Sumter, Jackson of Georgia, and some others in the Battle of Eutaw. I have supposed a citadel mined and blown up in the siege of York, and two ships of war grappled and blown up in the naval battle of Degrasse and Graves. It is presumed that these circumstances require no apology; as in the two latter cases the events are incidental to such situations, and they here serve the principal purpose, being meant to increase our natural horror for the havoc and miseries of war in general.

And with regard to the two former cases we ought to consider that, in the epic field, the interest to be excited by the action cannot be sustained by following the gazette, as Lucan has done. The desultory parts of the historical action must be brought together and be made to elevate and strengthen each other so as to press upon the mind with the full force of their symmetry and unity. Where the events are recent and the actors known, the only duty imposed by that circumstance on the poet is to do them historical justice and not ascribe to one hero the actions of another. But the scales of justice in this case are not necessarily accompanied by the calendar and the map.

It will occur to most of my readers that the modern modes of fighting, as likewise the instruments and terms now used in war, are not yet rendered familiar in poetical language. It is doubtless from an unwarrantable timidity, or want of confidence in their own powers of description, that modern poets have made so little use of this kind of riches that lay before them. I confess that I imbibed the common prejudice and remained a long time in the error of supposing that the ancients had a poetical advantage over us in respect to the dignity of the names of the weapons used in war, if not in their number and variety. And when I published a sketch of the present poem, under the title of *The Vision of Columbus,* I labored under the embarrassment of that idea. I am now convinced that the advantage, at least as to the weapons, is on the side of the moderns. There are better sounding names and more variety in the instruments, works, stratagems and other artifices employed in our war system than in theirs. In short, the modern military dictionary is more copious than the ancient and the words at least as poetical.

As to the mode of fighting, we have, poetically speaking, lost something in one respect, but we have gained much in another. Our battles indeed admit but few single combats or trials of individual prowess. They do admit them, however; and it is not impossible to describe them with as much detail and interest as the nature of the action requires. . . . Since our single combats must be insignificant in their consequences, not deciding anything as to the result of the battle, it would be inconvenient and misplaced to make much use of them in our descriptions. And here lies our disadvantage, compared with the ancients.

But in a general engagement, the shock of modern armies is, beyond comparison, more magnificent, more sonorous, and more discoloring to the face of nature than the ancient could have been, and is consequently susceptible of more pomp and variety of description. Our heaven and earth are not only shaken and tormented with greater noise but filled and suffocated with fire and smoke. . . .

With regard to naval battles the moderns have altogether the advantage. But there has been no naval battle described in modern poetry; neither is there any remaining to us from the ancients, except that in the bay of Marseilles by Lucan and that near Syracuse by Silius. It would seem strange indeed that Homer, whose wonderful powers of fiction were not embarrassed by historical realities, and who in other respects is so insatiable of variety, did not introduce a sea fight either in the defense of Troy or in the disastrous voyages of Ulysses. But the want of this in Homer's two poems amounts almost to a proof that in his time the nations had not yet adopted any method of fighting at sea, so that the poet could have no such image in his mind.

The business of war, with all its varieties, makes but a small part of the subject of my poem; it ought, therefore, to occupy but a small portion of its scenery. This is the reason why I have not been more solicitous to vary and heighten the descriptions of battles and other military operations. I make this observation to satisfy those readers who, being accustomed to see a long poem chiefly occupied with this sort of bustle, conceive that the life and interest of such compositions depend upon it. How far the majesty or interest of epic song really depends upon the tumultuous conflicts of war I will not decide; but I can assure the reader, so far as my experience goes, that these parts of the work are not the most difficult to write. They are scenes that exhibit those vigorous traits of human character which strike the beholder most forcibly and leave the deepest impression. They delight in violent attitudes; and, painting themselves in the strongest colors on the poet's fancy, they are easy at any time to recall. He varies them at pleasure; he adorns them readily with incidents and imparts them with spirit to the reader.

My object is altogether of a moral and political nature. I wish to encourage and strengthen, in the rising generation, a sense of the importance of republican institutions as being the great foundation of public and private happiness, the necessary aliment of future and permanent ameliorations in the condition of human nature.

This is the moment in America to give such a direction to poetry, painting, and the other fine arts, that true and useful ideas of glory may be implanted in the minds of men here, to take the place of the false and destructive ones that have degraded the species in other countries; impressions which have become so wrought into their most sacred institutions that it is there thought impious to detect them and dangerous to root them out, tho acknowledged to be false. Woe be to the republican principle and to all the institutions it supports when once the pernicious doctrine of the holiness of error shall creep into the creed of our schools and distort the intellect of our citizens.

The Columbiad, in its present form, is such as I shall probably leave it to its fate. Whether it be destined to survive its author is a question that gives me no other concern than what arises from the most pure and ardent desire of doing good to my country. To my country, therefore, with every sentiment of veneration and affection, I dedicate my labors.

POSTSCRIPT

I AM WELL AWARE that some readers will be dissatisfied in certain instances with my orthography. Their judgments are respectable; and as it is not a wanton deviation from ancient usage on my part, the subject may justify a moment's retrospect from this place. Since we have arrived at the end of a work that has given me more pleasure in the composition than it probably will in its reception by the public, they must pardon me if I thus linger awhile in taking leave. It is a favorite object of amusement as well as labor, which I cannot hope to replace.

Our language is constantly and rapidly improving. The unexampled progress of the sciences and arts for the last thirty years has enriched it with a great number of new words which are now become as necessary to the writer as his ancient mother tongue. The same progress which leads to farther extensions of ideas will still extend the vocabulary; and our neology must and will keep pace with the advancement of our knowledge. Hence will follow a closer definition and more accurate use of words, with a stricter attention to their orthography.

Such innovations ought undoubtedly to be admitted with caution; and they will of course be severely scrutinized by men of letters. A language is public property in the most extensive sense of the word; and readers as well as writers are its guardians. But they ought to have no objection to improving the estate as it passes thro their hands, by making a liberal tho rigid estimate of what may be offered as ameliorations. Some respectable philologists have proposed a total and immediate reform of our orthography and even of our alphabet; but the great body of proprietors in this heritage are of opinion that the attempt would be less advantageous than the slow and certain improvements which are going forward, and which will necessarily continue to attend the active state of our literature.

We have long since laid aside the Latin diphthongs *ae* and *oe* in common English words, and in some proper names, tho not in all. Uniformity in this respect is desirable and will prevail. Names of that description which occur in this work I have therefore written with the simple vowel, as *Cesar, Phenicia, Etna, Medea.*

Another class of our words are in a gradual state of reform. They are those Latin nouns ending in *or,* which having past thro France on their way from Rome, changed their *o* into *eu.* The Norman-English writers restored the Latin *o* but retained the French *u;* and tho the latter has been since rejected in most of these words, yet in others it is still retained by many writers. It is quite useless in pronunciation, and propriety as well as analogy requires that the reform should be carried thro. No writer at this day retains the *u* in *actor, author, emperor* and the far greater part, perhaps nine-tenths, of this class of nouns; why then should it be continued in the few that remain, such as *labor, honor?* The most accurate authors reject it in all these, and I have followed the example.

Courtesy, Museum of Fine Arts, Boston

Portrait of Joel Barlow by John Trumbull

I have also respectable authorities in prose as well as poetry for expunging the three last letters in *though* and *through;* they being totally disregarded in pronunciation and awkward in appearance. The long sound of *o* in many words, as *go, fro,* puts it out of doubt with respect to *tho;* and its sound of *oo,* which frequently occurs, as in *prove, move,* is an equal justification of *thro.* All the British poets, from Pope downward, and several eminent prose writers, including Shaftesbury and Staunton, have by their practice supported this orthography.

Some verbs in the past tense, where the usual ending in *ed* is harsh and uncouth, having long ago changed it for *t,* as *fixt, capt, meant, past, blest.* Poetry has extended this innovation to many other verbs which are necessarily uttered with the sound of *t,* tho in prose they may still retain for a while their ancient *ed.* I consider this reform as a valuable improvement in the language because it brings a numerous class of words to be written as they are spoken; and the proportion of the reformed ones is already so considerable that analogy, or regularity of conjugation, requires us to complete the list. I have not carried this reform much farther than other poets have done before me. Examples might perhaps be found for nearly all the instances in which I have indulged it, such as *perisht, astonisht,* tho I have not been solicitous to seek them. The correction might well be extended to several remaining verbs of the same class; but it is difficult in this particular case to fix the proper limit.

With regard to the apostrophe, as employed to mark the elision in the past tense of verbs, I have followed the example of the most accurate poets, who use it where the verb in the present tense does not end in *e,* as *furl'd,* because the *ed* would add a syllable and destroy the measure. But where the present tense ends in *e,* it is retained in the past with the *d,* as *robed,* because it does not add a syllable.

The letter *k* we borrowed from the Greek, and the *c* from the Latin. The power of each of these letters at the end of a word is precisely the same; and the power of one is the same as that of both. Yet our early writers placed them both at the end of certain words, with the *c* before the *k,* as *musick, publick;* why they did not put the *k* first, as being the most ancient character, does not appear. Modern authors have rejected the *k* at the end of this class of words; and no correct writer will think of replacing such an inconvenient appendage.

The idea of putting a stop to innovation in a living language is absurd, unless we put a stop to thinking. When a language becomes fixt it becomes a dead language. Men must leave it for a living one, in which they can express their ideas with all their changes, extensions and corrections. The duty of the critic in this case is only to keep a steady watch over the innovations that are offered, and require a rigid conformity to the general principles of the idiom. Noah Webster, to whose philological labors our language will be much indebted for its purity and regularity, has pointed out the advantages of a steady course of improvement and how it ought to be conducted. The Preface to his new dictionary is an able performance. He might advantageously give it more development, with some correction, and publish it as a prospectus to the great work he now has in hand.

The uniform tendency of our language is toward simplicity as well as regularity. With this view the final *e,* in words where it is quite silent and useless, is dropping off and will soon disappear. Having long since resigned the place it held in the greater part of these words, as *joye, ruine,* and more recently in some others, it must finally quit the remainder where it is still found a superfluous letter, as *active, decisive, determine.*

We may even hazard a prediction that our whole class of adjectives ending in *ous* will be reformed and brought nearer to their pronunciation by rejecting the *o.* A similar change may be expected in words ending in *ss.* These words have already undergone one reform; they were formerly written with a final *e,* as *wildernesse.* They have lost the *e* because it was useless; and as the final *s* has now become equally useless, it might be dismissed with as little violence to the language. But these two projected innovations have not yet been ventured upon in any degree; and it is not desirable to be the first in so daring an enterprise when it is not immediately important.

58.

The Embargo Act

Despite Federalist forebodings, the Jefferson administration was highly successful on the domestic front. However, difficulties in foreign affairs marred the record. The many victories of Napoleon over his British foes had resulted in French control over much of Europe, though Britain continued to dominate the seas. American ships headed for other than English ports were often stopped by British naval vessels, and between 1804 and 1807 more than 1,500 American seamen were captured. This state of affairs led most Americans to believe that war was imminent. Jefferson believed, or at least hoped, that peaceful solutions were still possible, and in December 1807, he urgently requested Congress to pass an Embargo Act that would deny both Britain and France the benefits of trade with the United States. This policy of "peaceful coercion," in Jefferson's view, would frustrate the belligerent nations and force them to respect American neutrality. The Act, passed December 22, 1807, was unfavorably received by merchants, shipowners, and farmers who had carried on a profitable trade despite the hazards involved, and pressure from all sections of the country forced Congress to repeal it in 1809.

Source: *Statutes,* II, pp. 451-453.

Be it enacted, by the Senate and House of Representatives of the United States of America in Congress assembled, that an embargo be, and hereby is laid on all ships and vessels in the ports and places within the limits or jurisdiction of the United States, cleared or not cleared, bound to any foreign port or place; and that no clearance be furnished to any ship or vessel bound to such foreign port or place, except vessels under the immediate direction of the President of the United States; and that the President be authorized to give such instructions to the officers of the revenue, and of the navy and revenue cutters of the United States, as shall appear best adapted for carrying the same into full effect; *provided,* that nothing herein contained shall be construed to prevent the departure of any foreign ship or vessel, either in ballast or with the goods, wares, and merchandise on board of such foreign ship or vessel. . . .

Section 2. *And be it further enacted,* that during the continuance of this act, no registered or sea letter vessel, having on board goods, wares, and merchandise, shall be allowed to depart from one port of the United States to any other within the same, unless the master, owner, consignee, or factor of such vessel shall first give bond, with one or more sureties to the collector of the district from which she is bound to depart, in a sum of double the value of the vessel and cargo, that the said goods, wares, or merchandise shall be relanded in some port of the United States, dangers of the seas excepted, which bond, and also a certificate from the collector where the same may be relanded, shall by the collector respectively be transmitted to the secretary of the treasury. All armed vessels possessing public commissions from any foreign power are not to be considered as liable to the embargo laid by this act.

1808

59.

Thomas Jefferson: On the Civil and Religious Powers of Government

One of the basic tenets of Thomas Jefferson's political creed was his belief in the fundamental freedom of religion from any interference by the state. This notion is today so much a part of our heritage that it is difficult to imagine the time when many openly combatted it. The early New England theocracies clearly would not have recognized such a separation, and this influence was still apparent there in the early nineteenth century. In the following letter, dated January 23, 1808, to Samuel Miller, a Presbyterian minister, Jefferson took the opportunity to defend his point of view, which he felt was strongly supported by the Constitution.

Source: Randolph, IV, pp. 106-107.

I HAVE DULY RECEIVED your favor of the 18th and am thankful to you for having written it, because it is more agreeable to prevent than to refuse what I do not think myself authorized to comply with.

I consider the government of the United States as interdicted by the Constitution from intermeddling with religious institutions, their doctrines, discipline, or exercises. This results not only from the provision that no law shall be made respecting the establishment, or free exercise, of religion, but from that also which reserves to the states the powers not delegated to the U.S. Certainly no power to prescribe any religious exercise, or to assume authority in religious discipline, has been delegated to the general government. It must then rest with the states, as far as it can be in any human authority.

But it is only proposed that I should *recommend* not prescribe a day of fasting and prayer. That is, that I should indirectly assume to the U.S. an authority over religious exercises which the Constitution has directly precluded them from. It must be meant, too, that this recommendation is to carry some authority, and to be sanctioned by some penalty on those who disregard it; not indeed of fine and imprisonment but of some degree of proscription. . . .

And does the change in the nature of the penalty make the recommendation the less a law of conduct for those to whom it is directed? I do not believe it is for the interest of religion to invite the civil magistrate to direct its exercises, its discipline, or its doctrines; nor of the religious societies that the general government should be invested with the power of effecting any uniformity of time or matter among them. Fasting and prayer are religious exercises; the enjoining them an act of discipline. Every religious society has a right to determine for itself the times for these exercises and the objects proper for them, according to their own particular tenets; and this right can never be safer than in their own hands, where the Constitution has deposited it.

I am aware that the practice of my predecessors may be quoted. But I have ever believed that the example of state executives led to the assumption of that authority by the general government, without due examination, which would have discovered that what might be a right in a state government was a violation of that right when assumed by another. Be this as it may, everyone must act according to the dictates of his own reason, and mine tells me that civil powers alone have been given to the President of the U.S. and no authority to direct the religious exercises of his constituents.

60.

George Hay: Aaron Burr's Conspiracy

"As to Burr these things are admitted, and indeed cannot be denied," wrote Hamilton in a letter of 1801, "that he is a man of extreme *and* irregular *ambition; that he is selfish to a degree which excludes all social affections, and that he is decidedly profligate." This description, probably in large part correct, of the man who was later, in 1804, to slay Hamilton in a duel, may help to explain why the talented Burr missed having a brilliant political career and instead came to the very threshold of treason. Aaron Burr's "conspiracy," the exact nature of which is still unknown, involved an apparent attempt on his part to establish an "empire" in the American Southwest. A key figure in the plot was General James Wilkinson, governor of the Louisiana Territory, who had promised support to Burr, but who in the end betrayed him to Jefferson. The ensuing trial was not so much a test of Burr's guilt as of the relative strength of the two great political foes, President Jefferson and Chief Justice John Marshall. The President, convinced of Burr's guilt, did everything in his power to bring about his conviction, but he was acquitted because the evidence did not fit a strict interpretation of the Constitution's definition of treason. The U.S. attorney for Virginia, George Hay, presented the following opening speech for the prosecution. The "facts" of the plot, and the legal interpretation of them, outlined here, are as much matters of dispute today as they were in 1808.*

Source: *Reports of the Trials of Aaron Burr, etc., etc.,* Philadelphia, 1808, Vol. I, pp. 433-451.

The prisoner at the bar is charged with treason in levying war against the United States. To this charge he has pleaded not guilty. It is your high and solemn duty to decide whether the charge be true or not; and you have sworn to decide it according to the evidence which shall be laid before you. If you attend to the obligation and the words of your oath, any admonitions from me with respect to the course which you

Carolina Art Association Collection; photo, Frick Art Reference Library

Aaron Burr, portrait by Washington Allston

ought to pursue will be entirely superfluous. If you decide according to the evidence, you will divest your minds of every bias, of all political prepossessions produced by extraneous statements and rumors which you may have seen and heard. You will enter upon the case with impartial attention and a firm determination to do justice between the United States and the prisoner. But, gentlemen, if, after that patient investigation of the evidence which the importance of the case requires, and which I am sure you will bestow, you be not satisfied of the guilt of the accused, it is your duty to say that he is not guilty. . . .

This indictment contains two counts: one for levying war against the United States, at Blannerhassett's Island, in the county of Wood. The other contains precisely the same charge, but goes on with this addition — that in order to levy it more effectually, he descended the Ohio and Mississippi, with an armed force, for the purpose of taking New Orleans. If either charge be supported by evidence, it will be your duty to find a verdict against him.

In Great Britain there are no less than ten different species of treason; at least that was the number when Blackstone wrote, and it is possible that the number may have been increased since. But in this country, where the principle is established in the Constitution, there are only two descriptions of treason; and the number being fixed in the Constitution itself can never be increased by the legislature, however important and necessary it should be, in their opinion, that the number should be augmented.

By the 3rd Section of the 3rd Article of the Constitution of the United States, "Treason against the United States shall consist only in levying war against them, or in adhering to their enemies, giving them aid and comfort." With respect to the latter description, there is no occasion to say anything, as the offense charged in the indictment is "levying war against the United States"; but it adds that "no person shall be convicted of treason unless on the testimony of two witnesses to the same *overt act*, or on confession in open court." . . .

What, then, is the point at which a treasonable conspiracy shall be said to be matured into treason? What shall be said to be an overt act of treason in this country? The answer is this, gentlemen of the jury, that an assemblage of men convened for the purpose of effecting by force a treasonable design, which force is intended to be employed before their dispersion, is treasonable; and the persons engaged in it are traitors. . . . If, then, the accused and his associates had met together for the purpose of effecting by force a dissolution of the government of the United States, at New Orleans, though no force had been used or battle fought to accomplish it, they would have been guilty of treason. . . .

It will perhaps be said on the other side (though I can hardly persuade myself that it will) that *arms* must be *used,* that *force* must be *employed,* before war shall be said to be levied. If they should contend that the conspirators must have arms and must employ force before they can incur the guilt of treason, observe the embarrassment in which their doctrine will involve them. If 10,000 men were to assemble together and march to the city of Washington for the express purpose of sending the President to Monticello, turning Congress out-of-doors, taking possession of the Capitol, and usurping the powers of the government, they would not be guilty of treason; because they had not yet struck a blow. They advance and proceed; they meet no opposition; the members of the government disperse through fear; and yet this is not treason! . . .

It is incumbent on those who prosecute to show: (1) that there was a treasonable design; and (2) that there was an assemblage of men for the purpose of effectuating that design. It will be proved to you, gentlemen of the jury, that the design of the prisoner was not only to wage war against the Spanish provinces but to take possession of the city of New Orleans as preparatory to that design; to detach the people of that country from this and establish an independent government there; and to dismember the Union, separate the Western from the Eastern states, making the Allegheny Mountains the boundary line. You will perceive from the evidence that he intended to take possession of New Orleans to excite the people there to insurrection, and to take advantage of the hostile sentiments which prevailed to the west of the Allegheny against the Spaniards.

If either of these be proved; if it be established that his design was to separate the states; or, after seizing New Orleans, to invade the Spanish provinces, he is guilty of treason. If, in fact, it be proved that he intended to take New Orleans at all, he is completely guilty of treason; whether he designed to take possession of the whole or of a part, he is equally guilty of treason.

It would be absurd to suppose that a man who had revolved in his mind a scheme so gigantic as this would communicate it to many persons. But he did disclose it to a few; and, fortunately for our country, he was mistaken in his opinion of those persons in whom he confided; and the evidences of his design have been disclosed to our government. I am warranted in saying, gentlemen of the jury, that evidence, the most positive and direct, and circumstances, numerous and conclusive, will prove to your satisfaction that the intentions of the accused were precisely such as I have mentioned.

For the purpose of accomplishing these great designs — of establishing an empire in the West, of which New Orleans was to be the capital and the accused was to be the chief — he made two long visits to the Western country. He went to Ohio, Tennessee, and Kentucky, in fact to all the Western world, and traveled in various directions, till he went finally to New Orleans. Wherever he went, he spoke disrespectfully of the government of his country, with a view to facilitate the consummation of his own designs. He represented it as destitute of energy to support or defend our national rights against foreign enemies, and of spirit to maintain our national character. He uniformly said that we had no character, either at home or abroad. To those in whom he confided, he asserted that all the men of property and influence were dissatisfied with its arrangements, because they were not in the proper situation to which they were entitled; that with 500 men he could effect a revolution by which he could send the President to Monticello, intimidate Congress, and take the government of the United States into his own hands; that the people of the United States had so little knowledge of their rights, and so little disposition to maintain them, that they would meanly and tamely acquiesce in this shameful usurpation.

This is the very language of the prisoner, about the government and people; representing the one as totally destitute of all energy and talents, and the other of their homes, under a belief that they would be speedily informed of the whole project. The information was promised but never imparted. The consequence was that, when Mr. Burr was apprehended, they were left to find the way back to their own homes, by any means in their power.

Chimerical as this project was, there was only one single thing wanting to its accomplishment — the cooperation of the commander in chief and of the American Army. If General Wilkinson had acted as some have represented, if he had acted the part of a traitor instead of performing the character of a patriot, I ask what would have been the situation of this country at this moment? There would have been a civil war raging in the West; and the people of the United States, united as they are, by interest, by sympathy, and blood, would have been involved in a sanguinary contest with one another; while our eastern coasts would have been insulted and ravaged by an insolent and rapacious foe, in consequence of their knowledge of our divided situation.

From this calamity in the West, we have been protected by the vigilance and integrity of the commander in chief. I care not how my declaration may be considered; but I will venture to assert that from the adoption of the federal Constitution till this time, no man has rendered more essential service to the people and government of the United States than General Wilkinson has done, by counteracting and defeating this project. Yet, for this service, eminent and important as it is, he has been as much censured, abused, and calumniated as if he had joined in it. . . .

I have observed that you would enter upon this inquiry with candor and patience and I must hope, too, with firmness. You will contemplate and decide this question on the same principles, under the same laws, and in the same manner as if the question were between the United States and the most ignorant and deluded of those concerned in the scheme. It is true that the prisoner has been vice-president of the United States; he has been the second in office in the government of this country, and perhaps the second in the confidence and affection of the people; and that he possesses talents and energies which at the approaching crisis might have been employed most honorably for himself and most usefully for his country; but these circumstances rather aggravate than extenuate his guilt, if he be guilty. . . .

I call upon you, gentlemen of the jury, to disregard all . . . distinctions in this land of liberty, equality, and justice; and to view this case in the same light in which you would regard it if any other man in the community were brought before you. I call on you to do justice and to decide the cause according to the evidence which will be produced before you.

1809

61.

Jacob Henry: Private Belief and Public Office

Two separate and conflicting articles in the constitution of North Carolina provided that elected officials accept "the truth of the Protestant religion" and, at the same time, allowed for freedom of religious belief. Jacob Henry, a Carteret County representative in the North Carolina House of Commons, was reelected in 1809. Because he was a Jew and hence denied "the divine authority of the New Testament, and refused to take the oath prescribed by law for his qualification" for that office, the Rockingham County representative, Hugh C. Mills, moved that Henry be refused his seat. During the discussion on Mills's motion, Henry addressed his colleagues in the following speech (it has been attributed by one North Carolina historian to Attorney General John Louis Taylor, a Roman Catholic). So impressive and convincing was Henry that the legislature voted to seat him. Though this was a significant victory for both Jews and Catholics, the executive and other sections of the state government remained closed to all except Protestants.

Source: *Publications of the American Jewish Historical Society,* No. 16, 1907, pp. 68-71.

I certainly, Mr. Speaker, know not the design of the declaration of rights made by the people of this state in the year 1776, if it was not to consecrate certain great and fundamental rights and principles which even the constitution cannot impair; for Section 44 of the latter instrument declares that the declaration of rights ought never to be violated on any pretense whatever. If there is any apparent difference between the two instruments, they ought, if possible, to be reconciled; but if there is a final repugnance between them, the declaration of rights must be considered paramount; for I believe it is to the constitution as the constitution is to law; it controls and directs it absolutely and conclusively.

If, then, a belief in the Protestant religion is required by the constitution to qualify a man for a seat in this House, and such qualification is dispensed with by the declaration of rights, the provision of the constitution must be altogether inoperative; as the language of the bill of rights is,

> that all men have a natural and inalienable right to worship Almighty God according to the dictates of their own consciences.

It is undoubtedly a natural right, and when it is declared to be an inalienable one by the people in their sovereign and original capacity, any attempt to alienate either by the constitution or by law must be vain and fruitless.

It is difficult to conceive how such a provision crept into the constitution, unless it is from the difficulty the human mind feels in suddenly emancipating itself from fetters by which it has long been enchained; and how adverse it is to the feelings and manners of the people of the present day every gentleman may satisfy himself by glancing at the religious belief of the persons who fill the various offices in this state: there are Presbyterians, Lutherans, Calvinists, Mennonists, Baptists, Trinitarians, and Unitarians. But, as far as my observation extends, there are fewer Protestants, in the strict sense of the word used by the constitution, than of any other persuasion; for I suppose that they meant by it the Protestant religion as established by the law in England. For other persuasions we see houses of worship in almost every part of the state, but very few of the Protestant; so few that, indeed, I fear that the people of this state would for some time remain unrepresented in this House if that clause of the constitution is supposed to be in force. So far from believing in the Thirty-Nine Articles, I will venture to assert that a majority of the people never have read them.

If a man should hold religious principles incompatible with the freedom and safety of the state, I do not hesitate to pronounce that he should be excluded from the public councils of the same; and I trust, if I know myself, no one would be more ready to aid and assist than myself. But I should really be at a loss to specify any known religious principles which are thus dangerous. It is surely a question between a man and his Maker, and requires more than human attributes to pronounce which of the numerous sects prevailing in the world is most acceptable to the Deity. If a man fulfills the duties of that religion, which his education or his conscience has pointed to him as the true one, no person, I hold, in this our land of liberty has a right to arraign him at the bar of any inquisition. And the day, I trust, has long passed when principles, merely speculative, were propagated by force; when the sincere and pious were made victims, and the light-minded bribed into hypocrites.

The purest homage man could render to the Almighty was in the sacrifice of his passions and the performance of his duties; that the Ruler of the universe would receive with equal benignity the various offerings of man's adoration, if they proceeded from the heart. Governments only concern the actions and conduct of man, and not his speculative notions. Who among us feels himself so exalted above his fellows as to have a right to dictate to them any mode of belief? Shall this free country set an example of persecution, which even the returning reason of enslaved Europe would not submit to? Will you bind the conscience in chains, and fasten convictions upon the mind in spite of the conclusions of reason and of those ties and habitudes which are blended with every pulsation of the heart? Are you prepared to plunge at once from the sublime heights of moral legislation into the dark and gloomy caverns of superstitious ignorance? Will you drive from your shores and from the shelter of your constitution all who do not lay their oblations on the same altar, observe the same ritual, and subscribe to the same dogmas? If so, which among the various sects into which we are divided shall be the favored one?

I should insult the understanding of this House to suppose it possible that they could ever assent to such absurdities; for all know that persecution, in all its shapes and modifications, is contrary to the genius of our government and the spirit of our laws, and that it can never produce any other effect than to render men hypocrites or martyrs.

When Charles V, emperor of Germany, tired of the cares of government, resigned his crown to his son, he retired to a monastery, where he amused the evening of his life in regulating the movements of watches, endeavoring to make a number to keep the same time; but, not being able to make any two to go exactly alike, it led him to reflect upon the folly and crimes he had committed in attempting the impossibility of making men think alike!

Nothing is more easily demonstrated than that the conduct alone is the subject of human laws, and that man ought to suffer civil disqualification for what he does and not for what he thinks. The mind can conceive laws only from Him, of whose divine essence it is a portion. He alone can punish disobedience; for who else can know its movements, or estimate their merits?

The religion I profess inculcates every duty which man owes to his fellowmen; it enjoins upon its votaries the practice of every virtue and the detestation of every vice; it teaches them to hope for the favor of heaven exactly in proportion as their lives have been directed by just, honorable, and beneficent maxims. This, then, gentlemen, is my creed; it was impressed upon my infant mind, it has been the director of my youth, the monitor of my manhood, and will, I trust, be the consolation of my old age. At any rate, Mr. Speaker, I am sure that you cannot see anything in this religion to deprive me of my seat in this House.

So far as relates to my life and conduct, the examination of these I submit with cheerfulness to your candid and liberal construction. What may be the religion of him who made this objection against me, or whether he has any religion or not, I am unable to say. I have never considered it my duty to pry into the belief of other members of this House. If their actions are upright and conduct just, the rest is for their own consideration, not for mine. I do not seek to make converts to my faith, whatever it may be esteemed in the eyes of my officious friend, nor do I exclude anyone from my esteem or friendship because he and I differ in that respect. The same charity, therefore, it is not unreasonable to expect, will be extended to myself, because in all things that relate to the state and to the duties of civil life, I am bound by the same obligations with my fellow citizens, nor does any man subscribe more sincerely than myself to the maxim, "Whatever ye would that men should do unto you, do ye so even unto them, for such is the law and the prophets."

Even to this day they never hear a thunderstorm of a summer afternoon about the Kaatskill, but they say Hendrick Hudson and his crew are at their game of nine-pins; and it is a common wish of all hen-pecked husbands in the neighborhood, when life hangs heavy on their hands, that they might have a quieting draught out of Rip Van Winkle's flagon.

Washington Irving, "Rip Van Winkle," 1809

62.

Thomas Campbell: Christian Union

Born in Ireland and ordained a Presbyterian minister in Glasgow, Scotland, Thomas Campbell from the outset of his religious career opposed religious sectarianism. Because of failing health and disillusionment with religious factionalism in Scotland, he journeyed to the United States in 1807 and became a parish preacher in western Pennsylvania. His sermons on Christian unity soon won him a large following. When he held an interdenominational celebration of the Lord's Supper, however, the Presbyterian Church forced his removal. Persisting in his efforts to foster Christian unity, Campbell founded the Christian Association of Washington, a voluntary movement "for the sole purpose of promoting simple evangelical Christianity, free from all mixture of human opinions and inventions of men." On September 7, 1809, Campbell issued a "Declaration and Address," a portion of which is reprinted here, which explained the principles of his group. His statement was significant for being an early formulation of the doctrines of the Disciples of Christ Church that grew out of his association.

Source: *Historical Documents Advocating Christian Union,* Charles A. Young, ed., Chicago, 1904, pp. 91-116.

The cause that we advocate is not our own peculiar cause, nor the cause of any party, considered as such; it is a common cause, the cause of Christ and our brethren of all denominations. All that we presume, then, is to do what we humbly conceive to be *our* duty in connection with our brethren; to each of whom it equally belongs, as to us, to exert himself for this blessed purpose. And as we have no just reason to doubt the concurrence of our brethren to accomplish an object so desirable in itself, and fraught with such happy consequences, so neither can we look forward to that happy event which will forever put an end to our hapless divisions, and restore to the church its primitive unity, purity, and prosperity, but in the pleasing prospect of their hearty and dutiful concurrence.

Dearly beloved brethren, why should *we* deem it a thing incredible that the Church of Christ, in this highly favored country, should resume that original unity, peace, and purity which belong to its constitution and constitute its glory? Or, is there anything that can be justly deemed necessary for this desirable purpose, both to conform to the model and adopt the practice of the primitive church, expressly exhibited in the New Testament? Whatever alterations this might produce in any or in all of the churches should, we think, neither be deemed inadmissible nor ineligible. Surely such alteration would be every way for the better, and not for the worse, unless we should suppose the divinely inspired rule to be faulty or defective. Were we, then, in our church constitution and managements, to exhibit a complete conformity to the apostolic church, would we not be, in that respect, as perfect as Christ intended we should be? And should not this suffice?

It is, to us, a pleasing consideration that all the Churches of Christ which mutually acknowledge each other as such are not only agreed in the great doctrines of faith and holiness but are also materially agreed as to the positive ordinances of the Gospel institution; so that our differences, at most, are about the things in which the kingdom of God does not consist; that is, about matters of private opinion or human invention. What a pity that the kingdom of God should be divided about such things! Who, then, would not be the first among us to give up human inventions in the worship of God and to cease from imposing his private opinions upon his brethren that our breaches might thus be healed? Who would not willingly conform to the original pattern laid down in the New Testament for this happy purpose?

Our dear brethren of all denominations will please to consider that we have our educational prejudices and particular customs to struggle against as well as they. But this we do sincerely declare, that there is nothing we have hitherto received as matter of faith or practice which is not expressly taught and enjoined in the word of God, either in express terms or approved precedent, that we would not heartily relinquish so that we might return to the original constitutional unity of the Christian Church; and in this happy unity enjoy full communion with all our brethren in peace and charity. The like dutiful condescension we candidly expect of all that are seriously impressed with a sense of the duty they owe to God, to each other, and to their perishing brethren of mankind. To this we call, we invite, our dear brethren of all denominations, by all the sacred motives which we have avouched as the impulsive reasons of our thus addressing them.

You are all, dear brethren, equally included as the objects of our love and esteem. With you all we desire to unite in the bonds of an entire Christian unity — Christ alone being the head, the center, His word the rule; an explicit belief of, and manifest conformity to it, in all things — the terms. More than this you will not require of us; and less we cannot require of you; nor, indeed, can we reasonably suppose any would desire it, for what good purpose would it serve? We dare neither assume nor propose the trite, indefinite distinction between essentials and nonessentials in matters of revealed truth and duty; firmly persuaded that whatever may be their comparative importance, simply considered, the high obligation of the divine authority revealing, or enjoining them, renders the belief or performance of them absolutely essential to us, insofar as we know them. And to be ignorant of anything God has revealed can neither be our duty nor our privilege. . . .

We hope, then, what we urge will neither be deemed an unreasonable nor an unseasonable undertaking. Why should it be thought unreasonable? Can any time be assigned, while things continue as they are, that would prove more favorable for such an attempt, or what could be supposed to make it so? Might it be the approximation of parties to a greater nearness, in point of public profession and similarity of customs? Or might it be expected from a gradual decline of bigotry?

As to the former, it is a well-known fact that where the difference is least the opposition is always managed with a degree of vehemence inversely proportioned to the merits of the cause. With respect to the latter, though, we are happy to say that, in some cases and places and, we hope, universally, bigotry is upon the decline; yet we are not warranted, either by the past or present, to act upon that supposition. We have, as yet, by this means seen no such effect produced; nor indeed could we reasonably expect it;

for there will always be multitudes of weak persons in the church, and these are generally most subject to bigotry. Add to this that while divisions exist there will always be found interested men who will not fail to support them; nor can we at all suppose that Satan will be idle to improve an advantage so important to the interests of his kingdom.

And let it be further observed, upon the whole, that, in matters of similar importance to our secular interests, we would by no means content ourselves with such kind of reasoning. We might further add that the attempt here suggested, not being of a partial but of general nature, it can have no just tendency to excite the jealousy or hurt the feelings of any party. On the contrary, every effort toward a permanent scriptural unity among the churches, upon the solid basis of universally acknowledged and self-evident truths, must have the happiest tendency to enlighten and conciliate, by thus manifesting to each other their mutual charity and zeal for the truth: "Whom I love in the truth," saith the apostle, "and not I only, but also all they that have known the truth; for the truth's sake, which is in us, and shall be with us forever."

Indeed, if no such divine and adequate basis of union can be fairly exhibited as will meet the approbation of every upright and intelligent Christian, nor such mode of procedure adopted in favor of the weak as will not oppress their consciences, then the accomplishment of this grand object upon principle must be forever impossible. There would, upon this supposition, remain no other way of accomplishing it but merely by voluntary compromise and good-natured accommodation. That such a thing, however, will be accomplished, one way or other, will not be questioned by any that allow themselves to believe that the commands and prayers of our Lord Jesus Christ will not utterly prove ineffectual.

Whatever way, then, it is to be effected, whether upon the solid basis of divinely revealed truth or the good-natured principle of Christian forbearance and gracious condescension, is it not equally practicable, equally eligible to us, as ever it can be to any; unless we should suppose ourselves destitute of that Christian temper and discernment which is essentially necessary to qualify us to do the will of our gracious Redeemer, whose express command to His people is that there be "no divisions among them; but that they all walk by the same rule, speak the same thing, and be perfectly joined together in the same mind and in the same judgment?" We believe, then, it is as practicable as it is eligible. Let us attempt it. "Up, and be doing, and the Lord will be with us." . . .

To you, therefore, it peculiarly belongs, as the professed and acknowledged leaders of the people, to go before them in this good work, to remove human opinions and the inventions of men out of the way, by carefully separating this chaff from the pure wheat of primary and authentic revelation; casting out that assumed authority, that enacting and decreeing power by which those things have been imposed and established. To this ministerial department, then, do we look with anxiety. Ministers of Jesus, you can neither be ignorant of nor unaffected with the divisions and corruptions of His church. His dying commands, His last and ardent prayers for the visible unity of His professing people, will not suffer you to be indifferent in this matter. You will not, you cannot, therefore, be silent upon a subject of such vast importance to His personal glory and the happiness of His people — consistently you cannot; for silence gives consent. You will rather lift up your voice like a trumpet to expose the heinous nature and dreadful consequences of those unnatural and antichristian divisions which have so rent and ruined the church of God. . . .

Let none imagine that the subjoined propositions are at all intended as an overture toward a new creed or standard for the church, or as in any wise designed to be made a term of communion; nothing can be further from our intention. They are merely designed for opening up the way, that we may come fairly and firmly to original ground upon clear and certain premises and take up things just as the apostles left them; that, thus disentangled from the accruing embarrassments of the intervening ages, we may stand with evidence upon the same ground on which the church stood at the beginning.

Having said so much to solicit attention and prevent mistake, we submit as follows:

1. That the Church of Christ upon earth is essentially, intentionally, and constitutionally one; consisting of all those in every place that profess their faith in Christ and obedience to Him in all things according to the Scriptures, and that manifest the same by their tempers and conduct, and of none else; as none else can be truly and properly called Christians.

2. That although the Church of Christ upon earth must necessarily exist in particular and distinct societies, locally separate one from another, yet there ought to be no schisms, no uncharitable divisions among them. They ought to receive each other as Christ Jesus has also received them, to the glory of God. And for this purpose they ought all to walk by the same rule, to mind and speak the same thing, and to be perfectly joined together in the same mind and in the same judgment.

3. That in order to this, nothing ought to be inculcated upon Christians as articles of faith nor required of them as terms of communion but what is expressly taught and enjoined upon them in the word of God. Nor ought anything to be admitted as of divine obligation, in their church constitution and managements, but what is expressly enjoined by the authority of our Lord Jesus Christ and His apostles upon the New Testament church, either in express terms or by approved precedent.

4. That although the Scriptures of the Old and New Testaments are inseparably connected, making together but one perfect and entire revelation of the divine will, for the edification and salvation of the church, and therefore in that respect cannot be separated; yet as to what directly and properly belongs to their immediate object, the New Testament is as perfect a constitution for the worship, discipline, and government of the New Testament church, and as perfect a rule for the particular duties of its members as the Old Testament was for the worship, discipline, and government of the Old Testament church and the particular duties of its members.

5. That with respect to the commands and ordinances of our Lord Jesus Christ, where the Scriptures are silent as to the express time or manner of performance, if any such there be, no human authority has power to interfere in order to supply the supposed deficiency by making laws for the church; nor can anything more be required of Christians in such cases but only that they so observe these commands and ordinances as will evidently answer the declared and obvious end of their institution. Much less has any human authority power to impose new commands or ordinances upon the church which our Lord Jesus Christ has not enjoined. Nothing ought to be received into the faith or worship of the church or be made a term of communion among Christians, that is not as old as the New Testament.

6. That although inferences and deductions from Scripture premises, when fairly inferred, may be truly called the doctrine of God's holy word, yet are they not formally binding upon the consciences of Christians farther than they perceive the connection, and evidently see that they are so; for their faith must not stand in the wisdom of men but in the power and veracity of God.

Therefore, no such deductions can be made terms of communion but do properly belong to the after and progressive edification of the church. Hence, it is evident that no such deductions or inferential truths ought to have any place in the Church's confession.

7. That although doctrinal exhibitions of the great system of divine truths and defensive testimonies in opposition to prevailing errors be highly expedient, and the more full and explicit they be for these purposes, the better; yet, as these must be in a great measure the effect of human reasoning, and of course must contain many inferential truths, they ought not to be made terms of Christian communion; unless we suppose, what is contrary to fact, that none have a right to the communion of the church but such as possess a very clear and decisive judgment, or are come to a very high degree of doctrinal information; whereas the church from the beginning did, and ever will, consist of little children and young men, as well as fathers.

8. That as it is not necessary that persons should have a particular knowledge or distinct apprehension of all divinely revealed truths in order to entitle them to a place in the church, neither should they, for this purpose, be required to make a profession more extensive than their knowledge; but that, on the contrary, their having a due measure of scriptural self-knowledge respecting their lost and perishing condition by nature and practice, and of the way of salvation through Jesus Christ, accompanied with a profession of their faith in and obedience to Him, in all things, according to His word, is all that is absolutely necessary to qualify them for admission into His church.

9. That all that are enabled through grace to make such a profession and to manifest the reality of it in their tempers and conduct should consider each other as the precious saints of God; should love each other as brethren, children of the same family and Father, temples of the same Spirit, members of the same body, subjects of the same grace, objects of the same divine love, bought with the same price, and joint heirs of the same inheritance. Whom God has thus joined together no man should dare to put asunder.

10. That division among the Christians is a horrid evil, fraught with many evils. It is antichristian, as it destroys the visible unity of the body of Christ; as if He were divided against Himself, excluding and excommunicating a part of Himself. It is antiscriptural, as being strictly prohibited by His sovereign authority, a direct violation of His express command. It is antinatural, as it excites Christians to contemn, to hate, and oppose one another, who are bound by the highest and most endearing obligations to love each other as brethren, even as Christ has loved them. In a word, it is productive of confusion and of every evil work.

11. That (in some instances) a partial neglect of the expressly revealed will of God, and (in others) an assumed authority for making the approbation of human opinions and human inventions a term of communion, by introducing them into the constitution, faith, or worship of the church, are and have been the immediate, obvious, and universally acknowledged causes of all the corruptions and divisions that ever have taken place in the church of God.

12. That all that is necessary to the highest state of perfection and purity of the church upon earth is: first, that none be received as members but such as having that due measure of scriptural self-knowledge described above, do profess their faith in Christ and obedience to Him in all things according to the Scriptures; nor, second, that any be retained in her communion longer than they continue to manifest the reality of their profession by their tempers and conduct; third, that her ministers, duly and scripturally qualified, inculcate none other

things than those very articles of faith and holiness expressly revealed and enjoined in the word of God; last, that in all their administrations they keep close by the observance of all divine ordinances, after the example of the primitive church, exhibited in the New Testament, without any additions whatsoever of human opinions or inventions of men.

13. Last, that if any circumstantials indispensably necessary to the observance of divine ordinances be not found upon the page of express revelation, such, and such only, as are absolutely necessary for this purpose should be adopted under the title of human expedients, without any pretense to a more sacred origin, so that any subsequent alteration or difference in the observance of these things might produce no contention nor division in the church.

From the nature and construction of these propositions, it will evidently appear that they are laid in a designed subserviency to the declared end of our association, and are exhibited for the express purpose of performing a duty of previous necessity, a duty loudly called for in existing circumstances at the hand of everyone that would desire to promote the interests of Zion; a duty not only enjoined, as has been already observed from Isaiah 57:13-14, but which is also there predicted of the faithful remnant as a thing in which they would voluntarily engage. "He that putteth his trust in me shall possess the land, and shall inherit my holy mountain; and shall say, Cast ye up, cast ye up, prepare the way, take up the stumbling block out of the way of my people."

To prepare the way for a permanent scriptural unity among Christians by calling up to their consideration fundamental truths, directing their attention to first principles, clearing the way before them by removing the stumbling blocks, the rubbish of ages which has been thrown upon it, and fencing it on each side, that in advancing toward the desired object they may not miss the way through mistake or inadvertency, by turning aside to the right hand or to the left, is, at least, the sincere intention of the above propositions. It remains with our brethren now to say how far they go toward answering this intention.

Do they exhibit truths demonstrably evident in the light of Scripture and right reason, so that to deny any part of them the contrary assertion would be manifestly absurd and inadmissible? Considered as a preliminary for the above purpose, are they adequate, so that, if acted upon, they would infallibly lead to the desired issue? If evidently defective in either of these respects, let them be corrected and amended, till they become sufficiently evident, adequate, and unexceptionable. In the meantime, let them be examined with rigor, with all the rigor that justice, candor, and charity will admit. If we have mistaken the way, we shall be glad to be set right; but if, in the meantime, we have been happily led to suggest obvious and undeniable truths, which, if adopted and acted upon, would infallibly lead to the desired unity and secure it when obtained, we hope it will be no objection that they have not proceeded from a General Council. It is not the voice of the multitude but the voice of truth that has power with the conscience; that can produce rational conviction and acceptable obedience.

A sharp tongue is the only edged tool that grows keener with constant use.
Washington Irving, "Rip Van Winkle," 1809

1810

63.

John Randolph: Against Trade Restrictions

Jefferson's embargo policy was a retaliatory measure against British and French interference with American shipping during the Napoleonic Wars. The obvious ineffectiveness of the policy and mounting opposition to it led to its repeal. Nevertheless, President Madison wished to continue Jefferson's policy of "peaceful coercion" in an effort to avoid war with Britain. Congress passed the Nonintercourse Act of 1809, a watered-down version of the Embargo Act, which allowed trade with all nations except France and England. This act, as well as the general policy of trade restrictions, incurred continuing opposition from the Federalist camp. Between March 31 and April 2, 1810, John Randolph of Virginia spoke in the House denouncing the assumptions behind the Act and advocating its repeal. The following selection contains excerpts from Randolph's impassioned speeches.

Source: *Debates,* 11 Cong., pp. 1702-1727.

We have . . . an act in subsistence which, for brevity's sake, I will call the nonintercourse law. This act has been reprobated and reviled by every man of every political description in this House and out of it, from one end of the continent to the other; and yet, sir, strange as it may appear, Congress has been in session near five months, and this law in relation to which everyone seems to concur, indeed, vie with each other in its reprobation, still remains upon our statute books. To answer what end, I beseech you, sir? Is it a sort of scarecrow, set up to frighten the great belligerents of Europe; or, is it a toy, a rattle, a bare plaything, to amuse the great children of our political world?

On whatsoever measures the nation may ultimately resolve — be it peace, be it war, be it (if there be such a thing) an intermediate state between these two — there is no difference of opinion as to the deleterious operation of this unfortunate law. I ought perhaps to call it fortunate; for, although it was introduced into the House without a single friend, although no man was found to lift up his voice in its defense, it actually passed by a majority of two to one, and is found nearly as difficult to repeal as the old Sedition Law of a former majority, even after all its abettors have become convinced of its mischievous tendency. I hope, sir, we shall profit of former experience, and not pertinaciously adhere to a measure which is daily diminishing the resources of the nation, and very justly impairing the public confidence in the wisdom and patriotism of the legislature.

But I beg pardon. I am entering into a discussion when my sole object is to submit a naked proposition to the House, and, if possible, to get the most speedy decision on it. I do not mean to reiterate (because they must present themselves to every man of common observation and common sense) the arguments by which the propriety of a speedy decision of the question is enforced.

If any member of the House will figure to himself the fair and bona fide American merchant whose ship has been lying at the wharf the greater part of the winter, laden with a cargo perishable in its nature, say flaxseed, which, if not exported now, becomes utterly worthless, he will conceive of the situation of those whom I wish to relieve. How our resources are to be enlarged, or the belligerents to be acted on by our produce perishing here, I cannot conceive. I mean the produce of the fair and bona fide trader; for the other description of men, we know, all send their produce when and where they please. We have had official information near five months ago that the law is wholly inoperative, except as to men of high character for probity and honor who cannot gain their own consent to violate the law. I therefore move that the act interdicting commercial intercourse, etc., ought to be immediately repealed. . . .

When a law has existed on our statute book for months, an acknowledged excrescence, I may move its repeal. If the nonintercourse be this manly resistance which

National Gallery of Art

Portrait of John Randolph by Gilbert Stuart

some gentlemen seem to suppose it, let us have a resolution to continue it — let us reenact it. If not, let us repeal it now, when the merchants and planters may receive some benefit from it. Instead of letting it die what may be called a natural death (although it will die on the gibbet) at the end of the session, I hope it will be now repealed. However the House may act, no part of the responsibility for its continuance can attach to me. . . .

When I return home, if I be asked why this system, which stands branded with infamy on the treasury books, which no man has the hardihood to advocate, is suffered to côntinue, if I had, like other men, sat sluggishly in my seat, and silently submitting to it, I should consider myself responsible for the mischief or disgrace resulting from a continuance of it. The moment the fate of the bill which has been lost was determined, I relieved myself from any part of the odium of continuing the system which might have attached to me. Gentlemen, on the contrary, are anxious that this glorious system should continue for three weeks; that we should adjourn and let it die. Well, sir; great is the Diana of the Ephesians! The House has it in its power to do as it pleases. If the system be prolonged, my anxiety is that it shall be no conduct of mine, passive or active, and I hope to have a direct vote on the question. The House can as well act on the subject in one day as in seven years. There is nothing *de novo;* every man's mind is long ago made up upon it. If gentlemen see something so charming in this system that they will not give it up till death do them part, so be it.

With respect to all the rest, as to the amendment proposed, for bolstering up our independence, etc., I have not a word to utter. I really could wish that less was said in this House about the independence of the United States. I do not think it creditable to us. It looks as if we had not an assurance of our independence, as if we doubted or were afraid of some flaw in our title; and I should be sorry to see that spirit which dictated it invoked, not for the purpose for which alone it should be called up but to answer the ordinary occasions of political life.

A great deal has been said, sir, about the Spirit of '76. What is it? A spirit which calls upon the nation to guard against abuse in government; a spirit which resisted the unconstitutional and arbitrary measures of the government of that day; a spirit which darts its penetrating eye always into abuses of government at home. It is the genius of investigation — the spirit of resistance; it has nothing to do with foreign prejudices and partialities. The very moment the Treaty of 1783 was signed, the spirit of the American Revolution became, as to foreign nations, neutralized. We took our rank among the nations of the earth, and stood upon equal ground with any of them.

I am sorry, sir, to be hurried into these observations; but I do think that the public mind ought not to be artfully led away, under a cry of the Spirit of '76, from objects to which that spirit would direct us — the union of military and civil offices in a single individual — a tyrannical Governor Gage at Boston, rendering the military superior to the civil power, and protecting them by mock trial from punishment; arbitrary and oppressive laws, cutting off our trade to all parts of the world — a legislature turning a deaf ear to petitioning citizens. These, sir, are the objects to which the Spirit of '76 and of the Revolution naturally guide us. The moment you invoke it to support your independence against Great Britain or any foreign power, you do by a sort of *ex post facto* act bastardize your own pedigree — you seem willing to concede that we are not an independent people. The spirit of the Revolution is invoked to induce you to resist — what? Great Britain.

Sir, it is not a spirit of opposition to foreign nations but a spirit of resistance to corruption and tyranny at home. We want no Revolutionary spirit to rouse us to assert and defend our right to a place among the nations of the earth, but to induce us to sift carefully and pertinaciously every abuse of the government at home. It is not worthwhile in a foreign contest to be repeating our Declaration of Independence. It is a black catalogue of crimes which never were nor never can be committed by a foreign government upon an independent state, but by a government upon its own people, and against these we ought to guard. Against foreign aggression we want nothing more to support our rights than the spirit of ordinary men.

The Granger Collection

The Granger Collection

Harvard University

(Above John Adams by John S. Copley; (top left) American cartoon on the XYZ Affair; the five-headed "Paris monster," representing the French Directory, demands money from the American representatives; (left) preparations for war at a Philadelphia shipyard, 1799

POLITICS

When John Adams succeeded Washington as President in 1797 he inherited domestic political problems — the schism between Federalists and Republicans and rifts within his own Federalist party, and problems of foreign relations — the continuing hostility of England and the growing hostility of France. To deal with France, Adams sent a commission, in 1797, to secure a trade and friendship treaty. The result was the XYZ Affair. The French agents, X, Y, and Z, essentially tried to blackmail the commission by suggesting that "loans" and bribes be paid to France. The meetings broke down, and undeclared war existed with France. There were few engagements in the war, except a few incidents at sea. Another American commission went to France, and by the Convention of 1800 (Treaty of Morfontaine) the U.S. and France ceased hostilities.

Festivities in the gardens at Morfontaine, celebrating the Franco-American Convention, 1800

Library of Congress

Library of Congress

Cartoon commenting unfavorably on the government's move to Washington by way of Philadelphia

Library of Congress

The Bank of the United States in Philadelphia, 1800

Yale Art Gallery

Oliver Wolcott, Jr., secretary of the treasury (1795-1800)

American Antiquarian Society

(Left) Federalist cartoon shows Jefferson offering up the Constitution to French despotism; (right) Sen. John Taylor, who introduced the Virginia Resolutions, was an early advocate of the Southern states' rights position, which denied Congress' right to interfere with slavery and denounced tariffs as sectional tyranny by the North

Commonwealth of Va.; photo, Valentine Museum

New York Historical Society

Metropolitan Museum of Art; gift of F. W. Stevens

(Left) Thomas Jefferson by Rembrandt Peale; Albert Gallatin, secretary of the treasury, 1801-14

Jefferson

The result of the Federalist rift was the election of the Republican Thomas Jefferson as the third President, backed by Hamilton and other Federalists. Jefferson was the first President to be inaugurated at the new capitol in Washington. Jefferson's administration engineered the Louisiana Purchase, sponsored the explorations of Lewis and Clark and Zebulon Pike, and waged war against the Barbary pirates of Tripoli, who were exacting tribute from American merchant ships in the Mediterranean. Jefferson believed in a conservative fiscal policy, and he re-echoed Washington's warning against entangling foreign alliances.

Library of Congress

(Above) American schooner paying to Tripoli, 1801; (below left) frigate "Philadelphia" under attack in the Tripolitan War, 1804-05; the war ended need for tribute to the Pasha of Tripoli, but payment to other Barbary states continued until 1816; (below) U.S. Custom House, N.Y.

Library of Congress

Stokes Collection, New York Public Library

The Granger Collection

"Mad Tom in a Rage," a Federalist cartoon attacking Jefferson

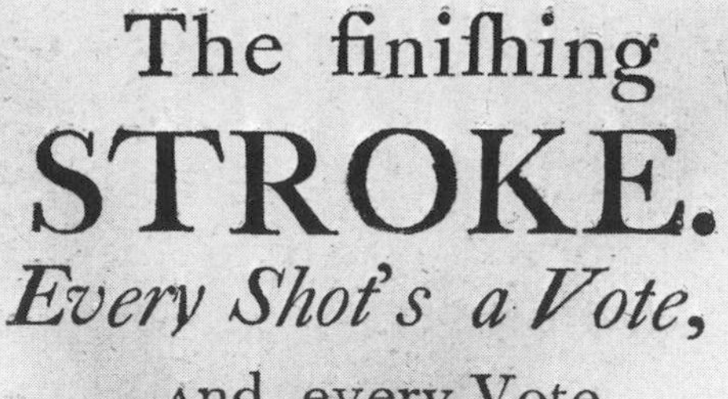

New-York Historical Society

Republican broadside linking the Federalists (Tories) with the "Kings and Tyrants of Britain," 1807

Fogg Art Museum, Harvard

The Granger Collection

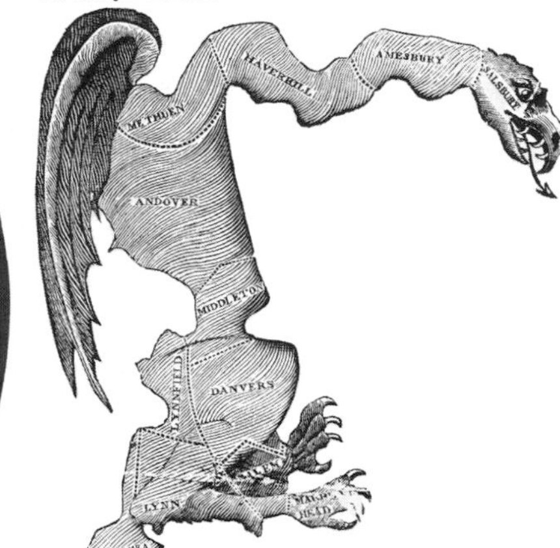

Gov. Elbridge Gerry of Massachusetts; "The Gerrymander," satirizing Gerry's redistricting scheme; cartoon, dedicated to "the butchers of the U.S.," chides Simon Snyder, Republican governor of Pennsylvania

During Jefferson's administration party politics were in full swing. Slogans were devised to pillory the opposition: Jefferson was linked with the devil as a threat to the federal government, and the Federalists were labeled monarchists in disguise. Elbridge Gerry, despite his long service, gained notoriety from a plan favoring his party.

Sen. Samuel Smith, who wrote the Non-Importation Act

Independence National Historical Park

Library of Congress

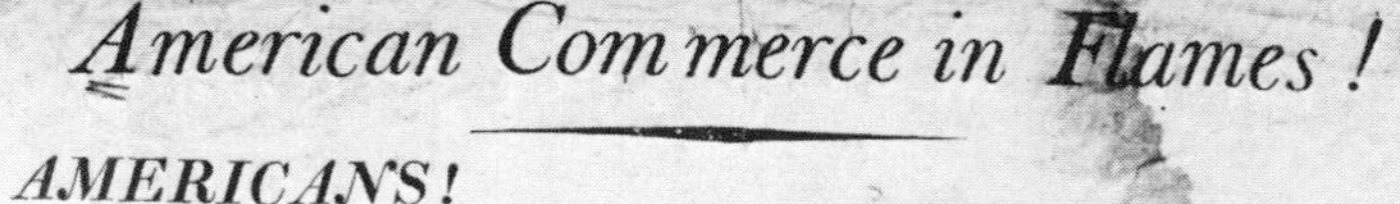

AMERICANS!

See the EXECUTION of BONAPARTE'S Orders to *Burn*, *Sink*, and *Destroy* your Ships!

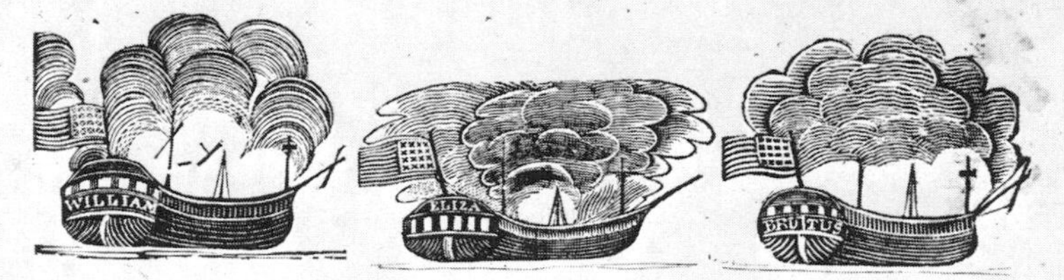

AMERICANS!

Look on this Picture! Read the transactions on which it is founded; and then Vote for SULLIVAN, or any other Partizan of *France*, if you can!!

BOSTON, MARCH 28, 1808.

Library of Congress

Federalist broadside publicizing French attacks and (bottom) Republican anti-British broadside

(Both) Library of Congress

The embargo turtle "Ograbme," harasses British shipping; (right) 1812 cartoon shows Columbia warning Bonaparte that she will deal with him after teaching John Bull (England) a lesson. Bull reads a book entitled "Might Makes Right"

During the administrations of both Jefferson and Madison, a political battle arose over the position of America in the conflicts between France and England. Neither country would recognize the neutrality of American ships, fearing the advantage that American shipping might give to the other. A non-importation policy on British goods failed to end their violations of this claimed neutrality. A later embargo on trade with both countries also failed. General agreement on the need to establish American rights in international politics was complicated by disagreement over whom to fight.

Library of Congress

British Barbarity and Piracy!!

The Federalists say that Mr. Christopher Gore ought to be supported as Governor—for *his attachment to Britain.*—If British influence is to effect the suffrages of a free people, let them read the following melancholy and outrageous conduct of British Piracy, and judge for themselves.

The "LEOPARD OUTSPOTTED" or Chesapeak Outrage outdone.

Springfield Art Museum

A "Patriotic Parade," Philadelphia, 1812; watercolor by John L. Krimmel

The "war hawks" shouted loudly in Congress, even though the real issues that led to the War of 1812 were maritime and many of the hawks were from agricultural areas. President Madison's maneuvering led inexorably toward conflict. After his declaration against Britain, the peace advocates referred to the war as "Mr. Madison's war" and deplored U.S. involvement as an extension of French hostility to England, and not in the best interests of the U.S. However, a mood of belligerence was developing.

James Madison, by Chester Harding; Mrs. Madison

Washington and Lee University; photo, Frick

New-York Historical Society

War hawks: (top) John C. Breckinridge and Henry Clay, Ky.; (bottom) Langdon Cheves and John C. Calhoun, S.C.

Dept. of Justice

Historical Society of Pennsylvania

U.S. Capitol

Corcoran Gallery of Art

New York Historical Society

(Above) Launch of the "Fulton," first steam warship, 1814; (right) cartoon lampooning the military, 1813

Library of Congress

The hawks judged that it was an opportune time to "teach England respect," since she was preoccupied with the Napoleonic wars. Peace advocates argued that attacking England constituted taking the side of France and that Napoleon's disregard for American neutrality claims had been just as blatant as England's. Opposition was chiefly among New England shippers, who stood to loose from wartime disruptions. These Federalists soon disappeared as a major party.

New York Historical Society

(Above) De Witt Clinton, N.Y., anti-war candidate for president, 1812; (below) Harrison Gray Otis, leader of the Hartford Convention, 1814

Vose Galleries, Boston

Josiah Quincy's extreme Federalist position in the Senate was satirized in this cartoon by William Charles (below)

Library Company of Philadelphia

Pennsylvania Academy of the Fine Arts

Library of Congress

Virulent British cartoon, 1819, lampoons Americans and attacks Jackson's execution of two Englishmen during his invasion of Florida

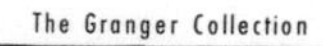

The Redwood Library

Alexander J. Dallas, by Stuart (top), and John Quincy Adams, by Harding

Peace and Politics

The war was over, and the government set about getting back in business. About six months after the war duties were lifted and trade again commenced with England. Secretary of the Treasury Alexander J. Dallas urged the formation of a new national bank to stabilize American currency, disrupted during the war. There were no further hostilities with England, and soon after taking office President Monroe traveled west as far as Detroit, marking peace on the frontier. In 1819 Spain ceded Florida to the United States as a result of the Adams-Onis Treaty, engineered by John Quincy Adams, secretary of state and destined to follow Monroe as president. Missouri applied for admission as a slave state, and Representative James Tallmadge tried to curb the growth of slavery in Missouri, but his amendment failed in the Senate.

(Left to right) James Tallmadge (1778-1853); Luther Martin, attorney general of Md., and Judge Spencer Roane of Va., both opponents of Marshall's extension of federal court jurisdiction

The Granger Collection

Johns Hopkins University; photo, Frick

Valentine Museum, Richmond

64.

ALBERT GALLATIN: The State of Manufacturing

At the request of Congress, the secretary of the treasury, Albert Gallatin, prepared a report on the progress of manufacturing in the United States. Submitted to the House of Representatives on April 19, 1810, the report discussed in some detail the textile industry, which at the time was growing faster than most others in the country.

Source: 11 Congress, 2 Session, House Report No. 325.

THE FOLLOWING MANUFACTURES are carried on to an extent which may be considered adequate to the consumption of the United States, the foreign articles annually imported being less in value than those of American manufacture belonging to the same general class which are annually exported, viz.: manufactures of wood, or of which wood is the principal material; leather and manufactures of leather; soap and tallow candles; spermaceti oil and candles; flaxseed oil; refined sugar; coarse earthenware; snuff, chocolate, hair powder, and mustard.

The following branches are firmly established, supplying in several instances the greater, and in all a considerable, part of the consumption of the United States, viz.: iron and manufactures of iron; manufactures of cotton, wool, and flax; hats; paper, printing types, printed books, playing cards; spirituous and malt liquors; several manufactures of hemp; gunpowder; window glass; jewelry and clocks; several manufactures of lead; straw bonnets and hats; wax candles.

Progress has also been made in the following branches, viz.: paints and colors; several chemical preparations and medicinal drugs; salt; manufactures of copper and brass; japanned and plated ware; calico printing; queens- and other earthen- and glasswares, etc. . . .

The substance of the information obtained on the most important branches is comprehended under the following heads:

Wood and Manufactures of Wood. All the branches of this manufacture are carried to a high degree of perfection, supply the whole demand of the United States, and consist principally of cabinetware and other household furniture, coaches and carriages either for pleasure or transportation, and shipbuilding.

The ships and vessels above 20 tons burden built in the United States during the years 1801 to 1807 measured 774,922 tons, making, on an average, about 110,000 tons a year, and worth more than $6,000,000. About two-thirds were registered for the foreign trade, and the remainder licensed for the coasting trade and fisheries.

Of the other branches, no particular account can be given, but the annual exportations of furniture and carriages amount to $170,000. The value of the whole, including shipbuilding, cannot be less than $20,000,000 a year.

Under this head may also be mentioned pot and pearl ash, of which, besides supplying the internal demand, 7,400 tons are annually exported.

Leather and Manufactures of Leather. Tanneries are established in every part of the United States, some of them on a very large scale: the capital employed in a single establishment amounting to $100,000. A few hides are exported, and it is stated that one-third of those used in the great tanneries of the Atlantic states are imported from Spanish America. Some superior or particular kinds of English leather and morocco are still imported, but about 350,000 lb. of American leather are annually exported. . . . Morocco is also made in several places, partly from imported goatskins, and principally from sheepskins. And it may be proper here to add that deerskins, which form an article of exportation, are dressed and manufactured in the United States to the amount required for the consumption of the country.

The principal manufactures of leather are those of shoes and boots, harness and saddles. Some inconsiderable quantities of the two last articles are both imported and exported. The annual importation of foreign boots and shoes amounts to 3,250 pairs of boots and 59,000 pairs of shoes, principally kid and morocco; the annual exportation of the same articles of American manufacture to 8,500 pairs of boots and 127,000 pairs of shoes. The shoe manufactures of New Jersey are extensive. That of Lynn, in Massachusetts, makes 100,000 pairs of women's shoes annually.

The value of all the articles annually manufactured in the United States which are embraced under this head (leather) may be estimated at $20,000,000.

Soap and Tallow Candles. A great portion of the soap and candles used in the United States is a family manufacture. But there are also several establishments on an extensive scale in all the large cities, and several other places. Those of the village of Roxbury, near Boston, employ alone a capital of $100,000, and make annually 370,000 lb. of candles, 380,000 lb. of brown soap, and 50,000 lb. of windsor and fancy soap, with a profit, it is said, of 15 percent on the capital employed.

The annual importations of foreign manufacture are: candles, 158,000 lb.; soap, 470,000 lb. The annual exportations of domestic manufacture are: candles, 1,775,000 lb.; soap, 2,220,000 lb. The annual value manufactured in the United States including the quantity made in private families for their own use cannot be estimated at less than $8,000,000.

Spermaceti Oil and Candles. The establishments for this manufacture are at Nantucket and New Bedford, in Massachusetts, and at Hudson, in New York. Besides supplying the whole of the domestic consumption, they furnished annually, for exportation to foreign countries, 230,000 lb. of candles and 44,000 gal. of oil. The whole quantity annually manufactured amounted to about $300,000. But the exclusion from foreign markets has lately affected the manufacture.

Refined Sugar. The annual importations of foreign refined sugar amount for the years 1803 to 1807 to 47,000 lb. The annual exportation of American refined sugar amounts for the same years to 150,000 lb.

The then existing duty was in the year 1801 collected on 3,827,000 lb.; and as the manufacture has kept pace with the increase of population, the quantity now annually made may be estimated at 5,000,000 lb., worth $1,000,000. The capital employed is stated at $3,500,000; and as the establishments have increased in number, some of them have declined in business. It is believed that if a drawback equivalent to the duty paid on the importation of the brown sugar used in the refined sugar exported was again allowed, the foreign demand, particularly of Russia, would give a great extension to this branch. A special report has been made on that subject to the committee of commerce and manufactures.

Cotton, Wool, and Flax

Spinning Mills and Manufacturing Establishments. The first cotton mill was erected in the state of Rhode Island in the year 1791; another in the same state in the year 1795; and two more in the state of Massachusetts in the years 1803 and 1804. During the three succeeding years, 10 more were erected or commenced in Rhode Island, and 1 in Connecticut; making altogether 15 mills erected before the year 1808, working at that time about 8,000 spindles, and producing about 300,000 lb. of yarn a year.

Returns have been received of 87 mills which were erected at the end of the year 1809; 62 of which (48 water and 14 horse mills) were in operation, and worked at that time 31,000 spindles. The other 25 will all be in operation in the course of this year and, together with the former ones (almost all of which are increasing their machinery) will, by the estimate received, work more than 80,000 spindles at the commencement of the year 1811.

The capital required to carry on the manufacture on the best terms is estimated at the rate of $100 for each spindle, including both the fixed capital applied to the purchase of the mill-seats and to the construction of the mills and machinery, and that employed in wages, repairs, raw materials, goods on hand, and contingencies. But it is believed that no more than at the rate of $60 for each spindle is generally actually employed. Forty-five pounds of cotton worth about 20 cents a pound are, on an average, annually used for each spindle; and these produce about 36 lb. of yarn of different qualities worth, on an average, $1.125 a pound. Eight hundred spindles employ 40 persons, viz.: 5 men and 35 women and children.

On those data, the general results for the year 1811 are estimated in the following table:

Mills	Spindles	Capital Employed $000	Cotton used	
			Pounds	Value
87	80,000	4,800	3,600,000	$720,000

Yarn spun		Persons employed		
Pounds	Value	Men	Women and Children	Total
2,880,000	$3,240,000	500	3,500	4,000

The increase of carding and spinning of cotton by machinery in establishments for that purpose and exclusively of that done in private families, has therefore been fourfold during the two last years, and will have been tenfold in three years. . . .

Manufacturing establishments for spinning and weaving flax are yet but few. In the state of New York there is one which employs a capital of $18,000 and 26 persons, and in which about 90,000 lb. of flax are annually spun and woven into canvas and other coarse linen. Information has been received respecting two in the vicinity of Philadelphia, one of which produces annually 72,000 yd. of canvas made of flax and cotton; in the other, the flax is both hackled and spun by machinery; 30 looms are employed, and it is said that 500,000 yd. of cotton bagging, sailcloth, and coarse linen may be made annually.

Hosiery may also be considered as almost exclusively a household manufacture. That of Germantown has declined, and it does not appear to have been attempted on a large scale in other places. There are, however, some exceptions; and it is stated that the island of Martha's Vineyard exports annually 9,000 pairs of stockings.

Household Manufactures. But by far the greater part of the goods made of those materials (cotton, flax, and wool) are manufactured in private families, mostly for their own use and partly for sale. They consist principally of coarse cloth, flannel, cotton stuffs, stripes of every description, linen, and mixtures of wool with flax or cotton. The information received from every state and from more than 60 different places concurs in establishing the fact of an extraordinary increase during the two last years, and in rendering it probable that about two-thirds of the clothing including hosiery, and of the house and table linen worn and used by the inhabitants of the United States who do not reside in cities is the product of family manufactures.

In the Eastern and Middle states, carding machines worked by water are everywhere established, and they are rapidly extending southward and westward. Jennies, other family spinning machines, and flying shuttles are also introduced in many places; and as many fulling mills are erected as are required for finishing all the cloth which is woven in private families.

Difficult as it is to form an estimate, it is inferred from a comparison of all the facts which have been communicated with the population of the United States (estimated at 6,000,000 white and 1,200,000 black persons) that the value of all the goods made of cotton, wool, and flax which are annually manufactured in the United States exceeds $40,000,000. . . .

Hats. The annual importations of foreign hats amount to $350,000. The annual exportation of American hats amounts to $100,000. The domestic manufacture is, therefore, nearly equal to the home consumption. The number made in the state of Massachusetts is estimated by the hat company of Boston at four times the number required for the consumption of the state; and from other information it would appear that in that state alone the capital applied to that branch is near $3,000,000, the number of persons employed about 4,000, and the number of hats annually made 1,550,000, of which 1,150,000 are fine hats worth, on an average, $4 each, and 400,000 felt hats worth $1 each. That the manufacture is still profitable appears from a late establishment on the Charles River, calculated to make annually 35,000 hats at $5 apiece and to employ 150 workmen.

The quantity made in Rhode Island is stated at 50,000, worth $5 each, exclusively of felt hats. Connecticut and New York make more than is necessary for their consumption, the largest establishment being that of Danbury, where 200 persons are employed and to the amount of $130,000 annually manufactured. In Vermont the manufacture supplies the consumption. It is stated by the hatters of Philadelphia that 92,000 hats worth $5 each are annually made there, in addition to which 50,000 country hats worth $3 each are annually sold in the city. In various quarters the scarcity of wool is complained of as preventing the making of a sufficient quantity of coarse hats. From all the information which has been received, it is believed that the value of all the hats annually made in the United States is near $10,000,000.

Paper and Printing. Some foreign paper is still imported, but the greater part of the consumption is of American manufacture; and it is believed that if sufficient attention was everywhere paid to the preservation of rags, a quantity equal to the demand would be made in the United States. Paper mills are erected in every part of the Union. There are 21 in the states of New Hampshire, Vermont, Rhode Island, and Delaware alone, and 10 in only 5 counties of the states of New York and Maryland. Eleven of those mills employ a capital of $200,000 and 180 workmen, and make annually $150,000 worth of paper.

Printing is carried on to an extent commensurate with the demand. Exclusive of the numerous newspapers, which alone form a considerable item in value, all the books for which there is an adequate number of purchasers are printed in the United States. But sufficient data have not been obtained to form an estimate of the annual aggregate value of the paper made, and of the printing and bookbinding executed in the United States other than what may be inferred from the population. The manufactures of hanging paper and of playing cards are also extensive; and that of printing types, of which there are two establishments, the principal at Philadelphia and another at Baltimore, was fully adequate to the demand, but has lately been affected by the want of regulus of antimony.

Manufactures of Hemp. The annual importations of foreign hemp amounted to 6,200 tons. But the interruption of commerce has greatly promoted the cultivation of that article in Massachusetts, New York, Kentucky, and several other places; and it is believed that a sufficient quantity will, in a short time, be produced in the United States. . . .

Spirituous and Malt Liquors. The duty on licensed stills amounted in 1801 to $372,000 and, on account of omissions, might be estimated at $450,000. As the duty actually paid on the spirits distilled in those stills did not on an average exceed 5 cents per gal., the quantity of spirits distilled during that year from grain and fruit (exclusive of the large gin distilleries in cities) must have amounted to about 9,000,000 gal., and may at present, the manufacturing having increased at least in the same ratio as the population, be estimated at 12,000,000 gal. To this must be added about 3,000,000 gal. of gin and rum distilled in cities; making an aggregate of 15,000,000 gal.

The importations of foreign spirits are, nevertheless, very considerable, having amounted during the years 1806 and 1807 to 9,750,000 gal. a year, and yielding a net annual revenue to the United States of $2,865,000. The quantity of malt liquors made in the United States is nearly equal to their consumption. The annual foreign importations amount only to 185,000 gal.; and the annual exportations of American beer and cider to 187,000 gal., but the amount actually made cannot be correctly stated. It has been said that the breweries of Philadelphia consumed annually 150,000 bu. of malt; and, exclusively of the numerous establishments on a smaller scale dispersed throughout the country, extensive breweries are known to exist in New York and Baltimore.

From those data the aggregate value of spirituous and malt liquors annually made in the United States cannot be estimated at less than $10,000,000.

Iron and Manufactures of Iron. The information received respecting that important branch is very imperfect. It is, however, well known that iron ore abounds, and that numerous furnaces and forges are erected throughout the United States. They supply a sufficient quantity of hollow ware and of castings of every description; but about 4,500 tons of bar iron are annually imported from Russia, and probably an equal quantity from Sweden and England together. A vague estimate states the amount of bar iron annually used in the United States at 50,000 tons, which would leave about 40,000 for that of American manufacture. Although a great proportion of the ore found in Vermont, Pennsylvania, Maryland, and Virginia is of a superior quality, and some of the iron manufactured there equal to any imported, it is to be regretted that, from the demand and from want of proper attention in the manufacture, much inferior American iron is brought to market. On that account the want of the ordinary supply of Russian iron has been felt in some of the slitting and rolling mills. But whilst a reduction of the duty on Russian iron is asked from several quarters, it is generally stated that a high or prohibitory duty on English bar, slit, rolled, and sheet iron would be beneficial; that which is usually imported on account of its cheapness being made with pit coal and of a very inferior quality.

The annual importations of sheet, slit, and hoop iron amount to 565 tons; and the quantity rolled and slit in the United States is estimated at 7,000 tons. In the state of Massachusetts alone are found 13 rolling and slitting mills in which about 3,500 tons of bar iron, principally from Russia, are annually rolled or slit. A portion is used for sheet iron and nail rods for wrought nails; but two-thirds of the whole quantity of bar iron flattened by machinery in the United States is used in the manufacture of cut nails, which has now extended throughout the whole country and, being altogether an American invention — substituting machinery to manual labor — deserves particular notice. . . .

It will be sufficient here to state that the annual product of that branch alone may be estimated at $1,200,000, and that, exclusive of the saving of fuel, the expense of manufacturing cut nails is not one-third part of that of forging wrought nails. About 280 tons are already annually exported, but the United States continue to import annually more than 1,500 tons of wrought nails and spikes. An increase of duty on these and a drawback on the exportation of the cut nails is generally asked for.

A considerable quantity of blistered and some refined steel are made in America; but the foreign importations exceed 11,000 cwt. a year.

The manufactures of iron consist principally of agricultural implements, and of all the usual work performed by common blacksmiths. To these may be added anchors, shovels and spades, axes, scythes and other edge tools, saws, bits and stirrups, and a great variety of the coarser articles of ironmongery; but cutlery and all the finer species of hardware and of steelwork are almost altogether imported from Great Britain. Balls, shells, and cannon of small caliber are cast in several places; and three foundries for casting solid, those of the largest caliber, together with the proper machinery for boring and finishing them are established at Cecil County, Maryland, near the city of Washington, and at Richmond, in Virginia; each of the two last may cast 300 pieces of artillery a year, and a great number of iron and brass cannon are made at that near the seat of government. Those of Philadelphia and near the Hudson River are not now employed. It may be here added that there are several iron foundries for casting every species of work wanted for machinery, and that steam engines are made at that of Philadelphia.

At the two public armories of Springfield and Harpers Ferry, 19,000 muskets are annually made. About 20,000 more are made at several factories, of which the most perfect is said to be that near New Haven, and which, with the exception of that erected at Richmond by the state of Virginia, are all private establishments. These may, if wanted, be immediately enlarged, and do not include a number of gunsmiths employed in making rifles and several other species of arms. Swords and pistols are also manufactured in several places.

Although it is not practicable to make a correct statement of the value of all the iron and manufactures of iron annually made in the United States, it is believed to be from $12,000,000 to $15,000,000. The annual importations from all foreign countries including bar iron and every description of manufactures of iron or steel are estimated at nearly $4,000,000.

Copper and Brass. Rich copper mines are found in New Jersey, in Virginia, and near Lake Superior, but they are not now wrought. The principal manufactures of that material are those of stills and other vessels; but the copper in sheets and bolts is almost universally imported; the only manufacture for that object, which is at Boston, not receiving sufficient encouragement, although a capital of $25,000 has been invested in a rolling mill and other apparatus. The true reason is that those articles are imported free of duty, and the owners seem to be principally employed in casting bells and other articles.

Zinc has been lately discovered in Pennsylvania, and there are a few manufactures of metal buttons and various brass wares.

Manufactures of Lead. Lead is found in Virginia and some other places, but the richest mines of that metal are found in upper Louisiana and also, it is said, in the adjacent country on the east side of the Mississippi. They are not yet wrought to the extent of which they are susceptible, and, after supplying the western country, do not furnish more than 200 tons annually to the Atlantic states. The annual importations from foreign countries of red and white lead amount to 1,150 tons, and those of lead itself, and of all other manufactures of lead, to 1,225 tons. The principal American manufactures are those of shot and colors of lead. Of the first, there are two establishments on a large scale at Philadelphia, and another in Louisiana, which are more than sufficient to supply the whole demand, stated at 600 tons a year. Five hundred and sixty tons of red and white lead, litharge, and some other preparations of that metal are made in Philadelphia alone. A repeal of the duty of 1 cent per lb. on lead, and an equalization of that on the manufactures of lead by charging them all with the 2 cents per lb. laid on white and red lead, is asked by the manufacturers. Various other paints and colors are also prepared in Philadelphia, and some other places.

Tin-, Japanned, Plated Wares. The manufacture of tinware is very extensive, and Connecticut supplies the greater part of the United States with that article, but the sheets are always imported. The manufacture of plated ware, principally for coach makers and saddlers, employs at Philadelphia 73 workmen; and the amount annually made there exceeds $100,000. There are other similar establishments at New York, Baltimore, Boston, and Charleston.

Gunpowder. Saltpeter is found in Virginia, Kentucky, and some other of the Western states and territories; but it is principally imported from the East Indies. The manufacture of gunpowder is nearly, and may at any moment be made altogether, adequate to the consumption, the importation of foreign powder amounting only to 200,000 lb., and the exportation of American powder to 100,000 lb. The manufacture of Brandywine, which employs a capital of $75,000 and 36 workmen and is considered as the most perfect, makes alone 225,000 lb. annually, and might make 600,000 lb. if there was a demand for it. Two others near Baltimore have a capital of $100,000 and make 430,000 lb. of a quality said lately to be equal to any imported. There are several other powder mills in Pennsylvania and other places; but the total amount of gunpowder made in the United States is not ascertained.

Earthen- and Glassware. A sufficient quantity of the coarser species of pottery is made everywhere; and information has been received of 4 manufactures of a finer kind lately established. One at Philadelphia, with a capital of $11,000, manufactures a species similar to that made in Staffordshire, England, and the others, in Chester County, Pennsylvania, in New Jersey, and on the Ohio, make various kinds of queensware.

Information has been obtained of 10 glass manufactures which employ about 140 glassblowers and make annually 27,000 boxes of window glass, containing each, 100 sq.ft. of glass. That of Boston makes crown glass equal to any imported; all the others make green or German glass, worth 15 percent less; that of Pittsburgh uses coal, and all the others wood for fuel. The annual importations of foreign window glass amount to 27,000 boxes, the extension of the domestic manufacture, which supplies precisely one-half of the consumption, being prevented by the want of workmen. Some of those manufactures make also green bottles and other wares; and two works, employing together 6 glassblowers, have been lately erected at Pittsburgh, and make decanters, tumblers, and every other description of flint glass of a superior quality.

Chemical Preparations. Copperas is extracted in large quantities from pyrites in Vermont, New Jersey, and Tennessee. About 200,000 lb. of oil of vitriol and other acids are annually manufactured in a single establishment at Philadelphia. Various other preparations and drugs are also made there and in some other places; and the annual amount exported exceeds $30,000 in value.

Salt. The salt springs of Onondaga and Cayuga in the state of New York furnish about 300,000 bu. a year, and the quantity may be increased in proportion to the demand. Those of the Western states and territories supply about an equal quantity; that known by the name of the Wabash Saline which belongs to the United States making now 130,000 bu. Valuable discoveries have also lately been made on the banks of the Kanawha. But the annual importation of foreign salt amounts to more than 3,000,000 bu., and cannot be superseded by American salt unless it be made along the seacoast. The works in the state of Massachusetts are declining and cannot proceed unless the duty on foreign salt should again be laid. It is necessary to shelter the works from the heavy summer rains by light roofs moving on rollers. This considerably increases the expense, and it appears that the erection of 10,000 superficial sq.ft. costs $1,000, and that they produce only 200 bu. a year. A more favorable result is anticipated on the coast of North Carolina on account of the difference in the climate; and works covering 275,000 sq. ft. have been lately erected there. . . .

From that imperfect sketch of American manufactures, it may with certainty be inferred that their annual product exceeds $120,000,000. And it is not improbable that the raw materials used and the provisions and other articles consumed by the manufacturers create a home market for agricultural products not very inferior to that which arises from foreign demand: a result more favorable than might have been expected from a view of the natural causes which impede the introduction and retard the progress of manufactures in the United States.

The most prominent of those causes are the abundance of land compared with the population, the high price of labor, and the want of a sufficient capital. The superior attractions of agricultural pursuits, the great extension of American commerce during the late European wars, and the continuance of habits after the causes which produced them have ceased to exist may also be enumerated. Several of those obstacles have, however, been removed or lessened. The cheapness of provisions had always, to a certain extent, counterbalanced the high price of manual labor; and this is now, in many important branches, nearly superseded by the introduction of machinery; a great American capital has been acquired during the last twenty years; and the injurious violations of the neutral commerce of the United States, by forcing industry and capital into other channels, have broken inveterate habits and given a general impulse, to which must be ascribed the great increase of manufactures during the two last years.

The revenue of the United States being principally derived from duties on the importation of foreign merchandise; these have also operated as a premium in favor of American manufactures whilst, on the other hand, the continuance of peace and the frugality of government have rendered unnecessary any oppressive taxes tending materially to enhance the price of labor or impeding any species of industry.

No cause, indeed, has perhaps more promoted in every respect the general prosperity of the United States than the absence of those systems of internal restrictions and monopoly which continue to disfigure the state of society in other countries. No law exists here directly or indirectly confining man to a particular occupation or place, or excluding any citizen from any branch he may at any time think proper to pursue. Industry is in every respect perfectly free and unfettered; every species of trade, commerce, art, profession, and manufacture being equally opened to all, without requiring any previous regular apprenticeship, admission, or license. Hence the progress of America has not been confined to the improvement of her agriculture and to the rapid formation of new settlements and states in the wilderness; but her citizens have extended their commerce through every part of the globe, and carry on with complete success even those branches for which a monopoly had heretofore been considered essentially necessary.

The same principle has also accelerated the introduction and progress of manufactures, and must ultimately give in that branch, as in all others, a decided superiority to the citizens of the United States over the inhabitants of countries oppressed by taxes, restrictions, and monopolies. It is believed that even at this time the only powerful obstacle against which American manufactures have to struggle arises from the vastly superior capital of the first manufacturing nation of Europe which enables her merchants to give very long credits, to sell on small profits, and to make occasional sacrifices.

The information which has been obtained is not sufficient to submit, in conformity with the resolution of the House, the plan best calculated to protect and promote American manufactures. The most obvious means are bounties, increased duties on importation, and loans by government. Occasional premiums might be beneficial, but a general system of bounties is more applicable to articles exported than to those manufactured for home consumption.

The present system of duties may in some respects be equalized and improved so as to protect some species of manufactures without affecting the revenue. But prohibitory duties are liable to the treble objection of destroying competition, of taxing the consumer, and of diverting capital and industry into channels generally less profitable to the nation than those which would have naturally been pursued by individual interest left to itself. A moderate increase will be less dangerous and, if adopted, should be continued during a certain period; for the repeal of a duty once laid materially injures those who have relied on its permanency, as has been exemplified in the salt manufacture.

Since, however, the comparative want of capital is the principal obstacle to the introduction and advancement of manufactures in America, it seems that the most efficient and most obvious remedy would consist in supplying that capital. For although the extension of banks may give some assistance in that respect, their operation is limited to a few places, nor does it comport with the nature of those institutions to lend for periods as long as are requisite for the establishment of manufactures. The United States might create a circulating stock bearing a low rate of interest, and lend it at par to manufacturers on principles somewhat similar to that formerly adopted by the states of New York and Pennsylvania in their loan offices. It is believed that a plan might be devised by which $5,000,000 a year, but not exceeding in the whole $20,000,000, might be thus lent without any material risk of ultimate loss, and without taxing or injuring any other part of the community.

65.

Thomas Jefferson: On Authorities Beyond the Law

At the end of his second term, Thomas Jefferson left Washington for his country home in Virginia. During his seventeen-year retirement at Monticello he carried on a voluminous correspondence. The following letter, dated September 20, 1810, was addressed to J. B. Colvin. Colvin was a friend in whom Jefferson must have had a great deal of confidence, as the tone of the letter suggests. Jefferson explained the reasons for some of the actions and policies of his administration, and at the same time expressed his understanding of the benefits and occasional limitations of the law.

Source: Randolph, IV, pp. 153-155.

Your favor of the 14th has been duly received, and I have to thank you for the many obliging things respecting myself which are said in it. If I have left in the breasts of my fellow citizens a sentiment of satisfaction with my conduct in the transaction of their business, it will soften the pillow of my repose through the residue of life.

The question you propose, whether circumstances do not sometimes occur which make it a duty in officers of high trust to assume authorities beyond the law, is easy of solution in principle, but sometimes embarrassing in practice. A strict observance of the written laws is doubtless one of the high duties of a good citizen, but it is not the highest. The laws of necessity, of self-preservation, of saving our country when in danger, are of higher obligation. To lose our country by a scrupulous adherence to written law would be to lose the law itself, with life, liberty, property, and all those who are enjoying them with us; thus absurdly sacrificing the end to the means.

When, in the battle of Germantown, General Washington's army was annoyed from Chew's house, he did not hesitate to plant his cannon against it, although the property of a citizen. When he besieged Yorktown, he leveled the suburbs, feeling that the laws of property must be postponed to the safety of the nation. While the army was before Yorktown, the governor of Virginia took horses, carriages, provisions, and even men by force, to enable that army to stay together till it could master the public enemy; and he was justified. A ship at sea in distress for provisions meets another having abundance, yet refusing a supply; the law of self-preservation authorizes the distressed to take a supply by force. In all these cases, the unwritten laws of necessity, of self-preservation, and of the public safety control the written laws of *meum* and *tuum*.

Further to exemplify the principle, I will state a hypothetical case. Suppose it had been made known to the executive of the Union in the autumn of 1805 that we might have the Floridas for a reasonable sum; that that sum had not indeed been so appropriated by law, but that Congress were to meet within three weeks and might appropriate it on the first or second day of their session. Ought he, for so great an advantage to his country, to have risked himself by transcending the law and making the purchase? The public advantage offered in this supposed case was indeed immense; but a reverence for law and the probability that the advantage might still be *legally* accomplished by a delay of only three weeks were powerful reasons against hazarding the act. But suppose it foreseen that a John Randolph would find means to protract the proceeding on it by Congress until the ensuing spring, by which time new circumstances would change the mind of the other party. Ought the executive in that case, and with that foreknowledge, to have secured the good to his country, and to have trusted to their justice for the transgression of the law? I think he ought, and that the act would have been approved.

After the affair of the *Chesapeake,* we thought war a very possible result. Our magazines were illy provided with some necessary articles, nor had any appropriations been made for their purchase. We ventured, however, to provide them and to place our country in safety; and stating the case to Congress, they sanctioned the act.

To proceed to the conspiracy of Burr and, particularly, to General Wilkinson's situation in New Orleans. In judging this case, we are bound to consider the state of the information, correct and incorrect, which he then possessed. He expected Burr and his band from above, a British fleet from below, and he knew there was a formidable conspiracy within the city. Under these circumstances, was he justifiable, first, in seizing notorious conspirators? On this, there can be but two opinions: one, of the guilty and their accomplices; the other, that of all honest men; second, in sending them to the seat of government, when the written law gave them a right to trial in the territory.

The danger of their rescue, of their continuing their machinations, the tardiness and weakness of the law, apathy of the judges, active patronage of the whole tribe of lawyers, unknown disposition of the juries, an hourly expectation of the enemy, salvation of the city and of the Union itself, which would have been convulsed to its center, had that conspiracy succeeded — all these constituted a law of necessity and self-preservation, and rendered the *salus populi* supreme over the written law.

The officer who is called to act on this superior ground does indeed risk himself on the justice of the controlling powers of the Constitution, and his station makes it his duty to incur that risk. But those controlling powers, and his fellow citizens generally, are bound to judge according to the circumstances under which he acted. They are not to transfer the information of this place or moment to the time and place of his action but to put themselves into his situation. We knew here that there never was danger of a British fleet from below, and that Burr's band was crushed before it reached the Mississippi. But General Wilkinson's information was very different, and he could act on no other.

From these examples and principles you may see what I think on the question proposed. They do not go to the case of persons charged with petty duties where consequences are trifling and time allowed for a legal course, nor to authorize them to take such cases out of the written law. In these, the example of overleaping the law is of greater evil than a strict adherence to its imperfect provisions. It is incumbent on those only who accept of great charges to risk themselves on great occasions when the safety of the nation or some of its very high interests are at stake. An officer is bound to obey orders; yet he would be a bad one who should do it in cases for which they were not intended and which involved the most important consequences. The line of discrimination between cases may be difficult; but the good officer is bound to draw it at his own peril and throw himself on the justice of his country and the rectitude of his motives.

I have indulged freer views on this question on your assurances that they are for your own eye only, and that they will not get into the hands of newswriters. I met their scurrilities without concern while in pursuit of the great interests with which I was charged. But in my present retirement, no duty forbids my wish for quiet.

66.

Charles J. Ingersoll: The National Character of Americans

Charles Ingersoll, a Philadelphia lawyer and ardent patriot, defied his Federalist family tradition by supporting Thomas Jefferson and later Andrew Jackson. He abhorred the critical accounts of the American people by Europeans, and even more distasteful to him were those Americans who bowed to the criticism or assumed airs of European aristocracy. Attempting to give an accurate and fair description of the United States and the American way of life, Ingersoll wrote a work to which he gave the title Inchiquin. *Published anonymously in 1810 as a series of letters, it was attributed to a traveling Jesuit. The last letter of the book, reprinted here, is a searching analysis of the national American character.*

Source: *Inchiquin, the Jesuits Letter, etc., etc.,* by "Some Unknown Author," New York, 1810, Letter VIII.

Though I have never been inattentive to the national characteristics of the American people, it was not my intention to write a separate account of them; but rather that you should glean these particulars from my communications generally. *Non hoc pollicitus* [this was not promised]. As, however, you enjoin it, I will cheerfully endeavor, from the scanty materials and little time I can command, to sketch their character; premising that I enter on the subject with more than ordinary diffidence, from the assurance I feel of its intrinsic difficulty and the many prejudices I know I must encounter.

To be as perspicuous as possible, I shall pursue the inquiry under the separate considerations of: (1) their origin and population; (2) their provincial diversities; (3) their natural and political association; (4) its moral results; and, last, their resources and prospects.

1. History affords no instance of a nation formed originally on such principles, or of such materials, as the American. It is a common opinion that these materials were of the worst species — vagabonds, mendicants, and convicts. But the fact is that the first settlers were mostly of reputable families and good character, who came to America under the auspices of intelligent and distinguished individuals, in the language of their own epic, "braving the dangers of untraversed seas," in an honorable and sacred cause. From these sources, the great currents of American population have proceeded, increased much more partially than is commonly supposed, from foreign streams. . . .

The white population of North America

is of European extraction, with scarcely any admixture with the Indian aborigines. At least three-fourths of the people of the United States derive their descent and national sympathies, through a tradition varying from one to two centuries, from neither conquerors, colonization, adventurers, nor savages but from sects of respectable exiles, by whom the basis of the population was broadly laid in principles and habits of virtue, independence, and toleration. . . .

From this origin, the augmentation has been prodigious; so much so as to confound the calculations of those who did not make allowance for the extraordinary circumstances of the country, but chose to apply the ordinary and established rules of political arithmetic to determine the increase of a country not within their principles. An exuberant and inexhaustible territory, healthy occupations, and temperate lives have impelled population at an incredible rate, notwithstanding the devastations of pestilence, which seems to be incidental to a new country. Where nature is bountiful of the inducements to marriage, the increase will be great, even in spite of the wars and follies of man. . . .

2. In point of origin, the people of this country are less homogeneous than many others. But the primary causes of their migration hither were the same; the liberality of their institutions, their intelligence and common interests, together with external pressure, have tended to approximate them; and though so small a population is scattered over so extensive a territory, including many varieties of climate, their provincial diversities are fewer and less striking than might be expected. About nine-tenths speak precisely the same language, which is a national unity probably not to be found without some variation of dialect among the same number, so largely diffused, in any other quarter of the world. The German is the only tongue spoken that forms an exception to this unity of language. That is gradually losing ground; and unless some unforeseen calamity should check the progress of natural increase, it is probable that in one century there will be 100 million people in America to whom the English speech, in its purity, will be vernacular.

The laws, manners, interests, religion, and opinions of the inhabitants of the different states, while they differ somewhat in detail, essentially correspond and coincide in principle; and it is rather from physical than moral circumstances that their diversities arise.

That demarcation, which the hand of Heaven has everywhere traced between natives of northern and those of southern latitudes, is aggravated here by the pernicious influence of subordinate slavery, with which the Southern Americans indulge their constitutional indolence. A transposition of labor upon slaves is incompatible with industry and morals, the most certain wealth of nations. Man will not labor where he can substitute slaves; and wherever man does not labor, he will abuse his time and faculties. Plutarch makes Alexander the Great say to his voluptuous officers, that nothing is so royal as to work; and certainly it may be said with emphatic propriety that nothing is so republican.

Not that there is anything in inferior servitude militant with republicanism. On the contrary, "where there is a vast multitude of slaves, as in Virginia and the Carolinas, those who are free are by far the most proud and jealous of their freedom. Freedom is to them not only an enjoyment but a kind of rank and privilege. Not seeing there that freedom, as in countries where it is a common blessing, and as broad and general as the air, may be united with much abject toil, with great misery, with all the exterior of servitude, liberty looks, amongst them, like something that is more noble and liberal. The people of the Southern colonies are much more strongly, and with a higher and more stubborn spirit, attached to liberty than those of the Northern. Such were all the ancient commonwealths; and such will be the masters of slaves who are not slaves themselves. In such a people the haughtiness of domination combines with the spirit of freedom, fortifies it, and renders it invincible."[1] But it relaxes the sinews of industry, corrupts the morals, and checks amelioration.

Fallow lands, in the titular possession of a few opulent individuals, defended from creditors by feudal tenures; the menial, the agricultural, and even the mechanic offices performed by unrewarded bondsmen; education, except among the rich, much neglected; religious exercises little attended to; commerce, as an unworthy employment, consigned to strangers; large fortunes and expensive establishments are some of the disadvantageous peculiarities by which the Southern are distinguished from the Eastern states. Equality of possessions, general information, simplicity of manners, sagacity, industry, frugality, enterprise, a rigorous observance of Presbyterian rites, a strong pervading tincture of puritanical tradition are prominent features of the latter — features which have expanded with their growth, but retain all the marked character of their original cast. . . .

The division, characteristic and territorial, into which the Americans themselves have separated their country is that of the Southern, Northern or Middle, and Eastern states. The Western, or those separated by the great intersecting ridge of mountains from the Atlantic states, is a natural allotment, scarcely yet acknowledged, exhibiting no moral varieties from the others, and formed by migrations from the East and the Atlantic side.

The Eastern and Southern sections of the Union are inhabited chiefly by natives. The population of the Middle states is more heterogeneous, partaking to a certain degree of the properties of the East and South, blended in different proportions with its own. Less profuse or fierce than those of the South, less hospitable or amiable than either; without the romantic lassitude, the lofty prejudices, and haughty republicanism of the Southern gentlemen, or the invincible enterprise of the Eastern people, without that boldness of characteristic and inveterate provincialism that are displayed in both; but richer, less prejudiced, more contented, and more thriving in population, agriculture, commerce, manufactures, and resources than either; their capitals being the emporia of the continent, the seat of its empire and its arts, the inhabitants of what are called the Middle states differ more from each other, and less from those of the East and South, and exhibit in our present view a much less interesting spectacle.

3. The lien of this "mighty continental nation" is commercial liberty; not mere political liberty but positive freedom; geographical absolution from all but the slightest restraints; the inherent and inalienable birthright of this adolescent people, upon the enjoyment of which they entered by a lineal title the moment they felt strength enough to cast off the trammels of infancy — a heritage as natural as the air they breathe, which, whether it sweeten the toil of New England, where the same farmer who sows and reaps his own field is also the mariner, who attends his produce on distant ventures, or inflate the pride of the South, where the poor black sows the ground and the rich white reaps the harvest, is still and everywhere the same "brave spirit" pervading the whole republic and binding it together by an influence, not the less powerful because its current is propelled by an animating contrariety. The American people, dispersed over an immense territory, abounding in all the means of commercial greatness, to whom an opportunity was presented at an early period of adapting their government to their cir-

1. Burke's speech on conciliation with America.

cumstances, followed the manifest order of nature when they adopted a free, republican, commercial federation.

The course and catastrophe of the French Revolution have cast a gloom over republicanism, which perhaps it may never shake off; and which, at least for the present, renders it in Europe repulsive and discreditable. But the American republic is the natural fruit of the American soil; the spirit of its freedom is impassioned, perhaps factious, but not furious or bloody. . . . The French had not the raw material. But the American federation is the natural offspring of commerce and liberty, whose correlative interests will bind it together in principle even after its formal dissolution.

What are the merits of those institutions which have been framed by the people of this country it is not necessary here to inquire, or whether the government be calculated for strength and durability. The states, as now organized, may be consolidated or dismembered, may fall asunder by the weight and weakness of the Union, or may separate in a convulsion. But it is the perfection of polity, when it rests on natural bases; and a disunion of the American states, whatever might be its political consequences, could not destroy or materially change their mutual commercial dependence and would not probably diminish the almost universal attachment of the people to republican institutions. The empire, in point of extent, is unwieldy. The East and the South are already jealous of each other, and the West regards them both with suspicion. But a community of language, of laws, of political attachments, and a reciprocity of interests are strong bonds of union. . . .

4. The prevailing character of these national elements is the natural result from their geographical and political combination. It is natural that a people descended so lately from pilgrims and sectaries should be enthusiasts; that a commercial people should be enterprising and ingenious; that a republican people, whose press is free and whose government is a government of laws and opinion, should be intelligent and licentious; that an adolescent and prosperous people should be aspiring, warlike, and vainglorious.

This is not the character the Americans bear in Europe. The question there is whether they have any national character at all; and the common impression is that they have not. . . . Reflecting men in Europe regard the American Revolution as a period when the American character shone forth with considerable distinction. Yet the same nation, in part the same men, after thirty years of peace and prosperity, are supposed to have lost the energy of patriotism they then displayed. An expansion of population, of resources, of territory, of power, of information, of freedom, of everything that tends to magnify man, is supposed to have degenerated the Americans. Is this the course of nature? . . .

According to the common course of events, the genius of the American people should be enhanced, not deteriorated, by the peace and prosperity they have enjoyed since the period of their birth as a nation. By sketches of the present state of their religion, legislation, literature, arts, and society, with an aspect never turned from their national characteristics and embracing no further details than are necessary for their exposition, I propose to endeavor to refute the false opinions inferred from their tranquillity, and at the same time to exhibit their national character.

In this age of infidelity and indifference, to call any people a religious people is a license which nothing but a comparative view of the state of religion in this and in other Christian countries can uphold. It is, however, true that the number of persons devoted to pious exercises, from reflection, independent of education and habit, is greater in the United States than in any other part of the world, in proportion to the population; and religious morality is more general and purer here than elsewhere. The political ordinance of religious toleration is one of those improvements in the science of politics for which mankind will acknowledge their obligations to America; and the divorce of church and state is an inestimable pledge for the purity and stability of republican government. . . .

Universal toleration has produced numberless particular sects, each maintained by enthusiastic proselytes. Thus the Americans are a nation of freethinkers; and having, moreover, not only no established church but being perfectly unrestrained in their belief, those persuasions are most followed which involve the utmost refinements of enthusiasm and rejection of ceremonial. After shaking off entirely the shackles of superstition, it is not easy to avoid the frenzy of fanaticism, for one begins where the other ends. But it is the advantage of the latter that, whereas superstition binds the soul in sloth and fear, fanaticism sets it free from their mortification; and though, for a time, it may float in an unsettled medium, it will settle at last on the right base.

The civil institutions of this country conduce equally with religious toleration to habits of intelligence and independence. Natural equality perhaps does not exist. Birth, affluence, and talents create distinctions, notwithstanding political regulations to the contrary. The pride of family, the vanity of wealth, and other adventitious advantages are not without their sensation in society, even in this young republic. But patrician and plebeian orders are unknown, and that third or middle class, upon which so many theories have been founded, is a section that has no existence here. Luxury has not yet corrupted the rich, nor is there any of that want which classifies the poor. There is no populace. All are people. What in other countries is called the populace, a compost heap, whence germinate mobs, beggars, and tyrants, is not to be found in the towns; and there is no peasantry in the country. Were it not for the slaves of the South, there would be but one rank. By the facility of subsistence and high price of labor, by the universal education and universal suffrage, almost every man is a yeoman or a citizen, sensible of his individual importance.

Not more than 350,000 of the 7 million composing the population of the American states reside in large towns. The remainder live on farms or in villages. Most of them are proprietors of the soil, and many of them the wealthiest and most influential natives. This great repartition of estate has necessarily a great and beneficial influence on the morals and sentiments of the people, which the laws are in general contrived to aid and confirm. The abolition of the rights of primogeniture and of entails, and the statutes for regulating the transmission of property are calculated to prevent the accumulation of the fortune of a family in the hands of any one of the children; and, by distributing it equally among them all, serve to exalt those sentiments of individual independence which are the roots of patriotism. They are most attached to the soil, who own a part of it; from which attachment spring love of country, glory, and that fine union of public with private feelings, which constitutes the strength and ornament of republics. . . .

Each individual feels himself rising in his fortunes; and the nation, rising with the concentration of all this elasticity, rejoices in its growing greatness. It is the perfection of civilized society, as far as respects the happiness of its members, when its ends are accomplished with the least pressure from government; and if the principle of internal corruption and the dangers of foreign aggression did not render necessary a sacrifice of some of this felicity to preserve and perpetuate the rest, the Americans might continue to float in undisturbed buoyancy. . . .

It would be practicable for the American government to give such encouragement to public festivals and recreations as might tend to allay popular restlessness, and to give the popular feeling an innocent and even a patriotic direction. But at present, with all their fondness for public meetings, which is indulged in a numberless variety of associations, religious, political, convivial, and social, greatly exceeding that of any other country, the Americans have few national festivals, and they are falling into disuse.

Perhaps this is not the scene for science, literature, and the fine arts. Business and tranquillity are not their elements. The poets, painters, architects, or philosophers of America are as yet neither very numerous nor eminent. But the Americans are by no means, as is often asserted in Europe, so absorbed in ignoble pursuits as to be insensible to the arts that polish and refine society. The natural genius of man is very similar in all climates, and literary excellence has had charms for all civilized men in their turn. Why, then, should a free, rich, and rising nation be lost to the noblest attractions, the groundwork for whose attachment to literature is broadly laid in a far more general dissemination of common learning than any other people enjoy? There are few Americans who cannot read and write, and who have not a competent knowledge of figures. Education is more a public concern here than in any other country. . . .

The literature of the country, to advance our view a grade higher, is rather solid than shining. But the vast number of newspapers and periodical publications, the immense importations from Europe of books of every description and their continual sale at very high prices, the printing presses, the public libraries, the philosophical and literary institutions, and, above all, the general education and intelligence of the community, most effectually refute the charges of indifference to literature and science. Germany and England are the only countries where more books are annually published; and in neither of these, though their original writers are more numerous, is the number of readers so great as in the United States. Nor in either of those or any other country whatever is a genius for writing or speaking a more useful or commanding endowment than in this. The talents displayed in the American state papers, both for composition and legislation, are seldom contested. Independent of several public literary works, of sterling and of brilliant merits, almost every state has its historian and other writers; and statistical, professional, commercial, scientific, and especially political, treatises are the offspring of every day, and multiply at a prodigious rate. . . .

In all the useful mechanic arts, in common and indispensable manufactures, as well as in not a few of the more curious and costly fabrications, in agriculture, both practically and scientifically, in the construction of houses and ships, they rank with the most advanced nations of Europe, and very far surpass some, who, upon no better pretension than a higher national ancestry, presume to consider the Americans as totally unacquainted with refinements, which in fact they understand and enjoy much better than themselves. Their architecture is always neat and commodious, often elegant, and, in some instances, grand and imposing. In their laborsaving machinery, in their implements of husbandry and domestic utensils, they are a century more improved than the inhabitants of France and Spain.

When we leave the province of utility and approach the regions of elegance, or the depths of erudition, it is true they are in a state of minority when compared with the most improved nations. Some arts and studies require leisure and patronage, perhaps luxury, to foster them into maturity. Though of these the American soil is not entirely unproductive, yet such shoots as have appeared are rare and spontaneous.

There are few individuals with the means and inclination to be patrons; and the government has hitherto afforded little protection or countenance to such improvements.

Most foreigners impute this barbarian niggardliness on the part of the government to the spirit of a republican people and the policy of their rulers; and I fear there are not wanting native Americans who consider the fine arts and republicanism incompatible. But how rude and false is such a sentiment! How offensive to the history and genius of republics!

Certain it is, however, that there is almost a total absence from this country of those magnificent memorials and incentives of distinction which the fine arts, particularly those of statuary and painting, create and sanctify. There is scarcely a statue, structure, or public monument to commemorate the achievements of their war for independence. The ground where the principal battles were fought remains unconsecrated; the ashes of the patriots who died for liberty, uninurned; and every disposition toward a suitable emblazonment of those events and characters, which should be perpetually present to the nation, in every captivating form, has been repressed as inimical to the thrifty policy of republicanism.

Thousands of pens, indeed, and tens of thousands of tongues vie with each other in their panegyric. And more than one native pencil, too, has been dedicated to their immortalizing; but these are private effusions. The nation has not the honor of their creation, and remains to this day with scarcely one of those great and splendid edifices, obelisks, and monuments which should be scattered over the land with munificent profusion, to attach and inspire its inhabitants, and embody, identify, and preserve their national feelings and character. Patriotism must have shrines or its ardor will relent. Permanent public memorials serve not only to invigorate the character of a country and incite the best emotions of its citizens but to embellish, civilize, and make it happy. . . .

In those efforts, which are the production of genius rather than erudition, particularly in the accomplishment of public speaking, the Americans have attained to greater excellence than other modern nations, their superiors in age and refinement. In the prevalence of oratory, as a common talent; in the number of good public speakers; in the fire and captivation of their public harangues, parliamentary, popular, forensic, and of the pulpit, the English are the only modern people comparable with the Americans, and the English are far from being their equals. . . .

There being few rich and no poor, there is less disparity, little luxury, and morals predominate over manners in this country. . . . Though there are few men of very large fortunes in the United States, a great proportion are in easy circumstances, and hospitality and politeness are common virtues. . . . The amusements of the Americans are gayer and less ferocious than those of the English. They are more addicted to dancing, for instance, and less to boxing, bull-baiting, and cockfighting. . . . The prevailing vice is inebriety, induced by the relaxing heats of the climate in the Southern and Middle states, by the absence of all restriction, and the high price of wages. From this odious imputation, New England is exempt. But, in every other part of the Union, the laborers and too many of the farmers are given up to a pernicious indulgence in spirituous liquors.

Marriages in the United States are contracted early and generally from disinterested motives. With very few exceptions they are sacred. Adultery is rare, and seduction seldom practised. The intercourse of the sexes is more familiar, without vice, than in any other part of the world; to which circumstance may, in great measure, be attributed the happy footing of society. This intercourse, in some countries, is confined, by cold and haughty customs, almost to the circles of consanguinity; in others, from opposite causes, it is unrestrained, voluptuous, and depraved. In the United States, it is free, chaste, and honorable. Women are said to afford a type of the state of civilization. In savage life, they are slaves. At the middle era of refinement, they are companions. With its excess, they become mistresses and slaves again.

North America is now at that happy mean, when well-educated and virtuous women enjoy the confidence of their husbands, the reverence of their children, and the respect of society, which is chiefly indebted to them for its tone and embellishments. The unobtrusive and insensible influence of the sex is in meridian operation at this time; and as the company of virtuous women is the best school for manners, the Americans, without as high a polish as some Europeans acquire, are distinguished for a sociability and urbanity that all nations, even the most refined, have not attained.

Commerce, which equalizes fortunes, levels ranks; and parade and stateliness can be kept up only where there is great disproportion of possessions. Expensive establishments, splendid equipages, and magnificent entertainments are sometimes copied after European models. But they are neither common nor popular. It is difficult and invidious to be magnificent in a republican country, where there is no populace and so many members of society have wherewithal to be generous and hospitable. A plentiful mediocrity, a hearty hospitality, a steadier and less ostentatious style of living are more congenial with the habits and fortunes of the Americans. . . .

A long interval of profound tranquillity and multiplied commerce may have tarnished the fame, perhaps relaxed somewhat the tone of this people. But it was the government, not the nation, who compromised with endurance for emolument; and the same spirit which was once displayed is still ready to show itself when summoned into action. The same valor, good faith, clemency, and patriotism still animate the bosoms of America, as the first burst of their hostilities, whenever it takes place, will convince their calumniators.

Legitimate commerce, instead of demoralizing or debasing a community, refines its sentiments, multiplies its intelligence, and sharpens its ingenuity. Where are the evidences to the contrary in this country? The Americans, far from being a sordid or venal, are not even a thrifty people. Subsistence is so easy and competency so common that those nice calculations of domestic economy, which are a branch almost of education in Europe, are scarcely attended to in America. And that long, disgusting catalog of petty offenses, through which the lower classes of other nations are driven by indigence and wretchedness, has hardly an existence here, though death is almost proscribed from the penal code.

Native Americans are very seldom to be met with in menial or the laborious occupations, which are filled by blacks and foreigners, mostly *Europeans*, who are also the common perpetrators of the smaller crimes alluded to. Though the government is supported by the customs, and the punishments for their contravention are merely pecuniary, yet such delinquencies are infinitely less frequent than in Europe or even Asia. The salaries of the public officers are very inconsiderable; yet malversation is a crime of rare occurrence; and that essential venality, which pervades almost every department of government in other countries, is altogether unpractised in this. . . .

5. A view of the resources and prospects of the United States necessarily involves some consideration of that commercial capacity by which they are connected, as regards their intercourse with the rest of the world, and as it affects them with the policy and revolutions of other great commercial

empires. I have endeavored to show that trade does not impoverish, deteriorate, or demoralize. But this must be understood with reference to spontaneous trade, the offspring of superfluous agriculture, or superior arts. The commerce which furnishes a national revenue, which cultivates an inexhaustible territory, and may at any moment be modified or suspended with no heavier grievance than a temporary deprivation of profit, should not be confounded with that exotic traffic, for whose products a nation neglects its agriculture, which is protected by navies that cost eternal wars and impoverishes the people that it may magnify the state. . . .

Whatever may be thought of their [the United States] national character or legislation, that they are eminently situated to become a great commercial people can hardly be denied. The extent and variety of their territories, the fruitfulness of their different soils, the prodigious structure of their internal navigation by means of the immense lakes and Western waters, the reciprocal dependence of the different parts of the continent on each other, the capacity of all parts to supply other countries with those superfluities they require, their remoteness and natural protection from the only powers that can injure them, their industry, freedom, and affluence, insure a rapid augmentation of population, strength, and prosperity.

67.

Timothy Dwight: The Restless Frontiersman

Timothy Dwight, influential teacher and president of Yale from 1795 to 1817, was one of the more prominent members of the New England establishment. His dislike of the frontiersmen who moved west whenever civilization impinged on them is manifested in many of his writings, and particularly in his most important work, Travels in New-England and New-York *(1821-1822). He was irritated by the unfavorable comments that Europeans continued to make about the United States, and he felt compelled to defend the New England that he loved on the ground that there, at least, was no lack of culture and of the amenities of life. Dwight's* Travels *is an entertaining book that provides a wealth of detail on the political, economic, social, and scenic aspects of New England in the early years of the last century. The selection on Vermont reprinted here was written in 1810.*

Source: *Travels in New-England and New-York,* London, 1823, Vol. II, pp. 437-443.

Vermont has been settled entirely from the other states of New England. The inhabitants have, of course, the New England character, with no other difference besides what is accidental. In the formation of colonies, those who are first inclined to emigrate are usually such as have met with difficulties at home. These are commonly joined by persons who, having large families and small farms, are induced for the sake of settling their children comfortably to seek for new and cheaper lands. To both are always added the discontented, the enterprising, the ambitious, and the covetous. Many of the first and some of all these classes are found in every new American country within ten years after its settlement has commenced. From this period, kindred, friendship, and former neighborhood prompt others to follow them. Others still are allured by the prospect of gain, presented in every new country to the sagacious from the purchase and sale of lands, while not a small number are influenced by the brilliant stories which everywhere are told concerning most tracts during the early progress of their settlement.

A considerable part of all those who begin the cultivation of the wilderness may be denominated foresters, or pioneers. The business of these persons is no other than to cut down trees, build log houses, lay open forested grounds to cultivation, and prepare the way for those who come after them. These men cannot live in regular society. They are too idle, too talkative, too passionate, too prodigal, and too shiftless to acquire either property or character. They are impatient of the restraints of law, religion, and morality; grumble about the taxes by which rulers, ministers, and schoolmasters are supported; and complain incessantly, as well as bitterly, of the extortions of mechanics, farmers, merchants, and physicians to whom they are always indebted. At the same time they are usually possessed, in their own view, of uncommon wisdom; understand medical science, politics, and religion better than those who have studied them through life; and, although they manage their own concerns worse than any other men, feel perfectly satisfied that they could manage those of the nation far better than the agents to whom they are committed by the public.

After displaying their own talents and worth, after censuring the weakness and wickedness of their superiors, after exposing the injustice of the community in neglecting to invest persons of such merit with public offices in many an eloquent harangue, uttered by many a kitchen fire, in every blacksmith's shop, and in every corner of the streets, and finding all their efforts vain, they become at length discouraged and under pressure of poverty, the fear of a jail, and the consciousness of public contempt, leave their native places and betake themselves to the wilderness.

Here they are obliged either to work or to starve. They accordingly cut down some trees and girdle others; they furnish themselves with an ill-built log house and a worse barn; and reduce a part of the forest into fields, half-enclosed and half-cultivated. The forests furnish browse; and their fields yield a stinted herbage. On this scanty provision they feed a few cattle; and with these and the penurious products of their labor, eked out by hunting and fishing, they keep their families alive.

A farm, thus far cleared, promises immediate subsistence to a better husbandman. A log house, thus built, presents, when repaired with moderate exertions, a shelter for his family. Such a husbandman is therefore induced by these little advantages, where the soil and situation please him, to purchase such a farm, when he would not plant himself in an absolute wilderness. The proprietor is always ready to sell, for he loves this irregular, adventurous, half-working and half-lounging life; and hates the sober industry and prudent economy by which his bush pasture might be changed into a farm and himself raised to thrift and independence.

The bargain is soon made. The forester, receiving more money for his improvements than he ever before possessed and a price for the soil somewhat enhanced by surrounding settlements, willingly quits his house to build another like it, and his farm to girdle trees, hunt, and saunter in another place. His wife accompanies him only from a sense of duty or necessity and secretly pines for the quiet, orderly, friendly society to which she originally bade a reluctant farewell. Her husband, in the meantime, becomes less and less a civilized man, and almost everything in the family which is amiable and meritorious is usually the result of her principles, care, and influence.

The second proprietor is commonly a farmer, and with an industry and spirit deserving no small commendation changes the desert into a fruitful field.

This change is accomplished much more rapidly in some places than in others, as various causes, often accidental, operate. In some instances a settlement is begun by farmers and assumes the aspect of regular society from its commencement. This, to some extent, is always the fact; and the greater number of the first planters are probably of this description; but some of them also are foresters, and sometimes a majority.

You must have remarked a very sensible difference in the character of different towns through which I have passed. This diversity is in no small degree derived from the original character of the planters in the different cases.

The class of men who have been the principal subject of these remarks have already straggled onward from New England, as well as from other parts of the Union, to Louisiana. In a political view their emigration is of very serious utility to the ancient settlements. All countries contain restless inhabitants, men impatient of labor; men who will contract debts without intending to pay them, who had rather talk than work, whose vanity persuades them that they are wise and prevents them from knowing that they are fools, who are delighted with innovation, who think places of power and profit due to their peculiar merits, who feel that every change from good order and established society will be beneficial to themselves, who have nothing to lose and therefore expect to be gainers by every scramble, and who, of course, spend life in disturbing others with the hope of gaining something for themselves. Under despotic governments they are awed into quiet; but in every free community they create, to a greater or less extent, continual turmoil, and have often overturned the peace, liberty, and happiness of their fellow citizens.

In the Roman commonwealth, as before in the republics of Greece, they were emptied out as soldiers upon the surrounding countries and left the sober inhabitants in comparative quiet at home. It is true they often threw these states into confusion and sometimes overturned the government. But if they had not been thus thrown off from the body politic, its life would have been of a momentary duration. As things actually were, they finally ruined all these states. For some of them had, as some of them always will have, sufficient talents to do mischief, at times very extensive. The Gracchi, Clodius, Marius, and Mark Antony were men of this character. Of this character is every demagogue, whatever may be his circumstances. Power and profit are the only ultimate objects which every such man with a direction as steady as that of the needle to the pole pursues with a greediness unlimited and inextinguishable.

Formerly, the energetic government established in New England, together with the prevailing high sense of religion and morals and the continually pressing danger from the French and the savages, compelled the inhabitants into habits of regularity and good order, not surpassed perhaps in the world; but since the American Revolution, our situation has become less favorable to the existence, as well as to the efficacy, of these great means of internal peace. The former exact and decisive energy of the government has been obviously weakened. From our ancient dangers we have been delivered, and the deliverance was a distinguished blessing; but the sense of danger regularly brings with it a strong conviction that safety cannot be preserved without exact order and a ready submission to lawful authority.

The institutions and the habits of New England, more I suspect than those of any other country, have prevented or kept down this noxious disposition, but they cannot entirely prevent either its existence or its effects. In mercy, therefore, to the sober, industrious, and well-disposed inhabitants, Providence has opened in the vast western wilderness a retreat sufficiently alluring to draw them away from the land of their nativity. We have many troubles even now; but we should have many more if this body of foresters had remained at home.

It is, however, to be observed that a considerable number even of these people become sober, industrious citizens merely by the acquisition of property. The love of property to a certain degree seems indispensable to the existence of sound morals. I have never had a servant in whom I could confide except such as were desirous to earn and preserve money. The conveniences and the character, attendant on the preservation of property, fix even these restless men at times when they find themselves really able to accumulate it, and persuade them to a course of regular industry. I have mentioned that they sell the soil of their first farms at an enhanced price, and that they gain for their improvements on them what, to themselves at least, is a considerable sum. The possession of this money removes, perhaps for the first time, the despair of acquiring property and awakens the hope and the wish to acquire more.

The secure possession of property demands, every moment, the hedge of law and reconciles a man, originally lawless, to the restraints of government. Thus situated, he sees that reputation also is within his reach. Ambition forces him to aim at it, and compels him to a life of sobriety and decency. That his children may obtain this benefit, he is obliged to send them to school, and to unite with those around him in supporting a schoolmaster. His neighbors are disposed to build a church and settle a minister. A regard to his own character, to the character and feelings of his family, and very often to the solicitations of his wife prompts him to contribute to both these objects; to attend, when they are compassed, upon the public worship of God; and perhaps to become in the end a religious man.

These lands are ours. No one has a right to remove us, because we were the first owners. The Great Spirit above has appointed this place for us, on which to light our fires, and here we will remain. As to boundaries, the Great Spirit knows no boundaries, nor will His red children acknowledge any.

Tecumseh, Chief of the Shawnees; to the messenger of the President of the United States in 1810

1811

68.

State Aid for Jewish Schools

Early American educational institutions were religiously oriented and were often wholly supported by the theocratic governments of the colonies. With the adoption of the Constitution, civil and religious spheres of interest were separated. However, the custom of state aid to denominational schools remained. Catholic schools had increased rapidly, owing to the large influx of Catholic immigrants, and they received a large portion of state funds. It was natural that other religious groups should also seek funds to support their educational efforts. In the following memorial to the state legislature, Congregation Shearith Israel of New York requested the appropriation of funds for Jewish schools. The petition, signed by the Congregation, was drafted by DeWitt Clinton, whose influence as mayor of New York City and as a state senator helped secure its approval.

Source: Alexander M. Dushkin, *Jewish Education in New York City,* New York, 1918, p. 452.

The petition of the trustees of the Congregation of Shearith Israel in the city of New York most respectfully represent:

That from the year 1793 a school has been supported from the funds of the said congregation for the education of their indigent children. That on the 8th of April, 1801, certain school monies were distributed among seven charity schools of the said city supported by religious societies. That the free school of the Roman Catholic Church and that of your memorialists were overlooked in this benevolent distribution.

That on the 21st of March, 1806, a law was passed placing the school of the former on the same footing as the others. That your memorialists also made application to the legislature, but did not succeed, owing, as they presume, to the pressure of business.

Your memorialists, fully persuaded that the legislature will look with an equal eye upon all occupations of people who conduct themselves as good and faithful citizens, and conscious that nothing has been omitted on their part to deserve the same countenance and encouragement which has been exhibited to others, do most respectfully pray your honorable body to extend the same relief to their charity school which has been granted to all others in this city.

69.

Josiah Quincy: Against the Admission of New States

Josiah Quincy, politician, wealthy municipal reformer, and president of Harvard College, was elected to Congress where he became the leader of the Federalist minority. He was a spokesman for his state, Massachusetts, as well as for the conservative forces that opposed the expansionist policies of Jefferson and Madison. Rising to speak against a bill before the House that would allow the Orleans (Louisiana) territory to adopt a constitution and form a state government, Quincy shocked his colleagues by openly suggesting the secession of those states that did not approve the bill. Quincy felt that the disequilibrium that the admission of new states would produce would be a deathblow to the Constitution. Part of his address of January 14, 1811, is reprinted here.

Source: *Debates,* 11 Cong., 3 Sess., pp. 524-542.

Mr. Speaker:

I address you, sir, with an anxiety and distress of mind, with me wholly unprecedented. The friends of this bill seem to consider it as the exercise of a common power; as an ordinary affair; a mere municipal regulation which they expect to see pass without other questions than those concerning details. But, sir, the principle of this bill materially affects the liberties and rights of the whole people of the United States. To me, it appears that it would justify a revolution in this country; and that, in no great length of time, may produce it. . . .

If this bill passes, it is my deliberate opinion that it is virtually a dissolution of this Union; that it will free the states from their moral obligation, and, as it will be the right of all, so it will be the duty of some, definitely to prepare for a separation, amicably if they can, violently if they must. . . . It is to preserve, to guard the Constitution of my country that I denounce this attempt. I would rouse the attention of gentlemen from the apathy with which they seem beset. These observations are not made in a corner; there is no low intrigue, no secret machinations. I am on the people's own ground; to them I appeal, concerning their own rights, their own liberties, their own intent in adopting this Constitution. . . .

The bill, which is now proposed to be passed, has this assumed principle for its basis — that the three branches of this national government, without recurrence to conventions of the people, in the states, or to the legislatures of the states, are authorized to admit new partners to a share of the political power in countries out of the original limits of the United States. Now, this assumed principle I maintain to be altogether without any sanction in the Constitution. I declare it to be a manifest and atrocious usurpation of power; of a nature, dissolving, according to undeniable principles of moral

Courtesy, Museum of Fine Arts, Boston; gift of Miss Eliza Susan Quincy

Portrait of Josiah Quincy by G. Stuart, 1826

law, the obligations of our national compact; and leading to all the awful consequences which flow from such a state of things.

Concerning this assumed principle, which is the basis of this bill, this is the general position on which I rest my argument — that if the authority, now proposed to be exercised, be delegated to the three branches of the government, by virtue of the Constitution, it results either from its general nature, or from its particular provisions. . . .

As the introduction of a new associate in political power implies, necessarily, a new division of power, and consequent diminution of the relative proportion of the former proprietors of it, there can, certainly, be nothing more obvious than that, from the general nature of the instrument, no power can result to diminish and give away to strangers any proportion of the rights of the original partners. If such a power exist, it must be found, then, in the particular provisions in the Constitution. The question now arising is in which of these provisions is given the power to admit new states, to be created in territories beyond the limits of the old United States. If it exist anywhere, it is either in the 3rd Section of the 4th Article of the Constitution, or in the treaty-making power. If it result from neither of these, it is not pretended to be found anywhere else.

That part of the 3rd Section of the 4th Article on which the advocates of this bill rely is the following: "New states may be admitted, by the Congress, into this Union; but no new states shall be formed or erected within the jurisdiction of any other state, nor any state be formed by the junction of two or more states, or parts of states, without the consent of the legislatures of the states concerned, as well as of the Congress." I know, Mr. Speaker, that the first clause of this paragraph has been read with all the superciliousness of a grammarian's triumph. "New states may be admitted, by the Congress, into this Union." Accompanied with this most consequential inquiry: "Is not this a new state to be admitted? And is not here an express authority?" . . .

The question concerns the proportion of power, reserved by this Constitution, to every state in the Union. Have the three branches of this government a right, at will, to weaken and outweigh the influence respectively secured to each state in this compact, by introducing, at pleasure, new partners, situated beyond the old limits of the United States? The question has not relation merely to New Orleans. The great objection is to the principle of the bill. If this bill be admitted, the whole space of Louisiana, greater, it is said, than the entire extent of the old United States, will be a mighty theater, in which this government assumes the right of exercising this unparalleled power. And it will be; there is no concealment; it is intended to be exercised. Nor will it stop until the very name and nature of the old partners be overwhelmed by newcomers into the confederacy.

Sir, the question goes to the very root of the power and influence of the present members of this Union. The real intent of this article is, therefore, an inquiry of most serious import; and is to be settled only by a recurrence to the known history and known relations of this people and their Constitution. These, I maintain, support this position: that the terms "new states," in this article, do intend new political sovereignties to be formed within the original limits of the United States; and do not intend new political sovereignties with territorial annexations to be erected without the original limits of the United States. . . .

But there is an argument stronger even than all those which have been produced to be drawn from the nature of the power here proposed to be exercised. Is it possible that such a power, if it had been intended to be given by the people, should be left dependent upon the effect of general expressions; and such, too, as were obviously applicable to another subject, to a particular exigency contemplated at the time? Sir, what is this power we propose now to usurp? Nothing less than a power changing all the proportion of the weight and influence possessed by the potent sovereignties composing this Union. A stranger is to be introduced to an equal share, without their consent. Upon a principle, pretended to be deduced from the Constitution, this government, after this bill passes, may and will multiply foreign partners in power, at its own mere motion, at its irresponsible pleasure; in other words, as local interests, party passions, or ambitious views may suggest. It is a power that, from its nature, never could be delegated; never was delegated; and as it breaks down all the proportions of power guaranteed by the Constitution to the states, upon which their essential security depends, utterly annihilates the moral force of this political contract. Would this people, so wisely vigilant concerning their rights, have transferred to Congress a power to balance, at its will, the political weight of any one state, much more of all the states, by authorizing it to create new states at its pleasure, in foreign countries, not pretended to be within the scope of the Constitution or the conception of the people, at the time of passing it?

This is not so much a question concerning the exercise of sovereignty as it is who shall be sovereign. Whether the proprietors of the good old United States shall manage their own affairs in their own way; or whether they and their Constitution and their political rights shall be trampled underfoot by foreigners introduced through a breach of the Constitution. The proportion of the political weight of each sovereign state constituting this Union depends upon the number of the states which have a voice under the compact. This number the Constitution permits us to multiply at pleasure, within the limits of the original United States, observing only the expressed limitations in the Constitution. But when, in order to increase your power of augmenting this number, you pass the old limits, you are guilty of a violation of the Constitution, in a fundamental point; and in one, also, which is totally inconsistent with the intent of the contract and the safety of the states which established the association.

What is the practical difference to the old partners, whether they hold their liberties at the will of a master, or whether, by admitting exterior states on an equal footing with the original states, arbiters are constituted, who by availing themselves of the contrariety of interests and views, which in such a confederacy necessarily will arise, hold the balance among the parties, which exist and govern us, by throwing themselves into the scale most conformable to their purposes? In both cases there is an effective despotism. But the last is the more galling, as we carry the chain in the name and gait of freemen.

I have thus shown, and whether fairly I am willing to be judged by the sound discretion of the American people, that the power, proposed to be usurped in this bill, results neither from the general nature nor the particular provisions of the federal Constitution; and that it is a palpable violation of it in a fundamental point; whence flow all the consequences I have intimated.

But, says the gentleman from Tennessee (Mr. Rhea), "These people have been seven years citizens of the United States." I deny it. Sir, as citizens of New Orleans, or of Louisiana, they never have been, and by the mode proposed, they never will be, citizens of the United States. They may be girt upon us for the moment, but no real cement can grow from such an association. What the real situation of the inhabitants of those foreign countries is, I shall have occasion to show presently. But, says the same gentleman, "If I have a farm, have not I a right to purchase another farm in my neighborhood, and settle my sons upon it, and in time admit them to a share in the management of my household?" Doubtless, sir. But are these cases parallel? Are the three branches of this government owners of this farm called the United States? I desire to thank heaven they are not.

I hold my life, liberty, and property, and the people of the state from which I have the honor to be a representative hold theirs, by a better tenure than any this national government can give. Sir, I know your virtue. And I thank the Great Giver of every good gift that neither the gentleman from Tennessee, nor his comrades, nor any, nor all the members of this House, nor of the other branch of the legislature, nor the good gentleman who lives in the palace yonder, nor all combined, can touch these my essential rights and those of my friends and constituents, except in a limited and prescribed form. No, sir. We hold these by the laws, customs, and principles of the Commonwealth of Massachusetts. Behind her ample shield we find refuge, and feel safety. I beg gentlemen not to act upon the principle that the Commonwealth of Massachusetts is their farm. . . .

As then the power in this bill proposed to be usurped is neither to be drawn from the general nature of the instrument, nor from the clause just examined, it follows that if it exist anywhere, it must result from the treaty-making power. This the gentleman from Tennessee (Mr. Rhea) asserts, but the gentleman from North Carolina (Mr. Macon) denies; and very justly. For what a monstrous position is this, that the treaty-making power has the competency to change the fundamental relations of the Constitution itself! That a power under the Constitution should have the ability to change and annihilate the instrument from which it derives all its power; and if the treaty-making power can introduce new partners to the political rights of the states, there is no length, however extravagant, or inconsistent with the end, to which it may not be wrested.

Father! You have got the arms and ammunition which our great father sent for his red children. If you have an idea of going away, give them to us, and you may go and welcome, for us. Our lives are in the hands of the Great Spirit. We are determined to defend our lands, and if it is His will, we wish to leave our bones upon them.

TECUMSEH, to the English, before the War of 1812. He was right — the English deserted the Indians, and the Indian Confederacy was destroyed in Nov. 1811, by General Harrison at Tippecanoe.

70.

JAMES MADISON: The Civil and Religious Functions of Government

Throughout his life, James Madison was deeply concerned with the relationship between religious establishments and civil government. He firmly believed that the Constitution, and especially the First Amendment, clearly separated church and state and, furthermore, that this separation was fundamental to the health of the nation as a whole. While he was President, a bill came before him calling for the chartering of an Episcopal church in Alexandria, Virginia. As would be expected from this great advocate of religious freedom, he vetoed the bill and sent the following message to the House of Representatives on February 21, 1811.

Source: Richardson, I, pp. 489-490.

HAVING EXAMINED AND CONSIDERED the bill entitled "An Act Incorporating the Protestant Episcopal Church in the Town of Alexandria, in the District of Columbia," I now return the bill to the House of Representatives, in which it originated, with the following objections:

Because the bill exceeds the rightful authority to which governments are limited by the essential distinction between civil and religious functions, and violates in particular the article of the Constitution of the United States which declares that "Congress shall make no law respecting a religious establishment." The bill enacts into and establishes by law sundry rules and proceedings relative purely to the organization and polity of the church incorporated, and comprehending even the election and removal of the minister of the same, so that no change could be made therein by the particular society or by the general church of which it is a member, and whose authority it recognizes. This particular church, therefore, would so far be a religious establishment by law, a legal force and sanction being given to certain articles in its constitution and administration. Nor can it be considered that the articles thus established are to be taken as the descriptive criteria only of the corporate identity of the society, inasmuch as this identity must depend on other characteristics, as the regulations established are in general unessential and alterable according to the principles and canons by which churches of that denomination govern themselves, and as the injunctions and prohibitions contained in the regulations would be enforced by the penal consequences applicable to a violation of them according to the local law.

Because the bill vests in the said incorporated church an authority to provide for the support of the poor and the education of poor children of the same, an authority which, being altogether superfluous if the provision is to be the result of pious charity, would be a precedent for giving to religious societies as such a legal agency in carrying into effect a public and civil duty.

71.

On a Northern Confederation

The correspondence between John Adams and Benjamin Waterhouse was filled with thoughtful commentaries on events of the day and was touched with the same humor that is apparent in Adams' epistolary exchanges with Jefferson. Waterhouse, the Boston physician who had introduced the Jenner method of smallpox vaccination to the United States, was one of Adams' dearest and most respected friends. The economic and political frustrations of the northern Federalist states just prior to the War of 1812 gave rise to speculation that these states might form a separate confederation. The following exchange of letters linking Hamilton and Burr to such plans is a fascinating appraisal of the ambitions of these adversaries. The first letter, from Waterhouse to Adams, was written from Cambridge, Massachusetts, on July 8, 1811; Adams replied to Waterhouse on July 12.

Source: *Statesman and Friend, Correspondence of John Adams with Benjamin Waterhouse 1784-1822,* Worthington C. Ford, ed., Boston, 1927, pp. 58-66.

I.

Benjamin Waterhouse to John Adams

I RECEIVED YOUR LETTER of the 5th with pleasure and read it with satisfaction, as I always do, because I understand your politics, and because I see in them one uniform and everlasting principle that does not bend to the fashions and caprices of the day. Foolish people have cried out, "Mr. Adams has changed his politics; he is no longer a Federalist, but is changed to a Republican." I have as constantly replied that I know of no man in the country who has changed less. . . .

What I long to see above all things is an exposition of what I call the "Hamiltonian Conspiracy." Whether I am perfectly correct I know not but my general idea is this: The British Party, or Tories, have long contemplated a separation of the states and a formation of a Northern confederacy, the end and aim of which was to be opposition to France and to the Southern states, and a sort of alliance with England. Old England was to hold one end of the golden chain of commerce and New England the other, while the devil and Bonaparte were to take our Southern brethren. Fisher Ames gave a toast in a certain assemblage several years ago indicating Hamilton as the military leader of this kingdom of the North. His sentiment was to this effect: Alex'r H——— may we not speedily want his great military and political talents, but when we do, *may we have them.* When Burr shot Hamilton, it was not Brutus killing Caesar in the Senate house; but it was killing him before he passed the Rubicon. Hence the anguish, the deep anguish of Geo. Cabot and company at their Caesar's death. Whether his plan of 50,000 foot and 10,000 horse was not a part of the scheme is a question I am not able to answer; but certain I am that their extreme disappointment at his death, which amounted to an agony, could not have arisen from a mere personal feeling, nor for the loss of his financiering talents.

This intriguing West Indian saw in the same city one man who watched his motions, and who was capable of counteracting his plans and the designs of his party; and this man he tried to destroy by the poisoned arrows of calumny, but (providentially for us) was destroyed himself; and with him fell, for that time, the hopes of the Northern confederacy. Hence we may account for his bust staring us in the face in the entries of some of our professors and clergymen! Washington himself is not spoken of in such terms of deep regret as is this New York lawyer! And your animadversions upon him in your printed correspondence created more disagreeable sensations than if you had spoken as much against Washington. How is all this to be accounted for, if it were not for the loss of their contemplated military leader?

Two years ago, when they brought forth their famous resolutions in the legislature, and when Gore talked so boldly of warring with France, Hamilton's death was again a melancholy subject of deep lamentation among the leaders of the party, and the separation of the states and a Northern confederacy was again alluded to, in private circles and "assemblages." They then began again "to speak daggers"; and it was observed that they brought forward and caressed General Brooks, of this neighborhood, and toasted him at a dinner they have in honor of the Spanish patriots; but they found that the general had grown old very fast and was spiritless, so that we have heard no more of him at their solemn feasts. All these things, and 100 other little things, such as half-uttered wishes and sentences, convince me that the party have been looking anxiously around for a military man as near like unto Alex'r Hamilton as possible, but they can find none. They can raise their eyes to nothing higher in Massachusetts than Captain I——— and Captain D————l S———r———t! Men "full of sound and fury." Some of them have avowed that they looked to H. as the savior of the country; but that now, there may be a dozen as good as he, but alas! there is not one with his reputation! So that unless they invite back and forgive Aaron Burr, the South and the North will not be divided immediately.

Now, sir, have I been dreaming, or writing romance, or true history, collected from their own words and actions? I am firmly of opinion that there are in ——— 200 or 300 of the assemblage on the verge of bankruptcy, and who would enlist under Catiline had Catiline the confidence to beat up for volunteers. I suspect that the governor has a similar idea; and I guess that the President and he view objects through the same glass and in the same light, but am doubtful if the council ever had a peep through it. Walsh has taken up the odious business of Ames, that of rendering us contemptible in our own eyes, and of magnifying and glorifying modern Babylon, the city of the Great King, while most of the clergy are like the ancient Augurs, uttering to the people just what their masters dictate, and several of these in Boston and its vicinity will groop in the guts of beast for hire. Now unless I am, like J. Lowell, politically mad, I can trace all these things up to the Hamiltonian Conspiracy that destroyed the federal administration.

If these things be truths, ought they not to be told to the people, instead of amusing them with the Berlin and Milan decrees, and orders of council? Ought not the people of this state to be told that their chief justice [Theophilus Parsons] is in league against their liberties, against their constitution? And ought they not to be told that a war with England is the only remedy against the evil, and against a greater one, a war among ourselves? Thus has the spirit moved me; and if I do not seal it up and send it off to the posthouse, I shall do with it as I hope you will — burn it.

II.

Adams to Waterhouse

The charge of "Change of politics" hinted in your letter of the 8th deserves no other answer than this, "the Hyperfederalists are become Jacobins, and the Hyperrepublicans are become Federalists." John Adams remains *semper idem,* both Federalist and Republican in every rational and intelligible sense of both those words.

What shall I say of Mr. Dexter? *Rara Avis in Terris nigroque Similima Cygno!* [as rare a bird on earth as a black swan!] (You see I have not forgotten my Lilly's Grammar.) I wish he was more acquainted with the governor, and the governor with him. He is destined, if his country has common sense and he is not too happy in his family, to be a very important character in our drama, before, at, or after the great denouement, if that should happen in his day. If he were pitted against Otis, who must hide his diminished head?

Of Pickering and Smith I have nothing to say at present but this: a secretary of state ought to have pierced into the remotest periods of ancient times and into the most distant regions of the earth; he should have studied the map of man, in his savage as well as civilized state. It is more necessary that a secretary of state should be omniscient than a President, provided the President be honest and judicious. Where can we find such men, either for presidents or secretaries?

If there ever was a "Hamiltonian Conspiracy," as you call it, and as you seem to suppose, I have reason to think its object was not "a Northern confederation." Hamilton's ambition was too large for so small an aim. He aimed at commanding the whole Union, and he did not like to be shackled even with an alliance with Great Britain. I know that Pickering was disappointed in not finding Hamilton zealous for an alliance with England when we were at swords' points with France, and I have information which I believe, but could not legally prove perhaps, that Pickering was mortified to find that neither Hamilton nor King would adopt the plan that he carried from Boston in his way to Congress after he was first chosen into the Senate, of a division of the states and a Northern confederacy. No! Hamilton had wider views! If he could have made a tool of Adams as he did of Washington, he hoped to erect such a government as he pleased over the whole Union and enter into alliance with France or England as would suit his convenience.

Hamilton and Burr, in point of ambition, were equal. In principle equal. In talents different. Hamilton superior in literary talents; Burr, in military. Hamilton, a Nevis adventurer; Burr, descended from the earliest, most learned, pious, and virtuous of our American nation, and buoyed up by prejudices of half the nation. He found himself thwarted, persecuted, calumniated by a wandering stranger. The deep malice of Hamilton against Burr, and his indefatigable exertions to defame him, are little known. I knew so much of it for a course of years that I wondered a duel had not taken place seven years before it did. I could have produced such a duel at any moment for seven years. I kept the secrets sacred and inviolable, and have kept them to this day.

What shall I say of [Robert] Walsh? His history, character, and connections are not sufficiently known. Popish Jesuits, French Loyalists, Scotish Reviewers are his closest friends. I wish our countrymen would not run after such meteors without inquiring into their natural history. Genius, talents, learning in such hands!

I can no more.

72.

Debate Over War with England

Two widely different developments brought on the War of 1812. One was a long series of violations by Great Britain of American maritime rights, which had come about as a by-product of the Napoleonic Wars. The other was an equally long series of depredations by Indians against frontier settlements beyond the Alleghenies — massacres, as now and then they were, which could have been laid to the encroachment of the settlers upon Indian lands, but were attributed instead to the inspiration (and the supplies) of British garrisons stationed south of Canada. These attacks were the more resented in that they conflicted with the rapidly growing expansionist sentiment of the frontier. A desire to drive the British from all of North America, even from Canada itself, made Americans from the West eager to have war declared. In pursuit of this object, a number of young War Hawks, as they were called, were elected to Congress in 1810. Among them were Henry Clay, John C. Calhoun, Felix Grundy of Tennessee, and Richard M. Johnson of Kentucky. At first the Hawks concealed their continental ambitions, and in an effort to win the support of maritime New England to their cause, cried out against British interference with American trade. But a naval war required a navy, whereas what the Hawks really wanted, and needed, was an army. The debate on military preparations thus forced them to reveal their expansionist aims, which then were challenged not only by the Federalists but by some members of their own Republican Party as well. In the following exchange, Grundy and Johnson were opposed by John Randolph of Virginia, better known as John Randolph of Roanoke, an old-line Republican who had broken with Jefferson and his successor, James Madison, over what he considered their betrayal of party principles. Having become an independent in politics, Randolph was making a career of opposition, both as a constitutional purist and as an unsparing castigator of iniquity. His vituperative, high-pitched voice was the most feared in the House. Eccentric, sickly, finally mad, he was for all his grave defects the last of the great revolutionary generation of Virginians. The following speeches were made in the House in December 1811.

Source: *Debates*, 12 Cong., 1 Sess., pp. 422-455.

I.

Felix Grundy: War as a Means of Continental Expansion

It is not the carrying trade, properly so called, about which this nation and Great Britain are at present contending. Were this the only question now under consideration, I should feel great unwillingness (however clear our claim might be) to involve the nation in war for the assertion of a right, in the enjoyment of which the community at large are not more deeply concerned. The true question in controversy is of a very different character; it involves the interest of the whole nation. It is the right of exporting the productions of our own soil and industry to foreign markets.

Sir, our vessels are now captured when destined to the ports of France, and condemned by the British Courts of Admiralty without even the pretext of having on board contraband of war, enemies' property, or having in any other respect violated the laws of nations. These depredations on our lawful commerce, under whatever ostensible pretense committed, are not to be traced to any maxims or rules of public law but to the maritime supremacy and pride of the British nation.

This hostile and unjust policy of that country toward us is not to be wondered at when we recollect that the United States are already the second commercial nation in the world. The rapid growth of our commercial importance has not only awakened the jealousy of the commercial interests of Great Britain but her statesmen, no doubt, anticipate with deep concern the maritime greatness of this republic.

The unjust and unprecedented demands now made by Great Britain, that we shall cause the markets of the Continent to be opened to her manufactures, fully justifies the views I have suggested.

That we as a neutral nation should interfere between belligerents in their municipal regulations will not be contended for by anyone. From the course pursued by that nation for some years past, it evidently appears that neither public law nor justice, but power alone, is made by her the test of maritime rights.

What, Mr. Speaker, are we now called on to decide? It is whether we will resist by force the attempt made by that government to subject our maritime rights to the arbitrary and capricious rule of her will; for my part I am not prepared to say that this country shall submit to have her commerce interdicted or regulated by any foreign nation. Sir, I prefer war to submission.

Over and above these unjust pretensions of the British government, for many years past they have been in the practice of impressing our seamen from merchant vessels; this unjust and lawless invasion of personal liberty calls loudly for the interposition of this government. To those better acquainted with the facts in relation to it, I leave it to fill up the picture. My mind is irresistibly drawn to the West. . . .

This war, if carried on successfully, will have its advantages. We shall drive the British from our continent — they will no longer have an opportunity of intriguing with our Indian neighbors, and setting on the ruthless savage to tomahawk our women and children. That nation will lose her Canadian trade, and, by having no resting place in this country, her means of annoying us will be diminished. The idea I am now about to advance is at war, I know, with sentiments of the gentleman from Virginia. I am willing to receive the Canadians as adopted brethren; it will have beneficial political effects; it will preserve the equilibrium of the government. When Louisiana shall be fully peopled, the Northern states will lose their power; they will be at the discretion of others; they can be depressed at pleasure; and then this Union might be endangered. I therefore feel anxious not only to add the Floridas to the South, but the Canadas to the North of this empire.

II.

Richard M. Johnson: For War with England

The gentleman from Virginia says we are identified with the British in religion, in blood, in language, and deeply laments our hatred to that country who can boast of so many illustrious characters. This deep-rooted enmity to Great Britain arises from her insidious policy, the offspring of her perfidious conduct toward the United States. Her disposition is unfriendly; her enmity is implacable; she sickens at our prosperity and happiness. If obligations of friendship do exist, why does Great Britain rend those ties asunder and open the bleeding wounds of former conflicts? Or does the obligation of friendship exist on the part of the United States alone? I have never thought that the ties of religion, of blood, of language, and of commerce would justify or sanctify insult and injury; on the contrary, that a premeditated wrong from the hand of a friend created more sensibility and deserved the greater chastisement and the higher execration.

What would you think of a man to whom you were bound by the most sacred ties who would plunder you of your substance, aim a deadly blow at your honor, and in the hour of confidence endeavor to bury a dagger in your bosom? Would you, sir, proclaim to the world your affection for this miscreant of society, after this conduct, and endeavor to interest your audience with the ties of kindred that bound you to each other? So let it be with nations, and there will be neither surprise nor lamentation that we execrate a government so hostile to our independence — for it is from the government that we meet with such multiplied injury, and to that object is our hatred directed.

As to individuals of merit, whether British or French, I presume no person would accuse the people of the United States of such hatred to them, or of despising individuals, who might not be instrumental in the maritime despotism which we feel; and this accounts for the veneration we have for Sidney and Russell, statesmen of whom the gentleman has spoken; they are fatal examples why we should love the British government. The records of that government are now stained with the blood of these martyrs in freedom's cause, as vilely as with the blood of American citizens; and certainly we shall not be called upon to love equally the murderer and the victim.

For God's sake, let us not again be told of the ties of religion, of laws, of blood, and of customs, which bind the two nations together, with a view to extort our love for the English government, and, more especially, when the same gentleman has acknowledged that we have ample cause of war against that nation; let us not be told of the freedom of that corrupt government whose hands are washed alike in the blood of her own illustrious statesmen, for a manly opposition to tyranny, and the citizens of every other clime.

But I would inquire into this love for the British government and British institutions, in the gross, without any discrimination. Why love her rulers? Why kiss the rod of iron which inflicts the stripes without a cause? When all admit we have just cause of war, such attachments are dangerous, and encourage encroachment. I will venture to say that our hatred of the British government is not commensurate with her depredations and her outrages on our rights, or we should have waged a deadly war against her many years past.

The subject of foreign attachments and British hatred has been examined at considerable length. I did not intend to begin that discussion, but I will pursue it; and though I make no charge of British attachments, I will, at all times, at every hazard, defend the administration and the Republican Party against the charge of foreign partialities — French or Spanish, or any other kind — when applied to the measures of our government. This foreign influence is a dangerous enemy; we should destroy the means of its circulation among us — like the fatal tunic, it destroys where it touches. It is insidious, invisible, and takes advantage of the most unsuspecting hours of social intercourse. I would not deny the goodwill of France nor of Great Britain to have an undue influence among us. But Great Britain alone has the means of this influence to an extent dangerous to the United States.

It has been said that Great Britain was fighting the battles of the world — that she stands against universal dominion threatened by the archfiend of mankind. I should be sorry if our independence depended upon the power of Great Britain. If, however, she would act the part of a friendly power toward the United States, I should never wish to deprive her of power, of wealth, of honor, of prosperity. But if her energies are to be directed against the liberties of this free and happy people, against my native country, I should not drop a tear if the fast-anchored isle would sink into the waves, provided the innocent inhabitants could escape the deluge and find an asylum in a more favorable soil. And as to the power of France, I fear it as little as any other power; I would oppose her aggressions, under any circumstances, as soon as I would British outrages.

The ties of religion, of language, of blood, as it regards Great Britain, are dangerous ties to this country, with her present hostile disposition; instead of pledges of friendship they are used to paralyze the strength of the United States in relation to her aggressions. There are other ties equally efficacious. The number of her commercial traders within our limits, her agents, etc., the vast British capital employed in our commerce and our moneyed institutions, connected with her language, ancestry, customs, habits, and laws. These are formidable means for estranging the affections of many from our republican institutions and producing partialities for Great Britain.

III.

John Randolph: Against War with England

An insinuation had fallen from the gentleman from Tennessee (Mr. Grundy) that the late massacre of our brethren on the Wabash had been instigated by the British government. Has the President given any such information? Has the gentleman received any such, even informally, from any officer of this government? Is it so believed by the administration? He [Randolph] had cause to think the contrary to be the fact; that such was not their opinion. This insinuation was of the grossest kind — a presumption the most rash, the most unjustifiable. Show but good ground for it, he would give up the question at the threshold — he was ready to march to Canada. It was indeed well calculated to excite the feelings of the Western people particularly, who were not quite so tenderly attached to our red brethren as some modern philosophers; but it was destitute of any foundation, beyond mere surmise and suspicion. What would be thought if, without any proof whatsoever, a member should rise in his place and tell us that the massacre in Savannah, a massacre perpetrated by civilized savages with French commissions in their pockets, was excited by the French government? There was an easy and natural solution of the late transaction on the Wabash, in the well-known character of the aboriginal savage of North America, without resorting to any such mere conjectural estimate.

He was sorry to say that for this signal calamity and disgrace the House was, in part, at least, answerable. Session after session, their table had been piled up with Indian treaties, for which the appropriations had been voted as a matter of course, without examination. Advantage had been taken of the spirit of the Indians, broken by the war which ended in the Treaty of Greenville. Under the ascendancy then acquired over them, they had been pent up by subsequent treaties into nooks, straightened in their quarters by a blind cupidity, seeking to extinguish their title to immense wildernesses, for which (possessing, as we do already, more land than we can sell or use) we shall not have occasion for half a century to come. It was our own thirst for territory, our own want of moderation that had driven these sons of nature to desperation, of which we felt the effects. . . .

This war of conquest, a war for the ac-

New York Historical Society

Portrait of John Randolph by John Wesley Jarvis

quisition of territory and subjects, is to be a new commentary on the doctrine that republics are destitute of ambition; that they are addicted to peace, wedded to the happiness and safety of the great body of their people. But it seems this is to be a holiday campaign — there is to be no expense of blood or treasure on our part. Canada is to conquer herself — she is to be subdued by the principles of fraternity. The people of that country are first to be seduced from their allegiance, and converted into traitors, as preparatory to the making them good citizens. Although he must acknowledge that some of our flaming patriots were thus manufactured, he did not think the process would hold good with a whole community. It was a dangerous experiment. We were to succeed in the French mode by the system of fraternization — all is French! but how dreadfully it might be retorted on the Southern and Western slaveholding states. He detested this subornation of treason. No, if he must have them, let them fall by the valor of our arms, by fair, legitimate conquest, not become the victims of treacherous seduction.

He was not surprised at the war spirit which was manifesting itself in gentlemen from the South. In the year 1805-6, in a struggle for the carrying trade of belligerent colonial produce, this country had been most unwisely brought into collision with the great powers of Europe. By a series of most impolitic and ruinous measures, utterly incomprehensible to every rational, sober-minded man, the Southern planters, by their own votes, had succeeded in knocking down the price of cotton to seven cents, and of tobacco (a few choice crops excepted) to nothing; and in raising the price of blankets (of which a few would not be amiss in a Canadian campaign) coarse woolens, and every article of first necessity, 300 or 400 percent. And now that, by our own acts, we have brought ourselves into this unprecedented condition, we must get out of it in any way but by an acknowledgement of our own want of wisdom and forecast.

But is war the true remedy? Who will profit by it? Speculators — a few lucky merchants who draw prizes in the lottery — commissaries and contractors. Who must suffer by it? The people. It is their blood, their taxes, that must flow to support it.

But gentlemen avowed that they would not go to war for the carrying trade, that is, for any other but the direct export and import trade — that which carries our native products abroad and brings back the return cargo. And yet they stickle for our commercial rights, and will go to war for them! He wished to know, in point of principle, what difference gentlemen could point out between the abandonment of this or that maritime right? Do gentlemen assume the lofty port and tone of chivalrous redressers of maritime wrongs, and declare their readiness to surrender every other maritime right, provided they may remain unmolested in the exercise of the humble privilege of carrying their own produce abroad, and bringing back a return cargo? Do you make this declaration to the enemy at the outset?

Do you state the minimum with which you will be contented, and put it in her power to close with your proposals at her option; give her the basis of a treaty ruinous and disgraceful beyond example and expression? And this too after having turned up your noses in disdain at the treaties of Mr. Jay and Mr. Monroe! Will you say to England, "End the war when you please, give us the direct trade in our own produce, we are content?" But what will the merchants of Salem, and Boston, and New York, and Philadelphia, and Baltimore, the men of Marblehead and Cape Cod say to this? Will they join in a war professing to have for its object what they would consider (and justly too) as the sacrifice of their maritime rights, yet affecting to be a war for the protection of commerce?

He was gratified to find gentlemen acknowledging the demoralizing and destructive consequences of the nonimportation law — confessing the truth of all that its opponents foretold when it was enacted. And will you plunge yourselves in war, because you have passed a foolish and ruinous law, and are ashamed to repeal it? But our good friend the French emperor stands in the way of its repeal, and as we cannot go too far in making sacrifices to him, who has given such demonstration of his love for the Americans, we must, in point of fact, become parties to his war. Who can be so cruel as to refuse him this favor? His imagination shrunk from the miseries of such a connection. He called upon the House to reflect whether they were not about to abandon all reclamation for the unparalleled outrages, insults, and injuries of the French government to give up our claim for plundered millions; and asked what reparation or atonement they could expect to obtain in hours of future dalliance, after they should have made a tender of their person to this great deflowerer of the virginity of republics.

We had by our own wise (he would not say *wiseacre*) measures so increased the trade and wealth of Montreal and Quebec that at last we began to cast a wistful eye at Canada. Having done so much toward its improvement by the exercise of "our restrictive energies," we began to think the laborer worthy of his hire, and to put in claim for our portion. Suppose it ours, are we any nearer to our point? As his minister said to the king of Epirus, "may we not as well take our bottle of wine before as after this exploit?" Go! March to Canada! Leave the broad bosom of the Chesapeake and her hundred tributary rivers — the whole line of seacoast from Machias to St. Mary's — unprotected! You have taken Quebec — have you conquered England? Will you seek for the deep foundations of her power in the frozen deserts of Labrador?

Her march is on the mountain wave,
Her home is on the deep!

Will you call upon her to leave your ports and harbors untouched, only just till you can return from Canada to defend them? The coast is to be left defenseless, while men of the interior are reveling in conquest and spoil. But grant for a moment, for mere argument's sake, that in Canada you touched the sinews of her strength instead of removing a clog upon her resources — an encumbrance, but one which, from a spirit of honor, she will vigorously defend. In what situation would you then place some of the best men of the nation? As Chatham and Burke, and the whole band of her patriots, prayed for her defeat in 1776, so must some of the truest friends to their country deprecate the success of our arms against the only power that holds in check the archenemy of mankind. . . .

Our people will not submit to be taxed for this war of conquest and dominion. The government of the United States was not calculated to wage offensive foreign war; it was instituted for the common defense and general welfare; and whosoever should embark it in a war of offense would put it to a test which it was by no means calculated to endure. Make it out that Great Britain had instigated the Indians on the late occasion, and he was ready for battle; but not for dominion. He was unwilling, however, under present circumstances, to take Canada at the risk of the Constitution; to embark in a common cause with France and be dragged at the wheels of the car of some Burr or Bonaparte. For a gentleman from Tennessee or Gennessee, or Lake Champlain there may be some prospect of advantage. Their hemp would bear a great price by the exclusion of foreign supply. In that too the great importers were deeply interested. The upper country on the Hudson and the Lakes would be enriched by the supplies for the troops, which they alone could furnish. They would have the exclusive market, to say nothing of the increased preponderance from the acquisition of Canada and that section of the Union which the Southern and Western states had already felt so severely in the apportionment bill.

Mr. R. adverted to the defenseless state of our seaports, and particularly of the Chesapeake. A single spot only, on both shores, might be considered in tolerable security — from the nature of the port and the strength of the population — and that spot unhappily governed the whole state of Maryland. His friend, the late governor of Maryland (Mr. Lloyd), at the very time he was bringing his warlike resolutions before the legislature of the state, was liable, on any night, to be taken out of his bed and carried off with his family by the most contemptible picaroon. Such was the situation of many a family in Maryland and lower Virginia.

Mr. R. dwelt on the danger arising from the black population. He said he would touch this subject as tenderly as possible — it was with reluctance that he touched it at all — but in cases of great emergency, the state physician must not be deterred by a sickly, hysterical humanity from probing the wound of his patient; he must not be withheld by a fastidious and mistaken humanity from representing his true situation to his friends, or even to the sick man himself, where the occasion called for it. What was the situation of the slaveholding states? During the war of the Revolution, so fixed were their habits of subordination that when the whole Southern country was over-run by the enemy, who invited them to desert, no fear was ever entertained of an insurrection of the slaves. During the war of seven years, with our country in possession of the enemy, no such danger was ever apprehended. But should we therefore be unobservant spectators of the progress of society within the last twenty years — of the silent but powerful change wrought by time and chance upon its composition and temper? When the fountains of the great deep of abomination were broken up, even the poor slaves had not escaped the general deluge. The French Revolution had polluted even them. Nay, there had not been wanting men in that House, witness their legislative *legendre*, the butcher who once held a seat there, to preach upon that floor these imprescriptible rights to a crowded audience of blacks in the galleries — teaching them that they are equal to their masters — in other words, advising them to cut their throats.

Similar doctrines were disseminated by pedlers from New England and elsewhere throughout the Southern country; and masters had been found so infatuated, as by their lives and conversation, by a general contempt of order, morality, and religion, unthinkingly to cherish these seeds of self-destruction to them and their families. What was the consequence? Within the last ten years, repeated alarms of insurrection among the slaves — some of them awful indeed. From the spreading of this infernal doctrine, the whole Southern country had been thrown into a state of insecurity. Men dead to the operation of moral causes had taken away from the poor slave his habits of loyalty and obedience to his master, which lightened his servitude by a double operation, beguiling his own cares and disarming his master's suspicions and severity; and now, like true empirics in politics, you are called upon to trust to the mere physical strength of the fetter which holds him in bondage.

You have deprived him of all moral restraint; you have tempted him to eat of the fruit of the tree of knowledge, just enough to perfect him in wickedness; you have opened his eyes to his nakedness; you have armed his nature against the hand that has fed, that has clothed him, that has cherished him in sickness; that hand, which before he became a pupil of your school, he had been accustomed to press with respectful affection. You have done all this — and then show him the gibbet and the wheel as incentives to a sullen, repugnant obedience. God forbid, sir, that the Southern states should ever see an enemy on their shores, with these infernal principles of French fraternity in the van! While talking of taking Canada, some of us were shuddering for our own safety at home. He spoke from facts when he said that the nightbell never tolled for fire in Richmond that the mother did not hug her infant more closely to her bosom. He had been a witness of some of the alarms in the capital of Virginia. . . .

Before this miserable force of 10,000 men was raised to take Canada, he begged them to look at the state of defense at home — to count the cost of the enterprise before it was set on foot, not when it might be too late — when the best blood of the country should be spilled, and nought but empty coffers left to pay the cost. . . . He would beseech the House, before they ran their heads against this post, Quebec, to count the cost. His word for it, Virginia planters would not be taxed to support such a war — a war which must aggravate their present distresses — in which they had not the remotest interest. Where is the Montgomery, or even the Arnold, or the Burr who is to march to Point Levi?

He called upon those professing to be Republicans to make good the promises held out by their Republican predecessors when they came into power — promises, which for years afterward they had honestly, faithfully fulfilled. We had vaunted of paying off the national debt, of retrenching useless establishments; and yet had now become as infatuated with standing armies, loans, taxes, navies, and war as ever were the Essex Junto. What Republicanism is this?

Be Always Sure You're Right — Then Go Ahead.

Davy Crockett, his motto; became motto of War of 1812

New Haven Colony Historical Society

WAR OF 1812

England's troubles with Napoleon caused her to impress American merchant sailors for naval service against France. England was also pressing on America's western frontier. In Congress the "war hawks" decried British abuses on land and sea, on one hand, and called for expansion and seizure of Canada and of Florida (belonging to England's ally Spain), on the other. War was declared on June 18, 1812. America had many important sea victories, especially with her prize ship "Constitution" ("Old Ironsides"), but land engagements did not go as well: the Canadian campaign failed, and British troops captured Washington and burned the White House to the ground. The war went badly for both sides, and international politics surrounding the war were complex. Finally, peace was reached with the signing of the Treaty of Ghent on Dec. 24, 1814. Andrew Jackson's troops drove the British away from New Orleans two weeks later. The war was truly America's second war of independence.

Maryland Historical Society

British Admiral Cockburn burning and plundering Havre de Grace on Chesapeake Bay

Metropolitan Museum of Art, Rogers Fund

The War of 1812 was a war on land and on sea, with land battles on virtually all possible American fronts. Fighting raged along the Canadian border, the Florida boundary, and the western frontiers. Fighting in the East began with a British landing in Maryland. As in the Revolutionary War, the Americans were faced with hostile Indians allied with the British. Two soldiers emerged from the struggle with great reputations, and both later became presidents — William Henry Harrison and Andrew Jackson. Battles in the South and West resulted in more rapid eviction of Indians from areas desired by white settlers. The Indians were relentlessly pushed westward.

White House; photo, National Geographic

(Above) Members of the City Troop of Philadelphia assembling for a parade; while the fighting accelerated in the East, Andrew Jackson (left) was leading the Tennessee militia against the Creek nations in the South. In the battle of Tohopeka, the Creeks were all but wiped out, opening Alabama to white settlement after the war

Library of Congress

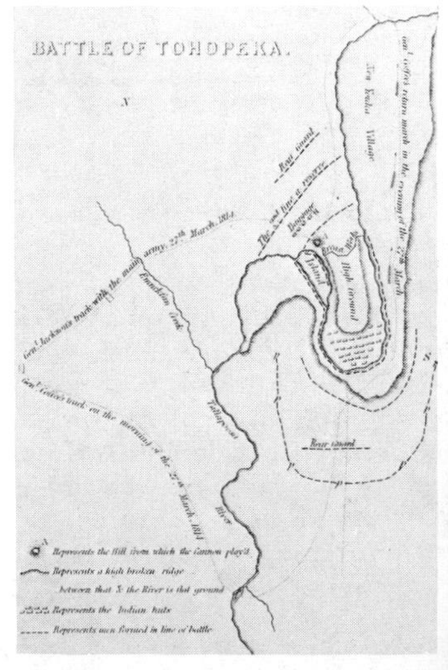

Library of Congress

An American cartoon attacking the alliance between the "Humane British" and the Indians

Francis Vigo Chapter, DAR; Vincennes, Indiana

In October, 1813, Brig. Gen. W. H. Harrison (left) defeated the British and the Indians at the Battle of the Thames (below); during the fight his Indian adversary, Tecumseh (right) was killed

Library of Congress

Library of Congress

Pennsylvania Academy of the Fine Arts

Fighting at sea was appropriate in a maritime war, and victories over the world's great naval power were wildly celebrated. The "Constitution" defeated the "Guerriere"; Commodore Perry vanquished the British in the Battle of Lake Erie. Nevertheless, as the war ground on, Britain's far greater sea power resulted in capture of most American vessels.

In September, 1813, Commodore O. H. Perry (below) defeated the British on Lake Erie (left and bottom)

Pennsylvania Historical Society

Pennsylvania Academy of the Fine Arts

For the most part the land war was fought to turn back invading British armies. The worst shock to the nation was the burning of Washington in 1814, carried out in retaliation for similar treatment of Toronto the year before. But a planned British invasion thrusting at New York was forestalled by a new naval victory on Lake Champlain.

Library of Congress

Library of Congress

The White House (above) and the Capitol were two of the buildings burned when the British set fire to Washington, D.C. (below)

Library of Congress

Library of Congress

Library of Congress

Library of Congress

The Battle of Lake Champlain was probably the most significant American victory in the war, because the total loss of the British ships made a planned British invasion impossible. Young Captain Thomas Macdonough was the hero of the hour for his brilliant success. Meanwhile an attack on Baltimore followed the burning of Washington. The British fleet bombarded Fort McHenry, the city's chief defense. The fort's refusal to surrender inspired Francis Scott Key to draft what later became the national anthem — the "Star-Spangled Banner."

Does That Banner Yet Wave?

Thomas Macdonough (above) was in command of the decisive American naval victory near Plattsburg on Lake Champlain (top and right)

Library of Congress

Chicago Historical Society

(Left) The bombing of Fort McHenry during the battle at Baltimore (bottom), which inspired Francis Scott Key to write our national anthem (the original copy is seen below)

Maryland Historical Society

Maryland Historical Society

O say can you see by the dawn's early light
What so proudly we hail'd at the twilight's last gleaming,
Whose broad stripes & bright stars through the perilous fight
O'er the ramparts we watch'd, were so gallantly streaming?
And the rocket's red glare, the bomb bursting in air,
Gave proof through the night that our flag was still there,
O say does that star spangled banner yet wave
O'er the land of the free & the home of the brave?

On the shore dimly seen through the mists of the deep,
Where the foe's haughty host in dread silence reposes,
What is that which the breeze, o'er the towering steep,
As it fitfully blows, half conceals, half discloses?
Now it catches the gleam of the morning's first beam,
In full glory reflected now shines in the stream,
'Tis the star-spangled banner — O long may it wave
O'er the land of the free & the home of the brave!

And where is that band who so vauntingly swore,
That the havoc of war & the battle's confusion
A home & a Country should leave us no more?
— Their blood has wash'd out their foul footstep's pollution.
No refuge could save the hireling & slave
From the terror of flight or the gloom of the grave,
And the star-spangled banner in triumph doth wave
O'er the land of the free & the home of the brave.

O thus be it ever when freemen shall stand
Between their lov'd home & the war's desolation!
Blest with vict'ry & peace may the heav'n rescued land
Praise the power that hath made & preserv'd us a nation!
Then conquer we must, when our cause it is just,
And this be our motto — "In God is our trust,"
And the star-spangled banner in triumph shall wave
O'er the land of the free & the home of the brave. —

Maryland Historical Society

New York Historical Society

Peace — Then Victory

Commissioners from Britain and the United States wrangled over terms for peace. Although the Americans were chiefly concerned with British impressment of American seamen, the issue was not resolved by the treaty. Andrew Jackson won the greatest victory of the war two weeks after the Treaty of Ghent.

Library of Congress

(Right) "A glorious tableau of the Peace of Ghent 1814, and Triumph of America"; and two divergent views of the Battle of New Orleans

Knox College, Galesburg, Ill.; the Preston Player Print Collection

1812

73.

David Hosack: On the Progress of Medical Education

Prior to 1800, few medical schools existed in the United States, where most physicians either served an American apprenticeship or were trained in European universities. Around the turn of the century, lectures and small discussion sessions held by eminent physicians led to the establishment of schools designed specifically for medical education. Among the first of these schools was Philadelphia College, which in 1792 was incorporated into the University of Pennsylvania. The New York College of Physicians and Surgeons (later Columbia University Medical School) was established in 1807. The following selection by David Hosack, a professor of the theory and practice of physic and clinical medicine, is an extract from an introductory lecture delivered to the College of Physicians and Surgeons. It was published in 1812.

Source: *The American Medical and Philosophical Register,* January 1812: "Sketch of the Origin and Progress of the Medical Schools of New York and Philadelphia."

In this country, medical schools are comparatively of recent date. Although the American colonies could boast of several medical characters, distinguished for general literature as well as professional erudition, no attempt was made to establish a regularly organized school for the purpose of medical instruction until the year 1762. As early, however, as 1750, the body of Hermannus Carroll, executed for murder, was dissected in this city by two of the most eminent physicians of that day, Drs. John Bard and Peter Middleton, and the blood vessels injected for the instruction of the youth then engaged in the study of medicine. This was the first essay made in the United States for the purpose of imparting medical knowledge by the dissection of the human body of which we have any record. But, notwithstanding this first laudable effort of individuals, a regularly constituted medical school was not completed in this city until the year 1769.

In the meantime, a few gentlemen, who had been distinguished for their literary and professional attainments, undertook an establishment of this kind in the city of Philadelphia. In 1762, Dr. William Shippen, the late eminent professor of anatomy of that city, returned from Europe, where he had finished his medical education under the direction of that celebrated anatomist and physician, Dr. William Hunter of London. The pupil, fired with the spirit of his master, resolved to extend the benefits of his instruction to the youth of his native city

The Society of the New York Hospital

Portrait of David Hosack, M.D. by John Trumbull

then engaged in medical study. His first class in 1764 consisted of ten pupils, but he lived to see that small beginning extend into an establishment that annually educated between 200 and 300.

In 1765, Dr. Morgan met a few students, in like manner unfolding to them the institutes or theory of medicine, including the materia medica and the principles of pharmaceutic chemistry. Dr. Adam Kuhn, who had been a pupil of the celebrated Linnaeus, upon his return to his native country was also appointed in 1768 to the joint professorship of botany and materia medica in the college of that city; and in 1769, Dr. Benjamin Rush, the present distinguished professor of the theory and practice of physic in the University of Pennsylvania, who had just completed his course of medical studies at the University of Edinburgh, first became a teacher of chemistry in the then College of Philadelphia. Long may his useful labors be continued to the advantage of his numerous pupils, the benefit of the profession, and the honor of our country.

While those gentlemen were all zealously occupied in the several departments of anatomy, surgery, the theory and practice of physic, materia medica, and chemistry, the venerable Dr. Thomas Bond exhibited to the pupils, at the bedside of the sick, in the Pennsylvania Hospital, a practical illustration of those principles in which they had been instructed, and these were the first clinical lectures that had been delivered in this country. The meed of praise is certainly due to the trustees of the College of Philadelphia, and the distinguished president of that body, Dr. Franklin, who at that early day established the *first* medical institution in this country.

New York did not long remain an inactive spectator of the important example set before her by her sister colony. As early as 1768, a similar establishment for medical education was opened in this city, in which were united the learning and abilities of Drs. Clossey, Jones, Middleton, Smith, Tennent, and the present president of this college.

About the same time, in consequence of a public address delivered by Dr. Samuel Bard at the first medical graduation in 1769, a very important addition was made to the means then afforded of medical education, by the establishment of the New York Hospital. The necessity and utility of a public infirmary, to use the language of Dr. Middleton, "was so warmly and pathetically set forth in that memorable discourse," that upon the same day on which it was delivered, a subscription was commenced by His Excellency Sir Henry Moore, then governor of this province, and the sum of £800 sterling collected for that establishment. The corporation of the city, animated by the same public spirit and active benevolence, in a short time added £3,000 sterling to the first subscription, when the united amount was employed in laying the foundation of that valuable institution, now the pride of our city, and alike devoted to the purposes of humanity and the promotion of medical science.

The Medical School of New York, thus provided with professors eminent for their abilities and learning and an infirmary for the purpose of clinical instruction, promised to be productive of all those advantages which were reasonably contemplated at its first institution; but these fair prospects, in common with those of every other literary institution in our land, were not only interrupted but totally destroyed by the Revolutionary War.

Shortly after the peace of 1783, the regents of the university attempted to revive the Medical School of this city, and created professors for that purpose. But this attempt, owing to circumstances which need not here be related, proved abortive. Although lectures upon many branches of medicine were afterward delivered by several gentlemen in their private capacity, no public measures were adopted for reorganizing the Medical School until the year 1791, when an act was passed by the legislature for the purpose of enabling the regents of the university to establish a College of Physicians and Surgeons within this state; but that power, thus vested in them by the state, the regents did not think it expedient to exercise until 1807.

In 1792, the trustees of Columbia College made another effort, by annexing a medical faculty to that institution. By this connection, it was supposed by its friends and patrons that the medical school thus restored would at least have recovered the celebrity it had attained previous to the revolution. How far the liberal views of the trustees of that college, or the expectations of the public have been realized, is too well known to require a single remark on this occasion.

About the same period of time, the present Medical School of Pennsylvania was revived, and, since that event, has acquired so much celebrity that in the number of its pupils it is probably not even surpassed by the University of Edinburgh. That institution has not only become a source of honor and emolument to its professors, and the means of advancing the literary reputation of the state of Pennsylvania, but has become no inconsiderable source of revenue to the city of Philadelphia. It is calculated that at least $150,000 are annually expended in that city by the students resorting to its medical school from the different parts of the United States.

Without dwelling upon the inquiry to what causes the comparative failure of the Medical School of Columbia College and the unexampled success of that of Philadelphia are to be ascribed, I proceed to observe that the honorable regents of the University of New York, after the most mature deliberation, after devoting the most serious attention to the respective rights and claims of the colleges of this state as well as to a remonstrance which was presented to them by certain individuals of this city in the year 1807, did unanimously resolve immediately to grant a charter for the establishment of the present College of Physicians and Surgeons as an institution which, in their opinion, would be calculated to reflect honor upon our city, and in its advantages would be commensurate with the wealth and commercial importance of this great and growing state. The legislature, actuated by the same spirit, and sensible of the benefit to be derived to the community at large from such an establishment, in the following year expressed their approbation of the proceedings of the regents by liberally appropriating $20,000 to its support.

During the first three years the success of this school exceeded the most sanguine expectations, and gave abundant evidence that the state of New York possesses the most ample resources for establishing a system of medical education, equal in all the means of instruction with any institution of this or any other country. Such, too, were the favorable impressions which had been created upon the minds of the regents, its founders, that upon receiving information of the events which had lately occurred to produce a temporary check to the progress and usefulness of this hitherto promising institution, they immediately, and with the same activity and zeal that led them to the first organization of the college, adopted the most efficient means, not only of removing out of the way every impediment to its prosperity but at the same time of reorganizing the institution in such manner as they conceived calculated to insure its permanent success and usefulness.

Such, young gentlemen, has been the solicitude manifested by the regents of the university and the legislature of the state in providing for you the means of medical education. But to the liberality of the legislature you are not only indebted for the appropriation which has been already noticed; by the purchase of the Botanic Garden, which has recently been placed by the regents under the direction of the professors and trustees of this college, you have also access to an additional source of instruction, which is enjoyed by no other medical seminary in the United States, and one highly necessary to every accomplished and well-educated physician.

Nor are these the only advantages which are now presented to the student of medicine in the city of New York. In the College of Physicians and Surgeons he has not only, by means of private dissection and an anatomical museum, the opportunity of obtaining a correct knowledge of the structure of the human frame; he not only enjoys the benefits of an extensive course of chemical experiments and, under the direction of the learned professor of natural history, of becoming acquainted with the various subjects which are embraced in that very interesting and extensive department of human learning, but in the New York Hospital, which encloses within its walls nearly 400 patients, he has more opportunities of observing the diseases which most frequently occur in this climate and country, and which he will have occasion most frequently to meet with in practice, than in any other similar establishment in the United States. Even the infirmary of Edinburgh, the Hotel Dieu of Paris, or the hospitals of London do not afford to their students more real advantages than are to be obtained at this well-regulated asylum.

In this excellent institution you also have access to an extensive medical library, consisting of the most respectable writings, both of ancient and modern times. I cannot pass by this circumstance without bearing testimony to the liberality of the gentlemen who compose the board of governors of that institution. Entertaining a due sense of the importance of that establishment as a place of instruction to the student of medicine, they have not only embraced every opportunity but they have eagerly sought for occasions by which they could render it most profitable to the pupils who attend the practice of the house, as well as a comfortable asylum to the sick, who are the objects of its charity.

Upon the advantages which the liberality and paternal care of the regents of the university, aided by the munificence of an enlightened legislature, have thus secured to our profession, I congratulate you with the utmost sincerity. Let us now by our exertions demonstrate to the world that the zeal and public spirit which those respective bodies have manifested for the general interests of learning have been no less honorable to themselves than beneficial to this community.

Although the city of New York, by its geographical position in the Union and the continued intercourse which it holds with the different states as well as with most of the commercial cities of Europe, is thereby entitled to many preeminent advantages, it must be acknowledged that it has not hitherto sustained that high literary character that has distinguished the metropolis of Pennsylvania; but we trust the time is at hand when the state of New York, and this otherwise flourishing city, will be rendered the literary, as it is now the commercial, emporium of our country.

Shall the state whose commerce renders her first in wealth, whose population amounts to nearly a million inhabitants, and whose annual revenue to the Union has exceeded $5 million not contribute her quota in wealth, talents, and exertions to the promotion of science? Shall her literature only consist in the means of increasing her number of dollars; shall the Tontine Coffee House be her only university; and the receipts of customs and insurance companies her colleges? Our patriotism, our pride of character, our love of life, or what is stronger, our love of gain, forbids such apathy. No, we will not consent that such negligence shall continue to mark the character of our state.

And I see in this auditory gentlemen whose talents and literary attainments have enabled them to appreciate the importance of this subject, and whose patriotism and merited influence in our public councils have given us every assurance that our exertions will continue to receive that support which a liberal and enlightened government has it in its power to bestow. Let us then be animated by these prospects, and redouble our exertions. With these impressions I enter upon the duties assigned me in this university.

74.

John Adams: Thoughts on Current Politics

Though retired from public affairs, John Adams was always mindful of current political activities and often wrote on the subject to his friend Benjamin Waterhouse. The occasion for the following letter, dated March 11, 1812, was the impending Massachusetts gubernatorial election. Adams perceived the advent of war with England and thus supported the incumbent Republican governor, Elbridge Gerry, who was not pro-British.

Source: *Statesman and Friend, Correspondence of John Adams with Benjamin Waterhouse 1784-1822*, Worthington C. Ford, ed., Boston, 1927, pp. 74-80.

The tumultuous crowd of thoughts that rushed into my head as I read your letter of yesterday would appear as gross a chaos and as wild an anarchy, if it could be described in writing, as the politics of our commonwealth appear to you, as described in your letter. If I hint at some of them, I shall study no tactics to marshal them in order.

In the first place, I absolutely forbid that this letter or any part of it should be published in my name, because instead of promoting Mr. Gerry's election, it would alienate from him thousands of votes. The least appearance of forwardness in me, to dictate or advise, would be imputed to selfish motives and produce a reaction.

In the second place, I hope your doubt of

the election of Mr. Gerry is unfounded; I see no reason why a single man who voted for Mr. Gerry last year should not vote for him this. On the contrary, I see many more and much stronger reasons for voting for him this year than last.

In the third place, not only "a slight speck" but a black cloud of war with England hangs over us. If such a war or any war should take place, Mr. Gerry is infinitely better fitted to conduct this commonwealth through it than Mr. Strong. I have known Mr. Gerry very nearly forty years, and I know him to possess a sagacity, a fortitude, an inflexibility, and an indefatigable application which few men can equal. Indeed, I know of none in the state. These are virtues, talents, and qualities which at this time are peculiarly requisite and indispensable.

In the fourth place, the party which supports Mr. Strong love Great Britain and hate France. Mr. Gerry hates neither. Nor loves either with more than general benevolence to all nations. To throw the government of the commonwealth into the hands of a party devoted to Great Britain at a time when we are in immediate danger of a war with that empire would be downright absurdity.

In the fifth place, you want my opinion of "modern politics generally" and "Governor Gerry's politics" in particular. My stars! to write these opinions would require a volume as large as Willard's *Body of Divinity!* But what signify the opinions of an individual? or a state? We must in such times as these cling to the national government as our only rock of safety against the storm, and endeavor to conform our state governments to the general government as much as we can. There were many things in Washington's administration, in my own, and in Jefferson's which I could not approve. I wished they were otherwise. But I could not prevent them nor alter them. I had no choice but to submit.

If I had a vote I should give it to Mr. Madison at the next election, because I know of no man who would do better. At present the general government are approaching nearer and nearer to my system. They are restoring the taxes that ought never to have been repealed. They are doing something by sea. Why do not the Republicans and Federalists, too, cry aloud for a navy? That is the only arm that can protect us or preserve the Union. This object I have pursued with unabated zeal for six-and-thirty years. Why do we not celebrate the American Navy of 1775, '76, '77, '78, '79, '80, etc.? Why are not held up to admiration the triumphs of Talbot, Truxtun, Little, Preble, and the two Decaturs? No! Toryism abhors all these exploits, and Whigs have not sense nor spirit to see the necessity of it, or to undertake the work. The landed interest in Holland depressed their navy. The landed interest in France always starved theirs. And we see the consequences. The landed interest in America has done the same, and we feel the effects.

In the sixth place, the necessity of a union of sentiment and affection between the national and state governments at this important juncture, the danger of being influenced by men who threaten to resist the laws and destroy the fabric of the Union is so obvious and palpable that the man who wants the opinion of John Adams to convince him of it must be destitute of common information or common understanding.

In the seventh place, I have been absent from this commonwealth from 1775 to 1778 in Congress, *four years;* from 1778 to 1788, in Europe, *ten years;* from 1789 to 1801, as vice-president and President, *twelve years;* and *eleven years* in a Hermitage in Quincy: *thirty-seven years.* In all this time I have had no opportunities to mix with the people of this state or to know much of men or things in it. How then is it possible, or how can it be decent, for me to come forward and preach and exhort upon the politics of the state? I have had opportunities to know something of the general affairs of the Union and of the foreign relations of the nation. I have learned to respect the rights of Kentucky, Tennessee, and Ohio, as much as those of Rhode Island, Massachusetts, or New Hampshire. I cannot enter into local feelings, low intrigues, or party flickerings.

In the eighth place, I have voted for Mr. Gerry and will vote for him this year, and most ardently hope he will be chosen, because I believe him to be incomparably the most independent, disinterested, and capable man for the office that now breathes the air of Massachusetts.

In the ninth place, *Massachusetts is her own worst enemy.* As soon as a man has done great services, made great sacrifices, and acquired a name, envy runs him down; Hancock, Adams, Gerry, Warren, James Otis are with them interested men. Washington and Franklin, with their $500,000 apiece, are disinterested ones. Hamilton is the idol, and his worshipers — Ames, Otis, etc. — are the saints. The Tories have done this, and they must be humbled as they are in New York and Pennsylvania; or Woe! Woe! Woe to Jerusalem! How opposite is the policy of Virginia! Washington, Jefferson, Madison, P. Henry, Monroe, Marshall, and even John Randolph [are] steadily supported and cried up to the stars!

In the tenth place, I regret the necessity Mr. Gerry has been under to remove so many officers. The predominant party have pushed him too hard and grasped at too much. Mr. Gerry has done the best in his power. I know by long experience that a governor checked by a council and a President checked by a Senate in appointments to executive offices cannot always do what he thinks is wisest and best.

The Federalists by their own selfishness, exclusion, and intolerance have provoked and deserved the retaliation; yet I cannot but wish that both parties, when in power, would be more generous and liberal.

Mr. Gerry's philosophy will support him whatever may be the event.

I have said nothing of banks, a system of injustice from the foundation, but it is now hard to say which party has been most culpable. I am as ever your friend.

Strike wherever we can reach the enemy, at sea and on land. But if we fail, let us fail like men, lash ourselves to our gallant tars, and expire together in one common struggle, fighting for free trade and seamen's rights.

HENRY CLAY, during War of 1812

75.

James Madison: War Message

It is one of the perversities of American history that while President Madison's message to Congress urging the commencement of hostilities against Great Britain in 1812 listed only maritime grievances as the cause and said nothing about expansionist aims in the Ohio Valley, the Treaty of Ghent, which in 1814 ended the war, dealt only with those expansionist aims and said nothing about maritime grievances. But this was only one of many contradictions in a conflict that began in confusion and unreadiness, was fought amid disagreements that all but tore the country to pieces, and then ended in triumph. What Madison really did was take a long chance. Bedeviled by a tangle of diplomatic and political problems he could not otherwise solve, and largely unprepared for war, he later admitted that he had "thrown forward the flag of the country, sure that the people would press forward." The President gave the following message to Congress on June 1, 1812.

Source: Richardson, I, pp. 499-505.

I communicate to Congress certain documents, being a continuation of those heretofore laid before them on the subject of our affairs with Great Britain. Without going back beyond the renewal in 1803 of the war in which Great Britain is engaged, and omitting unrepaired wrongs of inferior magnitude, the conduct of her government presents a series of acts hostile to the United States as an independent and neutral nation.

British cruisers have been in the continued practice of violating the American flag on the great highway of nations, and of seizing and carrying off persons sailing under it, not in the exercise of a belligerent right founded on the law of nations against an enemy but of a municipal prerogative over British subjects. British jurisdiction is thus extended to neutral vessels in a situation where no laws can operate but the law of nations and the laws of the country to which the vessels belong; and a self-redress is assumed which, if British subjects were wrongfully detained and alone concerned, is that substitution of force for a resort to the responsible sovereign which falls within the definition of war. Could the seizure of British subjects in such cases be regarded as within the exercise of a belligerent right, the acknowledged laws of war, which forbid an article of captured property to be adjudged without a regular investigation before a competent tribunal, would imperiously demand the fairest trial where the sacred rights of persons were at issue? In place of such a trial, these rights are subjected to the will of every petty commander.

The practice, hence, is so far from affecting British subjects alone that, under the pretext of searching for these, thousands of American citizens, under the safeguard of public law and of their national flag, have been torn from their country and from everything dear to them; have been dragged on board ships of war of a foreign nation and exposed, under the severities of their discipline, to be exiled to the most distant and deadly climes, to risk their lives in the battles of their oppressors, and to be the melancholy instruments of taking away those of their own brethren.

Against this crying enormity, which Great Britain would be so prompt to avenge if committed against herself, the United States have in vain exhausted remonstrances and expostulations; and that no proof might be wanting of their conciliatory dispositions, and no pretext left for a continuance of the practice, the British government was formally assured of the readiness of the United States to enter into arrangements such as could not be rejected if the recovery of British subjects were the real and the sole object. The communication passed without effect.

British cruisers have been in the practice, also, of violating the rights and the peace of our coasts. They hover over and harass our entering and departing commerce. To the most insulting pretensions they have added the most lawless proceedings in our very harbors, and have wantonly spilled American blood within the sanctuary of our territorial jurisdiction. The principles and rules enforced by that nation, when a neutral nation, against armed vessels of belligerents hovering near her coasts and disturbing her commerce are well known. When called on, nevertheless, by the United States to punish the greater offenses committed by her own vessels, her government has bestowed on their commanders additional marks of honor and confidence.

Under pretended blockades, without the presence of an adequate force and sometimes without the practicability of applying one, our commerce has been plundered in every sea, the great staples of our country have been cut off from their legitimate markets, and a destructive blow aimed at our agricultural and maritime interests. In aggravation of these predatory measures, they have been considered as in force from the dates of their notification, a retrospective effect being thus added, as has been done in other important cases, to the unlawfulness of the course pursued. And to render the outrage the more signal, these mock blockades have been reiterated and enforced in the face of official communications from the British government declaring as the true definition of a legal blockade "that particular ports must be actually invested and previous warning given to vessels bound to them not to enter."

Not content with these occasional expedients for laying waste our neutral trade, the cabinet of Britain resorted at length to the sweeping system of blockades, under the name of orders in council, which has been molded and managed as might best suit its political views, its commercial jealousies, or the avidity of British cruisers.

To our remonstrances against the complicated and transcendent injustice of this innovation, the first reply was that the orders were reluctantly adopted by Great Britain as a necessary retaliation on decrees of her enemy proclaiming a general blockade of the British Isles at a time when the naval force of that enemy dared not issue from his own ports. She was reminded, without effect, that her own prior blockades, unsupported by an adequate naval force actually applied and continued, were a bar to this plea; that executed edicts against millions of our property could not be retaliation on edicts confessedly impossible to be executed; that retaliation, to be just, should fall on the party setting the guilty example, not on an innocent party which was not even chargeable with an acquiescence in it.

When deprived of this flimsy veil for a prohibition of our trade with her enemy by the repeal of his prohibition of our trade with Great Britain, her cabinet, instead of a corresponding repeal or a practical discontinuance of its orders, formally avowed a determination to persist in them against the United States until the markets of her enemy should be laid open to British products; thus asserting an obligation on a neutral power to require one belligerent to encourage, by its internal regulations, the trade of another belligerent, contradicting her own practice toward all nations, in peace as well as in war, and betraying the insincerity of those professions which inculcated a belief that, having resorted to her orders with regret, she was anxious to find an occasion for putting an end to them.

Abandoning still more all respect for the neutral rights of the United States and for its own consistency, the British government now demands, as prerequisites to a repeal of its orders as they relate to the United States, that a formality should be observed in the repeal of the French decrees, nowise necessary to their termination nor exemplified by British usage, and that the French repeal, besides including that portion of the decrees which operates within a territorial jurisdiction as well as that which operates on the high seas against the commerce of the United States should not be a single and special repeal in relation to the United States but should be extended to whatever other neutral nations unconnected with them may be affected by those decrees. And as an additional insult, they are called on for a formal disavowal of conditions and pretensions advanced by the French government, for which the United States are, so far from having made themselves responsible that, in official explanations which have been published to the world and in a correspondence of the American minister at London with the British minister for foreign affairs, such a responsibility was explicitly and emphatically disclaimed.

It has become, indeed, sufficiently certain that the commerce of the United States is to be sacrificed, not as interfering with the belligerent rights of Great Britain; not as supplying the wants of her enemies, which she herself supplies; but as interfering with the monopoly which she covets for her own commerce and navigation. She carries on a war against the lawful commerce of a friend that she may the better carry on a commerce with an enemy — a commerce polluted by the forgeries and perjuries which are for the most part the only passports by which it can succeed.

Anxious to make every experiment short of the last resort of injured nations, the United States have withheld from Great Britain, under successive modifications, the benefits of a free intercourse with their market, the loss of which could not but outweigh the profits accruing from her restrictions of our commerce with other nations. And to entitle these experiments to the more favorable consideration, they were so framed as to enable her to place her adversary under the exclusive operation of them. To these appeals her government has been equally inflexible, as if willing to make sacrifices of every sort rather than yield to the claims of justice or renounce the errors of a false pride. Nay, so far were the attempts carried to overcome the attachment of the British cabinet to its unjust edicts that it received every encouragement within the competency of the executive branch of our government to expect that a repeal of them would be followed by a war between the United States and France, unless the French edicts should also be repealed. Even this communication, although silencing forever the plea of a disposition in the United States to acquiesce in those edicts originally the sole plea for them, received no attention.

If no other proof existed of a predetermination of the British government against a repeal of its orders, it might be found in the correspondence of the minister plenipotentiary of the United States at London and the British secretary for foreign affairs, in 1810, on the question whether the blockade of May 1806 was considered as in force or as not in force. It had been ascertained that the French government, which urged this blockade as the ground of its Berlin Decree, was willing, in the event of its removal, to repeal that decree, which, being followed by alternate repeals of the other offensive edicts, might abolish the whole system on both sides.

This inviting opportunity for accomplishing an object so important to the United States, and professed so often to be the desire of both the belligerents, was made known to the British government. As that government admits that an actual application of an adequate force is necessary to the existence of a legal blockade, and it was notorious that if such a force had ever been applied its long discontinuance had annulled the blockade in question, there could be no sufficient objection on the part of Great Britain to a formal revocation of it, and no imaginable objection to a declaration of the fact that the blockade did not exist. The declaration would have been consistent with her avowed principles of blockade, and would have enabled the United States to demand from France the pledged repeal of her decrees, either with success; in which case the way would have been opened for a general repeal of the belligerent edicts; or without success, in which case the United States would have been justified in turning their measures exclusively against France.

The British government would, however, neither rescind the blockade nor declare its nonexistence, nor permit its nonexistence to be inferred and affirmed by the American plenipotentiary. On the contrary, by representing the blockade to be comprehended in the orders in council, the United States were compelled so to regard it in their subsequent proceedings.

There was a period when a favorable change in the policy of the British cabinet was justly considered as established. The minister plenipotentiary of His Britannic Majesty here proposed an adjustment of the differences more immediately endangering the harmony of the two countries. The proposition was accepted with the promptitude and cordiality corresponding with the invariable professions of this government. A foundation appeared to be laid for a sincere and lasting reconciliation. The prospect, however, quickly vanished. The whole proceeding was disavowed by the British government without any explanations which could at that time repress the belief that the disavowal proceeded from a spirit of hostility to the commercial rights and prosperity of the United States; and it has since come into proof that at the very moment when the public minister was holding the language of friendship and inspiring confidence in the sincerity of the negotiation with which he was charged, a secret agent of his government was employed in intrigues having for their object a subversion of our government and a dismemberment of our happy Union.

In reviewing the conduct of Great Britain toward the United States, our attention is necessarily drawn to the warfare just renewed by the savages on one of our extensive frontiers — a warfare which is known to spare neither age nor sex and to be distinguished by features peculiarly shocking to humanity. It is difficult to account for the activity and combinations which have for some time been developing themselves among tribes in constant intercourse with British traders and garrisons, without connecting their hostility with that influence and without recollecting the authenticated examples of such interpositions heretofore furnished by the officers and agents of that government.

Such is the spectacle of injuries and indignities which have been heaped on our country, and such the crisis which its unexampled forbearance and conciliatory efforts have not been able to avert. It might at least have been expected that an enlightened nation, if less urged by moral obligations or invited by friendly dispositions on the part of the United States, would have found in its true interest alone a sufficient motive to respect their rights and their tranquillity on the high seas; that an enlarged policy would have favored that free and general circulation of commerce in which the British nation is at all times interested, and which in times of war is the best alleviation of its calamities to herself as well as to other belligerents; and more especially that the British cabinet would not, for the sake of a precarious and surreptitious intercourse with hostile markets, have persevered in a course of measures which necessarily put at hazard the invaluable market of a great and growing country, disposed to cultivate the mutual advantages of an active commerce.

Other counsels have prevailed. Our moderation and conciliation have had no other effect than to encourage perseverance and to enlarge pretensions. We behold our seafaring citizens still the daily victims of lawless violence, committed on the great common and highway of nations, even within sight of the country which owes them protection. We behold our vessels, freighted with the products of our soil and industry, or returning with the honest proceeds of them, wrested from their lawful destinations, confiscated by prize courts no longer the organs of public law but the instruments of arbitrary edicts, and their unfortunate crews dispersed and lost, or forced or inveigled in British ports into British fleets, whilst arguments are employed in support of these aggressions which have no foundation but in a principle, equally supporting a claim to regulate our external commerce in all cases whatsoever.

We behold, in fine, on the side of Great Britain, a state of war against the United States, and, on the side of the United States, a state of peace toward Great Britain.

Whether the United States shall continue passive under these progressive usurpations and these accumulating wrongs, or, opposing force to force in defense of their national rights, shall commit a just cause into the hands of the Almighty Disposer of Events, avoiding all connections which might entangle it in the contest or views of other powers, and preserving a constant readiness to concur in an honorable reestablishment of peace and friendship, is a solemn question which the Constitution wisely confides to the Legislative Department of the government. In recommending it to their early deliberations, I am happy in the assurance that the decision will be worthy the enlightened and patriotic councils of a virtuous, a free, and a powerful nation.

Having presented this view of the relations of the United States with Great Britain and of the solemn alternative growing out of them, I proceed to remark that the communications last made to Congress on the subject of our relations with France will have shown that since the revocation of her decrees, as they violated the neutral rights of the United States, her government has authorized illegal captures by its privateers and public ships, and that other outrages have been practised on our vessels and our citizens. It will have been seen, also, that no indemnity had been provided or satisfactorily pledged for the extensive spoliations committed under the violent and retrospective orders of the French government against the property of our citizens seized within the jurisdiction of France. I abstain at this time from recommending to the consideration of Congress definitive measures with respect to that nation, in the expectation that the result of unclosed discussions between our minister plenipotentiary at Paris and the French government will speedily enable Congress to decide with greater advantage on the course due to the rights, the interests, and the honor of our country.

76.

Obadiah German: Unprepared for War with England

The congressional debate that ensued after Madison's war message of June 1, 1812, lasted three weeks. The House voted for war, 79 to 49, on June 4. Those senators who were opposed to war, finding it difficult to deny that the United States had sufficient provocation, relied on delaying tactics and arguments designed to show what in fact was the case: that the United States was militarily unprepared, both on land and sea, to fight Britain. The following portions of a speech by Senator German of New York on June 13 stated this case. On June 18, the Senate voted for war, 19 to 13.

Source: *Debates,* 12 Cong., 1 Sess., pp. 272-283.

I am ready to allow, Mr. President, that both Great Britain and France have given us abundant cause for war. On this occasion, therefore, I shall dispense with using any argument which might serve to show that if we were even in a state of preparation, and possessed the means of insuring a favorable issue, it would be bad policy for this country, at the present time, to enter into war with Great Britain, although perhaps many weighty reasons might be adduced in support of such argument. . . .

Before we take the step proposed by the bill before us, I think we ought also to make some calculation on the general state of the nation. Except some trifling Indian war, it will be recollected we have been twenty-nine years at peace, and have become a nation, in a great degree, of active moneymakers. We have lost much of the spirit of war and chivalry possessed by our Revolutionary fathers; and we are a people, also, not overfond of paying taxes to the extent of our ability; and this because our purses have been sweated down by our restrictive system till they have become light.

I shall now beg leave to trespass on your attention, Mr. President, while I advert to the situation of our small but daring navy, the increase of which, it will be remembered, has been decided against by this Senate during the present session. It is true, provision has been made for rebuilding some three or four frigates, which had been deemed unworthy of repair; and that a small sum of money has been appropriated for the purchase of materials for building some vessels of war at a future day; but the appropriation is so scanty that very little can be expected from it. I am, however, ready to acknowledge that the few ships we have ready for service are good ones, and I have no doubt but they are kept in proper order for immediate and active employment. This, however, I am perfectly confident of, that there is not a braver set of officers and sailors in existence than those by whom they are commanded and manned; but we cannot, therefore, expect that this little fleet, if it may be so called, can be competent to hold in check any detachment that Great Britain is able to send upon our coast from her thousand ships. It would be a sacrifice of justice to imagine it. Prior to any declaration of war, Mr. President, my plan would be, and my first wish is, to prepare for it — to put the country in complete armor — in the attitude imperiously demanded in a crisis of war, and to which it must be brought before any war can be effective. This, too, would be agreeable to the recommendation of the executive; but I would not first rashly commit the nation by such a measure and then begin to look about us and try to make preparation for meeting the calamity we have, without consideration, brought upon ourselves.

It will be necessary, Mr. President, to take a view of the subject of ways and means on this occasion, and see what aspect the finances of the nation afford. It is well known to every member of the Senate that our treasury is empty, and that the government has been under the necessity of authorizing loans in time of peace; but has the sanguine expectations relative to the subscriptions for the $11 million loan, authorized this session, been at all answered? I believe not. If my recollection serves me faithfully, there is about $5 million still wanting to complete the subscription to the loan for the current year's expenditures; and here it is worthy of remark what quarter of the Union has been most remiss on this patriotic occasion. If I were to inquire how much the states beyond the Allegheny Mountains have subscribed to this loan, I believe the answer would be, not one dollar. But, sir, if the people in those states have not been found forward in their subscriptions toward carrying on the war, their representatives have made up for this deficiency by being forward and liberal enough in their war speeches. They have raised the war whoop equal to those of any section of the Union, and particularly the representation from the state of Kentucky, one of the gentlemen, in this Senate, only excepted.

After the war is once commenced, however, I presume gentlemen will find something more forcible than empty war speeches will be necessary. It will not be sufficient, then, to rely on war speeches, documents, nor proclamations to repel the attack of an enemy, or to carry war into their territory. And I have understood that the people of those states are not extremely partial to internal and direct taxes, nor were they very promptly collected and paid there, when formerly laid, under the administration of Mr. Adams.

In crossing the Alleghenies, we look almost in vain in the states of Georgia and South Carolina for that liberal spirit in contributing to the loan, which was no doubt so much relied on by their representation in the famous war speeches when they urged war on almost any terms. The banks and people of those states, in refusing to subscribe, have evinced a backwardness which, from the language of war held by their representation, was least to have been expected; although it is there perhaps that we may find the combustibles which have kindled this mighty war flame, and precipitated this nation to the verge of ruin.

We will now, sir, pass on to good old Virginia — the Ancient Dominion — that proud state which has governed this nation twenty years out of twenty-four; and there, sir, we may also look for her full proportion of the cause and origin of this untimely war measure, this fatal tragedy, which, before it is over, will cause the country to suffer pain in every member, and to bleed at every pore. Yes, sir, if Virginia's sons have not been as open and ardent in producing this fatal bill as those of some other states, they have no doubt acted their part well behind the curtain as prompters. But how stands this proud head of the nation on the books for the subscription to the loan? Has she, by the paltry sum she has subscribed, evinced her determination to avenge her country's wrongs? Or has she, by that, supported the zeal so strongly and so repeatedly professed? We shall find, sir, that these states will not be more liberal in furnishing soldiers to fight your battles than they have been in assisting in the means of maintaining and paying them. Their liberality and willingness to furnish your armies, and every other place in the government, with officers, I do not doubt; but further, or other aid, need be little expected.

If this representation I have been making to the Senate be facts, whence are we to expect subscriptions to fill the remainder of this loan, and where is the money to come from after this year? It is not, I believe, to be expected from those states whose representatives seem to be so liberal in votes and speeches for immediate war; but, if it is to be filled at all, it must be done by the states and people north of the Potomac. Yes, sir, both the money and men to carry on the war must mostly come from the Northern states, where the people are opposed to entering into the war in this blind and rash manner, without system or preparation. And, according to the calculation of the secretary of the treasury, who I imagine to possess as much sagacity as any of the cabinet, we have no reason to expect loans in future for carrying on the war short of 8 percent; and when that takes place, we may freely say we have seen nearly all the measures of Mr. Adams' administration revived.

Mr. President, I have now taken a view of the ability of the country we are about to make war upon, to sustain that war, and make it terrible to us. I have also shown the wretched, unprepared situation my country is in to repel the attacks of an enemy, much less of carrying war into the enemy's territory with a probability of success. If I have given a true statement of the situation of the disposable force of the two countries; if I have drawn a true picture (although a very disagreeable task for me to perform) of the situation of our country and of our present inability to make war upon Great Britain; and if I have not been deceived by my zeal and anxiety to check the passage of this bill and to avoid the evils which in my judgment it will bring upon my beloved country (and my honest conviction is that I have not) — can it be possible that as grave and discreet a body as this Senate, with the acknowledged justice of my statements before them, will, at this time, pass the bill under consideration? Can we look for a blessing without the use of rational means? Does God in His providence ever dispense His blessings on any but those who are vigilant in the use of means? Can we expect to reap if we neglect to sow? If we do, the crop will surely be briars, thorns, and thistles.

I must call on every member of this Senate to pause before he leaps into or crosses the Rubicon — declaring war is passing the Rubicon in reality, and you cannot recross it when you please. It must be remembered that when you once declare war, you must obtain the consent of your enemy before you can make peace. And gentlemen may be assured that if we do not pause and reflect before we act, the people will reflect and examine our deeds after we have acted; and if, contrary to every principle of prudence and common sense, we at this time declare war, the people, who are always governed by the rules of common sense, deduced from practical observation, will, after they have had time to reflect, dismiss us as unprofitable servants.

I do not, Mr. President, oppose the passage of the bill at this time, or press so hard for its postponement, because I doubt the justice of our cause or perfidy of the enemy we are about to declare war upon. Nor should I have doubted our own ability had our resources been well husbanded, for four or five past years, to make the war terrible to our enemy; but the tale of the bad management of our resources is too obvious and too lamentable to be told at this time; although, without subjecting myself to the charge of raising a cry against the executive,

I may assert, it is a notorious and lamentable fact that the President neglected to fill the ranks in the additional army, during the period between the adjournment of the last and the meeting of the present Congress. And he has also neglected to direct the purchase of the necessary munitions of war when appropriations had been made by the Eleventh Congress for both purposes. These neglects naturally created a suspicion of the sincerity of the President's War Message.

There is another fact — a serious, a material fact — which I have heard acknowledged by almost every member of this Senate: it is this, that the head of the War Department is in a great degree deficient in skill, unable to systematize, and wanting energy to execute the necessary business of that department. Why not place a man of competent ability at the head of your War Department, one who will reduce the business of that department to order, who will mark out a regular system of discipline and government for your army, and more particularly the staff of it; so that when your disposable force may be brought to act upon the enemy there may be a prospect of advantage or victory?

If the taking of Canada, Mr. President, is the real object of the war, no discreet executive would wish that war declared, until he saw a force raised, concentrated, and disciplined that would warrant the calculation of Montreal's being in our possession within six weeks after the declaration; for if Canada is not assailed in this manner, the conflict must be lengthy, and, consequently, more bloody, if not doubtful. If you commence the attack at Fort Malden, and pursue the enemy down the lakes and rivers, they will be falling back or retreating on their reinforcements, and constantly increasing and concentrating their forces; and would perhaps be able to hold your army in check before it reaches Montreal. But let your army be enabled by its strength to first possess itself of Montreal, and all the upper country must fall of course; you would then soon be able to draw the line dividing your army and that of your enemy between Montreal and Quebec, and when this is accomplished you have put an end to the Indian war by cutting the Indians off from any further succor from the British.

Did I wish, sir, to embarrass the Executive at the expense of the blood and treasure of my country, I would vote for the immediate passage of this bill; I would strive to bring on premature war, especially since he has recommended it; and I must, sir, be here permitted to ask, who displays the greatest friendship for the President — those that wish to plunge him and the nation down the precipice which presents itself to us, or those who wish to check this hazardous, this uncertain step?

I do not, Mr. President, draw all these discouraging pictures, or relate these lamentable facts, because I would shrink from the conflict or terrors of war, for the defense of the rights of my injured country, sooner than any gentleman of this Senate, nor with a wish that all these evils may be realized; my object is to avert them from my country. I do it, sir, to check the precipitate step of plunging my country prematurely into a war without any of the means of making the war terrible to our enemy, and with the certainty that it will be terrible to ourselves, or at least to our merchants, our seaports, and cities. Yes, sir, the millions that your merchants will lose in consequence of this rash, this premature step, will strike them with terror and dismay from New Orleans to Maine; and how lamentable it is that a war, which has for its avowed object the protection of commercial rights, should be commenced at a time and in a manner which will prove more destructive to commerce itself than all the plunderings and burnings of both France and England.

But I conclude the ostensible object of this war is to force the cotton and tobacco trade into the continent of Europe, and to support the executive in the declaration that the Berlin and Milan decrees are revoked; but it should be recollected that it will not only be necessary in order to enforce a market for our cotton and tobacco upon the Continent to obtain a repeal of the British orders; but it will be also necessary to force Napoleon to give up his continental system, or make an exception in it in our favor; and, even if he permits us to go to the Continent with the produce of our soil, his tariff of duties is an exclusion to our trade, for cotton and tobacco will scarcely pay freight and charges.

I must now ask, sir, with what force we are to effectuate all these desirable objects? Are our 6,000 men, and the few raw recruits of the new army spread over the vast extent of these United States and their territories, and our little fleet of four or five frigates, equal to the invasion of the Canadas, and the protection of our maritime frontiers, and to strike the British government and the inflexible Napoleon with such terrors that we are to expect they will abandon their system of warfare against each other? I presume no one will pretend to say they are. Well, then, why declare war at this time; why will gentlemen not defer until your new army of 25,000 men are raised and disciplined fit for service? It must be believed, sir, if we now declare war that the object of it is not for the reduction of Canada, because we have not the means provided; and I am somewhat at a loss to discover the real object; but if I dare indulge a suspicion that the real and avowed objects are different, I should say this war is to be declared, but not prosecuted, other than in a defensive manner, and, consequently, altogether within our own territory, and to operate as an enforcement of the restrictive system, and may with propriety be called the "Terrapin War," and be by some considered more popular than a continuance of the embargo.

I have heard some complaints and charges of inconsistency against those members of Congress who voted for raising the 25,000 men, because they would not now vote for war! I never once supposed, nor would anybody in their senses suppose, a vote to raise an army as a preparatory measure to coerce justice from a neighboring nation would impose the obligation of voting for a declaration of war before that army should be raised. For my part, sir, ever since I had the honor of a seat in this Senate, I have uniformly voted appropriations for the putting my country in a state of defense, and to prepare it for war. A country well prepared to meet war will scarcely find war necessary, but if it cannot be avoided, preparation does away half its terrors. And if gentlemen will show me an army of 25,000 men, well-formed, disciplined, and supplied, at the place of the grand rendezvous near Albany, give us a reasonable increase of our navy, and will place both the great belligerents on the same footing (as I consider them equal trespassers on our rights), then, I say, if Great Britain will not do us justice, I will vote at the proper time a declaration of war against her; and I will use my utmost exertions to make the war terrible to her. But to declare war without the means of making the enemy feel its horrors, and at a time when it must produce evil and terrors only to ourselves, strikes me with astonishment.

If war is declared before we have a force raised sufficient to subdue Canada, we shall have war upon our northern frontier, and perhaps it will be pushed into our territory. This will be particularly alarming and distressing to the inhabitants on the Canada line; and your militia will be called out from their usual business and avocations of life into the field, as soldiers for the protection of the frontier settlements, and you will have all the expense of a regular campaign without any of its benefits; besides that, the evils attending upon calling a large portion of the militia into actual service for any considerable time is almost incalculable. After a short time, sickness, death, and many other evils will teach you the impropriety of relying on them for the carrying on the war; and the discouraging effects, which these calamities naturally attendant on militia camps will have on the community, when those who survive return home to their families and friends, and tell the mournful tale, are to be seriously deprecated.

But, sir, when I look round this Senate and see a number of our Revolutionary patriots who have grown gray in the service of their country, my hopes are cheered. It is to them I look at this time; it is from their experience and discretion (venerable fathers of their country) that that country expects this impending evil to be averted. And can it be possible that the younger men of this Senate, who must have descended from so discreet and noble an ancestry as their Revolutionary fathers proved themselves to be, should suffer their judgment to be so misled as to vote against the postponement of this measure, which may, if it passes under the present circumstances, put to the test the very existence of the Constitution under which we have enjoyed so much liberty and happiness, and the attainment of which cost our fathers so much blood and treasure!

77.

John Adams: Party Divisions in America

John Adams' astute comments on the origin and growth of political parties were prompted by a pamphlet, Crisis, *which had been sent to him by its author, William Keteltas. Adams, who had followed Washington in the presidency, had been out of office for eleven years when he wrote this letter to Keteltas on November 25, 1812.*

Source: C. F. Adams, X, pp. 22-24.

I have received your polite letter of the 6th of the month and your present of the *Crisis.* You will excuse a question or two. In page first, you say, "Our administrations, with the exception of Washington's, have been party administrations." On what ground do you except Washington's? If by party you mean majority, his majority was the smallest of the four in all his legislative and executive acts, though not in his election.

You say, "our divisions began with Federalism and anti- Federalism." Alas! they began with human nature; they have existed in America from its first plantation. In every colony, divisions always prevailed. In New York, Pennsylvania, Virginia, Massachusetts, and all the rest, a court and country party have always contended. Whig and Tory disputed very sharply before the Revolution, and in every step during the Revolution. Every measure of Congress, from 1774 to 1787, inclusively, was disputed with acrimony, and decided by as small majorities as any question is decided in these days. We lost Canada then, as we are like to lose it now, by a similar opposition. Away, then, with your false, though popular, distinctions in favor of Washington.

In page eleventh, you recommend a

"constitutional rotation, to destroy the snake in the grass"; but the snake will elude your snare. Suppose your president in rotation is to be chosen for Rhode Island. There will be a Federal and a Republican candidate in that state. Every Federalist in the nation will vote for the former, and every Republican for the latter. The light troops on both sides will skirmish; the same Northern and Southern distinctions will still prevail; the same running and riding; the same railing and reviling; the same lying and libeling, cursing and swearing will still continue. The same caucusing, assemblaging, and conventioning.

In the same page eleventh, you speak of a "portion of our own people who palsy the arm of the nation." There is too much truth in this. When I was exerting every nerve to vindicate the honor, and demand a redress of the wrongs, of the nation against the tyranny of France, the arm of the nation was palsied by one party. Now, Mr. Madison is acting the same part, for the same ends, against Great Britain, the arm of the nation is palsied by the opposite party. And so it will always be while we feel like colonists, dependent for protection on France or England; while we have so little national public opinion, so little national principle, national feeling, national patriotism; while we have no sentiment of our own strength, power, and resources.

78.

"Ye Parliament of England"

Indian problems in the West, British trade restrictions, and the kidnapping of American seamen who were forced to serve England in her naval war with Napoleon were but some of the provocations that roused America to war with Great Britain in 1812. The indignation and defiance of American patriots is well expressed by a famous song of the period, "Ye Parliament of England." The vessels mentioned in the verses were all engaged in important naval actions, and the last line, sometimes written "Free Trade and Seamen's Rights," was the motto of the war in the United States.

Source: *Ballads Migrant in New England*, Helen H. Flanders and Marguerite Olney, eds., New York, 1953.

YE PARLIAMENT OF ENGLAND

Ye Parliament of England,
Ye Lords and Commons too,
Consider well what you're about,
What you're about to do;
For you're to war with Yankees,
And I'm sure you'll rue the day
You roused the sons of liberty
In North Ameri-cay!

You first confined our commerce,
You said our ships shan't trade,
You next impressed our seamen,
And used them as your slaves;
You then insulted Rodgers,
While ploughing o'er the main,
And had we not declared war,
You'd have done it o'er again.

You tho't our frigates were but few,
And Yankees could not fight,
Until brave Hull your *Guerrière* took,
And banished her from your sight.
The *Wasp* then took your *Frolic,*
We'll nothing say to that,
The *Poictiers* being of the line
Of course she took her back.

The next, your *Macedonian,*
No finer ship could swim,
Decatur took her gilt work off,
And then he sent her in.
The *Java,* by a Yankee ship
Was sunk you all must know;
The *Peacock* fine, in all her plume,
By Lawrence down did go.

Then, next you sent your *Boxer,*
To box us all about,
But we had an *Enterprising* brig
That boxed your *Boxer* out;
She boxed her up to Portland,
And moored her off the town,
To show the sons of liberty
The *Boxer* of renown.

The next upon Lake Erie,
Where Perry had some fun,
You own he beat your naval force,
And caused them for to run;
This was to you a sore defeat,
The like ne'er known before —
Your British squadron beat complete —
Some took, some run ashore.

There's Rodgers, in the *President,*
Will burn, sink, and destroy;
The *Congress,* on the Brazil coast,
Your commerce will annoy;
The *Essex,* in the South Seas,
Will put out all your lights,
The flag she waves at her masthead —
"Free Trade and Sailors' Rights!"

Wednesday, Aug. 19th, 1812, 6:30 P.M., *the Birth of a World Power.*

CHARLES FRANCIS ADAMS, title of essay in *American Historical Review,* 1880s. The date is that of the defeat of the *Guerrière* by the *Constitution.*

Don't give up the ship!

CAPTAIN JAMES LAWRENCE, command given as he lay dying aboard his frigate, the *Chesapeake,* June 1, 1813. The ship was taken by the British after a bloody fight. Another version of this famous quote: "Tell the men to fire faster and not to give up the ship; fight her till she sinks."

1813

79.

Henry Clay: For a Vigorous Prosecution of the War

After 1811, a large number of congressional seats were occupied by newly elected Republicans who were too young to have experienced British rule and whose strong sense of nationalism led them first to call for war with England and then to support it enthusiastically. Henry Clay was one of these "War Hawks" and was elected by them to be speaker of the House. By placing persons favorable to his policies on key committees, as it is the speaker's prerogative to do, Clay was able to bring before the House a number of bills that had the effect of strengthening the armed forces. In pursuance of these efforts, as well as in support of a vigorous prosecution of the war, Clay addressed the House in early January 1813.

Source: *Debates,* 12 Cong., 2 Sess., pp. 659-676.

The war was declared because Great Britain arrogated to herself the pretension of regulating foreign trade, under the delusive name of retaliatory Orders in Council — a pretension by which she undertook to proclaim to American enterprise, "Thus far shalt thou go, and no farther." Orders which she refused to revoke after the alleged cause of their enactment had ceased; because she persisted in the act of impressing American seamen; because she had instigated the Indians to commit hostilities against us; and because she refused indemnity for her past injuries upon our commerce. . . .

It is not to the British principle, objectionable as it is, that we are alone to look; it is to her practice — no matter what guise she puts on. It is in vain to assert the inviolability of the obligation of allegiance. It is in vain to set up the plea of necessity and to allege that she cannot exist without the impressment of her seamen. The truth is, she comes, by her press gangs, on board of our vessels, seizes our native seamen, as well as naturalized, and drags them into her service. It is the case, then, of the assertion of an erroneous principle, and a practice not conformable to the principle — a principle which, if it were theoretically right, must be forever practically wrong.

We are told by gentlemen in the opposition that government has not done all that was incumbent on it to do to avoid just cause of complaint on the part of Great Britain; that, in particular, the certificates of protection, authorized by the act of 1796, are fraudulently used. Sir, government has done too much in granting those paper protections. I can never think of them without being shocked. They resemble the passes which the master grants to his Negro slave: "Let the bearer, Mungo, pass and repass without molestation." What do they imply? That Great Britain has a right to take all who are not provided with them. . . .

The honorable gentleman from New York (Mr. Bleecker), in the very sensible speech with which he favored the committee, made one observation that did not comport with his usual liberal and enlarged views. It was that those who are most interested against the practice of impressment did not desire a continuance of the war on account of it, while those (the Southern and Western members) who had no interest in it, were zealous advocates of the American seaman. It was a provincial sentiment, unworthy of that gentleman. It was one which, in a change of condition, he would not express, because I know he could not feel it. Does not that gentleman feel for the unhappy victims of the tomahawk in the Western country, although his quarter of the Union may be exempted from similar barbarities? I am sure he does. If there be a description of rights which, more than any other, should unite all parties in all quarters of the Union, it is unquestionably the rights of the person. No matter what his vocation, whether he seeks subsistence amid the dangers of the deep, or draws it from the bowels of the earth, or from the humblest occupations of mechanic life, whenever the sacred rights of an American freeman are assailed, all hearts ought to unite and every arm should be braced to vindicate his cause.

The gentleman from Delaware sees in Canada no object worthy of conquest. According to him, it is a cold, sterile, and inhospitable region; and, yet, such are the allurements which it offers that the same gentleman apprehends that, if it be annexed to the United States, already too much weakened by an extension of territory, the people of New England will rush over the line and depopulate that section of the Union. That gentleman considers it honest to hold Canada as a kind of hostage; to regard it as a sort of bond, for the good behavior of the enemy. But he will not enforce the bond. The actual conquest of that country would, according to him, make no impression upon the enemy, and yet the very apprehension only of such a conquest would at all times, have a powerful operation upon him.

Other gentlemen consider the invasion of that country as wicked and unjustifiable. Its inhabitants are represented as unoffending, connected with those of the bordering states by a thousand tender ties, interchanging acts of kindness, and all the offices of good neighborhood. Canada innocent! Canada unoffending! Is it not in Canada that the tomahawk of the savage has been molded into its deathlike form? From Canadian magazines, Malden, and others, that those supplies have been issued which nourish and sustain the Indian hostilities? Supplies which have enabled the savage hordes to butcher the garrison of Chicago, and to commit other horrible murders? Was it not by the joint cooperation of Canadians and Indians that a remote American fort, Michilimackinac, was fallen upon and reduced while the garrison was in ignorance of a state of war?

But, sir, how soon have the opposition changed! When the administration was striving, by the operation of peaceful measures, to bring Great Britain back to a sense of justice, they were for old-fashioned war. And now that they have got old-fashioned war, their sensibilities are cruelly shocked, and all their sympathies are lavished upon the harmless inhabitants of the adjoining provinces. . . .

The disasters of the war admonish us, we are told, of the necessity of terminating the contest. If our achievements upon the land have been less splendid than those of our intrepid seamen, it is not because the American soldier is less brave. On the one element, organization, discipline, and a thorough knowledge of their duties exist on the part of the officers and their men. On the other, almost everything is yet to be acquired. We have, however, the consolation that our country abounds with the richest materials, and that, in no instance, when engaged in an action, have our arms been tarnished. . . .

It is alleged that the elections in England are in favor of the Ministry, and that those in this country are against the war. If, in such a cause (saying nothing of the impurity of their elections), the people of that country have rallied around their government, it affords a salutary lesson to the people here, who, at all hazards, ought to support theirs, struggling, as it is, to maintain our just rights. But the people here have not been false to themselves; a great majority approve the war, as is evinced by the recent reelection of the chief magistrate. Suppose it were even true that an entire section of the Union were opposed to the war, that section being a minority, is the will of the majority to be relinquished? In that section the real strength of the opposition had been greatly exaggerated. Vermont has, by two successive expressions of her opinion, approved the declaration of war. In New Hampshire, parties are so nearly equipoised that, out of 30,000 or 35,000 votes, those who approved and are for supporting it lost the election by only 1,000 or 1,500 votes. In Massachusetts alone have they obtained any considerable accession. If we come to New York, we shall find that other and local causes have influenced her elections.

What cause, Mr. Chairman, which existed for declaring the war has been removed? We sought indemnity for the past and security for the future. The Orders in Council are suspended, not revoked; no compensation for spoliations; Indian hostilities, which were before secretly instigated, now openly encouraged; and the practice of impressment unremittingly persevered in and insisted upon. Yet administration has given the strongest demonstrations of its love of peace. On the 29th of June, less than ten days after the declaration of war, the secretary of state writes to Mr. Russell authorizing him to agree to an armistice upon two conditions only. And what are they? That the Orders in Council should be repealed, and the practice of impressing American seamen cease, those already impressed being released. The proposition was for nothing more than a real truce; that the war should in fact cease on both sides. Again, on the 27th of July, one month later, anticipating a possible objection to these terms, reasonable as they are, Mr. Monroe empowers Mr. Russell to stipulate in general terms for an armistice, having only an informal understanding on these points. In return, the enemy is offered a prohibition of the employment of his seamen in our service, thus removing entirely all pretext for the practice of impressment.

The very proposition which the gentleman from Connecticut (Mr. Pitkin) contends ought to be made has been made. How are these pacific advances met by the other party? Rejected as absolutely inadmissible; cavils are indulged about the inadequacy of Mr. Russell's powers; and the want of an act of Congress is intimated. And yet the constant usage of nations, I believe, is where the legislation of one party is necessary to carry into effect a given stipulation, to leave it to the contracting party to provide the requisite laws. If he fails to do so, it is a breach of good faith, and a subject of subsequent remonstrance by the injured party. When Mr. Russell renews the overture, in what was intended as a more agreeable form to the British government, Lord Castlereagh is not content with a simple rejection, but clothes it in the language of insult. Afterward, in conversation with Mr. Russell, the moderation of our government is misinterpreted and made the occasion of a sneer, that we are tired of the war.

The proposition of Admiral Warren is submitted in a spirit not more pacific. He is instructed, he tells us, to propose that the government of the United States shall instantly recall their letters of marque and reprisal against British ships, together with all orders and instructions for any acts of hostility whatever against the territories of His Majesty or the persons or property of his subjects. That small affair being settled, he is further authorized to arrange as to the revocation of the laws which interdict the commerce and ships of war of His Majesty from the harbors and waters of the United States. This messenger of peace comes with one qualified concession in his pocket, not made to the justice of our demands, and is fully empowered to receive our homage, the contrite retraction of all our measures adopted against his master! And, in default, he does not fail to assure us the Orders in Council are to be forthwith revived.

Administration, still anxious to terminate the war, suppresses the indignation which such a proposal ought to have created, and in its answer concludes by informing Admiral Warren,

> that if there be no objection to an accommodation of the difference relating to impressment, in the mode proposed, other than the suspension of the British claim to impressment during the armistice, there can be none to proceeding, without the armistice, to an immediate discussion and arrangement of an article on that subject.

Thus it has left the door of negotiation unclosed, and it remains to be seen if the enemy will accept the invitation tendered to him.

The honorable gentleman from North Carolina (Mr. Pearson) supposes that if Congress would pass a law prohibiting the employment of British seamen in our service, upon condition of a like prohibition on their part, and repeal the act of nonimportation, peace would immediately follow. Sir, I have no doubt if such a law were passed, with all the requisite solemnities, and the repeal to take place, Lord Castlereagh would laugh at our simplicity. No, sir, administration has erred in the steps which it has taken to restore peace, but its error has been not in doing too little but in betraying too great a solicitude for that event. An honorable peace is attainable only by an efficient war.

My plan would be to call out the ample resources of the country, give them a judicious direction, prosecute the war with the utmost vigor, strike wherever we can reach the enemy, at sea or on land, and negotiate the terms of a peace at Quebec or Halifax. We are told that England is a proud and lofty nation; that disdaining to wait for danger, meets it halfway. Haughty as she is, we once triumphed over her, and if we do not listen to the councils of timidity and despair, we shall again prevail. In such a cause, with the aid of Providence, we must come out crowned with success; but if we fail, let us fail like men — lash ourselves to our gallant tars and expire together in one common struggle, fighting for "seamen's rights and free trade."

80.

Opposed Views on Aristocracy

There are no more interesting letters in American history than the correspondence between John Adams and Thomas Jefferson after both had retired from public life. Interesting and also moving, for the two men had become estranged during the late 1790s, when Adams thought Jefferson had helped to undermine his unhappy presidency, and when Jefferson thought Adams had been seduced by the idea of monarchy. For many years afterward there was almost no communication between them. In 1812, through the mediation of Dr. Benjamin Rush, who acted at Jefferson's request, the two renewed a correspondence that lasted up to their all but simultaneous deaths on July 4, 1826. Of their many letters, Adams' are perhaps the more remarkable, and the more important for his reputation. Except on the count of generosity, Jefferson could add little to his own fame with a pen that had already expressed itself fully in thousands of letters to others. But nowhere else did Adams so clearly reveal the variety of his tough, sharp mind, or show that he was by no means lacking, as he is often supposed to have been, in a dry but distinct Puritan wit. The conflicting views on aristocracy represented in the following letters of 1813 are all the more interesting in that they are illustrative of a deep division in American thought.

Source: C. F. Adams, X, pp. 49-52, 58-59, 64-65.
H. A. Washington, VI, pp. 221-228, 254-260.

I.

John Adams to Thomas Jefferson July 9

I RECOLLECT, near thirty years ago, to have said carelessly to you that I wished I could find time and means to write something upon aristocracy. You seized upon the idea and encouraged me to do it with all that friendly warmth that is natural and habitual to you. I soon began, and have been writing on that subject ever since. I have been so unfortunate as never to be able to make myself understood.

Your [aristocrats] are the most difficult animals to manage of anything in the whole theory and practice of government. They will not suffer themselves to be governed. They not only exert all their own subtlety, industry, and courage but they employ the commonalty to knock to pieces every plan and model that the most honest architects in legislation can invent to keep them within bounds. Both patricians and plebians are as furious as the workmen in England to demolish laborsaving machinery.

But who are these *aristoi*? Who shall judge? Who shall select these choice spirits from the rest of the congregation? Themselves? We must first find out and determine who themselves are. Shall the congregation choose? Ask Xenophon; perhaps hereafter I may quote you Greek. Too much in a hurry at present, English must suffice. Xenophon says that the ecclesia always chooses the worst men they can find because none others will do their dirty work. This wicked motive is worse than birth or wealth. Here I want to quote Greek again.

But the day before I received your letter of June 27, I gave the book to George Washington Adams, going to the academy at Hingham. The title is *Formation of Character*, a collection of moral sentences from all the most ancient Greek poets. In one of the oldest of them, I read in Greek that I cannot repeat a couplet, the sense of which was: "Nobility in men is worth as much as it is in horses, asses, or rams; but the meanest blooded puppy in the world, if he gets a little money, is as good a man as the best of them." Yet birth and wealth together have prevailed over virtue and talents in all ages. The many will acknowledge no other *aristoi*.

Your experience of this truth will not much differ from that of your old friend.

II.

Adams to Jefferson, August

Has science, or morals, or philosophy, or criticism, or Christianity advanced, or improved, or enlightened mankind upon this subject and shown them that the idea of the "well-born" is a prejudice, a phantom, a point-no-point, a Cape Fly-away, a dream?

I say it is the ordinance of God Almighty in the constitution of human nature and wrought into the fabric of the universe. Philosophers and politicians may nibble and quibble but they never will get rid of it. Their only resource is to control it. Wealth is another monster to be subdued. Hercules could not subdue both or either. To subdue them by regular approaches, and strong fortifications by a regular siege was not my object in writing on aristocracy, as I proposed to you in Grosvenor Square. If you deny any one of these positions, I will prove them to demonstration by examples drawn from your own Virginia, and from every other state in the Union, and from the history of every nation, civilized and savage, from all we know of the time of the Creation of the world. . . .

We may call this sentiment a prejudice, because we can give what names we please to such things as we please; but in my opinion it is a part of the natural history of man, and politicians and philosophers may as well project to make the animal live without bones or blood as society can pretend to establish a free government without attention to it.

III.

Adams to Jefferson, September 2

Now, my friend, who are the *aristoi?* Philosophers may answer, "the wise and good." But the world, mankind, have, by their practice, always answered, "the rich, the beautiful, and well-born." And philosophers themselves, in marrying their children, prefer the rich, the handsome, and the well-descended to the wise and good.

What chance have talents and virtues in competition with wealth and birth and beauty? . . .

> One truth is clear, by all the world
> confessed,
> Slow rises worth, by poverty oppressed.

The five pillars of aristocracy are beauty, wealth, birth, genius, and virtue. Any one of the three first can, at any time, overbear any one or both of the two last.

Let me ask again what a wave of public

opinion, in favor of birth, has been spread over the globe by Abraham, by Hercules, by Mohammed, by Guelphs, Ghibellines, Bourbons, and a miserable Scottish chief Stuart? By Genghis Khan, by, by, by a million others. And what a wave will be spread by Napoleon and by Washington? Their remotest cousins will be sought and will be proud and will avail themselves of their descent. Call this principle prejudice, folly, ignorance, baseness, slavery, stupidity, adulation, superstition, or what you will, I will not contradict you. But the fact in natural, moral, political, and domestic history I cannot deny or dispute or question.

And is this great fact in the natural history of man, this unalterable principle of morals, philosophy, policy, domestic felicity, and daily experience from the Creation to be overlooked, forgotten, neglected, or hypocritically waved out of sight by a legislator? By a professed writer upon civil government and upon constitution of civil government?

IV.

Jefferson to Adams, October 28

I AGREE WITH YOU that there is a natural aristocracy among men. The grounds of this are virtue and talents. Formerly, bodily powers gave place among the *aristoi.* But since the invention of gunpowder has armed the weak as well as the strong with missile death, bodily strength, like beauty, good humor, politeness, and other accomplishments, has become but an auxiliary ground of distinction.

There is also an artificial aristocracy, founded on wealth and birth, without either virtue or talents; for with these it would belong to the first class. The natural aristocracy I consider as the most precious gift of nature, for the instruction, the trusts, and government of society. And, indeed, it would have been inconsistent in Creation to have formed man for the social state and not to have provided virtue and wisdom enough to manage the concerns of the society. May we not even say that that form of government is the best which provides the most effectually for a pure selection of these natural *aristoi* into the offices of government? The artificial aristocracy is a mischievous ingredient in government, and provision should be made to prevent its ascendancy.

On the question, What is the best provision? you and I differ; but we differ as rational friends, using the free exercise of our own reason and mutually indulging its errors. You think it best to put the *pseudo-aristoi* into a separate chamber of legislation, where they may be hindered from doing mischief by their coordinate branches, and where also they may be a protection to wealth against the agrarian and plundering enterprises of the majority of the people. I think that to give them power in order to prevent them from doing mischief is arming them for it and increasing instead of remedying the evil. For if the coordinate branches can arrest their action, so may they that of the coordinates. Mischief may be done negatively as well as positively. Of this, a cabal in the Senate of the United States has furnished many proofs. Nor do I believe them necessary to protect the wealthy, because enough of these will find their way into every branch of the legislation to protect themselves. From fifteen to twenty legislatures of our own, in action for thirty years past, have proved that no fears of an equalization of property are to be apprehended from them. *I* think the best remedy is exactly that provided by all our constitutions: to leave to the citizens the free election and separation of the *aristoi* from the *pseudo-aristoi,* of the wheat from the chaff. In general they will elect the real good and wise. In some instances, wealth may corrupt and birth blind them, but not in sufficient degree to endanger the society.

It is probable that our difference of opinion may, in some measure, be produced by a difference of character in those among whom we live. From what I have seen of Massachusetts and Connecticut myself, and still more from what I have heard, and the character given of the former by yourself who know them so much better, there seems to be in those two states a traditionary reverence for certain families which has rendered the offices of the government nearly hereditary in those families. I presume that, from an early period of your history, members of those families happening to possess virtue and talents have honestly exercised them for the good of the people and by their services have endeared their names to them. In coupling Connecticut with you, I mean it politically only, not morally. For having made the Bible the common law of their land, they seemed to have modeled their morality on the story of Jacob and Laban. But although this hereditary succession to office with you may, in some degree, be founded in real family merit, yet in a much higher degree it has proceeded from your strict alliance of church and state. These families are canonized in the eyes of the people on common principles, "You tickle me, and I will tickle you." In Virginia we have nothing of this.

Our clergy, before the Revolution, having been secured against rivalship by fixed salaries, did not give themselves the trouble of acquiring influence over the people. Of wealth, there were great accumulations in particular families, handed down from generation to generation, under the English law of entails. But the only object of ambition for the wealthy was a seat in the king's council. All their court then was paid to the crown on its creatures; and they Philipized [were a fifth column] in all collisions between the king and the people. Hence they were unpopular; and that unpopularity continues attached to their names. A Randolph, a Carter, or a Burwell must have great personal superiority over a common competitor to be elected by the people even at this day.

At the first session of our legislature after the Declaration of Independence, we passed a law abolishing entails. And this was followed by one abolishing the privilege of primogeniture and dividing the lands of intestates equally among all their children or other representatives. These laws, drawn by myself, laid the ax to the foot of pseudo-aristocracy. And had another which I prepared been adopted by the legislature, our work would have been complete. It was a bill for the more general diffusion of learning. This proposed to divide every country into wards of five or six miles square, like your townships; to establish in each ward a free school for reading, writing, and common arithmetic; to provide for the annual selection of the best subjects from these schools, who might receive, at the public expense, a higher degree of education at a district school; and from these district schools to select a certain number of the most promising subjects, to be completed at an university, where all the useful sciences should be taught. Worth and genius would thus have been sought out from every condition of life and completely prepared by education for defeating the competition of wealth and birth for public trusts. My proposition had, for a further object, to impart to these wards those portions of self-government for which they are best qualified, by confiding to them the care of their poor, their roads, police, elections, the nomination of jurors, administration of justice in small cases, elementary exercises of militia; in short, to have made them little republics, with a warden at the head of each, for all those concerns which, being under their eye, they would better manage than the larger republics of the county or state. A general call of ward meetings by their wardens on the same day through the state would at any time produce the genuine sense of the people on any required point and would enable the state to act in mass, as your people have so often done, and with so much effect by their town meetings.

The law for religious freedom, which made a part of this system, having put down the aristocracy of the clergy, and restored to the citizen the freedom of the mind, and those of entails and descents nurturing an equality of condition among them, this on education would have raised the mass of the people to the high ground of moral respectability necessary to their own safety and to orderly government and would have completed the great object of qualifying them to select the veritable *aristoi* for the trusts of government, to the exclusion of the pseudalists; and the same Theognis who has furnished the epigraphs of your two letters assures us that "good men never destroyed any state." Although this law has not yet been acted on but in a small and inefficient degree, it is still considered as before the legislature, with other bills of the revised code, not yet taken up, and I have great hope that some patriotic spirit will, at a favorable moment, call it up and make it the keystone of the arch of our government.

With respect to aristocracy, we should further consider that, before the establishment of the American states, nothing was known to history but the man of the Old World, crowded within limits either small or overcharged and steeped in the vices which that situation generates. A government adapted to such men would be one thing; but a very different one than that for the man of these states. Here everyone may have land to labor for himself, if he chooses; or, preferring the exercise of any other industry, may exact for it such compensation as not only to afford a comfortable subsistence but wherewith to provide for a cessation from labor in old age.

Everyone, by his property, or by his satisfactory situation, is interested in the support of law and order. And such men may safely and advantageously reserve to themselves a wholesome control over their public affairs, and a degree of freedom which, in the hands of the canaille [rabble] of the cities of Europe, would be instantly perverted to the demolition and destruction of everything public and private. The history of the last 25 years of France, and of the last 40 years in America, nay, of its last 200 years, proves the truth of both parts of this observation.

But even in Europe a change has sensibly taken place in the mind of man. Science had liberated the ideas of those who read and reflect, and the American example had kindled feelings of right in the people. An insurrection has consequently begun of science, talents, and courage against rank and birth, which have fallen into contempt. It has failed in its first effort, because the mobs of the cities, the instrument used for its accomplishment, debased by ignorance, poverty, and vice, could not be restrained to rational action. But the world will recover from the panic of this first catastrophe. Science is progressive, and talents and enterprise on the alert.

Resort may be had to the people of the country, a more governable power from their principles and subordination; and rank, and birth, and tinsel-aristocracy will finally shrink into insignificance even there. This, however, we have no right to meddle with. It suffices for us if the moral and physical condition of our own citizens qualifies them to select the able and good for the direction of their government with a recurrence of elections at such short periods as will enable them to displace an unfaithful servant before the mischief he meditates may be irremediable.

I have thus stated my opinion on a point on which we differ, not with a view to controversy, for we are both too old to change opinions which are the result of a long life of inquiry and reflection, but on the suggestions of a former letter of yours that we ought not to die before we have explained ourselves to each other. We acted in perfect harmony through a long and perilous contest for our liberty and independence. A constitution has been acquired, which, though neither of us thinks perfect, yet both consider as competent to render our fellow citizens the happiest and the securest on whom the sun has ever shone. If we do not think exactly alike as to imperfections, it matters little to our country which, after devoting to it long lives of disinterested labor, we have delivered over to our successors in life, who will be able to take care of it and of themselves.

Of the pamphlet on aristocracy which has been sent to you, or who may be its author, I have heard nothing but through your letter. If the person you suspect, it may be known from the quaint, mystical, and hyperbolical ideas involved in affected, newfangled, and pedantic terms which stamp his writings. Whatever it be, I hope your quiet is not to be affected at this day by the rudeness or intemperance of scribblers; but that you may continue in tranquillity to live and to rejoice in the prosperity of our country, until it shall be your own wish to take your seat among the *aristoi* who have gone before you.

V.

Adams to Jefferson, November 15

I CANNOT APPEASE my melancholy commiseration for our armies in this furious snowstorm in any way so well as by studying your letter of Oct. 28.

We are now explicitly agreed upon one important point, viz., that there is a natural aristocracy among men, the grounds of which are virtue and talents. You very justly indulge a little merriment upon this solemn subject of aristocracy. I often laugh at it too, for there is nothing in this laughable world more ridiculous than the management of it by all the nations of the earth; but while we smile, mankind have reason to say to us, as the frogs said to the boys, what is sport to you are wounds and death to us. When I consider the weakness, the folly, the pride, the vanity, the selfishness, the artifice, the low craft and mean cunning, the want of principle, the avarice, the unbounded ambition, the unfeeling cruelty of a majority of those (in all nations) who are allowed an aristocratical influence, and, on the other hand, the stupidity with which the more numerous multitude not only become their dupes but even love to be taken in by their tricks, I feel a stronger disposition to weep at their destiny than to laugh at their folly. But though we have agreed in one point, in words, it is not yet certain that we are perfectly agreed in sense.

Fashion has introduced an indeterminate use of the word talents. Education, wealth, strength, beauty, stature, birth, marriage, graceful attitudes and motions, gait, air, complexion, physiognomy are talents, as well as genius, science, and learning. Any one of these talents that in fact commands or influences two votes in society gives to the man who possesses it the character of an aristocrat, in my sense of the word. Pick up the first hundred men you meet and make a republic. Every man will have an equal vote; but when deliberations and discussions are opened, it will be found that twenty-five, by their talents, virtues being equal, will be able to carry fifty votes. Every one of these twenty-five is an aristocrat in my sense of the word; whether he obtains his one vote in addition to his own by his birth, fortune, figure, eloquence, science, learning, craft, cunning, or even his character for good fellowship and a *bon vivant.*

What gave Sir William Wallace his amazing aristocratical superiority? His strength. What gave Mrs. Clark her aristocratical influence to create generals, admirals, and bishops? Her beauty. What gave Pompadour and Du Barry the power of making cardinals and popes? And I have lived for years in the Hotel de Valentinois with Franklin, who had as many virtues as any of them. In the investigation of the meaning of the word "talents," I could write 630 pages as pertinent as John Taylor's of Hazlewood; but I will select a single example, for female aristocrats are nearly as formidable as males.

A daughter of a greengrocer walks the streets in London daily with a basket of cabbage sprouts, dandelions, and spinach on her head. She is observed by the painters to have a beautiful face, an elegant figure, a graceful step, and a debonairness. They hire her to sit. She complies, and is painted by forty artists in a circle around her. The scientific Dr. William Hamilton outbids the painters, sends her to school for a genteel education, and marries her. This lady not only causes the triumphs of the Nile, Copenhagen, and Trafalgar but separates Naples from France and finally banishes the King and Queen from Sicily. Such is the aristocracy of the natural talent of beauty. Millions of examples might be quoted from history, sacred and profane, from Eve, Hannah, Deborah, Susanna, Abigail, Judith, Ruth, down to Helen, Mrs. de Mainbenor, and Mrs. Fitzherbert. For mercy's sake, do not compel me to look to our chaste states and territories to find women, one of whom let go would, in the words of Holofernes' guards, deceive the whole earth.

The proverbs of Theognis, like those of Solomon, are observations on human nature, ordinary life, and civil society, with moral reflections on the facts. I quoted him as a witness of the fact that there was as much difference in the races of men as in the breeds of sheep, and as a sharp reprover and censurer of the sordid, mercenary practice of disgracing birth by preferring gold to it. Surely no authority can be more expressly in point to prove the existence of inequalities, not of rights but of moral, intellectual, and physical inequalities in families, descents, and generations. If a descent from pious, virtuous, wealthy, literary, or scientific ancestors is a letter of recommendation, or introduction in a man's favor, and enables him to influence only one vote in addition to his own, he is an aristocrat; for a democrat can have but one vote. Aaron Burr has 100,000 votes from the single circumstance of his descent from President Burr and President Edwards.

Your commentary on the proverbs of Theognis reminded me of two solemn characters — the one resembling John Bunyan, the other Scarron; the one John Torrey, the other Ben Franklin. Torrey, a poet, an enthusiast, a superstitious bigot, once very gravely asked my brother whether it would not be better for mankind if children were always begotten by religious motives only? Would not religion in this sad case have as little efficacy in encouraging procreation as it has now in discouraging it? I should apprehend a decrease of population, even in our country where it increases so rapidly.

In 1775, Franklin made a morning visit at Mrs. Yard's, to Sam Adams and John. He was unusually loquacious. "Man, a rational creature!" said Franklin. "Come, let us suppose a rational man. Strip him of all his appetites, especially his hunger and thirst. He is in his chamber, engaged in making experiments, or in pursuing some problem. He is highly entertained. At this moment a servant knocks. 'Sir, dinner is on the table.' 'Dinner! pox! pough! but what have you for dinner?' 'Ham and chickens.' 'Ham, and must I break the chain of my thoughts to go down and gnaw a morsel of damned hog's arse? Put aside your ham; I will dine tomorrow.' " Take away appetite and the present generation would not live a month, and no future generation would ever exist; and thus the exalted dignity of human nature would be annihilated and lost, and in my opinion the whole loss would be of no more importance than putting out a candle, quenching a torch, or crushing a firefly, if in this world we only have hope.

Your distinction between natural and artificial aristocracy does not appear to me founded. Birth and wealth are conferred upon some men as imperiously by nature as genius, strength, or beauty. The heir to honors and riches and power has often no more merit in procuring these advantages than he has in obtaining a handsome face or an elegant figure. When aristocracies are established by human laws, and honor, wealth, and power are made hereditary by municipal laws and political institutions, then I acknowledge artificial aristocracy to commence; but this never commences till corruption in elections become dominant and uncontrollable. But this artificial aristocracy can never last. The everlasting envies, jealousies, rivalries, and quarrels among them, their cruel rapacity upon the poor ignorant people, their followers, compel them to set up Caesar, a demagogue, to be a monarch, a master; *pour mettre chacun à sa place* [to put each one in his place].

Here you have the origin of all artificial aristocracy, which is the origin of all monarchies. And both artificial aristocracy and monarchy and civil, military, political, and hierarchical despotism have all grown out of the natural aristocracy of virtues and talents. We, to be sure, are far remote from this. Many hundred years must roll away before we shall be corrupted. Our pure, virtuous, public-spirited, federative republic will last forever, govern the globe, and introduce the perfection of man — his perfectibility being already proved by Price, Priestley, Condorcet, Rousseau, Diderot, and Godwin. Mischief has been done by the Senate of the United States. I have known and felt more of this mischief than Washington, Jefferson, and Madison all together. But this has been all caused by the constitutional power of the Senate, in executive business, which ought to be immediately, totally, and essentially abolished.

Your distinction between the *aristoi* and *pseudo-aristoi* will not help the matter. I would trust one as well as the other with unlimited power. The law wisely refuses an oath, as a witness in his own case, to the saint as well as the sinner. No romance would be more amusing than the history of your Virginian and our New England aristocratical families. Yet even in Rhode Island there has been no clergy, no church, and I had almost said no state, and some people say no religion. There has been a constant respect for certain old families. Fifty-seven or fifty-eight years ago, in company with Colonel, Counselor, Judge John Chandler, whom I have quoted before, a newspaper was brought in. The old sage asked me to look for the news from Rhode Island and see how the elections had gone there. I read the list of Wanbous, Watrous, Greens, Whipples, Malboues, etc. "I expected as much," said the aged gentleman, "for I have always been of opinion that in the most popular governments, the elections will generally go in favor of the most ancient families." To this day, when any of these tribes — and we may add Ellerys, Channings, Champlins, etc. — are pleased to fall in with the popular current, they are sure to carry all before them.

You suppose a difference of opinion between you and me on the subject of aristocracy. I can find none. I dislike and detest hereditary honors, offices, emoluments established by law. So do you. I am for excluding legal, hereditary distinctions from the United States as long as possible. So are you. I only say that mankind have not yet discovered any remedy against irresistible corruption in elections to offices of great power and profit but making them hereditary.

But will you say our elections are pure? Be it so, upon the whole; but do you recollect in history a more corrupt election than that of Aaron Burr to be President, or that of De Witt Clinton last year? By corruption here, I mean a sacrifice of every national interest and honor to private and party objects. I see the same spirit in Virginia that you and I see in Rhode Island and the rest of New England. In New York it is a struggle of family feuds — a feudal aristocracy. Pennsylvania is a contest between German, Irish, and old England families. When Germans and Irish unite they give 30,000 majorities. There is virtually a white rose and a red rose, a Caesar and a Pompey, in every state in this Union, and contests and dissensions will be as lasting. The rivalry of Bourbons and Noaillises produced the French Revolution, and a similar competition for consideration and influence exists and prevails in every village in the world.

Where will terminate the *rabies agri* [rage for land]? The continent will be scattered over with manors much larger than Livingston's, Van Renselaers', or Philips'; even our Deacon Strong will have a principality among you southern folk. What inequality of talents will be produced by these land jobbers! Where tends the mania of banks? At my table in Philadelphia I once proposed to you to unite in endeavors to obtain an amendment of the Constitution prohibiting to the separate states the power of creating banks, but giving Congress authority to establish one bank with a branch in each state, the whole limited to $10 million. Whether this project was wise or unwise, I know not, for I had deliberated little on it then and have never thought it worth thinking of since. But you spurned the proposition from you with disdain. This system of banks begotten, brooded, and hatched by Duer, Robert and Gouverneur Morris, Hamilton, and Washington I have always considered as a system of national injustice. A sacrifice of public and private interest to a few aristocratical friends and favorites.

My scheme could have had no such effect. Verres plundered temples and robbed a few rich men, but he never made such ravages among private property in general, nor swindled so much out of the pockets of the poor and middle class of people as these banks have done. No people but this would have borne the imposition so long. The people of Ireland would not bear Wood's halfpence. What inequalities of talent have been introduced into this country by these aristocratical banks! Our Winthrops, Winslows, Bradfords, Saltonstalls, Quinceys, Chandlers, Leonards, Hutchinsons, Olivers, Sewalls, etc., are precisely in the situation of your Randolphs, Carters, Burwells, and Harrisons. Some of them unpopular for the part they took in the late Revolution, but all respected for their names and connections; and whenever they fell in with the popular sentiments are preferred, *ceteris paribus,* to all others.

When I was young the *summum bonum* in Massachusetts was to be of worth £10,000 sterling, ride in a chariot, be colonel of a regiment of militia, and hold a seat in His Majesty's Council. No man's imagination aspired to anything higher beneath the skies. But these plums, chariots, colonelships, and counselorships are recorded and will never be forgotten. No great accumulations of land were made by our early settlers. Mr. Baudoin, a French refugee, made the first great purchases, and your General Dearborne, born under a fortunate star, is now enjoying a large portion of the aristocratical sweets of them. As I have no amanuenses but females, and there is so much about generation in this letter that I dare not ask any of them to copy it, and I cannot copy it myself, I must beg of you to return it to me.

81.

Thomas Jefferson: Isolation and Independence

Baron von Humboldt, the great German naturalist and physical geographer, corresponded with Thomas Jefferson over many years. Humboldt's conception of physical nature as an organic whole governing the development of human communities fitted well with Jefferson's conception of the frontier farmer as one who, if unimpeded by kings and priests (as in Europe), would create a new society in harmony with natural law. This letter of Jefferson's, written on December 6, 1813, expresses ideas similar to those that were proclaimed in the Monroe Doctrine ten years later.

Source: Ford, IX, pp. 430-433.

The livraison of your astronomical observations, and the sixth and seventh on the subject of New Spain, with the corresponding atlases, are duly received. . . . For these treasures of a learning so interesting to us, accept my sincere thanks.

I think it most fortunate that your travels in those countries were so timed as to make them known to the world in the moment they were about to become actors on its stage. That they will throw off their European dependence I have no doubt; but in what kind of government their revolution will end I am not so certain. History, I believe, furnishes no example of a priest-ridden people maintaining a free civil government. This marks the lowest grade of ignorance, of which their civil as well as religious leaders will always avail themselves for their own purposes.

The vicinity of New Spain to the United States, and their consequent intercourse, may furnish schools for the higher, and example for the lower, classes of their citizens. And Mexico, where we learn from you that men of science are not wanting, may revolutionize itself under better auspices than the Southern provinces. These last, I fear, must end in military despotisms. The different castes of their inhabitants, their mutual hatreds and jealousies, their profound ignorance and bigotry, will be played off by cunning leaders and each be made the instrument of enslaving others. But of all this you can best judge, for in truth we have little knowledge of them to be depended on, but through you. But in whatever governments they end, they will be *American* governments, no longer to be involved in the never-ceasing broils of Europe.

The European nations constitute a separate division of the globe; their localities make them part of a distinct system; they have a set of interests of their own in which it is our business never to engage ourselves. America has a hemisphere to itself. It must have its separate system of interests, which must not be subordinated to those of Europe. The insulated state in which nature has placed the American continent should so far avail it that no spark of war kindled in the other quarters of the globe should be wafted across the wide oceans which separate us from them. And it will be so.

In fifty years more, the United States alone will contain 50 million inhabitants, and fifty years are soon gone over. The peace of 1763 is within that period. I was then twenty years old, and of course remember well all the transactions of the war preceding it. And you will live to see the epoch now equally ahead of us; and the numbers which will then be spread over the other parts of the American hemisphere, catching long before that the principles of our portion of it, and concurring with us in the maintenance of the same system. You see how readily we run into ages beyond the grave; and even those of us to whom that grave is already opening its quiet bosom. I am anticipating events of which you will be the bearer to me in the Elysian fields fifty years hence.

You know, my friend, the benevolent plan we were pursuing here for the happiness of the aboriginal inhabitants in our vicinities. We spared nothing to keep them at peace with one another; to teach them agriculture and the rudiments of the most necessary arts, and to encourage industry by establishing among them separate property. In this way they would have been enabled to subsist and multiply on a moderate scale of landed possession. They would have mixed their blood with ours, and been amalgamated and identified with us within no distant period of time. On the commencement of our present war, we pressed on them the observance of peace and neutrality, but the interested and unprincipled policy of England has defeated all our labors for the salvation of these unfortunate people. They have seduced the greater part of the tribes within our neighborhood, to take up the hatchet against us; and the cruel massacres they have committed on the women and children of our frontier, taken by surprise, will oblige us now to pursue them to extermination or drive them to new seats beyond our reach.

Already we have driven their patrons and seducers into Montreal, and the opening season will force them to their last refuge, the walls of Quebec. We have cut off all possibility of intercourse and of mutual aid, and may pursue at our leisure whatever plan we find necessary to secure ourselves against the future effects of their savage and ruthless warfare. The confirmed brutalization, if not the extermination, of this race in our America is therefore to form an additional chapter in the English history of the same colored man in Asia, and of the brethren of their own color in Ireland, and wherever else Anglo-mercantile cupidity can find a twopenny interest in deluging the earth with human blood.

No ill luck stirring but what lights upon Uncle Sam's shoulders.

ANON., editorial, Troy (New York) *Post*, Sept. 7, 1813. The earliest known use of the phrase "Uncle Sam." There is a legend that the original Uncle Sam was Samuel Wilson, of Troy, an army contractor, b. 1766, d. 1854.

1814

82.

John Taylor: True and False Aristocracies

John Taylor of Virginia, known after the county in which he lived as John Taylor of Caroline, was the philosopher and theorist of Jeffersonian Republicanism. In a variety of political and economic writings he set forth the anti-Federalist principles of agrarian democracy and states' rights on which the Jeffersonian party was founded, but from which increasingly it drew away. The critic first of Hamilton and then of Chief Justice Marshall, Taylor consistently opposed what he regarded as usurpations of power by the federal government in his lifetime. Particularly did he protest the growth, as he believed was taking place, of an exploitive commercial class, which he held to be as dangerous to the body politic as a nobility or a priesthood. His Inquiry into the Principles and Policy of the Government of the United States, *from which the following excerpt is taken, is representative of him. It was regarded by the historian Charles Beard as "among the two or three really historic contributions to political science which have been produced in the United States." Though not published until 1814, the book was originally planned by Taylor as a reply to John Adams'* Defense of the Constitutions of Government of the United States, *which appeared in 1787-1788.*

Source: *An Inquiry into the Principles and Policy of the Government of the United States,* Fredericksburg, Va., 1814, Ch. 1: "Aristocracy."

It will be an effort of this essay to prove that the United States have refuted the ancient axiom "that monarchy, aristocracy, and democracy are the only elements of government," by planting theirs in moral principles, without any reference to those elements; and that by demolishing the barrier hitherto obstructing the progress of political science they have cleared the way for improvement.

Mr. Adams' system promises nothing. It tells us that human nature is always the same; that the art of government can never change; that it is contracted into three simple principles; and that mankind must . . . suffer the evils of one of these simple principles. . . .

Do the Americans recognize themselves in a group of Goths, Vandals, Italians, Turks, and Chinese? If not, man is not al ways morally the same. If man is not always morally the same, it is not true that he requires the same political regimen. And thence a conclusion of considerable weight follows, to overthrow the groundwork of Mr. Adams' system; for by proving, if he had proved it, that his system was proper for those men and those times, resorted to by him for its illustration, he proves that it is not proper for men and times of dissimilar moral characters and circumstances.

The traces of intellectual originality and diversity; the shades and novelties of the human character between the philosopher and the savage, between different countries, different governments, and different eras, exhibit a complexity which the politician and philologist have never been able to unravel. Out of this intellectual variety arises the impossibility of contriving one form of government suitable for every nation; and also the fact that human nature, instead of begetting one form constantly, demonstrates its moral capacity in the vast variety of its political productions. . . .

The position first presenting itself is "that an aristocracy is the work of nature" — a position equivalent to the antiquated doctrine "that a king is the work of God." A particular attention will be now paid to this point, because Mr. Adams' theory is entirely founded upon it.

Superior abilities constitute one among the enumerated causes of a natural aristocracy. This cause is evidently as fluctuating as knowledge and ignorance; and its capacity to produce aristocracy must depend upon this fluctuation. The aristocracy of superior abilities will be regulated by the extent of the space between knowledge and ignorance. As the space contracts or widens, it will be diminished or increased; and if aristocracy may be thus diminished, it follows that it may be thus destroyed.

No certain state of knowledge is a natural or unavoidable quality of man. As an intellectual or moral quality, it may be created, destroyed, and modified by human power. Can that which may be created, destroyed, and modified by human power be a natural and inevitable cause of aristocracy? It has been modified in an extent which Mr. Adams does not even compute, by the art of printing, discovered subsequently to almost the whole of the authorities which have convinced Mr. Adams that knowledge, or as he might have more correctly asserted, ignorance, was a cause of aristocracy.

The peerage of knowledge or abilities, in consequence of its enlargement by the effects of printing, can no longer be collected and controlled in the shape of a noble order or a legislative department. The great body of this peerage must remain scattered throughout every nation by the enjoyment of the benefit of the press. By endowing a small portion of it with exclusive rights and privileges, the indignation of this main body is excited. If this endowment should enable a nation to watch and control an inconsiderable number of that species of peerage produced by knowledge, it would also purchase the dissatisfaction of its numberless members unjustly excluded; and would be a system for defending a nation against imbecility and inviting aggression from strength, equivalent to a project for defeating an army by feasting its vanguard.

If this reasoning is correct, the collection of that species of natural aristocracy (as Mr. Adams calls it) produced by superior abilities into a legislative department for the purpose of watching and controlling it is now rendered impracticable, however useful it might have been at an era when the proportion between knowledge and ignorance was essentially different; and this impracticability is a strong indication of the radical inaccuracy of considering aristocracy as an inevitable natural law. The wisdom of uniting exclusive knowledge by exclusive privileges that it may be controlled by disunited ignorance is not considered as being a hy-

New Britain Museum of American Art

"Gentleman with Negro Attendant," painting by Ralph Earl

pothetical question, since this aristocratical knowledge cannot now exist.

Similar reasoning applies still more forcibly to the idea of nature's constituting aristocracy by means of exclusive virtue. Knowledge and virtue both fluctuate. A steady effect, from fluctuating causes, is morally and physically impossible. And yet Mr. Adams infers a natural aristocracy from the error that virtue and knowledge are in a uniform relation to vice and ignorance; sweeps away by it every human faculty for the attainment of temporal or eternal happiness; and overturns the efficacy of law to produce private or public moral rectitude.

Had it been true that knowledge and virtue were natural causes of aristocracy, no fact could more clearly have exploded Mr. Adams' system, or more unequivocally have dissented from the eulogy he bestows on the English form of government. Until knowledge and virtue shall become genealogical, they cannot be the causes of inheritable aristocracy; and its existence, without the aid of superior knowledge and virtue, is a positive refutation of the idea that nature creates aristocracy with these tools. . . .

From the tyranny of aristocracy, Mr. Adams takes refuge under the protection of a king, and considers him as so essentially the ally and protector of the people as positively to declare, that, "instead of the trite saying, 'no bishop, no king,' it would be a much more exact and important truth to say, no people, no king, and no king, no people; meaning, by the word king, a first magistrate, possessed exclusively of executive power."

Throughout his system, Mr. Adams infers a necessity for a king, or (what is the same thing) of a "first magistrate, possessed exclusively of executive power," from the certainty of a natural aristocracy. But if aristocracy is artificial and not natural, it may be prevented by detecting the artifice, and by preventing aristocracy (the only cause for a king), the king himself becomes useless. His utility, according to Mr. Adams' system, consists in checking aristocratical power; but if no such power naturally exists, it would evidently be absurd to create a scourge (as Mr. Adams allows it to be) merely as a cause for a king. . . .

Admitting monarchy to be an evil, the ratio of the evil must be increased or diminished by its quantity, and it was evidently the comparative interest of the people to diminish the number of kings for the sake of contracting the oppressions of monarchy. In England, one king would be less mischievous than one hundred. This motive actuated the people to assist the great king to destroy the little kings; and ambition, not the popular interest, induced the great king to avail himself of this assistance.

But when the petty monarchies, which had excited the jealousy and produced the coalition of one king and the people, were destroyed, this jealousy transferred itself to the allies. Having acquired a complete victory, they became objects of danger to each other and resorted to mutual precautions. Representation, invented by the Crown to destroy the barons, was used by the people against the Crown; and is now used by the

Crown against the people. The conquered nobility, reduced from sovereigns to subjects, became the chief disciples of royal patronage; and having lost the power of annoying the king, revenged itself upon the people by uniting with the king to annoy them.

The result we obtain from this short history is that noble orders, divested of royalties and reduced to the degree of subjects, are the instruments of kings; but that such orders, chiefs of clans, and possessed of dominions are inimical to a monarchy sufficiently powerful to suppress their own. Thus these phenomena are reconciled, and the alliance between kings and nobles, in some cases, and their enmity, in others, accounted for. When the reasons inducing kings to destroy barons and to create lords are understood, the interest of the people to aid them in the first work and to oppose them in the second will be discerned. And Mr. Adams' system must sustain the shock of admitting that a king cannot be a good remedy against the evils of any species of aristocracy, created by himself for an instrument not for a check of monarchical power. . . .

Reader, pause and recollect several of the ingredients compounding aristocracy in the opinion of Mr. Adams. Do you behold them in the English peerage? Do you behold an exclusive mass of virtue, almost inducing you to exclaim "these are the sons of the Gods?" Do you behold an exclusive mass of talents compelling you to acknowledge "that these are sages qualified to govern?" Do you behold an exclusive mass of wealth, purchasing and converting into armies, clients, and followers? Or do you behold a band of warriors, inured to hardships, skilled in war, and inspiring fear and love? Truth compels you to acknowledge that you cannot discern a solitary particle of these qualities so essential to aristocracy according to Mr. Adams. And will you, against an acknowledgment which you cannot withhold, concur with Mr. Adams in believing that such a body of men as the English nobility ought to be placed in a legislative branch, that it may be guarded by a king and a House of Commons? . . .

And yet Mr. Adams has written three volumes to excite our jealousy against the aristocracy of motto and blazon, without disclosing the danger from the aristocracy of paper and patronage; that political hydra of modern invention whose arms embrace a whole nation, whose ears hear every sound, whose eyes see all objects, and whose hands can reach every purse and every throat. . . .

We are ready to acknowledge that extraordinary virtue, talents, and wealth, united, will govern and ought to govern; and yet it is denied that this concession is reconcilable with the system of King, Lords, and Commons. If a body of men which possesses the virtue, talents, and wealth of a nation ought to govern, it follows that a body of men which does not possess these attributes ought not to govern. . . .

Having thus conceded to Mr. Adams that wherever a few possess the mass of the renown, virtue, talents, and wealth of a nation that they will become an aristocracy, and probably ought to do so, it would be a concession, strictly reciprocal, to admit that wherever no such body is to be found an aristocracy ought not to be created by legal assignments of wealth and poverty. . . .

Talents and virtue are now so widely distributed as to have rendered a monopoly of either, equivalent to that of antiquity, impracticable; and if an aristocracy ought to have existed while it possessed such a monopoly, it ought not also to exist because this monopoly is irretrievably lost. The distribution of wealth produced by commerce and alienation is equal to that of knowledge and virtue produced by printing; but as the first distribution might be artificially counteracted, with a better prospect of success than the latter, aristocracy has abandoned a reliance on a monopoly of virtue, renown, and abilities, and resorted wholly to a monopoly of wealth by the system of paper and patronage. Modern taxes and frauds to collect money, and not ancient authors, will, therefore, afford the best evidence of its present character. . . .

Whenever the mass of wealth, virtue, and talents is lost by a few and transferred to a great portion of a nation, an aristocracy no longer retains the only sanctions of its claim; and wherever these sanctions deposit themselves, they carry the interwoven power. By spreading themselves so generally throughout a nation as to be no longer compressible into a legislative chamber, or inheritable by the aid of perpetuity and superstition, these ancient sanctions of aristocracy become the modern sanctions of public opinion. And as its will (now the rightful sovereign upon the selfsame principle, urged in favor of the best-founded aristocracy) can no longer be obtained through the medium of a hereditary order, the American invention of applying the doctrine of responsibility to magistrates is the only one yet discovered for effecting the same object which was effected by an aristocracy, holding the mass of national virtue, talents, and wealth. This mass, governed through such an aristocracy; this mass cannot now govern through any aristocracy; this mass has searched for a new organ as a medium for exercising the sovereignty to which it is on all sides allowed to be entitled — and this medium is representation.

When the principles and practice of the American policy come to be considered, one subject of inquiry will be whether public opinion, or the declaration of the mass of national virtue, talents, and wealth, will be able to exercise this its just sovereignty in union with the system of paper and patronage. . . .

It is not the mode by which this is effected but the effect which causes oppression. It is the same thing to a nation whether it is subjected to the will of a minority by superstition, conquest, or patronage and paper. Whether this end is generated by error, by force, or by fraud, the interest of the nation is invariably sacrificed to the interest of the minority.

If the oppressions of the aristocracies of the first and second ages arose from the power obtained by minorities, how has it happened that a nation which has rejoiced in their downfall should be joyfully gliding back into the same policy? How happens it that, while religious frauds are no longer rendered sacred by calling them oracles, political fraud should be sanctified by calling it national credit? Experience, it is agreed, has exploded the promises of oracles; does it not testify also to those of paper stock?

Paper stock always promises to defend a nation and always flees from danger. America and France saved themselves by physical power after danger had driven paper credit out of the field. In America, so soon as the danger disappeared, paper credit loudly boasted of its capacity to defend nations, and, though a deserter, artfully reaped the rewards due to the conqueror. . . .

Whatever destroys a unity of interest between a government and a nation infallibly produces oppression and hatred. Human conception is unable to invent a scheme more capable of afflicting mankind with these evils than that of paper and patronage. It divides a nation into two groups, creditors and debtors; the first supplying its want of physical strength by alliances with fleets and armies, and practising the most unblushing corruption. A consciousness of inflicting or suffering injuries fills each with malignity toward the other. This malignity first begets a multitude of penalties, punishments, and executions, and then vengeance.

A legislature, in a nation where the system of paper and patronage prevails, will be governed by that interest and legislate in its favor. It is impossible to do this without legislating to the injury of the other interest, that is, the great mass of the nation. Such a legislature will create unnecessary offices that themselves or their relations may be endowed with them. They will lavish the revenue to enrich themselves. They will borrow for the nation that they may lend. They will offer lenders great profits that they may share in them. As grievances gradually excite national discontent, they will fix the yoke more securely by making it gradually heavier. And they will finally avow and maintain their corruption by establishing an irresistible standing army, not to defend the nation but to defend a system for plundering the nation.

A uniform deception resorted to by a funding system, through legislative bodies, unites with experience in testifying to its uniform corruption of legislatures. It professes that its object is to pay debts. A government must either be the fraudulent instrument of the system or the system a fraudulent instrument of a government, or it would not utter this falsehood to deceive the people. This promise is similar to that of protecting property. It promises to diminish, and accumulates; it promises to protect, and invades. All political oppressors deceive in order to succeed. When did an aristocracy avow its purpose? . . .

A nation exposed to a paroxysm of conquering rage has infinitely the advantage of one subjected to this aristocratical system. One is local and temporary; the other is spread by law and perpetual. One is an open robber who warns you to defend yourself; the other, a sly thief who empties your pockets under a pretense of paying your debts. One is a pestilence, which will end of itself; the other, a climate deadly to liberty.

After an invasion, suspended rights may be resumed, ruined cities rebuilt, and past cruelties forgotten; but in the oppressions of the aristocracy of paper and patronage, there can be no respite. So long as there is anything to get, it cannot be glutted with wealth; so long as there is anything to fear,

Peabody Museum of Salem

Portrait of Elias Hasket Derby by J. Frothingham

it cannot be glutted with power; other tyrants die, this is immortal. . . .

The only two modes extant of enslaving nations are those of armies and the system of paper and patronage. The European nations are subjected by both, so that their chains are doubly riveted. The Americans devoted their effectual precautions to the obsolete modes of title and hierarchy, erected several barriers against the army mode, and utterly disregarded the mode of paper and patronage. The army mode was thought so formidable that military men are excluded from legislatures and limited to charters or commissions at will; and the paper mode so harmless that it is allowed to break the principle of keeping legislative, executive, and judicative powers separate and distinct, to infuse itself into all these departments, to unite them in one conspiracy, and to obtain charters or commissions for unrestricted terms, entrenched behind public faith and out of the reach, it is said, of national will; which it may assail, wound, and destroy with impunity. . . .

Thus, while a paper system pretends to make a nation rich and potent, it only makes a minority of that nation rich and potent at the expense of the majority, which it makes poor and impotent. Wealth makes a nation, a faction, or an individual powerful; and, therefore, if paper systems extracted the wealth they accumulate from the winds and not from property and labor, they would still be inimical to the principles of every constitution founded in the idea of national will; because the subjection of a nation to the will of individuals or factions is an invariable effect of great accumulation of wealth. But when the accumulation of a minority impoverishes a majority, a double operation doubly rivets this subjection. . . .

Hereditary aristocracy, supported by perpetuities, is preferable to a paper and patronage aristocracy because its taxation would be less oppressive, since its landed estate would furnish it with opulence and power; whereas eternal and oppressive taxation is necessary to supply the aristocracy of paper and patronage with these vital qualities.

83.

THOMAS JEFFERSON: On the Censorship of Religious Books

Behind Jefferson's insistence on the freedom of religious expression lay his more general belief that all censorship was unwise. False theories, he felt, would wither and die if exposed to the light of day, and the only real effect of censorship was to make attractive books that otherwise would be ignored or soon forgotten. The following letter of April 19, 1814, was written by Jefferson to his bookseller, N. G. Dufief, in Philadelphia, where the civil authorities had prevented the sale of a book on the origin of the world.

Source: H. A. Washington, VI, pp. 339-341.

YOUR FAVOR OF THE 6TH instant is just received, and I shall with equal willingness and truth state the degree of agency you had respecting the copy of M. de Becourt's book, which came to my hands. That gentleman informed me by letter that he was about to publish a volume in French, *Sur la Création du monde, un systeme d'organisation primitive,* which its title promised to be either a geological or astronomical work. I subscribed, and, when published, he sent me a copy; and as you were my correspondent in the book line in Philadelphia, I took the liberty of desiring him to call on you for the price, which, he afterwards informed me, you were so kind as to pay him for me, being, I believe, $2.00. But the sole copy which came to me was from himself directly and, as far as I know, was never seen by you.

I am really mortified to be told that, in the United States of America, a fact like this can become a subject of inquiry, and of criminal inquiry too, as an offense against religion; that a question about the sale of a book can be carried before the civil magistrate. Is this then our freedom of religion? And are we to have a censor whose imprimatur shall say what books may be sold and what we may buy? And who is thus to dogmatize religious opinions for our citizens? Whose foot is to be the measure to which ours are all to be cut or stretched? Is a priest to be our inquisitor, or shall a layman, simple as ourselves, set up his reason as the rule for what we are to read and what we must believe? It is an insult to our citizens to question whether they are rational beings or not, and blasphemy against religion to suppose it cannot stand the test of truth and reason.

If M. de Becourt's book be false in its facts, disprove them; if false in its reasoning, refute it. But, for God's sake, let us freely hear both sides if we choose. I know little of its contents, having barely glanced over here and there a passage and over the table of contents. From this, the Newtonian philosophy seemed the chief object of attack, the issue of which might be trusted to the strength of the two combatants, Newton certainly not needing the auxiliary arm of the government, and still less the holy Author of our religion, as to what in it concerns Him. I thought the work would be very innocent and one which might be confided to the reason of any man; not likely to be much read if let alone, but, if persecuted, it will be generally read. Every man in the United States will think it a duty to buy a copy in vindication of his right to buy and to read what he pleases. I have just been reading the new constitution of Spain. One of its fundamental bases is expressed in these words: "The Roman Catholic religion, the only true one is, and always shall be, that of the Spanish nation. The government protects it by wise and just laws, and prohibits the exercise of any other whatever." Now I wish this presented to those who question what you may sell or we may buy, with a request to strike out the words "Roman Catholic" and to insert the denomination of their own religion.

This would ascertain the code of dogmas which each wishes should domineer over the opinions of all others, and be taken, like the Spanish religion, under the "protection of wise and just laws." It would show to what they wish to reduce the liberty for which one generation has sacrificed life and happiness. It would present our boasted freedom of religion as a thing of theory only and not of practice, as what would be a poor exchange for the theoretic thralldom but practical freedom of Europe. But it is impossible that the laws of Pennsylvania, which set us the first example of the wholesome and happy effects of religious freedom, can permit the inquisitorial functions to be proposed to their courts. Under them you are surely safe.

At the date of yours of the 6th, you had not received mine of the 3rd instant asking a copy of an edition of Newton's *Principia,* which I had seen advertised. When the cost of that shall be known, it shall be added to the balance of $4.93 and incorporated with a larger remittance I have to make to Philadelphia. Accept the assurance of my great esteem and respect.

Now I lay me down to sleep,
I pray thee, Lord, my soul to keep;
If I should die before I wake,
I pray thee, Lord, my soul to take.

New England Primer, 1814

84.

THOMAS JEFFERSON: Elementary, General, and Professional Schools

"Enlighten the people, generally," wrote Jefferson in 1816, "and tyranny and oppressions of both mind and body will vanish like evil spirits at the dawn of day." To the ideal expressed in these words, Jefferson devoted himself throughout his life, but especially during the years of his retirement. From 1814, when he was appointed a trustee of Albemarle Academy, until 1825, when the University of Virginia opened under his rectorship, he worked indefatigably to produce a practical plan for a state-supported educational system. His famous letter to Peter Carr, written September 7, 1814, marks the beginning of these efforts. The letter was first published in the Richmond Enquirer.

Source: *Early History of the University of Virginia as Contained in the Letters of Thomas Jefferson and Joseph C. Cobell,* Richmond, 1856, pp. 384-390.

ON THE SUBJECT of the academy or college proposed to be established in our neighborhood, I promised the trustees that I would prepare for them a plan, adapted, in the first instance, to our slender funds, but susceptible of being enlarged either by their own growth or by accession from other quarters.

I have long entertained the hope that this, our native state, would take up the subject of education and make an establishment, either with or without incorporation into that of William and Mary, where every branch of science deemed useful at this day should be taught in its highest degree. With this view, I have lost no occasion of making myself acquainted with the organization of the best seminaries in other countries, and with the opinions of the most enlightened individuals on the subject of the sciences worthy of a place in such an institution. In order to prepare what I have promised our trustees, I have lately revised these several plans with attention; and I am struck with the diversity of arrangement observable in them — no two alike.

Yet I have no doubt that these several arrangements have been the subject of mature reflection by wise and learned men, who, contemplating local circumstances, have adapted them to the condition of the section of society for which they have been framed. I am strengthened in this conclusion by an examination of each separately, and a conviction that no one of them, if adopted without change, would be suited to the circumstances and pursuit of our country. The example they have set, then, is authority for us to select from their different institutions the materials which are good for us, and, with them, to erect a structure whose arrangement shall correspond with our own social condition and shall admit of enlargement in proportion to the encouragement it may merit and receive. . . .

In the first place, we must ascertain with precision the object of our institution, by taking a survey of the general field of science and marking out the portion we mean to occupy at first and the ultimate extension of our views beyond that, should we be enabled to render it, in the end, as comprehensive as we would wish.

Elementary Schools. It is highly interesting

to our country and it is the duty of its functionaries to provide that every citizen in it should receive an education proportioned to the condition and pursuits of his life. The mass of our citizens may be divided into two classes — the laboring and the learned. The laboring will need the first grade of education to qualify them for their pursuits and duties; the learned will need it as a foundation for further acquirements. A plan was formerly proposed to the legislature of this state for laying off every county into hundreds or wards of five or six miles square, within each of which should be a school for the education of the children of the ward, wherein they should receive three years' instruction gratis in reading, writing, arithmetic as far as fractions, the roots and ratios, and geography. The legislature, at one time, tried an ineffectual expedient for introducing this plan which, having failed, it is hoped they will someday resume it in a more promising form.

General Schools. At the discharging of the pupils from the elementary schools, the two classes separate — those destined for labor will engage in the business of agriculture or enter into apprenticeships to such handicraft art as may be their choice; their companions, destined to the pursuits of science, will proceed to the college, which will consist first of general schools and second of professional schools. The general schools will constitute the second grade of education.

The learned class may still be subdivided into two sections; first, those who are destined for learned professions, as a means of livelihood; and second, the wealthy, who, possessing independent fortunes, may aspire to share in conducting the affairs of the nation or to live with usefulness and respect in the private ranks of life. Both of these sections will require instruction in all the higher branches of science; the wealthy to qualify them for either public or private life; the professional section will need those branches especially which are the basis of their future profession, and a general knowledge of the others as auxiliary to that and necessary to their standing and associating with the scientific class. All the branches, then, of useful science ought to be taught in the general schools to a competent extent, in the first instance. These sciences may be arranged into three departments, not rigorously scientific, indeed, but sufficiently so for our purposes. These are I, Language; II, Mathematics; III, Philosophy.

I. *Language.* In the first department I would arrange a distinct science: (1) languages and history, ancient and modern; (2) grammar; (3) belles lettres; (4) rhetoric and oratory; (5) a school for the deaf, dumb, and blind. History is here associated with languages not as a kindred subject but on a principle of economy, because both may be attained by the same course of reading, if books are selected with that view.

II. *Mathematics.* In the department of mathematics, I should give place distinctly to, (1) pure mathematics; (2) physico-mathematics; (3) physics; (4) chemistry; (5) natural history, *to wit:* mineralogy; (6) botany; and (7) zoology; (8) anatomy; (9) the theory of medicine.

III. *Philosophy.* In the philosophical department, I should distinguish (1) ideology; (2) ethics; (3) the law of nature and nations; (4) government; (5) political economy.

But, some of these terms being used by different writers in different degrees of extension, I shall define exactly what I mean to comprehend in each of them.

I. (3) Within the term of belles lettres I include poetry and composition generally, and criticism.

II. (1) I consider pure mathematics as the science of numbers, and measure in the abstract; that of numbers comprehending arithmetic, algebra, and fluxions; that of measure (under the general appellation of geometry) comprehending trigonometry, plane and spherical, conic sections, and transcendental curves.

II. (2) physico-mathematics treat of physical subjects by the aid of mathematical calculation. These are mechanics, statics, hydrostatics, hydrodynamics, navigation, astronomy, geography, optics, pneumatics, acoustics.

II. (3) physics, or natural philosophy (not entering the limits of chemistry), treat of natural substances, their properties, mutual relations, and action. They particularly examine the subjects of motion, action, magnetism, electricity, galvanism, light, meteorology, with an etc. not easily enumerated. These definitions and specifications render immaterial the question whether I use the generic terms in the exact degree of comprehension in which others use them; to be understood is all that is necessary to the present object.

Professional Schools. At the close of this course the students separate; the wealthy retiring, with a sufficient stock of knowledge, to improve themselves to any degree to which their views may lead them, and the professional section to the professional schools, constituting the third grade of education, and teaching the particular sciences which the individuals of this section mean to pursue with more minuteness and detail than was within the scope of the general schools for the second grade of instruction. In these professional schools each science is to be taught in the highest degree it has yet attained. They are to be the:

First Department, the fine arts, to wit: civil architecture, gardening, painting, sculpture, and the theory of music.

Second Department, architecture, military and naval; projectiles; rural economy (comprehending agriculture, horticulture, and veterinary), technical philosophy; the practice of medicine, materia medica; pharmacy and surgery. . . .

Third Department, theology and ecclesiastical history; law, municipal and foreign.

To these professional schools will come those who separated at the close of their first elementary course, to wit: the lawyer to the school of law; the ecclesiastic to that of theology and ecclesiastical history; the physician to those of the practice of medicine, materia medica, pharmacy, and surgery; the military man to that of military and naval architecture and projectiles; the agricultor to that of rural economy; the gentleman, the architect, the pleasure gardener, painter, and musician to the school of fine arts. And to that of technical philosophy will come the mariner, carpenter, shipwright, pump maker, clockmaker, machinist, optician, metallurgist, founder, cutler, druggist, brewer, vintner, distiller, dyer, painter, bleacher, soapmaker, tanner, powder maker, salt maker, glassmaker, to learn as much as shall be necessary to pursue their art understandingly, of the sciences of geometry, mechanics, statics, hydrostatics, hydraulics, hydrodynamics, navigation, astronomy, geography, optics, pneumatics, acoustics, physics, chemistry, natural history, botany, mineralogy, and pharmacy.

The school of technical philosophy will differ essentially in its functions from the other professional schools. The others are instituted to ramify and dilate the particular sciences taught in the schools of the second grade on a general scale only. The technical school is to abridge those which were taught there too much *in extenso* for the limited wants of the artificer or practical man. These artificers must be grouped together according to the particular branch of science in which they need elementary and practical instruction; and a special lecture or lectures should be prepared for each group — and these lectures should be given in the evening so as not to interrupt the labors of the day. The school, particularly, should be maintained wholly at the public expense on the same principles with that of the ward schools.

Through the whole of the collegiate course, at the hours of recreation on certain days, all the students should be taught the manual exercise; military evolutions and maneuvers should be under a standing organization as a military corps, and with proper officers to train and command them. . . .

On this survey of the field of science, I recur to the question, what portion of it we mark out for the occupation of our institution? With the first grade of education we shall have nothing to do. The sciences of the second grade are our first object, and to adapt them to our slender beginnings, we must separate them into groups comprehending many sciences each, and greatly more in the first instance than ought to be imposed on or can be competently conducted by a single professor permanently. They must be subdivided from time to time as our means increase, until each professor shall have no more under his care than he can attend to with advantage to his pupils and ease to himself.

In the further advance of our resources, the professional schools must be introduced, and professorships established for them also. For the present, we may group the sciences into professorships as follows, subject, however, to be changed according to the qualifications of the persons we may be able to engage.

I. Professorship.
Language and History, Ancient and Modern.
Belles Lettres, Rhetoric and Oratory.

II. Professorship.
Mathematics pure — Physico-Mathematics.
Physics — Anatomy — Medicine — Theory.

III. Professorship.
Chemistry — Zoology — Botany — Mineralogy.

IV. Professorship.
Philosophy.

The organization of the branch of the institution which respects its government, police and economy, depending on principles which have no affinity with those of its institution, may be the subject of separate and subsequent consideration.

85.

Francis Scott Key: "The Star-Spangled Banner"

Francis Scott Key, a young Baltimore lawyer, had been commissioned by the American government to secure the release of William Beanes, a well-known Maryland physician, who had been captured by the British as they were retreating from their attack on Washington in August 1814. Beanes's freedom was obtained, but Key himself was held for several days prior to a planned attack on Baltimore. Watching the bombardment of Fort McHenry from a British ship during the night of September 13-14, he waited for some sign of victory from his country or from the enemy. When at dawn he saw the American flag still waving over the fort, the excitement and emotional relief that Key felt compelled him to write the verses of "The Star-Spangled Banner." The poem was printed in the Baltimore Patriot *on September 20, under the title of "The Defence of Fort M'Henry," and was sung to the tune of the English song, "To Anacreon in Heaven," by an actor, Ferdinand Durang. The American Revolutionary song, "Adams and Liberty," had been sung to the same tune.*

Source: "The Star Spangled Banner," Revised and Enlarged from the "Report" on the Above and Other Airs, issued in 1909, by Oscar G. T. Sonneck, Washington, 1914.

THE STAR-SPANGLED BANNER

Oh, say, can you see, by the dawn's early light,
What so proudly we hailed at the twilight's last gleaming,
Whose broad stripes and bright stars through the perilous fight,
O'er the ramparts we watched were so gallantly streaming?
And the rockets' red glare, the bombs bursting in air,
Gave proof through the night that our flag was still there.
Oh, say, does that star-spangled banner yet wave
O'er the land of the free, and the home of the brave?

On the shore, dimly seen through the mists of the deep,
Where the foe's haughty host in dread silence reposes,
What is that which the breeze, o'er the towering steep,
As it fitfully blows, half conceals, half discloses?
Now it catches the gleam of the morning's first beam,
In full glory reflected, now shines on the stream.
'Tis the star-spangled banner; oh, long may it wave
O'er the land of the free, and the home of the brave!

And where is that band who so vauntingly swore
That the havoc of war and the battle's confusion
A home and a country should leave us no more?
Their blood has washed out their foul footsteps' pollution.
No refuge could save the hireling and slave
From the terror of flight, or the gloom of the grave:
And the star-spangled banner in triumph doth wave
O'er the land of the free, and the home of the brave!

Oh! thus be it ever when freemen shall stand
Between their loved homes and the war's desolation!
Blest with victory and peace, may the heaven-rescued land
Praise the Power that hath made and preserved us a nation!
Then conquer we must, for our cause it is just,
And this be our motto: "In God is our trust!"
And the star-spangled banner in triumph shall wave,
O'er the land of the free, and the home of the brave!

86.

Daniel Webster: Against Conscription

The long public career of Daniel Webster began with his election to the House of Representatives in 1813 from New Hampshire. He early allied himself to the interests of New England, the stronghold of Federalism. As New England opposed the War of 1812, so Webster opposed it, and in the following speech, delivered on December 9, 1814, he spoke brilliantly against it. His subject was the conscription bill to which President Madison had resorted in the face of the Federalist refusal to encourage enlistments in the army, and upon the rejection by Congress of his requisitions for militia. But Webster enlarged this subject to consider the whole problem of dissent in a free society.

Source: *The Writings and Speeches of Daniel Webster, Hitherto Uncollected,* Boston, 1903, Vol. II, pp. 55-69.

After the best reflection which I have been able to bestow on the subject of the bill before you, I am of the opinion that its principles are not warranted by any provision of the Constitution. It appears to me to partake of the nature of those other propositions for military measures which this session, so fertile in inventions, has produced. . . .

Let us examine the nature and extent of the power which is assumed by the various military measures before us. In the present want of men and money, the secretary of war has proposed to Congress a military conscription. For the conquest of Canada, the people will not enlist; and if they would, the treasury is exhausted, and they could not be paid. Conscription is chosen as the most promising instrument both of overcoming reluctance to the service and of subduing the difficulties which arise from the deficiencies of the exchequer. The administration asserts the right to fill the ranks of the regular army by compulsion. It contends that it may now take one out of every twenty-five men, and any part, or the whole of the rest, whenever its occasions require. Persons thus taken by force and put into an army may be compelled to serve there during the war, or for life. They may be put on any service at home or abroad for defense or for invasion, according to the will and pleasure of the government. This power does not grow out of any invasion of the country, or even out of a state of war. It belongs to government at all times, in peace as well as in war, and it is to be exercised under all circumstances according to its mere discretion. This, sir, is the amount of the principle contended for by the secretary of war.

Is this, sir, consistent with the character of a free government? Is this civil liberty? Is this the real character of our Constitution? No, sir, indeed it is not. The Constitution is libeled, foully libeled. The people of this country have not established for themselves such a fabric of despotism. They have not purchased at a vast expense of their own treasure and their own blood a Magna Carta to be slaves. Where is it written in the Constitution, in what article or section is it contained, that you may take children from their parents, and parents from their children, and compel them to fight the battles of any war in which the folly or the wickedness of government may engage it? Under what concealment has this power lain hidden which now for the first time comes forth, with a tremendous and baleful aspect, to trample down and destroy the dearest rights of personal liberty? Who will show me any constitutional injunction which makes it the duty of the American people to surrender everything valuable in life, and even life itself, not when the safety of their country and its liberties may demand the sacrifice, but whenever the purposes of an ambitious and mischievous government may require it?

Sir, I almost disdain to go to quotations and references to prove that such an abominable doctrine has no foundation in the Constitution of the country. It is enough to know that that instrument was intended as the basis of a free government, and that the power contended for is incompatible with any notion of personal liberty. An attempt to maintain this doctrine upon the provisions of the Constitution is an exercise of perverse ingenuity to extract slavery from the substance of a free government. It is an attempt to show by proof and argument that we ourselves are subjects of despotism, and that we have a right to chains and bondage, firmly secured to us and our children by the provisions of our government. It has been the labor of other men at other times to mitigate and reform the powers of government by construction, to support the rights of personal security by every species of favorable and benign interpretation, and thus to infuse a free spirit into governments not friendly in their general structure and formation to public liberty.

The supporters of the measures before us act on the opposite principle. It is their task to raise arbitrary powers, by construction, out of a plain written charter of national liberty. It is their pleasing duty to free us of the delusion which we have fondly cherished that we are the subjects of a mild, free, and limited government, and to demonstrate by a regular chain of premises and conclusions that government possesses over us a power more tyrannical, more arbitrary, more dangerous, more allied to blood and murder, more full of every form of mischief, more productive of every sort and degree of misery than has been exercised by any civilized government, with a single exception, in modern times.

The secretary of war has favored us with an argument on the constitutionality of this power. Those who lament that such doctrines should be supported by the opinion of a high officer of government may a little abate their regret when they remember that the same officer, in his last letter of instructions to our ministers abroad, maintained the contrary. In that letter he declares that even the impressment of seamen, for which many more plausible reasons may be given than for the impressment of soldiers, is repugnant to our Constitution. It might therefore be a sufficient answer to his argument, in the present case, to quote against it the sentiments of its own author, and to place the two opinions before the House in a state of irreconcilable conflict. Further comment on either might then be properly forborne, until he should be pleased to inform us which he retracted and to which he adhered. But the importance of the subject may justify a further consideration of the arguments.

Congress having, by the Constitution, a power to raise armies, the secretary contends that no restraint is to be imposed on the exercise of this power, except such as is expressly stated in the written letter of the instrument. In other words, that Congress may execute its powers by any means it chooses, unless such means are particularly prohibited. But the general nature and object of the Constitution impose as rigid a restriction on the means of exercising power as could be done by the most explicit injunctions. It is the first principle applicable to such a case that no construction shall be admitted which impairs the general nature and character of the instrument. A free constitution of government is to be construed upon free principles, and every branch of its provisions is to receive such an interpretation as is full of its general spirit. No means are to be taken by implication which would strike us absurdly if expressed. And what would have been more absurd than for this Constitution to have said that to secure the great blessings of liberty it gave to government an uncontrolled power of military conscription? Yet such is the absurdity which it is made to exhibit under the commentary of the secretary of war.

But it is said that it might happen that an army could not be raised by voluntary enlistment, in which case the power to raise armies would be granted in vain, unless they might be raised by compulsion. If this reasoning could prove anything, it would equally show that whenever the legitimate power of the Constitution should be so badly administered as to cease to answer the great ends intended by them, such new powers may be assumed or usurped as any existing administration may deem expedient. This is the result of his own reasoning, to which the secretary does not profess to go. But it is a true result. For if it is to be assumed that all powers were granted which might by possibility become necessary, and that government itself is the judge of this possible necessity, then the powers of government are precisely what it chooses they should be.

Apply the same reasoning to any other power granted to Congress, and test its accuracy by the result. Congress has power to borrow money. How is it to exercise this power? Is it confined to voluntary loans? There is no express limitation to that effect, and, in the language of the secretary, it might happen, indeed it has happened, that persons could not be found willing to lend. Money might be borrowed then in any other mode. In other words, Congress might resort to a forced loan. It might take the money of any man by force, and give him in exchange exchequer notes or certificates of stock. Would this be quite constitutional, sir? It is entirely within the reasoning of the secretary, and it is a result of his argument, outraging the rights of individuals in a far less degree than the practical consequences which he himself draws from it. A compulsory loan is not to be compared, in point of enormity, with a compulsory military service.

If the secretary of war has proved the right of Congress to enact a law enforcing a draft of men out of the militia into the regular army, he will at any time be able to prove quite as clearly that Congress has power to create a dictator. The arguments which have helped him in one case will equally aid him in the other, the same reason of a supposed or possible state necessity which is urged now may be repeated then, with equal pertinency and effect. . . .

Nor is it, sir, for the defense of his own house and home that he who is the subject of military draft is to perform the task allotted to him. You will put him upon a service equally foreign to his interests and abhorrent to his feelings. With his aid you are to push your purposes of conquest. The battles which he is to fight are the battles of invasion, battles which he detests perhaps and abhors, less from the danger and the death that gather over them and the blood with which they drench the plain than from the principles in which they have their origin. Fresh from the peaceful pursuits of life, and yet a soldier but in name, he is to be opposed to the veteran troops, hardened under every scene, inured to every privation, and disciplined in every service.

If, sir, in this strife he fall; if, while ready to obey every rightful command of government, he is forced from his home against right, not to contend for the defense of his country but to prosecute a miserable and detestable project of invasion, and in that strife he fall, 'tis murder. It may stalk above the cognizance of human law, but in the sight of heaven it is murder; and though millions of years may roll away while his ashes and yours lie mingled together in the earth, the day will yet come when his spirit and the spirits of his children must be met at the bar of omnipotent justice. May God in His compassion shield me from any participation in the enormity of this guilt. . . .

It will be the solemn duty of the state governments to protect their own authority over their own militia, and to interpose between their citizens and arbitrary power. These are among the objects for which the state governments exist; and their highest obligations bind them to the preservation of their own rights and the liberties of their people.

I express these sentiments here, sir, because I shall express them to my constituents. Both they and myself live under a constitution which teaches us that "the doctrine of nonresistance against arbitrary power and oppression is absurd, slavish, and destructive of the good and happiness of mankind." With the same earnestness with which I now exhort you to forbear from these measures, I shall exhort them to exercise their unquestionable right of providing for the security of their own liberties.

In my opinion, sir, the sentiments of the free population of this country are greatly mistaken here. The nation is not yet in a temper to submit to conscription. The people have too fresh and strong a feeling of the blessings of civil liberty to be willing thus to surrender it. You may talk to them as much as you please of the victory and glory to be obtained in the enemy's provinces; they will hold those objects in light estimation if the means be a forced military service. You may sing to them the song of Canada conquest in all its variety, but they will not be charmed out of the remembrance of their substantial interests and true happiness. Similar pretenses, they know, are the grave in which the liberties of other nations have been buried, and they will take warning.

Laws, sir, of this nature can create nothing but opposition. If you scatter them abroad, like the fabled serpents' teeth, they will spring up into armed men. A military force cannot be raised in this manner but by the means of a military force. If administration has found that it cannot form an army without conscription, it will find, if it venture on these experiments, that it cannot enforce conscription without an army. The government was not constituted for such purposes. Framed in the spirit of liberty and in the love of peace, it has no powers which render it able to enforce such laws. The attempt, if we rashly make it, will fail; and having already thrown away our peace, we may thereby throw away our government.

Allusions have been made, sir, to the state of things in New England, and, as usual, she has been charged with an intention to dissolve the Union. The charge is unfounded. She is much too wise to entertain such purposes. She has had too much experience, and has too strong a recollection of the blessings which the Union is capable of producing under a just administration of government. It is her greatest fear that the course at present pursued will destroy it, by destroying every principle, every interest, every sentiment, and every feeling which have hitherto contributed to uphold it.

Those who cry out that the Union is in danger are themselves the authors of that danger. They put its existence to hazard by measures of violence which it is not capable of enduring. They talk of dangerous designs against government when they are overthrowing the fabric from its foundations. They alone, sir, are friends to the union of the states who endeavor to maintain the principles of civil liberty in the country and to preserve the spirit in which the Union was framed.

Philadelphia Museum of Art

"He That Tilleth His Land Shall Be Satisfied," by an unknown artist

CITY AND FARM

In 1790, when the first United States census was taken, only 5 percent of the population was urban. In spite of substantial growth in the cities since the Revolution, agriculture was still the primary source of livelihood for most Americans.

However, with available farmland in the East largely under cultivation by this time, a change in the patterns of life was imminent. For a young farmer, to stay put meant working a small farm or changing occupations. Meanwhile, in the West, rich, unused farmland beckoned and land speculators traveled the country, advertising the limitless opportunities awaiting anyone who would migrate. By 1820, the opening of the West and, increasingly, the spread of manufacturing in New England, already had begun to transform the Northeast. Cities, particularly New York, were beginning a period of enormous growth. Commercial activities and foreign trade dominated city life and plans were under way for canals to bring western agriculture to the East and eastern goods to the West. Competition from western farms and new jobs in manufacturing or at sea began to draw ever larger numbers of young men away from farming.

In the cities, the prosperity that these activities engendered freed a growing number of people for leisure activities. Even at this early date many of the wealthy, whose interests were in the city, built mansions in the suburbs to escape the congestion. At the same time the population of cities began to swell with the laborers, stevedores, construction workers, and numerous skilled and unskilled workers that city life requires.

Stokes Collection, New York Public Library

View of New York from Long Island, by St. Memin, 1796

New York Historical Society

Tontine Coffee House, at Wall and Water Streets, New York, 1797

St. Paul's Church, New York, from "New York Magazine," 1799

Library of Congress

New York

In spite of serving briefly as the national capital during Washington's first administration, New York's basic concerns were commercial. The harbor and easy connections with neighboring areas through Long Island Sound or up the Hudson River gave the city unique advantages as a port. At the same time, the city's business and banking traditions extended back into its colonial history and the descendants of the colonial patroons offered a ready source of capital. By 1820, New York had replaced Philadelphia as the nation's largest city and leading port.

Stokes Collection, New York Public Library

Elgin Botanical Garden, Fifth Avenue, New York, 1812

Metropolitan Museum of Art, Edward Arnold Collection

Bathing party on the East River, 1810; oil by W. Chappel

Library of Congress

John Stevens' home, Hoboken, N.J.

Library of Congress

View of the bridge over the Charles River, Boston; from "Massachusetts Magazine"

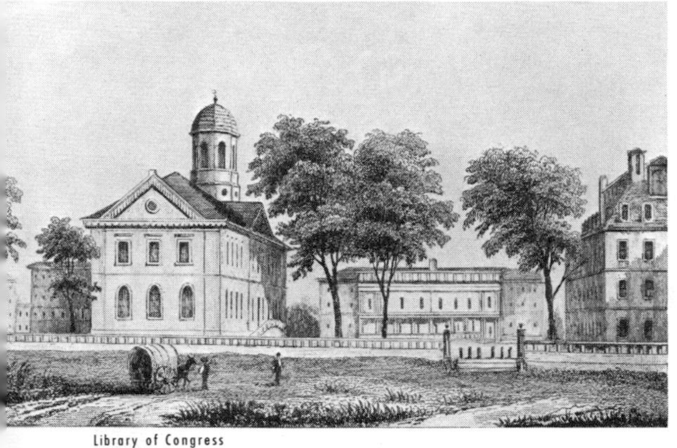
Library of Congress

Harvard University, Cambridge

Boston

The major source of prosperity in Boston at the end of the 18th century was shipping. Eventually, the depredations in international trade caused by the War of 1812 led many Boston merchants to invest in manufacturing and the city became a principal exporter of textiles. Boston's austere religious traditions and the relatively refined intellectualism emanating from Harvard contrasted increasingly with the rest of the country. To visitors it was the most "English" of American cities.

The Old Feather Store, Boston

Massachusetts Historical Society

The Peale Museum, Baltimore

"Exhuming the First American Mastodon," by C. W. Peale, 1806-1808

Leisure

The time and broadened interests that prosperity and the "pursuit of happiness" afforded brought forth a variety of activities. C. W. Peale's museum added a mastodon to its collection of birds and portraits. Theaters and art galleries were built in several cities and a few struggling American theatrical companies emerged. For those few with time to read, there was the first flourishing of American literary art, while more practical minds flooded the Patent Office with impractical schemes.

Library of Congress

(Above) A bogus "perpetual motion machine," exhibited in New York before it was exposed by Fulton

Two inventions that failed to make a fortune: a hot bath (below) and a hand-powered carriage (right)

National Archives

National Archives

Library of Congress

(Above) Free Public Library in Philadelphia, 1799; (center) the Pennsylvania Academy of Fine Arts, watercolor by Svinin; (bottom) State-House Garden, Philadelphia, in 1798

Metropolitan Museum of Art, Rogers Fund

Library of Congress

Yale Art Gallery

Amherst College

Free Library of Philadelphia

(Top) John Trumbull the poet, painting by John Trumbull, 1794; (center) Charles Brockden Brown, miniature by William Dunlap; Brown authored four novels between 1798 and 1800; (bottom) William Bartram, naturalist and supervisor of a botanical garden on the Schuylkill River near Philadelphia, 1777-1812

Library of Congress

(Above) New Theater on Chestnut Street; (right) oyster barrow in front of the theater; watercolor by Svinin

Metropolitan Museum of Art, Rogers Fund

Scene from a performance of "School for Scandal" as staged at the Park Theater in New York; painting by William Dunlap, manager of the theater

Harvard Theater Collection

Library of Congress

Harper Theater, Newport, R.I.; the theater was erected in 1793 following the repeal of the state's prohibitory law

Springfield Museum of Fine Arts

"Smithtown, Long Island," watercolor by A. Milne

The Country

Along most of the Atlantic seaboard, the patterns of rural life were settled. If the roads were bad and the outlook provincial, nature had been mastered, the Indians were long since gone, and most people could read. But the captured tranquility of the villages omits those restless souls departing for the West or the whaling ports.

Library of Congress

A view of Minisink, N. J. from "New York Magazine," 1800

A New England hillside, painted by an unknown artist

Museum of Fine Arts, Boston; Karolik Collection

Library of Congress

Henry Livingston's estate at Poughkeepsie, New York, 1797

Library of Congress

The ruins of Ft. Ticonderoga in 1818 seem to symbolize the end of insecurity

Rockefeller Coll., Colonial Williamsburg

"Connecticut House," by Rebecca Couch, 1800

Library of Congress

"A View of Campo Bello Island," in Maine

Garbisch Coll., National Gallery of Art

"The Sargent Family," painting by an unknown artist, 1800

Atkins Museum of Fine Arts

"George and Emma Eastman," by C. Balis

Courtesy, Edgar W. Garbisch

"The Wedding," painting by an unidentified artist

Engraving of a farmyard, 1796; from "Massachusetts Magazine"

Library of Congress

Addison Gallery of American Art

"View of Barnstable," by an unknown artist

Yale University Library

Playing ball on the grounds of Yale College, engraving by Doolittle, 1807

Market Street, Albany, N.Y., 1805; watercolor by James Eights

Albany Institute of History and Art

Essex Institute, Salem

Derby House, Salem, Mass.; designed by Bulfinch, 1799

Old Dartmouth Whaling Museum

A view of New Bedford, Mass., in 1807; painted by William Wall

Plan of the Town of Burlington in New Jersey

Library of Congress

1815

87.

New England and the Union

Dissatisfied with the progress of the war with England, and long resentful over the balance of political power that gave the South, and particularly Virginia, effective control of the national government, representatives of the New England states called a convention at Hartford in the fall of 1814. The more extreme among them were for considering secession, but others sought only to dictate amendments to the Constitution that would protect their interests. The latter course was decided upon, and the proposed amendments, along with some stringent criticisms of President Madison's administration, were agreed to by the convention on January 4, 1815. They were never presented to the government. Even as the convention finished its business, a British sloop-of-war was beating its way across the Atlantic with dispatches containing the peace terms that had been worked out in neutral Belgium. Moreover, as the convention's emissaries approached Washington, they were met by the news of General Andrew Jackson's unexpected victory at New Orleans. By the time the emissaries arrived, it was no longer possible to serve the kind of ultimatum contained in the convention's report. The war, along with the national crisis it had brought about, had ended.

Source: Theodore Dwight, *History of the Hartford Convention, etc., etc.*, New York, 1833, pp. 352-379.

If the Union be destined to dissolution by reason of the multiplied abuses of bad administrations, it should, if possible, be the work of peaceable times and deliberate consent. Some new form of confederacy should be substituted among those states which shall intend to maintain a federal relation to each other. Events may prove that the causes of our calamities are deep and permanent. They may be found to proceed, not merely from the blindness of prejudice, pride of opinion, violence of party spirit, or the confusion of the times but they may be traced to implacable combinations of individuals, or of states, to monopolize power and office, and to trample without remorse upon the rights and interests of commercial sections of the Union. Whenever it shall appear that these causes are radical and permanent, a separation, by equitable arrangement, will be preferable to an alliance by constraint, among nominal friends but real enemies, inflamed by mutual hatred and jealousy, and inviting, by intestine divisions, contempt and aggression from abroad.

But a severance of the Union by one or

Library of Congress

"The Hartford Convention or Leap No Leap," a cartoon depicting New England's sympathy for England in 1815

more states, against the will of the rest, and especially in a time of war, can be justified only by absolute necessity. These are among the principal objections against precipitate measures tending to disunite the states; and when examined in connection with the farewell address of the father of his country, they must, it is believed, be deemed conclusive.

Under these impressions, the Convention have proceeded to confer and deliberate upon the alarming state of public affairs, especially as affecting the interests of the people who have appointed them for this purpose. And they are naturally led to a consideration, in the first place, of the dangers and grievances which menace an immediate or speedy pressure, with a view of suggesting means of present relief; in the next place, of such as are of a more remote and general description, in the hope of attaining future security. . . .

In the catalogue of blessings which have fallen to the lot of the most favored nations, none could be enumerated from which our country was excluded — a free Constitution, administered by great and incorruptible statesmen, realized the fondest hopes of liberty and independence; the progress of agriculture was stimulated by the certainty of value in the harvest; and commerce, after traversing every sea, returned with the riches of every clime. A revenue, secured by a sense of honor, collected without oppression, and paid without murmurs, melted away the national debt; and the chief concern of the public creditor arose from its too rapid diminution. The wars and commotions of the European nations and their interruptions of the commercial intercourse afforded to those who had not promoted but who would have rejoiced to alleviate their calamities, a fair and golden opportunity, by combining themselves to lay a broad foundation for national wealth. Although occasional vexations to commerce arose from the furious collisions of the powers at war, yet the great and good men of that time conformed to the force of circumstances which they could not control, and preserved their country in security from the tempests which overwhelmed the Old World, and threw the wreck of their fortunes on these shores.

Respect abroad, prosperity at home, wise laws made by honored legislators, and prompt obedience yielded by a contented people had silenced the enemies of republican institutions. The arts flourished; the sciences were cultivated; the comforts and conveniences of life were universally diffused; and nothing remained for succeeding administrations but to reap the advantages and cherish the resources flowing from the policy of their predecessors.

But no sooner was a new administration established in the hands of the party opposed to the Washington policy than a fixed determination was perceived and avowed of changing a system which had already produced these substantial fruits. The consequences of this change, for a few years after its commencement, were not sufficient to counteract the prodigious impulse toward prosperity which had been given to the nation. But a steady perseverance in the new plans of administration at length developed their weakness and deformity, but not until a majority of the people had been deceived by flattery, and inflamed by passion, into blindness to their defects. Under the withering influence of this new system, the declension of the nation has been uniform and rapid. The richest advantages for securing the great objects of the Constitution have been wantonly rejected. While Europe reposes from the convulsions that had shaken down her ancient institutions, she beholds with amazement this remote country, once so happy and so envied, involved in a ruinous war and excluded from intercourse with the rest of the world.

To investigate and explain the means whereby this fatal reverse has been effected would require a voluminous discussion. Nothing more can be attempted in this report than a general allusion to the principal outlines of the policy which has produced this vicissitude. Among these may be enumerated:

First, a deliberate and extensive system for effecting a combination among certain states, by exciting local jealousies and ambition, so as to secure to popular leaders in one section of the Union the control of public affairs in perpetual succession; to which primary object most other characteristics of the system may be reconciled.

Second, the political intolerance displayed and avowed in excluding from office men of unexceptable merit for want of adherence to the executive creed.

Third, the infraction of the judiciary authority and rights by depriving judges of their offices in violation of the Constitution.

Fourth, the abolition of existing taxes, requisite to prepare the country for those changes to which nations are always exposed, with a view to the acquisition of popular favor.

Fifth, the influence of patronage in the distribution of offices, which in these states has been almost invariably made among men the least entitled to such distinction, and who have sold themselves as ready instruments for distracting public opinion, and encouraging administration to hold in contempt the wishes and remonstrances of a people thus apparently divided.

Sixth, the admission of new states into the Union, formed at pleasure in the Western region, has destroyed the balance of power which existed among the original states and deeply affected their interest.

Seventh, the easy admission of naturalized foreigners to places of trust, honor, or profit, operating as an inducement to the malcontent subjects of the Old World to come to these states in quest of executive patronage, and to repay it by an abject devotion to executive measures.

Eighth, hostility to Great Britain and partiality to the late government of France, adopted as coincident with popular prejudice and subservient to the main object, party power. Connected with these must be ranked erroneous and distorted estimates of the power and resources of those nations, of the probable results of their controversies, and of our political relations to them respectively.

Last and principally, a visionary and superficial theory in regard to commerce, accompanied by a real hatred but a feigned regard to its interests, and a ruinous perseverance in efforts to render it an instrument of coercion and war.

But it is not conceivable that the obliquity of any administration could, in so short a period, have so nearly consummated the work of national ruin, unless favored by defects in the Constitution. . . .

Therefore resolved: that it be and hereby is recommended to the legislatures of the several states represented in this Convention to adopt all such measures as may be necessary, effectually, to protect the citizens of said states from the operation and effects of all acts which have been or may be passed by the Congress of the United States which shall contain provisions subjecting the militia or other citizens to forcible drafts, conscriptions, or impressments not authorized by the Constitution of the United States.

Resolved, that it be, and hereby is, recommended to the said legislatures to authorize an immediate and earnest application to be made to the government of the United States requesting their consent to some arrangement whereby the said states may, separately or in concert, be empowered to assume upon themselves the defense of their territory against the enemy; and a reasonable portion of the taxes collected within said states may be paid into the respective treasuries thereof, and appropriated to the payment of the balance due said states, and to the future defense of the same. The amount so paid into the said treasuries to be credited, and the disbursements made as aforesaid to be charged to the United States.

Resolved, that it be, and hereby is, recommended to the legislatures of the aforesaid states to pass laws (where it has not already been done) authorizing the governors or commanders in chief of their militia to make detachments from the same, or to form voluntary corps, as shall be most convenient and conformable to their constitutions, and to cause the same to be well armed, equipped, and disciplined, and held in readiness for service; and, upon the request of the governor of either of the other states, to employ the whole of such detachment or corps, as well as the regular forces of the state, or such part thereof as may be required and can be spared consistently with the safety of the state, in assisting the state making such request to repel any invasion thereof which shall be made or attempted by the public enemy.

Resolved, that the following amendments of the Constitution of the United States be recommended to the states represented as aforesaid, to be proposed by them for adoption by the state legislatures, and, in such cases as may be deemed expedient, by a convention chosen by the people of each state.

And it is further recommended that the said states shall persevere in their efforts to obtain such amendments until the same shall be effected.

First, representatives and direct taxes shall be apportioned among the several states which may be included within this Union according to their respective numbers of free persons, including those bound to serve for a term of years, and excluding Indians not taxed and all other persons.

Second, no new state shall be admitted into the Union by Congress, in virtue of the power granted by the Constitution without the concurrence of two-thirds of both houses.

Third, Congress shall not have power to lay any embargo on the ships or vessels of the citizens of the United States, in the ports or harbors thereof, for more than sixty days.

Fourth, Congress shall not have power without the concurrence of two-thirds of both houses, to interdict the commercial intercourse between the United States and any foreign nation or the dependencies thereof.

Fifth, Congress shall not make or declare

war, or authorize acts of hostility against any foreign nation, without the concurrence of two-thirds of both houses, except such acts of hostility be in defense of the territories of the United States when actually invaded.

Sixth, no person who shall hereafter be naturalized shall be eligible as a member of the Senate or House of Representatives of the United States, nor capable of holding any civil office under the authority of the United States.

Seventh, the same person shall not be elected President of the United States a second time; nor shall the President be elected from the same state two terms in succession.

Resolved, that if the application of these states to the government of the United States, recommended in a foregoing resolution, should be unsuccessful and peace should not be concluded, and the defense of these states should be neglected, as it has been since the commencement of the war, it will, in the opinion of this Convention, be expedient for the legislatures of the several states to appoint delegates to another convention, to meet at Boston . . . with such powers and instructions as the exigency of a crisis so momentous may require.

88.

Noah Worcester: War and Popular Delusion

Noah Worcester, a clergyman and the first editor of the Christian Disciple (Christian Examiner), *was known as the "Friend of Peace." By nature he was a man of peace, believing that Christian love could be practically efficacious in abolishing war as a means of settling disputes. Long before the League of Nations, the International Court of Justice, or the United Nations had been conceived, Worcester suggested the establishment of international peace organizations in his book* A Solemn Review of the Custom of War; Showing that War Is the Effect of Popular Delusion, and Proposing a Remedy. *Until 1815, when the book was published, there were no formal organizations for the prevention of war. In the midst of popular reaction against the War of 1812, combined with the generally optimistic tone of the period, Worcester's book had an effect, and is said to have inspired the foundation of a number of peace societies. A portion of* A Solemn Review *is reprinted here.*

Source: *A Solemn Review of the Custom of War; Showing that War Is the Effect of Popular Delusion, and Proposing a Remedy,* Cambridge, 1815, pp. 5-27.

SECTION I

"Shall the sword devour forever?"

We regard with horror the custom of the ancient heathens in offering their children in sacrifice to idols. We are shocked with the customs of the Hindoos, in prostrating themselves before the car of an idol to be crushed to death; in burning women alive on the funeral piles of their husbands; in offering a monthly sacrifice by casting living children into the Ganges to be drowned. We read with astonishment of the sacrifices made in the papal crusades, and in the Mahometan and Hindoo pilgrimages. We wonder at the blindness of Christian nations, who have esteemed it right and honorable to buy and sell Africans as property, and reduce them to bondage for life. But that which is fashionable and popular in any country is esteemed right and honorable, whatever may be its nature in the views of men better informed.

But while we look back with a mixture of wonder, indignation, and pity on many of the customs of former ages, are we careful to inquire whether some customs which we deem honorable are not the effect of popular delusion; and whether they will not be so regarded by future generations? Is it not a fact that one of the most horrid customs of savage men is now popular in every nation in Christendom? What custom of the most barbarous nations is more repugnant to the feelings of piety, humanity, and justice than that of deciding controversies between nations by the edge of the sword, by powder and ball, or the point of the bayonet? What other savage custom has occasioned half the desolation and misery to the human race? And what but the grossest infatuation could render such a custom popular among rational beings?

SECTION II

That it is possible to produce such a state of society as to exclude national wars may appear probable from the following facts.

1. It is impossible for the rulers of any one nation to do much in carrying on a war with another without the aid of subjects, or the common people.

2. A war between two nations is generally produced by the influence of a small number of ambitious and unprincipled individuals; while the greater part of the nation has no hand in the business until war is proclaimed.

3. A vast majority of every civilized nation has an aversion to war; such an aversion that it requires much effort and management to work up their passions so far that they are willing personally to engage in such hazardous and bloody conflicts. The more any people are civilized and christianized, the greater is their aversion to war, and the more powerful exertions are necessary to excite what is called the war spirit. Were it not for the influence of a few ambitious or revengeful men, an offensive war could not be undertaken with any prospect of success, except when the mass of the people are either uncivilized, or slaves. If then, as great exertions should be made to excite a just abhorrence of war as have often been made to excite a war spirit, we may be very certain that rulers would find little encouragement to engage in any war which is not strictly defensive. And as soon as offensive wars shall cease, defensive wars will of course be unknown.

4. It is an affront to common sense to pretend that military officers and soldiers have no right to inquire whether a war be just or unjust; and that all they have to do is to obey the orders of government. Such a doctrine is fit to be taught only to slaves without souls. If a man is called to fight, he should be faithfully informed and fully satisfied that he is not to act the part of a murderer, that the blood of men may not be required at his hands. Every soldier ought to be impressed with the idea that offensive war is murderous, and that no government on earth has any right to compel him to shed blood in a wanton and aggressive war. Yet in the present state of general delusion, the soldiers and most of the citizens are treated as having no more right to judge of the justice or the injustice of a war than the horses employed in military service. On one side a war is certainly unjust and murderous. Yet on both sides it is considered as the duty of soldiers to submit to the orders of government and fight, whether it be murder, or not murder! With the same propriety it might be considered as the duty of a citizen to obey an order of government

for murdering an individual of his own nation.

5. National wars often originate from such petty offenses as would not justify the taking of a single life, and from false principles of honor, which every Christian should abhor. What can be more perfect delusion than to suppose the *honor* of a nation requires a declaration of war, for such offenses as would not justify one individual in taking the life of another? Or what can be more absurd than to suppose the honor of a nation requires going to war, while there is not even the prospect of advantage? Is such petulance as would disgrace a common citizen, or such a revengeful spirit as would disgrace a savage, becoming the dignity of a national government, or the ruler of a Christian people?

To sacrifice human beings to false notions of national honor, or to the ambition or avarice of rulers, is no better than to offer them to Moloch, or any other heathen deity. As soon as the eyes of people can be opened to see that war is the effect of delusion. it will then become as unpopular as any other heathenish mode of offering human sacrifices.

It is enough to fill the mind of any reflecting man with horror, to think of the millions of his fellow men who have been sacrificed to the ambition, the avarice, the petulance, or the profligacy of ungodly rulers. How shocking the thought of armies meeting under the influence of enmity, artificially excited, to plunge their bayonets into the breasts of each other; and thus to offer human sacrifices by thousands, to some idolized phantom of ambitious or revengeful men! In every war that has taken place, the soldiers on one side or the other have been either the slaves or the dupes of deluded or unprincipled rulers. The soldiers on each side often meet without ever having experienced the least injury from each other; with no enmity but what has been artificially excited, and without having the least ground to be offended with each other, any more than they had in a time of perfect peace. Yet those who never had any provocation from one another, nor any hand in proclaiming the war, are by art inspired with enmity, and made to thirst for each other's blood, and to perish by each other's hands. A more barbarous mode of offering human sacrifices was never practised by the most savage nations; nor one, it is believed, more abhorrent in the eyes of Heaven.

Public wars and private duels seem to be practised on similar principles. Gentlemen may fight and kill for petty offenses; but if common people do the same, they are hanged as murderers. Gentlemen of the sword cannot wait the slow operation of law for the redress of supposed wrongs, but must show themselves men of spirit, that is, ready to kill for an offensive word. What is deemed honorable virtue in them is shameful vice in other people. That benevolent, forbearing spirit, which is the glory of good people, is thought beneath the dignity of a gentleman of honor. First to give a challenge, and thus notify a man of a wish to kill him, is supposed to exclude the sin of murder. So in regard to war-makers, that magnanimity and forbearance which would adorn the character of a private Christian, is despised by the ambitious ruler in relation to himself. And that petulance, rashness, and disregard to the lives of others, which would render a private citizen the object of just and general abhorrence, are regarded by many as honorable traits in the character of one who is exalted to rule over men. If in the exercise of this haughty, unfeeling, and vindictive temper he declares war, this declaration, he fancies, will secure him from the guilt of murder. Thus thousands after thousands are sacrificed on the altar of his ungodly ambition; and every means which ingenuity can invent is employed to delude the unfortunate victims and make them believe that with such sacrifices God is well pleased.

There is, however, one circumstance usually attending public wars which renders them more detestable than private duels. The duelist usually has the generosity to do his own fighting; but war-makers usually have the meanness to avoid the dangers which they create, and to call on other people to fight their battles.

Dueling is indeed a horrible custom; but war is as much more horrible as it is more desolating and ruinous. As to the principles on which war is practised, it has no advantage of dueling. It is in fact *national dueling*, attended generally with this dishonorable circumstance: that those who give and accept the challenge call together a multitude of seconds, and then have not the magnanimity first to risk their own lives, but to involve their seconds in a bloody contest while they themselves stand remote from danger, as spectators, or at most as directors of the awful combat. Or perhaps more commonly, after issuing their bloody mandate, they indulge in pleasure, regardless of the sufferings of others. So "the king and Haman sat down to drink; but the city Sushan was perplexed."

SECTION III

In favor of war several pleas will probably be made.

First, some will plead that the Israelites were permitted, and even commanded, to make war on the inhabitants of Canaan. To this it may be answered that the Giver and Arbiter of life had a right, if He pleased, to make use of the savage customs of the age, for punishing guilty nations. If any government of the present day should receive a commission to make war, as the Israelites did, let the order be obeyed. But until they have such a commission, let it not be imagined that they can innocently make war. . . .

A second plea in favor of the custom of war may be this: that war is an advantage to a nation, as it usually takes off many vicious and dangerous characters. But does not war make two such characters for every one it removes? Is it not in fact the greatest school of depravity, and the greatest source of mischievous and dangerous characters, that ever existed among men? Does not a state of war lower down the standard of morality in a nation, so that a vast portion of common vice is scarcely observed as evil? Let anyone who was old enough to observe the state of morals prior to our Revolution ask himself, what was the effect of that war on the morals of New England?

Besides, is it not awful to think of sending vicious men beyond the means of reformation, and the hope of repentance! When they are sent into the army, what is this but consigning them to a state where they will rapidly fill up the measure of their iniquity, and become "fitted to destruction!"

Third, it will be pleaded that no substitute for war can be devised which will insure to a nation a redress of wrongs. In reply we may ask, is it common for a nation to obtain a redress of wrongs by war? As to redress, do not the wars of nations resemble boxing at a tavern, when both the combatants receive a terrible bruising, then drink a mug of flip together and make peace; each, however, bearing for a long time the marks of his folly and madness? A redress of wrongs by war is so uncommon, that unless revenge is redress, and multiplied injuries satisfaction, we should suppose that none but madmen would run the hazard.

But if the eyes of people could be opened in regard to the evils and delusions of war, would it not be easy to form a confederacy of nations and organize a high court of equity to decide national controversies? Why might not such a court be composed of some of the most eminent characters from each nation; and a compliance with the decision of the court be made a point of national honor, to prevent the effusion of blood, and to preserve the blessings of peace? Can any considerate person say that the probability of obtaining right in such a court, would be less than by an appeal to arms? When an individual appeals to a court of justice for the redress of wrongs, it is not always the case that he obtains his right. Still, such an appeal is more honorable, more safe, and more certain, as well as more benevolent, than for the individual to attempt to obtain a redress by his pistol or his sword. And are not the reasons for avoiding an appeal to the sword for the redress of wrongs, always great in proportion to the calamities which such an appeal must naturally involve? If this be a fact, then there is infinitely greater reason why two nations should avoid an appeal to arms, than usually exists against a bloody combat between two contending individuals.

In the fourth place, it may be urged that a spirit of forbearance on the part of a national government would operate as an invitation to repeated insult and aggression.

But is this plea founded on facts and experience? Does it accord with what is well known of human nature? Who are the persons in society that most frequently receive insult and abuse? Are they the meek, the benevolent, and the forbearing? Do these more commonly have reason to complain than persons of quick resentment, who are ready to fight on the least provocation?

There are two sects of professed Christians in this country, which, as sects, are peculiar in their opinions respecting the lawfulness of war, and the right of repelling injury by violence. These are the Quakers and the Shakers. They are remarkably pacific. Now we ask, does it appear from experience that their forbearing spirit brings on them a greater portion of injury and insult than what is experienced by people of other sects? Is not the reverse of this true in fact? There may indeed be some instances of such gross depravity, as a person's taking advantage of their pacific character to do them injury, with the hope of impunity. But in general, it is believed, their pacific principles and spirit command the esteem even of the vicious, and operate as a shield from insult and abuse.

The question may be brought home to every society. How seldom do children of a mild, forbearing temper experience insult or injury, compared with the waspish, who will sting if touched? The same inquiry may be made in respect to persons of these opposite descriptions of every age, and in every situation of life; and the result will be favorable to the point in question.

Should any deny the applicability of these examples to national rulers, we have the pleasure of being able to produce one example which is undeniably applicable.

When William Penn took the government of Pennsylvania he distinctly avowed to the Indians his forbearing and pacific principles, and his benevolent wishes for uninterrupted peace with them. On these principles the government was administered, while it remained in the hands of the Quakers. What then was the effect? Did this pacific character in government invite aggression and insult? Let the answer be given in the language of the *Edinburgh Review* of the *Life of William Penn.* Speaking of the treaty made by Penn with the Indians, the reviewer says:

> Such indeed was the spirit in which the negotiation was entered into, and the corresponding settlement conducted, that for the space of more than seventy years — and so long indeed as the Quakers retained the chief power in the government, the peace and amity which had been thus solemnly promised and concluded, never was violated; and a large though solitary example afforded, of the facility with which they, who are really sincere and friendly in their views, may live in harmony with those who are supposed to be peculiarly fierce and faithless.

Shall then this "solitary" but successful "example" never be imitated? "Shall the sword devour forever?"

SECTION IV

SOME OF THE EVILS OF WAR have already been mentioned, but the field is almost boundless. The demoralizing and depraving effects of war cannot be too seriously considered. We have heard much of the corrupting tendency of some of the rites and customs of the heathen; but what custom of the heathen nations had a greater effect in depraving the human character than the custom of war? What is that feeling usually called a war spirit, but a deleterious compound of enthusiastic ardor, ambition, malignity and revenge, a compound which as really endangers the soul of the possessor as the life of his enemy! Who, but a person deranged or deluded, would think it safe to rush into the presence of his Judge with his heart boiling with enmity, and his brothers' blood dripping from his hands! Yet in time of war, how much pain is taken to excite and maintain this bloodthirsty disposition as essential to success!

The profession of a soldier exposes him to sudden and untimely death, and at the same time burdens his heart, and renders him regardless of his final account. When a person goes into the army, it is expected of him that he will rise above the fear of death. In doing this he too commonly rises above the fear of God, and all serious concern for his soul. It is not denied that some men sustain virtuous characters amidst the contaminating vapors of a camp; and some may be reformed by a sense of the dangers to which they are exposed; but these are uncommon occurrences.

The depravity occasioned by war is not confined to the army. Every species of vice gains ground in a nation during a war. And when a war is brought to a close, seldom, perhaps, does a community return to its former standard of morals. In time of peace, vice and irreligion generally retain the ground they acquired by war. As every war augments the amount of national depravity, so it proportionably increases the dangers and miseries of society.

Among the evil effects of war, a wanton undervaluing of human life ought to be mentioned. This effect may appear in various forms. When a war is declared for the redress of some wrong, in regard to property, if nothing but property be taken into consideration, the result is not commonly better than spending $500 in a law suit to recover a debt of $10. But when we come to estimate human lives against dollars and cents, how are we confounded! "All that a man hath will he give for his life." Yet, by the custom of war, men are so deluded that a ruler may give 50,000 or 100,000 lives, when only a trifling amount of property is in question, and when the probabilities are as 10 to 1 against him, that even that small amount will not be secured by the contest. It must, however, again be remarked that war-makers do not usually give their own lives, but the lives of others. How often has a war been declared with the prospect that not less than 50,000 lives must be sacrificed; and while the chief agent in making the war would not have given his own life to secure to his nation everything that he claimed from the other? And are rulers to be upheld in thus gambling away the lives of others, while they are careful to secure their own? If people in general could obtain just views of this species of gambling, rulers would not make offensive wars with impunity. How little do they consider the misery and wretchedness which they bring on those, for whom they should exercise the kindness and care of a father! Does it not appear that they regard the lives of soldiers as mere property, which they may sacrifice, or barter away at pleasure? War is in truth the most dreadful species of gambling. Rulers are the gamblers. The lives and property of their subjects are the things they put to hazard in the game; and he that is most successful in doing mischief is considered as the best gamester.

If by the custom of war, rulers learn to undervalue the lives of their own subjects, how much more do they undervalue the lives of their enemies! As they learn to hear of the loss of 500, or 1,000 of their own men, with perhaps less feeling than they would hear of the death of a favorite horse or dog; so they learn to hear of the death of thousands after thousands on the side of the enemy, with joy and exultation. If their own men have succeeded in taking an unimportant fortress, or a frigate, with the loss of 50 lives on their own side, and 51 on the other, this is a matter of joy and triumph. This time they have got the game. But alas! At what expense to others! This expense, however, does not interrupt the joy of war-makers. They leave it to the wounded and the friends of the dead to feel and to mourn.

This dreadful depravity of feeling is not confined to rulers in time of war. The army becomes abandoned to such depravity. They learn to undervalue not only the lives of their enemies, but even their own, and will often wantonly rush into the arms of death, for the sake of military glory. And more or less of the same want of feeling, and the same undervaluing of human life, extends through the nation, in proportion to the frequency of battles and the duration of war.

If anything be done by the army of one nation, which is deemed by the other as contrary to the modern usages in war, how soon do we hear the exclamations of "Goths and Vandals!" Yet what are Christians at war, better than those barbarous tribes; and what is the war spirit in them, better than the spirit of "Goths and Vandals"? When the war spirit is excited, it is not always to be circumscribed in its operations by the refinements of civilization. It is at best a bloody and desolating spirit.

What is our boast of civilization, or christianization, while we tolerate as popular and justifiable the most horrid custom which ever resulted from human wickedness? Should a period arrive when the nations "shall learn war no more," what will posterity think of our claims, as Christians and civilized men? The custom of sacrificing men by war may appear to them as the blackest of all heathen superstitions. Its present popularity may appear as wonderful to ages to come, as the past popularity of any ancient custom now does to us. "What!" they may exclaim, "could those be Christians, who would sacrifice men by thousands to a point of honor, falsely so called; or to obtain a redress of a trifling wrong in regard to property! If such were the customs of Christians, what were they better than the heathens of their own time?"

Perhaps some apologist may rise up in that day, and plead that it appears from the history of our times that it was supposed necessary to the safety of a nation, that its government should be quick to assume a warlike tone and attitude, upon every infringement of their rights; that magnanimous forbearance was considered as pusillanimity, and that Christian meekness was thought intolerable in the character of a ruler.

To this others may reply: "Could these professed Christians imagine that their safety depended on displaying a spirit the reverse of their Master's? Could they suppose such a temper best calculated to insure the protection of Him, who held their destiny in His hands? Did they not know that wars were of a demoralizing tendency, and that the greatest danger to a nation resulted from its corruption and depravity? Did they not also know that a haughty spirit of resentment in our government was very sure to provoke a similar spirit in another? That one war usually paved the way for a repetition of similar calamities by depriving each of the contending parties, and by fixing enmities and jealousies, which would be ready to break forth on the most frivolous occasions?" . . .

SECTION VII

An important question now occurs. By what means is it possible to produce such a change in the state of society, and the views of Christian nations, that every ruler shall feel that his own honor, safety, and happiness, depend on his displaying a pacific spirit, and forbearing to engage in offensive wars? Is it not possible to form powerful peace societies in every nation of Christendom, whose object shall be to support government and secure the nation from war? . . .

Another means of advancing the object deserves particular consideration; namely, early education. This grand object should have a place in every plan of education, in families, common schools, academies and universities.

"Train up a child in the way he should go, and when he is old, he will not depart from it." The power of education has been tried to make children of a ferocious, bloodthirsty character. Let it now have a fair chance to see what it will do toward making mild, friendly and peaceful citizens. . . .

I have till now avoided the mention of our present war, that nothing should appear calculated to excite party feelings. But as the present calamity is severely felt, I must be permitted to express my hope that the affliction will favor the present object. If our distresses may be the occasion of opening the eyes of this people to see the delusions of war in general, and of exciting them to suitable exertions to prevent a return of such a calamity, an important benefit may result not only to posterity, but to the world. For if suitable exertions should be made in this country, the influence will not be bounded by the Atlantic; it will cross the ocean, and find its way in the Bible Societies, and other religious societies in Great Britain, and on the continents of Europe, Asia, and Africa. Nor will it be many years before it will find access to the houses of legislation and the palaces of kings.

Here Christians of every sect may find an object worthy of their attention, and in which they may cordially unite. For this object, they may with propriety leave behind all party zeal and party distinctions, and bury their animosities in one united effort to give peace to the world.

Let lawyers, politicians, and divines, and men of every class who can write or speak, consecrate their talents to the diffusion of light, and love, and peace. Should there be an effort such as the object demands, God will grant his blessing, posterity will be grateful, heaven will be filled with joy and praise, and "the sword shall *not* devour forever."

89.

THOMAS JEFFERSON: The Sphere of Religion

Thomas Jefferson believed firmly in the separation of church and state. In his Notes on the State of Virginia, *he had warned against the interference of the state in matters of religious belief. "Our rulers can have authority over such natural rights, only as we have submitted to them," he wrote in 1783. "The rights of conscience we never submitted. . . . We are answerable for them to our God. The legitimate powers of government extend to such acts only as are injurious to others. But it does me no injury for my neighbor to say there are twenty gods, or no god." In the following letter to P. H. Wendover, written on March 13, 1815, Jefferson examined the other side of the matter declaring that the interference of the church in affairs of state, under the guise of political sermons, is equally menacing.*

Source: Randolph, IV, pp. 259-262.

YOUR FAVOR OF JANUARY 30 was received after long delay on the road, and I have to thank you for the volume of discourses which you have been so kind as to send me. I have gone over them with great satisfaction, and concur with the able preacher in his estimate of the character of the belligerents in our late war, and lawfulness of defensive war. I consider the war, with him, as "made on good advice," that is, for just causes, and its dispensation as providential, inasmuch as it has exercised our patriotism and submission to order, has planted and invigorated among us arts of urgent necessity, has manifested the strong and the weak parts of our republican institutions and the excellence of a representative democracy compared with the misrule of kings, has rallied the opinions of mankind to the natural rights of expatriation and of a common property in the ocean, and raised us to that grade in the scale of nations which the bravery and liberality of our citizen soldiers, by land and by sea, the wisdom of our institutions, and their observance of justice, entitled us to in the eyes of the world.

All this Mr. McLeod has well proved, and from these sources of argument particularly which belong to his profession. On one question only I differ from him, and it is that which constitutes the subject of his first discourse, the right of discussing public affairs in the pulpit. I add the last words, because I admit the right in general conversation and in writing; in which last form it has been exercised in the valuable book you have now favored me with.

The mass of human concerns, moral and physical, is so vast, the field of knowledge requisite for man to conduct them to the best advantage is so extensive, that no human being can acquire the whole himself, and much less in that degree necessary for the instruction of others. It has of necessity, then, been distributed into different departments, each of which, singly, may give occupation enough to the whole time and attention of a single individual. Thus we have teachers of languages, teachers of mathematics, of natural philosophy, of chemistry, of medicine, of law, of history, of government, etc. Religion, too, is a separate department, and happens to be the only one deemed requisite for all men, however high or low.

Collections of men associate together, under the name of congregations, and employ a religious teacher of the particular sect of opinions of which they happen to be, and contribute to make up a stipend as a compensation for the trouble of delivering them, at such periods as they agree on, lessons in the religion they profess. If they want instruction in other sciences or arts, they apply to other instructors; and this is generally the business of early life. But I suppose there is not an instance of a single congregation which has employed their preacher for the mixed purposes of lecturing them from the pulpit in chemistry, in medicine, in law, in the science and principles of government, or in anything but religion exclusively. Whenever, therefore, preachers, instead of a lesson in religion, put them off with a discourse on the Copernican system, on chemical affinities, on the construction of government, or the characters or conduct of those administering it, it is a breach of contract, depriving their audience of the kind of service for which they are salaried, and giving them, instead of it, what they did not want, or, if wanted, would rather seek from better sources in that particular art or science. In choosing our pastor we look to his religious qualifications, without inquiring into his physical or political dogmas, with which we mean to have nothing to do. I am aware that arguments may be found which may twist a thread of politics into the cord of religious duties. So may they for every other branch of human art or science.

Thus, for example, it is a religious duty to obey the laws of our country; the teacher of religion, therefore, must instruct us in those laws, that we may know how to obey them. It is a religious duty to assist our sick neighbors; the preacher must, therefore, teach us medicine, that we may do it understandingly. It is a religious duty to preserve our own health; our religious teacher, then, must tell us what dishes are wholesome, and give us recipes in cookery, that we may learn how to prepare them. And so, ingenuity, by generalizing more and more, may amalgamate all the branches of science into any one of them, and the physician who is paid to visit the sick may give a sermon instead of medicine, and the merchant to whom money is sent for a hat may send a handkerchief instead of it.

But notwithstanding this possible confusion of all sciences into one, common sense draws lines between them sufficiently distinct for the general purposes of life, and no one is at a loss to understand that a recipe in medicine or cookery, or a demonstration in geometry is not a lesson in religion. I do not deny that a congregation may, if they please, agree with their preacher that he shall instruct them in medicine also, or law, or politics. Then, lectures in these, from the pulpit, become not only a matter of right, but of duty also. But this must be with the consent of every individual; because the association being voluntary, the mere majority has no right to apply the contributions of the minority to purposes unspecified in the agreement of the congregation.

I agree, too, that on all other occasions, the preacher has the right, equally with every other citizen, to express his sentiments, in speaking or writing, on the subjects of medicine, law, politics, etc., his leisure time being his own, and his congregation not obliged to listen to his conversation or to read his writings; and no one would have regretted more than myself, had any scruple as to this right withheld from us the valuable discourses which have led to the expression of an opinion as to the true limits of the right. I feel my portion of indebtedness to the reverend author for the distinguished learning, the logic, and the eloquence with which he has proved that religion, as well as reason, confirms the soundness of those principles on which our government has been founded and its rights asserted.

These are my views on this question. They are in opposition to those of the highly respected and able preacher, and are, therefore, the more doubtingly offered. Difference of opinion leads to inquiry, and inquiry to truth; and that, I am sure, is the ultimate and sincere object of us both. We both value too much the freedom of opinion sanctioned by our Constitution not to cherish its exercise even where in opposition to ourselves.

Unaccustomed to reserve or mystery in the expression of my opinions, I have opened myself frankly on a question suggested by your letter and present. And although I have not the honor of your acquaintance, this mark of attention, and still more the sentiments of esteem so kindly expressed in your letter, are entitled to a confidence that observations not intended for the public will not be ushered to their notice, as has happened to me sometimes. Tranquillity, at my age, is the balm of life. While I know I am safe in the honor and charity of a McLeod, I do not wish to be cast forth to the Marats, the Dantons, and the Robespierres of the priesthood; I mean the Parishes, the Ogdens, and the Gardiners of Massachusetts.

I pray you to accept the assurances of my esteem and respect.

90.

Richard Rush: Jurisprudence and the Common Law

The eminent position enjoyed by lawyers in the early years of the republic was partly a result of the fact that many distinguished figures graced the profession, but partly, too, the result of a more or less self-conscious campaign on the part of lawyers themselves to publicize and promote the law. One of the more memorable examples of this literature is Richard Rush's pamphlet, American Jurisprudence, *written in 1815. Rush was attorney general and had just completed the editing of his* Laws of the United States from 1789 to 1815 *(5 vols., 1815). Excerpts from* American Jurisprudence *are reprinted below.*

Source: *American Jurisprudence,* Philadelphia, 1815.

The law itself in this country is . . . a science of great extent. We have an entire substratum of common law as the broad foundation upon which everything else is built. It fills its thousand volumes like that of England, whose volumes in this respect are, at the same time, ours. But the extent of this law, its beginning, its termination; upon what subjects precisely it operates and where it falls short; where the analogy of situation holds and where not, with the shades under which it may do the one or the other . . . these start questions upon which the nicest discriminations of ingenuity and learning have been for a century at work.

Often, therefore, the American lawyer has gone through but half his task when he has

Library of Congress

An engraving of Richard Rush by an unknown artist

informed himself of what the common law is. The remaining and perhaps most difficult branch of inquiry is whether it does or does not apply to his case. Notwithstanding the determination of the Supreme Court in the case of the *United States* v. *Hudson and Goodwin,* it is still by no means certain that that tribunal would not sustain another and more full argument at this day on the question, in its nature so extensive and fundamental, as whether or not the federal government draws to itself the common law of England in criminal matters. When we speak of the great body of this system of law as a substratum, we mean of course as applied to the individual states.

The statute law of England during our provincial day, or anterior to it, is another great division, liable to much the same sort of counterargument at the hands of those who have been charged with the heavy task, at which they still toil, of rearing up the fabric of American jurisprudence. Next comes the prolific exuberance of our own statute law, superinducting its daily modifications upon the English code and giving birth to original systems to meet the new exigencies of our incessant enterprise, our growing population, and the genius of all our other institutions. The statutes and the lawsuits to which steamboats alone have given rise within the last two or three years would probably occupy several volumes. Those relative to turnpike roads and the contentions they have bred, taking all the states, would probably fill a dozen; and it would be difficult to limit the further illustrations we could give. Patents for new inventions would make an ample not to say curious figure.

But the most fruitful theme upon which the abundant and commanding stores of intellect may be poured out is what we understand by our constitutional law, and which is nearly peculiar to the United States. The apportionment of power between the national and state constitutions in the numerous channels in which it is made to flow was originally a work surrounded on all sides with difficulties of equal novelty and magnitude. To draw with accuracy the line of separate authority between these conflicting charters has often presented, and in all probability will long continue to present, complex problems, calling for the most artificial, untried, and elaborate, investigations. These must not infrequently borrow the lights of history as well as of law, of universal as well as of local jurisprudence, and, by affecting the rights or touching the passions of entire communities, they often rouse the mind to the highest stretch of vigorous and, in regard to the manifestation of its powers, of advantageous effort. This contrariety of jurisdiction between the federal and state governments has been prettily compared by a celebrated elementary jurist of our country to a line which "extends like the ecliptic, sometimes on one side and sometimes on the other of our political equator."

The judicial, the legislative, and the executive functions which, under the two systems in the numerous ranges of their exercise, are to be conciliated with an efficacious and harmonious whole, may well be supposed to open a wide field for the highest attributes of the understanding, where original strength must unite with the most complete state of improvement as to every kindred source of acquired knowledge. If we were to advert to a few instances occurring to us as lending countenance to the spirit of the remarks, they would be, such as the great case of the suability of a state, that of the British debts, that of the carriage tax, Colonel Burr's trial, [etc.].

Moreover, while we are led into an allusion to such cases as these, we will take upon us to say, without resorting to numerous others which the state as well as the national tribunals afford, that they are characterized by as universal and as splendid displays of appropriate genius and learning, both from the bench and bar, as any recorded judicial decisions with which we are acquainted will be found to boast. It is true, they are not yet much known or acknowledged abroad; but that is because the day of our being treated as provincial is hardly quite worn out. It is far from impossible that we may lately have been hastening the period of its obliteration, and that having become somewhat more known in our mere existence as a nation through our Jacksons, our Browns, our Biddles, our Blakeleys, and our Decaturs, we may be making more encouraging approximations than we could otherwise have flattered ourselves with the hope of doing toward the more diffusive fame of our Jays, our Ellsworths, and our Marshalls. . . .

In the structure of our judicature we have a multitude of different sorts of courts. We have courts of common law and courts of chancery, Admiralty and maritime courts, courts civil and courts criminal, sittings at *nisi prius* and full terms in bank, registers' courts, orphans' courts, escheators' courts, justices' courts, with the many gradations of some of them, and with others that might be made to swell the catalog. It may be said that this is nothing more than the judicial polity of other countries, particularly Britain, is liable to; that if you will begin at the piepoudre and go up to the peers in Parliament, you will run through, under some modification or other, as long an enumeration. This may be true. But the difference is that the profession here is not subdivided in any of the states in the ways that it is in England, and the American lawyer is called upon at one period or other of his life to understand the constitution of each of these forums; to be familiar at least with their principles if not with their forms as he passes on through the usual stages to the head of his profession.

It may be supposed that great labor is necessary to master such a range of knowledge. And such, undoubtedly, is the case. The men among us who reach the vantage ground of the science, who become as well the safe counselors as the eloquent advocates, are only those who in their early day explore its ways with repetitions of intense and, through all its dreadful discouragements to the young mind, unwearied assiduity; and who are afterward content to devote their days to business and their nights to study. Sparing indeed must be their relaxations. . . .

While the law with us is so copious, we are still willing to believe that it has all the essential characteristics of a good code; that its comprehensiveness is the unavoidable result of our wants and the glorious evidence of our freedom; that its occasional darkness, supposed or real, is nothing more than belongs to all free codes in a greater or less degree, and is generally to be dispelled by the penetrating rays of a comprehensive knowledge; that, above all, if in the unraveling and adjustment of complicated concerns, it may sometimes at first sight seem itself complicated, it never fails to throw a broad effulgence upon all the fundamental securities of the liberty and property of the citizen. . . .

If mind be the result of external stimuli forcing it into action, our jurisprudence is surrounded by what must provoke and improve its powers. There are reasons why it ought not to be expected of us to produce a Lord Byron, or a Walter Scott, a Dugal Stewart perhaps, or other men of like stamp with those who enrich the British press with such a copious and constant flow of profound or elegant literary and scientific productions. We are yet at some distance, though we trust not very great, from the age that can feed in any extent the merely classic mind into fullness and perfection. But we see no reasons at all why we may not breed Gibbses, and Garrows, and Saubeys, and Lawrences, and breed them in abundance. If we have not gained that stage of our growth when the luxury of the arts and sciences goes hand in hand with all other luxuries, we enjoy in a proud degree, to use an expression of the *Edinburgh Review,* "the luxury of liberty"; and it is not irrational to suppose that those who officiate so largely at her altars should arrive at a perfection in their duty.

In throwing out a conjectural sentiment, and one not altogether hasty, we presume to think that the law mind, if we may so speak, of the United States has, from adequate causes, forerun the general condition of literature, and already been accelerated and matured into as much force and discipline as it is likely to reach in any more distant period of the country's advancement. How it may be in medicine and in divinity, we do not presume on this occasion to intimate. If there be fit matter for reflection under these heads, it must be gone into in some separate disquisition. In painting there might be room to say something, keeping to the walk of native genius at least. We pass to our proper subject.

The profession of the law with us, then, seems to be absorbed by duties as numerous and as commanding at this day as it is probable that it can be at any more remote epoch of fuller population and greater riches. Those scenes of portentous convulsion which in their occasional visitations rouse the mind of a whole community into temporary and preternatural force, and which more frequently belong to a full than a slender population, and to age than to youth, may indeed form exceptions. But we speak of the settled and ordinary course of things. As our lonely territory continues to be overspread with cultivated fields and to glitter with the spires of villages and cities, we shall, to be sure, witness a corresponding increase in the professors of this science; but it does not appear to follow that their faculties will be tasked to a higher compass of exertion than the faculties of those who now flourish in the walks of full occupation. . . .

Endeavoring to divest ourselves as far as possible of the national feeling, we candidly think that the English lawyers, taken in the bulk, bear upon them, in the comparison with our own, something of the stamp of this rigidly exclusive occupation of the faculties. . . .

These are only opinions. We would by no means be understood as asserting them with any dogmatic confidence. The English have theirs upon all subjects, and no doubt will upon this. There can be no harm in having and expressing ours. Those who do not think our way of accounting for them good will not agree with us. It lately seemed strange, and to some inexplicable, that we should keep vanquishing their frigates, and their sloops of war, and their squadrons, with scarcely an exception, wherever we happened to find them; and yet so was the fact.

Now, as their jurisprudence has been as long and is as justly their boast as their Navy, who knows, if we could only get impartial arbiters, but that this country of their own peopling might also be thought in danger of tearing from them some of the laurels of the law? We leave others to talk about the causes or effects of the war, and for ourselves have nothing more to do with its events than barely to try, if we can draw from them some remote but possibly not imperceptible analogies, to mix with our speculations. Humbly supposing that we have gone near toward surpassing them in the one line, we do not know that it ought wholly to shock belief should anyone be bold enough to dream of our falling into the same unexpected sort of sacrilege in another! . . .

There is indeed at the present day in England a judge, perhaps their first, of the volumes containing whose decisions it has been said in the British House of Commons, "that they were no less valuable to the classical reader than to the student of law by perpetuating the style in which the judgments of the court were delivered." A man he is of dazzling mind. Born, we believe, a miller's son, he can talk of giving a *rusticum judicium*. Yet, surely, no judge upon the face of the earth was ever farther from having rendered such a one. His intellect is so polished that it has been called transparent. Some of his pages are as if diamond sparks were on them. When he deals in wit, it is like a sunbeam and gone as quick. . . .

There graces the first seat of judicial magistracy in this country a man of another stamp, and exhibiting different aspects of excellence. Venerable and dignified, laborious and intuitive, common law, chancery law, and admiralty law each make their demands upon his profound, his discriminating, and his well-stored mind. Universal in his attainments in legal science, prompt and patient, courteous and firm, he fills up, by a combination of rare endowments, the measure of his difficult, his extensive, and his responsible duties; responsible not to the dictates of an executive but, moving in a sphere of true independence, responsible to his conscience, to his country, and to his God. What a grand, and to a mind exalted and virtuous, what an awful sphere! How independent, how responsible! Vain would it be for us to expect to do justice to the full-orbed merit with which he moves in it.

Bred up in a state rich in great names, counting her Washingtons, her Jeffersons, her Madisons, he long sustained a career of the highest reputation at the bar. Passing to the bench of the Supreme Court of the United States, he carried to its duties a mind matured by experience and invigorated by long daily and successful toil. In the voluminous state of our jurisprudence, every portion of which is occasionally brought under his review, and in the novelties of our political state, often does it happen that questions are brought before him where the path is untrodden, where neither the book case nor the record exist to guide, and where the elementary writer himself glimmers dimly. . . .

Upon such occasions, as well as upon the entire body of commercial law so copiously in the last resort intermingled with his adjudications, his recorded opinions will best make known to the world the penetration of his views, the extent of his knowledge, and the solidity of his judgment. They are a national treasure. Posterity will read in them as well the rule of conduct as the monuments of a genius that would have done honor to any age or to any country.

Such is the sketch we would attempt of the judicial character of the Chief Justice of our country. That country is on a swift wing to greatness and to glory. To the world at large the early day of her jurisprudence may remain unknown until then; but then it will break into light, and his name, like the Fortescues and the Cokes of the early day of England, fill perhaps even a wider region from the less local foundations upon which it will rest. Let the courts of England boast of Sir William Scott. Those of America will boast of John Marshall.

91.

Thomas Jefferson: On the Constitutional Powers of the Branches of Government

When the Constitution was new, Jefferson expressed the wish that the Supreme Court had been invested with a veto power over the legislature. After it had been in force for almost three decades, and his own administration's policies had been strongly and persistently opposed by John Marshall's Court, Jefferson decided that each of the three branches of government should be the final judge of its own actions. The latter view, which Jefferson maintained for the rest of his life, was expressed in the following letter to W. H. Torrance, dated June 11, 1815.

Source: Ford, IX, pp. 516-519.

The . . . question, whether . . . judges are invested with exclusive authority to decide on the constitutionality of a law, has been heretofore a subject of consideration with me in the exercise of official duties. Certainly there is not a word in the Constitution which has given that power to them more than to the executive or legislative branches. Questions of property, of character, and of crime being ascribed to the judges, through a definite course of legal proceeding, laws involving such questions belong, of course, to them; and as they decide on them ultimately and without appeal, they of course decide *for themselves.* The constitutional validity of the law or laws again prescribing executive action, and to be administered by that branch ultimately and without appeal, the executive must decide *for themselves,* also, whether, under the Constitution, they are valid or not. So also as to laws governing the proceedings of the legislature, that body must judge *for itself* the constitutionality of the law, and, equally, without appeal or control from its coordinate branches.

And, in general, that branch which is to act ultimately, and without appeal, on any law, is the rightful expositor of the validity of the law, uncontrolled by the opinions of the other coordinate authorities. It may be said that contradictory decisions may arise in such case, and produce inconvenience. This is possible, and is a necessary failing in all human proceedings. Yet the prudence of the public functionaries, and authority of public opinion, will generally produce accommodation. Such an instance of difference occurred between the judges of England (in the time of Lord Holt) and the House of Commons, but the prudence of those bodies prevented inconvenience from it. So in the cases of Duane and of William Smith of South Carolina, whose characters of citizenship stood precisely on the same ground, the judges, in a question of *meum* and *tuum* which came before them, decided that Duane was not a citizen; and in a question of membership, the House of Representatives, under the same words of the same provision, adjudged William Smith to be a citizen. Yet no inconvenience has ensued from these contradictory decisions.

This is what I believe, myself, to be

sound. But there is another opinion entertained by some men of such judgment and information as to lessen my confidence in my own; that is, that the legislature alone is the exclusive expounder of the sense of the Constitution, in every part of it whatever. And they allege, in its support, that this branch has authority to impeach and punish a member of either of the others acting contrary to its declaration of the sense of the Constitution. It may indeed be answered that an act may still be valid although the party is punished for it, right or wrong. However, this opinion which ascribes exclusive exposition to the legislature merits respect for its safety, there being in the body of the nation a control over them, which, if expressed by rejection on the subsequent exercise of their elective franchise, enlists public opinion against their exposition, and encourages a judge or executive on a future occasion to adhere to their former opinion. Between these two doctrines, everyone has a right to choose, and I know of no third meriting any respect.

I have thus, sir, frankly, without the honor of your acquaintance, confided to you my opinion; trusting assuredly that no use will be made of it which shall commit me to the contentions of the newspapers. From that field of disquietude my age asks exemption and permission to enjoy the privileged tranquility of a private and unmeddling citizen. In this confidence accept the assurances of my respect and consideration.

92.

Thomas Jefferson: On the Balance of Power in Europe

"It cannot be to our interest," declared Jefferson early in 1814, "that all Europe should be reduced to a single monarchy." But this was before a victory over Napoleon promised to give Britain such sweeping powers as no single government had wielded since the fall of the Roman Empire. Thus, despite his natural hatred of despotism, Jefferson changed his mind, and expressed the hope that Napoleon would be victorious at least in part, and retain enough influence to produce a balance of power on the European continent. Among other things, Jefferson felt, this would help to insure the security as well as the neutrality of the United States. He discussed these matters in a letter to the Philadelphia merchant, Thomas Leiper, dated June 12, 1815. Napoleon was totally defeated by combined British and Prussian armies at Waterloo, in Belgium, exactly one week later.

Source: Randolph, IV, pp. 270-273.

In our principles of government we differ not at all; nor in the general object and tenor of political measures. We concur in considering the government of England as totally without morality, insolent beyond bearing, inflated with vanity and ambition, aiming at the exclusive dominion of the sea, lost in corruption, of deep-rooted hatred toward us, hostile to liberty wherever it endeavors to show its head, and the eternal disturber of the peace of the world.

In our estimate of Bonaparte, I suspect we differ. I view him as a political engine only, and a very wicked one; you, I believe, as both political and religious, and obeying, as an instrument, an unseen hand. I still deprecate his becoming sole lord of the continent of Europe, which he would have been had he reached in triumph the gates of Petersburg. The establishment in our day of another Roman Empire spreading vassalage and depravity over the face of the globe is not, I hope, within the purposes of heaven. Nor does the return of Bonaparte give me pleasure unmixed; I see in his expulsion of the Bourbons a valuable lesson to the world, as showing that its ancient dynasties may be changed for their misrule. Should the allied powers presume to dictate a ruler and government to France, and follow the example he had set of parceling and usurping to themselves their neighbor nations, I hope he will give them another lesson in vindication of the rights of independence and self-government, which himself had heretofore so much abused; and that in this contest he will wear down the maritime power of England to limitable and safe dimensions. So far, good.

It cannot be denied, on the other hand, that his successful perversion of the force (committed to him for vindicating the rights and liberties of his country) to usurp its government and to enchain it under a hereditary despotism is of baneful effect in encouraging future usurpations, and deterring those under oppression from rising to redress themselves. His restless spirit leaves no hope of peace to the world; and his hatred of us is only a little less than that he bears to England, and England to us. Our form of government is odious to him, as a standing contrast between republican and despotic rule; and as much from that hatred as from ignorance in political economy he had excluded intercourse between us and his people, by prohibiting the only articles they wanted from us; that is, cotton and tobacco. Whether the war we have had with England, the achievements of that war, and the hope that we may become his instruments and partisans against that enemy may induce him, in future, to tolerate our commercial intercourse with his people is still to be seen.

For my part, I wish that all nations may recover and retain their independence; that those which are overgrown may not advance beyond safe measures of power; that a salutary balance may be ever maintained among nations; and that our peace, commerce, and friendship may be sought and cultivated by all. It is our business to manufacture for ourselves whatever we can, to keep all markets open for what we can spare or want; and the less we have to do with the amities or enmities of Europe, the better. Not in our day, but at no distant one, we may shake a rod over the heads of all, which may make the stoutest of them tremble. But I hope our wisdom will grow with our power, and teach us that the less we use our power, the greater it will be. . . .

I rejoice exceedingly that our war with England was single-handed. In that of the Revolution, we had France, Spain, and Holland on our side; and the credit of its success was given to them. On the late occasion, unprepared and unexpecting war, we were compelled to declare it, and to receive the attack of England, just issuing from a general war, fully armed and freed from all other enemies, and have not only made her sick of it, but glad to prevent by a peace the capture of her adjacent possessions, which one or two campaigns more would infallibly have made ours. She has found that we can do her more injury than any other enemy on earth, and, henceforth, will better estimate the value of our peace. But whether her government has power, in opposition to the aristocracy of her Navy, to restrain their piracies within the limits of national rights may well be doubted. I pray, therefore, for peace, as best for all the world, best for us, and best for me, who have already lived to see three wars, and now pant for nothing more than to be permitted to depart in peace.

93.

Robert Finley: National Uniformity in Textbooks and Curricula

Nationalists like George Washington and Benjamin Rush had expressed the hope at the end of the eighteenth century that the new country would develop a truly American system of education. The idea continued to be popular during Jefferson's administration and until after the War of 1812, when Robert Finley, a Presbyterian minister and president of the University of Georgia, advocated the use of uniform textbooks throughout the nation's schools and colleges. Any such suggestion today would probably be met by charges of censorship, and in fact Finley was not successful in his campaign, but he had no desire to dictate to other educators. In his view, uniform textbooks would be a practical solution of the problems of critical shortages and poor quality of teaching materials in many of the country's schools.

Source: Isaac V. Brown, *Memoirs of the Rev. Robert Finley,* New Brunswick, N.J., 1819, pp. 347-360.

In a country like ours, where the interests of science do not experience extensively the benefits of legislative patronage, literature, left to depend upon her own contingent resources, must be expected to make slow progress in accomplishing her views. Her success will depend, in a very great degree, upon the wisdom, zeal, and energy which characterize the system pursued in the seminaries established for the promotion of literature.

The interests of classical science, in the United States, are suffering materially from that want of uniformity in elementary books which generally prevails. The variety exhibited by our schools and colleges, in this respect, corresponds fully with the varieties of climate, soil, and character which our country in general sustains. This want of uniformity exists, not only between the northern and southern districts of our country but is found, unfortunately, to prevail in the central regions, and in schools and seminaries situated quite contiguous to one another. It would facilitate the progress of youth in a collegiate course to make all their preparatory books of study, on every subject, bear as much general resemblance as circumstances would permit. . . .

To introduce entire uniformity into the American system of education, would it not be advisable for those colleges which can be brought to adopt the same elementary books in the several departments, classical, mathematical, and philosophical, to select, arrange, and publish a complete set of studies to be distinguished and known as the particular studies of these institutions? And, should this arrangement be found impracticable, would it not be highly advantageous for each college to make this selection for its own use, and as far as necessary for the accommodation of its subordinate schools? By this measure:

1. Money might be saved to the learner. Most of the books now used in schools and colleges are published in a style of execution more costly than necessary and are bought at too dear a rate. In many instances the expense of procuring a whole work is incurred, while only a small portion of it is read or studied. The paper is often thin and perishable, and the binding very slight and inferior. In the proposed publication, these disadvantages might easily be remedied. The materials and the workmanship should be of the most substantial and durable nature. All unnecessary matter it is proposed to leave out.

2. On the plan here contemplated, accuracy, in classical books, might be restored.

The Latin and Greek authors printed in this country abound so exceedingly with typographical errors that very great injury is sustained from the use of them in schools. When inaccuracies frequently occur, the teacher is incessantly harassed and the business of school interrupted by applications to have the classical text examined, and existing errors exposed and corrected. In this manner much time is lost and the school is injured; and, besides, the student, always ready to impute difficulty to inaccuracy and to suspend his efforts till doubt is removed, finds his diligence in application and independent exercise of thought much impaired. These disadvantages have been experienced so seriously that it has been judged expedient in some instances to keep a European edition of the principal authors read as a standard to refer to — a fact disgraceful and humiliating to American scholars!

3. The proposed publication might be made entirely free from those impurities, with which some of the best classical writers unhappily abound. Retaining passages which convey insinuations against religion and morals, and which are of an obscene and vitiating tendency in those books which are very early put into the hands of youth to be carefully studied, is very manifestly dangerous and improper. It would be a favor of no common magnitude to the principles and morals of literary youth to have everything licentious, low, and polluting removed from our classical authors. A remedy might thus be furnished for the evils and the dangers arising from making our young men whom we wish to lead to the knowledge of the one only living and true God, too early and too intimately acquainted with Grecian and Roman polytheism, with the fictions and absurdities of their mythology, and with the vices and follies of their imaginary deities.

4. This measure would contribute very extensively to that uniformity which is so much desired. Wherever this work would circulate, the plan of education pursued in the institution which had given it existence might be fully understood and easily followed. The public in general, teachers, and schools especially would know precisely in what manner the preliminary studies of a candidate for that college must be conducted to obtain for him an easy and honorable admission into it.

Might we not adopt with some prudent modifications in our literary institutions that part of the ancient Jewish system of education in which they trained their pupils to an acquaintance with mechanical pursuits, in connection with letters and science; and while they strengthened and enriched the minds of their scholars with literary culture, established them in the practical knowledge of the useful arts and mechanical employments of life? If acquiring practical knowledge of mechanics, of gardening, of agriculture could be made to occupy a portion of that time which is commonly spent in idleness and amusement, and be brought to answer the purpose of necessary exercise, several additional objects of considerable importance would be in some degree gained by the alteration. . . .

One great object contemplated in placing boys at school ought to be to ascertain the degree and the peculiar character of their talents, to discover toward what objects their genius tends most strongly, with a view to the judicious direction of their future and permanent pursuits in life. In order to bring this experiment to a successful issue, it ought not to be partially made; mechanic arts and manual employments in some measure ought to be placed before every pupil and some attention to them required. Had this plan been faithfully pursued heretofore, our academies and perhaps colleges too, would have produced more good *mechanics* and not so many *dull literati!*

The plan proposed might be rendered an excellent security against the noisy habits and, above all, many of the vices of which too much leisure and amusement are the fruitful source.

Could not the alteration here contemplated be so modified as to become a powerful auxiliary in the government of youth, and be made the means of preventing altogether the necessity of corporal punishment?

The last consideration is that every man, whatever his grade of talent, his degree of education, and his sphere in life, ought to have a practical acquaintance with some mechanic art. Should he never pursue any branch of mechanical employ, his progress through life, his respectability, ease and comfort will be greatly promoted by a general acquaintance with the common necessary and useful arts and occupations of men. . . .

Great exertions have recently been made to establish new colleges in several states in the Union, and measures have been adopted in some of the best institutions in our country to enlarge and ameliorate their capacity for the accommodation and instruction of youth. But, notwithstanding, a university located near the center of the United States, amply endowed, and extensively patronized by the national government, is a desideratum of great magnitude. The wise and patriotic Washington suggested an idea of this nature in his last will and testament, and the reasons on which he founded that intimation are still applicable in all their force.

> It has been [says he] my ardent wish to see a plan devised on a liberal scale which would have a tendency to spread systematic ideas through all parts of this rising empire, thereby to do away local attachments and state prejudices, as far as the nature of things would or, indeed, ought to admit from our national councils. Looking anxiously forward to the accomplishment of so desirable an object as this is, in my estimation, my mind has not been able to contemplate any plan more likely to effect the measure than the establishment of a university in a central part of the United States, to which the youths of fortune and talents, from all parts thereof, might be sent for the completion of their education, in all the branches of polite literature, in the arts and sciences, in acquiring knowledge in the principles of politics and good government; and, as a matter of infinite importance, in my judgment, by associating with each other and forming friendships in juvenile years, be enabled to free themselves, in a proper degree, from those local prejudices and habitual jealousies . . . which, when carried to excess, are never failing sources of disquietude to the public mind and pregnant of mischievous consequences.

The colleges of the United States are so circumscribed in their resources and restricted in their views as to embrace in their system of instruction only those subjects which are most common and essential in a literary course. Other objects, hitherto neglected, are becoming highly interesting. A university, established on a widely extended scale so as to comprehend them all, would be truly worthy of national attention, and extensively conducive to national honor and interest.

This institution, besides the classical, mathematical, and philosophical professorships, ought to possess:

1. A theological department, amply endowed for the purpose of teaching the ele-

ments of natural and revealed religion, biblical and ecclesiastical history, moral and theological science in general.

2. It ought to include a professorship for the languages of modern Europe.

This would be a great convenience to young men of talent and enterprise seeking education principally as an auxiliary in the honorable pursuits of foreign commerce. It would afford to American genius a more direct and easy access to those stores of polite and accomplished literature which have been accumulating for centuries in the south of Europe, but from which our sons must be excluded while ignorant of the languages which are the only key to their depositories. And it would be an important accommodation to that part of our citizens who inhabit the regions in the south and west, where the French and Spanish especially are becoming almost vernacular tongues.

3. A professorship for the purpose of extending the knowledge of the languages of the various nations of America, Asia, and Africa.

This would facilitate the necessary intercourse with the American tribes both in treaty and in traffic; it would furnish a ready and happy assistant in carrying on the lucrative commerce with the Eastern world; it would extensively aid the glorious cause of foreign missions, in promoting which every American statesman and philanthropist should feel a pride and an interest; it would enlarge the compass of human knowledge by extending the sphere of education in this Western land; and, in the course of time, by its indirect operation on the aborigines of India, Africa, and America, it might have extensive influence in producing that community of sentiment and manners, that amelioration of aspect and condition, which will soon, we hope, be exhibited by the human race.

4. In this institution, provision should be made, in the best manner practicable, for exciting, directing, and aiding the efforts of American genius in the cultivation of the fine arts.

With success in this department of science, the honor of the nation is closely connected. Europe claims preeminence in the arts, and looks down upon the United States with disdain. Let every encouragement and facility for the successful cultivation of American talent and taste be afforded by a liberal and enlightened government, jealous of its own honor, and anxious for the best improvement of its own sons in those arts and accomplishments which peculiarly liberalize, elevate, and adorn the human character.

5. This establishment ought to afford to American youth the means of obtaining accurate theoretic and practical knowledge of agriculture.

The course of improvement which this country seems destined to undergo, by means of canals, turnpikes, bridges, fortifications, etc., will demand increasing skill in mechanic arts and operations. The American people have also manifested a strong predilection for manufacturing pursuits of various kinds. These objects respectively are highly deserving of national patronage. But, from the extent of our territory, the excellence of our climate, the fertility of our soil, the ideas, habits, and necessities of the people, agriculture appears likely to be the general and predominant occupation of the American states. And as a warrant for making a system of instruction on this subject an appendage of a great literary institution, it may be recollected that the example has been set in many of the most celebrated universities of Europe. . . .

6. Considering the infant state of eloquence and political knowledge in the American republic, it appears reasonable and necessary that, in the contemplated institution, the duty of affording to American youth profound and expanded instruction,

in civil and national law, in political economy, and on the whole science of government, should receive special attention. The spirit of our government, the nature of our climate, the lofty and independent sentiments of our citizens, and the peculiar character and power of genius which they have already manifested, at the bar and in the legislative hall, inspire us with the pleasing expectation that the United States will soon possess many orators and statesmen who *will* be the pride of their country and *may* be the admiration of mankind.

Animated by this hope, should not the genius of our sons be excited and fostered in the most efficient manner practicable? Can anything be conceived more worthy the attention of the supreme legislature of an enlightened and liberal people than providing suitable motives and facilities for this progress to national honor, greatness, and glory?

94.

Hezekiah Niles: National Unity and Prosperity

Hezekiah Niles's Weekly Register *was one of the most influential periodicals in America during the first half of the last century. Founded by Niles in 1811 and published by him in Baltimore until 1836, the paper consistently favored policies that, in the opinion of its editor, were likely to contribute both to the unity and to the prosperity of the country. At the beginning of his career, Niles was one of the leading spokesmen of "the era of good feeling," as the period between the War of 1812 and the panic of 1820 was called by him and his contemporaries. In his editorial of September 2, 1815, Niles helped get the era under way. Entitled "The Prospect Before Us," the editorial is typical of its author's ardent nationalism.*

Source: *Niles' Weekly Register,* September 2, 1815.

It is so much the custom for editors of works like this, to make an occasional stop and hold a little familiar chat with their patrons, that I might be supposed to want due respect for the numerous readers of the *Weekly Register* if I were to omit an observance of it.

The existing state of things, as well as the "prospect before us," is most happy for the American people. *The republic, reposing on the laurels of a glorious war, gathers the rich harvest of an honorable peace.* Everywhere the sound of the axe is heard, opening the forest to the sun and claiming for agriculture the range of the buffalo. Our cities grow and towns rise up as by magic; commerce expands her proud sails in safety, and the "striped bunting" floats with majesty over every sea. The busy hum of 10,000 wheels fills our seaports, and the sound of the spindle and the loom succeeds the yell of the savage or screech of the night owl in the late wilderness of the interior. The lord of the soil, who recently deserted the plow to meet the enemies of his country on its threshold and dispute the possession, has returned in quiet to his fields, exulting that the *republic lives,* and in honor! The hardy hunter, whose deadly rifle lately brought the foeman to the earth, has resumed his

Maryland Historical Society

Portrait of Hezekiah Niles by an unknown artist

former life, and, in the trackless forest, employs the same weapon, with unerring aim, to stop the fleet deer in his course. Plenty crowns the works of peace with abundance, and scatters from her cornucopia all the good things of this life, with prodigal bounty.

A high and honorable feeling generally prevails, and the people begin to assume, more and more, a *national character;* and to look at home for the only means, under divine goodness, of preserving their religion and liberty, with all the blessings that flow from their unrestricted enjoyment. The "bulwark" of these is in the sanctity of their principles, and the virtue and valor of these who profess to love them, and need no guarantee from the bloodstained and profligate princes and powers of Europe. Morality and good order ever prevail — canting hypocrisy has but few advocates, for the Great Architect of the universe is worshiped on the altar of men's hearts, in the way that each believes most acceptable to Him. . . .

The progress of our country in population, wealth, and resources is without parallel. The census of 1820 will give us not less than 10,000,000 people, of which a large and unexpected portion will be found westward of the Alleghenies, having emigrated from the East, with a *tripled* proportion of wealth and resources compared with what they were in 1810, the "calamities of the war" notwithstanding. The great ease with which a livelihood is obtained in the republic will continue a like increase of the first for many generations, and the others will go on with a geometrical ratio. And much assistance to each may be expected from war-worn Europeans, seeking a place of rest from oppression and chains. It is hardly possible to imagine, with any degree of certainty, the value annually created by the recently applied industry of the people to manufactures, aided by the various labor-saving machinery adapted to large institutions or household establishments. We are friendly to the former to a given extent, but it is on the latter that we chiefly rely to accomplish a sublime independence of the New World. . . .

A reduction and general modification of the existing duties, as well as a relinquishment of all the indirect taxes, is expected at the end of a year after the close of the war; but still, the national income will amply supply all its wants, and diminish the public debt as fast, perhaps, as true policy may require; for the national securities present us with a medium of commerce, as well foreign as domestic, that, it is possible, might be too suddenly withdrawn. That is, supposing we shall have peace, of which there is the happiest prospect, in the late news received of a commercial treaty being signed with England, the nation most likely to involve us in war. But the demand for foreign manufactures will be small compared with what it would have been, if the orders and decrees of the late belligerents had not driven us into the idea of being independent of them. It is not less easy to abandon habits that do *very well* than adopt others with the prospect of doing so.

A general spirit for manufacturing was got up with great difficulty, and cannot now be laid aside without immense exertion and sacrifice. The money that has been invested in our various branches of manufacture, including the rearing of sheep and cultivation of the cane to make sugar, within the last eight or ten years, and now employed in them, far exceeds that occupied by foreign trade. And, happily, it is so; for if the weight of the power of the "legitimates" of Europe shall settle the people down into the calm of despotism, and a general peace lasts for five years, the shipping interest of the United States, now or recently engaged in trading with that part of the world and its colonies, will suffer a diminution of 40 or 50 percent. And the demand for some of our most valuable and bulky staple articles of agriculture will be exceedingly reduced. The fact is, we had a great deal more of the commerce of the world than our share, as they who would have sold every honorable feeling to England for a miserable part of it will soon ascertain. But this is of little consequence to the bulk of the people who would rather have peace and quietness than Boston memorials, insurrection resolutions, or Hartford conventions.

In the general prosperity, we behold the downfall of that faction which would have made a common interest with the British during the late war — a faction that, for the profligacy of its proceedings, all things considered, stands without precedent; a faction that would have raised itself to power on the broken fasces of the Union! *It falls as its country rises* — the stability of the republic is arsenic to its hopes and wishes. Miserable, in the honorable result of the war; miserable, that Great Britain did not reduce us to "unconditional submission"; miserable, that Mr. Madison was not "deposed" by a foreign force; miserable, that they are despised by the people they would have given soul and body to serve; miserable, that they are laughed at by all who consider them too contemptible for serious rebuke — they drink the very dregs of the cup of mortification but alter their ways with bitterness and cursings. These men had no pride in the name of an "American," and it may be right to treat them as *aliens* when we speak of the affairs of the republic. But, if they must be considered as of our people, we have the satisfaction to say that they are a small, and the only portion of the population whose heart does not leap with gratitude to heaven for its munificence to the United States. . . .

Let us then, fellow citizens, cherish our republican institutions, and hold up as "objects for scorn to point her slow unmoving finger at" anyone that would jeopardize them, or bring them into disrepute. We have a strong monarchical party among us, whose principle is imported from England, that must be carefully watched. Let us recollect the saying of the sage who declared that he who gives up essential liberty to purchase temporary safety deserves neither liberty nor safety; and, always acting up to it, fix the disposition in our mind as a part of our existence that these United States are, of God and by our right, free, sovereign and independent; and, in this persuasion, also feel a determination to obey the injunction of Washington, "and frown indignantly on the first drawing of an attempt to alienate one portion of our country from the rest, or to enfeeble the sacred ties that now link together the various parts."

95.

Hugh H. Brackenridge: Should Beasts Vote?

H. H. Brackenridge's contribution to America's fiction stands out mainly because of the otherwise meager production of the years from 1789 to 1830, during which he edited the Pittsburgh Gazette *and published a number of books. One of them,* Modern Chivalry, *which he wrote at for more than twenty years (from 1792 to 1815), has achieved a measure of fame. Little escaped its author's biting satire, but Brackenridge's favorite targets were probably democratic politics (with a small "d") and the already developing mystique of the frontier. "Universal Suffrage," a chapter of the book, typifies the attitude of Brackenridge to the successes and failures of democracy in America.*

Source: *Modern Chivalry,* Philadelphia, 1857, Pt. 2, Vol. IV, Ch. 20.

The new Constitution had hardly gone into operation before new discussions took place. Various questions were agitated. One of the first was the propriety of universal suffrage; that is, whether every poll should poll or have a vote; or that *property* should also vote. If property alone, the question would arise, whether *soil* only; or also goods and chattels. If soil only, to what quantity or quality shall the suffrage be attached? A hundred acres of soil of a bad quality may not have the intrinsic worth of one of good. How should an inspector or judge of an election determine on the quality unless the owner brings a sample with him, as the man who had his house to sell brought a brick. This would be an inconvenience and would render it impracticable to escape frauds; for a man might dig a sample from his neighbor's and pass it for his own. And as to quantity, the occupier of the greater quantity is the less valuable citizen, especially who holds more than he cultivates, because he neither eats the hay nor lets another eat it. It is preposterous that *soil* should vote. A dumb field; a dead tree with a crow's nest upon it; a hazel bush; a morass or a barren mountain; or even a hill with a tuft of oaks upon it — these are all inanimate substances; how can they vote?

For goods and chattels, something might be said. A *live beast* particularly, as the animal could not speak, not with a *viva voce* vote, like a man; *more humano,* like a human creature; but with some gutteral sound from the throat, or fauces, which might be called its own; and not like the tree with a turkey buzzard on it, and which is not its own voice. I mean that of the tree, said the speaker, who was running on this manner; and yet it is advocated that stocks and stones that go with the soil shall have a vote. There might be some reason in improvements voting — a brick house or a Dutch barn — but none at all in the *mere brutum tellus* of an estate.

This had led the way to an hypothesis that property in moveables should alone entitle; and this, after some debate, began to be narrowed down to property in *living animals;* especially to useful quadrupeds, and those of full growth, and who had come to years, I will not say of discretion, but of maturity. From the light thrown upon the subject, the right of suffrage to grown cattle had become so popular that there was no resisting it; not that, *viva voce,* it was proposed or thought of, that inarticulating, speaking creatures should speak out, or name their representatives, nor even that they give in a ballot, but that they should be brought upon the ground to show their faces that there might be no imposition, the voters alleging that they had cattle when they had not.

But it was not to every owner's beast that it was advisable to extend the right; but only to the more valuable animals, or such as were of a good breed; Virginia horses that are fit for the saddle or the turf.

It may seem very strange; but actually the thing took; and at a polling, some time after, it began to be carried into effect that beasts should be constituents and have their representatives. It was not to the principle but the individual beast that some exceptions took place; as, for instance, an English bull was brought upon the hustings to give his vote. We will have no English bull, said the inspectors. Not that a brute beast is not entitled to a vote, nor that a bull cannot vote or be voted for; but this is an *English bull.* No English bull can vote. You might as well bring an Englishman himself to the polls. It is in right of the bull keeper, or bull owner, that the bull claims the suffrage. If an Englishman himself, not naturalized, is excluded, how can his bull or his horse or any other quadruped be admitted? It would be sufficient to set aside the election if his ticket was introduced. A bull indeed! The name of John Bull is appropriate to an Englishman. An Irish bull is quite *another matter.* John Bull shall have no voter here.

In the meantime, a man on an iron-gray horse rode up to the window, which was open for receiving tickets, and unequivocally insisted on a vote for his horse. Vouchers stood by, who averred that he was foaled in the county; that, horse and colt, they had known him many years; that, as to his paying taxes, they could not so well say, unless his labor on the farm could be considered as paying tax. And now, the horse putting his nose in at the window, taking it for a rack, an inspector gave him a fillip on the snout, which resenting, the owner wheeling round, the horse wheeling under him, he rode over one or more of the bystanders who were in the way.

It may be material to mention that the horse's mane and tail were black, to distinguish him from a gray horse that belonged to another person. A warm controversy arose on the subject, some taking the one side and some the other. Some also stood mute, not choosing to take part in election disputes. Others were very positive and violent. Such is the result of strong passions when not under the control of reason and reflection. Weak persons are always the most positive because they cannot afford the acknowledgment of an error. It will not do to admit fallibility, for there is no knowing how far the inference may be drawn.

Another man came up who brought a sheep to the polls; a Merino ram, who, he said, was entitled to a vote, having resided in the country since he had been brought in by Humphreys, representing him to be of the breed of the great Fezzen ram, though there were those who thought it might be what is called a Yankee trick; not but that all Americans may be capable of substituting a thing for what it is not; and all are called Yankees by the British; but New England men are distinguished and called Yankee Doodles.

The ram is not entitled to a vote, said the inspector, nor ought he to be permitted to put in a ticket were he of the breed of the Golden Fleece guarded by the fiery dragons whom Jason overcame and brought away the wool. No, not if he was the very ram that was caught in the thicket; or that Daniel saw in his vision coupled with the he goat. But he is a Spanish ram, born under despotism — how can he be expected to give a republican vote? Of papist origin, he may bring the Inquisition with him, coming here to vote. Besides, this is a very real sheep that is offered, and not one whom we call a sheep in a figurative sense of the word. Where we call men horses, or asses, we do not mean always that they are so, *puris naturalibus,* without overalls on, with the horn and the hoof about them, but shadowing forth the same thing under a veil of metaphor, as the case may be. But not on this ground altogether do I reject him, and because he has wool on his back; but because he is of Barbary origin. The Moors brought the breed into Spain. You may cast a *sheep's eye* at the window as long as you please, Master Ram, but not a vote shall you have as long as *I* am here. I do not know whether you are not a half-breed, and no genuine Merino. So away with him, as the song says,

To the ewe-boughts, Marian.

Another person coming up brought a large ox, which he called Thomas Jefferson, not out of respect to the ox but to the man, as having a good name and reputation. Make way, said the voters, for Thomas Jefferson. We will have no Thomas Jefferson, said the inspector; he is out of his district. I assert the contrary, said the owner; he was calved in this settlement. He is called the mammoth ox, and I had thought of driving him to Washington; but that I knew that if he were he might be made a present to Jefferson, the Congress would eat him, as they did the mammoth cheese; so that the President would scarcely get a slice of him. For there are parasites in all countries, and the worthless are chiefly those who dance attendance upon men in office; and how can it be avoided to invite them to partake of civilities?

You will certainly allow a vote to Thomas Jefferson. No, not if he was the real Jefferson from Monticello, said the inspector. How can I tell but he may introduce the same politics? That is true, said another; break judges, abolish taxes, dismantle navies, build gunboats, lay embargoes, depress armies, pay no tributes to Barbary powers, issue proclamations, wear red breeches, receive ambassadors in pantaloons and slippers, collect prairie dogs and horned frogs, dream of salt mountains, walk with pedometers, and be *under French influence.* We will have no Thomas Jefferson. You may drive off your ox. He shall have no vote here.

No doubt the judges and inspectors, being men of sense, saw the absurdity of carrying the principle so far into practice as to admit the representation of property, by this property being itself and in its own individual existence the constituent. But not thinking it safe or practicable to resist this temporary frenzy and misrepresentation of things by a direct resistance, it became necessary, by indirect means, to avoid it. To lay it down in the face of the multitude that these new voters had not a right would not have been endured; but parrying it by questioning the right in a particular case gave no umbrage. It was saving the principle, though it denied the exercise.

The man that had rode down the bystanders and was taken up for a horse thief was pardoned by the governor. This was done to get quit of the investigation, the governor thinking it for the credit of the country that there should be nothing said about the occasion and manner of the felony, or the mistake under which the imputation had arisen.

But, party spirit continued to run high; some insisting on the right of suffrage to their cattle, and others considering it a burlesque. You might have seen shillelaghs in the air, and several bullocks were knocked down that were brought up to the polls. A lad was tumbled from his palfry as he was riding him to water, under an idea that he was bringing him to aid the adverse ticket. The ram that had been offered, seeing arrive the sheep, cried "baa"; and it was insisted that he had given his vote, which the candidate against whom it was taken down resented, and hit the tup [ram] a stroke, that, in the sailor's phrase, brought him on his beam ends. The blow struck a pig in a poke, which a man was carrying home, and which was heard to squeal. What, said the assailant, are you bringing here the swinish multitude to vote?

Nevertheless, it was not so much the admitting quadrupeds but unqualified cattle that became the subject of the controversy, intelligent persons arguing that it was a thing shameful in itself and unjust. Because it was a fraud upon the whole community that stragglers should be brought forward, which the individual concerned in the fraud reconciled to himself on the score of serving the party; that it required some refinement to be aware of the indelicacy of urging an improper vote.

Was it reasonable to suppose that a horse creature could give an independent vote, that was in the power of his owner to be stinted of his oats, and rode faster or slower as he thought proper on a journey? Was it to be supposed that he could judge wisely of the comparative merits of candidates, or of the party principles or policy involved in his vote? But the same question might be asked of the greater part of the rational voters. Was it reasonable to expect that the ox would think differently on political subjects from his master? Should he venture to dissent, a crack of the whip or the point of the goad would bring him to his senses.

Even a rational creature, that may be supposed to have more fortitude, is usually in subjection to the master, in matter of opinion, where he is a slave. It is for this reason that slaves are excluded. Whatever might plausibly be said as to the expediency of extending the privilege of citizenship to those animals that are *ferae naturae,* and are at their own hands in a forest, it is quite another matter as far as it respects domesticated animals that have no will of their own, but are under dominion, whether subjugated to a plough or a team.

The wild animals that roam have some spirit of independence. They would starve before they would tamely submit themselves to arbitrary rule and government. Hence it is that traps are used. It requires shooting to bring some to terms. But an ox may be goaded into acquiescence. He does not drink whiskey, it is true; and, for that reason, it cannot be said that whiskey will purchase him; but is there nothing to be done with good grass? The encitements are various that might be held out to allure from the independence of his own judgment.

As to horses voting on the occasion we are speaking of, so far as matter of fact is concerned, I admit it has been denied. For that though a great number of horses were seen to be ridden up, yet it is usual to go on horseback to elections, especially when the voters have to come from some distance; so that the mere circumstance of being on the ground is no conclusive evidence of having given a vote. And this, I am the more careful to note, as in the case of a new government that, like an individual, has a character in some measure to establish, it is of moment that what is groundlessly alleged be explained. At the same time, I am aware of the impolicy of denying a thing *in toto* where there is no foundation — were there no other reason that would induce an historian to adhere to the truth. For even where a man is pressing a matter that is difficult to be believed, and he has nothing in truth to concede, he will yield a little, skilfully, in order to give the impression of candor and secure belief to the more important points.

How much more does it behoove a writer to be careful of insisting on the freedom from all blame on the part of those whom he advocates, lest that he bring in question the veracity of his relation, when he has everything on his side. I do not, therefore, say positively that the inspectors and judges of the election, in some districts, were not deceived and their vigilance baffled, or that they did not connive; for that would be saying too much, considering the nature of affairs. The most vigilant cannot always watch; and the most severe in their notions of the rights of persons may indulge.

But, granting that some horse creatures did vote, with their riders on their backs, does it follow that the inspectors had notice of it, or that the persons who usually stand by and vouch for the right of suffrage to the individual were not to blame? They may have announced their names as rational, and, under that idea, may have got their votes taken. I have been the more careful in throwing out these hints because if it were once admitted that such votes did pass, unless surreptitiously and *sub silentio,* it might grow into precedent. And we well know that in matters of political and legal law precedent has the force of authority.

It may be suggested as not fairly presumable that inspectors and judges could be deceived. I have seen too much of elections not to think that practice to be unfair, where an individual, powerful for wealth or family, is a candidate, or where there is a contest of party somewhat violent; and unprincipled and daring individuals will take their stations and act as common vouchers on an election day, as to the name, age, freedom, or estate of the person who offers a vote. He will be supported by pugilists, or persons prepared with clubs, who, though they do not actually strike, will menace with this appearance of force and intimidate those who might dispute the vouching that is given. And, in the course of time, violence may be actually used, when ruffians and gladiators will keep away from the polls the more feeble or peaceful citizens.

I consider all this as immoral and unbecoming. I have seen even inspectors and judges intimidated by this show of hostility; and I would not wonder if I were to hear that, under this awe, in some place, improper votes were taken. Not that I would excuse this timidity of officers as lessening it from a misdemeanor to a mere neglect of duty. I reprehend both the overawing and being overawed in the discharge of a public trust. It will be a sad day for the people when the elective franchise, this divine essence, the life of liberty, shall be crushed out by the foot of violence! In that day we shall call upon the rocks of despotism to fall down and cover us.

But in justice to the character of the country, I incline to think, after all that has been reported to the contrary, that instances of beasts voting were more rare than is imagined; and that a considerable foundation of what has gone abroad on this head was the epithets bestowed by the contending parties, calling one another beasts — such as horses, asses, sheep, buffaloes, oxen, and the names of other cattle. All this metaphorically, just as persons of a less polished education, where they dispute on literary or theological subjects, call each other geese, sucking pigs, or turkey buzzards. I have heard even well-bred persons speak of their antagonists, after a warm debate, as woodpeckers and mire snipes. In political controversies, it is no uncommon thing to bestow the epithet of jackass. I have heard even an accomplished lady use the term "monkey," speaking of an individual of the other sex. It would be endless to enumerate the application of such terms that do not in themselves import the natural form or metamorphose of any person.

96.

"Hunters of Kentucky"

The Battle of New Orleans, fought on January 8, 1815, was America's most signal victory in the War of 1812, even though it occurred some two weeks after the Treaty of Ghent had been signed, ending the war. (Word of the signing did not reach the combatants in time.) Sir Edward Pakenham led the British forces in the battle, Andrew Jackson the American; Pakenham's troops were roundly defeated by Jackson's well-entrenched volunteers. Some 2,000 British soldiers were killed, and but a handful of Americans — some say 6, some say 13. The victory brought great fame to Jackson and his men, who were memorialized in the song, "Hunters of Kentucky," a rollicking set of verses to a surprisingly lovely tune. The words were written by Samuel Woodworth, better known as the author of "The Old Oaken Bucket," in 1822.

HUNTERS OF KENTUCKY

Ye gentlemen and ladies fair,
Who grace this famous city,
Just listen if you've time to spare,
While I rehearse this ditty;
And for the opportunity
Conceive yourselves quite lucky,
For 'tis not often that you see
A hunter of Kentucky.

We are a hardy, free-born race,
To fear each man a stranger;
Whatever the game we join in chase,
Despoiling time and danger;
And if a daring foe annoys,
Whatever his strength and forces,
We'll show him that Kentucky boys
Are alligator horses.

I s'pose you've read it in the prints,
How Packenham attempted
To make Old Hickory Jackson wince,
But soon his scheme repented;
For we, with rifles ready cocked,
Thought such occasion lucky,
And soon around the general flocked
The hunters of Kentucky.

You've heard, I s'pose, how New Orleans
Is famed for wealth and beauty,
There's girls of every hue it seems,
From snowy white to sooty.
So Packenham he made his brags,
If he in fight was lucky,
He'd have their girls and cotton bags,
In spite of old Kentucky.

But Jackson he was wide awake,
And was not scared at trifles,
For well he knew what aim we take
With our Kentucky rifles.
So he led us down to Cypress swamp,
The ground was low and mucky;
There stood John Bull in martial pomp,
And here was old Kentucky.

A bank was raised to hide our breasts,
Not that we thought of dying,
But that we always like to rest,
Unless the game is flying.
Behind it stood our little force,
None wished it to be greater,
For every man was half a horse,
And half an alligator.

They did not let our patience tire,
Before they showed their faces;
We did not choose to waste our fire,
So snugly kept our places.
But when so near we saw them wink,
We thought it time to stop 'em,
And 'twould have done you good I think,
To see Kentuckians drop 'em.

They found, at last, 'twas vain to fight,
Where lead was all the booty,
And so they wisely took to flight,
And left us all our beauty.
And now, if danger e'er annoys,
Remember what our trade is,
Just send for us Kentucky boys,
And we'll protect ye, ladies.

97.

Alexander J. Dallas: Proposal for a National Bank

The successful termination of the War of 1812 brought with it a surge of nationalism, and many of the discarded ideas of Washington and Hamilton gained new currency even among Republicans. One idea was to reestablish the National Bank, a proposal for which was formulated in 1814, only to be rejected as too weak. President Madison asked Congress to prepare a stronger bill, and John C. Calhoun, chairman of the Committee on the National Currency, sought the advice of Secretary of the Treasury Dallas. Dallas responded on December 24, 1815; his letter, reprinted below, describes the main features of the bill that finally became law on April 10, 1816.

Source: *Debates,* 14 Cong., 1 Sess., pp. 505-511.

It affords much satisfaction to find that the policy of establishing a national bank has received the sanction of the committee; and the decision, in this respect, renders it unnecessary to enter into a comparative examination of the superior advantages of such an institution for the attainment of the objects contemplated by the legislature. Referring, therefore, to the outline of a national bank, which is subjoined to this letter, as the result of an attentive consideration bestowed upon the subjects of your inquiry, I proceed, with deference and respect, to offer some explanation of the principles upon which the system is founded.

1. It is proposed that, under a charter for twenty years, the capital of the national bank shall amount to $35,000,000; that

Congress shall retain the power to raise it to $50,000,000; and that it shall consist three-quarters of public stock and one-quarter of gold and silver.

First, with respect to the amount of the capital. The services to be performed by the capital of the bank are important, various, and extensive. They will be required through a period almost as long as is usually assigned to a generation. They will be required for the accommodation of the government in the collection and distribution of its revenue, as well as for the uses of commerce, agriculture, manufactures, and the arts, throughout the Union. They will be required to restore and maintain the national currency; and, in short, they will be required, under every change of circumstances, in a season of war, as well as in the season of peace, for the circulation of the national wealth, which augments with a rapidity beyond the reach of ordinary calculation.

In the performance of these national services, the local and incidental cooperation of the state banks may undoubtedly be expected; but it is the object of the present measure to create an independent, though not a discordant, institution. And while the government is granting a monopoly for twenty years, it would seem to be improvident and dangerous to rely upon gratuitous or casual aids for the enjoyment of those benefits which can be effectually secured by positive stipulation.

Nor is it believed that any public inconvenience can possibly arise from the proposed amount of the capital of the bank with its augmentable quality. The amount may, indeed, be a clog upon the profits of the institution, but it can never be employed for any injurious purpose (not even for the purpose of discount accommodation beyond the fair demand) without an abuse of trust, which cannot, in candor, be anticipated, or which, if anticipated, may be made an object of penal responsibility.

The competition which exists at present among the state banks will, it is true, be extended to the national bank; but competition does not imply hostility. The commercial interests and the personal associations of the stockholders will generally be the same in the state banks and in the national bank. The directors of both institutions will naturally be taken from the same class of citizens. And experience has shown not only the policy but the existence of those sympathies by which the intercourse of a national bank and the state banks has been, and always ought to be, regulated, for their common credit and security.

At the present crisis it will be peculiarly incumbent upon the national bank, as well as the treasury, to conciliate the state banks; to confide to them, liberally, a participation in the deposits of public revenue, and to encourage them in every reasonable effort to resume the payment of their notes in coin. But, independent of these considerations, it is to be recollected that when portions of the capital of the national bank shall be transferred to its branches, the amount invested in each branch will not, probably, exceed the amount of the capital of any of the principal state banks, and will certainly be less than the amount of the combined capital of the state banks operating in any of the principal commercial cities.

The whole number of the banking establishments in the United States may be stated at 260, and the aggregate amount of their capitals may be estimated at $80,000,000. But the services of the national bank are also required in every state and territory, and the capital proposed is $35,000,000, of which only one-fourth part will consist of gold and silver.

Second, with respect to the composition of the capital of the bank. There does not prevail much diversity of opinion upon the proposition to form a compound capital for the national bank, partly of public stock and partly of coin. The proportions now sug-

New York Historical Society

Portrait of Alexander J. Dallas by John W. Jarvis

gested appear also to be free from any important objections. Under all the regulations of the charter, it is believed that the amount of gold and silver required will afford an adequate supply for commencing and continuing the payments of the bank in current coin; while the power which the bank will possess to convert its stock portion of capital into bullion or coin, from time to time, is calculated to provide for any probable augmentation of the demand. This object being sufficiently secured, the capital of the bank is next to be employed, in perfect consistency with the general interests and safety of the institution, to raise the value of the public securities, by withdrawing almost one-fifth of the amount from the ordinary stock market. Nor will the bank be allowed to expose the public to the danger of a depreciation, by returning any part of the stock to the market, until it has been offered, at the current price, to the Commissioners of the Sinking Fund; and it is not an inconsiderable advantage, in the growing state of the public revenue, that the stock subscribed to the capital of the bank will become redeemable at the pleasure of the government.

The subscription to the capital of the bank is opened to every species of funded stock. The estimate that the revenues of 1816 and 1817 will enable the treasury to discharge the whole of the treasury note debt furnishes the only reason for omitting to authorize a subscription in that species of debt.

Thus, the old and new 6 percent stocks are receivable at par; the 7 percent stock, upon a valuation referring to the 30th of September, 1816, is receivable at 106.51 percent; the 3 percent stock, which can only be redeemed for its nominal or certificate value, may be estimated, under all circumstances, to be worth about 62 percent when the 6 percent stock is at par. But as it is desirable to accomplish the redemption of this stock upon equitable terms, it is made receivable at 65 percent, the rate sanctioned by the government, and in part accepted by the stockholders in the year 1807.

Of the installments for paying the subscriptions, it is only necessary to observe that they are regulated by a desire to reconcile an early commencement of the operations of the bank with the existing difficulties in the currency, and with the convenience of the subscribers. In one of the modes proposed for discharging the subscription of the government, it is particularly contemplated to aid the bank with a medium which cannot fail to alleviate the first pressure for payments in coin.

2. It is proposed that the national bank shall be governed by twenty-five directors, and each of its branches by thirteen directors; that the President of the United States, with the advice and consent of the Senate, shall appoint five of the directors of the bank, one of whom shall be chosen as president of the bank by the board of directors; that the resident stockholders shall elect twenty of the directors of the national bank, who shall be resident citizens of the

United States, and that the national bank shall appoint the directors of each branch (being resident citizens of the United States), one of whom shall be designated by the secretary of the treasury, with the approbation of the President of the United States, to be president of the branch bank.

The participation of the President and Senate of the United States in the appointment of directors appears to be the only feature in the proposition for the government of the national bank which requires an explanatory remark.

Upon general principles, wherever a pecuniary interest is to be effected by the operations of a public institution, a representative authority ought to be recognized. The United States will be the proprietors of one-fifth of the capital of the bank, and in that proportion, upon general principles, they should be represented in the direction. But an apprehension has sometimes been expressed lest the power of the government thus inserted into the administration of the affairs of the bank should be employed eventually to alienate the funds, and to destroy the credit of the institution. Whatever may have been the fate of banks in other countries, subject to forms of government essentially different, there can be no reasonable cause for apprehension here. Independent of the obvious improbability of the attempt, the government of the United States cannot, by any legislative or executive act, impair the rights, or multiply the obligations of a corporation, constitutionally established, as long as the independence and integrity of the judicial power shall be maintained. Whatever accommodation the treasury may have occasion to ask from the bank can only be asked under the license of a law; and whatever accommodation shall be obtained must be obtained from the voluntary assent of the directors, acting under the responsiblity of their trust.

Nor can it be doubted that the department of the government which is invested with the power of appointment to all the important offices of the state is a proper department to exercise the power of appointment in relation to a national trust of incalculable magnitude. The national bank ought not to be regarded simply as a commercial bank. It will not operate upon the funds of the stockholders alone but much more upon the funds of the nation. Its conduct, good or bad, will not affect the corporate credit and resources alone but much more the credit and resources of the government. In fine, it is not an institution created for the purposes of commerce and profit alone but much more for the purposes of national policy, as an auxiliary in the exercise of some of the highest powers of the government. Under such circumstances, the public interests cannot be too cautiously guarded, and the guards proposed can never be injurious to the commercial interests of the institution. The right to inspect the general accounts of the bank may be employed to detect the evils of a maladministration; but an interior agency in the direction of its affairs will best serve to prevent them.

3. It is proposed that, in addition to the usual privileges of a corporation, the notes of the national bank shall be received in all payments to the United States, unless Congress shall hereafter otherwise provide by law; and that, in addition to the duties usually required from a corporation of this description, the national bank shall be employed to receive, transfer, and distribute the public revenue, under the directions of the proper department.

The reservation of a legislative power on the subject of accepting the notes of the national bank in payments to the government is the only new stipulation in the present proposition. It is designed not merely as one of the securities for the general conduct of the bank but as the means of preserving entire the sovereign authority of Congress relative to the coin and currency of the United States. Recent occurrences inculcate the expediency of such a reservation, but it may be confidently hoped that an occasion to enforce it will never arise.

It is not proposed to stipulate that the bank shall in any case be bound to make loans to the government; but, in that respect, whenever a loan is authorized by law, the government will act upon the ordinary footing of an applicant for pecuniary accommodation.

4. It is proposed that the organization of the national bank shall be effected with as little delay as possible; and that its operations shall commence and continue upon the basis of payments in the current coin of the United States, with a qualified power under the authority of the government to suspend such payments.

The proposition now submitted necessarily implies an opinion that it is practicable to commence the operations of the national bank upon a circulation of gold and silver coin; and, in support of the opinion, a few remarks are respectfully offered to the consideration of the committee:

First, the actual receipts of the bank, at the opening of the subscription, will amount to the sum of $8,400,000; of which the sum of $1,400,000 will consist of gold and silver, and the sum of $7,000,000 will consist of public stock convertible by sale into gold and silver. But the actual receipts of the bank, at the expiration of six months from the opening of the subscription, will amount to the sum of $16,800,000; of which the sum of $2,800,000 will be in gold and silver, and the sum of $14,000,000 will be in public stock convertible by sale into gold and silver. To the fund thus possessed by the bank, the accumulations of the public revenue and the deposits of individuals being added, there can be little doubt, from past experience and observation in reference to similar establishments, that a sufficient foundation will exist for a gradual and judicious issue of bank notes payable on demand in the current coin; unless, contrary to all probability, public confidence should be withheld from the institution, or sinister combinations should be formed to defeat its operations, or the demands of an unfavorable balance of trade should press upon its metallic resources.

Second, the public confidence cannot be withheld from the institution. The resources of the nation will be intimately connected with the resources of the bank. The notes of the bank are accredited in every payment to the government, and must become familiar in every pecuniary negotiation. Unless, therefore, a state of things exist in which gold and silver only can command the public confidence, the national bank must command it. But the expression of the public sentiment does not, even at this period, leave the question exposed to difficulty and doubt; it is well known that the wealth of opulent and commercial nations requires for its circulation something more than a medium composed of the precious metals. The incompetency of the existing paper substitutes to furnish a national currency is also well known. Hence, throughout the United States, the public hope seems to rest, at this crisis, upon the establishment of a national bank; and every citizen, upon private or upon patriotic motives, will be prepared to support the institution.

Third, sinister combinations to defeat the operations of a national bank ought not to be presumed, and need not be feared. It is true that the influence of the state banks is extensively diffused; but the state banks, and the patrons of the state banks, partake of the existing evils; they must be conscious of the inadequacy of state institutions to restore and maintain the national currency; they will perceive that there is sufficient space in the commercial sphere for the movement of the state banks and the national bank; and, upon the whole, they will be ready to act upon the impulse of a common duty and a common interest. If, however, most unexpectedly, a different course should be pursued, the concurring powers of the national treasury and the national bank will be sufficient to avert the danger.

Fourth, the demand of an unfavorable balance of trade appears to be much overrated. It is not practicable, at this time, to ascertain either the value of the goods imported since the peace or the value of the property employed to pay for them. But when it is considered that a great proportion of the importations arose from investments of American funds previously in Europe; that a great proportion of the price has been paid by American exports; that a great proportion has been paid by remittances in American stocks; and that a great proportion remains upon credit to be paid by gradual remittances of goods, as well as in coin, it cannot be justly concluded that the balance of trade has hitherto materially affected the national stock of the precious metals. So far as an opportunity has occurred for observation, the demand for gold and silver to export appears rather to have arisen from the expectation of obtaining a higher price in a part of Europe, and from the revival of commerce with the countries beyond the Cape of Good Hope, than from any necessity to provide for the payment of the recent importations of goods into the United States. The former of these causes will probably soon cease to operate, and the operation of the latter may, if necessary, be restrained by law.

The proposition now under consideration further provides for a suspension of the bank payments in coin upon any future emergency. This is merely a matter of precaution; but, if the emergency should arise, it must be agreed on all hands that the power of suspension ought rather to be confided to the government than to the directors of the institution.

5. It is proposed that a bonus be paid to the government by the subscribers to the national bank in consideration of the emoluments to be derived from an exclusive charter, during a period of twenty years.

The amount of the bonus should be in proportion to the value of the charter grant; or, in other words, to the net profits which the subscribers will probably make, in consequence of their incorporation. The average rate of the dividends of the state banks, before the suspension of payments in coin, was about 8 percent per annum. It appears by a report from this department to the House of Representatives, dated the 3rd of April, 1810, that the annual dividends of the late bank of the United States, averaged, throughout the duration of its charter, the rate of 8 13/36 percent. But under all the circumstances which will attend the establishment and operations of the proposed national bank, its enlarged capital, and the extended field of competition, it is not deemed reasonable, for the present purpose, to rate the annual dividends of the institution higher than 7 percent upon its capital of $35,000,000.

Allowing, therefore, two, three, and four years for the payment of the bonus, a sum of $1,500,000 would amount to about 4 percent upon the capital of the bank, and would constitute a just equivalent for the benefits of its charter.

Our country! In her intercourse with foreign nations may she always be in the right; but our country, right or wrong!

STEPHEN DECATUR, toast, April, 1816. G. K. Chesterton, *The Defendant,* opined that " 'My country, right or wrong,' is a thing no patriot would think of saying except in a desperate case. It is like saying, 'My mother, drunk or sober.' "

1816

98.

Thomas Jefferson: On the Present Need to Promote Manufacturing

"Those who labor in the earth are the chosen people of God," Jefferson wrote in his Notes on the State of Virginia. *This belief in the superior virtue of agricultural life was fundamental to his political philosophy, and it went with a consequent distrust of manufacturers, which he regarded as a corrupting influence. But Jefferson lived long enough to see his countrymen become manufacturers all the same, while in the course of time and by virtue of certain historical events he came to view their doing so in a more approving light. All of this he explained in the following letter, dated January 9, 1816, to Benjamin Austin, a Republican leader in Massachusetts. What Jefferson referred to when he wrote, "Yet all this has taken place," were the illegal restrictions placed upon American commerce by Britain and France before the War of 1812 — restrictions that forced a rapid development of American industry.*

Source: Randolph, IV, pp. 276-279.

You tell me I am quoted by those who wish to continue our dependence on England for manufactures. There was a time when I might have been so quoted with more candor, but within the thirty years which have since elapsed, how are circumstances changed! We were then in peace. Our independent place among nations was acknowledged. A commerce which offered the raw material in exchange for the same material after receiving the last touch of industry was worthy of welcome to all nations. It was expected that those especially to whom manufacturing industry was important would cherish the friendship of such customers by every favor, by every inducement, and particularly cultivate their peace by every act of justice and friendship.

Under this prospect the question seemed legitimate whether, with such an immensity of unimproved land courting the hand of husbandry, the industry of agriculture, or that of manufactures would add most to the national wealth. And the doubt on the utility of the American manufactures was entertained on this consideration chiefly, that to the labor of the husbandman a vast addition is made by the spontaneous energies of the earth on which it is employed. For one grain of wheat committed to the earth, she renders twenty-, thirty-, and even fiftyfold, whereas to the labor of the manufacturer nothing is added. Pounds of flax, in his hands, yield but pennyweights of lace. This exchange, too, laborious as it might seem — what a field did it promise for the occupation of the ocean; what a nursery for that class of citizens who were to exercise and maintain our equal rights in that element!

This was the state of things in 1785, when the *Notes on Virginia* were first published; when, the ocean being open to all nations, and their common right in it acknowledged and exercised under regulations sanctioned by the assent and usage of all, it was thought that the doubt might claim some consideration. But who in 1785 could foresee the rapid depravity which was to render the close of that century a disgrace of the history of men? Who could have imagined that the two most distinguished in the rank of nations for science and civilization would have suddenly descended from that honorable eminence, and setting at defiance all those moral laws established by the Author of nature between nation and nation, as between man and man, would cover earth and sea with robberies and piracies, merely because strong enough to do it with temporal impunity; and that under this disbandment of nations from social order, we should have been despoiled of a thousand ships, and have thousands of our citizens reduced to Algerine slavery.

Yet all this has taken place. The British interdicted to our vessels all harbors of the globe without having first proceeded to some one of hers, there paid a tribute proportioned to the cargo, and obtained her license to proceed to the port of destination. The other declared them to be lawful prize if they had touched at the port, or been visited by a ship of the enemy nation. Thus were we completely excluded from the ocean. Compare this state of things with that of '85, and say whether an opinion founded in the circumstances of that day can be fairly applied to those of the present. We have experienced what we did not then believe, that there exists both profligacy and power enough to exclude us from the field of interchange with other nations; that to be independent for the comforts of life we must fabricate them ourselves. We must now place the manufacturer by the side of the agriculturist.

The former question is suppressed, or rather assumes a new form.

The grand inquiry now is, shall we make our own comforts or go without them at the will of a foreign nation? He, therefore, who is now against domestic manufacture must be for reducing us either to dependence on that foreign nation, or to be clothed in skins and to live like wild beasts in dens and caverns. I am not one of these; experience has taught me that manufactures are now as necessary to our independence as to our comfort; and if those who quote me as of a different opinion will keep pace with me in purchasing nothing foreign where an equivalent of domestic fabric can be obtained, without regard to difference of price, it will not be our fault if we do not soon have a supply at home equal to our demand, and wrest that weapon of distress from the hand which has wielded it. If it shall be proposed to go beyond our own supply, the question of '85 will then recur, will our surplus labor be then most beneficially employed in the culture of the earth or in the fabrications of art?

We have time yet for consideration before that question will press upon us; and the maxim to be applied will depend on the circumstances which shall then exist; for in so complicated a science as political economy, no one axiom can be laid down as wise and expedient for all times and circumstances, and for their contraries. Inattention to this is what has called for this explanation, which reflection would have rendered unnecessary with the candid, while nothing will do it with those who use the former opinion only as a stalking-horse to cover their disloyal propensities to keep us in eternal vassalage to a foreign and unfriendly people.

99.

Thomas Jefferson: The Rulers and the Ruled

Pierre S. du Pont de Nemours, French economist and father of the founder of the Du Pont powder works in Wilmington, Delaware, was an early supporter of the French Revolution and a persistent worker in the cause of good relations between France and the United States. He had dealings with Jefferson from the beginning of the latter's presidency, and corresponded with him for many years. In the spring of 1816, Du Pont was engaged in writing constitutions for several new South American republics, and he asked his friend's opinion of representative government. In his reply, written April 24, 1816, Jefferson took the opportunity to expound on his favorite subject, Republicanism, and explained that in a good government, the enlightened and educated, "the natural aristocracy," as he called them, should rule — but not without a check by the people.

Source: Ford, X, pp. 22-25.

Distinguishing between the structure of the government and the moral principles on which you prescribe its administration, with the latter we concur cordially, with the former we should not. We of the United States, you know, are constitutionally and conscientiously democrats. We consider society as one of the natural wants with which man has been created; that he has been endowed with faculties and qualities to effect its satisfaction by concurrence of others having the same want; that when, by the exercise of these faculties, he has procured a state of society, it is one of his acquisitions which he has a right to regulate and control, jointly indeed with all those who have concurred in the procurement, whom he cannot exclude from its use or direction more than they him. We think experience has proved it safer for the mass of individuals composing the society to reserve to themselves personally the exercise of all rightful powers to which they are competent, and to delegate those to which they are not competent to deputies named, and removable for unfaithful conduct, by themselves immediately.

Hence, with us, the people (by which is meant the mass of individuals composing the society) being competent to judge of the facts occurring in ordinary life, they have retained the functions of judges of facts under the name of jurors; but being unqualified for the management of affairs requiring intelligence above the common level, yet competent judges of human character, they chose for their management representatives, some by themselves immediately, others by electors chosen by themselves.

Thus, our President is chosen by ourselves, directly in *practice,* for we vote for *A* as elector only on the condition he will vote for *B;* our representatives by ourselves immediately; our Senate and judges of law through electors chosen by ourselves. And we believe that this proximate choice and power of removal is the best security which experience has sanctioned for ensuring an honest conduct in the functionaries of society. . . .

But when we come to the moral principles on which the government is to be administered, we come to what is proper for all conditions of society. I meet you there in all the benevolence and rectitude of your native character; and I love myself always most where I concur most with you. Liberty, truth, probity, honor are declared to be the four cardinal principles of your society.

I believe with you that morality, compassion, generosity are innate elements of the human constitution; that there exists a right independent of force; that a right to property is founded in our natural wants, in the means with which we are endowed to satisfy these wants, and the right to what we acquire by those means without violating the similar rights of other sensible beings; that no one has a right to obstruct another exercising his faculties innocently for the relief of sensibilities made a part of his nature; that justice is the fundamental law of society; that the majority, oppressing an individual, is guilty of a crime, abuses its strength, and by acting on the law of the strongest, breaks up the foundations of society; that action by the citizens in person, in affairs within their reach and competence, and in all others by representatives chosen immediately and removable by themselves, constitutes the essence of a republic; that all governments are more or less republican in proportion as this principle enters more or less into their composition; and that a government by representation is capable of extension over a greater surface of country than one of any other form. These, my friend, are the essentials in which you and I agree; however, in our zeal for their maintenance, we may be perplexed and divaricate as to the structure of society most likely to secure them. . . .

Enlighten the people generally, and tyranny and oppressions of body and mind will vanish like evil spirits at the dawn of day. Although I do not, with some enthusiasts, believe that the human condition will ever advance to such a state of perfection as that there shall no longer be pain or vice in the world, yet I believe it susceptible of much improvement, and most of all in matters of government and religion; and that the diffusion of knowledge among the people is to be the instrument by which it is to be effected.

100.

THOMAS JEFFERSON: On Republican Government

John Taylor of Caroline, who had stood with Jefferson through twenty years of political conflict, completed his magnum opus, An Enquiry into the Principles and Policy of the Government of the United States, *in 1814. Taylor intended the work to be a definitive answer to the theories of government of John Adams and the Federalists, and he sent a copy to his old friend and political ally. Jefferson read the book carefully and wrote a letter containing his comments to the author. The letter, dated May 28, 1816, contains a statement of Jefferson's mature thinking on the subject of Republican government. The indirect method of electing senators to which Jefferson refers was in effect until 1913, when it was changed by the Seventeenth Amendment.*

Source: Randolph, IV, pp. 285-288.

ON MY RETURN from a long journey and considerable absence from home, I found here the copy of your *Enquiry into the Principles of Our Government,* which you had been so kind as to send me; and for which I pray you to accept my thanks. The difficulties of getting new works in our situation, inland and without a single bookstore, are such as had prevented my obtaining a copy before; and letters which had accumulated during my absence, and were calling for answers, have not yet permitted me to give to the whole a thorough reading. Yet, certain that you and I could not think differently on the fundamentals of rightful government, I was impatient, and availed myself of the intervals of repose from the writing table to obtain a cursory idea of the body of the work.

I see in it much matter for profound reflection; much which should confirm our adhesion, in practice, to the good principles of our Constitution, and fix our attention on what is yet to be made good. The sixth section on the good moral principles of our government I found so interesting and replete with sound principles as to postpone my letter writing to its thorough perusal and consideration. Besides much other good matter, it settles unanswerably the right of instructing representatives, and their duty to obey. The system of banking we have both equally and ever reprobated. I contemplate it as a blot left in all our constitutions, which, if not covered, will end in their destruction, which is already hit by the gamblers in corruption, and is sweeping away in its progress the fortunes and morals of our citizens. Funding I consider as limited, rightfully, to a redemption of the debt within the lives of a majority of the generation contracting it; every generation coming equally, by the laws of the Creator of the world, to the free possession of the earth

He made for their subsistence, unencumbered by their predecessors, who, like them, were but tenants for life.

You have successfully and completely pulverized Mr. Adams' system of orders, and his opening the mantle of republicanism to every government of laws, whether consistent or not with natural right. Indeed, it must be acknowledged that the term "republic" is of very vague application in every language. Witness the self-styled republics of Holland, Switzerland, Genoa, Venice, Poland. Were I to assign to this term a precise and definite idea, I would say that, purely and simply, it means a government by its citizens in mass, acting directly and personally according to rules established by the majority; and that every other government is more or less republican, in proportion as it has in its composition more or less of this ingredient of the direct action of the citizens. Such a government is evidently restrained to very narrow limits of space and population. I doubt if it would be practicable beyond the extent of a New England township.

The first shade from this pure element, which, like that of pure vital air, cannot sustain life of itself, would be where the powers of the government, being divided, should be exercised each by representatives chosen by the citizens either *pro hâc vice*, or for such short terms as should render secure the duty of expressing the will of their constituents. This I should consider as the nearest approach to a pure republic, which is practicable on a large scale of country or population. And we have examples of it in some of our state constitutions, which, if not poisoned by priestcraft, would prove its excellence over all mixtures with other elements; and, with only equal doses of poison, would still be the best.

Other shades of republicanism may be found in other forms of government, where the executive, judiciary, and legislative functions, and the different branches of the latter, are chosen by the people more or less directly, for longer terms of years, or for life, or made hereditary; or where there are mixtures of authorities, some dependent on, and others independent of, the people. The further the departure from direct and constant control by the citizens, the less has the government of the ingredient of republicanism; evidently none where the authorities are hereditary, as in France, Venice, etc., or self-chosen, as in Holland; and little, where for life, in proportion as the life continues in being after the act of election.

The purest republican feature in the government of our own state is the House of Representatives. The Senate is equally so the first year, less the second, and so on. The executive still less, because not chosen by the people directly. The judiciary, seriously antirepublican, because for life; and the national arm wielded, as you observe, by military leaders, irresponsible but to themselves. Add to this the vicious constitution of our county courts (to whom the justice, the executive administration, the taxation, police, the military appointments of the county, and nearly all our daily concerns are confided) — self-appointed, self-continued, holding their authorities for life, and with an impossibility of breaking in on the perpetual succession of any faction once possessed of the bench. They are in truth the executive, the judiciary, and the military of their respective counties, and the sum of the counties makes the state.

And add, also, that one-half of our brethren who fight and pay taxes are excluded, like Helots, from the rights of representation, as if society were instituted for the soil and not for the men inhabiting it; or one-half of these could dispose of the rights and the will of the other half, without their consent.

What constitutes a State?
Not high-raised battlements, or labored
mound,

Thick wall, or moated gate;
Not cities proud, with spires and turrets crowned;
No: men, high-minded men,
Men, who their duties know;
But know their rights; and, knowing, dare maintain.
These constitute a State.

In the general government, the House of Representatives is mainly republican; the Senate scarcely so at all, as not elected by the people directly, and so long secured even against those who do elect them; the executive more republican than the Senate, from its shorter term, its election by the people, *in practice* (for they vote for A only on an assurance that he will vote for B), and because, *in practice also,* a principle of rotation seems to be in a course of establishment; the judiciary independent of the nation, their coercion by impeachment being found nugatory.

If, then, the control of the people over the organs of their government be the measure of its republicanism, and I confess I know no other measure, it must be agreed that our governments have much less of republicanism than ought to have been expected; in other words, that the people have less regular control over their agents than their rights and their interest require. And this I ascribe, not to any want of republican dispositions in those who formed these constitutions but to a submission of true principle to European authorities, to speculators on government, whose fears of the people have been inspired by the populace of their own great cities, and were unjustly entertained against the independent, the happy, and, therefore, orderly citizens of the United States.

Much I apprehend that the golden moment is past for reforming these heresies. The functionaries of public power rarely strengthen in their dispositions to abridge it, and an unorganized call for timely amendment is not likely to prevail against an unorganized opposition to it. We are always told that things are going on well; why change them? *"Chi sta bene, non si muove,"* says the Italian, "let him who stands well, stand still." This is true; and I verily believe they would go on well with us under an absolute monarch, while our present character remains, of order, industry, and love of peace, and restrained, as he would be, by the proper spirit of the people. But it is while it remains such, we should provide against the consequences of its deterioration. And let us rest in the hope that it will yet be done, and spare ourselves the pain of evils which may never happen.

On this view of the import of the term "republic," instead of saying, as has been said, "that it may mean anything or nothing," we may say with truth and meaning that governments are more or less republican, as they have more or less of the element of popular election and control in their composition; and believing, as I do, that the mass of the citizens is the safest depository of their own rights, and especially, that the evils flowing from the duperies of the people are less injurious than those from the egoism of their agents, I am a friend to that composition of government which has in it the most of this ingredient. And I sincerely believe, with you, that banking establishments are more dangerous than standing armies; and that the principle of spending money to be paid by posterity, under the name of funding, is but swindling futurity on a large scale.

101.

THOMAS JEFFERSON: On Civil and Natural Rights

Francis Walker Gilmer, a lawyer and author, was one of Jefferson's numerous correspondents in the years after 1812. In the following letter to Gilmer of June 7, 1816, Jefferson discoursed on the extent to which natural rights must be relinquished in civil society, and expressed his profound disagreement with the Hobbesian view that justice is conventional only, and not natural. The letter reflected Jefferson's abiding faith in Republican government, the main if not the sole function of which was, in his view, to preserve those rights that man has, ideally, in the state of nature.

Source: Randolph, IV, pp. 288-290.

I RECEIVED A FEW DAYS AGO from Mr. Du Pont the enclosed manuscript, with permission to read it, and a request, when read, to forward it to you, in expectation that you would translate it. It is well worthy of publication for the instruction of our citizens, being profound, sound, and short.

Our legislators are not sufficiently apprised of the rightful limits of their powers; that their true office is to declare and enforce only our natural rights and duties, and to take none of them from us. No man has a natural right to commit aggression on the equal rights of another; and this is all from which the laws ought to restrain him. Every man is under the natural duty of contributing to the necessities of the society; and this is all the laws should enforce on him. And, no man having a natural right to be the judge between himself and another, it is his natural duty to submit to the umpirage of an impartial third. When the laws have declared and enforced all this, they have fulfilled their functions, and the idea is quite unfounded that on entering into society we give up any natural right. The trial of every law by one of these texts would lessen much the labors of our legislators, and lighten equally our municipal codes.

There is a work of the first order of merit . . . by Destutt Tracy on the subject of political economy. . . . In a preliminary discourse on the origin of the right of property, he coincides much with the principles of the present manuscript; but is more developed, more demonstrative. He promises a future work on morals, in which I lament to see that he will adopt the principles of Hobbes, or humiliation to human nature; that the sense of justice and injustice is not derived from our natural organization but founded on convention only. I lament this the more as he is unquestionably the ablest writer living, on abstract subjects.

Assuming the fact that the earth has been created in time, and, consequently, the dogma of final causes, we yield, of course, to this short syllogism. Man was created for social intercourse; but social intercourse cannot be maintained without a sense of justice; then man must have been created with a sense of justice.

There is an error into which most of the speculators on government have fallen, and which the well-known state of society of our Indians ought, before now, to have corrected. In their hypothesis of the origin of government, they suppose it to have commenced in the patriarchal or monarchical form. Our Indians are evidently in that state of nature which has passed the association of a single family; and not yet submitted to the authority of positive laws, or of any acknowledged magistrate. Every man, with them, is perfectly free to follow his own inclinations. But if, in doing this, he violates the rights of another, if the case be slight, he is punished by the disesteem of his society, or, as we say, by public opinion; if serious, he is tomahawked as a dangerous enemy. Their leaders conduct them by the influence of their character only; and they follow or not, as they please, him of whose character for wisdom or war they have the highest opinion. Hence the origin of the parties among them adhering to different leaders, and governed by their advice, not by their command.

The Cherokees, the only tribe I know to be contemplating the establishment of regular laws, magistrates, and government, propose a government of representatives, elected from every town. But of all things, they least think of subjecting themselves to the will of one man. This, the only instance of actual fact within our knowledge, will be then a beginning by republican, and not by patriarchal or monarchical government, as speculative writers have generally conjectured.

102.

William Plumer: State Control of Dartmouth College

The feud that developed in the early years of the last century between John Wheelock, second president of Dartmouth College, and its board of trustees, was to have far-reaching consequences. The school had been established in 1769, and its original charter gave the president the right to name his successor with the approval of the board. Personal differences led to Wheelock's dismissal by the trustees on August 26, 1815, whereupon he published a pamphlet, Sketches of the History of Dartmouth College, *by means of which he hoped to enlist Republican support in his fight to regain his post. The newly elected Republican governor of New Hampshire, William Plumer, asked the legislature (also Republican) to reorganize the college administration. The legislature responded by changing the name of the college to Dartmouth University, giving the state veto power over the trustees, and reinstating Wheelock, all of which in effect made Dartmouth a state institution. The enactment of this law led to the famous case of* Dartmouth *v.* Woodward. *Plumer's message to the legislature of June 6, 1816, is reprinted below.*

Source: *New-Hampshire Patriot,* (Concord), June 11, 1816.

There is no system of government where the general diffusion of knowledge is so necessary as in a republic. It is therefore not less the duty than the interest of the state to patronize and support the cause of literature and the sciences. So sensible were our ancestors of this that they early made provision for schools, academies, and a college, the good effects of which we daily experience.

But all literary establishments, like everything human, if not duly attended to, are subject to decay; permit me, therefore, to invite your consideration to the state and condition of Dartmouth College, the head of our learned institutions. As the state has contributed liberally to the establishment of its funds, and as our constituents have a deep interest in its prosperity, it has a strong claim to our attention. The charter of that college was granted December 30, 1769, by John Wentworth, who was then governor of New Hampshire under the authority of the British king. As it emanated from royalty, it contained, as was natural it should, principles congenial to monarchy. Among others it established trustees, made seven a quorum, and authorized a majority of those present to remove any of its members which they might consider unfit or incapable, and the survivors to perpetuate the board by themselves electing others to supply vacancies.

This last principle is hostile to the spirit and genius of a free government. Sound policy therefore requires that the mode of election should be changed, and that trustees in future should be elected by some other body of men. To increase the number of trustees would not only increase the security of the college but be a mean of interesting more men in its prosperity. If it should be made in future the duty of the president, annually in May, to report to the governor a full and particular account of the state of the funds, their receipts and expenditures, the number of students and their progress, and generally the state and condition of the college, and the governor to communicate this statement to the legislature in their June session — this would form a check upon the proceedings of the trustees, excite a spirit of attention in the officers and students of the college, and give to the legislature such information as would enable them to act with greater propriety upon whatever may relate to that institution.

The college was formed for the public good, not for the benefit or emolument of its trustees; and the right to amend and improve acts of incorporation of this nature has been exercised by all governments, both monarchical and republican. . . .

A number of the states have passed laws that made material changes in the charters of their colleges. And, in this state, acts of incorporation of a similar nature have frequently been amended and changed by the legislature. By the several acts incorporating towns, their limits were established; but whenever the legislature judged that the public good required a town to be made into two, they have made the division, and in some instances against the remonstrance of a majority of its inhabitants.

In the charter of Dartmouth College, it is expressly provided that the president, trustees, professors, tutors, and other officers shall take the oath of allegiance to the British king; but if the laws of the United States, as well as those of New Hampshire, abolished by implication that part of the charter, much more might they have done it directly and by express words. These facts show the authority of the legislature to interfere upon this subject; and I trust you will make such further provisions as will render this important institution more useful to mankind.

It is . . . a small college, and yet there are those who love it.

Daniel Webster, Dartmouth College case, 1819

103.

Thomas Jefferson: The Roots of Democracy

To Jefferson, the best form of government, the government that provided the greatest liberty to all citizens, was direct democracy. Jefferson realized, however, that direct democracy, or Republicanism (as he often called it), was not feasible in a country as large as the United States, and that some system of representation was required. In a letter dated July 12, 1816, to Samuel Kercheval, who had sought his views concerning the approaching constitutional convention in Virginia, Jefferson discussed these matters and, in the portion of the letter reprinted here, measured the U.S. Constitution against his Republican ideal.

Source: Randolph, IV, pp. 293-300.

At the birth of our republic . . . we imagined everything republican which was not monarchy. We had not yet penetrated to the mother principle, that "governments are republican only in proportion as they embody the will of their people and execute it." Hence, our first constitutions had really no leading principle in them. But experience and reflection have but more and more confirmed me in the particular importance of the equal representation then proposed. . . .

But inequality of representation in both houses of our legislature is not the only republican heresy in this first essay of our revolutionary patriots at forming a constitution. For let it be agreed that a government is republican in proportion as every member composing it has his equal voice in the direction of its concerns (not, indeed, in person, which would be impracticable beyond the limits of a city or small township, but) by representatives chosen by himself, and responsible to him at short periods, and let us bring to the test of this canon every branch of our Constitution.

In the legislature, the House of Representatives is chosen by less than half the people, and not at all in proportion to those who do choose. The Senate are still more disproportionate, and for long terms of irresponsibility. In the executive, the governor is entirely independent of the choice of the people and of their control; his Council equally so, and at best but a fifth wheel to a wagon. In the judiciary, the judges of the highest courts are dependent on none but themselves. In England, where judges were named and removable at the will of a hereditary executive, from which branch most misrule was feared and has flowed, it was a great point gained, by fixing them for life to make them independent of that executive.

But in a government founded on the public will, this principle operates in an opposite direction and against that will. There, too, they were still removable on a concurrence of the executive and legislative branches. But we have made them independent of the nation itself. They are irremovable but by their own body for any depravities of conduct, and even by their own body for the imbecilities of dotage.

The justices of the inferior courts are self-chosen, are for life, and perpetuate their own body in succession forever, so that a faction once possessing themselves of the bench of a county can never be broken up, but hold their county in chains forever indissoluble. Yet these justices are the real executive, as well as judiciary, in all our minor and most ordinary concerns. They tax us at will; fill the office of sheriff, the most important of all the executive officers of the county; name nearly all our military leaders, which leaders, once named, are removable but by themselves. The juries, our judges of all fact, and of law when they choose it, are not selected by the people, nor amenable to them. They are chosen by an officer named by the court and executive. Chosen, did I say? Picked up by the sheriff from the loungings of the courtyard after everything respectable has retired from it.

Where, then, is our republicanism to be found? Not in our Constitution certainly, but merely in the spirit of our people. That would oblige even a despot to govern us republicanly. Owing to this spirit, and to nothing in the form of our Constitution, all things have gone well. But this fact, so triumphantly misquoted by the enemies of reformation, is not the fruit of our Constitution but has prevailed in spite of it. Our functionaries have done well, because generally honest men. If any were not so, they feared to show it.

But it will be said it is easier to find faults than to amend them. I do not think their amendment so difficult as is pretended. Only lay down true principles, and adhere to them inflexibly. Do not be frightened into their surrender by the alarms of the timid or the croakings of wealth against the ascendancy of the people. If experience be called for, appeal to that of our fifteen or twenty governments for forty years, and show me where the people have done half the mischief in these forty years that a single despot would have done in a single year; or show half the riots and rebellions, the crimes and the punishments, which have taken place in any single nation, under kingly government, during the same period.

The true foundation of republican government is the equal right of every citizen in his person and property and in their management. Try by this, as a tally, every provision of our Constitution and see if it hangs directly on the will of the people. Reduce your legislature to a convenient number for full but orderly discussion. Let every man who fights or pays exercise his just and equal right in their election. Submit them to approbation or rejection at short intervals. Let the executive be chosen in the same way, and for the same term, by those whose agent he is to be; and leave no screen of a council behind which to skulk from responsibility.

It has been thought that the people are not competent electors of judges learned in the law. But I do not know that this is true, and, if doubtful, we should follow principle. In this, as in many other elections, they would be guided by reputation which would not err oftener, perhaps, than the present mode of appointment. In one state of the Union at least, it has long been tried, and with the most satisfactory success. The judges of Connecticut have been chosen by the people every six months, for nearly two centuries, and I believe there has hardly ever been an instance of change, so powerful is the curb of incessant responsibility. If prejudice, however, derived from a monarchical institution, is still to prevail against the vital elective principle of our own, and if the existing example among ourselves of periodical election of judges by the people be still mistrusted, let us at least not adopt the evil and reject the good of the English precedent; let us retain amovability on the concurrence of the executive and legislative branches, and nomination by the executive alone.

Nomination to office is an executive function. To give it to the legislature, as we do, is a violation of the principle of the separation of powers. It swerves the members from correctness by temptations to intrigue for office themselves, and to a corrupt barter of votes; and destroys responsibility by dividing it among a multitude. By leaving nomination in its proper place among executive functions, the principle of the distribution of power is preserved and responsibility weighs with its heaviest force on a single head.

The organization of our county administrations may be thought more difficult. But follow principle and the knot unties itself. Divide the counties into wards of such size as that every citizen can attend, when called on, and act in person. Ascribe to them the government of their wards in all things relating to themselves exclusively. A justice chosen by themselves in each, a constable, a military company, a patrol, a school, the care of their own poor, their own portion of the public roads, the choice of one or more jurors to serve in some court, and the delivery, within their own wards, of their own votes for all elective officers of higher sphere will relieve the county administration of nearly all its business, will have it better done, and by making every citizen an acting member of the government, and in the offices nearest and most interesting to him, will attach him by his strongest feelings to the independence of his country and its republican Constitution.

The justices thus chosen by every ward would constitute the county court, would do its judiciary business, direct roads and bridges, levy county and poor rates, and administer all the matters of common interest to the whole county. These wards, called townships in New England, are the vital principle of their governments, and have proved themselves the wisest invention ever devised by the wit of man for the perfect exercise of self-government, and for its preservation.

We should thus marshal our government into: (1) the general federal republic for all concerns foreign and federal; (2) that of the state, for what relates to our own citizens exclusively; (3) the county republics, for the duties and concerns of the county; and (4) the ward republics, for the small and yet numerous and interesting concerns of the neighborhood. And in government, as well as in every other business of life, it is by division and subdivision of duties alone that all matters, great and small, can be managed to perfection. And the whole is cemented by giving to every citizen, personally, a part in the administration of the public affairs.

The sum of these amendments is: (1) general suffrage; (2) equal representation in the legislature; (3) an executive chosen by the people; (4) judges elective or amovable; (5) justices, jurors, and sheriffs elective; (6) ward divisions; and (7) periodical amendments of the Constitution.

I have thrown out these, as loose heads of amendment, for consideration and correction; and their object is to secure self-government by the republicanism of our Constitution, as well as by the spirit of the people, and to nourish and perpetuate that spirit. I am not among those who fear the people. They, and not the rich, are our dependence for continued freedom.

And to preserve their independence, we must not let our rulers load us with perpetual debt. We must make our election between *economy and liberty,* or *profusion and servitude.* If we run into such debts, as that we must be taxed in our meat and in our drink, in our necessaries and our comforts, in our labors and our amusements, for our callings and our creeds, as the people of England are, our people, like them, must come to labor sixteen hours in the twenty-four, give the earnings of fifteen of these to the government for their debts and daily expenses; and the sixteenth being insufficient to afford us bread, we must live, as they now do, on oatmeal and potatoes; have no time to think, no means of calling the mismanagers to account; but be glad to obtain subsistence by hiring ourselves to rivet their chains on the necks of our fellow sufferers. Our landholders too, like theirs, retaining indeed the title and stewardship of estates called theirs, but held really in trust for the treasury, must wander, like theirs, in foreign countries, and be contented with penury, obscurity, exile, and the glory of the nation.

This example reads to us the salutary lesson that private fortunes are destroyed by public as well as by private extravagance. And this is the tendency of all human governments. A departure from principle in one instance becomes a precedent for a second; that second, for a third; and so on, till the bulk of the society is reduced to be mere automatons of misery, to have no sensibilities left but for sinning and suffering. Then begins, indeed, the *bellum omnium in omnia* [war of all against all], which some philosophers, observing to be so general in this world, have mistaken it for the natural instead of the abusive state of man. And the fore horse of this frightful team is public debt. Taxation follows that, and, in its train, wretchedness and oppression.

Some men look at constitutions with sanctimonious reverence and deem them, like the Ark of the Covenant, too sacred to be touched. They ascribe to the men of the preceding age a wisdom more than human and suppose what they did to be beyond amendment. I knew that age well; I belonged to it and labored with it. It deserved well of its country. It was very like the present, but without the experience of the present; and forty years of experience in government is worth a century of book reading. And this they would say themselves were they to rise from the dead. I am certainly not an advocate for frequent and untried changes in laws and constitutions. I think moderate imperfections had better be borne with because, when once known, we accommodate ourselves to them, and find practical means of correcting their ill effects.

But I know also that laws and institutions must go hand in hand with the progress of the human mind. As that becomes more developed, more enlightened, as new discoveries are made, new truths disclosed, and manners and opinions change with the change of circumstances, institutions must advance also, and keep pace with the times. We might as well require a man to wear still the coat which fitted him when a boy, as civilized society to remain ever under the regimen of their barbarous ancestors. . . .

Let us [not] weakly believe that one generation is not as capable as another of taking care of itself and of ordering its own affairs. Let us, as our sister states have done, avail ourselves of our reason and experience to correct the crude essays of our first and unexperienced, although wise, virtuous, and well-meaning, councils. And lastly, let us provide in our Constitution for its revision at stated periods. What these periods should be, nature herself indicates. By the European tables of mortality, of the adults living at any one moment of time, a majority will be dead in about nineteen years. At the end of that period, then, a new majority is come into place; or, in other words, a new generation.

Each generation is as independent of the one preceding as that was of all which had gone before. It has then, like them, a right to choose for itself the form of government it believes most promotive of its own happiness; consequently, to accommodate to the circumstances in which it finds itself, that received from its predecessors; and it is for the peace and good of mankind that a solemn opportunity of doing this every nineteen or twenty years should be provided by the Constitution, so that it may be handed on with periodical repairs from generation to generation, to the end of time, if anything human can so long endure.

It is now forty years since the constitution of Virginia was formed. The same tables inform us that, within that period, two-thirds of the adults then living are now dead. Have, then, the remaining third, even if they had the wish, the right to hold in obedience to their will, and to laws heretofore made by them, the other two-thirds, who, with themselves, compose the present mass of adults? If they have not, who has? The dead? But the dead have no rights. They are nothing; and nothing cannot own something. Where there is no substance, there can be no accident.

This corporeal globe and everything upon it belong to its present corporeal inhabitants during their generation. They alone have a right to direct what is the concern of themselves alone, and to declare the law of that direction; and this declaration can only be made by their majority. That majority, then, has a right to depute representatives to a convention and to make the Constitution what they think will be the best for themselves.

But how collect their voice? This is the real difficulty. If invited by private authority to county or district meetings, these divisions are so large that few will attend; and their voice will be imperfectly, or falsely, pronounced. Here, then, would be one of the advantages of the ward divisions I have proposed. The mayor of every ward, on a question like the present, would call his ward together, take the simple yea or nay of its members, convey these to the county court, who would hand on those of all its wards to the proper general authority; and the voice of the whole people would be thus fairly, fully, and peaceably expressed, discussed, and decided by the common reason of the society.

If this avenue be shut to the call of sufferance, it will make itself heard through that of force, and we shall go on, as other nations are doing, in the endless circle of oppression, rebellion, reformation; and oppression, rebellion, reformation, again; and so on forever.

These, sir, are my opinions of the governments we see among men and of the principles by which alone we may prevent our own from falling into the same dreadful track. I have given them at greater length than your letter called for; but I cannot say things by halves; and I confide them to your honor so to use them as to preserve me from the gridiron of the public papers. If you shall approve and enforce them, as you have done that of equal representation, they may do some good. If not, keep them to yourself, as the effusions of withered age and useless time.

104.

John Randolph: Against a Protective Tariff

The rapid development of American industry after the War of 1812 led to the replacement of shipping by manufacturing as the primary commercial interest of New England. The Fourteenth Congress (the first to be elected after the war) was anxious to support the country's economy, and various commercial factions, mainly in the North, strongly advocated high tariffs to protect their markets. The Tariff Act of 1816 was duly passed, but not without continuing opposition from Southern congressmen. John Randolph of Roanoke, whose speech against the bill in January 1816 is reprinted here in part, summed up the South's case when he proclaimed his refusal "to lay a duty on the cultivator of the soil to encourage exotic manufactures."

Source: *Debates,* 14 Cong., 1 Sess., pp. 685-688.

We hear much said about taxes, about our funds being pledged to the public creditors; and about the national faith being violated with respect to those creditors if we should repeal the double taxes, oppressive as they are to the people. To this I answer that the public faith never was broken when I had a share in the councils of the country; and, yet, we did repeal an entire system of taxation, though the whole of it was pledged for the public debt; and here, sir, we have another proof that the present government have renounced the true republican principles of Jefferson's administration on which they raised themselves to power, and that they have taken up, in their stead, those of John Adams.

At that time — I mean when we repealed that system of taxation — the Federalists were against the repeal, as these men are now, and, like these, insisted that the taxes were pledged to the public creditors. This, sir, is another plain indication that they have changed the principle by their pretenses to which they have gulled the people and obtained their ascendency, and that, as I have somewhere else remarked, their principle now is old Federalism, vamped up into a something bearing the superficial appearance of republicanism. Yes, we repealed those taxes upon the ground that so long as the nation should punctually pay the public creditor his due, the latter had no right to inquire out of what fund it came.

Suppose, sir, I borrow a sum of money and promise to pay my creditor out of the sales of my next crop of cotton, and that I should think fit to raise corn enough to pay him, and choose to reserve my cotton in store for a more advantageous market — will any man be absurd enough to say that I violate the faith I had pledged to that creditor if I do not sell my cotton? The Federalists at that time said that we had violated the public faith; while we, on the other hand, contended that so long as the creditor was paid his just demand, he had no right to ask where we got the means; whether we drew them, like the Federalists, from internal taxes, or, like the Republicans of that day, from our import duties, and the funds of the customhouse. . . .

My honorable colleague (Mr. Sheffey) has said that the case of the manufacturers is not fairly before the House. True! it is not fairly before the House. It never can be fairly before the House. Whenever it comes before us, it must come unfairly, not as "a spirit of health — but a goblin damned"; not "bringing with it airs from Heaven but blasts from Hell" — it ought to be exorcised out of the House; for, what do the principles about which such a contest is maintained amount to but a system of bounties to manufacturers, in order to encourage them to do that which, if it be advantageous to do at all, they will do, of course, for their own sakes; a largess to men to exercise their own customary callings for their own emolument; and government devising plans, and bestowing premiums out of the pockets of the hard-working cultivator of the soil, to mold the productive labor of the country into a thousand fantastic shapes; barring up, all the time, for that perverted purpose, the great, deep, rich stream of our prosperous industry.

Such a case, sir, I agree with the honorable gentleman, cannot be fairly brought before the House. It eventuates in this: whether you, as a planter, will consent to be taxed in order to hire another man to go to work in a shoemaker's shop, or to set up a spinning jenny. For my part I will not agree to it, even though they should, by way of return, agree to be taxed to help us to plant tobacco; much less will I agree to pay all and receive nothing for it. No, I will buy where I can get manufactures cheapest. I will not agree to lay a duty on the cultivators of the soil to encourage exotic manufactures; because, after all, we should only get much worse things at a much higher price, and we, the cultivators of the country, would in the end pay for all. Why do not gentlemen ask us to grant a bounty for the encouragement of making flour? The reason is too plain for me to repeat it; then, why pay a man much more than the value for it to work up our own cotton into clothing, when, by selling my raw material, I can get my clothing much better and cheaper from Dacca?

Sir, I am convinced that it would be impolitic, as well as unjust, to aggravate the burdens of the people for the purpose of favoring the manufacturers; for this government created and gave power to Congress to regulate commerce and equalize duties on the whole of the United States, and not to lay a duty but with a steady eye to revenue. With my goodwill, sir, there should be none but an ad valorem duty on all articles, which would prevent the possibility of one interest in the country being sacrificed by the management of taxation to another. What is there in those objects of the honorable gentlemen's solicitude to give them a claim to be supported by the earnings of the others? The agriculturists bear the whole brunt of the war and taxation, and remain poor, while the others run in the ring of pleasure, and fatten upon them. The agriculturists not only pay all but fight all, while the others run. The manufacturer is the citizen of no place or any place; the agriculturist has his property, his lands, his all, his household gods to defend; and, like that meek drudge, the ox, who does the labor and plows the ground, and, then, for his reward, takes the refuse of the farmyard, the blighted blades and the moldy straw, and the mildewed shocks of corn for his support; while the commercial speculators live in opulence, whirling in coaches, and indulging in palaces — to use the words of Dr. Johnson, "coaches, which fly like meteors, and palaces, which rise like exhalations."

Even without your aid, the agriculturists are no match for them. Alert, vigilant, enterprising, and active, the manufacturing interest are collected in masses, and ready to associate at a moment's warning for any purpose of general interest to their body. Do but ring the fire bell, and you can assemble all the manufacturing interest of Philadelphia in fifteen minutes. Nay, for matter of that, they are always assembled; they are always on the Rialto; and Shylock and Antonio meet there every day, as friends, and compare notes, and lay plans, and possess in trick and intelligence what, in the goodness of God to them, the others can never possess. It is the choicest bounty to the ox that he cannot play the fox or the tiger. So it is to one of the body of agriculturists that he cannot skip into a coffee house and shave a note with one hand, while with the other he signs a petition to Congress portraying the wrongs and grievances and sufferings he endures, and begging them to relieve him; yes, to relieve him out of the pockets of those whose labors have fed and enriched, and whose valor has defended them. The cultivators, the patient drudges of the other orders of society, are now waiting for your resolution. For, on you it depends whether they shall be left further unhurt or be, like those in Europe reduced, *gradatim* [gradually] and subjected to another squeeze from the hard grasp of power.

105.

Hints to Emigrants from Europe

The end of the Napoleonic Wars and the growing awareness of opportunities in America led to a new wave of immigration after 1815. However, the influx glutted the labor market, and many immigrants, especially those from Ireland, were unable to find jobs. To help these people, a number of Irish who had already established themselves in the new land formed the Shamrock Friendly Association. The organization was both an employment and a welfare agency; it provided temporary subsistence while helping immigrants to find work. In July 1816, the Shamrock Society of New York published Hints to Emigrants from Europe, *a booklet intended to acquaint newcomers from Ireland with economic and political conditions in the United States. Extracts from the booklet are reprinted here.*

Source: *Hints to Emigrants from Europe, etc., etc.,* London, 1817.

THAT HOSPITALITY WHICH, as Mr. Jefferson says, the savages of the wilderness extended to the first settlers arriving in this land, cannot be denied by a free, civilized, and Christian people to brethren emigrating from the countries of their common fathers; and the exercise of it is peculiarly agreeable to us who have (some of us) been induced by a similarity of fate and fortunes with your own to quit the lands of our nativity and seek freedom and happiness in America. That hospitality which the wild Arab never violates, and which the American Indian so often exercises to strangers, that sacred virtue is dear to our hearts which we open to address you in the frankness of friendship and sincerity of truth. We bid you welcome to a land of freedom; we applaud your resolution; we commend your judgment in asserting the right of expatriation — a right acknowledged and practised by people of all nations from the earliest ages to the present time (England, with her absurd pretensions, not excepted), a right indispensable to liberty and happiness, and which ought never to be surrendered. The free states once established in Asia recognized it; Greece adopted it. Emigration from thence was uncontrolled; and naturalization, which puts the emigrants, civilly, on a level with the native, was there a thing of course. The Romans avowed and vindicated the right in all its latitude; and this memorable declaration composed part of their code: "Every man has a right to choose the state to which he will belong."

It is a law of nature that we may go whither we list to promote our happiness. It is thus, indeed, that the arts, sciences, laws, and civilization itself have journeyed with colonies from one region to another; from Asia and Egypt to Europe, and from Europe to America. In making this country your home, your choice does you honor; and we doubt not but your conduct will be equally correct, judicious, and honorable. That the laws and institutions of America may be from this moment the objects of your constant respect, we will quote what a European philosopher has said of America, as compared politically with Europe. "Whilst almost all the nations of Europe," says the Abbé de Mably, "are ignorant of the constituent principles of society, and regard the people as beasts of a farm, cultivated for the benefit of the owner, we are astonished, we are edified, that your thirteen republics should know, at once, the dignity of man, and should have drawn from the sources of the wisest philosophy the principles by which they are disposed to be governed."

Even in your state of probation here, as aliens, you will soon perceive that the laws (and ours is a government of laws) are made by the will of the people, through agents called representatives. The will of a majority passes for, and requires the consent of all. Entire acquiescence in the decisions of the majority is the vital principle of republics, from which there is no legitimate appeal; for resistance to those decisions is an appeal to force, the vital principle and immediate parent of despotism. It is a fundamental truth in nature, and for those not held in servitude it is a law in America, that men are born equal, and endowed with inalienable rights, of which they can neither divest themselves nor be deprived by others. Slaves may be ruled by the will of one, or a few; but freemen are governed only by the general will.

Strangers as you are, you may derive benefit from the counsel and guidance of friends. If one who has gone the road you are about to travel, by only showing you how it winds beyond the next hill, does you an act of civility, how much more important would be some information that must influence your welfare and future fortune? And when you reflect that circumstances apparently trivial may make the one or mar the other, you will not disregard a communication which relates to the business of life.

All that a first conversation with an emigrant can properly embrace will fall under three heads: first, what relates to his personal safety in a new climate; second, his interests as a probationary resident; and, third, his future rights and duties as a member of a free state. Under the first will be comprised some directions for your mode of living, and the preservation of your health. The second would demand some description of this extensive country, which may direct your choice and industry. Under the third should be contained a brief abstract of . . . civil or political matters. . . .

Emigrants from Europe usually arrive here during summer; and, everything considered, it is best they should; for in the middle and eastern states the winter is long, fuel very dear, and employment comparatively scarce at that season. In winter they will expend more and earn less. But if arriving at this time bear more upon their pocket, the heats of the summer are undoubtedly more trying to their health. In the middle states, namely, New York, New Jersey, Pennsylvania, and Maryland, a northern European usually finds the climate intensely hot from about the middle of June till toward the 1st of October. The thermometer frequently ranges from 84 to 90, and sometimes to 96 in the middle of the day; this, to a stranger who works in the open air exposed to the burning sun, is certainly dangerous, and requires some precautions on his part.

First of all, he should regulate his diet, and be temperate in the quantity of his food. The American laborer or working mechanic who has a better and more plentiful table than any other man in the world of his class is, for the most, a small eater; and we recommend to you his example. The European of the same condition who receives meat or fish and coffee, at breakfast, meat at dinner, and meat or fish and tea at supper — an abundance of animal food to which he was unaccustomed — insensibly falls into a state of too great repletion, which exposes him to the worst kind of fever during the heats of summer and autumn. He should, therefore, be quite as abstemious in the quantity of food as of strong drink; and in addition to this method of preventing sickness, he should take a dose of active physic, every now and then, especially in the hotter months of July and August. By this prudent course an ardent climate will have no terrors; and, after some residence here, he may preserve his health by regimen and exercise alone.

The laborer or mechanic should put off his ordinary clothes, and wear next his skin a loose flannel shirt while he works; it should be taken off again when he is done. . . .

Do you ask by this time with a view to the ordinary business of life, What is America? What sort of people may be expected to succeed in it? The immortal Franklin has answered these questions; "America is the land of labor." But it is, emphatically, the best country on earth for those who will labor. By industry they can earn more wages here than elsewhere in the world. Our governments are more frugal; they demand few taxes so that the earnings of the poor man are left to enrich himself; they are nearly all his own, and not expended on kings or their satellites.

Idlers are out of their element here, and the being who is technically called a man of rank in Europe is despicable in America. He must become a useful member of society, or he will find no society; he will be shunned by all decent people. Franklin, whose sage counsel is the best that can be given or observed, has said that it is not advisable for a person to come hither "who has no other quality to recommend him but his birth." In Europe, indeed, it may have its value; but it is a commodity which cannot be carried to a worse market than that of America where people do not inquire concerning a stranger, What is he? but, What can he do? If he has any useful art, he is welcome; and if he exercises it and behaves well, he will be respected by all who know him. The husbandman is in honor here, and so is the mechanic because their employments are useful. "And the people," he adds, "have a saying, that 'God Almighty is himself a mechanic, the greatest in the universe.' " Franklin further illustrates the generality of industrious habits by the Negro's observation, "that the white man makes the black man work, the horses work, the oxen work, and everything work except the hog, which alone walks about, goes to sleep when he pleases, and lives like a gentleman.

"The only encouragements we hold out to strangers are a good climate, fertile soil, wholesome air and water, plenty of provisions, good pay for labor, kind neighbors, good laws, a free government, and a hearty welcome. The rest depends on a man's own industry and virtue."

It would be very prudent for newcomers, especially laborers or farmers, to go into the country without delay, as they will save both money and time by it, and avoid several inconveniences of a seaport town. By spending some time with an American farmer in any capacity, they will learn the method of tillage, or working a plantation peculiar to this country. No time can be more usefully employed than a year in this manner. In that space any smart, stout man can learn how woodland may be cleared, how clear land is managed; he will acquire some knowledge of crops and their succession, of usages and customs that ought to be known, and perhaps save something into the bargain. Many European emigrants who brought money with them have heretofore taken this wise course, and found it greatly to their advantage; for at the end of the year they knew what to do with it. They had learned the value of lands in old settlements and near the frontiers, the prices of labor, cattle, and grain, and were ready to begin the world with ardor and confidence. Multitudes of poor people from Ireland, Scotland, and Germany have by these means, together with industry and frugality, become wealthy farmers, or, as they are called in Europe, estated men who, in their own countries, where all the lands are fully occupied and the wages of labor low, could never have emerged from the condition wherein they were born.

In the west, in Pennsylvania, there is a custom which the farmers there call *cropping,* and which is as beneficial to the owner as to the tiller of the ground in the present state of this country. The cropper performs the labor of the plantation, as spring and fall ploughings, sowing, harrowing, or other work, and receives a certain share of the crop, as agreed on, for his pains. But he must be an expert farmer before he can undertake, or be entrusted with the working of the farm. None but a poor man undertakes it, and that only until he can save money to buy land of his own.

It is invariably the practice of the American, and well suited to his love of independence, to purchase a piece of land as soon as he can and cultivate his own farm, rather than live at wages. It is equally in the power of an emigrant to do the same after a few years of labor and economy. From that moment he secures all the means of happiness. He has a sufficiency of fortune without being exempt from moderate labor; he feels the comfort of independence and has no fear of poverty in his old age. He is invested with the powers as well as the rights of a freeman, and may in all cases, without let or apprehension, exercise them according to his judgment. He can afford to his children a good education, and knows that he has thereby provided for their wants. Prospects open to them far brighter than were his own; and in seeing all this, he is surely blest.

Industrious men need never lack employment in America. Laborers, carpenters, masons, bricklayers, stonecutters, tailors, and shoemakers, and the useful mechanics generally are always sure of work and wages. Stonecutters now receive in this city (New York) $2 a day, equal to 9*s.* sterling; carpenters, $1.87½; bricklayers, $2; laborers, from $1 to $1.25; others in proportion. At this time (July 1816), house carpenters, bricklayers, masons, and stonecutters are paid $3 per day in Petersburg, Virginia. The town was totally consumed by fire about a year since, but it is now rising from its ashes in more elegance than ever. Mechanics will find ample employment there for perhaps two years to come.

Artisans receive better pay in America than in Europe, and can live with less exertion and more comfort, because they put an additional price on their work equal to the cost of freight and commission charged by the merchant on importation. But there are not many of the laborious classes whom we would advise to reside, or even loiter, in great towns; because as much will be spent during a long winter as can be made through a toilsome summer, so that a man may be kept a moneyless drudge for life. But this is not perhaps the worst; he is tempted to become a tippler by the cheapness and plenty of liquors, and then his prospects are blasted forever. In few countries is drunkenness more despised than in this. The drunkard is viewed as a person socially dead, shut out from decent intercourse, shunned, despised, or abhorred. . . .

Men of science who can apply their knowledge to useful and practical purposes, may be very advantageously settled; but mere literary scholars who have no profession, or only one which they cannot profitably practise in this country, do not meet with much encouragement; in truth, with little or none unless they are willing to devote themselves to the education of youth. The demand for persons who will do this is obviously increasing; although many excellent preceptors are everywhere to be found among the native Americans, there is still considerable room for competition on the part of well-qualified foreigners. In the seminaries for classical education, it is very common to find the preceptors natives of Ireland. In the southern states, where a thin population is spread over an extensive country, good schools are but few; but there are rich planters in those districts, in whose families foreigners of genteel address and good knowledge of the classics, English, and arithmetic will find employment and a good salary as private tutors. It does not detract from a man's personal respectability or future prospects to have been thus engaged. The Americans are too wise to treat that condition as mean which is essential to the honor and prosperity of the nation, and which supposes in its possessor natural talents and acquired knowledge. It is not unusual in this country to see young men who taught school until they accumulated some property, and who then turn to the professions of law, medicine, or divinity, or who become farmers or merchants. The practice and feelings of the Americans in this particular may be judged from the fact that many gentlemen who begin their career as schoolmasters pass through all the gradations of state honors, are appointed to foreign embassies, promoted to the head of departments of the federal government, and have as good prospects as others of attaining the presidency. Several instances of this nature might be quoted from this unprejudiced people.

In what part of this extensive country can an emigrant from the northern or western parts of Europe most advantageously settle? If he be undecided until his arrival, his choice will be agreeably perplexed or suspended by the different invitations offered by various sections of this empire. It covers an area between the 31st and 46th degrees of N. latitude, and from the Atlantic Ocean to the westward indefinitely. In time our settlements will reach the borders of the Pacific. The productions of the soil are as various as the climates. The middle states produce grain of all kinds. Maryland and Virginia afford wheat and tobacco; North Carolina, naval stores; and South Carolina and Georgia, rice, cotton, indigo, and tobacco; to these products Louisiana and Mississippi add sugar and indigo, which are now cultivated in Georgia likewise. Tennessee, Kentucky, Indiana, and Ohio are productive of the chief part of these great and principal staples, together with hemp, coal, and such plants as are found in the northern and middle states, to the westward of the Allegheny Mountains. Over this great tract, the finest fruits grow in perfection; grain of every sort is in plenty; and "he who puts a seed into the earth is recompensed, perhaps, by receiving forty out of it." We are of opinion that those parts of the United States between the 35th and 43rd, or 37th and 42nd degrees of N. latitude will be found most congenial to the constitutions of

Europeans. New York (principally), Pennsylvania, Maryland, Virginia, Kentucky, Ohio, Indiana, the Illinois and Missouri territories are spread within these parallels. As the European is more patient of cold than of heat, he will be apt to prefer the middle and western, or northwestern states, to the southern. There he will form connections with inhabitants whose manners most resemble his own. In some one of them we would advise him, after a proper examination, to pitch his tent and fix his residence.

Farther to the south, where Negro slaves are the only or principal laborers, some white men think it disreputable to follow the plough. Far be it from us to cast censure on our southern neighbors; yet, in choosing a settle, we would have emigrants take slavery, with all other circumstances, into their consideration.

It is the opinion of some judicious men that though persons newly arrived ought to go without loss of time into the country, yet it would not be prudent for them to retire all at once to the remote parts of the west; that they ought to stop nearer the seashore, and learn a little of the mode of doing business. Perhaps this, in some instances, may be advisable; but we think that young men whose habits are not fixed cannot pass too speedily to the fine regions beyond the Allegheny. The laborer, however, will find great difference between them and Europe in everything. The man who was accustomed to the spade must now use the axe; he who used to dig ditches will learn to maul rails and make fences. These are the extremes that must be met; and the sooner, perhaps, the better.

We omit annexing to these directions a table of roads; as almanacs are everywhere to be had for a trifle, and they contain accurate lists with the principal stages from east to west; there are also people always willing to direct the stranger on his path.

If a European has previously resolved to go to the western country near the Allegheny or Ohio rivers, he will save much expense and travel by landing at Baltimore; from thence to Pittsburgh, at the head of the Ohio, is about 200 miles direct, perhaps not more than 240 by the course of the road. A few days' journey will bring him along a fine turnpike from Baltimore, nearly to Cumberland in Allegheny county (Md.) from whence the public road, begun by the United States, crosses the mountains, and is to touch the Ohio at Wheeling. A smart fellow, in a little time, will reach Union, in Fayette county, Pennsylvania. Here is a flourishing county adjoining Green, Washington, and Westmoreland, in either of which may be found almost everything that is desirable, and a population hospitable and intelligent. From Union to Pittsburgh is but a day's journey. There, one may ascend the Allegheny River to the upper counties, or he may follow the current and descend the Ohio to the state of that name, cross it to Indiana, or continue his voyage to Kentucky. He may proceed to the Mississippi River, and go up it to St. Louis, in the Missouri Territory, or he may proceed a little farther up, and ascend the Illinois River, in the Illinois Territory. Such are the facilities of going by water from Pittsburgh to various parts of the west; and those states and territories named are among the most fertile in America.

From Philadelphia to Pittsburgh is about 300 miles, chiefly through a fine, plentiful, and well-cultivated country. A gentleman of Pennsylvania, of high standing and information, writes to a member of this society: "Pennsylvania, after all, is, perhaps, the best field for Irish capacity and habits to act in, with prospects for a family, or for individual reward. Lands of the finest quality may be had in this state for barely settling and remaining five years; the advantage derived from the grant being the encouragement of others to settle and purchase." That is, by the laws of Pennsylvania, warrantees must make an actual settlement on the land they hold by deeds from the land office. Hence, trusty persons obtain a deed for a part, on condition of clearing a certain quantity, and building a house and residing there.

In our state (of New York) the advantages are great, whether we regard soil, or situation, or roads, lakes, and rivers. Few, if any, states in the Union have finer land than the great western district of New York. It has risen exceedingly in a few years, and the price will be much increased as soon as the intended canal from Lakes Erie and Champlain to the Hudson River shall be completed. These most useful and magnificent works will probably be begun next summer, and afford for several years to come, to many thousands of industrious poor men an opportunity of enriching themselves. If prudent, they may realize their earnings on the spot and become proprietors in fee of landed estates in the beautiful country they shall have so greatly improved.

From no other city in the Atlantic can a person sooner reach the country than by means of the Hudson and the roads that branch from its towns on either of its banks. Lands of good quality may be still purchased, even in the midland parts of New York, at a reasonable rate.

As every emigrant does not mean to turn farmer, and our wish is to furnish hints to various classes, we will here, at the risk of repetition, state the ideas of a gentleman of much experience, respectability, and intelligence concerning the pursuits of different persons.

Those who have acquired useful trades will, in general, find little difficulty either in our large cities or the towns and villages all over the country. . . .

Clerks, shopkeepers, or attendants in stores are seldom wanted; their occupation is an uncertain one; it requires some time, too, for such persons to acquire the mode of doing business with the same expertness as natives or long residents. In most cases a sort of apprenticeship is to be served; and it would be well for persons newly arrived to engage for some months at low wages, with a view to procure the necessary experience. Six months or a year spent in this manner, and for this purpose, will fit a man for making better use of his future years; and he will have no occasion to repent his pains. We would press this on your consideration.

The same observations are applicable, but in a less degree, to persons who mean to apply themselves to husbandry. Some local peculiarities must be learned even by them, the neglect of which would be so much the more inexcusable as the knowledge may be shortly and easily acquired.

Those who have money and intend to settle here in any business would do well to invest their funds in some public stock, or deposit them in a bank, until they have acquired such a knowledge of the country, the modes of life and business as shall enable them to launch into trade, commerce, or manufactures with safety. To loan money securely needs great care. It has been often seen that persons arriving in America with some property lose it all before they prosper in the world. The reason of which is that in the first place, they begin some kind of business without knowing how to conduct it; and in the next that with less skill, they are less frugal and industrious than their competitors. It is equally observable that persons who arrive here with little to depend on beside their personal exertions become prosperous at last; for by the time they have earned some money in the employ of others, they will have learned there, likewise, how to secure and improve it. . . .

It is fit the emigrant should be distinctly apprised (for it will conciliate his attachment and gratitude to the country of his adoption) that nowhere in the world is a well-conducted foreigner received into the bosom of the state with equal liberality and readiness as in America. When, on the 4th of July, 1776, the Congress unanimously adopted a Declaration of Independence and delivered their country from the dominion of the King of England, this was one of the complaints alleged against him: "He has endeavored to prevent the population of these states; for that purpose obstructing the laws for naturalization of foreigners." The same liberal feeling has prevailed in the government of the United States from that memorable day to this, with one exception, during the administration of President Adams. The stranger, however, is certainly exposed to incidents which may lead him to doubt the truth of this assertion. He may light upon an ignorant, a prejudiced, or illiberal wretch who will manifest an ill will toward him because he is a foreigner, and perhaps revive British and royalists' taunts in a new form; but these, the scum of a country, are totally insignificant when compared with the mass of the people. The best men in America have always been ready to welcome the valuable emigrant, the stranger of moral and industrious habits. An author, eminent as a statesman, a scholar, and philosopher, speaking in his discourse to the Philosophical Society of New York of the advantages which Cicero boasted that Rome had derived from Athens, adds:

> We are perhaps more favored in another point of view. Attica was peopled from Egypt; but we can boast of our descent from a superior stock. I speak not of families or dynasties; I refer to our origin from those nations where civilization, knowledge, and refinement have erected their empire, and where human nature has attained its greatest perfection. Annihilate Holland, Great Britain, Ireland, France, and Germany, and what would become of civilized man? This country, young as it is, would be the great Atlas remaining to support the dignity of the world. And perhaps our mingled descent from various nations may have a benign influence upon genius. We perceive the improving effects of an analogous state upon vegetables and inferior animals. The extraordinary character which the United States have produced may be in some measure ascribed to the mixed blood of so many nations flowing in our veins; and it may be confidently said the operation of causes, acting with irresistible effect, will carry, in this country, all the improvable faculties of human nature to the highest state of perfection.

You will, however, observe that the privilege of citizenship is not granted without proper precautions; to secure that, while the worthy are admitted, the unworthy should, if practicable, be rejected. You will from hence deduce the importance of good moral habits, even to the acquisition of political rights.

The steps to be taken by a foreigner preparatory to and for the purpose of his being naturalized are these:

1. He must, at least five years before he can be admitted a citizen of the United States, report himself at the office of one of the courts of record within the state or territory where he may be; and in that report set forth his name, birthplace, age, nation, and prior allegiance, together with the country which he has left to come into the United States, and the place of his intended settlement. In general, forms of this report will be furnished by the clerk of the court who will also give a certificate under the seal of the court that the report has been made and filed. This certificate must be carefully kept for the purpose of being produced at the time of application for admission to citizenship.

This step of reporting one's arrival is indispensable, and ought to be taken as soon as possible because the five years of probation begin to be counted only from the date of the report; and the time which a foreigner may have previously spent in the country cannot be rendered of any service toward his naturalization.

2. At least three years before the alien can be naturalized, he must appear before

some one of the courts of record within the state or territory where he may be and there declare, on oath, that it is in good faith his intention to become a citizen of the United States; to renounce forever all allegiance and fidelity to any sovereign prince, potentate, state, or sovereignty whatever, and particularly, by name, to the prince, potentate, state or sovereign, whereof he may at the time be a citizen or subject. This oath or affirmation, which must have been made at least three years before the admission or citizenship, may be made at any convenient time after the report of arrival. . . .

3. At this period the applicant, after producing both those certificates, must declare on oath, or affirmation before some of the same courts that he will support the Constitution of the United States. He must also satisfy the court (which cannot be done by the affidavit of the applicant himself, and is usually done by the affidavits of two respectable citizens, who know and can testify to the facts) that he has resided within the United States five years at least, and within the state or territory where he applies to be admitted at least one year, and that during such time he has behaved as a man of good moral character, attached to the principles of the Constitution of the United States, and well-disposed to the good order and happiness of the same. The clerk will thereupon make out a certificate of naturalization under the seal of the court, which should be carefully kept and ready to be produced whenever it may be requisite.

The liberality of Congress has extended the benefits of this admission to citizenship beyond those who perform these requisites; for the children of a person so naturalized, being under age, and dwelling in the United States at the time of their parents' naturalization, also become citizens. And still further, if any alien who shall have regularly reported himself, and made oath or affirmation declaratory of his intentions (which, as we have seen, must precede his own admission by three years), should unfortunately die before he was actually naturalized, his widow and children would thenceforth be considered as citizens of the United States and be entitled to all rights and privileges as such, upon taking the oaths prescribed by law. This provision, therefore, furnishes a very strong inducement for losing no time in taking the oath declaratory of the party's intention.

In the interval between the emigrant's choosing a place of abode and completing the five years of probationary residence which must elapse before he can become a citizen of the United States, he will do well to familiarize himself with the state of parties, and acquire a correct knowledge of our constitutions of civil government. He will become a respectable and capable citizen in proportion to his information and virtue. Liberality and justice are the leading principles of our government which, as it secures liberty and property, and neither makes nor suffers religious distinctions, better deserves the fidelity of good men than the tyrannical governments of Europe. Ours maintains the rights of the people; theirs, the absolute power of princes.

No emigrant ought to stay more than one week in the country without endeavoring to procure the Constitution of the United States and, at least, that of the state in which he means to reside. The federal Constitution, and those of the several states, are printed and bound together in a neat pocket volume with the Declaration of Independence and form a political bible, well deserving the study of every reflecting republican. . . .

The source of every blessing, and itself the most valuable of all which America offers to the emigrant, is a degree of civil and political liberty more ample and better secured in this republic than anywhere in the whole world besides. The persecutions of kings and priests, and the denial of rights, which drove a freedom-loving race from Europe to these shores, the same continue to operate to the present day. This is all to our gain; for they who escape from the dungeons of tyranny there will here be zealous to support the noble edifice of liberty; while the private welfare of each man, fairly pursued, forms the benefit of all and constitutes the public good.

The principles of liberty which are embodied in our frame of government and in our laws branch out likewise through every department of society, mold our manners, and determine the character even of our domestic relations. They have the effect of producing, generally, in the deportment of individuals who know neither superiors nor inferiors, a certain degree of ease and dignity that is equally removed from servility and arrogance. It is one of the practical results of those principles that the poorer classes in this community are more civilized, more polite and friendly, though not so submissive, as persons of the same fortunes in Europe. They are also usually followed by impartial justice in the equal distribution of family property. Hence opulence is rarely seen to accumulate in one branch, while others languish in genteel beggary. As there is nowhere an aristocratic establishment, the amplitude of the community is never broken up into little compartments, envious and contemptuous of each other. Every man's range of occupation is extended, while every state is held worthy of respect. Honest industry nowhere derogates, but the facility of providing for a family is everywhere enlarged.

Nothing is more worthy of regard than the contrast between the general demeanor of Europeans living here, and what is alleged of the same people, and others similar to them, whilst under the yoke of transatlantic governments. In New York City alone there are supposed to be not less than 12,000 Irish, and the number of all other foreigners may probably be as many. The other great cities of the United States have an equal proportion according to their population; and emigrants from the Old World are settled and in progress of settlement everywhere throughout the Union; yet here they are never accused of sedition, or rebellion, or conspiracy against the government. They are never disarmed by a military force; and no magistrate trembles when they provide themselves with ammunition. They are, indeed, the most strenuous supporters of the government; and it is evident that a country may exist in the utmost good order, peace, and prosperity under such a system of law as they are willing to maintain with their lives. It is manifest, therefore, that if the laws were in Europe what they are here, Europe need not drive her children into exile. The same men who are called rebels there are esteemed and tranquil citizens here, without having changed their nature or their sentiments. But here the law is made by the majority for the good of the great number; and for this reason it is essentially equal and impartial. It prohibits nothing but what is in itself morally wrong. Hence there are fewer laws and fewer transgressions; but when a real transgression happens, an offended community is always prompt to support the law; for it then vindicates its own decision and its own safety.

You then who left the abject condition of European subjects, who will never encounter the persecution of kings, lords, or hierarchies, who are now beyond the fantastic tyranny of those governments that exterminate Catholics in one country, and connive at the massacre of Protestants in another, what more is requisite to engage your love and veneration of the free Constitution of America than to remember what you were, what you have witnessed, what you have suffered, and to reflect on what you are about to become, and the blessings you have it in your power to enjoy?

Peabody Museum of Salem

Nathaniel Bowditch, a self-educated insurance executive, also wrote a definitive navigator's guide

TRADE AND ENTERPRISE

At the beginning of the 19th century the diverse talents of many men played a part in the commercial growth of the country. Nathaniel Bowditch published "The New American Practical Navigator" (1802), which was an indispensable aid to merchant sailors. Bowditch was also an important insurance man and as such helped underwrite commercial ventures.

To become a commercial nation, America had to manufacture; to manufacture, America needed technology — machines. Steam engines and water power were at first used to run the machines.

One of the most important early machines in America was Eli Whitney's cotton gin (patented 1794). With it, cotton fiber could quickly be separated from the seeds. The gin transformed cotton from an unprofitable crop into the mainstay of Southern economy. Whitney later turned to gun making. At his factory near New Haven, Conn., he introduced a system of interchangeable parts for his weapons. Mass production was born in the marriage of machine speed and uniform interchangeability.

The agricultural fair became a useful way of encouraging farm improvements. The fairs introduced new farming techniques and the latest farm equipment. Imported breeds of cattle and sheep were introduced that helped farmers improve their stock, and the prizes and high prices for champion stock that the fairs promised made improvement all the more rewarding. The American fair became a kind of exhibition, rather than a bazaar, as was the European fair. Americans liked to compete.

On the Sea

The importance of shipping and sea trade to the United States was reflected in the foreign policy of the period. The Jay Treaty tried, unsuccessfully, to establish the right of neutrality for American ships. Merchant ships from American ports carried tea, spices, and cotton from the Orient to European ports. This "middle-man" trade augmented the usual exchange of American raw materials for finished goods from Europe and Negro slaves from Africa.

The New-York Gazette General Advertiser.

Published (Daily) by John Lang,

For London,

For Norfolk, Petersburg and Richmond,

For Savannah,

For Boston,

WINES

Pilot Bread.

For Norfolk,

New York Historical Society

Commercial advertising in the "New York Gazette," Dec. 21, 1799; the border marks Washington's death

"Columbia Seizing the Trident of Neptune"; design by Sully

Library of Congress

The Philadelphia waterfront; watercolor by Thomas Birch, about 1800

Museum of Fine Arts, Boston; Karolik Collection

Peabody Museum of Salem

Crowninshield's Wharf, Salem, Mass.; painted by George Ropes, 1806

This flourishing commerce was disrupted during the War of 1812 and faced vigorous European competition after peace was restored.

After 1815 the whaling industry began to grow. Whale oil became the common lamp fuel, spermaceti was used in candles and cosmetics, and whalebone was used in corsets and fans. Whaling ships processed and stored the whale products on board and stayed at sea for several years at a time, reaping the whale harvest. At the industry's peak, in the 1840s, voyages often returned as much as 1,000 percent on investment.

Shelburne Museum

"A Ship's Boat Attacking a Whale"

Launching of the "Fame," built at the Becket shipyard, Salem, 1802

Essex Institute, Salem

Banner of the N.Y. Society of Pewterers, used in the Federal Procession, July 23, 1788

New York Historical Society

National Archives

Machine for splitting hides and shaving leather, 1809

In the early 19th century a period of transition began in the system of manufacture. Previously, one man created his product alone, but now the work was divided among several people. The factories of the new system demanded large investments of capital and placed owners and laborers in a relationship much different from that between a shop-owner and his journeymen.

Seals of the Boston Chair-makers Society

Warshaw Collection

Pamphlet reporting the Boot and Shoemakers' trial, 1806

New York Public Library

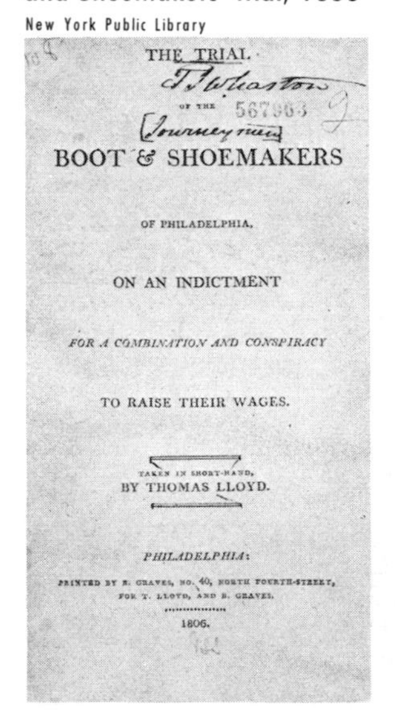

THE TRIAL

OF THE

BOOT & SHOEMAKERS

OF PHILADELPHIA,

ON AN INDICTMENT

FOR A COMBINATION AND CONSPIRACY

TO RAISE THEIR WAGES.

TAKEN IN SHORT-HAND,

BY THOMAS LLOYD.

PHILADELPHIA:

PRINTED BY B. GRAVES, NO. 40, NORTH FOURTH-STREET,

FOR T. LLOYD, AND B. GRAVES.

1806.

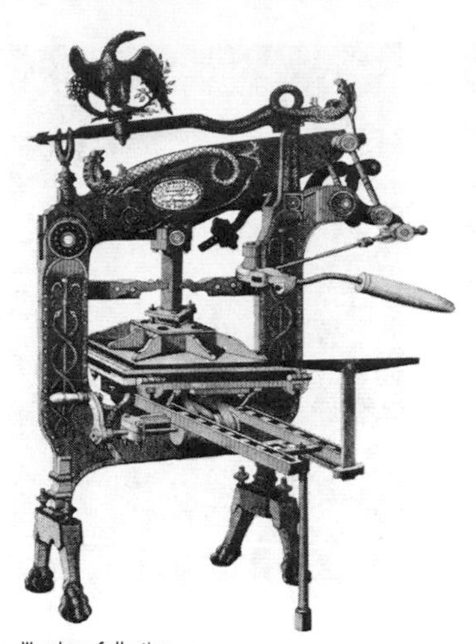

Warshaw Collection

The "Columbian Press," invented in 1813 by George Clymer

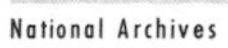

National Archives

Machine for boring wheel hubs, patented in 1810

National Archives

Shovel and scraper for use in road-making, patented in 1819 by Nathan Whiting

Trip-hammer patented in 1807 for use in forging and heavy metal-working

National Archives

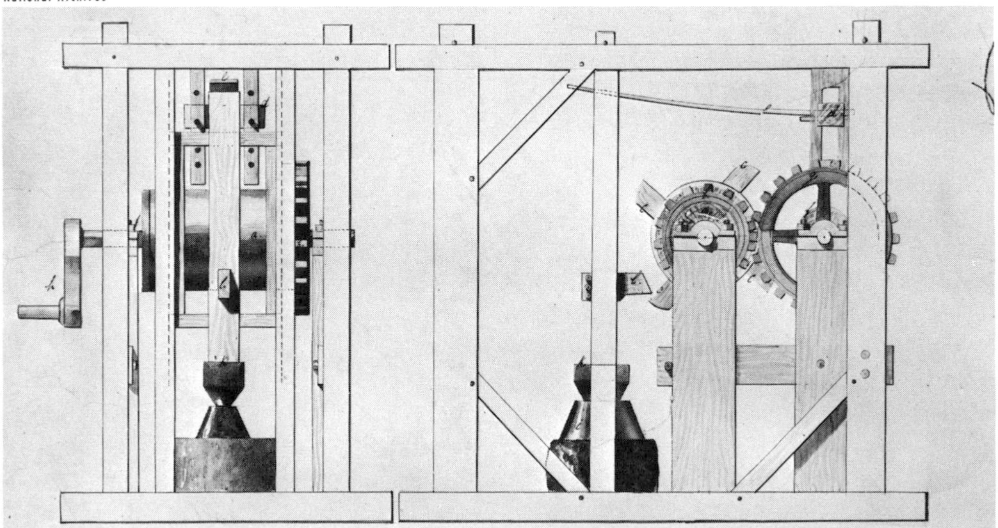

a The cylinder 32 inches diameter
4 feet stroke;
b The condenser 32 inches diameter
3 feet deep.
d. The air pump.
c The passage from the air pump to the condenser, this is cast in the foundation or iron bed, e, f is the seat of the condenser g, the seat of the air pump, this bed is screwed to the bottom of the boat. The air pump condenser and cylinder screwed on it so that the whole will form one strong and solid mass and render much of the present timber unnecessary.
Such an engine making 17 strokes a minute with steam one pound to the inch will drive a boat 16 feet wide drawing 2 feet of water 5 miles an hour [illegible] to Albany in 27 or 30 hours.
R. F.
July 1808

R Fulton July 24th 1808

New York Historical Society

Drawing of a steam engine by Robert Fulton, 1808

N.Y. State Historical Association

Robert Fulton, portrait by Benjamin West

Amherst College

Robert Livingston, partner in Fulton's monopoly

Steam

Americans were quick to realize the potentialities of steam power. Internal transportation was largely confined to the waterways, and the steamboat's ability to move upstream easily produced interest, invention, and commercial plans. At least 30 steamboats had been built in America by the time Robert Fulton launched his "Clermont" in 1807. However, the commercial beginnings of steam transportation can be traced to the competition between Fulton and Isaac Stevens for monopoly of steamboat travel on the Hudson River. In less than a decade steamboat lines plied the Eastern rivers and coast and were operating as far west as the Ohio and Mississippi Rivers.

Fulton's drawing of some of his proposals for using mines and torpedoes in warfare

The "Clermont" passing West Point on its way from New York to Albany in 1809

Stokes Collection, New York Public Library

Library of Congress

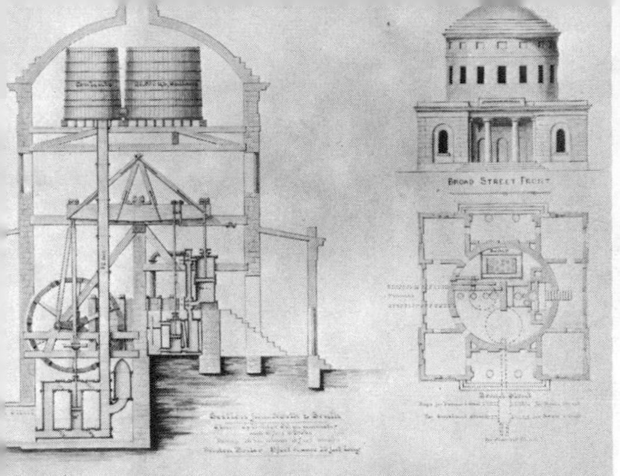

Pennsylvania Historical Society

The Philadelphia waterworks, in use 1798-1815, employed steam pumps to draw water

Library of Congress

Design by Jonathan Hull, an Englishman, for a steam-powered tugboat, 1787

Drawing of the crude steam engine used by Oliver Evans in his experiments

Library of Congress

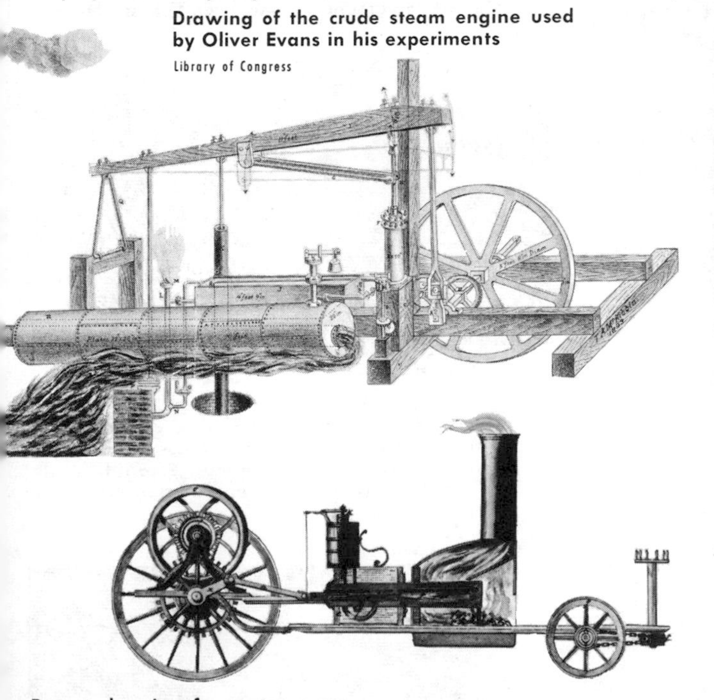

Stevens Institute; photo, Frick

Col. John Stevens, Fulton's rival, built the first ocean-going steamer, 1809, and later pioneered in railroads

Patent drawing for a steam carriage, 1817; it never was built

National Archives

Oliver Evans' "Amphibdros," an amphibious dredge, successfully operated in 1803

University of Michigan, Engineering Library

Granger Collection

"The Country Fair" by John Woodside, 1824; the sheep in the foreground are imported Spanish Merino

Agriculture

Major changes were also taking place in agriculture. Elkanah Watson and the Berkshire Agricultural Society sponsored the first county fair in 1811. The "Berkshire system" offered a forum for new ideas and popularized competitive stock breeding. Eli Whitney's cotton gin was the most important of a number of inventions affecting agriculture.

Library of Congress

Warshaw Collection

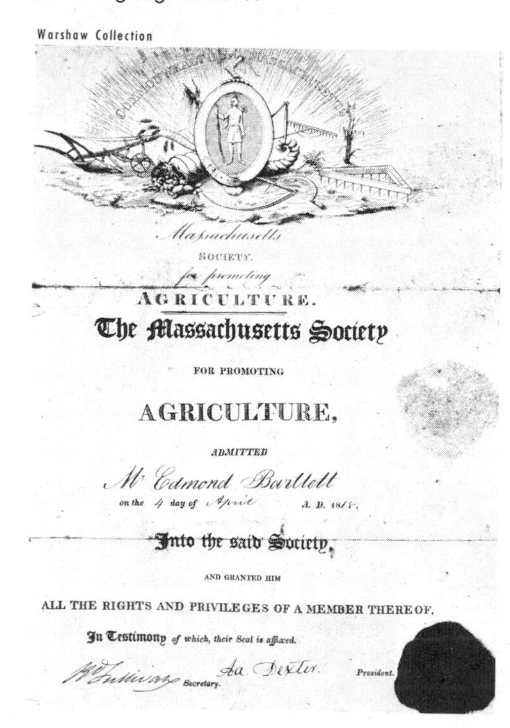

Massachusetts SOCIETY for promoting AGRICULTURE.

The Massachusetts Society

FOR PROMOTING

AGRICULTURE,

ADMITTED

Mr Edmond Bartlett

on the 4 day of April A. D. 1818.

Into the said Society,

AND GRANTED HIM

ALL THE RIGHTS AND PRIVILEGES OF A MEMBER THEREOF.

In Testimony of which, their Seal is affixed.

Secretary. Aa. Dexter. President.

(Above) Harvesting wheat with a cradle; (left) membership certificate of the Mass. Society for Promoting Agriculture; (below) Elkanah Watson, merchant, canal promoter, and agriculturist

Granger Collection

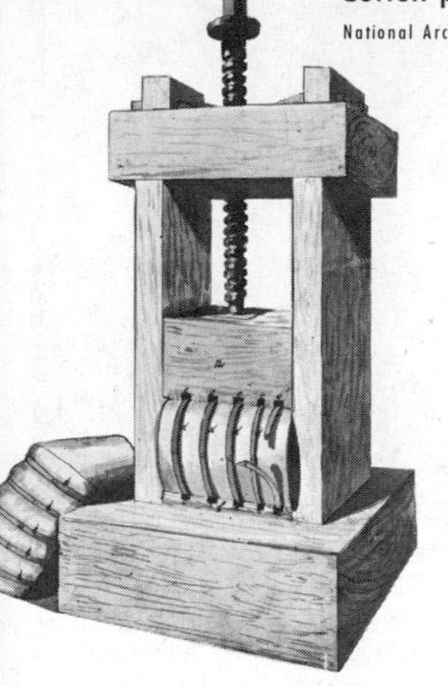

Cotton press and bale binder, 1809

National Archives

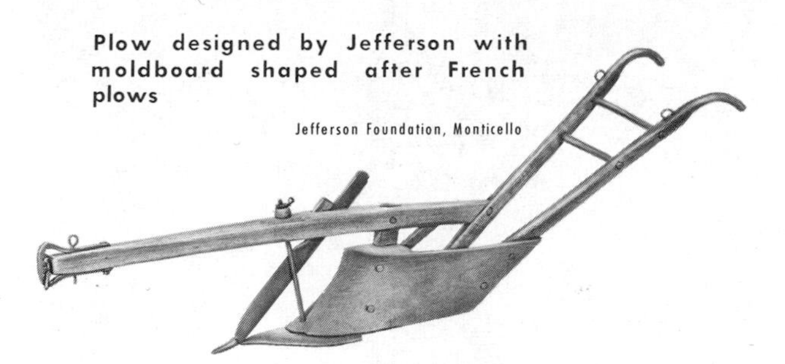

Plow designed by Jefferson with moldboard shaped after French plows

Jefferson Foundation, Monticello

Whitney's gin to remove seed from cotton, a job formerly done by hand

Smithsonian Inst.

Eli Whitney by Morse

Yale Art Gallery

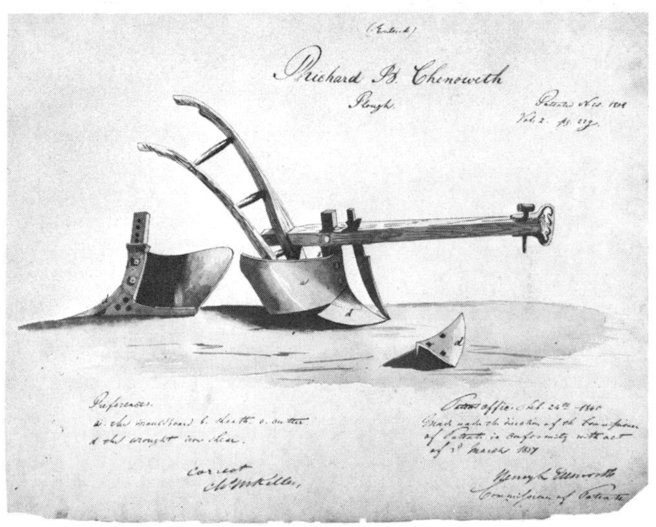

National Archives

(Above) Richard Chenoweth's patented plow with replaceable wrought iron shears, 1808; (below) Newbold plow, 1797

National Archives

Charles Newbold
Cast Iron Plough

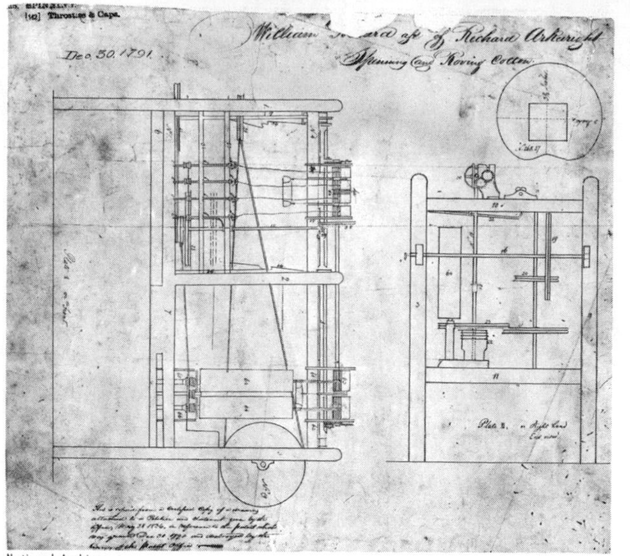

National Archives

New Britain Museum

Richard Arkwright (above) by Mather Brown; (left) sketch of Arkwright's spinning device, registered at the U.S. Patent Office in 1791

Textiles

The first American textile mill was built by an immigrant from England, Samuel Slater, at Pawtucket, R.I., in 1793. Slater had circumvented British restrictions on the export of technological data by memorizing the details of Richard Arkwright's spinning machines before coming to America. Within a generation water-powered machinery had been developed to handle every phase of cloth making, from fiber processing to textile finishing. New England became the center of the textile industry by virtue of its greater capital and willing labor.

National Archives

(Above) John Thorp's water-powered loom, 1812; (right) carding and spinning machine devised by Alanson Holmes, 1810; (below) Pennington's Mills, near Baltimore, about 1800

National Archives

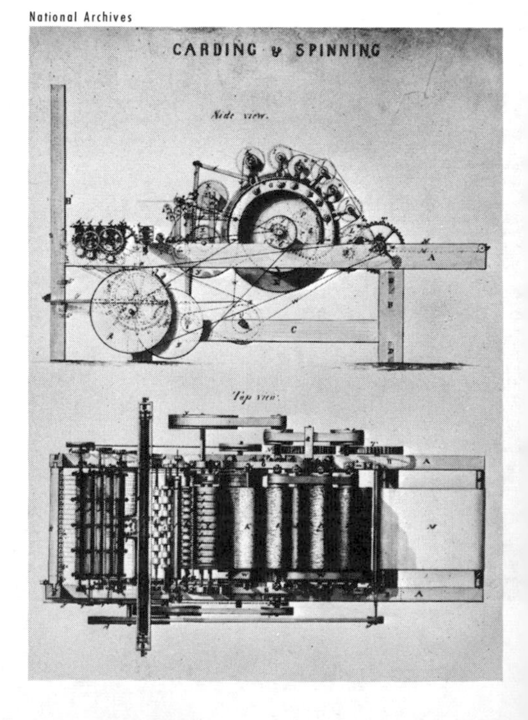

Baltimore Museum of Art

106.

Jacob Bigelow: The Future of the Arts and Sciences

Jacob Bigelow, physician and botanist, held the Rumford chair of the application of science to the useful arts at Harvard from 1816 to 1827. His professorship suited Bigelow exactly, for he was a passionate believer in the promise of what he was the first to call "technology" (his Rumford lectures appeared under the title Elements of Technology *in 1829), as well as in America's capacity to make significant contributions to scientific progress. Bigelow delivered his inaugural address as Rumford professor on December 11, 1816; part of the speech appears below.*

Source: *North American Review,* January 1817.

If anyone here despair of successfully cultivating those branches of physical science which are pursued by learned men in other parts of the globe with large establishments and expensive endowments, let him see if there are not subjects within the circle of his own walks which are neither arduous in their character nor expensive in their cultivation, and which lie open to his unassisted industry. A multitude of such subjects he may find in the face and features of our continent: its structure and composition; its capacity for the different branches of agriculture, the improvements of which its present appropriations are susceptible; its geography; its climate and meteorology; its influence on the human body and the human mind; its diseases; its natural productions, minerals, plants, and animals; the resources which it has already derived from these, and those which it has yet to discover; the local exigences and wants which may be supplied by the application of foreign inventions and known improvements, or by the contrivance and adaptation of new ones; in short, whatever may tend to increase the facilities of subsistence and the welfare of those among whom we live.

Motives of philanthropy may urge the pursuit of subjects like these, but the calls of patriotism prefer even a stronger claim. The place of our birth and residence is the proper sphere and object of our exertions. It does not become us to complain of its disadvantages and descant upon the superiority of more favored spots. We should rather consider how we may overcome its defects and improve its real advantages. We should also see whether its irremediable faults are not in some instances productive to us of good as well as of evil.

The portion of country in which it is our fortune to live is not one of exuberant soil and spontaneous plenty. The summer of New England does not elicit a second burden from our trees, nor is even our annual harvest exempt from the contingency of failure. Winter maintains here a long and late influence upon the seasons, and frosts are visiting us in the latest breezes of spring.

Our territory is interrupted by extensive masses of rock and broken by mountains intractable to cultivation. Our thin and penurious soil rests upon beds of granite, upon flint and sand which drain it of its moisture, while themselves afford no pabulum for its vegetation. Whatever is raised from the bosom of the earth must be extorted by assiduous and painful culture, and a laborious vigilance is necessary to insure the fruits of the year.

Yet has this part of our country become the most populous and enlightened in the continent upon which we live. The very causes which seemed at variance with our prosperity have proved its most powerful promoters. A vigor and hardihood of character have grown up out of the evils which they had to combat; and a spirit of enterprise and perseverance unknown in more luxurious climates has become the characteristic of our population. The intelligence and the untiring application which were at first the offspring of necessity have eventually exhibited ample fruits in the features of our land. Cultivated grounds and ornamental dwellings, wealthy cities, and flourishing institutions have arisen upon a spot where nature was never lavish of her gifts. A spirit of frugality and a talent of invention have more than supplied the disadvantages of our natural situation. Around us is comfort, and plenty, and health. Our faculties are not exhausted by the debilitating heats of a sultry summer, nor our constitutions assailed by the miasmata of pestilential marshes. In our climate youth is active, and manhood is hardy. A spirit of adventure carries us everywhere in pursuit of the means of living, and there is no part of the world in which the New England character is not represented. The means of information are cherished in our humblest villages; our cities are but little infested with the crimes of the older continent, and among us to an extent perhaps unexampled, the reign of intelligence and of principle supersedes the coercion of law.

Under so distinguished advantages, let us not complain of our lot in a country which gives us natural talents, and a climate which calls them into action. We should rather consider that the health and alacrity which we possess are not the common tenants of a rank and luxuriant clime; that the sultry and tepid breezes which multiply the fruits of the earth and render their qualities more exquisite do not bring with them a keener relish, a more healthy circulation, or a more vigorous frame. Few countries can boast of being what Italy was in the time of her ancient poets, at once the parent of fruits and of men. Luxury and indolence are the well-known concomitants of a torrid atmosphere and an exuberant soil. If, in our northern and wintry climate, we are strangers to the rich profusion of a southern soil, we have the consolation that this climate, while it yields us but a scanty harvest for a laborious cultivation, yields us at the same time a blessing for which there can be no equivalent, the capacity of enjoyment that results from vigor of body and activity of mind.

In science and the arts, notwithstanding the infancy of our institutions and the embarrassment which most individuals experience from the necessity of attending to the calls of business, we have not been wholly without improvement, and are perhaps not destitute of a name. The researches of most of our ingenious men have had utility for their object. They have been performed in intervals taken from professional duties, and have been impeded by a deficiency of books and means. We have had little of the parade of operation, yet we have sometimes seen the fruits of silent efficiency and perseverance. We have had few learned men, but many useful ones. We have not often seen individuals among us like the laborious Germans, spending their lives in endless acquisitions while perhaps themselves add little to the general stock of knowledge; yet we have had men of original talents who have been fortunate enough to discover some province in which they were qualified to be serviceable to their country and mankind. We have had ingenious mechanics, skilful projectors, profound mathematicians, and men well-versed in the useful learning of their time.

The progress of our internal improvements and the high state of the mechanic arts among us, as well as in our sister states, has entitled us to the character of a nation of inventors. The individuals who have originated and promoted such improvements have often been men unambitious of fame, whose lives have passed in obscurity; yet there have sometimes been those among us whose labors have attracted the honorable notice of foreigners, and reflected luster upon the country of their birth. It has even been our fortune to impose obligations on others, and there are services of our citizens which are now better known than their names. There are some things which, if gathered from the ashes of obscurity, might serve to shed a gleam upon our literary reputation, and to make known at least the light they have kindled for others. It is a fact, perhaps not generally realized, that the American Philosophical Society at Philadelphia, the Royal Society of Great Britain, and the Royal Institution of London are all of them in a measure indebted for their birth and first foundation to natives or inhabitants of New England.

107.

Displacement of Free Negroes

For those who recognized the threat to the Union posed by the institution of slavery, the possibility of colonizing the Negro often seemed a solution. Jefferson considered the idea in 1801 but felt it should be left to the state governments to execute. The American Colonization Society was formed in December 1816 for the purpose of transporting free Negroes to Africa to be colonized in the state of Liberia. The Society, composed of many prominent white people from both North and South, was supported by local groups, churches, and some state legislatures. Though designed to colonize only "free people of color," the Society opened an easy and safe channel for emancipation to those masters (and there were some) who desired to free their slaves. The Negroes themselves were, for the most part, opposed to deportation to a land no longer familiar to their people. The following selection is an account of the organizational meeting of the Society on December 21, 1816.

Source: Isaac V. Brown, *Biography of the Rev. Robert Finley,* 2nd edition, Philadelphia, 1857, pp. 103-120.

At the first meeting in the Congressional Hall, on the 21st of December, the Hon. Henry Clay was called to the chair. Before taking his seat, he addressed the meeting in the following terms, as reported in the *Intelligencer,* viz:

He understood the object of the present meeting to be to consider the propriety and practicability of colonizing the *free people of color* in the United States, and of forming an association in relation to that object. That class of the mixed population of our country was peculiarly situated. They neither enjoyed the immunities of freemen nor were they subject to the incapacities of slaves, but partook in some degree of the qualities of both. From their condition, and the unconquerable prejudices resulting from their color, they never could amalgamate with the free whites of this country. It was desirable, therefore, both as it respected them and the residue of the population of the country to draw them off.

Various schemes of colonization had been thought of, and a part of our own continent, it was thought by some, might furnish a suitable establishment for them, but for his part he had a decided preference for some part of the coast of Africa. There, ample provision might be made for the colony itself, and it might be rendered instrumental to the introduction into that extensive quarter of the globe of the arts, civilization, and Christianity. There was a peculiar, a moral fitness, in restoring them to the land of their fathers. And if, instead of the evils and sufferings which we have been the innocent cause of inflicting upon the inhabitants of Africa, we can transmit to her the blessings of our arts, our civilization, and our religion, may we not hope that America will extinguish a great portion of that moral debt which she has contracted to that unfortunate continent?

We should derive much encouragement in the prosecution of the object which had assembled us together by the success which had attended the colony at Sierra Leone. The establishment had commenced about twenty or tweny-five years ago under the patronage of private individuals in Great Britain. The basis of the population of the colony consisted of the fugitive slaves of the Southern states during the Revolutionary War, who had first been carried to Nova Scotia, and who afterward, about the year 1792, upon their own application, almost en masse, had been transferred to the western coast of Africa. The colony, after struggling with the most unheard of difficulties — difficulties resulting from the ignorance, barbarity, and prejudice of the natives, from the climate (which were however found to be not at all insurmountable), from wars, African as well as European, and such as are incidental to all new settlements, had made a gradual and steady progress until it has acquired a strength and stability which promises to crown the efforts of its founders with complete success. We have their experience before us; and can there be a nobler cause than that which, while it proposes to rid our own country of a useless and pernicious if not a dangerous portion of its population, contemplates the spreading of the arts of civilized life, and the possible redemption from ignorance and barbarism of a benighted portion of the globe?

It was proper and necessary distinctly to state that he understood it constituted no part of the object of this meeting to touch or agitate in the slightest degree a delicate question connected with another portion of the colored population of our country. It was not proposed to deliberate on, or consider at all, any question of emancipation, or that which was connected with the abolition of slavery. It was upon that condition alone, he was sure, that many gentlemen from the South and West whom he saw present had attended, or could be expected to cooperate. It was upon that condition that he himself attended.

He would only further add that he hoped in their deliberations they would be guided by that moderation, politeness, and deference for the opinion of each other which were essential to any useful result. But when he looked around and saw the respectable assemblage, and recollected the humane and benevolent purpose which had produced it, he felt it unnecessary to insist further on this topic.

Elias B. Caldwell, Esq., secretary of the Supreme Court of the United States, next addressed the meeting in substance as follows, viz:

I feel peculiar embarrassment in obtruding myself upon the notice of so large and respectable a meeting in which I find some of the most distinguished characters of our country. I ask your indulgence in offering to the consideration of the meeting the resolution which I hold in my hand, and to a few explanatory observations. The objects of the meeting have been feelingly and correctly stated by the honorable chairman. The subject seems to be divided into first, the expediency; and second, the practicability of the proposed plan.

The expediency of colonizing the free people of color in the United States may be considered in reference to its influence on our civil institutions, on the morals and habits of the people, and on the future happiness of the free people of color. It has been a subject of unceasing regret and anxious solicitude, among many of our best patriots and wisest statesmen, from the first establishment of our independence, that this class of people should remain a monument of reproach to those sacred principles of civil liberty which constitute the foundations of all our constitutions. We say in the Declaration of Independence "that all men are created equal, and have certain unalienable rights." Yet it is considered impossible, consistently with the safety of the state, and it is certainly impossible with the present feelings toward these people, that they can ever be placed upon this equality or admitted to the enjoyment of these "unalienable rights" while they remain mixed with us.

Some persons may declaim and call it prejudice. No matter! Prejudice is as powerful a motive, and will as certainly exclude them, as the soundest reason. Others may say they are free enough. If this is a matter of opinion, let them judge — if of reason, let it be decided by our repeated and solemn declarations in all our public acts. This state of society unquestionably tends, in various ways, to injure the morals and destroy the habits of industry among our people. This will be acknowledged by every person who has paid any attention to the subject, and it seems to be so generally admitted that it would promote the happiness and the interests of the people to provide a place where these people might be settled by themselves that it is unnecessary to dwell on this branch of the subject.

As to the blacks, it is manifest that their interest and happiness would be promoted by collecting them together where they would enjoy equal rights and privileges with those around them. A state of degradation is necessarily a state of unhappiness. It debases the mind, it damps the energies of the soul, and represses every vigorous effort toward moral or intellectual greatness. How can you expect from them anything great or noble without the motives to stimulate or the rewards to crown great and noble achievements? It not only prevents their climbing the steep and rugged paths of fame but it prevents the enjoyment of the true happiness of calm contentment, satisfied with enjoying but a part of what we possess, of using only a portion of what is in our power. Take away, however, the portion that is not used, and it immediately becomes the object of our fondest desires.

The more you endeavor to improve the condition of these people, the more you cultivate their minds (unless by religious instruction), the more miserable you make them, in their present state. You give them a higher relish for those privileges which they can never attain, and you turn what we intend for a blessing into a curse. No, if they must remain in their present situation, keep them in the lowest state of degradation and ignorance. The more you bring them to the condition of brutes, the better chance do you give them of possessing their apathy. Surely, Americans ought to be the last people on earth to advocate such slavish doctrines; to cry peace and contentment to those who are deprived of the privileges of civil liberty. They who have so largely partaken of its blessings, who know so well how to estimate its value, ought to be the foremost to extend it to others. . . .

I will consider the practicability of colonization under three heads — the territory, the expense, and the probability of obtaining their consent.

1. The territory. Various plans have been mentioned by different persons. A situation within our own territory would certainly possess some considerable advantage. It would be more immediately under the eye and control of our own government. But there are some real and some apprehended evils to encounter. Many apprehend that they might hereafter join the Indians, or the nations bordering on our frontiers, in case of war, if they were placed so near us — that the

colony would become the asylum of fugitives and runaway slaves. Added to these difficulties, there are inveterate prejudices against such a plan, in so large a portion of the country, which it would be impossible to overcome or remove. Upon mature reflection, with all the light that has yet been shed upon the subject, I believe it will be found that Africa will be liable to the fewest objections. A territory might, no doubt, be procured there; the climate is best adapted to their constitution, and they could live cheaper.

But, Mr. Chairman, I have a greater and nobler object in view in desiring them to be placed in Africa. It is the belief that through them civilization and the Christian religion would be introduced into that benighted quarter of the world. It is the hope of redeeming many millions from the lowest state of superstition and ignorance, and restoring them to the knowledge and worship of the true God. Great and powerful as are the other motives of this measure (and I acknowledge them to be of sufficient magnitude to attract the attention and to call for the united efforts of this nation), in my opinion, and you will find it the opinion of a large class of the community, all other motives are small and trifling compared with the hope of spreading among them the knowledge of the Gospel.

From the importance of this view of the subject, permit me to enlarge a little upon it. Whatever may be the difference of opinion among the different denominations of Christians, I believe they will all be found to unite in the belief that the Scriptures predict a time when the Gospel of Jesus Christ shall be spread over every part of the world — shall be acknowledged by every nation, and perhaps shall influence every heart. The opinion is perhaps as general that this glorious and happy day is near at hand. The great movements and mighty efforts in the moral and religious world seem to indicate some great design of Providence on the eve of accomplishment. The unexampled and astonishing success attending the numerous and various plans which have been devised, and which are in operation now in different parts of the world, and the union and harmony with which Christians of different denominations unite in promoting these plans, clearly indicate a divine hand in their direction.

Nay, sir, the subject on which we are now deliberating has been brought to public view, nearly at the same time, in different parts of our country. In New Jersey, New York, Indiana, Tennessee, Virginia, and perhaps other places not known to me, the public attention seems to have been awakened, as from a slumber, to this subject. The belief that I have mentioned leads Christians to look with anxious solicitude and joyful hope to every movement which they believe to be instrumental in accomplishing the great designs of Providence. They will receive your proposal with joy and support it with zeal; and, permit me to say, that it will be of no small consequence to gain the zealous support and cooperation of this portion of the community.

On the subject of expense, I should hope there would not be much difference of opinion. All are interested, though some portions are more immediately so than others. We should consider that what affects a part of our country is interesting to the whole. Besides, it is a great national object and ought to be supported by a national purse. And, as has been justly observed by the honorable gentlemen in the chair, there ought to be a national atonement for the wrongs and injuries which Africa has suffered. For, although the state legislatures commenced early after our independence to put a stop to the slave trade, and the national government interfered as soon as the Constitution would permit, yet as a nation we cannot rid ourselves entirely from the guilt and disgrace attending that iniquitous traffic until we, as a nation, have made every reparation in our power. If, however, more funds are wanting than it is thought expedient to appropriate out of the public treasury, the liberality and humanity of our citizens will not suffer it to fail for want of pecuniary aid. I should be sorry, however, to see our government dividing any part of the glory and honor which cannot fail of attending the accomplishment of a work so great, so interesting, and which will tend so much to diffuse the blessings of civil liberty and promote the happiness of man.

Among the objections which have been made, I must confess that I am most surprised at one which seems to be prevalent, to wit, that these people will be unwilling to be colonized. What, sir, are they not men? Will they not be actuated by the same motives of interest and ambition which influence other men? Or will they prefer remaining in a hopeless state of degradation for themselves and their children, to the prospect of the full enjoyment of their civil rights and a state of equality? What brought our ancestors to these shores? They had no friendly hand to lead them — no powerful arm to protect them. They left the land of their nativity, the sepulchers of their fathers, the comforts of civilized society, and all the endearments of friends and relatives and early associations to traverse the ocean, to clear the forests, to encounter all the hardships of a new settlement, and to brave the dangers of the tomahawk and scalping knife. How many were destroyed! Sometimes whole settlements cut off by disease and hunger, by the treachery and cruelty of the savages; yet were they not discouraged.

What is it impels many Europeans daily to seek our shores and to sell themselves — for the prime of their life — to defray the expenses of their passages? It is that ruling, imperious desire planted in the breast of every man — the desire of liberty, of standing upon an equality with his fellowmen. If we were to add to these motives, the offer of land, and to aid in the expense of emigration and of first settling — they cannot be so blind to their own interests, so devoid of every generous and noble feeling, as to hesitate about accepting the offer. It is not a matter of speculation and opinion only. It has been satisfactorily ascertained that numbers will gladly accept of the invitation. And when once the colony is formed and flourishing, all other obstacles will be easily removed.

It is for us to make the experiment and the offer; we shall then, and not till then, have discharged our duty. It is a plan in which all interests, all classes and descriptions of people may unite, in which all discord and feelings may be lost in those of humanity — in promoting "peace on earth and goodwill to men."

This speaker having concluded, the Hon. John Randolph followed, and began by saying:

That it had been properly observed by the chairman that there was nothing in the proposition submitted to consideration which, in the smallest degree, touched another very important and delicate question which ought to be left as much out of view as possible. But it appeared to him that it had not been sufficiently insisted on, with a view to obtain the cooperation of all the citizens of the United States — not only that this meeting does not, in anywise, affect the question of Negro slavery but, as far as it goes, must materially tend to secure the property of every master in the United States over his slaves. It appeared to him that this aspect of the question had not been sufficiently presented to the public view. It was a notorious fact that the existence of this mixed and intermediate population of free Negroes was viewed by every slaveholder as one of the greatest sources of the insecurity and unprofitableness of slave property; that they serve to excite in their fellow beings a feeling of discontent, of repining at their situation, and they act as channels of communication, not only between different slaves but between the slaves of different districts — that they are the depositories of stolen goods and the promoters of mischief.

In a worldly point of view, then, without entering into the general question, and apart from those higher and nobler motives which had been presented to the meeting, the owners of slaves were interested in providing a retreat for this part of our population. There was no fear that this proposition would alarm them; they had been accustomed to think seriously of the subject. There was a popular work on agriculture by John Taylor, of Caroline County, which was widely circulated and much confided in, in Virginia. In that book, much read, because coming from a practical man this description of people was pointed out as a great evil. If a place could be provided for their reception, and a mode of sending them hence, there were hundreds, nay, thousands of citizens who would, by manumitting their slaves, relieve themselves from the cares attendant upon their possession.

The Hon. Robert Wright of Maryland added a few remarks, as follows:

That he could not withhold his approbation from a measure that had for its object the melioration of the lot of any portion of the human race, particularly of the free people of color, whose degraded state robs them of the happiness of self-government, so dear to the American people. And . . . as I discover the most delicate regard to the rights of property, I shall with great pleasure lend my aid to restore this unfortunate people to the enjoyment of their liberty; but I fear gentlemen are too sanguine in their expectations — that they would be willing to abandon the land of their nativity, so dear to man. However, I have the disposition to give them that election by furnishing all the means contemplated. But while we wish to promote the happiness of these free people of color, we ought to take care not to furnish the means of transporting out of the reach of the master his property.

These addresses being concluded, Elias B. Caldwell, Esq., offered the following resolutions, to wit:

Resolved, that an association or society be formed for the purpose of collecting information and to assist in the formation and execution of a plan for the colonization of the free people of color, with their consent, in Africa, or elsewhere, as may be thought most advisable by the constituted authorities of the country.

Resolved, that Elias B. Caldwell, John Randolph, Richard Rush, Walter Jones, Francis S. Key, Robert Wright, James H. Blake, and John Peter be a committee to present a respectful memorial to Congress requesting them to adopt such measures as may be thought most advisable for procuring a territory in Africa, or elsewhere, suitable for the colonization of the free people of color.

Resolved, that Francis S. Key, Bushrod Washington, Elias B. Caldwell, James Breckinridge, Walter Jones, Richard Rush, and William G. D. Worthington be a committee to prepare a constitution and rules for the government of the association or society above-mentioned, and report the same to the next meeting for consideration.

1817

108.

John C. Calhoun: Roadways and Waterways

John C. Calhoun is traditionally identified with the South that he supported with increasing rigidity over the last twenty-five years of his life. As a young man, however, he was as fervent a nationalist as the country possessed. Elected to Congress in 1811 from the western region of South Carolina, he revealed the usual frontier passion for what were known as internal improvements, chiefly roads and waterways. As these were proposed for the whole country, they implied an exercise of national power that violated everything the Republican Party had previously stood for. But this was precisely the political turnabout after 1815, when Jefferson's Republicans became the party of nationalist visions and federal programs rather than of local autonomy and federal restraint. Calhoun even offered a bill to finance such improvements by a bonus and by dividends from a new National Bank, though the old Bank, created by Alexander Hamilton, had been the bête noire *of the earlier Republicans. It was too much for President Madison, who in a last and rather contradictory assertion of Jeffersonian principles, vetoed the so-called Bonus Bill on the day he left office, March 3, 1817. The following speech, reported in the third person, was given by Calhoun before the House on February 4, 1817, when he presented the Bonus Bill. The bill passed both Houses of Congress the same month.*

Source: *Debates,* 14 Cong., 2 Sess., pp. 851-858.

Mr. Calhoun rose and observed that it seemed to be the fate of some measures to be praised but not adopted. Such, he feared, would be the fate of that on which we are now deliberating. From the indisposition manifested by the House to go into committee on the bill, there was not much prospect of its success; yet it seemed to him, when he reflected how favorable was the present moment, and how confessedly important a good system of roads and canals was to our country, he might reasonably be very sanguine of success. At peace with all the world, abounding in pecuniary means, and, what was of the most importance, and at what he rejoiced as most favorable to the country, party, and sectional feelings immerged in a liberal and enlightened regard to the general concerns of the nation — such, said he, are the favorable circumstances under which we are now deliberating.

Thus situated, to what can we direct our resources and attention more important than internal improvements? What can add more to the wealth, the strength, and the political prosperity of our country? The manner in which facility and cheapness of intercourse added to the wealth of a nation had been so often and ably discussed by writers on political economy, that he presumed the House to be perfectly acquainted with the subject. It was sufficient to observe that every branch of national industry — agricultural, manufacturing, and commercial — was greatly stimulated and rendered by it more productive. The result is, said he, that it tends to diffuse universal opulence. It gives to the interior the advantages possessed by the parts most eligibly situated for trade. It makes the country price, whether in the sale of the raw product or in the purchase of the articles for consumption, approximate to that of the commercial towns. In fact, if we look into the nature of wealth, we will find that nothing can be more favorable to its growth than good roads and canals. An article, to command a price, must not only be useful but must be the subject of demand; and the better the means of commercial intercourse the larger is the sphere of demand.

The truth of these positions, said Mr. C., is obvious, and has been tested by all countries where the experiment has been made. It has particularly been strikingly exemplified in England, and if the result there, in a country so limited and so similar in its products, has been to produce a most uncommon state of opulence, what may we not expect from the same cause in our country, abounding as it does in the greatest variety of products, and presenting the greatest facility for improvements?

Let it not be said that internal improvements may be wholly left to the enterprise of the states and of individuals. He knew, he said, that much might justly be expected to be done by them; but in a country so new and so extensive as ours, there is room enough, said he, for all the general and state governments and individuals in which to exert their resources. But many of the improvements contemplated, said Mr. C., are on too great a scale for the resources of the states or individuals; and many of such a nature that the rival jealousy of the states, if left alone, might prevent. They required the resources and the general superintendence of this government to effect and complete them.

But, said Mr. C., there are higher and more powerful considerations why Congress ought to take charge of this subject. If we were only to consider the pecuniary advantages of a good system of roads and canals, it might indeed admit of some doubt whether they ought not to be left wholly to individual exertions; but when we come to consider how intimately the strength and political prosperity of the republic are connected with this subject, we find the most urgent reasons why we should apply our resources to them. In many respects, no country of equal population and wealth possesses equal materials of power with ours. The people, in muscular power, in hardy and enterprising habits, and in a lofty and gallant courage are surpassed by none. In one respect, and, in my opinion, in one only, are we materially weak. We occupy a surface prodigiously great in proportion to our numbers. The common strength is brought to bear with great difficulty on the point that may be menaced by an enemy. It is our duty, then, as far as in the nature of things it can be effected, to counteract this weakness.

Good roads and canals, judiciously laid out, are the proper remedy. In the recent war, how much did we suffer for the want of them! Besides the tardiness and the consequential inefficacy of our military movements, to what an increased expense was the country put for the article of transportation alone! In the event of another war, the saving in this particular would go far toward indemnifying us for the expense of constructing the means of transportation.

It is not, however, in this respect only, that roads and canals add to the strength of the country. Our power of raising revenue, in war particularly, depends, said he, mainly on them. In peace, our revenue depends principally on the imposts; in war, this source, in a great measure, fails, and internal taxes, to a great amount, become necessary. Unless the means of commercial intercourse are rendered much more perfect than they now are, we shall never be able, in war, to raise the necessary supplies. If taxes were collected in kind; if, for instance, the farmer and mechanic paid in their surplus produce, then the difficulty would not exist, as, in no country on earth, is there so great a surplus, in proportion to its population, as in ours. But such a system of taxes is impossible. They must be paid in money; and, by the Constitution, must be laid uniformly.

What, then, is the effect? The taxes are raised in every part of this extensive country uniformly; but the expenditure must, in its nature, be principally confined to the scene of military operations. This drains the circulating medium from one part and accumulates it in another, and perhaps a very distant one. The result, said he, is obvious. Unless it can return through the operation of trade, the parts from which the constant drain takes place must ultimately be impoverished. Commercial intercourse is the true remedy to this weakness; and the means by which that is to be effected are roads, canals, and the coasting trade. On these, combined with domestic manufactures, does the moneyed capacity of this country, in war, depend. Without them, not only will we be unable to raise the necessary supplies but the currency of the country must necessarily fall into the greatest disorder — such as we lately experienced.

But on this subject of national power, what, said Mr. C., can be more important than a perfect unity in every part, in feelings and sentiments? And what can tend more powerfully to produce it than overcoming the effects of distance? No country, enjoying freedom, ever occupied anything like as great an extent of country as this republic. One hundred years ago, the most profound philosophers did not believe it to be even possible. They did not suppose it possible that a pure republic could exist on as great a scale even as the island of Great Britain. What then was considered as chimerical, said Mr. C., we now have the felicity to enjoy; and, what is most remarkable, such is the happy mold of our government, so well are the state and general powers blended, that much of our political happiness draws its origin from the extent of our republic. It has exempted us from most of the causes which distracted the small republics of antiquity.

Let it not, however, be forgotten; let it, said he, be forever kept in mind that it exposes us to the greatest of all calamities, next to the loss of liberty, and even to that in its consequence — *disunion.* We are great, and rapidly — he was about to say fearfully — growing. This, said he, is our pride and danger — our weakness and our strength. Little, said Mr. C., does he deserve to be entrusted with the liberties of this people who does not raise his mind to these truths. We are under the most imperious obligation to counteract every tendency to disunion. The strongest of all cements is, undoubtedly, the wisdom, justice, and, above all, the moderation of this House; yet the great subject on which we are now deliberating, in this respect, deserves the most serious consideration. Whatever, said Mr. C., impedes the intercourse of the extremes with this, the center of the republic, weakens the Union. The more enlarged the sphere of commercial circulation, the more extended that of social intercourse; the more strongly are we bound together; the more inseparable are our destinies. Those who understand the human heart best know how powerfully distance tends to break the sympathies of our nature. Nothing, not even dissimilarity of language, tends more to estrange man from man. Let us then, said Mr. C., bind the republic together with a perfect system of roads and canals. Let us conquer space. It is thus the most distant parts of the republic will be brought within a few days travel of the center; it is thus that a citizen of the West will read the news of Boston still moist from the press.

The mail and the press, said he, are the nerves of the body politic. By them the slightest impression made on the most remote parts is communicated to the whole system; and the more perfect the means of transportation, the more rapid and true the vibration. To aid us in this great work, to maintain the integrity of this republic, we inhabit a country presenting the most admirable advantages. Belted around, as it is, by lakes and oceans, intersected in every direction by bays and rivers, the hand of industry and art is tempted to improvement. So situated, said he, blessed with a form of government at once combining liberty and strength, we may reasonably raise our eyes to a most splendid future if we only act in a manner worthy of our advantages. If, however, neglecting them, we permit a low, sordid, selfish, and sectional spirit to take possession of this House, this happy scene will vanish. We will divide, and in its consequences will follow misery and despotism.

To legislate for our country, said Mr. C., requires not only the most enlarged views but a species of self-devotion not exacted in any other. In a country so extensive and so various in its interests, what is necessary for the common good may apparently be opposed to the interest of particular sections. It must be submitted to as the condition of our greatness. But were we a small republic, were we confined to the ten miles square, the selfish instincts of our nature might in most cases be relied on in the management of public affairs.

Such, then, being the obvious advantages of internal improvements, why, said Mr. C., should the House hesitate to commence the system? He understood there were, with some members, constitutional objections. The power of Congress is objected to — first, that they have none to cut a road or canal through a state without its consent; and, next, that the public moneys can only be appropriated to effect the particular powers enumerated in the Constitution. The first of these objections, it is plain, does not apply to this bill. No particular road or canal is proposed to be cut through any state. The bill simply appropriates money to the general purpose of improving the means of communication. When a bill is introduced to apply the money to a particular object in any state, then, and not till then, will the question be fairly before us. Mr. C. gave no opinion on this point. In fact, he scarcely thought it worth the discussion, since the good sense of the states might be relied on. They will in all cases readily yield their assent.

The fear is in a different direction; in a too great solicitude to obtain an undue share to be expended within their respective limits. In fact, he said he understood that this was not the objection insisted on. It was mainly urged that the Congress can only apply the public money in execution of the enumerated powers. He was no advocate for refined arguments on the Constitution. The instrument was not intended as a thesis for the logician to exercise his ingenuity on. It ought to be construed with plain, good sense; and what can be more express than the Constitution on this very point? . . .

Let it not be urged that the construction for which he contended gave a dangerous extent to the powers of Congress. In this point of view, he conceived it to be more safe than the opposite. By giving a reasonable extent to the money power, it exempted us from the necessity of giving a strained and forced construction to the other enumerated powers. For instance, he said, if the public money could be applied to the purchase of Louisiana, as he contended, then there was no constitutional difficulty in that purchase; but, if it could not, then were we compelled either to deny that we had the power to purchase, or to strain some of the enumerated powers to prove our right? It had, for instance, been said that we had the right to purchase, under the power to admit new states — a construction, he would venture to say, far more forced than the one for which he contended. Such are my views, said he, on our right to pass this bill.

He believed that the passage of the bill would not be much endangered by a doubt of the power, as he conceived on that point there were not many who were opposed. The mode is principally objected to. A system, it is contended, ought to be presented before the money is appropriated. He thought differently. To set apart the fund appeared to him to be naturally the first act; at least he took it to be the only practicable course. A bill filled with details would have but a faint prospect of passing. The enemies to any possible system in detail and those who are opposed in principle would unite and defeat it. Though he was unwilling to incorporate details in the bill, yet he was not adverse to presenting his views on that point.

The first great object was to perfect the communication from Maine to Louisiana. This might be fairly considered as the principal artery of the whole system. The next was the connection of the Lakes with the Hudson River. In a political, commercial, and military point of view, few objects could be more important. The next object of chief importance was to connect all the great commercial points on the Atlantic — Philadelphia, Baltimore, Washington, Richmond, Charleston, and Savannah — with the Western states; and, finally, to perfect the intercourse between the West and New Orleans. These seemed to him to be the great objects. There were others, no doubt of great importance, which would receive the aid of government.

The fund proposed to be set apart in this bill was about $650,000 a year, which was doubtless too small to effect such great objects of itself; but it would be a good beginning; and he had no doubt, when it was once begun, the great work will be finished. If the bill succeeds at the next session, the details can be arranged, and the system commenced. He could not consider those who objected merely to the mode to be very hearty in favor of the system. Every member must know that in all great measures it is necessary to concede something — as it is impossible to make all think alike in the minutiae of the measure who are agreed in principle. A deep conviction of the importance of the thing itself is almost sure to be accompanied with a liberal spirit of concession. The committee who introduced this bill gave it the shape in their opinion the most proper in itself and the most likely to succeed. If it cannot pass in its present form and under the present circumstances, it is certainly very doubtful whether it ever will. . . .

Uninfluenced by any other considerations than love of country and duty, said he, let us add this to the many useful measures already adopted. The money cannot be appropriated to a more exalted use. Every portion of the community — the farmer, mechanic, and merchant — will feel its good effects; and, what is of the greatest importance, the strength of the community will be augmented, and its political prosperity rendered more secure.

109.

JAMES MADISON: On the Commerce Clause

It has always been hard to understand just why Madison, in his last act as President, should have vetoed Calhoun's Bonus Bill for internal improvements. The reasons he gave, in a famous message reprinted here, might have been supposed to apply with equal force to the bill creating a second National Bank, or to the Tariff Act of 1816 giving protection to new industry, or to various measures strengthening the permanent military establishment — all of which he had lately approved. Every one of these acts appeared on the face of it to violate Jeffersonian principles, and as offered in different form by Hamilton twenty years before, they had been opposed by Madison. The difference was that where Hamilton's program had been designed for the sake of one *interest at the expense of others, these later measures could be regarded by Madison as an attempt to preserve the* balance *of interests that he had all along thought it the chief purpose of government to maintain. To this end, any exercise of governmental power was in his view legitimate; to Hamilton's end, none was, unless backed by an explicit authority such as a constitutional amendment that would indicate that the single interest had become a general one. In these terms, the internal improvements program assumed a desire in the country to alter the balance between federal and state authority as Madison conceived the Constitution to define it. But lacking formal evidence of that desire, he would not accept the assumption of its existence. So the Bonus Bill was lost, and with it went an interesting chance for the federal control of national development. Never again until the Civil War would nationalist sentiment be so strong in Congress, and by then internal improvements had long since become the preserve of private enterprise.*

Source: Richardson, I, pp. 584-585.

HAVING CONSIDERED THE BILL this day presented to me entitled "An act to set apart and pledge certain funds for internal improvements," and which sets apart and pledges funds

> for constructing roads and canals, and improving the navigation of water courses, in order to facilitate, promote, and give security to internal commerce among the several states, and to render more easy and less expensive the means and provisions for the common defense,

I am constrained by the insuperable difficulty I feel in reconciling the bill with the Constitution of the United States to return it with that objection to the House of Representatives, in which it originated.

The legislative powers vested in Congress are specified and enumerated in the eighth section of the first article of the Constitution, and it does not appear that the power proposed to be exercised by the bill is among the enumerated powers, or that it falls by any just interpretation within the power to make laws necessary and proper for carrying into execution those or other powers vested by the Constitution in the government of the United States.

"The power to regulate commerce among the several states" cannot include a power to construct roads and canals, and to improve the navigation of water courses in order to facilitate, promote, and secure such a commerce without a latitude of construction departing from the ordinary import of the terms strengthened by the known inconveniences which doubtless led to the grant of this remedial power to Congress.

To refer the power in question to the clause "to provide for the common defense and general welfare" would be contrary to the established and consistent rules of interpretation, as rendering the special and careful enumeration of powers which follow the clause nugatory and improper. Such a view of the Constitution would have the effect of giving to Congress a general power of legislation instead of the defined and limited one hitherto understood to belong to them, the terms "common defense and general welfare" embracing every object and act within the purview of a legislative trust. It would have the effect of subjecting both the Constitution and laws of the several states in all cases not specifically exempted to be superseded by laws of Congress, it being expressly declared

> that the Constitution of the United States and laws made in pursuance thereof shall be the supreme law of the land, and the judges of every state shall be bound thereby, anything in the constitution or laws of any State to the contrary notwithstanding.

Such a view of the Constitution, finally, would have the effect of excluding the judicial authority of the United States from its participation in guarding the boundary between the legislative powers of the general and the state governments, inasmuch as questions relating to the general welfare, being questions of policy and expediency, are unsusceptible of judicial cognizance and decision.

A restriction of the power "to provide for the common defense and general welfare" to cases which are to be provided for by the expenditure of money would still leave within the legislative power of Congress all the great and most important measures of government, money being the ordinary and necessary means of carrying them into execution.

If a general power to construct roads and canals, and to improve the navigation of water courses, with the train of powers incident thereto, be not possessed by Congress, the assent of the states in the mode provided in the bill can not confer the power. The only cases in which the consent and cession of particular states can extend the power of Congress are those specified and provided for in the Constitution.

I am not unaware of the great importance of roads and canals and the improved navigation of water courses, and that a power in the national legislature to provide for them might be exercised with signal advantage to the general prosperity. But seeing that such a power is not expressly given by the Constitution, and believing that it can not be deduced from any part of it without an inadmissible latitude of construction and a reliance on insufficient precedents; believing also that the permanent success of the Constitution depends on a definite partition of powers between the general and the state governments, and that no adequate landmarks would be left by the constructive extension of the powers of Congress as proposed in the bill, I have no option but to withhold my signature from it, and to cherish the hope that its beneficial objects may be attained by a resort for the necessary powers to the same wisdom and virtue in the nation which established the Constitution in its actual form and providently marked out in the instrument itself a safe and practicable mode of improving it as experience might suggest.

110.

John Quincy Adams: On the Revolutions in Latin America

Revolutions in Spain's colonies in Central and South America aroused the sympathy of the American people for the cause of liberty and the right to self-government. Ever since Washington's Neutrality Proclamation of 1793, the United States had followed a policy of nonintervention in the affairs of other nations. It was President Monroe's intent to continue this policy in the present instance, for, as he observed, "if they cannot beat Spain, they do not deserve to be free." However, certain persons in the government who were interested for political reasons in embarrassing the President called for immediate recognition and support of the revolutionary governments, even before they had been established. John Quincy Adams, who had consistently supported the policy of nonintervention, foresaw the pressures that would be put on the President concerning Latin America. On December 21, 1817, he wrote to his father about his premonitions.

Source: *Writings of John Quincy Adams*, Worthington C. Ford, ed., Vol. VI, New York, 1916, pp. 274-276.

There are, however . . . several subjects of no small importance upon which opinions are not well settled, and some upon which the divisions will soon awaken the antagonizing feelings of party spirit. The Abbé de Pradt, whose pamphlet on the Bourbon restoration you have read, has since published, in July last, another pamphlet, called *Les trois derniers mois de l'Amérique Méridionale*, in which he says that South America has now taken in the world the place which the French Revolution had held for twenty years before. It is very much so here. The republican spirit of our country not only sympathizes with people struggling in a cause so nearly if not precisely the same which was once our own, but it is working into indignation against the relapse of Europe into the opposite principle of monkery and despotism. And now, as at the early stage of the French Revolution, we have ardent spirits who are for rushing into the conflict without looking to the consequences. Others are for proceeding more deliberately, and for waiting to ascertain what the nature and character of the governments in South America are to be with whom we are to associate as members of the community of nations. Spain, on the one hand, by her mode of negotiating provokes us to take a part against her; and the colonies, by the irregular and convulsive character of their measures, and by their internal elements of the exterminating war between black and white, present to us the prospect of very troublesome and dangerous associates, and still more fearful allies. Such are the ingredients of the caldron, which will soon be at boiling heat.

1818

111.

John Adams: The Meaning of the American Revolution

John Adams sent the following lucid essay to Hezekiah Niles, editor of the Weekly Register, *on February 13, 1818, and Niles praised it three weeks later. "Those who delight to trace the early dawnings of the American Revolution," wrote Niles in an editorial note, ". . . will be grateful for this tribute to the memory of the illustrious dead, from the pen of such a distinguished co-adjutor and co-patriot, as John Adams." The essay may have produced more than gratitude; it is thought that it inspired Niles to collect and publish his monumental* Principles and Acts of the Revolution in America *(1822), a leading source of our knowledge of the period.*

Source: *Niles' Weekly Register,* March 7, 1818.

The American Revolution was not a common event. Its effects and consequences have already been awful over a great part of the globe. And when and where are they to cease?

But what do we mean by the American Revolution? Do we mean the American War? The Revolution was effected before the War commenced. The Revolution was in the minds and hearts of the people, a change in their religious sentiments of their duties and obligations. While the king, and all in authority under him, were believed to govern in justice and mercy according to the laws and constitution derived to them from the God of nature, and transmitted to them by their ancestors, they thought themselves bound to pray for the king and queen and all the royal family, and all in authority under them, as ministers ordained of God for their good. But when they saw those powers renouncing all the principles of authority, and bent upon the destruction of all the securities of their lives, liberties, and properties, they thought it their duty to pray for the Continental Congress and all the thirteen state congresses, etc.

There might be, and there were, others who thought less about religion and conscience, but had certain habitual sentiments of allegiance and loyalty derived from their education; but believing allegiance and protection to be reciprocal, when protection was withdrawn, they thought allegiance was dissolved.

Another alteration was common to all. The people of America had been educated in a habitual affection for England as their mother country; and while they thought her a kind and tender parent (erroneously enough, however, for she never was such a mother) no affection could be more sincere. But when they found her a cruel beldam, willing, like Lady Macbeth, to "dash their brains out," it is no wonder if their filial affections ceased and were changed into indignation and horror.

This radical change in the principles, opinions, sentiments, and affections of the people was the real American Revolution.

By what means this great and important alteration in the religious, moral, political, and social character of the people of thirteen colonies, all distinct, unconnected, and independent of each other, was begun, pursued, and accomplished, it is surely interesting to humanity to investigate and perpetuate to posterity.

To this end it is greatly to be desired that young gentlemen of letters in all the states, especially in the thirteen original states, would undertake the laborious, but certainly interesting and amusing, task of searching and collecting all the records, pamphlets, newspapers, and even handbills which in any way contributed to change the temper and views of the people and compose them into an independent nation.

The colonies had grown up under constitutions of government so different; there was so great a variety of religions; they were composed of so many different nations; their customs, manners, and habits had so little resemblance; and their intercourse had been so rare and their knowledge of each other so imperfect that to unite them in the same principles in theory and the same system of action was certainly a very difficult enterprise. The complete accomplishment of it in so short a time and by such simple means was perhaps a singular example in the history of mankind. Thirteen clocks were made to strike together: a perfection of mechanism which no artist had ever before effected.

In this research, the glorioles of individual gentlemen and of separate states is of little consequence. The means and the measures are the proper objects of investigation. These may be of use to posterity, not only in this nation, but in South America and all other countries. They may teach mankind that revolutions are no trifles; that they ought never to be undertaken rashly; nor without deliberate consideration and sober reflection; nor without a solid, immutable, eternal foundation of justice and humanity; nor without a people possessed of intelligence, fortitude, and integrity sufficient to carry them with steadiness, patience, and perseverance through all the vicissitudes of fortune, the fiery trials, and melancholy disasters they may have to encounter.

The town of Boston early instituted an annual oration on the 4th of July, in commemoration of the principles and feelings which contributed to produce the Revolution. Many of those orations I have heard, and all that I could obtain I have read. Much ingenuity and eloquence appears upon every subject except those principles and feelings. That of my honest and amiable neighbor Josiah Quincy appeared to me the most directly to the purpose of the institution. Those principles and feelings ought to be traced back for 200 years and sought in the history of the country from the first plantations in America. Nor should the principles and feelings of the English and Scots toward the colonies through that whole period ever be forgotten. The perpetual discordance between British principles and feelings and those of America, the next year after the suppression of the French power in America, came to a crisis and produced an explosion.

It was not until after the annihilation of the French dominion in America that any British ministry had dared to gratify their own wishes, and the desire of the nation, by projecting a formal plan for raising a national revenue from America by parliamentary taxation. The first great manifestation of this design was by the order to carry into strict execution those acts of Parliament which were well-known by the appellation of the Acts of Trade, which had lain a dead letter, unexecuted for half a century — and some of them, I believe, for nearly a whole one.

This produced, in 1760 and 1761, an awakening and a revival of American principles and feelings, with an enthusiasm which went on increasing till in 1775 it burst out in open violence, hostility, and fury.

The characters the most conspicuous, the most ardent and influential in this revival, from 1760 to 1766, were first and foremost, before all and above all, James Otis; next to him was Oxenbridge Thatcher; next to him Samuel Adams; next to him John Hancock; then Dr. Mayhew; then Dr. Cooper and his brother. Of Mr. Hancock's life, character, generous nature, great and disinterested sacrifices, and important services, if I had forces, I should be glad to write a volume. But this I hope will be done by some younger and abler hand.

Mr. Thatcher, because his name and merits are less known, must not be wholly omitted. This gentleman was an eminent barrister at law, in as large practice as anyone in Boston. There was not a citizen of that town more universally beloved for his learning, ingenuity, every domestic and social virtue, and conscientious conduct in every relation of life. His patriotism was as ardent as his progenitors had been ancient and illustrious in this country. Hutchinson often said, "Thatcher was not born a plebeian, but he was determined to die one." In May 1768, I believe, he was chosen by the town of Boston one of their representatives in the legislature, a colleague with Mr. Otis, who had been a member from May 1761, and he continued to be reelected annually till his death in 1765, when Mr. Samuel Adams was elected to fill his place, in the absence of Mr. Otis then attending the congress at New York. Thatcher had long been jealous of the unbounded ambition of Mr. Hutchinson, but when he found him not content with the office of lieutenant governor, the command of the castle and its emoluments, of judge of probate for the county of Suffolk, a seat in his Majesty's Council in the legislature, his brother-in-law secretary of state by the king's commission, a brother of that secretary of state a judge of the Supreme Court and a member of Council; now in 1760 and 1761 soliciting and accepting the office of chief justice of the Superior Court of Judicature, he concluded, as Mr. Otis did, and as every other enlightened friend of his country did, that he sought that office with the determined purpose of determining all causes in favor of the ministry at St. James's and their servile Parliament.

His indignation against him henceforward, to 1765 when he died, knew no bounds but truth. I speak from personal knowledge, for, from 1758 to 1765, I attended every superior and inferior court in Boston, and recollect not one in which he did not invite me home to spend evenings with him, when he made me converse with him as well as I could on all subjects of religion, morals, law, politics, history, philosophy, belle-lettres, theology, mythology, cosmogony, metaphysics (Locke, Clark, Leibniz, Bolingbroke, Berkeley), the preestablished harmony of the universe, the nature of matter and of spirit, and the eternal establishment of coincidences between their operations, fate, foreknowledge, absolute. We reasoned on such unfathomable subjects as high as Milton's gentry in pandemonium; and we understood them as well as they did, and no better. To such mighty mysteries he added the news of the day, and the tittle-tattle of the town.

But his favorite subject was politics, and the impending threatening system of parliamentary taxation and universal government over the colonies. On this subject he was so anxious and agitated that I have no doubt it occasioned his premature death. From the time when he argued the question of writs of assistance to his death, he considered the king, ministry, Parliament, and nation of Great Britain as determined to new-model the colonies from the foundation; to annul all their charters, to constitute them all royal governments; to raise a revenue in America by parliamentary taxation; to apply that revenue to pay the salaries of governors, judges, and all other Crown officers; and after all this, to raise as large a revenue as they pleased, to be applied to national purposes at the exchequer in England; and further to establish bishops and the whole system of the Church of England, tithes and all, throughout all British America. This system, he said, if it was suffered to prevail, would extinguish the flame of liberty all over the world; that America would be employed as an engine to batter down all the miserable remains of liberty in Great Britain and Ireland, where only any semblance of it was left in the world. To this system he considered Hutchinson, the Olivers, and all their connections, dependants, adherents, and shoelickers entirely devoted. He asserted that they were all engaged with all the Crown officers in America and the understrappers of the ministry in England in a deep and treasonable conspiracy to betray the liberties of their country for their own private, personal, and family aggrandizement.

His philippics against the unprincipled ambition and avarice of all of them, but especially of Hutchinson, were unbridled, not only in private, confidential conversations but in all companies and on all occasions. He gave Hutchinson the sobriquet of "Summa Potestatis," and rarely mentioned him but by the name of "Summa." His liberties of speech were no secrets to his enemies. I have sometimes wondered that they did not throw him over the bar, as they did soon afterwards Major Hawley. They hated him worse than they did James Otis, or Samuel Adams, and they feared him more, because they had no revenge for a father's disappointment of a seat on the superior bench to impute to him, as they did to Otis; and Thatcher's character through life had been so modest, decent, unassuming, his morals so pure, and his religion so venerated that they dared not attack him. In his office were educated to the bar two eminent characters, the late Judge Lowell and Josiah Quincy, aptly called the Boston Cicero.

Mr. Thatcher's frame was slender, his constitution delicate; whether his physicians overstrained his vessels with mercury when he had the smallpox by inoculation at the castle, or whether he was overplied by public anxieties and exertions, the smallpox left him in a decline from which he never recovered. Not long before his death he sent for me to commit to my care some of his business at the bar. I asked him whether he had seen the Virginia Resolves:

> Oh yes, they are men! They are noble spirits! It kills me to think of the lethargy and stupidity that prevails here. I long to be out. I will go out. I will go out. I will go into court and make a speech which shall be read after my death as my dying testimony against this infernal tyranny they are bringing upon us.

Seeing the violent agitation into which it threw him, I changed the subject as soon as possible, and retired. He had been confined for some time. Had he been abroad among the people he would not have complained so pathetically of the "lethargy and stupidity that prevailed," for town and country were all alive, and in August became active enough and some of the people proceeded to unwarrantable excesses, which were more lamented by the patriots than by their enemies. Mr. Thatcher soon died, deeply lamented by all the friends of their country.

Another gentleman who had great influence in the commencement of the Revolution was Dr. Jonathan Mayhew, a descendant of the ancient governor of Martha's Vineyard. This divine had raised a great reputation both in Europe and America by the publication of a volume of seven sermons in the reign of King George II, 1749, and by many other writings, particularly a sermon in 1750 on January 30, on the subject of passive obedience and nonresistance, in which the saintship and martyrdom of King Charles I are considered, seasoned with wit and satire superior to any in Swift or Franklin. It was read by everybody, celebrated by friends, and abused by enemies.

During the reigns of King George I and King George II, the reigns of the Stuarts (the two Jameses and the two Charleses) were in general disgrace in England. In America they had always been held in abhorrence. The persecutions and cruelties suffered by their ancestors under those reigns had been transmitted by history and tradition, and Mayhew seemed to be raised up to revive all their animosity against tyranny in church and state, and at the same time to destroy their bigotry, fanaticism, and inconsistency. David Hume's plausible, elegant, fascinating, and fallacious apology, in which he varnished over the crimes of the Stuarts, had not then appeared.

To draw the character of Mayhew would be to transcribe a dozen volumes. This transcendent genius threw all the weight of his great fame into the scale of his country in 1761, and maintained it there with zeal and ardor till his death in 1766. In 1763 appeared the controversy between him and Mr. Apthorp, Mr. Caner, Dr. Johnson, and Archbishop Secker on the charter and conduct of the society for propagating the gospel in foreign parts. To form a judgment of this debate I beg leave to refer to a review of the whole, printed at the time and written by Samuel Adams, though by some very absurdly and erroneously ascribed to Mr. Apthorp. If I am not mistaken, it will be found a model of candor, sagacity, impartiality, and close correct reasoning.

If any gentleman supposes this controversy to be nothing to the present purpose, he is grossly mistaken. It spread a universal alarm against the authority of Parliament. It excited a general and just apprehension that bishops and dioceses and churches and priests and tithes were to be imposed upon us by Parliament. It was known that neither king, nor ministry, nor archbishops could appoint bishops in America without an act of Parliament; and if Parliament could tax us they could establish the Church of England with all its creeds, articles, tests, ceremonies, and tithes, and prohibit all other churches as conventicles and schism shops.

Nor must Mr. Cushing be forgotten. His good sense and sound judgment, the urbanity of his manners, his universal good character, his numerous friends and connections, and his continual intercourse with all sorts of people, added to his constant attachment to the liberties of his country, gave him a great and salutary influence from the beginning in 1760.

Let me recommend these hints to the consideration of Mr. Wirt, whose life of Mr. Henry I have read with great delight. I think that after mature investigation he will be convinced that Mr. Henry did not "give the first impulse to the ball of independence," and that Otis, Thatcher, Samuel Adams, Mayhew, Hancock, Cushing, and thousands of others were laboring for several years at the wheel before the name of Mr. Henry was heard beyond the limits of Virginia.

If you print this, I will endeavor to send you something concerning Samuel Adams, who was destined to a longer career, and to act a more conspicuous and, perhaps, a more important part than any other man. But his life would require a volume.

112.

Elias Pym Fordham: Opportunities in the West

Following the War of 1812, westward expansion proceeded at a greatly increased rate. "The Atlantic states," a traveler wrote at this time, "seem to have had their day. . . . The people who partake of youth, enterprise and hardihood . . . are looking more and more to the West." The war's end also brought a renewed influx of immigrants from Europe. Of all the immigrants those from England enjoyed the greatest advantages, owing to their possession of a common language, advanced agricultural skills, and higher social status. In the following letters, Elias Pym Fordham, an English immigrant who settled in Illinois, offers a detailed and often vivid account of conditions in the West and opportunities for settlement there.

Source: *Personal Narrative of Travels in Virginia, Maryland, Pennsylvania, Ohio, Indiana, Kentucky; and of a Residence in the Illinois Territory: 1817-1818,* Frederic A. Ogg, ed., Cleveland, 1906, pp. 170-175, 226-229.

February 18, 1818

I TAKE A HASTY OPPORTUNITY of sending you a few lines by a gentleman who is going to Scotland from this place. He will start tomorrow morning early; and I have to give a dozen orders to the engineer, smiths, and founders in the course of the day; so you will excuse a very hastily written scrawl.

We are all in good health and spirits and are more accustomed to American manners — therefore more comfortable. It is useless for emigrants to think of retaining English manners or English feelings in this country of liberty and equality. But, to do the Americans justice, they respect the love which every man of generous feeling has for his native country, and they are pretty in expressing their contempt of a renegade. There are too many of this character; and I have been more hurt by their conduct than by all the rudeness of the Ohioans or the pride and haughtiness of the Kentuckians.

The western Americans generally feel great hostility to the British government, but toward the English emigrants, they are, with few exceptions, kind and hospitable. They are in most respects different from their brethren in the East, for whom they do not entertain much respect or affection.

Military courage is here considered to be the prince of all the virtues. Even Quakers talk like soldiers, and frequently the younger members turn out with their fellow citizens.

The Indians in the South, who were making a great head against General Gaines, have now proposed a friendly talk and, probably, peace will be concluded before this reaches you. I am glad of this, because there was some danger of the spirit of hostility spreading among the tribes who live on the western banks of the Mississippi and the northern tribes. In that case we must have fortified our dwellings; and we young men, though not called upon by law, should have looked small if we had not volunteered.

The Prophet chief, brother of Tecumseh, is still living beyond the Missouri. The Missouri Territory is peopling so fast that very soon our country will be backed up on that side. The banks of the Okaw and the Little Muddy, about 80 miles westward of us, are being entered very fast, though unluckily by speculators as well as settlers. We have as yet, however, been fortunate enough to keep the former away from our immediate neighborhood.

An English gentleman of fortune, a Mr. Q———, is gone down the river with his family, with the intention of buying land close to us.

Mr. Birkbeck is laying out a farm of 1,600 acres in the midst of his estate of 4,000 acres. He has entered the whole of the Bolton house prairie; with the exception of three quarters on the southwest side, and one quarter on the north side of Mr. Flower's land, which I have entered for myself.

My little estate lies on and between two small hills, from which descend several small streams that unite in the valley and flow on through the prairie. An arm of the prairie runs up this valley and extends itself on the heights. I suppose I have about 100 acres of meadow and 60 of timber land. The timber is white oak, walnut, and hickory. There are some persimmons, a most delicious fruit, growing on straight and rather lofty trees, a good many grapes, and hazels.

I am getting the iron work for a windmill and other machinery. Iron costs 12½ cents per lb. and the working is charged at 12½ cents more. I have bought anvils, bellows, and all the tools of a blacksmith's, millwright's, and carpenter's shop. I can get work done here as well as in London at from 50 to 100 percent advance upon London prices.

I am going down the river in a boat of which I shall take the command. I went down last autumn in two boats, in one of which I had two horses. To confess the truth, I nearly lost the boats and all the property would have been gone if my lads had not made uncommon exertions. It was in the night and a most tremendous thunderstorm came on. The intervals between the flashes of lightning were so dark that we could not see some rocks, which we ran foul of and hung to all night.

I am boarding in a very respectable Quaker family, who do not in general take in boarders. But I was recommended by a gentleman of this town, with whom I had traveled, and to whom we are all well known. Introductions into respectable families are as necessary in this country as in any other; and as much is thought of steadiness of conduct, though more latitude is given to speech.

I have consciously avoided giving to my young friends in England colored descriptions of this country; but I must beg leave to assure you that you cannot do a greater favor to any young man, who possesses from £800 to £5,000, with a proper degree of spirit, than by sending him out here. But if he has no money, if he knows no mechanical trade, and if he cannot work, he had better stay in a countinghouse in England.

Any young man who wishes to marry, but dare not enter into business and the expenses of a family in England, if he can command £1,000, may choose his trade here. If he is a plain working farmer, £500 will make him more independent than an English gentlemen with £1,000 per annum.

An emigrant who is rich may settle near a large town, find society, libraries, and a great many comforts. If he does not object to holding slaves, Kentucky offers him great advantages. But if he is not rich, or is ambitious, the Illinois and Missouri territories, and, from what I have heard, I may say, the

Alabama country, will hold out advantages that will pay him for all sacrifices.

A bill is in Congress for making a state of the Illinois Territory. We shall be citizens as soon as it passes, and eligible, I believe, to any office.

Men of education and manners are much respected; and there is a large proportion of the people who have a great deal of information; which, though acquired more by conversation and observation than by reading, makes them good judges of character, and enables them to value literary and scientific acquirements.

I have had interest offered me to procure an election to a command in a militia regiment in Indiana; but I have declined the offer.

August 24, 1818

You ask me, can a farmer with a capital of £250 live comfortably in this country? Certainly much more comfortably than he can in England, if he has only £250 and no friends to lend him £2,000 in addition to it, or his friends are unwilling to help him. It is only a matter of choice then between servitude and independence. But there is no comfort here for the poor man beyond coarse food in plenty, coarse clothing, log huts, and the pleasure of repose earned by hard work. If the industrious farmer invest his capital in land and hogs in Illinois, these will pay him 50 percent, and that 25 percent per annum for several succeeding years. But perhaps he must carry his horse-load of wheat thirty miles to the mill, and his wife, if he have one, must make biscuits of it on his return. This is not consistent with English notions of comfort, but it is certain the backsettler is happier than the wretch who is condemned to crouch to haughty landlords, to dread the oft repeated visit of the titheman, the taxgatherer, and the overseer.

If a man can live within his income without losing his rank in society, and without being forced to borrow of those who think they oblige by lending; if he can pay the overwhelming taxes which the English ministry have so thoughtlessly squandered in making the English name hated to the uttermost parts of the earth; there are in England comforts, nay, sources of happiness, which will for ages be denied to these half-savage countries: good houses, good roads, a mild and healthy climate — healthy, because the country is old — society, and the arts of life carried almost to perfection, and laws well administered. . . .

I will loosely classify English emigrants, and point out the sections of country in which each will find the greatest number of advantages.

The English country gentleman may settle in Virginia, District of Columbia, Maryland, New Jersey, and the lower part of Pennsylvania; the genteel farmer in Kentucky; the rich yeoman in Kentucky, Missouri, Tennessee, and Apalachicola; the poor farmer, with a capital of £300 and upwards in Illinois and Indiana; ditto, if unmarried, in Missouri, the lower parts of Kentucky, and Appalouchia, because in these countries he can have servants; mechanics, if masters of the most useful trade, and capitalists, always in the most settled parts of the western country, and generally in the slave states; ditto, inferior workmen, or men without money, in the new towns on the frontiers; engineers, smiths, founders, millwrights, and turners may find employment in the larger towns on the Ohio; shopkeepers and makers and dealers of articles of luxury should never cross the mountains.

I cannot think that any elderly man, especially if he have a family delicately brought up, would live comfortably in a free state. In a slave state, if he have wealth, say £5,000 and upwards, he may raise upon his own farm all the food and raiment, the latter manufactured at home, necessary to supply the wants of his own family.

This has been, till lately, the universal economy of the first Kentucky families. Thus, without living more expensively than in a free state, a family may have the comforts of domestic services, and yet find plenty of employment within doors; not sordid slavery that wears out the health and depresses the spirits of Ohio, but useful yet light labors, that may be remitted and resumed at pleasure.

There is more difference between the manners of the female sex on the east and west sides of the Ohio River than on the east and west shores of the Atlantic Ocean. Servitude in any form is an evil, but the structure of civilized society is raised upon it. If the minds of women are left unimproved, their morals will be at the mercy of any man. It is much worse where there is no superior rank to influence them by example, or to awe them by disapprobation. I am conscious that I repeat again and again the same arguments — or rather I state similar facts; but it is an important subject.

Society may suffer more by the abjectness of slaves than by the want of servants, and a father of a family would prefer to live where there are good free servants as in Europe, or where slaves have more liberty of action than servants, as in Kentucky. The question in these wildernesses is this: shall we have civilization and refinement or sordid manners and semi-barbarism till time shall produce so much inequality of condition that the poor man must serve the rich man for his daily bread?

113.

Land Sale Advertisement

Between 1815 and 1819, the desire to exploit the territories acquired during the recent war led to a new boom in the sale of public lands. Such sales were regulated by the Land Acts of 1796 and 1800, which provided that land should be sold by townships divided into half sections (320 acres), at public auction, with a minimum price of $2 an acre. The acts also made credit available to interested buyers, who had only to look in the local newspaper to discover where the next auction would take place. The following land sale advertisement, which is typical of the period, appeared in a Shelbyville, Tennessee, paper in February 1818. Cotton Port was a neighboring town.

Source: *Tennessee Herald,* February 21, 1818.

On March 16, 1818 (being the next Monday after the close of the Public Land Sales at Huntsville), will be offered for sale to the highest bidder on the premises, a part of the lots laid out for the new town of Cotton Port.

The town is laid out on the west bank of Limestone River, one mile above its junction with the Tennessee and a little below the south Beaver Dam and the Piney Fork.

The situation is high and dry, promises to be as healthy as any other place in the Alabama Territory, is near the Tennessee, is sufficiently level, and elevated above the reach of the highest floods of the Tennessee.

Engraving by J. Hill after painting by J. Shaw, "Picturesque Views of American Scenery," 1820

Within the limits of the town are two never-failing springs of good water. The appearance of the land and the success of similar experiments in the country adjacent justify a belief that on almost every lot a well of good water may be had at a moderate depth without blowing rock.

Limestone River, from the Tennessee to this place, is navigable at all seasons of the year by the largest keel and flat bottomed boats used in the navigation of the Tennessee. Limestone here affords a safe harbor of deep, still water, in which, the greatest floods, boats will be entirely free from the dangers to be at such times apprehended from the strong and rapid current and sudden risings and fallings of the Tennessee. The situation at which Cotton Port is laid out has in fact long since been proved, by the observation and experience of the planters of the western and the northwestern parts of Madison County, to be the place which nature has distinctly marked out for the commercial center of the very fertile country adjacent. It includes the well-known old boat landing, Limestone. At this place for several years past, not an inconsiderable part of the cotton from these parts of Madison County has been imbarked in flat-bottomed boats, which ascended with ease from the Tennessee, and with full cargoes descended from this place to New Orleans. The saving in the expense of land carriage, although the country for more than fifteen miles around the boat landing was then unsettled and the Indian claim to it unextinguished, caused the produce of this quarter of Madison County to be embarked at this place in preference to any other. The same reason must naturally render Cotton Port the place of embarkation for all the produce of the country north of it, as far as the southern boundary of the state of Tennessee, and for a considerable distance to the west and to the east.

The country whose trade seems decreed by nature to center here includes one of the finest cotton districts north of the Tennessee River. Of its fertility and probable wealth and produce something like definite ideas may be formed when it is known that at the public sales now going on at Huntsville, the lands in the township in which Cotton Port has been laid out, and the next to the north, sold at from $2 to $70 per acre and at an average of $16 per acre; in the two next townships to the east and northeast at about the same prices. The two nearest townships to the west and northwest of Cotton Port are to be sold during the present week. The greater part of the land in these is not less fertile and inviting to wealthy and industrious settlers. To people at a distance who may not have inquired into the system pursued in surveying and selling public lands of the United States, it may be proper to observe that a township is six miles square, in each of which, after the reservation for schools, there are 22,400 acres to be sold in quarter-sections of 160 each. Of the rich and high-priced lands just mentioned, the most remote is but twelve miles from Cotton Port.

Men of industry, enterprise, and judgment in almost every walk of life, who seek to better their condition in a new and unoccupied field of action, will not be slow in forming their conclusions if they can rely upon these statements. Let them examine the records of the land office and see if they are correct; let them examine the account of sales and calculate what must in all probability be the produce of a district in one half of which capital to so large an amount has been vested by prudent men in the purchase of lands at the public sales of government; let them examine a map of the country and ascertain the point at which the commerce of this district must center.

To the merchant it must occur that for the exportation of the produce of such a country there must be buyers at the point where it will be collected, and that to supply such a country in foreign articles of consumption there must be sellers at the place to which the consumers come to sell their produce.

Trade cannot stagnate here. Industrious and ingenious mechanics must see that the inhabitants of such a country will want houses, furniture, farming utensils, leather, saddles, boots, shoes, etc., and will be able to pay good prices for them. The upper country on the Tennessee and Holston rivers and their branches will afford, at a very trifling expense for water carriage down the river, abundant supplies of provisions, iron, lumber, and other raw materials.

A good dry road can be had from Cotton Port north to Elk River. The proprietors of the land laid out for the town intend to build a bridge across Limestone, and to make a good road for several miles towards the rich country about the Big Prairie.

From Cotton Port to Falls of the Black Warrior, as good a road can probably be had as from any place on Tennessee River. The distance is about 100 miles.

The trustees of the town will reserve for public benefit two lots including the two springs, two or more lots for a place of public worship, a schoolhouse, and such other public buildings as the prospects of the place may seem to require.

In the plan of the town the trustees have endeavored to avoid everything which will tend to bring all its population and business into one span and leave the rest of the lots unoccupied. They have endeavored to arrange the streets, lots, etc., so as to secure to the future inhabitants, as far as practicable, the benefits of shade and a free circulation of air, and to every family a piece of garden ground.

A plan of the town and a map of the adjacent country will be left for public inspection at John H. Smith's store in Nashville, and a plan of the town with Brice M. Garner, Fayetteville, Tenn., and with John Brahan in Huntsville as soon as they can be prepared.

The sale will commence precisely at 12 o'clock. The trustees are induced to commence the sale at so short a notice in order to meet the wishes of many now waiting and anxious to commence improvements in the town immediately. If the demand for lots requires it, the sale will be continued from day to day.

Terms eight months credit. Bond and approved security to be given.

114.

An Irish Colony in Illinois

When a group of French immigrants known as the Society of the Olive and Vine was granted generous terms of credit in purchasing land on which to colonize, other immigrant groups petitioned Congress for similar favors. One of the largest of these groups, the Irish Emigrant Associations of New York, Philadelphia, Baltimore, and Pittsburgh sent the following request to the Committee on Public Lands for extended credit on land in Illinois. The Committee refused the request on February 25, 1818, on the grounds that it was unwise to create ethnic political units. "Probably no decision in the history of American immigration policy," wrote Marcus Lee Hansen in 1935, "possesses more profound significance. By its terms the immigrant was to enjoy no special privileges to encourage his coming; also he was to suffer no special restrictions. His opportunities were those of a native, nothing more, nothing less."

Source: 15 Congress, 1 Session, House Report No. 119.

The Committee on the Public Lands, to whom was referred the petition of the Irish Emigrant Associations of New York, Philadelphia, Baltimore, and Pittsburgh, have had the same under consideration, and report that the petitioners ask that a portion of the public land lying in the Illinois Territory may be set apart for the purpose of being settled by emigrants from Ireland, to whom it is requested the lands may be sold on an extended credit. For the reasons urged in favor of this application, the committee refer the House to the petitions themselves.

The following specific propositions were also submitted to the consideration of the committee by the agents of the petitioners, viz:

1. That the Secretary of the Treasury should be authorized to designate and set apart ——— townships, each of six miles square, in the Illinois Territory, east of the military bounty lands, each alternate section thereof to be settled by emigrants from Ireland, and sold to them at $2 per acre, on a credit of four years for one-third, eight years for one-third, and twelve years for the last installment, with interest upon the several sums.

2. That the Secretary of the Treasury should be at liberty to reject applications, unless the applicant emigrants should be satisfactorily recommended by some of the Irish Emigrant Associations, as moral and industrious men.

3. That no contract should be made with any emigrant, unless he would engage to improve at least 20 of each 100 acres, and erect a tenement suitable for his abode.

4. That no contract should be binding upon the United States, nor title vest in any emigrant settler, unless he had made the improvement and settlement abovementioned, and fully paid for the land contracted for.

5. That no contract should be made, or patent issued, to any settler, or his heirs, for more than 640 acres.

6. That in every instance in which the conditions of improvement, settlement, and payment should not be complied with at the expiration of the term of twelve years, the Secretary of the Treasury should cause the lands so forfeited to be sold, for the benefit of the United States: provided, that in every case in which payment in part had been made, the sum or sums paid should be refunded to the emigrant settler, or his heirs.

The committee refer to their reports on several analogous cases, some of which have been sanctioned by the House, and others which still lie on the table, for the reasons that induce them to recommend the following resolution:

Resolved, that the prayer of the petitioners ought not to be granted.

115.

Daniel Webster: Contracts and Corporate Charters

When the New Hampshire law that transformed Dartmouth College into a state university became effective, the original trustees refused to recognize the new institution. Though they were ousted from the school itself, they moved, along with part of the student body and faculty, to nearby buildings in which the old "college" continued to function. However, the secretary and treasurer, William H. Woodward, who sympathized with President Wheelock and the new university faction, refused to give up the seal and records to the old trustees. They sued Woodward but lost the case in the state court. The trustees then asked Daniel Webster to take their appeal before the Supreme Court. The significant portions of his argument, presented to the Court on March 10, 1818, are reprinted here.

Source: 4 Wheaton 551.

The charter, or letters patent . . . create . . . a corporation and . . . appoint twelve persons to constitute it, by the name of the "Trustees of Dartmouth College"; to have perpetual existence, as such corporation, and with power to hold and dispose of lands and goods for the use of the college, with all the ordinary powers of corporations. . . .

After the institution thus created and constituted had existed uninterruptedly and usefully nearly fifty years, the legislature of New Hampshire passed the acts in question. The first act makes the twelve trustees, under the charter, and nine other individuals to be appointed by the governor and council a corporation, by a new name; and to this new corporation transfers all the *property, rights, powers, liberties, and privileges* of the old corporation, with further power to establish *new colleges and an institute,* and to apply all or any part of the funds to these purposes, subject to the power and control of a board of twenty-five overseers to be appointed by the governor and council. The second act makes further provisions for executing the objects of the first; and the last act authorizes the defendant, the treasurer of the plaintiffs, to retain and hold their property against their will.

If these acts are valid, the old corporation is abolished and a new one created. The first act does, in fact, if it can have effect, *create a new corporation* and transfer to it all the property and franchises of the old. The two corporations are not the same in anything which essentially belongs to the existence of a corporation. They have different names, and different powers, rights, and duties. Their organization is wholly different. The powers of the corporation are not vested in the same or similar hands. In one, the trustees are twelve, and no more; in the other, they are twenty-one. In one, the power is a single board; in the other, it is divided between two boards. Although the act professes to include the old trustees in the new corporation; yet that was without their assent and against their remonstrance; and no person can be compelled to be a member of such a corporation against his will. It was neither expected nor intended, that they should be members of the new corporation.

The act itself treats the old corporation as at an end, and going on the ground that all its functions have ceased, it provides for the first meeting and organization of the new corporation. It expressly provides, also, that the new corporation shall have and hold all the property of the old, a provision which would be quite unnecessary upon any other ground than that the old corporation was dissolved. But if it could be contended that the effect of these acts was not entirely to abolish the old corporation, yet it is manifest that they impair and invade the rights, property, and powers of the trustees under the charter *as a corporation,* and the legal rights, privileges, and immunities which belong to them *as individual members* of the corporation.

The twelve trustees were the sole legal owners of all the property acquired under the charter. By the acts, others are admitted, against their will, to be joint owners. The twelve individuals who are trustees were possessed of all the franchises and immunities conferred by the charter. By the acts, nine other trustees and twenty-five overseers are admitted, against their will, to divide these franchises and immunities with them. If, either as a corporation or as individuals, they have any legal rights, this forcible intrusion of others violates those rights as manifestly as an entire and complete ouster and dispossession. These acts alter the whole constitution of the corporation. They affect the rights of the whole body, as a corporation, and the rights of the individuals who compose it. They revoke corporate powers and franchises. They alienate and transfer the property of the college to others.

By the charter, the trustees had a right to fill vacancies in their own number. This is now taken away. They were to consist of twelve, and by express provision, of no more. This is altered. They and their successors, appointed by themselves, were forever to hold the property. The legislature has found successors for them before their seats are vacant. The powers and privileges which the twelve were to exercise *exclusively* are now to be exercised by others. By one of the acts, they are subjected to heavy penalties if they exercise their offices, or any of those powers and privileges granted them by charter, and which they had exercised for fifty years. They are to be punished for not accepting the new grant and taking its benefits. This, it must be confessed, is rather a summary mode of settling a question of constitutional right.

Not only are new trustees forced into the corporation but new trusts and uses are created. The college is turned into a university. Power is given to create new colleges; and to authorize any diversion of the funds which may be agreeable to the new boards, sufficient latitude is given by the undefined power of establishing an institute. To these new colleges, and this institute, the funds contributed by the founder, Dr. Wheelock, and by the original donors, the Earl of Dartmouth and others, are to be applied, in plain and manifest disregard of the uses to which they were given. The president, one of the old trustees, had a right to his office, salary, and emoluments, subject to the twelve trustees alone. His title to these is now changed, and he is made accountable to new masters. So also all the professors and tutors.

If the legislature can at pleasure make these alterations and changes in the rights and privileges of the plaintiffs, it may, with equal propriety, abolish these rights and privileges altogether. The same power which can do any part of this work can accomplish the whole. And, indeed, the argument on which these acts have been hitherto defended goes altogether on the ground that this is such a corporation as the legislature may abolish at pleasure; and that its members have no rights, liberties, franchises, property, or privileges which the legislature may not revoke, annul, alienate, or transfer to others whenever it sees fit.

It will be contended by the plaintiffs that these acts are not valid and binding upon them without their assent: (1) because they are against common right and the constitution of New Hampshire; (2) because they are repugnant to the Constitution of the United States. . . .

It is not too much to assert that the legislature of New Hampshire would not have been competent to pass the acts in question and to make them binding on the plaintiffs without their assent, even if there had been, in the constitution of New Hampshire, or of the United States, no special restriction on their power; because these acts are not the exercise of a power properly legislative. Their object and effect is to take away from one rights, property, and franchises and to grant them to another. This is not the exercise of a legislative power. . . .

Corporate franchises can only be forfeited by trial and judgment. In case of a new charter or grant to an existing corporation, it may accept or reject it as it pleases. It may accept such part of the grant as it chooses and reject the rest. In the very nature of things, a charter cannot be forced upon anybody. . . .

But there are prohibitions in the constitution and bill of rights of New Hampshire, introduced for the purpose of limiting the legislative power, and of protecting the rights and property of the citizens. One prohibition is "that no person shall be deprived of his property, immunities, or privileges, put out of the protection of the law, or deprived of his life, liberty, or estate, but by judgment of his peers, or the law of the land." In the opinion, however, which was given in the court below, it is denied that the trustees, under the charter, had any property, immunity, liberty, or privilege in this corporation within the meaning of this prohibition in the bill of rights. It is said that it is a *public corporation* and *public property;* that the trustees have no greater interest in it than any other individuals; that it is not private property which they can sell or transmit to their heirs, and that, therefore, they have no interest in it; that their office is a public trust like that of the governor or a judge, and that they have no more concern in the property of the college than the governor in the property of the state, or than the judges in the fines which they impose on the culprits at their bar; that it is nothing to them whether their powers shall be extended or lessened, any more than it is to the courts whether their jurisdiction shall be enlarged or diminished. It is necessary, therefore, to inquire into the true nature and character of the corporation which was created by the charter of 1769. . . .

The corporation in question is not a civil, although it is a lay, corporation. It is an eleemosynary corporation. It is a private charity, originally founded and endowed by an individual, with a charter obtained for it at his request for the better administration of his charity. "The eleemosynary sort of corporations are such as are constituted for the perpetual distributions of the free alms or bounty of the founder of them to such persons as he has directed. Of this are all hospitals for the maintenance of the poor, sick, and impotent; and all colleges both in our universities and out of them." Eleemosynary corporations are for the management of private property, according to the will of the donors. They are private corporations. A college is as much a private corporation as a hospital; especially a college founded as this was, by private bounty. . . .

The case before the Court is clearly that of an eleemosynary corporation. It is, in the strictest legal sense, a private charity. In *King* v. *St. Catharine's Hall,* that college is called a "private eleemosynary lay corporation." It was endowed by a private founder and incorporated by letters patent. And in the same manner was Dartmouth College founded and incorporated. Dr. Wheelock is declared by the charter to be its founder. It was established by him on funds contributed and collected by himself. As such founder, he had a right of visitation, which he assigned to the trustees, and they received it by his consent and appointment, and held it under the charter. He appointed these trustees visitors, and in that respect to take place of his heir; as he might have appointed devisees to take his estate instead of his heir. Little, probably, did he think, at that time, that the legislature would ever take away this property and these privileges, and give them to others. Little did he suppose that this charter secured to him and his successors no legal rights. Little did the other donors think so. If they had, the college would have been what the university is now, a thing upon paper, existing only in name. . . .

The privilege, then, of being a member of a corporation, under a lawful grant, and of exercising the rights and powers of such member, is such a privilege, liberty, or franchise as has been the object of legal protection and the subject of a legal interest, from the time of Magna Carta to the present moment. The plaintiffs have such an interest in this corporation, individually, as they could assert and maintain in a court of law, not as agents of the public but in their own right. Each trustee has a franchise, and if he be disturbed in the enjoyment of it, he would have redress, on appealing to the law, as promptly as for any other injury. If the other trustees should conspire against any one of them to prevent his equal right and voice in the appointment of a president or professor, or in the passing of any statute or ordinance of the college, he would be entitled to his action for depriving him of his franchise.

It makes no difference that this property is to be held and administered and these franchises exercised for the purpose of diffusing learning. No principle and no case establishes any such distinction. The public may be benefited by the use of this property. But this does not change the nature of the property or the rights of the owners. . . . That all property of which the use may be beneficial to the public belongs, therefore, to the public is quite a new doctrine. It has no precedent and is supported by no known principle.

Dr. Wheelock might have answered his purposes, in this case, by executing a private deed of trust. He might have conveyed his property to trustees for precisely such uses as are described in this charter. Indeed, it appears that he had contemplated the establishing of his school in that manner, and had made his will and devised the property to the same persons who were afterward appointed trustees in the charter. Many literary and other charitable institutions are founded in that manner, and the trust is renewed and conferred on other persons, from time to time, as occasion may require. In such a case, no lawyer would or could say that the legislature might divest the trustees constituted by deed or will, seize upon the property, and give it to other persons for other purposes. And does the granting of a charter, which is only done to perpetuate the trust in a more convenient manner, make any difference? Does or can this change the nature of the charity and turn it into a public, political corporation? . . .

The granting of the corporation is but making the trust perpetual and does not alter the nature of the charity. The very object sought in obtaining such charter, and in giving property to such a corporation, is to make and keep it private property, and to clothe it with all the security and inviolability of private property. The intent is that there shall be a legal private ownership, and that the legal owners shall maintain and protect the property for the benefit of those for whose use it was designed. Who ever endowed the public? . . .

I hope enough has been said to show that the trustees possessed vested liberties, privileges, and immunities under this charter; and that such liberties, privileges, and immunities, being once lawfully obtained and vested, are as inviolable as any vested rights of property whatever. Rights to do certain acts, such, for instance, as the visitation and superintendence of a college, and the appointment of its officers, may surely be *vested rights,* to all legal intents, as completely as the right to possess property. . . .

The plaintiffs contend . . . that the acts in question are repugnant to the 10th Section of the 1st Article of the Constitution of the United States. The material words of that section are: "No state shall pass any bill of attainder, ex post facto law, or law impairing the obligation of contracts." . . .

The charter recites that the founder, on his part, has agreed to establish his seminary in New Hampshire and to enlarge it beyond its original design, among other things, for the benefit of that province; and thereupon a charter is given to him and his associates, designated by himself, promising and assuring to them, under the plighted faith of the state, the right of governing the college and administering its concerns in the manner provided in the charter. There is a complete and perfect grant to them of all the power of superintendence, visitation, and government. Is not this a contract? If lands or money had been granted to him and his associates for the same purposes, such grant could not be rescinded. And is there any difference, in legal contemplation, between a grant of corporate franchises and a grant of tangible property? No such difference is recognized in any decided case, nor does it exist in the common apprehension of mankind.

It is therefore contended that this case falls within the true meaning of this provision of the Constitution, as expounded in the decisions of this Court; that the charter of 1769 is a contract, a stipulation, or agreement; mutual in its considerations, express and formal in its terms, and of a most binding and solemn nature. That the acts in question impair this contract has already been sufficiently shown. They repeal and abrogate its most essential parts. . . .

The case before the Court is not of ordinary importance, nor of everyday occurrence. It affects not this college only but every college and all the literary institutions of the country. They have flourished, hitherto, and have become in a high degree respectable and useful to the community. They have all a common principle of existence — the inviolability of their charters. It will be a dangerous, a most dangerous experiment, to hold these institutions subject to the rise and fall of popular parties and the fluctuations of political opinions. If the franchise may be at any time taken away, or impaired, the property also may be taken away, or its use perverted. Benefactors will have no certainty of effecting the object of their bounty; and learned men will be deterred from devoting themselves to the service of such institutions from the precarious title of their officers. Colleges and halls will be deserted by all better spirits and become a theater for the contention of politics. Party and faction will be cherished in the places consecrated to piety and learning. These consequences are neither remote nor possible only. They are certain and immediate.

116.

Henry Clay: Internal Improvements and the Powers of Congress

The economic expansion as well as the movement westward that followed the War of 1812 required, in the minds of nationalists, an improved system of roads and canals to connect the interior with eastern markets. The issue that arose once more of the proper role of the federal government in such internal improvements turned on diverse interpretations of the Constitution. While some insisted that private enterprise should finance internal improvements, Henry Clay, whose "American System" depended on an interconnecting system of roadways, favored support by the national government. In a speech to the House of Representatives on March 13, 1818, Clay argued the constitutionality of his plan.

Source: *The Life and Speeches of Henry Clay,* New York, 1844, Vol. I, pp. 55-78.

That there are two classes of powers in the Constitution, I believe has never been controverted by an American politician. We cannot foresee and provide specifically for all contingencies. Man and his language are both imperfect. Hence the existence of construction and of constructive powers. Hence, also, the rule that a grant of the end is a grant of the means. If you amend the Constitution a thousand times, the same imperfection of our nature and our language will attend our new works.

There are two dangers to which we are exposed. The one is that the general government may relapse into the debility which existed in the old Confederation, and finally dissolve from the want of cohesion. The denial to it of powers plainly conferred, or clearly necessary and proper to execute the conferred powers, may produce this effect. And I think, with great deference to the gentlemen on the other side, this is the danger to which their principles directly tend. The other danger, that of consolidation, is by the assumption of powers not granted nor incident to granted powers, or the assumption of powers which have been withheld or expressly prohibited. This was the danger of the period of 1798-99. For instance, that in direct contradiction to a prohibitory clause of the Constitution, a Sedition Act was passed; and an Alien Law was also passed, in equal violation of the spirit, if not of the express provisions of the Constitution. . . .

It is agreed that there is no power in the general government but that which is expressly granted, or which is impliable from an express grant. . . . The gentleman from Virginia, who has favored the House with so able an argument on the subject, has conceded, though somewhat reluctantly, the existence of incidental powers, but he contended that they must have a direct and necessary relation to some specified power. Granted. But who is to judge of this relation? And what rule can you prescribe different from that which the Constitution has required that it should be necessary and proper? Whatever may be the rule, in whatever language you may choose to express it, there must be a certain degree of discretion left to the agent who is to apply it. But gentlemen are alarmed at this discretion — that law of tyrants on which they contend there is no limitation.

It should be observed, in the first place, that the gentlemen are brought, by the very course of reasoning which they themselves employ, by all the rules which they would lay down for the Constitution, to cases where discretion must exist. But is there no limitation, no security against the abuse of it? Yes, there is such security in the fact of our being members of the same society, equally affected ourselves by the laws we promulgate. There is the further security in the oath which is taken to support the Constitution, and which will tend to restrain Congress from deriving powers which are not proper and necessary. There is the yet further security that, at the end of every two years, the members must be amenable to the people for the manner in which their trusts have been performed. And there remains also that further, though awful, security, the last resort of society, which I contend belongs alike to the people and to the states in their sovereign capacity, to be exercised in extreme cases, and when oppression becomes intolerable — the right of resistance. . . .

I have contended that the power to construct post roads is expressly granted in the power to establish post roads. If it be, there is an end of the controversy; but if not, the next inquiry is whether that power may be fairly deduced, by implication, from any of the special grants of power. To show that the power is expressly granted, I might safely appeal to the arguments already used to prove that the words establish — in this case can mean only one thing — the right of making. Several gentlemen have contended that the word has a different sense; and one has resorted to the Preamble of the Constitution to show that the phrase "to establish justice," there used, does not convey the power of creation. If the word "establish" is there to be taken in the sense which gentlemen claim for it, that of adoption or designation, Congress could have a choice only of systems of justice preexisting. Will any gentleman contend that we are obliged to take the Justinian Code, the Napoleon Code, the code of civil or the code of common or canon law? Establishment means in the Preamble, as in other cases, construction, formation, creation. . . .

Now let us review those opinions [of the President] as communicated at different periods. It was the opinion of Mr. Jefferson that, although there was no general power vested by the Constitution in Congress to construct roads and canals without the consent of the states, yet such a power might be exercised with their assent. Mr. Jefferson not only held this opinion in the abstract but he practically executed it in the instance of the Cumberland Road; and how? First by a compact made with the state of Ohio for the application of a specified fund, and then by compacts with Virginia, Pennsylvania, and Maryland to apply the fund so set apart within their respective limits. If, however, I rightly understood my honorable friend the other day, he expressly denied (and in that I concur with him) that the power could be acquired by the mere consent of the state. Yet he defended the act of Mr. Jefferson, in the case referred to.

It is far from my intention to misstate the gentleman. I certainly understood him to say that, as the road was first stipulated for in the compact with Ohio, it was competent afterward to carry it through the states mentioned, with their assent. Now, if we have not the right to make a road in virtue of one compact made with a single state, can we obtain it by two contracts made with several states? The character of the fund cannot affect the question. It is totally immaterial whether it arises from the sales of the public lands or from the general revenue. Suppose a contract made with Massachusetts, that a certain portion of the revenue collected at the port of Boston from foreign trade should be expended in making roads and canals leading to that state, and that a subsequent compact should be made with Connecticut or New Hampshire for the expenditure of the fund on these objects, within their limits. Can we acquire the power, in this manner, over internal improvements if we do not possess it independently of such compacts? I conceive, clearly not. And I am entirely at a loss to comprehend how gentlemen, consistently with their own principles, can justify the erection of the Cumberland Road. No man is prouder than I am of that noble monument of the provident care of the nation, and of the public spirit of its projectors; and I trust that, in spite of all constitutional and other scruples, here or elsewhere, an appropriation will be made to complete that road. I confess, however, freely that I am entirely unable to conceive of any principle on which that road can be supported that would not uphold the general power contended for.

I will now examine the opinion of Mr. Madison. Of all the acts of that pure, virtuous, and illustrious statesman, whose administration has so powerfully tended to advance the glory, honor, and prosperity of this country, I most regret, for his sake and for the sake of the country, the rejection of the bill of the last session. I think it irreconcilable with Mr. Madison's own principles — those great, broad, and liberal principles on which he so ably administered the government. And, sir, when I appeal to the members of the last Congress, who are now in my hearing, I am authorized to say, with regard to the majority of them, that no circumstance, not even an earthquake that should have swallowed up one-half of this city, could have excited more surprise than when it was first communicated to this House that Mr. Madison had rejected his own bill. I say his own bill, for his message at the opening of the session meant nothing if it did not recommend such an exercise of power as was contained in that bill. . . .

It is impossible, moreover, to disguise the fact that the question is now a question between the executive on the one side and the representatives of the people on the other. So it is understood in the country, and such is the fact. Mr. Madison enjoys, in his retreat at Montpelier, the repose and the honors due to his eminent and laborious services; and I would be among the last to disturb it. However painful it is to me to animadvert upon any of his opinions, I feel perfectly sure that the circumstance can only be viewed by him with an enlightened liberality. What are the opinions which have been expressed by Mr. Madison on this subject? I will not refer to all the messages wherein he has recommended internal improvements, but to that alone which he addressed to Congress at the commencement of the last session, which contains this passage:

> I particularly invite *again* the attention of Congress to the expediency of exercising *their existing powers,* and, where necessary, of resorting to the prescribed mode of enlarging them, in order to *effectuate a comprehensive system of roads and canals,* such as will have the effect of drawing more closely together every part of our country, by promoting intercourse and improvements, and by increasing the share of every part in the common stock of national prosperity.

In the examination of this passage, two positions force themselves upon our attention. The first is the assertion that there are existing powers in Congress to effectuate a comprehensive system of roads and canals, the effect of which would be to draw the different parts of the country more closely together. And I would candidly admit, in the second place, that it was intimated that, in the exercise of those existing powers, some defect might be discovered which would render an amendment of the Constitution necessary. Nothing could be more clearly affirmed than the first position; but in the message of Mr. Madison returning the bill, passed in consequence of his recommendation, he has not specified a solitary case to which those existing powers are applicable; he has not told us what he meant by those existing powers; and the general scope of his reasoning, in that message, if well founded, proves that there are no existing powers whatever. It is apparent that Mr. Madison himself has not examined some of those principal sources of the Constitution from which, during this debate, the power has been derived. . . .

I come now to the message of Mr. Monroe; and if, by the communication of his opinion to Congress he intended to prevent discussion, he has most woefully failed. I know that, according to a most venerable and excellent usage, the opinion, neither of the President nor of the Senate, upon any proposition depending in this House, ought to be adverted to. Even in the Parliament of Great Britain, a member who would refer to the opinion of the sovereign, in such a case, would be instantly called to order; but under the extraordinary circumstances of the President having, with, I have no doubt, the best motives, volunteered his opinion on this head, and inverted the order of legislation by beginning where it should end, I am compelled, most reluctantly, to refer to that opinion. I cannot but deprecate the practice of which the President has, in this instance, set the example to his successors.

The constitutional order of legislation supposes that every bill originating in one house shall be there deliberately investigated, without influence from any other branch of the legislature; and then remitted to the other house for a like free and unbiased consideration. Having passed both houses, it is to be laid before the President; signed if approved, and if disapproved, to be returned, with his objections, to the originating house. In this manner, entire freedom of thought and of action is secured, and the President finally sees the proposition in the most matured form which Congress can give to it. The practical effect, to say no more, of forestalling the legislative opinion, and telling us what we may or may not do, will be to deprive the President himself of the opportunity of considering a proposition so matured, and us of the benefit of his reasoning applied specifically to such proposition. For the Constitution further enjoins it upon him to state his objections upon returning the bill. The originating house is then to reconsider it, and deliberately to weigh those objections; and it is further required, when the question is again taken — shall the bill pass, those objections notwithstanding? that the votes shall be solemnly spread, by ayes and noes, upon the record.

Of this opportunity of thus recording our opinions, in matters of great public concern, we are deprived, if we submit to the innovation of the President. I will not press this part of the subject further. I repeat, again and again, that I have no doubt but that the President was actuated by the purest motives. I am compelled, however, in the exercise of that freedom of opinion, which, so long as I exist I will maintain, to say that the proceeding is irregular and unconstitutional. Let us, however, examine the reasoning and opinion of the President.

> A difference of opinion has existed from the first formation of our Constitution to the present time, among our most enlightened and virtuous citizens, respecting the right of Congress to establish a system of internal improvement. Taking into view the trust with which I am now honored, it would be improper, after what has passed, that this discussion

> should be revived, with an uncertainty of my opinion respecting the right. Disregarding early impressions, I have bestowed on the subject all the deliberation which its great importance and a just sense of my duty required, and the result is, a settled conviction in my mind that Congress does not possess the right. It is not contained in any of the specified powers granted to Congress: nor can I consider it incidental to, or a necessary mean, viewed on the most liberal scale, for carrying into effect any of the powers which are specifically granted. In communicating this result, I cannot resist the obligation which I feel to suggest to Congress the propriety of recommending to the states the adoption of an amendment to the Constitution which shall give the right in question. In cases of doubtful construction, especially of such vital interest, it comports with the nature and origin of our institutions, and will contribute much to preserve them, to apply to our constituents for an explicit grant of power. We may confidently rely that, if it appears to their satisfaction that the power is necessary, it will always be granted.

In this passage the President has furnished us with no reasoning, no argument in support of his opinion — nothing addressed to the understanding. He gives us, indeed, a historical account of the operations of his own mind, and he asserts that he has made a laborious effort to conquer his early impressions, but that the result is a settled conviction against the power, without a single reason. In his position that the power must be specifically granted, or incident to a power so granted, it has been seen that I have the honor to entirely concur with him; but, he says the power is not among the specified powers. Has he taken into consideration the clause respecting post roads, and told us how and why that does not convey the power? If he had acted within what I conceive to be his constitutional sphere of rejecting the bill, after it had passed both houses, he must have learned that great stress was placed on that clause, and we should have been enlightened by his comments upon it. As to his denial of the power, as an incident to any of the express grants, I would have thought that we might have safely appealed to the experience of the President, during the late war, when the country derived so much benefit from his judicious administration of the duties of the War Department, whether roads and canals for military purposes were not essential to celerity and successful result in the operations of armies.

This part of the message is all assertion, and contains no argument which I can comprehend, or which meet the points contended for during this debate. Allow me here to say, and I do it without the least disrespect to that branch of the government on whose opinions and acts it has been rendered my painful duty to comment; let me say, in reference to any man, however elevated his station, even if he be endowed with the power and prerogatives of a sovereign, that his acts are worth infinitely more, and are more intelligible, than mere paper sentiments or declarations.

And what have been the acts of the President? During his tour of the last summer, did he not order a road to be cut or repaired from near Plattsburgh to the St. Lawrence? My honorable friend will excuse me if my comprehension is too dull to perceive the force of that argument which seeks to draw a distinction between repairing an old and making a new road.

Certainly no such distinction is to be found in the Constitution or exists in reason. Grant, however, the power of reparation, and we will make it do. We will take the post roads, sinuous as they are, and put them in a condition to enable the mails to pass, without those mortifying delays and disappointments to which we, at least in the West, are so often liable. The President, then, ordered a road of considerable extent to be constructed or repaired, on his sole authority, in a time of profound peace, when no enemy threatened the country, and when, in relation to the power as to which alone that road could be useful in time of war, there exists the best understanding and a prospect of lasting friendship greater than at any other period. On his sole authority the President acted, and we are already called upon by the chairman of the Committee of Ways and Means to sanction the act by an appropriation. This measure has been taken, too, without the consent of the state of New York; and what is wonderful, when we consider the magnitude of the state rights which are said to be violated, without even a protest. . . .

On the contrary, I understand, from some of the military officers who are charged with the execution of the work, what is very extraordinary, that the people through whose quarter of the country the road passes do not view it as a national calamity; that they would be very glad that the President would visit them often, and that he would order a road to be cut and improved, at the national expense, every time he should visit them. Other roads, in other parts of the Union, have, it seems, been likewise ordered, or their execution, at the public expense, sanctioned by the executive, without the concurrence of Congress.

If the President has the power to cause these public improvements to be executed at his pleasure, whence is it derived? If any member will stand up in this place and say the President is clothed with this authority, and that it is denied to Congress, let us hear from him; and let him point to the clause of the Constitution which vests it in the executive and withholds it from the legislative branch.

There is no such clause; there is no such exclusive executive power. The power is derivable by the executive only from those provisions of the Constitution which charge him with the duties of commanding the physical force of the country and the employment of that force in war, and the preservation of the public tranquillity, and in the execution of the laws. But Congress has paramount power to the President. It alone can declare war, can raise armies, can provide for calling out the militia, in the specified instances, and can raise and appropriate the ways and means necessary to those objects. Or is it come to this, that there are to be two rules of construction for the Constitution — one, an enlarged rule, for the executive, and another, a restricted rule, for the legislature? Is it already to be held that, according to the genius and nature of our Constitution, powers of this kind may be safely entrusted to the executive, but when attempted to be exercised by the legislature are so alarming and dangerous that a war with all the allied powers would be less terrible, and that the nation should clothe itself straightway in sackcloth and ashes!

No, sir, if the power belongs only by implication to the chief magistrate, it is placed both by implication and express grant in the hands of Congress. I am so far from condemning the act of the President, to which I have referred, that I think it deserving of high approbation. That it was within the scope of his constitutional authority I have no doubt; and I sincerely trust that the secretary at war will, in time of peace, constantly employ in that way the military force. It will at the same time guard that force against the vices incident to indolence and inaction, and correct the evil of subtracting from the mass of the labor of society, where labor is more valuable than in any other country, that portion of it which enters into the composition of the army. But I most solemnly protest against any exercise of powers of this kind by the President which are denied to Congress. And, if the opinions expressed by him, in his message, were communicated, or are to be used here, to influence the judgment of the House, their authority is more than countervailed by the authority of his deliberate acts. . . .

117.

Henry Clay: Recognition for Latin American Governments

President Monroe was opposed to recognizing the new revolutionary governments in Latin America on the grounds that such recognition, even if not accompanied by active support of the rebels, might draw the nation into war with Spain. One of those who opposed Monroe, and who favored particularly the recognition of the United Provinces of the Rio de la Plata, was Henry Clay of Kentucky. In a speech to Congress given on March 25, 1818, Clay sought to have additional monies appropriated for an expedition to Buenos Aires. He took the opportunity to explain his support of the new governments and to arouse sympathy for their cause, holding that, unlike the revolutions in Europe, the revolts in the American hemisphere were intimately linked with the national interest of the United States.

Source: *Debates,* 15 Cong., 1 Sess., pp. 1474-1499.

Mr. C.[lay] said he was no propagandist. He would not seek to force upon other nations our principles and our liberty if they did not want them. He would not disturb the repose even of a detestable despotism. But if an abused and oppressed people willed their freedom; if they sought to establish it; if, in truth, they had established it, we had a right as a sovereign power, to notice the fact, and to act as circumstances and our interest required. He would say, in the language of the venerated Father of His Country: "Born in a land of liberty, my anxious recollections, my sympathetic feelings, and my best wishes are irresistibly excited, whensoever, in any country, I see an oppressed nation unfurl the banners of freedom." For his own part, Mr. C. said, that whenever he thought of Spanish America the image irresistibly forced itself upon his mind of an elder brother whose education had been neglected, whose person had been abused and maltreated, and who had been disinherited by the unkindness of an unnatural parent. And when he contemplated the glorious struggle which that country was now making, he thought he beheld that brother rising, by the power and energy of his fine native genius, to the manly rank which nature and nature's God intended for him.

If Spanish America were entitled to success from the justness of her cause, we had no less reason to wish that success from the horrible character which the royal arms have given to the war. More atrocities than those which had been perpetrated during its existence were not to be found even in the annals of Spain herself. . . .

In the establishment of the independence of Spanish America, the United States have the deepest interest. He had no hesitation in asserting his firm belief that there was no question, in the foreign policy of this country, which had ever arisen, or which he could conceive as ever occurring, in the decision of which we had so much at stake. This interest concerned our politics, our commerce, our navigation. There could not be a doubt that Spanish America, once independent, whatever might be the form of the governments established in its several parts, those governments would be animated by an American feeling and guided by an American policy. They would obey the laws of the system of the New World, of which they would compose a part, in contradistinction to that of Europe. Without the influence of that vortex in Europe, the balance of power between its several parts, the preservation of which had so often drenched Europe in blood, America is sufficiently remote to contemplate the new wars which are to afflict that quarter of the globe as a calm, if not a cold and indifferent, spectator. In relation to those wars, the several parts of America will generally stand neutral. And as, during the period when they rage, it would be important that a liberal system of neutrality should be adopted and observed, all America will be interested in maintaining and enforcing such a system.

The independence, then, of Spanish America is an interest of primary consideration. Next to that, and highly important in itself, was the consideration of the nature of their governments. That was a question, however, for themselves. They would, no doubt, adopt those kinds of governments which were best suited to their condition, best calculated for their happiness. Anxious as he was that they should be free governments, we had no right to prescribe for them. They were, and ought to be, the sole judges for themselves. He was strongly inclined to believe that they would in most, if not all, parts of their country, establish free governments. We were their great example. Of us they constantly spoke as of brothers, having a similar origin. They adopted our principles, copied our institutions, and, in some instances, employed the very language and sentiments of our revolutionary papers. . . .

Mr. C. continued, having shown that the cause of the patriots was just, and that we had a great interest in its successful issue, he would next inquire what course of policy it became us to adopt. He had already declared that to be one of strict and impartial neutrality. It was not necessary for their interest, it was not expedient for our own that we should take part in the war. All they demanded of us was a just neutrality. It was compatible with this pacific policy — it was required by it — that we should recognize any established government if there were any established government in Spanish America. Recognition alone, without aid, was no just cause of war. With aid it was, not because of the recognition but because of the aid, as aid without recognition was cause of war. The truth of these propositions he would maintain upon principle, by the practice of other states, and by the usage of our own. There was no common tribunal among the nations to pronounce upon the fact of the sovereignty of a new state. Each power must and does judge for itself. It was an attribute of sovereignty so to judge. A nation, in exerting this incontestable right — in pronouncing upon the independence, in fact, of a new state — takes no part in the war. It gives neither men, nor ships, nor money. It merely pronounces that in so far as it may be necessary to institute any relations or to support any intercourse with the new power, that power is capable of maintaining those relations and authorizing that intercourse.

118.

THOMAS JEFFERSON: The Education of Women

Although Jefferson spent much of his later life developing plans for an institution of higher education — they eventually culminated in the University of Virginia — he did not consider systematic schooling for females in the same light as for males. Some of his thoughts on the subject were expressed in a letter to a very close friend, Nathaniel Burwell, written March 14, 1818.

Source: Ford, X, pp. 104-106.

YOUR LETTER OF FEBRUARY 17 found me suffering under an attack of rheumatism, which has but now left me at sufficient ease to attend to the letters I have received. A plan of female education has never been a subject of systematic contemplation with me. It has occupied my attention so far only as the education of my own daughters occasionally required. Considering that they would be placed in a country situation, where little aid could be obtained from abroad, I thought it essential to give them a solid education which might enable them, when [they] become mothers, to educate their own daughters, and even to direct the course for sons, should their fathers be lost, or incapable, or inattentive. My surviving daughter accordingly, the mother of many daughters as well as sons, has made their education the object of her life, and being a better judge of the practical part than myself, it is with her aid and that of one of her *élèves* that I shall subjoin a catalogue of the books for such a course of reading as we have practised.

A great obstacle to good education is the inordinate passion prevalent for novels and the time lost in that reading which should be instructively employed. When this poison infects the mind, it destroys its tone and revolts it against wholesome reading. Reason and fact, plain and unadorned, are rejected. Nothing can engage attention unless dressed in all the figments of fancy, and nothing so bedecked comes amiss. The result is a bloated imagination, sickly judgment, and disgust toward all the real businesses of life. This mass of trash, however, is not without some distinction; some few, modeling their narratives, although fictitious, on the incidents of real life, have been able to make them interesting and useful vehicles of a sound morality. Such, I think, are Marmontel's new moral tales, but not his old ones, which are really immoral. Such are the writings of Miss Edgeworth, and some of those of Madame Genlis. For a like reason, too, much poetry should not be indulged. Some is useful for forming style and taste. Pope, Dryden, Thompson, Shakespeare, and of the French, Molière, Racine, the Corneilles, may be read with pleasure and improvement.

The French language, become that of the

general intercourse of nations, and from their extraordinary advances now the depository of all science, is an indispensable part of education for both sexes. In the subjoined catalogue, therefore, I have placed the books of both languages indifferently, according as the one or the other offers what is best.

The ornaments, too, and the amusements of life are entitled to their portion of attention. These, for a female, are dancing, drawing, and music. The first is a healthy exercise, elegant and very attractive for young people. Every affectionate parent would be pleased to see his daughter qualified to participate with her companions, and without awkwardness at least, in the circles of festivity of which she occasionally becomes a part. It is a necessary accomplishment, therefore, although of short use for the French rule is wise that no lady dances after marriage. This is founded in solid physical reasons, gestation and nursing leaving little time to a married lady when this exercise can be either safe or innocent. Drawing is thought less of in this country than in Europe. It is an innocent and engaging amusement, often useful, and a qualification not to be neglected in one who is to become a mother and an instructor. Music is invaluable where a person has an ear. Where they have not, it should not be attempted. It furnishes a delightful recreation for the hours of respite from the cares of the day, and lasts us through life. The taste of this country, too, calls for this accomplishment more strongly than for either of the others.

I need say nothing of household economy, in which the mothers of our country are generally skilled, and generally careful to instruct their daughters. We all know its value, and that diligence and dexterity in all its processes are inestimable treasures. The order and economy of a house are as honorable to the mistress as those of the farm to the master, and if either be neglected, ruin follows, and children destitute of the means of living.

This, sir, is offered as a summary sketch on a subject on which I have not thought much. It probably contains nothing but what has already occurred to yourself, and claims your acceptance on no other ground than as a testimony of my respect for your wishes, and of my great esteem and respect.

119.

Baron de Montlezun: American Women and American Character

Baron de Montlezun, an ultra-royalist who had of course disapproved of the French Revolution but who also was displeased by the character of French society under the restored Bourbon, Louis XVIII, made a voyage to the West Indies and to the United States. While in America, he viewed the people, the society, and the democratic government with a disgust and contempt that on the whole was typical of his class. He published a book in 1818 that recorded his impressions of the country; the portion reprinted here reveals the kind of attitude that so disturbed American nationalists.

Source: *Voyage fait dans les années 1816 et 1817, de New-Yorck à la Nouvelle-Orléans, etc., etc.,* Paris, 1818 [TWA, pp. 128-131].

Philadelphia is no more gay than last year. It seemed to me there were fewer strangers and less trade. As in the other American cities, most of the women wore black, no doubt so as not to vary the endless monotony of the country.

The women spend their days shopping; that is their favorite occupation. The men who are not now fully occupied with business hardly know what to do with their time. Almost all the Frenchmen one meets here, merchants, traders, and travelers, are infected with revolutionary poison. The natives, with a few exceptions among those who have seen European society, are strongly democratic.

Their zealotry, although in appearance everywhere, is, however, genuine only in the lower classes; everyone agrees that there is great hypocrisy in the upper. Men in the United States are, so to speak, compelled to adopt a certain outward humility from the fear of being suspected of a deficiency in republican principles. Any man may be compelled to prove in a disagreeable manner that the lowest individual in the lowest class has the same rights as he. The result is that the highest social classes, whether by rank or fortune, act with a certain air of restraint, nature being the same everywhere and the same causes producing the same effects, particularly when it comes to such natural human sentiments as pride and pomp.

The further result is that the women are deprived of the possibility of satisfying their immense vanity by the disdainful countenances and the superior air of their husbands and of the people with whom they appear in public. Not being able to stifle that passion, they trample under foot their modesty, that irresistible charm with which nature endowed them, and assume a masculine, severe, haughty air. Their natural graces disappear beneath the severity of their appearance and the affectation of male manners, as ridiculous as disgusting. This is to say nothing of the fact that they are generally thin and ugly, with enormous feet, an attribute of the lower classes which wealth cannot alter in one or two generations and which often gives away the low birth of respectable persons.

People of good birth (an advantage praised by Homer, and before Homer, and destined to be praised to the end of the world) have larger fortunes than the traders, have dignity and knowledge unattainable by those who spend all their time in the pursuit of profits and the calculation of interests. In addition, the wellborn are generally physically superior, more urbane, more polished, and have a better tone. Yet they seem so often simple and unpretentious as to stand out by that alone.

The cause is simple. The esteem they enjoy has deep roots, nourished through centuries. It is so well established and so undisputed that it gives birth to a modesty that causes those who witness it to be lavish in devotion with which they would have been miserly had it been demanded of them.

By contrast, when money alone raises us above the common herd, into which we may relapse at the slightest accident and from which fortune may raise the most obscure to our own level, the result is a ridiculous arrogance by which we accord to ourselves that which no one else will accord to us. And in this case, the obstacles, multiplied and increased, offend those who encounter them, harden their hearts, and make of them the most detestable individuals that society can possibly be infested with.

Art Museum, Princeton University

Portrait of wife of Captain George of Haverhill, Mass., about 1820, by an unknown artist

In New York in the middle of October winter descends upon us. My eyes, accustomed to the blueness of Southern skies, can hardly adjust themselves to the clouds that roll in from the sea. While the wise man devotes himself to his studies under his solitary roof, society gathers itself, coteries form, the idle are themselves again. Boxes fill up, Cupid unlooses his arrows, passions clash, the public places are full, the crowd sounds its bells, and stupidity tricked out in triangles and squares, in ribbons and in gravely ridiculous toys, draws a prolific breath, and, blindfolded, aspires to the honor of producing light; a miserable opaque mass surrounded by the blackest shadows!

In this country, where the word liberty never is omitted in conversation, there is the greatest tyranny of opinion; that is, of political opinion, for that is the only kind that seems important. You are pursued by such talk for twenty-seven years, you flee from Europe to escape it, and you fall here into a veritable whirlpool of it. You try hard to call off the hounds, speak vaguely, and turn away the conversation, but it always comes back. Good taste, bad taste, they must absolutely know if you are for the Federalists or for the Democrats. Are you convinced the American sailors will whip the English? Does your heart bleed for the independence of the Latin-American colonies or do you think it unjust to interfere in that quarrel? Can you doubt that the United States in twenty-five years will have a population of 40 million, and be the first country in the world? At the slightest deviation from the line of the fanatics, you are a marked man. You will be met coldly, the rules of politeness will be suspended in your case, and you will encounter unexpected reverses in your business, the origin of which only the inexperienced would find it difficult to guess.

Ease here is only superficial, but misery shows itself in all reality in its most hideous form. Yesterday, a white woman, nude on one side to the waist, sat on the sidewalk near Broadway exposing her sores to the view of the public and begging for alms. This country is hard and difficult, as much from a disgraceful climate, from its sandy soil, as from the disposition of almost all its inhabitants. One finds here some people distinguished by education, culture, politeness, and knowledge of how to live; but the number is infinitely small. . . .

The dominant character of Americans is arrogance carried to an extreme by various causes. In the case of most, lack of education is the root. Others know the political impotence of their country and moreover know the opinion that Europeans have of them because of their recent origin. These people can have no illusions about themselves. Their self-love is thus deeply wounded, and since nothing can wipe out this recollection or remedy this illness, this arrogance, born of desperation, is easily imitated by the people and inoculated among them by a crass ignorance. To arrogance is joined a great deal of superstition and fanaticism, of grandiloquent words about the rights of man and of the people, although slavery flourishes in most of their country; and declamations without end against tyrants and nobles, although there are none as bad as among them and although the aristocracy of riches, acquired God knows how, affects the most ridiculous pretensions. Joined to that is also a pronounced intolerance, a propensity for masonic stupidities and foolishness, a continual turgidity, a vanity born of the idea of their own merit and of the pretended superiority of a clownish population made up of odds and ends, of blacks, of yellows, and of whites, of European adventurers and their obscure descendants, scattered over a wretched land stolen from the peaceful Indian peoples. And all that is supported by an army of 10,000 raw troops, a navy of eight or ten frigates, three ships of the line, and some brigs of war, no forts, provinces open to attack from every side. Yet the end result is an insatiable greed that satisfies itself at no matter what cost, a ridiculous presumption, a self-love that is more than comic. There you have a picture of the Americans and of their country.

120.

French Emigrants to America

Among the French immigrants in the United States were a number of prominent political refugees. They petitioned the government after the War of 1812 to sell them some land on which they could establish a community that, they claimed, would be useful to the nation. They argued that the U.S. economy as a whole would benefit if they were allowed to plant vines and olive trees and take steps toward establishing domestic industries in these agricultural specialties. Congress agreed to the plan and sold several townships to the newly formed Society for the Olive and the Vine in 1817. The terms of sale were so lenient that it was referred to, by those who did not entirely approve of it, as a grant. The scheme failed, in part because the new owners engaged in the land speculation that was the will-o-the-wisp of so many at the time. An editorial in the Weekly Register *— probably written by its editor, Hezekiah Niles — discussed the situation in August 1818.*

Source: *Niles' Weekly Register,* August 8, 1818.

Among the splendid fooleries which have at times amused a portion of the American people, as well as their representatives in Congress, was that of granting, on most favorable terms to certain emigrants from France, a large tract of land in the Alabama Territory to encourage the cultivation of the vine and olive, passed the 3rd of March, 1817.

This tract contains 92,000 acres, and was sold at $2 per acre, payable without interest, in fourteen years — in truth, much better than a mere gratuity of so much land considering the license of selection, and which could not, at this time, probably be purchased of the proprietors for less than $2 million. What was honestly intended as a common benefit to a number of unfortunate persons is understood to have immediately centered, like banking, into the benefit of a few; and I am told that one man's gains by this speculation are estimated at from $500,000 to $1 million.

The act of Congress by which this grant was made contains many provisions to prevent the public munificence from being converted into a private monopoly. And one of our objects in referring to it is to excite some member of Congress to a rigid inquiry to ascertain if the letter of the law has been satisfied, seeing that its spirit has been violated — in order to a reclamation of the immunities granted, if justice requires it.

So much, indeed, has the beneficence of Congress been abused, that two or three of the oldest and most respectable members told me, when at Washington last winter, that there was nothing against which they should hereafter be so much upon their guard as those acts called liberal — and one of them observed he never had voted for any law that was intended by him as an advantage to a class of people which he had not sincerely repented of, because the advantages designed for all had uniformly been perverted to the benefit of a few scheming individuals; and he instanced a series of speculations "too tedious to mention." It was the abuse of the Alabama grant that caused the rejection of the petition of the Irish Emigrant Associations for the laying off of a tract of land in the Illinois, though everybody felt satisfied that their design was an honest one.

By the way, however, I very much question the policy of any act of government that has a tendency to introduce and keep up among us a foreign national language or dialect, manners or character, as every large and compact settlement of emigrants from any particular country must necessarily occasion. Though some have seemed almost ready to quarrel with me for the often-repeated assertion, I still assert and will maintain it, that the people of the United States are yet wretchedly deficient of a national character, though it is rapidly forming, and in a short time will be as the vanguard of the national strength. Its progress, however, is retarded by the influx of foreigners, with manners and prejudices favorable to a state of things repugnant to our rules and notions of right, since few enlightened men may be called citizens of the world; but most men's ideas are narrowed to the spot or country, with its habits of thinking and of acting, where they received their education, which it requires at least the mixture of a generation to remove.

These prejudices extend as well to the religious as to the political supremacy of certain poor, weak, and miserable individuals; and considerably prevent an exercise of the right which man has to worship God after the dictates of his own heart, and are at open war with the power that he has, in its liberal sense, to manage all his own concerns in his own way. To lessen the force of prejudices so hostile to our free institutions, it is important that those subject to them should be cast into the common stock of the people; in which, if they do not get more expanded ideas and fall in with the general habits of the nation of which they are members, their scattered condition will measurably forbid them from retarding the growth of a general feeling — or at least, prevent a powerful action against it.

These remarks might be illustrated by many well-known examples; but the case does not require it at present, and would be to travel from the point that is now aimed at. I am notoriously the friend of all persons seeking happiness in this land of liberty, and designing to lay their bones among us; and would afford to them every facility that they may become Americans, indeed — but it is only upon the condition of their becoming so that I wish the presence of any. I most sincerely despise the creature that, rioting in his ease possessed here, adheres to those institutions which drove him from his country. If any love a king better than freedom, let them lick his feet "at home" as long as his majesty will condescend to suffer it — but it is knavery, or folly, in a man who voluntarily takes up his abode in America, this "despicable country," to be always telling us of the roast beef and happiness that he left. And it ought to be resented by advising him to go back again as quickly as possible — adding that we will cheerfully part with him.

121.

Robert Lee: A Society for a National Literature

Men like Noah Webster and Benjamin Rush had called, in the post-Revolutionary period, for a second or cultural revolution that in their view would solidify the gains of the political revolution and make permanent the separation from Europe. There was relatively little response to their plea at the time, but after the War of 1812 the cry went up again for a "national literature" when harsh English attacks on the quality of America's cultural achievement helped bring on the so-called Paper War. The conflict was furious and bitter, its weapons magazine articles, editorials, and letters to the editors. An example of the last, which appeared in Niles' Weekly Register *in May 1818, appears here. Its author, Robert Lee, advocated the establishment of a society to foster all kinds of native art and science.*

Source: *Niles' Weekly Register,* May 16, 1818.

Among the various events which have tended most essentially to change the face of human affairs may justly be ranked the discovery and colonization of America, the revolt of the colonies of North America from British dominion, and the establishment of a new empire in that portion of the New World which had disdained any longer being subjected to European domination.

Nor was the mere change of foreign rulers for rulers chosen from among and by ourselves the only change which we experienced. New modes of thinking were adopted; new principles of government were established. Out of that chaos, darkness, and night from which we emerged has been brought order, light, and the beauty of a glorious morn.

But, have we, the American people, done all that is required at our hands? Have we improved all the glorious opportunities offered us by our emancipation from European domination? Do we appreciate the extent of the blessings which we enjoy? Or have we considered the best means of securing these blessings to ourselves, of diffusing them among our contemporaries, or of transmitting them to posterity?

And have we, in fact, considered how infinitely important is the present crisis of human affairs? That upon what has recently been done and upon what is now transpiring depend the destinies of all future generations of men; and that next to the honor of having performed a part in the late glorious Revolution, will be the honor of having contributed to the promotion of literature, the arts and sciences in the New World, and from thence diffusing them — and with them the principles of our admirable system of government — to every distant land and among all the scattered tribes of the earth.

If anything can console my regret at not having been here, an actor in the Revolution, or at having been precluded by my youth from participating in the establishment of our generous systems of government, it is the reflection that a work almost as glorious yet remains to be performed; a work in which an infinite number may be engaged, in which every capacity and extent of genius may be usefully employed, in which every extent of lawful ambition may be gratified, and from which a wreath of unfading laurels may be gathered.

Shall we remain where we are, shall we be content to see only the dawn, nor wish to behold the splendor of the midday sun? Or shall we, by a noble and glorious effort, call forth all that remains of latent genius among us, and establish upon an immovable basis the justness of our claims as a literary and scientific people?

Have we considered the high destinies which await our country; the vast extent of territory and variety of soil which it embraces, the countless millions which are destined to inhabit it, the long vista of ages through which its course is, doubtless, to run, or the mighty influence which its systems of government, its modes of thinking and manner of acting, are to have over the destinies of other nations? If we have, we shall be irresistibly compelled to believe that the American people are called upon to act a most distinguished part upon the great theater of the universe.

In proposing the establishment of a society of the kind and for the objects here suggested, I have had equally in view to open wide the doors of the temple of fame to all who, with a laudable ambition, desire to distinguish themselves by rendering essential service to their country, to induce a national manner of thinking and acting on all important matters, and to transfer to other countries and to transmit to distant ages the influence of this manner of thinking and acting, so far as the same is connected with and may tend to perpetuate those rules and principles by which our country is now distinguished from the rest of the world, and from which it derives so many blessings.

I want to establish a society with ample means to reward every exertion of genius which may be displayed, and to call forth every latent genius which our country may possess, to give every possible encouragement to literature, the arts and sciences, and to give to them the stamp and character of America; to wipe away that reproach which foreigners have unjustly cast upon us, and to build up for our country a solid pyramid of fame.

I therefore propose that a national society be established for the encouragement of American literature, and for the promotion of arts and sciences;

That the original subscription for each member be $100, and the annual subscription $25 or $50;

That the number of shares be without limit, and that the original and annual subscriptions be called in only as they are wanted to reward or compensate any extraordinary display of genius;

That the funds of the society be appropriated, under the directions of a committee of the society, in purchasing the copyrights of every valuable literary production, and the patent right of every valuable invention;

That means be adopted by the society to publish and to diffuse over the American empire, and throughout the world, all such works as they become possessed of by purchase, and to make known every useful invention the patent for which may be transferred to them.

I am induced to believe that in time, the sale of copyrights of valuable literary productions, and the sale of patent rights to useful inventions, would more than repay the society what it in the first instance might be required to expend. Suppose $100,000 had been paid for the invention of the method of propelling vessels by steam, would not that right for fourteen years be worth (in the United States only) $1 million?

I will ask, what would be the value of a complete treatise on education, that education obtained in schools, academies, and colleges, and a complete series of books of instruction for every class and grade of learners, provided such treatise on education and such series of books of instruction were universally used in our schools, academies, and colleges? Would not the copyright of such works be cheaply purchased at $100,000?

One grand desideratum in the formation of a society of the nature of the one contemplated would be to give to the American people American modes and habits of thinking and acting; and no time so proper to begin as with the first lessons of instruction; no medium so proper in which to convey these first principles to the mind and fix them there, as in elementary treatises on education.

I can only hope in this short essay to call the attention of my fellow citizens to the importance of the subjects. I do not ever pretend to give the general outlines of the plan, nor so much as notice of many of the effects that would result from its adoption. All that I can hope for at present is to induce them to give a thought toward it.

The thing is new, but, by thinking men, will be anticipated all the mighty consequences to result from the influence of a society holding in its hand $1 million wherewith to reward every exertion of intellect; and, by the munificence of its bounty, calling forth every latent spark of genius; putting under requisition our whole national stock of mental energy; and by hand as liberal, distributing the fair fruits thereof, not only throughout our widely extended empire but to the remotest dwelling of man.

For myself, I can only say, I am ready to advance to a society of this kind, whenever formed, $1,000; and I think I can venture to promise for the counties of Middlesex and Monmouth in New Jersey at least $20,000. A subscription equally liberal throughout the United States would raise a capital of $3 million.

122.

Anonymous: Opposition to Paper Money

The chronic problem of the country during its early years was a scarcity of capital, which went hand in hand with a shortage of hard money (specie). The obvious solution was to print paper currency and other instruments of credit, but these always rapidly depreciated for lack of any regulation. Thus men were divided on the question, whether an absence of specie or an excess of paper was the greater evil. When Hamilton attempted to establish a central credit system by creating the First Bank of the United States, he was opposed both from fear that the Bank's paper would become inflated (it didn't) and on the ground that the credit system would be manipulated to the advantage of specie-holding merchant capitalists (it was). As the First Bank did not solve the money problem for the rest of the country, it was allowed to die when its charter expired in 1811. Its place was taken by state and private banks, of which more than 300 were established. They loaned money freely, but their paper was often unnegotiable even in neighboring communities. After the War of 1812, when a passion for land speculation swept the country, the amount of paper in circulation rose to $100 million, most of it in wildly inflated values. In 1816 the federal government created the Second Bank of the United States to bring order into the financial chaos. But the Second Bank, unlike the First, had to compete with the state banks, which continued to exist beside it. To establish itself, it lent money even more generously than they did, and this only made the situation worse. The result was that in 1818, when the Second Bank was forced to put a brake on its credit, the crash came. By 1819, the entire country was in a severe depression. Before this happened, numerous protests against the banks appeared in newspapers everywhere. The following, from the Niles' Weekly Register, *was published in May 1818. Its claim that "the paper system" was seducing the farmers from the path of virtue was consistent with old Jeffersonian doctrine. Agrarians with fixed capital in land favored hard money. Jefferson himself, in the inflation of post-Revolutionary times, had once been forced to sell a farm to buy an overcoat.*

Source: *Niles' Weekly Register,* May 9, 1818.

The cultivators of the earth constitute the American nation. The products of the soil are its only real and substantial wealth. They furnish the food of man; they give to the merchant the staples of his trade; to the manufacturer, the materials of his workmanship; to the laborer, his most wholesome and virtuous occupation; and to the mechanic, his employment and his bread. Agriculture is the only lasting source of national wealth, because it is independent of those political changes that turn the course of commerce and manufactures into new channels; and its history never presents such examples of short-lived grandeur, founded by permanent decay, as are exhibited by Tyre, Venice, Genoa, and many other states.

An agricultural people belong exclusively to their own country; and are, in a great degree, out of the reach of those regulations made at the pleasure of governments, over which they have no control; which exercise a decisive influence on the well-being of merchants, and render those dependent on commerce almost as much the subjects of every other commercial state as of their own.

Agriculture is, most emphatically, the employment becoming a republican people, since it introduces none of those tremendous inequalities of wealth and poverty that create the materials of tyranny — nobles and beggars, oppressors and slaves. Its gains are moderate and sure; it enriches by salutary degrees, and by the exercise of industry and frugality, the two great pillars of a virtuous state. Its inviolable operation is, in short, to produce a beautiful system of equality — equally removed from the splendid, corrupting prodigality of unbounded wealth, and the debasing wretchedness of pinching poverty. It was *agriculture* that changed the earth from a wilderness to a garden, and man from a brute to a civilized being. Its virtuous labors, while they mellowed the soil, humanized his manners, and turned him from war and plunder, hitherto his only occupations, to cultivate social feelings, to cherish social rights and that sacred good-fellowship which arises from the influence of neighborhood — the interchange of friendly offices and the sense of mutual dependence. . . .

The two boasted benefits which the farmers are said to derive from the paper-rag system are the facility of procuring money from the banks, wherewith to improve their lands, and the increased price of the land, as well as of its produce. As to the first, sir, I am one of those desperate unbelievers who doubt whether the virtue, the happiness, or the prosperity of a people are enhanced by the facility of running in debt. I believe that the only true and lasting basis of honorable and salutary independence, to the laboring classes, is industry and frugality; for I know, by experience, that a dependence on any other props is sure to be followed by idleness, debauchery, extravagance, and ruin. Whenever a state of public feeling is produced, where men are not ashamed of being in debt, the mind loses its proper sense of manly independence; and whenever the salutary obstacles to borrowing money are removed, and men are *invited* to become debtors by the facility of borrowing, the axe is laid to the root of national industry, which is the foundation of national virtue and prosperity. In no well-organized state of society ought the generality of men to become borrowers; and in no class of any community can borrowing become general, without ultimately ending in its ruin. . . .

There *was* a time — I speak in the melancholy *past tense* when recurring to the days of agricultural prosperity — there was a time, when it was disgraceful in a farmer to borrow money, and his respectability was seriously injured by becoming a dependent on banks. These honest people had a just and instinctive abhorrence to these institutions, and, without exactly reasoning on the subject, they arrived at just conclusions. They saw that the art of becoming rich, without either capital or industry — the power of creating wealth from *rags* — must, in the end, inevitably prove highly injurious to every man possessed of real property. It was plain that if men could grow rich by such means, the value of industry and land must continue to diminish insensibly, because it is impossible to give a fictitious value to any imaginary and worthless commodity without diminishing, in the like proportion, the value of what is real.

The farmer had earned dearly the money with which he purchased this land; and when he saw the facility with which land could be acquired without labor or silver or gold, he could not fail to be struck with a conviction of the truth. He saw and felt that the system of rags must either be destroyed or that he must become an accomplice or a victim. These truths are every day coming home to the farmers . . . and we now every day see them, either selling their lands to invest their proceeds in banks; or to flee to some sequestered region where none are to be found; or we see them driven to sacrifice their inheritance to pay their discounts.

Of all men living, the *American farmer* had the least occasion to borrow money. If he was born to the inheritance of a farm, that farm would support him as it did his father before him — if, like him, he was frugal and industrious. If he had no land of his own, he could get it in his neighborhood; he could buy it without money; and pay for it by his industry. The payments were always so proportioned as to give him a fair chance of meeting them from the profits of his land; and, being aware of this, he lost every other dependence but that becoming a man — a dependence on his own exertions. The different periods of payment were distant and certain, and he knew the precise time that they would be demanded. He gave no security but a mortgage on his farm, and he allowed no extraordinary premium on the score of the uncertainty of being able to pay. He could, therefore, pursue the even tenor of his industry without being drawn off every sixty days to raise the ways and means for paying his sixty-day bank accommodations; and seldom, if ever, did it happen that he was forced, as nowadays, to sacrifice his farm and his produce, at half price, to some hungry bank director, to pay a loan, unexpectedly demanded, upon some frivolous pretense. If, in short, he was prudent and industrious — and, without these, even bank loans will not enrich the farmer — he soon became independent; for he did not rely on the conscience of brokers, or the goodwill of the petty directors of a petty village bank, thirsting for his land, because they were poor, and careless of the means of acquiring it — because they were unprincipled.

Or if, sir, he found it difficult to procure a farm on these terms in his more immediate neighborhood, the fertile regions of the West and South, where land was cheap and labor the source of wealth, were open to his enterprise and industry. Here he was certain of independence, and sure to grow moderately rich, as rapidly as it is salutary for a man to become so. He required not a shilling to buy a farm, for his labor was sure to make it his own; and his landlord knew his interest too well not to render the situation of his settlers as easy as possible. There was a contest for settlers, and not for lands on which to settle. I assert, therefore, that the farmers wanted no greater facilities in raising money than they possessed before the erection of a single bank; and I appeal to their present declining state that the facilities they now possess, in consequence of the multiplication of these mischievous and unprincipled institutions, are the sources of their speedy and inevitable decay.

123.

James Madison: Agriculture and Conservation

After leaving the White House Madison remained active, taking part in numerous minor political groups and societies. In 1817 he accepted the presidency of the Albemarle (Virginia) Agricultural Society, a pet project of Jefferson's and one of the first American organizations designed to promote improvements in the field of agriculture. The following selection comprises excerpts from an address delivered to the Society by Madison on May 12, 1818.

Source: *Niles' Weekly Register,* July 18, 1818.

In proportion as we relax the hypothesis which makes the aggregate number of mankind unsusceptible to change, and believe that the resources of our country may not only contribute to the greater happiness of a given number but to the augmentation of the number enjoying a greater happiness, the motives become stronger for the improvement and extension of them.

But, whilst all are sensible that agriculture is the basis of population and prosperity, it cannot be denied that the study and practice of its true principles have hitherto been too generally neglected in the United States; and that this state has at least its full share of the blame. Now only, for the first time, notwithstanding several meritorious examples of earlier date, a general attention seems to be awakened to the necessity of a reform. Patriotic societies, the best agents for effecting it, are pursuing the object with the animation and intelligence which characterize the efforts of a self-governed people, whatever be the objects to which they may be directed.

Among these promising institutions, I cannot glance at all the names of those composing that of Albemarle without being assured that its full quota of information will be furnished to the general stock. I regret only that my own competency bears so little proportion to my wishes to cooperate with them. That I may not be thought, however, deficient in goodwill, as well as in other requisites, I shall venture on the task, a task the least difficult, of pointing out some of the most prevalent errors in our husbandry and which appear to be among those which may merit the attention of the society, and the instructive examples of its members.

I. The error first to be noticed is that of cultivating land, either naturally poor or impoverished by cultivation. This error, like many others, is the effect of habit, continued after the reason for it has failed. Whilst there was an abundance of fresh and fertile soil, it was the interest of the cultivator to spread his labor over as great a surface as he could. Land being cheap and labor dear, and the land cooperating powerfully with the labor, it was profitable to draw as much as possible from the land. Labor is now comparatively cheaper and land dearer. Where labor has risen in price fourfold land has risen tenfold. It might be profitable, therefore, now, to contract the surface over which labor is spread, even if the soil retained its freshness and fertility. But this is not the case. Much of the fertile soil is exhausted, and unfertile soils are brought into cultivation; and both cooperating less with labor in producing the crop, it is necessary to consider how far labor can be profitably exerted on them; whether it ought not to be applied toward making them fertile, rather than in further impoverishing them, or whether it might not be more profitably applied to mechanical occupations, or to domestic manufactures?

In the old countries of Europe, where labor is cheap and land dear, the object is to augment labor, and contract the space on which it is employed. In the new settlements taking place in this country, the original practice here may be rationally pursued. In the old settlements, the reason for the practice in Europe is becoming daily less inapplicable; and we ought to yield to the change of circumstances by forebearing to waste our labor on land which, besides not paying for it, is still more impoverished, and rendered more difficult to be made rich. The crop which is of least amount gives the blow most mortal to the soil. It has not been a very rare thing to see land under the plough not producing enough to feed the ploughman and his horse, and it is in such cases that the death blow is given. The goose is killed, without even obtaining the coveted egg.

There cannot be a more rational principle in the code of agriculture than that every farm which is in good heart should be kept so; that everyone not in good heart should be made so; and that what is right as to the farm, generally, is so as to every part of every farm. Any system therefore, or want of system, which tends to make a rich farm poor, or does not tend to make a poor farm rich, cannot be good for the owner, whatever it may be for the tenant or superintendent, who has transient interest only in it. The profit, where there is any, will not balance the loss of intrinsic value sustained by the land.

II. The evil of pressing too hard upon the land has also been much increased by the bad mode of ploughing it. Shallow ploughing, and ploughing up and down hilly land, have, by exposing the loosened soil to be carried off by rains, hastened more than anything else the waste of its fertility. When the mere surface is pulverized, moderate rains on land but little uneven, if ploughed up and down, gradually wear it away. And heavy rains on hilly land ploughed in that manner soon produce a like effect, notwithstanding the improved practice of deeper ploughing. How have the beauty and value of this red ridge of country suffered from this cause? And how much is due to the happy improvement introduced by a member of this society, whom I need not name, by a cultivation in horizontal drills with a plough adapted to it? Had the practice prevailed from the first settlement of the country, the general fertility would have been more than the double of what the red hills, and indeed all other hilly lands, now possess; and the scars and sores now defacing them would nowhere be seen. Happily, experience is proving that this remedy, aided by a more rational management in other respects, is adequate to the purpose of healing what has been wounded, as well as of preserving the health of what has escaped the calamity. It is truly gratifying to observe how fast the improvement is spreading from the parent example. The value of our red hills, under a mode of cultivation which guards their fertility against wasting rains, is probably exceeded by that of no uplands whatever; and without that advantage they are exceeded in value by almost all others. They are little more than a lease for years.

Besides the inestimable advantage from horizontal ploughing in protecting the soil against the wasting effect of rains, there is a great one in its preventing the rains themselves from being lost to the crop. The Indian corn is the crop which most exposes the soil to be carried off by the rains; and it is at the same time the crop which most needs them. Where the land is not only hilly but the soil thirsty (as is the case particularly throughout this mountainous range), the preservation of the rain as it falls between the drilled ridges is of peculiar importance, and its gradual setting downward the roots is the best possible mode of supplying them with moisture. In the old method of ploughing shallow, with the furrows up and down, the rain as well as the soil was lost.

III. The neglect of manures is another error which claims particular notice. It may be traced to the same cause with our excessive cropping. In the early stages of our agriculture, it was more convenient, and more profitable, to bring new land into cultivation than to improve exhausted land. The failure of new land has long called for the improvement of old land; but habit has kept us deaf to the call. . . .

But the most eligible mode of preserving the richness, and of enriching the poverty of a farm, is certainly that of applying to the soil a sufficiency of animal and vegetable matter in a putrefied state or a state ready for putrefaction; in order to procure which, too much care cannot be observed in saving every material furnished by the farm. This resource was among the earliest discoveries of men living by agriculture, and a proper use of it has been made a test of good husbandry, in all countries, ancient and modern, where its principles and profits have been studied. . . .

With so many consumers of the fertility of the earth, and so little attention to the means of repairing their ravages, no one can be surprised at the impoverished face of the country; whilst everyone ought to be desirous of aiding in the work of reformation.

The first main step toward it is to make the thieves restore as much as possible of the stolen fertility. On this, with other improvements which may be made in our husbandry, we must depend for the rescue of our farms from their present degraded condition. . . .

IV. Among the means aiding the productiveness of the soil which have not received merited attention is irrigation. In scarcely any country does this resource abound more than in the United States; nor is there any where there is so little sensibility to its value. . . .

V. A more manifest error in the husbandry of the older settlements is that of keeping too many neat cattle on their farms. As a farm should not be cultivated farther than it can be continued in good heart, the stock of cattle should not be in greater number than the resources of food will keep in good plight. If a poor farm be unprofitable, so are poor cattle. It is particularly the case with the milch cows. When the whole of the food given them is necessary to support a lean existence, no part can be spared for the milk pail. The same food given to the proper number will not only keep them in a thrifty state but enable them to supply the dairy. Even the manure from several poor cattle is worth less than that from a single fat one. The remark holds equally good with respect to the hide.

The misjudged practice in question is another effect of inattention of the change of circumstances through which our country has passed. Originally the forest abounded in rich herbage which fed and fatted, without expense, all the cattle that could be brought through the winter into the spring.

It was natural at that time to keep as large a stock as could be preserved through the winter. For a long time past, the forest is scarcely anywhere a resource for more than two or three months, and in many places, no resource at all. A greater difficulty is often felt in finding summer, than winter, subsistence. And yet where no inclosed pasturage is provided to take the place of the extinct one in the forest, the habit, founded in reasons which have entirely ceased, is but too generally retained. The same number of cattle is aimed at as if the forest was as ready to receive and fatten them now as formerly. The size and appearance of our neat cattle, compared with those for which nature or good husbandry has provided sufficient food, are proofs that their food is not in proportion to their number, and that where the food cannot be increased, the number ought to be reduced.

VI. Of all the errors in our rural economy none is perhaps so much to be regretted, because none is so difficult to be repaired, as the injudicious and excessive destruction of timber and firewood. It seems never to have occurred that the fund was not inexhaustible, and that a crop of trees could not be raised as quickly as one of wheat or corn.

Here again we are presented with a proof of the continuance of a practice for which the reasons have ceased. When our ancestors arrived, they found the trees of the forest the great obstacle to their settlement and cultivation. The great effort was, of course, to destroy the trees. It would seem that they contracted and transmitted an antipathy to them; for the trees were not even spared around the dwellings, where their shade would have been a comfort and their beauty an ornament; and it is of late years only that these advantages have been attended to. In fact, such has been the inconsiderate and indiscriminate use of the axe that this country is beginning to feel the calamity as much as some of the old countries of Europe; and it will soon be forced to understand the difficulty of curing it. A vast proportion of the farms on the eastern side of the Blue Ridge, and some even on the other side, have but a scanty fund for present use, and are without a fund for permanent use. And to increase the evil, the remnant of timber and fuel on many farms, inadequate as it is, is left in situations remote from the dwelling, and incapable of being divided, according to the divisions and subdivisions into which all the larger farms must be rapidly forced by the law of descents, the impulses of parental affection, and other causes.

It is high time for many farmers, even in this quarter, and still more so in the country below us, to take this subject into serious consideration. Prudence will no longer delay to economize what remains of woodland, to foster the second growths where taking place in convenient spots, and to commence, where necessary, plantations of the trees recommended by their utility and quickness of growth.

I wish I could more satisfactorily estimate the proportion of woodland which ought to belong to every farm as a permanent fund of timber for building and repairing houses; for fences, where live or stone ones may not be introduced; for wheel carriages, and the other apparatus needed on farms. The estimate is the more difficult because it must be varied according to many circumstances; particularly, according to the nature of the soil and the kind of trees at once suited to it and to the uses to be made of them.

Estimating the crop of wood yielded by an acre at twenty cords, the period of reproduction at twenty years, and the average number of cords annually consumed at a fireplace, including the culinary consumption, at ten cords, every fireplace on a farm will require ten acres for a permanent supply of fuel. For the other necessities of a farm several acres more ought to be added.

An estimate in a very sensible publication, entitled *The New England Farmer,* makes seventeen acres necessary for a fireplace. The winters there are longer, and the climate may be less favorable to the quick growth of trees. But their houses are generally closer than with us; to say nothing of a more judicious management than can be forced on most of our farms.

To this catalogue of errors in our rural economy, considerable as it is, many, I fear, might be added. The task of pointing them out I gladly leave to others less incapable than I have shown myself to be, by the very imperfect manner in which I have performed the one on which I ventured.

124.

A Christian Indictment of Slavery

Many Christians in both North and South could not in good conscience reconcile their faith with the institution of slavery. During the nineteenth century the Presbyterian Church played a leading role in the Abolitionist movement. As early as 1787, the Presbyterian Synod of New York and Philadelphia had officially opposed slavery, and in May 1818, the General Assembly of the church issued the following revised and more adamant demand for abolition. The Assembly, which included many Southern members, adopted the report unanimously. Prior to 1820 there was significant anti-slavery sentiment in the South, hence the fact that wholehearted support for the Assembly's position came from the Southern members was not unusual.

Source: *A Collection of the Acts, Deliverances, and Testimonies of the Supreme Judicatory of the Presbyterian Church,* Samuel J. Baird, ed., Philadelphia, 1855, pp. 820-822.

The General Assembly of the Presbyterian Church, having taken into consideration the subject of slavery, think proper to make known their sentiments upon it to the churches and people under their care.

We consider the voluntary enslaving of one part of the human race by another as a gross violation of the most precious and sacred rights of human nature; as utterly inconsistent with the law of God which requires us to love our neighbor as ourselves; and as totally irreconcilable with the spirit and principles of the Gospel of Christ, which enjoin that "all things whatsoever ye would that men should do to you, do ye even so to them." Slavery creates a paradox in the moral system. It exhibits rational, accountable, and immortal beings in such circumstances as scarcely to leave them the power of moral action. It exhibits them as dependent on the will of others whether they shall receive religious instruction, whether they shall know and worship the true God, whether they shall enjoy the ordinances of the gospel, whether they shall perform the duties and cherish the endearments of husbands and wives, parents and children, neighbors and friends, whether they shall preserve their chastity and purity, or regard the dictates of justice and humanity. Such are some of the consequences of slavery, consequences not imaginary but which connect themselves with its very existence.

The evils to which the slave is *always* exposed, often take place in fact, and in their very worst degree and form; and where all of them do not take place, as we rejoice to say that in many instances, through the influence of the principles of humanity and religion on the minds of masters they do not, still the slave is deprived of his natural right, degraded as a human being, and exposed to the danger of passing into the hands of a master who may inflict upon him all the hardships and injuries which inhumanity and avarice may suggest.

From this view of the consequences resulting from the practice into which Christian people have most inconsistently fallen of enslaving a portion of their brethren of mankind, for "God hath made of one blood all nations of men to dwell on the face of the earth," it is manifestly the duty of all Christians who enjoy the light of the present day, when the inconsistency of slavery, both with the dictates of humanity and religion, has been demonstrated, and is generally seen and acknowledged, to use their honest, earnest, and unwearied endeavors to correct the errors of former times, and as speedily as possible to efface this blot on our holy religion, and to obtain the complete abolition of slavery throughout Christendom, and if possible throughout the world.

We rejoice that the church to which we belong commenced as early as any other in this country the good work of endeavoring to put an end to slavery, and that in the same work, many of its members have ever since been, and now are, among the most active, vigorous, and efficient laborers. We do, indeed, tenderly sympathize with those portions of our church and our country where the evil of slavery has been entailed upon them; where a great, and the most virtuous part of the community abhor slavery and wish its extermination as sincerely as any others, but where the number of slaves, their ignorance, and their vicious habits generally render an immediate and universal emancipation inconsistent alike with the safety and happiness of the master and the slave. With those who are thus circumstanced, we repeat that we tenderly sympathize. At the same time, we earnestly exhort them to continue and, if possible, to increase their exertions to effect a total abolition of slavery. We exhort them to suffer no greater delay to take place in this most interesting concern than a regard to the public welfare truly and indispensably demands.

As our country has inflicted a most grievous injury upon the unhappy Africans by bringing them into slavery, we cannot, indeed, urge that we should add a second injury to the first by emancipating them in such manner as that they will be likely to destroy themselves or others. But we do think that our country ought to be governed in this matter by no other consideration than an honest and impartial regard to the happiness of the injured party; uninfluenced by the expense or inconvenience which such a regard may involve. We therefore warn all who belong to our denomination of Christians against unduly extending this plea of necessity, against making it a cover for the love and practice of slavery, or a pretense for not using efforts that are lawful and practicable to extinguish the evil.

And we, at the same time, exhort others to forbear harsh censures and uncharitable reflections on their brethren who unhappily live among slaves whom they cannot immediately set free, but who, at the same time, are really using all their influence, and all their endeavors, to bring them into a state of freedom as soon as a door for it can be safely opened.

Having thus expressed our views of slavery, and of the duty indispensably incumbent on all Christians to labor for its complete extinction, we proceed to recommend (and we do it with all the earnestness and solemnity which this momentous subject demands) a particular attention to the following points.

1. We recommend to all our people to patronize and encourage the society, lately formed, for colonizing in Africa, the land of their ancestors, the free people of color in our country. We hope that much good may result from the plans and efforts of this society. And while we exceedingly rejoice to have witnessed its origin and organization among the holders of slaves, as giving an unequivocal pledge of their desires to deliver themselves and their country from the calamity of slavery; we hope that those portions of the American Union whose inhabitants are by a gracious Providence more favorably circumstanced will cordially, and liberally, and earnestly cooperate with their brethren in bringing about the great end contemplated.

2. We recommend to all the members of our religious denomination not only to permit but to facilitate and encourage the instruction of their slaves in the principles and duties of the Christian religion, by granting them liberty to attend on the preaching of the gospel when they have the opportunity, by favoring the instruction of them in Sabbath schools, wherever those schools can be formed, and by giving them all other proper advantages for acquiring the knowledge of their duty both to God and man. We are perfectly satisfied that as it is incumbent on all Christians to communicate religious instruction to those who are under their authority, so that the doing of this in the case before us, so far from operating, as some have apprehended that it might, as an excitement to insubordination and insurrection would, on the contrary, operate as the most powerful means for the prevention of those evils.

3. We enjoin it on all church sessions and presbyteries, under the care of this Assembly, to discountenance, and, as far as possible, to prevent, all cruelty of whatever kind in the treatment of slaves; especially the cruelty of separating husband and wife, parents and children, and that which consists in selling slaves to those who will either themselves deprive these unhappy people of the blessings of the gospel, or who will transport them to places where the gospel is not proclaimed, or where it is forbidden to slaves to attend upon its institutions.

And if it shall ever happen that a Christian professor in our communion shall sell a slave who is also in communion and good standing with our church contrary to his or her will and inclination, it ought immediately to claim the particular attention of the proper church judicature; and unless there be such peculiar circumstances attending the case as can but seldom happen, it ought to be followed, without delay, by a suspension of the offender from all the privileges of the church till he repent and make all the reparation in his power to the injured party.

125.

Report on the Proposed University of Virginia

"We wish to establish in the upper and healthier country, and more centrally for the state," wrote Thomas Jefferson to Joseph Priestley in 1800, "a university on a plan so broad and liberal and modern, as to be worth patronizing with the public support, and be a temptation to the youth of other states to come, and drink the cup of knowledge and fraternize with us." However, it was nineteen years before Jefferson's dream became a reality. His plans for the school included a student government and a course of elective studies — very progressive ideas for the time. The Rockfish Gap Commission, which included Jefferson and Madison, was charged in 1818 with deciding on a suitable location for the University of Virginia. Reprinted here is a portion of the commission's report, which faithfully echoed Jefferson's ideas on education. When the University was finally chartered in 1819, Jefferson was appointed its first rector.

Source: *Report of the Commissioners Appointed to Fix the Scite of the University of Virginia*, Richmond, 1818.

In proceeding to the third and fourth duties prescribed by the legislature of reporting "the branches of learning which should be taught in the university, and the number and description of the professorships they will require," the commissioners were first to consider at what point it was understood that university education should commence. Certainly not with the alphabet, for reasons of expediency and impracticability as well as from the obvious sense of the legislature, who, in the same act, make other provision for the primary instruction of poor children, expecting doubtless that, in other cases, it would be provided by the parent or become, perhaps, a subject of future and further attention for the legislature. The objects of this primary education determine its character and limits. These objects would be:

To give to every citizen the information he needs for the transaction of his own business.

To enable him to calculate for himself, and to express and preserve his ideas, his contracts and accounts in writing.

To improve, by reading, his morals and faculties.

To understand his duties to his neighbors and country, and to discharge with competence the functions confided to him by either.

To know his rights; to exercise with order and justice those he retains; to choose with discretion the fiduciaries of those he delegates; and to notice their conduct with diligence, with candor, and judgment.

And, in general, to observe with intelligence and faithfulness all the social relations under which he shall be placed.

To instruct the mass of our citizens in these their rights, interests, and duties as men and citizens, being then the objects of education in the primary schools, whether private or public, in them should be taught reading, writing, and numerical arithmetic, the elements of mensuration (useful in so many callings), and the outlines of geography and history. And this brings us to the point at which are to commence the higher branches of education, of which the legislature require the development; those, for example, which are:

To form the statesmen, legislators, and judges on whom public prosperity and individual happiness are so much to depend.

To expound the principles and structure of government; the laws which regulate the intercourse of nations; those formed municipally for our own government; and a sound spirit of legislation which, banishing all arbitrary and unnecessary restraint on individual action, shall leave us free to do whatever does not violate the equal rights of another.

To harmonize and promote the interests of agriculture, manufactures, and commerce, and, by well-informed views of political economy, to give a free scope to the public industry.

To develop the reasoning faculties of our youth, enlarge their minds, cultivate their morals, and instill into them the precepts of virtue and order.

To enlighten them with mathematical and physical sciences which advance the arts and administer to the health, the subsistence, and comforts of human life.

And generally to form them to habits of reflection and correct action, rendering them examples of virtue to others and of happiness within themselves.

These are the objects of that higher grade of education, the benefits and blessings of which the legislature now propose to provide for the good and ornament of their country, the gratification and happiness of their fellow citizens, of the parent especially and his progeny on which all his affections are concentrated.

In entering on this field, the commissioners are aware that they have to encounter much difference of opinion as to the extent which it is expedient that this institution should occupy. Some good men, and even of respectable information, consider the learned sciences as useless acquirements; some think that they do not better the condition of man; and others that education, like private and individual concerns, should be left to private and individual effort, not reflecting that an establishment, embracing all the sciences which may be useful and even necessary in the various vocations of life, with the buildings and apparatus belonging to each, are far beyond the reach of individual means and must either derive existence from public patronage or not exist at all. This would leave us, then, without those callings which depend on education, or send us to other countries to seek the instruction they require.

But the commissioners are happy in considering the statute under which they are assembled as proof that the legislature is far from the abandonment of objects so interesting. They are sensible that the advantages of well-directed education, moral, political, and economical, are truly above all estimate. Education generates habits of application, of order, and the love of virtue, and controls, by the force of habit, any innate obliquities in our moral organization. We should be far, too, from the discouraging persuasion that man is fixed by the law of his nature at a given point, that his improvement is a chimera, and the hope delusive of rendering ourselves wiser, happier, or better than our forefathers were. As well might it be urged that the wild and uncultivated tree, hitherto yielding sour and bitter fruit only, can never be made to yield better. Yet we know that the grafting art implants a new tree on the savage stock, producing what is most estimable both in kind and degree.

Education in like manner engrafts a new man on the native stock, and improves what in his nature was vicious and perverse into qualities of virtue and social worth; and it cannot be but that each generation, succeeding to the knowledge acquired by all those who preceded it, adding to it their own acquisitions and discoveries, and handing the mass down for successive and constant accumulation, must advance the knowledge and well-being of mankind; not infinitely, as some have said, but indefinitely, and to a term which no one can fix or foresee. Indeed, we need look back half a century, to times which many now living remember well, and see the wonderful advances in the sciences and arts which have been made within that period. Some of these have rendered the elements themselves subservient to the purposes of man, have harnessed them to the yoke of his labors, and effected the great blessings of moderating his own, of accomplishing what was beyond his feeble force, and extending the comforts of life to a much enlarged circle, to those who had before known its necessaries only.

That these are not the vain dreams of sanguine hope, we have before our eyes real and living examples. What but education has advanced us beyond the condition of our indigenous neighbors? And what chains them to their present state of barbarism and wretchedness but a bigoted veneration for the supposed superlative wisdom of their fathers and the preposterous idea that they are to look backward for better things and not forward, longing, as it should seem, to return to the days of eating acorns and roots rather than indulge in the degeneracies of civilization. And how much more encouraging to the achievements of science and improvement is this than the desponding view that the condition of man cannot be ameliorated, that what has been must ever be, and that to secure ourselves where we are, we must tread with awful reverence in the footsteps of our fathers.

This doctrine is the genuine fruit of the alliance between church and state, the tenants of which, finding themselves but too well in their present position, oppose all advances which might unmask their usurpations and monopolies of honors, wealth, and power, and fear every change as endangering the comforts they now hold. Nor must we omit to mention, among the benefits of education, the incalculable advantage of training up able counselors to administer the affairs of our country in all its departments, legislative, executive, and judiciary, and to bear their proper share in the councils of our national government; nothing more than education, advancing the prosperity, the power and the happiness of a nation.

Encouraged, therefore, by the sentiments of the legislature, manifested in this statute, we present the following . . . statement of the branches of learning which we think should be taught in the university. . . .

A professor is proposed for ancient languages — the Latin, Greek, and Hebrew, particularly — but these languages being the foundation common to all the sciences, it is difficult to foresee what may be the extent of this school. At the same time, no greater obstruction to industrious study could be proposed than the presence, the intrusions, and the noisy turbulence of a multitude of small boys; and if they are to be placed here for the rudiments of the languages, they may be so numerous that its character and value as a university will be merged in those of a grammar school. It is, therefore, greatly to be wished that preliminary schools, either on private or public establishment, could be distributed in districts through the state as preparatory to the entrance of students into the university.

The tender age at which this part of education commences, generally about the tenth year, would weigh heavily with parents in sending their sons to a school so distant as the central establishment would be from most of them. Districts of such extent as that every parent should be within a day's journey of his son at school would be desirable in cases of sickness, and convenient for supplying their ordinary wants, and might be made to lessen sensibly the expense of this part of their education. And where a sparse population would not, within such a compass, furnish subjects sufficient to maintain a school, a competent enlargement of district must, of necessity, there be submitted to. . . .

Until this preparatory provision shall be made, either the university will be overwhelmed with the grammar school, or a separate establishment, under one or more ushers for its lower classes, will be advisable, at a mile or two distance from the general one, where, too, may be exercised the stricter government necessary for young boys, but unsuitable for youths arrived at years of discretion.

The considerations which have governed the specification of languages to be taught by the professor of modern languages were that the French is the language of general intercourse among nations, and as a depository of human science is unsurpassed by any other language, living or dead; that the Spanish is highly interesting to us as the language spoken by so great a portion of the inhabitants of our continents with whom we shall probably have great intercourse ere long, and is that also in which is written the greater part of the earlier history of America. The Italian abounds with works of very superior order, valuable for their matter, and still more distinguished as models of the finest taste in style and composition; and the German now stands in a line with that of the most learned nations in richness of erudition and advance in the sciences. It is, too, of common descent with the language of our own country, a branch of the same original Gothic stock, and furnishes valuable illustrations for us.

But in this point of view, Anglo-Saxon is of peculiar value. We have placed it among the modern languages because it is in fact that which we speak, in the earliest form in which we have knowledge of it. It has been undergoing, with time, those gradual changes which all languages, ancient and modern, have experienced, and, even now, needs only to be printed in the modern character and orthography to be intelligible, in a considerable degree, to an English reader. It has this value, too, above the Greek and Latin, that, while it gives the radix of the mass of our language, they explain its innovations only. Obvious proofs of this have been presented to the modern reader in the disquisitions of Horn Tooke, and Fortescue Aland has well explained the great instruction which may be derived from it toward a full understanding of our ancient common law, on which, as a stock, our whole system of law is engrafted.

It will form the first link in the chain of an historical review of our language through all its successive changes to the present day; will constitute the foundation of that critical instruction in it which ought to be found in a seminary of general learning, and thus reward amply the few weeks of attention which would alone be requisite for its attainment. A language already fraught with all the eminent science of our parent country, the future vehicle of whatever we may ourselves achieve, and destined to occupy so much space on the globe claims distinguished attention in American education.

Medicine, where fully taught, is usually subdivided into several professorships, but this cannot well be without the accessory of a hospital where the student can have the benefit of attending clinical lectures and of assisting at operations of surgery. With this accessory the seat of our university is not yet prepared, either by its population or by the numbers of poor who would leave their own houses and accept of the charities of a hospital. For the present, therefore, we propose but a single professor for both medicine and anatomy. By him the elements of medical science may be taught, with a history and explanations of all its successive theories from Hippocrates to the present day: and anatomy may be fully treated. Vegetable pharmacy will make a part of the botanical course, and mineral and chemical pharmacy, of those of mineralogy and chemistry.

This degree of medical information is

such as the mass of scientific students would wish to possess, as enabling them, in their course through life, to estimate with satisfaction the extent and limits of the aid to human life and health which they may understandingly expect from that art. And it constitutes a foundation for those intended for the profession, that the finishing course of practice at the bedsides of the sick, and at the operations of surgery in a hospital, can neither be long nor expensive. To seek this finishing elsewhere must therefore be submitted to for awhile.

In conformity with the principles of our constitution, which places all sects of religion on an equal footing, with the jealousies of the different sects in guarding that equality from encroachment and surprise, and with the sentiments of the legislature in favor of freedom of religion manifested on former occasions, we have proposed no professor of divinity; and the rather, as the proofs of the being of a God, the Creator, Preserver, and Supreme Ruler of the universe, the Author of all the relations of morality, and of the laws and obligations these infer, will be within the province of the professor of ethics; to which, adding the developments of these moral obligations, of those in which all sects agree, with a knowledge of the languages Hebrew, Greek, and Latin, a basis will be formed common to all sects. Proceeding thus far without offense to the constitution, we have thought it proper, at this point, to leave every sect to provide as they think fittest the means of further instruction in their own peculiar tenets.

We are further of opinion that, after declaring by law that certain sciences shall be taught in the university, fixing the number of professors they require, which we think should at present be ten, limiting (except as to the professors who shall be first engaged in each branch) a maximum for their salaries (which should be a certain but moderate subsistence, to be made up by liberal tuition fees, as an excitement to assiduity), it will be best to leave to the discretion of the visitors the grouping of these sciences together, according to the accidental qualifications of the professors; and the introduction also of other branches of science, when enabled by private donations or by public provision, and called for by the increase of population or other change of circumstances; to establish beginnings, in short, to be developed by time as those who come after us shall find expedient. They will be more advanced than we are in science and in useful arts, and will know best what will suit the circumstances of their day.

We have proposed no formal provision for the gymnastics of the school, although a proper object of attention for every institution of youth. These exercises with ancient nations constituted the principal part of the education of their youth. Their arms and mode of warfare rendered them severe in the extreme; ours, on the same correct principle, should be adapted to our arms and warfare; and the manual exercise, military maneuvers, and tactics generally should be the frequent exercises of the students in their hours of recreation. It is at that age of aptness, docility, and emulation of the practices of manhood that such things are soonest learned and longest remembered.

The use of tools, too, in the manual arts is worthy of encouragement, by facilitating to such as choose it an admission into the neighboring workshops. To these should be added the arts which embellish life, dancing, music, and drawing; the last more especially as an important part of military education. These innocent arts furnish amusement and happiness to those who, having time on their hands, might less inoffensively employ it. Needing, at the same time, no regular incorporation with the institution, they may be left to accessory teachers, who will be paid by the individuals employing them, the university only providing proper apartments for their exercise.

126.

Public Works in the State of Virginia

Virginia was one of the first states to undertake a public works program for internal improvements as well as economic development. In order to design and execute its program, the Virginia Board of Public Works called on the services of Loammi Baldwin, Jr., a famous civil engineer from Boston, acclaimed by a biographer as the "father of civil engineering in America." In December 1818, the Board submitted the following annual report, based on Baldwin's recommendations to the Virginia legislature.

Source: *North American Review*, December 1818.

EVER SINCE OUR ANCESTORS founded this new family among nations, we have been in a continual bustle and stir to supplant the old tenants, to arrange our great and increasing household, and to dispose of its members among the departments and recesses of this extensive and fair domain. No sooner had a small number fixed themselves in a comfortable situation than a spirit of inquiry and boldness of enterprise rendered them restless. New discoveries led to new emigration; love of safety and of social ties yielded to a love of territory and power; and the consequent dispersion of the early colonists has been continued among their descendants to the present day, when the limits of our territory and population are scarcely discernible toward the west.

It is remarkable that, in spite of this spreading emigration which so powerfully counteracts the growth of useful arts, we should, in two centuries, be so little behind Europe, where a thousand years have been spent in labor, invention, and experience to bring them to their present state of improvement. But we must not be too proud of our advantages, nor mistake the cause which produced them.

We should recollect that Europe has been at work many ages for our benefit, and that our philosophy, our science, our literature, and our arts come from her, ready made up for our use. Our habits, manners, fashions, modes of worship, morals, laws, and forms of government, as well as ourselves, have all sprung from the great European fountain, whence has flowed, and still flows, a rich and constant stream of learning and intellect. Our social and moral powers are excited and brightened by the familiar intercourse between this country and Europe; but many of our inventive faculties are inactive because we have few occasions for invention. In its place a habit of copying, and of copying well, has grown up with us. Our mechanic arts are devoted to the imitation or manufacturing of articles or fabrics from models taken out of foreign workshops; we make roads and canals, and improve rivers; build docks and improve our harbors from plans of similar works in France and England. We do all these as the means of acquiring wealth; in Europe wealth has produced them. Here we endeavor to add them to the natural advantages of our country, and begin in our infancy to construct works which are there considered as the monuments of extensive opulence, population, and refinement. . . .

If we examine ourselves as a nation, we shall be at no loss to discover that it is our limited application of this principle — the division of labor — which has placed us behind Europe in arts, science, and literature. But the examination neither excites our regret nor wounds our pride. Industry, in civil society, is as natural as the love of light; it is always striving to multiply and magnify its products, and tends as steadily to separate workmen into classes as the love of independence to separate them into families. All this, however, is the result of individual, unassociated effort; it is slow, but sure in its progress, and does not spring at once into being from any combination or compact; it is founded in self-love, which will act, and which no moral or political power can check or control.

There are other means of promoting the public prosperity which are not so obvious, and depend in some way or other on the good will, sanction, and assistance of the community. These are the works of ingenious and literary men; of men who study the laws of motion and the constitution of things; who improve our moral capacities; who reveal the occult laws of nature, and instruct us how to apply discoveries in science to the useful arts; who teach us how to think, to reason, to feel, and how to labor and how to be happy; of men who toil for the public, and get little or no return for their exertions.

We would gladly proceed to extend these remarks, and exemplify them in detail; but we must, for the present, forgo that pleasure, and introduce to the notice of our readers the important, wise and effectual plan for the improvement of our country which gave rise to them, and which, in our opinion, is better suited to the existing calls of the nation, and will do more for the encouragement of useful science and for the development of our physical resources than any institution in the United States.

The Board of Public Works in the State of Virginia was established by an act of the General Assembly, passed February 1816, entitled "An Act creating a fund for internal improvement." Thirteen members constitute the Board, who are called by the act, "The President and Directors of the Board of Public Works." Of these, the governor, the attorney general, and the treasurer of the commonwealth are *ex officio* members, and the governor is the president of the Board. The ten other members are elected annually by the assembly, in certain proportions, from different sections of the state. They hold their annual meetings at Richmond, during the session of the General Assembly, and receive the same pay and compensation as the members of the House of Delegates. The Board has the control and management of the fund for internal improvement, which will be presently noticed; they have power to fill any vacancy that may happen during the year, and to appoint a treasurer, secretary, principal engineer and assistants, etc., and to fix the salaries of the different officers. In short, the Board has the usual powers of corporations, and are bound by the act to make an annual report to the legislature of all their proceedings.

The objects of internal improvement, in aid of which the Board is authorized to subscribe in behalf of the state, are canals, roads, opening river navigation, etc. For these purposes, the act prescribes the circumstances under which the application of the funds shall be made. On the request of any company or commissioners for carrying into effect any project for internal improvement, the Board directs their engineer to make the preliminary surveys, examination, levels, and estimates, and if, upon his report, it shall appear to them that the proposed work will be of public utility, and promises a reimbursement, by tolls, etc., of the expense, the Board are allowed to subscribe two-fifths of the amount of stock necessary to complete the work.

But the most effectual and liberal assistance arises from the condition of this subscription, which is that no toll, interest, or dividend is to be received by the Board on their two-fifths until the other, private stockholders of the company shall have received a net profit of 6 percent on their three-fifths of the stock; and when the net proceeds of the work shall amount to more than 6 percent on three-fifths of the stock, and not until then, does the public receive any share in the profit.

The first annual report of the Board to the General Assembly was made on the 19th of December, 1816. It contains a statement of the funds committed to their management; observations upon the nature of the works which the Board think important to the public; with documents relative to the Little River Turnpike, Dismal Swamp Canal, Appomattox Canal, Potomac Canal, and James River Canal companies, together with the resolutions of the Board concerning the objects of primary importance in internal improvement, and the correspondence in which the Board had previously been engaged concerning the election of a principal engineer. . . .

On the 12th day of November, 1816, the president and directors proceeded to the appointment of a principal engineer, when Loammi Baldwin, Esq., of Massachusetts was chosen, and we cannot give a better account of the objects and policy of the Board than by showing how the engineer has been employed in their service.

The first object to which he was called was the examination and survey of the Rappahannock and Rapidan rivers, for the purpose of opening the navigation from the tidewater at Fredericksburg, about forty miles on each stream. His report, with a plan, was made to the Board, in which the engineer recommends a system of navigation for small rivers, uninterrupted and complete through the whole season, for boats carrying from fifteen to twenty tons. This, however, was considered by the Rappahannock Company as too expensive for their means, and he was again called upon by a committee of the Board to revise his report, and reduce the estimate to a scale of navigation similar to that now used on the James River. Accordingly he made out a new estimate, by which the cost of the work was reduced to $200,000. This was perfectly satisfactory to the Board and the company, and the Board immediately subscribed for two-fifths of the stock, and the work has already been, or soon will be, commenced.

It appears that Mr. Baldwin's scheme was to erect dams across the rivers at suitable places, with locks, and thus to deepen the water over the rocks and other obstructions, and, as far as possible, to convert the rivers into canals. This is certainly an excellent plan, and in many parts of our country may be adopted with more ease and safety than is generally supposed. But it will require great judgment and experience in the engineer to determine where this system can be successfully adopted. The quantity of water which the stream discharges, its depth, width, velocity, bed, and all its physical characters must be carefully ascertained before any safe result can be predicated. . . .

The next duty to which the engineer was called by the Board of Public Works was the survey and examination of a route for a road and water communication between the eastern and western borders of the state. . . .

The duty assigned to the engineer by the direction of the Board occupied him above three months. His report to the Board accompanies theirs to the legislature, and fills almost thirty pages. He began his survey at Looney's Creek. This is the highest point to which the navigation of James River has been opened by the James River Company, and is about 230 miles above Richmond.

From Looney's Creek to the mouth of the Cowpasture River, the head of James River, the distance is over 24 miles, and the ascent 234 feet; thence up Jackson's River to the mouth of Dunlap's Creek, 36 miles, the ascent is 170 feet. From the mouth of Dunlap's Creek, the line for a road to the great falls of the Kanawha is nearly 100 miles, and the Kanawha River, from the foot of the falls to its junction with the Ohio, is 91 miles, having a fall of 100 feet.

A water communication from the Roanoke River, across the country to the Appomattox near Petersburg, or to the James River, has long engaged the attention of gentlemen interested in the intermediate territory, and the merchants in Petersburg concerned in the interior trade of Virginia and the northwest part of North Carolina. Upon an application of the citizens of Petersburg, the Board of Public Works directed their engineer to make the survey, and run the levels for a canal to connect the waters of the Roanoke with those of the Appomattox, the expenses of the survey to be defrayed by the applicants.

In examining the country over which this canal was contemplated, many difficulties presented themselves. The Roanoke, the Meherrin, the Nottoway, and the Appomattox rivers descend from the highlands in the vicinity of the Blue Ridge and the Allegheny mountains, in nearly parallel directions. To open a water communication from the first to the last mentioned river, the Meherrin and the Nottoway rivers, with many smaller streams, must be crossed; and the land between them rises in high ridges, some of which, especially that between the Roanoke and Meherrin, must be tunneled After exploring the left bank of the Roanoke, from Goode's Ferry in Mecklenburg County 20 miles to the boundary line of North Carolina, no place was found so eligible for communicating with the Roanoke as by Miles Creek, which empties into that river at Goode's Ferry. Here the survey was begun, and carried over the ridge and down Mountain Creek to the Meherrin. The distance was 18 miles, the highest part of the ridge 232 feet, and the surface of the Meherrin 10 feet above the level of the Roanoke. A level was then taken 20 feet above the Meherrin and carried down the left bank of that stream to Brunswick Court House, and then over the intermediate ridge between Rose Creek and Sturgeon Creek to the Nottoway at Cut Bank Bridge. From this place to Petersburg, there appears to be little difficulty in executing a canal, the distance being 30 miles.

The whole line surveyed is about 90 miles, and the estimated expense $2,000,000. It is expected an application will be made to the General Assembly next winter for an act of incorporation. The report and plan of this survey have been made to the Board by the engineer, and will be communicated to the legislature and the public in their next annual report. . . .

We have given this sketch of the views of the government in establishing the Board, the funds set apart and devoted to objects of internal improvement, the organization of the Board and the services in which their principal engineer has been employed, that our readers may form a general notion of this new and important institution. Indeed, whatever view we take of the Board of Public Works in Virginia, we consider it not only honorable to that state, as being the first establishment of the kind in the United States, but also as leading the way to the most valuable, permanent, and economical scale of national improvement the country is susceptible of. Like all new projects, however high and honorable their objects, this Board has met with opposition; in the General Assembly last winter, a resolution was introduced for abolishing the Board and transferring their duties to the governor and Council. The reasons on which the motion was made, we deem it unnecessary to state, as the report of the committee appointed to take the subject into consideration, although favorable to the views of the mover, was rejected by a powerful majority, and the Board consequently more firmly established in the good opinion and confidence of the public.

Before we lay aside this report of the Board, we feel a strong inclination to recommend this establishment to the attention and careful examination of our readers. We shall proceed to state some of the beneficial influences which similar institutions in every state would have upon the interior improvement of the country.

The profession of a civil engineer is scarcely known among us. Whenever any new work is to be undertaken, it is no difficult task to find men of strong minds, good sense, with a little practice and skill, to superintend the execution. Such men are numerous and generally have moderate pay. Their labors, though not always judicious, are for the most part successful; but whether the best plan has been adopted, or whether much expense might not have been avoided, excites no inquiry or criticism where so few are qualified to judge. In bridge architecture, our country abounds with beautiful specimens both in carpentry and mechanical invention. But we do not build in stone or iron, and scarcely has one wooden bridge been erected where the plan, with the number and adjustment of parts, has been founded on purely scientific principles. Our ingenious artificers pursue the right onward path of practice, without minute investigations of the strength of materials, center of oscillation, or the balance of forces; and it is certainly an honorable evidence of the general improvement of the people that such men are so frequently found, and that their works are so promptly and effectually accomplished.

In hydraulic architecture, opportunities seldom arise for the application of much genius or science. To construct a canal, it would hardly be thought necessary now to employ a regular engineer. Digging a wide ditch, blasting rocks, and laying a few short walls for locks are things of everyday experience, and when one undertaking is finished, the laborers, masons, carpenters, superintendents, and all retire to their usual occupations from which for a short time they have thus been called. All the advantages which practice has thus bestowed are lost to the public, without one individual having acquired any information that can be useful to the community in similar works.

In the construction of roads, a proposition to employ a professed engineer would excite laughter. Every able-bodied man in the community is considered as competent to such work, and after the surveyor has staked or blazed out the line, the work is commenced by a great many individuals, and executed in as many different manners as there are contractors. Our highways, especially in New England, are certainly very good, but there are many which might have been better constructed at first, and much of the subsequent expense of keeping them in repair avoided. From this carelessness about the adoption of proper forms and materials, no good plan or safe mode of working has been adopted, nor any general fund or depository established where useful and safe information, science, or practice can be procured.

Hydraulic structures in rivers and currents of water are attended with greater embarrassments. In this branch of engineering, workmen are not so easily found. Bold and enterprising contractors, so frequently met with to undertake any part of roads and navigable canals, are too cautious to combat the subtle operation of hydraulic laws, and in no department of the profession are there so many instances of failure. But even the great faults daily committed by inexperienced and ill-informed workmen have their use. Whoever consults the works of European engineers will perceive that the failures in labors of this kind have taught useful lessons to those who have followed the unsuccessful projectors; but knowledge thus acquired is necessarily limited in its application, and perhaps a plan altogether bad for one situation may be the best for another place near it on the same river. From the want of that union of sound science and extensive practice which constitutes a good engineer, serious injuries to the navigation of rivers have frequently occurred. The operation of hydraulic principles is superficially understood by many people who presume to change their effects without a single correct notion of their laws. . . .

From this view of the manner in which the profession of an engineer has been kept from rising to the notice and encouragement its importance demands, we may perceive why so little information can be procured, and so few men found capable of directing costly and difficult works. Few minds are competent to the arduous studies, critical observation, and philosophical mechanics on which alone a valuable artist can be formed. No school has been opened, no board of works created, no society of engineers established, nor any constant, profitable employment offered in the United States for the encouragement of this highly valuable but unaspiring profession.

Whatever experience has or might have taught is scattered among a multitude of ingenious and contriving men, without anyone having been employed long enough to rise into prominent reputation. In the acquisition of science still fewer are to be met with. Many little tracts are published and read upon different subjects, where a hasty and superficial knowledge only can be gathered, and all that is thus acquired rises only a little above the ordinary contents of newspapers. The valuable experiments and analytical investigations of French and English philosophers and engineers are scarcely known in this country, and whoever would make the profession a study must be at great expense in collecting books. The works of the early Italian writers must be followed with great caution, the French abound with elegant and deep mathematical analyses, and the English books upon the subject are few and incomplete. . . .

Under these circumstances, there is little to flatter the hope or awaken the pride of anyone disposed to follow the profession; and to these difficulties may be ascribed the want of scientific, safe, practical, civil engineers in the United States. . . .

Without a knowledge of the theory of rivers, we hazard much in setting about any of the works usually built in them. If we have occasion to build dams; to improve the navigation of rivers; build piers and abutments for bridges; construct weirs or overfalls; contract the bed or deepen the channel; defend lands from freshes; construct dikes for reclaiming our salt marshes from the sea, or other purposes; erect mills; calculate the quantity of water a river, pond, or other source will furnish; ascertain what is the effect of a dam or other obstruction upon the stream, either above or below it; fix the dimensions of a conduit pipe to bring water to towns or houses; change the direction of currents; remove bars or other obstructions which injure river navigation; determine the dimensions of canals and the forms of boats to navigate them; if we wish to do any of these and many other things of the kind, we must go back to scientific researches and experiments for a satisfactory solution. Let any man attend our courts of law, and witness the trials arising under the Mill Act, as it is called, in Massachusetts, and he will see how little is understood by the parties, their witnesses, or counsel of the real cause of the evil, or the laws of hydraulics, which alone can furnish a correct decision.

For want of extensive acquaintance with this science, many bridges, having been injudiciously placed and erected over rivers, have been swept away by freshes, and examples might easily be named where attempts to remove sandbars and improve river navigation have not only failed but greater evils have been created by the unsuccessful trials.

We shall now recur again to the Board of Public Works in Virginia, and recommend it, as a novel experiment to be sure, but an experiment, in our opinion, admirably calculated in all its relations to society, as a model for similar institutions in each state, that would combine and concentrate all the science and experience relative to civil engineering. We will not inquire whether the Virginia Board is, in all respects, founded on the best plan, and organized in the best manner the nature of the establishment would admit. It is new and, probably, has not yet come to its proper bearing, either in its labors, its tendency, or public opinion; therefore, all criticism would be premature and unfair. As far as we can judge from the eminent and enlightened men who brought forward this subject in the Virginia legislature, and from the caution, wisdom, activity, and perseverance which have marked the proceedings of that Board hitherto — we speak from personal acquaintance with most of the members, as well as with the acts of the Board — we have no hesitation in believing it will be extremely useful to that commonwealth, that it is in every respect worthy of public confidence, and is being imitated in every state in the Union.

Let us then suppose a Board of Public Works, or some establishment of the kind, to be founded in Massachusetts, with powers and duties like those given to the Virginia Board; and who can doubt of its utility and extensive influence? Some of the leading advantages we will state, because we are persuaded that there are many intelligent men in our legislature who would take pride in advocating and promoting a rational plan for improving the condition of our country.

In the first place, there would be at least one engineer of the commonwealth who might devote all his time to the study and practice of his profession, whose salary and occasional employment by private companies or individuals would give him a sufficient and honorable support. There would thus be a professional character, to whom the public might confidently resort for surveys, plans, estimates, etc., in all great undertakings and public buildings.

Second, the office of the Board would collect all the records, reports, plans, etc., of canals, roads, docks, and every species of labor connected with internal communications. Surveys of towns and roads, all the documents relative to canals either begun or contemplated, schemes for the improvement of rivers either for navigation or manufactures, and plans of bridges, docks, etc., might be collected in one place, from which could be obtained important information concerning the commercial and internal improvement of the state.

Third, the Board should gradually collect books and instruments connected with the science and practice of engineering. Neither of these are possessed by individuals in great numbers, and if any person seeks for them in the shops or bookstores in the United States, he will be disappointed. He must import them for his own use at great expense. Small appropriations of money for these several objects can surely be no objection in the beginning, but a beginning is indispensable. We are not advocating the cause of any individuals or class of men, for we have no engineers; we wish only to excite inquiry and to produce in the public mind a conviction of the advantages that must result from the plan we recommend, and to place within reach of the community all the knowledge and practice of the science, if we are unwilling to encourage engineers. . . .

1819

127.

John Marshall: *Dartmouth College* v. *Woodward*

Daniel Webster's famous speech before the Supreme Court in Dartmouth College *v.* Woodward *is said to have brought tears to the eyes of Chief Justice John Marshall. Marshall's majority opinion in favor of the college was not based on sentiment but rather on his strong views concerning the contract clause in the Constitution. He had previously set forth the principle in* Fletcher *v.* Peck *that contracts could not be impaired by state rulings. In the Dartmouth case he extended this principle to corporate charters such as the one at hand. This new doctrine was to be a turning point in constitutional law. Since business corporations were now free from state interference, investors were more willing to support such enterprises. Thus, the whole field of business was encouraged to expand, with far-reaching effects on the American economy. Half a century later, Justice Miller remarked that "it may be doubted whether any decision ever delivered by any court has had such a pervading operation and influence in controlling legislation as this."*

Source: 4 Wheaton 624.

It can require no argument to prove that the circumstances of this case constitute a contract. An application is made to the Crown for a charter to incorporate a religious and literary institution. In the application it is stated that large contributions have been made for the object, which will be conferred on the corporation as soon as it shall be created. The charter is granted, and on its faith the property is conveyed. Surely in this transaction every ingredient of a complete and legitimate contract is to be found.

The points for consideration are:

1. Is this contract protected by the Constitution of the United States?

2. Is it impaired by the acts under which the defendant holds?

On the first point, it has been argued that the word "contract," in its broadest sense, would comprehend the political relations between the government and its citizens, would extend to offices held within a state for state purposes and to many of those laws concerning civil institutions, which must change with circumstances and be modified by ordinary legislation; which deeply concern the public, and which, to preserve good government, the public judgment must control — that even marriage is a contract, and its obligations are affected by the laws respecting divorces; that the clause in the Constitution, if construed in its greatest latitude, would prohibit these laws.

Taken in its broad, unlimited sense, the clause would be an unprofitable and vexatious interference with the internal concerns of a state, would unnecessarily and unwisely embarrass its legislation, and render immutable those civil institutions which are established for purposes of internal government, and which, to subserve those purposes, ought to vary with varying circumstances. That as the framers of the Constitution could never have intended to insert in that instrument a provision so unnecessary, so mischievous, and so repugnant to its general spirit, the term "contract" must be understood in a more limited sense. That it must be understood as intended to guard against a power of at least doubtful utility, the abuse of which had been extensively felt; and to restrain the legislature in future from violating the right to property. That anterior to the formation of the Constitution, a course of legislation had prevailed in many, if not in all, of the states which weakened the confidence of man in man and embarrassed all transactions between individuals by dispensing with a faithful performance of engagements.

To correct this mischief, by restraining the power which produced it, the state legislatures were forbidden "to pass any law impairing the obligation of contracts," that is, of contracts respecting property, under which some individual could claim a right to something beneficial to himself; and that since the clause in the Constitution must in construction receive some limitation, it may be confined, and ought to be confined, to cases of this description; to cases within the mischief it was intended to remedy. . . .

The provision of the Constitution never has been understood to embrace other contracts than those which respect property, or some object of value, and confer rights which may be asserted in a court of justice. It never has been understood to restrict the general right of the legislature to legislate on the subject of divorces. Those acts enable some tribunal not to impair a marriage contract but to liberate one of the parties because it has been broken by the other. When any state legislature shall pass an act annulling all marriage contracts, or allowing either party to annul it without the consent of the other, it will be time enough to inquire whether such an act be constitutional.

The parties in this case differ less on general principles, less on the true construction of the Constitution in the abstract than on the application of those principles to this case and on the true construction of the charter of 1769. This is the point on which the cause essentially depends. If the act of incorporation be a grant of political power, if it create a civil institution to be employed in the administration of the government, or if the funds of the college be public property, or if the state of New Hampshire, as a government, be alone interested in its transactions, the subject is one in which the legislature of the state may act according to its own judgment, unrestrained by any limitation of its power imposed by the Constitution of the United States.

But if this be a private, eleemosynary institution, endowed with a capacity to take property for objects unconnected with government, whose funds are bestowed by individuals on the faith of the charter; if the donors have stipulated for the future disposition and management of those funds in the manner prescribed by themselves, there may be more difficulty in the case, although neither the persons who have made these stipulations nor those for whose benefit they were made should be parties to the cause. Those who are no longer interested in the property may yet retain such an interest in the preservation of their own arrangements as to have a right to insist that those arrangements shall be held sacred. Or, if they have themselves disappeared, it becomes a subject of serious and anxious inquiry whether those whom they have legally empowered to represent them forever

Dartmouth College Collection

Participants in the Dartmouth College case: (left) John Wheelock, president of Dartmouth who was removed from office by the trustees in a dispute over the college charter; (center) Daniel Webster, attorney for the trustees of Dartmouth; (right) William Henry Woodward, secretary of the second Board of Trustees appointed by the state in an attempt to make Dartmouth a public institution and restore Wheelock to office

may not assert all the rights which they possessed, while in being; whether, if they be without personal representatives who may feel injured by a violation of the compact, the trustees be not so completely their representatives, in the eye of the law, as to stand in their place, not only as respects the government of the college but also as respects the maintenance of the college charter. . . .

A corporation is an artificial being, invisible, intangible, and existing only in contemplation of law. Being the mere creature of law, it possesses only those properties which the charter of its creation confers upon it, either expressly or as incidental to its very existence. These are such as are supposed best calculated to effect the object for which it was created. Among the most important are immortality, and, if the expression may be allowed, individuality; properties by which a perpetual succession of many persons are considered as the same, and may act as a single individual. They enable a corporation to manage its own affairs and to hold property without the perplexing intricacies, the hazardous and endless necessity of perpetual conveyances for the purpose of transmitting it from hand to hand. It is chiefly for the purpose of clothing bodies of men, in succession, with these qualities and capacities that corporations were invented and are in use.

By these means, a perpetual succession of individuals are capable of acting for the promotion of the particular object, like one immortal being. But this being does not share in the civil government of the country, unless that be the purpose for which it was created. Its immortality no more confers on it political power, or a political character, than immortality would confer such power or character on a natural person. It is no more a state instrument than a natural person exercising the same powers would be.

If, then, a natural person, employed by individuals in the education of youth, or for the government of a seminary in which youth is educated, would not become a public officer, or be considered as a member of the civil government, how is it that this artificial being, created by law for the purpose of being employed by the same individuals for the same purposes, should become a part of the civil government of the country? Is it because its existence, its capacities, its powers are given by law? Because the government has given it the power to take and to hold property in a particular form, and for particular purposes, has the government a consequent right substantially to change that form or to vary the purposes to which the property is to be applied? This principle has never been asserted or recognized and is supported by no authority. Can it derive aid from reason? . . .

From the fact, then, that a charter of incorporation has been granted, nothing can be inferred which changes the character of the institution or transfers to the government any new power over it. The character of civil institutions does not grow out of their incorporation but out of the manner in which they are formed and the objects for which they are created. The right to change them is not founded on their being incorporated but on their being the instruments of government, created for its purposes. The same institutions, created for the same objects though not incorporated, would be public institutions and, of course, be controllable by the legislature. The incorporating act neither gives nor prevents this control. Neither, in reason, can the incorporating act change the character of a private, eleemosynary institution. . . .

From this review of the charter, it appears that Dartmouth College is an eleemosynary institution, incorporated for the purpose of perpetuating the application of the bounty of the donors to the specified objects of that bounty; that its trustees or governors were originally named by the founder and invested with the power of perpetuating themselves; that they are not public officers, nor is it a civil institution, participating in the administration of government, but a charity school, or a seminary of education, incorporated for the preservation of its property, and the perpetual application of that property to the objects of its creation.

Yet a question remains to be considered, of more real difficulty, on which more doubt has been entertained than on all that have been discussed. The founders of the college, at least those whose contributions were in money, have parted with the property bestowed upon it, and their representatives have no interest in that property. The donors of land are equally without interest so long as the corporation shall exist. Could they be found, they are unaffected by any alteration in its constitution, and probably regardless of its form, or even of its existence. The students are fluctuating, and no individual among our youth has a vested interest in the institution, which can be asserted in a court of justice. Neither the founders of the college nor the youth for whose benefit it was founded, complain of the alteration made in its charter or think themselves injured by it. The trustees alone complain, and the trustees have no beneficial interest to be protected. Can this be such a contract, as the constitution intended to withdraw from the power of state legislation? Contracts, the parties to which have a vested beneficial interest, and those only, it has been said, are the objects about which the Constitution is solicitous, and to which its protection is extended. . . .

According to the theory of the British constitution, their Parliament is omnipotent. To annul corporate rights might give a shock to public opinion, which that government has chosen to avoid; but its power is not questioned. Had Parliament, immediately after the emanation of this charter, and the execution of those conveyances which followed it, annulled the instrument, so that the living donors would have witnessed the disappointment of their hopes, the perfidy of the transaction would have been universally acknowledged. Yet then, as now, the donors would have had no interest in the property; then, as now, those who might be students would have had no rights to be violated; then, as now, it might be said that the trustees, in whom the rights of all were combined, possessed no private, individual, beneficial interest in the property confided to their protection. Yet the contract would at that time have been deemed sacred by all. What has since occurred to strip it of its inviolability? Circumstances have not changed it. In reason, in justice, and in law, it is now what it was in 1769.

This is plainly a contract to which the donors, the trustees, and the Crown (to whose rights and obligations New Hampshire succeeds) were the original parties. It is a contract made on a valuable consideration. It is a contract for the security and disposition of property. It is a contract on the faith of which real and personal estate has been conveyed to the corporation. It is then a contract within the letter of the Constitution, and within its spirit also, unless the fact that the property is invested by the donors in trustees for the promotion of religion and education, for the benefit of persons who are perpetually changing, though the objects remain the same, shall create a particular exception, taking this case out of the prohibition contained in the Constitution.

It is more than possible that the preservation of rights of this description was not particularly in the view of the framers of the Constitution when the clause under consideration was introduced into that instrument. It is probable that interferences of more frequent recurrence, to which the temptation was stronger and of which the mischief was more extensive, constituted the great motive for imposing this restriction on the state legislatures. But although a particular and a rare case may not, in itself, be of sufficient magnitude to induce a rule, yet it must be governed by the rule, when established, unless some plain and strong reason for excluding it can be given.

It is not enough to say that this particular case was not in the mind of the Convention when the article was framed, nor of the American people when it was adopted. It is necessary to go further and to say that, had this particular case been suggested, the language would have been so varied as to exclude it, or it would have been made a special exception. The case, being within the words of the rule, must be within its operation likewise, unless there be something in the literal construction so obviously absurd, or mischievous, or repugnant to the general spirit of the instrument as to justify those who expound the Constitution in making it an exception.

On what safe and intelligible ground can this exception stand? There is no expression in the Constitution, no sentiment delivered by its contemporaneous expounders which would justify us in making it. In the absence of all authority of this kind, is there, in the nature and reason of the case itself, that which would sustain a construction of the Constitution not warranted by its words? Are contracts of this description of a character to excite so little interest that we must exclude them from the provisions of the Constitution as being unworthy of the attention of those who framed the instrument? Or does public policy so imperiously demand their remaining exposed to legislative alteration as to compel us, or rather permit us, to say that these words, which were introduced to give stability to contracts, and which in their plain import comprehend this contract, must yet be so construed as to exclude it?

Almost all eleemosynary corporations, those which are created for the promotion of religion, of charity, or of education, are of the same character. The law of this case is the law of all. In every literary or charitable institution, unless the objects of the bounty be themselves incorporated, the whole legal interest is in trustees and can be asserted only by them. The donors, or claimants of the bounty, if they can appear in court at all, can appear only to complain of the trustees. In all other situations, they are identified with, and personated by, the trustees; and their rights are to be defended and maintained by them. Religion, charity, and education are, in the law of England, legatees or donees, capable of receiving bequests or donations in this form. They appear in court and claim or defend by the corporation. . . .

The opinion of the Court, after mature deliberation, is that this is a contract, the obligation of which cannot be impaired without violating the Constitution of the United States. This opinion appears to us to be equally supported by reason and by the former decisions of this Court.

We next proceed to the inquiry whether its obligation has been impaired by those acts of the legislature of New Hampshire to which the special verdict refers. . . .

By the Revolution, the duties as well as the powers of government devolved on the people of New Hampshire. It is admitted that among the latter was comprehended the transcendent power of Parliament, as well as that of the Executive Department. It is too clear to require the support of argument that all contracts and rights respecting property remained unchanged by the Revolution.

The obligations, then, which were created by the charter to Dartmouth College were the same in the new that they had been in the old government. The power of the government was also the same. A repeal of this charter at any time prior to the adoption of the present Constitution of the United States would have been an extraordinary and unprecedented act of power, but one which could have been contested only by the restrictions upon the legislature to be found in the constitution of the state. But the Constitution of the United States has imposed this additional limitation, that the legislature of a state shall pass no act "impairing the obligation of contracts."

It has been already stated that the act "to amend the charter, and enlarge and improve the corporation of Dartmouth College" increases the number of trustees to twenty-one, gives the appointment of the additional members to the executive of the state, and creates a board of overseers to consist of twenty-five persons, of whom twenty-one are also appointed by the executive of New Hampshire, who have power to inspect and control the most important acts of the trustees.

On the effect of this law, two opinions cannot be entertained. Between acting directly and acting through the agency of trustees and overseers, no essential difference is perceived. The whole power of governing the college is transferred from trustees, appointed according to the will of the founder, expressed in the charter, to the executive of New Hampshire. The management and application of the funds of this eleemosynary institution, which are placed by the donors in the hands of trustees named in the charter and empowered to perpetuate themselves, are placed by this act under the control of the government of the state. The will of the state is substituted for the will of the donors in every essential operation of the college.

This is not an immaterial change. The founders of the college contracted, not merely for the perpetual application of the funds which they gave to the objects for which those funds were given; they contracted, also, to secure that application by the constitution of the corporation. They contracted for a system, which should, as far as human foresight can provide, retain forever the government of the literary institution they had formed in the hands of persons approved by themselves.

This system is totally changed. The charter of 1769 exists no longer. It is reorganized; and reorganized in such a manner as to convert a literary institution, molded according to the will of its founders and placed under the control of private literary men, into a machine entirely subservient to the will of government. This may be for the advantage of this college in particular, and may be for the advantage of literature in general, but it is not according to the will of the donors, and is subversive of that contract, on the faith of which their property was given.

In the view which has been taken of this

interesting case, the Court has confined itself to the rights possessed by the trustees, as the assignees and representatives of the donors and founders, for the benefit of religion and literature. Yet it is not clear that the trustees ought to be considered as destitute of such beneficial interest in themselves as the law may respect. In addition to their being the legal owners of the property, and to their having a freehold right in the powers confided to them, the charter itself countenances the idea that trustees may also be tutors with salaries. The first president was one of the original trustees; and the charter provides that in case of vacancy in that office "the senior professor or tutor, *being one of the trustees,* shall exercise the office of president until the trustees shall make choice of, and appoint a president."

According to the tenor of the charter, then, the trustees might, without impropriety, appoint a president and other professors from their own body. This is a power not entirely unconnected with an interest. Even if the proposition of the counsel for the defendant were sustained; if it were admitted that those contracts only are protected by the Constitution, a beneficial interest in which is vested in the party, who appears in court to assert that interest; yet it is by no means clear that the trustees of Dartmouth College have no beneficial interest in themselves. But the Court has deemed it unnecessary to investigate this particular point. . . .

It results from this opinion that the acts of the legislature of New Hampshire, which are stated in the special verdict found in this cause, are repugnant to the Constitution of the United States; and that the judgment on this special verdict ought to have been for the plaintiffs. The judgment of the state court must therefore be reversed.

128.

Apprentice Labor Act

The apprentice system has its roots in ancient times, and was at first a simple agreement between a child (or his parents) and an experienced workman for the purpose of teaching the child a trade in return for his labor. As the system evolved, laws were passed regulating the relationship, and contracts, known as indentures, set the terms of the agreement. Most early state laws, designed to control abuses of the contractual agreements, were based on the principles set forth in an English statute of 1563. The following act was passed by the Illinois state legislature on February 6, 1819, only a few months after the state had been admitted to the Union.

Source: *Laws of the State of Illinois,* 1819, pp. 4-6.

Section 1. *Be it enacted by the people of the state of Illinois represented in the General Assembly, and it is hereby enacted by the authority of the same,* that if any white person within the age of twenty-one years, who now is, or hereafter shall be bound by an indenture of his or her own free will and accord, and by and with the consent of his or her father, or in the case of the death of his father, with the consent of his or her mother or guardian, to be expressed on such indenture, and signified by such parent or guardian, sealing and signing the said indenture and not otherwise, to serve as apprentices in any art or mystery [craft], service, trade, employment, manual occupation, or labor, until he or she arrives, males till the age of twenty-one, and females till the age of eighteen years (as the case may be), or for any shorter time; then the said apprentice, so bound as aforesaid, shall serve accordingly.

Section 2. If any master or mistress shall be guilty of any misusage, refusal of necessary provision or clothes, unreasonable correction, cruelty, or other ill-treatment, so that his or her said apprentice shall have any just cause to complain; or if the said apprentice shall absent himself or herself from the service of his or her master or mistress, or be guilty of any misdemeanor, miscarriage, or ill-behavior; then the said master or mistress, or apprentice being aggrieved, and having just cause of complaint, shall repair to some justice of the peace, unconnected with either of the parties, within the county where the said master or mistress dwell; who, having heard the matters in difference, shall have authority to discharge if he think proper, by writing under his hand and seal, the said apprentice of and from his or her apprenticeship; and such writing as aforesaid shall be a sufficient discharge for the said apprentice against his or her master or mistress, and his or her executors or administrators, the said indenture, or any law to the contrary notwithstanding.

And if default shall be found to be in the said apprentice, then the said justice shall cause such due correction to be administered unto him or her, as he shall deem to be just and reasonable; and if any person shall think himself or herself aggrieved by such adjudication of the said justice, he or she may appeal to the next circuit court in and for the county where such adjudication shall have been made, such person giving ten days notice of his or her intention of bringing such appeal, and of the cause and matter thereof, to the adverse party; and entering into a recognizance within five days after such notice, before some justice of the peace of the county, with sufficient surety, conditioned to try such appeal at, and abide the order or judgment of, and pay such costs as shall be awarded by the said court. Which said court, at their said term, upon due proof upon oath or affirmation of such notice having been given, and of entering into such recognizance as aforesaid shall be and are hereby empowered and directed to proceed in and hear, and determine the cause and matter of such appeal, and give and award such judgment therein, with costs to either party, appellant or respondent, as they, in their discretion, shall judge proper and reasonable.

Section 3. No writ of certiorari or other process shall issue or be issuable to remove into the superior court any proceeding had in pursuance of this act before any justice of the peace, or before any circuit court.

129.

John Marshall: *M'Culloch* v. *Maryland*

Feeling ran high against the Second Bank of the United States during the depression of 1818-1819, and several state legislatures laid taxes on such of the Bank's branches as were within their jurisdiction with the intent of limiting or even destroying its business. The Baltimore branch determined, however, to ignore a law of this sort, whereupon Maryland brought suit against the cashier, James M'Culloch. M'Culloch appealed the Maryland court's decision upholding the state law to the Supreme Court. Two questions were to be decided by the Court: Did Congress have the right to incorporate a bank, and was a state tax upon such a bank constitutional? In holding that the answer to the first question was yes and to the second no, Chief Justice Marshall, for the Court, gave one of the most important opinions of his long career. The Constitution said nothing explicit about establishing banks, nor was Congress authorized to grant charters of incorporation. Hence such powers could only be supposed by the logic of the Tenth Amendment to lie in the states, and Maryland would thus have seemed within its rights to legislate a banking tax. But Marshall bypassed these objections with his interpretation of the "necessary and proper" clause of the Constitution. It was no long step from there to the so-called contract cases, including Dartmouth College *v.* Woodward, *in which Marshall served notice that the Tenth Amendment was a dead letter insofar as property rights were concerned. Indeed, he gave notice that he would construe it as meaning just the opposite of what it said when the question of those rights came before his Court.*

Source: 4 Wheaton 400.

The first question made in the cause is — Has Congress power to incorporate a bank?

It has been truly said that this can scarcely be considered as an open question, entirely unprejudiced by the former proceedings of the nation respecting it. The principle now contested was introduced at a very early period of our history, has been recognized by many successive legislatures, and has been acted upon by the Judicial Department, in cases of peculiar delicacy, as a law of undoubted obligation. . . .

In discussing this question, the counsel for the State of Maryland have deemed it of some importance, in the construction of the Constitution, to consider that instrument not as emanating from the people but as the act of sovereign and independent states. The powers of the general government, it has been said, are delegated by the states, who alone are truly sovereign; and must be exercised in subordination to the states, who alone possess supreme dominion.

It would be difficult to sustain this proposition. The Convention which framed the Constitution was indeed elected by the state legislatures. But the instrument, when it came from their hands, was a mere proposal, without obligation or pretensions to it. It was reported to the then existing Congress of the United States with a request that it might "be submitted to a Convention of Delegates, chosen in each state by the people thereof, under the recommendation of its legislature, for their assent and ratification." This mode of proceeding was adopted; and by the Convention, by Congress, and by the state legislatures the instrument was submitted to the people. They acted upon it in the only manner in which they can act safely, effectively, and wisely, on such a subject — by assembling in convention.

It is true, they assembled in their several states; and where else should they have assembled? No political dreamer was ever wild enough to think of breaking down the lines which separate the states, and of compounding the American people into one common mass. Of consequence, when they act, they act in their states. But the measures they adopt do not, on that account, cease to be the measures of the people themselves, or become the measures of the state governments.

From these conventions the Constitution derives its whole authority. The government proceeds directly from the people; is "ordained and established" in the name of the people; and is declared to be ordained "in order to form a more perfect union, establish justice, ensure domestic tranquillity, and secure the blessings of liberty to themselves and to their posterity." The assent of the states, in their sovereign capacity, is implied in calling a convention, and thus submitting that instrument to the people. But the people were at perfect liberty to accept or reject it; and their act was final. It required not the affirmance, and could not be negatived, by the state governments. The Constitution, when thus adopted, was of complete obligation, and bound the state sovereignties.

It has been said that the people had already surrendered all their powers to the state sovereignties, and had nothing more to give. But, surely, the question whether they may resume and modify the powers granted to government does not remain to be settled in this country. Much more might the legitimacy of the general government be doubted had it been created by the states. The powers delegated to the state sovereignties were to be exercised by themselves, not by a distinct and independent sovereignty created by themselves. To the formation of a league, such as was the Confederation, the state sovereignties were certainly competent. But when, "in order to form a more perfect union," it was deemed necessary to change this alliance into an effective government, possessing great and sovereign powers, and acting directly on the people, the necessity of referring it to the people, and of deriving its powers directly from them, was felt and acknowledged by all.

The government of the Union, then (whatever may be the influence of this fact on the case), is emphatically and truly, a government of the people. In form and in substance it emanates from them. Its powers are granted by them and are to be exercised directly on them and for their benefit.

This government is acknowledged by all to be one of enumerated powers. The principle that it can exercise only the powers granted to it would seem too apparent to have required to be enforced by all those arguments which its enlightened friends, while it was depending before the people, found it necessary to urge. That principle is now universally admitted. But the question respecting the extent of the powers actually granted is perpetually arising, and will probably continue to arise as long as our system shall exist.

In discussing these questions, the conflicting powers of the general and state governments must be brought into view, and the supremacy of their respective laws, when they are in opposition, must be settled.

If any one proposition could command the universal assent of mankind, we might expect it would be this — that the government of the Union though limited in its powers is supreme within its sphere of action. This would seem to result necessarily from its nature. It is the government of all; its powers are delegated by all; it represents all; and acts for all. Though any one state may be willing to control its operations, no state is willing to allow others to control them. The nation, on those subjects on which it can act, must necessarily bind its component parts.

But this question is not left to mere reason: the people have, in express terms, decided it by saying, "this Constitution, and the laws of the United States, which shall be made in pursuance thereof, shall be the supreme law of the land," and by requiring that the members of the state legislatures, and the officers of the Executive and Judicial departments of the states shall take the oath of fidelity to it.

The government of the United States, then, though limited in its powers is supreme; and its laws, when made in pursuance of the Constitution, form the supreme law of the land, "anything in the constitution or laws of any state to the contrary notwithstanding." . . .

A constitution, to contain an accurate detail of all the subdivisions of which its great powers will admit, and of all the means by which they may be carried into execution, would partake of the prolixity of a legal code, and could scarcely be embraced by the human mind. It would probably never be understood by the public. Its nature, therefore, requires that only its great outlines should be marked, its important objects designated, and the minor ingredients which compose those objects be deduced from the nature of the objects themselves. That this idea was entertained by the framers of the American Constitution is not only to be inferred from the nature of the instrument but from the language. Why else were some of the limitations found in the 9th Section of the 1st Article introduced? It is also, in some degree, warranted by their having omitted to use any restrictive term which might prevent its receiving a fair and just interpretation. In considering this question, then, we must never forget that it is *a constitution* we are expounding.

Although, among the enumerated powers of government, we do not find the word "bank" or "incorporation," we find the great powers to lay and collect taxes; to borrow money; to regulate commerce; to declare and conduct a war; and to raise and support armies and navies. The sword and the purse, all the external relations, and no inconsiderable portion of the industry of the nation are entrusted to its government. It can never be pretended that these vast powers draw after them others of inferior importance, merely because they are inferior. Such an idea can never be advanced. But it may with great reason be contended that a government, entrusted with such ample powers, on the due execution of which the happiness and prosperity of the nation so vitally depends, must also be entrusted with ample means for their execution. The power being given, it is the interest of the nation to facilitate its execution. It can never be their interest, and cannot be presumed to have been their intention, to clog and embarrass its execution by withholding the most appropriate means.

Throughout this vast republic, from the St. Croix to the Gulf of Mexico, from the Atlantic to the Pacific, revenue is to be collected and expended, armies are to be marched and supported. The exigencies of the nation may require that the treasure raised in the North should be transported to the South, *that* raised in the East conveyed to the West, or that this order should be reversed. Is that construction of the Constitution to be preferred which would render these operations difficult, hazardous, and expensive? Can we adopt that construction (unless the words imperiously require it) which would impute to the framers of that instrument, when granting these powers for the public good, the intention of impeding their exercise by withholding a choice of means? If, indeed, such be the mandate of the Constitution, we have only to obey; but that instrument does not profess to enumerate the means by which the powers it confers may be executed; nor does it prohibit the creation of a corporation if the existence of such a being be essential to the beneficial exercise of those powers. It is then the subject of fair inquiry, how far such means may be employed.

It is not denied that the powers given to the government imply the ordinary means of execution. That, for example, of raising revenue and applying it to national purposes is admitted to imply the power of conveying money from place to place, as the exigencies of the nation may require, and of employing the usual means of conveyance. But it is denied that the government has its choice of means; or, that it may employ the most convenient means, if, to employ them, it be necessary to erect a corporation.

On what foundation does this argument rest? On this alone: The power of creating a corporation is one appertaining to sovereignty, and is not expressly conferred on Congress. This is true. But all legislative powers appertain to sovereignty. The original power of giving the law on any subject whatever is a sovereign power; and if the government of the Union is restrained from creating a corporation, as a means for performing its functions, on the single reason that the creation of a corporation is an act of sovereignty; if the sufficiency of this reason be acknowledged, there would be some difficulty in sustaining the authority of Congress to pass other laws for the accomplishment of the same objects.

The government which has a right to do an act, and has imposed on it the duty of performing that act, must, according to the dictates of reason, be allowed to select the means; and those who contend that it may not select any appropriate means, that one particular mode of effecting the object is excepted, take upon themselves the burden of establishing that exception.

The creation of a corporation, it is said, appertains to sovereignty. This is admitted. But to what portion of sovereignty does it appertain? Does it belong to one more than to another? In America, the powers of sovereignty are divided between the government of the Union and those of the states. They are each sovereign with respect to the objects committed to it, and neither sovereign with respect to the objects committed to the other. We cannot comprehend that train of reasoning which would maintain that the extent of power granted by the people is to be ascertained, not by the nature and terms of the grant but by its date. Some state constitutions were formed *before*, some *since* that of the United States. We cannot believe that their relation to each other is in any degree dependent upon this circumstance. Their respective powers must, we think, be precisely the same as if they had been formed at the same time. Had they been formed at the same time, and had the people conferred on the general government the power contained in the Constitution, and on the states the whole residuum of power, would it have been asserted that the government of the Union was not sovereign with respect to those objects which were entrusted to it, in relation to which its laws were declared to be supreme? If this could not have been asserted, we cannot well comprehend the process of reasoning which maintains that a power appertaining to sovereignty cannot be connected with that vast portion of it which is granted to the general government, so far as it is calculated to subserve the legitimate objects of that government.

The power of creating a corporation, though appertaining to sovereignty, is not, like the power of making war or levying taxes or of regulating commerce, a great substantive and independent power, which cannot be implied as incidental to other powers, or used as a means of executing them. It is never the end for which other powers are exercised, but a means by which other objects are accomplished. No contributions are made to charity for the sake of an incorporation, but a corporation is created to administer the charity; no seminary of learning is instituted in order to be incorporated, but the corporate character is conferred to subserve the purposes of education. No city was ever built with the sole object of being incorporated, but is incorporated as affording the best means of being well governed. The power of creating a corporation is never used for its own sake, but for the purpose of effecting something else. No sufficient reason is, therefore, perceived why it may not pass as incidental to those powers which are expressly given, if it be a direct mode of executing them.

But the Constitution of the United States has not left the right of Congress to employ the necessary means for the execution of the powers conferred on the government to general reasoning. To its enumeration of powers is added that of making "all laws which shall be necessary and proper, for carrying into execution the foregoing powers, and all other powers vested by this Constitution, in the government of the United States, or in any department thereof."

The counsel for the State of Maryland have urged various arguments to prove that this clause, though in terms a grant of power, is not so in effect, but is really restrictive of the general right, which might otherwise be implied, of selecting means for executing the enumerated powers. In support of this proposition, they have found it necessary to contend that this clause was inserted for the purpose of conferring on Congress the power of making laws. That, without it, doubts might be entertained whether Congress could exercise its powers in the form of legislation.

But could this be the object for which it was inserted? A government is created by the people, having legislative, executive, and judicial powers. Its legislative powers are vested in a Congress, which is to consist of a Senate and House of Representatives. Each house may determine the rule of its proceedings; and it is declared that every bill which shall have passed both houses, shall, before it becomes a law, be presented to the President of the United States. The 7th Section describes the course of proceedings by which a bill shall become a law; and, then, the 8th Section enumerates the powers of Congress. Could it be necessary to say that a legislature should exercise legislative powers in the shape of legislation? After allowing each house to prescribe its own course of proceeding, after describing the manner in which a bill should become a law, would it have entered into the mind of a single member of the Convention that an express power to make laws was necessary to enable the legislature to make them? That a legislature, endowed with legislative powers, can legislate is a proposition too self-evident to have been questioned.

But the argument on which most reliance is placed is drawn from the peculiar language of this clause. Congress is not empowered by it to make all laws which may have relation to the powers conferred on the government, but such only as may be "*necessary and proper*" for carrying them into execution. The word "*necessary*" is considered as controlling the whole sentence, and as limiting the right to pass laws for the execution of the granted powers, to such as are indispensable and without which the power would be nugatory. That it excludes the choice of means, and leaves to Congress, in each case, that only which is most direct and simple.

Is it true that this is the sense in which the word "necessary" is always used? Does it always import an absolute physical necessity, so strong that one thing to which another may be termed necessary cannot exist without that other? We think it does not. If reference be had to its use, in the common affairs of the world or in approved authors, we find that it frequently imports no more than that one thing is convenient, or useful, or essential to another. To employ the means necessary to an end is generally understood as employing any means calculated to produce the end, and not as being confined to those single means without which the end would be entirely unattainable.

Such is the character of human language that no word conveys to the mind, in all situations, one single definite idea; and nothing is more common than to use words in a figurative sense. Almost all compositions contain words which, taken in their rigorous sense, would convey a meaning different from that which is obviously intended. It is essential to just construction that many words which import something excessive should be understood in a more mitigated sense — in that sense which common usage justifies. The word "necessary" is of this description. It has not a fixed character peculiar to itself. It admits of all degrees of comparison, and is often connected with other words, which increase or diminish the impression the mind receives of the urgency it imports. A thing may be necessary, very necessary, absolutely or indispensably necessary. To no mind would the same idea be conveyed by these several phrases.

This comment on the word is well illustrated by the passage cited at the bar, from the 10th Section of the 1st Article of the Constitution. It is, we think, impossible to compare the sentence which prohibits a state from laying "imposts, or duties on imports or exports, except what may be *absolutely* necessary for executing its inspection laws," with that which authorizes Congress "to make all laws which shall be necessary and proper for carrying into execution" the powers of the general government, without feeling a conviction that the Convention understood itself to change materially the meaning of the word "necessary" by prefixing the word "absolutely." This word, then, like others, is used in various senses; and, in its construction, the subject, the context, the intention of the person using them are all to be taken into view.

Let this be done in the case under consideration. The subject is the execution of those great powers on which the welfare of a nation essentially depends. It must have been the intention of those who gave these powers to insure, as far as human prudence could insure, their beneficial execution. This could not be done by confiding the choice of means to such narrow limits as not to leave it in the power of Congress to adopt any which might be appropriate, and which were conducive to the end. This provision is made in a constitution intended to endure for ages to come, and, consequently, to be adapted to the various *crises* of human affairs. To have prescribed the means by which government should, in all future time, execute its powers, would have been to change, entirely, the character of the instrument, and give it the properties of a legal code. It would have been an unwise attempt to provide, by immutable rules, for exigencies which, if foreseen at all, must have been seen dimly, and which can be best provided for as they occur. To have declared that the best means shall not be used, but those alone without which the power given would be nugatory, would have been to deprive the legislature of the capacity to avail itself of experience, to exercise its reason, and to accommodate its legislation to circumstances. . . .

But the argument which most conclusively demonstrates the error of the construction contended for by the counsel for the State of Maryland is founded on the intention of the Convention, as manifested in the whole clause. To waste time and argument in proving that, without it, Congress might carry its powers into execution would be not much less idle than to hold a lighted taper to the sun. As little can it be required to prove that, in the absence of this clause, Congress would have some choice of means; that it might employ those which, in its judgment, would most advantageously effect the object to be accomplished; that any means adapted to the end, any means which tended directly to the execution of the constitutional powers of the government, were in themselves constitutional.

This clause, as construed by the State of Maryland, would abridge, and almost annihilate, this useful and necessary right of the legislature to select its means. That this could not be intended is, we should think, had it not been already controverted, too apparent for controversy. . . .

The result of the most careful and attentive consideration bestowed upon this clause is that if it does not enlarge, it cannot be construed to restrain the powers of Congress, or to impair the right of the legislature to exercise its best judgment in the selection of measures to carry into execution the constitutional powers of the government. If no other motive for its insertion can be suggested, a sufficient one is found in the desire to remove all doubts respecting the right to legislate on that vast mass of incidental powers which must be involved in the Constitution, if that instrument be not a splendid bauble.

We admit, as all must admit, that the powers of the government are limited, and that its limits are not to be transcended. But we think the sound construction of the Constitution must allow to the national legislature that discretion, with respect to the means by which the powers it confers are to be carried into execution, which will enable that body to perform the high duties assigned to it, in the manner most beneficial to the people. Let the end be legitimate, let it be within the scope of the Constitution, and all means which are appropriate, which are plainly adapted to that end, which are not prohibited, but consist with the letter and spirit of the Constitution, are constitutional. . . .

If a corporation may be employed indiscriminately with other means to carry into execution the powers of the government, no particular reason can be assigned for excluding the use of a bank, if required for its fiscal operations. To use one must be within the discretion of Congress, if it be an appropriate mode of executing the powers of government. That it is a convenient, a useful, and essential instrument in the prosecution of its fiscal operations is not now a subject of controversy. All those who have been concerned in the administration of our finances have concurred in representing its importance and necessity; and so strongly have they been felt that statesmen of the first class, whose previous opinions against it had been confirmed by every circumstance which can fix the human judgment, have yielded those opinions to the exigencies of the nation. Under the Confederation, Congress, justifying the measure by its necessity, transcended perhaps its powers to obtain the advantage of a bank; and our own legislation attests the universal conviction of the utility of this measure. The time has passed away when it can be necessary to enter into any discussion in order to prove the importance of this instrument as a means to effect the legitimate objects of the government.

But, were its necessity less apparent, none can deny its being an appropriate measure; and if it is, the degree of its necessity, as has been very justly observed, is to be discussed in another place. Should Congress, in the execution of its powers, adopt measures which are prohibited by the Constitution; or should Congress, under the pretext of executing its powers, pass laws for the accomplishment of objects not entrusted to the government, it would become the painful duty of this tribunal, should a case requiring such a decision come before it, to say that such an act was not the law of the land. But where the law is not prohibited, and is really calculated to effect any of the objects entrusted to the government, to undertake here to inquire into the degree of its necessity would be to pass the line which circumscribes the Judicial Department, and to tread on legislative ground. This court disclaims all pretensions to such a power.

After this declaration, it can scarcely be necessary to say that the existence of state banks can have no possible influence on the question. No trace is to be found in the Constitution of an intention to create a dependence of the government of the Union on those of the states for the execution of the great powers assigned to it. Its means are adequate to its ends; and on those means alone was it expected to rely for the accomplishment of its ends. To impose on it the necessity of resorting to means which it cannot control, which another government may furnish or withhold, would render its course precarious, the result of its measures uncertain, and create a dependence on other governments, which might disappoint its most important designs, and is incompatible with the language of the Constitution. But were it otherwise, the choice of means implies a right to choose a national bank in preference to state banks, and Congress alone can make the election.

After the most deliberate consideration, it is the unanimous and decided opinion of this Court that the act to incorporate the Bank of the United States is a law made in pursuance of the Constitution, and is a part of the supreme law of the land. . . .

It being the opinion of the Court that the act incorporating the bank is constitutional; and that the power of establishing a branch in the State of Maryland might be properly exercised by the bank itself, we proceed to inquire whether the State of Maryland may, without violating the Constitution, tax that branch.

That the power of taxation is one of vital importance; that it is retained by the states; that it is not abridged by the grant of a similar power to the government of the Union; that it is to be concurrently exercised by the two governments are truths which have never been denied. But, such is the paramount character of the Constitution that its capacity to withdraw any subject from the action of even this power is admitted. The states are expressly forbidden to lay any duties on imports or exports, except what may be absolutely necessary for executing their inspection laws. If the obligation of this prohibition must be conceded, if it may restrain a state from the exercise of its taxing power on imports and exports, the same paramount character would seem to restrain, as it certainly may restrain, a state from such other exercise of this power as is in its nature incompatible with, and repugnant to, the constitutional laws of the Union. A law, absolutely repugnant to another, as entirely repeals that other as if express terms of repeal were used.

On this ground the counsel for the bank place its claim to be exempted from the power of a state to tax its operations. There is no express provision for the case, but the claim has been sustained on a principle which so entirely pervades the Constitution, is so intermixed with the materials which compose it, so interwoven with its web, so blended with its texture as to be incapable of being separated from it without rending it into shreds.

This great principle is that the Constitution and the laws made in pursuance thereof are supreme; that they control the constitution and laws of the respective states, and cannot be controlled by them. From this, which may be almost termed an axiom, other propositions are deduced as corollaries, on the truth or error of which, and on their application to this case, the cause has been supposed to depend. These are (1) that a power to create implies a power to preserve; (2) that a power to destroy, if wielded by a different hand, is hostile to, and incompatible with, these powers to create and to preserve; (3) that where this repugnancy exists, that authority which is supreme must control, not yield to, that over which it is supreme. . . .

The power of Congress to create, and of course to continue, the bank, was the subject of the preceding part of this opinion; and is no longer to be considered as questionable.

That the power of taxing it by the states may be exercised so as to destroy it is too obvious to be denied. But taxation is said to be an absolute power which acknowledges no other limits than those expressly prescribed in the Constitution, and like sovereign power of every other description, is trusted to the discretion of those who use it. . . .

The argument on the part of the State of Maryland is, not that the states may directly resist a law of Congress but that they may exercise their acknowledged powers upon it, and that the Constitution leaves them this right in the confidence that they will not abuse it. . . .

That the power to tax involves the power to destroy; that the power to destroy may defeat and render useless the power to create; that there is a plain repugnance in conferring on one government a power to control the constitutional measures of another, which other, with respect to those very measures, is declared to be supreme over that which exerts the control, are propositions not to be denied. But all inconsistencies are to be reconciled by the magic of the word "confidence." Taxation, it is said, does not necessarily and unavoidably destroy. To carry it to the excess of destruction would be an abuse, to presume which would banish that confidence which is essential to all government.

But is this a case of confidence? Would the people of any one state trust those of another with a power to control the most insignificant operations of their state government? We know they would not. Why, then, should we suppose that the people of any one state should be willing to trust those of another with a power to control the operations of a government to which they have confided their most important and most valuable interests? In the legislature of the Union alone are all represented. The legislature of the Union alone, therefore, can be trusted by the people with the power of controlling measures which concern all, in the confidence that it will not be abused. This, then, is not a case of confidence, and we must consider it as it really is.

If we apply the principle for which the State of Maryland contends, to the Constitution generally, we shall find it capable of changing totally the character of that instrument. We shall find it capable of arresting all the measures of the government, and of prostrating it at the foot of the states. The American people have declared their Constitution, and the laws made in pursuance thereof, to be supreme; but this principle would transfer the supremacy, in fact, to the states. . . .

The question is, in truth, a question of supremacy; and if the right of the states to tax the means employed by the general government be conceded, the declaration that the Constitution, and the laws made in pursuance thereof, shall be the supreme law of the land is empty and unmeaning declamation. . . .

It has also been insisted that, as the power of taxation in the general and state governments is acknowledged to be concurrent, every argument which would sustain the right of the general government to tax banks chartered by the states will equally sustain the right of the states to tax banks chartered by the general government.

But the two cases are not on the same reason. The people of all the states have created the general government, and have conferred upon it the general power of taxation. The people of all the states, and the states themselves, are represented in Congress, and, by their representatives, exercise this power. When they tax the chartered institutions of the states, they tax their constituents; and these taxes must be uniform. But, when a state taxes the operations of the government of the United States, it acts upon institutions created, not by their own constituents but by people over whom they claim no control. It acts upon the measures of a government created by others as well as themselves, for the benefit of others in common with themselves. The difference is that which always exists, and always must exist, between the action of the whole on a part, and the action of a part on the whole — between the laws of a government declared to be supreme, and those of a government which, when in opposition to those laws, is not supreme. . . .

The Court has bestowed on this subject its most deliberate consideration. The result is a conviction that the states have no power, by taxation or otherwise, to retard, impede, burden, or in any manner control the operations of the constitutional laws enacted by Congress to carry into execution the powers vested in the general government. This is, we think, the unavoidable consequence of that supremacy which the Constitution has declared.

We are unanimously of opinion, that the law passed by the legislature of Maryland, imposing a tax on the Bank of the United States, is unconstitutional and void.

This opinion does not deprive the states of any resources which they originally possessed. It does not extend to a tax paid by the real property of the bank, in common with the other real property within the state, nor to a tax imposed on the interest which the citizens of Maryland may hold in this institution, in common with other property of the same description throughout the state. But this is a tax on the operations of the bank, and is consequently a tax on the operation of an instrument employed by the government of the Union to carry its powers into execution. Such a tax must be unconstitutional.

130.

Spencer Roane: Defense of the Power of State Courts

Had the health of Chief Justice Oliver Ellsworth allowed him to serve six months longer than he did, Jefferson rather than Adams would have appointed his successor; and Jefferson would not have appointed John Marshall but (as he later said) Judge Spencer Roane of the Virginia Supreme Court to lead the United States Supreme Court. If this had happened, the subsequent history of the United States might have been very different, for Roane's position was directly opposed to that of Marshall: Roane was a strict constructionist of the Constitution, an advocate of limited governmental powers, and a firm believer in states' rights. The following abbreviated version of two articles, written by him under the pseudonym "Hampden," originally appeared in the Richmond Enquirer *on June 11 and 15, 1819. The articles were inspired by and directed against Marshall's decision in* M'Culloch *v.* Maryland.

Source: *The John P. Branch Historical Papers of Randolph-Macon College,* June 1905, pp. 77-93.

I BEG LEAVE TO ADDRESS my fellow citizens . . . on a momentous subject. . . . Although some of them will, doubtless, lend a more willing ear than others to the important truths I shall endeavor to articulate, none can hear them with indifference. None of them can be prepared to give a *carte blanche* to our federal rulers, and to obliterate the state governments, forever, from our political system.

It has been the happiness of the American people to be connected together in a confederate republic; to be united by a system which extends the sphere of popular government and reconciles the advantages of monarchy with those of a republic; a system which combines all the internal advantages of the latter with all the force of the former. It has been our happiness to believe that, in the partition of powers between the general and state governments, the former possessed only such as were expressly granted, or passed therewith as necessary incidents, while all the residuary powers were reserved by the latter. It was deemed by the enlightened founders of the Constitution as essential to the internal happiness and welfare of their constituents to reserve some powers to the state governments; as to their external safety, to grant others to the government of the Union. This, it is believed, was done by the Constitution, in its original shape; but such were the natural fears and jealousies of our citizens, in relation to this all-important subject, that it was deemed necessary to quiet those fears by the Tenth Amendment to the Constitution. It is not easy to devise stronger terms to effect that object than those used in that amendment.

Such, however, is the proneness of all men to extend and abuse their power — to "feel power and forget right" — that even this article has afforded us no security. That legislative power, which is everywhere extending the sphere of its activity and drawing all power into its impetuous vortex, has blinked even the strong words of this amendment. That judicial power, which, according to Montesquieu is "in some measure, next to nothing"; and whose province this great writer limits to "punishing criminals and determining the disputes which arise between individuals"; that judiciary which, in Rome, according to the same author, was not entrusted to decide questions which concerned "the interests of the state, in the relation which it bears to its citizens"; and which, in England, has only invaded the Constitution in the worst of times, and then, always, on the side of arbitrary power, has also deemed its interference necessary in our country. It will readily be perceived that I allude to the decision of the Supreme Court of the United States, in the case of M'Culloch against the State of Maryland.

The warfare carried on by the legislature of the Union against the rights of "the states" and of "the people" has been with various success and always by detachment. *They* have not dared to break down the barriers of the Constitution by a *general* act declaratory of their power. That measure was too bold for these ephemeral duties of the people. The people hold them in check by a short rein, and would consign them to merited infamy, at the next election. . . . They have adopted a safer course. *Crescit eundo* is their maxim; and they have succeeded in seeing the Constitution expounded, not by what it actually contains but by the *abuses* committed under it.

A new mode of amending the Constitution has been added to the ample ones provided in that instrument, and the strongest checks established in it have been made to yield to the force of precedents! The time will soon arrive, if it is not already at hand, when the Constitution may be expounded without ever looking into it — by merely reading the acts of a renegade Congress, or adopting the outrageous doctrines of Pickering, Lloyd, or Sheffey!

The warfare waged by the judicial body has been of a bolder tone and character. It was not enough for them to sanction, in former times, the detestable doctrines of Pickering & Co., as aforesaid; it was not enough for them to annihilate the freedom of the press by incarcerating all those who dare, with a manly freedom, to canvass the conduct of their public agents; it was not enough for the predecessors of the present judges to preach political sermons from the bench of justice and bolster up the most unconstitutional measures of the most abandoned of our rulers; it did not suffice to do the business in detail, and ratify, one by one, the legislative infractions of the Constitution. That process would have been too slow, and perhaps too troublesome. . . .

They resolved, therefore, to put down all discussions of the kind, in future, by a judicial *coup de main;* to give a *general* letter of attorney to the future legislators of the Union; and to tread under foot all those parts and articles of the Constitution which had been, heretofore, deemed to set limits to the power of the federal legislature. That man must be a deplorable idiot who does not see that there is no earthly difference between an *unlimited* grant of power and a grant limited in its terms, but accompanied with *unlimited* means of carrying it into execution.

The Supreme Court of the United States have not only granted this *general* power of attorney to Congress, but they have gone out of the record to do it, in the case in question. It was only necessary, in that case, to decide whether or not the bank law was "necessary and proper," within the meaning of the Constitution, for carrying into effect some of the granted powers; but the Court have, in effect, expunged those words from the Constitution. . . . The power of the Supreme Court is indeed great, but it does not extend to everything; it is not great enough to *change* the Constitution. . . .

According to the regular course of legal proceedings I ought, in the first place, to urge my plea in abatement to the jurisdiction of the Court. As, however, we are not now in a court of justice, and such a course might imply some want of confidence in the merits of my cause, I will postpone that inquiry, for the present, and proceed directly to the merits. In investigating those merits, I shall sometimes discuss particular points stated by the Supreme Court, and at others, urge propositions inconsistent with them. I pledge myself to object to nothing in the opinion in question which does not appear to me to be materially subject to error.

I beg leave to lay down the following propositions as being equally incontestable in themselves, and assented to by the enlightened advocates of the Constitution at the time of its adoption.

1. That that Constitution conveyed only a limited grant of powers to the general government, and reserved the residuary powers to the governments of the states and to the people; and that the Tenth Amendment was merely declaratory of this principle, and inserted only to quiet what the Court is pleased to call "the excessive jealousies of the people."

2. That the limited grant to Congress of certain enumerated powers only carried with it such additional powers as were *fairly incidental* to them, or, in other words, were necessary and proper for their execution.

3. That the insertion of the words "necessary and proper," in the last part of the 8th Section of the 1st Article, did not enlarge the powers previously given, but were inserted only through abundant caution.

On the first point it is to be remarked that the Constitution does not give to Congress *general* legislative powers but the legislative powers "*herein granted.*" . . . So it is said in *The Federalist,* that the jurisdiction of the general government extends to certain enumerated objects only and leaves to the states a residuary and inviolable sovereignty over all other objects; that in the *new* as well as the old government, the general powers are limited, and the states, in all the unenumerated cases, are left in the enjoyment of their sovereign and independent jurisdiction; that the powers given to the general government are few and defined; and that all authorities of which the states are not *explicitly* divested, in favor of the Union, remain with them in full force; as is admitted by the affirmative grants to the general government, and the prohibitions of some powers by negative clauses to the state governments.

It was said by Mr. Madison, in the convention of Virginia, that the powers of the general government were enumerated and that its legislative powers are on defined objects, beyond which it cannot extend its jurisdiction; that the general government has no power but what is given and delegated, and that the delegation alone warranted the power; and that the powers of the general government are but *few,* and relate to external objects, whereas those of the states relate to those great objects which immediately concern the prosperity of the people. It was said by Mr. Marshall that Congress cannot go beyond the delegated powers, and that a law not warranted by any of the enumerated powers would be void; and that the powers not given to Congress were *retained* by the states, and that without the aid of implication. Mr. Randolph said that every power not given by this system is left with the states. And it was said by Mr. Geo. Nicholas that the people retain the powers not conferred on the general government, and that Congress cannot meddle with a power not enumerated.

It was resolved in the legislature of Virginia, in acting upon the celebrated report of 1799 (of which Mr. Madison, the great patron of the Constitution, was the author), that the powers vested in the general government result from the *compact,* to which the *states* are the parties; that they are limited by the plain sense of that instrument (the Constitution), and extend no further than they are authorized by the grant; that the Constitution had been constantly discussed and justified by *its friends* on the ground that the powers not given to the government were withheld from it; and that if any doubts could have existed on the original text of the Constitution. they are removed by the Tenth Amendment; that if the powers granted be valid, it is only because they are *granted,* and that all others are retained; that both from the original Constitution and the Tenth Amendment, it results that it is incumbent on the general government to *prove,* from the Constitution, that it grants the *particular* powers; that it is *immaterial* whether unlimited powers be exercised under the name of unlimited powers, or under that of unlimited means of carrying a limited power into execution; that, in all the discussions and ratifications of the Constitution, it was urged as a characteristic of the government that powers not given were retained, and that none were given but those which were *expressly* granted, or were fairly incident to them; and that in the ratification of the Constitution by Virginia, it was expressly asserted that every power *not granted* by the Constitution remained with them (the people of Virginia), and *at their will.*

I am to show in the second place that by the provisions of the Constitution (taken in exclusion of the words "necessary and proper" in the 8th [Section] of the 1st Article) such powers were only conveyed to the general government as were expressly granted or were (to use the language of the report) fairly incident to them. I shall afterward show that the insertion of those words, in that article, made no difference whatever and created no extension of the powers previously granted.

I take it to be a clear principle of universal law — of the law of nature, of nations, of war, of reason, and of the common law — that the general grant of a thing or power carries with it all those means (and those only) which are necessary to the perfection of the grant or the execution of the power. All those entirely concur in this respect, and are bestowed upon a clear principle. That principle is one which, while it completely effects the object of the grant or power, is a safe one as it relates to the reserved rights of the other party.

This is the true principle, and it is a universal one, applying to *all* pacts and conventions, high or low, or of which nature or kind soever. It cannot be stretched or extended even in relation to the American government; although, for purposes which can easily be conjectured, the Supreme Court has used high-sounding words as to it. They have stated it to be a government extending from St. Croix to the Gulf of Mexico, and from the Atlantic to the Pacific Ocean. This principle depends on a basis which applies to all cases whatsoever, and is inflexible and universal. . . .

We are told in *The Federalist* that all powers *indispensably necessary* are granted by the Constitution, though they be not expressly; and that all the particular powers *requisite* to carry the enumerated ones into effect would have resulted to the government by unavoidable implications *without* the words "necessary and proper"; and that when a power is given, every particular power *necessary* for doing it is included. Again, it is said that a power is nothing but the ability or faculty of doing a thing, and that that ability includes the means *necessary* for its execution.

It is laid down in the report before mentioned that Congress under the terms "necessary and proper" have only all incidental powers necessary and proper, etc., and that the only inquiry is whether the power is properly an *incident* to an express power and *necessary* to its execution, and that, if it is not, Congress cannot exercise it; and that this Constitution provided during all the discussions and ratifications of the Constitution, and is *absolutely necessary to consist* with the idea of defined or particular powers. Again, it is said, that none but the express powers and those *fairly incident* to them were granted by the Constitution.

The terms "incident" and "incidental powers" are not only the terms used in the early stages and by the *friends* of the Constitution but they are the terms used by the *Court* itself, in more passages than one, in relation to the power in question. . . . Can it be then said that means which are of an independent or paramount character can be implied as incidental ones? Certainly not, unless, to say the least, they be absolutely necessary.

Can it be said, after this, that we are at liberty to invent terms at our pleasure in relation to this all-important question? Are we not tied down to the terms used by the founders of the Constitution; terms, too, of limited, well-defined, and established signification? On the contrary, I see great danger in using the *general* term now introduced; it may cover the latent designs of ambition and change the nature of the general government. It is entirely unimportant, as is before said, by what means this end is effected.

I come in the third place to show that the words "necessary and proper," in the Constitution, add nothing to the powers before given to the general government. They were only added (says *The Federalist)* for greater caution, and are tautologous and redundant, though harmless. It is also said, in the report aforesaid, that these words do not amount to a grant of *new* power, but for the removal of all uncertainty the declaration was made that the means were included in the grant. I might multiply authorities on this point to infinity; but if these do not suffice, neither would one were he to arise from the dead. If this power existed in the government before these words were used, its repetition or reduplication, in the Constitution, does not increase it. The "expression of that which before existed in the grant, has no operation." So these words, "necessary and proper," have no power or other effect than if they had been annexed to and repeated in every specific grant; and in that case they would have been equally unnecessary and harmless. As a friend, however, to the just powers of the general government, I do not object to them, considered as merely declaratory words, and inserted for greater caution. I only deny to them an extension to which they are not entitled, and which may be fatal to the reserved rights by the states and of the people.

131.

William Ellery Channing: An Attack on Orthodox Calvinism

Calvinism was slow to die in New England. But by 1815 its main doctrines — of original sin, of man's innate depravity, and of a jealous God whose doubtful grace is all that stands between men and their damnation — had come to seem repugnant to the new breed of liberal theologians. Precisely opposite doctrines took the place of those of Calvin: that man like God is good, that he can comprehend divinity with reason, and that by the exercise of his free will he can bring God's grace upon himself for his salvation. There was no real meeting ground between the two modes of thought. Unitarians regarded Calvinism as giving too dim a portrayal of human nature, while to traditional theology it seemed that religion had grown sentimental — for, as they were inclined to ask: What was man that he should presume to make sense of his Creator? The somewhat unwilling spokesman for Unitarianism was William Ellery Channing, who defined his position and that of liberal New England in a famous sermon delivered at the ordination of a fellow minister, Jared Sparks. A portion of Channing's sermon, which was given in Baltimore on May 5, 1819, is reprinted here.

Source: *The Works of William E. Channing,* 6th edition, Boston, 1846, Vol. III, pp. 59-103.

Prove all things; hold fast that which is good.
I Thess. 5:21

The peculiar circumstances of this occasion not only justify but seem to demand a departure from the course generally followed by preachers at the introduction of a brother into the sacred office. It is usual to speak of the nature, design, duties, and advantages of the Christian ministry; and on these topics I should now be happy to insist, did I not remember that a minister is to be given this day to a religious society, whose peculiarities of opinion have drawn upon them much remark and, may I not add, much reproach. Many good minds, many sincere Christians, I am aware, are apprehensive that the solemnities of this day are to give a degree of influence to principles which they deem false and injurious. The fears and anxieties of such men I respect; and, believing that they are grounded in part on mistake, I have thought it my duty to lay before you, as clearly as I can, some of the distinguishing opinions of that class of Christians in our country who are known to sympathize with this religious society.

I must ask your patience, for such a subject is not to be dispatched in a narrow compass. I must also ask you to remember that it is impossible to exhibit, in a single discourse, our views of every doctrine of revelation, much less the differences of opinion which are known to subsist among ourselves. I shall confine myself to topics on which our sentiments have been misrepresented, or which distinguish us most widely from others. May I not hope to be heard with candor? God deliver us all from prejudice and unkindness, and fill us with the love of truth and virtue.

There are two natural divisions under which my thoughts will be arranged. I shall endeavor to unfold, first, the principles which we adopt in interpreting the Scriptures; and second, some of the doctrines which the Scriptures, so interpreted, seem to us clearly to express.

I. We regard the Scriptures as the records of God's successive revelations to mankind, and particularly of the last and most perfect revelation of His will by Jesus Christ. Whatever doctrines seem to us to be clearly taught in the Scriptures, we receive without reserve or exception. We do not, however, attach equal importance to all the books in this collection. Our religion, we believe, lies chiefly in the New Testament. The dispensation of Moses, compared with that of Jesus, we consider as adapted to the childhood of the human race, a preparation for a nobler system, and chiefly useful now as serving to confirm and illustrate the Christian Scriptures. Jesus Christ is the only master of Christians, and whatever He taught, either during His personal ministry or by His inspired apostles, we regard as of divine authority and profess to make the rule of our lives.

This authority which we give to the Scriptures is a reason, we conceive, for studying them with peculiar care, and for inquiring anxiously into the principles of interpretation by which their true meaning may be ascertained. The principles adopted by the class of Christians in whose name I speak need to be explained because they are often misunderstood. We are particularly accused of making an unwarrantable use of reason in the interpretation of Scripture. We are said to exalt reason above revelation, to prefer our own wisdom to God's. Loose and undefined charges of this kind are circulated so freely that we think it due to ourselves, and to the cause of truth, to express our views with some particularity.

Our leading principle in interpreting Scripture is this, that the Bible is a book written for men, in the language of men, and that its meaning is to be sought in the same manner as that of other books. We believe that God, when He speaks to the human race, conforms, if we may so say, to the established rules of speaking and writing. How else would the Scriptures avail us more than if communicated in an unknown tongue?

Now, all books and all conversation require in the reader or hearer the constant exercise of reason; or their true import is only to be obtained by continual comparison and inference. Human language, you well know, admits various interpretations; and every word and every sentence must be modified and explained according to the subject which is discussed; according to the purposes, feelings, circumstances, and principles of the writer; and according to the genius and idioms of the language which he uses. These are acknowledged principles in the interpretation of human writings; and a man, whose words we should explain without reference to these principles, would reproach us justly with a criminal want of candor and an intention of obscuring or distorting his meaning. . . .

Enough has been said to show in what sense we make use of reason in interpreting Scripture. From a variety of possible interpretations, we select that which accords with the nature of the subject and the state of the writer, with the connection of the passage, with the general strain of Scripture, with the known character and will of God, and with the obvious and acknowledged laws of nature. In other words, we believe that God never contradicts, in one part of Scripture, what He teaches in another; and never contradicts, in revelation, what He teaches in His works and providence. And we therefore distrust every interpretation which, after deliberate attention, seems repugnant to any established truth.

We reason about the Bible precisely as civilians do about the Constitution under which we live; who, you know, are accustomed to limit one provision of that venerable instrument by others, and to fix the precise import of its parts by inquiring into its general spirit, into the intentions of its authors, and into the prevalent feelings, impressions, and circumstances of the time when it was framed. Without these principles of interpretation, we frankly acknowledge that we cannot defend the divine authority of the Scriptures. Deny us this latitude and we must abandon this book to its enemies. . . .

We object strongly to the contemptuous manner in which human reason is often spoken of by our adversaries, because it leads, we believe, to universal skepticism. If reason be so dreadfully darkened by the fall that its most decisive judgments on religion are unworthy of trust, then Christianity, and even natural theology, must be abandoned; for the existence and veracity of God, and the divine original of Christianity, are conclusions of reason and must stand or fall with it. If revelation be at war with this faculty, it subverts itself; for the great question of its truth is left by God to be decided at the bar of reason. It is worthy of remark how nearly the bigot and the skeptic approach. Both would annihilate our confidence in our faculties, and both throw doubt and confusion over every truth. We honor revelation too highly to make it the antagonist of reason, or to believe that it calls us to renounce our highest powers . . .

We ought, indeed, to expect occasional obscurity in such a book as the Bible, which was written for past and future ages as well as for the present. But God's wisdom is a pledge, that whatever is necessary for *us* and necessary for salvation is revealed too plainly to be mistaken, and too consistently to be questioned, by a sound and upright mind. It is not the mark of wisdom to use an unintelligible phraseology, to communicate what is above our capacities, to confuse and unsettle the intellect by appearances of contradiction. We honor our Heavenly Teacher too much to ascribe to Him such a revelation. A revelation is a gift of light. It cannot thicken our darkness and multiply our perplexities.

Bostonian Society

Portrait of William Ellery Channing by an unknown artist

II. Having thus stated the principles according to which we interpret Scripture, I now proceed to the second great head of this discourse, which is to state some of the views which we derive from that sacred book, particularly those which distinguish us from other Christians.

1. In the first place, we believe in the doctrine of God's unity, or that there is one God, and one only. . . .

We object to the doctrine of the Trinity that, while acknowledging in words, it subverts in effect, the unity of God. According to this doctrine, there are three infinite and equal persons possessing supreme divinity, called the Father, Son, and Holy Ghost. Each of these persons, as described by theologians, has his own particular consciousness, will, and perceptions. They love each other, converse with each other, and delight in each other's society. They perform different parts in man's redemption, each having his appropriate office, and neither doing the work of the other. The Son is mediator and not the Father. The Father sends the Son, and is not himself sent; nor is he conscious, like the Son, of taking flesh. Here, then, we have three intelligent agents, possessed of different consciousnesses, different wills, and different perceptions, performing different acts and sustaining different relations; and if these things do not imply and constitute three minds or beings, we are utterly at a loss to know how three minds or beings are to be formed.

It is difference of properties, and acts, and consciousness which leads us to the belief of different intelligent beings, and, if this mark fails us, our whole knowledge falls; we have no proof that all the agents and persons in the universe are not one and the same mind. When we attempt to conceive of three Gods, we can do nothing more than represent to ourselves three agents, distinguished from each other by similar marks and peculiarities to those which separate the persons of the Trinity. And when common Christians hear these persons spoken of as conversing with each other, loving each other, and performing different acts, how can they help regarding them as different beings, different minds?

We do, then, with all earnestness, though without reproaching our brethren, protest against the irrational and unscriptural doctrine of the Trinity. . . .

We think, too, that the peculiar offices ascribed to Jesus by the popular theology make him the most attractive person in the Godhead. The Father is the depositary of the justice, the vindicator of the rights, the avenger of the laws of the Divinity. On the other hand, the Son, the brightness of the divine mercy, stands between the incensed Deity and guilty humanity, exposes His meek head to the storms and His compassionate breast to the sword of the divine justice, bears our whole load of punishment, and purchases with His blood every blessing which descends from heaven. Need we state the effect of these representations, especially on common minds, for whom Christianity was chiefly designed and whom it seeks to bring to the Father as the loveliest being? We do believe that the worship of a bleeding, suffering God tends strongly to absorb the mind and to draw it from other objects, just as the human tenderness of the Virgin Mary has given her so conspicuous a place in the devotions of the Church of Rome. We believe, too, that this worship, though attractive, is not most fitted to spiritualize the mind, that it awakens human transport rather than that deep veneration of the moral perfections of God, which is the essence of piety.

2. Having thus given our views of the unity of God, I proceed, in the second place, to observe that we believe in the unity of Jesus Christ. We believe that Jesus is one mind, one soul, one being, as truly one as we are, and equally distinct from the one God. We complain of the doctrine of the Trinity that, not satisfied with making God three beings, it makes Jesus Christ two beings, and thus introduces infinite confusion into our conceptions of His character. This corruption of Christianity, alike repugnant to common sense and to the general strain of Scripture, is a remarkable proof of the power of a false philosophy in disfiguring the simple truth of Jesus. . . .

Trinitarians profess to derive some important advantages from their mode of viewing Christ. It furnishes them, they tell us, with an infinite atonement, for it shows them an infinite being suffering for their sins. The confidence with which this fallacy is repeated astonishes us. When pressed with the question whether they really believe that the infinite and unchangeable God suffered and died on the cross, they acknowledge that this is not true, but that Christ's human mind alone sustained the pains of death. How have we, then, an infinite sufferer? This language seems to us an imposition on common minds and very derogatory to God's justice, as if this attribute could be satisfied by a sophism and a fiction. . . .

But not only does their doctrine, when fully explained, reduce Christ's humiliation to a fiction, it almost wholly destroys the impressions with which His cross ought to be viewed. According to their doctrine, Christ was comparatively no sufferer at all. It is true, his human mind suffered; but this, they tell us, was an infinitely small part of Jesus, bearing no more proportion to His whole nature than a single hair of our heads to the whole body, or than a drop to the ocean. The divine mind of Christ, that which was most properly Himself, was infinitely happy at the very moment of the suffering of His humanity. While hanging on the cross, He was the happiest being in the universe, as happy as the infinite Father; so that His pains, compared with His felicity, were nothing.

This, Trinitarians do, and must, acknowledge. It follows, necessarily, from the immutableness of the divine nature which they ascribe to Christ; so that their system, justly viewed, robs His death of interest, weakens our sympathy with His sufferings, and is, of all others, most unfavorable to a love of Christ, founded on a sense of His sacrifices for mankind.

We esteem our own views to be vastly more affecting. It is our belief that Christ's humiliation was real and entire; that the whole Savior, and not a part of Him, suffered; that His crucifixion was a scene of deep and unmixed agony. As we stand round His cross, our minds are not distracted nor our sensibility weakened by contemplating Him as composed of incongruous and infinitely differing minds, and as having a balance of infinite felicity. We recognize in the dying Jesus but one mind. This, we think, renders His sufferings, and His patience and love in bearing them, incomparably more impressive and affecting than the system we oppose.

3. Having thus given our belief on two great points, namely, that there is one God, and that Jesus Christ is a being distinct from, and inferior to, God, I now proceed to another point, on which we lay still greater stress. We believe in the *moral perfection of God.* We consider no part of theology so important as that which treats of God's moral character; and we value our views of Christianity chiefly as they assert His amiable and venerable attributes. . . .

We believe that God is infinitely good, kind, benevolent, in the proper sense of these words; good in disposition as well as in act; good, not to a few but to all; good to every individual as well as to the general system.

We believe, too, that God is just; but we never forget that His justice is the justice of a good being, dwelling in the same mind and acting in harmony with perfect benevolence. By this attribute, we understand God's infinite regard to virtue or moral worth expressed in a moral government; that is, in giving excellent and equitable laws, and in conferring such rewards, and inflicting such punishments, as are best fitted to secure their observance. God's justice has for its end the highest virtue of the creation, and it punishes for this end alone, and thus it coincides with benevolence; for virtue and happiness, though not the same, are inseparably conjoined. . . .

To give our views of God in one word, we believe in His parental character. We ascribe to Him not only the name but the dispositions and principles of a father. We believe that He has a father's concern for His creatures, a father's desire for their improvement, a father's equity in proportioning His commands to their powers, a father's joy in their progress, a father's readiness to receive the penitent, and a father's justice for the incorrigible. We look upon this world as a place of education in which He is training men by prosperity and adversity, by aids and obstructions, by conflicts of reason and passion, by motives to duty and temptations to sin, by a various discipline suited to free and moral beings, for union with Himself, and for a sublime and ever growing virtue in heaven.

Now, we object to the systems of religion which prevail among us that they are adverse, in a greater or less degree, to these purifying, comforting, and honorable views of God; that they take from us our Father in heaven and substitute for Him a being whom we cannot love if we would, and whom we ought not to love if we could. We object, particularly on this ground, to that system which arrogates to itself the name of "Orthodoxy," and which is now industriously propagated through our country. This system, indeed, takes various shapes, but in all it casts dishonor on the Creator.

According to its old and genuine form, it teaches that God brings us into life wholly depraved, so that under the innocent features of our childhood is hidden a nature averse to all good and propense to all evil, a nature which exposes us to God's displeasure and wrath, even before we have acquired power to understand our duties or to reflect upon our actions. According to a more modern exposition, it teaches that we came from the hands of our Maker with such a constitution, and are placed under such influences and circumstances, as to render certain and infallible the total depravity of every human being from the first moment of his moral agency. And it also teaches that the offense of the child who brings into life this ceaseless tendency to unmingled crime exposes him to the sentence of everlasting damnation. Now, according to the plainest principles of morality, we maintain that a natural constitution of the mind, unfailingly disposing it to evil and to evil alone, would absolve it from guilt; that to give existence under this condition would argue unspeakable cruelty; and that to punish the sin of this unhappily constituted child with endless ruin would be a wrong unparalleled by the most merciless despotism. . . .

The false and dishonorable views of God which have now been stated we feel ourselves bound to resist unceasingly. Other errors we can pass over with comparative indifference. But we ask our opponents to leave to us a God worthy of our love and trust, in whom our moral sentiments may delight, in whom our weaknesses and sorrows may find refuge. We cling to the divine perfections. We meet them everywhere in creation, we read them in the Scriptures, we see a lovely image of them in Jesus Christ; and gratitude, love, and veneration call on us to assert them. Reproached, as we often are, by men, it is our consolation and happiness that one of our chief offenses is the zeal with which we vindicate the dishonored goodness and rectitude of God. . . .

Another important branch of virtue we believe to be love to Christ. The greatness of the work of Jesus, the spirit with which He executed it, and the sufferings which He bore for our salvation we feel to be strong claims on our gratitude and veneration. We see in nature no beauty to be compared with the loveliness of His character, nor do we find on earth a benefactor to whom we owe an equal debt. We read His history with delight, and learn from it the perfection of our nature. We are particularly touched by His death, which was endured for our redemption, and by that strength of charity which triumphed over His pains. His resurrection is the foundation of our hope of immortality. His intercession gives us boldness to draw nigh to the throne of grace; and we look up to heaven with new desire when we think that, if we follow Him here, we shall there see His benignant countenance, and enjoy His friendship forever.

I need not express to you our views on the subject of the benevolent virtues. We attach such importance to these that we are sometimes reproached with exalting them above piety. We regard the spirit of love, charity, meekness, forgiveness, liberality, and beneficence as the badge and distinction of Christians, as the brightest image we can bear of God, as the best proof of piety. On this subject, I need not and cannot enlarge.

But there is one branch of benevolence which I ought not to pass over in silence, because we think that we conceive of it more highly and justly than many of our brethren. I refer to the duty of candor, charitable judgment, especially toward those who differ in religious opinion. We think that in nothing have Christians so widely departed from their religion as in this particular. We read with astonishment and horror the history of the church; and sometimes, when we look back on the fires of persecution and on the zeal of Christians in building up walls of separation and in giving up one another to perdition, we feel as if we were reading the records of an infernal rather than a heavenly kingdom. An enemy to every religion, if asked to describe a Christian, would, with some show of reason, depict him as an idolater of his own distinguishing opinions, covered with badges of party, shutting his eyes on the virtues, and his ears on the arguments, of his opponents; arrogating all excellence to his own sect and all saving power to his own creed; sheltering under the name of pious zeal the love of domination, the conceit of infallibility, and the spirit of intolerance; and trampling on men's rights under the pretense of saving their souls.

We can hardly conceive of a plainer obligation on beings of our frail and fallible nature, who are instructed in the duty of candid judgment, than to abstain from condemning men of apparent conscientiousness and sincerity, who are chargeable with no crime but that of differing from us in the interpretation of the Scriptures, and differing, too, on topics of great and acknowledged obscurity. We are astonished at the hardihood of those who, with Christ's warnings sounding in their ears, take on them the responsibility of making creeds for His church, and cast out professors of virtuous lives for imagined errors, for the guilt of thinking of themselves.

We know that zeal for truth is the cover for this usurpation of Christ's prerogative; but we think that zeal for truth, as it is called, is very suspicious, except in men whose capacities and advantages, whose patient deliberation, and whose improvements in humility, mildness, and candor give them a right to hope that their views are more just than those of their neighbors. Much of what passes for a zeal for truth, we look upon with little respect, for it often appears to thrive most luxuriantly where other virtues shoot up thinly and feebly; and we have no gratitude for those reformers who would force upon us a doctrine which has not sweetened their own tempers, or made them better men than their neighbors.

We are accustomed to think much of the difficulties attending religious inquiries; difficulties springing from the slow development of our minds, from the power of early impressions, from the state of society, from human authority, from the general neglect of the reasoning powers, from the want of just principles of criticism and of important helps in interpreting Scripture, and from various other causes. We find that on no subject have men, and even good men, ingrafted so many strange conceits, wild theories, and fictions of fancy as on religion; and remembering, as we do, that we ourselves are sharers of the common frailty, we dare not assume infallibility in the treatment of our fellow Christians, or encourage in common Christians, who have little time for investigation, the habit of denouncing and contemning other denominations, perhaps more enlightened and virtuous than their own.

Charity, forbearance, a delight in the virtues of different sects, a backwardness to censure and condemn, these are virtues which, however poorly practised by us, we admire and recommend; and we would rather join ourselves to the church in which they abound than to any other communion, however elated with the belief of its own orthodoxy, however strict in guarding its creed, however burning with zeal against imagined error.

I have thus given the distinguishing views of those Christians in whose names I have spoken. We have embraced this system, not hastily or lightly but after much deliberation; and we hold it fast, not merely because we believe it to be true but because we regard it as purifying truth, as a doctrine according to godliness, as able to "work mightily" and to "bring forth fruit" in them who believe. That we wish to spread it, we have no desire to conceal; but we think that we wish its diffusion because we regard it as more friendly to practical piety and pure morals than the opposite doctrines; because it gives clearer and nobler views of duty and stronger motives to its performance; because it recommends religion at once to the understanding and the heart; because it asserts the lovely and venerable attributes of God; because it tends to restore the benevolent spirit of Jesus to His divided and afflicted church; and because it cuts off every hope of God's favor, except that which springs from practical conformity to the life and precepts of Christ. We see nothing in our views to give offense, save their purity; and it is their purity which makes us seek and hope their extension through the world.

My friend and brother, you are this day to take upon you important duties; to be clothed with an office which the Son of God did not disdain; to devote yourself to that religion which the most hallowed lips have preached and the most precious blood sealed. We trust that you will bring to this work a willing mind, a firm purpose, a martyr's spirit, a readiness to toil and suffer for the truth, a devotion of your best powers to the interests of piety and virtue. I have spoken of the doctrines which you will probably preach; but I do not mean that you are to give yourself to controversy. You will remember that good practice is the end of preaching, and will labor to make your people holy livers rather than skillful disputants. Be careful lest the desire of defending what you deem truth, and of repelling reproach and misrepresentation, turn you aside from your great business, which is to fix in men's minds a living conviction of the obligation, sublimity, and happiness of Christian virtue.

The best way to vindicate your sentiments is to show, in your preaching and life, their intimate connection with Christian morals, with a high and delicate sense of duty, with candor toward your opposers, with inflexible integrity, and with a habitual reverence for God. If any light can pierce and scatter the clouds of prejudice, it is that of a pure example. My brother, may your life preach more loudly than your lips. Be to this people a pattern of all good works, and may your instructions derive authority from a well-grounded belief in your hearers, that you speak from the heart, that you preach from experience, that the truth which you dispense has wrought powerfully in your own heart, that God and Jesus and heaven are not merely words on your lips but most affecting realities to your mind, and springs of hope and consolation and strength in all your trials. Thus laboring, may you reap abundantly and have a testimony of your faithfulness, not only in your own conscience but in the esteem, love, virtues, and improvements of your people.

132.

Henry M. Brackenridge: A Vindication of Civil Rights for Jews

Attempts to repeal an old Maryland law that forbade Jews to practise law or hold elective office had failed repeatedly since 1797. The thirty-year struggle for civil rights for Jews was finally won in 1825, under the leadership of Thomas Kennedy, a Washington County state legislator whose agitation in favor of the Jews at one point cost him his seat in the Maryland House of Delegates. But there had been notable moments before that. One such moment was the speech in support of the Maryland "Jew Bill," as it was known at the time, by Judge Henry M. Brackenridge, given in January 1819. The portions of the speech reprinted here give the main arguments of those who advocated equal rights for all in the state.

Source: *Speeches on the Jew Bill in the House of Delegates of Maryland,* Philadelphia, 1829, pp. 59-100.

Could I, for a moment, suppose it possible for the bill on your table to lessen, in the slightest degree, by its passage the attachment we all profess for the religion in which we have been educated; or could I bring myself to believe that even those innocent and harmless prejudices which more or less influence the opinions of the most liberal are treated with disrespect by bringing the subject before this House, I should be the last person to urge it on your consideration.

But, sir, I feel a firm conviction that there is no room for any such apprehensions. The known public and private worth (if I may be allowed thus to express myself in this place), as well as the firm and fixed religious principles of the gentleman with whom the bill has originated and who has supported it in a manner so becoming the enlightened American statesman and the tolerant Christian, must necessarily repel the suspicion of any but the most generous, disinterested, and philanthropic motives. In the theological view he has just taken of this interesting subject, he has most satisfactorily proved to my mind that there is nothing in the religious faith which we profess that enjoins us to hold to the arbitrary test engrafted as a principle on the constitution of this state, at this day, when it is converted into a stain by the progressive wisdom of the political world.

To the test of that wisdom I will, nevertheless, endeavor to bring the question now before the House. I will endeavor to show that the objectionable provision in our own constitution is at variance with all the sound and well-established political creed of the present enlightened age. For this I will refer to the opinions publicly avowed and successfully maintained by every distinguished statesman, not only of America but throughout the civilized world. In addition to this, I will show that the principles for which I this day contend have received the unequivocal sanction of the most enlightened and respectable political bodies of our country.

The subject, although of a most fruitful nature, properly resolves itself into three questions. 1. Have the Jews a *right* to be placed on a footing with other citizens? 2. Is there any urgent reason of state policy which requires that they should be made an exception? 3. Is there anything incompatible with the respect we owe to the Christian religion in allowing them a participation in civil offices and employments?

In ascending to first principles (and in examining institutions supposed to be founded upon them, we must often do so) I find that we have duties to perform to our Creator as well as to society, but which are so distinct in their nature that unless their corresponding obligations be clearly understood we shall in vain attempt to lay the foundation of a solid and satisfactory argument.

It is unquestionably the right of society to compel everyone who enjoys its protection to conform to its ordinances and laws. It is its right so to restrain his *actions* as to conduce to the general happiness and prosperity. But I contend that after having exercised this control over his actions, the temporal power has reached its limit; and when it dares to pass that limit, it opens the way to oppression, persecution, and cruelty, such as the history of the world has furnished but too many melancholy examples — not for our imitation, but abhorrence. Opinion, when merely such, when prompting to no act inconsistent with the laws and peace of society, should be encountered only by opinion; and on such occasions the interposition of the temporal arm is improper, however mildly interposed. For it is not the extent or degree of compulsion which renders it improper, but the unjust and arbitrary interference itself.

If, as members of society, we have duties whose performance the temporal power may justly enforce, we have, as rational beings, other duties of a much higher nature to our Creator, of which He is the judge, and to whom, alone, should be referred the punishment or reward of their fulfilment or neglect. Religion, therefore, merely as such, is a matter entirely between man and his God.

If my position, then, be correct, it will follow that it must be left to every citizen, as he is to stand or fall by his own merits or demerits, to entertain that belief or offer that worship which in his conscience he thinks most acceptable; and should any of his fellow citizens desire to release him from what he conceives to be the bondage of error, let it be by an appeal to the reason, and not by a resort to coercion — a coercion which can only affect outward actions, and serve to exhibit power on the one side and feebleness on the other. He that is thus convinced will be of the same opinion still. The human frame may be bound in chains; it may be imprisoned and enslaved; it may yield to the dagger of the assassin, or the murderer's bowl; but the immortal mind soars beyond the reach of earthly violence.

Upon the self-evident truths which I have spoken (and on no others can they safely rest) are built the *rights of conscience,* so little understood, or at least respected, in most countries; not so well, I confess it with regret, in Maryland, as they ought to be, but perfectly so in the Constitution of the United States, an instrument for which we are indebted as a nation to the high estimation of enlightened men, and which has conferred on our country the reputation of being the land of freedom and toleration.

And here I find it necessary to encounter an argument of those gentlemen who oppose the passage of the bill; they tell us, that no *force* or coercion is resorted to by the constitution of Maryland in consequence of religious faith; that everyone is secured in his civil rights, no matter what religion he may profess; that no one can be molested on account of his religious belief; that no one has a right to complain of being denied some common benefit, or being excluded from holding offices, when he does not think proper to conform to the prevailing religious tenets of the community of which he is admitted a member.

Sir, I contend that in conformity to the reasons I have advanced, *every* citizen is entitled to *all* the privileges of citizenship; that the religious opinions of no one can be justly visited upon him, either directly or indirectly, as the immediate or remote consequence of that opinion. If, on account of my religious faith, I am subjected to disqualifications from which others are free, while there is no paramount reason drawn from a regard to the safety of society why I should be thus excepted, I cannot but consider myself a persecuted man. The persecution may be but slight in its character, but still it must bear the detested name of persecution. It is true, it is not the fagot or the wheel, but it is applied for the same reason, because my opinions do not conform to those of the more numerous or the more powerful.

An odious exclusion from any of the benefits common to the rest of my fellow citizens is a persecution differing only in degree, but of a nature equally unjustifiable with that whose instruments are chains and torture. In our land of equal rights and equal pretensions to the dignity and emolument of office, to be subjected to a degrading exception is by no means a nominal punishment.

Sir, in the sentiments which I have uttered on this occasion, I have done nothing more than repeat what has already been so often and so much better expressed by the enlightened statesmen of our country. There is hardly a distinguished American who has not in some mode or other given to these ideas his decided approbation. They are deeply engraven on the tablets of those political doctrines which are considered as eternal and immutable. They are among the first lessons inculcated on our youthful minds; they are interwoven in the texture of our political constitutions; and so deeply are we impressed with their truth that every American who aspires to the character of liberality, as well as to a proper knowledge of the spirit of our institutions, must subscribe to this proposition as the test of the progress of his attainments: THAT RELIGION IS A MATTER BETWEEN MAN AND HIS GOD — THAT THE TEMPORAL ARM SHOULD BE INTERPOSED TO DIRECT THE ACTIONS OF MEN AND NOT THEIR THOUGHTS. . . .

I have hitherto, Mr. Speaker, considered rather what ought to be the right of the citizen than what it really is, as guaranteed by the recorded monument of his liberties; for it is our pride that for these we are not indebted to the charter of a sovereign. And here I do not hesitate to assert that could this question be brought before some tribunal competent to decide, I would undertake to maintain that the right which this bill professes to give is already *secured* by our national compact. I would boldly contend that the state of Maryland has deprived, and still continues to deprive, American citizens of their just political rights. If we cannot find it in the express letter of the instrument, can we hesitate for a moment in believing that it has at least virtually abrogated every part of state laws or constitutions, whose tendency is to infringe the *rights of conscience?*

But first let me ask what says your own declaration of rights on this subject? It emphatically declares, not merely that it is the right but that it is the *duty of every man to worship God in such a manner as he thinks most acceptable to him.* It is true, this is narrowed by the subsequent clause of the sentence, which would seem to confine that worship to the professors of Christianity; and I will not trouble you with a vindication of the enlightened men who drew up that declaration, from the charge of narrowness of mind, in supposing it impossible for anyone conscientiously to worship God, excepting through the medium of Christianity.

I firmly believe that the subsequent expressions were intended to apply to all who *worship the Deity,* and that it was not the intention to discriminate as to the mode: Wherefore,

> no person ought by any law to be molested in his person or estate on account of his religious persuasion or profession or for his religious practice, unless, under color of religion, any man shall disturb the good order, peace, or safety of the state, or shall infringe the laws of morality, or injure others in their natural, civil, or religious rights.

I will ask whether the religious test in the constitution of this state can stand for a moment when construed by the spirit of this declaration? No, sir, they are utterly incompatible. Let us now turn to the 1st Amendment of the Constitution of the United States; we find that Congress is expressly forbidden *to pass any law respecting an establishment of religion.* Does not this speak volumes? And is it not morally certain that if a declaration of rights had preceded that instrument, the right to worship God free from all human control or reflection would have been unequivocally declared? No test oath is required in that instrument; and can there be a clearer, although but a negative exposition?

It is true, the Constitution of the United States, as a form of government, is confined in its operation to the specific objects for which it was instituted. But there are certain broad and fundamental principles entitled to universal respect; and, without respecting them, it is impossible for the general and state governments to move in harmony in their respective orbits. This, I contend, is one of them, and not the least important.

Let us look at the consequence of the contrary in the practical operation. The citizen, who cannot hold the most trivial office in the state of Maryland, may be chosen to preside over its destinies as the chief magistrate of the nation! He may be called to the command of your armies, and lead you to battle against the enemy who has dared to invade your shores; and, yet, he cannot be an ensign or a lieutenant of the smallest company in the mighty host! He may sit on the bench, and, in the federal courts, be called to decide upon the fortune or the life of the citizen of Maryland; and, yet, your constitution forbids him, as a justice of the peace, to decide the most trifling dispute? He may be juror in the circuit courts of the United States and be the arbiter of the reputation, the life, or the liberty of the first among you; yet, under the laws of Maryland, he cannot sit in the same box to deal out the measure of justice to the pilfering slave! He may be marshal of the district, and, in that highly respectable and responsible situation, be entrusted with your most important interests, at the same time that he is disqualified from performing the duties of a constable!

Can it be believed that such glaring inconsistencies could have been foreseen or imagined when our political system was put in motion, attuned, as it was supposed, to move in unison and harmony? This clashing discord of general and state government could not have been foreseen. Still less could it have been supposed that discord would have been produced by such a cause. Supported, then, by the spirit of the law and the strong argument of inconvenience, I would contend in behalf of the citizen, *that in requiring him to subscribe to a religious test, for any purpose, his just, constitutional rights are infringed and violated. . . .*

Let me not be understood, sir, to contend that there may not be sound reason and policy for withholding from certain classes of citizens, or people, the rights or benefits of citizens, in their utmost latitude. The existence of servitude, an evil beyond our power to remedy, has given rise to certain ideas and policy which would be useless in us to attempt to counteract. On this subject, and that of not throwing open to naturalized citizens the whole career of public offices, there are reasons of state policy, so fully established by our laws and received opinions that it would be presumptuous in me to call them in question. But, I have seen no reason of state, nor has any been suggested, why the naturalized Jew should not be placed on the same footing with any other naturalized citizen; or why a *native* Jew should be cast into a lower order than even the naturalized foreigner of any country on the globe! Is it because there is something in the nature of his race which necessarily renders the Jew a less valuable citizen?

Then, sir, ought we to form a graduated scale for the different nations of the world, and regulate the term of their admission, or the extent of their privilege, according to the merits or demerits of their national character! And would it not, on the same principle, be necessary to establish different castes among our own citizens, and lay aside that wholesome republican respect for individual merit which has hitherto been our guide? No, sir, such odious discrimination is practically impossible. The citizen of Jewish origin, whether naturalized or native, ought to be entitled to all the rights of citizenship that may be claimed under like circumstances by an Englishman, a Frenchman, or a Spaniard. . . .

Were it necessary for the support of this bill, I would undertake to vindicate the Jewish character from its commonly imputed vices and defects. But the question before the House has nothing to do with these considerations. I will ask those Christians who now hear me, candidly and dispassionately to examine their own minds and to say how much of their opinions on the subject of the Jewish character is the offspring of prejudice? Most of us have been taught from earliest infancy to look upon them as a depraved and wicked people. The books put into our hands, and even the immortal Shakespeare himself, have contributed to fix in our minds this unchristian hatred to a portion of our fellowmen. It is true, we have witnessed some honorable exceptions; a modern character (I rejoice to say it for the honor of Christendom) ventured to be their advocate and, what is more, with success.

We have seen, sir, that in the same country, in proportion as science and civilization have advanced, the condition of the Jew has improved, while his moral character has as uniformly risen to the level of that condition. Will anyone seriously compare the Jews of England of the present day with the same people a few centuries ago, when degraded and oppressed by the British kings? Will the Jews of Portugal or Turkey bear a comparison with those of the more liberal governments of Europe?

To come nearer home, I will ask whether the American Jew is distinguished by those characteristics so invidiously ascribed to his race by its enemies? Sir, I have had the honor of being acquainted with a number of American Jews and do not hesitate to say that I have found at least an equal proportion of estimable individuals to that which might be expected in any other class of men. None, sir, appeared to me more zealously attached to the interests and happiness of our common country; the more so as it is the only one on earth they can call by that endearing name. None have more gallantly espoused its cause both in the late and Revolutionary War; none feel a livelier sense of gratitude and affection for the mild and liberal institutions of this country, which not only allow them, publicly and freely, the enjoyment and exercise of their religion but also, with the exception of the state of Maryland, have done away all those odious civil and political discriminations by which they are elsewhere thrown into an inferior and degraded caste.

In the city which I have the honor to represent, there are Jewish families which, in point of estimation and worth, stand in the first rank of respectability, who are scarcely remarked as differing from their Christian brethren in their religious tenets, and whose children are educated in the same schools with our youth, AND, LIKE THEM, GLORY IN BEING AMERICANS AND FREEMEN. Have we hitherto had any cause to repent of our liberality, rather of our justice?

Sir, I abhor intolerance, *whether it be political or religious;* and, yet, I can scarcely regard religious *tolerance* as a virtue. What! Has weak and erring man a right to give *permission* to his fellow mortal to offer his adorations to the Supreme Being after his own manner? Did I not feel myself somehow restrained from pursuing this subject, I would endeavor to demonstrate that the idea of such permission, or toleration, is not better than impiety.

But I content myself with calling your attention to what has been the effect, in this country, at least, of leaving religion to be taught from the pulpit, or to be instilled by early education. Is there, let me ask, less genuine Christianity in America than in any other Christian country? For, if the interference of government be necessary to uphold it, such ought to be the natural consequence. Certainly we are not disposed to confess an inferiority in this particular. Sir, I believe there is more.

And I am well convinced that if the success of true religion were the only end in view, other nations would follow our example of universal toleration. I believe that in no countries are there more atheists and deists than in those where but one mode of worship is sanctioned or permitted. In my opinion it is the natural inclination of man to seek support and refuge in religious feelings; and if he find a religion which his judgment approves, or to which his affections attach him, he will cling to it as his brightest hope. The man who cannot subscribe to all the doctrines and discipline of Catholicism may still be a Protestant; the Protestant may be a Churchman, a Presbyterian, a Friend, or a Methodist. But the Inquisition allows him no choice; he must either embrace that which is tendered him or be nothing.

No, sir, it does not enter into the duties of this body to guard and preserve the religious faith of Maryland from schism and innovation; otherwise, we have been grossly remiss in the performance of that duty. I do not recollect a single statute or resolution on the records of this House for this purpose. Sir, the propagation of error has never been prevented by force; but force has sometimes given permanence to what would otherwise have been ephemeral.

Were we about to attempt the conversion of the Jews to Christianity, the true mode, in my opinion, would be to treat them with kindness and to allow them a full participation of political and social rights. When men are proscribed for their opinions, those opinions become dear to them; like the traveler in the storm, they draw the mantle closer about them, but on the return of the warm and genial sun, they cast it carelessly away. . . .

It has been asserted and repeated that there is no intolerance in withholding from the Jews the common privileges of citizenship. It is asked — Are they not protected in the free exercise of their religion? Are they not permitted to hold property and to pursue the occupations most agreeable to them, with one only exception, that of the legal profession, which requires them to sign the test? Are they not permitted to vote at elections and thus to have a voice in the formation of the laws? I own, sir, that this is true; but why allow them even these privileges? It is the principle against which I contend and not the extent of the injustice.

Suppose the Jews were allowed one privilege *less* than they at present enjoy, for instance, the right to vote at elections (and now, for the first time, it was sought to be given them); would not the same arguments be urged in opposition to that just request that we have heard this day against placing them entirely on a footing with their fellow citizens? To go further, let us suppose them on a footing with the Jews of England, and an attempt were now made to extend to them some trivial privilege of citizenship; would not the same arguments still be urged against it? Pursuing this train of thought, to what result would it conduct us? Sir, it would end in consigning the Jews to the dungeons of the Inquisition.

The selfsame arguments that have been arrayed this day against the passage of the bill on your table have been heard from the lips of those who were engaged in preparing the rack, the chains, the fires for the persecuted Jew. Such arguments are unworthy of free Americans, and ought to be abhorred, if for no other reason that they are the constant theme of such as perpetrate the most horrid crimes in the name of religion — of those, to use the words of a celebrated orator, *whose banner is stolen from the altar of God, and whose forces are congregated from the abysses of hell.* . . .

I call upon any gentleman to produce the dictum or opinion of an American statesman of note or celebrity in favor of a religious test for political purposes; or *the example of any state of the Union which withholds from American citizens of Jewish origin all eligibility to office.* In one of the states (Massachusetts), we find something like a test, but confined to a few of the higher offices; but I entertain no doubt that it will be done away in that enlightened republic whenever it shall be proposed. From every state constitution formed since that of the United States, the test has been rejected; and some of them have gone so far as to say that none shall ever be required.

In the state of North Carolina there is a memorable instance on record of an attempt to expel Mr. [Jacob] Henry, a Jew, from the legislative body of which he had been elected a member. The speech delivered on that occasion I hold in my hand; it is published in a collection called the *American Orator;* a book given to your children at school, and containing those republican truths you wish to see earliest implanted in their minds. . . . Mr. Henry prevailed, and it is a part of our education, as Americans, to love and cherish the sentiments uttered by him on that occasion. . . .

There is but one remaining objection to the passage of the bill, and this I will endeavor also to meet, and yet it is not without reluctance. It has been repeated that the passage of the bill is incompatible with the respect we owe to the Christian religion; that this a Christian land, that the Christian religion ought here to be, at least, legally avowed and acknowledged; and that the respect which is due to that institution may be weakened by abolishing the test. Sir, I can see no disrespect offered to any system of religion where the government simply declares that every man may enjoy his own, provided he discharges his social duties; and that the only support of religion should be derived from the zeal, affection, and faith of those who profess it. Sir, I do firmly believe that it is an insult to the Christian religion to suppose that it needs the temporal arm for its support. It has flourished in spite of temporal power; by the interference of temporal power in its behalf, has its progress ever been retarded or its principles perverted.

But, we are told that this is a Christian land, and that we are Christians! I rejoice to hear it, and I hope we will prove ourselves worthy of the name by acting on this, and on every other occasion, with Christian spirit. The Great Author of that sublime religion teaches us charity and forbearance to the errors and failings of our fellowmen. To His followers, He promised no worldly benefits, but crowns of glory in heaven; for He emphatically declared that His kingdom was not of this world. Far from inculcating unkindness and resentment to those of the Jews who did not believe in

Him, He even forgave those among them who were His persecutors and enemies. Do we find any injunction bequeathed to His followers to pursue those enemies with vengeance? No; His last words were a prayer for their forgiveness; and shall we dare to punish where He has been pleased to forgive?

But this is a Christian land! And let me inquire of the page of history, by what means it became so? Was it through the instrumentality of peace and goodwill to our fellowmen? Perhaps we may say with a clear conscience that we violated no principle of justice or Christianity in our dealings with the poor heathen whom we found in possession of the soil. . . .

No, sir, the soil we inhabit yields its fruit to the just and to the unjust; the sun which gives us life sheds his glorious beams impartially on all. But the great majority of the dwellers in this land are Christians; therefore is it a Christian land! For the same reason, it might be a Catholic, Episcopal, or Presbyterian land. Our political compacts are not entered into as brethren of the Christian faith, but as men, as members of a civilized society. In looking back to our struggle for independence, I find that we engaged in that bloody conflict for the RIGHTS OF MAN, and not for the purpose of enforcing or defending any particular religious creed.

If the accidental circumstance of our being for the greater part Christians could justify us in proscribing other religions, the same reason would justify any one of the sects of Christianity in persecuting the rest. But, sir, all persecution for the sake of opinions is tyranny; and the first speck of it that may appear should be eradicated as the commencement of a deadly gangrene, whose ultimate tendency is to convert the body politic into a corrupt and putrid mass.

Mr. Speaker, if I were required to assign a reason why, in the course of events, it was permitted by Providence that this continent should have become known to Europe, the first and most striking, according to my understanding, would be *that it was the will of heaven to open here* AN ASYLUM TO THE PERSECUTED OF EVERY NATION! We are placed here to officiate in that magnificent temple; to us is assigned the noble task of stretching forth the hand of charity to all those unfortunate men whom the political tempests of the world may have cast upon our shores. We, as Americans, should feel a generous exultation when we behold even the Jew, to whom the rest of the world is dark and cheerless, overjoyed to find a HOME in this *Christian land;* in finding here one sunny spot at last!

In perusing an elegant pamphlet from the pen of an American Jew, and lately published in New York, I felt proud to find myself the citizen of a republic whose benevolent conduct deserved such a eulogium. "Let us turn, then," says he,

> from Europe and her errors of opinion, on points of faith, to contemplate a more noble prospect — OUR COUNTRY, the bright example of universal tolerance, of liberality, true religion, and good faith. In the formation and arrangement of our civil code, the sages and patriots, whose collected wisdom adopted them, closed the doors upon that great evil which has shaken the world to its center. They proclaimed freedom of conscience, and left the errors of the heart to be judged at that tribunal whose rights should never have been usurped. Here no inquiry of privileges, no asperity of opinion, no invidious distinctions exist; dignity is blended with equality; justice administered impartially; merit alone has a fixed value; and each man is stimulated by the same laudable ambition — an ambition of doing his duty and meriting the goodwill of his fellowmen. Until the Jews can recover their ancient rights and dominions, and take their rank among the governments of the earth, THIS IS THEIR CHOSEN COUNTRY; here they can rest with the persecuted from every clime, secure in their persons and property, protected from tyranny and oppression, and participating of equal rights and immunities.

Sir, I have done. I trust I have satisfied every member of this House of the justice of the positions I have undertaken to maintain. I hope we shall no longer persevere in withholding from the Jews privileges to which they are constitutionally entitled, and which are not controlled by any paramount reason of state policy arising from a regard to our own safety and welfare. We surely run into no danger by following the example of the enlightened framers of the federal compact with the great Washington at their head. Let us boldly, then, adopt that course, the only one which can steer clear of error and inconsistency, and enable us to square our conduct by the immutable rules of justice. Let us sever at once, and forever, the unnatural union between force and opinion, between temporal power and religious faith. Let us give unto Caesar those things that are Caesar's, and unto God, those things that are God's.

133.

Giovanni Antonio Grassi: Observations on the United States

The Italian Jesuit Giovanni Grassi, who came to the United States in 1810, served as president of Georgetown College from 1812 to 1817. When he returned to Rome, in the latter year, he recorded his experiences in America in a book entitled Notizie varie sullo stato presente della repubblica degli Stati Uniti dell'America *(1819), portions of which, as translated by Oscar Handlin, are reprinted here. The book contained the sympathetic observations of a man who had attempted to overcome his natural bias for his homeland and to give a careful and fair description of the America he saw.*

Source: *Notizie varie sullo stato presente della repubblica degli Stati Uniti dell'America settentrionale scritte al principio del 1818,* Milan, 1819 [TWA, pp. 137-150].

The American cities have the rare advantage of being built according to well-designed and uniform plans. The streets are wide and straight, with poplars now and then along the way. Along the sides are convenient walks which spare the pedestrians the inconveniences they meet in most European cities from wagons, carriages, and horses. Except for some government buildings and a few banks, the architecture is simple and monotonous. The facades of the houses are of red bricks, with little intervals of white. In the rooms there are few pictures, statues, or decorated furniture; instead they prefer mahogany furniture and fine carpets on the floors. If these lack the Italian magnificence, they have, in general, an air of ease, of simplicity, and of cleanliness.

In the cities the window glass, the floors, and the thresholds of the doors are washed at least once a week. The buildings seem rather weak and always are built with a very large amount of wood, which accounts for the frequency of fires. But the safeguards for extinguishing them are effective, since each quarter has its night watchmen, and there are also men appointed to appear at first sound of the alarm, bringing pumps, ladders, pails, axes, and other instruments that may be needed.

Palaces like the Italian are altogether unknown. The houses are made in such a manner that each is used exclusively by one family; the rooms each occupies may be one above another and not all on the same floor. It would seem very strange to an American to learn that in Europe one family lives on the first floor of a house, another on the second, and still another on the third. And it would seem even stranger to see horses and carriages come out of the houses.

No plazas or fountains or the other ornaments familiar in Italy are to be seen in American cities. Water is abundant. There are frequently pumps in the street for public use, and there are underground pipes that carry water to the various houses. In the interest of quiet and cleanliness, the slaughterhouses are on the outskirts of the city and only the meat ready for sale may be brought to shops and markets.

Civil order and public tranquillity are generally well maintained. The abundance of bread makes certain that those who are not lazy will not be poor and will not beg in public. However, many artisans spend as much as they earn, and whenever they are ill find themselves reduced to the most deplorable misery.

English is the language universally spoken, and it is not corrupted here as in England by a variety of dialects. Weights and measures follow the English manner, but there is a decimal money and the dollar is worth one Spanish piece. To avoid the inconvenience of carrying around coins, they use a great deal of bank notes.

Among the inhabitants of the United States, those from New England, called the Yankees, are regarded as the most knavish and capable of the most ingenious impositions. The large volume of business that they carry on in all the other states, and the tricks they resort to for profits have fixed this conception on them. It is certain that to deal with such people one needs much sagacity and an exact knowledge of their laws of trade. But it seems to me unfair to extend this reputation, which may fit some individuals or even a whole class of people, to all the inhabitants of those states.

The limitless liberty that reigns here, the frequent drunkenness, the intermixture of so many adventurers, the number of Negroes held in slavery, the variety of sects that take hold everywhere, the slight knowledge of the true religion, the incredible quantities of novels read, and the eager pursuit of profits are, in truth, elements that stand in the way of a proper view of American customs. At first view, it is hard to realize the waste that is common in this country, since it is often covered over by a veil of superficial well-being. But that waste is not difficult to discover when one becomes a little familiar with these people, especially in the cities.

The sight of gambling and of drunkenness is more frequent here than in Italy, if that may be believed, and the consequences are fatal to individuals and to entire families. Behavior is generally civil, but one will find many deficiencies in the niceties. It is, for example, not regarded as uncivil to cut the fingernails and comb the hair in the presence of others, or to remain seated, feet on the next chair or propped up high against the wall. When a stranger is introduced to a group by an acquaintance, the latter will point out and name each person individually. Friends who meet again after many years will not embrace each other; they are content to shake hands. Mothers have the praiseworthy custom of suckling their offspring themselves; they would be even more worthy of praise if they were to do it more modestly.

The custom of binding babies has altogether been given up in the United States. The complexion of the natives is rather pale, although few lamed and deformed people are seen here. Even a wealthy man will not be above handling the plough and the pick in the fields, or eating there with the day laborers. Luxury in clothing has reached a degree unknown even in Europe; in the country they dress as well as in the city, and the cost of a holiday garment is no index of the condition of the persons who wear them. Balls are the most common entertainment of Americans; the mania for jumping about in this manner is not less powerful here than in France itself.

Points of honor occasion frequent duels. To evade the laws, the combatants go to the borders of some neighboring state to settle their quarrels in this barbarous, foolish, and superstitious manner, in which the aggressor always wins, and in which the innocent bear the heaviest burden of injuries. To reprimand such madness, and to excite the public authorities to more zeal in suppressing it, one need only think of the tragic accidents which were fatal both to individuals and to the public, such, for instance, as the killing of Hamilton by Burr. On the site of this death a monument was erected as a constant warning to the duelists of New York. Two years ago, two young officials in Virginia lost their lives in a duel with pistols, the method ordinarily used here. These are the advantages which result from such affairs of honor.

The observers of American customs have always deplored the fact that the fathers, especially in the South, yield sadly and foolishly to their children whom they seem unable to contradict and whose capricious wishes they do not restrain. Education is, however, far from neglected, especially insofar as it helps to maintain status or to earn a fortune. To facilitate that training, even for the poor, parents and guardians are, by law, authorized to put young people under some artisan who binds himself to hold them as apprentices until the age of twenty-one, and to teach them a trade, reading, writing, and reckoning. The laws insist very strongly on the last points, so important for the public good. Such education is so highly esteemed that a father will use almost all the capital which will be the portion of his son to give him a literary education. A rich farmer will often send one of his sons to the university and keep another with him at the plough. Finally, some young men of narrow fortunes will spend a winter teaching in rural elementary schools in order to earn enough to maintain themselves at some college.

There are two sorts of literary education, one classical, the other simple English. The first includes belles-lettres, Greek and Latin, rhetoric, mathematics, and the various branches of philosophy, and is designed for those who intend to practise law or medicine. The second, for those destined for agriculture or trade, consists of the study of good reading and correct writing in their own language, arithmetic, a little geography, and similar subjects. In New England the laws compel every town of fifty families to maintain a public school. The Lancastrian system is common in America. When it was first introduced even the genteel parents of good position sent their children there, but these were compelled to withdraw very soon because of the rusticity of the customs and the corruption of manners that came from contact with the dregs of the low common people. The education of girls rarely permits them to handle well the needle and the spindle, but never lacks instruction in the dance. Sometimes a few lessons in music, in drawing, and perhaps even in French top off their education. It is a matter of prestige for the ladies to be able to say they have studied music, drawing, and French.

The European instructors brought to teach in America have always admired the docility and modesty with which girls behave whenever they find themselves in a school with a regular discipline, at least if they are not spoiled to begin with. These qualities are united to a certain freeness and maturity of judgment rarely found elsewhere. But, especially among those born and raised among Negroes, there are rarely found noble and disinterested thoughts and sentiments, generosity, honor, or gratitude.

Instability of fortunes seems more common to Americans than to the youth of other countries; they frequently have the misfortune to see the finest hopes betrayed by tragic changes. When they reach a certain age they become impatient with suggestions, at least with those that do not coincide with their own. The liberty that they assume often descends to insubordination and to violent revolts against superiors. Such uprisings are not unusual in American colleges, and have lately occurred in Princeton in New Jersey and in William and Mary in Virginia; the students broke windows, chairs, furniture, and everything that came to their hands, and were at the point of destroying the very buildings. Since the people who preside over such places are concerned only with the injection of a little knowledge into the students, it is not surprising that the latter bring themselves to certain excesses of misbehavior which are condemned by honest Americans.

In the United States, where the spirit of trade and avidity for profits distinguishes all classes, it is not surprising that the flowers of poetic genius fail to flourish. There is no lack there of gifted men; but a wide acquaintance with many subjects is more characteristic than a profound knowledge of any single field. A kind of superficial tincture of learning is perhaps more widespread and more common in America than elsewhere. The well-educated man is continually surprised to hear the decisive and certain tone with which all manner of subjects are discussed. There is probably not a house in which will not be seen instructive books, stories, and novels; even if there is no Bible or catechism, there will infallibly be a newspaper. These are in America the most common fonts of erudition, the universal encyclopedias that speak on every subject, the tribunals in which literary controversies are brought to the judgment of the public, the heralds that announce everything that happens in the four corners of the world — declarations of war and treaties of peace and commerce, the expenses of government, the decisions of the courts, the prices of all sorts of merchandise, accidents, deaths, marriages, and new inventions.

A European can sometimes hardly restrain his scorn and laughter when he reads in the same issue an enthusiastic eulogy of liberty and the advertisement of the sale of a number of slaves, or a notice that a certain Negro is in prison for having attempted to become, through flight, one of those heroes of liberty. An incredible number of these newspapers are published, and, to encourage circulation, the government charges only 1 cent for carrying a large issue 100 miles. To the continual and universal reading of newspapers must be attributed the purity of the English language, even among the vulgar people. Another consequence is that politics is one of the most frequent subjects of conversation and every man thinks and talks as does the paper he reads.

There are also some scientific and general journals, but these rarely continue for many years. The one that has best survived is the edition of the *Edinburgh Review* reprinted in New York. Greek and Latin literature are commonly cultivated, but, with few exceptions, not well enough to bring a true knowledge of the beauties of the original masterpieces. Otherwise, could their public prints hail Barlow's *Columbiad* as a poem equal or even superior to those of Homer and Virgil? Would they speak of their public oratory as superior to that of Demosthenes and Cicero?

I will not deny that Americans express themselves with much facility and elegance and now and then produce pieces of fine eloquence. Eloquence is, in fact, after gold their highest ideal. But of all the parts which, according to the great masters, make up the art of speaking well, they cultivate elocution with most zeal. A speech with elegant expressions, ornate phrases, and harmonious periods will be considered a great oration although undistinguished in originality of invention, beauty of thought, weight of ideas, force of argument, regularity of development, or movement of the emotions. In view of the encomiums of American eloquence, I wished to procure at least a single example worthy of presentation in Europe and to posterity as equal to that developed among us across the Atlantic; but no one could give me one, and frequently those which were cited as masterpieces by some were rejected by others as of slight worth.

There are many students of medicine in all parts of the United States, but from the point of view of the quality of studies there is an important distinction between the Northern and the Southern states. In the former there are wise regulations for the study and the practice of this noble art, in the latter it is often only necessary that a young man assist a licensed doctor for some time, to qualify himself for a license. The use of mercury is common enough, and what in Italy would seem even stranger, the doctors themselves also act as apothecaries, so that it may well be imagined how much must be paid for medicines. The United States already glory in having produced Doctor Rush, whose works are highly esteemed in Europe.

What might be called the material parts of literature are more advanced than is thought in Italy. The printing establishments are numerous and turn out books of remarkable elegance, embellished with fine engravings. The series of Latin authors published in Boston, the American ornithology with fine colored plates in Philadelphia, and an edition of Barlow's *Columbiad* are fine examples and will always be monuments of the excellence of American typography.

Trade in books is brisk. There are also many circulating libraries from which each one may borrow for a given time by paying a certain sum. But unhappily the most popular reading is in novels which serve to deprave hearts and minds. As far as the various public libraries are concerned, that at Philadelphia is the largest, and that of the college in Cambridge reputed to have the best collection. On hearing that the government library in Washington cost $24,000 an Italian would be well impressed, but he would be quite disillusioned if he actually saw and examined it.

Painting, sculpture, and the arts of ornamentation are on the whole in their infancy in the United States. They are not regarded with respect or esteem. In Philadelphia and in New York there are academies of fine arts, and the success in painting of two Americans, West and Trumbull, is proof sufficient that the natives of the United States are not lacking in the genius needed to succeed in the arts, if they wished to cultivate them. The philosophical society established in Philadelphia in 1769 is already well recognized in Europe for the transactions it publishes from time to time.

The sciences more immediately useful are well and much cultivated in America; mathematics, even in the more abstract branches, physics, mineralogy, and chemistry are taught by professors of high ability. Until now they have not yet made of astronomy as a science as much as might be expected of a people concerned with navigation; they are content simply to reprint the *Nautical Almanack* for the use of their seamen. Yet there is no lack of individuals very proficient in both the theory and the practice of that science whose efforts have thrown new light on the field. The work of Nathaniel Bowditch on practical navigation and the various articles and treatises by Father Wallace of the Society of Jesus prove that assertion. I may add that the government has already acquired astronomical instruments of the best construction, for lack of which it has not been possible to determine the exact longitude of Washington. The investigations that many other people carry on into perpetual motion, if they do no honor to a knowledge of mechanics, nevertheless illustrate a certain spirit of inquiry that is prevalent in the United States. In surveying they make use of the magnetized needle, but the slight heed they pay to the variations of the pole will some day be the source of innumerable law suits, to which they are in any case inclined.

The ingenious Americans make up for the lack of hands to do their work by the invention of mechanical tools. To encourage this branch of industry a patent office is established in Washington, through which the government gives inventors the exclusive privilege of using or selling their machines, of which they must present models preserved to satisfy the curiosity of the public. It cannot be denied that among the great abundance of these models (many are considered new which in reality are old) there are some of very great ingenuity. Particularly worthy of attention is a water saw that cuts the trunk of a tree, sets it in position, and saws the boards. There is also a machine which cuts an iron wire into pieces, bends it as desired, inserts it into leather, and in a short time forms a very exact card. The construction of mills is also very ingenious, and proper tools almost always conserve labor.

Nothing is more striking to the Italian at his arrival in America than the state of religion. By virtue of an article in the federal Constitution every religion and every sect is fully tolerated, is equally protected, and equally treated in the United States, at least if its principles or practices do not disturb the civil order and established law. Or, to put it more precisely, the government will not interfere in purely religious matters.

The number of those who openly deny the revelations is not as large as might be supposed, considering that this country is the refuge of all sorts of European wretches. The bulk of atheists is restricted to the French, who abandon the religion of their ancestors but rarely assume a non-Catholic belief.

Indifference, which is so common in the Europe of our times, takes on a special character in America. It does not consist of despising and giving up all practice of religion; many people continue to speak of religion and, generally, with respect. What then? They act as if God had never manifested His will to men, never pointed out the narrow path to salvation that is followed by a few, had never warned that there are other, broader, easier ones traveled by many whose principles seem correct but which ultimately lead to inevitable perdition — in a word, as if the Bible, so highly esteemed, so often read, and seized by all as rule of their religion, does not speak of an infallible God. Every sect there is held as good, every road as correct, and every error as the insignificant weakness of poor mortals.

In accordance with such principles, it is not surprising if America gives birth to innumerable sects which daily subdivide and multiply. Although how can one speak of sects? Those who describe themselves as members of one or another of the sects do not thereby profess an abiding adherence to the doctrines of the founders of the sect; they simply call themselves by the name of the sect to express the fact that they are not without any religion and that they frequent assemblies of a certain kind, or that they are brought up within a certain persuasion, whatever may be the actual state of their thoughts. Thus the Anglicans of today no longer take much account of their Thirty-Nine Articles, nor the Lutherans of the Confession of Augsburg, nor the Presbyterians of the teachings of Calvin or of Knox. On the contrary, imitating the example of their masters, they examine, change, and decide as seems best at the time.

The very word sect does not have in America the derogatory meaning that etymology and usage have given it among us, so that a man there does not have the slightest hesitation in saying, "I belong to such a sect." Among the peculiarities of America, not the most extreme is that of finding persons who live together for several years without knowing each other's religion. And many, when asked, do not answer, "I believe," but simply, "I was brought up in such a persuasion."

Better to explain how religion is regarded here, I will give a few examples. In Georgetown, a suburb of Washington, there was a militia regiment which was, in accordance with its regulations, obliged to go to church each Sunday. But since the members belonged to various sects it was not easy to decide to which church or meeting to go. The matter was diplomatically adjusted as follows: they would go one Sunday to the Catholic Church, another to the Methodist, a third to the Anglican, then to the Calvinist, and so on until they completed the circle, when they would start over again.

The impartiality of the government in religious matters is observed in practice, as was solemnly promised. This was never more clearly illustrated than in the following incident which occurred in 1813. At that time a considerable theft was brought to the notice of the police, who searched for the criminal; but the latter, penitent for his misdeed, went to confess to the Jesuit Father, Anthony Kohlmann, and in the act of confession gave to his confessor that which he had stolen to be restored to its owner, whom he named. The priest quickly acted and returned the property. The owner informed the police. A non-Catholic magistrate, having learned that the restitution took place through Father Kohlmann, hurriedly demanded the name of the thief. The priest answered that, having learned that through the sacred confession, he could not in any way violate a confidence that natural law and the Catholic religion impose on confessors as most sacred and inviolable. The magistrate answered that the civil law made no exceptions, but ordered under heavy penalties that anyone who knew the perpetrator of a crime must make him known. To this the priest replied that he had every respect for the civil laws but that those same laws guaranteed the free exercise of the Catholic religion which obliged a confessor never to reveal the secrets of his confessional.

Not being able to agree, a solemn trial was held on the matter. On the appointed day, Father Kohlmann, accompanied by non-Catholic lawyers, appeared before the supreme court of the city. The tribunal opened with a demand on the priest for the reasons why he did not believe himself obliged to reveal the name of the thief, and these were briefly set forth. Then the lawyers began to speak, and in excellent orations answered the objection of the prosecutor and demonstrated that such a revelation could not be demanded of Father Kohlmann without an open violation of the laws which guaranteed freedom to every sect and did not restrain in any respect the Catholic religion, so old, so much the same throughout the world, so well known in its principles, so useful in the public welfare, as the facts of the case well proved.

When it came to the verdict, Judge Clinton, according to English practice, delivered a summation in which he concluded, after emphasizing the spirit of the country's laws and its well-known principles of liberality, that it would not be just to oblige a Catholic priest to reveal a criminal made known through the medium of the confession, and that therefore Father Kohlmann was free of any crime. This decision was everywhere applauded, and was recorded so that it may in the future serve to determine similar cases. The speeches of the attorney and of Clinton, together with the facts of the case, were printed in a volume entitled, *The Catholick Question in America.* At the end of this book, in the form of an appendix, was added a little tract on the sacred confession, which helped much to confirm Catholics on this article of faith and to diminish the prejudices and make known the errors of the non-Catholics.

Despite the indifference as to sect, there is, especially in the North, much show of piety. Everyone reads the Bible, and in New England they will not permit a traveler or allow a messenger to continue his journey on a Sunday. Also, almost every year petitions are presented to Congress to prohibit by law journeys on the Lord's Day. The captain of the ship on which I sailed from America to Europe would not allow the passengers to play dominoes or to sing on Sunday. Yet when we arrived in port on a Sunday morning he made the sailors work the whole day without the slightest reason. The observation of holidays in the North was formerly carried to truly extravagant rigor. In certain states religious laws still remain on the statute book, particularly those which insist on the observation of the third commandment. These laws, although not repealed, are no longer rigorously enforced, and are called the Blue Laws.

From the arbitrary interpretation of the Holy Scriptures come results often truly lamentable. People with the best of wills are agitated by all the winds of doctrine. In Southington, Connecticut, there are some who read in the Bible that God commands the sanctification of the Sabbath; they observe precisely the Sabbath and not Sunday. There is a sect in Pennsylvania called the Harmony Society, which is directed by a chief who explains the Bible to them. Several years ago, having found in Saint Paul that virginity is better than matrimony, he promulgated an ordinance that all should observe chastity. There were sharp remonstrances that *melius est nubere quam uri* [it is better to marry than to burn], but all was in vain; the leader was inflexible. In Virginia, in the spring of 1812, a preacher announced from his pulpit the fatal prediction that on the fourth of July of that year would come the end of the world. The people believed it true, and let the season go by without planting or cultivating their fields, saying, why should they trouble to work since the end of the world would surely come before the harvest.

134.

William Cobbett: A Year in the United States

William Cobbett ("Peter Porcupine") is best known as an English journalist, pamphleteer, and politician, but he came to the United States twice as a political refugee. During his first stay (1792-1800) he was a vehement opponent of the French Revolution and of its supporters in this country. He returned to America in May 1817 and remained until October 1819. A Year's Residence in the United States, *published in London in 1820, was one of the results of this second visit. Though Cobbett preferred his homeland to his place of temporary exile, the work was an amiable account of the society and the customs that he observed in the United States. A selection is reprinted below.*

Source: *A Year's Residence in the United States of America,* London, 1820, Pt. 2, pp. 204-223.

Now, then, my dear sir, this people contains very few persons very much raised in men's estimation above the general mass; for, though there are some men of immense fortunes, their wealth does very little indeed in the way of purchasing even the outward signs of respect; and, as to adulation, it is not to be purchased with love or money. Men, be they what they may, are generally called by their two names, without anything prefixed or added. I am one of the greatest men in this country at present; for people in general call me "*Cobbett*," though the Quakers provokingly persevere in putting the *William* before it, and my old friends in Pennsylvania use even the word *Billy*, which, in the very sound of the letters, is an antidote to every thing like thirst for distinction. . . .

The causes of hypocrisy are the fear of loss and the hope of gain. Men crawl to those whom, in their hearts, they despise, because they fear the effects of their ill will and hope to gain their goodwill. The circumstances of all ranks are so easy here that there is no cause for hypocrisy; and the thing is not of so fascinating a nature that men should love it for its own sake.

The boasting of wealth, and the endeavoring to disguise poverty, these two acts, so painful to contemplate, are almost total strangers in this country; for, no man can gain adulation or respect by his wealth, and no man dreads the effects of poverty, because no man sees any dreadful effects arising from poverty.

That anxious eagerness to get on, which is seldom accompanied with some degree of envy of more successful neighbors, and which has its foundation first in a dread of future want, and next in a desire to obtain distinction by means of wealth; this anxious eagerness, so unamiable in itself, and so unpleasant an inmate of the breast, so great a sourer of the temper, is a stranger to America, where accidents and losses, which would drive an Englishman half mad, produce but very little agitation.

From the absence of so many causes of uneasiness, of envy, of jealousy, of rivalship, and of mutual dislike, society, that is to say, the intercourse between man and man, and family and family, becomes easy and pleasant; while the universal plenty is the cause of universal hospitality. I know, and have ever known, but little of the people in the cities and towns in America; but the difference between them and the people in the country can only be such as is found in all other countries. As to the manner of living in the country, I was, the other day, at a gentleman's house, and I asked the lady for her bill of fare for the year. I saw fourteen fat hogs, weighing about twenty score a piece, which were to come into the house the next Monday; for here they slaughter them all in one day. This led me to ask, "Why, in God's name, what do you eat in a year?" The bill of fare was this, for this present year: about this same quantity of hog meat; four beeves; and forty-six fat sheep! Besides the sucking pigs (of which we had then one on the table), besides lambs, and besides the produce of seventy hen fowls, not to mention good parcels of geese, ducks, and turkeys, but, not to forget a garden of three-quarters of an acre and the butter of ten cows, not one ounce of which is ever sold! What do you think of that? Why you will say, this must be some great overgrown farmer, that has swallowed up half the country; or some nabob sort of merchant. Not at all. He has only 154 acres of land (all he consumes is of the produce of this land), and he lives in the same house that his English-born grandfather lived in.

When the hogs are killed, the house is full of work. The sides are salted down as pork. The hams are smoked. The lean meats are made into sausages, of which, in this family, they make about two hundredweight. These latter, with broiled fish, eggs, dried beef, dried mutton, slices of ham, tongue, bread, butter, cheese, shortcakes, buckwheat cakes, sweetmeats of various sorts, and many other things, make up the breakfast fare of the year, and a dish of beefsteaks is frequently added.

When one sees this sort of living, with the houses full of good beds, ready for the guest as well as the family to sleep in, we cannot help perceiving that this is that "English hospitality" of which we have read so much; but, which boroughmongers' taxes and pawns have long since driven out of England. . . .

It is not with a little bit of dry toast so neatly put in a rack; a bit of butter so round and small; a little milkpot so pretty and so empty; an egg for you, the host and hostess not liking eggs. It is not with looks that seem to say, "don't eat too much, for the tax gatherer is coming." It is not thus that you are received in America. You are not much asked, not much pressed, to eat and drink; but, such an abundance is spread before you, and so hearty and so cordial is your reception, that you instantly lose all restraint, and are tempted to feast whether you be hungry or not. And, though the manner and style are widely different in different houses, the abundance everywhere prevails. This is the strength of the government — a happy people — and no government ought to have any other strength.

But, as you may say, perhaps that plenty, however great, is not all that is wanted. Very true; for the mind is of more account than the carcass. But, here is mind too. These repasts, amongst people of any figure, come forth under the superintendence of industrious and accomplished housewives, or their daughters, who all read a great deal, and in whom that gentle treatment from parents and husbands, which arises from an absence of raking anxiety, has created a habitual and even a hereditary good humor. These ladies can converse with you upon almost any subject, and the ease and gracefulness of their behavior are surpassed by those of none of even our best-tempered English women. They fade at an earlier age than in England; but, till then, they are as beautiful as the women in Cornwall, which contains, to my thinking, the prettiest women in our country. However, young or old, blooming or fading, well or ill, rich or poor, they still preserve their good humor. . . .

There are very few really ignorant men in America of native growth. Every farmer is more or less of a reader. There is no brogue, no provincial dialect. No class like that which the French call peasantry, and which degrading appellation the miscreant spawn of the Funds have, of late years, applied to the whole mass of the most useful of the people in England, those who do the work and fight the battles. And, as to the men who would naturally form *your* acquaintances, they, I know from experience, are as kind, frank, and sensible men as are, on the general run, to be found in England, even with the power of selection. They are all well-informed, modest without shyness, always free to communicate what they know, and never ashamed to acknowledge that they have yet to learn. You never hear them boast of their possessions, and you never hear them complaining of their wants. They have all been readers from their youth up; and there are few subjects upon which they cannot converse with you, whether of a political or scientific nature. At any rate, they always hear with patience. I do not know that I ever heard a native American interrupt another man while he was speaking. Their sedateness and coolness, the deliberate manner in which they say and do everything, and the slowness and reserve with which they express their assent; these are very wrongly estimated, when they are taken for marks of a want of feeling. It must be a tale of woe indeed, that will bring a tear from an American's eye; but any trumped-up story will send his hand to his pocket, as the ambassadors from the beggars of France, Italy, and Germany can fully testify.

However, you will not, for a long while, know what to do for want of the quick responses of the English tongue, and the decided tone of the English expression. The loud voice; the hard squeeze by the hand; the instant assent or dissent; the clamorous joy; the bitter wailing; the ardent friendship; the deadly enmity; the love that makes people kill themselves; the hatred that makes them kill others; all these belong to the characters of Englishmen, in whose mind and hearts every feeling exists in the extreme. To decide the question, which character is, upon the whole, best, the American or the English, we must appeal to some third party. But it is no matter; we cannot change our natures. For my part, who can in nothing think or act by halves, I must belie my very nature, if I said that I did not like the character of my own countrymen best. We all like our own parents and children better than other people's parents and children; not because they are better, but because they are *ours;* because they belong to us and we to them, and because we must resemble each other. There are some Americans that I like full as well as I do any man in England; but, if, nation against nation, I put the question home to my heart, it instantly decides in favor of my countrymen. . . .

There is one thing in the Americans, which though its proper place was further back, I have reserved, or rather kept back, to the last moment. It has presented itself several times; but I have turned from the thought, as men do from thinking of any mortal disease that is at work in their frame. It is not covetousness; it is not niggardliness; it is not insincerity; it is not enviousness; it is not cowardice, above all things; it is *drinking*. Aye, and that too, amongst but too many men who, one would think, would loathe it. You can go into hardly any man's house without being asked to drink wine or spirits, even in the morning. They are quick at meals, are little eaters, seem to care little about what they eat, and never talk about it. This, which arises out of the universal abundance of good and even fine eatables, is very amiable. You are here disgusted with none of those eaters by reputation that are found, especially amongst the Parsons, in England: fellows that unbutton at it. Nor do the Americans sit and tope much after dinner, and talk on till they get into nonsense and smut, which last is a sure mark of a silly and, pretty generally, even of a base mind. But, they tipple; and the infernal spirits they tipple too! The scenes that I witnessed at Harrisburg I shall never forget. I almost wished (God forgive me!) that there were boroughmongers here to tax these drinkers: they would soon reduce them to a moderate dose. Any nation that feels itself uneasy with its fullness of good things has only to resort to an application of boroughmongers. These are by no means nice feeders or of contracted throat; they will suck down anything from the poor man's pot of beer to the rich man's lands and tenements.

The Americans preserve their gravity and quietness and good humor even in their drink; and so much the worse. It were far better for them to be as noisy and quarrelsome as the English drunkards; for then the odiousness of the vice would be more visible, and the vice itself might become less frequent. Few vices want an apology, and drinking has not only its apologies but its praises; for, besides the appellation of "generous wine," and the numerous songs, some in very elegant and witty language, from the pens of debauched men of talents, drinking is said to be necessary, in certain cases at least, to raise the spirits, and to keep out cold. Never was anything more false. Whatever intoxicates must enfeeble in the end, and whatever enfeebles must chill. It is very well known, in the northern countries, that if the cold be such as to produce danger of frostbiting, you must take care *not* to drink strong liquors.

To see this beastly vice in young men is shocking. At one of the taverns at Harrisburg there were several as fine young men as I ever saw. Well-dressed, well-educated, polite, and everything but sober. What a squalid, drooping, sickly set they looked in the morning!

Even little boys at, or under, twelve years of age go into stores, and tip off their drams! I never struck a child in anger in my life, that I recollect; but, if I were so unfortunate as to have a son to do this, he having had an example to the contrary in me, I would, if any other means of reclaiming him failed, whip him like a dog, or, which would be better, make him an outcast from my family.

However, I must not be understood as meaning that this tippling is universal amongst gentlemen; and God be thanked, the women of any figure in life do by no means give in to the practice; but, abhor it as much as well-bred women in England, who in general no more think of drinking strong liquors than they do of drinking poison.

I shall be told that men in the harvest field must have something to drink. To be sure, where perspiration almost instantly carries off the drink, the latter does not remain so long to burn the liver, or whatever else it does burn. But, I must question the utility even here; and I think that in the long run a water drinker would beat a spirit drinker at anything, provided both had plenty of good food. And, besides, beer, which does not burn, at any rate, is within everyone's reach in America, if he will but take the trouble to brew it. . . .

The soldiers, in the regiment that I belonged to, many of whom served in the American war, had a saying, the Quakers used the word "tired" in place of the word "drunk." Whether any of them do ever get tired themselves, I know not; but at any rate they most resolutely set their faces against the common use of spirits. They forbid their members to retail them; and, in case of disobedience, they disown them.

However, there is no remedy but the introduction of beer, and, I am very happy to know that beer is everyday becoming more and more fashionable. In Bristol in Pennsylvania, I was pleased to see excellent beer in clean and nice pewter pots. Beer does not kill. It does not eat out the vitals and take the color from the cheek. It will make men "tired," indeed, by midnight; but it does not make them half dead in the morning. . . .

There are persons who question the right of man to pursue and destroy the wild animals, which are called game. Such persons, however, claim the right of killing foxes and hawks; yet, these have as much right to live and to follow their food as pheasants and partridges have. This, therefore, in such persons, is nonsense.

Others, in their mitigated hostility to the sports of the field, say that it is wanton cruelty to shoot or hunt; and that we kill animals from the farmyard only because their flesh is necessary to our own existence. Prove that. No, you cannot. If you could, it is but the "tyrant's plea;" but you cannot; for we know that men can, and do, live without animal food, and, if their labor be not of an exhausting kind, live well, too, and longer than those who eat it. It comes to this, then, that we kill hogs and oxen because we *choose* to kill them; and we kill game for precisely the same reason.

A third class of objectors, seeing the weak position of the two former, and still resolved to eat flesh, take their stand upon this ground: that sportsmen send some game off wounded and leave them in a state of suffering. These gentlemen forget the operations performed upon calves, pigs, lambs and sometimes on poultry. . . .

Taking it for granted, then, that sportsmen are as good as other folks on the score of humanity, the sports of the field, like everything else done in the fields, tend to produce or preserve health. I prefer them to all other pastime, because they produce early rising; because they have no tendency to lead young men into vicious habits. It is where men congregate that the vices haunt. A hunter or a shooter may also be a gambler and a drinker; but, he is less likely to be fond of the two latter, if he be fond of the former. Boys will take to something in the way of pastime; and it is better that they take to that which is innocent, healthy, and manly than that which is vicious, unhealthy, and effeminate. Besides, the scenes of rural sport are necessarily at a distance from cities and towns. This is another great consideration; for though great talents are wanted to be employed in the hives of men, they are very rarely acquired in these hives: the surrounding objects are too numerous, too near the eye, too frequently under it, and too artificial. . . .

This chapter will be a head without a body; for it will not require much time to give an account of the rural sports of America. The general taste of the country is to kill the things in order to have them to eat, which latter forms no part of the sportsman's objects.

There cannot be said to be anything here which we in England call hunting. The deer are hunted by dogs, indeed, but the hunters do not follow. They are posted at their several stations to shoot the deer as he passes. This is only one remove from the Indian hunting. I never saw, that I know of, any man that had seen a pack of hounds in America, except those kept by old John Brown, in Bucks County, Pennsylvania, who was the only hunting Quaker that I ever heard of, and who was grandfather of the famous General Brown. In short, there is none of what we call hunting; or so little that no man can expect to meet with it.

No coursing. I never saw a greyhound here. Indeed, there are no hares that have the same manners that ours have or anything like their fleetness. The woods, too, or some sort of cover, except in the singular instance of the plains in this island, are too near at hand.

But of shooting the variety is endless. Pheasants, partridges, woodcocks, snipes, grouse, wild ducks of many sorts, teal, plover, rabbits.

There is a disagreement between the North and the South as to the naming of the two former. North of New Jersey, the pheasants are called partridges and the partridges are called quails. To the South of New Jersey, they are called by what I think are their proper names, taking the English names of those birds to be proper. For, pheasants do not remain in coveys but mix, like common fowls. The intercourse between the males and females is promiscuous, and not by pairs as in the case of partridges. And these are the manners of the American pheasants, which are found by ones, twos, and so on, and never in families, except when young, when, like chickens, they keep with the old hen. The American partridges are not quails, because quails are gregarious. They keep in flocks like rooks (called crows in America), or like larks, or starlings; of which the reader will remember a remarkable instance in the history of the migration of those grumbling vagabonds, the Jews, soon after their march from Horeb, when the quails came and settled upon each other's backs to a height of two cubits, and covered a superficial space of two days' journey in diameter. It is a well-known fact that quails flock. It is also well known that partridges do not, but that they keep in distinct families, which we call coveys from the French *couvée,* which means the eggs or brood, which the hen covers at one time.

The American partridges live in coveys. The cock and his [mate] pair in the spring. They have their brood by sitting alternately on the eggs, just as the English partridges do; the young ones, if none are killed or die, remain with the old ones till spring; the covey always live within a small distance of the same spot; if frightened into a state of separation, they call to each other and reassemble; they roost altogether in a round ring, as close as they can sit, the tails inward and the heads outward; and are, in short, in all their manners, precisely the same as the English partridge, with this exception, that they will sometimes alight on a rail or a bough, and that, when the hen sits, the cock, perched at a little distance, makes a sort of periodical whistle, in a monotonous, but very soft and sweet tone.

The size of the pheasant is about the half of that of the English. The plumage is by no means so beautiful; but the flesh is far more delicate. The size of the partridge bears about the same proportion. But its plumage is more beautiful than that of the English, and its flesh is more delicate. Both are delightful, though rather difficult, shooting. The pheasant does not tower, but darts through the trees; and the partridge does not rise boldly, but darts away at no great height from the ground. Some years they are more abundant than other years. This is an abundant year. There are, perhaps, fifty coveys within half a mile of my house.

The woodcocks are, in all respects, like those in England, except that they are only about three-fifths of the size. They breed here; and are in such numbers that some men kill twenty brace or more in a day. Their haunts are in marshy places or woods. The shooting of them lasts from the 4th of July till the hardish frosts come. The last we killed this year was killed on the 21st of November. So that here are five months of this sport; and pheasants and partridges are shot from September to April.

The snipes are called English snipes, which they resemble in all respects, and are found in great abundance in the usual haunts of snipes.

The grouse is precisely like the Scotch grouse. There is only here and there a place where they are found. But, they are, in those places, killed in great quantities in the fall of the year.

As to wild ducks and other waterfowl, which are come at by lying in wait, and killed most frequently swimming, or sitting, they are slaughtered in whole flocks. An American counts the cost of powder and shot. If he is deliberate in everything else, this habit will hardly forsake him in the act of shooting. When the sentimental flesh-eaters hear the report of his gun, they may begin to pull out their white handkerchiefs; for death follows the pull of the trigger, with, perhaps, even more certainty than it used to follow the lancet of Doctor Rush.

The plover is a fine bird, and is found in great numbers upon the plains, and in the cultivated fields of this island, and at a mile from my house. Plovers are very shy and wary; but they have ingenious enemies to deal with. A wagon, or carriage of some sort, is made use of to approach them; and then they are easily killed.

Rabbits are very abundant in some places. They are killed by shooting; for all here is done with the gun. No reliance is placed upon a dog.

As to game laws there are none except those which appoint the times for killing. People go where they like, and, as to wild animals, shoot what they like. There is the common law, which forbids trespass, and the statute law, I believe, of "malicious trespass," or trespass after warning. And these are more than enough; for nobody, that I ever hear of, warns people off. So that, as far as shooting goes, and that is the sport which is the most general favorite, there never was a more delightful country than this island. The sky is so fair, the soil so dry, the cover so convenient, the game so abundant, and the people, go where you will, so civil, hospitable, and kind.

135.

Emma Hart Willard: Education and the Weaker Sex

In the early nineteenth century, public funds were increasingly used to raise educational standards in men's schools, but institutions for women remained private, profit-making organizations, poor in their facilities and teaching staffs, with curriculums lacking in substantial subject matter. In addition, there were at this time no colleges or universities that would admit women. This state of affairs came forcibly to the attention of Emma Willard, who had already successfully established an academy for women, when, through the good offices of a nephew who was boarding with her while attending Middlebury College, she took the opportunity to scrutinize the course of study at what was then a typical men's college. Hoping to interest the public as well as legislators in female education, Mrs. Willard traveled to New York, a state that she felt would be more sympathetic to her cause than Vermont, and there addressed the legislature. A selection from her remarks on this occasion is reprinted here.

Source: *Woman and the Higher Education,* Anna C. Brackett, ed., New York, 1893, pp. 1-46.

In inquiring concerning the benefits of the plan proposed, I shall proceed upon the supposition that female seminaries will be patronized throughout our country.

Nor is this altogether a visionary supposition. If one seminary should be well organized, its advantages would be found so great that others would soon be instituted; and that sufficient patronage can be found to put one in operation may be presumed from its reasonableness and from the public opinion with regard to the present mode of female education. It is from an intimate acquaintance with those parts of our country whose education is said to flourish most that the writer has drawn her picture of the present state of female instruction; and she knows that she is not alone in perceiving or deploring its faults. Her sentiments are shared by many an enlightened parent of a daughter who has received a boarding school education.

Counting on the promise of her childhood, the father had anticipated her maturity as combining what is excellent in mind with what is elegant in manners. He spared no expense that education might realize to him the image of his imagination. His daughter returned from her boarding school, improved in fashionable airs and expert in manufacturing fashionable toys; but, in her conversation, he sought in vain for that refined and fertile mind which he had fondly expected. Aware that his disappointment has its source in a defective education, he looks with anxiety on his other daughters, whose minds, like lovely buds, are beginning to open. Where shall he find a genial soil in which he may place them to expand? Shall he provide them male instructors? Then the graces of their persons and manners, and whatever forms the distinguishing charm of the feminine character, they cannot be expected to acquire. Shall he give them a private tutoress? She will have been educated at the boarding school, and his daughters will have the faults of its instruction second-handed. Such is now the dilemma of many parents; and it is one from which they cannot be extricated by their individual exertions. May not then the only plan which promises to relieve them expect their vigorous support?

Let us now proceed to inquire what benefits would result from the establishment of female seminaries.

They would constitute a grade of public education superior to any yet known in the history of our sex; and through them, the lower grades of female instruction might be controlled. The influence of public seminaries over these would operate in two ways: first by requiring certain qualifications for entrance; and second by furnishing instructresses initiated in these modes of teaching and imbued with their maxims. Female seminaries might be expected to have important and happy effects on common schools in general; and in the manner of operating on these would probably place the business of teaching children into hands now nearly useless to society; and take it from those whose services the state wants in many other ways.

That nature designed for our sex the care of children, she has made manifest by mental as well as physical indications. She has given us, in a greater degree than men, the gentle arts of insinuation to soften their minds and fit them to receive impressions; a greater quickness of invention to vary modes of teaching to different dispositions; and more patience to make repeated efforts. There are many females of ability to whom the business of instructing children is highly acceptable; and who would devote all their faculties to their occupation. For they would have no higher pecuniary object to engage their attention; and their reputation as instructors they would consider as important. Whereas, whenever able and enterprising men engage in this business, they consider it merely as a temporary employment to further some object, to the attainment of which their best thoughts and calculations are all directed. If, then, women were properly fitted by instruction, they would be likely to teach children better than the other sex; they could afford to do it cheaper; and those men who would otherwise be engaged in this employment might be at liberty to add to the wealth of the nation, by any of those thousand occupations from which women are necessarily debarred.

But the females who taught children would have been themselves instructed either immediately or indirectly by the seminaries. Hence through these, the government might exercise an intimate and most beneficial control over common schools. Anyone who has turned his attention to this subject must be aware that there is great room for improvement in these, both as to the modes of teaching and the things taught; and what method could be devised so likely to effect this improvement as to prepare by instruction a class of individuals whose interest, leisure, and natural talents would combine to make them pursue it with ardor! Such a class of individuals would be raised up by female seminaries. And therefore they would be likely to have highly important and happy effects on common schools.

It is believed that such institutions would tend to prolong or perpetuate our excellent government.

An opinion too generally prevails that our present form of government, though good, cannot be permanent. Other republics have failed, and the historian and philosopher have told us that nations are like individuals; that at their birth, they receive the seeds of their decline and dissolution. Here, deceived by a false analogy, we receive an apt illustration of particular facts for a general truth. The existence of nations cannot, in strictness, be compared with the duration

Emma Willard School

Portrait of Emma H. Willard by Daniel Huntington, 1869

of animate life; for by the operation of physical causes, this, after a certain length of time, must cease. But the existence of nations is prolonged by the succession of one generation to another, and there is no physical cause to prevent this succession's going on, in a peaceable manner, under a good government, till the end of time. We must then look to other causes than necessity for the decline and fall of former republics. If we could discover these causes and seasonably prevent their operation, then might our latest posterity enjoy the same happy government with which we are blessed; or if but in part, then might the triumph of tyranny be delayed, and a few more generations be free.

Permit me, then, to ask the enlightened politician of any country whether, amid his researches for these causes, he cannot discover one in the neglect which free governments, in common with others, have shown to whatever regarded the formation of the female character.

In those great republics which have fallen of themselves, the loss of republican manners and virtues has been the invariable precursor of their loss of the republican form of government. But is it not the power of our sex to give society its tone, both as to manners and morals? And if such is the extent of female influence, is it wonderful that republics have failed when they calmly suffered that influence to become enlisted in favor of luxuries and follies wholly incompatible with the existence of freedom?

It may be said that the depravation of morals and manners can be traced to the introduction of wealth as its cause. But wealth will be introduced; even the iron laws of Lycurgus could not prevent it. Let us then inquire if means may not be devised to prevent its bringing with it the destruction of public virtue. May not these means be found in education? in implanting in early youth habits that may counteract the temptations to which, through the influence of wealth, mature age will be exposed? and in giving strength and expansion to the mind, that it may comprehend and prize those principles which teach the rigid performance of duty? Education, it may be said, has been tried as a preservative of national purity. But was it applied to every exposed part of the body politic? For if any part has been left within the pestilential atmosphere of wealth without this preservative, then that part, becoming corrupted, would communicate the contagion to the whole; and if so, then has the experiment, whether education may not preserve public virtue, never yet been fairly tried. Such a part has been left in all former experiments.

Females have been exposed to the contagion of wealth without the preservative of a good education; and they constitute that part of the body politic least endowed by nature to resist, most to communicate it. Nay, not merely have they been left without the defense of a good education, but their corruption has been accelerated by a bad one. The character of women of wealth has been, and in the old governments of Europe now is, all that this statement would lead us to expect. Not content with doing nothing to promote their country's welfare, like pampered children they revel in its prosperity and scatter it to the winds with a wanton profusion. And still worse, they empoison its source, by diffusing a contempt for useful labor. To court pleasure their business, within her temple in defiance of the laws of God and man, they have erected the idol fashion; and upon her altar they sacrifice, with shameless rites, whatever is sacred to virtue or religion. Not the strongest ties of nature, not even maternal love can restrain them! Like the worshiper of Moloch, the mother, while yet yearning over the newborn babe, tears it from the bosom which God has swelled with nutrition for its support, and casts it remorseless from her, the victim of her unhallowed devotion!

But while with an anguished heart I thus depict the crimes of my sex, let not the other stand by and smile. Reason declares that you are guiltier than we. You are our natural guardians, our brothers, our fathers, and our rulers. You know that our ductile minds readily take the impressions of education. Why then have you neglected our education? Why have you looked with lethargic indifference on circumstances ruinous to the formation of other characters which you might have controlled?

But it may be said the observations here made cannot be applied to any class of females in our country. True, they cannot yet; and if they could, it would be useless to make them; for when the females of any country have become thus debased, then is that country so corrupted that nothing but the awful judgments of heaven can arrest its career of vice. But it cannot be denied that our manners are verging toward those described; and the change, though gradual, has not been slow; already do our daughters listen with surprise when we tell them of the republican simplicity of our mothers. But our manners are not as yet so altered, but that throughout our country they are still marked with republican virtues.

The inquiry to which these remarks have conducted us is this: what is offered by the plan of female education here proposed, which may teach or preserve among females of wealthy families that purity of manners which is allowed to be so essential to national prosperity, and so necessary to the existence of a republican government?

1. Females, by having their understandings cultivated, their reasoning powers developed and strengthened, may be expected to act more from the dictates of reason and less from those of fashion and caprice.

2. With minds thus strengthened they would be taught systems of morality, enforced by the sanctions of religion; and they might be expected to acquire juster and more enlarged views of their duty, and stronger and higher motives to its performance.

3. This plan of education offers all that can be done to preserve female youth from a contempt of useful labor. The pupils would become accustomed to it in conjunction with the high objects of literature and the elegant pursuits of the fine arts; and it is to be hoped that, both from habit and association, they might in future life regard it as respectable.

To this it may be added that if housewifery could be raised to a regular art, and taught upon philosophical principles, it would become a higher and more interesting occupation; and ladies of fortune, like wealthy agriculturists, might find that to regulate their business was an agreeable employment.

4. The pupils might be expected to acquire a taste for moral and intellectual pleasures, which would buoy them above a passion for show and parade, and which would make them seek to gratify the natural love

of superiority, by endeavoring to excel others in intrinsic merit, rather than in the extrinsic frivolities of dress, furniture, and equipage.

5. By being enlightened in moral philosophy and in that which teaches the operations of the mind, females would be enabled to perceive the nature and extent of that influence which they possess over their children, and the obligation which this lays them under, to watch the formation of their characters with unceasing vigilance, to become their instructors, to devise plans for their improvement, to weed out the vices from their minds, and to implant and foster the virtues. And surely, there is that in the maternal bosom which, when its pleadings shall be aided by education, will overcome the seductions of wealth and fashion, and will lead the mother to seek her happiness in communing with her children and promoting their welfare, rather than in a heartless intercourse with the votaries of pleasure: especially when, with an expanded mind, she extends her views to futurity, and sees her care to her offspring rewarded by peace of conscience, the blessings of her family, the prosperity of her country, and finally with everlasting pleasure to herself and to them.

Thus laudable objects and employments would be furnished for the great body of females who are not kept by poverty from excesses. But among these, as among the other sex, will be found master spirits who must have preeminence at whatever price they acquire it. Domestic life cannot hold these because they prefer to be infamous rather than obscure. To leave such without any virtuous road to eminence is unsafe to the community; for not unfrequently are the secret springs of revolution set in motion by their intrigues. Such aspiring minds we will regulate by education; we will remove obstructions to the course of literature which has heretofore been their only honorable way to distinction; and we offer them a new object, worthy of their ambition; to govern and improve the seminaries for their sex.

In calling on my patriotic countrymen to effect so noble an object, the consideration of national glory should not be overlooked. Ages have rolled away; barbarians have trodden the weaker sex beneath their feet; tyrants have robbed us of the present light of heaven, and fain would take its future. Nations calling themselves polite have made us the fancied idols of a ridiculous worship, and we have repaid them with ruin for their folly. But where is that wise and heroic country which has considered that our rights are sacred, though we cannot defend them? that though a weaker, we are an essential part of the body politic, whose corruption or improvement must effect the whole? and which, having thus considered, has sought to give us by education that rank in the scale of being to which our importance entitles us?

History shows not that country. It shows many whose legislatures have sought to improve their various vegetable productions and their breeds of useful brutes; but none whose public councils have made it an object of their deliberations to improve the character of their women. Yet though history lifts not her finger to such a one, anticipation does. She points to a nation which, having thrown off the shackles of authority and precedent, shrinks not from schemes of improvement because other nations have never attempted them; but which, in its pride of independence, would rather lead than follow in the march of human improvement: a nation, wise and magnanimous to plan, enterprising to undertake, and rich in resources to execute. Does not every American exult that this country is his own? And who knows how great and good a race of men may yet arise from the forming hand of mothers, enlightened by the bounty of that beloved country, to defend her liberties, to plan her future improvement, and to raise her to unparalleled glory.

136.

Rufus King: Against the Extension of Slavery to the New States

Slavery was permitted by French and Spanish law in the territory of the Louisiana Purchase. After the War of 1812, therefore, no opposition arose when Southern slave owners took their property into the region. Nor did they hesitate to include slavery in their constitution when they asked to be admitted to the Union as the State of Missouri. But when a bill for this purpose came before the House in February 1819, James Tallmadge of New York surprised and angered the Southern members by offering an amendment prohibiting the further introduction of slaves into the area, and providing for the eventual emancipation of those who were already there. The amended bill passed the House but was lost in the Senate, and thus was put over to the next session of Congress. What was at stake was the tacit political balance between North and South that had prevailed since 1787. The North in the interval had drawn ahead in population, and therefore in the number of members it sent to the House. But the balance was maintained in the Senate, which in the admission of new states to the Union had always accepted free and slave states alternately; after the admission of Alabama in 1819 there were just eleven of each kind. The Missouri debate was not on the morals of slavery but on the question of sectional power and prestige. Senator Rufus King of New York, who in the following remarks argued for the Missouri restriction, was an old Federalist. He but uttered the long-standing resentment of his party at the dominance of the South, particularly Virginia, in national politics. King sent the substance of two of his speeches on the Missouri bill to Hezekiah Niles, who published them in December 1819.

Source: *Niles' Weekly Register,* December 4, 1819.

The Constitution declares "that Congress shall have power to dispose of, and make all needful rules and regulations respecting the territory and other property of the United States." Under this power, Congress have passed laws for the survey and sale of the public lands, for the division of the same into separate territories; and have ordained for each of them a constitution, a place of temporary government, whereby the civil and political rights of the inhabitants are regulated, and the rights of conscience and other natural rights are protected.

The power to make all needful regulations includes the power to determine what regulations are needful; and if a regulation prohibiting slavery within any territory of the United States be, as it has been, deemed needful, Congress possess the power to make the same, and, moreover, to pass all laws necessary to carry this power into execution.

The territory of Missouri is a portion of

Louisiana, which was purchased of France, and belongs to the United States in full dominion; in the language of the Constitution, Missouri is their territory, or property, and is subject, like other territories of the United States, to the regulations and temporary government which has been, or shall be, prescribed by Congress. The clause of the Constitution, which grants this power to Congress, is so comprehensive and unambiguous, and its purpose so manifest, that commentary will not render the power, or the object of its establishment, more explicit or plain.

The Constitution further provides, that "new states may be admitted by Congress into the Union."

As this power is conferred without limitation, the time, terms, and circumstances of the admission of new states are referred to the discretion of Congress, which may admit new states, but are not obliged to do so — of right no new state can demand admission into the Union unless such demand be founded upon some previous engagement with the United States.

When admitted by Congress into the Union, whether by compact or otherwise, the new state becomes entitled to the enjoyment of the same rights, and bound to perform the like duties, as the other states, and its citizens will be entitled to all privileges and immunities of citizens in the several states.

The citizens of each state possess rights and owe duties that are peculiar to and arise out of the constitution and laws of the several states. These rights and duties differ from each other in the different states, and among these differences, none is so remarkable or important as that which proceeds from the constitution and laws of the several states respecting slavery; the same being permitted in some states, and forbidden in others.

The question respecting slavery in the old thirteen states had been decided and settled before the adoption of the Constitution, which grants no power to Congress to interfere with or to change what had been previously settled. The slave states, therefore, are free to continue or to abolish slavery. Since the year 1808, Congress has possessed power to prohibit, and have prohibited, the further migration or importation of slaves into any of the old thirteen states, and at all times under the Constitution have had power to prohibit such migration or importation into any of the new states or territories of the United States. The Constitution contains no express provisions respecting slavery in a new state that may be admitted into the Union; every regulation upon this subject belongs to the power whose consent is necessary to the formation and admission of such state. Congress may, therefore, make it a condition of the admission of a new state that slavery shall be forever prohibited within the same. We may, with the more confidence, pronounce this to be the construction of the Constitution, as it has been so amply confirmed by the past decisions of Congress. . . .

Although Congress possess the power of making the exclusion of slavery a part or condition of the act admitting a new state into the Union, they may, in special cases, and for sufficient reasons, forbear to exercise this power. Thus, Kentucky and Vermont were admitted as new states into the Union without making the abolition of slavery the condition of their admission. In Vermont, slavery never existed, her laws excluding the same. Kentucky was formed out of, and settled by, Virginia, and the inhabitants of Kentucky, equally with those of Virginia, by fair interpretation of the Constitution, were exempt from all such interference of Congress as might disturb or impair the security of their property in slaves. . . .

If Congress possess the power to exclude slavery from Missouri, it still remains to be shown that they ought to do so. The examination of this branch of the subject, for obvious reasons, is attended with peculiar difficulty, and cannot be made without passing over arguments which to some of us might appear to be decisive, but the use of which, in this place, would call up feelings the influence of which would disturb, if not defeat, the impartial consideration of the subject.

Slavery unhappily exists within the United States. Enlightened men in the states where it is permitted, and everywhere out of them, regret its existence among us, and seek for the means of limiting and of mitigating it. The first introduction of slaves is not imputable to the present generation, nor even to their ancestors. Before the year 1642, the trade and ports of the colonies were open to foreigners equally as those of the mother country, and as early as 1620, a few years only after planting the colony of Virginia, and the same in which the first settlement was made in the old colony of Plymouth, a cargo of Negroes was brought into and sold as slaves in Virginia by a foreign ship. From this beginning the importation of slaves was continued for nearly two centuries. To her honor, Virginia, while a colony, opposed the importation of slaves, and was the first state to prohibit the same by a law passed for this purpose in 1778, thirty years before the general prohibition enacted by Congress in 1808. The laws and customs of the states in which slavery has existed for so long a period must have had their influence on the opinions and habits of the citizens, which ought not to be disregarded on the present occasion.

Omitting, therefore, the arguments which might be urged, and which by all of us might be deemed conclusive, were this an original question, the reasons which shall be offered in favor of the interposition of the power of Congress to exclude slavery from Missouri shall be only such as respect the common defense, the general welfare, and that wise administration of government which as far as possible may produce the impartial distribution of benefits and burdens throughout the Union.

By the Articles of Confederation, the common treasury was to be supplied by the several states according to the value of the land, with the houses and improvements thereon, within the respective states. From the difficulty in making this valuation, the old Congress were unable to apportion the requisitions for the supply of the general treasury, and obliged the states to propose an alteration of the Articles of Confederation, by which the whole number of free persons, with three-fifths of the slaves contained in the respective states, should become the rule of such apportionment of the taxes. A majority of the states approved of this alteration, but some of them disagreed to the same; and for want of a practicable rule of apportionment, the whole of the requisitions of taxes made by Congress during the Revolutionary War, and afterward, up to the establishment of the Constitution of the United States, were merely provisional and subject to revision and correction as soon as such rules should be adopted. The several states were credited for their supplies, and charged for the advances made to them by Congress, but no settlement of their accounts could be made, for the want of a rule of apportionment, until the establishment of the Constitution.

When the general convention that formed the Constitution took the subject into their consideration, the whole question was once more examined; and while it was agreed that all contributions to the common treasury should be made according to the ability of the several states to furnish the same, the old difficulty recurred in agreeing upon a rule whereby such ability should be ascertained, there being no simple standard by which the ability of individuals to pay taxes can be ascertained. A diversity in the selection of taxes has been deemed requisite to their equalization. Between communities this difficulty is less considerable, and although the rule of relative numbers would not accurately measure the wealth of nations, in states in the circumstances of the United States, whose institutions, laws, and employments are so much alike, the rule of number is probably as nearly equal as any other simple and practicable rule can be expected to be (though between the old and new states its equity is defective). These considerations, added to the approbation which had already been given to the rule by a majority of the states, induced the convention to agree that direct taxes should be apportioned among the states according to the whole number of free persons, and three-fifths of the slaves which they might respectively contain.

The rule for apportionment of taxes is not necessarily the most equitable rule for the apportionment of representatives among the states; property must not be disregarded in the composition of the first rule, but frequently is overlooked in the establishment of the second. A rule which might be approved in respect to taxes would be disapproved in respect to representatives; one individual, possessing twice as much property as another, might be required to pay double the taxes of such other; but no man has two votes to another's one; rich or poor, each has but one vote in the choice of representatives.

In the dispute between England and the colonies, the latter denied the right of the former to tax them, because they were not represented in the English Parliament. They contended that, according to the law of the land, taxation and representation were inseparable. The rule of taxation being agreed upon by the convention, it is possible that the maxim with which we successfully opposed the claim of England may have had an influence in procuring the adoption of the same rule for the apportionment of representatives. The true meaning, however, of this principle of the English constitution is that a colony or district is not to be taxed

Independence National Historical Park

Portrait of Rufus King by C. W. Peale, 1818

which is not represented; not that its number or representative shall be ascertained by its quota of taxes. If three-fifths of the slaves are virtually represented, or their owners obtain a disproportionate power in legislation and in the appointment of the president of the United States, why should not other property be virtually represented, and its owners obtain a like power in legislation and in the choice of the President? Property is not confined to slaves but exists in houses, stores, ships, capital in trade, and manufactures. To secure to the owners of property in slaves, greater political power than is allowed to the owners of other and equivalent property seems to be contrary to our theory of the equality of personal rights, inasmuch as the citizens of some states thereby become entitled to other and greater political power than citizens of other states.

The present House of Representatives consists of 181 members, which are apportioned among the states in a ratio of 1 representative for every 35,000 federal members, which are ascertained by adding to the whole number of free persons three-fifths of the slaves. According to the last census, the whole number of slaves within the United States was 1,191,364, which entitled the states possessing the same to 20 representatives and 20 presidential electors, more than they would be entitled to were the slaves excluded. By the last census, Virginia contained 582,104 free persons and 392,518 slaves. In any of the states where slavery is excluded, 582,104 free persons would be entitled to elect only 16 representatives, while in Virginia, 582,104 free persons, by the addition of three-fifths of her slaves, become entitled to elect, and do in fact elect, 23 representatives, being 7 additional ones on account of her slaves. Thus, while 35,000 free persons are requisite to elect 1 representative in a state where slavery is prohibited, 25,559 free persons in Virginia may, and do, elect a representative — so that 5 free persons in Virginia have as much power in the choice of representatives to Congress, and in the appointment of presidential electors, as 7 free persons in any of the states in which slavery does not exist.

This inequality in the apportionment of representatives was not misunderstood at the adoption of the Constitution, but as no one anticipated the fact that the whole of the revenue of the United States would be derived from indirect taxes (which cannot be supposed to spread themselves over the several states, according to the rule for the apportionment of direct taxes), but it was believed that a part of the contribution to the common treasury would be apportioned among the states by the rule for the apportionment of representatives. The states in which slavery is prohibited, ultimately, though with reluctance, acquiesced in the disproportionate number of representatives and electors that was secured to the slaveholding states. The concession was, at the time, believed to be a great one, and has proved to have been the greatest which was made to secure the adoption of the Constitution.

Great, however, as this concession was, it was definite, and its full extent was comprehended. It was a settlement between the thirteen states. The considerations arising out of their actual condition, their past connection, and the obligation which all felt to promote a reformation in the federal government were peculiar to the time and to the parties, and are not applicable to the new states, which Congress may now be willing to admit into the Union.

The equality of rights, which includes an equality of burdens, is a vital principle in our theory of government, and its jealous preservation is the best security of public and individual freedom; the departure from this principle in the disproportionate power and influence, allowed to the slaveholding states, was a necessary sacrifice to the establishment of the Constitution. The effect of this Constitution has been obvious to the preponderance it has given to the slaveholding states over the other states. Nevertheless, it is an ancient settlement, and faith and honor stand pledged not to disturb it. But the extension of this disproportionate power to the new states would be unjust and odious. The states whose power would be abridged, and whose burdens would be increased by the measure, cannot be expected to consent to it; and we may hope that the other states are too magnanimous to insist on it.

The existence of slavery impairs the industry and the power of a nation; and it does so in proportion to the multiplication of its slaves: where the manual labor of a country is performed by slaves, labor dishonors the hands of freemen.

If her laborers are slaves, Missouri may be able to pay money taxes, but will be unable to raise soldiers or to recruit seamen; and experience seems to have proved that manufactures do not prosper where the artificers are slaves. In case of foreign war or domestic insurrection, misfortunes from which no states are exempt, and against which all should be seasonably prepared, slaves not only do not add to but diminish the faculty of self-defense; instead of increasing the public strength, they lessen it, by the whole number of free persons whose place they occupy, increased by the number of freemen that may be employed as guards over them.

The motives for the admission of new states into the Union are the extension of the principles of our free government; the equalizing of the public burdens; and the consolidation of the power of the confederated nation. Unless these objects be promoted by the admission of new states, no such admission can be expedient or justified.

The states in which slavery already exists are contiguous to each other; they are also the portion of the United States nearest to the European colonies in the West Indies — colonies whose future condition can hardly be regarded as problematical. If Missouri, and the other states that may be formed to the west of the River Mississippi, are permitted to introduce and establish slavery, the repose, if not the security, of the Union may be endangered; all the states south of the River Ohio and west of Pennsylvania and Delaware, will be peopled with slaves, and the establishment of new states west of the River Mississippi will serve to extend slavery instead of freedom over that boundless region.

Such increase of the states, whatever other interests it may promote, will be sure to add nothing to the security of the public liberties; and can hardly fail hereafter to require and produce a change in our government.

On the other hand, if slavery be excluded from Missouri, and the other new states which may be formed in this quarter, not only will the slave markets be broken up, and the principles of freedom be extended and strengthened, but an exposed and important frontier will present a barrier which will check and keep back foreign assailants, who may be as brave and, as we hope, will be as free as ourselves. Surrounded in this manner by connected bodies of freemen, the states where slavery is allowed will be made more secure against domestic insurrection, and less liable to be affected by what may take place in the neighboring colonies.

It ought not to be forgotten that the first and main object of the negotiation which led to the acquisition of Louisiana was the free navigation of the Mississippi — a river that forms the sole passage from the Western states to the ocean. This navigation, although of general benefit, has been always valued and desired as of peculiar advantage to the Western states, whose demands to obtain it were neither equivocal nor unreasonable. But with the River Mississippi, by a sort of coercion, we acquired by ill or good fortune, as our future measures shall determine, the whole province of Louisiana. As this acquisition was made at the common expense, it is very fairly urged that the advantages to be derived from it should also be common. This, it is said, will not happen if slavery be excluded from Missouri, as the citizens of states where slavery is permitted will be shut out, and none but citizens of states where slavery is prohibited can become inhabitants of Missouri.

But this consequence will not arise from the proposed exclusion of slavery. The citizens of states in which slavery is allowed, like all other citizens, will be free to become the inhabitants of the Missouri, in like manner as they have become inhabitants of Ohio, Indiana, and Illinois, in which slavery is forbidden. The exclusion of slavery from Missouri will not, therefore, operate unequally among the citizens of the United States. The Constitution provides "that the citizens of each state shall be entitled to enjoy all the rights and immunities of citizens of the several states" — every citizen may therefore remove from one to another state, and there enjoy the rights and immunities of its citizens — the proposed provision excludes slaves, not citizens, whose rights it will not and cannot impair.

Besides, there is nothing new or peculiar in a provision for the exclusion of slavery; it has been established in the states northwest of the River Ohio, and has existed from the beginning in the old states where slavery is forbidden. The citizens of states where slavery is allowed may become inhabitants of Missouri, but cannot hold slaves there, nor in any other state where slavery is prohibited. As well might the laws prohibiting slavery in the old states become the subject of complaint as the proposed exclusion of slavery in Missouri; but there is no foundation for such complaint in either case. It is further urged that the admission of slaves into Missouri would be limited to the slaves already within the United States; that their health and comfort would be promoted by their dispersion; and that their numbers would be the same, whether they remain confined to the states where slavery exists, or are dispersed over the new states that are admitted into the Union.

That none but domestic slaves would be introduced into Missouri, and the other new and frontier states, is most fully disproved by the thousands of fresh slaves which, in violation of our laws, are annually imported into Alabama, Louisiana, and Mississippi.

We may renew our efforts, and enact new laws with heavier penalties, against the importation of slaves; the revenue cutters may more diligently watch our shores; and the naval force may be employed on the coast of Africa and on the ocean to break up the slave trade, but these means will not put an end to it. So long as markets are open to the purchase of slaves, so long they will be supplied; and so long as we permit the existence of slavery in our new and frontier states, so long slave markets will exist. The plea of humanity is equally inadmissible; since no one who has ever witnessed the experiment will believe that the condition of slaves is made better by the breaking up and separation of their families, nor by their removal from the old states to the new ones; and the objection to the provision of the bill, excluding slavery from Missouri, is equally applicable to the like prohibition of the old states; these should be revoked in order that, the slaves, now confined to certain states, may, for their health and comfort and multiplication be spread over the whole Union.

That the condition of slaves within the United States has been improved, and the rigors of slavery mitigated by the establishment and progress of our free governments, is a fact that imparts consolation to all who have taken pains to inquire concerning it. The disproportionate increase of free persons of color can be explained only by the supposition that the practice of emancipation is gaining ground; a practice which there is reason to believe would become more general if a plan could be devised by which the comforts and morals of the emancipated slaves could be satisfactorily provided for. For it is not to be doubted that public opinion everywhere, and especially in the oldest state of the Union, is less favorable than formerly to the existence of slavery. Generous and enlightened men in the states where slavery exists have discovered much solicitude on the subject, a desire has been manifested that emancipation might be encouraged by the establishment of a place or colony, without the United States, to which free persons of color might be removed; and great efforts for that purpose are making, with corresponding anxiety for their success. Those persons, enlightened and humane as they are known to be, surely will be unwilling to promote the removal of slaves from the old states to the new ones, where their comforts will not be multiplied, and where their fetters may be riveted forever.

Slavery cannot exist in Missouri without the consent of Congress; the question may, therefore, be considered, in certain lights, as a new one, it being the first instance in which an inquiry respecting slavery, in a case so free from the influence of the ancient laws and usages of the country, has come before the Senate.

The territory of Missouri is beyond our ancient limits, and the inquiry whether slavery shall exist there is open to many of the arguments that might be employed had slavery never existed within the United States. It is a question of no ordinary importance. Freedom and slavery are the parties which stand this day before the Senate; and upon its decision the empire of the one or the other will be established in the new state which we are about to admit into the Union.

If slavery be permitted in Missouri, with the climate and soil and in the circumstances of this territory, what hope can be entertained that it will ever be prohibited in any of the new states that will be formed in the immense region west of the Mississippi? Will the coextensive establishment of slavery and of new states throughout this region lessen the danger of domestic insurrection or of foreign aggression? Will this manner of executing the great trust of admitting new states into the Union contribute to assimilate our manners and usages, to increase our mutual affection and confidence, and to establish that equality of benefits and burdens which constitutes the true basis of our strength and union? Will the militia of the nation, which must furnish our soldiers and seamen, increase as slaves increase; will the actual disproportion in the military service of the nation be thereby diminished — a disproportion that will be, as it has been, readily borne, as between the original states, because it arises out of their compact of union, but which may become a badge of inferiority, if required for the protection of those who, being free to choose, persist in the establishment of maxims; the inevitable effect of which will deprive them of the power to contribute to the common defense, and even of the ability to protect themselves?

There are limits within which our federal system must stop; no one has supposed that it could be indefinitely extended — we are now about to pass our original boundary; if this can be done without affecting the principles of our free government, it can be accomplished only by the most vigilant attention to plant, cherish, and sustain the principles of liberty in the new states that may be formed beyond our ancient limits. With our utmost caution in this respect, it may still be justly apprehended that the general government must be made stronger as we become more extended.

But if, instead of freedom, slavery is to prevail and spread as we extend our dominion, can any reflecting man fail to see the necessity of giving to the general government greater powers; to enable it to afford the protection that will be demanded of it; powers that will be difficult to control and which may prove fatal to the public liberties?

Talking for Buncombe.

Felix Walker, speech on the Missouri Bill, House of Representatives, Feb. 25, 1820. Walker was representative from North Carolina, and Buncombe County was part of his district. Toward the close of the debate, Walker rose to speak and was asked not to so the vote could be taken, but he refused, saying he was bound to make "a speech for Buncombe."

137.

Anonymous: Against Restriction of Slavery to the Southern States

The antislavery speeches of Rufus King on the Missouri bill excited a barrage of bitter comments in the Southern press. The Richmond Enquirer, *one of the most influential newspapers in the South, ran a series of articles opposing King's position. According to the Southern view, the Constitution guaranteed new states the same rights as it did the old, and, consequently, Congress had no right to ban slavery as a qualification for admission. Though moral issues were certainly involved, many Southerners, like the anonymous author of the following selection, believed that the Northern Federalists were using the Missouri question to enhance the position of their party. The article which appeared in the* Enquirer *at the end of December 1819, was signed "A Southron."*

Source: *Richmond Enquirer,* December 23, 1819.

The Congress of the United States have again before them the deeply interesting Missouri question. In my judgment, the petty concern of an acquisition of barren territory and even the danger of a war with a decrepit foe, in comparison with it, sink into insignificance. The matter is to preserve the happiness we already possess; to perpetuate this noble confederacy; to brighten the chain which binds together a band of brothers, instead of lighting up the torch of discord which will blaze like a bale fire from one end of the continent to the other. The harmony of the present moment, the happiness of the future, the independence of the states, the continuance of their Union, even the preservation of the unimpaired sovereignty of this ancient and venerable member of the confederacy may perhaps hang upon the decision to this interesting question.

Let not then a disgraceful supineness possess us; let not "the fatal coma," which has been eloquently declared to have seized upon the people, overcome us longer with lethargic slumber; let not a legislative body, which has hitherto been distinguished "for auguring maladministration at a distance and scenting the approach of tyranny in every tainted breeze," sleep upon their posts at this interesting moment when the enemies of our institutions are throwing up outworks which, at a period not remote, may be used for the subversion of our sovereignty and independence.

It were charity to hope that the motives which have dictated the late attempt to introduce restrictions into the constitution of Missouri were as praiseworthy as they affect to be. But we cannot "wink so hard" as to be insensible to the political object which some of the statesmen of the East would fain conceal. The pretexts of humanity and a love of liberty are too flimsy a veil to hide from our view the political hostility which governs these.

Humanity! Where is the humanity of resisting the only feasible plan of future emancipation? Can we expect an event so desirable in the Southern states, while their numbers so far exceed the numbers of whites? Shall we oppose that dispersion of them through the Western states, which, by lessening the excess, may at a future day render practicable the schemes of philanthropy for their relief? Shall we adopt the barbarous principles of affected benevolence in imposing a check on the increase of black population by excluding them from an emigration to a country more salubrious and fertile than they now inhabit, and affording more abundantly the means of subsistence and comfort? Admirable philanthropists, who have religion and humanity on their lips, and look to the diminution of slave population from the combined operations of pestilence and famine!

But while humanity cannot offer an apology for this outrage upon the rights of the South, it is easily explained by the antipathies of certain politicians, and their jealousy of the influence of the Southern states in the councils of the nation. Rob us of our just portion of the territory which has been jointly purchased by the treasures of the nation and the valley of the Mississippi will be settled by the sons of the Eastern people, the inheritors of their fathers' prejudices; new states will spring up, emulous of setting new limits to Southern domination; swarms of "Southern slaveholders" will no longer crowd the halls of Congress and "sear the eyeballs" of their jealous countrymen; "the scepter will depart from Judah"; and Virginia influence — so magnified and deprecated — will be heard of no more!

If rumor has not deceived us, there may be other objects more immediate to be attained by this modern crusade against the rights of the people of the South. Some master spirit of the North may expect to ride on this popular wave to the lofty pinnacle of his ambition. Whatever is indecorous in personality or unparliamentary in abuse has been abundantly poured forth by those frothy declaimers against the unavoidable domestic slavery of the South. They have assumed to themselves the power of making a form of government for others, and have supported so insolent a pretension by arguments and language no less insolent and offensive.

And when they have succeeded in excluding from the Western settlements every Southern man, and shall have sent forth in every direction swarms from the Northern hive, and missionary preachers against the cruelties and inhumanities of Southern slavery, a universal emancipation may be the next scheme suggested by visionary philanthropists or promoted by designing politicians.

With dangers such as these in prospect, can Virginia look on with stoical indifference because it is not her own case? Shall she console herself with the hope that she may be the last to be devoured? Shall she be silent when the great principles of the Constitution are assailed, when the rights of her sons, now peopling a western clime, are invaded, and principles asserted which may one day be turned with fatal effect against her own institutions?

I am not one of those who upon every trivial occasion would have the legislative body exert its rights as a member of the confederacy to protest against the acts of the general government. I would not, it is true, make this medicine of the Constitution our daily bread. But I have known no subject more important than the present, none on which the firm yet dignified and moderate language of this sovereignty was more imperiously demanded. . . .

It behooves us to contest at the threshold a pretension which violates the compact of the states; which sets at nought the great principle of self-government; which will prove an apple of discord among the sisters of this confederacy, and threaten to subvert our free and happy Constitution by a deadly blow at the rights of a part of the nation, and a destruction of the harmony and tranquility of the whole.

1820

138.

John Quincy Adams: Slavery and the Constitution

The complexity of the issues involved in the debate about the Missouri Compromise is revealed in the selection that appears below from the diary of John Quincy Adams, dated March 3, 1820, only three days before the Missouri Enabling Act went into effect. President Monroe had assembled his cabinet (Adams was secretary of state) for advice before signing the bills admitting Maine and Missouri, and Adams recommended their acceptance. He did so despite the fact that he believed that slavery was a profound moral evil. At the same time, however, he was convinced that the Constitution did not give the federal government the power to abolish the institution. "The abolition of slavery where it is established must be left entirely to the people of the state itself," he declared in a letter of the same date to Governor Jonathan Jennings of Indiana. "The healthy have no right to reproach or to prescribe for the diseased."

Source: *Memoirs of John Quincy Adams, Comprising Portions of his Diary from 1795 to 1848,* Charles Francis Adams, ed., Vol. V, Philadelphia, 1875, pp. 4-12.

When I came this day to my office, I found there a note requesting me to call at one o'clock at the President's house. It was then one, and I immediately went over. He expected that the two bills — for the admission of Maine, and to enable Missouri to make a constitution — would have been brought to him for his signature, and he had summoned all the members of the administration to ask their opinions, in writing, to be deposited in the Department of State, upon two questions: (1) whether Congress had a constitutional right to prohibit slavery in a territory; and (2) whether the 8th Section of the Missouri bill (which interdicts slavery *forever* in the territory north of thirty-six and a half latitude) was applicable only to the territorial state, or could extend to it after it should become a state. . . .

After this meeting, I walked home with Calhoun, who said that . . . in the Southern country . . . domestic labor was confined to the blacks; and such was the prejudice that if he, who was the most popular man in his district, were to keep a white servant in his house, his character and reputation would be irretrievably ruined.

I said that this confounding of the ideas of servitude and labor was one of the bad effects of slavery; but he thought it attended with many excellent consequences. It did not apply to all kinds of labor — not, for example, to farming. He himself had often held the plough; so had his father. Manufacturing and mechanical labor was not degrading. It was only manual labor — the proper work of slaves. No white person could descend to that. And it was the best guarantee to equality among the whites. It produced an unvarying level among them. It not only did not excite but did not even admit of inequalities, by which one white man could domineer over another.

I told Calhoun I could not see things in the same light. It is, in truth, all perverted sentiment — mistaking labor for slavery, and dominion for freedom. The discussion of this Missouri question has betrayed the secret of their souls. In the abstract they admit that slavery is an evil, they disclaim all participation in the introduction of it, and cast it all upon the shoulders of our old Grandam Britain. But when probed to the quick upon it, they show at the bottom of their souls pride and vainglory in their condition of masterdom. They fancy themselves more generous and noblehearted than the plain freemen who labor for subsistence. They look down upon the simplicity of a Yankee's manners, because he has no habits of overbearing like theirs and cannot treat Negroes like dogs.

It is among the evils of slavery that it taints the very sources of moral principle. It establishes false estimates of virtue and vice; for what can be more false and heartless than this doctrine which makes the first and holiest rights of humanity to depend upon the color of the skin? It perverts human reason, and reduces man endowed with logical powers to maintain that slavery is sanctioned by the Christian religion, that slaves are happy and contented in their condition, that between master and slave there are ties of mutual attachment and affection, that the virtues of the master are refined and exalted by the degradation of the slave; while at the same time they vent execrations upon the slave trade, curse Britain for having given them slaves, burn at the stake Negroes convicted of crimes for the terror of the example, and writhe in agonies of fear at the very mention of human rights as applicable to men of color. The impression produced upon my mind by the progress of this discussion is that the bargain between freedom and slavery contained in the Constitution of the United States is morally and politically vicious, inconsistent with the principles upon which alone our Revolution can be justified; cruel and oppressive, by riveting the chains of slavery, by pledging the faith of freedom to maintain and perpetuate the tyranny of the master; and grossly unequal and impolitic, by admitting that slaves are at once enemies to be kept in subjection, property to be secured or restored to their owners, and persons not to be represented themselves, but for whom their masters are privileged with nearly a double share of representation. The consequence has been that this slave representation has governed the Union.

Benjamin portioned above his brethren has ravined as a wolf. In the morning he has devoured the prey, and at night he has divided the spoil. It would be no difficult matter to prove, by reviewing the history of the Union under this Constitution, that almost everything which has contributed to the honor and welfare of the nation has been accomplished in spite of them or forced upon them, and that everything unpropitious and dishonorable, including the blunders and follies of their adversaries, may be traced to them.

I have favored this Missouri Compromise,

believing it to be all that could be effected under the present Constitution, and from extreme unwillingness to put the Union at hazard. But perhaps it would have been a wiser as well as a bolder course to have persisted in the restriction upon Missouri, till it should have terminated in a convention of the states to revise and amend the Constitution. This would have produced a new Union of thirteen or fourteen States, unpolluted with slavery, with a great and glorious object to effect; namely, that of rallying to their standard the other states by the universal emancipation of their slaves. If the Union must be dissolved, slavery is precisely the question upon which it ought to break. For the present, however, this contest is laid asleep.

139.

Missouri Enabling Act

The admission of Alabama in 1819 brought the total number of states to 22, half slave and half free. The appeals for statehood of Maine, free, and Missouri, slave — as it was supposed — seemed to be routine until the question arose of excluding slavery from Missouri. This would make the count in the Senate 13 free states to 11 slave, which, along with the Northern preponderance in the House, would have given that section clear dominance. By the Missouri Compromise, Maine was admitted as a free state on March 3, 1820, and the Missouri Enabling Act, part of which is reprinted here, went into effect on March 6. But a year of bitter debate had still to occur before Missouri's statehood became official. The Missouri Compromise endured for a generation, but the controversy surrounding it had revealed the deep division in the country, and it was the occasion of dire prophecies. As John Quincy Adams noted in his diary: "Take it for granted that the present is a mere preamble — a title page to a great, tragic volume."

Source: *Statutes,* III, pp. 545-548.

Be it enacted by the Senate and House of Representatives of the United States of America, in Congress assembled, that the inhabitants of that portion of the Missouri territory included within the boundaries hereinafter designated be, and they are hereby authorized to form for themselves a constitution and state government, and to assume such name as they shall deem proper; and the said state, when formed, shall be admitted into the Union, upon an equal footing with the original states in all respects whatsoever.

Section 2. *And be it further enacted,* that the said state shall consist of all the territory included within the following boundaries, to wit: Beginning in the middle of the Mississippi River, on the parallel of 36° N latitude; thence west, along that parallel of latitude, to the St. Francois River; thence up, and following the course of that river, in the middle of the main channel thereof, to the parallel of latitude of 36°30′; thence west, along the same, to a point where the said parallel is intersected by a meridian line passing through the middle of the mouth of the Kansas River, where the same empties into the Missouri River; thence, from the point aforesaid, north, along the said meridian line, to the intersection of the parallel of latitude which passes through the rapids of the River Des Moines, making the said line to correspond with the Indian boundary line; thence east, from the point of intersection last aforesaid, along the said parallel of latitude, to the middle of the channel of the main fork of the said River Des Moines; thence down and along the middle of the main channel of the said River Des Moines to the mouth of the same, where it empties into the Mississippi River; thence due east, to the middle of the main channel of the Mississippi River; thence down, and following the course of the Mississippi River, in the middle of the main channel thereof, to the place of beginning: *Provided,* the said state shall ratify the boundaries aforesaid; *And provided also,* that the said state shall have concurrent jurisdiction on the River Mississippi and every other river bordering on the said state, so far as the said rivers shall form a common boundary to the said state; and any other state or states, now or hereafter to be formed and bounded by the same, such rivers to be common to both; and that the River Mississippi, and the navigable rivers and waters leading into the same, shall be common highways and forever free, as well to the inhabitants of the said state as to other citizens of the United States, without any tax, duty, impost, or toll, therefor, imposed by the said state.

Section 3. *And be it further enacted,* that all free, white, male citizens of the United States who shall have arrived at the age of twenty-one years and have resided in said territory three months previous to the day of election, and all other persons qualified to vote for representatives to the General Assembly of the said territory, shall be qualified to be elected; and they are hereby qualified and authorized to vote and choose representatives to form a convention, who shall be apportioned among the several counties. . . .

Section 6. *And be it further enacted,* that the following propositions be, and the same are hereby, offered to the convention of the said territory of Missouri, when formed, for their free acceptance or rejection, which, if accepted by the convention, shall be obligatory upon the United States.

First, that section numbered sixteen in every township, and when such section has been sold, or otherwise disposed of, other lands equivalent thereto, and as contiguous as may be, shall be granted to the state for the use of the inhabitants of such township for the use of schools. . . .

Third, that 5 percent of the net proceeds of the sale of lands lying within the said territory or state, and which shall be sold by Congress, from and after the 1st day of January next, after deducting all expenses incident to the same, shall be reserved for making public roads and canals, of which three-fifths shall be applied to those objects within the state, under the direction of the legislature thereof; and the other two-fifths in defraying, under the direction of Congress, the expenses to be incurred in making of a road or roads, canal or canals, leading to the said state. . . .

Section 8. *And be it further enacted,* that in all that territory ceded by France to the United States, under the name of Louisiana, which lies north of 36°30′ N latitude, not included within the limits of the state, contemplated by this act, slavery and involuntary servitude, otherwise than in the punishment of crimes, whereof the parties shall have been duly convicted, shall be, and is hereby, forever prohibited: *Provided always,* that any person escaping into the same, from whom labor or service is lawfully claimed, in any state or territory of the United States, such fugitive may be lawfully reclaimed and conveyed to the person claiming his or her labor or service as aforesaid.

Library of Congress

Watercolor by Benjamin Latrobe of his design for the west elevation of the Capitol

TRANSITION IN THE ARTS

The first decades of the 19th century represent a period of tentative experiment in American art. In painting, the principal traditions were in portraiture, and the only sure market was in that field. Celebrations of the Revolution were widely popular for a time, particularly in engraved reproductions, but the work of imaginative artists aroused little interest. A few such as Washington Allston and John Vanderlyn were deeply influenced by long years of study in Europe and attempted to carry this experience to America. Both ended as portraitists, when their romantic landscapes and classical scenes proved irrelevant to life in America. In response to a consistent demand, American portraiture achieved international stature, but, for many artists, painting likenesses for a living was an embittering experience.

In architecture, the first trained, professional architects began working in America during this period. Prosperity brought a demand for mansions and public buildings of unassailable stature and dignity. In attempting to respond to this demand, most American designers turned to Greek models. The basic classical forms were borrowed, almost intact in some cases, for banks and government buildings of marble or stone. In other instances, most notably Southern plantation houses, the characteristic columns and triangular pediments were adapted to private dwellings built of wood. The Greek revival spread even to the Midwest, where simple houses were often embellished with a columned doorway. Neo-classicism remained the norm for government buildings and Gothic examples soon became popular for church architecture.

Primitive Art

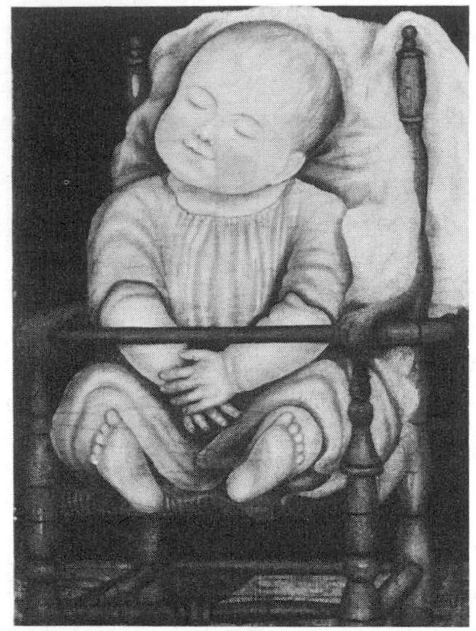

Rockefeller Collection, Colonial Williamsburg

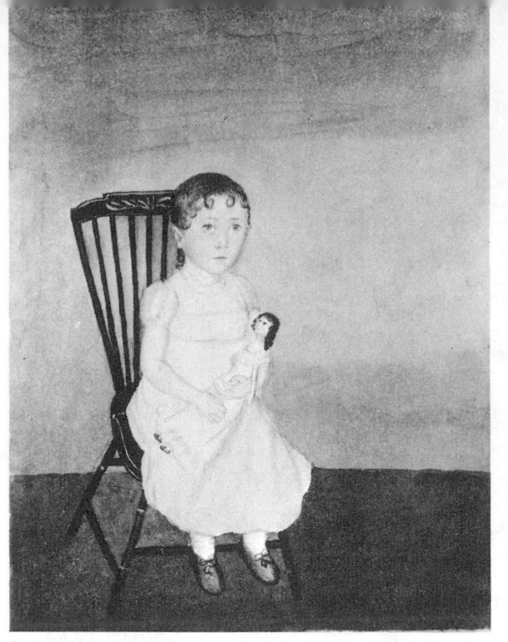

Courtesy, Edgar W. Garbisch

Of all the artists working in America at the time, only those now classified as primitive were clearly American in subject and style. Because they were untutored and provincial in outlook, these painters were able to recreate their time and place with simplicity and directness. The itinerant portraitists, amateur water-colorists, and ambitious signpainters who made these works responded to their environment in a way that their professionally trained counterparts could not, and certainly the paintings represent the uncomplicated tastes of the people who bought them.

National Gallery of Art, Garbisch Collection

Princeton University

(From top right) "Eliza Roxberry," "Baby in Red Chair," "Joseph and Anna Raymond," and "Girl in Mauve, Stockbridge, Massachusetts"

Metropolitan Museum of Art, Garbisch Collection

Courtesy, Edgar W. Garbisch

Rockefeller Collection, Colonial Williamsburg

(Top) "The Picnic" by an unknown artist, c. 1800; (left) "General Schumaker" by Jacob Mantel, c. 1812; (above) "The Prodigal Son Reclaimed," anonymous

Metropolitan Museum of Art, Jesup Fund

Established Modes

Museum of the City of New York

At the beginning of the 19th century there were three principal traditions in American painting: colonial portraiture as carried on by Ralph Earl; the richer, more cosmopolitan portraiture represented by Gilbert Stuart; and the school of Benjamin West, which sought to move beyond portraiture to grand historical or biblical scenes. Even among those artists who studied abroad and sought alternative models, there was little consciousness of trying to create a distinctive "American" style.

(Top) "Return of the Prodigal Son" by West; (left) Mrs. Alexander Hamilton sat for Ralph Earl to get him out of debtor's prison; (bottom left) copying the masters at the British Institution, London; (below) Mrs. Richard Yates by Stuart

Metropolitan Museum of Art

National Gallery of Art

Detroit Institute of Arts

Peale

The work of Rembrandt Peale (1778-1860) represents one response to the existing traditions in American painting. He was taught by his father, Charles Willson Peale, and although he later spent two years in France his early training remained his principal influence. His paintings of Washington and the Revolution are refinements of his father's approach, while his few experiments with classical subjects were uninspired and were soon abandoned. Peale lived out his long life writing art books, painting portraits, and selling copies of his own earlier successes.

(Top) "The Court of Death"; (right) "Washington Before Yorktown"; (below, from left) "Self-Portrait by Candlelight," "Jean Houdon," "Dr. Joseph Priestley"

Corcoran Gallery of Art

orth Atheneum, Hartford

Pennsylvania Academy of the Fine Arts

New York Historical Society

Museum of Fine Arts, Boston; Karolik Collection

"Landscape with a Lake" (left) is characteristic of Allston's romantic response to Italy; (below) Allston; portrait by Chester Harding

Allston

Massachusetts Historical Society

Unlike Peale, Washington Allston (1779-1843), after his graduation from Harvard in 1800, spent most of the next 18 years in Europe. He was greatly influenced by Renaissance Italian painting, which he approached with a genuine romantic vision. The landscapes, often of biblical scenes, that he painted in Europe earned him a modest reputation, particularly in London. However, after returning to America, public disinterest and his failure to relate this romantic style to American life, as was later done by Thomas Cole, soon reduced Allston to portraiture.

Addison Gallery of American Art

"Italian Landscape," by Allston, is again typical of his quiet romanticism

Pennsylvania Academy of Fine Arts

(Left) "Ariadne Asleep on the Island of Naxos," by Vanderlyn, the first nude shown in America; (center) Cadwallader D. Colden, by Jarvis; (below) self-portraits by Vanderlyn (left) and Jarvis (right)

New York Historical Society

The lives of John Vanderlyn and John Wesley Jarvis also illustrate, in different ways, the difficulties encountered by American artists. Vanderlyn spent a total of 14 years in Paris and Rome between 1796 and 1815. His ambition was to establish a school of American painting based on the current French vogue for enormous, idealized interpretations of history. He failed in this and ended as a portraitist. Jarvis, a nephew of John Wesley, was a skilled engraver and a popular portraitist in New York and the South. Both Henry Inman and Thomas Sully worked in his studio, but by his death in 1839, Jarvis' bohemian way of life and heavy drinking left him destitute.

Metropolitan Museum of Art; Stephens Bequest

Museum of Fine Arts, Boston; Karolik Collection

(Both) Massachusetts Historical Society

Jefferson's final version of Monticello (1803), drawn by Robert Mills while studying architecture with Jefferson; (below) sketch by Jefferson of his original conception for the house, 1771

Courtesy, Mrs. F. C. Latrobe; photo, Frick

Benjamin Latrobe by C.W. Peale

Greek Revival

American architects also looked to Europe for guidance, but, unlike the painters, they were consciously seeking a style suited to their interpretation of America. Jefferson was actively involved in these early experiments and gave them a Republican coloring. British traditions were rejected, while Jefferson's attraction to France influenced him in favor of the classical revival taking place there. Benjamin Latrobe, a friend of Jefferson's, argued that Greek models, as products of the world's first republic, would best represent America's democratic spirit. Latrobe was a major force behind the Greek revival in America and taught both Robert Mills and William Strickland. He was also active in the plans for Washington.

Library of Congress

(Left) The first Philadelphia Water Works, 1797, and the Bank of Pennsylvania, 1798, both by Benjamin Latrobe, in Greek revival style

Historical Society of Pennsylvania

New York Historical Society

The Merchant's Exchange in Philadelphia, designed by William Strickland, 1836

The three leading architects of the early Greek revival, in addition to Latrobe, were Robert Mills, William Strickland, and John Haviland. These men formed the first group of professional architects in America and all three remained active until the 1850s. The Greek revival style that they helped popularize was particularly suited to government buildings, churches, banks, and buildings of similar stature.

Gothic church architecture began to interest some architects prior to 1820 and shortly thereafter served as one basis for the eclectic styles now called Victorian.

Avery Library, Columbia University

Sansom Street Church, Philadelphia, designed by Robert Mills, 1808, in the Greek revival mode; was distinguished by a circular baptistry under a central dome

Maryland Historical Society

Chapel of St. Mary's Seminary, Baltimore, 1807, designed by Maximilian Godefroy and considered the first Gothic revival church in America

Library of Congress

Design for the Capitol by James Diamond

Library of Congress

Samuel Dobie's competition design

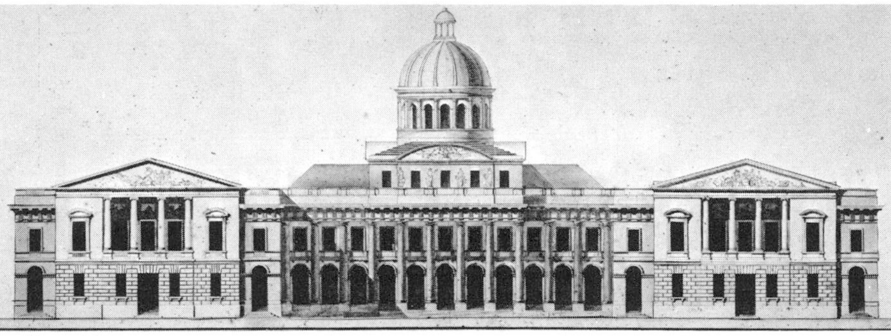

Library of Congress

The dome and proportions of Stephen Hallet's design foreshadow the Capitol's present look

Capitol Competition

A major stimulus to interest in architecture and the Greek revival was the design competition held for the Capitol building in Washington. Dr. William Thornton, an amateur designer, won, although several proposals were by trained architects, including a newly arrived Frenchman, Stephen Hallet. Most of the designs submitted derived their sense of what a capitol should be from classical sources. George Washington approved the plans.

During the course of construction there was considerable controversy over details, but Thornton's plan was followed in general.

U.S. Capitol; photo, Library of Congress

William Thornton

The design by William Thornton that won the Capitol competition and was the basis for construction

Library of Congress

140.

Thomas Jefferson: A Firebell in the Night

The Missouri Compromise, by the terms of which slavery was henceforth excluded from the territories north of latitude 36°30′ (the southern boundary of Missouri), alarmed Thomas Jefferson, as he told John Holmes in this famous letter, "like a firebell in the night." The vividness of the image was in keeping with the passions of the time. Jefferson disapproved deeply of slavery; but he even more strongly disapproved of any action on the part of Congress that, in his view, exceeded its constitutional authority. Slavery, Jefferson felt, would die a natural death if left alone; but the very life of the Union depended on maintaining a due measure in legislative acts. In addition, the Compromise had drawn a line across the country on the basis of a principle, and not of geography; such a line, held up, as Jefferson put it, to the angry passions of men, could have no other ultimate effect than the disastrous rending of the body politic. Holmes, a Massachusetts man, was one of the few Northern congressmen to vote against the Tallmadge Amendment that would have excluded slavery from Missouri itself; Jefferson's prophetic letter to him was written April 22, 1820, a short month after the passage of the Missouri Compromise.

Source: Randolph, IV, pp. 323-333.

I thank you, dear sir, for the copy you have been so kind as to send me of the letter to your constituents on the Missouri question. It is a perfect justification to them. I had for a long time ceased to read newspapers, or pay any attention to public affairs, confident they were in good hands, and content to be a passenger in our bark to the shore from which I am not distant. But this momentous question, like a firebell in the night, awakened and filled me with terror. I considered it at once as the knell of the Union. It is hushed, indeed, for the moment. But this is a reprieve only, not a final sentence. A geographical line, coinciding with a marked principle, moral and political, once conceived and held up to the angry passions of men, will never be obliterated; and every new irritation will mark it deeper and deeper. I can say, with conscious truth, that there is not a man on earth who would sacrifice more than I would to relieve us from this heavy reproach, in any *practicable* way.

The cession of that kind of property, for so it is misnamed, is a bagatelle which would not cost me a second thought, if, in that way, a general emancipation and *expatriation* could be effected; and gradually, and with due sacrifices, I think it might be. But as it is, we have the wolf by the ears, and we can neither hold him, nor safely let him go. Justice is in one scale, and self-preservation in the other. Of one thing I am certain, that as the passage of slaves from one state to another would not make a slave of a single human being who would not be so without it, so their diffusion over a greater surface would make them individually happier, and proportionally facilitate the accomplishment of their emancipation, by dividing the burden on a greater number of coadjutors. An abstinence too, from this act of power, would remove the jealousy excited by the undertaking of Congress to regulate the condition of the different descriptions of men composing a state. This certainly is the exclusive right of every state, which nothing in the Constitution has taken from them and given to the general government. Could Congress, for example, say that the non-freemen of Connecticut shall be freemen, or that they shall not emigrate into any other state?

I regret that I am now to die in the belief that the useless sacrifice of themselves by the generation of 1776, to acquire self-government and happiness to their country, is to be thrown away by the unwise and unworthy passions of their sons, and that my only consolation is to be that I live not to weep over it. If they would but dispassionately weigh the blessings they will throw away against an abstract principle more likely to be effected by union than by scission, they would pause before they would perpetrate this act of suicide on themselves, and of treason against the hopes of the world. To yourself, as the faithful advocate of the Union, I tender the offering of my high esteem and respect.

141.

Against a Protective Tariff

When the War of 1812 ended, the resumption of foreign trade threatened to engulf the new American industries that had arisen in its absence. But these industries were ambitious, not only to survive but also to expand. Pittsburgh mills hoped to replace British and Swedish iron, Kentucky hemp wished to beat out the Scotch bagging industry, sheepherders in Vermont and Ohio had their eye on the demand for English woolens, and the wheat growers of central New York, shut out of England by the Corn Laws, wished the same protection for their own home market. The result was that in 1816 Congress passed a new tariff raising the customs duties on imports from abroad. This tariff was not everywhere approved. Commercial interests in New England (as distinct from the newer industrial interests) were against it. So were Southern planters, who were forced to buy from New England mills the cloth they had hitherto imported at a quarter of the cost. Certain of these groups, two of which are represented in the following selection, formally protested to Congress. The remonstrances of the Virginia Agricultural Society of Fredericksburg and of merchants and other townspeople of Salem, Massachusetts, were presented on January 3 and 31, 1820, respectively.

Source: *Debates,* 16 Cong., 1 Sess., pp. 2296-2299, 2335-2348.

I.

Fredericksburg Remonstrance

The remonstrance of the Virginia Agricultural Society of Fredericksburg against the attempts now making, by our domestic manufacturers and their friends, to increase the duties upon foreign goods, wares, and merchandise, respectfully represents:

That it is the indisputable right of every free people to petition and remonstrate, either individually or collectively, not only against grievances actually inflicted, but against such also as are either seriously threatened or meditated.

That hostility, resulting from true republican principles, to partial taxation, exclusive privileges, and monopolies created by law was the primary cause of our glorious and ever memorable Revolution.

That, although most of us are only the descendants of those patriots who achieved that Revolution by the lavish expenditure of their treasure and their blood, yet that we inherit enough of their spirit to feel equal aversion to similar oppressions; at the same time, we confidently trust that neither we, nor our sons after us, will ever be found backward or reluctant in offering up at the shrine of national good and national happiness any sacrifices, however great, which their promotion and preservation may obviously and necessarily require. But we have been taught to believe that a parental government — a government founded upon the immutable and sacred principles of truth, justice, and liberty — if she required sacrifices at all from those whom she is so solemnly bound to protect, would make them such as should operate equally upon every member of the community.

That we view with great concern, both nationally and individually, certain late attempts on the part of various descriptions of domestic manufacturers to induce your honorable body to increase the duties upon imports, already so high as to amount, upon many articles, nearly to a prohibition. The increased cost upon some of these may truly be designated a tax upon knowledge, if not a bounty to ignorance; such, for example, as the duty upon books in foreign languages, and upon philosophical, mathematical, surgical, and chemical instruments.

That, although these attempts are sustained under the plausible pretext of "promoting national industry," they are calculated (we will not say in *design* but certainly in *effect*) to produce a tax highly impolitic in its nature, partial in its operation, and oppressive in its effect; a tax, in fact, to be levied principally on the great body of agriculturists, who constitute a large majority of the whole American people, and who are the chief consumers of all foreign imports.

That such a tax would be a flagrant violation of the soundest and most important principles of political economy, among which we deem the following to be incontrovertibly true: that, as the interests of dealers and consumers necessarily conflict with each other, the first always aiming to *narrow*, while the latter, who form the majority of every nation, as constantly endeavor to *enlarge* competition; by which enlargement alone extravagant prices and exorbitant profits are prevented, it is the duty of every wise and just government to secure the consumers against both exorbitant profits and extravagant prices by leaving competition as free and open as possible.

That in this way alone can the benefits of good government be equalized among the various orders and classes of society, the prosperity and happiness of which depend not upon immunities, privileges, and monopolies granted to one class or order at the expense of another but upon the unfettered exercise of talent, skill, and industry, directed and employed in whatever manner, and upon whatsoever objects of pursuit each individual may select for himself; provided, always, that such objects be not incompatible with the public good; for so to use your own rights as not to injure the rights of others is not less the dictate of common sense and common honesty than it is a cardinal maxim of all legitimate government.

That national industry is best promoted by leaving every member of society free to apply his labor and his knowledge according to his own choice, exempt from all restraints but such as the public good requires, and burdened with no tax but such as shall be both impartial and as moderate as the exigencies of the state will permit.

That, according to the natural progress of society in every country favorably situated for agriculture, the class of manufacturers is the last to spring up; but that it will necessarily do so, as soon as either the natural or artificial wants of the people create a demand for their labors.

That any legislative interference to force either this or any other class into existence by the strong arm of power, exercised in levying taxes to support the forced class, contrary to the wishes and interests of the other members of the community, is not only bad policy, but oppression; because taxes of any kind, to be rightfully levied, should be equal, and should be imposed, not for the emolument of any one portion of society at the expense of the rest but for the support of government alone.

That either to exclude foreign manufactures or to tax them very heavily, under a notion of improving those of domestic fabric, lessens the profits of agriculture; diminishes the public revenue, either by augmenting the number of smugglers, or by enabling the domestic manufacturer to pocket that sum which otherwise would go into the public treasury, under the form of an import duty; and at the same time secures to him the power of practising upon the community the double imposition of deteriorating his goods and selling them at a higher price; because that competition which constitutes the only security for skill, industry, and moderate prices is either entirely removed or so limited as not to be felt.

That all free trade, of whatever description, must be a mutual benefit to the parties engaged in it, notwithstanding the profits arising therefrom may be somewhat unequally divided; because by free trade alone can supply and demand (the two circumstances upon which trade of every kind depends) be kept nearly equal to each other.

That, instead of struggling against the dictates of reason and nature, and madly attempting to produce everything at home, countries should study to direct their labors to those departments of industry for which their situation and circumstances are best adapted.

That the use of capital should be left, as much as possible, to the care of those to whom it belongs; because they will be most likely to discover in what line it can be employed to the greatest advantage.

And that the best-regulated and happiest communities are those wherein all the various trades, professions, and callings enjoy equal rights, and contribute equally to the necessary support of their common government; but that if anyone should be thought to have superior claims to the fostering care of the national legislature, it should be "the tillers of the earth — the fountainhead of all wealth, of all power, and of all prosperity."

The sagacious and patriotic Franklin has said (and we believe he never uttered a better or wiser remark) "that most of the statutes or acts, edicts, arrets, and placards, of parliaments, princes, and states for regulating, directing, or restraining trade have, we think, been either political blunders or jobs obtained by artful men for private advantage, under pretense of public good."

Your petitioners have thus freely, but respectfully, endeavored to represent to your honorable body their views of a policy which you are so importunately urged to adopt, but upon which we should have said nothing, having due confidence both in your willingness and ability to protect the great landed interests of our country, had we not been apprehensive that silence might possibly be construed into consent, if all who are attached to those interests had forborne to speak, when so clamorously and powerfully assailed. To guard against the possibility of misapprehension, we take this occasion to say that we are incapable of feeling anything like enmity toward either manufacturers or any other useful description of our fellow citizens, but heartily wish them all the success to which their skill and industry may entitle them, in whatsoever way applied, provided, always, that such application be not made at our risk, and continued at our cost.

We will go further, and pledge ourselves to prefer whatever they may manufacture at anytime that they will make the price and the quality the same with the quality and price of similar articles of foreign fabric. To give more for any article simply because it is made at home may suit the feelings of political enthusiasm, but it can never promote the interests either of individuals or of nations. To buy as cheap as you can, no matter where, and to sell as dear is the maxim which should regulate the commerce of both; for if competition be left free, neither can be exorbitant in their demands.

We ask no tax upon manufacturers for our benefit; neither do we desire anything of government to enable us to cultivate the soil as profitably as we could wish, but to leave us free, so far as it depends on them, to carry our products to the best market we can find, and to purchase what we want in return, on the best terms we can, either at home or abroad. We will ever support the government of our choice in all just and rightful undertakings, both with our fortunes and our lives; but we will never voluntarily contribute to maintain either manufacturers, or any other class of citizens, by the payment of unequal and partial taxes, by awarding to them exclusive privileges, or by sustaining them in the enjoyment of oppressive monopolies, which are ultimately to grind both us and our children after us "into dust and ashes."

II.

Salem Memorial

The undersigned memorialists, merchants, and inhabitants of Salem, in the Commonwealth of Massachusetts, and of the towns in its vicinity, beg leave most respectfully to represent:

That they have seen, with unfeigned regret and surprise, some propositions recently brought forward in Congress, and others advocated by respectable portions of the community, which, in their humble opinions, are calculated seriously to injure, if not eventually to destroy, some of the most important branches of the commerce and navigation of the United States. The memorialists have not the slightest intention of casting any imputation of unworthy motives upon those from whom, on this occasion, they feel themselves compelled to differ in the most decided manner. They are ready to admit that many of those who were inclined to revive commercial prohibitions and restrictions, and to change some of the fundamental rules of our financial policy, are governed by motives solely suggested, by their own views of the national interest. They are free also to admit that the manufacturing interests of the country deserve to receive the fostering care and patronage of the government. But while they make these admissions, they also beg leave to suggest that the interests of commerce are not less vital to the welfare and prosperity of the Union than manufactures; and that it never can be a sound or safe policy to build up the one upon the ruins of the other.

Under a wise and enlightened revenue system, the commerce of our country has hitherto advanced with a rapidity and force which have exceeded the most sanguine expectations of its friends. This commerce has contributed largely to the employment of the capital, the industry, and the enterprise of our citizens. It has quickened the march of agriculture, and, by increasing the value as well as amount of its products, has given to the planter and husbandman a reward in solid profit for their toils. It has also materially sustained the credit and finances of the nation by insuring a regular and growing revenue through a taxation scarcely felt, and cheerfully borne by all classes of our citizens. It has also given birth to our naval power by fostering a hardy race of seamen, and patronizing those arts which are essential to the building, preservation, and equipment of ships. It has greatly enlarged, and the memorialists had almost said created, the moneyed capital of the country. And the memorialists believe that it cannot be too frequently or deeply inculcated as an axiom in political economy that productive capital, in whatever manner added to the stock of the country, is equally beneficial to its best interests. Its real value can never be ascertained by the sources from whence it flows but from the blessings which it dispenses. A million dollars added to the productive capital by commerce is at least as useful as the same sum added by manufactures.

The benefits of the commerce of the United States, which have been enumerated, are not deduced from theoretical reasoning; they are established by thirty years' experience, since the Constitution was adopted. At that time our capital was small and had suffered for a series of years a continual diminution. Our agriculture was depressed, and our finances were embarrassed. The changes, which a thrifty commerce during this period has contributed to produce, are so striking that they scarcely require to be stated. There is not a single portion of the country that has not felt its beneficial influence. On the seaboard we have everywhere flourishing towns and cities — the busy haunts of industry where the products of our soil are accumulated on their transit to foreign countries. In the interior, hundreds of towns have arisen, which but a few years since were desolate wastes or dreary forests. The agriculture of the old states has grown up and spread itself into a thousand new directions; and our cotton and our wheat, our tobacco and our provisions are administering to the wants of millions, to whom even our very name was but a short time ago utterly unknown.

The memorialists would respectfully ask if it be not a part of the duty of a wise nation to profit by the lessons of experience. Is it just, is it salutary, is it politic to abandon a course which has so eminently conduced to our welfare for the purpose of trying experiments, the effect of which cannot be fully ascertained, which are founded upon mere theoretical doctrines, at best complex and questionable, and it may be, in practice, ruinous as well to morals as to property? Suppose it were practicable to arrest the present course of commerce, to narrow its limits, and even reduce it to the mere coasting trade of the nation; is it clear that the capital, thus withdrawn from commercial pursuits, could be as usefully or as profitably employed in any other branch of business? It is perfectly certain that such a change must be attended with severe losses to the merchants and with ruin to numerous classes of our citizens, to our seamen and shipwrights, and other artisans, whose business depends on or is connected with commerce. Cases may possibly arise in which the interests of a respectable portion of the community may be justly sacrificed; but they are cases of extreme public necessity, not cases where the rivalry and the interest of one class of men seek to sustain themselves by destruction to another.

In a free country, too, it may well be asked if it be a legitimate end of government to control the ordinary occupations of men, and compel them to confine themselves to pursuits in which their habits, their feelings, or their enterprise forbid them to engage. While the manufacturers are left free to engage in their own peculiar pursuits, enjoying in common with others a reasonable protection from the government, the memorialists trust it is no undue claim on their own part to plead for the freedom of commerce also, as the natural ally of agriculture and naval greatness. Nothing, however, can be more obvious than that many of the manufacturers and their friends are attempting, by fallacious statements, founded on an interested policy, or a misguided zeal, or very shortsighted views, to uproot some of the fundamental principles of our revenue policy, and to compel our merchants to abandon some of the most lucrative branches of commerce — branches which alone enable us to contend with success against the monopoly and the competition of foreign nations.

It is not a little remarkable, too, that these attempts, to which the memorialists allude, are not only repugnant to those maxims of free trade which the United States have hitherto so forcibly and perseveringly contended for as the sure foundation of national prosperity, but they are pressed upon us at a moment when the statesmen of the Old World, in admiration of the success of our policy, are relaxing the rigor of their own systems, and yielding themselves to the rational doctrine that national wealth is best promoted by a free interchange of commodities upon principles of perfect reciprocity. May the memorialists be permitted to say, that it would be a strange anomaly in America to adopt a system which sound philosophy is exploding in Europe; to attempt a monopoly of the home market, and yet claim an entire freedom of commerce abroad; to stimulate our own manufactures to an unnatural growth by the exclusion of foreign manufactures, and yet to expect that no retaliatory measures would be pursued by other nations? If we are unwilling to receive foreign manufactures, we cannot reasonably suppose that foreign nations will receive our raw materials; we may force other nations to seek an inferior market for their productions, but we cannot force them to become buyers when they are not sellers, or to consume our cottons when they cannot pay the price in their own fabrics. We may compel them to use the cotton of the West Indies, or of the Brazils, or of the East Indies, or the wheat of the Mediterranean — an experiment in itself sufficiently dangerous to some of our most vital interests; but we cannot expect them to carry on with us a ruinous trade when the profit is all on one side. Nations, like individuals, will pursue their own interests, and sooner or later abandon a trade, however fixed may be its habits, where there is no reciprocity of benefit.

There is another consideration which the memorialists would respectfully suggest that is entitled, in their opinion, to great weight on questions of this nature; and that is the dangers and inconveniences which fluctuations in the commercial policy of a nation unavoidably produce. The trade of a nation is of gradual growth, and forms its channels by slow and almost imperceptible degrees. Time and confidence, and protection and experience are necessary to give it a settled course. It insinuates itself into the general commerce of the world with difficulty, and, when incorporated into the mass, its ramifications are so numerous and intricate that they cannot be suddenly withdrawn without immense losses and injuries. Even the temporary stoppage of but a single branch of trade throws thousands out of employment, and, by pressing the mass of capital and shipping which it held engaged in its service into other branches, it is sure to produce embarrassment and depression, and not unfrequently ruin to the shipholders and the merchants.

Besides all this, men are slow to engage their capital in new pursuits. They have a natural timidity in embarking in enterprises to which they are not accustomed; and if the commercial policy of the nation is fluctuating, they feel so much insecurity in it that they are unwilling to yield themselves up even to prospects apparently inviting. No nation ever prospered in commerce until its own policy became settled and the channels of its trade were worn deep and clear. It is to this state of things that the capitalist looks with confidence, because he may conclude that if his profits are but small, they are subject to a reasonable certainty of calculation. Another state of things may suit the young and enterprising speculators; but it can never be safe for a nation to found its revenue upon a trade that is not uniform in its operations. The memorialists most sincerely believe that it is a sound political maxim that the more free trade is, and the more widely it circulates, the more sure will be its prosperity and that of the nation. Every restriction, which is not indispensable for purposes of revenue is a shoal which will impede its progress, and not unfrequently jeopard its security. . . .

The memorialists are no enemies to manufactures; but they most sincerely express it as their deliberate judgment that no manufactures ought to be patronized in the country which will not grow up and support themselves in every competition in the market, under the ordinary protecting duty; that the only manufactures which can ultimately flourish here are those which are of slow growth and moderate profit, such as can be carried on by capitalists with economy and steadiness; and that a change of system, which should suddenly introduce great profits, by encouraging undue speculation, and the expectation of inordinate gain, would end in the deepest injuries even to manufacturing establishments.

The history of the cotton manufactories in New England completely demonstrates the truth of these positions. They grew up gradually, under the protection of our ordinary duties, in a time of peace, and were profitable to those engaged in them. But when the embargo and nonimportation systems produced a deficiency in the foreign supply, a feverish excitement was produced; manufactories were established without sufficient capital; extravagant expenditures in buildings and machinery followed; for a while the demand was great and the profits high, but, upon the return of the ordinary state of things, many of these establishments sunk, one after another, and involved their owners in ruin. And such, in the opinion of the memorialists, would be the scene acted over again in a few years, if the manufacturers could now succeed in accomplishing their present objects. For a short time their establishments would flourish; but in a free country like ours, there would be a reaction of the other great interests of the community, and the national distress and national policy would soon require a repeal of the monopolizing system. A moderate protecting duty is the best support of domestic manufactures, for the very reason that it may be safely calculated on as permanent. It may not encourage speculation, but it will encourage the employment of capital, as fast as safety and a reasonable profit are connected with it.

Nor will the high prices and eventual insecurity to domestic manufactures be the only evils attendant upon this prohibitory system. It will encourage smuggling and frauds to an extent truly formidable, and never yet practised in our country; and the same effect will arise, though in a more limited degree, from the abolition of drawbacks and credit on duties. The utter impossibility of suppressing frauds and smuggling, where the markets are very high and the prohibitions very extensive, has been demonstrated by the experience of all Europe. During the most rigorous enforcement of the continental exclusion of British manufactures, aided by civil vigilance and military bayonets and despotic power, these manufactures found their way into every part of Europe, from the cottage to the throne. Great Britain herself, insulated as she is, and with a naval force adequate to every object, has not been able to suppress smuggling. Prohibited goods find their way into the United Kingdom, notwithstanding the vigilance of her custom houses and the unwearied jealousy of her manufacturers.

In the United States, with a thousand miles of seacoast, indented with innumerable bays and harbors, how can it be reasonably expected that the temptations to illicit traffic will not soon outweigh the habits of obedience to the laws, especially when those laws shall become odious, as the supposed instruments of one class to oppress another? Hitherto our country has exhibited a spectacle not unworthy of a free people. Frauds upon the revenue have been comparatively few; and smuggling has been repressed by the general sense of the mercantile community. What system could be more disastrous than that which should hold out permanent temptations to smuggling, connected with a sense of the impolicy and injustice of the laws? The memorialists believe that one of the first objects of legislation is to become auxiliary to the preservation of the morals of the people by interfering as little as possible with pursuits consonant with their habits and feelings, lawful in their objects, and adapted to their wants.

Upon the whole, the memorialists would respectfully state their unequivocal opinion that all the measures to which they have alluded are calculated to impair our naval strength and glory; to injure our most profitable commerce; to diminish, in an alarming degree, the public revenue; to promote unjustifiable speculation; to enhance the prices of manufactures; to throw the great business and trade of the nation into the hands of a few capitalists, to the exclusion of the industrious and enterprising of other classes; to introduce general distress among commercial artisans and agriculturists; to aggravate the present distress of the other classes of the community; to provoke and extend an undue appetite for fraud and smuggling; and, in fine, to destroy many of the great objects for which the Constitution of the United States was originally framed and adopted.

The memorialists, therefore, most respectfully ask the interposition of Congress to prevent these great evils, and to promote the general good, by a perseverance in that system under the protection of which our commerce and navigation and agriculture have flourished; a system conceived in political wisdom, justified by experience, and approved by the soundest maxims of national economy.

142.

HENRY CLAY: Manufacturing and a Protective Tariff

Even more than that of John C. Calhoun, the name of Henry Clay is associated with the idea of internal improvements. Clay, who had begun to promote such a program in 1810, called it the American System. As the speaker of the House, in which he was the most powerful figure of his day, he had much to do with getting the charter of the Second Bank of the United States and the Tariff Act of 1816 passed — measures that suited the nationalistic spirit of his home state of Kentucky. The failure of Calhoun's Bonus Bill removed the chance for federal subsidy of the canals and roads Clay wanted, however, and as the Tariff of 1816 had proved inadequate to protect home industries, he thought both ends might be achieved by a new and higher tariff. In the following speech of April 26, 1820, he supported a bill (which as speaker he could not originate) introduced into the House for this purpose. The bill was ultimately defeated in the Senate — by two votes.

Source: *The Life and Speeches of Henry Clay,* New York, 1844, pp. 139-161.

THE FIRST IMPORTANT INQUIRY that we should make is whether it be desirable that such a portion of the capital and labor of the country should be employed in the business of manufacturing, as would furnish a supply of our necessary wants. Since the first colonization of America, the principal direction of the labor and capital of the inhabitants has been to produce raw materials for the consumption or fabrication of foreign nations. We have always had, in great abundance, the means of subsistence, but we have derived chiefly from other countries our clothes, and the instruments of defense. Except during those interruptions of commerce arising from a state of war, or from measures adopted for vindicating our commercial rights, we have experienced no very great inconvenience, heretofore, from this mode of supply. The limited amount of our surplus produce, resulting from the smallness of our numbers, and the long and arduous convulsions of Europe, secured us good markets for that surplus in her ports or those of her colonies. But those convulsions have now ceased, and our population has reached nearly 10 million.

A new epoch has arisen; and it becomes us deliberately to contemplate our own actual condition and the relations which are likely to exist between us and the other parts of the world. The actual state of our population, and the ratio of its progressive increase when compared with the ratio of the increase of the population of the countries which have hitherto consumed our raw produce, seem to me, alone, to demonstrate the necessity of diverting some portion of our industry from its accustomed channel. We double our population in about the term of twenty-five years. If there be no change in the mode of exerting our industry, we shall double, during the same term, the amount of our exportable produce. Europe, including such of her colonies as we have free access to, taken altogether, does not duplicate her population in a shorter term, probably, than one hundred years. The ratio of the increase of her capacity of consumption, therefore, is, to that of our capacity of production, as one is to four. And it is manifest, from the simple exhibition of the powers of the consuming countries, compared with those of the supplying country, that the former are inadequate to the latter. It is certainly true that a portion of the mass of our raw produce which we transmit to her reverts to us in a fabricated form, and that this return augments with our increasing population. This is, however, a very inconsiderable addition to her actual ability to afford a market for the produce of our industry.

I believe that we are already beginning to experience the want of capacity in Europe to consume our surplus produce. Take the articles of cotton, tobacco, and breadstuffs. For the latter we have scarcely any foreign demand. And is there not reason to believe that we have reached, if we have not passed, the maximum of the foreign demand for the other two articles? Considerations connected with the cheapness of cotton, as a raw material, and the facility with which it can be fabricated, will probably make it be more and more used as a substitute for other materials. But, after you allow to the demand for it the utmost extension of which it is susceptible, it is yet quite *limited* — limited by the number of persons who use it, by their wants, and their ability to supply them. If we have not reached, therefore, the maximum of the foreign demand (as I believe we have), we must soon fully satisfy it. With respect to tobacco, that article affording an enjoyment not necessary, as food and clothes are, to human existence, the foreign demand for it is still more precarious, and I apprehend that we have already passed its limits. It appears to me, then, that if we consult our interest merely, we ought to encourage home manufactures. But there are other motives to recommend it, of not less importance.

The wants of man may be classed under three heads — food, raiment, and defense. They are felt alike in the state of barbarism and of civilization. He must be defended against the ferocious beasts of prey in the one condition, and against the ambition, violence, and injustice incident to the other. If he seeks to obtain a supply of those wants without giving an equivalent, he is a beggar or a robber; if by promising an equivalent which he cannot give, he is fraudulent; and if by a commerce, in which there is perfect freedom on his side, while he meets with nothing but restrictions on the other, he submits to an unjust and degrading inequality.

What is true of individuals is equally so of nations. The country, then, which relies upon foreign nations for either of these great essentials is not, in fact, independent. Nor is it any consolation for our dependence upon other nations that they are also dependent upon us, even were it true. Every nation should anxiously endeavor to establish its absolute independence, and consequently be able to feed and clothe and defend itself. If it rely upon a foreign supply that may be cut off by the caprice of the nation yielding it, by war with it, or even by war with other nations, it cannot be independent.

But it is not true that any other nations depend upon us in a degree anything like equal to that of our dependence upon them for the great necessaries to which I have referred. Every other nation seeks to supply itself with them from its own resources; and so strong is the desire which they feel to accomplish this purpose that they exclude the cheaper foreign article for the dearer home production. Witness the English policy in regard to corn. So selfish, in this respect, is the conduct of other powers that, in some instances, they even prohibit the produce of the industry of their *own* colonies, when it comes into competition with the produce of the parent country. All other countries but our own exclude, by high duties or absolute prohibitions, whatever they can respectively produce within themselves. The truth is, and it is in vain to disguise it, that we are a sort of independent colonies of England — politically free, commercially slaves. Gentlemen tell us of the advantages of a free exchange of the produce of the world. But they tell us of what has never existed, does not exist, and perhaps never will exist. They invoke us to give perfect freedom on our side, while in the ports of every other nation, we are met with a code of odious restrictions, shutting out entirely a great part of our produce, and letting in only so much as they cannot possibly do without.

I will hereafter examine their favorite maxim, of leaving things to themselves, more particularly. At present I will only say that I, too, am a friend to free trade, but it must be a free trade of perfect reciprocity. If the governing consideration were cheapness; if national independence were to weigh nothing; if honor nothing — why not subsidize foreign powers to defend us? Why not hire Swiss or Hessian mercenaries to protect us? Why not get our arms of all kinds, as we do, in part, the blankets and clothing of our soldiers, from abroad? We should probably consult economy by these dangerous expedients.

But, say gentlemen, there are to the manufacturing system some inherent objections, which should induce us to avoid its introduction into this country; and we are warned by the example of England, by her pauperism, by the vices of her population, her wars, etc. It would be a strange order of Providence, if it were true, that He should create necessary and indispensable wants, and yet should render us unable to supply them without the degradation or contamination of our species.

Pauperism is, in general, the effect of an overflowing population. Manufactures may undoubtedly produce a redundant population; but so may commerce, and so may agriculture. In this respect they are alike; and from whatever cause the disproportion of a population to the subsisting faculty of a country may proceed, its effect of pauperism is the same. Many parts of Asia would exhibit, perhaps, as afflicting effects of an extreme prosecution of the agricultural system as England can possibly furnish, respecting the manufacturing. It is not, however, fair to argue from these extreme cases against either the one system or the other. There are abuses incident to every branch of industry, to every profession. It would not be thought very just or wise to arraign the honorable professions of law and physic, because the one produces the pettifogger, and the other the quack.

Even in England it has been established . . . from the most authentic evidence — the judicial records of the country — that the instances of crime were much more numerous in the agricultural than in the manufacturing districts; thus proving that the cause of wretchedness and vice in that country was to be sought for, not in this or that system so much as in the fact of the density of its population. France resembles this country more than England, in respect to the employments of her population; and we do not find that there is anything in the condition of the manufacturing portion of it which ought to dissuade us from the introduction of it into our own country. But even France has not that great security against the abuses of the manufacturing system, against the effects of too great a density of population, which we possess in our wastelands. While this resource exists, we have nothing to apprehend.

Do capitalists give too low wages; are the laborers too crowded, and in danger of starving? The unsettled lands will draw off the redundancy, and leave the others better provided for. If an unsettled province, such as Texas, for example, could, by some convulsion of nature, be wafted alongside of and attached to the island of Great Britain, the instantaneous effect would be to draw off the redundant portion of the population, and to render more comfortable both the emigrants and those whom they would leave behind.

I am aware that while the public domain is an acknowledged security against the abuses of the manufacturing, or any other system, it constitutes, at the same time, an impediment, in the opinion of some, to the success of manufacturing industry by its tendency to prevent the reduction of the wages of labor. Those who urge this objection have their eyes too much fixed on the ancient system of manufacturing, when manual labor was the principal instrument which it employed. During the last half century, since the inventions of Arkwright, and the long train of improvements which followed, the labor of machinery is principally used. I have understood, from sources of information which I believe to be accurate, that the combined force of all the machinery employed by Great Britain in manufacturing is equal to the labor of 100 million able-bodied men. If we suppose the aggregate of the labor of all the individuals which she employs in that branch of industry to be equal to the united labor of 2 million able-bodied men (and I should think it does not exceed it) machine labor will stand to manual labor, in the proportion of 100 to 2. There cannot be a doubt that we have skill and enterprise enough to command the requisite amount of machine power.

There are, too, some checks to emigration from the settled parts of our country to the wastelands of the West. Distance is one, and it is every day becoming greater and greater. There exists, also, a natural repugnance (felt less, it is true, in the United States than elsewhere, but felt even here) to abandoning the place of our nativity. Women and children, who could not migrate and who would be comparatively idle if manufactures did not exist, may be profitably employed in them. This is a very great benefit. I witnessed the advantage resulting from the employment of this description of our population in a visit which I lately made to the Waltham manufactory, near Boston. There, some hundreds of girls and boys were occupied in separate apartments. The greatest order, neatness, and apparent comfort reigned throughout the whole establishment. The daughters of respectable farmers — in one instance I remember the daughter of a senator in the state legislature, were usefully employed. They would come down to the manufactory, remain perhaps some months, and return with their earnings to their families, to assist them throughout the year. But one instance had occurred, I was informed by the intelligent manager, of doubtful conduct on the part of any of the females, and, after she was dismissed, there was reason to believe that injustice had been done her.

Suppose that establishment to be destroyed, what would become of all the persons who are there engaged so beneficially to themselves, and so usefully to the state? Can it be doubted that, if the crowds of little mendicant boys and girls who infest this edifice and assail us every day at its very thresholds, as we come in and go out, begging for a cent, were employed in some manufacturing establishment, it would be better for them and the city? Those who object to the manufacturing system should recollect that constant occupation is the best security for innocence and virtue, and that idleness is the parent of vice and crime. They should contemplate the laboring poor with employment, and ask themselves what would be their condition without it.

If there are instances of hard taskmasters among the manufacturers, so also are there in agriculture. The cause is to be sought for, not in the nature of this or that system but in the nature of man. If there are particular species of unhealthy employment in manufactures, so there are in agriculture also. There has been an idle attempt to ridicule the manufacturing system, and we have heard the expression, "spinning-jenny tenure." It is one of the noblest inventions of human skill. It has diffused comforts among thousands who without it would never have enjoyed them; and millions yet unborn will bless the man by whom it was invented.

Three important inventions have distinguished the last half century, each of which, if it had happened at long intervals of time from the other, would have been sufficient to constitute an epoch in the progress of the useful arts. The first was that of Arkwright; and our own country is entitled to the merit of the other two. The world is indebted to Whitney for the one, and to Fulton for the other. Nothing is secure against the shafts of ridicule. What would be thought of a man who should speak of a "cotton-gin tenure," or a "steamboat tenure?"

In one respect there is a great difference in favor of manufactures when compared with agriculture. It is the rapidity with which the whole manufacturing community avail themselves of an improvement. It is instantly communicated and put in operation. There is an avidity for improvement in the one system; an aversion from it in the other. The habits of generation after generation pass down the long track of time in perpetual succession without the slightest change in agriculture. The plowman who fastens his plow to the tails of his cattle will not own that there is any other mode equal to his. An agricultural people will be in the neighborhood of other communities, who have made the greatest progress in husbandry, without advancing in the slightest degree. Many parts of our country are one hundred years in advance of Sweden in the cultivation and improvement of the soil.

It is objected that the effect of the encouragement of home manufactures, by the proposed tariff, will be to diminish the revenue from the customs. The amount of the revenue from that source will depend upon the amount of importations, and the measure of these will be the value of the exports from this country. The quantity of the exportable produce will depend upon the foreign demand; and there can be no doubt that, under any distribution of the labor and capital of this country, from the greater allurements which agriculture presents than any other species of industry, there would be always a quantity of its produce sufficient to satisfy that demand. If there be a diminution in the ability of foreign nations to consume our raw produce, in the proportion of our diminished consumption of theirs, under the operation of this system, that will be compensated by the substitution of a home for a foreign market, in the same proportion. It is true that we cannot remain in the relation of seller, only to foreign powers, for any length of time; but if, as I have no doubt, our agriculture will continue to supply, as far as it can profitably, to the extent of the limits of foreign demand, we shall receive not only in return many of the articles on which the tariff operates, for our own consumption, but they may also form the objects of trade with South America and other powers, and our comforts may be multiplied by the importation of other articles. Diminished consumption, in consequence of the augmentation of duties, does not necessarily imply diminished revenue. The increase of the duty may compensate the decrease in the consumption, and give you as large a revenue as you before possessed.

Can anyone doubt the impolicy of government resting solely upon the precarious resource of such a revenue? It is constantly fluctuating. It tempts us, by its enormous amount, at one time, into extravagant expenditure; and we are then driven, by its sudden and unexpected depression, into the opposite extreme. We are seduced by its flattering promises into expenses which we might avoid; and we are afterward constrained by its treachery to avoid expenses which we ought to make. It is a system under which there is a sort of perpetual war between the interest of the government and the interest of the people. Large importations fill the coffers of government and empty the pockets of the people. Small importations imply prudence on the part of the people and leave the treasury empty. In war, the revenue disappears; in peace, it is unsteady. On such a system the government will not be able much longer exclusively to rely. We all anticipate that we shall have shortly to resort to some additional supply of revenue within ourselves.

I was opposed to the total repeal of the internal revenue. I would have preserved certain parts of it, at least, to be ready for emergencies such as now exist. And I am, for one, ready to exclude foreign spirits altogether, and substitute for the revenue levied on them a tax upon the spirits made within the country. No other nation lets in so much of foreign spirits as we do. By the encouragement of home industry, you will lay a basis of internal taxation, when it gets strong, that will be steady and uniform, yielding alike in peace and in war. We do not derive our ability from abroad to pay taxes. That depends upon our wealth and our industry; and it is the same, whatever may be the form of levying the public contributions.

But it is urged that you tax other interests of the state to sustain manufacturers. The business of manufacturing, if encouraged, will be open to all. It is not for the sake of the particular individuals who may happen to be engaged in it that we propose to foster it; but it is for the general interest. We think that it is necessary to the comfort and well-being of society that fabrication, as well as the business of production and distribution, should be supported and taken care of. Now, if it be even true that the price of the home fabric will be somewhat higher, in the first instance, than the rival foreign articles, that consideration ought not to prevent our extending reasonable protection to the home fabric. Present temporary inconvenience may be well submitted to for the sake of future permanent benefit. If the experience of all other countries be not utterly fallacious; if the promises of the manufacturing system be not absolutely illusory, by the competition which will be elicited in consequence of your parental care, prices will be ultimately brought down to a level with that of the foreign commodity.

Now, in a scheme of policy which is devised for a nation, we should not limit our views to its operation during a single year, or for even a short term of years. We should look at its operation for a considerable time, and in war as well as in peace. Can there be a doubt, thus contemplating it, that we shall be compensated by the certainty and steadiness of the supply in all seasons, and the ultimate reduction of the price for any temporary sacrifices we make?

Take the example of salt, which the ingenious gentleman from Virginia (Mr. Archer) has adduced. He says, during the war, the price of that article rose to $10 per bushel, and he asks if you would lay a duty, permanent in its duration, of $3 per bushel to secure a supply in war. I answer, no, I would not lay so high a duty. That which is now proposed, for the encouragement of the domestic production, is only 5 cents per bushel. In forty years the duty would amount only to $2.

If the recurrence of war shall be only after intervals of forty years' peace (and we may expect it probably oftener), and if, when it does come, the same price should again be given, there will be a clear saving of $8 by promoting the domestic fabrication.

All society is an affair of mutual concession. If we expect to derive the benefits which are inherent to it, we must sustain our reasonable share of burdens. The great interests which it is intended to guard and cherish must be supported by their reciprocal action and reaction. The harmony of its parts is disturbed, the discipline which is necessary to its order is incomplete when one of the three great and essential branches of its industry is abandoned and unprotected. . . .

The manufacturing system is not only injurious to agriculture but, say its opponents, it is injurious also to foreign commerce. We ought not to conceal from ourselves our present actual position in relation to other powers. During the protracted war which has so long convulsed all Europe, and which will probably be succeeded by a long peace, we transacted the commercial business of other nations, and largely shared with England the carrying trade of the world. Now, every other nation is anxiously endeavoring to transact its own business, to rebuild its marine, and to foster its navigation. The consequence of the former state of things was that our mercantile marine and our commercial employment were enormously disproportionate to the exchangeable domestic produce of our country. And the result of the latter will be that, as exchanges between this country and other nations will hereafter consist principally, on our part of our domestic produce, that marine and that employment will be brought down to what is necessary to effect those exchanges. I regret exceedingly this reduction. I wish the mercantile class could enjoy the same extensive commerce that they formerly did. But if they cannot, it would be a folly to repine at what is irrecoverably lost, and we should seek rather to adapt ourselves to the new circumstances in which we find ourselves.

If, as I think, we have reached the maximum of our foreign demand for our three great staples — cotton, tobacco, and flour — no man will contend that we should go on to produce more and more, to be sent to the glutted foreign market and consumed by devouring expenses, merely to give employment to our tonnage and to our foreign commerce. It would be extremely unwise to accommodate our industry to produce not what is wanted abroad but cargoes for our unemployed ships. I would give our foreign trade every legitimate encouragement, and extend it whenever it can be extended profitably. Hitherto it has been stimulated too highly by the condition of the world and our own policy, acting on that condition. And we are reluctant to believe that we must submit to its necessary abridgement. The habits of trade; the tempting instances of enormous fortunes which have been made by the successful prosecution of it are such that we turn with regret from its pursuit; we still cherish a lingering hope; we persuade our selves that something will occur, how and what it may be, we know not, to revive its former activity; and we would push into every untried channel, grope through the Dardanelles into the Black Sea to restore its former profits.

I repeat it, let us proclaim to the people of the United States the incontestable truth, that our foreign trade must be circumscribed by the altered state of the world; and, leaving it in the possession of all the gains which it can now possibly make, let us present motives to the capital and labor of our country to employ themselves in fabrication at home. There is no danger that, by a withdrawal of that portion which is unprofitably employed on other objects, and an application of it to fabrication, our agriculture would be too much cramped. The produce of it will always come up to the foreign demand. Such are the superior allurements belonging to the cultivation of the soil to all other branches of industry that it will always be preferred when it can profitably be followed. The foreign demand will, in any conceivable state of things, limit the amount of the exportable produce of agriculture. The amount of our exportations will form the measure of our importations, and, whatever these may be, they will constitute the basis of the revenue derivable from customs.

The manufacturing system is favorable to the maintenance of peace. Foreign commerce is the great source of foreign wars. The eagerness with which we contend for every branch of it; the temptations which it offers, operating alike upon us and our foreign competitors, produce constant collisions. No country on earth, by the extent of its superficies, the richness of its soil, the variety of its climate, contains within its own limits more abundant facilities for supplying all our rational wants than ours does. It is not necessary or desirable, however, to cut off all intercourse with foreign powers. But, after securing a supply, within ourselves, of all the great essentials of life, there will be ample scope still left for preserving such an intercourse. If we had no intercourse with foreign states, if we adopted the policy of China, we should have no external wars. And in proportion as we diminish our dependence upon them, shall we lessen the danger of the recurrence of war. . . .

The tendency of reasonable encouragement to our home industry is favorable to the preservation and strength of our confederacy. Now our connection is merely political. For the sale of the surplus of the produce of our agricultural labor, all eyes are constantly turned upon the markets of Liverpool. There is scarcely any of that beneficial intercourse, the best basis of political connection, which consists of the exchange of the produce of our labor. On our maritime frontier, there has been too much stimulus, an unnatural activity; in the great interior of the country, there exists a perfect paralysis. Encourage fabrication at home, and there will instantly arise animation and a healthful circulation throughout all the parts of the republic. The cheapness, fertility, and quantity of our wastelands offer such powerful inducements to cultivation that our countrymen are constantly engaging in it. I would not check this disposition by hard terms in the sale of it. Let it be easily accessible to all who wish to acquire it. But I would countervail this predilection by presenting to capital and labor motives for employment in other branches of industry.

Nothing is more uncertain than the pursuit of agriculture, when we mainly rely upon foreign markets for the sale of its surplus produce. In the first place, it is impossible to determine, *a priori*, the amount of this surplus; and, in the second, it is equally impossible to anticipate the extent of the foreign demand. Both the one and the other depend upon the seasons. From the fluctuations incident to these, and from other causes, it may happen that the supplying country will, for a long series of years, have employed a larger share of its capital and labor than is wise in production to supply the wants of the consuming countries, without becoming sensible of its defect of policy. The failure of a crop, or the failure of a market, does not discourage the cultivator. He renews his labors another year, and he renews his hopes. It is otherwise with manufacturing industry. The precise quantum of its produce, at least, can with some accuracy be previously estimated. And the wants of foreign countries can be with some probability anticipated.

I am sensible, Mr. Chairman, if I have even had a success, which I dare not presume, in the endeavor I have been making to show that sound policy requires a diversion of so much of the capital and labor of this country from other employments as may be necessary, by a different application of them, to secure, within ourselves, a steady and adequate supply of the great necessaries of life, I shall have only established one-half of what is incumbent upon me to prove. It will still be required by the other side that a second proposition be supported, and that is, that government ought to present motives for such a diversion and new application of labor and capital by that species of protection which the tariff holds out. Gentlemen say, We agree with you; you are right in your first proposition; but, "let things alone," and they will come right in the end.

Now, I agree with them, that things would ultimately get right; but not until after a long period of disorder and distress, terminating in the impoverishment and, perhaps, ruin of the country. Dissolve government, reduce it to its primitive elements, and, without any general effort to reconstruct it, there would arise out of the anarchy which would ensue partial combinations for the purpose of individual protection, which would finally lead to a social form, competent to the conservation of peace within and the repulsion of force from without. Yet no one would say, in such a state of anarchy, "Let things alone!" If gentlemen, by their favorite maxim, mean only that within the bosom of the state things are to be left alone, and each individual and each branch of industry allowed to pursue their respective interests without giving a preference to either, I subscribe to it. But if they give it a more comprehensive import; if they require that things be left alone, in respect not only to interior action but to exterior action also; not only as regards the operation of our own government upon the mass of the interests of the state but as it relates to the operation of foreign governments upon that mass, I dissent from it.

This maxim, in this enlarged sense, is, indeed, everywhere proclaimed, but nowhere practised. It is truth in the books of European political economists. It is error in the practical code of every European state. It is not applied where it is most applicable; it is attempted to be introduced here, where it is least applicable; and even here its friends propose to limit it to the single branch of manufacturing industry, while every other interest is encouraged and protected according to the policy of Europe. The maxim would best suit Europe, where each interest is adjusted and arranged to every other by causes operating during many centuries. Everything there has taken and preserved its ancient position. The house that was built centuries ago is occupied by the descendants of its original constructor. If one could rise up, after the lapse of ages, and enter a European shop, he would see the same hammer at work on the same anvil or last, and almost by the same hand. There, everything has found its place and its level, and everything, one would think, might there be safely left alone. But the policy of the European states is otherwise. Here everything is new and unfixed. Neither the state, nor the individuals who compose it, have settled down in their firm and permanent positions. There is a constant tendency, in consequence of the extent of our public domain, toward production for foreign markets.

The maxim, in the comprehensive sense in which I am considering it, requires, to entitle it to observation, two conditions, neither of which exists. First, that there should be perpetual peace, and second, that the maxim should be everywhere respected. When war breaks out, that free and general circulation of the produce of industry among the nations which it recommends is interrupted, and the nation that depends upon a foreign supply of its necessaries must be subjected to the greatest inconvenience. If it be not everywhere observed, there will be, between the nation that does not and the nation that does conform to it, an inequality alike condemned by honor and by interest. If there be no reciprocity; if, on the one side, there is perfect freedom of trade, and on the other a code of odious restrictions, will gentlemen still contend that we are to submit to such an unprofitable and degrading intercourse? Will they require that we shall act upon the social system, while every other power acts upon the selfish? Will they demand of us to throw widely open our ports to every nation, while all other nations entirely or partly exclude theirs against our productions? It is, indeed, possible, that some pecuniary advantage might be enjoyed by our country in prosecuting the remnant of the trade which the contracted policy of other powers leaves to us. But what security is there for our continuing to enjoy even that? And is national honor, is national independence to count as nothing? . . .

But this maxim, according to which gentlemen would have us abandon the home industry of the country, so the influence of the restrictive systems of other countries, without an effort to protect and preserve it, is not itself observed by the same gentlemen in regard to the great interests of the nation. We protect our fisheries by bounties and drawbacks. We protect our tonnage by excluding or restricting foreign tonnage, exactly as our tonnage is excluded or restricted by foreign states. We passed, a year or two ago, the bill to prohibit British navigation from the West India colonies of that power to the United States, because ours is shut out from them. The session prior to the passage of that law, the gentleman from South Carolina and I, almost alone, urged the House to pass it. But the subject was postponed until the next session, when it was passed by nearly a unanimous vote — the gentleman from South Carolina and the two gentlemen from Virginia . . . voting with the majority.

We have now upon our table other bills connected with that object, and proposing restriction upon the French tonnage to countervail theirs upon ours. I shall, with pleasure, vote for these measures. We protect our foreign trade by consuls, by foreign ministers, by embargoes, by nonintercourse, by a navy, by fortifications, by squadrons constantly acting abroad, by war, and by a variety of commercial regulations in our statute book. The whole system of the general government, from its first formation to the present time, consists almost exclusively in one unremitting endeavor to nourish and protect and defend the foreign trade. Why have not all these great interests been left to the operation of the gentlemen's favorite maxim? Sir, it is perfectly right that we should have [afforded] this protection. And it is perfectly right, in my humble opinion, that we should extend the principle to the home industry. I am a friend to foreign trade, but I protest against its being the monopolist of all the parental favor and care of this government.

But, sir, friendly as I am to the existence of domestic manufactures, I would not give to them unreasonable encouragement by protecting duties. Their growth ought to be gradual, but sure. I believe all the circumstances of the present period highly favorable to their success. But they are the youngest and the weakest interest of the state. Agriculture wants but little or no protection against the regulations of foreign powers. The advantages of our position, and the cheapness and abundance and fertility of our land afford to that greatest interest of the state almost all the protection it wants. As it should be, it is strong and flourishing; or, if it be not, at this moment, prosperous, it is not because its produce is not ample but because, depending, as we do altogether, upon a foreign market for the sale of the surplus of that produce, the foreign market is glutted. Our foreign trade, having almost exclusively engrossed the protecting care of government, wants no further legislative aid. And, whatever depression it may now experience, it is attributable to causes beyond the control of this government. The abundance of capital, indicated by the avidity with which loans are sought at the reduced rate of 5 percent; the reduction in the wages of labor; and the decline in the price of property of every kind, as well as that of agricultural produce, all concur favorably for domestic manufactures.

Now, as when we arranged the existing tariff, is the auspicious moment for government to step in and cheer and countenance them. We did too little then, and I endeavored to warn this House of the effects of inadequate protection. We were called upon, at that time, by the previous pledges we had given, by the inundation of foreign fabrics, which was to be anticipated from their free admission after the termination of the war, and by the lasting interests of this country, to give them efficient support. We did not do it; but let us not now repeat the error. Our great mistake has been in the irregularity of the action of the measures of this government upon manufacturing industry. At one period it is stimulated too high, and then, by an opposite course of policy, it is precipitated into a condition of depression too low. First there came the embargo; then nonintercourse and other restrictive measures followed; and, finally, that greatest of all stimuli to domestic fabrication, war.

During all that long period, we were adding to the positive effect of the measures of government all the moral encouragement which results from popular resolves, legislative resolves, and other manifestations of the public will and the public wish to foster our home manufactures, and to render our confederacy independent of foreign powers. The peace ensued, and the country was flooded with the fabrics of other countries; and we, forgetting all our promises, coolly and philosophically talk of leaving things to themselves; making up our deficiency of practical good sense by the stores of learning which we collect from theoretical writers. I, too, sometimes amuse myself with the visions of these writers (as I do with those of metaphysicians and novelists), and, if I do not forget, one of the best among them enjoins it upon a country to protect its industry against the injurious influence of the prohibitions and restrictions of foreign countries which operate upon it. . . .

Mr. Chairman, I frankly own that I feel great solicitude for the success of this bill. The entire independence of my country on all foreign states, as it respects a supply of our essential wants, has ever been with me a favorite object. The war of our Revolution effected our political emancipation. The last war contributed greatly toward accomplishing our commercial freedom. But our complete independence will only be consummated after the policy of this bill shall be recognized and adopted. We have, indeed, great difficulties to contend with; old habits, colonial usages, the obduracy of the colonial spirit, the enormous profits of a foreign trade, prosecuted under favorable circumstances which no longer continue. I will not despair; the cause, I verily believe, is the cause of the country. It may be postponed; it may be frustrated for the moment; but it must finally prevail.

143.

Daniel Raymond: The Role of Labor in the National Wealth

Daniel Raymond is remembered today for his original Thoughts on Political Economy *(1820), a chapter of which is reprinted here, and in which, more than a century before F.D.R. and the New Deal, he argued for some measure of deliberate government regulation of the economy, yet his thought is clearly a product of the nationalism of his time. He provided a theoretic base for the policies of men like Clay, whose "American System" of tariffs, expansion, and a central Bank was designed to balance national interests. Raymond, however, opposed the National Bank.*

Source: *Thoughts on Political Economy,* Baltimore, 1820, pp. 278-294.

The first question that presents itself to the political economist is whether one species of labor[1] is better calculated to promote national wealth than another. Whether it be the duty of government to encourage one species of labor in preference to another, or in other words, whether agricultural or manufacturing labor is most conducive to national wealth, or whether they stand upon equal ground in point of utility.

The most effectual mode of augmenting a nation's capacity for acquiring the necessaries and comforts of life is the proper subject of inquiry for the political economist. . . .

The only rational division that can be made of labor is into that which produces the necessaries and that which produces the comforts of life. No man ever has or ever will be able to draw the line of distinction between the comforts and luxuries of life. . . .

There is another distinction vastly more important to have established. The distinction between the labor that tends to preserve and that which tends to corrupt the morals of society. Let political economists cease their disputes about productive and unproductive labor, and employ their talents in ascertaining what kinds of labor have a moral and what an immoral tendency, and then they may render some service to mankind.

Whether one species of labor is more productive to national wealth than another depends entirely upon the circumstances of each particular nation. At one period agricultural labor may be the most productive, at another manufacturing labor. Nor can there be any rules laid down beforehand for ascertaining whether the one or the other kind will be most productive.

Suppose the comforts of life not taken into the definition of national wealth, and it be defined a capacity for acquiring the necessaries of life alone. Even according to this

1. Although there is, in fact, but one species of labor, yet there are different subjects upon which it may be bestowed, which produces a difference in the effect; and the established laws of rhetoric authorize a figure of speech which puts the effect for the cause. By different species of labor, therefore, is not meant any difference in labor itself, but in the effect produced, according to the subject upon which the labor is bestowed.

definition, it would not by any means follow that manufacturing labor was unproductive of national wealth. According to this definition, manufacturers for home consumption would be unproductive laborers; but manufacturers for foreign consumption would not. So far as national wealth is concerned, a nation may as well export manufactures as provisions; it may as well purchase provisions by exporting manufactures as to raise those provisions by agriculture. If the same quantity of labor which would be necessary to raise 100,000 bushels of wheat, by being bestowed on manufactures, could always procure the same quantity of wheat from foreign countries, what difference can it make, so far as national wealth is concerned, in which way the labor is employed? It may make a material difference as to the moral character of the people and the political safety of the nation; and for these reasons, agricultural labor may be preferable, though not on the score of its being more productive or profitable.

As a general rule manufacturing labor is the most profitable because it requires the most skill. A man can, ordinarily, earn more corn in a day by spinning and weaving than by plowing, notwithstanding all that economists may say of the unproductiveness of manufacturing labor. And if an individual can do this, so may a nation.

So long as the comforts and luxuries of life constitute a portion of our natural or artificial wants, so long will every species of labor which contributes to their gratification be productive; and as a general rule, the more refined the luxury, and the more unnecessary the gratification, the better will the labor be paid which produces it. Hence, stage players and mountebanks are always better paid than the cultivators of the soil, dancing masters and fiddlers better paid than teachers of the sciences. In a rude and unsophisticated state of society, one would naturally enough suppose that dancing and stage playing were a species of labor not very well adapted to the production of corn; but in this refined age, they are found to be more productive of that article than turning up the virgin soil.[2]

But although it is perfectly immaterial so far as national wealth is concerned whether the people raise their own corn by cultivating the earth or whether they manufacture toys and trinkets to purchase it with, so long as toys and trinkets will purchase it, yet in regard to national security and independence, there is a vast difference between the two modes. A nation that raises its own corn need not fear having its supplies cut off. A nation that depends on purchasing it from foreign nations by a sale of its manufactures is liable to two very probable, and very fatal, contingencies: that of having its supplies interrupted by foreign hostility, and that of losing the market for its manufactures, which would deprive it of the means of purchasing corn. Their occupation is liable to be usurped or interfered with by others. . . .

There is, however, this material difference between the effects which the same causes have produced in this country and in England. The difference arises from the different kinds of labor most prevalent in the two countries. The exports of England consist principally of the comforts of life, or the product of manufacturing labor. The exports of the United States consist of the necessaries of life, or the product of agricultural labor. Destroying the market for these different kinds of products causes the same mercantile embarrassment and distress, but it does not cause the same distress to the people. The commercial embarrassments are probably as great in this country as in En-

2. The labor of the fiddler and stage player produces a comfort of life, real or imaginary, to the audience, who are the consumers, and who pay for it, as much as labor bestowed in manufacturing lace produces a comfort of life to those who wear or consume the lace. In both cases, the labor produces a comfort of life to the consumer, and the price paid for the labor is a certain portion of the necessaries of life. This kind of labor, therefore, produces the comforts of life to the consumer, and the necessaries to the producer: strange result! but no more strange than true.

gland, because commercial prosperity depends on the facility with which one commodity can be exchanged for another, and not on the kind of commodities exchanged. But a surplus of the product of agricultural labor has a very different effect upon the laborers who produce it from what a surplus of the product of manufacturing labor has upon those by whose labor it is produced. The latter is useless, unless it can be sold; the former may be eaten and will sustain life. As a general rule manufactures are as useless to those whose labor produces them as gold and silver would have been to Robinson Crusoe. This is not the case with the surplus of agricultural labor; if it cannot be sold or exchanged, it can be eaten. We may be obliged to forgo some of the comforts of life, according to our refined notions, but we are not obliged to forgo life itself.

We are very much in the habit of confounding embarrassments in trade and commerce with national distress. We are perpetually mistaking a few prominent noisy individuals in a nation for the nation itself. There is a great stagnation in trade and commerce, the facility of exchanging commodities is interrupted or constrained, and the merchants make a great outcry which we mistake for the moanings of national distress. This, however, is not always the case. Mercantile distress may be the distress of the nation, or it may not. When the surplus produce which the merchants cannot dispose of consists of manufactures or the comforts of life, then the embarrassment and distress of the merchants will be the distress of the nation. But when that surplus consists of the necessaries of life, then the distress of the merchants will not be the distress of the nation. National distress consists in the want of the necessaries of life. Pauperism and starvation are the signs of national distress. But half the merchants in the country may fail and still pauperism not prevail to any uncommon extent. Commercial embarrassment of itself is not a species of distress which touches life. Merchants are not a class of people likely to want the necessaries of life, whatever may be the extent of their embarrassments. National distress must always be sought for among the laboring poor. Distress among them is a distress which touches life.

Whether agricultural or manufacturing labor will be most productive of national wealth for the time being depends entirely on accidental, arbitrary circumstances which no political economist can foresee. It would have been impossible in 1814 to have told whether in 1818 agricultural or manufacturing labor would be most productive of national wealth in England.

The demand, however, for agricultural labor, that is for the produce of it, is not liable to such fluctuations as the demand for manufacturing labor; nor are the fluctuations, when they happen, so fatal in their consequences. The former has, therefore, a great advantage over the latter as regards national security and independence.

It has also a great advantage as to its moral effect upon the people. Agriculturists are a superior class of men to manufacturers. They enjoy more vigorous health, and possess more personal courage. They have more elevated and liberal minds. It is much more congenial to man's nature to be abroad in the fields, breathing a pure air, and admiring the works of creation and the beauties of nature, than to be confined in the unwholesome, impure air of a workshop. The former softens the heart and liberalizes the mind; the latter hardens the heart, contracts the mind, and corrupts the passions.

It does not, however, follow that agricultural labor should be encouraged and patronized by the government and manufacturing labor neglected or discouraged. Universal experience proves that the two species of labor are a mutual advantage to each other, and that those nations are the most flourishing and prosperous where a proper medium is preserved between them. They produce a reaction upon each other and in this way infuse into the body politic a much greater degree of energy than would otherwise be produced. To encourage manufactures is often the most effectual mode of encouraging agriculture. Agriculture is never carried to so great a degree of perfection in countries exclusively agricultural as in countries where agriculture and manufactures flourish together and receive the equal protection and encouragement of the government. This is manifest not only from experience, but also from the very nature of things.

Nature, when she planted in the breast of man a desire for the comforts of life, intended this desire should be gratified upon the same terms and conditions that his desire for the necessaries of life was to be gratified. It is, therefore, in pursuance of the dictate of nature that man labors for the comforts of life! This is the provision of nature for raising man from a state of savagism to civilization. If nature had not planted in the breast of man a desire for the comforts and luxuries of life, the arts and sciences would never have been cultivated. Had such been the case, manufacturing labor would have been unproductive, and there would have been none of it; there would have been no employment for man but agriculture, hunting, and fishing. With human nature thus modified, mankind would always have remained in a state of barbarism, for there could have been no motive for the exertion of his faculties for any other purpose than to obtain the necessaries of life. Every man must have provided his own food by his own labor, for there would have been nothing which he would give in exchange for it.

Among a people whose wants are confined to the necessaries of life, as is almost entirely the case with all savage nations, it is notorious that agriculture is never carried to any degree of perfection. Our industry is always in proportion to our wants, or to our motives to labor; and where his wants are confined to the mere necessaries of life, man is an indolent, slothful animal. But the case is entirely changed when the comforts and luxuries of life come to constitute a portion of his wants. Skill in the arts then becomes a means of acquiring food; manufactures come to have a value; manufacturing labor becomes productive; its product stimulates the agriculturist to greater exertion; a reaction is produced; the wilderness is converted into a fruitful field; and savage man into the polished enlightened citizen.

In this way artisans and manufacturers perform their full share in multiplying the fruits of the earth, and in ameliorating the condition of man; not, however, by accumulating the surplus product of labor but by consuming it.

That is the best regulated community where agriculture and manufacturing labor bear a due proportion to each other; and when one preponderates in too great a degree, as is often the case, it becomes the duty of the government to interpose and restore the equilibrium by encouraging and protecting the other.

In England, manufactures have acquired too great a preponderance, either from the particular circumstances of the times, or from an unwise interposition of the government in their behalf. In the United States agriculture has acquired too great a preponderance, from the particular situation of our country, and from the unwonted demand for the product of agriculture, in consequence of the unexampled condition of the world for the last thirty years. In both cases ought the government to interpose to restore that just equilibrium so essential to the health of the body politic and so conducive to national prosperity and wealth.

The principal, or at least one of the principal, objects of government should be to preserve the body politic from the disease of accumulation, not by stifling industry or preventing production (for that would be like a physician who should think to preserve the vigor of the human body by constant depletion), but by making effectual provision for the complete consumption, within the time which nature dictates, of the whole product of industry. . . .

If all the manufactures are worn out, and all the provisions are eaten up clean annually, we shall have no occasion to trouble ourselves about their value, or the price they would sell for; nor any occasion to inquire whether money is plenty or scarce; whether interest is high or low; whether the circulating medium be paper or gold; whether the national debt be great or small; or whether one kind of labor be more productive than another. We may be very sure, whatever be the case in these other respects, that in the present condition of the civilized world, the nation will be in a prosperous and flourishing condition. . . .

The wants of civilized man . . . . are innumerable and insatiable. The necessaries of life constitute a very small portion of them. The wants of the humblest individual in civil life are so numerous that the labor of himself could supply but a very small portion of them. Could any one man build the house he lives in, and prepare the materials of which it is built? Could he make the furniture for it? Could he make even the clothes which he considers necessary to his comfort? What man is there in civil society who would not think himself in a deplorable state of poverty if his articles of food were limited to the production of his own labor — if he could obtain no greater variety than that which contents the savage?

But great as is the difference between the wants of the savage and the citizen, the difference between the manner in which they are supplied is still greater. This difference places them in such totally different circumstances that the principles which govern the one cannot govern the other.

The savage supplies all his wants by his own labor. He depends on the labor of others for no part of them. His individuality is in this respect as complete as if he did not belong to any nation or tribe. Unless he hunts or fishes for himself, he goes without food. In such a state of things it is very manifest that no evil consequences can arise from accumulation. He can accumulate nothing but the necessaries of life, the benefit of which he is to enjoy himself, and if he fails to accumulate, he suffers the consequence of a dearth, famine, or other casualty.

The case, however, is very different with a man in civil society. Not one in 500 of his wants is, or can be, supplied by his own labor. He depends on the labor of others, perhaps, for all the necessaries of life, and, perhaps, for 99 in 100 of the comforts of life, and these he probably depends on being able to procure, by his own labor, on an article which is to him neither a necessary or a comfort of life. If then the article accumulates upon his hands, and he cannot sell or exchange it for the necessaries of life, he must starve, or live upon the bounty of others. What is true of one individual is true of thousands of others, and of a nation. . . .

Although it is a matter of indifference by whom the annual product of labor is consumed, provided there is a certainty that it always will be consumed, yet it is all-important to guard against probable, or even possible, contingencies which may affect this certainty of consumption. For this reason, domestic is preferable to foreign consumption — the latter depending in some measure on the will of others; the former, on the nation's own will alone. Home consumption, and a home market, is, therefore, always to be preferred to a foreign one.

This affords a solution of that much vexed and long agitated question of free trade. . . . The true principles upon which that question ought to be settled have never yet been developed. The question whether individuals should be permitted to sell where they can sell dearest and buy where they can buy cheapest ought not to be decided upon the narrow, contemptible principles of private interests but upon the more expanded and noble principles of public interests. Public and private interests are often directly at variance; but when at variance, I presume, it is not to be made a question, which ought to prevail.

It is the duty of legislators to foresee the public evil consequences of any particular policy, and guard against them. Private citizens can only be expected to be wise for themselves. It is not their duty to look after the public interests; they are not the conservators of national wealth. This belongs to the department of legislation.

If, from particular circumstances, from a state of war or a state of peace, one species of industry is more profitable than another, it must be expected that individuals will embark in it without any regard to the evil consequences it may produce to succeeding generations; but it does not become a legislator either to be blind to their consequences or not to guard against them.

Hitherto, individuals have found it extremely profitable to import slaves from Africa to cultivate their lands in America; and in the earlier periods of this accursed traffic, when there was a scarcity of laborers in America, it was no doubt greatly conducive both to public and private wealth. This being the case, and admitting that there was no injustice or moral iniquity in the trade, it could not have been expected of individuals to forgo the advantages to themselves on account of the pernicious effects of slavery upon future generations. No man can be expected to forgo a present advantage to himself, provided there is no immorality in the enjoyment of it, upon the ground that it may be prejudicial to posterity. He may have no posterity, or if he has, their interests at the distance of two or three generations is too remote to influence his conduct. The influence of self-interest on human conduct, like the laws of gravitation, is in the inverse compound ratio of distance and quantity.

Legislators, however, are not permitted to take such limited, short-sighted views of things; they are placed on a more elevated station; they move in a higher sphere; they are traitors to their high trust if they do not look to the future as well as the present. . . .

Had the legislators of former ages been as just and as wise as they ought to have been, they would have foreseen the dreadful consequences of slavery to succeeding generations; and foreseeing them, it would have been their imperious duty (admitting slavery to be innocent in itself) to have abolished the slave trade and slavery. . . .

It does not, however, follow (as some have absurdly supposed) that because the legislators of those days were not as wise or as just as they should have been, or because they neglected their duty in not abolishing the slave trade, that those persons concerned in it were guiltless. Our forefathers are not exonerated from the guilt of carrying on the slave trade upon the ground that the English government permitted it. They were, on the contrary, guilty of the most atrocious crimes against both God and man. They violated the law of God written upon the heart of every human being. The nation, or state, as contradistinguished from the people, may not have been guilty because it may not have had the power of offending, but the people themselves were not the less guilty on that account.

What is true, as it respects the duty of government in regard to the slave trade, so far as national interests alone are concerned, is true of every other measure relating to national industry which has a remote tendency to affect national wealth and prosperity. The true policy for every wise legislator is to consider the nation immortal, and to legislate for it as though it was to exist forever; but, unfortunately, most legislators act as though they thought the nation as short-lived as themselves. And instead of adopting a policy which looks prospectively to future generations and centuries, they adopt one which looks only to themselves and the present race; and, too frequently, one which looks only to the interests of some particular individuals or classes in the community instead of the interests of the nation.

Legislation should always be national and not individual; instead of which, it is more frequently individual than national. This is not to be wondered at, when we consider what a mass of stupidity and ignorance is ordinarily selected for the administration of public affairs. It seems almost to have grown into a maxim that "when a man is fit for nothing else, he is fit for a legislator" — that neither talents, education, or experience are at all necessary to qualify a man to take charge of a nation's interests. . . .

WAR AFFORDS A STIMULUS to industry by increasing the demand for labor. The consumption of the product of labor by an army prevents accumulation, and often causes a still greater increase of population. This explains the phenomenon of England's always increasing in wealth during a period of war with the maritime nations of Europe. Having a naval superiority on the ocean, war gives her the commerce of the world and, in addition to the excitement and energy which war is calculated to infuse into the body politic, she enjoys the additional advantage of supplying the world, or the greater part of it, with her manufactures, which gives an impulse to the industry of the nation and causes an increase of production much greater than the war expenditure. War may, therefore, enrich England while it impoverishes other nations.

It is altogether a mistaken notion to suppose that the evils of war consist in a useless consumption of the product of labor. If this was the only evil, war would be a very harmless amusement or, perhaps, a useful luxury. The devastation and desolation which it occasions is of quite a different character. In this respect, it has an immediate and lasting effect to diminish national wealth. It has also an injurious effect on public morals and, therefore, tends to enervate and weaken the arm of industry. The influence of war also is irregular and fluctuating in its operation. It furnishes, for a time, a strong demand for particular species of labor; but as war cannot be permanent or lasting, that demand may be suddenly withdrawn, and then distress is produced among those classes of people to whom it had given employment. All fluctuations are unfavorable to national wealth and happiness; the more permanent the demand for any article, the better. This is one cause of the present distress in England and this country. An unnatural demand had been occasioned by war for the product of the labor of the two countries. Peace has interrupted the demand, and thousands of people are thrown out of employment in consequence of it.

Public Works. The expenditure of public money in public works frequently has not a less invigorating influence than war on national industry.

It is a common opinion that all expenditures in public works of all descriptions, whether in building fortifications, ships, making roads, canals, or any other permanent improvement, is a real tax upon the community, to the amount of money expended, and that the public can only be remunerated by the advantage it may derive from the use of the building or improvement. . . .

If the fortification or ship should be destroyed the day they were finished, it would not follow that national wealth would have been lessened in consequence of building them. Should a road or canal be perfectly useless when finished, it would not follow that the nation was the poorer for the money expended upon them. It would, undoubtedly, be better for the nation that the fortification or ship should remain, when built, than be destroyed; nevertheless, it may be better for the nation to have built than not to have built them, even though they should be immediately destroyed. The capacity of the nation for acquiring the necessaries and comforts of life may be none the less for having built a ship that sinks to the bottom of the ocean as soon as she is off the stocks, or for having made a road or canal which are perfectly useless. If public money is to be expended, it is no doubt better that it should be expended prudently than imprudently, profitably than unprofitably; although it does not follow that national wealth is lessened by its being expended either imprudently or unprofitably. To those who have been in the habit of confounding national with individual wealth, and of considering national wealth to consist in the accumulation of superfluous labor, or, in other words, of idleness, these may seem to be strange opinions, although they are perfectly reconcilable with those theories which make national wealth to consist in the surplus of production above consumption, or in the accumulation of gold and silver.

If a canal is made with a nation's own means, there will be just as much money in the nation after as before it was made, or, as there would have been had it not been made, even though it should be perfectly useless when made. The money may belong to different individuals in consequence of making the canal; still, it will belong to the nation; and so far as national wealth is concerned, even upon the principles of accumulation, it matters not whether it be in the possession of A or B; and as there will be just as much money in the country after as before building the useless canal, or road, or a ship that is sunk to the bottom of the ocean; so there may be just as much, or as great a surplus of production above consumption.

If the expenditure of the public money in these public works has caused an increase of the quantity of labor equal to what was required to build them, then the production will be just as great with as it would have been without building them. The number of people to be supported out of the product of labor is not increased; and, therefore, the surplus, if any, will be as great in the one case as in the other. In this case, the expenditure affords such a stimulus to national industry as to augment the quantity of labor equal to what was required in the public works; and of course, there will not be a bushel less of wheat, or a pound less of tobacco, cotton, or sugar than there would have been but for the public works. It is very clear that this may be the case in all countries. There is not a country on earth that has not a large quantity of surplus labor, or, in other words, a large number of people who are either idle the whole or some part of their time and who might be employed in labor.

As every nation, therefore, possesses a quantity of unexerted, or unexpended, labor or power, a measure of government which shall have the effect to call this labor into action may expend it in the erection of public works without diminishing the annual product of labor or preventing as great an accumulation of the surplus of it as would have taken place without such expenditure. Suppose the United States was to employ 10,000 men during the next ten years, at an annual expense of $2 million, in making roads, canals, and other permanent improvements in the country. Is there any reason to suppose that any portion of that labor would be withdrawn from other branches of industry? The particular individuals employed upon the public works would, no doubt, be withdrawn from other branches of industry; but others would either take their places, or those who remained would labor more; so that the quantity of labor would be as great as though none had been withdrawn. . . .

But this is not all. The expenditure of labor and money in this way may be the means of augmenting public wealth in other respects; it may cause a greater annual product of labor than there would otherwise have been; it may make the necessaries and comforts of life still more abundant among the people. It may produce this effect by infusing into the nation a degree of industry which will more than supply the labor expended upon the public works. It may excite the energies of the nation to a much greater degree than is required for the performance of this additional labor, and thereby augment the annual product of the necessaries and comforts of life.

Was the state of Maryland to expend $1 million in making a canal from the Susquehanna to Baltimore, there is not the slightest reason to suppose there would be a bushel less of wheat or corn, or a pound less of tobacco, raised in the state in consequence of the labor bestowed upon the canal; nor would there be a dollar less money in the state. It might, on the contrary, be the means of augmenting the quantity of both. The canal then would cost the state in reality nothing. Public wealth would be just as great after the canal was made, exclusive of the canal itself, as it would have been, had the canal not been made, and the national wealth would, therefore, at all events be augmented to an amount equal to the value[3] of the canal to the public.

If making the canal should cause an increase of industry equal only to half the labor bestowed on it, then public wealth would be augmented only to half the amount of the value of the canal to the public. In other words, if the labor expended in building the canal was equal to the value of $1 million, and in consequence of building it, labor should be withdrawn from other branches of industry to the value of $500,000, which would cause a diminished product of wheat, corn, tobacco, etc., equal to $500,000, then the actual expense to the state of the canal would be $500,000. . . .

This is taking it for granted that making the canal would withdraw a quantity of labor equal to half the quantity expended on the canal from other branches of industry. But upon the supposition that no labor would be withdrawn from other branches of industry, which would probably be the case, should the canal, when finished, be of no value to the state, still public wealth would not be diminished.

There is every reason to believe that the New York canals will increase the quantum of industry in the state equal to the whole amount of labor bestowed upon them, and that the product of labor in agriculture, manufactures, and commerce will be as great as it would have been had the canals not been built, so that in reality they will cause no drain on public wealth, even though they should be worth nothing to the state when finished; and it is even more than probable that these enterprises have infused into the body politic a degree of energy and industry which will more than supply all the labor required to build the canals, and that there will be a greater product of labor in other branches of industry in consequence of making them. The public wealth of the state will, therefore, be augmented, independent of the value of the canals.

The body politic, like the natural body, is liable to fall into a state of comparative lethargy and torpor. It then becomes necessary to arouse its dormant energies by administering stimulants. The expenditure of public money in public works will often produce this effect.

3. The word value is here used in its popular or figurative sense, for a canal can have no value in the technical sense of the word, any more than national territory.

144.

James Flint: The Panic in Indiana

The years of postwar prosperity came to a sudden halt with the economic depression of 1819. European demand for American exports had lessened, and the Bank of the United States, which had previously extended generous credit, began to demand payment from the state banks. Because of this sudden demand, a number of banks were forced to close, setting off a chain reaction: Farmers lost their land, and speculators, unable to repay government loans, had to give up their claims. The nation was embittered and in large part blamed the Bank of the United States. A Scottish traveler, James Flint, was in America when the panic broke out and wrote the following letter from Jefferson, Indiana, on May 4, 1820, commenting on its effects.

Source: *Early Western Travels 1748-1846,* Reuben Gold Thwaites, ed., Cleveland, 1904, Vol. IX, pp. 224-229.

The accounts [I have] given . . . of the depredations committed by bankers will make you suppose that affairs are much deranged here. Bankruptcy is now a sin prohibited by law. In the Eastern states and in Europe our condition must be viewed as universal insolvency. Who, it may be asked, would give credit to a people whose laws tolerate the violation of contracts? Mutual credit and confidence are almost torn up by the roots. It is said that in China knaves are openly commended in courts of law for the adroitness of their management. In the interior of the United States, law has removed the necessity of being either acute or honest.

The money in circulation is puzzling to traders, and more particularly to strangers; for besides the multiplicity of banks, and the diversity in supposed value, fluctuations are so frequent and so great that no man who holds it in his possession can be safe for a day. The merchant, when asked the price of an article, instead of making a direct answer, usually puts the question, "What sort of money have you got?" Supposing that a number of bills are shown, and one or more are accepted of, it is not till then that the price of the goods is declared; and an additional price is uniformly laid on to compensate for the supposed defect in the quality of the money.

Trade is stagnated, produce cheap, and merchants find it difficult to lay in assortments of foreign manufactures. I have lately heard that if a lady purchases a dress in the city of Cincinnati, she has to call at almost all the shops in town before she can procure trimmings of the suitable colors. It is only about three years ago that an English traveler asserted that in Cincinnati "English goods abound in as great profusion as in Cheapside."

Merchants in Cincinnati, as elsewhere, have got into debt by buying property or by building houses, but are now secure in the possession. Such people, notwithstanding, complain of the badness of the times, finding that the trade of buying without paying cannot be continued. Those who have not already secured an independence for life may soon be willing to have trade and fair dealing as formerly. Property laws deprive creditors of the debts now due to them; but they cannot force them to give credit as they were wont to do.

Agriculture languishes — farmers cannot find profit in hiring laborers. The increase of produce in the United States is greater than any increase of consumption that may be pointed out elsewhere. To increase the quantity of provisions, then, without enlarging the numbers of those who eat them will be only diminishing the price further. Land in these circumstances can be of no value to the capitalist who would employ his funds in farming. The spare capital of farmers is here chiefly laid out in the purchase of lands.

Laborers and mechanics are in want of employment. I think that I have seen upward of 1,500 men in quest of work within eleven months past, and many of these declared that they had no money. Newspapers and private letters agree in stating that wages are so low as 18¾ cents (about 10*d.*) per day, with board, at Philadelphia and some other places. Great numbers of strangers lately camped in the open field near Baltimore, depending on the contributions of the charitable for subsistence. You have no doubt heard of emigrants returning to Europe without finding the prospect of a livelihood in America. Some who have come out to this part of the country do not succeed well.

Laborers' wages are at present a dollar and an eighth part per day. Board costs them two three-fourths or three dollars per week, and washing three-fourths of a dollar for a dozen of pieces. On these terms, it is plain that they cannot live two days by the labor of one, with the other deductions which are to be taken from their wages. Clothing, for example, will cost about three times its price in Britain: and the poor laborer is almost certain of being paid in depreciated money; perhaps from 30 to 50 percent under par. I have seen several men turned out of boardinghouses where their money would not be taken. They had no other resource left but to lodge in the woods, without any covering except their clothes. They set fire to a decayed log, spread some boards alongside of it for a bed, laid a block of timber across for a pillow, and pursued their labor by day, as usual.

A still greater misfortune than being paid with bad money is to be guarded against, namely, that of not being paid at all. Public improvements are frequently executed by subscription, and subscribers do not in every case consider themselves dishonored by nonpayment of the sum they engage for. I could point out an interesting work, where a tenth part of the amount on the subscription book cannot now be realized. The treasurer of a company so circumstanced has only to tell undertakers or laborers that he cannot pay them. I have heard of a treasurer who applied the funds entrusted to him to his own use, and who refused to give any satisfaction for his conduct. It is understood that persons who are agents for others frequently exchange the money put into their hands for worse bills, and reserve the premium obtained for themselves. Employers are also in the habit of deceiving their workmen by telling them that it is not convenient to pay wages in money, and that they run accounts with the storekeeper, the tailor, and the shoemaker; and that from them they may have all the necessaries they want very cheap. The workman who consents to this mode of payment procures orders from the employer, on one or more of these citizens, and is charged in a higher price for the goods than the employer actually pays for them. This is called "paying in trade."

You have often heard that extreme poverty does not exist in the United States. For some time after my arrival in the country supposed to be exempt from abject misery, I never heard the term "poor" (a word, by the by, not often used) without imagining that it applied to a class in moderate circumstances, who had it not in their power to live in fine houses, indulge in foreign luxuries, and wear expensive clothing; and on seeing a person whose external appearance would have denoted a beggar in Britain, I concluded that the unfortunate must have been improvident or dissipated, or perhaps possessed of both of these qualities. My conjectures may have on two or three occasions been just, as people of a depressed appearance are very rarely to be seen, but I now see the propriety of divesting myself of such a hasty and ungenerous opinion. Last winter a Cincinnati newspaper advertised a place where old clothes were received for the poor, and another where cast shoes were collected for children who could not, for want of them, attend Sunday schools. The charitable measure of supplying the poor with public meals has lately been resorted to at Baltimore; but . . . most of the people who are relieved in this way are Europeans recently come into America.

In the western country, poor rates are raised in the form of a county tax. They are, however, so moderate as to be scarcely felt. Contracts for boarding the permanently poor are advertised and let to the lowest bidder, who has a right to employ the pauper in any light work suited to the age or ability of the object of charity. They are said to be well treated. This sort of public exposure must create a repugnance against becoming a pauper.

In the Eastern states, workhouses are established. It is to be wished that those who follow this plan will not lose sight of the example of England. The operations of bankers and the recent decline in trade have been effective causes of poverty; and it seems probable that the introduction of manufacturing industry, and a reduction of base paper, would soon give effectual relief.

145.

Daniel Webster: Property and Political Power

The debate about the extension of the suffrage raged throughout the 1820s and resulted in liberalization of the voting qualifications in every state of the union. (Even in 1830, however, no state allowed all *male adults to vote; and of course women could not vote in any state until much later.) These gains were strongly opposed by conservatives, who felt that a property qualification for voters was necessary to insure a responsible electorate. Daniel Webster eloquently stated the conservative viewpoint in a speech in the Massachusetts Constitutional Convention on December 15, 1820. Massachusetts' state constitution, which had originally been drafted by John Adams in 1780 and is still in effect today, was changed despite Webster's wishes in the 1820s, and has been changed many times since.*

Source: *The Works of Daniel Webster,* 16th edition, Boston, 1872, Vol. III, pp. 8-25.

The subject before us is the manner of constituting the Legislative Department of government. We have already decided that the legislative power shall exist as it has heretofore existed, in two separate and distinct branches — a Senate and a House of Representatives. We propose, also, at least I have heard no intimation of a contrary opinion, that these branches shall, in form, possess a negative on each other. I presume

I may also take it for granted that the members of both these houses are to be chosen annually.

The immediate question now under discussion is — In what manner shall the senators be elected? They are to be chosen in districts; but shall they be chosen in proportion to the number of inhabitants in each district, or in proportion to the taxable property of each district, or, in other words, in proportion to the part which each district bears in the public burdens of the state? The latter is the existing provision of the Constitution; and to this I give my support.

The resolution of the honorable member from Roxbury proposes to divide the state into certain legislative districts, and to choose a given number of senators and a given number of representatives in each district, in proportion to population. This I understand. It is a simple and plain system. The honorable member from Pittsfield and the honorable member from Worcester support the first part of this proposition; that is to say, that part which provides for the choice of senators according to population, without explaining entirely their views as to the latter part, relative to the choice of representatives. They insist that the questions are distinct, and capable of a separate consideration and decision. I confess myself, sir, unable to view the subject in that light. It seems to me, there is an essential propriety in considering the questions together, and in forming our opinions of them, as parts, respectively, of one legislative system. . . .

In my opinion, sir, there are two questions before the committee. The first is — Shall the Legislative Department be constructed with any other *check* than such as arises simply from dividing the members of this department into two houses? The second is — If such other and further check ought to exist, *in what manner* shall it be created?

If the two houses are to be chosen in the manner proposed by the resolutions of the member from Roxbury, there is obviously no other check or control than a division into separate chambers. The members of both houses are to be chosen at the same time, by the same electors, in the same districts, and for the same term of office. They will, of course, all be actuated by the same feelings and interests. Whatever motives may at the moment exist to elect particular members of one house will operate equally on the choice of the members of the other. There is so little of real utility in this mode that, if nothing more be done, it would be more expedient to choose all the members of the legislature, without distinction, simply as members of the legislature, and to make the division into two houses, either by lot or otherwise, after these members thus chosen should have come up to the capital.

I understand the reason of checks and balances in the legislative power to arise from the truth that, in representative governments, that department is the leading and predominating power; and if its will may be at any time suddenly and hastily expressed, there is great danger that it may overthrow all other powers. Legislative bodies naturally feel strong, because they are numerous, and because they consider themselves as the immediate representatives of the people. They depend on public opinion to sustain their measures, and they undoubtedly possess great means of influencing public opinion. With all the guards which can be raised by constitutional provisions, we are not likely to be too well secured against cases of improper, or hasty, or intemperate legislation. It may be observed, also, that the executive power, so uniformly the object of jealousy to republics, has in the states of this Union been deprived of the greater part both of its importance and its splendor by the establishment of the general government. . . .

Nor has it been found easy, nor in all cases possible, to preserve the Judicial Department from the progress of legislative encroachment. Indeed, in some of the states all judges are appointed by the legislature; in others, although appointed by the executive, they are removable at the pleasure of the legislature. In all, the provision for their maintenance is necessarily to be made by the legislature. As if Montesquieu had never demonstrated the necessity of separating the departments of governments; as if Mr. Adams had not done the same thing, with equal ability and more clearness, in his "Defense of the American Constitutions"; as if the sentiments of Mr. Hamilton and Mr. Madison were already forgotten — we see, all around us, a tendency to extend the legislative power over the proper sphere of the other departments. And as the legislature, from the very nature of things, is the most powerful department, it becomes necessary to provide, in the mode of forming it, some check which shall insure deliberation and caution in its measures.

If all legislative power rested in one house, it is very problematical whether any proper independence could be given either to the executive or the judiciary. Experience does not speak encouragingly on that point. If we look through the several constitutions of the states, we shall perceive that generally the departments are most distinct and independent where the legislature is composed of two houses, with equal authority and mutual checks. If all legislative power be in one popular body, all other power, sooner or later, will be there also.

I wish, now, sir, to correct a most important mistake in the manner in which this question has been stated. It has been said that we propose to give to property, merely as such, a control over the people, numerically considered. But this I take not to be at all the true nature of the proposition. The Senate is not to be a check on the people, but on the House of Representatives. It is the case of an authority, given to one agent, to check or control the acts of another. The people, having conferred on the House of Representatives powers which are great, and, from their nature, liable to abuse, require, for their own security, another house, which shall possess an effectual negative on the first. This does not limit the power of the people, but only the authority of their agents. It is not a restraint on their rights, but a restraint on that power which they have delegated. It limits the authority of agents in making laws to bind their principals.

And if it be wise to give one agent the power of checking or controlling another, it is equally wise, most manifestly, that there should be some difference of character, sentiment, feeling, or origin in that agent who is to possess this control. Otherwise, it is not at all probable that the control will ever be exercised. To require the consent of two agents to the validity of an act, and yet to appoint agents so similar, in all respects, as to create a moral certainty that what one does the other will do also, would be inconsistent and nugatory. There can be no effectual control without some difference of origin, or character, or interest, or feeling, or sentiment. And the great question in this country has been where to find, or how to create, this difference in governments. . . .

Various modes have been attempted in various states. In some, a difference of qualification has been required in the persons to be elected. This obviously produces little or no effect. All property qualification, even the highest, is so low as to produce no exclusion, to any extent, in any of the states. A difference of age in the persons elected is sometimes required; but this is found to be equally unimportant. Neither has it happened that any consideration of the relative rank of the members of the two houses has had much effect on the character of their constituent members. Both in the state governments and in the United States government, we daily see persons elected into the House of Representatives who have been members of the Senate. Public opinion does not attach so much weight and importance to the distinction as to lead individuals greatly to regard it.

In some of the states, a different sort of qualification in the electors is required for the two houses; and this is probably the most proper and efficient check. But such has not been the provision in this Commonwealth, and there are strong objections to introducing it. In other cases, again, there is a double election for senators; electors being first chosen, who elect senators. Such is the case in Maryland, where the senators are elected for five years by electors appointed in equal numbers by the counties; a mode of election not unlike that of choosing representatives in the British Parliament for the boroughs of Scotland. In this state, the qualification of the voters is the same for the two houses, and there is no essential difference in that of the persons chosen. But, in apportioning the Senate to the different districts of the state, the present constitution assigns to each district a number proportioned to its public taxes. Whether this be the best mode of producing a difference in the construction of the two houses is not now the question; but the question is whether this be better than no mode.

The gentleman from Roxbury called for authority on this subject. He asked what writer of reputation had approved the principle for which we contend. I should hope, sir, that even if this call could not be answered, it would not necessarily follow that the principle should be expunged. Governments are instituted for practical benefit, not for subjects of speculative reasoning merely. The best authority for the support of a particular principle or provision in government is experience; and of all experience, our own, if it have been long enough to give the principle a fair trial, should be most decisive. This provision has existed for forty years, and while so many gentlemen contend that it is wrong in theory, no one has shown that it has been either injurious or inconvenient in practice. No one pretends that it has caused a bad law to be enacted, or a good one to be rejected. To call on us, then, to strike out this provision because we should be able to find no authority for it in any book on government would seem to be like requiring a mechanic to abandon the use of an implement, which had always answered all the purposes designed by it, because he could find no model of it in the patent office.

But, sir, I take the *principle* to be well established by writers of the greatest authority. In the first place, those who have treated of natural law have maintained, as a principle of that law, that, as far as the object of society is the protection of something in which the members possess unequal shares, it is just that the weight of each person in the common councils should bear a relation and proportion to his interest. Such is the sentiment of Grotius, and he refers, in support of it, to several institutions among the ancient states. Those authors who have written more particularly on the subject of political institutions have, many of them, maintained similar sentiments. Not, indeed, that every man's power should be in exact proportion to his property, but that, in a general sense and in a general form, property, as such, should have its weight and influence in political arrangement. . . .

To this sentiment, sir, I entirely agree. It seems to me to be plain that, in the absence of military force, political power naturally and necessarily goes into the hands which hold the property. In my judgment, therefore, a republican form of government rests not more on political constitutions than on those laws which regulate the descent and transmission of property.

If the nature of our institutions be to found government on property, and that it should look to those who hold property for its protection, it is entirely just that property should have its due weight and consideration in political arrangements. Life and personal liberty are no doubt to be protected by law; but property is also to be protected by law, and is the fund out of which the means for protecting life and liberty are usually furnished. We have no experience that teaches us that any other rights are safe where property is not safe. Confiscation and plunder are generally, in revolutionary commotions, not far before banishment, imprisonment, and death. It would be monstrous to give even the name of government to any association in which the rights of property should not be completely secured. The disastrous revolutions which the world has witnessed, those political thunderstorms and earthquakes which have shaken the pillars of society to their very deepest foundations, have been revolutions against property. . . .

The English Revolution of 1688 was a revolution in favor of property, as well as of other rights. It was brought about by the men of property for their security; and our own immortal Revolution was undertaken not to shake or plunder property but to protect it. The acts of which the country complained were such as violated rights of property. An immense majority of all those who had an interest in the soil were in favor of the Revolution; and they carried it through, looking to its results for the security of their possessions. It was the property of the frugal yeomanry of New England, hard earned but freely given, that enabled her to act her proper part and perform her full duty in achieving the independence of the country.

I would not be thought, Mr. Chairman, to be among those who underrate the value of military service. My heart beats, I trust, as responsive as anyone's, to a soldier's claim for honor and renown. It has ever been my opinion, however, that while celebrating the military achievements of our countrymen in the Revolutionary contest, we have not always done equal justice to the merits and the sufferings of those who sustained, on their property and on their means of subsistence, the great burden of the war. Anyone who has had occasion to be acquainted with the records of the New England towns knows well how to estimate those merits and those sufferings. Nobler records of patriotism exist nowhere. Nowhere can there be found higher proofs of a spirit that was ready to hazard all, to pledge all, to sacrifice all in the cause of the country. Instances were not infrequent in which small freeholders parted with their last hoof and the last measure of corn from their granaries to supply provisions for the troops and hire service for the ranks.

The voice of Otis and of Adams in Faneuil Hall found its full and true echo in the little councils of the interior towns; and if within the Continental Congress patriotism shone more conspicuously, it did not there exist more truly, nor burn more fervently; it did not render the day more anxious, or the night more sleepless; it sent up no more ardent prayer to God for succor; and it put forth in no greater degree the fullness of its effort, and the energy of its whole soul and spirit, in the common cause, than it did in the small assemblies of the towns.

I cannot, therefore, sir, agree that it is in favor of society, or in favor of the people, to constitute government with an entire disregard to those who bear the public burdens in times of great exigency. This question has been argued as if it were proposed only to give an advantage to a few rich men. I do not so understand it. I consider it as giving property, generally, a representation in the Senate, both because it is just that it should have such representation, and because it is a convenient mode of providing that *check* which the constitution of the legislature requires. I do not say that such check might not be found in some other provision; but this is the provision already established, and it is, in my opinion, a just and proper one.

I will beg leave to ask, sir, whether property may not be said to deserve this portion of respect and power in the government? It pays, at this moment, I think, five-sixths of all the public taxes; one-sixth only being raised on persons. Not only, sir, do these taxes support those burdens which all governments require, but we have in New England from early times held property to be subject to another great public use — I mean the support of schools. Sir, property, and the power which the law exercises over it for the purpose of instruction, are the basis of the system. It is entitled to the respect and protection of government, because, in a very vital respect, it aids and sustains government.

The honorable member from Worcester, in contending for the admission of the mere popular principle in all branches of the government, told us that our system rested on the intelligence of the community. He told us truly. But allow me, sir, to ask the honorable gentleman what, but property, supplies the means of that intelligence? What living fountain feeds this ever flowing, ever refreshing, ever fertilizing stream of public instruction and general intelligence? If we take away from the towns the power of assessing taxes on property, will the schoolhouses remain open? If we deny to the poor the benefit which they now derive from the property of the rich, will their children remain on their forms, or will they not, rather, be in the streets, in idleness and in vice? . . .

I will now proceed to ask, sir, whether we have not seen, and whether we do not at this moment see, the advantage and benefit of giving security to property, by this and all other reasonable and just provisions. The constitution has stood on its present basis forty years. Let me ask — What state has been more distinguished for wise and wholesome legislation? I speak, sir, without the partiality of a native, and also without intending the compliment of a stranger; and I ask — What example have we had of better legislation? No violent measures affecting property have been attempted. Stop laws, suspension laws, tender laws, all the tribe of these arbitrary and tyrannical interferences between creditor and debtor, which, wheresoever practised, generally end in the ruin of both, are strangers to our statute book. An upright and intelligent judiciary has come in aid of wholesome legislation; and general security for public and private rights has been the result. I do not say that this is peculiar; I do not say that others have not done as well. It is enough that, in these respects, we shall be satisfied that we are not behind our neighbors.

No doubt, sir, there are benefits of every kind, and of great value, in an organization of government, both in legislative and judicial administration, which well secures the rights of property; and we should find it so, by unfortunate experience, should that character be lost. There are millions of personal property now in this Commonwealth which are easily transferable, and would be instantly transferred elsewhere, if any doubt existed of its entire security. I do not know how much of this stability of government, and of the general respect for it, may be fairly imputed to this particular mode of organizing the Senate. It has, no doubt, had some effect. It indicates a respect for the rights of property, and may have operated on opinion as well as upon measures. Now to strike out and obliterate it, as it seems to me, would be in a high degree unwise and improper.

As to the *right* of apportioning senators upon this principle, I do not understand how there can be a question about it. All government is a modification of general principles and general truths, with a view to practical utility. Personal liberty, for instance, is a clear right, and is to be provided for; but it is not a clearer right than the right of property, though it may be more important. It is, therefore, entitled to protection. But property is also to be protected; and when it is remembered how great a portion of the people of this state possess property, I cannot understand how its protection or its influence is hostile to their rights and privileges. For these reasons, sir, I am in favor of maintaining that check in the constitution of the legislature which has so long existed there.

146.

For Wider Suffrage

The first state constitutions limited the suffrage to property holders. By the first decade of the nineteenth century, when those early constitutions came under review, there existed a new class of Americans, who did not own land, but who nevertheless felt a vital interest in government and were ready to press for the right to vote. Men like John Adams, Joseph Story, Daniel Webster, James Madison, and James Monroe defended the status quo: They foresaw a society divided along economic lines, rent by conflict between rich and poor, and they feared that extension of the suffrage would provide the masses with a political weapon with which to attack the rights of property. Liberals denied that the masses had any desire for class conflicts. The following editorial from the Niles' Weekly Register *of October 21, 1820, supports the liberal view, one that was ultimately to prevail in the impending Jacksonian era — the age, as it has been called, of the common man.*

Source: *Niles' Weekly Register,* October 21, 1820.

We observe that, in several of the states, discussions are going on which have for their purpose an extension of the right of suffrage, to which we wish success. In looking at some of the state constitutions, we have much cause to wonder that, in this enlightened day, so many barriers should be placed between the people at large and their local governments, as though it were necessary to have a body of patricians to stand between the plebeians and power!

But, yet, the right of suffrage is so common in other states that it is not valued as it should be. Whatsoever is most estimable, whatsoever most delightful — even the enjoyment of health, the acquisition of wealth, or the society of lovely woman — loses a large part of its zest from complete possession; and hence it is that that which nations have waded through oceans of blood to obtain, that for which America contended in a seven years' cruel war with the "mother country" to secure to herself, is, in some places, enjoyed so much as a matter of course that very little reverence or respect is paid to it. The inestimable right is exercised with indifference or from favoritism. The choice of a sheriff to execute the law produces ten times the bustle of the election of an officer who is to make the law. This should not be so. We may have our friends at elections but never ought to forget that our first duty is to serve ourselves in a serious selection of persons best qualified by their wisdom to discern the wants and wishes of the people of a state, and vested with virtue sufficient to pursue its interests to their consummation in defiance of the intrigues of party or the clamors of unworthy men.

When the ballot is thus used, it brings about revolutions without confusion, which cannot be accomplished in a different state of things except through force and arms. In the state of Massachusetts a convention is about to be chosen to change the constitution of the commonwealth; and so quietly has this great affair proceeded that nothing more than the simple fact that a convention is to be called is known out of the state. There is no anxiety about the matter, no convulsion is expected to grow out of it, for the people are acting for themselves. . . .

We hold it to be the natural right of every citizen, who is bound by the law to render personal services to the state or aid its revenue by money drawn from his pocket, to vote for those who may require such services or cause such exactions, and that persons so elected are responsible to such electors for their good conduct, legislative or executive. The possession of a certain quantity of property is by no means necessary to an acquirement of the right of suffrage.

If the law for such purpose relates to things of small value, it tempts to fraud; if it respects large amounts, it forms an aristocracy. Party and partisans can make freeholders by hundreds without hazard or loss, and when personal property is the criterion, a single watch may make fifty voters in one day. We know that such things have been done, and must believe that they will continue to be done, so long as offices are desired by men who ought not to have them. So every man liable to fight the battles of his country, or to pay taxes to support its government, should be a qualified voter.

In Virginia (the names of states are mentioned only for examples) none but freeholders have the right of suffrage. In New York the same description of persons elect the governor and senate. In Pennsylvania all vote who pay taxes. In Maryland nothing but citizenship is required — not even a record of the voter as such. Objections may lie to either of these modes: the freehold suffrage represents property, always best able to protect itself, at the cost of liberty, and even life, to be involved in its legislation; poll taxes may not be desirable, and without them many must be disfranchised; and universal suffrage, without check or control but the opinions of the judges of election, is liable to the most disgraceful frauds, for a minority may easily rule, if resolved to appear as the majority, in populous districts where the places of polling are adjacent to one another.

In corporate cities and towns, it has been contended by many that their local government should represent property only. There is some feasibility in this proposition, but it will not bear the touchstone of truth. Property is nothing unless it is occupied and made productive; and it must be defended to render it valuable. It is the consumer that pays the tax on every article subject to taxation; thus, the tenant pays the tax of the landlord, and even the boarder the rent of the tenant. A house makes nothing; it will not, of itself, produce one cent's value in a hundred years; it is the occupant that gives value to it, the income which it brings for the accommodation afforded. No prudent man will build a house without estimating the taxes to which it is to be liable, as well as the rent which it may produce, unless he builds it for his own use; and then he estimates the taxes in its cost to him, just as if he imported a bag of coffee for his own table on which he knew he would have to pay five cents per pound duty. And yet the right of suffrage should not be made too cheap; some act should be done by which a person may become possessed of it.

As a general principle, then, we hold it to be equitable that every citizen who may be called into the military service of a state, at the hazard of his life, by privation or exposure in battle, or who is liable to a poll or other taxes on his person or property, should have the right of voting for any office in the gift of the people; and a vote in one district should have the same weight as a vote in another district, not as it is in Maryland, etc., where one vote, in certain counties, has twenty times the influence of a like vote in other counties; but this high privilege should be carefully guarded that it may be rightfully exercised.

Something should be done by which the legal voters should be recorded and known to those they elect as responsible to perform the duties of citizens. In Pennsylvania, etc., this is accomplished by a small poll tax; and no one can vote who has not paid a tax which was assessed six months previous to the election, except the sons of persons so qualified, between the ages of twenty-one and twenty-two years. If a state wants revenue, and will admit people to vote on paying their portion of it, perhaps a poll tax, as one means of a system, is as proper a mode of raising it as any other; but, if that be thought inexpedient, the names of all the voters should at least be recorded, at their own expense or that of the state, in their respective districts, say, six months anterior to an election, which record should be handed over to the judges of their election districts, and if the name of an applicant to vote should not be found thereon (unless in special and well-defined exceptions), his vote should not be received. And every person offering his name for record should prove his citizenship and qualify that he had not had it recorded in any other district, except in the case of a removal, when he should distinctly state the same, of which a proper entry should be made.

This procedure would cause little trouble. Persons paying taxes would be electors *ipso facto,* their names being recorded; and all others would have to give in their names but once in their lifetime, but in consequence of a removal. It would affect transient persons only who have nothing at stake and prevent them and others from voting several times, at different polls, at the same election, as may easily be done in large cities or populous districts. Thus would the purity of suffrage be defended, the poor citizen be protected in his rights, and wandering persons be debarred the privilege that exclusively belongs to settled inhabitants.

147.

John Quincy Adams: On America and European Alliances

John Quincy Adams, sixth President of the United States, was the son of the second. He had a long and distinguished political and diplomatic career. When the War of 1812 came to an end, he was his country's most experienced figure in foreign affairs. It was natural that President Monroe should appoint him secretary of state, in which post he served from 1817 to 1824, when he was elected President. The letter that follows was written July 5, 1820, to Henry Middleton, a South Carolinian who was then minister to Russia. In the letter Adams expressed views that prefigure the principles of the Monroe Doctrine, promulgated three years later.

Source: *A Digest of International Law,* John B. Moore, ed., Washington, 1906, Vol. VI, pp. 376-379.

The League of Peace, so far as it was a covenant of organized governments, has proved effectual to its purposes by an experience of five years. Its only interruption has been in this hemisphere, (though between nations strictly European) by the invasion of the Portuguese on the territory claimed by Spain but already lost to her, on the eastern shore of the Rio de la Plata. This aggression, too, the European alliance have undertaken to control; and in connection with it they have formed projects hitherto abortive of interposing in the revolutionary struggle between Spain and her South American colonies.

As a compact between governments it is not improbable that the European alliance will last as long as some of the states who are parties to it. The warlike passions and propensities of the present age find their principal aliment not in the enmities between nation and nation but in the internal dissensions between the component parts of all. The war is between nations and their rulers.

The Emperor Alexander may be considered as the principal patron and founder of the League of Peace. His interest is the more unequivocal in support of it. His empire is the only party to the compact free from that internal fermentation which threatens the existence of all the rest. His territories are the most extensive, his military establishment the most stupendous, his country the most improvable and thriving of them all. He is therefore naturally the most obnoxious to the jealousy and fears of his associates, and his circumstances point his policy to a faithful adhesion to the general system, with a strong reprobation of those who would resort to special and partial alliances, from which any one member of the league should be excluded.

This general tendency of his policy is corroborated by the mild and religious turn of his individual character. He finds a happy coincidence between the dictates of his conscience and the interest of his empire. And as from the very circumstance of his preponderancy, partial alliances might be most easily contracted by him from the natural resort of the weak for succor to the strong, by discountenancing all such partial combinations, he has the appearance of discarding advantages entirely within his command and reaps the glory of disinterestedness while most efficaciously providing for his own security.

Such is accordingly the constant indication of the Russian policy since the peace of Paris in 1815. The neighbors of Russia which have the most to dread from her overshadowing and encroaching power are Persia, Turkey, Austria, and Prussia; the two latter of which are members of the European and even of the Holy Alliance, while the two former are not only extra-European in their general policy, but of religions which excluded them from ever becoming parties, if not from ever deriving benefit from that singular compact.

The political system of the United States is also essentially extra-European. To stand in firm and cautious independence of all entanglement in the European system has been a cardinal point of their policy under every administration of their government, from the peace of 1783 to this day. If at the original adoption of their system there could have been any doubt of its justice or its wisdom, there can be none at this time. Every year's experience rivets it more deeply in the principles and opinions of the nation.

Yet in proportion as the importance of the United States as one of the members of the general society of civilized nations increases in the eyes of the others, the difficulties of maintaining this system and the temptations to depart from it increase and multiply with it. The Russian government has not only manifested an inclination that the United States should concur in the general principles of the European league, but a direct though unofficial application has been made by the present Russian minister here that the United States should become formal parties to the Holy Alliance. It has been suggested, as inducement to obtain their compliance, that this compact bound the parties to no specific engagement of anything; that it was a pledge of mere principles; that its real as well as its professed purpose was merely the general preservation of peace. And it was intimated that if any question should arise between the United

States and other governments of Europe, the Emperor Alexander, desirous of using his influence in their favor, would have a substantial motive and justification for interposing if he could regard them as *his allies,* which, as parties to the Holy Alliance, he would.

It is possible that overtures of a similar character may be made to you; but, whether they should be or not, it is proper to apprise you of the light in which they have been viewed by the President. No direct refusal has been signified to Mr. Poletica. It is presumed that none will be necessary. His instructions are not to make the proposal in form unless with a prospect that it will be successful. It might, perhaps, be sufficient to answer that the organization of our government is such as not to admit of our acceding formally to that compact. But it may be added that the President, approving its general principles and thoroughly convinced of the benevolent and virtuous motives which led to the conception and presided at the formation of this system by the Emperor Alexander, believes that the United States will more effectually contribute to the great and sublime objects for which it was concluded by abstaining from a formal participation in it than they could as stipulated members of it.

As a general declaration of principles, disclaiming the impulses of vulgar ambition and unprincipled aggrandizement and openly proclaiming the peculiarly Christian maxims of mutual benevolence and brotherly love to be binding upon the intercourse between nations no less than upon that of individuals, the United States not only give their hearty assent to the articles of the Holy Alliance but will be among the most earnest and conscientious in observing them. But independent of the prejudices which have been excited against this instrument in the public opinion, which time and an experience of its good effects will gradually wear away, it may be observed that, for the repose of Europe as well as of America, the European and American political system should be kept as separate and distinct from each other as possible.

If the United States as members of the Holy Alliance could acquire a right to ask the influence of its most powerful member in their controversies with other states, the other members must be entitled in return to ask the influence of the United States for themselves or against their opponents. In the deliberations of the league they would be entitled to a voice, and in exercising their right must occasionally appeal to principles which might not harmonize with those of any European member of the bond. This consideration alone would be decisive for declining a participation in that league, which is the President's absolute and irrevocable determination, although he trusts that no occasion will present itself rendering it necessary to make that determination known by an explicit refusal.

148.

ROBERT MILLS: The Beginnings of American Architecture

The so-called Greek revival in architecture found its way to America in the first decades of the nineteenth century. The initial enthusiasm for this style has been attributed to Benjamin Latrobe, but Robert Mills, a student of Latrobe and one of the few native-born architects of the period, also gave it considerable impetus — for example, he was the architect of the Washington Monument. In the selection reprinted below, Mills argued against those in his time who held that classical architecture was not suitable for America. The piece cannot be dated accurately; it was intended as the introduction for a book about his own work that Mills never completed. It is placed here because the year 1820 marked the apex of the Greek revival in the United States.

Source: H. M. Pierce Gallagher, *Robert Mills, Architect of the Washington Monument, 1781-1855*, New York, 1935, pp. 168-171.

THE AUTHOR, HAVING THE HONOR of being the first native American who directed his studies to architecture as a profession, may have some claim to the favorable mention of his fellow citizens, and having acted as a pioneer in the cause, his more enlightened brethren of the profession will be less severe in their criticisms than they would otherwise be on these, his original efforts.

The author is altogether American in his views — his studies having never been out of the United States — and consequently had very little advantage of and from a personal examination of the celebrated works of antiquity, or of more modern date, except that which is to be found in books, and even these were few and difficult to procure at the time he was a student, as architecture was then in its infancy in this country and no invitation was held out for the importation of works of art.

Fortunately for the author, Mr. Jefferson, then President of the United States, befriended him, to whose library he had the honor of having access, where he found some few works of eminent Roman architects, but no Grecian writers.

Mr. Jefferson was an amateur and a great admirer of architecture. He was therefore much gratified to find an American turning his attention to its study, and he gave him every encouragement in the pursuit of his profession. Through his recommendation and advice, the author entered into the office of that celebrated architect and engineer Benjamin H. Latrobe, whom Mr. Jefferson had lately appointed surveyor of the public buildings. With this gentleman, the author pursued and completed his studies and practised in both branches of his profession, as Mr. Latrobe was, at this time, acting engineer of the Chesapeake and Delaware Canal.

The talents of this gentleman were of the first order; his style was purely Greek, and for the first time in this country was it introduced by him in the Bank of Pennsylvania, a building much admired for its chasteness of design and execution.

It was fortunate that this style was so early introduced into our country, both on the ground of economy and of correct taste, as it exactly suited the character of our political institutions and pecuniary means. Mr. Jefferson was a Roman in his views of architecture, as evidenced in Monticello House, his late residence, which was designed by him, and for the execution of which he furnished with his own hands all the detail drawings.

The example and influence of Mr. Jefferson at first operated in favor of the introduction of the Roman style into the country, and it required all the talents and good taste of such a man as Mr. Latrobe to correct it by introducing a better. The natural good taste and the unprejudiced eye of our citizens required only a few examples of the Greek style to convince them of its superiority over the Roman for public structures, and its simplicity recommended its introduction into their private dwellings.

During this period, also, Europe, which for centuries had adapted the Roman and mixed style, began to emerge out of its prejudices, and the light which had been thrown upon the Greek architecture by such men as Stewart caused it to be early substituted in their place. Since then it has been universally approved throughout civilized Europe, and in our own country we now find the simple and chaste style of the Grecian buildings generally adopted.

The author has contributed his mite in this important work, and has acted as a pioneer in the undertaking. He had many and great difficulties to contend against which those who may succeed him in the profession will never be subject to. In a new country like ours, where everything had to be done and little means to accomplish it with, it will readily be seen that the architect would receive little encouragement and the value of his labors be little appreciated. The increasing prosperity of the Union, the wealth and good taste of our citizens are every day aiding the cause of the fine arts, and we may anticipate the time when the United States will rival the most enlightened country of the Old World, if not in the splendor, yet in the magnitude, utility, and good taste of its public works.

The nature of our public institutions, the independent character of our people, their liberal education, and the wide field for successful enterprise opened in the various pursuits of life all tend to enlarge the mind and give the most exalted views on every subject of art and science. Taken in the aggregate, there is not a more liberal and enlightened people on the face of the globe than the people of the United States.

The professional labors of the author are distributed in various parts of the Union. The principal part of the designs found in his work were executed in Philadelphia, Baltimore, Washington, Richmond, Charleston, Columbia, Camden and other towns of South Carolina, Augusta, Ga., New Orleans, Mobile, etc., etc.

Utility and economy will be found to have entered into most of the studies of the author, and little sacrificed to display; at the same time his endeavors were to produce as much harmony and beauty of arrangement as practicable. The principle assumed and acted upon was that beauty is founded upon order, and that convenience and utility were constituent parts. In the cases of private buildings, it is of special importance that convenience, utility, and economy should be associated, and the author was generally successful in developing these. European works of architecture were, some years ago, very deficient in plans for private houses, and those laid down were both unsuitable and wanting in economy and convenience.

The author experienced no aid . . . and was obliged to refer to his own resources for assistance. The subject of domestic economy in the arrangement of private houses has since undergone considerable improvement, particularly in France, and many useful hints now are to be gathered from French works on architecture; but the author has made it a rule never to consult books when he had to design a building. His considerations were: first, the object of the building; second, the means appropriated for its construction; third, the situation it was to occupy. These served as guides in forming the outline of his plan. Books are useful to the student, but when he enters upon the practice of his profession, he should lay them aside and only consult them upon doubtful points, or in matters of detail or as mere studies, not to copy buildings from.

The science of architecture is perhaps the most difficult, important, and interesting of all branches of study where it is intended to form the groundwork of practice. There is no other profession that embraces so wide a field of research and practical operation. Some idea may be formed of the nature of these researches when the requisites to constitute an accomplished architect are taken into consideration. The student, after going through the usual collegiate course, will find himself on the threshold of the temple. Besides having an intimate acquaintance with the different styles of building, ancient and modern, and a thorough knowledge of the five orders (as they are termed), which necessarily demand an acquaintance with drawing, he must study the infinite detail which makes up the endless variety of parts constituting the higher class of structure.

There is not a mechanic art, from the laborer who excavates the foundation to the highest artisan who decorates the interior of the building, but should acquire such knowledge as would enable him to give direction and judge whether the work executed is done in proper manner. There is scarcely a science but is embraced in greater or less degree in this profession: mathematics, natural philosophy, chemistry, geology, botany, natural history, jurisprudence, and theology. In short, to be an accomplished architect is to be not only an accomplished scholar but an accomplished artist and mechanic. There is not a more fascinating study in the whole range of the liberal professions than that of architecture, even considered in the light of study only; but when its utility is examined, and that it offers one of the most honorable pursuits, it cannot be too highly commended to our youth.

If it constituted a part of liberal education, we should see a better taste and a more attractive character of buildings adopted in our country. Until our citizens can distinguish between the crude drawings of the illiterate artist and the designs of the regular bred architect, it is not to be expected that a judicious selection of plans would always be made. It is all-important, therefore, that architecture should constitute one of the sciences taught in our colleges and academies.

149.

James Kirke Paulding: On the Scarcity of Romantic Fiction in America

James Kirke Paulding, though he is not considered today among the leading American authors, had a large following among his contemporaries. Like many of them, he expressed the wish for a national literature, and he himself, as author and critic, produced a number of works on American subjects. With his friend Washington Irving he edited, during 1807-1808, an entertaining and informative periodical in New York, the Salmagundi; *the magazine lapsed but was revived in 1819-1820, when Paulding contributed an article on "National Literature," a portion of which is reprinted here. It was his contention that America was as much a breeding ground for great literature as any other land, and he chided those who merely elaborated on American characteristics without attempting to discover the universality that, in his view, gave depth and grandeur to fiction.*

Source: *Salmagundi,* 2nd series, New York, 1835, Vol. II, pp. 265-272.

It has been often observed by such as have attempted to account for the scarcity of romantic fiction among our native writers that the history of the country affords few materials for such works, and offers little in its traditionary lore to warm the heart or elevate the imagination. The remark has been so often repeated that it is now pretty generally received with perfect docility as an incontrovertible truth, though it seems to me without the shadow of a foundation. It is, in fact, an observation that never did nor ever will apply to any nation, ancient or modern.

Wherever there are men, there will be materials for romantic adventure. In the misfortunes that befall them, in the sufferings and vicissitudes which are everywhere the lot of human beings, in the struggles to counteract fortune, and in the conflicts of the passions — in every situation of life, he who studies nature and draws his pictures from her rich and inexhaustible sources of variety will always find enough of those characters and incidents which give relish to works of fancy. The aid of superstition, the agency of ghosts, fairies, goblins, and all that antiquated machinery which till lately was confined to the nursery, is not necessary to excite our wonder or interest our feelings; although it is not the least of incongruities that, in an age which boasts of having by its scientific discoveries dissipated almost all the materials of superstition, some of the most popular fictions should be founded upon a superstition which is now become entirely ridiculous, even among the ignorant.

The best and most perfect works of imagination appear to me to be those which are founded upon a combination of such characters as every generation of men exhibits, and such events as have often taken place in the world, and will again. Such works are only fictions because the tissue of events which they record never perhaps happened in precisely the same train, and to the same number of persons, as are exhibited and associated in the relation. Real life is fraught with adventures, to which the wildest fictions scarcely afford a parallel; and it has this special advantage over its rival, that these events, however extraordinary, can always be traced to motives, actions, and passions arising out of circumstances no way unnatural, and partaking of no impossible or supernatural agency.

Hence it is, that the judgment and the fancy are both equally gratified in the perusal of this class of fictions, if they are skilfully conducted; while in those which have nothing to recommend them but appeals to the agency of beings in whose existence nobody believes, and whose actions of course can have no alliance either with nature or probability, it is the imagination alone that is satisfied, and that only by the total subjection of every other faculty of the mind.

It must be acknowledged, however, that these probable and consistent fictions are by far the most difficult to manage. It is easy enough to bring about the most improbable, not to say impossible catastrophe, by the aid of beings whose power is without limit, and whose motives are inscrutable, though in my opinion it is always a proof of want of power in the writer when he is thus compelled to call upon Hercules to do what he cannot perform himself. It is either an indication that his judgement is inadequate to the arrangement of his materials and the adjustment of his plans, or that he is deficient in the invention of rational means to extricate himself from his difficulties. . . .

That these materials have as yet been little more than partially interwoven into the few fictions which this country has given birth to is not owing to their being inapplicable to that purpose, but to another cause entirely. We have been misled by bad models, or the suffrages of docile critics, who have bowed to the influence of rank and fashion, and given testimony in favor of works which their better judgment must have condemned. We have cherished a habit of looking to other nations for examples of every kind, and debased the genius of this New World by making it the ape and the tributary of that of the Old. We have imitated where we might often have excelled; we have overlooked our own rich resources, and sponged upon the exhausted treasury of our impoverished neighbors; we were born rich, and yet have all our lives subsisted by borrowing. Hence it has continually occurred that those who might have gone before had they chosen a new path have been content to come last, merely by following the old track.

Many a genius that could and would have attained an equal height in some new and unexplored region of fancy has dwindled into insignificance and contempt by stooping to track some inferior spirit, to whom fashion had assigned a temporary elevation. They ought to be told that though fashion may give a momentary popularity to works that neither appeal to national attachments, domestic habits, or those feelings which are the same yesterday, today, and forever, and everywhere, still it is not by imitation that they can hope to equal anything great. It appears to me that the young candidate for the prize of genius in the regions of invention and fancy has but one path open to fame. He cannot hope to wing his way above those immortal works that have stood the test of ages and are now with one consent recognized as specimens beyond which the intellect of man is not permitted to soar. But a noble prize is yet within his grasp and worthy of the most aspiring ambition.

By freeing himself from a habit of servile imitation; by daring to think and feel and express his feelings; by dwelling on scenes and events connected with our pride and our affections; by indulging in those little peculiarities of thought, feeling, and expression which belong to every nation; by borrowing from nature and not from those who disfigure or burlesque her, he may and will in time destroy the ascendancy of foreign taste and opinions, and elevate his own in the place of them. These causes lead to the final establishment of a national literature, and give that air and character of originality which it is sure to acquire, unless it is debased and expatriated by a habit of servile imitation. . . .

It is my delight to furnish occasionally such hints as may turn the attention of those who have leisure, health, youth, genius, and opportunities to domestic subjects on which to exercise their powers. Let them not be disheartened, even should they sink into a temporary oblivion in the outset.

This country is not destined to be always behind in the race of literary glory. The time will assuredly come when that same freedom of thought and action which has given such a spur to our genius in other respects will achieve similar wonders in literature. It is then that our early specimens will be sought after with avidity, and that those who led the way in the rugged discouraging path will be honored, as we begin to honor the adventurous spirits who first sought, explored, and cleared this Western wilderness.

150.

Joseph Rodman Drake: "The American Flag"

Joseph Rodman Drake's "The American Flag" is the only one of the numerous productions of this young poet — he died shortly after his twenty-fifth birthday — to survive. It not only reflects Drake's own nationalistic impulses, but it is also a good example of the patriotic literature that flourished during the early nineteenth century. The last verse of the poem has been attributed to Fitz-Greene Halleck, who joined with his friend in publishing a series of witty poems in the New York Evening Post *under the name "Croaker and Co.," and who composed a celebrated elegy on Drake, "Green be the turf above thee." The first edition of Drake's poems was not published until 1835, and the first complete edition appeared in 1935.*

Source: *Immortal Songs of Camp and Field,* Cleveland, 1899, pp. 17-19.

THE AMERICAN FLAG

When freedom, from her mountain height,
Unfurled her standard to the air,
She tore the azure robe of night,
And set the stars of glory there!
She mingled with its gorgeous dyes
The milky baldric of the skies,
And striped its pure celestial white
With streakings of the morning light;
Then, from his mansion in the sun,
She called her eagle bearer down,
And gave into his mighty hand
The symbol of her chosen land!

Majestic monarch of the cloud!
  Who rear'st aloft thy regal form,
To hear the tempest trumpings loud,
And see the lightning lances driven,
  When stride the warriors of the storm
And rolls the thunder drum of heaven!
Child of the sun! to thee 'tis given
  To guard the banner of the free,
To hover in the sulphur smoke,
To ward away the battle stroke,
And bid its blendings shine afar
Like rainbows on the cloud of war,
  The harbingers of victory.

Flag of the brave! thy folds shall fly,
The sign of hope and triumph high!
When speaks the signal trumpet tone
And the long line comes gleaming on
(Ere yet the life-blood, warm and wet,
Has dimmed the glistening bayonet),
Each soldier eye shall brightly turn
To where thy sky-born glories burn,
And, as his springing steps advance,
Catch war and vengeance from the glance.
And when the cannon mouthing cloud
Heaves in wild wreaths the battle shroud,
And gory sabers rise and fall,
Like shoots of flame on midnight's pall;
There shall thy meteor glances glow,
  And cowering foes shall shrink beneath
Each gallant arm that strikes below
  That lovely messenger of death.

Flag of the seas! on ocean wave
Thy stars shall glitter o'er the brave;
When death, careering on the gale,
Sweeps darkly round the bellied sail,
And frighted waves rush wildly back
Before the broadside's reeling rack,
Each dying wanderer of the sea
Shall look at once to heaven and thee,
And smile to see thy splendors fly
In triumph o'er his closing eye.

Flag of the free heart's hope and home,
  By angel hands to valor given;
Thy stars have lit the welkin dome
  And all thy hues were born in heaven!
Forever float that standard sheet!
  Where breathes the foe but falls before us?
With freedom's soil beneath our feet,
  And freedom's banner streaming o'er us?

Index of Authors

The numbers in brackets indicate selection numbers in this volume

ADAMS, ABIGAIL (Nov. 22, 1744-Oct. 28, 1818), wife of John Adams and mother of John Quincy Adams. [46] See also Author Index, Vols. 2, 3.

ADAMS, JOHN (Oct. 30, 1735-July 4, 1826), lawyer and journalist. Second President of the United States (1797-1801); representative (1770-71) to the Massachusetts General Court; member (1774-78) of the Continental Congress; signed the Declaration of Independence; commissioner to France (1778); helped draft the Massachusetts state constitution (1780); foreign minister to Great Britain (1785-88); Vice-President of the United States under Washington. [48, 71, 74, 77, 80, 111] See also Author Index, Vols. 2, 3.

ADAMS, JOHN QUINCY (July 11, 1767-Feb. 23, 1848), diplomat and statesman. Sixth President of the United States (1825-29); U.S. senator from Massachusetts (1803-08); minister to St. Petersburg (1809-14); minister to Great Britain (1815); secretary of state under Monroe; U.S. representative (1831-48). [110, 138, 147] See also Author Index, Vols. 5, 6.

ALLEN, "LONG JOHN" (June 12, 1763-July 31, 1812), public official. U.S. representative from Connecticut (1797-99). [11]

AMES, FISHER (April 9, 1758-July 4, 1808), orator, essayist, and public official. U.S. representative from Massachusetts (1789-97). [14, 50]

AUSTIN, MOSES (Oct. 4, 1761-June 10, 1821), mine owner and merchant. Organized (1816) the first Bank of St. Louis; established American colonies in Missouri and Texas. [1]

BARLOW, JOEL (March 24, 1754-Dec. 24, 1812), lawyer and poet. Founded (1784) the *American Mercury;* wrote *Hasty Pudding* (1796) as humorous evocation of New England life. [57] See also Author Index, Vol. 3.

BIGELOW, JACOB (Feb. 27, 1786-Jan. 10, 1879), physician and botanist. Professor (from 1815) at Harvard Medical School; professor of the application of science to the fine arts (1816-27) at Harvard College; president (1847-63) of the American Academy of Arts and Sciences. [106]

BRACKENRIDGE, HENRY M. (May 11, 1786-Jan. 18, 1871), jurist and author. Son of Hugh H. Brackenridge. Author of studies on Missouri, Louisiana, and South America. [132]

BRACKENRIDGE, HUGH H. (1748-June 25, 1816), author, jurist, and public official. Friend of Philip Freneau and James Madison; wrote *The Battle of Bunker's Hill* (1776), *The Death of General Montgomery* (1777), *Modern Chivalry* (1792-1815). [95] See also Author Index, Vols. 2, 3.

BROWN, CHARLES BROCKDEN (Jan. 17, 1771-Feb. 21, 1810), author. Wrote *Wieland* (1798), *Ormond* (1799), *Edgar Huntly* (1799), *Arthur Mervyn* (1799-1800); his pioneer use of the Gothic style won for him the title "Father of the American Novel." [9]

CALHOUN, JOHN C. (March 18, 1782-March 31, 1850), political philosopher, lawyer, and statesman. U.S. representative from South Carolina (1811-17); secretary of war under Monroe; Vice-President of the United States (1825-32) under J. Q. Adams and Jackson; U.S. senator (1833-43, 1845-50); secretary of state (1844-45) under Tyler. **[108]** See also Author Index, Vols. 5, 6, 7, 8.

CAMPBELL, THOMAS (1763-1854), clergyman. With his son, Alexander Campbell, founded the Church of the Disciples of Christ (Campbellites) in 1832. **[62]**

CHANNING, WILLIAM ELLERY (April 7, 1780-Oct. 2, 1842), clergyman and author. Pastor (1803-42) of Boston Federal Street Church; founded (1825) the American Unitarian Association; wrote *Negro Slavery* (1835) in behalf of the Abolitionist cause, *Remarks on National Literature* (1830), *Self Culture* (1838). **[131]** See also Author Index, Vols. 5, 6.

CLAY, HENRY (April 12, 1777-June 29, 1852), lawyer and statesman. U.S. senator from Kentucky (1806-07, 1810-11, 1831-42, 1849-52); U.S. representative (1811-14, 1815-21, 1823-25); House speaker in all years but 1821; secretary of state under J. Q. Adams. **[79, 116, 117, 142]** See also Author Index, Vols. 5, 6, 8.

COBBETT, WILLIAM (March 9, 1763-June 18, 1835), English political essayist and journalist under the pseudonym "Peter Porcupine." Published (1797-99) *Porcupine's Gazette* in Philadelphia; editor (1802-35) of the British *Political Register*. **[134]**

CUMING, FORTESCUE (Feb. 26, 1762-1828), author and traveler. Wrote *Sketches of a Tour to the Western Country* (1810) describing the Mississippi Valley, Louisiana, and Florida territories. **[56]**

DALLAS, ALEXANDER J. (June 21, 1759-Jan. 16, 1817), lawyer and financier. Editor (1787-89) of the *Columbian Magazine;* secretary of the Commonwealth of Pennsylvania (1791-1801); secretary of the treasury (1814-16) under Madison. **[97]**

DOW, LORENZO (Oct. 16, 1777-Feb. 2, 1834), evangelist. Preached the first Protestant sermon ever heard in Alabama; carried on evangelistic missions from Boston to Natchez, Miss. **[52]**

DRAKE, JOSEPH RODMAN (Aug. 7, 1795-Sept. 21, 1820), physician and poet. Wrote "The Culprit Fay," "The American Flag," and "Niagara," collected and published in 1835. **[150]**

DUANE, WILLIAM (May 17, 1760-Nov. 24, 1835), journalist. Editor (1798-1822) of the *Philadelphia Aurora;* indicted (1799) under the Sedition Act for articles on the conduct of federal troops in crushing Fries's Rebellion. **[23]** See also Author Index, Vol. 5.

DWIGHT, TIMOTHY (May 14, 1752-Jan. 11, 1817), Congregational clergyman and author. Grandson of Jonathan Edwards; chaplain (1777-78) in the Revolutionary Army; president (1795-1817) of Yale College. **[8, 67]**

FENNO, JOHN WARD (fl. 1778-1800), journalist. Editor (1798-1800) of the *Gazette of the United States,* a Federalist newspaper founded in 1789 by his father, John Fenno. **[22]**

FINLEY, ROBERT (Feb. 15, 1772-Oct. 3, 1817), Presbyterian clergyman and educator. Founder (1816) of the American Colonization Society, which hoped to solve the slavery problem by sending Negroes to a colony in Africa; president (1817) of the University of Georgia. **[93]**

FLINT, JAMES (fl. 1820), Scottish traveler and letter writer. **[144]**

FORDHAM, ELIAS PYM (fl. 1817-1818), traveler and letter writer. **[112]**

GALLATIN, ALBERT (Jan. 29, 1761-Aug. 12, 1849), financier and diplomat. U.S. representative from Pennsylvania (1795-1801); secretary of the treasury (1801-14) under Jefferson and Madison; minister to France (1816-23); minister to Great Britain (1826-27). **[4, 11, 64]** See also Author Index, Vols. 5, 7.

GERMAN, OBADIAH (April 22, 1766-Sept. 24, 1842), U.S. senator from New York (1809-15). **[76]**

GRASSI, GIOVANNI ANTONIO (1775-1849), Jesuit priest and scholar. President (1812-17) of Georgetown College. **[133]**

Grundy, Felix (Sept. 11, 1777-Dec. 19, 1840), public leader, lawyer, and jurist. U.S. representative from Kentucky (1811-14); U.S. senator (1829-38, 1839-40); U.S. attorney general (1838-39) under Van Buren. **[72]** See also Author Index, Vol. 5.

Hamilton, Alexander (?Jan. 11, 1755-July 12, 1804), soldier, lawyer, and statesman. Member (1782-83) of the Congress of the Confederation; New York delegate to the Constitutional Convention (1787); author with James Madison and John Jay of *The Federalist* (1787-88); secretary of the treasury (1789-95) under Washington and creator of the first Bank of the United States. Mortally wounded in a duel with Aaron Burr. **[19]** See also Author Index, Vols. 2, 3.

Hay, George (Dec. 15, 1765-Sept. 21, 1830), jurist. Member of the Virginia House of Delegates; U.S. district attorney for Virginia; judge of the U.S. District Court of eastern Virginia; son-in-law and confidante of James Monroe. **[60]**

Henry, Jacob (fl. 1809), first Jewish member of the North Carolina legislature. **[61]**

Hewitt, James (June 4, 1770-*c.* Aug. 1, 1827), violinist and composer. Composed *Tammany* (1794), one of the first ballad operas composed in the U.S. with libretto by Ann Julia Hatton. **[17]**

Hopkinson, Joseph (Nov. 12, 1770-Jan. 15, 1842), jurist, public official, and author. U.S. representative from Pennsylvania (1815-19); judge of the U.S. District Court of eastern Pennsylvania; author of the patriotic song "Hail Columbia!" (1798). **[17]**

Hosack, David (Aug. 31, 1769-Dec. 22, 1835), physician. Professor of botany and of materia medica (1795-1811) at Columbia University; professor of theory and practice of physic (1811-35) at New York College of Physicians and Surgeons. **[73]**

Ingersoll, Charles J. (Oct. 3, 1782-May 14, 1862), lawyer, public official, and author. U.S. representative from Pennsylvania (1813-15, 1841-49); U.S. district attorney for Pennsylvania (1815-29); wrote *View of the Rights and Wrongs, Power and Policy, of the United States of America* (1808). **[66]** See also Author Index, Vol. 5.

Jefferson, Thomas (April 13, 1743-July 4, 1826), lawyer, architect, agriculturalist, educator, political philosopher, diplomat, and statesman. Third President of the United States (1801-09); member (1775-76) of the Continental Congress; author of the Declaration of Independence; governor of Virginia (1779-81); minister to France (1785-89); secretary of state (1790-93) under Washington; Vice-President of the United States under John Adams; founder of the University of Virginia. **[24, 32, 34, 36, 37, 40, 42, 43, 55, 59, 65, 80, 81, 83, 84, 89, 91, 92, 98, 99, 100, 101, 103, 118, 140]** See also Author Index, Vols. 2, 3, 5.

Johnson, Richard M. (1780-Nov. 19, 1850), lawyer and public official. U.S. representative from Kentucky (1807-19, 1829-37); U.S. senator (1819-29); Vice-President of the United States under Van Buren. **[72]** See also Author Index, Vol. 5.

Key, Francis Scott (Aug. 1, 1779-Jan. 11, 1843), lawyer and author. Wrote U.S. national anthem, "The Star-Spangled Banner" (Sept. 13-14, 1814). **[85]**

King, Rufus (March 24, 1755-April 29, 1827), public official and diplomat. Member (1784-87) of the Congress of the Confederation and (1787) of the Constitutional Convention; U.S. senator from New York (1789-96, 1813-25); minister to Great Britain (1796-1803, 1825-26). **[136]**

Kosciuszko, Tadeusz (Feb. 4, 1746-Oct. 15, 1817), soldier and engineer. Born Poland; volunteered services in American Revolutionary Army (1776-82); granted honorary U.S. citizenship (1783). **[5]**

Latrobe, Benjamin H. (May 1, 1764-Sept. 3, 1820), architect and engineer. Surveyor of Washington, D.C. (from 1803); designed south wing of Capitol, made alterations in the White House, remodeled Patent Office, designed Marine Hospital; rebuilt Capitol after it was burned by British in 1814. **[6, 51]**

LEE, ROBERT (fl. 1818), promoter of an American national literature. **[121]**

LIVINGSTON, EDWARD (May 28, 1764-May 23, 1836), lawyer and public official. U.S. representative from New York (1795-1801) and from Louisiana (1823-29); mayor of New York City (1801-03); U.S. senator from Louisiana (1829-31); secretary of state (1831-33) under Jackson; minister to France (1833-35). **[10]** See also Author Index, Vol. 5.

MADISON, JAMES (March 16, 1751-June 28, 1836), statesman. Fourth President of the United States (1809-17); member (1780-81) of the Continental Congress, (1781-83) of the Congress of the Confederation, and (1787) of the Constitutional Convention; author with John Jay and Alexander Hamilton of *The Federalist* (1787-88); U.S. representative from Virginia (1789-97); secretary of state under Jefferson; rector (1826-36) of the University of Virginia. **[28, 70, 75, 109, 123]** See also Author Index, Vols. 3, 5, 6.

MANNING, WILLIAM (1747-1814), farmer and essayist. Wrote *The Key of Libberty* (1798), a series of anti-aristocratic essays. **[18]**

MARSHALL, JOHN (Sept. 24, 1755-July 6, 1835), public official and jurist. Member (1782-95) of the Virginia Executive Council and (1782-88) of the House of Burgesses; U.S. representative from Virginia (1799-1800); secretary of state (1800-01) under John Adams; chief justice (1801-35) of the U.S. Supreme Court. **[41, 127, 129]** See also Author Index, Vol. 5.

MICHAUX, FRANCOIS ANDRÉ (1770-1855), French botanist and traveler. Wrote of his botanical expeditions west of the Alleghenies and along the Atlantic Coast. **[39]**

MILLS, ROBERT (Aug. 12, 1781-March 3, 1855), architect. Designed (1836-51) U.S. Treasury Building, General Post Office, Patent Office, and Washington Monument in Washington, D.C. **[148]**

MONTLEZUN, ?LOUIS-ELIZABETH, Baron de (fl. 1815-1817), French traveler and essayist. **[119]**

MORRIS, GOUVERNEUR (Jan. 31, 1752-Nov. 6, 1816), lawyer, diplomat, and statesman. Member of the revolutionary provincial congress of New York (1776-77); signed the Articles of Confederation (1781); member (1777-79) of the Continental Congress and (1787) of the Constitutional Convention; commissioner to Great Britain (1790-91); minister to France (1792-94); U.S. senator from New York (1800-03). **[26, 38]** See also Author Index, Vol. 2.

NILES, HEZEKIAH (1777-1839), editor (1805-11) of the *Baltimore Evening Post* and (1811-36) of *Niles' Weekly Register*. **[94]**

NONES, BENJAMIN (1757-1826), broker. Leader of the Jewish community in Philadelphia. **[31]**

PAINE, ROBERT TREAT (1773-1811), poet and songwriter. Founded and edited (1794-96) *Federal Orrery*. **[17]**

PAULDING, JAMES KIRKE (Aug. 22, 1778-1860), public official and author. Secretary of the navy (1838-41) under Van Buren; satirized English conduct in *The Diverting History of John Bull* (1812), and employed typically American themes in *Westward Ho!* (1832) and *A Life of Washington* (1835). **[149]** See also Author Index, Vol. 6.

PICKERING, TIMOTHY (July 17, 1745-Jan. 29, 1829), Revolutionary War soldier, lawyer, and public official. Indian commissioner (1790-95), postmaster general (1791-95), and secretary of war (1795-96) under Washington, as well as secretary of state (1795-1800) under Washington and John Adams; U.S. senator (1803-11) and U.S. representative (1813-17) from Massachusetts. **[45]** See also Author Index, Vol. 3.

PLUMER, WILLIAM (1759-1850), public official. U.S. senator (1802-07); governor of New Hampshire (1812-13 , 1816-19). **[102]**

QUINCY, JOSIAH (Feb. 4, 1772-July 1, 1864), public official and educator. U.S. representative from Massachusetts (1805-13); mayor of Boston (1823-29); president (1829-45) of Harvard College. **[69]**

RANDOLPH, JOHN, "of Roanoke" (June 2,

1773-May 24, 1833), Virginia planter and public official. U.S. representative (1799-1813, 1815-17, 1819-25, 1827-29); U.S. senator (1825-27); minister to Russia (1830). **[63, 72, 104]** See also Author Index, Vol. 5.

RAYMOND, DANIEL (1786-?1849), lawyer and economist. Wrote *Thoughts on Political Economy* (1820). **[143]**

RED JACKET (*c.* 1758-Jan. 20, 1830), Seneca Indian chief; Indian name, Sagoyewatha. Gained popularity among the Iroquois nation by opposing white civilization. **[47]**

ROANE, SPENCER (April 4, 1762-Sept. 4, 1822), political writer and jurist. Member (1783-84) of the Virginia House of Delegates; judge (1794-1821) of the Virginia Supreme Court of Appeals; founded (1804) the *Richmond Enquirer*. **[130]**

RUSH, BENJAMIN (1745-April 19, 1813), physician, medical educator, and public official. Signed the Declaration of Independence; member (1776-77) of the Continental Congress; treasurer of the United States (1797-1813); his *Medical Inquiries and Observations Upon the Diseases of the Mind* (1812) was the first systematic American work on that subject. **[7, 49]** See also Author Index, Vols. 2, 3.

RUSH, RICHARD (Aug. 29, 1780-July 30, 1859), lawyer, diplomat, and public official. Comptroller of the U.S. Treasury (1811); U.S. attorney general (1814-17) and secretary of state (1817) under Madison; minister to Great Britain (1817-25); secretary of the treasury under J. Q. Adams; secured the Smithson bequest to found the Smithsonian Institution (1836-38); minister to France (1847-49). **[90]** See also Author Index, Vol. 5.

SMITH, JAMES (Sept. 17, 1757-July 28, 1800), Methodist clergyman. Published three journals of his travels through Kentucky and the Northwest Territory (1783, 1795, 1797). **[2]**

TAYLOR, JOHN (?Dec. 19, 1753-Aug. 21, 1824), political writer and public official. Member (1779-81, 1783-85, 1796-1800) of the Virginia House of Delegates; U.S. senator (1792-94, 1803, 1822-24); author of *An Enquiry into the Principles and Policy of the Government of the United States* (1814), *Tyranny Unmasked* (1822). **[82]** See also Author Index, Vol. 5.

WASHINGTON, GEORGE (Feb. 22, 1732-Dec. 14, 1799), surveyor, planter, soldier, and statesman. First President of the United States (1789-97); member (1759-74) of the Virginia House of Burgesses; delegate (1774-75) to the Continental Congress; commander (1775-83) of all Continental armies; president of the Constitutional Convention (1787); commander in chief (1798-99) of the U.S. Army. **[15, 25]** See also Author Index, Vols. 2, 3.

WATERHOUSE, BENJAMIN (March 4, 1754-Oct. 2, 1846), physician. Professor of theory and practice of physic (1783-1812) at Harvard College; U.S. pioneer in vaccination against smallpox (from 1800). **[71]**

WEBSTER, DANIEL (Jan. 18, 1782-Oct. 24, 1852), lawyer, orator, and statesman. U.S. representative from New Hampshire (1813-17) and from Massachusetts (1823-27); U.S. senator from Massachusetts (1827-41, 1845-50); secretary of state (1841-43) under Tyler and (1850-52) under Fillmore. **[86, 115, 145]** See also Author Index, Vols. 5, 6, 7, 8.

WHITE, SAMUEL (Dec. 1770-Nov. 4, 1809), lawyer and public official. U.S. senator from Delaware (1801-09). **[44]**

WILLARD, EMMA HART (Feb. 23, 1787-April 15, 1870), educator and poetess. Pioneer in women's education; founded Waterford (N.Y.) Academy (1819) and Troy (N.Y.) Female Seminary (1821); wrote "Rocked in the Cradle of the Deep." **[135]** See also Author Index, Vol. 5.

WORCESTER, NOAH (Nov. 25, 1758-Oct. 31, 1837), clergyman and editor. Pastor (1787-1810) of the Thornton, N.H., Congregational Church; editor (1813-18) of the Unitarian periodical *Christian Disciple* and (1819-28) of the pacifist magazine *The Friend of Peace*. **[88]**

WORTMAN, TUNIS (fl. 1800), lawyer and political writer. **[30]**